INTRODUCTION TO SOCIAL WORK AND SOCIAL WELFARE

Seventh Edition

Charles Zastrow
University of Wisconsin—Whitewater

Brooks/Cole • Wadsworth Publishing Company

I(T)P® An International Thomson Publishing Company

Belmont, CA • Albany, NY • Boston • Cincinnati
Johannesburg • London • Madrid • Melbourne
Mexico City • New York • Pacific Grove, CA
Scottsdale, AZ • Singapore • Tokyo • Toronto

Social Work Editor: *Lisa Gebo*
Editorial Assistant: *Susan Wilson*
Marketing Manager: *Jennie Burger*
Project Editor: *Christal Niederer*
Print Buyer: *Karen Hunt*
Permissions Editor: *Bob Kauser*
Production: *New Leaf Publishing Services*

Designer: *Wendy LaChance, Laurie Albrecht*
Copyeditor: *Frank Hubert*
Cover Design: *Ellen Pettengell*
Cover Image: *Stock Illustration Source, Inc.*
Compositor: *G & S Typesetters, Inc.*
Printer: *R. R. Donnelley & Sons/Crawfordsville*

Printed in the United States of America
3 4 5 6 7 8 9 10

Wadsworth Publishing Company
10 Davis Drive
Belmont, CA 94002

International Thomson Editores
Seneca, 53
Colonia Polanco
11560 México D.F. México

International Thomson Publishing Europe
Berkshire House
168-173 High Holborn
London, WC1V 7AA, United Kingdom

International Thomson Publishing Asia
60 Albert Street #15-01
Albert Complex
Singapore 189969

Nelson ITP, Australia
102 Dodds Street
South Melbourne
Victoria 3205 Australia

International Thomson Publishing Japan
Hirakawa-cho Kyowa Building, 3F
2-2-1 Hirakawa-cho, Chiyoda-ku
Tokyo 102, Japan

Nelson Canada
1120 Birchmount Road
Scarborough, Ontario
Canada M1K 5G4

International Thomson Publishing Southern Africa
Building 18, Constantia Square
138 Sixteenth Road, P.O. Box 2459
Halfway House, 1685 South Africa

Library of Congress Cataloging-in-Publication Data

Zastrow, Charles.
    Introduction to social work and social welfare / Charles Zastrow.
—7th ed.
        p.   cm.
    Includes bibliographical references and index.
    ISBN 0-534-36698-8
    1. Social service—United States.   2. Social service—Vocational
guidance—United States.   3. Public welfare—United States.
I. Title.
HV91.Z37 1999
362—dc21   99-26101

Instructor's Edition ISBN: 0-534-36991-X

To Kathy

About the Author

CHARLES ZASTROW, MSW and PhD, is Professor in the Social Work Department, University of Wisconsin–Whitewater. He has worked as a practitioner in a variety of public and private social welfare agencies and has chaired 13 social work accreditation site visit teams for the Council on Social Work Education (CSWE). He is currently a member of the Accreditation Commission of CSWE. He is a member of the National Association of Social Workers, the Council on Social Work Education, and NASW Register of Clinical Social Workers. He is certified as an Independent Clinical Social Worker in Wisconsin. In addition to *Introduction to Social Work and Social Welfare,* Dr. Zastrow has written five other textbooks: *The Practice of Social Work* (6th ed.), *Social Work with Groups* (4th ed.), *Social Problems: Issues and Solutions* (4th ed.), *Understanding Human Behavior and the Social Environment* (4th ed.) (with Dr. Karen Kirst-Ashman), and *You Are What You Think: A Guide to Self-Realization.*

Contributing Author

DON NOLAN
Social Worker
Jefferson County Public School System
Wisconsin

CONTENTS

PREFACE

This book is designed to stimulate student interest in social work and to provide an experiential "flavor" of what the fields of social welfare and social work are really like. Using a social problems approach, the book describes how people are affected by poverty, child abuse, emotional difficulties, sexism, alcoholism, crime, AIDS, physical and mental disabilities, racism, overpopulation, sexual assault, and other problems. Information on the nature, extent, and causes of such problems is also presented. In teaching introductory courses in social work, a number of my colleagues and I have found that students tend to be more interested when they come face-to-face with the tragic social conditions that people experience. This book also includes case examples through which the reader is able to identify with people in need of help.

Knowledge about social problems prepares and motivates the student to read the sections of the text that cover current services, merits and shortcomings of those services, and new programs that are needed to fill service gaps.

In addition, *Introduction to Social Work and Social Welfare* is designed to:

- Provoke the reader's thinking about some of the controversial contemporary issues in social welfare. I believe developing the student's critical thinking capacities is much more important than teaching unimportant facts to be recited on exams.

- Convey material on social work intervention approaches that the reader can use in working with people to facilitate positive changes.

- Present material on both sides of major social issues confronting our society that the reader can use in arriving at informed positions.

- Provide case examples of the functions, roles, responsibilities, gratifications, and frustrations of social workers that will help the student who is considering a social work major to make an informed career decision.

- Provide a brief historical review of the development of social welfare, social work, and various social services.

- Facilitate the reader in acquiring an international perspective by presenting, in practically every chapter, information on social problems and social services not only in the United States but also in other countries.

- Inform the reader of the Council on Social Work Education's (CSWE) conceptualization of social work education at the baccalaureate and master's levels as delineated in CSWE's Curriculum Policy Statements.

- Help the reader "sort out" his or her value structure in relation to welfare recipients, single parents, ex-convicts, the mentally ill, the divorced, persons with AIDS, abusive parents, minority groups, those who are prejudiced, and so on. The aim is not to sell any particular set of values but to help the reader arrive at a value system that she or he will be comfortable with and find functional in interacting with others.

Plan of the Book

Part I introduces the student in the fields of social welfare, social work, and human services. These terms are defined, and their relationships to sociology, psychology, and other disciplines are described. A brief history of social welfare and social work is provided, and the future is examined. A discussion of social work as a career and as a profession is included, and this gives the reader a basis for deciding whether to pursue a career in social work.

This part also describes generalist social work practice with systems of all sizes, including individuals, groups, families, organizations, and communities. This conceptualization introduces readers to the knowledge, skills, and values needed for effective social work practice.

Part II focuses on the most common social problems served by the field of social welfare. This part constitutes the main emphasis of the text and describes:

- Contemporary social problems in our society.

- Current social services for meeting these problems.

- Gaps in current services.

- Controversial issues in each service area.

- Proposed new programs to meet current gaps in services.

Numerous case examples provide the reader with a "feeling" awareness of how the problems affect people and convey what it is really like to be a social worker.

This seventh edition updates information in all of the chapters. Several chapters have been extensively revised in accordance with suggestions from a number of faculty members who reviewed and commented on the sixth edition. New topics include: the welfare reform act of 1996, the strengths perspective in social work, the Africentric perspective and worldview, ethnic-sensitive social work practice, managed mental health care, the devolution revolution, respect for the spiritual and religious beliefs of others, managed health care, family preservation programs, critical theory of crime, changes in affirmative action, and the developmental approach to social welfare.

The Council on Social Work Education is the national organization that accredits baccalaureate and master's degree programs in social work education in the United States. In 1992 CSWE adopted revisions in its Curriculum Policy Statements for undergraduate and graduate programs. A major thrust of *Introduction to Social Work and Social Welfare* is to present material that is consistent with the revisions of these policy statements. Three additional themes around which content is organized in this text are vignettes of a "day in the life" of social workers, generalist practice, and ecological perspectives.

The book is intended for use in introductory social work and social welfare courses. It introduces prospective social work majors to the field of social welfare and will help them arrive at career decisions and prepare for future social work courses. For nonmajors, the book provides information about current social problems and social services; the text also gives a framework for analyzing policy issues and for making citizenship decisions on social issues.

Supplements

InfoTrac® College Edition

With this Wadsworth exclusive, students receive four months of real-time access to InfoTrac College Edition's on-line database of continuously-updated, full-length articles from more than 900 journals and periodicals. By doing a simple keyword search, users can quickly generate a powerful list of related articles from thousands of possibilities, then select relevant articles to explore and/or print out for reference or further study. For professors, InfoTrac College Edition articles offer opportunities to ignite discussions or augment their lectures with the latest developments in the discipline. For students, InfoTrac College Edition's virtual library allows Internet access to sources that extend their learning far beyond the pages of a text.

Instructor's Manual (0-534-36701-1)

The Instructor's Manual contains a brief summary, suggestions for discussion topics, essay questions, guest speakers, class exercises, objective test questions, and relevant Web sites for each chapter in the main text. It is also available in ASCII format for your convenience in both Macintosh (0-534-36700-3) and Windows (0-534-36699-6) platforms.

On-line Test Items

Test items for each chapter will be available on-line for students to practice and apply their knowledge. Please visit us at *http://socialwork.wadsworth.com/* for access to the on-line quizzes and for other text information.

Acknowledgments

I wish to express my deep appreciation to the various people who made this book possible. Special thanks to Don Nolan (contributing author) and to the photo researcher, Suzi Howard. I would like to thank the following colleagues who provided comments on the manuscript for this edition:

> Margaret Martin, Eastern Connecticut State University
> Lois Shane, Western Illinois University
> David Wilson, Florida Atlantic University

Previous editions were similarly enhanced by the insights of the following reviewers:

> Mich Barbezat, Elgin Community College
> Gloria Carpenter, University of Texas
> Bruce Friedman, Wayne State University
> Mary Hart, University of Wyoming
> Ken Herrmann, State University of New York at Brockport
> Janine Mariscotti, LaSalle University
> Ann Boydston Park, Cabrini College
> William Roberts
> David Storm, Central Missouri State University
> Carolyn Tice, Ohio University at Athens

A sincere thank you to Vicki Vogel for helping in a number of ways with the writing of this text. I especially want to thank Lisa Gebo (Social Work Editor at Brooks/Cole • Wadsworth) who helped substantially in conceptualizing this revision and who is a pleasure to work with. A final thank you to the staff at Brooks/Cole • Wadsworth for their support and highly professional assistance with the texts I've authored.

Charles Zastrow

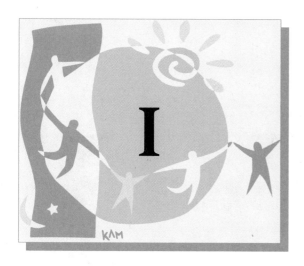

INTRODUCTION: SOCIAL WELFARE AND SOCIAL WORK

SOCIAL
WELFARE:
ITS BUSINESS,
HISTORY,
AND FUTURE

In our industrialized, complex, and rapidly changing society, social welfare activities have become important functions in terms of the money spent, the human misery treated, and the number of people served.[1] This chapter will:

- Define social welfare and describe its goals.

- Describe the relationship between social welfare and the following disciplines: sociology, psychology, social work, and human services.

- Provide a history of social welfare.

- Describe how the future of social welfare will be affected by technological advances.

- Illustrate that the future of social welfare will also be partially affected by changes in the American family system. A summary of many of the changes that are occurring in the American family is provided.

GOAL OF SOCIAL WELFARE

The goal of social welfare is to fulfill the social, financial, health, and recreational requirements of all individuals in a society. Social welfare seeks to enhance the social functioning of all age groups, both rich and poor. When other institutions in our society, such as the market economy and the family, fail at times to meet the basic needs of individuals or groups of people, then social services are needed and demanded.

In less industrialized societies, people's basic needs have been fulfilled in more direct and informal ways. Even in this country, fewer than 150 years ago most Americans lived on farms or in small towns with extended families and relatives close by. If financial or other needs arose, relatives, the church, and neighbors were there to "lend a helping hand." Problems were visible and personal; everyone knew everyone else in the community. When a need arose, it was taken for granted that those with resources would do whatever they could to alleviate the difficulty. If, for example, the need was financial, personal ac-

quaintance with the storekeeper or banker usually was sufficient to obtain needed goods or money.

Clearly, we are now living in a different era. Our technology, economic base, social patterns, and living styles have changed dramatically. Our commercial, industrial, political, educational, and religious institutions are considerably larger and more impersonal. We tend to live in large urban communities—away from families or relatives—frequently without even knowing our neighbors. We have become much more mobile, often having few roots and limited knowledge of the community in which we live. Vocationally, we have specialized and become more interdependent on others, and as a result we have diminishing control over major aspects of our lives. Our rapidly changing society is a breeding ground for exacerbating former social ills and creating new problems, such as the expanding number of homeless people, higher crime rates, recurring energy crises, terrorism, and the destruction of our environment. Obviously, the old rural-frontier methods of meeting social welfare needs are no longer viable.

It is the business of social welfare:

- To find homes for parentless children.

- To rehabilitate people who are addicted to alcohol or drugs.

- To treat those with emotional difficulties.

- To make life more meaningful for the elderly.

- To provide vocational rehabilitation services to persons with a physical or mental disability.

- To meet the financial needs of the poor.

- To rehabilitate juveniles and adults who have committed criminal offenses.

- To end all types of discrimination and oppression.

- To provide child-care services for parents who work outside the home.

- To counteract violence in families, including child abuse and spouse abuse.

- To fulfill the health and legal exigencies of those in financial need.

- To counsel individuals and groups experiencing a wide variety of personal and social difficulties.

- To provide services to persons with AIDS and to their families and friends.

- To provide recreational and leisure-time services to all age groups.

- To educate and provide socialization experiences to children who have a cognitive disability* or an emotional disorder.

- To serve families struck by such physical disasters as fires and tornadoes.

- To provide adequate housing for the homeless.

- To provide programs that support and enhance the normal growth and development of all children and adults.

- To provide vocational training and employment opportunities to the unskilled and unemployed.

- To meet the special needs of people of color, migrant workers, and other minority groups.

SOCIAL WELFARE AS AN INSTITUTION AND AS A DISCIPLINE

The term *social welfare* has different meanings, as it is both an *institution* and an *academic discipline.* The National Association of Social Workers (the primary professional organization for social workers) gives the following definition of social welfare as an institution:

> A nation's system of programs, benefits, and services that helps people meet those social, economic, educational, and health needs that are fundamental to the maintenance of society.[2]

---

*The term *cognitive disability* is used in this text in lieu of *mental retardation,* which has negative connotations.

Examples of social welfare programs and services are foster care, adoption, day care, Head Start, probation and parole, financial assistance programs for low-income parents and their children, services to the homeless, public health nursing, sex therapy, suicide counseling, recreational services such as Boy Scouts and YWCA programs, services to minority groups, services to veterans, school social services, medical and legal services to the poor, family planning services, Meals on Wheels, nursing-home services, shelters for battered spouses, protective services for child abuse and neglect, assertiveness-training programs, encounter groups and sensitivity training, public housing projects, family counseling, Alcoholics Anonymous, runaway services, services to persons with a developmental disability, and rehabilitation services.

Social welfare programs and social service organizations are sometimes referred to as "social welfare institutions." The purposes of social welfare institutions are to prevent, alleviate, or contribute to the solution of recognized social problems in order to directly improve the well-being of individuals, groups, families, organizations, and communities. Social welfare institutions are established by policies and laws, with the programs and services being provided by voluntary (private) and governmental (public) agencies.

The term *social welfare institution* is applied to various levels of complexity and abstraction. It may be applied to a single program or organization—for example, foster care or Planned Parenthood. Or the term may be applied to a group of services or programs. For example, child welfare services is a social welfare institution that includes such services as adoption, foster care, juvenile probation, protective services, runaway services, day care, school social services, and residential treatment. The highest aggregate level to which the term *social welfare institution* is applied includes *all* of the social programs and organizations in a country that are designed to prevent, alleviate, or contribute to the solution of recognized social problems.

Another meaning of social welfare derives from its role as an academic discipline. In this context, social welfare is "the study of agencies, programs, personnel, and policies which focus on the delivery of social services to individuals, groups, and communities."[3] One of the functions of the social welfare discipline is to educate and train social workers. (Some colleges and universities call their professional preparation programs for social work practice "social work," and others call their programs "social welfare.")

SOCIAL WELFARE'S RELATIONSHIP TO SOCIOLOGY AND TO OTHER ACADEMIC DISCIPLINES

Social welfare has often been confused with "sociology" and "human services." In addition, many people are confused about how social welfare and social work relate to psychology, psychiatry, and other related disciplines. The next few sections seek to clarify these relationships.

Several academic disciplines seek to develop a knowledge base about social problems, their causes, and their alleviation. The most common disciplines are social welfare, sociology, psychology, political science, economics, psychiatry, and cultural anthropology. Figure 1.1 shows the relationship of these disciplines to social welfare.

Each of these disciplines has a distinct focus. The following definitions highlight the similarities and differences among these disciplines:

Sociology: The study of human social behavior, especially the study of the origins, organizations, institutions, and development of human society.

Psychology: The study of mental processes and behavior.

Psychiatry: The study of the diagnosis, treatment, and prevention of mental illness.

Political science: The study of the processes, principles, and structure of government and of political institutions.

FIGURE 1.1

Overlap of Knowledge Base of Social Welfare with Other Disciplines

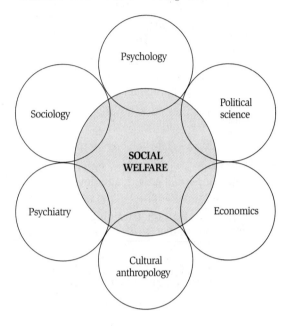

Economics: The study of the production, distribution, and consumption of commodities.

Cultural anthropology: The study of human culture based on archeological, ethnographic, linguistic, social, and psychological data and methods of analysis.[4]

Theories and research in these disciplines may or may not, depending on the nature of the content, be considered part of the knowledge base of social welfare. When the theories and research have direct application to the goal of enhancing the social functioning of people, such knowledge can also be considered part of the knowledge base of social welfare. In the past, social welfare has been more of an applied science than a pure science; that is, it has formed its knowledge base primarily from the theories and research of other disciplines and has focused on applying such knowledge through social programs. In recent years, the academic discipline of social welfare (called social work at many campuses) has been active in research projects and in theory development. This increased research and theory development activity is an indication that social welfare is a discipline that is maturing, as it is now developing much of its own knowledge base.

A few examples may be useful in illustrating how the knowledge base of other disciplines overlaps with social welfare. Sociological research on and conceptualization of the causes of social problems (for example, juvenile delinquency, mental illness, poverty, and racial discrimination) may be considered part of the knowledge base of social welfare. Only through an understanding of such problems can social welfare effectively prevent and control such problems. Sociological studies on the effects of institutions (for example, mental hospitals and prisons) on individuals are currently of considerable interest to and have important application in social welfare. Sociological investigations of other subjects, such as mobility, urbanization, secularization, group formation, race relations, prejudice, and the process of acculturation, have also become part of social welfare's knowledge base because such investigations are directly applicable to enhancing people's social well-being. However, research in other sociological areas, such as studies of social organizations among nonliterate tribes, is usually considered outside the knowledge base of social welfare because such research usually does not have direct applications to the goal of social welfare.

Comparable overlap occurs between social welfare and the other previously mentioned disciplines. Using psychology as an example, studies and theory development in such areas as personality growth and therapeutic techniques can be considered part of the knowledge base of social welfare because they have direct social welfare applications. On the other hand, experimental investigations of, for example, the perceptions and thinking processes of animals do not, at least presently, have such applications and would not therefore be considered part of the social welfare knowledge base.

SOCIAL WELFARE'S RELATIONSHIP TO SOCIAL WORK

The previously given institutional definition of social welfare is applicable when the relationship between social welfare and social work is examined. *Social welfare* is a more comprehensive term than *social work;* social welfare encompasses social work. Social welfare and social work are primarily related at the level of practice. *Social work* has been defined by the National Association of Social Workers as follows:

> *Social work is the professional activity of helping individuals, groups, or communities to enhance or restore their capacity for social functioning and to create societal conditions favorable to their goals.*
>
> *Social work practice consists of the professional application of social work values, principles, and techniques to one or more of the following ends: helping people obtain tangible services; providing counseling and psychotherapy for individuals, families, and groups; helping communities or groups provide or improve social and health services; and participating in relevant legislative processes.*
>
> *The practice of social work requires knowledge of human development and behavior; of social, economic, and cultural institutions; and of the interaction of all these factors.*[5]

The term *social worker* has been defined by the National Association of Social Workers as:

> *Graduates of schools of social work (with either bachelor's or master's degrees), who use their knowledge and skills to provide social services for clients (who may be individuals, families, groups, communities, organizations, or society in general). Social workers help people increase their capacities for problem solving and coping and help them obtain needed resources, facilitate interactions between individuals and between people and their environments, make organizations responsible to people, and influence social policies.*[6]

CASE EXAMPLE 1.1   What It's All About

Shortly after their marriage in the fall of 1966, Frank Lund, age 24, and his wife, Jean, age 22, moved from their rural farm area in northern Wisconsin to a large midwestern city. They had bright hopes for their future. Frank obtained a well-paying job on the assembly line of an auto manufacturing company. Jean worked part-time as a file clerk until her first pregnancy in the spring of 1968. In the next 4 years, they had three children and also purchased a three-bedroom home in a suburb. Then, in 1973, while on a hunting trip, Frank was accidentally killed. Ms. Lund was never quite the same. She suffered periodic bouts of depression and had considerable difficulty in finding the energy to care for her three young children.

By 1974 the Lunds' financial resources were depleted. Unable to make the payments on the house, they were forced to move to a rundown two-bedroom apartment closer to the center of the city. In the winter of 1974, Ms. Lund applied for financial assistance under the Aid to Families with Dependent Children program. The state in which the Lunds lived had negative attitudes toward welfare, and consequently, the monthly payments the Lunds received were barely sufficient to meet their basic needs. In addition, the neighbors never attempted to understand the Lunds' plight. They were more concerned about their tax dollars being spent for "such people." Ms. Lund felt she was a second-class citizen, stigmatized because she was a "welfare" case. She also soon became aware that some of her neighbors would not permit their children to play with hers. When her children entered school, they began to feel different from other youngsters; they were poorly dressed, the lunches they brought from home usually consisted of cheese sandwiches, and they had no father. A few years later, Ms. Lund dated a salesman for a while; being lonely, she permitted him to stay over some evenings at the apartment. The neighbors frowned upon this behavior and made moral accusations. Several months later, Ms. Lund ended the relationship after she realized she would be unable to change the man's drinking problem. (When intoxicated, he was sometimes abusive to Ms. Lund and the children.)

When the oldest child, Tom, was 15, he was arrested for starting three fires in the neighborhood. Perhaps he just wanted attention, or maybe it was his way of demonstrating that he needed help. Anyway, he was judged to have emotional difficulties and was sent to a residential treatment center. At the age of 20, he was released. He applied for several semiskilled jobs but, partly because of potential employers' concerns about his past, someone else was always hired. He therefore obtained a series of odd jobs as a maintenance man, dishwasher, store clerk, and so forth. Not finding more stimulating work, he began drinking, sometimes to excess. At the age of 25 he married and within the next few years fathered four children. Because of his family responsibilities, low-paying job, and drinking problem, he and his family are now locked into poverty.

The second child, Corine, wanted to escape from her home and from school when she became a teenager. She ran away several times but was always returned by the police. At age 16 she became involved with Mike, a high school dropout, and became pregnant. Mike's parents would not give their consent to a marriage. Corine dropped out of school, delivered the baby, and decided to keep it. For the next 6 years she continued to live with her mother, even though there were frequent arguments. At age 22 she met and within a year married Bill Loomans, a seasonal construction worker and a widower with three children. Already Bill and Corine were close to being locked into poverty for the rest of their lives due to their large family and limited incomes. The two additional children they had after marriage did not help.

Ms. Lund's youngest child, Dave, was also a problem for her. In the early years of school, he had considerable difficulty learning to read. He soon fell behind the rest of his classmates. By the fourth grade, he felt self-conscious about being unable to read. In class he no longer would put forth much effort to do academic work and instead spent most of his time clowning around. Psychological testing indicated Dave had average mental ability and suggested he had developed an "emotional block" to academic work that appeared to be related to his home environment. On entering the fifth grade, he was placed in a special class for children with cognitive disabilities. Dave was very sensitive about this and became involved in several fights when referred to as a "dummy" by his peers. At age 16 he dropped out of school and was fortunate to obtain a job pumping gas. Two years later, he was "forced" to marry Terri Fernandez after she became pregnant. Terri and Dave had a stormy marriage, with frequent disputes. Within a year and a half they had two children. Six months later they separated, and Dave was ordered by the court to pay child support until the children were 18. Two years later, on being named as the father of another child borne by a different woman, Dave was ordered to make monthly support payments for this child as well. He tried to meet these responsibilities, but his income would not stretch; he therefore wrote some checks that "bounced." Recently, he was arrested and placed on probation for 2 years. He now appears to be solidly locked into poverty for the remainder of his life. His chances of securing a better-paying job are slight because of his past, his lack of training for a skilled job, his inability to read, and his financial obligations.

The story of the Lund family raises a number of questions for social welfare. Who is to "blame" for the difficulties of this family? Or is no one at fault? Is this cycle of poverty (which has been transmitted from one generation to the next) and the social difficulties associated with it likely to be continued among the grandchildren of Frank and Jean Lund? What should be done now to help the members of the Lund family? Who should pay for the help provided? What kind of help (both services and money), if provided to Jean Lund when her husband was accidentally killed, could have prevented the social difficulties experienced by her children and those that her grandchildren will probably face?

FIGURE 1.2

Examples of Professional Groups within the Field of Social Welfare

Almost all social workers are working in the field of social welfare. There are, however, many other professional and occupational groups that may be working in this field, as illustrated in Figure 1.2. Professional people providing social welfare services include attorneys who offer legal services to the poor; urban planners in social-planning agencies; physicians in public health agencies; teachers in residential treatment facilities for the emotionally disturbed; psychologists, nurses, and recreational therapists in mental hospitals; and psychiatrists in mental health clinics.

SOCIAL WELFARE'S RELATIONSHIP TO OTHER INSTITUTIONS

Social welfare overlaps with such institutions as the family, education, religion, and politics. One of the functions of the family is raising and caring for children. Social welfare assists families by provid-

ing services such as counseling, day care, foster care, and adoption. Certain educational courses have both educational and social welfare aspects; for example, social science and physical education courses provide socialization experiences and are important in the social development of youth. Structured religion has long been interested in people's social well-being and has provided such social welfare services as counseling, financial assistance, day care, and recreation. The overlap between politics and social welfare primarily involves the political processes that occur in regard to the funding of social service programs. Some social welfare programs (for example, public assistance) are controversial political topics. Securing the necessary funding for essential social welfare programs is a crucial component of the social welfare system in any country.

SOCIAL WELFARE'S RELATIONSHIP TO HUMAN SERVICES

Human services may be defined as those systems of services and allied occupations and professions that concentrate on improving or maintaining the physical and mental health and general well-being of individuals, groups, or communities in our society. Alfred Kahn has conceptualized human services as composed of the following four service categories:[7]

1. Personal services (casework, counseling, recreation, rehabilitation, religion, therapy).

2. Protection services (consumer protection, corrections, courts, fire prevention/fire fighting, housing-code enforcement, law enforcement, public health services).

3. Information/advising services (consulting, consumer information, education, financial counseling, hotlines, and library services).

4. Maintenance services (child care, unemployment assistance, institutional services, public welfare programs, retirement plans, and Social Security programs).

Kahn indicates that there is a tendency to use the term *human services* for what in the past has been called social welfare.[8] Actually, *human services* is a broader term because it includes services (such as library services, law enforcement, housing-code enforcement, consumer protection, and fire prevention and fire fighting) that are usually not considered social welfare services. The term *social welfare* is thus more limited because it focuses on conceptualizing and resolving social problems. *Human services* is a broader term that encompasses social welfare programs. The two terms relate at a *program* level.

RESIDUAL VIEW VERSUS INSTITUTIONAL VIEW OF SOCIAL WELFARE

The present social welfare scene is substantially influenced by the past. Currently, there are two conflicting views of the role of social welfare in our society.[9] One of these roles has been termed *residual*—a gap-filling or first-aid role. This view holds that social welfare services should be provided only when an individual's needs are not properly met through other societal institutions, primarily the family and the market economy. According to the residual view, social services and financial aid should not be provided until all other measures or efforts have been exhausted, including the individual's and his or her family's resources. In addition, this view asserts that funds and services should be provided on a short-term basis (primarily during emergencies) and should be withdrawn when the individual or the family again becomes capable of being self-sufficient.

The residual view has been characterized as "charity for unfortunates."[10] Funds and services are seen not as a right (something that one is entitled to) but as a gift, with the receiver having certain obligations; for example, to receive financial aid, recipients may be required to perform certain low-grade work assignments. Associated with the residual view is the belief that the causes of clients' difficulties are rooted in their own malfunctioning—that is, clients are to blame for their

predicaments because of personal inadequacies, ill-advised activities, or sins.

Under the residual view, there is usually a stigma attached to receiving services or funds. The prevalence of the residual stigma can be shown by asking, "Have you ever felt a reluctance to seek counseling for a personal or emotional situation you faced because you were wary of what others might think of you?" For almost everyone the answer is yes. An example of this stigma in American society was evidenced in 1968, when Senator Thomas Eagleton was dropped as the vice presidential candidate on the Democratic ticket after it became known that he had once received psychiatric counseling.

The opposing point of view, which has been coined the *institutional view,** holds that social welfare programs are to be "accepted as a proper, legitimate function of modern industrial society in helping individuals achieve self-fulfillment."[11] Under this view, there is no stigma attached to receiving funds or services; recipients are viewed as being entitled to such help. Associated with this view is the belief that an individual's difficulties are due to causes largely beyond his or her control (for example, a person may be unemployed because of a lack of employment opportunities). When difficulties arise, causes are sought in the environment (society), and efforts are focused on improving the social institutions within which the individual functions.

The residual approach characterized social welfare programs from our early history to the depression of the 1930s. Since the Great Depression, both approaches have been applied to social welfare programs, with some programs largely residual in nature and others more institutional in design and implementation. Social insurance programs, such as Old Age, Survivors, Disability, and Health Insurance (described in Chapter 4), are examples of institutional programs. Public assistance programs (also described in Chapter 4) are examples of residual programs.

---

*The term *institutional view of social welfare* is distinctly different from, and not to be confused with, the term *social welfare institutions*.

Blaming the Victim

Jerry Jorgenson and Joyce Mantha decided to get married after dating for 3 years. Both looked forward to a big wedding and a happy future. They had met in college, and now both were working in Mayville, a small town that Jerry had grown up in. Joyce was a kindergarten teacher, and Jerry was manager of a grocery store. Against Jerry's wishes, Joyce drove one weekend to a nearby city to attend a bridal shower with some of her women college friends. The party was still going strong at 2:00 A.M., when Joyce thought it was time to go back to her motel in order to return to Mayville early on Sunday. In the parking lot, Joyce was sexually assaulted. She tried to fight off the assailant and suffered a number of bruises and abrasions. After the assault, a passerby called the police and an ambulance. Joyce called Jerry the next day. At first he was angry at the rapist. But the more he thought about it, the more he assigned blame to Joyce: She went to the party against his wishes, and he erroneously speculated that she dressed and acted in such a way as to interest the rapist (especially since Jerry further assumed that she had been intoxicated).

The weeks that followed became increasingly difficult for Jerry and Joyce. Joyce sensed that Jerry was blaming her for being raped. She tried to talk it out with Jerry, but it did not help. Their sexual relationship became practically nil, as Jerry felt his "sexual rights" had been violated, and the few times he made sexual advances he had images of Joyce being attacked by a stranger. They postponed the marriage.

When they first heard about the rape, many townspeople also thought that Joyce had "asked for it" while partying in the big city. Postponement of the marriage was interpreted by the townspeople as evidence for this belief, and they began shunning Joyce. After several months of such treatment, Joyce began to believe that she was at

LIBERALISM VERSUS CONSERVATISM

The two prominent political philosophies in the United States are liberalism and conservatism. The Republican party is considered relatively conservative and the Democratic party is considered relatively liberal. (It should be noted, however, that there are some Democrats who are primarily conservative in ideology and some Republicans who are primarily liberal in ideology.)

Conservatives (derived from the verb "to conserve") tend to resist change. They emphasize tradition and believe that rapid change usually results in more negative than positive consequences.

In economic matters, conservatives feel that government should not interfere with the workings of the marketplace. They encourage the government to support (for example, through tax incentives), rather than regulate, business and industry in society. A free-market economy is thought to be the best way to ensure prosperity and fulfillment of individual needs. Conservatives embrace the old adage that "Government governs best which governs least." They believe that most government activities constitute grave threats to individual liberty and to the smooth functioning of the free market.

Conservatives generally view individuals as autonomous (that is, as self-governing). Regardless of what a person's situation is, or what his or fault and increasingly blamed herself for her predicament. She became despondent and moved back with her parents for refuge.

This story is only one illustration of the tendency in American culture to blame the victim. Others abound. If an adult is unemployed for a long time, often that person is believed to be "lazy" or "unmotivated." Parents who are receiving welfare benefits are erroneously stereotyped as being promiscuous, irresponsible, and lazy. When a marriage breaks up, either the husband or the wife or both are blamed, rather than the relationship being viewed as having deteriorated. When unfortunate circumstances occur (for example, lightning striking someone's home), some people believe it is a punishment for sinful activity. Slapping one's wife is justified by some segments of the population as being a way to "keep her in line" and to "show her who's boss." People living in poverty are often inaccurately viewed as being personally inadequate, incompetent, or lazy or as having a culture that holds them in poverty. The problems of slum housing in inner cities are sometimes traced to the characteristics of "southern rural migrants" not yet "acculturated" to life in the big city. Such blaming of the victim sometimes sadly leads to acceptance by the general public of the original victimization, with few efforts then being made to assist current victims or to prevent victimizations in the future.

But perhaps the saddest feature of victim blaming is that the erroneous explanation often becomes a self-fulfilling prophecy. If a teacher is told that a child is a poor learner, that teacher will interact with the child as if he or she were a slow learner. Unfortunately, the child will eventually come to believe the teacher is correct and learn little. Labeling people as lazy, criminal, immoral, or mentally ill strongly influences the expectations others hold for them and simultaneously influences the victims themselves in their expectations and self-definition.

her problems are, each person is thought to be responsible for his or her own behavior. People are thought to choose whatever they are doing, and they therefore are viewed as responsible for whatever gains or losses result from their choices. People are thought to possess free will, and thus can choose to engage in behaviors such as hard work that help them get ahead or activities such as excessive leisure that contribute to failure (or poverty). Poverty and other personal problems are seen as the result of laziness, irresponsibility, or lack of self-control. Conservatives believe that social welfare programs force hardworking, productive citizens to pay for the consequences of the irresponsible behavior of recipients of social welfare services.

Conservatives generally advocate a residual approach to social welfare programs. They believe that dependency is a result of personal failure and that it is natural for inequality to exist among humans. They assert that the family, the church, and gainful employment should be the primary defenses against dependency. Social welfare should be only a temporary function that is used sparingly; prolonged social welfare assistance will lead recipients to become permanently dependent. Conservatives also believe that charity is a moral virtue and that the "fortunate" are obligated to help the "less fortunate" become productive, contributing citizens in a society. If government funds are provided for health and social welfare services, conservatives advocate that such funding should go to private organizations, which are thought to be more effective and efficient than public agencies in providing services.

Conservatives revere the "traditional" nuclear family and try to devise policies to preserve it. They see the family as a source of strength for individuals and as the primary unit of society. They oppose abortion, sex education in schools, rights for homosexuals, public funding of day-care centers, birth control counseling for minors, and other measures that might undermine parental authority or support alternative family forms such as single parenthood.

In contrast, liberals believe that change is generally good, as it usually brings progress. Moderate change is best. They view society as needing regulation to ensure fair competition among various interests. In particular, a free-market economy is viewed as needing regulation to ensure fairness. Government programs, including social welfare programs, are necessary to help meet basic human needs. Liberals advocate government action to remedy social deficiencies and to improve human welfare. They feel that government regulation and intervention are often required to safeguard human rights, to control the excesses of capitalism, and to provide equal chances for success. They emphasize egalitarianism and the rights of minorities.

Liberals generally adhere to an institutional view of social welfare. They assert that, because modern society has become so fragmented and complex and because traditional institutions (such as the family) have been unable to meet emerging human needs, few individuals can now function without the help of social services (including work training, job placement services, child care, health care, and counseling). Liberals believe that the personal problems encountered by someone are generally due to causes beyond that person's control. Causes are generally sought in the person's environment. For example, a child with a learning disability is thought to be at risk only if he or she is not receiving appropriate educational services to accommodate the disability. In such a situation, liberals would seek to develop educational services to meet the child's learning needs.

Liberals view the family as an evolving institution and therefore are willing to support programs that assist emerging family forms such as single-parent families and same-sex marriages.

DEVELOPMENTAL VIEW OF SOCIAL WELFARE

For years, liberals have criticized the residual approach to social welfare as being incongruent with society's obligation to provide long-term assistance to those who have long-term health, welfare, social, and recreational needs. Conservatives, on the other hand, have been highly critical of the institutional approach. They claim it creates a welfare state with many recipients then deciding to become dependent on the government to meet their health, welfare, social, and recreational needs without seeking to work and without contributing in other ways to the well-being of society. It is clear that conservatives will stop the creation of any major new social program that moves our country in the direction of a welfare society. They have the political power (that is, the necessary legislative votes) to stop the enactment of programs that are "marketed" to society as being consistent with the institutional approach.

Is there a view of social welfare that can garner the support of both liberals and conservatives? Midgley contends that the developmental view (or perspective) offers an alternative approach that appears to appeal to liberals, conservatives, and the general public.[12] He defines this approach as a "process of planned social change designed to promote the well-being of the population as a whole in conjunction with a dynamic process of economic development."[13]

This perspective appeals to liberals because it supports the development and expansion of needed social welfare programs. The perspective appeals to conservatives because it asserts that the development of certain social welfare programs will have a positive impact on the economy. (In the past, conservative politicians have opposed the development of many social welfare programs because they claimed such programs would have a negative impact on economic development.) The general public also would be apt to support the developmental perspective. Many voters oppose welfarism because they believe it causes economic problems (for example, recipients choosing to be on the government dole rather than contributing to society by working). Asserting, and documenting, that certain proposed social welfare programs will directly benefit the economy is attractive to voters.

Midgley and Livermore note that the developmental approach is presently not very well defined.[14] It has its roots in the promotion of the growth of social programs in developing (Third World) countries. Advocates for social welfare programs in developing countries have been successful in getting certain social welfare programs enacted by asserting, and documenting, that such programs will have a beneficial impact on the overall economy of the country. Midgley and Livermore note, "the developmental perspective's global relevance began in the Third World in the years of decolonization after World War II."[15] The developmental approach was later used by the United Nations in its efforts in developing countries to promote the growth of social programs, as the United Nations asserted such programs had the promise of improving the overall economies of these Third World countries.

What are the characteristics of the developmental approach? It advocates social interventions that contribute positively to economic development. It thus promotes harmony between economic and social institutions. The approach regards economic progress as a vital component of social progress. It promotes the active role of the government in economic and social planning. This is in direct opposition to the residual approach, which advocates that the government should seek to minimize its role in the provision of social welfare programs. Finally, the developmental approach focuses on integrating economic and social development for the benefit of all members of society.

The developmental approach can be used in advocating for the expansion of a wide range of social welfare programs. It can be argued that any social program that assists a person in becoming employable contributes to the economic well-being of a society. It can also be argued that any social program that assists a person in making significant contributions to his or her family, or to his or her community, contributes to the economic well-being of a society. Functional families and functional communities are good for businesses; members of functional families tend to be better employees, and businesses want to locate in prosperous communities that have low rates of crime and other social problems.

A few examples will be cited to illustrate how the developmental approach can be used to advocate for the expansion of social welfare programs. It can be argued that the following programs will be beneficial for the economy because they assist unemployed single parents in obtaining employment: job training; quality child-care programs for children of these parents; and adequate health insurance for these parents and their children so that care is provided to keep them healthy, which will facilitate the parents' ability to work. It can be argued that providing mentoring programs and other social services in school systems will help at-risk children stay in school and eventually contribute to society. When they become adults, these individuals are likely to get jobs and contribute to their families and communities. It can be argued that rehabilitative programs in the criminal justice system will help correctional clients become contributing members to society. It can be argued that the following programs can assist individuals to better handle certain issues and thereby increase their likelihood of becoming contributors to the economy and well-being of society: alcohol and other drug abuse treatment programs, domestic violence services, mental health counseling, nutritional programs, eating disorder intervention programs, stress management programs, and grief management programs.

HISTORY OF SOCIAL WELFARE

Early European History

All societies must develop ways to meet the needs of those who are unable to be self-sufficient—the orphaned, the blind, persons with a physical or mental disability, the poor, and the sick. Before the Industrial Revolution, this responsibility was met largely by the family, by the church, and by neighbors. An important value of the Judeo-Christian tradition throughout history—and one that has considerable relevancy for social welfare—is humanitarianism: ascribing a high value to human life and benevolently helping those in need.

With the development of the feudal system in Europe, when a tenant family was unable to meet a relative's basic needs, the feudal lord usually provided whatever was necessary.

The Elizabethan Poor Law

In the Middle Ages, famines, wars, crop failures, pestilence, and the breakdown in the feudal system all contributed to substantial increases in the number of people in need. Former approaches, primarily through the church and the family, were unsuccessful at meeting the needs of many who were unable to be self-sufficient. As a result, many of these individuals were forced to resort to begging. To attempt to solve this social problem, England passed several Poor Laws between the mid-1300s and the mid-1800s. The most significant of these was the Elizabethan Poor Law of 1601, enacted during the reign of Queen Elizabeth I. The fundamental provisions of this Poor Law were incorporated into the laws of the American colonies and have had an important influence on our current approaches to public assistance and other social legislation. (It is interesting to observe that the social problem that these Poor Laws were designed to alleviate was conceptualized not as poverty but, rather, as the ruling class's annoyance with begging.)

The Elizabethan Poor Law established three categories of relief recipients:

1. The able-bodied poor. This group was given low-grade employment, and citizens were prohibited from offering them financial help. Anyone who refused to work was placed in stocks or in jail.

2. The impotent poor. People unable to work composed this group—the elderly, the blind, the deaf, mothers with young children, and those with a physical or mental disability. They were usually placed together in an almshouse (institution). If the impotent poor had a place to live and if it appeared less expensive to maintain them there, they were permitted to live outside the almshouse, where they were granted "outdoor relief," usually "in kind" (food, clothing, and fuel).

3. Dependent children. Children whose parents or grandparents were unable to support them were apprenticed out to other citizens. Boys were taught the trade of their master and had to serve until their 24th birthday. Girls were brought up as domestic servants and were required to remain until they were 21 or married.

This Poor Law did not permit the registration of a person as being in need of charity if his or her parents, spouse, children, or other relatives were able to provide support. Although the law was passed by the English Parliament, the parish (town or local community) was assigned the responsibility of implementing its provisions, with the program expenses to be met by charitable donations and a tax in the parish on lands, houses, and tithes. The Poor Law also stated that the parish's responsibility extended only to those who had legal residence in the parish, which was variously defined as having been born in the parish or having lived in the parish for 3 years. (Residence requirements are still part of current public assistance programs.) The Poor Law of 1601 set the pattern of public relief under governmental responsibility in both Great Britain and the United States for the next 300 years.

Most of the provisions of the Elizabethan Poor Law were incorporated into the social welfare policies of colonial America. Towns were assigned the responsibility of providing for the needy, almshouses were built to house the unemployable, orphaned children were apprenticed out, and a system of legal residency was established to make it clear that towns were not responsible for meeting the needs of destitute strangers. Conditions in almshouses, it should be noted, were unbelievably deplorable. Into almshouses were packed not only the poor but also the sick, the emotionally disturbed, the blind, the alcoholic, and dependent children. Straw and old cots served for beds, there were no sanitary facilities, and the dilapidated buildings were barely heated in winter.

The Industrial Revolution

In the 17th, 18th, and 19th centuries, the Industrial Revolution flourished in Europe and America. A major reason for its growth was technological advances, such as the development of the steam engine. But the revolution was also made possible by the *Protestant ethic* and the *laissez-faire economic view.* These two themes also had important effects on social welfare. The Protestant ethic emphasized *individualism,* the view that one is master of one's own fate. Hard work and self-ambition were highly valued. An overriding goal for human beings set by the Protestant ethic was to acquire material goods. People were largely judged not on the basis of their personalities and other attributes but on how much wealth they had acquired. To be poor was thought to be one's own moral fault.

The laissez-faire economic theory asserted that the economy and society in general would best prosper if businesses and industries were permitted to do whatever they desired to make a profit. Any government regulation of business practices (for example, setting safety standards, passing minimum-wage laws, prohibiting child labor) was discouraged. The Protestant ethic and laissez-faire economics, together, justified such business practices as cutthroat competition, formation of monopolies, deplorable safety and working conditions, and exploitation of the working class through low pay, long hours, and child labor.

The social welfare implications of the Protestant ethic reached their most inhumane level in the theory of *social Darwinism,* which was based on Charles Darwin's theory of evolution. Darwin theorized that higher forms of the life evolved from lower forms by the process of survival of the fittest; he had seen in the animal world a fierce struggle for survival that destroyed the weak, rewarded the strong, and produced evolutionary change. Herbert Spencer extended this theory to humanity: Struggle, destruction, and survival of the fit were thought to be essential to progress in human society as well. The theory stated in its most inhumane form that the strong (the wealthy) survived because they were superior, whereas the weak (the needy) deserved to perish; it would be a mistake to help the weak survive. Although leaving the weak to perish was never advocated on a wide scale, the theory did have a substantial influence in curbing the development of innovative and more humane social welfare programs.

Prior to the Industrial Revolution, there were few communities in Europe or America with a population larger than a few thousand. One of the consequences of the Industrial Revolution was the development of large urban areas close to factories. Because employment opportunities were limited in rural areas, many workers moved to cities. With such movement, family and kinship ties were broken, and those who were unable to adapt faced a loss of community identity, alienation, and social breakdown. In an attempt to meet the needs of people living in urban areas, private social welfare services began to spring up in the 1800s— primarily at the initiation of the clergy and religious groups. (A public social welfare agency receives its funds through tax dollars, whereas a private or voluntary agency generally receives a large part of its funds from charitable contributions.*) Because of the lack of development of

---

*Some private agencies are now contracting with public agencies to receive public funds to provide services to certain clients. Public agencies are established and administered by governmental units, whereas private agencies are established and administered by nongovernmental groups or private citizens.

public social services, private agencies provided most of the funds and services to the needy until the 1930s. In the 1800s, social services and funds were usually provided by upper-middle-class volunteers who combined "charity" with religious admonitions.

Turn of the 20th Century

Around 1880 various segments of the population became aware of the evils of unlimited competition and of abuses by those with economic power. It became clear that a few leaders of industry were becoming very wealthy, whereas the standard of living for the bulk of the population was remaining static and only slightly above the subsistence level. One of the theorists who objected to social Darwinism was Lester Ward, who in *Dynamic Sociology* (1883) drew a sharp distinction between purposeless animal evolution and human evolution.[16] Ward asserted that humans, unlike animals, could and should provide social welfare programs to help the needy and that humans have the capacity for regulation through social and economic controls. Ward declared that such programs and controls would benefit everyone. This new thinking was in direct opposition to social Darwinism and laissez-faire economics. It called on the federal government to take on new functions, to establish legislation to regulate business practices, and to provide social welfare programs. As a result, around 1900 there was an awakening to social needs, with the federal government beginning to place some (although limited) funds into such programs as health, housing, and slum clearance.

In the early 1900s, social welfare became more professionalized. Prior to this time, such services were generally provided by well-meaning but untrained volunteers (do-gooders) from the middle and upper socioeconomic groups. At this time, people with more formalized training were employed in some positions, and there was an increased interest in developing therapeutic skills and methods in counseling clients. In this era, some of our present patterns of specialization in social welfare programs also developed, such as

family services and probation and parole. It was also at this time that the first schools of social work and social welfare were founded in universities.

The Great Depression and the Social Security Act

Before 1930 social services were provided primarily by churches and voluntary organizations, as was financial assistance for people in need. Some cities and some counties had local relief directors who distributed public tax money financed by local governments. In those days, poverty was associated with laziness and immorality. Public relief money was viewed as "pauper aid," and receiving it was a huge social disgrace.

The Roaring Twenties was largely a time of prosperity and festivities. Then, in October 1929, the New York Stock Exchange crashed. Many investors lost their businesses, homes, and life savings. The crash of the stock market was a significant sign that our economy (along with the whole world's economy) was heading for a severe depression.

The number of people who were unemployed rose from 3 million in the spring of 1929 to 15 million in January 1933.[17] More than 20% of workers were jobless in 1933.[18] Many banks closed. Many farmers and business owners went bankrupt.

In 1931 some states began providing unemployment relief to prevent starvation among the jobless and their families. Herbert Hoover, who was president at the time, believed that only private charity should meet the needs of the unemployed. He thought public relief (state and federal money) would demoralize people and make them permanently dependent on the state and federal governments. His attitude was graphically illustrated in December 1930, when he approved a $45 million bill to feed starving livestock in Arkansas but opposed a $25 million bill to feed starving farmers and their families in the same state.[19]

Chapters of the Community Chest and the Red Cross, as well as other volunteer organizations, were unable to meet the demand for financial assistance in the early 1930s. Because so many

Nearly 15 million people were unemployed at the height of the Great Depression. These formerly unemployed workers are selling apples as part of a plan devised by the International Apple Association to help meet the demand for jobs.

people were unemployed, private charity also had trouble raising the funds necessary to help the jobless.

Local and state funds proved inadequate to protect the growing millions of unemployed against hunger, cold, and despair. Many sick people could not pay for, and therefore did not receive, medical care. Children were passed around among neighbors because their parents had no food or were out looking for jobs. The number of suicides increased, as did the incidence of tuberculosis and malnutrition in children. Many middle-class people became penniless, factories lay idle, and stores had few customers.

In 1933, when President Franklin D. Roosevelt took office, 40% of the population in some states was receiving local and state public relief money.[20] Pressure grew for the federal government to bail out the states and counties by helping finance public relief for those living in poverty. Conditions were so desperate that our political leaders became concerned that there might be a Socialist or Communist revolution in this country.

President Roosevelt immediately proposed, and Congress passed, temporary emergency programs to provide paid work for some unemployed workers. For those unable to obtain a job, the federal government provided financial assistance.

The depression of the 1930s brought about profound changes in social welfare. Until that time, the belief in individualism was still widely held—that is, the belief that one is master of one's fate. The depression shattered this myth. It became clear that situations and events beyond individual control can cause deprivation, misery, and poverty. It also became clear that the federal government must play a role in providing financial assistance and social services.

The experience with emergency relief and work programs during the Great Depression demonstrated the need for more permanent federal efforts in dealing with some of the critical problems of unemployment, aging, disability, illness, and dependent children. As a result, in 1935 the Social Security Act was passed, which forms the basis of most of our current public social welfare programs, and federal legislation for the following three major categories of programs was enacted.

SOCIAL INSURANCE

This category was set up with an institutional orientation and provided insurance for unemployment, retirement, or death. It has two main programs: (a) Unemployment Compensation, which provides weekly benefits for a limited time to workers who lose their jobs, and (b) Old Age, Survivors, Disability, and Health Insurance, which provides monthly payments to individuals and their families when a worker retires, becomes disabled, or dies. In everyday conversation, this program is generally referred to as *Social Security.*

PUBLIC ASSISTANCE

This category has many residual aspects. To receive benefits, an individual must undergo a "means test" in which one's assets and expenses are reviewed to determine if there is a financial need. There were four programs under this category, with the titles indicating eligible groups: (a) Aid to the Blind (people of any age whose vision is 20/200 or less with correction), (b) Aid to the Disabled (people between the ages of 18 and 65 who are permanently disabled), (c) Old Age Assistance* (people 65 and older), and (d) Aid to Families with Dependent Children (AFDC) (primarily mothers with children under age 18 and no father in the home). Public assistance programs incorporated several features of the English Poor Laws: There were residence requirements and a means test, some of the aid was "in kind" (such as food), and the benefits were viewed as "charity" rather than aid to which recipients were entitled. Public assistance, particularly the AFDC program, has been frequently criticized and stigmatized by politicians and the general public. An inaccurate public perception is that "welfare" means public assistance *only*. In actuality, public assistance is but one of several hundred social welfare programs. A frequent complaint is that too much money is being spent on public assistance, yet it is generally unknown that five to six times more money is spent annually on social insurance programs than on public assistance! [21]

PUBLIC HEALTH AND WELFARE SERVICES

Whereas the first two categories provided financial benefits, this category established the role of the federal government in providing social services (for example, adoption, foster care, services to children with a disability, protective services, and services to single parents).

Following the enactment of the Social Security Act, public social welfare services became dominant in terms of expenditures, people served, and personnel. The private role shifted from financial aid to certain specialized service areas. One of the roles of private agencies has been to test the value of new services and approaches. If such new services are found to be cost effective and successful in alleviating human problems, public funds are sometimes requested to provide them on a large-scale basis.

The programs established by the Social Security Act have been controversial. Some authorities credit the act with bringing economic stability to our country and helping to bring us out of the worst depression we have ever seen. Other authorities, including fiscal conservatives, view Social Security expenditures as perpetuating poverty by making people dependent on government for their livelihood. It has been claimed for many years that people would rather live it up on welfare than work. It is also claimed that the expenditures are highly inflationary, as they represent a sizable portion of our federal government's budget.

The basic intent of the Social Security Act was to provide a decent standard of living to every American. President Roosevelt believed that financial security (including public assistance) should not be a matter of charity but a matter of justice. He asserted that every individual has a right to a minimum standard of living in a civilized society. He believed that liberty and security are synonymous; without financial security, people will eventually despair and revolt. Therefore, Roosevelt held the conviction that the very existence of a democratic society depended on the health and welfare of its citizens. [22]

From the 1930s to the 1980s, the federal government gradually expanded its role in providing financial assistance and social programs to Americans suffering from social problems.

The Great Society and War on Poverty

A major push for expansion of social welfare programs came in the 1960s, when President Lyndon Johnson declared a War on Poverty and sought to

---

*In January 1974, three programs—Aid to the Blind, Aid to the Disabled, and Old Age Assistance—were combined into one program, Supplemental Security Income (see Chapter 4).

EXHIBIT 1.1

How Welfare Became a Dirty Word

Linda Gordon notes:

> *In the last half-century, the American definition of "welfare" has been reversed. A term that once meant prosperity, good health, good spirits, and social respect now implies poverty, bad health, despondency, and social disrespect. A word used to describe the health of the body politic now evokes images of its disease—slums, depressed single mothers, neglected children, crime, despair.[a]*

How did this reversal of the concept of welfare occur? The term *welfare* could logically apply to hundreds of society's programs that enhance citizens' well-being: pollution control, schools, parks, counseling, recreational programs, regulation of food and drugs, and so on. Yet the general public today views "welfare" as Aid to Families with Dependent Children (AFDC). (The 1996 welfare reform legislation recently abolished AFDC.) For the past three decades, the AFDC program and its recipients were stigmatized.

AFDC was one of the programs enacted by the 1935 Social Security Act. The program was not intended by the writers of that act to be inferior to the other Social Security programs that were created. AFDC was intended to be small in terms of number of recipients and temporary, because the framers believed that the model of the family in which the male was the breadwinner and the female the homemaker would be the standard. AFDC was intended to serve the most deserving of all needy groups—namely, helpless mothers left alone with children by heartless men. In 1935 it was believed that mothers should stay home to raise their children; the vast majority of women were married, and it was considered the obligation of the husband to support the family. Unmarried or abandoned mothers, it was thought, should be

helped by the government to stay at home for the *welfare* (well-being) of their children.

Linda Gordon notes that the stigmatization of the AFDC program first began on a large scale in the 1950s and 1960s. There were three main reasons.

The role of women began to be redefining in the 1950s and 1960s. More women were entering the workforce, and it began to be expected that women would work outside the home. As a consequence, single mothers on AFDC began to be shamed for being on the welfare rolls. Negative terms such as "lazy," "undeserving," and "charity cases" were hurled at them.

Another development that contributed to the stigmatization was the increasing divorce rate, which left more women alone to raise their children. With AFDC rolls expanding, the general public became more critical of using taxpayers' money to support single mothers and their children.

A third development in the 1950s that contributed to the stigmatization was that African American women began to assert that AFDC was a right they were entitled to as citizens, just like the right to vote. The success of this claim increased not only the number of AFDC recipients but also the proportion of African Americans among the recipients. As a consequence, the stigma attached to welfare intensified, strengthened now by racist animosity toward the growing number of welfare recipients among minority groups.

Responding to the public outrage about the AFDC program, President Clinton (a Democrat) and the Republican-controlled Congress abolished AFDC in 1996 and replaced it with the Personal Responsibility and Work Opportunity Reconciliation Act. This program is described later in this chapter and in Chapter 4.

---

[a]Linda Gordon, "How 'Welfare' Became a Dirty Word," *The Chronicle of Higher Education,* Jul. 20, 1994, p. B1.

create what he called a "Great Society." In 1964 Johnson noted in his State of the Union address that one-fifth of our population was living in poverty and that nearly half of all African Americans were poor. Funding for existing social welfare programs was sharply increased, and many new programs were created (such as Head Start, Medicare, and Medicaid*).

The early 1960s was characterized by optimism; there was a feeling that we were on our way to a golden era in which poverty would gradually disappear, racial integration would occur, and other social problems would be smoothly and painlessly solved. The late 1960s was therefore a shock: Martin Luther King, Jr., and Robert Kennedy were assassinated; many of our inner cities were torched and burned to the ground during protests against racial discrimination; there were substantial increases in crime; there were student protests and riots on campuses over the Vietnam War and other issues; racial minorities and poor people organized to demand their piece of the national financial pie; there was a revolution in sexual values and behaviors; and there was a recognition of other social ills such as the drug problem and the need to preserve the environment.

In the social welfare field, the late 1960s brought a renewed interest in changing the environment, or "the system," to better meet the needs of clients (sociological approach) rather than enabling clients to better adapt and adjust to their life situations (the psychological approach). Social action again became an important part of social work, with some social workers becoming active as advocates of clients, community organizers, and political organizers for social reform.

Conservatism in the 1970s and 1980s

In the 1970s, after the end of the Vietnam War, the turmoil of the late 1960s was replaced for several years with an atmosphere of relative calm on both the foreign and domestic fronts. In contrast to the

hope of the 1960s that government programs could cure our social ills, the opposing philosophy emerged that many problems were beyond the capacity of the government to alleviate. Hence, the liberalism of the 1960s, which resulted in the expansion and development of new social programs, was replaced by a more conservative approach in the 1970s and 1980s. Practically no new, large-scale social welfare programs were initiated in the 1970s, 1980s, or early 1990s. Unfortunately, other crises (including Vietnam, Watergate, inflation, recession, the Israeli–Arab conflict, energy crises, political turmoil in Iran, the Iran–Contra affair, the 1991 war against Iraq, political turmoil in Haiti, and the large federal budget deficit) have received more attention in the last 30 years than our ongoing social problems. These social problems include dismal living conditions in the inner cities, the AIDS crisis, homelessness, racial discrimination, increasing crime rates, prison conditions, family violence, the high divorce rate, overpopulation, and the increasing number of people living in poverty.

During President Jimmy Carter's administration (1976–1980), there was increased recognition that the federal government simply did not have the power—no matter how much money it spent—to cure *all* the country's social ills. But instead of a desire for the government to partially allay *many* of these problems, there appears to have been a complete turnaround in philosophy: Many citizens, and many business leaders, began despairing and demanding that government sharply reduce the amount of tax money it was spending on social welfare programs.

In 1980 our domestic economy was in a mess. The rates of both unemployment and inflation were high, and the country had been in a recession for several years. Ronald Reagan was elected president that year and proceeded, as he had promised during his campaign, to make a number of changes to revitalize the economy and to strengthen the military. The following changes were implemented:

■ Taxes were sharply cut for both individuals and corporations. These tax cuts resulted in businesses and consumers having more

---

*Medicare and Medicaid are described in Chapter 15.

money to spend, which stimulated the economy and led to a reduction in the unemployment rate.

■ Military expenditures were sharply increased, which resulted in a strengthening of our armed forces.

■ Expenditures for social programs were sharply cut. This massive cutback was the first large-scale federal reduction in social welfare expenditures in our country's history.

In 1988 George Bush was elected president on a conservative platform, and he continued the social welfare policies of the Reagan administration. Bush believed (as did Reagan) that the federal government is not a solution to social problems but in fact is part of the problem. Reagan and Bush held that federally funded social welfare programs led recipients to become dependent on the government rather than industrious and productive. The Reagan and Bush administrations endorsed an economic program that cut taxes and government spending, eliminated cumbersome federal regulations and red tape that restricted the growth of business and industry, and provided incentives to the private sector for expansion and greater employment. The stated objective was to create a period of prosperity that would "trickle down" to the lowest stratum so that everyone would benefit. The result, however, was that the gap between the rich and the poor widened, with the poor failing to benefit from the improved financial circumstances of the rich.[23] The people who were hurt the most by cutbacks in federally financed social welfare programs were current and former recipients.

What have been the longer-term effects of these cutbacks? Many of our present social problems intensified: The proportion of people living in poverty increased,[24] the income gap between the rich and the poor widened, efforts to reduce racial discrimination slowed, prisons became overcrowded, many of the chronically mentally ill were released from mental hospitals and became homeless without receiving supportive services, the plight of people living in our inner cities worsened, there was an increase in single-parent fam-

ilies, environmental problems (such as acid rain and chemical waste hazards) increased in severity, and the overall number of homeless and hungry skyrocketed.

A Move Toward Liberalism — and Back — in the 1990s

Throughout history the predominant philosophy in our society has swung back and forth like a pendulum between the two poles of liberalism and conservatism. Bill Clinton was elected president in 1992. His views on resolving social problems are consistent with a moderate (middle-of-the-road) to liberal orientation. His liberal proposals included a universal health insurance program for all Americans. (This proposal was extensively debated but eventually defeated by a Republican-controlled Congress.)

The move toward liberalism in the early 1990s was short-lived. In the congressional elections of 1994, the Republicans (most with a conservative orientation) won majority control of both the Senate and the House of Representatives. (This was the first time in 40 years that Republicans held a majority in the House). These Republicans have a conservative political agenda and have been successful in passing legislation that has shifted spending from crime prevention to prison construction, eliminated welfare benefits for unmarried teens who have children, abolished the AFDC program, and cut the capital gains tax (a tax cut that primarily benefits the rich).

The Devolution Revolution

Presently, there is a "devolution revolution" occurring with regard to the provision of human services in our society. The term *devolution revolution* refers to the fact that decisions about the provision of key social welfare programs are being transferred from the federal government to the state level. One of the major programs affected by the devolution revolution is AFDC.

From 1935 to the mid-1990s, the federal government required all states to provide the AFDC program to eligible families. (The program was

Because decisions about key social welfare programs are being transferred from the federal government to the state level, federal programs such as AFDC that primarily benefit low-income mothers are being dismantled.

created by the 1935 Social Security Act.) This was a public assistance program that provided monthly checks primarily to low-income mothers with children under age 18. The precise parameters of eligibility for AFDC varied from state to state. Payments were made for both the parent (or parents) and the children in eligible families. Financing and administration of the AFDC program were shared by federal and state governments. In many states, counties also participated in the financing and administration. In 1996 federal legislation was enacted that is dismantling the AFDC program. The concept of poor families being entitled to health and human services as a basic right is shifting back to the assumption that both having jobs and charity can respond more cheaply to local social problems than public services can. The new legislation (the Personal Responsibility and Work Opportunity Reconciliation Act) calls for the following: (a) Each state sets its own eligibility rules and amounts for financial assistance. The federal government provides block grants to

states to assist in financing the programs that are developed. (b) Recipients of financial benefits receive no more than 2 years of assistance without working, and there is a 5-year lifetime limit of benefits for adults.

In 1935, when the AFDC program was enacted, it was thought best for single mothers to stay at home to raise their children. The 1996 welfare reform legislation asserts that such single mothers (and fathers) have an obligation to work for a living. The safety net for poor families with young children now has some major holes. Clearly, the legislation marks a shift by our society to the residual approach. What will happen to a poor parent who is unable to support her or his children after the time limit on financial benefits ends? A minimum-wage job for the breadwinner(s) in low-income families will not provide enough money to sustain most poor families. Will such families become homeless, turn to crime, or have their children removed from the home by the state? These questions are now confronting our society. The profession of social work is being challenged to confront the devolution revolution and to respond to the needs of those who are falling through the holes in the safety net.

Where Do We Stand Today?

Although many people's perception is that the United States spends more on social welfare than any other country in the world, this is far from accurate. Among industrialized nations, we rank very low in the percentage of gross national product spent on social welfare programs.[25] Sweden, for example, proportionately spends over twice as much as the United States.[26]

The status of social welfare today offers more questions than answers. As indicated in the preceding section, the recent enactment of the 1996 welfare reform legislation raises a number of questions. Here are some additional issues that need to be addressed.

Should some of the cutbacks in federal support for social welfare programs that occurred in the 1980s be restored? What services and programs should be developed to combat the AIDS crisis? How can drug abuse (such as alcohol and cocaine abuse) be more effectively controlled? What new programs should be developed for the homeless? What new services should be provided to the chronically mentally ill, especially those living on the streets of our cities? How can crime be curbed more effectively and the correctional system be made more rehabilitative? What measures should be taken to eliminate racial discrimination? How can we meet the problems of our inner cities?

Should transracial adoptions be encouraged? How should we remedy broken treaties to Native Americans, and what kinds of services need to be developed for Native Americans to alleviate the wide range of social problems they face? Should abortion laws be made more or less restrictive? Should a national health insurance program be established? How can child pornography be prevented? How can we prevent the Social Security system from going bankrupt? How can we curb fraud in Medicaid, Medicare, and other social welfare programs? How can child abuse, sexual abuse, and spousal abuse be curbed? How can we prevent suicides, especially the increasing number among teenagers? Should prostitution be legalized? What should be done about the teenage runaway problem?

Should busing to achieve racial integration be expanded or cut back? Do some affirmative action programs involve reverse discrimination against White males? What programs are needed to prevent rape? How can retirement living be made more meaningful? What measures should be taken to protect the civil rights of gays and lesbians? Should legislation be enacted to curb the sale of handguns? Do we really want to provide the funds and services that are necessary to break the cycle of poverty, or do we still believe that many poor people are undeserving in the sense that they would rather be on welfare than working?

THE FUTURE

The future direction and nature of social services will be determined largely by technological advances. In the past 60 years, the following advances have resulted in dramatic changes in our lifestyles: auto and air travel, nuclear power, television, birth control devices, automation, new electrical appliances, shopping centers, the discovery of penicillin and other wonder drugs, and computers.

The relationship between technological breakthroughs and changes in social welfare programs generally follows this format: Technological advances foster changes in our lifestyles; lifestyle changes affect changes in our future social, financial, health, and recreational needs; and the latter changes largely determine what changes will be demanded in social service programs.

Predicting what technological breakthroughs will occur and how these advances will affect our lifestyles is highly speculative. A number of advances are being predicted: space travel to other planets; computers capable of thinking; chip-enhanced brains to increase intelligence; the end of aging; vaccines that will prevent most forms of cancer; artificial hearts and kidneys; vaccines to prevent HIV infection; and weather and climate control. Because there are more scientists involved in technological research and development now than at any other time in the history of civilization, future technological breakthroughs are likely to occur even more rapidly than in the past. Adjusting psychologically to rapid lifestyle changes is currently a major problem and will continue to be one of the most difficult adjustments people will have to make in future years.

At the same time, environmentalists are predicting that our civilization is in serious danger due to overpopulation, depletion of energy resources, excessive use of toxic chemicals, likelihood of mass famines and starvation, and dramatic declines in the quality of life.

What the future will hold is difficult to predict accurately. The worst mistake, however, is to take the "ostrich head in the sand" approach, in which no effort is made to plan and control the future.

A key concern for social welfare in the future is changes in the American family. When there is family breakdown, social services are generally needed. As the needs of families change, there is a corresponding demand to change social services.

DRAMATIC CHANGES FORESEEN IN THE AMERICAN FAMILY

In viewing the future of the American family, it is helpful to gain a perspective by taking a quick glance at some of the changes that have occurred in the past. Two hundred years ago marriages were primarily arranged by parents, with economic considerations being the most important determinant of who married whom. Divorce was practically unheard of; now one of two marriages ends in divorce or annulment.[27] Two hundred years ago women did not work outside the home, and children were an economic asset; now, about 60% of married women work outside the home, and children are a financial liability.[28] Since colonial days, the family has lost (or there has been a sharp decline in) a number of functions: educational, economic production, religious, protective, and recreational.[29] Today the two main functions that remain are the affectional or companionship and the child-rearing functions.

In our fast-paced society, the family is likely to change even more dramatically in the future. As in the past, the family will be affected significantly by technological changes. Labor-saving devices in the home (for example, electrical appliances) have been and still are an important factor in making it possible for both spouses to work outside the home. Birth control devices have undoubtedly been an important factor in leading to an increase in premarital sexual relationships and in extramarital affairs.

The increased use of abortions has been a factor in sharply reducing the number of children available for adoption. Many adoption agencies have suspended taking applications from couples desiring healthy White infants. An ethically questionable business has developed in which women are paid to deliver and give up their babies for adoption to meet the demands of infertile couples who want a child. Women willing to bypass the normal adoption channels may sell an unwanted infant for as much as $20,000.[30]

In the future, the American family is likely to be substantially affected by technological break-throughs in biology and medicine. Let's look at a few developments in these areas—developments that are as alarming as they are intriguing.

Biomedical Technology

ARTIFICIAL INSEMINATION

Thousands of babies are born annually in the United States through the process of artificial insemination, with the usage expected to continue to increase in the future.[31] The process of artificial insemination has long been used with livestock because it eliminates all the problems associated with breeding. A breeder can transport a prized animal's frozen sperm across the world and raise a whole new herd of animals almost effortlessly.

Human sperm can be frozen for long periods of time (the length of time has not been determined; it is generally acknowledged that 5 years would be safe with close to 100% assurance). The sperm can then be thawed and used to impregnate a female. This new technology has led to the development of a unique new institution, the sperm bank. Sperm banks are usually private institutions. They collect and maintain sperm, which is withdrawn at some later date to impregnate (with a physician's assistance) a woman.

The sperm used in artificial insemination may be the husband's (called AIH, for artificial insemination—husband). There may be several reasons for using AIH. It is possible to pool several ejaculations from a man with a low sperm count and to inject them simultaneously into the vaginal canal of his spouse, thus vastly increasing the chance of pregnancy. AIH may also be used for family planning purposes; for example, a man might deposit his sperm in the bank, then undergo a vasectomy, and later withdraw the sperm to have children. High-risk jobs (such as those with a danger of being exposed to radioactive material) might prompt a man to make a deposit in case of sterility or untimely death.

A second type of artificial insemination is called AID (artificial insemination—donor), in which the donor of the sperm is someone other than the husband. AID has been used for several decades to circumvent male infertility. It is also used when it is known that the husband is a

CASE EXAMPLE 1.3   **Unethical Use of Technology**

Dr. Cecil Jacobson was well known for having introduced amniocentesis in the United States for diagnosing defects in unborn babies. For many years he operated an infertility clinic in Virginia. In March 1992, a federal jury found him guilty of 52 counts of fraud and perjury. He was charged with defrauding patients by artificially inseminating them with his own sperm while claiming to use other donors. He also was charged with tricking patients into believing they were pregnant when they were not. The prosecution alleged that Jacobson may have fathered as many as 75 children through artificial insemination. He was sentenced to 5 years in prison, ordered to pay $116,805 in fines and restitution, and required to serve 3 years probation after release from prison. This case example illustrates that the new biomedical reproductive technology can be used unscrupulously.

Dr. Cecil Jacobson

carrier of a genetic disease (such as hemophilia). In recent years an increasing number of single women who want a child but do not (at least for the near future) want a husband are requesting the services of a sperm bank. The woman specifies the general genetic characteristics she wants from the father, and the bank then tries to match those requests from the information known about donors.

A third type of artificial insemination is of recent origin and has received considerable publicity. Some married couples, in which the wife is infertile, have contracted for another woman to be artificially inseminated with the husband's sperm. Under the terms of the contract, this "surrogate mother" is paid and is expected to give the infant to the married couple shortly after birth. (Surrogate motherhood is the topic of the next section.)

A number of ethical, social, and legal questions have been raised about artificial insemination. There are objections from religious leaders that this practice is wrong—that God did not mean for people to reproduce in this way. In

the case of AID, there are certain psychological stresses placed on husbands and on marriages; the procedure emphasizes the husband's infertility and involves having a baby that he has not fathered. On a broader scale, artificial insemination raises other questions: What are the purposes of marriage and of sex? What will happen to male–female relationships if we do not even have to see each other to reproduce?

Some unusual court cases point to the need for new laws to resolve the questions that are arising. For instance, consider the case of Mr. and Mrs. John M. Prutting. Mr. Prutting was determined by doctors to be sterile as a result of radiation exposure received at work. Without her husband's knowledge, Mrs. Prutting was inseminated. After the birth of the baby, he sued her for divorce on the grounds of adultery.[32]

In another case, a wife was artificially inseminated with the husband's consent by AID. The couple later divorced. When the husband requested child visitation privileges, his wife took him to court on the grounds that he was not the father and thus had no such right. In New York, he won; but she moved to Oklahoma, where the decision was reversed.[33]

Finally, there was a reported case of an engaged couple whose mothers were discovered to have had the same artificial insemination donor. The couple were thus biologically half-brother and half-sister. The marriage would have been incestuous and was therefore canceled.[34]

There are other possible legal implications. What happens if the AIH sperm at a bank is not paid for? Would it become the property of the bank? Could it be auctioned off? If a woman was artificially inseminated by a donor and the child was later found to have genetic defects, could the parents bring suit against the physician, the donor, or the sperm bank? Does the child have a right to know the identity of the donor father?

Sperm banks can also be used in genetic engineering. In the spring of 1980, it was disclosed that Robert Graham had set up an exclusive sperm bank to produce exceptionally bright children. Graham stated that at lease five Nobel prize winners had donated sperm. A number of women have already given birth through the services of this bank.[35] This approach raises questions about whether reproductive technology should be used to produce "superior" children, and what characteristics should be defined as "superior."

SURROGATE MOTHERHOOD

Thousands of married couples who want children but are unable to reproduce because the wife is infertile have turned to surrogate motherhood. With this type of motherhood, a surrogate gives birth to a baby conceived by artificial insemination using the husband's sperm. (Often the surrogate mother is paid for her services.) At birth the surrogate mother terminates her parental rights, and the child is then legally adopted by the sperm donor and his wife.

Couples using the services of a surrogate mother are generally delighted with this medical technique and believe it is a highly desirable solution to their personal difficulty of being unable to bear children. However, other groups assert that surrogate motherhood raises a number of moral, legal, and personal issues.

EXHIBIT 1.2

Mr. Mom: Men Can Give Birth

Scientists say that the technology now exists to enable men to give birth! Male pregnancy would involve fertilizing a donated egg with sperm outside the body. The embryo would then be implanted into the bowel area, where it could attach itself to a major organ, such as a kidney or the wall of the large intestine. In addition, to achieve pregnancy, men would have to receive hormone treatment to stimulate changes that occur naturally in women during pregnancy. Because the embryo creates the placenta, the embryo theoretically would receive sufficient nourishment. The baby would be delivered by cesarean section.

Any attempt at male pregnancy would carry risks (perhaps some as-yet-unknown risks) for both the man and the embryo. Will some men try it? If people risk their lives climbing Mt. Everest, someone is likely to try this.

Source: "Mr. Mom," *Wisconsin State Journal*, May 9, 1986, sec. 1, p. 2.

Many theologians and religious leaders firmly believe that God intended conception to occur only among married couples through sexual intercourse. These religious leaders view surrogate motherhood as ethically wrong because the surrogate mother is not married to the sperm donor and because artificial insemination is viewed as "unnatural." Some religious leaders also assert that it is morally despicable for a surrogate mother to accept a fee (often between $5000 and $10,000). They maintain that procreation is a blessing from God and should not be commercialized.

Surrogate motherhood also raises complicated legal questions that have considerable social consequences. For example, surrogate mothers usually sign a nonbinding contract stipulating that the mother will give up the child for adoption at birth. What if the surrogate mother changes her mind shortly before birth and decides to keep the baby? Women who have been surrogate mothers usually report that they become emotionally attached to the child during pregnancy.[36]

Most surrogate mothers to date are married and already have children. A number of issues are likely to arise. How does the husband of a surrogate mother feel about his wife being pregnant by another man's sperm? How does such a married couple explain to their children that their half-brother or half-sister will be given up for adoption to another family? How does such a married couple explain what they are doing to relatives, neighbors, and the surrounding community? If the child is born with a severe mental or physical disability, who will care for the child and pay for the expenses? Will it be the surrogate mother and her husband, the contracting adoptive couple, or society?

In 1983 a surrogate mother gave birth in Michigan to a baby who was born with microcephaly, a condition in which the head is smaller than normal and mental retardation is likely. At first, neither the surrogate mother nor the contracting adoptive couple wanted to care for the child. The adoptive couple refused to pay the $10,000 fee to the surrogate mother. A legal battle ensued. Blood tests were eventually taken that indicated the probable father was not the contracting adoptive father but rather the husband of the surrogate mother. Following the blood tests, the surrogate mother and her husband assumed the care of the child. (This example illustrates another problem with the surrogate motherhood approach: If the surrogate mother engages in sexual intercourse with her partner/husband at about the same time that artificial insemination occurs, it becomes difficult to determine who is actually the genetic father of the child that is conceived.)

In 1986 Mary Beth Whitehead was a surrogate mother who gave birth to a child. She refused to give up the baby for adoption by the genetic father and his wife, even though she had signed a $10,000 contract in which she agreed to give up the child. The genetic father, William Stern, took the case to court, demanding that Whitehead honor the contract she had signed. Whitehead claimed she was the mother of the child and therefore had maternal rights to the child. The

case received national attention. In April 1987, in the nation's first judicial ruling on a disputed surrogate contract, the judge ruled that the contract was valid. Just as men have a constitutional right to sell their sperm, women can decide what to do with their wombs.[37] Whitehead appealed this decision to the New Jersey State Supreme Court. In 1988 this court ruled that the contract between Whitehead and the Sterns was invalid because it involved the sale of a mother's right to her child, which violates state laws prohibiting child selling. This decision voided the adoption of the baby by Mrs. Stern; Mr. Stern was given custody, and Whitehead was granted visitation rights. Whether this decision will become the legal guideline for disputed surrogate contracts will be determined by future court decisions about surrogate contracts. At the time of this writing, the legal issues of who will be recognized as "the parents" in disputed surrogate contract cases have not been resolved by the courts.

TEST-TUBE BABIES

In England, on July 24, 1978, Mrs. Lesley Brown gave birth to the first "test-tube baby." An egg taken from her reproductive system had been externally artificially impregnated using AIH and then implanted in her uterus to complete the normal process of pregnancy. The technique, called embryo transfer, was developed for women whose fallopian tubes are so damaged that the fertilized egg cannot pass through the tubes to the womb as is necessary for it to develop and grow until birth. Following the announcement of this birth, there was a surge of applications from thousands of childless couples asking fertility experts for similar implants.[38]

Another breakthrough in this area occurred in 1984, when an egg donated by one woman was fertilized and then implanted in another woman. Australian researchers in January 1984 reported the first successful birth resulting from a procedure in which an embryo was externally conceived and then implanted in the uterus of a surrogate.[39] This type of surrogate motherhood is a modern-day twist on the wet nurse (a woman who cares for and breast-feeds a child not her own) of earlier times. An unusual application of

CASE EXAMPLE 1.4   Embryo Case Gains International Attention

A South American–born couple, Elsa and Mario Rios, amassed a fortune of several million dollars in real estate in Los Angeles. In 1981 they enrolled in a "test-tube baby" program at Queen Victoria Medical Center in Melbourne, Australia, after their young daughter died. Several eggs were removed from Mrs. Rios and fertilized by her husband's sperm, which had been collected in a laboratory container. One of the fertilized eggs was implanted in Mrs. Rio's womb, but she had a miscarriage 10 days later. The two remaining embryos were frozen so that doctors could try implantation at a later time.

On April 2, 1983, the couple was killed in the crash of a private plane in Chile. Because doctors have successfully thawed and implanted frozen embryos (which have resulted in births), a number of social and legal questions arise:

■ Should the embryos be implanted in the womb of a surrogate mother in the hope that they will develop to delivery?

■ Are the embryos legal heirs to the multimillion-dollar estate?

■ Does life legally begin at conception? If a surrogate mother carries the embryo to birth, is she legally the mother, and is she entitled to some of the inheritance?

■ Do embryos conceived outside the womb have rights? If so, what rights? Should these rights be the same as those accorded born humans? (An Australian court ruled in 1987 that the embryos must be thawed and carried to term if a volunteer surrogate could be found. However, the offspring will not be viewed as legally entitled to inherit their biological parents' estate.)

This case highlights how the rapid advancement of *in vitro* fertilization (fertilization outside the human body) has outstripped attitudes and laws.

Sources: "Embryo Case Opens New Debate," *Wisconsin State Journal,* June 19, 1984, pp. 1–2; Stephen Budiansky, "The New Rules of Reproduction," *U.S. News & World Report,* Apr. 18, 1988, pp. 66–67.

---

this new technology occurred in South Africa in 1987, when a grandmother, Pat Anthony, gave birth to her own grandchildren. The daughter was infertile, so her eggs (which had been fertilized in a lab) were implanted into Ms. Anthony. Several months later, Ms. Anthony gave birth to triplets.[40]

This type of surrogate motherhood differs from the earlier version in which the surrogate mother contributes half of the genetic characteristics through the use of her egg. Here the surrogate contributes neither her own egg nor any of the genetic characteristics of the child.

Surrogate pregnancies can, in one respect, be seen as the final step in the biological liberation of women. Like men, women can "sire" children without the responsibility of pregnancy and childbirth.

However, surrogate pregnancies promise to create a legal nightmare. Do the genetic mother and father have any binding legal rights? Can the genetic parents place reasonable restrictions on health, medical care, and diet during the pregnancy? Can the genetic parents require the surrogate mother not to smoke or drink? Could the ge-

<table>
<tr><td>

CASE EXAMPLE 1.5

</td><td>

Redefining Motherhood

</td></tr>
</table>

In August 1990, surrogate mother Anna Johnson filed legal papers seeking parental rights to a child created from the sperm and egg of Mark and Crispina Calvert in California. Ms. Johnson gave birth to the child under a $10,000 surrogacy contract. She was the first surrogate mother to seek custody of a child not genetically related to her. In October 1990, the judge handling the case ruled that Ms. Johnson had no parental rights under California law. The judge assigned permanent custody of the child to the genetic parents. If the judge's ruling stands, it could lead to a new definition of motherhood—one in which genetics is the primary criterion for determining parentage when a surrogate carries a child genetically unrelated to her. (At the time of this writing, court decisions have tended to disagree with one another as to who should be recognized as "the parents.")

Anna Johnson

Source: From Susan Peterson and Susan Kelleher, "Surrogate's Loss Could Redefine Motherhood," *Wisconsin State Journal,* Oct. 23, 1990, p. 4A.

netic parents require the surrogate to abort? Could the surrogate abort without the genetic parents' consent? Whose child is it if both the genetic mother and the surrogate mother want to be recognized as the legal mother after the child is born? Will low-income women tend to serve as "holding tanks" for upper-class women's children? Legal experts see far-reaching changes in family law, inheritance, and the concept of legitimacy if laboratory fertilization and child-rearing by surrogate mothers become accepted practices.

Human embryo transplants, when combined with principles of genetic selection, allow people who want "superhuman" children to select embryos in which the resultant infant has a high probability of being free of genetic defects. The technology also allows parents to choose, with a high probability of success, the genetic character-

istics they desire—such as the child's sex, color of eyes and hair, skin color, probable height, probable muscular capabilities, and probable IQ. A superhuman embryo can be formed by combining the sperm and egg of a male and female who are thought to have the desired genetic characteristics.

This breakthrough will raise a number of personal and ethical questions. Couples desiring children may be faced with the decision of having a child through natural conception or of preselecting superhuman genetic characteristics through embryo transplants. Another question that will arise is whether our society will attempt to use this new technology to control human evolutionary development. If the answer is affirmative, decisions will need to be made about which genetic characteristics should be considered "desirable," and questions will arise about who should have the authority to make such decisions. Although our country may not want to control human evolutionary development in this manner, will we not feel it necessary to do so if a rival nation begins a massive evolutionary program? In addition, will parents have the same or somewhat different feelings toward children who result from embryo transplants compared to children who result from natural conception?

GENETIC SCREENING

Practically all states now require mandatory genetic screening programs for various disorders. There are about 2000 human disorders caused by defective genes, and it is estimated that each of us carries two or three of them.[41] Mass genetic screening could eliminate some of these disorders. One screening approach that is increasingly being used with pregnant women is amniocentesis, which is the surgical insertion of a hollow needle through the abdominal wall and uterus of a pregnant female to obtain amniotic fluid for the determination of chromosomal abnormality. More and more pregnant women are being pressured to terminate the pregnancy of a high-risk or proven genetically inferior fetus. In addition, some genetic disorders can be corrected if diagnosed in time.

Genetic screening programs raise serious questions. Which fetuses should be allowed to continue to grow and which should be aborted? Who shall be allowed to have children? Who shall make such decisions? Is this a direction our country ought to take?

Genetic screening during pregnancy can be used to detect a wide variety of inherited disorders. For example, Huntington's chorea is an inherited disease whose principal symptoms are involuntary movements—either rapid, forcible, and jerky or smooth and sinuous. This disorder is often associated with loss of intellectual abilities. Its onset is usually evidenced during middle age. If a fetus is diagnosed as having the gene for this disorder, which usually results in serious mental and physical deterioration in midlife, the pregnant woman and her partner would then be faced with the heart-wrenching decision of whether it would be best to terminate the pregnancy.

The eugenics (scientific breeding) movement was proposed late in the 19th century and embraced by many scientists and government officials. Similar to today, eugenics was designed to improve humanity or individual races by encouraging procreation by those deemed "most desirable" and discouraging it in those judged "deficient." The movement fell into disfavor for a while when Adolf Hitler used it to justify the Holocaust, in which millions of Jews, Gypsies, homosexuals, persons with a cognitive disability, and others were exterminated. Are we headed in a similar direction again?

CLONING

This term refers to the process whereby a new organism is reproduced from the nucleus of a single cell. The resultant new organism has the same genetic characteristics of the organism that contributes the nucleus. In effect, it is now possible to make biological copies of humans from a single cell. Biologically, each cell is a blueprint containing all the genetic code information for the design of the organism. Cloning has already been used to reproduce frogs, mice, cattle, sheep, and other animals.[42]

One type of cloning amounts to a nuclear transplant. The nucleus of an unfertilized egg is destroyed and removed. The egg is then injected with the nucleus of a body cell by one means or another. It should then start to take orders from the new nucleus, begin to reproduce cells, and eventually manufacture a baby with the same genetic features as the donor. The embryo would need a place to develop into a baby—either an artificial womb or a woman willing to supply her own. (The technology for a complete artificial womb is not yet in sight.) The resultant clone would start life with a genetic endowment identical to that of the donor, although learning experiences might alter physical development and personality. The possibilities are as fantastic as they are repulsive. With a quarter-inch piece of skin, one could produce 1000 genetic copies of any noted scientist or of anyone else! Imagine a professional basketball team composed of two Shaquille O'Neals and three Michael Jordans!

In 1993 a university researcher in the state of Washington cloned human embryos using a technique that already was widely used to clone animal embryos. The process involves taking a single human embryo and splitting it into identical twins.[43] Because human embryos can be frozen and gestated at a later date, it is now possible for parents to have a child and then, years later, use a frozen cloned embryo to give birth to an identical twin. It is also possible for parents to save identical copies of embryos so that, if a child ever needed an organ transplant, the mother could give birth to the child's identical twin, who would be a perfect match for organ donation.

In 1998 Dr. Richard Seed (a physicist in Chicago) announced that he was initiating a program to clone humans using the same procedures that were used to clone Dolly, a sheep (see Exhibit 1.3). Dr. Seed stated that human cloning will help infertile couples and spur genetic advances that could lead to the cure for diseases such as cancer.

Cloning could, among other things, be used to resolve the ancient controversy of heredity versus environment. But there are grave dangers and undreamed-of complications. What is to prevent the Adolf Hitlers from making copies of themselves? Will cloning fuel the population explosion? What legal rights will clones be accorded (regarding inheritance, for example)? Will religions recognize clones as having a "soul"? Who will decide which individuals can make clones of themselves? Couples may face the choice of having children naturally or raising children who are copies of themselves.

BREAKING THE GENETIC CODE

Biochemical genetics is the discipline that studies the mechanisms whereby genes control the development and maintenance of the organism. Current research focuses on understanding more precisely the roles of DNA (deoxyribonucleic acid) and messenger RNA (ribonucleic acid) in affecting the growth and maintenance of humans. When genes, DNA, and RNA are more fully understood, it may become possible to keep people alive, young, and healthy almost indefinitely. It is predicted that aging will be controlled, and any medi-

EXHIBIT 1.3

Clones: Dolly (a Sheep) and Gene (a Calf)

Early in 1997, scientists in Scotland announced they had cloned Dolly, a sheep. In August 1997, scientists in Windsor, Wisconsin, announced they had cloned Gene, a Holstein calf. The process used to make Gene will be briefly described.

Gene was the result of cloning a stem cell from a calf fetus. Stem cells are "blank slates" that have not yet specialized their function. (Examples of specialized cells are liver cells and muscle cells.) Researchers took the nucleus of a cell from the fetus of a calf and inserted the nucleus into a stem cell from a cow in which the genetic material had been removed. The new cell grew into an embryo and was implanted into a cow where it grew into Gene. The process used by ABS Global, Inc., in Wisconsin allows for an *infinite* number of copies of a clone to be produced. ABS Global, Inc., indicated that the technique will allow for fast, reliable duplication of cattle that produce impressive amounts of either beef or milk.

Can the same technique be used to clone a human? Probably.

Source: Rick Barret, "Calf Cloning May Lead to Food, Drug Advances," *Wisconsin State Journal*, Aug. 8, 1997, p. 1A.

cal condition (for example, an allergy, obesity, cancer, arthritic pain) will be relatively easy to treat and eradicate. Such possibilities stagger the imagination.

In January 1989, the National Institutes of Health launched a project to map the *human genome*—that is, to identify and list in order all of the genome's (the full set of chromosomes that carries all of the inherited traits of an organism) approximately 3 billion base pairs. Once completed, this map may permit scientists to predict an individual's vulnerability to genetic diseases, to treat genetically caused diseases, and possibly

EXHIBIT 1.4

Will Fetal Tissue Be Used for Medical Treatments?

Pioneering surgery has demonstrated that fetal tissue transplants can be used successfully to replace damaged nerve cells in victims of Parkinson's disease. Parkinson's disease is a neurological disorder that causes severe shaking and eventually death. Transplants of insulin-producing cells from fetuses also show promise in treating diabetes as well.

Would some women seek to abort a fetus so that its tissue could be used for such medical purposes? In January 1988, a woman appeared on Ted Koppel's *Nightline* television show and declared that she wanted to get pregnant for the sole purpose of aborting the fetus and using its tissue to treat her Parkinson's disease–stricken father.

Budiansky reported a case of a woman seeking to conceive in order to abort the fetus, whose tissue could then be used to treat her own diabetes.[a]

Many people would find this use of reproductive technology to be horrifying. Yet most states have no legal means to stop such activities—or even to prohibit the sale of fetal tissue.

---

[a]Stephen Budiansky, "The New Rules of Reproduction," *U.S. News & World Report,* Apr. 18, 1988, pp. 66–67.

---

to "enhance" a person's genetic potential through the introduction of gene modifications.[44]

Scientists have already discovered the genes that cause a variety of illnesses, such as cystic fibrosis, and demonstrated that gene therapy can be used to correct the underlying defect.[45] The approach uses genetically engineered cold viruses to ferry healthy genes into the body. (Cystic fibrosis results from a mutation in the gene that produces a protein called cystic fibrosis transmembrane conductive regulator. When the protein is missing, thick mucus builds up in the lungs, causing lung damage and eventually death, often by age 30.)

With this potential to break the genetic code to keep people alive and healthy indefinitely, we will be faced with many legal and ethical issues. Perhaps the most crucial issues will be who will live and who will die and who will be permitted to have children. A fountain of youth may occur within our lifetime.

New Family Forms

As we've seen, technology has had profound effects on the family. Now we'll look at some changes in the social structure of our society that are also causing us to redefine our notion of what a family is.

CHILDLESS COUPLES

Traditionally, our society has fostered the perception that there is something wrong with a couple who decides not to have children. Parenthood is regarded legally and religiously as one of the central components of a marriage. In some states, deceiving one's spouse before marriage about the desire to remain childless is grounds for an annulment. Perhaps in the future this myth of procreation will be shattered by the concern about overpopulation and by the high cost of raising children; the average cost of raising a child from birth to age 18 is estimated to be $161,000 in low-income families, $225,000 in middle-income families, and $315,000 in upper-income families.[46]

POSTPONEMENT OF PARENTHOOD UNTIL MIDDLE AGE OR LATER

Biological innovations, such as embryo transfers, are now making it possible for women in their fifties and even their sixties to give birth. As a result, couples have more leeway in deciding at what age they wish to raise children. Young couples today are often torn in their time commitments between their children and their careers. In our society, most couples now have children at the busiest time of their lives. Deferring raising children until later in life provides substantial activity and meaning to later adulthood. A major question, of course, is whether such a family pattern will lead to an increase in the number of orphans, as older parents have a higher death rate than younger parents. (An increase in the number of orphans would significantly impact adoption and foster-care services.) Additional questions are whether having older parents would lead to even more gaps in values between the older parents and their young children and whether the older parents would have sufficient energy to keep up with their young children.

PROFESSIONAL PARENTS

Alvin Toffler predicted that our society will develop a system of professional, trained, and licensed parents to whom a number of natural parents (bioparents) will turn to raise their children.[47] The natural parents would, of course, be permitted frequent visits, telephone contacts, and time to care for the children whenever they desire. Toffler stated: "Even now millions of parents, given the opportunity, would happily relinquish their parental responsibilities—and not necessarily through irresponsibility or lack of love. Harried, frenzied, up against the wall, they have come to see themselves as inadequate to the tasks."[48] The high rates of child abuse, child neglect, and teenage runaways seem to bear out the assertion that in a large number of families the parent–child relationship is more dissatisfying than satisfying. Many parents already hire part-time professional parents in the form of nannies and day-care center workers.

In our society, there is currently a belief system that bioparents should care for their children, even if they find the responsibility unrewarding. Only a tiny fraction of bioparents currently terminate their parental rights. Why? Could it be that many parents who have an unsatisfying relationship with their children are reluctant to give up their parenting responsibilities because of the stigma that would be attached? Two hundred years ago, divorces were rare mainly because of a similar stigma. Now, with increased acceptance of divorce, one of two marriages is being terminated. Is it not also feasible that a number of parents who cannot choose the characteristics of their children may also find the relationships with some of their children to be more dissatisfying than satisfying? The point is reinforced when it is remembered that a number of pregnancies are unplanned *and* unwanted.

SERIAL AND CONTRACT MARRIAGES

Culturally, religiously, and legally speaking, marriages are still expected to be permanent (that is, for a lifetime). Such a view implies that the two partners made the right decision when they married, that their personalities and abilities complement each other, and that their personalities and interests will develop in tandem for the rest of their lives. All of these suppositions (along with the concept of permanency) are being called into question, however.

With the high rates of divorce and remarriage, a number of sociologists have pointed out that a small proportion of our population is entering (perhaps unintentionally) into serial marriages— that is, a pattern of successive, temporary marriages.[49] Serial marriages among celebrities have been widely publicized for a number of years. Viewing marriage as temporary in nature may help reduce some of the embarrassment and pain still associated with divorce and perhaps result in an increase in the number of unhappily married people who will seek a divorce. Divorce per se is neither good nor bad; if both partners find that their lives are happier and more satisfying following legal termination, the end result may be viewed as desirable.

The growing divorce rate has resulted in the development of extensive services involving premarital counseling, marriage counseling, divorce counseling, single-parent services and programs, and remarriage counseling for spouses and the children involved. If marriage is increasingly viewed as temporary in nature, divorce may become even more frequent and result in an expansion of related social services.

Several sociologists have proposed that the concept of marriage as temporary be legally institutionalized through a contract marriage. For example, a couple would be legally married for a 2-year period, and (only in marriages where there are no children) the marriage would automatically be terminated unless they filed legal papers for a continuation.[50] A closely related type of contract is the prenuptial agreement in which a couple prior to marriage specify how their financial assets will be divided if they divorce. (Prenuptial agreements have been criticized as a factor in psychologically setting up an expectation that a divorce is apt to occur.)

Another arrangement embodying the temporary concept is "trial marriage," which is increasingly being tested out by young people. They live together on a day-by-day basis and share expenses. Closely related—and perhaps more common—is the arrangement in which the two maintain separate addresses and domiciles but for several days a month actually live together. (Perhaps this latter form is more accurately described as a "serial honeymoon" than a "trial marriage.") Acceptance of trial marriage is currently being advocated by some religious philosophers, and many states no longer define cohabitation as illegal.

Increasingly, courts are ruling that cohabiting couples who dissolve their living arrangements have certain legal obligations to each other quite similar to the obligations of a married couple.

OPEN MARRIAGES

O'Neill and O'Neill contrast traditional marriages with "open marriages," of which they are advocates.[51] A traditional or "closed" marriage, the O'Neills assert, embodies concepts such as (a) possession or ownership of mate; (b) denial or stifling of self; (c) playing the "couples game" by doing everything together during leisure time; (d) the husband being dominant and out in the world and the wife being domestic and passive and staying at home with the children; and (e) absolute fidelity. An open marriage, in contrast, offers freedom to pursue individual interests, flexible roles in meeting financial responsibilities, shared domestic tasks, and expansion and growth through openness. Such a marriage is based on communication, trust, and respect, and it is expected that one partner's growth will facilitate the other partner's development.

Marriage counselors increasingly report that couples have serious interaction difficulties because one spouse has a traditional orientation whereas the other has an open-marriage orientation. The feminist movement and the changing roles of women have brought the conflict between open and closed marriages into public awareness. Marriage counselors now see large numbers of couples in which the wife wants a career, her own identity, and a sharing of domestic responsibilities, but the husband, traditionally oriented, wants his wife to stay home and take care of domestic tasks.

GROUP MARRIAGES

Group marriage provides insurance against isolation. In the 1960s and 1970s, communes of young people flourished. In the later 1970s and in the 1980s, most communes disbanded. The goals, as well as the structure, of these communes varied widely, involving diverse social, political, religious, sexual, or recreational objectives.

Interestingly, geriatric communes (which have many of the characteristics and obligations of group marriages) are being advocated by a number of sociologists.[52] Such arrangements may be a solution to a number of social problems of the elderly. They may provide companionship, new meaning, and interest to the participants' lives, as well as an arrangement in which elderly people with reduced functioning capacities can be of mutual assistance to one another. The elderly can thereby band together, pool resources, hire nursing or domestic help if needed, and feel that "life begins at 60." In nursing homes, retirement communities, group homes for the elderly, and assisted-living residences, some of the elderly are presently developing relationships that are similar to group marriage.

HOMOSEXUAL MARRIAGES AND ADOPTIONS

Gay liberation groups seek to inform the public about the "naturalness" of homosexual expression and attempt to change current legislation that defines homosexual behavior between consenting adults as illegal. England has already rewritten its statutes: Homosexual relations between consenting adults in that country are no longer considered a crime. A number of marriages between homosexuals have taken place in churches in the United States, in Europe, and in other countries. (It should be noted, however, that no state in America yet recognizes homosexual marriages as legal.)

Adoption agencies and the courts are now facing decisions about whether to allow homosexual couples to adopt children. Single people are already being permitted by some agencies and courts to adopt children, so the argument that a child needs both a male and a female figure in the family is diluted.

TRANSRACIAL ADOPTIONS

Asian and Native American children have been adopted by White parents for more than four decades.[53] About 35 years ago, some White couples began adopting African American children. A number of questions have arisen about the desirability of placing African American children in White adoptive homes. To answer some of these questions, I conducted a study comparing the satisfactions derived and problems encountered between transracial adoptive parents and inracial adoptive parents.[54] Transracial adoptions were found to be as satisfying as inracial adoptions. In addition, transracial adoptive children were found to have been accepted by relatives, friends, neighbors, and the general community following placement. The transracial adoptive parents reported that substantially fewer problems had arisen due to the race of the child than even they anticipated before the adoption. They also indicated that they had parental feelings that the child was really their own. They reported becoming "color-blind" following placement—that is, they came to see the child not as African American but as a member of their family.

Unfortunately, none of the children in the study was older than 6. Some observers, a number of whom are African American, have raised questions about whether Black children reared by White parents will experience serious identity problems as they grow older. For example, will they experience difficulty in deciding which race to identify with, in learning how to cope with racial discrimination due to being raised in a White home, and in interacting with both Whites and Blacks due to a (speculated) confused sense of who they are? On the other hand, advocates of transracial adoption respond by asserting that the parent–child relationship is more crucial to identity formation than the racial composition of the family members. The question, of course, is critical, especially because there are a large number of homeless African American children and a shortage of African American adoptive parents.

One organization that has been strongly opposed to the adoptive placement of African American children in White homes is the National Association of Black Social Workers. This group views such placements as "cultural genocide."[55]

In 1971 Rita J. Simon began studying 204 White families who had adopted children of color. Joined later by Howard Altstein and many generations of graduate students, she went back to talk to the families over a period of 20 years.[56] The researchers interviewed the families in 1971, 1979, 1983, and 1991. Most of the children they studied now live away from their parents' homes. The majority of adoptees, despite occasional family conflicts, believe that their parents raised them well. If anything, some felt that the parents had overdone it a bit in trying to educate them about their heritage. African American adoptees, for example, complained that too many dinnertime conversations turned into lectures on Black history. The parents, although also acknowledging occasional conflicts, reported satisfaction with their decisions to adopt across racial lines. Fully 90% said they recommended transracial adoption for families planning to adopt. The researchers concluded that children of color who grow up in White families do not become confused about their identities, racial or otherwise.

COMARITAL SEX

The term *comarital sex* refers to mate swapping and other organized extramarital relations in which both spouses agree to participate. Comarital sex is distinctly different from a traditional extramarital affair, which is usually clandestine, with the straying spouse trying to hide the relationship.

Although some couples appear able to integrate comarital agreements into their lives successfully, others find their marriages breaking up as a consequence.[57] According to marriage counselors, a major reason couples drop out of comarital relationships, and sometimes end their marriage, is because of jealousy, competition, and possessiveness.[58]

The interest in comarital sex and extramarital sex raises the age-old question of whether any *one* individual can satisfy all of the intimate, sexual, and interpersonal needs of another. In the future (and perhaps now), there may be a decrease in comarital and extramarital relationships due to the increasing fear of AIDS.

SINGLE PARENTHOOD

Although in many people's minds marriage and parenthood "go together," single parenthood is emerging as a prominent form in our society. In many states, it is possible for unmarried people to adopt a child. In addition, an unmarried pregnant woman can refuse to marry and yet keep her child after it is born. Some unmarried fathers have been successful in obtaining custody of their child. Today, although the stigma attached to being single and pregnant is not as strong as it once was, this situation is still seriously frowned on by some.

Similar to single parenthood is the one-parent family, in which a person divorces or legally separates, assumes custody of one or more children, and chooses not to remarry. Although traditionally the mother has been awarded custody of the children, today the courts are occasionally granting custody to fathers. Another arrangement is shared custody, wherein both mother and father have the children part of the time.

Do single parents and one-parent families pose a serious problem? Are children adversely affected by being raised in a one-parent family? Papalia and Olds summarize some of the problems children face in growing up in one-parent families:

> Children growing up in one-parent homes undoubtedly have more problems and more adjustments to make than children growing up in homes where there are two adults to share the responsibilities for child rearing, to provide a higher income, to more closely approximate cultural expectations of the "ideal family," and to offer a counterpoint of sex-role models and an interplay of personalities. But the two-parent home is not always ideal, and the one-parent home is not necessarily pathological.[59]

Research indicates that it is better for children to be raised in a non-tension-laden one-parent family than in a tension-laden two-parent family.[60]

BLENDED FAMILIES

Many terms have been used to describe two families joined by the marriage of one parent to another: *stepfamilies, blended families, reconstituted families,* and *nontraditional families.* Here we will use the term *blended families.*

One of two marriages ends in divorce, and many divorcees have children. Most people who divorce remarry someone else within a few years. Moreover, some individuals who are marrying for the first time may have a child born outside of marriage. Thus, a variety of blended families are now being formed in our society.

In blended families, one or both spouses have biologically produced one or more children with someone else prior to their current marriage. Often, the newly married couple give birth to additional children. In yet other blended families, the children are biologically a combination of "his, hers, and theirs."

Blended families are increasing in number and proportion in our society, and the family dynamics and relationships are much more complex than in the traditional nuclear family. Blended families, in short, are burdened by much more "baggage" than are two childless adults marrying for the first time. Blended families must deal with stress that arises from the loss (through divorce or death) experienced by both adults and children, which can make them afraid to love and to trust. Previously established bonds between children and their biological parents, or loyalty to a dead or absent parent, may interfere with the formation of ties to the stepparent. If children go back and forth between two households, conflicts between stepchildren and stepparents may be intensified. Sometimes, divorced spouses continue to feud; in these cases, the children are likely to be used as "pawns," thus generating additional strife in the recently formed blended family.

Some difficulties in adjustment for the children are to be expected.[61] Jealousies may arise because the child resents sharing parental attention with the new spouse and with new siblings. Another issue for children is the adjustment to a new parent who may have different ideas, values, rules, and expectations. Sharing space with new people can be a source of stress as well. In addition, if one member of the couple enters the marriage with no child-rearing experience, an adjustment will be necessary by all family members to allow time for the new parent to learn and adapt.

People come into a blended family with ideas and issues based on past experiences. Old relationships and ways of doing things still have their impacts. In discussing blended families, Stuart and Jacobson note that marrying a new partner involves marrying a whole new family.[62] A blended family differs from a traditional family in that more people are involved, including ex-spouses, former in-laws, and an assortment of cousins, uncles, and aunts. The married couple may have both positive and negative interactions with this large supporting cast. If a prior marriage ended bitterly, the unresolved emotions that remain (such as anger and insecurity) will affect the present relationship.

The area of greatest stress for most stepparents is that of child-rearing. A stepchild, used to being raised in a certain way, may balk at having to conform to new rules or at accepting the stepparent as a parental figure. Such difficulty is more likely to arise if the stepchild feels remorse over the missing parent. If the husband and wife disagree about how to raise children, the chances of conflict are substantially increased. Stepparents and stepchildren also face the problem of adjusting to each other's habits and personalities. Kompara recommends that stepparents not rush into establishing a relationship with stepchildren; proceeding gradually is more likely to result in a trusting and positive relationship.[63] Kompara also notes that becoming a stepparent is usually more difficult for a woman because children tend to be emotionally closer to their biological mother and to have spent more time with her than with the father.

Three myths about blended families need to be addressed.[64] First, there is the myth of the "wicked stepmother"—the idea that the stepmother is not really concerned about what is best for the children but only about her own well-being. A scene from the children's story *Cinderella* comes to mind.

Here, the "wicked stepmother" cruelly keeps Cinderella from going to the ball in hopes that her own biological daughters will have a better chance at nabbing the handsome prince. In reality, stepmothers have been found to establish positive and caring relationships with their stepchildren, provided that the stepmothers have a positive self-concept and the affirmation of their husband.[65]

A second myth is that "step is less."[66] In other words, stepchildren will never hold the same place in the hearts of parents that biological children do. The fact is that people can learn to love each other and are motivated to bind members of their new family together.

The third myth is that the moment families are joined, they will have instant love for each other.[67] Relationships take time to develop and grow. The idea of instantly strong love bonds is unrealistic. People involved in any relationship need time to get to know each other, test each other out, and grow to feel comfortable with each other.

Stinnet and Walters reviewed the research literature on stepparenthood and came to the following conclusions: (a) integration tends to be easier in families that have been split by divorce rather than by death, perhaps because the children realize the first marriage did not work out; (b) stepparents and stepchildren come to the blended family with unrealistic expectations that love and togetherness will occur rapidly; (c) children tend to see a stepparent of the opposite sex as playing favorites with their own children; (d) most children continue to miss and admire the absent biological parent; (e) male children tend more readily to accept a stepparent, particularly if the new parent is a male; and (f) adolescents have greater difficulty accepting a stepparent than do young children or adult children.[68]

Berman and Visher and Visher offer the following suggestions to parents in blended families for increasing the chances of positive relationships between adults and children.[69]

1. *Maintain a courteous relationship with the former spouse or spouses.* Children adjust best after a divorce when there is a harmonious relationship between former spouses. Problems are intensified when former spouses continue to insult

each other and when the children are used as weapons ("pawns") for angry former spouses to hurt each other.

2. *Understand the emotions of children.* Although the newlyweds in a recently blended family may be fairly euphoric about their relationship, they need to be perceptive and responsive to the fears, concerns, and resentments of their children.

3. *Allow time for loving relationships to develop between stepparents and stepchildren.* Stepparents need to be aware that their stepchildren will probably have emotional ties to their absent biological parent and that the stepchildren may resent the breakup of the marriage between their biological parents. Some children may even feel responsible for their biological parents' separation. Others may try to make life difficult for the stepparent so that he or she will leave, with the hope that the biological parents will then reunite. Stepparents need to be perceptive and understanding of such feelings and patiently allow the stepchildren to work out their concerns and take time in bonding.

4. *New rituals, traditions, and ways of doing things need to be developed that seem right and enjoyable for all members of the blended family.* Sometimes it is helpful to move to a new residence that does not hold memories of the past. Leisure time should be structured so that the children spend time alone with the biological parent, with the stepparent, with both, and with the absent parent or parents. In addition, the new spouses need to spend some time alone with each other. New rituals should be developed for holidays, birthdays, and other special days.

5. *Seek social support.* Parents in blended families should seek to share their concerns, feelings, frustrations, experiences, coping strategies, and triumphs with other stepparents and stepchildren. Such sharing allows them to view their own situations more realistically and to learn from the experiences of others.

6. *Provide organization for the family.* Children need to have their limits defined and consistently upheld. One of the difficulties is that children are faced with a new stepparent attempting to gain control when they have not as yet enjoyed many supportive and positive experiences with their new stepparent. Therefore, it is important for this new stepparent to provide nurturance and positive feedback to stepchildren in addition to making rules and maintaining control.

THE SINGLE LIFE

In our society, women—and, to a lesser extent, men—are brought up to believe that one of their most important goals is to marry. Women who remain unmarried are labeled "old maids." Elaborate rituals have been developed to romanticize engagement and marriage. Unfortunately, many couples discover after the honeymoon that marriage is not always romantic or exciting. Many people deal with unfulfilled marriages with a series of divorces and remarriages. In the 1970s and early 1980s, an increasing number of adults turned away from the responsibilities and restrictions of marriage by choosing to remain single. Temporary and sometimes long-term deep emotional relationships were entered without the duties and restrictions imposed by a legal arrangement.

At present there appears to be a shift in sexual values. The sexual revolution that began in the 1960s and that glamorized multiple recreational sexual relationships appears to be on the decline. The current renewed interest in sharply limiting the number of sexual partners is largely due to the fear of acquiring AIDS. People are recognizing that the more sexual partners they have, the greater their chances of being exposed to the AIDS virus.

It is unclear at this point whether the threat of AIDS will lead to a decline in the number of people who choose to remain single. It should be noted that increases in the number of people who remain single have significant implications for social welfare: Statistics show higher rates of depression, loneliness, alcoholism, suicide, drug abuse, and alienation among those who are single.[70]

Concluding Comments

To summarize, it appears that the family of tomorrow will face a future shock. Technological developments (particularly in biology and medicine, for example, cloning and human embryo implants) may dramatically affect the family, raising a number of ethical, legal, social, and personal questions. In addition, the family is assuming a number of different forms that may dramatically alter the central characteristics of future families. We are now seeing childless couples, postponement of child-rearing until middle age or later, professional parents, serial and contract marriages, one-parent families, blended families, comarital sex, open marriages, group marriages for all age groups, homosexual marriages and adoptions, transracial adoptions, and a growing number of unmarrieds.

Other experiments are with interracial marriages and marriages involving partners of very different ages. Because of technological advances and the experimentation with new family forms, the style of living for all families may be substantially changed. Some individuals will probably find these changes exciting, personally satisfying, and functional; others may be less adaptable and find such changes extremely difficult and perhaps even overwhelming, resulting in personal disintegration. In any case, changes that are made in the American family will have important implications for the field of social welfare.

SUMMARY

The goal of social welfare is to fulfill the social, financial, health, and recreational needs of everyone in a society. The provision of social services has become one of the most important activities in our society in terms of the money spent, the human misery treated, and the number of people served.

Social welfare overlaps with sociology, psychology, and other disciplines on a knowledge-base level. When theories and research in other academic disciplines have direct applications to the social welfare goal of enhancing the social functioning of people, then this knowledge is also part of the knowledge base of social welfare.

Social welfare overlaps with social work at a practice (service) level. Almost all social workers work in the field of social welfare, but there are also many other professional and occupational groups that work within this field. Social welfare is erroneously conceived at times as synonymous with public assistance, but public assistance is only one of several hundred social welfare programs.

Social welfare institutions are composed of social service programs and social service organizations. The purposes of social welfare institutions are to prevent, alleviate, and contribute to the solution of recognized social problems so as to directly improve the well-being of individuals, groups, families, organizations, and communities.

Currently there are two conflicting views of the role of social welfare in our society: the residual versus the institutional orientations. The residual approach characterized social welfare programs from early history to the depression of the 1930s, at which time programs with an institutional orientation began to be implemented. Social welfare programs have in the past been influenced (and to some extent still are) by the Protestant ethic, the laissez-faire economic view, social Darwinism, individualism, the Industrial Revolution, and humanitarian ideals. The two prominent political philosophies in the United States are liberalism and conservatism. Liberals generally adhere to an institutional orientation, whereas conservatives tend to adhere to a residual orientation.

There are likely to be important changes in the social welfare field in the future primarily due to anticipated technological advances. In summary form, technological advances largely determine changes in our lifestyles; lifestyle changes largely determine changes in our future social, financial, health, and recreational needs; and the latter changes largely determine changes in needed social service programs.

Dramatic changes are also anticipated in the American family of the future due to technological advances in biology and medicine and to the current experimentation with new family forms. Some of these new forms will be found dysfunctional and will be discarded, whereas others will be found satisfying and functional and will probably be incorporated into the "typical" family of the future. The anticipated technological advances and the adoption of new family forms will result in the creation of new social service programs and the expansion of certain existing programs. Unless such changes are carefully examined and planned, our society faces a future shock.

NOTES

1. Andrew W. Dobelstein, *Social Welfare: Policy and Analysis,* 2nd ed. (Chicago: Nelson-Hall, 1996).

2. Robert L. Barker, *The Social Work Dictionary,* 3rd ed. (Washington, DC: NASW, 1995).

3. *The American Heritage Dictionary,* 2nd college ed. (Boston: Houghton Mifflin, 1982), p. 1103.

4. Ibid.

5. National Association of Social Workers, *Standards for Social Service Manpower* (New York: NASW, 1983), pp. 4–5.

6. Barker, *The Social Work Dictionary,* p. 358.

7. Alfred Kahn, *Shaping the New Social Work* (New York: Columbia University Press, 1973), pp. 12–34.

8. Ibid., p. 10.

9. Harold Wilensky and Charles Lebeux, *Industrial Society & Social Welfare* (New York: Free Press, 1965).

10. Ibid., p. 138.

11. Ibid., p. 139.

12. James Midgley, *Social Development: The Developmental Perspective in Social Welfare.* (Thousand Oaks, CA: Sage, 1995).

13. Ibid., p. 25.

14. James Midgley and Michelle Livermore, "The Developmental Perspective in Social Work: Educational Implications for a New Century," *Journal of Social Work Education,* 33, no. 3 (Fall 1997), pp. 573–585.

15. Ibid., p. 576.

16. Lester F. Ward, *Dynamic Sociology;* reprint of 1883 ed. (New York: Johnson Reprint, 1968).

17. Walter Trattner, *From Poor Law to Welfare State: A History of Social Welfare in America* (New York: Free Press, 1974).

18. Beulah Compton, *Introduction to Social Welfare & Social Work* (Homewood, IL: Dorsey Press, 1980).

19. Trattner, *From Poor Law to Welfare State.*

20. J. M. Romanyshyn, *Social Welfare: Charity to Justice* (New York: Random House, 1971).

21. U.S. Bureau of the Census, *Statistical Abstract of the United States, 1997* (Washington, DC: U.S. Government Printing Office, 1997).

22. Romanyshyn, *Social Welfare: Charity to Justice.*

23. "Poverty Gap Widens, Studies Reveal," *NASW News,* Jan. 1990, p. 19.

24. William Kornblum and Joseph Julian, *Social Problems,* 7th ed. (Englewood Cliffs, NJ: Prentice Hall, 1992), pp. 221–226.

25. Dick Polman, "Swedes Shaken As the Welfare State Shrinks," *Wisconsin State Journal,* July 3, 1994, p. 18.

26. Ibid.

27. U.S. Bureau of the Census, *Statistical Abstract of the United States, 1997.*

28. Ibid.

29. W. F. Ogburn and M. F. Nimkoff, *Technology and the Changing Family* (New York: Houghton Mifflin, 1955).

30. Alfred Kadushin and Judith A. Martin, *Child Welfare Services,* 4th ed. (New York: Macmillan, 1988).

31. Janet S. Hyde, *Understanding Human Sexuality,* 5th ed. (New York: McGraw-Hill, 1994), p. 654.

32. L. Rifken, *Who Should Play God?* (New York: Dell, 1977).

33. Ibid.

34. Ibid.

35. Art Caplan, "Superbaby Sperm Bank Morally Bankrupt," *Wisconsin State Journal,* Nov. 28, 1989, p. 9A.

36. Rita Christopher, "Mother's Little Helper," *Maclean's Magazine,* Mar. 10, 1980, p. 10.

37. "Dad Wins Custody of Baby M," *Wisconsin State Journal,* Apr. 1987, p. 1.

38. Hyde, *Understanding Human Sexuality,* pp. 189–190.

39. "Healthy Baby Is Born from Donated Embryo," *Wisconsin State Journal,* Feb. 4, 1984, sec. 1, p. 2.

40. Stephen Budiansky, "The New Rules of Reproduction," *U.S. News & World Report,* Apr. 18, 1988, pp. 66–69.

41. Philip Reilly, *Genetics, Law, and Social Policy* (Cambridge, MA: Harvard University Press, 1977).

42. William R. Wineke, "Calves Cloned Successfully in UW Experiment," *Wisconsin State Journal,* Sept. 9, 1987, p. 1.

43. Gina Kolata, "Human Clones," *Wisconsin State Journal,* Oct. 23, 1993, p. 3A.

44. Barbara M. Newman and Philip R. Newman, *Development Through Life,* 6th ed. (Pacific Grove, CA: Brooks/Cole, 1995), p. 142.

45. Daniel O. Haney, "Cystic Fibrosis Therapy Promising," *Wisconsin State Journal,* Oct. 29, 1993, p. 7A.

46. R. V. Kail and J. C. Cavanaugh, *Human Development* (Pacific Grove, CA: Brooks/Cole, 1996), p. 363.

47. Alvin Toffler, *Future Shock* (New York: Bantam Books, 1970).

48. Ibid., pp. 243–244.

49. Ethel Alpenfels, "Progressive Monogamy: An Alternate Pattern?" in *The Family in Search of a Future,* Herbert Otto, ed. (New York: Appleton-Century-Crofts, 1970), pp. 67–74.

50. Ibid.
51. George O'Neill and Nena O'Neill, *Open Marriage* (New York: M. Evans, 1971).
52. Victor Kassel, "Polygamy After Sixty," *Geriatrics,* 21 (Apr. 1966).
53. David Fanshel, *Far from the Reservation* (Metuchen, NJ: Scarecrow Press, 1972).
54. Charles Zastrow, *Outcome of Black Children–White Parents Transracial Adoptions* (San Francisco: R & E Research Associated, 1977).
55. David L. Wheeler, "Black Children, White Parents: The Difficult Issue of Transracial Adoption," *Chronicle of Higher Education,* Sept. 15, 1993, p. A16.
56. Ibid., p. A9.
57. Hyde, *Understanding Human Sexuality,* pp. 349–350.
58. Ibid.
59. Diane E. Papalia and Sally W. Olds, *Human Development,* 2nd ed. (New York: McGraw-Hill, 1981), p. 326.
60. Diane E. Papalia and Sally W. Olds, *Human Development,* 6th ed. (New York: McGraw-Hill, 1995), p. 328.
61. C. Janzen and O. Harris, *Family Treatment in Social Work Practice,* 2nd ed. (Itasca, IL: F. E. Peacock, 1986), p. 273.
62. R. B. Stuart and B. Jacobson, *Second Marriage: Make It Happy! Make It Last!* (New York: Norton, 1985).
63. D. Kompara, "Difficulties in the Socialization Process of Step-Parenting," *Family Relations,* 29 (1980), pp. 69–73.
64. Janzen and Harris, *Family Treatment,* pp. 275–276.
65. G. L. Shulman, "Myths That Intrude on the Adaptation of the Step-Family," *Social Casework,* 53, no. 3 (1972), pp. 131–139.
66. E. Wald, *The Remarried Family* (New York: Family Service Association of America, 1981).
67. Ibid.
68. N. Stinnet and J. Walters, *Relationships in Marriage and Family* (New York: Macmillan, 1977).
69. C. Berman, *Making It As a Stepparent: New Roles/ New Rules* (New York: Bantam, 1981); E. Visher and J. Visher, "Stepparenting: Blending Families," in *Stress and the Family: Vol. I. Coping with Normative Transitions,* H. I. McCubbin and C. R. Figley, eds. (New York: Brunner/Mazel, 1983), pp. 87–98.
70. William Kornblum and Joseph Julian, *Social Problems,* 8th ed. (Englewood Cliffs, NJ: Prentice Hall, 1985).

2

SOCIAL
WORK AS
A PROFESSION
AND A
CAREER

Social work is one of the primary professions that provide social welfare services. This chapter will:

- Define the profession of social work.
- Provide a brief history of social work.
- Describe the following social work activities: casework, case management, group work, group therapy, family therapy, and community organization.
- Describe the person-in-environment conceptualization for social work practice.
- Specify the goals of social work practice.
- Describe the strengths perspective.
- Summarize societal stereotypes of social workers.
- Summarize employment settings and career opportunities in social work.
- Briefly describe international social work.

A BRIEF HISTORY OF SOCIAL WORK

Social work as a profession is of relatively recent origin. The first social welfare agencies began in the early 1800s in an attempt to meet the needs of people living in urban areas. These agencies, or services, were private agencies developed primarily at the initiation of the clergy and religious groups. Until the early 1900s, these services were provided exclusively by members of the clergy and wealthy "do-gooders" who had no formal training and little understanding of human behavior. The focus was on meeting such basic physical needs as food and shelter and attempting to "cure" emotional and personal difficulties with religious admonitions.

An illustration of an early social welfare organization was the Society for the Prevention of Pauperism, founded by John Griscom in 1820.[1] This society's goals were to investigate the habits and circumstances of the poor, to suggest plans by which the poor could help themselves, and to encourage the poor to save and economize. Toward these ends, they conducted house-to-house visitation of the poor (a very elementary type of social work).

By the last half of the 1800s, a fairly large number of private relief agencies had been established in large cities to help the unemployed, the poor, the ill, persons with a physical or mental disability, and orphans. These agencies' programs were uncoordinated and sometimes overlapped. Therefore, an English innovation—the Charity Organization Society (COS)—caught the interest of a number of American cities.[2] Starting in Buffalo, New York, in 1877, COS was rapidly adopted in many cities. In charity organization societies, private agencies joined together to (a) provide direct services to individuals and families—in this respect, they were forerunners of social casework and of family counseling approaches—and (b) plan and coordinate the efforts of private agencies to meet the pressing social problems of cities—in this respect, they were precursors of community organization and social planning approaches. Charity organizations conducted a detailed investigation of each applicant for services and financial help, maintained a central system of registration of clients to avoid duplication, and used volunteer "friendly visitors" to work with those in difficulty. The friendly visitors were primarily "doers of good works"; they generally gave sympathy rather than money and encouraged the poor to save and to seek employment. Poverty was looked on as the result of a personal shortcoming. Most of the friendly visitors were women.

Concurrent with the COS movement was the establishment of settlement houses in the late 1800s. In 1884 Toynbee Hall became the first settlement house in London; many others were soon formed in larger U.S. cities. Many of the early settlement house workers were daughters of ministers, usually from the middle and upper classes. In contrast to friendly visitors, they lived in the impoverished neighborhoods and used the missionary approach of teaching residents how to live moral lives and improve their circumstances. They sought to improve housing, health, and living conditions; find jobs for neighborhood residents; teach English, hygiene, and occupational skills; and change environmental surroundings through cooperative efforts. Settlement houses used change techniques that are now referred to as social group work, social action, and community organization.

Settlement houses emphasized "environmental reform." At the same time, "they continued to struggle to teach the poor the prevailing middle-class values of work, thrift, and abstinence as the keys to success."[3] In addition to dealing with local problems by local action, settlement houses played important roles in drafting legislation and in organizing to influence social policy and legislation. The most noted leader in the settlement house movement was Jane Addams of Hull House in Chicago (see Case Example 2.1).

It appears that the first paid social workers were executive secretaries of charity organization societies in the late 1800s.[4] At that time, COSs received some contracts from the cities in which they were located to administer relief funds. They then hired people as executive secretaries to organize and train the friendly visitors and to establish bookkeeping procedures to account for the funds received. To improve the services of friendly visitors, executive secretaries established standards and training courses. The first such training course was offered for charity workers in 1898 by the New York Charity Organization Society. By 1904 a 1-year program was offered by the New York School of Philanthropy. Soon many colleges and universities were offering training programs in social work.

Richard Cabot introduced medical social work at Massachusetts General Hospital in 1905.[5] Gradually, social workers were employed in schools, courts, child guidance clinics, and other settings.

Early training programs in social work focused both on environmental reform efforts and on efforts to help individuals adjust better to society. In 1917 Mary Richmond published *Social Diagnosis*, the first text to present a theory and methodology for social work.[6] The book focused on how the worker should intervene with individuals. The process is still used today and involves study (collecting information), diagnosis (stating what is wrong), prognosis (stating the prospect of improvement), and treatment planning (stating what should be done to help clients improve). This text was important because it formulated a common body of knowledge for casework.

In the 1920s, Sigmund Freud's theories of personality development and therapy became popular. The concepts and explanations of psychiatrists appeared particularly appropriate for social workers, who also worked in one-to-one relationships with clients. The psychiatric approach emphasized intrapsychic processes and focused on enabling clients to adapt and adjust to their social situations. Thus, most social workers switched their emphasis from "reform" to "therapy" for the next three decades.

In the 1960s, however, there was a renewed interest in sociological approaches, or reform, by social workers. Several reasons account for this change. Questions arose about the relevance and appropriateness of "talking" approaches with low-income clients who have urgent social and economic pressures. Furthermore, the effectiveness of many psychotherapeutic approaches was questioned.[7] Other reasons for the renewed interest included an increase in the status of sociology and the mood of the 1960s, which raised questions about the relevancy of social institutions in meeting the needs of the population. Social work at present embraces both the reform approach and the therapy approach.

Not until the end of World War I did social work begin to be recognized as a distinct profession. The depression of the 1930s and the enactment of the Social Security Act in 1935 brought about an extensive expansion of public social services and job opportunities for social workers. Throughout the 20th century there has been a growing awareness by social agency boards and the public that professionally trained social workers are needed to provide social services competently. In 1955 the National Association of Social Workers (NASW) was formed, which represents the social work profession in this country. The purpose of this association is to improve social conditions in society and promote high quality and effectiveness in social work practice. The association publishes (a) several professional journals, most notably *Social Work;* (b) *The Encyclopedia of Social Work;* and (c) a monthly newsletter titled *NASW News.* The newsletter publishes current social work news

CASE EXAMPLE 2.1   Jane Addams: A Prominent Founder of Social Work

Jane Addams was born in 1860 in Cedarville, Illinois, the daughter of a successful couple who owned a flour mill and a wood mill. Jane graduated from Rockford Seminary (a college in Rockford, Illinois). She briefly attended medical school but was forced to leave because of illness. She then traveled for a few years in Europe, perplexed about what her life work should be. At the age of 25, she joined the Presbyterian Church, which helped her find a focus for her life: religion and humanitarianism—in particular, serving the poor. (Later in her life, she joined the Congregational Church, now known as the United Church of Christ.) Addams heard about the establishment of Toynbee Hall in England and returned to Europe to study this approach. Its staff was composed of college students and graduates, mainly from Oxford, who lived in the slums of London to learn conditions firsthand and to contribute to improving life in the slums with their own financial and personal resources.

Jane Addams

Addams returned to the United States and rented a two-story house (later called Hull House) in an impoverished Chicago neighborhood. With a few friends, Addams initiated a variety of group and individual activities for the community. She started a literature reading group for young women and a kindergarten. There were groups focusing on social relationships, sports, music, painting, art, and current affairs. Hull House also provided services to individuals who came asking for immediate help, such as food, shelter, information, and referrals for other services. A Hull House Social Science Club was formed, which studied social problems in a scientific manner and then became involved in social action efforts to improve living conditions. One of its successful efforts was to work for passage of Illinois legislation to prevent the employment of children in area sweatshops. Addams also became interested in the different ethnic groups in the neighborhood. She was fairly successful in bringing the various nationalities together at Hull House, where they could interact and exchange cultural values.

The success of Hull House served as a model for the establishment of settlement houses in other areas of Chicago and in many large cities in the United States. Settlement house leaders believed that, by improving neighborhoods, they would improve communities; by altering communities, they would develop a better society. For her extraordinary contributions, Jane Addams received the Nobel Prize for Peace in 1931.

Source: Adapted from "Jane Addams," by Herbert Stroup, pp. 1–29, in *Social Welfare Pioneers.* Copyright © 1986 by Nelson-Hall Publishers. Reprinted by permission.

as well as a list of job vacancies throughout the country.

In recent years, there has been considerable activity in developing a system of certification, or licensing of social workers. Such a system both helps assure the public that qualified personnel are providing social work services and advances the recognition of social work as a profession. All states have now passed legislation to license or regulate the practice of social work. Although a young profession, social work is growing and gaining respect and recognition.

A MULTISKILLED PROFESSION

Social work is the professional activity of helping individuals, groups, families, organizations, and communities to enhance or restore their capacity for social functioning and to create societal conditions favorable to their goals.[8] The term *social worker* has been defined by the National Association of Social Workers as:

> *Graduates of schools of social work (with either bachelor's or master's degrees), who use their knowledge and skills to provide social services for* clients *(who may be individuals, families, groups, communities, organizations, or society in general). Social workers help people increase their capacities for problem solving and coping and help them obtain needed resources, facilitate interactions between individuals and between people and their environments, make organizations responsible to people, and influence social policies.*[9]

Social work is distinct from other professions (such as psychology and psychiatry) by virtue of its responsibility and mandate to provide social services.

A social worker needs training and expertise in a wide range of areas to handle effectively the problems faced by individuals, groups, families, organizations, and the larger community. Whereas most professions are becoming more specialized (for example, nearly all medical doc-

tors now specialize in one or two areas), social work continues to emphasize a generic (broad-based) approach. The practice of social work is analogous to the old, now-fading practice of general medicine. A general practitioner in medicine was trained to handle a wide range of common medical problems; a social worker is trained to handle a wide range of common social and personal problems. Case Example 2.2 highlights some of the skills needed by social workers. This "success" story (in most cases, the outcome is not as promising) documents the range of abilities displayed by a social worker: interviewing skills, knowledge of how to counsel people with sexual problems and feelings of depression, ability to work effectively with other agencies, premarital counseling skills, research and grant-writing skills, program development and fund-raising skills, and knowledge of how to handle ethical/legal issues.

Perhaps the most basic skill that a social worker needs is the ability to counsel clients effectively. Anyone who is unable to do this should probably not be in social work—certainly not in direct service. The second most important skill is the ability to interact effectively with other groups and professionals in the area. A social worker, like a general practitioner, requires a wide range of skills that will enable him or her to intervene effectively in (a) the common personal and emotional problems of clients and (b) the common social problems faced by groups, organizations, and the larger community. Social workers also need an accurate perception of their professional strengths and weaknesses. If a situation arises that a worker knows she or he does not have the training or expertise to handle, then the worker needs to be a "broker" and link those affected with available services.

A Problem-Solving Approach

In working with individuals, families, groups, organizations, and communities, social workers use a problem-solving approach. Steps in the problem-solving process can be stated in a variety of ways. Here is a simple description of the process:

1. Identify as precisely as possible the problem or problems.
2. Generate possible alternative solutions.
3. Evaluate the alternative solutions.
4. Select a solution or solutions to be used and set goals.
5. Implement the solution(s).
6. Follow up to evaluate how the solution(s) worked.

(Another conceptualization of the problem-solving approach is the change process of social work practice, which is described in Chapter 3.)

Generalist Social Work Practice

The Council on Social Work Education (the national accrediting entity for baccalaureate and master's programs in social work) requires all undergraduate and graduate programs to train their students in generalist social work practice. (MSW programs, in addition, usually require their students to select and study in an area of specialization. MSW programs generally offer several specializations, such as family therapy, administration, corrections, and clinical social work.)

A generalist social worker is trained to use the problem-solving process to assess and intervene with the problems confronting individuals, families, groups, organizations, and communities. Because of the importance of generalist practice, Chapter 3 is devoted to this topic.

MICRO-, MEZZO-, AND MACROPRACTICE

Social workers practice at three levels: (a) micro—working on a one-to-one basis with an individual; (b) mezzo—working with families and other small groups; and (c) macro—working with organizations and communities or seeking changes in statutes and social policies.

The specific activities performed by workers include, but are not limited to, the following.

Social Casework

Aimed at helping individuals on a one-to-one basis to resolve personal and social problems, casework may be geared to helping clients adjust to their environment or to changing certain social and economic pressures that are adversely affecting them. Social casework services are provided by nearly every social welfare agency that offers direct services to people.

Social casework encompasses a wide variety of activities, such as counseling runaway youths, helping unemployed people secure training or employment, counseling someone who is suicidal, placing a homeless child in an adoptive or foster home, providing protective services to abused children and their families, finding nursing homes for stroke victims who no longer require hospitalization, counseling individuals with sexual dysfunctions, helping alcoholics to acknowledge that they have a drinking problem, counseling those with a terminal illness, serving as a probation or parole officer, providing services to single parents, and working in medical and mental hospitals as a member of a rehabilitation team.

Case Management

Recently a number of social service agencies have labeled their social workers *case managers.* The tasks performed by case managers are similar to those of caseworkers. The job descriptions of case managers vary from service area to service area. For example, case managers in a juvenile probation setting are highly involved in supervising clients, providing some counseling, monitoring clients to make certain they are following the rules of probation, linking clients and their families with needed services, preparing court reports, and testifying in court. On the other hand, case managers at a sheltered workshop are likely to be involved in providing job training to clients, counseling clients, arranging transportation, disciplining clients for unacceptable behavior, acting

A Case Involving Suicide and Sexual Deviancy

Dr. John Pritchard referred Dick Cherwenka to the Riverland Counseling Center (a mental health center). Mr. Cherwenka had briefly been hospitalized after slashing his wrists. This case was assigned to Tom Tounsend, MSW (master's degree in social work), who in the recent past had counseled most of the agency's attempted suicide cases. At the first two sessions, Mr. Cherwenka presented an unusual account of the events that led to his slashing his wrists.

His main problem centered around his desire to fondle the genitals of young girls (9 to 12 years old) whenever he felt depressed, tense, or at a "low tide." In the past 4 years, he had been arrested on three occasions for this offense. The last time, 11 months ago, he was placed on probation for 2 years, and the judge warned that he would be sentenced to prison for an indeterminate sentence as a "sex deviant" if there was a recurrence.

The day he slashed his wrists, he had felt quite depressed. While driving home from work, he stopped at a playground and began talking to a young girl. He offered her a ride home, and she accepted. But he drove out into the country, where he fondled her. The girl was terrified. Mr. Cherwenka then drove her back, dropped her off a few blocks from her home, and informed her that serious harm would come to her if she told anyone. Mr. Cherwenka, after thinking about what he had done, became even more depressed and slashed his wrists a few hours later.

The social worker at this point informed Mr. Cherwenka that he (the social worker) faced an ethical/legal question of whether the police should be informed and that he would have to discuss his obligations with the director of the agency. Mr. Cherwenka indicated that he understood and proceeded to relate the following account of why he believed he had developed the desire to fondle young girls.

He had normal childhood experiences until age 8, when his mother died. After his mother's death, his father continued to raise him and his sister, who was 14 months older. However, his father changed; he became bitter toward life and began drinking heavily. In the evening, he was at times in a drunken stupor. During these times, he would be abusive, verbally and physically, to his children. Dick and his sister became very fearful of their father when he was drunk and sought ways to hide from him. Gradually, they learned to hide together under a blanket. While fearful and tense under the blanket, they sought ways to occupy their time and reduce their fear. As a result, they began fondling each other. Mr. Cherwenka indicated that this activity of hiding and fondling under a blanket when their father was drunk lasted for nearly 3 years, until an aunt moved into their home and began raising them.

as an advocate for clients, and acting as liaison with the people who supervise clients during their nonwork hours (such as at a group home, foster home, residential treatment facility, or the parents' home). Hepworth, Rooney and Larsen describe the role of a case manager as follows:

A person designated to assume primary responsibility for assessing the needs of a client, arranging and coordinating the delivery of essential goods and services provided by other resources, and working directly with the client to ensure that the goods and services are provided

The social worker agreed with Mr. Cherwenka that his present desire to fondle young girls apparently resulted from his past learning experiences of coping with unwanted emotions. The problems that needed to be dealt with now were: (a) what ethical/legal obligations Mr. Tounsend and the mental health center had in regard to this admitted offense; (b) how to prevent Mr. Cherwenka from fondling young girls in the future; (c) how to help Mr. Cherwenka handle unwanted emotions; and (d) how to prevent Mr. Cherwenka from trying to take his life in the future. Because Mr. Cherwenka was engaged and planned to marry in 2 months, an additional situation that needed to be handled was his future relationship with his fiancée.

The following treatment plan was developed and then implemented. Mr. Tounsend discussed the ethical/legal obligations of this case with the agency's director. It was decided that the probation department needed to be informed. Mr. Tounsend discussed this decision with Mr. Cherwenka. Mr. Tounsend then arranged a meeting with Mr. Cherwenka and his probation officer. Following this meeting, it was agreed that the offense would be noted, but proceedings to revoke Mr. Cherwenka's probation would not be initiated as long as Mr. Cherwenka remained in counseling and no other offenses occurred.

The problems of preventing Mr. Cherwenka from fondling young girls and from committing suicide in the future were then addressed. It was agreed that, whenever Mr. Cherwenka had strong desires to fondle young girls or to take his life, he should immediately come to the center and voluntarily admit himself as an inpatient for a few hours or a few days until his desires subsided. (During the next 14 months, Mr. Cherwenka did voluntarily admit himself on three occasions.)

Gradually, by using rational therapy (described in Chapter 5), Mr. Cherwenka gained better control of his feelings of depression and his other unwanted emotions. Several meetings with Mr. Cherwenka and his fiancée were also held. After the initial shock of learning about Mr. Cherwenka's interest in young girls, his fiancée agreed to postpone the marriage for a year, while continuing the engagement.

As indicated earlier, this was only one of several potential suicide cases that Mr. Tounsend was handling. These cases led him to the conclusion that an emergency telephone number was needed that would be widely publicized and staffed 24 hours a day with professional counselors. He gathered data on the number of suicides in the area in the past year and obtained information from hospitals in the community about the number of attempted suicides. These data supported the need for an emergency intervention service. Mr. Tounsend then wrote a grant proposal, and after 10 months of searching for funding, his proposal was funded by a joint grant from the United Way and the Easter Seals Society.

in a timely manner. Case managers must maintain close contact with clients (including sometimes acting to provide direct casework services) and with other service providers to ensure that plans for service delivery are in place and are subsequently delivered as planned.[10]

Barker defines case management as follows:

A procedure to plan, seek, and monitor services from a variety of agencies and staff on behalf of a client. Usually one agency takes primary responsibility for the client and assigns a case

EXHIBIT 2.1

Playing a Poor Hand Well

Many adults who are currently enjoying a happy and productive life grew up under very difficult and stressful conditions. They may have been raised in a high-crime, distressed neighborhood. They may have been abused physically, sexually, or emotionally by a family member. They may have been raised in a series of foster homes. They may have a significant physical or learning disability. Some of these individuals have managed to escape serious emotional damage entirely. Others struggled as children and teenagers with school and had emotional and behavioral difficulties but then turned their lives around in their twenties.

What turned things around for them? Why were they able to play a poor hand well, while many others in similar situations succumbed and lived a life full of despair? In *On Playing a Poor Hand Well,* Mark Katz asserts that by identifying why some people have learned to play a poor hand well, we will then learn to provide avenues through which turning-point experiences and second-chance opportunities can occur for those experiencing severe adversity.

Katz summarizes evidence that a variety of *protective influences* are key to helping a young person find a way to enjoy a happy and productive life. For example, a close-knit family living in a distressed neighborhood can be protective; children may not feel safe on the street, but they feel safe at home. Homeless mothers who see their prime necessity as ensuring that their child was outside waiting for the school bus each morning have been protective influences for some homeless children. Parents advocating for a child with special needs and trying to ensure that those needs are met provide protection. The protective influence may be an older brother or sister helping a younger family member understand a parent's illness. Or it may be an aunt, uncle, or grandparent helping to raise a child because the child's parents may be unable to do so. A school that offers smaller class sizes, which can address each child's unique learning needs and highlight each child's special strengths, talents, and interests, can be protective. Also protective are high-quality recreational programs in distressed neighborhoods that children and teenagers go to after school and stay at for hours.

Mentors and special role models whom children get to know at school, during after-school activities, or through involvement in church or youth groups are protective. Those who overcome childhood adversities often identify a special person in their lives—a teacher, social worker, coach, parent, counselor—who was always there when needed.

Protection can also come from within. Some children have qualities that draw others toward them in times of need. They may be sparkly. They may excel at developing safety nets for themselves, and when adversity arises, their safety net is there to catch them. Some children are strong academically, or very skilled socially, so that success in the neighborhood and in school comes rather easily. Some children are more resilient, having the capacity to withstand the effects of exposure to known risk factors; for example, having the tendency to reframe adversities as being challenges that they know they have the capacities to overcome.

In working with individuals, groups, and families, social workers can often be a protective influence!

Source: Mark Katz, *On Playing a Poor Hand Well* (New York: Norton, 1997).

Group work is utilized by a wide variety of institutions with equally wide-ranging objectives. This community center offers emergency shelter, counseling, support groups, recreational activities, and educational and career guidance to homeless teenagers in the San Francisco Bay Area.

manager, who coordinates services, advocates for the client, and sometimes controls resources and purchases services for the client. The procedure makes it possible for many social workers in the agency, or different agencies, to coordinate their efforts to serve a given client through professional teamwork, thus expanding the range of needed services offered. Case management may involve monitoring the progress of a client whose needs require the services of many different professionals, agencies, health care facilities, and human service programs.[11]

Group Work

Group work seeks to facilitate the intellectual, emotional, and social development of individuals through group activities. In contrast to casework or group therapy, it is not primarily therapeutic except in a broad sense.

Different groups have different objectives, such as improving socialization, exchanging information, curbing delinquency, providing recreation, changing socially unacceptable values, helping to achieve better relations among cultural and racial groups, or explaining adoption procedures and helping applicants prepare for becoming adoptive parents. Activities and focuses of groups vary: arts and crafts, dancing, games, dramatics, music, photography, sports, nature study, woodworking, first aid, home management, information exchange, and discussion of such topics as politics, sex, marriage, religion, and career choice.

Group Therapy

Group therapy is aimed at facilitating the social, behavioral, and emotional adjustment of individuals through the group process. Participants in group therapy usually have emotional, interactional, or behavioral difficulties. Group therapy has several advantages over one-to-one counseling, such as the operation of the *helper therapy* principle, which maintains that it is therapeutic for the helper (who can be any member of a group) to feel he or she has been helpful to others.[12] Group pressure is often more effective than one-to-one counseling in changing maladaptive behavior of individuals, and group therapy is a time-saver in that it enables the therapist to treat several people at the same time. Group therapy has been especially effective for individuals who are severely depressed, have a drinking problem, are victims of rape, are psychologically addicted to drugs, have a relative who is terminally ill, are single and pregnant, are recently divorced, or have an eating disorder.

Family Therapy

Family therapy (a type of group therapy aimed at helping families with interactional, behavioral, and emotional problems) can be used with parent–child interaction problems, marital conflicts, and conflicts with grandparents. Some of the problems dealt with in family therapy or family counseling include disagreements between parents and youths on choice of friends, drinking and other drug use, domestic tasks, curfew hours, communication problems, sexual values and behavior, study habits and grades received, and choice of dating partners.

Community Organization

The aim of community organization is stimulating and assisting the local community to evaluate, plan, and coordinate efforts to provide for the community's health, welfare, and recreation needs. It perhaps is not possible to define precisely the activities of a community organizer, but such activities are likely to include encouraging and fostering citizen participation, coordinating efforts between agencies or between groups, performing public relations, providing public education, conducting research, planning, and being a resource person. A community organizer acts as a catalyst in stimulating and encouraging community action.

Agency settings where such specialists are employed include community welfare councils, social planning agencies, health planning councils, and community action agencies. The term *community organization* is now being replaced in some settings by labels such as *planning, social planning, program development, policy development,* and *macropractice.*

Barker defines community organization as follows:

> *An intervention process used by social workers and other professionals to help individuals, groups, and collectives of people with common interests or from the same geographic areas to deal with social problems and to enhance social well-being through planned collective action. Methods include identifying problem areas, analyzing causes, formulating plans, developing strategies, mobilizing necessary resources, identifying and recruiting community leaders, and encouraging interrelationships between them to facilitate their efforts.*[13]

Administration

Administration involves directing the overall program of a social service agency. Administrative functions include setting agency and program objectives, analyzing social conditions in the community, making decisions relating to what services will be provided, hiring and supervising staff members, setting up an organizational structure, administering financial affairs, and securing funds for the agency's operations. Administration also involves coordinating efforts to achieve selected goals, monitoring and revising internal procedures to improve effectiveness and efficiency, and performing whatever functions are required to transform social policy into social services. In social work, the term *administration* is often used synonymously with *management.* In a small agency, administrative functions may be carried out by one person; in a large agency, several people may be involved in administrative affairs.

Other areas of professional activity in social work include research, consulting, supervision, planning, program development, policy development, and teaching (primarily at the college level). Social casework, case management, group work, group therapy, family therapy, and community organization constitute the primary professional activities that beginning social workers are likely to provide. All of these activities require counseling skills. (Counseling involves helping individuals or groups resolve social and personal problems through the process of developing a relationship, exploring the problem[s] in depth, and exploring alternative solutions; this process is described in Chapter 5.) Caseworkers, case managers, group workers, group therapists, and family therapists obviously need a high level of counseling skills in working with individuals and groups. Community organizers need to have relationship skills, to be perceptive, and to be able to assess problems and develop resolution strategies—abilities that parallel or are analogous to counseling skills.

Additionally, caseworkers must be able to do social histories and link clients with other human services. In some agencies, they are required to do public speaking, to prepare and present reports to courts and other agencies, to teach parents better parenting techniques, and so forth. Knowledge of evaluative procedures for assessing one's own effectiveness and the effectiveness of social programs is also helpful for the social worker. (Essential skills needed for social work practice are described in more detail in Chapter 3.)

A MEDICAL VERSUS A SYSTEMS MODEL OF HUMAN BEHAVIOR

From the 1920s to the 1960s, most social work programs used a medical-model approach to assess and change human behavior. This approach was developed by Sigmund Freud. It views clients as "patients." The task of the provider of services is first to diagnose the causes of a patient's problems and then to provide treatment. The patient's problems are viewed as being inside the patient.

People with emotional or behavioral problems are given medical labels, such as schizophrenic, psychotic, borderline personality, or insane. Adherents of the medical approach believe that the disturbed person's mind is affected by some generally unknown internal condition. That unknown internal condition is thought to be due to a variety of possible causative factors: genetic endowment, metabolic disorders, infectious diseases, internal conflicts, chemical imbalances, unconscious use of defense mechanisms, or traumatic early experiences that cause emotional fixations and prevent future psychological growth.

The medical model provided a humane approach to treating people with emotional and behavioral problems. Prior to Freud, the emotionally disturbed were thought to be possessed by demons, viewed as "mad," blamed for their disturbances, and often treated by being beaten or locked up. The medical-model approach emphasized intrapsychic processes and focused on enabling patients to adapt and adjust to their social situations.

In the 1960s, social work began questioning the usefulness of the medical model. Environmental factors were shown to be at least as important in causing a client's problems as internal factors. Research also demonstrated that psychoanalysis was probably ineffective in treating clients' problems.[14] Social work thus shifted some of its emphasis to a reform approach.

A reform approach seeks to change systems to benefit clients. Antipoverty programs (such as Head Start) are examples of efforts to change systems to benefit clients.

Since the 1960s, social work has primarily used a systems approach to assessing human behavior. Social workers are now trained to have a systems perspective in their work with individuals, groups, families, organizations, and communities. The systems perspective emphasizes looking beyond the client's presenting problems to assess the complexities and interrelationships of the client's life situation. A systems perspective is based on systems theory. Key concepts of general systems theory are *wholeness, relationship,* and *homeostasis.*

The concept of wholeness means that the objects or elements within a system produce an entity that is greater than the additive sums of the separate parts. Systems theory is antireductionist; it asserts that no system can be adequately understood or totally explained once it has been broken down into its component parts. (For example, the central nervous system is able to carry out thought processes that would not occur if only the parts were observed.)

The concept of relationship asserts that the patterning and structuring among the elements in a system are as important as the elements themselves. For example, Masters and Johnson found that sexual dysfunctions occur primarily because of the nature of the relationship between husband and wife rather than the psychological makeup of individual partners in a marriage system.[15]

Systems theory opposes simple cause-and-effect explanations. For example, whether a child will be abused in a family is determined by a variety of variables as well as by the patterning of these variables: parents' capacity to control their anger, relationships between child and parents, relationships between parents, degree of psychological stress, characteristics of the child, and opportunities for socially acceptable ways for parents to vent anger.

The concept of homeostasis suggests that most living systems seek a balance to maintain and preserve the system. Jackson, for example, has noted that families tend to establish a behavioral balance or stability and to resist any change from that predetermined level of stability.[16] Emergence of the state of imbalance (generated either within or outside the marriage) ultimately acts to restore the homeostatic balance of the family. If one child is abused in a family, that abuse often serves a function in the family (as indicated by the fact that, if that child is removed, a second child is often abused). Or if one family member improves through counseling, that improvement will generally upset the balance within the family; as a result, other family members will have to make

changes (adaptive or maladaptive) to adjust to the new behavior of the improved family member.

We turn now to a subcategory of systems theory known as ecological theory, which has become prominent in social work practice.

AN ECOLOGICAL MODEL OF HUMAN BEHAVIOR

In recent years, social work has focused increasingly on using an ecological approach. This approach integrates both treatment and reform by conceptualizing and emphasizing the dysfunctional transactions between people and their physical and social environments. Human beings are viewed as developing and adapting through transactions with all elements of their environments. An ecological model explores both internal and external factors. It views people not as passive reactors to their environments but rather as dynamic and reciprocal interactors with those environments.

An ecological model tries to improve coping patterns so that a better match can be attained between an individual's needs and the characteristics of his or her environment. One emphasis of an ecological model is on the person-in-environment. This is depicted in Figure 2.1, which shows that people interact with many systems. With this conceptualization, social work can focus on three separate areas. First, it can focus on the person and seek to develop his or her problem-solving, coping, and developmental capacities. Second, it can focus on the relationship between a person and the systems he or she interacts with and link the person with needed resources, services, and opportunities. Third, it can focus on the systems and seek to reform them to meet the needs of the individual more effectively.

The ecological model views individuals, families, and small groups as having transitional problems and needs as they move from one life stage to another. Individuals face many changes as they grow older. Examples of some of the transitions are learning to walk, entering first grade, adjusting to puberty, graduating from school, finding a

FIGURE 2.1

Person-in-Environment Conceptualization

People in our society continually interact with many systems, some of which are depicted in this figure.

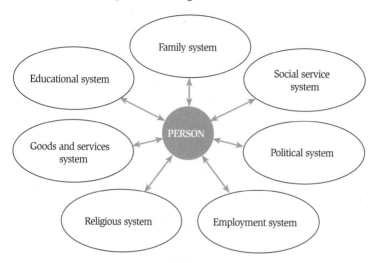

job, getting married, having children, seeing one's children leave home, and retiring.

Families also experience transitions. The following are only a few of the events that require adjustment: engagement, marriage, birth of children, parenting, children starting school, children leaving home, and loss of a parent (perhaps through death or divorce).

Small groups also have transitional phases of development. Members of a small group spend time getting acquainted, gradually learn to trust one another, begin to self-disclose more, learn to work together on tasks, develop approaches to handle interpersonal conflict, and face adjustments to the group eventually terminating or to some members leaving.

A central concern of an ecological model is to articulate the transitional problems and needs of individuals, families, and small groups. Once these problems and needs are identified, intervention approaches are selected and applied to help the individuals, families, and small groups resolve the transitional problems and meet their needs.

An ecological model can also focus on maladaptive interpersonal problems and needs. It can seek to articulate the maladaptive communication processes and dysfunctional relationship patterns of families and small groups. These difficulties cover an array of areas, including interpersonal conflicts, power struggles, double binds,* distortions in communicating, scapegoating, and discrimination. An ecological model seeks to identify such interpersonal obstacles and then apply appropriate intervention strategies. For example, some parents set too high a price on honesty for their children. In such families, children gradually learn to hide certain behaviors and thoughts and even learn to lie. If the parents discover such dishonesty, an uproar usually occurs. An appropriate intervention in such a family is to open up communication patterns and help the parents to understand that, if they really want honesty from

---

* A double bind is a psychological dilemma in which the receiver of a message gets conflicting interpersonal communications from the sender or faces disparagement no matter what her or his response to a situation is.

their children, they need to learn to be more accepting of their children's thoughts and actions.

Two centuries ago, people interacted primarily within the family system. Families were nearly self-sufficient. In those days, the "person-in-family" was a way of conceptualizing the main system that individuals interacted with. Our society has become much more complex. Today a person's life and quality of life are interwoven and interdependent on many systems, as shown in Figure 2.1.

GOALS OF SOCIAL WORK PRACTICE

The National Association of Social Workers has conceptualized social work practice as having four major goals.[17] We'll discuss each of them in turn.

Goal 1: Enhance the Problem-Solving, Coping, and Developmental Capacities of People

Using the person-in-environment concept, the focus of social work practice at this level is on the "person." With this focus, a social worker serves primarily as a *facilitator*. In this role, the worker may take on activities of a counselor, teacher, caregiver (that is, providing supportive services to those who cannot fully solve their problems and meet their own needs), and changer of specific behavior.

Goal 2: Link People with Systems That Provide Them with Resources, Services, and Opportunities

Using the person-in-environment concept, the focus of social work practice at this level is on the relationships between persons and the systems they interact with. With this focus, a social worker serves primarily as a *broker*.

Goal 3: Promote the Effectiveness and Humane Operation of Systems That Provide People with Resources and Services

Using the person-in-environment concept, the focus of social work practice at this level is on the systems people interact with. One role a worker may fill at this level is that of an *advocate*. Additional roles at this level are:

- *Program developer:* The worker needs to promote or design programs or technologies to meet social needs.
- *Supervisor:* The worker seeks to increase the effectiveness and efficiency of the delivery of services through supervising other staff.
- *Coordinator:* The worker seeks to improve a delivery system through increasing communications and coordination among human service resources.
- *Consultant:* The worker seeks to provide guidance to agencies and organizations by suggesting ways to increase the effectiveness and efficiency of services.

Goal 4: Develop and Improve Social Policy

As in Goal 3, the focus of social work practice at this level is on the systems people interact with. The distinction between Goal 3 and Goal 4 is that Goal 3 focuses on the available resources for serving people, whereas Goal 4 focuses on the statutes and broader social policies that underlie such resources. Social workers at this level are *planners* and *policy developers*. In these roles, workers develop and seek adoption of new statutes or policies and propose elimination of those that are ineffective or inappropriate. In these planning and policy development processes, social workers may take an advocate role and, in some instances, an activist role.

A closely related, but somewhat different, conceptualization of the purpose (which incorporates the goals) of social work practice has recently been formulated by the Council on Social Work Education (CSWE), the national accrediting body for social work education in the United States. The CSWE has defined the purpose of social work as follows:

The profession of social work is committed to the enhancement of human well-being and to the alleviation of poverty and oppression. The social work profession receives its sanction from public and private auspices and is the primary profession in the provision of social services. Within its general scope of concern, professional social work is practiced in a wide variety of settings and has four related purposes:

1. *The promotion, restoration, maintenance, and enhancement of the functioning of individuals, families, groups, organizations, and communities by helping them to accomplish tasks, prevent and alleviate distress, and use resources.*

2. *The planning, formulation, and implementation of social policies, services, resources, and programs needed to meet basic human needs and support the development of human capacities.*

3. *The pursuit of policies, services, resources, and programs through organizational or administrative advocacy and social or political action, so as to empower groups at risk and promote social and economic justice.*

4. *The development and testing of professional knowledge and skills related to these purposes.**

This definition of the purpose of social work differs from NASW's definition in the following

* Reprinted from *Curriculum Policy Statement for Baccalaureate Degree Programs in Social Work Education*, Final Draft July 8, 1992, by permission of the Council on Social Work Education, Alexandria, VA.

important ways. First, it emphasizes that social work has a commitment to "the enhancement of human well-being and to the alleviation of poverty and oppression." Second, it identifies the client systems of social work practice as "individuals, families, groups, organizations, and communities." This definition, in effect, adds two goals of social work practice to NASW's listing: (a) to empower groups at risk and promote social and economic justice and (b) to develop and test professional knowledge and skills.

Goal 5: Empower Groups at Risk and Promote Social and Economic Justice

A partial listing of groups at risk includes people of color, women, gays and lesbians, the elderly, persons with physical or mental disabilities, the poor, persons with AIDS, and oppressed religious groups. Social justice represents an ideal condition in which all members of a society have the same basic rights, protection, opportunities, obligations, and social benefits. Economic justice also represents an ideal condition in which all members of a society have the same opportunities for attaining material goods, income, and wealth. This goal of social work practice asserts that social workers are obligated to help groups at risk increase their personal, interpersonal, socioeconomic, and political strength and influence by improving their life circumstances. Empowerment-focused social workers seek to achieve a more equitable distribution of resources and power among the various groups in a society.

Goal 6: Develop and Test Professional Knowledge and Skills in Social Work

Social workers are expected to contribute to the knowledge and skill base of social work practice. Included in this expectation is the responsibility of social workers to objectively assess their own practice, their programs, and the services they provide.

THE STRENGTHS PERSPECTIVE

For most of the past several decades, social work and the other helping professions have had a primary focus on diagnosing the pathology, shortcomings, and dysfunctions of clients. One reason may be that Freudian psychology was the primary theory used in analyzing human behavior. Freudian psychology is based on a medical model and thereby has concepts that are geared to identify illness or pathology. It has very few concepts to identify strengths. As described earlier in this chapter, social work is now shifting to a systems model in assessing human behavior. This model focuses on identifying both strengths and weaknesses.

It is essential that social workers include clients' strengths in the assessment process. In working with clients, social workers focus on the strengths and resources of clients to help them resolve their difficulties. To utilize clients' strengths effectively, social workers must first identify those strengths.

There is a danger that a primary focus on weaknesses will impair a worker's capacity to identify a client's growth potential. Social workers strongly believe that clients have the right (and should be encouraged) to develop their potentialities fully. Focusing on pathology often undermines this value commitment.

Another reason for attending to clients' strengths is that many clients need help in enhancing their self-esteem. Many have feelings of worthlessness and inadequacy, a sense of being a failure, and a lack of self-confidence and self-respect. Glasser noted that low self-esteem often leads to emotional difficulties, withdrawal, or crime.[18] To help clients view themselves more positively, social workers must first view them as having considerable strengths and competencies.

The *strengths perspective* is closely related to the concept of "empowerment." Empowerment has been defined by Barker as "the process of helping individuals, families, groups, and communities to increase their personal, interpersonal, socioeconomic, and political strength and to develop influence toward improving their circumstances."[19] The strengths perspective is useful across the life cycle and throughout the assessment, intervention, and evaluation stages of the helping process. It emphasizes people's abilities, values, interests, beliefs, resources, accomplishments, and aspirations.[20]

According to Saleebey, five principles guide the strengths perspective:[21]

1. *Every individual, group, family, and community has strengths.* The strengths perspective is about discerning these resources. Saleebey notes:

> *In the end, clients want to know that you actually care about them, that how they fare makes a difference to you, that you will listen to them, that you will respect them no matter what their history, and that you believe that they can build something of value with the resources within and around them. But most of all, clients want to know that you believe they can surmount adversity and begin the climb toward transformation and growth.*[22]

2. *Trauma and abuse, illness and struggle may be injurious, but they may also be sources of challenge and opportunity.* Clients who have been victimized are seen as active and developing individuals who, through their traumas, learn skills and develop personal attributes that assist them in coping with future struggles. There is dignity to be drawn in having prevailed over obstacles. We often grow more from crises that we have handled effectively than from contented and comfortable periods in our lives.

3. *Assume that you do not know the upper limits of the capacity to grow and change and take individual, group, and community aspirations seriously.* This principle means workers need to hold high their expectations of clients and form alliances with their visions, hopes, and values. Individuals, families, and communities have the capacity for restoration and rebounding. When workers connect with clients' hopes and dreams,

Every community has strengths and resources. Arthur Mitchell, center, challenged the dance world's stereotypes and boundaries when he created the Dance Theatre of Harlem in 1969.

clients are apt to have greater faith in themselves and then put forth the kinds of efforts that can make their hopes and dreams become self-fulfilling prophecies.

4. *We best serve clients by collaborating with them.* A worker is more effective when seen as a collaborator or consultant to a client than when seen as an expert or a professional. A collaborative stance by a worker makes her or him less vulnerable to many of the adverse effects of an expert–inferior relationship, including paternalism, victim blaming, and preemption of client views.

5. *Every environment is full of resources.* In every environment (no matter how harsh), there are individuals, groups, associations, and institutions that have something to give and something that others may desperately need. The strengths perspective seeks to identify these resources and make them available to benefit individuals, families, and groups in a community.

SOCIAL WORK STEREOTYPES

The image of the social worker has undergone a more rapid change than that of perhaps any other professional. Sixty years ago, there was a stereotype of a social worker as a moralistic upper-middle-class older woman who carried a basket of food and had little understanding of the people she tried to help. The image is much more positive today, reflecting the improved professional nature of the training and services provided. The image is also much more varied.

Dolgoff, Feldstein, and Skolnik summarize some of the current social work stereotypes:

> Depending upon who is doing the "name calling," social workers are referred to in many ways: do-gooders, bleeding hearts, radicals intent on changing our society, captives of and apologists for "the establishment," organizers of the poor, and servers of the middle class. All these are ways in which people stereotype social workers and the functions they perform in society.[23]

EMPLOYMENT SETTINGS AND OPPORTUNITIES IN SOCIAL WORK

There are currently more employment opportunities in social work than in many other fields. Social services and their delivery are becoming an integral part of our fast-paced existence, and the demand for qualified personnel is expected to expand. If you are looking for the challenge of working with people to improve their social and personal difficulties, then you should seriously consider a career in social work.

From 1960 to 1994, the number of employed social workers grew by nearly 600%—from 95,000 to 557,000.[24] About two of five social workers are employed by public social welfare agencies.[25] The Bureau of Labor Statistics projects the following job outlook for social work positions:

Employment of social workers is expected to increase faster than the average for all occupations through the year 2005. The number of older people, who are more likely to need social services, is growing rapidly. In addition, rising crime and juvenile delinquency as well as increasing concern about services for the mentally ill, the mentally retarded, AIDS patients, and individuals and families in crisis will spur demand for social workers. . . .

Projected employment growth among social workers in hospitals reflects greater emphasis on discharge planning, which facilitates early discharge of patients by assuring that the necessary medical services and social supports are in place when individuals leave the hospital . . .

Social worker employment in home health care services is growing, not only because hospitals are releasing patients more quickly, but because a large and growing number of people have impairments or disabilities that make it difficult to live at home without some form of assistance.

Opportunities for social workers in private practice will expand because of the anticipated availability of funding from health insurance and public-sector contracts. Also, with increasing affluence, people will be better able to pay for professional help to deal with personal problems. The growing popularity of employee assistance programs is also expected to spur demand for private practitioners, some of whom provide social work services to corporations on a contractual basis.

Employment of school workers is expected to grow, due to expanded efforts to respond to the adjustment problems of immigrants, children from single-parent families, and rising rates of teen pregnancy. Moreover, continued emphasis

on integrating disabled children into the general school population—a requirement under the Education for All Handicapped Children Act—will lead to more jobs.[26]

A wide variety of employment settings are available for social workers, including foster care, adoption, probation and parole, public assistance, counseling, services to single parents, day-care services, school social services, services to populations at risk, services to veterans, recreational services such as Boy Scouts and YWCA programs, social services in a medical or mental hospital, antipoverty programs, social services in nursing homes and other services to the elderly, marital counseling, drug and alcohol counseling, services to the emotionally disturbed, abortion counseling, family planning services, services to persons with a physical disability, sexual counseling, equal rights services, protective services, services in rehabilitation centers, research, social action, and fund-raising. (These settings will be described in detail in the chapters that follow.) In addition to these direct services, there are employment opportunities for those with experience and advanced professional training in social planning, community organization, consultation, supervision, teaching, and administration.

Social work majors who are most likely to secure employment in social work following graduation are those who are outgoing, dynamic, and able to "sell" themselves during an interview as having the competence, confidence, and skills to perform the job they are applying for. Involvement in groups and extracurricular activities while at college facilitates the development of these capacities, as does volunteer work at one or more social service agencies. A high number of our students secure employment through the relationships they develop with staff during their field placement. If they do well at their field placement and a vacancy occurs, they have an inside track in being hired. Also, through acquaintances with staff at an agency, they hear about employment opportunities at other agencies and frequently receive a positive letter of reference from their field placement staff.

Students who consider majoring in social work frequently ask: "Is a graduate degree needed to get a job in social work?" It definitely is not. The vast majority of employed social workers hold only a baccalaureate degree. In fact, some agencies prefer to hire a person with a bachelor's degree because it is less expensive. Of course, as in most fields, a master's degree provides higher status, greater promotion opportunities, and perhaps more gratifying work.

PRIVATE PRACTICE OF SOCIAL WORK

Although the vast majority of social workers are employed by agencies (financed by either public or private funds), a growing number of social workers in the past two decades have opted to provide counseling (also called psychotherapy) and group therapy on a fee basis. This type of *private practice* is similar to the arrangement in which private physicians provide services to patients.

The social worker may conduct a private practice on a part-time basis in addition to working full time for an agency. Or the individual may work full time in private practice. Sometimes social workers form a partnership with psychologists and/or psychiatrists to provide psychotherapy and group therapy through a private for-profit clinic. In yet another arrangement, social workers may be employed by a private clinic (which may be owned by a psychologist or psychiatrist) to provide therapy to individuals and groups.

Different states have different laws regulating the structure and operation of private clinics and private practice. Such legislation is intended to protect the public. These laws usually require that the social worker in private practice have a master's degree from an accredited school of social work as well as a few years of supervised practice in counseling individuals and groups.

In most cases, fees for therapy are paid by recipients' health insurance policies. If recipients do not have health insurance coverage, they are expected to pay their own fees for the therapy they receive.

INTERNATIONAL SOCIAL WORK

Social work is a recognized profession in Great Britain, Canada, the United States, India, and numerous other countries. There is a growing recognition that people in all nations are interdependent. In many ways, the world has become, as futurist Marshall McLuhan put it, a "global village."[27] The crises and problems experienced by one country often affect other countries. There is a trend in colleges and universities in many countries to "internationalize" the curriculum. Students need an understanding and appreciation of the diversity that exists internationally.

Social work educational programs in the United States are increasingly seeking to foster an international perspective for social work majors. This is being done through student exchange programs with other countries, faculty exchange programs with other countries, study-abroad programs (including internship) for social work majors, and new curriculum content on social problems and innovative services in other countries. The revised curriculum Policy Statements of the Council on Social Work Education in 1992 for the first time mentioned the importance of an international perspective. The CSWE[28] also has a commission on international social work education that is composed of educators from around the country who are actively involved in teaching international content and initiating cross-national exchange programs. (This text seeks to facilitate readers acquiring an international perspective by presenting, in practically every chapter, information on social problems and social services in not only the United States but also in other countries.)

The International Federation of Social Workers (IFSW) is an organization comprising more than 50 professional membership associations, including the National Association of Social Workers.[29] Healy describes the goals of IFSW:

> The goals of the federation are to promote social work as a profession with professional standards, training, and ethics; to support the involvement of national associations of social work in policy development; to encourage communications among social workers in various countries; and to present the views of the profession internationally to intergovernment organizations . . . A valuable part of the federation's work has been its human rights advocacy for social workers who are held as political prisoners in various parts of the world.[30]

People of all countries are experiencing many of the social problems described in this text, including poverty, mental illness, crime, divorce, family violence, births outside of marriage, AIDS, rape, incest, drug abuse, worker alienation, international terrorism, unemployment, racism, sexism, medical problems, physical and mental disabilities, overpopulation, and misuse of the environment. By studying and analyzing how other countries are combating these problems, social service policymakers and providers in every country can learn to identify more effective programs and service delivery systems. Indeed, some of these problems (such as overpopulation and international terrorism) can be resolved only by coordinated international efforts. Social workers in the future will increasingly need an international perspective in analyzing and combating social problems.

Some international employment opportunities are available for social workers. The United Nations employs some social workers in staff positions for UNESCO (United Nations Educational, Scientific, and Cultural Organization), UNICEF (United Nations Children's Fund), and refugee work. Some units of government in other countries, and some private organizations as well, contract with social workers in the United States to be consultants. Some private national or international organizations (such as Catholic Charities, Worldwide

Adoptions, and the Red Cross) have utilized social workers in their international programs.

SELF-AWARENESS AND IDENTITY DEVELOPMENT

As stated earlier, perhaps the key skill needed to be a competent social worker is the capacity to relate to and counsel individuals. Increasingly, when training social work students, educators are finding that the students who are best able to counsel others are those who know themselves; that is, they have a high level of self-awareness. A counselor has to be perceptive regarding what clients are thinking and feeling. To be perceptive, the counselor must be able to place himself or herself in the client's situation and determine (with the client's values and pressures) what that person is really feeling and thinking. Unless the counselor has a high level of self-awareness, it is very unlikely that she or he will be able to perceive what others are thinking and feeling.

A variety of approaches have been developed to increase self-awareness, including biofeedback, transcendental meditation, muscle relaxation, Gestalt therapy, identity formation, sensitivity training, and encounter groups.* (Some programs in social work are now offering interpersonal skills courses that are designed to develop self-awareness and interpersonal awareness capacities.)

Identity Formation

One approach to self-awareness—identity formation—will be explored here.† Identity formation is the process of determining who you are and what

---

* A review of the specific techniques used in these approaches is contained in Charles Zastrow, *The Practice of Social Work*, 6th ed. (Pacific Grove, CA: Brooks/Cole, 1999).
† This material on identity formation is adapted from an article I wrote entitled, "Who Am I: Quest for Identity," in *The Personal Problem Solver*, Charles Zastrow and Dae Chang, eds. (Englewood Cliffs, NJ: Prentice Hall, 1977), pp. 365–370.

you want out of life. Arriving at an identity you will be comfortable with is one of the most important tasks you will ever have to face. Whether or not you pursue a social work career, the following information on identity could have considerable importance for your future. As noted, it is especially significant for those considering a social work career because knowing oneself substantially enhances one's ability to counsel others.

Identity development is a lifelong process; there are gradual changes in our identity throughout our lifetime. During the early years, our sense of who we are is largely determined by the reactions of others (the looking-glass self-concept). For example, if neighbors, for whatever reason, perceive a young male to be a "troublemaker" or a "delinquent," they are then likely to accuse the youth of delinquent acts, treat him with suspicion, and label many of his activities "delinquent." Although frequently accused and criticized, the youth, to some extent, soon begins to realize that enacting the delinquent role also brings certain rewards; it gives him a type of status and prestige, at least from other youths. In the absence of objective ways to determine whether he is a delinquent, he relies on the subjective evaluations of others. Gradually, a vicious cycle develops: The more he is related to as a delinquent, the more likely he is to view himself as a delinquent and the more likely he is to enact the delinquent role.

Glasser indicates that a useful perspective for viewing identity is in terms of a success-versus-failure orientation.[31] Those who develop a success identity view themselves as being generally successful; people who develop a success identity do so through the pathways of *love* and *worth*. People who view themselves as a success must feel that at least one other person loves them and also that they love at least one other person. They must feel that at least one other person believes they are worthwhile, and they must feel they (themselves) are worthwhile.

To develop a success identity, a person must experience both love and worth, particularly during childhood. A person can feel loved but not feel worthwhile. Worth comes through accomplishing tasks and achieving success in the accomplishment of those tasks. A person can feel worthwhile through accomplishing tasks (for example, a successful businessperson) but believe she is unloved because she cannot name someone she loves and who loves her. Experiencing only one of these elements (worth or love) without the other can lead to a failure identity.

A failure identity is likely to develop when a child has received inadequate love or been made to feel worthless. People with a failure identity are likely to be depressed, lonely, anxious, reluctant to face everyday challenges, and indecisive. Escape through drugs or alcohol, withdrawal, criminal behavior, and the development of emotional problems are common.

However, because identity is a lifelong process, significant positive changes can be achieved, even by those with a serious failure identity. An important principle is: *Although we cannot change the past, what we want out of the future, along with our motivation to achieve what we want, is more important (than our past experiences) in determining what our future will be.*

Some of the most important issues you will ever have to face are these:

1. What kind of person do you want to be?

2. What do you want out of life?

3. Who are you?

Without answers to these questions, you will not be prepared to make such major decisions as selecting a career, choosing where to live and what type of lifestyle you want, and deciding whether to marry and whether to have children. Unfortunately, many people muddle through life without ever arriving at answers to these questions. The answers don't come easily. They require considerable thought and much trial and error. During the time you are searching for a sense of who you are, a great deal of anxiety may arise. However, if you are to lead a satisfying, fulfilling life, it is imperative that you know what you want and who you are. Here are some additional questions to aid in identity formation.

Questions for Arriving at a Sense of Identity

To determine who you are, answer the following more specific questions:

1. What do you find satisfying/enjoyable? Only after you identify what is meaningful and gratifying will you be able to consciously seek involvement in activities that will make your life fulfilling and avoid activities that are meaningless or stifling.

2. What are your religious beliefs?

3. What is your moral code? One possible code is to attempt to fulfill your needs and do what you find enjoyable without depriving others of the ability to fulfill their needs.

4. What are your sexual mores? All of us should develop a consistent code that we are comfortable with and that helps us meet our needs without exploiting others. There is no one right code—what works for me may not work for you because of differences in lifestyle, life goals, and personal values.

5. What kind of a career do you desire? Ideally, you should seek work that is stimulating and satisfying, that you are skilled at, and that earns you enough money to support the lifestyle you desire.

6. What area of the country or world do you want to live in? Variables to be considered are climate, geography, type of dwelling, rural or urban setting, proximity to relatives or friends, and characteristics of the neighborhood.

7. Do you hope to marry? If yes, to what type of person? When? How consistent are your answers here with your other life goals?

8. Do you want to have children? If yes, how many? When? How consistent are your answers here with your other life goals?

9. What kind of image do you want to project to others? Your image consists of your dressing style and grooming habits, emotions, personality, degree of assertiveness, capacity to communicate, material possessions, moral code, physical features, and voice patterns. You need to honestly assess your strengths and shortcomings in this area and try to make improvements in the latter. Seeking counseling in problem areas may be desirable.

10. What do you enjoy doing in your leisure time?

11. Do you desire to improve the quality of your life and that of others? If yes, in what ways? How do you hope to achieve these goals?

12. What type of people do you enjoy being with? Why?

13. What kind of a relationship do you want to have with your relatives, friends, neighbors, and people you meet for the first time?

14. What are your thoughts about death and dying?

15. What do you hope to be doing in 5 years? in 10 years? in 20 years? What are your plans for achieving these goals in these time periods?

To have a fairly well-developed sense of identity, you need to have answers to most, but not all, of these questions. Very few people are able to arrive at rational, fully consistent answers to all the questions.

Be honest about your strengths and shortcomings. Realize that for practically any shortcoming there are specific intervention strategies to bring about improvement.

In addition, expect some changes in your life goals as time goes on. As you grow as a person, changes will occur in your beliefs, attitudes, and values and in the activities that you find enjoyable.

Your life is shaped by different events that result from the decisions you make and the decisions that are made for you. Without a sense of identity, you will not know what decisions are best, and your life will be unfulfilled. With a sense of identity, you will be able to direct your life toward the goals you select and find personally meaningful.

SUMMARY

A social worker is a multiskilled professional. The social worker needs training and expertise in a wide range of areas to be able to deal effectively with problems faced by individuals, groups, families, organizations, and the larger community. Like the general practitioner in medicine, a social worker should acquire a wide range of skills and intervention techniques. Social work is distinct from other careers in that it is the profession that has the responsibility and mandate to provide social services.

The ability to counsel clients effectively is perhaps the most basic skill a social worker needs. Second in importance is probably the ability to interact effectively with other groups and professionals in the community.

Social work as a profession is of relatively recent origin. Individuals were first hired as social workers around 1900, and formalized training in social work was first offered at universities in the early 1900s.

Social workers work with individuals, groups, families, organizations, and communities. The social worker helps people increase their capacities for problem solving and coping, helps them obtain needed resources, facilitates interactions between individuals and between people and their environments, helps make organizations responsible to people, and influences social policies. There are several types of professional social work activities: casework, case management, group work, group therapy, family therapy, community organization, administration, research, consulting, planning, supervision, and teaching.

The six goals of social work practice are to (a) enhance the problem-solving, coping, and developmental capacities of people; (b) link people with systems that provide them with resources, services, and opportunities; (c) promote the effectiveness and humane operation of systems that provide people with resources and services; (d) develop and improve social policy; (e) empower groups at risk and promote social and eco-

nomic justice; and (f) develop and test professional knowledge and skills.

Social work emphasizes a strengths perspective (rather than a focus on pathology) in working with individuals, groups, families, organizations, and communities.

Sixty years ago, the stereotype of a social worker was that of a moralistic upper-middle-class older woman carrying a basket of food and having little understanding of the people she tried to help. With the rapid development of social work as a profession, there are now many stereotypes (generally more positive) of what a social worker is.

Currently there are more employment opportunities available in social work than in many other fields. A wide variety of employment settings are available for social workers. A majority of people employed as social workers do not have a graduate degree. As in most fields, however, individuals with a master's degree in social work generally have higher status and greater promotion opportunities.

It is crucial for social workers to have a high level of self-awareness and a sense of who they are and what they want out of life. Arriving at a sense of identity is one of the most important and difficult quests in life—for everyone. With a sense of identity, you will be able to direct your life toward the goals you select and find personally meaningful.

NOTES

1. Robert M. Bremner, "The Rediscovery of Pauperism," *Current Issues in Social Work Seen in Historical Perspective* (New York: Council on Social Work Education, 1962), p. 13.
2. Nathan E. Cohen, *Social Work in the American Tradition* (Hinsdale, IL: Dryden Press, 1958), p. 66.
3. Dorothy G. Becker, "Social Welfare Leaders As Spokesmen for the Poor," *Social Casework*, 49, no. 2 (Feb. 1968), p. 85.
4. Ralph Dolgoff and Donald Feldstein, *Understanding Social Welfare* (New York: Harper & Row, 1980), pp. 233–234.

5. Ibid., p. 235.
6. Mary E. Richmond, *Social Diagnosis* (New York: Free Press, 1965).
7. H. J. Eysenck, "The Effects of Psychotherapy," in *Handbook of Abnormal Psychology*, H. J. Eysenck, ed. (New York: Basic Books, 1961), pp. 697–725.
8. Robert L. Barker, *The Social Work Dictionary*, 3rd ed. (Washington, DC: NASW, 1995), p. 357.
9. Ibid., p. 358.
10. Dean H. Hepworth, Ronald H. Rooney, and Jo Ann Larsen, *Direct Social Work Practice: Theory and Skills*, 5th ed. (Pacific Grove, CA: Brooks/Cole, 1997), pp. 27–28.
11. Barker, *The Social Work Dictionary*, p. 47.
12. Frank Riessman, "The 'Helper Therapy' Principle," *Journal of Social Work*, 10, no. 2 (Apr. 1965), pp. 27–34.
13. Barker, *The Social Work Dictionary*, p. 69.
14. Richard Stuart, *Trick or Treatment: How and When Psychotherapy Fails* (Champaign, IL: Research Press, 1970).
15. William H. Masters and Virginia E. Johnson, *Human Sexual Inadequacy* (Boston: Little, Brown, 1970).
16. D. D. Jackson, "The Study of the Family," *Family Process*, 4 (1965), pp. 1–20.
17. National Association of Social Workers, *Standards for the Classification of Social Work Practice* (Washington, DC: NASW, 1982), p. 17.
18. William Glasser, *The Identity Society* (New York: Harper & Row, 1972).
19. Barker, *The Social Work Dictionary*, p. 20.
20. A. Weick, C. Rapp, W. P. Sullivan, and W. Kisthardt, "A Strengths Perspective for Social Work Practice," *Social Work*, 34 (1989), pp. 350–354.
21. Dennis Saleebey, *The Strengths Perspective in Social Work Practice*, 2nd ed. (New York: Longman, 1997), pp. 12–15.
22. Ibid., p. 12.
23. Ralph Dolgoff, Donald Feldstein, and Louise Skolnik, *Understanding Social Welfare*, 4th ed. (New York: Longman, 1997), p. 295.
24. U.S. Department of Labor, *Occupational Outlook Handbook: 1996–97 Edition* (Washington, DC: U.S. Department of Labor, 1996), p. 133.
25. Ibid.
26. Ibid., pp. 133–134.
27. See William Kornblum and Joseph Julian, *Social Problems*, 7th ed. (Englewood Cliffs, NJ: Prentice Hall, 1992), p. 468.
28. *Curriculum Policy Statement for Baccalaureate Degree Programs in Social Work Education* (Alexandria, VA: Council on Social Work Education, 1992); *Curriculum Policy Statement for Master's Degree Programs in Social Work Education* (Alexandria, VA: Council on Social Work Education, 1992).
29. Lynne M. Healy, "International Social Welfare: Organizations and Activities," *Encyclopedia of Social Work*, 19th ed. (Washington, DC: NASW, 1995), p. 1505.
30. Ibid.
31. Glasser, *The Identity Society*.

GENERALIST
SOCIAL
WORK
PRACTICE

The focus of this chapter will be on generalist social work practice. This chapter will:

- Define generalist social work practice.
- Summarize the change process in social work practice.
- Describe roles assumed by social workers in social work practice.
- Discuss social work practice with individuals, families, groups, organizations, and the community.
- Summarize the knowledge, skills, and values needed for social work practice.
- Briefly describe educational training for social work practice.

GENERALIST SOCIAL WORK PRACTICE DEFINED

The traditional perception of the social worker has been that of a caseworker, group worker, or community organizer. Practicing social workers know that their roles are more complex than that; every social worker is involved as a change agent (someone who assists in promoting positive changes) in working with individuals, groups, families, organizations, and the larger community. The amount of time spent at these levels varies from worker to worker. But every worker will, at times, be assigned and expected to function effectively at all these levels and therefore needs training in all of them.

The Council on Social Work Education (CSWE) (the national accrediting entity for baccalaureate and master's programs in social work) requires all bachelor's and master's programs to train their students in generalist social work practice. (MSW programs, in addition, usually require their students to select and study in an area of specialization. These programs generally offer several specializations, such as family therapy, administration, corrections, and clinical social work.)

Anderson has identified three characteristics of a generalist social worker: (a) The generalist is often the first professional to see clients as they enter the social welfare system; (b) the worker must therefore be competent to assess their needs and to identify their stress points and problems; and (c) the worker must draw on a variety of skills and methods in serving clients.[1]

D. Brieland, L. B. Costin, and C. R. Atherton define and describe generalist practice as follows:

The generalist social worker, the equivalent of the general practitioner in medicine, is characterized by a wide repertoire of skills to deal with basic conditions, backed up by specialists to whom referrals are made. This role is a fitting one for the entry-level social worker.

The generalist model involves identifying and analyzing the interventive behaviors appropriate to social work. The worker must perform a wide range of tasks related to the provision and management of direct service, the development of social policy, and the facilitation of social change. The generalist should be well grounded in systems theory that emphasizes interaction and independence. The major system that will be used is the local network of services. . . .

The public welfare worker in a small county may be a classic example of the generalist. He or she knows the resources of the county, is acquainted with the key people, and may have considerable influence to accomplish service goals, including obtaining jobs, different housing, or emergency food and clothing. The activities of the urban generalist are more complex, and more effort must be expended to use the array of resources.[2]

G. Hull defines generalist practice as follows:

The basic principle of generalist practice is that baccalaureate social workers are able to utilize the problem solving process to intervene with various size systems including individuals, families, groups, organizations, and communities. The generalist operates within a systems and person-in-the-environment framework (sometimes referred to as an ecological model). The generalist expects that many problems will require intervention with more than one system (e.g., individual work with a delinquent adolescent plus work with the family or school) and that single explanations of problem situations are frequently unhelpful. The generalist may play several roles simultaneously or sequentially, depending upon the needs of the client (e.g., facilitator, advocate, educator, broker, enabler, case manager, and/or mediator). They may serve as leaders/facilitators of task groups, socialization groups, information groups, and self-help groups. They are capable of conducting needs assessments and evaluating their own practice and the programs with which they are associated. They make referrals when client problems so dictate and know when to utilize supervision from more experienced staff. Generalists operate within the ethical guidelines prescribed by the NASW Code of Ethics and must be able to work with clients, coworkers, and colleagues from different ethnic, cultural, and professional orientations. The knowledge and skills of the generalist are transferable from one setting to another and from one problem to another.[3]

The crux of generalist practice involves (a) viewing a problem situation in terms of the person-in-environment conceptualization (described in Chapter 2) and (b) being willing and able to intervene at several different levels, if necessary, while assuming any number of roles. The next section describes the change process in social work practice and illustrates the approach of responding at different levels in a variety of roles.

THE CHANGE PROCESS

Social workers use the *change process* in working with clients. (Clients include individuals, groups, families, organizations, and communities.) The CSWE, in its curriculum policy statements, identifies the following eight skills that are needed for social work practice:

1. *Defining issues;*
2. *Collecting and assessing data;*
3. *Planning and contracting;*
4. *Identifying alternative interventions;*
5. *Selecting and implementing appropriate courses of action;*
6. *Using appropriate research to monitor and evaluate outcomes;*
7. *Applying appropriate research-based knowledge and technological advances; and*
8. *Termination.*[4]

These eight skills, interestingly, provide an excellent framework for conceptualizing the phases of the change process in social work. I'll use a case example to illustrate this change process.

Carlos Ramirez is a social worker at a high school in a midwestern state. Four teenagers are suspended for 2 weeks (consistent with school board policy) for drinking alcoholic beverages at school. The case is referred to Mr. Ramirez for intervention.

Phase 1: Defining Issues

Defining issues, the first step in the change process, often becomes fairly complex. In this case example, there are a number of issues (questions, concerns, problems) that the school social worker, Carlos Ramirez, identifies: Do the youths have a drinking problem? Were the boys disenchanted with the school system and displaying their discontent by breaking school rules? What short-term and long-term adverse effects might the suspensions have on the youths? (For example, the suspensions could have a labeling effect, giving these youths a reputation as "troublemakers"; this label could lead them to become further involved in delinquent behavior.) What will be the reactions of the parents to the drinking and to the suspensions? What effects will the suspensions have on other students at the school? (A possible positive effect is that the suspensions may be a deterrent to other students who are considering violating school rules; a possible negative consequence is that the suspensions may encourage other students to violate school rules and get suspended so they can avoid having to attend school.) Will the suspensions create problems for merchants in the community because the suspended youths are now likely to spend their days on the street? Is the school policy of suspending youths for drinking on school grounds a constructive or destructive educational policy? Does the school system have a responsibility to add an educational program on substance abuse to the curriculum? Are there aspects about the school system that encourage youths to rebel? If so, should these aspects be changed?

The issues identified then serve as a guide for the next phase (data collection and assessment). During this initial phase (as well as during the other phases), it is essential that the social worker seeks to establish and continue a working relationship with the client(s).

Phase 2: Collecting and Assessing Data

Here the social worker does an in-depth collection and analysis of data to find answers to the questions raised in Phase 1. For some of the issues, useful information can be obtained directly from the clients. (In this case example, the clients would certainly include the youths with a drinking problem. Another client is the school system that employs Mr. Ramirez, as Mr. Ramirez has an obligation to serve the needs of the school system for which he works. The parents of the suspended youths are potential clients as some may want services for family dynamics that are contributing to the drinking behavior of their teenagers.) For instance, the question of whether the youths have a drinking problem can perhaps be answered by meeting individually with each boy, forming a trusting relationship, and then asking how often the youth drinks, how much he consumes when drinking, and what problems he has encountered while drinking. For other issues raised in Phase 1, useful information will need to be collected from other sources. For example, the short- and long-term adverse effects of the suspensions on the youths might be determined by researching the literature on this topic.

Assessment is the process of analyzing the data to make sense of it. Phase 2 also involves an assessment of the degree of match, or fit, between the client's needs and the agency's eligibility requirements and resources. The service may be terminated for lack of fit. The client may be referred elsewhere for service, perhaps because of the specialization of some other agency's resources. If the fit is deemed appropriate, the social worker and the client then move on to the next phase.

Phase 3: Planning and Contracting

Planning includes formulating initial objectives (goals) and deciding which objectives to pursue. One objective may be to explore with the youths whether they have a drinking problem. Another objective may be to have the youths reinstated in school. Still another might be to change the out-of-school suspension policy to in-school suspension. Or perhaps an objective would be to add educational material on substance abuse to the curriculum. Often the social worker will use a technique like cost-benefit analysis (weighing resources expended against estimated potential benefits) to make decisions about which objective(s) to pursue. (In real-life situations, social workers rarely are able to pursue all worthy objectives because of time and resource constraints.)

Contracting involves making arrangements with the client(s), or with organizations that are providing funding for the client(s), for what services (often with a specification of the objectives) will be offered and at what cost (with a specification of financial arrangements).

Phase 4: Identifying Alternative Interventions

Carlos Ramirez, social worker at the high school the youths were suspended from, selects (in Phase 3) as one of his objectives the preventative approach of seeking to add educational material on substance abuse to the curriculum. Numerous questions related to this objective now arise for him. What specific material should be covered in a drug education program? Which drugs should be included? (Mr. Ramirez is aware that certain drugs, such as LSD, are seldom used in the community; some parents may thus question whether educational material about these drugs might actually encourage some youths to experiment with them.) Where should this educational component be added into the curriculum—in large assemblies with all students being required to attend, in health classes, in social science classes, or elsewhere? Will the administration, faculty, school board, students, and parents be supportive of adding this component to the curriculum? What will be the most effective strategy for gaining the support of these various groups?

As a first step in this phase, Mr. Ramirez meets with his immediate supervisor, Dr. Marie Lee, Director of Pupil Services at the high school, to discuss these issues and to generate a list of alternative strategies for how to proceed. Three strategies are considered: (a) Students could be anonymously surveyed to determine the extent of alcohol and other drug use and abuse at the school. Such survey results could document the need for a drug education program. (b) A committee of professional staff in the Pupil Services Department could be appointed to develop a drug education program. (c) The Pupil Services Department could request that the administration and school board appoint a committee—composed of representatives from the school board, school administration, faculty, students, parents, and Pupil Services—to explore the need for and feasibility of a drug education program.

Phase 5: Selecting and Implementing Appropriate Courses of Action

Mr. Ramirez and Dr. Lee decide that the best way to obtain broad support for a drug education program is to pursue the third option listed in Phase 4. Dr. Lee meets with the high school principal, Mary Powell. After some contemplation, Ms. Powell agrees that the need for such a program should be explored, and she asks the school board to support the formation of such a committee. The board agrees. A committee is eventually formed, and it begins to hold meetings. Mr. Ramirez is appointed by Dr. Lee to be Pupil Services' representative to this committee.

Phase 6: Using Appropriate Research to Monitor and Evaluate Outcomes

One of the first questions raised by committee members during initial deliberations is which specific drugs should be covered in the program. As a result, the Pupil Services Department is asked to conduct a survey of all the students to identify which drugs are currently being used and to what extent.

A second (related) issue that arises in the committee is the broader question of whether a drug education program really would have preventative value or would have the undesired outcome of promoting illegal drug use. To obtain information on this issue, staff in the Pupil Services Department research the literature on the preventative value of drug education programs nationally, as well as on the most effective formats for such programs.

After 14 months of planning and deliberation, the committee presents a proposal to the school board for a drug education program. The program is designed to become part of the curriculum of health classes in middle schools and high schools throughout the school district. One component of the proposal requires that the Pupil Services Department conduct an annual survey of a random sample of students to obtain (a) information on the extent of drug use/abuse and (b) students' thoughts about the merits and shortcomings of the program. Such a survey provides a way of monitoring and evaluating the outcomes of the drug education program.

Phase 7: Applying Appropriate Research-Based Knowledge and Technological Advances

The drug education program that is implemented contains the latest research-based knowledge on commonly used drugs by young people in the community. The following topics are covered: mind-altering effects, physical and psychological dependency, withdrawal, and long-term effects on health. The curriculum also contains research-based information on the most effective treatment approaches, ways of coping when someone in the family is abusing, ways to confront a friend or relative who is abusing, dangers of driving when using drugs, associations between drug use and sexually transmitted diseases (including AIDS), steps to take if one has concerns about his or her own drug use, and ways of saying "no" to peer pressure to use drugs.

Several technological advances are used for this drug education program. Computers search databases for information on effective drug programs in other school systems in the country; they also process data from the surveys on drug use by middle and high school students in the district. Educational films and videotapes are also integrated into the curriculum.

Phase 8: Termination

The committee that developed the drug education program holds its final meeting after the school board approves the proposal. Most members experience mixed emotions—delight that their task is successfully completed but sad that this important and meaningful part of their lives is now ending.

If a close working relationship has formed between the worker and the client, termination is often a painful process, especially for the client but sometimes for the worker as well. In the change process, sensitive issues are often addressed, considerable effort is expended on making constructive changes, and dependency may develop. As a result, the client is likely to experience a sense of loss when termination occurs. The client may also feel angry and rejected.

A final evaluation is usually a part of terminating. The final evaluation involves more than the assessment of what occurred during monitoring; it emphasizes the usefulness of the entire change process. The final evaluation is also extremely significant to the agency because it indicates whether the agency's services have been

beneficial. Each agency needs composite evaluations of all their services to all clients that provide documentation to funding sources to justify continued funding.

A VARIETY OF ROLES

In working with individuals, groups, families, organizations, and communities, a social worker is expected to be knowledgeable and skillful in a variety of roles. The particular role that is selected should (ideally) be determined by what will be most effective, given the circumstances. The following material identifies some, but certainly not all, of the roles assumed by social workers.

ENABLER

In this role, a worker *helps* individuals or groups to articulate their needs, to clarify and identify their problems, to explore resolution strategies, to select and apply a strategy, and to develop their capacities to deal with their own problems more effectively. This is perhaps the most frequently used approach in counseling individuals, groups, and families. The model is also used in community practice primarily when the objective is to help people organize to help themselves.

It should be noted that this definition of the term *enabler* is very different from the one used in the area of chemical dependency. There the term refers to a family member or friend who facilitates the substance abuser's continued use and abuse of a drug.

BROKER

A broker links individuals and groups who need help (and do not know where it is available) with community services. For example, a wife who is often physically abused by her husband might be referred to a shelter for battered women. Nowadays even moderate-sized communities have 200 or 300 social service agencies/organizations providing community services. Even human services professionals may be only partially aware of the total service network in their community.

ADVOCATE

The role of advocate has been borrowed from the legal profession. It is an active, directive role in which the social worker advocates for a client or for a citizens' group. When a client or a citizens' group is in need of help and existing institutions are uninterested (or even openly negative and hostile) in providing services, then the advocate's role may be appropriate. In such a role, the advocate provides leadership for collecting information, for arguing the correctness of the client's need and request, and for challenging the institution's decision not to provide services. The objective is not to ridicule or censure a particular institution but to modify or change one or more of its service policies. In this role, the advocate is a partisan who is exclusively serving the interests of a client or a citizens' group.

ACTIVIST

An activist seeks institutional change; often the objective involves a shift in power and resources to a disadvantaged group. Activists are concerned about social injustice, inequity, and deprivation, and their strategies include conflict, confrontation, and negotiation. The goal is to change the social environment to better meet the recognized needs of individuals. Using assertive and action-oriented methods (for example, organizing concerned citizens to work toward improvements in services in a community for persons with AIDS), social workers engage in fact finding, analysis of community needs, research, the dissemination and interpretation of information, mobilization, and other efforts to promote public understanding and support on behalf of existing or proposed social programs. Social action activity can be geared toward a problem that is local, statewide, or national in scope.

MEDIATOR

The mediator role involves intervention in disputes between parties to help them find compromises, reconcile differences, or reach mutually satisfactory agreements. Social workers have used their value orientations and unique skills in many forms of mediation. Examples of target groups in which mediation has been used include disputes that involve divorcing spouses, neighbors in conflict, landlord–tenant disputes, labor–management disputes, and child custody disputes. Mediators remain neutral, not siding with either party, and make sure they understand the positions of both parties. They may help to clarify positions, identify miscommunication about differences, and help those involved present their cases clearly.

NEGOTIATOR

A negotiator brings together those who are in conflict over one or more issues and seeks to achieve bargaining and compromise to arrive at mutually acceptable agreements. Somewhat like mediation, negotiation involves finding a middle ground that all sides can live with. However, unlike a mediator, which is a neutral role, a negotiator usually is allied with one of the sides involved.

EDUCATOR

The educator role involves giving information to clients and teaching them adaptive skills. To be an effective educator, the worker must first be knowledgeable. Additionally, she or he must be a good communicator so that information is clearly conveyed and readily understood by the receiver. Examples include teaching parenting skills to young parents, providing job-hunting strategies to the unemployed, and teaching anger-control techniques to individuals with bad tempers.

INITIATOR

An initiator calls attention to a problem—or even to a potential problem. It is important to realize that some problems can be recognized in advance. For example, a proposal to renovate a low-income neighborhood by building middle-income housing units may result in the current residents' becoming homeless. If the proposal is approved, the low-income families won't be able to afford the costs of the middle-income units. Usually the initiator role must be followed by other functions; merely calling attention to problems usually does not resolve them.

EMPOWERER

A key goal of social work practice is empowerment, which is the process of helping individuals, families, groups, organizations, and communities increase their personal, interpersonal, socioeconomic, and political strength and influence through improving their circumstances. Social workers who engage in empowerment-focused practice seek to develop the capacity of clients to understand their environment, make choices, take responsibility for their choices, and influence their life situations through organization and advocacy. Empowerment-focused social workers also seek to gain a more equitable distribution of resources and power among different groups in society. This focus on equity and social justice has been a hallmark of the social work profession, as evidenced through the early settlement workers such as Jane Addams (see Chapter 2).

COORDINATOR

Coordinators bring components together in some kind of organized manner. For example, for a multiproblem family it is often necessary for several agencies to work together to meet the complicated financial, emotional, legal, health, social, educational, recreational, and interactional needs of the family members. Someone at an agency needs to assume the role of case manager to coordinate the services from the different agencies to avoid duplication and to prevent the diverse services from having conflicting objectives.

RESEARCHER

Every social worker is at times a researcher. Research in social work practice includes studying the literature on topics of interest, evaluating the outcomes of one's practice, assessing the merits and shortcomings of programs, and studying community needs.

GROUP FACILITATOR

A group facilitator is one who serves as a leader for group activity. The group may be a therapy group, an educational group, a self-help group, a sensitivity group, a family therapy group, or a group with some other focus.

PUBLIC SPEAKER

Social workers occasionally are recruited to talk to various groups (such as high school classes, public service organizations such as Kiwanis, police officers, staff at other agencies) to inform them of available services or to advocate for new services. In recent years, a variety of needed services have been identified (for example, runaway centers, services for battered spouses, rape crisis centers, services for persons with AIDS, and group homes for youths). Social workers who have public-speaking skills can explain services to groups of potential clients.

As indicated earlier, a generalist social worker is a change agent (someone who assists in facilitating positive changes) who works with individuals, groups, families, organizations, and the community. To give you a flavor of social work practice in each of these areas, some brief practice-oriented information will be presented.

SOCIAL WORK WITH INDIVIDUALS

A majority of social workers spend most of their time working with individuals in public or private agencies or in private practice. Social work with individuals is aimed at helping people, on a one-to-one basis, to resolve personal and social problems. Social work with individuals encompasses a wide variety of activities, such as counseling runaway youths, helping unemployed people secure training or employment, counseling someone who is suicidal, placing a homeless child in an adoptive or foster home, providing protective services to abused children and their families, finding nursing homes for stroke victims who no longer need to be confined in a hospital, counseling individuals with sexual dysfunctions, helping alcoholics to acknowledge that they have a drinking problem, counseling those with a terminal illness, supervising individuals on probation or parole, providing services to single parents, and coordinating services for individuals who have AIDS.

All of us at times face personal problems that we cannot resolve by ourselves. Sometimes other family members, relatives, friends, or acquaintances can help. At other times we need more skilled intervention to help us handle emotional problems, obtain resources in times of crisis, deal with marital or family conflicts, resolve problems at work or school, or cope with a medical emergency. Furnishing skilled personal help is what social work with individuals is all about.

In their role as change agents in working with individuals, social workers perform many of the functions discussed earlier: enabler, broker, advocate, educator, and so on. An essential skill and role of a social worker is counseling. (Some authorities assert that counseling and relationship skills are the most important abilities needed by social workers.[5] Future chapters will illustrate that social workers counsel people with a wide variety of personal and social problems. See Chapter 5 for guidelines on counseling individuals.)

SOCIAL WORK WITH FAMILIES

Often the focus of social work services is on the family. A family is an interacting interdependent system. The problems faced by any individual are usually influenced by the dynamics within a family. Because a family is an interacting system, change in one member affects other members. For example, it has been noted that the abused child is at times a scapegoat on whom the parents vent their anger and hostility. If the abused child is removed from such a home, another child within the family is likely to be selected as the scapegoat.[6]

Another reason for focusing on the family is that the participation of all members is often needed in the treatment process. For example, other family members can put pressure on an alcoholic to make her or him acknowledge that a problem exists. The family members may all need counseling (or support from a self-help group) to assist them in coping with the alcoholic when she or he is drinking, and these family members may play important roles in providing emotional support for the alcoholic's efforts to stop drinking.

Family Problems

The following is a small listing of some of the infinite number of problems that may occur in families:

- Divorce
- Alcohol or drug abuse
- Unwanted pregnancy
- Bankruptcy
- Poverty
- Terminal illness
- Chronic illness
- Death
- Desertion
- Empty-shell marriage
- Emotional problems of one or more members
- Behavioral problems of one or more members
- Child abuse
- Child neglect
- Sexual abuse
- Spouse abuse
- Elder abuse
- Unemployment of wage earners
- Money management difficulties
- Injury from serious automobile accident involving one or more members
- Cognitive disability in one or more members
- Incarceration or institutionalization of one or more members
- Compulsive gambling by one or more members
- Crime victimization
- Forced retirement of a wage earner
- Alzheimer's disease in an elderly relative
- Involvement of a child in delinquent and criminal activities

- Illness of a member who acquires AIDS
- Runaway teenager
- Sexual dysfunctions of one or more members
- Infidelity
- Infertility

When there are problems in a family, social services are often needed. Many types and forms of service are provided by social workers to troubled families. These services require the social worker to perform a variety of roles (broker, educator, advocate, case manager, mediator, and so on). Chapter 6 describes family problems and some of the services to families, including protective services, services to single parents, and marriage counseling.

Satir's Family Therapy Approach

One important social service provided to families is family therapy (also called family counseling). A substantial amount of literature on family therapy has been developed in social work. Numerous theoretical frameworks for family therapy have been advanced. One of the most prominent was developed by Virginia Satir, a psychiatric social worker. Satir's approach to family therapy will be briefly summarized.[7]

Satir stresses clarification of family communication patterns. She notes, in particular, that communication patterns among troubled families tend to be vague and indirect. In other words, rather than speaking clearly for themselves, a marital pair may avoid talking with each other about their needs and desires, or perhaps they talk to each other about what they want through their children. The children are thus maneuvered into the stressful position of speaking for, and therefore allying with, one parent or the other, which precipitates fear of loss of the other parent.

In Satir's view, indirect communication in the troubled family begins with courtship of the marital pair (if not before) and is due to the low self-esteem of the individuals involved. Each spouse-to-be feels worthless but hides these feelings by acting confident and strong. Neither person talks about feeling worthless for fear of driving the potential mate away. So each sees in the other a strong person who will take care of him or her. They marry to gain an extension of the self, but a stronger self who will be able to meet all felt needs; in other words, each marries to "get."[8]

Unfortunately, after marriage some of the illusions must fall away. Each spouse is forced to realize at some level that the other spouse is not just an extension of the self. One insists on using a separate toothbrush, for example, while the other wants to share the same one. Such incidents force perceptions of difference, and difference is experienced as bad because it leads to arguments. A desire to fuse and to be cared for conflicts with the other's different felt needs. Facing this difference feels frightening and might lead to arguments that could result in the other's leaving.

Hence each frightened spouse with low self-esteem and high need for the other tries to mask differences as much as possible. On one level, they attempt to please the other to keep him or her; on another level, they fear and resent expressed needs from the other that may be experienced as undesirable.

Since both spouses are in the same uncomfortable position of resenting differences yet needing the other, interpersonal communication gradually becomes more and more indirect. Rather than risk a clear statement such as, "I'd like to get a dog," the spouse desiring a pet might say something like, "Aunt Matilda likes dogs." The hope is that the other spouse will mind read the intended message and then spontaneously agree to get a dog for the family. However, the receiver of this particular message will more likely communicate a response dealing with Aunt Matilda, bringing disappointment to the speaker. The speaker isn't able to negotiate the desired dog with this type of communication and is left with angry feelings toward the spouse and a sense of unfulfilled needs. However, this state of affairs is experienced as preferable to risking a point-blank denial. Meanwhile, the receiver of the message may become aware of the disappointment or anger of the speaker through nonverbal channels but have no idea what caused it. The spouse who is also afraid to deal with conflict will not ask the reason for the apparent upset. So the misunderstanding and tension build.

Satir also notes that communication involves far more than the literal meaning of any words used. First of all, much communication is nonverbal—gestures, facial expressions, voice tone, posture, and the like. Nonverbal communication that matches the meaning of any words used (the words "I am sad" are accompanied by tears and a downturned mouth) is considered *congruent*. The receiver is not likely to misunderstand the meaning of this message because the verbal and nonverbal components agree. However, messages are often *incongruent*. For example, the statement "I am sad" may be accompanied by a grin. Which message should the receiver believe—the words or the facial expression? The receiver is likely to misinterpret unless he or she explicitly asks the sender to explain.

But the person who feels safe only with indirect communication is not likely to ask. Moreover, the sender who becomes skilled at sending incongruent communication for self-protection may even be unaware of the action and will be unable to explain if asked. Satir believes that incongruent communication can lead to misunderstanding in troubled families. Mother, for example, may say to Father in words, "I'm angry with you." However, since she fears rejection if she sends this message too forcefully, she smiles sweetly as she says it. Father may then choose to believe the smile, not take Mother's words seriously, and continue the very behavior that made her use the word *angry*. This is likely to make her angrier, but she may not feel safe enough to express the feeling more congruently. As a result, the communication that is driving the spouses apart goes on.

Another kind of incongruent communication is one that places the receiver in a *double bind*. That is, no matter how one responds, the sender will criticize. Father may say, on the one hand, that all good children should keep their toys picked up, but on the other hand, he tells his son that all "real" boys are messy. The boy who receives both messages will be unable to please Father whether he keeps his toys neat or messy. He may solve the problem by refusing to listen at all. At the extreme, he may pull away from reality to such a degree that he develops a severe emotional disturbance.

Satir's therapeutic goals and techniques are based on her assumption that people have the inherent ability (even drive) to grow and to mature. She feels that we can choose to take responsibility for our own lives and actions and that the mature person will:

a. *Manifest himself clearly to others.*

b. *Be in touch with signals from his internal self, thus letting himself know openly what he thinks and feels.*

c. *Be able to see and hear what is outside himself as differentiated from himself and as different from anything else.*

d. *Behave toward another person as someone who is separate and unique.*

e. *Treat the presence of differentness as an opportunity to learn and explore rather than as a threat or signal of conflict.*[9]

To help the members of a troubled family differentiate from one another and learn to own their special unique beings, Satir patiently teaches each person to speak for himself or herself and to send "I-messages." I-messages are nonblaming messages that communicate only how the sender believes the receiver is adversely affecting him or her. For example, suppose a father becomes frightened while riding in a car with his 17-year-old son who is driving over the speed limit. An I-message that the father might use is, "John, going this fast in a car scares me."

In counseling families, Satir serves as an active, directive, loving role model. She teaches that differentness is normal and should be viewed as a catalyst for growth. She points out incongruent messages and double binds and teaches family members to send clear, congruent messages instead. She uses touch and other nonverbal means, such as family sculpting, to help illustrate to families the unverbalized assumptions they operate by. These techniques take the burden of labeling off the identified client and reveal his or her symptomatic behavior as a product of the family system as a whole.

Family sculpting is used for both assessment and treatment purposes. It involves a physical arrangement of the members of a family, with the placement of each person determined by an individual family member acting as "director." The resulting tableau represents that person's symbolic view of family relationships. Goldenberg and Goldenberg describe family sculpting as follows:

> The procedure calls for each member to arrange the bodies of all the other family members in a defined space, according to his or her perception of their relationships either at present or at a specific point in the past. Who the sculptor designates as domineering, meek and submissive, loving and touching, belligerent, benevolent, clinging, and so on, and how those people relate to each other becomes apparent to all who witness the tableau. The sculptor is invited to explain the creation, and a lively debate between members may follow. The adolescent boy who places his parents at opposite ends of the family group while he and his brothers and sisters are huddled together in the center conveys a great deal more about his views of the workings of the family system than he would probably be able to state in words. By the same token, his father's sculpture—placing himself apart from all others, including his wife—may reveal his sense of loneliness, isolation, and rejection by his family. The mother may present herself as a confidante of her daughter but ignored by the males in the family, and so forth.[10]

Satir also analyzes rules in the family. She helps clarify them in the context that some rules may be bad, but the people setting the rules or bound by them are not. She teaches that bad rules can be changed and has the family members negotiate new ones. She insists that each member be heard in her presence, thus teaching respect for each person and each point of view.

Clearly, then, Satir views the family as a system. Working with the family as a whole is the means of relieving the distress of the identified client or of the family itself due to the dysfunctional behavior of the identified client. Her major emphasis in intervention with the family as a system is to clarify their communication patterns and to help them become direct and congruent. Basi-

cally, Satir's therapeutic goal of improving methods of communication involves three outcomes: (a) Each member should be able to report congruently, completely, and obviously on what he or she sees, hears, feels, and thinks about himself or herself and others. (b) Each person should relate to his or her uniqueness so that decisions are made in terms of exploration and negotiation rather than in terms of power. (c) Differentness should be openly acknowledged and used for growth.[11]

SOCIAL WORK WITH GROUPS

A group may be defined as:

> Two or more individuals in face-to-face interaction, each aware of his or her membership in the group, each aware of the others who belong to the group, and each aware of their positive interdependence as they strive to achieve mutual goals.[12]

Group social work has its historical roots in informal recreational organizations such as the YWCA and YMCA, scouting, Jewish centers, settlement houses, and 4-H clubs.

George Williams established the Young Men's Christian Association in London in 1844 for the purpose of converting young men to Christian values.[13] Recreational group activities and socialization activities were a large part of the early YMCA's programs. In 1851 YMCAs were founded in Baltimore and Boston. The Young Women's Christian Association began in Boston in 1866.[14]

Settlement houses, which were established in many large cities of this country in the late 1800s, are largely credited for providing the roots of social group work.[15] Settlement houses sought to use the power of group associations to educate, reform, and organize neighborhoods; to preserve religious and cultural identities; and to give emotional support and assistance to newcomers both from the farm and from abroad.

Today almost every social service agency provides one or more of the following types of groups:

recreation-skill, education, socialization, and therapy. Most undergraduate and graduate social work programs offer practice courses to train students to lead groups, particularly socialization and therapy groups. There is a national social group work organization, the Association for the Advancement of Social Work with Groups, that holds a yearly symposium and publishes a journal.

The following summary describes a variety of groups in social work: social conversation, recreation, recreation-skill, education, task, problem solving and decision making, self-help, socialization, therapy, and sensitivity.

SOCIAL CONVERSATION GROUPS

Conversation in these groups is often loose and tends to drift aimlessly. There is no formal agenda. If one topic is dull, the subject is likely to change. Individuals may have some goal (perhaps only to establish an acquaintanceship), but such individual goals may not become the agenda for the entire group. Social conversation is often used for "testing" purposes—for example, to determine how deep a relationship might develop with people we do not know very well. In social work, social conversation with other professionals is frequent, but groups involving clients generally have objectives other than conversation.

RECREATION GROUPS

The objective of these groups is to provide activities for enjoyment and exercise. Often such activities are spontaneous and the groups are practically leaderless. The group service agency (such as YMCA, YWCA, or neighborhood center) may offer little more than physical space and the use of some equipment. Spontaneous playground activities, informal athletic games, and an open game room are examples. Some group agencies that provide such physical space claim that recreation and interaction with others help build "character" and prevent delinquency among youths by offering an alternative to the street.

RECREATION-SKILL GROUPS

The objective of these groups is to improve a set of skills while at the same time providing enjoyment. In contrast to recreation groups, an adviser, coach, or instructor is generally present, and there is more of a task orientation. Examples of activities include golf, basketball, needlework, arts and crafts, and swimming. Competitive team sports and leagues may emerge. Frequently such groups are led by professionals with recreational training rather than social work training. Social service agencies that provide such services include the YMCA, YWCA, Boy Scouts, Girl Scouts, neighborhood centers, and school recreational departments.

EDUCATION GROUPS

The focus of such groups is for members to acquire knowledge and learn more complex skills. The leader generally is a professional with considerable training and expertise in the topic area. Examples of topics include child-rearing practices, parent training, preparation for adoption, and volunteer training for specialized tasks in a social service agency. These groups may resemble a class, with considerable group interaction and discussion encouraged.

TASK GROUPS

Task groups exist to achieve a specific set of tasks or objectives. The following are just a few examples of task groups that social workers are likely to interact with or become involved in. A *board of directors* is an administrative group charged with responsibility for setting the policy that governs agency programs. A *task force* is a group established for a special purpose; it is usually disbanded after the task is completed. A *committee* of an agency or organization is a group that is formed to deal with specific tasks or matters. An *ad hoc committee*, like a task force, is set up for one purpose and usually ceases functioning after completion of its task. (An ad hoc committee and a task force are essentially the same.)

PROBLEM-SOLVING AND DECISION-MAKING GROUPS

Both providers and consumers of social services may become involved in problem-solving and decision-making groups. (There is considerable overlap between task groups and this category; in fact, problem-solving and decision-making groups could be viewed as a subcategory of task groups.) Providers of services use group meetings for such objectives as developing a treatment plan for a client or a group of clients, deciding how best to allocate scarce resources, deciding how to improve the delivery of services to clients, arriving at policy decisions for the agency, deciding how to improve coordination efforts with other agencies, and so on.

Potential consumers of services may form a group to meet some current community need. Data on the need may be gathered, and the group may be used as a vehicle either to develop a program or to influence existing agencies to provide services. Social workers may function as stimulators and organizers of such group efforts.

In problem-solving and decision-making groups, each participant often has some interest or stake in the process and stands to gain or lose personally by the outcome. Usually there is a formal leader of some sort, and other leaders sometimes emerge during the process.

SELF-HELP GROUPS

Self-help groups are very popular and are often successful in helping individuals with certain social or personal problems. Alfred Katz and Eugene Bender provide a comprehensive definition of self-help groups:

Self-help groups are voluntary, small group structures for mutual aid, and the accomplishment of a special purpose. They are usually formed by peers who have come together for mutual assistance in satisfying a common need, overcoming a common handicap or life-disrupting problem, and bringing about desired social and/or personal change. The initiators and members of such groups perceive that their needs are not, or cannot be, met by or through existing social institutions. Self-help groups emphasize face-to-face social interactions and the assumption of personal responsibility by members. They often provide material assistance, as well as emotional support. They are frequently "cause"-oriented, and promulgate an ideology or values through which members may attain an enhanced sense of personal identity.[16]

Alcoholics Anonymous, developed by two former alcoholics, was the first self-help group to demonstrate substantial success. A number of other such groups have since been formed. In a text entitled *Help: A Working Guide to Self-Help Groups*, Alan Gartner and Frank Riessmen describe over 200 self-help groups that are now active,[17] some of which are listed in Exhibit 3.1.

Many self-help groups stress (a) a confession to the group by every member that she or he has a problem, (b) a testimony to the group recounting past experiences with the problem and plans for handling it in the future, and (c) phone calls to another member whenever one feels a crisis (for example, an abusive parent having an urge to abuse a child); the person who is called stays with the member until the crisis subsides.

There appear to be several reasons why self-help groups are successful. All members have an internal understanding of the problem, which helps them to help others. Having experienced the misery and consequences of the problem, they are highly motivated and dedicated to find ways to help themselves and others who are fellow sufferers. The participants also benefit from the "helper therapy principle"—that is, the helper also gains psychological rewards.[18] Helping others leads the helper to feel "good" and worthwhile and also to put his or her own problems into perspective by seeing that others have problems that may be as serious or even more serious.

Some self-help groups, such as the National Organization for Women, focus on social advocacy and attempt to make legislative and policy changes in public and private institutions. Some groups (such as associations of parents of children with a cognitive disability) raise funds and operate community programs. Many people with a personal problem use self-help groups in the same way that others use social agencies. An additional advantage of self-help groups is that they are generally able to operate with a minimal budget.

SOCIALIZATION GROUPS

The objective of such groups generally is to seek to change members' attitudes and behaviors in a more socially acceptable direction. Developing

EXHIBIT 3.1

Examples of Existing Self-Help Groups

Organization	Service Focus
Abused Women's Aid in Crisis	For battered wives and other abused women
Adoptees' Liberty Movement Association	For adoptees searching for their natural parents
Alcoholics Anonymous	For adult alcoholics
American Diabetes Association	Clubs for diabetics, their families, and friends
Brain Tumor Support Group	For people with brain tumors or their loved ones
Burns Recovered	For burn victims
Cesarean Birth Association	For those expecting a cesarean delivery
Candlelighters	For parents of young children with cancer
Checks Anonymous	For people in debt
Concerned United Birthparents	For parents who have surrendered children for adoption
Depressives Anonymous	For depressed people
Divorce Anonymous	For divorced people
Emotions Anonymous	For people with emotional problems
Emphysema Anonymous	For those with emphysema
Fly Without Fear	For people who are afraid of flying
Fortune Society	For ex-offenders and their families
Gam-Anon	For families of gamblers
Gray Panthers	An intergenerational group
Make Today Count	For people with cancer and their families
Mensa	For people of high IQs
Naim Conference	For widowed people
National Council of Stutterers	For adult stutterers
National Organization for Women	For advocates of equal rights for women
Overeaters Anonymous	For compulsive overeaters
Parents Anonymous	For parents of abused children
Phobia Self-Help Groups	For people with phobias
Prison Families Anonymous	For family members of prisoners
Resolve	For infertile people
Stroke Clubs	For those who have had strokes and their families
Survivors of Suicide Victims	For the relatives and friends of suicide victims
We Care	For divorced and separated people

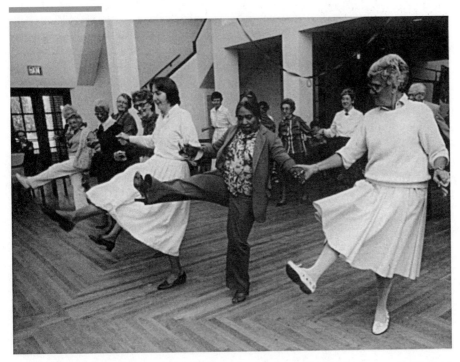

A senior citizens' dance illustrates socialization, a primary focus of group work. Motivating the elderly to become more socially active requires a special skill for using groups to foster individual growth.

social skills, increasing self-confidence, and planning for the future are other focuses. Leaders of such groups might work with predelinquent youths in group activities to curb delinquency, work with youths of diverse ethnic backgrounds to reduce racial tensions, work with "at-risk" young children in an elementary school to improve their interpersonal and problem-solving skills and to motivate them to succeed in the school setting, work with elderly residents at a nursing home to remotivate them and get them involved in various activities, or work with youths at a correctional school to help them make plans for returning to their home community. Leadership of such groups requires considerable skill and knowledge in using the group to foster individual growth and change. Socialization groups are frequently led by social workers.

THERAPY GROUPS

Therapy groups are generally composed of members with rather severe emotional or personal problems. Leaders must be highly skilled; they need to be perceptive, to understand human behavior and group dynamics, to have group counseling capacities, to use the group to bring about behavioral changes, to be aware at all times of how each member is affected by what is happening, and to develop and maintain a constructive atmosphere within the group. As with one-to-one counseling, the goal of therapy groups is generally to have members explore their problems in depth and then develop one or more strategies for resolving them. The group therapist often uses one or more of the following psychotherapy approaches as a guide for changing attitudes and behaviors: reality therapy, learning theory, rational

EXHIBIT 3.2

A Socialization Group at a Shelter for Runaways

New Horizons is a private temporary shelter facility for runaways in a large midwestern city. It is in a large house that was built 84 years ago. Youths on the run can stay for up to 2 weeks. State law requires that parents be contacted and parental permission received for New Horizons to provide shelter overnight. Services offered include temporary shelter care, individual and family counseling, and a 24-hour hotline for youths in crisis. The facility is licensed to house up to eight youths. Because the average stay is 9 days, the population is continually changing. Intensive counseling is provided for the youths (and often their parents), focusing on reducing family conflicts and on making future living plans. The 14-day limit helps convey to youths and their families, beginning with day one, that they must work to resolve the reasons for leaving home.

Every evening at 7 P.M. a group meeting is held. All the residents and the two or three staff members on duty are expected to attend. The meetings are convened and led by the staff. This meeting has four main objectives. One is providing a vehicle for residents to express their satisfactions and dissatisfactions with the facilities and program at New Horizons. Sometimes the meeting appears to be primarily a "gripe" session, but the staff members make conscientious efforts to improve those aspects in which the youths' concerns are legitimate. For example, a youth may indicate that the past few days have been "boring," and staff and residents then jointly plan activities for the next few days.

A second objective is to deal with interaction problems that arise between residents or between staff and residents. One resident may be preventing others from sleeping; some youths may refuse to do their "fair share" of domestic tasks; there may be squabbles about which TV program to watch; some residents may be overly aggressive. Because most of the youths face a variety of crises associated with being on the run, many tend to be anxious and under stress. In such an emotional climate, interaction problems are likely to arise. Staff are sometimes intensely questioned about their actions, decisions, and policies. For example, one policy at New Horizons is that each resident must agree not to use alcohol or illegal drugs while staying at the shelter, with the penalty being expulsion. Occasionally a few youths use some drugs and are caught and expelled. Removing a resident from this facility has an immense impact on the others, and at the following group meeting, staff are expected to clarify and explain such decisions.

A third objective is for staff to present material on topics requested by residents. Examples of topics include sex, drugs, homosexuality, physical and sexual abuse (a fair number of residents are abused by family members), ways to avoid being raped, ways to deal with depression and other unwanted emotions, sexually transmitted diseases, legal rights of youths on the run, assertiveness training, ways to make relatives and friends understand why they ran away, and availability of other human services in the community. During such presentations, discussion with residents is encouraged and generally occurs.

The final objective of these group meetings is to convey information about planned daily activities and changes in the overall program at New Horizons.

A Therapy Group

Several years ago, when I was employed as a social worker at a maximum security hospital for the criminally insane, my supervisor requested that I develop and lead a therapy group. When I asked such questions as "What should the group's objectives be?" and "Who should be selected to join?" my supervisor indicated that those decisions would be mine. No one else was doing any group therapy at this hospital, and the hospital administration thought it would be desirable, for accountability reasons, for group therapy programs to be developed.

Being newly employed at the hospital and wary because I had never led a therapy group before, I asked myself, "Who is in the greatest need of group therapy?" and "If the group members do not improve, or even deteriorate, how will I be able to explain this—that is, cover my tracks?" I concluded that I should select those persons identified as being the "sickest" (those labeled as chronic schizophrenics) for the group. Chronic schizophrenics are generally expected to show little improvement. Thus, if they did not improve, I felt I would not be blamed. However, if they did improve, I thought their progress would be viewed as a substantial accomplishment.

My next step was to invite those persons to join the group. I met with each individually and explained the purpose of the group and the probable topics that would be covered. Eight of the eleven I contacted decided to join. Some of the eight stated frankly that they were joining primarily because it would look good on their record and increase their chances for an early release. The approach I used with the group members was based on reality therapy,[a] as described in the following material.

At the first meeting, I again presented and described the purpose and focus of the group. The purpose was not to review the members' past but to help them make their present life more enjoyable and meaningful and to help them make plans for the future. Topics to be covered included how to convince the hospital staff they no longer needed to be hospitalized, how to prepare themselves for returning to their home community (for example, learning an employable skill while at the institution), what to do when they felt depressed or had some other unwanted emotion, and what actions they should take following their release if they had an urge to do something that would get them into trouble again. I further explained that occasional films covering some of these topics would be shown and discussed. I indicated that the group would meet for about an hour each week for the next 12 weeks (until the fall, when I had to return to school).

This focus on improving their current circumstances stimulated their interest, but soon they found it uncomfortable and anxiety producing to examine what the future might hold for them. Being informed that they had some responsibility and some

[a] William Glasser, *Reality Therapy* (New York: Harper & Row, 1965).

control of that future also created anxiety. Their reaction to this discomfort was to state that, because they were labeled mentally ill, they therefore had an internal condition that was causing their strange behavior. Because they were aware that a cure for schizophrenia had not yet been found, they concluded that they could do little to improve their situation.

The members were told their excuses were "garbage" (stronger terms were used), and we spent a few sessions on getting them to understand that the label "chronic schizophrenic" was meaningless. I spent considerable time explaining (as discussed in Chapter 5) that mental illness is a myth; that is, people do not have a "disease of the mind," even though they may have emotional/behavioral problems. I went on to explain that what had gotten them locked up was their deviant behavior, and the only way for them to get out was to stop exhibiting their strange behavior and to convince the other staff that they would not exhibit deviant behavior if released. I added that they held the key for getting released—that key was simply to act "sane."

The next set of excuses they tried held that their broken homes or inferior schools or broken romances or something else in their past had "messed them up," and therefore, they could do little about their situation. They were told that such excuses were also "garbage." True, their past experiences were relevant to their being in the hospital. But it was emphasized that what they wanted out of the future, along with their motivation to do something about achieving their goals, was more important than their past experiences in determining what their future would be like.

Finally, after we had worked through a number of excuses, we were able to focus on how they could better handle specific problems: how to handle being depressed, how to stop exhibiting behavior considered "strange," how to present themselves as "sane" to increase their chances of an early release, how they would adjust to returning to their home communities, what kind of work or career they desired on their release, how they could prepare themselves by learning a skill or trade while at this institution, how to examine what they wanted in the future and determine the specific steps they would have to take to achieve their goals, why it was important to continue taking the psychoactive medication that had been prescribed, and so on.

The results of this approach were very encouraging. Instead of idly spending much of the time brooding about their situation, they became motivated to improve their lives. At the end of the 12 weeks, the eight members of the group spontaneously stated that the meetings were resulting in positive changes in their lives. They requested that another social worker from the hospital be assigned to continue the group after my return to college. This was arranged. Three years later, on a return visit to the hospital, I was informed that five of the eight group members had been released to their home communities. Two of the others were considered to have shown improvement. The final group member's condition was described as "unchanged."

therapy, transactional analysis, client-centered therapy, psychodrama, and feminist therapy.*

Group therapy is widely used in counseling. It has several advantages over one-to-one therapy. The helper therapy principle generally is operative; members interchange roles and sometimes become the "helper" for someone else's problems. Helping others provides psychological rewards. Groups also help members put their problems into perspective by realizing that others have problems as serious as their own. Groups help members who are having interaction problems to test out new patterns of interacting. Research has shown that it is generally easier to change an individual's attitude in a group than individually.[19] Group pressure can have a substantial effect on changing attitudes and beliefs.[20] Furthermore, group therapy permits the social worker to treat more than one person at a time and thus maximizes the use of professional staff.

In essence, a group therapist uses the principles of one-to-one counseling (discussed in Chapter 5) and of group dynamics to help clients change dysfunctional attitudes and behavior. Often the traditional comprehensive psychotherapy approaches are combined with certain specialized treatment techniques (such as parent effectiveness training and assertiveness training) to help clients resolve personal and emotional problems. The selection of treatment techniques is based on the nature of the problems.

SENSITIVITY GROUPS

Encounter groups, T (training)-groups, and sensitivity training (these terms are used somewhat synonymously) refer to group experiences in which people relate to one another in an intimate manner requiring self-disclosure. The goal is to improve interpersonal awareness. An encounter group may meet for a few hours or for a few days.

---

*These psychotherapy approaches are described in Charles Zastrow, *The Practice of Social Work*, 6th ed. (Pacific Grove, CA: Brooks/Cole, 1999).

EXHIBIT 3.3

Contrasting Goals of Therapy Versus Sensitivity Groups

Therapy Groups	Sensitivity Groups
Step 1 Examine problem(s) in depth	**Step 1** Help each person become more aware of himself or herself and how he or she affects others in interpersonal interactions
Step 2 Explore and then select (from various resolution approaches) a strategy to resolve the problem	**Step 2** Help a person to then develop more effective interaction patterns

The goal of sensitivity groups provides an interesting contrast to those of therapy groups (see Exhibit 3.3). In therapy the goal is to have each member explore personal or emotional problems in depth and then develop a strategy to resolve them. In comparison, sensitivity groups seek to increase each member's personal and interpersonal awareness and then develop more effective interaction patterns. Sensitivity groups generally do not directly attempt to identify or change specific emotional or personal problems that people have (such as drinking problems, feelings of depression, sexual dysfunctions, and so on). The philosophy behind sensitivity groups is that, with increased personal and interpersonal awareness, people will be better able to avoid, cope with, and/or handle specific personal problems that arise.

Sensitivity groups are used in our society for a wide variety of purposes: to train professional counselors to be more perceptive and effective in interpersonal interactions with clients and with other professionals, to train people in management positions to be more effective in their business interactions, to help clients with overt relationship problems become more aware of how they affect others and to develop more effective interaction patterns, and to train interested citizens in becoming more aware and effective in their interactions.

Although encounter, marathon, and sensitivity groups are popular and have received considerable publicity, they remain controversial. In some cases, inadequately trained and incompetent individuals have become self-proclaimed leaders and have enticed people to join through sensational advertising. If mishandled, sensitivity groups can intensify personal problems. Many authorities on sensitivity training disclaim the use of encounter groups as a form of psychotherapy and discourage people with serious personal problems from joining such groups.

SOCIAL WORK WITH ORGANIZATIONS

An organization is a collectivity of individuals gathered together to serve a particular purpose. The types of purposes (or goals) that people organize themselves to achieve are infinite in number and can range from obtaining basic necessities to attaining world peace. Organizations exist because people working together can accomplish tasks and achieve goals that cannot be achieved as well (or even at all) by an individual.

The importance of organizations in our lives is described by Etzioni:

> We are born in organizations, educated by organizations, and most of us spend much of our lives working for organizations. We spend much of our leisure time paying, playing, and praying in organizations. Most of us will die in an organization, and when the time comes for burial, the largest organization of all—the state—must grant official permission.[21]

Netting, Kettner, and McMurtry have summarized the importance of organizations for social work practice:

> As social workers, our roles within, interactions with, and attempts to manipulate organizations define much of what we do. Clients often come to us seeking help because they are not able to obtain help from organizations that are critical to their survival or quality of life. In turn, the resources we attempt to gain for these clients usually come from still other organizations: . . . Social workers with little or no idea of how organizations operate, how they interact, or how they can be influenced and changed from both outside and inside are likely to be severely limited in their effectiveness.[22]

Many disciplines (including business, psychology, political science, and sociology) have generated a prodigious amount of theory and research on organizations. However, in spite of the importance of organizations to social work practice, the amount of social work literature devoted to this topic is limited. One significant reference in this area is *Social Work Macro Practice*, by Netting, Kettner, and McMurtry.[23]

Earlier in this chapter, in the section entitled "The Change Process," we saw an example of the processes a social worker used to achieve organizational change. That section described how a new educational component on alcohol and other drug abuse was added to the curriculum in a school district in a midwestern state. The remainder of this section will present material on how social workers can survive and thrive in bureaucratic systems. A bureaucracy is a type of organization or a subcategory of an organization. Distinctive characteristics of a bureaucracy include a vertical hierarchy with power centered at the top; a task-specific division of labor; clearly defined rules; formalized channels of communication; and selection, compensation, promotion and retention of personnel based on technical competency.

There are basic structural conflicts between helping professionals and the bureaucratic systems in which they work. Helping professionals

EXHIBIT 3.4

Analyzing a Human Services Organization

It is essential that a social worker understand and analyze not only the agency/organization that she or he works for but also the other agencies and organizations that she or he interacts with. Some questions that are useful in analyzing an agency or organization are:

1. What is the mission statement of the organization?

2. What are the major problems of the organization's clients?

3. What services are provided by the organization?

4. How are client needs determined?

5. What percentage of clients are people of color, women, gays or lesbians, elderly, or members of other at-risk populations?

6. What was the total cost of services of this organization in the past year?

7. How much money is spent on each program?

8. What are the organization's funding sources?

9. How much and what percentage of funds are received from each source?

10. What types of clients does the organization refuse?

11. What other organizations provide the same services in the community?

12. What is the organizational structure? For example, does the organization have a formal chain of command?

13. Is there an informal decision-making process and structure at the organization? (That is, are there people who are quite influential and thus exert more influence than would be expected for their formal positions in the bureaucracy of the organization?)

14. How much input do the direct-service providers at the organization have on major policy decisions?

15. Does the organization have a board that oversees its operations? If so, what are the backgrounds of the board members?

16. Do employees at every level feel valued?

17. What is the morale among employees?

18. What are the major unmet needs of the organization?

19. Does the organization have a handbook of personnel policies and procedures?

20. What is the public image of the organization in the community?

21. What has been the rate of turnover in recent years among the staff at the organization? What were departing staff members' major reasons for leaving?

22. Does the organization have a process for evaluating the outcomes of its services? If so, what is the process and what are the outcome results?

---

place a high value on creativity and change. Bureaucracies resist change and are most efficient when no one is "rocking the boat." Helping professionals seek to personalize services by conveying to each client "You count as a person."

Bureaucracies are highly depersonalized, emotionally detached systems that view every employee and every client as a tiny component of a large system. In a large bureaucracy, employees *don't* count as "persons"—only as functional parts of

EXHIBIT 3.5

Value Conflicts Between a Helping Professional and Bureaucracies

Orientations of a Helping Professional	Orientations of Bureaucratic Systems
Desires democratic system for decision making.	Most decisions are made autocratically.
Desires that power be distributed equally among employees (horizontal structure).	Power is distributed vertically.
Desires that clients have considerable power in the system.	Power is held primarily by top executives.
Desires a flexible, changing system.	System is rigid and stable.
Desires that creativity and growth be emphasized.	Emphasis is on structure and the status quo.
Desires that focus be client oriented.	System is organization centered.
Desires that communication be on a personalized level from person to person.	Communication is from level to level.
Desires shared decision making and shared responsibility structure.	A hierarchical decision-making structure and hierarchical responsibility structure are characteristic.
Desires that decisions be made by those having the most knowledge.	Decisions are made in terms of the decision-making authority assigned to each position in the hierarchy.
Desires shared leadership.	System uses autocratic leadership.
Believes feelings of clients and employees should be highly valued by the system.	Procedures and processes are highly valued.

a system. Exhibit 3.5 lists additional conflicting value orientations between a helping professional and bureaucratic systems.

Any of these differences in value orientations can become an arena for conflict between helping professionals and the bureaucracies in which they work. Knopf has concisely summarized the potential areas of conflict:

> The trademarks of a BS (bureaucratic system) are power, hierarchy, and specialization; that is, rules and roles. In essence, the result is depersonalization. The system itself is neither "good" nor "bad"; it is a system. I believe it to be amoral. It is efficient and effective, but in order to be so it must be impersonal in all of its functionings. This then is the location of the stress. The hallmark of the helping professional is a highly individualized, democratic, human-

> ized, relationship-oriented service aimed at self-motivation. The hallmark of a bureaucratic system is a highly impersonalized, valueless (amoral), emotionally detached, hierarchical structure of organization. The dilemma of the HP (helping person) is how to give a personalized service to a client through a delivery system that is not set up in any way to do that.[24]

Many helping professionals respond to these orientation conflicts by erroneously projecting a "personality" onto the bureaucracy. They describe it using expressions like red tape, officialism, uncaring, cruel, the enemy. Officials of the bureaucracy may be viewed as paper shufflers, rigid, deadwood, inefficient, and unproductive. Knopf states:

> The HP (helping person) . . . may deal with the impersonal nature of the system by projecting

values onto it and thereby give the BS (bureaucratic system) a "personality." In this way, we fool ourselves into thinking that we can deal with it in a personal way. Unfortunately, projection is almost always negative and reflects the dark or negative aspects of ourselves. The BS then becomes a screen onto which we vent our anger, sadness, or fright, and while a lot of energy is generated, very little is accomplished. Since the BS is amoral, it is unproductive to place a personality on it.[25]

A bureaucratic system is neither good nor bad. It has neither a personality nor a value system of its own. It is simply a structure developed to carry out various tasks.

A helping person may experience various emotional reactions to conflicts with bureaucratic systems.* Common reactions are anger at the system, self-blame ("It's all my fault"), sadness and depression ("Poor me"; "Nobody appreciates all I've done"), and fright and paranoia ("They're out to get me"; "If I mess up, I'm gone").

Knopf has identified several types of behavior patterns that helping professionals choose in dealing with bureaucracies.[26]

The *warrior* leads open campaigns to destroy and malign the system. A warrior discounts the value of the system and often enters into a win–lose conflict. She or he generally loses and is dismissed.

The *gossip* is a covert warrior who complains to others (including clients, politicians, and the news media) about how terrible the system is. A gossip frequently singles out a few officials to focus criticism on. Bureaucratic systems often make life very difficult for the gossip by assigning distasteful tasks, refusing to promote, giving very low salary increases, and perhaps even dismissing.

The *complainer* resembles a gossip but confines complaints to other helping persons, to in-house staff, and to family members. A complainer wants people to agree in order to find comfort in shared misery. Complainers want to stay with the system, and they generally do.

The *dancer* is skillful at ignoring rules and procedures. Dancers frequently are lonely. They are often reprimanded for incorrectly filling out forms, and they have low investment in the system or in helping clients.

The *defender* is timid, dislikes conflict, and therefore defends the rules, the system, and bureaucratic officials. Defenders often are supervisors and are viewed by others as being "bureaucrats."

The *machine* is a "bureaucrat" who takes on the orientation of the bureaucracy. Often a machine has not been involved in providing direct services for years. Machines are frequently named to head study committees and policy groups and to chair boards.

The *executioner* attacks persons within an organization with enthusiasm and vigor. An executioner usually has a high energy level and is impulsive. He or she abuses power by indiscriminately attacking and dismissing not only employees but also services and programs. Executioners have power and are angry (although the anger is disguised/denied). They are committed neither to the value orientation of helping professionals nor to the bureaucracy.

Knopf has listed 66 tips on how to survive in a bureaucracy.[27] Some of the most useful suggestions are summarized here:

---

*This description highlights a number of the negatives about bureaucratic systems, particularly their impersonalization. In fairness, it should be noted that an advantage of being part of a large bureaucracy is that the potential is there for changing a powerful system to the advantage of clients. In tiny or nonbureaucratic systems, the social worker may have lots of freedom but little opportunity or power to influence large systems or mobilize extensive resources on behalf of clients.

1. Whenever your needs, or the needs of your clients, are not met by the bureaucracy, use the following problem-solving approach: (a) Precisely identify which of your needs (or the needs of clients) are in conflict with the bureaucracy; this step is defining the problem. (b) Generate a list of possible solutions. Be creative in generating a wide range of ideas.

(c) Evaluate the merits and shortcomings of the possible solutions. (d) Select a solution. (e) Implement the solution. (f) Evaluate the solution.

2. Learn how your bureaucracy is structured and how it functions. Such knowledge will reduce fear of the unknown, make the system more predictable, and help in identifying rational ways to best meet your needs and those of your clients.

3. Remember that bureaucrats are people, too, and they have feelings. Communication gaps are often most effectively reduced if you treat them with as much respect and interest as you treat clients.

4. If you are at war with the bureaucracy, declare a truce. The system will find a way to dismiss you if you remain at war. With a truce, you can identify and use the strengths of the bureaucracy as an ally, rather than having the strengths used against you as an enemy.

5. Know your work contract and job expectations. If the expectations are unclear, seek clarity.

6. Continue to develop your knowledge and awareness of specific helping skills. Take advantage of continuing-education opportunities (workshops, conferences, courses). Among other advantages, your continued professional development will assist you in being able to contract from a position of competency and skill.

7. Seek to identify your professional strengths and limitations. Knowing your limitations will increase your ability to avoid undertaking responsibilities that are beyond your competencies.

8. Be aware that you can't change everything, so stop trying. In a bureaucracy, focus your change efforts on those aspects that most need change and that you also have a fair chance of changing. Stop thinking and complaining about those aspects you cannot change. It is irrational to complain about things that you cannot change or to complain about those things that you do not intend to make an effort to change.

9. Learn how to control your emotions in your interactions with the bureaucracy. Emotions that are counterproductive (such as most angry outbursts) particularly need to be controlled. Doing a rational self-analysis on your unwanted emotions (see Chapter 5) is one way of gaining control of them. Learning how to respond to stress in your personal life will also prepare you to handle stress better at work.

10. Develop and use a sense of humor. Humor takes the edge off adverse conditions and reduces negative feelings.

11. Learn to accept your mistakes and perhaps even laugh at some of them. No one is perfect.

12. Take time to enjoy and develop a support system with your coworkers.

13. Acknowledge your mistakes and give in sometimes on minor matters. You may not be right, and giving in allows other people to do the same.

14. Keep yourself physically fit and mentally alert. Learn to use approaches that will reduce stress and prevent burnout. (See Chapter 15 for a description of approaches to reduce stress.)

15. Leave your work at the office. If you have urgent unfinished bureaucratic business, do it before leaving work.

16. Occasionally take your supervisor and other administrators to lunch. Socializing prevents isolation and facilitates your involvement with and understanding of the system.

17. Do not seek self-actualization or ego satisfaction from the bureaucracy. A depersonalized system is incapable of providing these rewards; you must achieve them on your own.

18. In speeches to community groups, accentuate the positives about your agency. Ask after speeches that a thank-you letter be sent to your supervisor or agency director.

19. If you have a problem with the bureaucracy, discuss it with other employees, with the focus

on problem solving rather than on complaining. Groups are much more powerful and productive than an individual working alone for making changes in a system.

20. No matter how high you rise in a hierarchy, maintain direct service contact. Direct contact keeps you abreast of changing client needs, prevents you from getting stale, and keeps you attuned to the concerns of employees in lower levels of the hierarchy.

21. Do not try to change everything in the system at once. Attacking too much will overextend you and lead to burnout. Start small, and be selective and specific. Double-check your facts to make certain they accurately prove your position before you confront bureaucratic officials.

22. Identify your career goals and determine whether they can be met within this system. If the answer is no, then (a) change your goals, (b) change the bureaucracy, or (c) seek a position elsewhere in which your goals can be met.

SOCIAL WORK WITH THE COMMUNITY

Most social work students do not consider a career in community practice; they feel that they would rather work directly with people. Many believe that community practice involves skills and techniques that are too complex and too abstract to learn. In addition, they perceive community practice as having too few rewards and as involving a lot of boring, unenjoyable work. All of these beliefs are erroneous. The realities are that (a) the most basic skill needed in community practice is the ability to work effectively with people; (b) community practice primarily involves working with individuals and with groups; (c) every practicing social worker occasionally becomes involved in community practice projects; (d) seeing a community project developed, approved, and implemented is immensely gratifying; and (e) community practice efforts are often fun.

Workers in direct practice with individuals or groups are likely to become involved in community development activities when gaps in services or unmet needs are identified for clients they are working with. For example, if there is a rapid increase in teenage pregnancy in a community, a school social worker may become involved in efforts to establish a sex education program in the school system. If there are a number of terminally ill patients and their families are complaining about the way they are treated in a hospital, a medical social worker may become involved in efforts to establish a hospice. If a juvenile probation officer notes a sharp increase in juvenile offenses, the officer may become involved in efforts to have young offenders visit a prison and hear from inmates what prison life is like (as depicted in Scared Straight programs).

Workers involved in developing needed new services are aware of the human benefits that will result. These payoffs, and the time and effort workers put into community practice projects, often lead them to become highly "ego involved." Success in establishing new services is experienced as a deeply gratifying political victory. On a negative note, a reality is that the development of new services generally involves a number of unanticipated obstacles and requires several times as much time and effort as initially anticipated.

As yet, there is no widely accepted definition of the term *community practice.* The modes of practice performed under this heading have a variety of labels: social planning, community planning, locality development, community action, social action, macropractice, community organization, and community development.

Community practice will be defined here as the process of stimulating and assisting the local community to evaluate, plan, and coordinate its efforts to provide for the community's health, welfare, and recreation needs. In community practice, a worker's activities include encouraging and stimulating citizen organization around one or more issues, specifying the nature of the problem, coordinating efforts among concerned groups, fact-finding, formulating realizable goals, becoming involved in public relations and public education, conducting research, planning, identifying financial resources, developing strategies to achieve a goal, and being a resource person. Agency settings that employ community practice workers include community welfare councils, the United Way, social planning agencies, health planning councils, neighborhood councils, city planning councils, community action groups, and occasionally some other private or public organization.

Community practice workers become involved in a wide variety of social issues, including civil rights, welfare reform, the needs of poor people, education and health issues, housing, improvement of leisure-time services, race relations, minority-group employment, development of services to counteract alienation of youths, urban redevelopment programs, development of services for teenage runaways and drug users, development of services for the homeless, and development of services for people who are HIV positive or have AIDS.

Disciplines in addition to social work provide training in community practice. These include community psychology, urban and regional planning, health planning, corrections planning, recreation, and public administration.

In recent years, American citizens have organized around a number of issues. Some that have received national attention include labor–management disputes, women's rights issues, problems of farmers, the abortion question, capital punishment, rights for homosexuals, tax cuts, school closings in many cities, the national defense budget, nuclear energy, decriminalization of marijuana, massage parlors, nude dancing, affirmative action guidelines on hiring, and environmental concerns.

A Brief History of Community Practice

For centuries people have organized to change social and political conditions. In the 1700s, for example, Americans organized to revolt against the British and fought what has come to be called the Revolutionary War.

Community practice in social work began in the 1800s with the charity organization movement and the settlement house movement.[28]

In the 19th century, private philanthropy bore the major responsibility for the relief of poverty in the United States. During the early 1800s, a wide range of private health and welfare agencies was established to provide funds and services (generally combined with religious conversion efforts) to those in need. To avoid duplication of services to the same families, the Charity Organization Society was formed to *coordinate* efforts and to *plan* for meeting unmet needs.

Reformers associated with the settlement house movement based many of their programs on *social action* to promote legislation for providing needed services to neighborhoods. These reformers also encouraged neighborhood residents to work together to improve living conditions.

Community welfare councils were first organized in 1908.[29] Continuing the efforts begun by the charity organization movement, these councils served as coordinating organizations for voluntary agencies. The functions of these councils have continued to the present time and include planning, coordinating, avoiding duplication of services, setting standards for services, and improving efficiency and accountability.

Community Chests (now called United Way) were formed around 1920 to serve as centralized campaigns for raising funds for voluntary agencies.[30] In many communities, United Way has been combined with community welfare councils for fund-raising and for the allocation of funds to voluntary agencies.

All social welfare agencies and organizations become involved at times in community practice efforts.

Models of Community Practice

A variety of approaches have been developed to bring about community change. In reviewing these approaches, Jack Rothman and John Tropman categorized them into three models: locality development, social planning, and social action.[31]

The Locality Development Model

Robert McKearn, a social worker for a juvenile probation department, noticed in 1991 that an increasing number of school-age children were being referred to his office by the police department, school system, and parents from a small city of 11,000 people in the county served by his agency. The charges included status offenses (such as truancy) and delinquent offenses (such as shoplifting and burglary). He noted that most of these children were from single-parent families.

Mr. McKearn contacted the community mental health center, the self-help organization Parents Without Partners, the Pupil Services Department of the public school system, the county Social Services Department, and some members of the clergy in the area. Nearly everyone he talked with saw an emerging need to better serve children in single-parent families. The Pupil Services Department mentioned that these children were performing less well academically in school and tended to display more serious disciplinary problems.

Mr. McKearn arranged a meeting of representatives from all the groups and organizations that had been contacted. At the initial meeting, a number of concerns were expressed about the problematic behaviors being displayed by children who had single parents. The school system considered these children to be "at risk" for high rates of truancy, dropping out of school, delinquent activities, suicide, emotional problems, and unwanted pregnancies. Although a number of problems were identified, no one at this initial meeting was able to suggest a viable strategy to better serve single parents and their children. The community was undergoing an economic recession; therefore, funds were unavailable for an expensive new program.

These models are "ideal types." Actual approaches to community change tend to blend characteristics of all three models. Advocates of the social planning model, for example, may at times use community change techniques (such as extensive discussion and participation by a variety of groups) that are characteristic of the other two models. For analytical purposes, however, we'll view the three models as "pure" forms. (Examples of these three models are found in Case Examples 3.2, 3.3, and 3.4.)

LOCALITY DEVELOPMENT MODEL

The locality development (also called community development) model asserts that community change can best be brought about through broad-based participation by a wide spectrum of people at the local community level. The approach seeks to involve a cross section of individuals (including the disadvantaged and the power structure) in identifying and solving problems. Some themes emphasized in this model are democratic procedures, a consensus approach, voluntary cooperation, development of indigenous leadership, and self-help.

The roles of the community practitioner in this approach include enabler, catalyst, coordinator, and teacher of problem-solving skills and ethical values. It is assumed that any conflicts among various groups can be creatively and constructively resolved. People are encouraged to express their differences freely but to put aside self-interests to further the interests of their community. The basic theme of this approach is, "To-

Three more meetings were held. At the first two, several suggestions for providing services were discussed, but all were viewed as either too expensive or impractical. At the fourth meeting of the group, a single mother representing Parents Without Partners mentioned that Big Brothers and Big Sisters programs in some communities reportedly were of substantial benefit to children raised in single-parent families. This idea seemed to energize the group, and suggestions began to "piggyback." However, members determined that no funds were available to hire staff to run a Big Brothers and Big Sisters program. Then, Rhona Quinn, a social worker in the Public Services Department, offered to identify at-risk younger children in single-parent families and to supervise qualified volunteers in a Big Buddy program.

Mr. McKearn mentioned that he was currently supervising a student in an undergraduate field placement from an accredited social work program in a nearby college. Mr. McKearn suggested that perhaps undergraduate social work students could be recruited to be Big Buddies to fulfill their required volunteer experience. Rhona Quinn said she would approve the suggestion if she could have the freedom to screen interested applicants. Arrangements were made over the next 2 months for social work students to be Big Buddies for at-risk younger children from single-parent families. After a 2-year experimental period, the school system found the program to be sufficiently successful that it assigned Ms. Quinn to supervise it half time. Her duties included selecting at-risk children, screening volunteer applicants, matching children with Big Buddies, monitoring the progress of each matched pair, and conducting follow-up to ascertain the outcome of each pairing.

gether we can figure out what to do and then do it." The locality development model seeks to use discussion and communication among different factions to reach consensus on which problems to focus on and which strategies or actions to use to resolve these problems. A few examples of such efforts include neighborhood work programs conducted by community-based agencies; Volunteers in Service to America; village-level work in some overseas community development programs, including the Peace Corps; and a variety of activities performed by self-help groups.

SOCIAL PLANNING MODEL

The social planning approach emphasizes the process of problem solving. It assumes that community change in a complex industrial environment requires highly trained and skilled planners who can guide complex change processes. The role of the expert is crucial to identifying and resolving social problems. The expert or planner is generally employed by a segment of the power structure, such as an area planning agency, city or county planning department, mental health center, United Way board, Community Welfare Council, and so on. Because the social planner is employed by the power structure, there is a tendency for him or her to serve the interests of that structure. Marshaling community resources and facilitating radical social change are generally not emphasized in this approach.

The planner's roles in this approach include gathering facts, analyzing data, and serving as program designer, implementer, and facilitator.

The Social Planning Model

In 1991 the board of directors of Lincoln County Social Planning Agency authorized its staff to conduct a feasibility study on establishing a centralized information and referral center. Donald Levi (social planner on the staff) was assigned to direct the study. Mr. Levi collected data showing the following:

■ There were over 350 community service agencies and organizations in this largely metropolitan county of one-half million people. Not only clients but also service providers were confused about what services were available from this array of agencies.

■ There was a confusing array of specialized information and referral (I&R) services being developed. (Specialized information and referral services provided I&R services in only one or two areas.) Specialized I&R services were developing in suicide prevention, mental health, mental retardation, day care, adoption services, and alcohol and drug treatment.

Mr. Levi then designed a program model for providing a centralized information and referral service. The model described a service that would provide I&R services on *all* human and community services in the county. For example, I&R would provide information not only on what day-care services were available but also on where to find public tennis courts and whom to call to remove a stray cat killed in front of your house. The centralized information and referral service number would be widely publicized on television, radio, and billboards and in newspapers and telephone directories. A budget was developed by Mr. Levi for the program costs.

The board of directors of the Lincoln County Social Planning Agency concluded that such a centralized information and referral service would be more efficient and

Community participation may vary from little to substantial, depending on the community's attitudes toward the problems being addressed. For example, an effort to design and fund a community center for the elderly may or may not generate a lot of participation by interested community groups, depending on the politics surrounding such a center. Much of the focus of the social planning approach is on identifying needs and on arranging and delivering goods and services to people who need them. In effect, the philosophy is, "Let's get the facts and take the next rational steps."

SOCIAL ACTION MODEL

The social action model assumes that there is a disadvantaged (often oppressed) segment of the population that needs to be organized, perhaps in alliance with others, to pressure the power structure for increased resources or for social justice. Social action approaches seek basic changes in major institutions or in basic policies of formal organizations. The objective is redistribution of power and resources. Whereas locality developers envision a unified community, social action advocates see the power structure as the opposition—the target of action. Perhaps the besteconomical than the confusing array that had been developing. The board therefore authorized Mr. Levi to pursue the development of this centralized service.

Mr. Levi conducted a questionnaire survey of all the human service agencies and all the clergy in the county. The results showed that both groups strongly supported the development of a centralized I&R service. In addition, the Easter Seal Society felt so strongly that such a service was needed that they contacted Mr. Levi to indicate that they were willing to donate funds for the new program. Mr. Levi was delighted, and an arrangement was worked out for the Easter Seal Society to fund the program for a 3-year demonstration period.

Only one barrier remained. The proposal for this new service needed to be approved by the county board of supervisors, as the proposal required the county to fund the program (beginning 3 years in the future) if the service proved to be effective during the 3-year demonstration phase. Mr. Levi and two members of the board of the Lincoln County Social Planning Agency presented the program proposal to the county board of supervisors. The presentation included graphs showing the savings of a centralized I&R service over specialized I&R services and contained written statements of support from a variety of sources, including city council members, the United Way, human service agencies, and members of the clergy. It was also indicated that there would be no cost to the county for a 3-year demonstration period. At the end of that time, there would be an evaluative study of the merits and shortcomings of the program. Mr. Levi fully expected approval and was speechless when the county board of supervisors said "no." They turned the proposal down because they felt a centralized I&R meant that more people would be referred to county social service agencies, which would raise costs to the county, and because this board was opposed to making a commitment to funding any new social welfare program in the future.

The county continues to be served by less effective specialized I&R services. This case example realistically illustrates that some planning efforts are unsuccessful.

known social activist was Saul Alinsky, who advised: "Pick the target, freeze it, personalize it, and polarize it."[32]

The roles of the community practitioner in this approach include advocate, agitator, activist, partisan, broker, and negotiator. Tactics used in social action projects are protests, boycotts, confrontation, and negotiation. The change strategy is one of "Let's organize to overpower our oppressor."[33] The client population is viewed as being "victimized" by the oppressive power structure. Examples of the social action approach include boycotts during the civil rights movement of the 1960s, strikes by unions, protests by antiabortion groups, and protests by African American and Native American groups.

The social action model is not widely used by social workers at present. Involvement in social action activities may lead employing agencies to penalize those social workers with unpleasant work assignments, low merit increases, and withholding of promotions. Many agencies will accept minor and moderate changes in their service delivery systems but are threatened by the prospect of such radical changes as are often advocated by the social action approach.

The Social Action Model

Saul Alinsky, a nationally noted social action strategist, provides an example of a creative social action effort. The example also shows that social action efforts are often enjoyable:

> *I was lecturing at a college run by a very conservative, almost fundamentalist Protestant denomination. Afterward some of the students came to my motel to talk to me. Their problem was that they couldn't have any fun on campus. They weren't permitted to dance or smoke or have a can of beer. I had been talking about the strategy of effecting change in a society and they wanted to know what tactics they could use to change their situation. I reminded them that a tactic is doing what you can with what you've got. "Now, what have you got?" I asked. "What do they permit you to do?" "Practically nothing," they said, "except—you know—we can chew gum."*
> *I said, "Fine, Gum becomes the weapon. You get 200 or 300 students to get two packs of gum each, which is quite a wad. Then you have them drop it on the campus walks. This will cause absolute chaos. Why, with 500 wads of gum I could paralyze Chicago, stop all the traffic in the Loop." They looked at me as though I was some kind of nut. But about two weeks later I got an ecstatic letter saying, "It worked! It worked! Now we can do just about anything so long as we don't chew gum."*

Source: Saul Alinsky, *Rules for Radicals* (New York: Random House, 1972), pp. 145–146.

Exhibit 3.6 summarizes the three models that have been discussed.

KNOWLEDGE, SKILLS, AND VALUES FOR SOCIAL WORK PRACTICE

Knowledge Base

The knowledge needed for effective social work practice has been identified by NASW as follows:

■ Knowledge *of casework and group work theory and techniques.*

■ Knowledge *of community resources and services.*

■ Knowledge *of basic federal and state social service programs and their purposes.*

■ Knowledge *of community organization theory and the development of health and welfare services.*

■ Knowledge *of basic socioeconomic and political theory.*

■ Knowledge *of racial, ethnic, and other cultural groups in society—their values and lifestyles and the resultant issues in contemporary life.*

■ Knowledge *of sources of professional and scientific research appropriate to practice.*

■ Knowledge *of the concepts and techniques of social planning.*

■ Knowledge *of the theories and concepts of supervision and the professional supervision of social worker practice.*

■ Knowledge *of theories and concepts of personnel management.*

EXHIBIT 3.6

Three Models of Community Organization
Practice According to Selected Practice Variables

Characteristic	Locality Development Model	Social Planning Model	Social Action Model
1. Goals	Self-help; improve community living; emphasis on process goals	Using problem-solving approach to resolve community problems; emphasis on task goals	Shifting of power relationships and resources to an oppressed group; basic institutional change; emphasis on task and process goals
2. Assumptions concerning community	Everyone wants community living to improve and is willing to contribute to the improvement	Social problems in the community can be resolved through the efforts of planning experts	The community has a power structure and one or more oppressed groups; social injustice is a major problem
3. Basic change strategy	Broad cross section of people involved in identifying and solving their problems	Experts using fact gathering and the problem-solving approach	Members of oppressed groups organizing to take action against the power structure, which is the enemy
4. Characteristic change tactics and techniques	Consensus: communication among community groups and interests; group discussion	Consensus or conflict	Conflict or contest: confrontation, direct action, negotiation
5. Practitioner roles	Catalyst; facilitator; coordinator; teacher of problem-solving skills	Expert planner; fact gatherer; analyst; program developer and implementer	Activist; advocate; agitator; broker; negotiator; partisan
6. Views about power structure	Members of power structure as collaborators in a common venture	Power structure as employers and sponsors	Power structure as external target of action, oppressors to be coerced or overturned
7. Views about client population	Citizens	Consumers	Victims
8. Views about client role	Participants in a problem-solving process	Consumers or recipients	Employers, constituents

- Knowledge *of common social and psychological statistical and other research methods and techniques.*

- Knowledge *of the theories and concepts of social welfare administration.*

- Knowledge *of social and environmental factors affecting clients to be served.*

- Knowledge *of the theories and methods of psychosocial assessment and intervention and of differential diagnosis.*

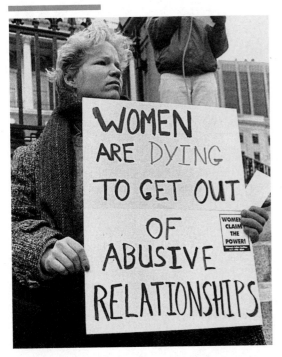

Social activists seek basic institutional change. Their tactics range from negotiation and advocacy to confrontation and protests.

- Knowledge *of the theory and behavior of organizational and social systems and of methods for encouraging change.*

- Knowledge *of community organization theory and techniques.*

- Knowledge *of the theories of human growth and development and of family and social interaction.*

- Knowledge *of small-group theory and behavioral dynamics.*

- Knowledge *of the theories of group interaction and therapeutic intervention.*

- Knowledge *of crisis intervention theories and techniques.*

- Knowledge *of advocacy theory and techniques.*

- Knowledge *of the ethical standards and practices of professional social work.*

- Knowledge *of teaching and instructional theories and techniques.*

- Knowledge *of social welfare trends and policies.*

- Knowledge *of local, state, and federal laws and regulations affecting social and health services.**

The Council on Social Work Education has categorized the knowledge needed by social workers into ten broad content areas. Every accredited social work educational program is expected to provide the following content, which is excerpted from the 1992 Curriculum Policy Statements.[34]

Liberal Arts Perspective. A liberal arts perspective enriches understanding of the person-environment context of professional social work practice and is integrally related to the mastery of social work content. The baccalaureate professional program in social work is built upon a liberal arts perspective.

A liberal arts perspective provides an understanding of one's cultural heritage in the context of other cultures; the methods and limitations of various systems of inquiry; and the knowledge, attitudes, ways of thinking, and means of communication that are characteristic of a broadly educated person. Students must be capable of thinking critically about society, about people and their problems, and about such expressions of culture as art, literature, science, history, and philosophy. Students must have direct knowledge about social, psychological, and biological determinants of human behavior and of diverse cultures, social conditions, and social problems.

Social Work Values and Ethics. Programs of social work education must provide specific knowledge about social work values and their ethical implications and must provide opportunities for students to demonstrate their application in professional practice. Students must be assisted to develop an awareness of their personal values and to clarify conflicting values and ethical dilemmas.

---

*Source: From Standards for the Classification of Social Work Practice, p. 17. Copyright © 1996 National Association of Social Workers, Inc. Reprinted by permission.

Diversity. Professional social work education is committed to preparing students to understand and appreciate human diversity. Programs must provide curriculum content about differences and similarities in the experiences, needs, and beliefs of people. The curriculum must include content about differential assessment and intervention skills that will enable practitioners to serve diverse populations.

Each program is required to include content about population groups that are particularly relevant to the program's mission. These include, but are not limited to, groups distinguished by race, ethnicity, culture, class, gender, sexual orientation, religion, physical or mental ability, age, and national origin.

Promotion of Social and Economic Justice. Programs of social work education must provide an understanding of the dynamics and consequences of social and economic injustice, including all forms of human oppression and discrimination. They must provide students with the skills to promote social change and to implement a wide range of interventions that further the achievement of individual and collective social and economic justice. Theoretical and practice content must be provided about strategies of intervention for achieving social and economic justice and for combating the causes and effects of institutionalized forms of oppression.

Populations-at-Risk. Programs of social work education must present theoretical and practice content about patterns, dynamics, and consequences of discrimination, economic deprivation, and oppression. The curriculum must provide content about people of color, women, and gay and lesbian persons. Such content must emphasize the impact of discrimination, economic deprivation, and oppression upon these groups.

Each program must include content about populations-at-risk that are particularly relevant to its mission. In addition to those mandated above, such groups include, but are not limited to, those distinguished by age, ethnicity, culture, class, religion, and physical or mental ability.

Human Behavior and the Social Environment. Programs of social work education must provide content about theories and knowledge of human bio-psycho-social development, including theories and knowledge about the range of social systems in which individuals live (families, groups, organizations, institutions, and communities). The human behavior and the social environment curriculum must provide an understanding of the interactions between and among human biological, social, psychological, and cultural systems as they affect and are affected by human behavior. The impact of social and economic forces on individuals and social systems must be presented. Content must be provided about the ways in which systems promote or deter people in the maintenance or attainment of optimal health and well-being. Content about values and ethical issues related to bio-psycho-social theories must be included. Students must be taught to evaluate theory and apply theory to client situations.

Social Welfare Policy and Services. Social welfare policy and services content must include the history, mission, and philosophy of the social work profession. Content must be presented about the history and current patterns of provision of social welfare services, the role of social policy in helping or deterring people in the maintenance or attainment of optimal health and well-being, and the effect of policy on social work practice. Students must be taught to analyze current social policy within the context of historical and contemporary factors that shape policy. Content must be presented about the political and organizational processes used to influence policy, the process of policy formulation, and the frameworks for analyzing social policies in light of the principles of social and economic justice.

Social Work Practice. At the baccalaureate level, professional social work education prepares students for generalist practice with systems of all sizes. Practice content emphasizes professional relationships that are characterized by mutuality, collaboration, and respect for the client system. Content on practice assessment focuses on the examination of client strengths and problems in the interactions among individuals and between people and their environments.

Social work practice content must include knowledge, values, and skills to enhance the *well-being of people and to help ameliorate the environmental conditions that affect people adversely. Practice content must include the following skills: defining issues; collecting and assessing data; planning and contracting; identifying alternative interventions; selecting and implementing appropriate courses of action; using appropriate research to monitor and evaluate outcomes; applying appropriate research-based knowledge and technological advances; and termination. Practice content also includes approaches and skills for practice with clients from differing social, cultural, racial, religious, spiritual, and class backgrounds and with systems of all sizes.*

Research. *The research curriculum must provide an understanding and appreciation of a scientific, analytic approach to building knowledge for practice and for evaluating service delivery in all areas of practice. Ethical standards of scientific inquiry must be included in the research content.*

The research content must include quantitative and qualitative research methodologies; analysis of data, including statistical procedures; systematic evaluation of practice; analysis and evaluation of theoretical bases, research questions, methodologies, statistical procedures, and conclusions of research reports; and relevant technological advances.

Each program must identify how the research curriculum contributes to the student's use of scientific knowledge for practice.

Field Practicum. *The field practicum is an integral component of the curriculum in social work education. It engages the student in supervised social work practice and provides opportunities to apply classroom learning in the field setting.*

The baccalaureate practicum must provide the student with opportunities for:

a. *The development of an awareness of self in the process of intervention.*

b. *Supervised practice experience in the application of knowledge, values and ethics, and practice skills to enhance the well-being of people and to work toward the amelioration of environmental conditions that affect people adversely.*

c. *Use of oral and written professional communications which are consistent with the language of the practicum setting and of the profession.*

d. *Use of professional supervision to enhance learning.*

e. *Critical assessment, implementation, and evaluation of agency policy within ethical guidelines.* *

The curriculum at the master's level in social work also must be based on a liberal arts perspective. The definition of this perspective is very similar to that for the baccalaureate level. The curriculum at the master's level is mandated by the Curriculum Policy Statement of the Council on Social Work Education to be composed of (a) professional foundation content and (b) concentration content in an area.

The professional foundation includes content on social work values and ethics, diversity, promotion of social and economic justice, populations-at-risk, human behavior and the social environment, social welfare policy and services, social work practice, research, and field practicum. The description of these areas in the master's-level Policy Statement is nearly identical to the description in the baccalaureate Curriculum Policy Statement; therefore, it will not be repeated here.

Concentration content includes knowledge, values, and skills for advanced practice in an identifiable area. Identifiable areas that are frequently offered by master's programs include fields of practice, problem areas, populations-at-risk, and intervention methods or roles.

Skill Base

Many efforts have been made to articulate the essential skills for entry-level social work positions. We'll look at a few of these conceptualizations to illustrate contemporary thinking about core prac-

---

* Reprinted from *Curriculum Policy Statement for Baccalaureate Degree Programs in Social Work Education*, Final Draft July 8, 1992, by permission of the Council on Social Work Education, Alexandria, VA.

tice skills. Be aware, however, that, despite the similarities among these conceptualizations, there is *not* full agreement on these core skills.

Federico has indirectly described social work skills by outlining roles and activities:

1. Outreach worker—*reaching out into the community to identify need and follow up referrals to service contexts.*

2. Broker—*knowing services available and making sure those in need reach the appropriate services.*

3. Advocate—*helping specific clients obtain services when they might otherwise be rejected, and helping to expand services to cover more needy persons.*

4. Evaluation—*evaluating needs and resources, generating alternatives for meeting needs, and making decisions between alternatives.*

5. Teacher—*teaching facts and skills.*

6. Mobilizer—*helping to develop new services.*

7. Behavior changer—*changing specific parts of a client's behavior.*

8. Consultant—*working with other professionals to help them be more effective in providing services.*

9. Community planner—*helping community groups plan effectively for the community's social welfare needs.*

10. Care giver—*providing supportive services to those who cannot fully solve their problems and meet their own needs.*

11. Data manager—*collecting and analyzing data for decision-making purposes.*

12. Administrator—*performing the activities necessary to plan and implement a program of services.*[35]

Baer has identified the following ten competencies as being essential for successfully performing the responsibilities of entry-level positions:

1. *Identify and assess situations in which the relationship between people and social institutions needs to be initiated, enhanced, restored, protected, or terminated.*

2. *Develop and implement a plan for improving the well-being of people, based on problem assessment and the exploration of obtainable goals and available options.*

3. *Enhance the problem-solving, coping, and developmental capacities of people.*

4. *Link people with systems that provide them with resources, services, and opportunities.*

5. *Intervene effectively on behalf of populations most vulnerable and discriminated against.*

6. *Promote the effective and humane operation of the systems that provide people with services, resources, and opportunities.*

7. *Actively participate with others in creating new, modified, or improved service, resource, or opportunity systems that are more equitable, just, and responsive to consumers of services; work with others to eliminate unjust systems.*

8. *Evaluate the extent to which the objectives of the intervention plan were achieved.*

9. *Continually evaluate one's professional growth and development through assessment of practice behaviors and skills.*

10. *Contribute to the improvement of service delivery by adding to the knowledge base of the profession as appropriate and supporting and upholding the standards and ethics of the profession.*[36]

These ten competencies were originally developed by Baer and Federico.[37]

NASW has identified the essential skills for social work practice as follows:

■ Skill *in listening to others with understanding and purpose.*

■ Skill *in eliciting information and in assembling relevant facts to prepare a social history, assessment, and report.*

■ Skill *in creating and maintaining professional helping relationships and in using oneself in relationships.*

■ Skill *in observing and interpreting verbal and nonverbal behavior and in using a knowledge of personality theory and diagnostic methods.*

- Skill *in engaging clients in efforts to resolve their own problems and in gaining trust.*
- Skill *in discussing sensitive emotional subjects in a nonthreatening, supportive manner.*
- Skill *in creating innovative solutions to clients' needs.*
- Skill *in determining the need to end therapeutic relationships and how to do so.*
- Skill *in interpreting the findings of research studies and professional literature.*
- Skill *in mediating and negotiating between conflicting parties.*
- Skill *in providing interorganizational liaison services.*
- Skill *in interpreting or communicating social needs to funding sources, the public, or legislators.* *

Closely related to the conceptualization of essential skills, NASW has identified the following abilities as being needed for social work practice:

- Ability *to speak and write clearly.*
- Ability *to teach others.*
- Ability *to respond supportively in emotion-laden or crisis situations.*
- Ability *to serve as a role model in a professional relationship.*
- Ability *to interpret complex psychosocial phenomena.*
- Ability *to organize a workload to meet designated responsibilities.*
- Ability *to identify and obtain resources needed to assist others.*
- Ability *to assess one's performance and feelings, and to use help or consultation.*
- Ability *to participate in and lead group activities.*
- Ability *to function under stress.*

- Ability *to deal with conflict situations or contentious personalities.*
- Ability *to relate social and psychological theory to practice situations.*
- Ability *to identify the information necessary to solve a problem.*
- Ability *to conduct research studies of agency services or one's practice.* *

In its 1992 Curriculum Policy Statements for both the baccalaureate and master's programs, the Council on Social Work Education mandated that social work programs provide content on the following skills:

- Defining issues.
- Collecting and assessing data.
- Planning and contracting.
- Identifying alternative interventions.
- Selecting and implementing appropriate courses of action.
- Using appropriate research to monitor and evaluate outcomes.
- Applying appropriate research-based knowledge and technological advances.
- Termination.

(These skills were elaborated on earlier in this chapter.)

The acquisition of social work skills depends partly on people's innate abilities and partly on learning experiences. Social work educational programs facilitate learning of such skills by presenting theoretical material to students (for example, material on how to interview), by monitoring and critiquing students who are practicing these skills (for example, videotaping students in simulated counseling situations), and by extensively supervising students in practicum courses.

Value Base

Should the primary objective of imprisonment be rehabilitation or punishment? Should a father who commits incest be prosecuted, with the likelihood that publicity in the community will lead to family breakup, or should an effort first be made, through counseling, to stop the incest and keep the family intact? Should a wife who is occasionally abused by her husband be encouraged to remain living with him? Should abortion be suggested as one alternative for resolving the problems of someone who is single and pregnant? Should youths who are claimed by their parents to be uncontrollable be placed in correctional schools? If a client informs a social worker that he intends to severely injure some third party, what should the worker do? Suppose a client indicates he is HIV positive but refuses to reveal his condition to his partner, thereby placing the partner in peril through unprotected sexual relations. What action should the social worker take? All of these questions involve making decisions that are based largely on values. Much of social work practice is dependent on making value-based decisions.

Allen Pincus and Anne Minahan concisely define *values* and describe differences between values and knowledge:

> *Values are beliefs, preferences, or assumptions about what is desirable or good for [humans].*
> *An example is the belief that society has an obligation to help each individual realize his fullest potential. They are not assertions about how the world is and what we know about it, but how it should be. As such, value statements cannot be subjected to scientific investigation; they must be accepted on faith. Thus we can speak of a value as being right or wrong only in relation to the particular belief system or ethical code being used as a standard.*
>
> *What we will refer to as knowledge statements, on the other hand, are observations about the world and [humans] which have been verified or are capable of verification. An example is that black people have a shorter life expectancy than white people in the United States. When we speak of a knowledge statement as*
> *being right or wrong, we are referring to the extent to which the assertion has been confirmed through objective empirical investigation.*[38]

The National Association of Social Workers (NASW) has formulated a Code of Ethics that summarizes important practice ethics for social workers; this code is presented in Appendix A.

RESPECT FOR THE DIGNITY AND UNIQUENESS OF THE INDIVIDUAL

This value or principle has also been called *individualization*, which means viewing and treating each person as unique and worthwhile. The social work profession firmly believes that everyone has inherent dignity, which is to be respected.

Every human being is unique in a variety of ways—value system, personality, goals in life, financial resources, emotional and physical strengths, personal concerns, past experiences, peer pressures, emotional reactions, self-identity, family relationships, and behavioral patterns. In working with a client, a social worker needs to perceive and respect the uniqueness of the client's situation.

Individualization is relatively easy for a social worker to achieve when clients have values, goals, behavioral patterns, and personal characteristics that are similar to those of the worker. It is harder to achieve when clients have values or behavioral patterns that the worker views as unpleasant. For example, a worker holding traditional middle-class values may have difficulty in respecting a client who has killed someone, has raped someone, is filthy, or continually uses vulgar language. A general guideline in such situations is that the worker should seek to accept and respect the client but not the deviant behavior that needs to be changed. If a worker is not able to convey that she or he accepts the client (but not the deviant behavior), a helping relationship will not be established. In that case, the worker will have practically no opportunity to help the client make constructive changes. A second guideline is that, if a worker views a client as being unpleasant and is unable to establish a working relationship, then the case should be transferred to another worker. The original social worker need not feel disgrace or embarrassment in having to transfer a case for such reasons; it is irrational to expect to like every client or to be liked by every client.[39]

Social workers occasionally encounter "raw" situations. I have worked with clients who have committed a wide range of asocial and bizarre acts, including incest, rape, murder, sodomy, sexual exhibitionism, and grave robbing. Achieving an attitude of respect for people who commit bizarre actions is difficult at times, but rehabilitation will not occur unless the worker develops respect.

Social psychologists have firmly established that our images of ourselves develop largely out of our interactions and communications with others. A long time ago, Charles Cooley labeled this process the "looking glass self-concept."[40] People develop their self-concept in terms of how other people relate to them, as if others were a looking glass or mirror. For example, if you receive respect from others and are praised for your positive qualities, you will feel good about yourself, will gradually develop a positive sense of worth, will be happier, and will seek responsible and socially acceptable ways to continue to maintain the respect of others.

On the other hand, if you are related to by others as if you are irresponsible, you will begin to view yourself as irresponsible and will gradually develop a negative self-concept. With such a view of yourself, you decrease your efforts to act responsibly. In both these examples, the ways that others relate to you (positively or negatively) become a self-fulfilling prophecy.[41]

The principle of individualization also plays a key role in social work treatment. Various problems, needs, goals, and values of clients require different patterns of relationships with workers and different methods of helping. For example, a teenage male who is placed in a group home because his parents find him "uncontrollable" may need an understanding but firm counselor who sets and enforces strict limits. At times the youth may need encouragement and guidance in how to perform better at school. If conflicts develop between the youth and other residents at the group home, the counselor may need to play a mediating role. If the boy is shy, assertiveness training may be needed. If his parents are fairly ineffective in their parenting role, the counselor may seek to have them enroll in a Parent Effectiveness Training (PET) program.[42] If the youth is being treated unfairly at school or by the juvenile court, the counselor may play an advocate role for him and attempt to change the system. If the youth has behavior problems, the social worker will need to explore the underlying reasons and develop an intervention program.

CLIENTS' RIGHT TO SELF-DETERMINATION

This principle asserts that clients have the right to hold and express their own opinions and to act on them, as long as doing so does not infringe on the rights of others. This principle is in sharp contrast to the layperson's perception that social workers seek to "remold" clients into a pattern chosen by the workers. Rather, the efforts of social workers are geared to enhancing the capability of clients to help themselves. Client self-determination derives logically from the belief in the inherent dignity of each person. If people have dignity, then it follows that they should be permitted to determine their own lifestyles as far as possible.

Making clients' decisions and doing everything for them are self-defeating; these actions lead to increased dependency rather than to self-reliance and self-sufficiency. For people to grow, to mature, and to become responsible, they need to make their own decisions and take responsibility for the consequences. Mistakes and emotional pain will at times occur. But that is part of life. We learn by our mistakes and by trial and error. Respect for the client's decision-making ability is associated with the principle that social work is a cooperative endeavor between client and worker (client participation). Social work is done *with* a client, not *to* a client. Plans imposed on people without their active involvement have a way of not turning out well.

Self-determination implies that clients should be made aware that there are alternatives for resolving their personal or social problems. They can choose from several courses of action. (If there is only one course of action, there is no choice and therefore no self-determination.) As we've seen, the role of a social worker in helping clients involves (a) building a helping relationship, (b) exploring problems with clients in depth, and (c) exploring alternative solutions, with the clients then choosing a course of action. This third step is the implementation of the principle of self-determination.

Social workers need to recognize that it is the client who *owns* the problem and therefore has the chief responsibility to resolve it. In this respect, social work differs markedly from most other professions. Most professionals, such as physicians and attorneys, advise clients about what they ought to do. Doctors, lawyers, and dentists are viewed as experts. Clients' decision making in such situations is generally limited to the professional's advice.

In sharp contrast, social workers seek to establish not an expert–inferior relationship but rather a relationship between equals. The expertise of the social worker does *not* lie in knowing or recommending what is best for the client; it lies in assisting clients to define their problems, to identify and examine alternatives for resolving the problems, to maximize their capacities and opportunities to make decisions for themselves, and to implement the decisions they make. Many students, when they first enter social work or some other helping profession, mistakenly see their role as that of "savior" or "rescuer." Mathew Dumont is highly critical of the rescuer role:

> · *The most destructive thing in psychotherapy is a "rescue fantasy" in the therapist—a feeling that the therapist is the divinely sent agent to pull a tormented soul from the pit of suffering and adversity and put him back on the road to happiness and glory. A major reason this fantasy is so destructive is that it carries the conviction that the patient will be saved only through and by the therapist. When such a conviction is communicated to the patient, verbally or otherwise, he has no choice other than to rebel and leave or become more helpless, dependent, and sick.*[43]

The principle of self-determination is complex and has some limitations. If a client decides to take a course of action that the social worker believes will have adverse effects, the social worker must decide whether to intervene. For example, if an elderly female client chooses to live alone in her home when there is serious concern about her physical capacities to live independently, a social worker has the obligation to point out the dangers and to suggest alternative living arrangements. In this situation, the social worker may decide not to take further action to force her into a safer living environment. On the other hand, if a client tries to commit suicide, the social worker should do everything possible to prevent another attempt.

Furthermore, if a client discusses an intention to harm another person, a social worker must make a judgment about whether to intervene to prevent the client from carrying out his or her intended actions. For example, if a client indicates that he plans to shoot someone and then bolts out of the social worker's office, the worker may choose (and may have a legal obligation) to inform the police and the intended victim.

CONFIDENTIALITY

Confidentiality is the implicit or explicit agreement between a professional and a client to maintain the privacy of information about the client. An "absolute" implementation of this principle means that disclosures made to the professional are not shared with anyone else, except when authorized by the client in writing or required by law. Because of the principle of confidentiality, professionals can be sued if they disclose unauthorized information that has a damaging effect on the client.

Confidentiality is important because clients are not likely to share their "hidden secrets," personal concerns, and asocial thoughts and actions with a professional who might reveal that information to others. A basic principle of counseling is that clients must feel comfortable in fully revealing themselves to the professional, without fear that their revelations will be used against them.

Confidentiality is absolute when information revealed to a professional is *never* passed on to anyone in any form. Such information would never be shared with other agency staff, fed into a computer, or written in a case record. A student or beginning practitioner tends to think in absolutes and may even naively promise clients "absolute confidentiality."

In reality, absolute confidentiality is seldom achieved. Social workers today generally function as part of a larger agency. In agencies much of the communication is written into case records and shared orally with other staff as part of the service-delivery process. Social workers share details with supervisors; many work in teams and are expected to share information with other team members. Thus it is more precise to describe confidentiality in social work practice as "relative confidentiality."

Confidentiality is a legal matter, and at present there is a fair amount of uncertainty about what legally constitutes a violation and what does not. There have been few test cases in court to define violations of confidentiality.

Today it is generally permissible to discuss a client's circumstances with other professionals within the agency. In some agencies, such as a mental hospital, the input of many professionals (psychiatrists, psychologists, social workers, nurses, physical therapists, and so on) is used in assessing a client and developing a treatment plan.

Many agencies consider it inappropriate to share or discuss the client's case with a secretary. (Yet the secretary does the typing and usually knows as much about each client as the professional staff.)

Most agencies believe it is inappropriate to discuss a client's case with professionals at another agency, unless the client first signs a release form. (However, professionals employed by different agencies do at times informally share information about a client without the client's authorization.)

At the present time, nearly all agencies share case information with social work interns. (Whether it is legally permissible to share information with student interns has not yet been determined.)

It is certainly permissible to discuss a case with others for educational purposes if the client

is not specifically identified. Yet this is another "gray" area, because the person talking about the case will not be able to determine precisely when identifying information is being given. Take the following example.

Some years ago, I was employed at a maximum security hospital for the criminally insane and had on my caseload a young male who had decapitated his 17-year-old girlfriend. Such a criminal offense is indeed shocking and rare. People in the client's local area will never forget the crime. If I were to discuss this case in a class at a university, I could never be fully certain that no one would be able to identify the offender. There is always the chance that one of the students may be from the client's home community and could recognize the offender.

Another problem area is the thorny question of when a professional should violate confidence and inform others. Again, there are many gray areas surrounding this question.

Most state laws permit or require the professional to inform the appropriate people when a client admits to a past or intended *serious* criminal act. Yet the question of how serious a crime must be before there is an obligation to report it has not been resolved. On the extreme end of the "severity" continuum (for example, when a client threatens to kill someone), it has been established that a professional *must* inform the appropriate people —such as the police and the intended victims.[44]

In regard to the question of how serious a crime must be before it is reported, S. J. Wilson notes:

> How serious must a crime be in order for the professional to take protective measures? Obviously, crimes involving someone's life are sufficiently serious. But what about destruction of personal property, theft, and the hundreds of misdemeanors that are so minor that they are rather easily overlooked? Unfortunately, there seems to be no clear-cut definition of what constitutes a serious crime, and it appears that this will have to be determined by the courts in individual case rulings.[45]

Without guidelines, a professional must use his or her own best judgment about when a client's actions or communications warrant protective measures and about what those measures should be. Student interns and beginning practitioners are advised to consult their supervisors when questions in this area arise.

A few years ago, I was the faculty supervisor for a student in a field placement at a public assistance agency. The intern had an unmarried AFDC mother on his caseload. A trusting working relationship between the intern and the mother was developed. The woman then informed the intern that she was dating a man who was sometimes abusive to her when drunk. She further indicated that there was a warrant for this man's arrest in another state for an armed robbery charge. The student contacted me, inquiring whether it was his obligation to inform the police, thereby violating confidentiality. My response was that he should discuss this with his agency supervisor to find out the agency's policy. The student informed the agency supervisor. The supervisor consulted with the attorney for the agency, who advised that the student should inform the woman that the information she revealed would have to be provided to the authorities. Upon being informed, the woman stomped out of the office, presumably to warn her partner. The police were immediately informed and proceeded to arrest him. The woman was outraged and ended all communication with the professional staff at this agency, as she felt she could no longer trust them. (When professionals are legally obligated to violate confidentiality, the clients involved are apt to react as this mother did.)

Wilson has researched this issue and concludes:

In summary, a professional whose client confesses an intended or past crime can find himself in a very delicate position, both legally and ethically. There are enough conflicting beliefs on how this should be handled, so that clear guidelines are lacking. Social workers who receive a communication about a serious criminal act by a client would be wise to consult an attorney for a detailed research of appropriate state statutes and a review of recent court rulings that might help determine the desired course of action.[46]

There are a number of other circumstances when a professional is permitted, expected, or required to violate confidentiality.* These include:

■ When a client formally (usually in writing) authorizes the professional to release information.

■ When a professional is called to testify in a criminal case. (State statutes vary regarding guidelines on what information may be kept confidential in criminal proceedings; practitioners must research their own particular statutes in each instance.)

■ When a client files a lawsuit against a professional (such as for malpractice).

■ When a client threatens suicide. A professional may then be forced to violate confidentiality to save the client's life. Although the treating professional is encouraged to violate confidentiality in such circumstances, there is not necessarily a legal requirement to do so.

■ When a client threatens to harm his or her therapist.

■ When a professional becomes aware that a minor has committed a crime, when a minor is used by adults as an accessory in a crime, or when a minor is a victim of criminal actions. In such situations, most states require that counselors inform the legal authorities. Again, the question arises of how serious the crime must be before it is reported.

■ When there is evidence of child abuse or neglect. Most states require professionals to report the evidence to the designated child protection agency.

■ When a client's emotional or physical condition makes his or her employment a clear danger to himself or herself or to others (for example, when a counselor discovers that a client who is an airplane pilot has a serious drinking problem).

---

*An extended discussion of these circumstances is contained in Suanna J. Wilson, *Confidentiality in Social Work: Issues and Principles* (New York: Free Press, 1978) and in Donald T. Dickson, *Confidentiality and Privacy in Social Work* (New York: Free Press, 1998).

All these instances require professional judgment in deciding when the circumstances justify violating confidentiality.

ADVOCACY AND SOCIAL ACTION FOR THE OPPRESSED

Social work recognizes an obligation to advocate for the powerless, oppressed, and the dispossessed. Social work believes that society has a responsibility to all of its members to provide security, acceptance, and satisfaction of basic cultural, social, and biological needs. Only when our basic needs are met can we develop our maximum potentials. Because social work believes in the value of the individual, it has a special responsibility to protect and secure civil rights for all oppressed persons and groups. Social workers have a moral responsibility to work toward eradicating discrimination. The civil rights of clients need to be protected to preserve human dignity and self-respect.

ACCOUNTABILITY

Increasingly, federal and state governmental units and private funding sources are requiring that the effectiveness of service programs be measured. Programs found to be ineffective are being phased out. Although some social workers view accountability with trepidation and claim that the paperwork involved interferes with serving clients, social work has an obligation to funding sources to provide the highest-quality services. Accountability studies have yielded some valuable information. For example, they have demonstrated that orphanages are not the best places to serve homeless children, that long-term hospitalization is not the best way to help the emotionally disturbed, that probation generally has higher rehabilitative value than long-term confinement in prison, that the Job Corps program of the 1960s was too expensive for the outcomes achieved, that most children with a cognitive disability can be better served in their home communities through local programs than by confinement in an institution, and that runaways fare better in runaway centers than in detention or in jail.

Social workers need to become skilled at evaluating their effectiveness in providing services.

A wide variety of evaluation techniques are now available to assess effectiveness of current services and to identify unmet needs and service gaps. One of the most useful approaches is management by objectives (MBO). This technique involves identifying the objectives of each program, specifying in measurable terms how and when these objectives are met, and then periodically measuring the extent to which the objectives are met.

Management by objectives is also one of the most useful approaches that every social worker can use to assess his or her own effectiveness. Many agencies are now requiring each of their workers, *with the involvement of their clients*, to (a) identify and specify what the goals will be for each client (generally this is done together with clients during the initial interviews), (b) have the client and the worker then write down in detail what each will do to accomplish the goals (deadlines for accomplishing these tasks are also set), and (c) assess the extent to which the goals have been achieved when the intervention is terminated (and perhaps periodically during the intervention process).

If goals are not being achieved, the worker needs to examine the underlying reasons. Perhaps unrealistic goals are being set. Perhaps the program or the intervention techniques are ineffective. Perhaps certain components of the intervention program are having an adverse effect. Perhaps other factors account for the low success rate. Depending on the cause, appropriate changes need to be made.

On the other hand, if the goals are being met, the worker can use this information to document to funding sources and to supervisors that high-quality services are being provided.

THE INSTITUTIONAL ORIENTATION

There are currently two conflicting views of the role of social welfare in our society: the residual orientation versus the institutional orientation. These two views were described at length in Chapter 1. Social work believes in the institutional approach and seeks to develop and provide programs with this orientation. Society must provide opportunities for growth and development that will allow each person to realize his or her fullest potential. Social work believes that society has a responsibility to all its members to provide security, acceptance, and satisfaction of basic cultural and biological needs. Social workers reject the views of rugged individualism and Social Darwinism.

RESPECT FOR THE SPIRITUAL AND RELIGIOUS BELIEFS OF OTHERS

A major thrust of social work education is to prepare students for culturally sensitive practice. Since religion and spirituality play important roles in all cultures, it is essential that social workers comprehend the influence of religion and spirituality in human lives. The Curriculum Policy Statements of the Council on Social Work Education now require that accredited baccalaureate and master's programs provide practice content in these areas so that students develop approaches and skills for working with clients with differing spiritual backgrounds.

Spirituality and religion are separate, though often related, dimensions. Spirituality can be defined as "the general human experience of developing a sense of meaning, purpose, and morality."[47] Key components of spirituality are the personal search for meaning in life, a sense of identity (discussed in Chapter 2), and a value system. In contrast, religion refers to the formal institutional contexts of spiritual beliefs and practices.

Social work's historical roots in religious organizations originated under the inspiration of the Judeo-Christian religious traditions of its philanthropic founders. Jewish scriptures and religious law requiring the emulation of God's creativity and caring have inspired social welfare activities for many centuries. Similarly, the Christian biblical command to love one's neighbor as oneself has been interpreted as a sense of moral responsibility for social service and inspired the development of charity organizations and philanthropy in the United States during the 19th century. Social workers need to be trained for effective practice with religiously oriented clients because many social issues today have religious dimensions, such as abortion, use of contraceptives, acceptance of gays and lesbians, cloning, reproductive technology, roles of women, prayer in public schools, and physician-assisted suicide.

It is essential that social workers comprehend the influence of religion and spirituality in their clients' lives.

Social workers need an appreciation and respect for religious beliefs that differ from their own. There is a danger that those who believe that their religion is the "one true religion" will tend to view people with divergent beliefs as ill-guided, evil, mistaken, or in need of being "saved." More wars have been fought over religious differences than for any other cause. A major source of intolerance, discrimination, and oppression is the belief that "my religion is the one true religion; those who believe as I do will go to heaven, while those who believe in some other religion are heathens who will go to eternal damnation" (see Chapter 12).

Furman notes, "The goal of incorporating religious and spiritual beliefs in social work curricula should include a broad array of knowledge of many different religious and spiritual beliefs, primarily to expand students' understanding and sensitivity."[48] Exhibit 3.7 summarizes information on four prominent world religions.

EXHIBIT 3.7

Four Prominent Religions: Judaism, Christianity, Islam, and Buddhism

Practicing social workers need a knowledge and appreciation of the religious beliefs and value systems of their clients. The four religions in this exhibit were selected because of their prominence. Readers should know that there are hundreds of other religions in the world.

JUDAISM

Judaism is the religion of the Jews. Jews believe in one God, the creator of the world who delivered the Israelites out of their bondage in Egypt. The Hebrew Bible is the primary source of Judaism. (The Hebrew Bible was adopted by Christians as part of their sacred writings, and they now call it the Old Testament.) God is believed to have revealed his law (Torah) to the Israelites; part of this law was the Ten Commandments which were given to Moses by God. The Israelites believe God chose them to be a light to all humankind.

Next in importance to the Hebrew Bible is the Talmud, which is an influential compilation of rabbinic traditions and discussions about Jewish life and law. It consists of the Mishnah (the codification of the oral Torah) and a collection of extensive early rabbinical commentary. Various later commentaries and the standard code of Jewish law and ritual (Halakhah) produced in the later Middle Ages have been important in shaping Jewish practice and thought.

Abraham (who lived roughly 2000 years before Christ) is viewed as an ancestor or father of the Hebrew people. According to Genesis, he came from the Sumerian town of Ur (now part of modern Iraq) and migrated with his family and flocks via Haran (the ancient city of Nari on the Euphrates River) to the "Promised Land" of Canaan, where he settled at Shechem (modern Nablus). After a sojourn in Egypt, he lived to be 175 years old and was buried with his first wife, Sarah. By

Sarah he was the father of Isaac (whom he was prepared to sacrifice at the behest of the Lord) and grandfather of Jacob ("Israel"). By his second wife, Hagar (Sarah's Egyptian handmaiden), he was the father of Ismael, the ancestor of 12 clans. By his third wife, Keturah, he had six sons who became the ancestors of the Arab tribes. He was also the uncle of Lot. (Interestingly, Abraham is regarded by Judaism, Christianity, and Islam as an important ancestor or father in their religions.)

All Jews see themselves as members of a community that originated around the time in which Abraham lived. This past lives on in its rituals. The family is the basic unit of Jewish ritual, although the synagogue has come to play an increasingly important role. The Sabbath, which begins at sunset on Friday and ends at sunset on Saturday, is the central religious worship. The synagogue is the center for community worship and study. Its main feature is the "ark" (a cupboard) containing the hand-written scrolls of the Pentateuch (the five books of Moses in the Hebrew Bible, comprising Genesis, Exodus, Leviticus, Numbers, and Deuteronomy). A rabbi is primarily a teacher and spiritual guide.

There is an annual cycle of religious festivals and days of fasting. The first of these is Rosh Hashanah, the Jewish New Year, which falls in September or October. During this New Year's Day service, a ram's horn is blown as a call to repentance and spiritual renewal. The holiest day in the Jewish year is Yom Kippur, the Day of Atonement, which comes at the end of 10 days of penitence following Rosh Hashanah; Yom Kippur is a day devoted to fasting, prayer, and repentance for past sins. Another important festival is Hanukkah, held in December, commemorating the rededication of Jerusalem after the victory of Judas Maccabees over the Syrians. Pesach is the Passover festival,

(continued)

EXHIBIT 3.7   *(continued)*

occurring in March or April, commemorating the exodus of the Israelites from Egypt; the festival is named after God's passing over the houses of Israelites when he killed the first-born children of the Egyptian families.

CHRISTIANITY

Christianity is a religion practiced in numerous countries that is centered on the life and work of Jesus of Nazareth in Israel. It developed out of Judaism. The earliest followers were Jews who, after the death and resurrection of Jesus, believed him to be the Messiah, or Christ, promised by the prophets in the Old Testament. He was declared to be the Son of God. During his life, he chose 12 men as disciples, who formed the nucleus of the church. This communion of followers believed that Jesus would come again to inaugurate the "kingdom of God." God is believed to be one in essence but threefold in person, comprising the Father, Son, and Holy Spirit or Holy Ghost (together known at the Trinity). Jesus Christ is also wholly human because of his birth to Mary. The Holy Spirit is the touch or "breath" of God that inspires people to follow the Christian faith. The Bible is thought to have been written under the Holy Spirit's influence.

Jesus Christ was the son of Mary and Joseph, yet also the Son of God created by a miraculous conception by the Spirit of God. He was born in Bethlehem (near Jerusalem) but began his ministry in Nazareth. The main records of his ministry are the New Testament gospels, which show him proclaiming the coming of the kingdom of God and in particular the acceptance of the oppressed and the poor into the kingdom. The duration of his public ministry is uncertain, but it is from John's Gospel that one gets the impression of a 3-year period of teaching. He was executed by crucifixion under the order of Pontius Pilate, a Roman ruler. The date of death is uncertain but is considered to be when Jesus was in his early thirties.

At the heart of the Christian faith is the conviction that through Jesus's death and resurrection, God has allowed humans to find salvation. Belief in Jesus as the Son of God, along with praying for forgiveness of sin, brings absolution of all sin. Christians believe that Jesus will return at the end of the world to judge between the good and the bad, with the good joining him in heaven and the bad being consigned to hell. The gospel of Jesus was proclaimed at first by word of mouth, but by the end of the first century A.D., it was written and became accepted as the authoritative scripture of the New Testament. Through the witness of the 12 earliest leaders (apostles) and their successors, the Christian faith, despite sporadic persecution, spread through the Greek and Roman world. In A.D. 315, it was declared by Emperor Constantine to be the official religion of the Roman Empire. It survived the breakup of the Empire and the "Dark Ages," largely through the life and witness of groups of monks in monasteries. The religion helped form the basis of civilization in the Middle Ages in Europe. Since the Middle Ages, major denominations of Christianity have formed as a result of differences in doctrine and practice.

ISLAM

Islam is the Arabic word for "submission" to the will of God (Allah). It is also the name of the religion originating in Arabia during the seventh century through the prophet Muhammad. Followers of Islam are known as Muslims, or Moslems.

Muhammad was born in Mecca. He was the son of Abdallah, a poor merchant of the powerful tribe of Quaraysh, hereditary guardians of the shrine in Mecca. Muhammad was orphaned at 6 and raised by his grandfather and uncle. His uncle Abu Talib trained him to be a merchant. At the age of 24, he entered the service of a rich widow, Khadijah, whom he eventually married. They had six children. While continuing as a trader, Muhammad became increasingly drawn to religious

(continued)

EXHIBIT 3.7 *(continued)*

contemplation. Soon afterward, he began to receive revelations of the word of Allah, the one and only God. These revelations given to Muhammad by the angel Gabriel over a period of 20 years were eventually codified into the Quran (Koran). The Quran commanded that the numerous idols of the shrine should be destroyed and that the rich should give to the poor. This simple message attracted some support but provoked a great deal of hostility from those who felt their interests threatened. When his wife and uncle died, Muhammad was reduced to poverty, but he began making a few converts among the pilgrims to Mecca. He eventually migrated to Hegira, the name of which was changed to Medina, "the City of the Prophet." This migration marks the beginning of the Muslim era. After a series of battles with warring enemies of Islam, Muhammad was able to take control of Mecca, which recognized him as chief and prophet. By A.D. 360, he had control over all Arabia. Two years later, he fell ill and died in the home of one of his nine wives. His tomb in the mosque at Medina is venerated throughout Islam.

Islam embraces every aspect of life. Muslims believe that individuals, societies, and governments should all be obedient to the will of God as set forth in the Quran. The Quran teaches there is one God, who has no partners. He is the creator of all things and has absolute power over them. All persons should commit themselves to lives of giving praise and grateful obedience to God, as everyone will be judged on the day of resurrection. Those who have obeyed God's commandments will dwell forever in paradise, whereas those who have sinned against God and have not repented will be condemned eternally to the fires of hell. Since the beginning of time, God has sent prophets (including Abraham, Moses, and Jesus) to provide the guidance necessary for the attainment of eternal reward.

There are five essential religious duties known as "the pillars of Islam." (a) The *shahadah* (pro-

fession of faith) is the sincere recitation of the twofold creed: "There is no god but God and Muhammad is the Messenger of God." (b) The *salat* (formal prayer) must be performed at fixed hours five time a day while facing toward the holy city of Mecca. (c) Almsgiving through the payment of *zakat* ("purification") is regarded primarily as an act of worship and is the duty of sharing one's wealth out of gratitude for God's favor, according to the uses stated in the Quran. (d) There is a duty to fast (*saum*) during the month of Ramadan. (Ramadan is the ninth month of the Muslim year during which Muslims abstain from eating and drinking between sunrise and sunset.) (e) The pilgrimage to Mecca is to be performed if at all possible at least once during one's lifetime.

Shariah is the sacred law of Islam and applies to all aspects of life, not just religious practices. This sacred law is found in the Quran and the sunnah (the sayings and acts of Muhammad).

BUDDHISM

Buddhism originated in India about 2500 years ago. The religion derived from the teaching of Buddha (Siddharta Gautama). Buddha is regarded as one of a continuing series of enlightened beings.

Buddha was born the son of the rajah of the Sakya tribe in Kapilavastu, north of Benares. His personal name was Siddharta, but he was also known by his family name of Gautama. At about age 30, he left the luxuries of the court, his beautiful wife, and all earthly ambitions. He became an ascetic, as he practiced strict self-denial as a measure of personal and spiritual discipline. After several years of severe austerities, he saw in meditation and contemplation the way to enlightenment. For the next four decades, he taught, gaining many followers and disciples. He died at Kusinagara in Oudh.

The teaching of Buddha is summarized in the four noble Truths, the last of which asserts the ex-

(continued)

EXHIBIT 3.7   *(continued)*

istence of a path leading to deliverance from the universal human experience of suffering. A central tenet of Buddhism is the law of karma, by which good and evil deeds result in appropriate rewards or punishments in this life or in a succession of rebirths. It is believed that the sum of a person's actions is carried forward from one life to the next, leading to an improvement or deterioration in that person's fate. Through a proper understanding of the law of karma, and by obedience to the right path, humans can break the chain of karma.

The Buddha's path to deliverance is through morality (*sila*), meditation (*samadhi*), and wisdom (*panna*). The goal is nirvana, which is the "blowing out" of the fires of all desires and the absorption of the self into the infinite. All Buddhas are greatly revered, with a place of special accordance being given to Gautama.

There are two main branches of Buddhism dating from its earliest history. Theravada Bud-

dhism adheres to the strict and narrow teachings of the early Buddhist writings; in this branch, salvation is possible for only the few who accept the severe discipline and effort to achieve it. Mahayana Buddhism is more liberal and makes concessions to popular piety; it teaches that salvation is possible for everyone. It introduced the doctrine of the bodhisattva (or personal savior). A bodhisattva is one who has attained the enlightenment of a Buddha but chooses not to pass into nirvana and voluntarily remains in the world to help lesser beings attain enlightenment; this view emphasizes charity toward others. Mahayana buddhism asserts that all living beings have the inner potential of Buddha nature. Buddha nature is a kind of spiritual embryo that holds out the promise to all people that they can eventually become Buddhas because they all have the potential for Buddhahood.

Source: Dictionary of Beliefs and Religions, Rosemary Goring, ed. (New York: Larousse, 1994).

VALUES SPECIFIED BY THE COUNCIL ON SOCIAL WORK EDUCATION

The 1992 Curriculum Policy Statements for both the baccalaureate and master's programs in social work education assert:

> *Among the values and principles that must be infused throughout every social work curriculum are the following:*

1. *Social workers' professional relationships are built on regard for individual worth and dignity and are furthered by mutual participation, acceptance, confidentiality, honesty, and responsible handling of conflict.*

2. *Social workers respect people's right to make independent decisions and to participate actively in the helping process.*

3. *Social workers are committed to assisting client systems to obtain needed resources.*

4. *Social workers strive to make social institutions more humane and responsive to human needs.*

5. *Social workers demonstrate respect for and acceptance of the unique characteristics of diverse populations.*

6. *Social workers are responsible for their own ethical conduct, the quality of their practice, and seeking continuous growth in the knowledge and skills of their profession.**

---

*Reprinted from *Curriculum Policy Statement for Baccalaureate Degree Programs in Social Work Education,* Final Draft, July 8, 1992 (Alexandria, VA: Council on Social Work Education, 1992). Reprinted from *Curriculum Policy Statement for Master's Degree Programs in Social Work Education,* Final Draft, July 8, 1992 (Alexandria, VA: Council on Social Work Education, 1992).

Because values play a key role in social work practice, it is essential that social work educational programs (a) help students clarify their values and (b) foster in students the development of values that are consistent with professional social work practice.

SOCIAL WORK EDUCATION

Two-Year Associate Programs

During the past two decades, a number of community colleges and technical schools have begun offering 2-year associate programs related to social work education. These programs provide training for a wide range of associate degrees with such titles as:

- Social Work Aide/Social Service Associate/ Social Service Technician
- Probation and Parole Aide
- Mental Health Associate/Mental Health Aide
- Human Services Technician/Human Services Aide
- Child-Care Technician/Residential Child-Care Aide
- Community Service Assistant/Community Services Technician/Community Social Service Worker

All of these degrees are considered preprofessional. The programs seek to achieve two simultaneous goals: training for employment and provision of some basic courses that *may* transfer to 4-year educational programs.

As yet, associate degrees are not accredited by the Council on Social Work Education (CSWE). (This council presently reviews social work baccalaureate and master's programs throughout the United States to determine whether individual programs meet the standards to warrant accreditation.) Standardization of associate programs in social work probably will not be achieved unless CSWE decides to review associate programs for accreditation.

Undergraduate Education

Like graduation programs, undergraduate programs are accredited by the CSWE, which sets standards for social work education and promotes and improves the quality of education in social work programs. Students who attend schools with accredited programs are assured that the quality of education meets national standards and generally have an advantage in securing employment following graduation because social welfare agencies prefer hiring graduates from accredited programs.

Until the early 1970s, undergraduate study in social work was generally recognized as an academic or preprofessional education; only the master's degree was recognized as the professional degree in social work. However, because a majority of people employed as social workers did not (and still do not) have a graduate degree, the need for professional training at the baccalaureate level was recognized. Effective July 1, 1974, accreditation requirements for undergraduate programs were substantially changed to emphasize professional preparation. In fact, the CSWE required that an accredited baccalaureate program "shall have as its primary stated educational objective preparation for beginning professional social work practice."[49] Secondary objectives for baccalaureate programs include (a) preparation of students for graduate professional education in social work and (b) preparation for intelligent, informed citizenship that brings an understanding of a wide range of social problems, intervention techniques to resolve such problems, and an understanding of social welfare concepts.

The 1992 revised Curriculum Policy Statement of CSWE identifies the following specific competencies for graduates of a baccalaureate social work program:

1. *Apply critical thinking skills within the context of professional social work practice.*

2. *Practice within the values and ethics of the social work profession and with an understanding of and respect for the positive value of diversity.*

3. *Demonstrate the professional use of self.*

4. *Understand the forms and mechanisms of oppression and discrimination and the strategies of change that advance social and economic justice.*

5. *Understand the history of the social work profession and its current structures and issues.*

6. *Apply the knowledge and skills of generalist social work to practice with systems of all sizes.*

7. *Apply knowledge of bio-psycho-social variables that affect individual development and behavior, and use theoretical frameworks to understand the interactions among individuals and between individuals and social systems (i.e., families, groups, organizations, and communities).*

8. *Analyze the impact of social policies on client systems, workers, and agencies.*

9. *Evaluate research studies and apply findings to practice, and, under supervision, evaluate their own practice interventions and those of other relevant systems.*

10. *Use communication skills differentially with a variety of client populations, colleagues, and members of the community.*

11. *Use supervision appropriate to generalist practice.*

12. *Function within the structure of organizations and service delivery systems, and, under supervision, seek necessary organizational change.**

Graduate Education

Master of Social Work (MSW) programs as a rule require 2 years of academic study. However, a number of graduate programs are granting advanced standing to students holding an undergraduate major in social work. Advanced standing (up to one academic year of credit) is given on the basis of the number of "core" courses taken as an undergraduate. Core courses are those that are required in both undergraduate and graduate programs and include classes in social welfare policy and services, social work practice, human behavior and the social environment, social research, and field placement.†

Because of the professional preparation focus of graduate programs, fieldwork is an important component of all MSW programs. Students spend an average of 2 to 3 days per week at an agency while receiving intensive supervision.

Although there is some variation in the format and structure of master's programs, almost all of them have the following two components: (a) Part of the program has a generic social work practice focus. Courses taken to meet this generic practice focus are similar (and at some schools identical) to the core courses of an undergraduate program. Some schools offer this generic focus during the first year, a few offer it during the first semester, and others have course content in this area for both years. (b) For the second part of the program, the student selects a concentration area from several available options and then takes courses in this study area. There is considerable variation among graduate schools in the concentration options that are offered. The CSWE annually publishes *Summary Information on Master of Social Work Programs*, which summarizes the concentration options at each school. Some of the concentration options are policy analysis, planning, research and administration, community

---

* Reprinted from *Curriculum Policy Statement for Baccalaureate Degree Programs in Social Work Education,* Final Draft July 8, 1992, by permission of the Council on Social Work Education, Alexandria, VA.

† Guidelines for granting advanced standing in MSW programs differ among schools; interested students should therefore consult with the graduate schools they want to attend.

organization, direct practice with individuals and small groups, direct practice with large groups, program development, community mental health, family functioning, health care, inner-city neighborhood services, social work in school systems, child welfare, consultation, aging, and crime and delinquency.[50]

Individuals with MSW degrees often, within a year or two following graduation, assume supervisory or administrative responsibilities.

The 1992 revised Curriculum Policy Statement of CSWE specifies the following competencies for graduates of a master's program:

Graduates of a master's social work program are advanced practitioners who can analyze, intervene, and evaluate in ways that are highly differentiated, discriminating, and self-critical. They must synthesize and apply a broad range of knowledge as well as practice with a high degree of autonomy and skill. They must be able to refine and advance the quality of their practice as well as that of the larger social work profession. These advanced competencies must be appropriately integrated and reflected in all aspects of their social work practice, including their ability to:

1. *Apply critical thinking skills within professional contexts, including synthesizing and applying appropriate theories and knowledge to practice interventions.*

2. *Practice within the values and ethics of the social work profession and with an understanding of and respect for the positive value of diversity.*

3. *Demonstrate the professional use of self.*

4. *Understand the forms and mechanisms of oppression and discrimination and the strategies and skills of change that advance social and economic justice.*

5. *Understand the history of the social work profession and its current structures and issues.*

6. *Apply the knowledge and skills of a generalist social work perspective to practice with client systems of all sizes.*

7. *Apply the knowledge and skills of advanced social work practice in an area of concentration.*

8. *Critically analyze and apply knowledge of bio-psycho-social variables that affect individual development and behavior, and use theoretical frameworks to understand the interactions among and between individuals and social systems (i.e., families, groups, organizations, and communities).*

9. *Analyze the impact of social policies on client systems, workers, and agencies and demonstrate skills for influencing policy formulation and change.*

10. *Evaluate relevant research studies and apply findings to practice, and demonstrate skills in quantitative and qualitative research design, data analysis, and knowledge dissemination.*

11. *Conduct empirical evaluations of their own practice interventions and those of other relevant systems.*

12. *Use complex communication skills differentially with a variety of client populations, colleagues, and members of the community.*

13. *Use supervision and consultation appropriate to advanced practice in an area of concentration.*

14. *Function within the structure of organizations and service delivery systems and seek necessary organizational change.* *

These outcomes (or competencies) constitute the knowledge, skills, and values needed for beginning and advanced social work practice.

At the advanced graduate level, two additional programs are offered by some schools: (a) a "third-year" program aimed at strengthening the professional skills of the student and (b) a Doctor of Social Work (DSW) or Doctor of Philosophy (PhD)

---

* Reprinted from *Curriculum Policy Statement for Baccalaureate Degree Programs in Social Work Education*, Final Draft July 8, 1992, by permission of the Council on Social Work Education, Alexandria, VA.

degree. The doctoral program requires 2 or more years of postgraduate studies.

SUMMARY

A generalist social worker is trained to use the problem-solving process to assess and intervene with the problems confronting clients. (Clients include individuals, groups, families, organizations, and communities.) A social worker uses a change process in working with clients. The change process can be conceptualized as involving eight phases: defining issues, collecting and assessing data, planning and contracting, identifying alternative interventions, selecting and implementing appropriate courses of action, using appropriate research to monitor and evaluate outcomes, applying appropriate research-based knowledge and technological advances, and termination.

Social workers are expected to be knowledgeable and skillful in filling a variety of roles, including enabler, broker, advocate, activist, empowerer, mediator, negotiator, educator, initiator, coordinator, researcher, group facilitator, and public speaker.

Social work with individuals is aimed at helping people on a one-to-one basis to resolve personal and social problems.

When there are problems in a family, social services are often needed. There is extensive variation in the types and forms of services that are provided by social workers to troubled families. One of the many social services provided to families is family therapy.

Almost every social service agency now provides some group services. The focus of social work groups has considerable variation, including social conversation, recreation, recreation-skill development, education, task, problem solving and decision making, self-help, socialization, therapy, and sensitivity training. The goal in therapy groups is generally to have each member explore, in depth, his or her personal or emotional problems and to develop a strategy to resolve those

problems. In contrast, sensitivity groups seek to foster increased personal and interpersonal awareness and to develop more effective interaction patterns.

An organization is a collectivity of individuals gathered together to serve a purpose. The roles of social workers within organizations, and their interactions with organizations (including their attempts to manipulate organizations), define much of what social workers do. There are basic structural conflicts between helping professionals and the bureaucratic systems in which they work. A number of suggestions have been offered on how social workers can survive and thrive in a bureaucracy.

Community practice is the process of stimulating and assisting the local community to evaluate, plan, and coordinate efforts to meet its needs. Social work is one of several disciplines that provides training in community practice. Practically all social workers, in one capacity or another, become involved in community practice efforts. Three models of community practice are locality development, social planning, and social action. The locality development model asserts that community change can best be brought about through broad participation of a wide spectrum of people at the local community level. The basic theme is, "Together we can figure out what to do and then do it." The social planning model emphasizes the process of problem solving. The role of the expert is stressed in identifying and resolving social problems. The theme of this approach is, "Let's get the facts and take the next rational steps." The social action model seeks to organize an oppressed group to pressure the power structure for increased resources or for social justice. The basic theme of this approach is, "Let's organize to overpower our oppressor."

To provide clients with competent service, social workers must have knowledge, skills, and values that are consistent with effective practice. The value base of social work includes respect for the dignity and uniqueness of each individual, clients' right to self-determination, confidentiality, advocacy and social action to ensure the rights of those who are oppressed, accountability, an institutional orientation, and respect for the spiritual and religious beliefs of others.

The primary educational objective for undergraduate social work programs accredited by the Council on Social Work Education (CSWE) is preparation for beginning professional social work practice. All accredited undergraduate and graduate social work programs are required to train their students for generalist practice. (MSW programs, in addition, usually require their students to select and study in an area of specialization.)

Whether or not you decide to pursue social work as a career, you can get involved in combating human problems.

NOTES

1. Joseph Anderson, *Social Work Methods and Processes* (Belmont, CA: Wadsworth, 1981).

2. Donald Brieland, Lela B. Costin, and Charles R. Atherton, *Contemporary Social Work: An Introduction to Social Work and Social Welfare,* 3rd ed. (New York: McGraw-Hill, 1985), pp. 120–121.

3. G. H. Hull, *Social Work Internship Manual* (Eau Claire: University of Wisconsin–Eau Claire, Department of Social Work, 1990), p. 17.

4. *Curriculum Policy Statement for Baccalaureate Degree Programs in Social Work Education* (Alexandria, VA: Council on Social Work Education, 1992); *Curriculum Policy Statement for Master's Degree Programs in Social Work Education* (Alexandria, VA: Council on Social Work Education, 1992).

5. Felix P. Biestek, *The Casework Relationship* (Chicago: Loyola University Press, 1957).

6. Alfred Kadushin, *Child Welfare Services,* 3rd ed. (New York: Macmillan, 1980).

7. Virginia Satir, *Conjoint Family Therapy,* rev. ed. (Palo Alto, CA: Science & Behavior Books, 1967); Virginia Satir, *Peoplemaking* (Palo Alto, CA: Science & Behavior Books, 1972).

8. Satir, *Conjoint Family Therapy,* pp. 8–10.

9. Ibid., p. 92.

10. Irene Goldenberg and Herbert Goldenberg, *Family Therapy,* 3rd ed. (Pacific Grove, CA: Brooks/Cole, 1991), p. 242.

11. B. Okun and L. Rappaport, *Working with Families: An Introduction to Family Therapy* (North Scituate, MA: Duxbury Press, 1980), p. 93.

12. David W. Johnson and Frank P. Johnson, *Joining Together: Group Theory and Group Skills,* 5th ed. (Boston: Allyn & Bacon, 1994), p. 13.

13. Gerald L. Euster, "Services to Groups," in *Contemporary Social Work,* Donald Brieland, Lela B. Costin, and Charles R. Atherton, eds. (New York: McGraw-Hill, 1975), p. 227.

14. Ibid.

15. Ralph Dolgoff and Donald Feldstein, *Understanding Social Welfare* (New York: Harper & Row, 1980), pp. 27–42.

16. Alfred H. Katz and Eugene I. Bender, *The Strength in Us: Self-Help Groups in the Modern World* (New York: Franklin-Watts, 1976), p. 9.

17. Alan Gartner and Frank Riessman, *Help: A Working Guide to Self-Help Groups* (New York: Franklin-Watts, 1980).

18. Frank Riessman, "The 'Helper Therapy' Principle," *Journal of Social Work* (Apr. 1965), pp. 27–34.

19. Johnson and Johnson, *Joining Together.*

20. Ibid.

21. A. Etzioni, *Modern Organizations* (Englewood Cliffs, NJ: Prentice Hall, 1964), p. 1.

22. F. E. Netting, P. M. Kettner, and S. L. McMurtry, *Social Work Macro Practice* (New York: Longman, 1993), p. 123.

23. Ibid.

24. R. Knopf, *Surviving the BS (Bureaucratic System)* Wilmington, NC: Mandala Press, 1979), pp. 21–22.

25. Ibid., p. 25.

26. Ibid.

27. Ibid.

28. A. Panitch, "Community Organization," in *Contemporary Social Work,* 2nd ed., Donald Brieland, Lela Costin, and Charles Atherton, eds. (New York: McGraw-Hill, 1980), pp. 124–125.

29. Neil Gilbert and Harry Specht, "Social Planning and Community Organization: Approaches," *Encyclopedia of Social Work,* 17th ed. (Washington, DC: NASW, 1977), pp. 1412–1425.

30. Ibid.

31. Jack Rothman and John E. Tropman, "Models of Community Organization and Macro Practice Perspectives: Their Mixing and Phasing," in *Strategies of Community Organization,* 4th ed., Fred Cox, John Erlich, Jack Rothman, and John E. Tropman, eds. (Itasca, IL: F. E. Peacock, 1987), pp. 3–26.

32. Saul Alinsky, *Rules for Radicals* (New York: Random House, 1972), p. 130.

33. Saul Alinsky, *Reveille for Radicals* (New York: Basic Books, 1969), p. 72.

34. *Curriculum Policy Statement for Baccalaureate Degree Programs in Social Work Education; Curricu-*

lum Policy Statement for Master's Degree Programs in Social Work Education.

35. Ronald Federico, *The Social Welfare Institution* (Lexington, MA: Heath, 1973), pp. 146–147.

36. Betty L. Baer, "Developing a New Curriculum for Social Work Education," in *The Pursuit of Competence in Social Work*, Frank Clark and Morton Arkava, eds. (San Francisco: Jossey-Bass, 1979), p. 106.

37. Betty L. Baer and Ronald Federico, *Educating the Baccalaureate Social Worker* (Cambridge, MA: Ballinger, 1978), pp. 92–95.

38. Allen Pincus and Anne Minahan, *Social Work Practice: Model and Method* (Itasca, IL: F. E. Peacock, 1973), p. 38.

39. Albert Ellis and R. Harper, *A New Guide to Rational Living* (North Hollywood, CA: Wilshire Books, 1975).

40. C. H. Cooley, *Human Nature and the Social Order* (New York: Scribner's, 1902).

41. William Glasser, *The Identity Society* (New York: Harper & Row, 1972).

42. Thomas Gordon, *Parent Effectiveness Training* (New York: Wyden, 1973).

43. Mathew Dumont, *The Absurd Healer* (New York: Viking, 1968), p. 60.

44. "Tarsoff v. Regents of University of California: The Psychotherapist's Peril," *University of Pittsburgh Law Review,* 37 (1975), pp. 159–164.

45. Suanna J. Wilson, *Confidentiality in Social Work: Issues and Principles* (New York: Free Press, 1978), pp. 116–117.

46. Ibid., p. 121.

47. K. Miley, *Religion and Spirituality as Central Social Work Concerns.* Paper presented at Midwest Biennial Conference on Social Work Education, LaCrosse, WI, Apr. 9–10, 1992, p. 2.

48. L. E. Furman, *Religion and Spirituality in Social Work Education.* Paper presented at Midwest Biennial Conference on Social Work Education, St. Paul, MN, Apr. 28–29, 1994, p. 10.

49. *Standards for the Accreditation of Baccalaureate Degree Programs in Social Work* (New York: Council on Social Work Education, 1974), p. 13.

50. *Summary Information on Master of Social Work Programs: 1997* (Alexandria, VA: Council on Social Work Education, 1997).

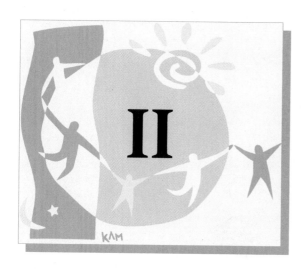

II

SOCIAL
PROBLEMS
AND
SOCIAL
SERVICES

POVERTY
AND
PUBLIC
WELFARE

P overty has always been one of the most serious social problems in the United States. (In most other countries, it is even more severe.) In our modern, civilized society, one of seven Americans is poor.[1] This chapter will:

- Describe the extent of poverty and the effects of living in poverty.
- Discuss the income and wealth gaps between the rich and the poor in the United States.
- Summarize the causes of poverty and identify the population groups with the lowest income levels.
- Outline current programs to combat poverty and discuss their merits and shortcomings.
- Describe and refute some of the myths about public welfare.
- Present strategies to reduce poverty in the future.
- Describe the role of social work in public welfare.

THE PROBLEM

In 1997 over 36 million people, about 14% of our population, were living below the poverty line.[2] (The poverty line is the level of income that the federal government considers sufficient to meet basic requirements of food, shelter, and clothing.) A cause for alarm is that the rate of poverty is higher now than it was in 1980, and the poverty rate in 1997 was nearly as high as it was in 1966.[3]

Poverty does not mean simply that poor people in the United States are living less well than those of average income. It means that the poor are often hungry. Many are malnourished, with some turning to dog food or cat food for nourishment. Poverty may mean not having running water, living in substandard housing, and being exposed to rats, cockroaches, and other vermin. It means not having sufficient heat in the winter and being unable to sleep because the walls are too thin to deaden the sounds from the people living next door. It means being embarrassed about the few ragged clothes that one has to wear. It means great susceptibility to emotional disturbances, alcoholism, and victimization by criminals, as well as a shortened life expectancy. It means lack of opportunity to advance oneself socially, economically, or educationally. It often means slum housing, unstable marriages, and few chances to enjoy the finer things in life—traveling, dining out, movies, plays, concerts, and sports events.

The infant mortality rate of the poor is almost double that of the affluent.[4] The poor have less access to medical services and receive lower quality health care from professionals. The poor are exposed to higher levels of air pollution, water pollution, and unsanitary conditions. They have higher rates of malnutrition and disease. Schools in poor areas are of lower quality and have fewer resources. As a result, the poor achieve less academically and are more likely to drop out of school. They are also more likely to be arrested, indicted, and imprisoned, and they are given longer sentences for the same offenses committed by the nonpoor. They are less likely to receive probation, parole, or suspended sentences.[5]

Poverty also often leads to despair, low self-esteem, and stunted growth—including physical, social, emotional, and intellectual growth. Poverty hurts most when it leads to a view of the self as inferior or second class.

We like to think that the United States is a land of equal opportunity and that there is considerable upward class mobility for those who put forth effort. The reality is the opposite of this myth. Extensive research has shown that poverty is almost "escape proof." Children raised in poor families are likely to live in poverty in their adult years. Most people have much the same social status their parents had. Movement to a higher social status is an unusual happening in practically all societies, including the United States.[6]

A BRIEF HISTORY OF OUR RESPONSE TO THE POOR

The way a society cares for its needy reflects its values. In nonliterate societies, the needs of those who were not self-sufficient were met by family or

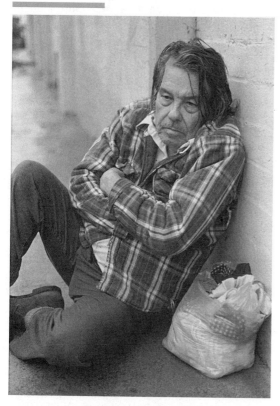

We like to think that we live in a land of equal opportunity and that upward mobility today is possible for all those who put forth the effort. But the reality is otherwise: Poverty is virtually "escape proof."

other tribal members. During the medieval period in Europe, poor relief was a church responsibility.

The famous Elizabethan Poor Law of 1601 in England combined humanitarianism with the Protestant ethic. This law was enacted because the general public viewed begging (not poverty) as a social problem. The law established three separate programs: (a) The able-bodied poor were offered work. If they refused, they were whipped, imprisoned, or sent back to their birthplace. (b) The impotent poor (the elderly and disabled) were either given public relief or placed in almshouses. (c) Children whose parents could not provide for them were bound out as apprentices to other adults. This Poor Law established the principles

of categorical relief by distinguishing between the able-bodied (undeserving) poor and the impotent (deserving) poor. Nearly all the principles contained within this Poor Law became incorporated into the "relief" programs of colonial America.

In the 19th century, a controversy raged in both England and the United States between advocates of workhouses and supporters of "outdoor relief" (assistance to people in their own homes). Outdoor relief raised concerns about fraud, and citizens feared that cash handouts might destroy moral fiber. On the other hand, workhouses (also called almshouses) were generally overcrowded and unsanitary; contrary to their stated goal, they offered no activity for the able-bodied. Also in the 19th century, the first social service organizations sprang up in urban areas to serve the needy. These organizations were private and church sponsored and primarily offered food and shelter. They attempted to solve personal problems with religious admonitions.

As you will recall from the discussions in Chapters 1 and 2, Americans, until the Great Depression, believed in the myth of individualism—that is, each person is master of his or her own fate. Those in need were viewed as lazy, as unintelligent, or as justly punished for their sinful ways (see Exhibit 4.1).

The Great Depression of the 1930s called into question the individualism myth. Nearly one-third of the workforce was unemployed.[7] With large numbers of people out of work, including those from the middle class, a new view of relief applicants developed: These people were not essentially different from others who were caught up in circumstances beyond their control. Private relief agencies (including private agencies receiving funding support from local governing entities) were unable to meet the financial needs of the unemployed. There was a rapid breakdown in traditional local methods of aiding the poor.

Harry Hopkins, a social worker from Iowa, was appointed by President Franklin Roosevelt to oversee national employment programs and emergency assistance. Hopkins became one of Roosevelt's closest advisers and exerted considerable influence in designing and enacting the 1935 Social Security program. As indicated in Chapter 1,

EXHIBIT 4.1

The Ideology of Individualism

Wealth is generally inherited in this country; few individuals actually move up the social-status ladder on their own. Having wealth opens up many doors (through education and contacts) for children to make large sums of money when they become adults. For children living in poverty, there is little chance to escape when they become older. Yet the individualism myth is held by many. It states that the rich are personally responsible for their success and that the poor are to blame for their failure. The main points of this individualism myth are:

1. Each individual should work hard and strive to succeed in competition with others.

2. Those who work hard should be rewarded with success (such as wealth, property, prestige, and power).

3. Because of extensive employment opportunities and because of equal opportunity legislation, those who work hard will in fact be rewarded with success.

4. Economic failure is an individual's own fault and reveals lack of effort and other character defects.

In our society, the poor are blamed for their circumstances. As a result, a stigma has been attached to poverty, particularly to those who receive public assistance (welfare). Although the belief in individualism is less strongly held now than it was prior to the Great Depression of the 1930s, remnants still remain today.

this program was of major significance because it initiated the federal government's role in three areas: (a) social insurance programs, (b) public assistance, and (c) social services.

After 1935 the economy of our country slowly began to recover. Some of those who had been

living in poverty began to enjoy a more affluent lifestyle—even though many other Americans remained in poverty. The poor were left behind and forgotten. Public concern shifted to World War II in the early 1940s and then to other issues, such as the feared spread of communism and the Korean War. From the 1940s through the 1950s, poverty was no longer recognized or addressed as a major problem—even though large segments of the population continued to live in abject poverty.

In 1960 John Kennedy saw large numbers of people in many states living in degrading circumstances due to poverty. He made this a central issue in his national presidential campaign. Hence, poverty was once again defined as a major social problem.

In 1962 Michael Harrington published *The Other America*, which graphically described the plight of the fifth of our population who were living in poverty.[8] The media publicized the poverty issue, and public concern about this problem increased dramatically.

In 1965 President Lyndon Johnson launched his War on Poverty and his plan for creating the "Great Society." Eliminating poverty became one of our nation's highest priorities. A variety of programs were established: Head Start, VISTA (Volunteers in Service to America), Job Corps, Title I Educational Funding, Community Action Program, Youth Corps, and Neighborhood Legal Services.

Although these programs reduced poverty somewhat, the optimistic hope of the early 1960s that poverty could be eradicated was short-lived. In the late 1960s, the Vietnam War drained resources that would otherwise have been spent on domestic programs. It also turned attention away from poverty and finally drove Johnson from office. During periods of economic growth, it is easier for a society to allocate resources to the poor in an effort to share the national wealth.

In the mid-1970s, after the end of the Vietnam War, the turmoil of the late 1960s was replaced for several years by an atmosphere of relative calm on both the foreign and domestic levels. In contrast to the hope of the 1960s that government programs could cure our social ills, the opposing philosophy emerged that many problems were beyond the capacity of the government to alleviate. Hence the liberalism of the 1960s, which resulted in the expansion and development of new social programs, was replaced by a more conservative approach in the 1970s and 1980s. Practically no new, large-scale social welfare programs were initiated in those two decades.

It again appears that poverty is taking a back seat to other issues. Government interest in helping the poor has waned considerably. Ronald Reagan was elected in 1980, partly on a program designed to give tax cuts to the rich and to provide decreased funds and services to the poor. Allegations of welfare fraud, high tax rates, and increasing relief roles replaced poverty as a national concern. Welfare again became a political "whipping boy." Since the 1970s, there has been a shift away from a liberalized extension of public responsibility to help the poor.

Past history suggests that, as government expenditures to help the poor (and the marginally poor) decrease, the proportion of the population living in poverty increases. Since 1980 there have been significant cutbacks in federal funding of programs for the poor, and the proportion of people living in poverty has risen.[9]

In 1988 George Bush was elected president on a conservative platform, and he continued the social welfare policies of his predecessor. The Reagan and Bush administrations endorsed an economic program that cut taxes (which primarily benefited the rich) and cut government spending on social welfare programs (which primarily hurt the poor). The result was that the income gap between the rich and the poor widened.[10] The people who were hurt the most were recipients of federally financed social welfare programs who received reduced services and sharp reductions in financial assistance.

Bill Clinton was elected president in 1992. During his campaign, Clinton promised "to end welfare as we know it." He was referring specifically to federal entitlement programs, particularly Aid to Families of Dependent Children (AFDC). AFDC was a major component of the so-called social safety net of measures designed to prevent poverty from turning into starvation and abject destitution. The conservative sweep of both houses of Congress in 1994 and President Clinton's endorsement of welform reform legislation prior to the 1996 presidential election were important political steps toward the most far-reaching changes in support for poor families and individuals since the 1930s. The 1996 welfare reform legislation (also known as the Personal Responsibility and Work Opportunity Reconciliation Act) ended the 60-year-old AFDC program.

Under 1996 welfare reform legislation, parents whose household incomes fall below a given level (depending on the size of the household) are no longer entitled to federal funds administered through state and county welfare agencies. Instead, states now receive block grants (that is, large sums of money earmarked for assistance to the poor) from the federal government. Federal requirements of these block grants specify that recipients of financial benefits cannot receive more than 2 years of financial assistance without working, and there is a 5-year limit on benefits for adults. In 1935, when the AFDC program was enacted as a component of the Social Security Act, it was thought best for single mothers to stay at home to raise their children. The 1996 welfare reform legislation asserts that single mothers (and fathers) now have an obligation to work for a living.

What will be the long-term effects of this recent welfare to work legislation? Will the legislation harm poor people, particularly poor children? It is too early to tell, but even conservative critics of the old welfare system are worried that drastic cuts in welfare benefits and the new punitive measures will create additional social problems and a potential backlash against the 1996 welfare reform legislation.[11]

Kornblum and Julian note:

Welfare critics on the liberal or left side of the political spectrum have been asking with increasing frequency why it is that the public and political leaders have been so determined to attack AFDC since it was a relatively small federal program. It never cost more than about 1 percent of the federal budget, and fewer than 5 million people are on the rolls, a number that has not changed appreciably since the 1970s. One answer is that beginning in the early 1980s, the welfare poor have been targeted as examples of the failure of liberal antipoverty politics. To afford tax cuts and budget reductions it has been necessary to cut programs for the most vulnerable and politically powerless segments of the population. The poor are foremost among those groups. So are immigrants, whose benefits are also scheduled for cuts under the new policies being formulated in many states. The idea that some people could subsist on payments that transferred funds from the more well-to-do to the poor, and that in some cases they could live that way for years without any work requirement, became an easy target for those who wished to decrease federal spending.[12]

The 1996 welfare reform legislation and other programs to combat poverty are discussed in greater detail later in this chapter.

THE RICH AND THE POOR

Throughout most countries in the world, wealth is concentrated in the hands of a few individuals and families. Poverty and wealth are closely related in that abundance for a few is often created through deprivation of others.

There are two ways of measuring the extent of economic inequality. *Income* refers to the amount of money a person makes in a given year. *Wealth* refers to a person's total assets—real estate holdings, cash, stocks, bonds, and so forth.

The distribution of wealth and income is highly unequal in our society. Like most countries, the United States is characterized by *social stratification;* that is, it has social classes, with the upper classes having by far the greatest access to the pleasures that money can buy.

Although this chapter focuses on poverty in the United States, it is important to note that there is a growing gap between the rich and the poor in most countries. In the world today, there are about 170 billionaires and about 2 million millionaires, but there are approximately 100 million homeless people.[13] Americans spend about $5 billion per year on diets to lower their caloric intake while 400 million people around the world are

EXHIBIT 4.2

Personal Income Disparities Are Astounding

In some countries in the world, the average per capita income is less than $500 per year. In the United States, over 36 million people (nearly 14% of the population) are living in poverty. (In 1996 the poverty threshold for a family of four was $16,036.)

In the fall of 1997, Kevin Garnett signed a 6-year deal for $123 million with the Minnesota Timberwolves (a professional team in the National Basketball Association). The deal of $20.5 million annual average was (at the time) the richest long-term sports contract. Kevin Garnett was only 20 years old when he signed. He joined the NBA after high school, without ever attending (or playing basketball in) college.

From 1996 to 1997, according to *Forbes* magazine, Bill Gates's net worth more than doubled. His net worth in October 1997 was $39.8 billion. During this 1-year period, he made an astounding average of $400 million per week, which is over $50 million per day! Bill Gates is the chairman of Microsoft Corporation.

Sources: U.S. Bureau of the Census, *Statistical Abstract of the United States, 1997* (Washington, DC: U.S. Government Printing Office, 1997); Randolph E. Schmid, "Census Bureau: Poor Lose, Rich Win," *Wisconsin State Journal,* Sept. 30, 1997, p. 2A; Eric R. Quinones, "Rich Get Richer: *Forbes* Lists 170 Billionaires," *Wisconsin State Journal,* Oct. 14, 1997, p. 2A.

undernourished to the point of physical deterioration.[14] Kornblum and Julian note:

These growing disparities between rich and poor throughout the world have a direct bearing on the situation of the poor in the United States because American jobs are being "exported" to areas where extremely poor people are willing to accept work at almost any wage. World poverty also contributes to environmental degradation, political instability, and violence—all problems that drain resources that could be used to meet the nation's domestic needs.[15]

In the United States, the wealthiest 1% of all households hold about 34% of all personal wealth.[16] (Net worth refers to the value of all assets minus debts; assets include savings and checking accounts, automobiles, real estate, and stocks and bonds.) The distribution of income is also unequal. The wealthiest 20% of households in the United States receive nearly 50% of all income, whereas the poorest 20% receive less than 5% of all income.[17]

In the words of a pastoral letter issued by a committee of Roman Catholic bishops, "The level of inequality in income and wealth in our society . . . must be judged morally unacceptable."[18] Paul Samuelson, an economist, provides a dramatic metaphor of the disparity between the very rich and most people in the United States:

If we made an income pyramid out of a child's blocks, with each layer portraying $1,000 of income, the peak would be far higher than the Eiffel Tower, but almost all of us would be within a yard of the ground.[19]

Given the enormous wealth of the richest 20%, it is clear that a simple redistribution of some of the wealth from the top one-fifth to the lowest one-fifth could easily wipe out poverty. Of course, that is not politically acceptable to members of the top fifth, who have the greatest control of the government. It should also be noted that many of these rich families avoid paying income taxes by taking advantage of tax loopholes and tax shelters.

An estimated 30 million Americans are hungry, due to lack of financial resources, at least some period of time each month.[20] Millions of those who go hungry in the United States are children.

Hunger can have devastating effects on young children, including causing mental retardation. The brain of an infant grows to 80% of its adult size within the first 3 years of life. If supplies of protein are inadequate during this period, the brain stops growing, the damage is irreversible, and the child will be permanently retarded.[21]

Coleman and Cressey describe the respective effects of wealth and poverty:

The economic differences between the rich, the poor, and the middle class have profound effects on lifestyles, attitudes toward others, and even attitudes toward oneself. The poor lack the freedom and autonomy so prized in our society. They are trapped by their surroundings, living in run-down, crime-ridden neighborhoods that they cannot afford to leave. They are constantly confronted with things they desire but have little chance to own. On the other hand, wealth provides power, freedom, and the ability to direct one's own fate. The wealthy live where they choose and do as they please, with few economic constraints. Because the poor lack education and money for travel, their horizons seldom extend beyond the confines of their neighborhood. In contrast, the world of the wealthy offers the best education, together with the opportunity to visit places that the poor haven't even heard of.

The children of the wealthy receive the best that society has to offer, as well as the assurance that they are valuable and important individuals. Because the children of the poor lack so many of the things everyone is "supposed" to have, it is much harder for them to develop the cool confidence of the rich. In our materialistic society people are judged as much by what they have as by who they are. The poor cannot help but feel inferior and inadequate in such a context.[22]

DEFINING POVERTY IS A POLICY PROBLEM

Despite all the research on poverty, we have yet to agree on how to define the condition. A family of four living on a farm that earns $15,000 per year may not view themselves as being "poverty stricken," especially if they have no rent to pay, are able to grow much of their own food, and are frugal and creative in securing essential needs. On

| CASE EXAMPLE 4.1 | Wealth Perpetuates Wealth and Poverty Perpetuates Poverty |

The following summaries of the life experiences of two people illustrate that in the United States wealth perpetuates wealth and poverty perpetuates poverty.

Tim Mills is the son of wealthy parents (both of whom also had parents in the upper social class). Tim Mills's mother, Suzanne, is a successful stock broker, and his father, David, is a successful attorney. (Their household income is in excess of $300,000 per year.) After Tim was born, he was always dressed in the finest clothes money could buy, and his parents focused on providing extensive early stimulation and the highest quality educational experiences. He attended expensive private schools in kindergarten, elementary school, middle school, and high school. The schools had low student-to-teacher ratios, so Tim Mills received extensive attention from his teachers. Tim's parents were always highly involved in the parent–teacher associations in the school systems, which encouraged the teachers to give Tim extra attention, and also to praise him frequently, which contributed to Tim developing a positive self-concept and a high level of self-confidence.

Tim's parents liked to travel to other countries two or three times a year, and they always took Tim along, which contributed to his learning to understand and appreciate diversity and other cultures. It also led Tim to understand that he needed to attain a college education to secure a high-paying position and have the privileges that money can buy.

Tim's mother and father had friends who were also in their community's power elite. Tim was introduced to this higher circle and made friends with the children of the parents in this power elite. In this sphere of the power elite, he acquired skills and confidence in his ability to socialize and to increasingly participate in the decisions made by this power elite. After graduating from high school, he attended a prestigious private college on the East Coast, which many of his high school friends also attended. Upon graduation from the 4-year college, he attended a prestigious law school and graduated with honors. His father's connections helped him join a distinguished law firm as a corporate attorney upon receiving his law degree. A year after graduating from law school, he married Virginia DeMarco, a lawyer he met in law

---

the other hand, a family of four earning $20,000 per year in a city with a high cost of living may be deeply in debt, especially if they pay high rent and are confronted with unexpected medical bills.

The usual definitions of poverty are based on lack of money, and annual income is the measure most commonly applied. There are two general approaches to defining poverty: the absolute approach and the relative approach.

The *absolute approach* holds that a certain amount of goods and services is essential to an individual's or family's welfare. Those who do not

have this minimum amount are viewed as poor. The fundamental problem with this approach is that there is no agreement as to what constitutes "minimum" needs. Depending on the income level selected, the number and percentage of the population who are poor change substantially, along with the characteristics of those defined as poor.

A serious problem with the absolute definition of poverty is that it does not take into account the fact that people are poor not only in terms of their own needs but also in relation to others who are not poor. That is, poverty is relative to time school who had a similar upper-class background. Five years later, their annual household income was in excess of $500,000.

In contrast, the following summary of Marcee Calvello's life describes how poverty and dismal living conditions lead to despair, hopelessness, and failure.

Marcee Calvello was born and raised in New York City. Her father had trouble holding a job because he was addicted to cocaine, and her mother was an alcoholic who divorced her husband when Marcee was 3 years old. Marcee's mother at first sought to provide a better home for Marcee and her three brothers. She worked part-time and also went on AFDC. However, her addiction to alcohol consumed most of her time and money. Neighbors reported the children were living in abject neglect, and Protective Services removed Marcee and her brothers to foster care. Marcee was placed in a series of 17 different foster homes. In one of these homes her foster father sexually assaulted her, and in another a foster brother assaulted her. Being moved from foster home to foster home resulted in frequent school changes. Marcee grew distrustful of the welfare system, schoolteachers and administrators, males, and anyone else who sought to get close to her.

When she turned 18, the state no longer paid for her foster care. She got a small efficiency apartment that cost her several hundred dollars a month. Because she dropped out of school at age 16, she had few marketable job skills. She worked for a while at some fast-food restaurants. The minimum wage she received was insufficient to pay her bills. Eight months after she moved into her apartment, she was evicted. Unable to afford another place, she started living in the subway system of New York City. She soon lost her job at McDonald's because of poor hygiene and an unkempt appearance.

Unable to shower and improve her appearance, she has not been able to secure another job. For the past 2 years she has been homeless, living on the street and in the subway. She has given up hope of improving her situation. She now occasionally shares IV needles and has been sexually assaulted periodically at night in the subway by men. She realizes she is at high risk for acquiring the AIDS virus but no longer cares very much. Death appears to be, to her, the final escape from a life filled with victimization and misery.

and place. Those Americans labeled poor today would certainly not be poor by the standards of 1850; nor would they be viewed as poor by standards existing in India or in other less developed countries. In the 1890s, no one felt particularly poor because of not having electric lights; yet today a family without electricity is usually considered poor.

It is important to realize that the experience of poverty is based on conditions in one's own society. People feel poor or rich with reference to others around them, not with reference to very poor or very rich people elsewhere in the world. To the poor in the United States, it is of little comfort to be informed that they would be regarded as well off (according to their income and wealth) if they lived in Ethiopia (or some other impoverished country).

The *relative approach* states, in essence, that a person is poor when his or her income is substantially less than the average income of the population. For example, anyone in the lowest one-fifth (or tenth or fourth) of the population is regarded as poor. By defining poverty in these terms, we

A woman living in a New York City tenement goes to a fire hydrant to get water. She may be considered poor by both the absolute approach and the relative approach to defining poverty.

WHO ARE THE POOR?

An encouraging trend is that the proportion of the population below the poverty line has gradually decreased in the past 100 years. Prior to the 20th century, a majority of Americans lived in poverty. In 1937 Franklin D. Roosevelt stated: "I see one-third of a nation ill-housed, ill-clad, ill-nourished."[24] In 1962 the President's Council of Economic Advisors estimated that one-fifth of the population was living in poverty.[25] In 1996 about 14% of the nation was estimated to be below the poverty line. An alarming concern is that, since 1978, there has been an increase in the proportion of the population that is poor.[26]

Poverty is concentrated in certain population categories, including one-parent families, children, the elderly, large families, and people of color. Educational level, unemployment, and place of residence are also related to poverty.

ONE-PARENT FAMILIES

Most one-parent families are headed by a female, and 37% of female-headed families are in poverty, compared to 12% for two-parent families.[27] Single mothers who are members of a racial minority (for example, African Americans, Latinos, Native Americans) are particularly vulnerable to poverty, as they are subjected to double discrimination (race and sex) in the labor market.

Women who work full time are paid on the average only about 75% of what men who work full time are paid.[28] Many single mothers are unable to work due to lack of transportation, the high cost of day-care facilities, and inadequate training. Of the families living in poverty, approximately half are headed by a single mother.[29] About one of every five children in this country is now living apart from one parent, and because of increasing divorce rates, separations, and births outside marriage, it is estimated that nearly one of two children born today will spend part of the first 18 years in a family headed by a single mother.[30] Single-parent families now constitute more than 20% of all families in the United States.[31] The increase in one-parent families has led to an increase in the feminization of poverty.

avoid having to define absolute needs, and we also put more emphasis on the inequality of incomes. With a relative approach, poverty will persist as long as income inequality exists. The major weakness with a relative approach is that it tells us nothing about how badly, or how well, the people at the bottom of the income distribution actually live. With poverty measures, ideally, we want to know not only how many people are poor but also how desperate their living conditions are.

The federal government has generally chosen the absolute approach in defining poverty. The poverty line is raised each year to adjust for inflation. In 1996 the government set the poverty line at $16,036 for a family of four.[23]

CHILDREN

Twenty percent of children under the age of 18 are living in poverty, and nearly 40% of the poor are children under 16.[32] More than one-half of these children live in families with an absentee father.[33] When the 1996 welfare reform legislation was passed, two-thirds of the nation's welfare recipients were children.[34] The 1996 welfare reform legislation focuses on putting adult welfare recipients to work. With two-thirds of the recipients being children, there are concerns about what will happen to the children in those families in which the parents use up their eligibility for benefits and yet do not obtain employment that provides enough income to support them and their children.

THE ELDERLY

Many of the elderly depend on Social Security pensions or public assistance (in the form of Supplemental Security Income) for their basic needs. Since the initiation of the 1964 War on Poverty programs, the population group that has benefited most has been the elderly. Programs such as Medicare and Supplemental Security Income, as well as increases in monthly payments under the Old Age, Survivors, Disability, and Health Insurance Program, have reduced the poverty rate among the elderly from over 25% in 1964 to around 11% at the present time.[35]

LARGE FAMILIES

Large families are more likely than smaller ones to be poor, partly because more income is needed as family size increases. It now costs an estimated $161,000 to raise a child from birth to age 18 in low-income families.[36]

PEOPLE OF COLOR

Contrary to popular stereotypes, most poor people (over 60%) are White.[37] But members of most minority groups are disproportionately likely to be poor. African Americans, for example, constitute about 12% of the total population, but over 25% of all the poor.[38] One of every three African Americans is poor, compared to one of ten White persons.[39] Approximately one-third of Native American families live below the poverty line, and about one of every three Latinos live in poverty.[40] Racial discrimination is a major reason most racial minorities are disproportionately poor.

EDUCATION

Attainment of less than a ninth-grade education is a good predictor of poverty. A high school diploma, however, is not a guarantee that one will earn wages adequate to avoid poverty, as many of the poor have graduated from high school. A college degree is an excellent predictor of avoiding poverty; only a small proportion of those with a college degree are impoverished.[41]

EMPLOYMENT

Being unemployed is, of course, associated with being poor. However, being employed is not a guarantee of avoiding poverty; over 1.5 million heads of families work full time, but their income is below the poverty level.[42] The general public (and many government officials) wrongly assumes that employment is the key to ending poverty. However, jobs alone cannot end poverty.

PLACE OF RESIDENCE

People who live in rural areas have a higher incidence of poverty than those in urban areas. In rural areas, wages are low, unemployment is high, and work tends to be seasonal. The Ozarks, Appalachia, and the South have pockets of rural poverty with high rates of unemployment.[43]

People who live in urban slums constitute the largest geographical group in terms of numbers of poor people. The decaying cities of the Northeast and Midwest have particularly large urban slums. Poverty is also extensive on Native American reservations and among seasonal migrant workers.

All these factors indicate that some people are more vulnerable to poverty than others. Michael Harrington, who coined the term *other America* for the poor in the United States, notes that the poor made the simple mistake of:

being born to the wrong parents, in the wrong section of the country, in the wrong industry, or in the wrong racial or ethnic group. Once that mistake has been made, they could have been paragons of will and morality, but most of them

*would never even have had a chance to get out
of the other America.*[44]

CAUSES OF POVERTY

There are a number of possible causes of poverty.

- High unemployment
- Poor physical health
- Physical disabilities
- Emotional problems
- Extensive medical bills
- Alcoholism
- Drug addiction
- Large families
- Job displacements due to automation
- Lack of an employable skill
- Low educational level
- Households with young children headed by females only
- Lack of cost-of-living increases for people on fixed incomes
- Racial discrimination
- Being labeled an "ex-convict" or "crazy"
- Residence in a geographic area where jobs are scarce
- Divorce, desertion, or death of a spouse
- Gambling
- Budgeting problems and mismanagement of resources
- Sex discrimination
- Consequences of being a crime victim
- Anti-work-ethic values
- Underemployment
- Low-paying jobs
- Mental retardation
- Retirement

This list is not exhaustive. However, it shows that
there are many causes of poverty, that eliminating
the causes of poverty would require a wide range

of social programs, and that poverty interacts with
almost all other social problems—emotional problems, alcoholism, unemployment, racial and sex
discrimination, medical problems, crime, gambling, mental retardation, and so on. The interaction between poverty and these other social
problems is complicated. As indicated, these other
social problems are contributing causes of poverty. Yet, for some social problems, poverty is also
a contributing *cause* of those problems (such as
emotional problems, alcoholism, and unemployment). Being poor intensifies the effects (the hurt)
of all social problems.

THE CULTURE OF POVERTY

To some extent, poverty is passed on from generation to generation in a cycle (Figure 4.l). Why?
Some authorities argue that the explanation can
be found in a "culture of poverty." Oscar Lewis,
an anthropologist, is one of the chief proponents
of this cultural explanation.[45]

Lewis examined poor neighborhoods in various parts of the world and concluded that people
are poor because they have a distinct culture or
lifestyle. The culture of poverty arises after extended periods of economic deprivation in highly
stratified capitalistic societies. Such economic
deprivation is brought about by high rates of unemployment for unskilled labor and by low wages
for those who are employed. Such economic deprivation leads to the development of attitudes and
values of despair and hopelessness. Lewis describes these attitudes and values as follows:

> The individual who grows up in this culture has
> a strong feeling of fatalism, helplessness, dependence, and inferiority, a strong present-time orientation with relatively little disposition to defer
> gratification and plan for the future, a high tolerance for psychological pathology of all kinds.[46]

Once developed, this culture continues to exist, even when the economic factors that created it
(for example, lack of employment opportunities)
no longer exist. The culture's attitudes, norms,
and expectations serve to limit opportunities and

FIGURE 4.1

Cycle of Poverty

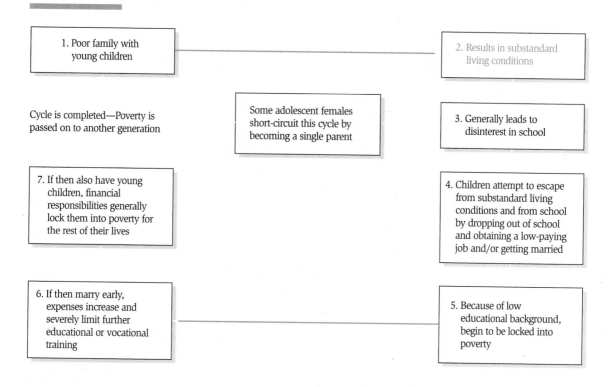

prevent escape. A major reason the poor remain locked into their culture is that they are socially isolated. They have few contacts with groups outside their own culture and are hostile toward the social services and educational institutions that might help them escape poverty. They reject such institutions because they perceive them as belonging to the dominant class. Furthermore, because they view their financial circumstances as private and hopeless and because they lack political and organizational skills, they do not take collective action to resolve their problems.

The culture-of-poverty theory has been controversial and widely criticized. Eleanor Leacock argues that the distinctive culture of the poor is not the *cause* but the *result* of their continuing poverty.[47] She agrees that the poor tend to emphasize "instant gratification," which involves spending and enjoying one's money while it lasts.

But she argues that instant gratification is a result of being poor, because it makes no sense to defer gratification when one is pessimistic about the future. Deferred gratification is a rational response only when one is optimistic that postponing pleasures today by saving money will reap greater benefits in the future. (Interestingly, studies have found that, when ghetto residents obtain a stable, well-paying job, they then display the middle-class value of deferred gratification.[48]) Because of poverty, Leacock argues, the poor are forced to abandon middle-class attitudes and values, which are irrelevant to their circumstances.

In an even stronger indictment, William Ryan criticizes the culture-of-poverty theory as being simply a classic example of "blaming the victim."[49] Blaming the poor for their circumstances is a convenient excuse, according to Ryan, for refusing to endorse the programs and policies thought necessary to eradicate poverty. The real culprit is the social system that allows poverty to exist. Ryan says bluntly that the poor are not poor because of their culture but because they do not have enough money.

Pro and con arguments for the culture-of-poverty theory persist. There are many reasons, both external and internal, why a person may be poor. External reasons include high rates of unemployment and underemployment; racial discrimination; automation, which throws people out of work; lack of job training programs; sex discrimination; a shortage of antipoverty programs; and inflation. Internal reasons include physical or mental impairment, alcoholism, obsolete job skills, early parenthood, lack of education, and lack of interest in taking available jobs.

FUNCTIONS OF POVERTY

Obviously, poverty is dysfunctional—mainly to the poor themselves, but also to the affluent. However, the realization that poverty also has some functions in society can help us understand why some decision makers are not actively seeking to eradicate it.

Eleven functions are provided by the poor to affluent groups:

1. They are available to do the unpleasant jobs no one else wants to do.

2. Their activities subsidize the more affluent (for example, domestic service for low pay).

3. They help create jobs (for example, jobs for social workers who provide services to the poor).

4. They purchase poor-quality goods that otherwise could not be sold.

5. They serve as examples of deviance to be frowned on by the majority, thereby supporting dominant norms.

6. They provide an opportunity for others to practice their "Christian duty" of helping the less fortunate.

7. They make mobility more likely for others because they are removed from the competition for good education and good jobs.

8. They contribute to cultural activities (for example, by providing cheap labor for the construction of monuments and works of art).

9. They create cultural forms (such as jazz and the blues) that are often adopted by the affluent.

10. They serve as symbolic opponents for some political groups and as constituents for others.

11. They often absorb the costs of change (for example, by being the victims of high levels of unemployment that result from technological advances).[50]

Furthermore, denigrating the poor has the psychological function for some Americans of making them feel better about themselves.

Partly because poverty is functional, our society makes only a halfhearted effort to eliminate—or even reduce—it. To do so would result in a redistribution of income from the rich to the poor, a policy generally seen as undemocratic (sometimes communistic) even by the not-so-affluent. Because the rich control the political power, proposals that would eliminate poverty (such as guaranteed annual income programs) have generally met with opposition. Gans emphasizes this point:

Legislation in America tends to favor the interests of the businessman, not the consumers, even though the latter are a vast majority; of landlords, not tenants; of doctors, not patients. Only organized interest groups have the specific concerns and the time, staff, and money to bring their demands before government officials. . . . The poor are powerless because they are a minority of the population, are not organized politically, are often difficult to organize, and are not even a homogeneous group with similar interests that could be organized into a single pressure group. . . . Given the antagonism toward them on the part of many Americans, any programs that would provide them with significant gains are likely to be voted down by a majority. Legislative proposals for a massive

antipoverty effort . . . have always run into con-
certed and united opposition in Washington.[51]

Our government has the resources to eliminate poverty—but not the will. In the 20th century, our country has been able to find billions of
dollars in resources within a few months when
we go to war (which has happened several times).
But our government has not been willing to allocate similar funds to improve living conditions for
the homeless and for millions of other people who
are living in poverty in this country.

SOCIAL INSURANCE PROGRAMS

Because poverty relates to nearly every other
social problem, almost every existing social service—to some extent—works to combat poverty
(including Alcoholics Anonymous, health-care
programs, vocational rehabilitation, Parents Without Partners, foster care, adoption, day care, Head
Start, housing programs, urban renewal, and community action programs). Such programs indirectly reduce poverty by alleviating related social
problems. These programs are too numerous to
describe fully in this text. This section will instead
describe social insurance programs, and the next
section will describe public assistance programs.
(Social insurance programs are financed by taxes
on employees, on employers, or on both. Public
assistance program benefits are paid from general
government revenues.)

Old Age, Survivors, Disability, and Health Insurance (OASDHI)

This social insurance program was created by the
1935 Social Security Act. Generally, OASDHI is referred to as "Social Security" by the public. It is the
largest income insurance program and is designed
to partially replace income that is lost when a
worker retires or becomes disabled. Cash benefits
are also paid to survivors of "insured" workers.

Payments to beneficiaries are based on previous earnings. The rich as well as the poor are eligible if insured. Benefits are provided to fully
insured workers at age 65 or older (somewhat
smaller benefits can be taken at age 62). Dependent husbands or wives over age 62 and dependent children under age 18 (there is no age limit
on disabled children who become disabled before
18) are also covered under the retirement benefits.

Participation in this insurance program is
compulsory for most employees. The program is
financed by a payroll tax assessed equally to employer and employee. The rate has gone up gradually. Eligibility for benefits is based on the number of years in which Social Security taxes have
been paid.

A major concern has been the financial soundness of OASDHI. Since 1935 the Social Security
(FICA) tax has led to a buildup in the trust fund
for OASDHI. But the liberalization of benefits and
the increased number of recipients in recent years
have raised concern about the system paying out
more than it takes in. In times of high unemployment and recession, the number of workers paying into OASDHI is decreased. The decline in the
birthrate, along with a steady increase in the
retired population, may jeopardize the financial
soundness of the program; the number of recipients is increasing at a faster rate than the number
of workers paying into the system. If OASDHI is to
remain financially sound, benefits may have to be
scaled back, FICA taxes increased, or both.

Medicare

In 1965 Congress enacted Title XVIII (Medicare)
to the Social Security Act. Medicare has two parts:
hospital insurance and medical insurance. Hospital insurance helps pay for inpatient hospital care,
inpatient care in a skilled nursing facility, home
health care, and hospice care. Medical insurance
helps pay for medically necessary doctors' services, outpatient hospital services, and a number
of other medical services and supplies that are not
covered by the hospital insurance part of Medicare. The hospital insurance part is financed by
a surcharge on the Social Security taxes paid by
employers and employees. The medical insurance

part is a voluntary insurance plan for which enrollees are charged a monthly premium. (More than two-thirds of the costs of the medical insurance premium is paid from general revenues of the federal government.) Medicare, a public health insurance program, is described more fully in Chapter 15.

Unemployment Insurance

This program was also created by the 1935 Social Security Act and provides benefits to workers who have been laid off or, in certain cases, fired. Unemployment insurance is financed by a tax on employers. The amount and duration of weekly benefits vary from state to state. In many states, the unemployed are eligible for benefits for about a year. To be eligible in most states, a person must (a) have worked a certain number of weeks in covered employment; (b) be ready, willing, and able to work; (c) file a claim for benefits and be registered in a public employment office; and (d) demonstrate that unemployment is due to a lack of work for which she or he is qualified.

Unemployment insurance benefits help individuals and families who become unemployed due to a lack of work. In our society, in which employment is valued highly, being without work can be a demeaning experience. In the past two decades, the unemployment rate has ranged from 4% to 11% of able-bodied workers. High rates clearly indicate a lack of available jobs. Yet the unemployment insurance program has been sharply criticized by claims that some of the unemployed would rather collect insurance benefits than make a concerted effort to obtain employment.

Workers' Compensation Insurance

This program provides both income and assistance in meeting medical expenses for injuries sustained on a job. The program was enacted after a series of lawsuits by injured employees against employers—the only recourse employees had. The first workers' compensation program was the Federal Employees Compensation Act of 1908. Individual states gradually passed workers' compensation laws modeled after the program for federal employees. By 1920 all but six states had such laws, but it was not until 1948 that all states had adequate coverage.[52] Cash benefits are paid for total or temporary disability or death. Medical benefits cover hospital and doctors' fees. Rehabilitation benefits are also available for those needing aftercare and retraining to again become employable. Workers' compensation is financed by a tax on employers.

PUBLIC ASSISTANCE PROGRAMS

Public assistance is sometimes viewed as synonymous with "welfare" by the general public, yet there are hundreds of other social welfare programs. Public assistance has primarily residual aspects, and applicants must undergo a "means test" that reviews their assets and liabilities to determine their eligibility for benefits.

Adherents of the residual view of public assistance generally hold the following opinions:

1. Assistance should be made as unpleasant as possible to discourage its use. This is to be accomplished by giving relief in kind (for example, food or clothes) rather than money, by threatening prosecution, by continually reevaluating need, by making it only temporary, by stopping it if illegitimacy is involved, and by removing children from their own homes when these homes do not meet minimal standards.

2. Relief should also be made unpleasant by requiring recipients to work for it regardless of what the nature of the work may be, how depressed the wage, or whether the requirement would be used as a means for securing cheap labor; notwithstanding, income from this work is still labeled relief.

3. Assistance should be discouraged by making payments too low for anyone to really want it. It is argued by advocates of this approach that assistance in amounts greater than would be received by the lowest paid, most menial worker

would encourage individuals to seek assistance in lieu of employment.

4. Outsiders should be prevented from seeking help (they may receive only emergency aid and only for short periods).

5. People should be forced to remain on their jobs or to return to employment; this is accomplished by denying assistance to anyone who is guilty of a "voluntary quit."[53]

In contrast, the institutional view of public assistance (generally held by social workers) assumes or advocates the following:

1. Adequate income and the elimination of hunger and destitution should be provided for all citizens as an instrument of social policy.

2. Relief should be extended to applicants who can qualify under eligibility requirements; that is, subjective, biased, and capricious considerations should be removed. Relief should be based on need as it is determined to exist by objective, rather than subjective, criteria and as a legally determined right.

3. It is assumed that workers generally prefer income from employment over public welfare and that motivations to work are built into the economy in the form of social, cultural, and economic advantages to the employed man or woman.

4. Psychological and social barriers sometimes stand in the way of rehabilitation and employment. Counseling and other services may be needed to restore certain individuals to economic and social self-sufficiency.

5. Preservation of the independence and self-respect of the applicant for assistance is a prime consideration in the administration of programs of relief.

6. A punitive approach defeats the purpose for which assistance is used—namely, the restoration of the individual to normal functioning; it deepens feelings of inadequacy and dependency, causes embarrassment and humiliation, and brings destructive psychological defenses into play.

7. There are many pulls in society that make work more appealing than public welfare, such as

a higher standard of living and the prestige and sense of importance one receives from gainful employment.[54]

Public assistance programs have several distinguishing features:

■ *Programs have a means test.* Individuals applying for assistance have their income and assets examined to determine whether their financial needs meet the eligibility requirements. The means test is designed to ensure that individuals receiving assistance do not already have sufficient resources for a minimum level of subsistence. Resources that are examined include both earned and unearned income. Earned income is money in the form of salary or wages. Unearned income includes benefits from other public and private financial programs, gifts, life insurance annuities, stock dividends, rental income, inheritances, support payments from relatives, and so on.

■ *Eligibility and benefit levels are determined on a case-by-case basis.* All applications for assistance are closely reviewed on an individual basis. Although there are federal, state, and local guidelines on eligibility and on allowable benefits, the staff who administer public assistance have substantial discretion in deciding whether a client will receive special allowances in addition to basic benefits. Staff also have discretion in deciding which social services and other resources might be mobilized on behalf of the client. Eligibility determination, along with benefit-level determination, is a cumbersome, lengthy process involving extensive review of documents.

■ *Benefits are viewed as charity.* In contrast to social insurance benefits, to which recipients are viewed as legally entitled, public assistance benefits are perceived as charity. In this country, poor people are not considered to have a constitutionally established right to a minimum income. (In comparison, some foreign countries, such as Great Britain, recognize the right of those in poverty to be maintained and protected by government.)

■ *Program benefits are paid from general government revenues.* Public assistance benefits at the federal, state, and local levels are financed through taxes on personal income and on property.

The main public assistance programs include Supplemental Security Income, General Assistance, Medicaid, food stamps, housing assistance, and the Personal Responsibility and Work Opportunity Reconciliation Act (which was enacted in 1996 to replace Aid to Families with Dependent Children).

Supplemental Security Income (SSI)

Under the SSI program, the federal government pays monthly checks to people in financial need who are 65 years of age and older or who are blind or disabled at any age. To qualify for payments, applicants must have no (or very little) regular cash income, own little property, and have little cash or few assets that could be turned into cash (such as stocks, bonds, jewelry, or other valuables).

The SSI program became effective January 1, 1974, and replaced the following programs that were created by the 1935 Social Security Act: Old-Age Assistance, Aid to the Blind, and Aid to the Permanently and Totally Disabled. SSI is the first federally administered assistance program. All other public assistance programs are administered through state and local governments. The word *supplemental* refers to the fact that, in most cases, payments *supplement* whatever income may be available to the claimant. Even OASDHI benefits are supplemented by this program.

SSI provides a guaranteed minimum income (an income floor) for the aged, the blind, and the disabled. Aged, blind, and disabled are defined as follows:

Aged: 65 or over.

Blind: Vision no better than 20/200 (even with glasses) or tunnel vision (limited visual field of 20° or less).

Disabled: A physical or mental disability that prevents a person from doing any substantial gainful work and is expected to last at least 12 months or result in death.

Administration of SSI has been assigned to the Social Security Administration. Financing of the program is through federal tax dollars, primarily income taxes.

General Assistance

The General Assistance (GA) program is supposed to serve those needing temporary, rather than long-term, financial support. It is designed to provide financial help to those in need who are ineligible for any other income-maintenance program. No clearly stated eligibility requirements exist for general assistance. GA is the only public assistance program that receives no federal funds. It is usually funded by property taxes. In some large cities, the state contributes substantially toward meeting the costs of GA. In most localities, however, the program is financed and administered at the local level through the county or township or by a village or city. In many local governmental units, a political official has arbitrary jurisdiction over whether an applicant receives help. Most expenditures for GA are for medical care. In-kind payments (food, medical care, clothes, and items other than money) are frequent. Whenever feasible, communities usually attempt to move GA recipients into federally funded public aid programs to reduce local expenses.

Payments for GA tend to be minimal and grudgingly made to discourage people from applying and from becoming dependent on welfare. With in-kind and voucher payments, GA conveys to recipients the suspicion that they are incapable of managing their own affairs. Because able-bodied unemployed men and women sometimes find it necessary to seek GA benefits, GA has been viewed as a public assistance program for the "undeserving poor." In some parts of the country, GA has demoralizing effects because many local program directors hold—and convey to recipients—a negative attitude about providing assistance.

In recent years, some states and counties have terminated their GA program.

Medicaid

This program provides hospital and medical care to certain poverty-stricken people. Those eligible are individuals who have very low income and assets. Because Medicaid is a joint federal/state program, the laws governing eligibility and benefits vary in different geographic areas. Generally, recipients of SSI and other public assistance programs are eligible. In addition, states have the option to include people who are able to provide for their own daily living but whose income and resources are not sufficient to meet all their medical costs.

Medicaid is administered by the states, with financial participation by the federal government. Direct payments are made to providers of services. As is required for every public assistance program, Medicaid applicants must undergo a means test.

Food Stamps

Tragically, an estimated 30 million people in the United States (the most powerful and one of the richest countries in the world) do not have enough food to eat.[55] Many of those with inadequate diets are poor. Not only does an insufficient diet affect the individual, but research suggests that severe nutritional deficits in expectant mothers also may lead to irreversible brain defects in their children.

The food stamp program is designed to combat hunger. Food stamps are available to public assistance recipients and to other low-income families. These stamps are traded in for groceries. With millions of Americans going hungry, the food stamp program is obviously underfunded.

Housing Assistance

Similar to food stamps and Medicaid, housing assistance is an "in-kind" program rather than a cash program. Generally, such assistance is provided in the form of public housing, usually large housing projects that are owned and operated by the government. In a public housing project, the tenants have lower, subsidized rents. Because they pay less than the market value of their apartments, they are effectively receiving an income transfer.

There are also housing assistance programs for low-income people who are renting and even buying their homes and apartments in the private market. In these programs, the rent or mortgage payment is reduced, with the Department of Housing and Urban Development (HUD) making up the difference.

Aid to Families with Dependent Children (AFDC)

With the passage of the 1996 welfare reform legislation, this program has been phased out and replaced by the Personal Responsibility and Work Opportunity Reconciliation Act. For readers to understand the differences between these two programs, both will be described here.

The AFDC program was created by the 1935 Social Security Act. It was originally entitled Aid to Dependent Children (ADC) and, a few decades later, was renamed Aid to Families with Dependent Children. When first enacted, one of ADC's objectives was to enable mothers with young children to remain at home so that their children would be raised well. But since 1935, our values surrounding working mothers have changed. There now is the expectation that single mothers (and single fathers) should obtain gainful employment. (The Personal Responsibility and Work Opportunity Reconciliation Act was largely created in 1996 to emphasize this change in expectation from welfare to work.)

The precise parameters of eligibility for AFDC varied from state to state. Payments were made for both the parent (or parents) and the children in eligible families. To be eligible, the children must have been deprived of parental support or care because of a parent's death or continued absence from the home (through desertion, divorce, or separation) or because the parent was never married. AFDC payments were also made to low-income two-parent families in which both parents were unemployed. In this situation, the breadwinner (or breadwinners) had to agree to seek work actively, to register with the state unemployment service, and to participate in job training programs. Most AFDC families were headed by a single parent, usually the mother because the father was absent from the home.

Financing and administration of the AFDC program were shared by federal and state governments. In many states, counties also participated in the financing and administration. The federal government, through the Department of Health and Human Services, wrote regulations to implement the Social Security laws. States, and often counties, then wrote their own regulations, within federal guidelines, relating to eligibility criteria, benefit standards, and qualifications of public assistance staff.

Decisions about eligibility criteria for AFDC benefits were made by the executive, legislative, and judicial branches of government and at federal, state, and local levels. As a result, the program was cumbersome, slow to change to meet emerging needs, and heavily bogged down by red tape and bureaucratic processes.

AFDC became the most stigmatized public assistance program. The general public's concept of welfare was the AFDC program. More money was spent on AFDC than on any other public assistance program. Concern arose about the fact that many adult recipients of AFDC had parents who were also recipients; AFDC was criticized as being a "way of life" for some people who chose to be on welfare rather than work.[56] In addition, it was found that the longer a family received AFDC, the higher the rate of social problems their children manifested in their teenage years (births outside marriage, early marriage, emotional problems, truancy, delinquency, and dropping out of school).[57] Some authorities asserted it was not AFDC per se that led to an increase in social problems displayed by some recipients but the fact that AFDC recipients were often stigmatized and viewed as "second-class citizens."[58] The program was also criticized for keeping most recipients in poverty by inadequate assistance grants that averaged well below the poverty level.[59]

AFDC MYTHS VERSUS FACTS

One of the main reasons the AFDC program was discontinued in 1996 was that a number of erroneous myths had arisen about it. This section summarizes these myths and presents facts that refute them. The myths and facts are summarized by Coleman and Cressey and by Kornblum and Julian.[60]

Myth 1: Most welfare children are "illegitimate."

Fact: A sizable majority of the children who received AFDC benefits were "legitimate." (This author strongly objects to labeling any child "illegitimate." The marital status of one's parents has nothing to do with one's value as a human being.)

Myth 2: Welfare makes it profitable for women to have illegitimate babies.

Fact: Because it costs over $160,000 to raise a child from birth to age 18, the "profit" from AFDC that a mother might expect to realize from having an additional child was minuscule, even if she minimized all expenditures for the child. Having more babies makes a family poorer.

Myth 3: Give them more money and they'll spend it on alcohol and drugs.

Fact: When AFDC families received extra funds (which rarely occurred), they almost always spent it on essentials.

Myth 4: Most welfare recipients are cheaters and frauds.

Fact: If fraud is defined as a deliberate and knowing attempt by a client to deceive the agency, then the incidence of fraud is remarkably low. A national survey found that 1 of every 20 AFDC recipients received checks for which he or she was ineligible. Less than half of 1% of welfare cases were referred for prosecution for fraud.[61] Because determining eligibility was a cumbersome, complex process, most of these errors were identified as honest mistakes made by state and local public assistance bureaucrats or by recipients. Contrasted with tax fraud, the welfare system was squeaky clean. The Internal Revenue Service estimates a 20% to 25% error rate in payment of income taxes, most of which is attributable to underreporting of income by taxpayers.[62]

Myth 5: The welfare rolls are soaring out of control.

Fact: Most caseload growth in the AFDC program occurred before 1973, with dramatic increases between 1970 and 1973. From early 1976 to 1996, the number of people on AFDC increased minimally each year.

Myth 6: Welfare is just a money handout—a dole.

Fact: Most families on AFDC received one or more social services designed to meet personal and social problems and to make them self-supportive. Available social services varied widely from area to area. Possible services included health care, financial counseling, counseling on home management, employment counseling, day care, vocational rehabilitation, homemaker services, consumer education, assistance in child rearing, Head Start, job training, and marriage counseling. The provision of social services to low-income families was one of the three programs enacted by the 1935 Social Security Act.

Myth 7: People on welfare are able-bodied loafers.

Fact: Contrary to public opinion, few able-bodied persons received assistance; the vast majority of AFDC recipients were children. Less than 1% of welfare recipients were able-bodied, unemployed males. The largest group of able-bodied adults was composed of AFDC mothers, most of whom headed families in which no able-bodied male was present. Many of these mothers were already working or actively seeking work, receiving work training, or waiting to be called back after a layoff. Other AFDC mothers faced serious barriers to obtaining employment: very young children to rear, lack of money for child care, lack of job skills, and lack of extensive medical or rehabilitative services to become employable. Contrary to the stereotype of the "welfare mother" as shiftless, lazy, and unwilling to take a job, even long-term AFDC mothers continued to have a strong work ethic but lacked the skills and confidence to obtain a job.

Myth 8: Most welfare families are African American.

Fact: The number of White families receiving AFDC was approximately the same as the number of African American families. Because African Americans constituted about 12% of the U.S. population and over 45% of all AFDC recipients, the stigma attached to AFDC may have been associated with racial prejudice.

Myth 9: "Why work when you can live it up on welfare?"

Fact: In most states, AFDC payments were below the established poverty level. Living in poverty is not "living it up."

Myth 10: Once on welfare, always on welfare.

Fact: In the early 1990s, only 10% of the households received AFDC benefits for 10 years or longer. Half the families on welfare had been receiving assistance for 20 months or less and two-thirds for less than 3 years.

Myth 11: Welfare is eating up tremendous chunks of our tax money, causing inflation, and "bleeding the country dry."

Fact: At the federal level, about 1% of the federal budget was allocated to AFDC. The largest single item in the national budget is defense spending.

Myth 12: Welfare is only for the poor.

Fact: The United States pays out much more to the rich than to the poor. These payments are not called welfare but research grants, training grants, tax loopholes, compensation, low-interest loans, and parity. Dale Tussing notes that the United States has two welfare systems:

> *Two welfare systems exist simultaneously in this country. One is well known. It is explicit, poorly funded, stigmatized and stigmatizing, and is directed at the poor. The other, practically unknown, is implicit, literally invisible, is nonstigmatized and nonstigmatizing, and provides vast but unacknowledged benefits for the nonpoor. . . . Our welfare systems do not distribute benefits on the basis of need. Rather, they distribute benefits on the basis of legitimacy. Poor people are viewed as less legitimate than nonpoor people . . . by and large, welfare programs for the poor are obvious, open and clearly labeled, and those for the nonpoor are either concealed (as in tax laws, for instance) and ill understood, or are clothed in protective language. . . . Whether or not a person is poor can often be determined*

by the names of his welfare programs. If his programs are called "relief," "welfare," "assistance," "charity," or the like, he is surely poor; but if they are called "parity," "insurance," "compensation," or "compulsory saving," he is surely a member of the large majority of nonpoor persons who do not even think of themselves as receiving welfare payments.[63]

Eleanor Clift adds:

If one counts a broad range of federal spending and tax programs, an average upper-income person will get more than a typical poor person.

It's no secret that middle- and upper-income families enjoy the benefit of tax breaks and entitlement programs like social security. But such families, many of whom complain bitterly these days that government is ignoring them, may be surprised to learn how much more they get than their poorer counterparts. In some ways, such benefits remain the holiest of sacred cows.[64]

Personal Responsibility and Work Opportunity Reconciliation Act

In 1986 Charles Murray proposed in his controversial book *Losing Ground* that the government should eliminate welfare benefits for all working-age adults.[65] He contended that court decisions, bureaucratic reforms, and antipoverty programs in our society have actually made the poor worse off by creating a dependency. In essence he asserted people on welfare decide that being on the government dole is better than working.

Murray was especially critical of the AFDC program. He asserted that it provided an incentive for single women to want to have children in order to receive welfare payments. He also asserted that increases in crime and drug abuse, poor educational performance in schools, and deteriorating conditions in inner cities stem largely from the increase in single-parent families, which he attributed to government programs that support such

families. His solution to overhauling the AFDC program was simple: "If you want to cut illegitimate births among poor people, . . . I know how to do that. You just rip away every kind of government support there is."[66]

Critics of this approach were horrified. They argued that Murray's plan would make innocent children suffer for their parents' inadequacies, which seems doubly unfair, given that two of three AFDC beneficiaries were children. If the AFDC program were eliminated without any program to replace it, many more children undoubtedly would end up homeless and hungry. Murray's response was that single mothers who are unable to care for their children should place them for adoption. He further asserted that terminating the AFDC program would force single women to think twice about getting pregnant and would force more low-income males to refrain from fathering children outside of marriage.

Although there was little support for eliminating the AFDC program without replacing it, political decision makers in the early 1990s became more interested in replacing AFDC with a program that forced unemployed single mothers (and single fathers) to take a job.

In the 1994 elections, Republicans (mostly conservatives) won a majority of seats in the House of Representatives for the first time in 40 years and had control of both houses of Congress. The new House speaker, Newt Gingrich, proposed there be no AFDC benefits for unmarried teens and their children. In addition, he proposed that AFDC recipients be prohibited from receiving benefits for more than 5 years, with states having the option of reducing the time limit for welfare benefits to 2 years.

When Bill Clinton was campaigning for the presidency in 1992, he promised to "end welfare as we know it." In 1994 he proposed attacking the costly national problem of welfare dependency with a plan that would force growing numbers of young welfare mothers into public or private jobs. The objective of the plan was to make young single mothers self-sufficient by giving them money and child care while they received job training—but then to cut off their cash benefits after no more than 24 months. Those who

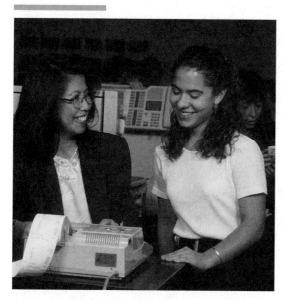

Under the 1996 welfare reform act, states are responsible for job training programs that lead to employment within 2 years of receiving benefits.

were unable to find jobs would be given temporary tax-subsidized work, usually at the minimum wage, either in the private sector or in community service.

In 1996 President Clinton and the Democrats and Republicans in Congress compromised on welfare reform and passed the Personal Responsibility and Work Opportunity Reconciliation Act. Key provisions of this act are:

■ The federal guarantee of cash assistance for poor families with children (under the AFDC program) is ended. Each state now receives a capped block grant (lump sum) to run its own welfare and work programs.

■ The head of every family has to work within 2 years, or the family loses its benefits. After receiving welfare for 2 months, adults have to perform community service unless they have found regular jobs. (States can choose not to have a community service requirement.)

■ Lifetime public welfare assistance is limited to 5 years. (States can establish stricter limits.)

Hardship exemptions from this requirement are available for up to 20% of recipients in a state.

■ States can provide payments to unmarried teenage parents only if a mother under 18 is living at home or in another adult-supervised setting and attends high school or an alternative educational or training program as soon as the child is 12 weeks old.

■ States are required to maintain their own spending on public welfare at 75% of their 1994 level or 80% if they failed to put enough public welfare recipients to work.

■ States cannot penalize a woman on public welfare who does not work because she cannot find day care for a child under 6 years old.

■ States are required to deduct benefits from welfare mothers who refuse to help identify the fathers. States may deny Medicaid to adults who lose welfare benefits because of a failure to meet work requirements.

■ A woman on public welfare who refuses to cooperate in identifying the father of her child must lose at least 25% of her benefits.

■ Future legal immigrants who have not yet become citizens are ineligible for most federal welfare benefits and social services during their first 5 years in the United States. SSI benefits and food stamp eligibility end for noncitizens, including legal immigrants, receiving benefits in 1996.[67]

At the time of this writing, states were in the process of designing and implementing their welfare systems within the federal guidelines for the Personal Responsibility and Work Opportunity Reconciliation Act. It is too early to determine the long-term effects of this act. An initial positive result was that the number of Americans on cash assistance plummeted in the first year of the program by 1.7 million, by far the biggest 1-year decline in the history of welfare.[68] The new law's tough provisions may be chasing away recipients who can more or less afford to leave public assistance (at least temporarily) because they have undisclosed income from friends, family, or under-the-table jobs. Glastris notes, "Far from living in

CASE EXAMPLE 4.2   ## Will Welfare Reform End the Poverty Trap?

Elaine Johnson, age 35, has recently become a grandmother. Her oldest daughter, Sylvia, is a 16-year-old unmarried mother. Today, October 13, 1997, is a significant day in their lives because Elaine and Sylvia are applying at Milwaukee's Public Welfare Office to place baby Tony's name on America's welfare rolls. He will represent the third successive generation in the Johnson family to receive public assistance benefits.

Elaine's parents migrated from Mississippi to Milwaukee in 1962, shortly after Elaine's birth. Her father got a job as a janitor in the school system, and her mother has been a part-time nurse's aide at a hospital. Elaine started high school and received above-average grades, She had hopes of getting a student loan to go to college. She wanted to get out of the inner city where she was being raised.

At the age of 17, however, Elaine became pregnant. Her parents talked her out of an abortion, and she gave birth to Sylvia. Two months after the birth, she signed up for AFDC at the urging of her parents and friends. It would only be temporary, she thought, until she could get a better handle on her life. But going to school and caring for a baby were too much work, so Elaine dropped out of high school in her senior year. She no longer had the same interests as her former friends who did not have children. At times Elaine found it a joy to care for Sylvia, but at other times she found caring for the baby frustrating. Elaine went out as much as she could, when she had a little extra money and when she could find someone to babysit for her. Over the next 15 years, Elaine had three other children. Only one of the four different fathers married her, and that marriage lasted only two and a half years. The husband left home one day, complaining about children and responsibilities. He never returned, and Elaine has never heard from him.

Elaine has tried a variety of jobs while on AFDC—nurse's aide, dishwasher, waitress, and service station attendant. But the costs of transportation, uniforms, and babysitting left her no better off financially than if she stayed home and received her monthly AFDC checks. Life has been hard for Elaine. Because she is on welfare, she feels like a second-class citizen and a "charity" case. She has had to pinch pennies all her life to try to make ends meet. On countless days, she has fed her children beans and rice. She sharply regrets not being able to give her children the material things that many other kids have. While some parents are buying computers for their chil-

royal luxury, however, most of these 'cheaters' have been struggling to make ends meet." [69]

Many unanswered questions remain about this 1996 welfare reform act. Will the program be successful in getting adult welfare recipients into decent paying jobs that will enable their families to leave public assistance? Even if adult welfare recipients obtain employment, will their children be cared for in healthy child-care arrangements while the parents are working? How difficult will it be for single parents with one or more of the following issues to obtain gainful employment: lack of a marketable job skill, a drug habit, a chronic medical problem, a child at home with a mental or physical disability, a lack of convenient transportation, being in a violent domestic relationdren, she takes her kids to Goodwill's clothing store to try to find bargains on second-hand sneakers, shirts, jeans, and jackets.

She is living in a deteriorated inner-city neighborhood and is alarmed that her oldest son, Marvin, is experimenting with cocaine and other drugs. The school system is another concern: A high percentage of students drop out, the windows in the buildings are boarded up, vandalism is frequent, physical attacks on teachers sometimes occur, and the educational quality is known to be inferior.

When Elaine discovered that Sylvia was sexually active at 15, she pleaded with her daughter not to make the mistake she had made. Elaine even took her to Planned Parenthood to get birth control pills. Sylvia took her pills for several months. When the supply ran out, she never got around to going back to Planned Parenthood to get her prescription refilled.

Elaine's remaining dream is that her children will have a better life than hers. Tears often come to her eyes when she sees her children getting caught in the same poverty trap that she is in.

Yes, today is a significant day for Elaine. Upon entering the welfare office, she is informed she must immediately enter work training and will soon be expected to be searching for employment. She also is informed of the 1996 welfare reform act and that all public assistance benefits for her will be terminated in a few years. Furthermore, Sylvia and Elaine are informed that Sylvia must continue to attend high school to be eligible for public assistance benefits. Sylvia is also informed there now is a maximum lifetime limit of 5 years for which she and Tony can receive these benefits. Elaine is overwhelmed and starts to cry. Her life is already in disarray. Now she is informed that both she and Sylvia have only a few years of eligibility left for public assistance and that both of them must immediately start learning a marketable job, making child-care arrangements for Tony for when they are receiving training or looking for a job, getting their lives in order, finding ways to help Marvin stop his drug experimentation, finding efficient forms of transportation, and finding decent paying jobs within a year or two. Elaine is clueless how all this can be accomplished.

Will the 1996 welfare reform legislation help Elaine and Sylvia and their family members escape the cycle of poverty? Or will the 1996 welfare reform legislation result in increased stress for this family and gradually result in further family deterioration?

---

ship, failure to have a strong work ethic, and having a chronic emotional or behavioral problem? Will some states design a punitive welfare system that cuts welfare benefits to the minimum allowed by federal guidelines in order to accomplish two things: to avoid becoming magnets for the poor and to minimize state taxes? Will the new legislation increase the number of homeless persons be-cause adult recipients are forced off public assistance when they reach the limit on the number of years they are eligible to receive public assistance without obtaining employment? Will this program add extensive additional stress to the lives of adult recipients and thereby result in increased incidents of child abuse (that is, will some adult recipients take out their frustrations and feelings of stress on their children)? If rates of child abuse and neglect increase, will more children be placed into the expensive foster-care system? Will some adult recipients who reach their term eligibility limits on public assistance without obtaining a decent paying job turn to prostitution or to theft? How can jobs be found or created in geographic areas having high unemployment rates?

AFDC was originally created to provide a stable, safe, and healthy living environment for the children of single unemployed parents. What assurance is there that the 1996 welfare reform act will continue to seek to provide a stable, safe, and healthy living environment for children in these families? The 1935 Social Security Act created a social safety net of programs for children and others in need. Has the 1996 welfare reform act ripped major holes in this social safety net?

PROPOSED WELFARE ALTERNATIVES

If the 1996 welfare reform act becomes recognized as a failure, what other systems may be enacted? This section will examine three proposals: offering family allowances, guaranteeing a basic annual income, and eliminating or reducing the causes of poverty.

Offer Family Allowances

The United States is the only Western industrialized country without a family allowance program. Under a family allowance program, the government pays each family a set amount based on the number of children in the household. If payments were large enough, a program like this could aid in eliminating poverty, particularly in large families.

There are some strong criticisms of family allowance plans. If payments were made to all children, the program would be very expensive and much of the money would go to nonpoor families. This problem could be solved (as Denmark has done) by varying the family allowance payments with income and terminating payments after a certain income is reached. (However, such an approach would then involve a means test and continue to stigmatize recipients.) A second criticism is that such a program would provide an incentive to increase the birthrate at a time when overpopulation is a major concern. A final criticism is that it would not provide payments to single individuals and childless couples who are poor.

Guarantee a Basic Annual Income

A variety of proposals to guarantee every American a certain annual income have been put forth, including proposals by Presidents Nixon and Carter. The base level could conceivably be set slightly above the poverty line and adjusted each year to account for inflation. Such a proposal, if implemented, would eradicate poverty.

Practically all guaranteed-income proposals are based on the concept of a "negative income tax." That is, persons earning above a certain level would pay income tax, whereas those earning below that level would receive a grant—the negative tax—to bring their income up to the guaranteed level. Most negative income tax plans also contain an incentive-to-work provision that allows recipients to keep a proportion of their earnings above the guaranteed base level.

Many variations of the negative income tax are possible, and some have been tested by the federal government. The minimum-income guarantee for a family of four, for example, could be set at the poverty line, and the incentive-to-work factor (the tax-back rate) could range widely. But such plans could be very expensive.

Using a hypothetical example, with a guaranteed base level of $16,000 for a family of four and the tax-back rate at 50%—allowing a family to keep $50 of every $100 earned—the family would receive subsidies until the break-even point of $32,000. The mathematics of this guaranteed base level and tax-back rate can be illustrated as follows:

If Your Annual Income from a Paying Job Is:	Then Your Annual Income from the Govern- ment Is:	So Your Total Income Is:
$ 0	$16,000	$16,000
5,000	13,500	18,500
10,000	11,000	21,000
15,000	8,500	23,500
20,000	6,000	26,000
25,000	3,500	28,500
30,000	1,000	31,000
32,000	0	32,000

There are a number of advantages to negative income tax plans. They would shift the focus of income maintenance programs from "charity" to a "right" of entitlement to a guaranteed income. The stigma of being a recipient would be sharply reduced. Such programs would be relatively simple to administer, as eligibility would be based on income tax returns. Furthermore, such a program would serve everyone who is poor; if the base level is at the poverty line, poverty would be eradicated. Another advantage would be to reduce equity problems that have occurred under present programs, in which nonworking people are eligible for several types of benefits (for example, food stamps and Medicaid) and may be able to achieve a higher standard of living than a low-income employed person who is eligible for few, if any, benefits. A negative income tax plan could also replace practically all other public assistance programs and thereby reduce the expense and complexity of administering a variety of programs.

Several unanswered questions and concerns have been raised about a negative income tax plan:

■ Such plans are based on the filing of income tax forms. If a family has little or no income (and no assets), must they wait nearly a year until their tax form is filed before being eligible for benefits?

■ Will a guaranteed income destroy the incentive to work?

■ The cost of living varies greatly between urban and rural areas and in different parts of the

country. Should financial adjustments be made for this?

■ Perhaps the biggest problem with a negative income tax plan involves what has been called the "unholy triangle"—that is, developing a plan that:

1. Has an adequate guaranteed base level.

2. Allows low-income workers to keep a sufficiently high percentage of their earnings above the guaranteed base level so that the incentive to work is not destroyed.

3. Is not exorbitantly expensive, so that our national economy is not severely affected.

The federal government in the past showed considerable interest in negative income tax programs, as evidenced by the passage in 1973 of the Supplemental Security Income (SSI) program, which has a guaranteed income base. But proposed negative income tax plans for unemployed, impoverished adults with children have not received much support in Congress. Liberals argued that the guaranteed base level of payments was too low and would not move families above the poverty line. Conservatives objected that the plans would be too costly and would provide financial payments to many more poor families than do current public assistance programs. Conservatives also opposed the plans because they feared they would destroy the incentive to work and would provide "something for nothing."

Eliminate or Reduce the Causes of Poverty

As noted earlier, a number of factors cause and perpetuate poverty. Another way of combating poverty is to develop and expand programs to alleviate its major causes.

Laws to end racial and sex discrimination can be more vigorously enforced. Programs to curb alcohol and drug abuse can be expanded to reach out and serve more of those who are addicted. Higher quality educational programs (and more resources) are needed in pockets of poverty (for example, urban inner cities) to inspire students, to help them stay in school, and to help them achieve higher academic levels. Sex education and family planning services need to be provided to more teenagers and young adults to teach responsible sexuality and prevent unwanted pregnancies, which play a role in locking young people into poverty. Family planning services also need to be expanded to help couples who do not want, and cannot afford, large families. An expanded public housing program is needed to provide adequate living quarters for the poor. A national health insurance program is needed to pay for unusually high medical bills, which at present wipe out the savings of some families and plunge them deep into debt.

Some families need financial counseling to help them more effectively manage and spend within the limits of their financial resources. Many middle-aged adults need educational programs to teach them to plan for their retirement years— what lifestyle they want, how to remain healthy, and how to prepare financially.

Jobs for able-bodied workers is a key to reducing the number of people in poverty. In recent years, high unemployment rates have forced many of the unemployed and their families into poverty. A variety of suggestions have been advanced to progress toward a full-employment society.

Able-bodied adults who do not have marketable job skills (perhaps because their skills have become obsolete) need training for jobs that are available. (In Germany adults are paid by the government during the weeks or months they are receiving job training or job retraining.) Our government should have a program to financially assist workers and their families to relocate from areas of high unemployment to booming areas where jobs are readily available. Many areas need more quality day-care centers that charge reasonable rates so that single parents (and also two-parent families) can work. For the unemployed able-bodied, the government could be a "last resort" employer. In many other countries, the government offers tax incentives to industries to locate in depressed areas. Another suggestion is to encourage industries to hire workers who have been unemployed

for a long time by reimbursing the employers for a portion of the new workers' salaries.

SOCIAL WORK AND PUBLIC WELFARE

The preamble to the Code of Ethics of the National Association of Social Workers states:

> *The primary mission of the social work profession is to enhance human well-being and help meet basic human needs of all people, with particular attention to the needs and empowerment of people who are vulnerable, oppressed and living in poverty.*[70]

The Curriculum Policy Statements of the Council on Social Work Education state:

> *The purpose of social work education is to prepare competent, effective social work professionals who are committed to practice that includes services to the poor and oppressed, and who work to alleviate poverty, oppression, and discrimination.*[71]

These two statements clearly assert that the profession of social work and social work professionals have an obligation to work toward alleviating poverty.

Since the enactment of the 1935 Social Security Act, numerous social services have been provided to public assistance recipients. The particular services provided vary widely from area to area (depending on state and county decisions) but include counseling, day care, protective services, foster care, services to people with a physical or mental disability, information and referral, homemaker services, financial counseling, assistance in child rearing, family planning, health services, vocational training, and employment counseling. A large number of social workers are employed to provide such services.

Until 1972 social services and financial assistance were combined, and social workers were involved in financial eligibility determination. The 1972 Amendments to the Social Security Act separated services and assistance. Now public assistance recipients are informed of available social services and of their right to request such services. Financial eligibility is determined by staff who generally are not social workers.

Social workers find many gratifications in helping people with personal or social problems. Yet social work is frequently frustrating. The sources of these frustrations include:

■ Having extensive paperwork.

■ Trying to meet the needs of clients when those needs are not served by existing programs.

■ Trying to change the huge public welfare bureaucratic structure to better meet the needs of clients. (The public welfare system is slow to change to meet emerging needs and is filled with extensive "red tape.")

■ Having a larger caseload than one can optimally and effectively serve.

■ Trying to keep informed about the numerous changes (program, organizational, and eligibility determination) that occur on an ongoing basis.

■ Dealing with discouraged clients who lack the necessary motivation to work toward improving their circumstances. Social work "interns" in field placement and new social workers frequently report this as their greatest frustration and a severe "reality shock." They anticipate that, after carefully working out an "intervention plan" with a client to resolve some problem, the client will follow through. Unfortunately, in many cases this does not happen. Future appointments may be broken by the client, and even if the client responsibly keeps appointments, she or he is likely to have excuses for not following through on the commitment. These excuses can usually be interpreted to represent a lack of motivation.

Working with Discouraged People

The key variable in determining if clients will make positive changes in their lives is whether they have the motivation to make the efforts necessary to improve their circumstances. Failure in counseling or social work generally occurs when clients do not become motivated.

Many public assistance recipients are discouraged. Continued economic pressures and generally a long series of past "failure" experiences when they have tried to improve their circumstances frequently have sapped their motivation. Discouraged people tend to travel through life in an unhappy "rut" that is dull, stagnating, and generally unfulfilling but that is seen by them as normal and predictable. For them, extensive efforts to improve their circumstances are viewed as risky and frightening. Many feel it is safer to remain in their rut than to try something new that might further expose their weaknesses and result in psychological "hurt."

Seeking a job, finding transportation, and making day-care arrangements could be seen as overwhelmingly difficult for an unskilled single mother (on public assistance) who has never been employed previously. For a wife with five children who periodically is physically beaten by her husband, seeking counseling or making separation arrangements may be seen as highly risky because the future would be uncertain; she may also fear that such actions would only make her husband more abusive. For a person with a drinking problem who has recently lost his last two jobs, giving up drinking may be seen as giving up his main "crutch."

To motivate a discouraged person, the social worker has to be an "encouraging person." According to Lewis Losoncy, an encouraging person does the following:[72]

Has complete acceptance for the discouraged person and conveys "I accept you exactly as you are, with no conditions attached." (She or he should not, however, convey acceptance of the deviant behavior that needs to be changed.)

Has a nonblaming attitude so that the discouraged person no longer feels a need to lie, pretend, or wear a mask.

Conveys empathy that she or he is aware and can to some extent feel what the discouraged person is feeling.

Conveys to the discouraged person that she or he is genuinely interested in the counselee's progress and conveys that the counselee is an important, worthwhile person. In order for discouraged people to believe in themselves, they generally need an encouraging person who conveys the idea that they are important and worthwhile.

Notices (rewards) every small instance of progress—for example, if the person is wearing something new, the counselor says "That's new, isn't it? It really looks good on you." This is particularly valuable during the beginning of the relationship.

Conveys to the discouraged person that she or he has confidence in that person's capacity to improve.

Conveys sincere enthusiasm about the discouraged person's interests, ideas, and risk-taking actions.

Has the capacity to be a nonjudgmental listener so that the discouraged person's real thoughts and feelings can be expressed freely, without fear of censure.

Has the time to spend listening and understanding the discouraged person as fully as possible. Motivating a discouraged person takes a long, long time. Discouraged people generally have a long history of failures.

Has a sincere belief in the discouraged person's ability to find a purpose in life.

Allows the person to take risks without judging him or her.

Reinforces efforts made by the discouraged person. The important thing is that one tries and not necessarily whether one succeeds. By making efforts to improve, there is hope.

Helps the discouraged person to see the falsehood and negative consequences of self-defeating statements, such as "I'm a failure." Every person has skills and deficiencies, and every person should be encouraged to improve both strengths and weaknesses.

Recognizes that all that can be done is to give one's best efforts in trying to motivate a discouraged person. Success in motivating a discouraged person is not guaranteed. To give up hope of motivating a discouraged person means *one will no longer be effective in working with that person.*

Is skilled at looking for uniquenesses and strengths in an individual. These uniquenesses are communicated to the discouraged person so that the person begins to realize she or he is special and worthwhile. This process leads to a sense of improved self-worth and strengthens the courage to take risks and change.

Helps the discouraged person to develop perceptual alternatives (other ways of looking at life). For example, for a woman who is periodically physically beaten by her husband, it is appropriate to point out that other women in similar situations have separated from their husbands, which has led eventually either to an improved marital relationship or to a happier, independent life.

Is aware of the negative consequences of overdependency in a relationship. When the discouraged person is on the way to taking risks and making constructive changes, one should start to help the discouraged person to develop "self-encouragement," in which the client is encouraged to make and trust his or her own decisions and is encouraged to take more risks.

The Future

With the passage of the 1996 welfare reform act, our country is embarking on a critically important new course. The people who will be most affected by this new legislation will be the adult recipients and their children who are in this program. Will most of these families be successful in making this shift from welfare to work? Even if the adult recipients are successful in attaining employment, will their children be placed in quality child-care arrangements so that their lives are not adversely impacted?

Past experiences with the enactment of a major new social program suggest that, at first, there are apt to be significant difficulties that require some adjustments in the design of the program. For example, the 1935 Social Security Act has been amended numerous times to adjust to changing human needs. It appears our political leaders will give considerable attention to making the 1996 welfare reform program viable for a variety of reasons. The general public strongly supports the concept of welfare to work for unemployed single parents. Both Republican and Democratic political leaders have agreed this is the welfare program that should be provided in this country for unemployed parents with children, and these political leaders are committed to making the changes needed to make the program viable. Yet another reason that our political leaders will give considerable attention to making this program viable is because alternative programs for combating poverty (such as a family allowance program or a guaranteed-income program) are much more expensive. Other countries, such as Sweden, that have similar programs to assist public assistance recipients in obtaining employment have been able to make their programs viable.[73]

Make no mistake, however. We will soon be hearing heartbreaking stories about families who will be adversely impacted by this program. Adjustments will have to be made to alleviate these adverse effects.

Currently, the United States is experiencing social welfare changes as profound as those in the 1930s, when the Social Security Act inaugurated federally funded public assistance programs. In Chapter 1, it was noted that there is a "devolution revolution" occurring in the United States in regard to the provision of social services. Political leaders view block grants as a means of transferring decision-making power about social programs and human services from the federal government to the state and local levels.

It is clear that local communities will play increasingly important roles in developing programs and services for the poor and for other vulnerable populations. It is also clear that social work will be one of the primary professions called upon in local communities to develop approaches to meet the needs of populations-at-risk. Social work faces extraordinary challenges in the current era of diminishing federal responsibility. Social workers are being called upon to respond to the needs of people who are in dire straits resulting from the dismantling of the federal safety net.

In responding to the devolution revolution, social work practice will need to stress community building. Churches, civic clubs, and other institutions in the local community are being asked to "take up the slack" created by the federal government downsizing its support for social welfare programs. Healthy communities are able to respond to social problems by providing a web of support for families and individuals and fill the holes in the social service safety net that are resulting from the devolution revolution.

Poverty is interrelated to most other social problems. Therefore, if the poverty problem intensifies, there will probably be increases in crime, emotional disorders, infant mortality, inadequate health care, inner-city problems, substandard housing, alcoholism, the school dropout rate, malnutrition, child neglect, and suicide. If the 1996 welfare reform act fails, the poverty problem will be intensified, and there will be an escalation in the severity of many other problems.

SUMMARY

About 14% of our population lives below the poverty line. Poverty is relative to time and place. An agreed-on definition of poverty does not exist. The usual definitions are based on a lack of money, with annual income most commonly used to gauge who is poor. Income is defined using either an absolute approach or a relative approach. The pain of poverty involves not only financial hardships but also the psychological implications that being "poverty stricken" have for a person.

Huge income and wealth gaps exist between the highest fifth and lowest fifth in our society, and social mobility (movement up the social-status ladder) occurs rarely. Wealth perpetuates wealth and poverty perpetuates poverty. The ideology of individualism and the Protestant ethic still stigmatize the poor in our society.

Those most likely to be poor include female heads of households, children, people of color, the elderly, large families, those with limited education, the unemployed, and those living in pockets of poverty and high unemployment.

The causes of poverty are numerous. Poverty is interrelated to all other social problems. Therefore, almost every social service combats poverty to some extent. Some researchers have noted that the poor have a set of values and attitudes that constitutes a culture of poverty. There is now considerable controversy about whether this culture *perpetuates* poverty or is simply an *adaptation* to being poor.

In some ways, poverty is functional for society. For this and other reasons, some decision makers are not actively seeking to eradicate it.

The major income maintenance programs to combat poverty were created by the 1935 Social Security Act. The federal government's role in providing social insurance programs and public assistance programs was initiated by this act.

Social insurance programs (which are consistent with the institutional view of income transfers) receive less criticism than public assistance programs (which are consistent with the residual view of income transfers). There are many negative myths about public assistance programs, especially the now defunct AFDC program. A danger of punitive, stigmatized public assistance programs is that poverty and dependency may be passed on to succeeding generations.

In 1996 welfare reform legislation was enacted, which focuses on putting adult public assistance recipients with children to work. In 1935, when the AFDC program was enacted, it was thought best for single mothers to stay at home to raise their children. The 1996 welfare reform act maintains that single mothers (and fathers) must work.

Although the profession of social work has gratifications, it also has frustrations, including dealing with mounds of paperwork and red tape, working in a bureaucratic structure that is slow to respond to emerging needs, and working with discouraged people who do not follow through on "intervention plans" to improve their circumstances. To motivate discouraged clients, the social worker has to be an "encouraging person."

NOTES

1. William Kornblum and Joseph Julian, *Social Problems*, 9th ed. (Upper Saddle River, NJ: Prentice Hall, 1998), pp. 227–230.
2. Randolph E. Schmid, "Census Bureau: Poor Lose, Rich Win," *Wisconsin State Journal*, Sept. 30, 1997, 2A.
3. Kornblum and Julian, *Social Problems*, pp. 227–230.
4. Ibid., pp. 32–35.
5. Ibid.
6. Ibid., pp. 235–237.
7. Marilyn Flynn, "Public Assistance," in *Contemporary Social Work*, 2nd ed., Donald Brieland, Lela Costin, and Charles Atherton, eds. (New York: McGraw-Hill, 1980), p. 165.
8. Michael Harrington, *The Other America* (New York: Macmillan, 1962).
9. Schmid, "Census Bureau: Poor Lose, Rich Win," p. 2A.
10. Ibid.
11. Kornblum and Julian, *Social Problems*, p. 253.
12. Ibid., p. 253.
13. James W. Coleman and Donald R. Cressey, *Social Problems*, 6th ed. (New York: HarperCollins, 1996), pp. 156–159.
14. Kornblum and Julian, *Social Problems*, p. 229.
15. Ibid.
16. Ibid., pp. 227–231.
17. Ibid.
18. Quoted in Kornblum and Julian, *Social Problems*, p. 232.
19. Paul Samuelson, quoted in Kornblum and Julian, *Social Problems*, p. 230.
20. Coleman and Cressey, *Social Problems*, p. 162.
21. Ian Robertson, *Social Problems*, 2nd ed. (New York: Random House, 1980), p. 31.
22. James W. Coleman and Donald R. Cressey, *Social Problems*, 4th ed. (New York: Harper & Row, 1990), p. 161.
23. Schmid, "Census Bureau: Poor Lose, Rich Win," p. 2A.
24. Second inaugural address of President Franklin D. Roosevelt (Jan. 20, 1937).
25. President's Council of Economic Advisors, *Economic Report of the President* (Washington, DC: U.S. Government Printing Office, 1964), pp. 56–57.

26. Schmid, "Census Bureau: Poor Lose, Rich Win," p. 2A.
27. U.S. Bureau of the Census, *Statistical Abstract of the United States, 1997* (Washington, DC: U.S. Government Printing Office, 1997), p. 478.
28. Kornblum and Julian, *Social Problems,* p. 293.
29. *Statistical Abstract of the United States, 1997.*
30. Kornblum and Julian, *Social Problems,* pp. 240–242.
31. Ibid.
32. *Statistical Abstract of the United States, 1997,* p. 475.
33. Ibid.
34. *The Future of Children,* 7, no. 1 (Los Altos, CA: Center for the Future of Children, 1997).
35. American Association of Retired Persons, *A Profile of Older Americans, 1996* (Washington, DC: AARP, 1996).
36. R. V. Kail and J. C. Cavanaugh, *Human Development,* (Pacific Grove, CA: Brooks/Cole, 1996).
37. *Statistical Abstract of the United States, 1997.*
38. Ibid.
39. Kornblum and Julian, *Social Problems,* pp. 227–232.
40. Ibid.
41. *Statistical Abstract of the United States, 1997.*
42. Ibid.
43. Kornblum and Julian, *Social Problems,* pp. 242–243.
44. Harrington, *The Other America,* p. 21.
45. Oscar Lewis, "The Culture of Poverty," *Scientific American,* 215 (Oct. 1966), pp. 19–25.
46. Ibid., p. 23.
47. Eleanor Leacock, ed., *The Culture of Poverty: A Critique* (New York: Simon & Schuster, 1971).
48. Elliott Liebow, *Tally's Corner: A Study of Negro Street-Corner Men* (Boston: Little, Brown, 1967); Ulf Hannertz, *Soulside: An Inquiry into Ghetto Culture and Community* (New York: Columbia University Press, 1969); Leacock, *The Culture of Poverty.*
49. William Ryan, *Blaming the Victim,* rev. ed. (New York: Vintage Books, 1976).
50. Thomas Sullivan, Kendrick Thompson, Richard Wright, George Gross, and Dale Spady, *Social Problems* (New York: Wiley, 1980), p. 390.
51. Herbert J. Gans, *More Equality* (New York: Pantheon, 1968), pp. 133–135.
52. Helen M. Crampton and Kenneth K. Keiser, *Social Welfare: Institution and Process* (New York: Random House, 1970), p. 73.
53. These conservative views are summarized by Samuel Mencher, "Newburgh: The Recurrent Crisis in Public Assistance," *Social Work,* 7 (Jan. 1962), pp. 3–4.
54. Rex A. Skidmore and Milton G. Thackeray, *Introduction to Social Work,* 2nd ed. (Englewood Cliffs, NJ: Prentice Hall, 1976), pp. 111–112.
55. Coleman and Cressey, *Social Problems,* p. 162.
56. Charles Murray, *Losing Ground* (New York: Basic Books, 1986).
57. Ibid.
58. Kornblum and Julian, *Social Problems,* pp. 243–245.
59. Ibid.
60. Coleman and Cressey, *Social Problems,* pp. 166–179; Kornblum and Julian, *Social Problems,* pp. 243–245.
61. Kornblum and Julian, *Social Problems,* pp. 243–245.
62. Ibid.
63. A. Dale Tussing, "The Dual Welfare System," *Society,* 11 (Jan.–Feb. 1974), pp. 50–57.
64. Eleanor Cliff, "Benefits 'R' Us," *Newsweek,* Aug. 10, 1992, p. 56.
65. Charles Murray, *Losing Ground.*
66. Quoted in David Whitman, "The Next War on Poverty," *U.S. News & World Report,* Oct. 5, 1992, p. 38.
67. Ralph Dolgoff, Donald Feldstein, and Louise Skolnik, *Understanding Social Welfare,* 4th ed. (White Plains, NY: Longman, 1997), pp. 217–218.
68. Paul Glastris, "Was Reagan Right?" *U.S. News & World Report,* Oct. 20, 1997, p. 30.
69. Ibid.
70. Preamble to the Code of Ethics of the National Association of Social Workers, as adopted by the Delegate Assembly of Aug. 1966.
71. *Curriculum Policy Statement for Baccalaureate Degree Programs in Social Work Education* (Alexandria, VA: Council on Social Work Education, 1992); *Curriculum Policy Statement for Master's Degree Programs in Social Work Education* (Alexandria, VA: Council on Social Work Education, 1992).
72. Lewis Losoncy, *Turning People On* (Englewood Cliffs, NJ: Prentice Hall, 1977).
73. James Midgley and Michelle Livermore, "The Developmental Perspective in Social Work: Educational Implications for a New Century," *Journal of Social Work Education,* 33, no. 3 (Fall 1997), pp. 573–585.

5

EMOTIONAL/
BEHAVIORAL
PROBLEMS
AND
COUNSELING

Everyone, at times, has emotional problems and/or behavioral difficulties. This chapter will:

- Describe the nature and extent of such difficulties.
- Discuss the concept of mental illness.
- Present a theory about the causes of chronic mental illness.
- Present information about the homeless.
- Discuss controversial issues in the mental health field.
- Present research on the relationship between social structure and the rate of mental illness.
- Present a brief history of our society's treatment of the emotionally disturbed.
- Describe treatment approaches for emotional and behavioral problems.
- Describe the role of social work in the mental health field.

A PERSPECTIVE ON EMOTIONAL AND BEHAVIORAL PROBLEMS

Several years ago, I worked as a counselor at a maximum security hospital for the "criminally insane." A number of the residents at this hospital had committed bizarre crimes due to emotional and behavioral problems. I'll describe a few of these situations to give you an idea of what I encountered.

In one case, a 22-year-old male had decapitated his 17-year-old friend. In another, a married male with four children had been arrested for the fourth time for exposing himself. In still another, a male had dug up several graves and used corpses to "redecorate" his home. Another married man had been committed after it was discovered that he was involved in incestuous relationships with his 11- and 12-year-old daughters. Another man had been committed after trying to deliver sermons in local taverns and after repeatedly main-

taining that clouds followed him around in whatever direction he was going. Another inmate had brutally killed his father with an ax. Bizarre? Yes, definitely!

Is there a way to explain why these men did what they did? A variety of interpretations have been offered by different authorities, most of whom assert that they acted strangely because they were mentally ill.

Albert Ellis, a prominent psychologist, has advanced a different explanation that offers considerable promise for understanding and treating people who commit bizarre offenses. Ellis asserts that, if we look at what the offenders were thinking when they committed unusual offenses, we will be able to gain an understanding of (a) why the bizarre actions occurred, (b) what would have prevented them from happening, and (c) what services are now needed to prevent the offenders from again getting into trouble after their release.[1] In a nutshell, Ellis asserts the primary determinant of all of our actions are our thoughts (that is, thoughts → actions).

At the maximum security hospital, Ellis's interpretation was applied to the gravedigger's case. Jim Schmidt (the name has been changed) was 46 years old when he began digging up graves and redecorating his home. His mother had died three and a half years earlier. Unfortunately, his mother was the only person who had provided meaning to his life. He was shy and had no other friends, and the two had lived together in a small rural community for the past 22 years. After his mother's death, he became even more isolated. Being very lonely, he wished his mother were still alive. As happens with many people who lose someone close, he began dreaming that she was still alive. His dreams appeared so real that, on awakening, he found it difficult to believe his mother was definitely dead. He then began thinking that his mother could in fact be brought back to life and that bringing corpses of females to his home would help bring his mother back. (Now, to us this idea certainly appears irrational. But being isolated, Jim had no way of checking what was real and what was not.) He decided to give the idea a try.

EXHIBIT 5.1

Eating Disorders: A Continuing Problem

Eating disorders are recognized as very serious afflictions. As many as 20% of college females are estimated to have an eating disorder.

The three primary eating disorders are anorexia nervosa, bulimia nervosa, and compulsive overeating. Both anorexics and bulimics have an excessive concern with food and fatness, but their techniques for staying thin vary greatly. On the one hand, an anorexic eats very little food and is near starvation much of the time. Bulimics, on the other hand, binge and purge themselves.

Although the average American's food intake is around 3000 calories a day, bulimics may devour 40,000 to 60,000 calories a day. They typically binge on high-calorie junk food, such as sweets and fried foods. Because bulimics also want to stay thin, they purge themselves in a variety of ways, the most common of which is vomiting. Vomiting may be induced initially by putting the fingers down the throat. Some bulimics use cotton swabs or drink copious amounts of fluids. With practice, many bulimics gain control of their esophageal muscles so they can induce vomiting at will. Other methods of purging include excessive intake of laxatives; fasting; enemas; spitting out rather than swallowing food after it is chewed; and compulsive exercise, such as swimming, running, and working out with barbells and weights.

Bulimia, although it is much more common than anorexia, went unrecognized for a long time because the binging and purging cycle is almost always done in secret. Bulimics dread being exposed; as a result, very few will report their malady.

Bulimics tend to avoid forming close relationships with others, as they are aware it is difficult to conceal their binging and purging from close friends. They are often overachievers and in college tend to attain high academic averages. Purging often becomes a purification rite to overcome self-loathing. Through purging, they feel completely fresh and clean again, but these feelings of self-worth are only temporary. They are extremely sensitive to minor insults and frustrations, which are often used as excuses to initiate another food binge.

Anorexia nervosa is a disorder characterized by the relentless pursuit of thinness through voluntary starvation. Anorexics have a distorted body image. They refuse to accept the fact that they are too thin; they will not eat, even when experiencing intense hunger. They stubbornly insist that they need to lose even more weight from their already emaciated bodies. They also erroneously believe that having a perfect body (defined by society as a thin body) will ensure happiness and success. About 95% of all anorexia nervosa cases are females.

Compulsive overeating is the irresistible urge to consume excessive amounts of food; it is eating irrationally, chewing and digesting excessive amounts of food on a long-term basis. Treatment for compulsive overeating is recommended for individuals whose body weight is more than 20% over desirable weight.

Michael O. Koch, Virginia L. Dotson, and Thomas P. Troast describe the relationships among these eating disorders:

Eating disorders seem to exist on a continuum. On one end are the anorexics, who achieve drastic weight loss by severely restricting food intake. In the middle are the anorexic bulimics, who eat and even binge on occasion, but who still maintain a much lower than normal weight by a combination of strict dieting and purging. Also included are normal-weight bulimics who binge and purge but who are not significantly underweight. These bulimics usually diet when they are not binging and may repeatedly gain and lose ten or more pounds because of their food behaviors. At the other end of the continuum, the compulsive overeater will repeatedly binge,

(continued)

EXHIBIT 5.1 *(continued)*

gaining significant amounts of weight without engaging in any of the purging behaviors associated with anorexia or bulimia nervosa. Individuals may move back and forth along this continuum, alternatively restricting or binging, depending on their circumstances.

Anorexics and bulimics have some similarities. For example, both are likely to have been brought up in middle-class, upwardly mobile families in which the mothers were overinvolved in their lives and the fathers were preoccupied with work outside the home. For the most part, bulimics and anorexics were good children, eager to obtain the love and approval of others. Both tend to lack self-esteem, feel ineffective, and have a distorted body image that causes them to view themselves as fatter than others perceive them.

Anorexics and bulimics differ in that anorexics are generally younger, far less socially competent, and much more isolated from and dependent on the family. The anorexic stays away from food. In contrast, bulimics, during times of stress, turn toward food; they binge and then purge. Bulimics are usually able to function in social and work contexts. Their health may be gravely affected by binging and purging, but their lives are not necessarily in imminent danger, as is often the case with anorexics. Anorexics are also *very* thin, whereas bulimics are not as underweight and may even be overweight.

Why are bulimics and anorexics primarily women? One key reason is that our society places more pressure on women than on men to be slender and trim. Our socialization practices also overemphasize the importance of women being slender.

Anorexia, bulimia, and compulsive overeating are dangerous health disorders. Anorexics risk starvation, and both bulimics and anorexics risk serious health problems. Fat synthesis and accumulation are necessary for survival. Fatty acids are a major source of energy. When fat levels are depleted, the body must draw on carbohydrates (sugar). When sugar supplies dwindle, body metabolism decreases, which often leads to drowsiness, inactivity, pessimism, depression, dizziness, and fatigue. For compulsive overeaters, as one's weight increases over that recommended for one's body build, mortality rates increase as well. Obesity is a contributing factor to such health problems as hypertension, heart attacks, and diabetes.

For bulimics and anorexics, psychotropic drugs (tranquilizers and antidepressants) have variable effects on the body due to changes in metabolism. Abnormalities have been found in the electroencephalograms of people with eating disorders. Chronic vomiting may lead to gum disease and cavities due to the hydrochloric acid content of vomit. Vomiting can also lead to severe tearing and bleeding in the esophagus. Chronic vomiting may result in a potassium deficiency, which then may lead to muscle fatigue, weakness, numbness, erratic heartbeat, kidney damage, and in severe instances, paralysis.

A variety of treatment programs are available for anorexics, bulimics, and compulsive overeaters. Individual and group therapy programs have been developed to change the psychological thinking patterns that initiated and are sustaining the undesirable eating patterns. For those for whom severe health problems have already developed, medical care is essential. Therapy for eating disorders includes instruction in establishing and maintaining a nutritious diet. Some elementary, secondary, and higher-education school systems are now developing preventative programs that inform students about the risks of eating disorders and identify and provide services for students who have developed an eating disorder.

Source: Michael O. Koch, Virginia L. Dotson, and Thomas P. Troast, "Interventions with Eating Disorders," in *Social Work with Groups*, 4th ed., Charles Zastrow, ed. (Chicago: Nelson-Hall, 1997), pp. 463–484. Quotation is from pp. 465–466.

Jim, of course, needed counseling (then and now). Such services would help him adjust to his mother's death, find new interests in life, become more involved with other people, and exchange thoughts with others to check out what is real and what is not.

NATURE AND EXTENT OF EMOTIONAL AND BEHAVIORAL PROBLEMS

Emotional and behavioral problems are two comprehensive labels covering an array of disturbances: depression, excessive anxiety, feelings of inferiority or isolation, alienation, sadistic or masochistic tendencies, marital difficulties, broken romances, parent–child relationship difficulties, hyperactivity, unusual or bizarre behavior, aggressiveness, phobias, child or spousal abuse, compulsive or obsessive behavior, guilt, shyness, violent displays of temper, vindictiveness, nightmares or insomnia, sexual deviations, eating disorders, and so on.

Each problem has unique and sometimes numerous potential causes. Depression, for example, may stem from the loss of a loved one or of something highly valuable, from feelings of guilt or shame, from knowledge of an undesirable impending event (for example, discovery of a terminal illness), from aggression turned inward, from certain physical factors such as menopause, from feelings of inadequacy or inferiority, from self-denigrating thoughts, or from feelings of loneliness or isolation. Literally hundreds of thousands of books have been published on the causes and treatments of the wide array of emotional and behavioral problems.

One of every four Americans experiences some form of emotional or behavioral disorder at some point during any given year.[2] These disorders range from mild depression and anxiety to suicide ideation or a severe eating disorder such as anorexia. Every year more than 6 million people receive mental health care in the United States.[3]

WHAT IS MENTAL ILLNESS?

Much of the language relating to emotional and behavioral disturbances has become a part of everyday conversation. We use a number of terms to express a judgment (often unfavorable) about someone's unusual behavior or emotions; for example, we say that he or she is *crazy, weird, psychotic, neurotic, insane, sick, uptight,* or *mad,* or is having a *nervous breakdown* or acting like a *space cadet.* Amazingly, we act as if the label accurately describes the person, and we then relate to that person as if the label were correct and all-encompassing. However, it is impossible to precisely define any of these terms. What, for example, are the specific characteristics that distinguish a "psychotic" or a "space cadet" from other people?

There are two general approaches to viewing and diagnosing people who display emotional disturbances and abnormal behaviors: the medical model and the interactional model (which asserts that mental illness is a myth).

Medical Model

This model views emotional and behavioral problems as mental illness, comparable to physical illness. Medical labels (for example, schizophrenia, paranoia, psychosis, insanity) are thus applied to emotional problems. Adherents of the medical approach believe that the disturbed person's mind is affected by some generally unknown internal condition. That condition, they assert, might be due to genetic endowment, metabolic disorders, infectious diseases, internal conflicts, unconscious use of defense mechanisms, or traumatic early experiences that cause emotional fixations and prevent future psychological growth.

The medical-model approach arose in reaction to the historical notion that emotionally disturbed individuals were possessed by demons, were mad, were to be blamed for their disturbances, and were to be "treated" by being beaten, locked up, or killed. The medical model led to a perception of the disturbed as in need of help. It also stimulated research into the nature of emotional and behavioral problems and promoted the development of therapeutic approaches.

The major evidence for the validity of the medical-model approach comes from studies suggesting that some mental disorders, such as schizophrenia, may be influenced by genetics (heredity). The bulk of the evidence for the significance of heredity comes from studies of twins. For example, identical twins have been found to have a concordance rate (that is, if one has it, both have it) for schizophrenia of about 50%.[4] The rate of schizophrenia in the general population is about 1%.[5] So when one identical twin is schizophrenic, the other is 50 times more likely than the average to be schizophrenic. This suggests a causal influence of genes, but not genetic determination, since concordance for identical twins is only 50%, not 100%.

The medical model has a lengthy classification of mental disorders that are defined by the American Psychiatric Association (see Exhibit 5.2). Several specific mental disorders are discussed in the following material.[6]

SCHIZOPHRENIA

This malady encompasses a large group of disorders, usually of psychotic proportion, manifested by disturbances of language and communication, thought, perception, affect, and behavior and lasting longer than 6 months.

DELUSIONAL DISORDER

The essential feature is the presence of one or more delusions that persist for at least 1 month. A delusion is something that is falsely believed or propagated. An example is the persecutory type, in which an individual erroneously believes that he or she is being conspired against, cheated, spied on, followed, poisoned or drugged, maliciously maligned, harassed, or obstructed in the pursuit of long-term goals.

HYPOCHONDRIASIS

This is a chronic maladaptive style of relating to the environment through preoccupation with shifting somatic concerns and symptoms, a fear or conviction that one has a serious physical illness, the search for medical treatment, inability to accept reassurance, and either hostile or dependent relationships with caregivers and family.

BIPOLAR DISORDER

This is a major affective disorder characterized by episodes of both mania and depression; it was formerly called manic-depressive psychosis. Bipolar disorder may be subdivided into manic, depressed, or mixed types on the basis of currently presenting symptoms.

PHOBIA

A phobia is characterized by an obsessive, persistent, unrealistic, intense fear of an object or situation. A few common phobias are *acrophobia* (fear of heights), *algophobia* (fear of pain), *claustrophobia* (fear of closed spaces), and *erythrophobia* (fear of blushing).

PERSONALITY DISORDERS

Some of the most common personality disorders and their characteristics are:

■ *Paranoid.* A pattern of distrust and suspiciousness such that others' motives are interpreted as malevolent.

■ *Schizoid.* A pattern of detachment from social relationships and a restricted range of emotional expression.

■ *Schizotypal.* A pattern of acute discomfort in close relationships, cognitive or perceptual distortions, and eccentricities of behavior.

■ *Antisocial.* A pattern of disregard for, and violation of, the rights of others.

■ *Borderline.* A pattern of instability in interpersonal relationships, self-image, and affect; also characterized by marked impulsivity.

■ *Histrionic.* A pattern of excessive emotionality and attention seeking.

■ *Narcissistic.* A pattern of grandiosity, need for admiration, and lack of empathy.

■ *Avoidant.* A pattern of social inhibition, feelings of inadequacy, and hypersensitivity to negative evaluation.

EXHIBIT 5.2

Major Mental Disorders as Defined by the American Psychiatric Association

DISORDERS USUALLY DIAGNOSED IN INFANCY, CHILDHOOD, OR ADOLESCENCE

These include, but are not limited to, mental retardation, learning disorders, communication disorders (such as stuttering), autism, attention-deficit/hyperactivity disorders, and separation-anxiety disorder.

DELIRIUM, DEMENTIA, AND AMNESTIC AND OTHER COGNITIVE DISORDERS

These include delirium due to alcohol and other drug intoxication, dementia due to Alzheimer's disease or Parkinson's disease, dementia due to head trauma, and amnestic disorder.

SUBSTANCE-RELATED DISORDERS

This category includes mental disorders related to abuse of alcohol, caffeine, amphetamines, cocaine, hallucinogens, nicotine, and other mind-altering substances.

SCHIZOPHRENIA AND OTHER PSYCHOTIC DISORDERS

This category includes delusional disorders and all forms of schizophrenia (such as paranoid, disorganized, and catatonic).

MOOD DISORDERS

These include emotional disorders such as depression and bipolar disorders.

ANXIETY DISORDERS

This category includes phobias, posttraumatic stress disorder, generalized anxiety disorder, acute stress disorder, and substance-induced anxiety disorder.

SOMATOFORM DISORDERS

These are psychological problems that manifest themselves as symptoms of physical disease (for example, hypochondria).

DISSOCIATIVE DISORDERS

This category includes problems in which part of the personality is dissociated from the rest, such as dissociative identity disorder (formerly called multiple personality disorder).

SEXUAL AND GENDER IDENTITY DISORDERS

This category includes sexual dysfunctions (such as hypoactive sexual desire, premature ejaculation, male erectile disorder, male and female orgasmic disorders, and vaginismus), exhibitionism, fetishism, pedophilia (child molestation), sexual masochism, sexual sadism, voyeurism, and gender identity disorders (such as cross-gender identification).

EATING DISORDERS

This category includes anorexia nervosa, bulimia nervosa, and compulsive overeating.

SLEEP DISORDERS

This classification includes insomnia and other problems with sleep (such as nightmares and sleepwalking).

IMPULSE-CONTROL DISORDERS

These disorders relate to the inability to control certain undesirable impulses (for example, kleptomania, pyromania, and pathological gambling).

(continued)

EXHIBIT 5.2   *(continued)*

ADJUSTMENT DISORDERS

These involve difficulty in adjusting to the stress created by such common events as unemployment or divorce.

PERSONALITY DISORDERS

This category refers to an enduring pattern of inner experience and behavior that deviates markedly from the expectations of the individual's culture, is pervasive and inflexible, has an onset in adolescence or early adulthood, is stable over time, and leads to distress or impairment. Examples include paranoid personality disorder, antisocial personality disorder, and obsessive-compulsive personality disorder.

OTHER CONDITIONS

This category covers a variety of other disorders that may be a focus of clinical attention. The category includes parent–child relational problems; partner relational problems; sibling relational problems; child victimization of physical abuse, sexual abuse, and neglect; adult victimization of physical and sexual abuse; malingering; bereavement; academic problems; occupational problems; identity problems; and religious or spiritual problems.

Source: DSM-IV (The Diagnostic and Statistical Manual of Mental Disorders), 4th ed. (Washington, DC: American Psychiatric Association, 1994).

■ *Dependent.* A pattern of submissive and clinging behavior related to an excessive need to be taken care of.

■ *Obsessive-Compulsive.* A pattern of preoccupation with orderliness, perfectionism, and control.

The DSM-IV categories are used in the systems of reimbursement from health insurance policies to mental health providers for the provision of psychotherapy to individuals and groups.

Interactional Model

Critics of the mental-illness approach assert that medical labels have no diagnostic or treatment value and frequently have an adverse effect.

Thomas Szasz, in the 1950s, was one of the first authorities to state that mental illness is a myth—that it does not exist.[7] Szasz's theory is interactional; it focuses on the processes of everyday social interaction and the effects of labeling on people. Beginning with the assumption that the term *mental illness* implies a "disease in the mind," Szasz categorizes all of the so-called mental illnesses into three types of emotional/behavioral disorders and discusses the inappropriateness of calling such human difficulties "mental illnesses":

1. *Personal disabilities,* such as excessive anxiety, depression, fears, and feelings of inadequacy. Another term for personal disabilities is *unwanted emotions.* Szasz says these so-called mental illnesses may appropriately be considered "mental" (in the sense that thinking and feeling are considered "mental" activities), but they are not diseases.

2. *Antisocial acts,* such as bizarre homicides and other social deviations. Homosexuality used to be in this category but was removed from the American Psychiatric Association's list of mental illnesses in 1974. Szasz says such antisocial acts are only social deviations; they are neither "mental" nor "diseases."

3. *Deterioration of the brain with associated personality changes.* This category includes the

CASE
EXAMPLE 5.1 A Mental-Illness Model Interpretation

Dan Vanda was arrested for stabbing his parents to death. He was 22 years old and had always been described as a "loner" by neighbors. In elementary school, junior high, and high school, he was frequently absent, had no close friends, and received mostly failing grades. School records showed that teachers had informed protective services on three occasions that they believed his parents were abusing and neglecting him. Protective services' records indicated that his parents were uncooperative but that sufficient evidence could not be found to justify placement in a foster home.

At the time of his arrest, Dan appeared confused. He said he was in communication with King David (the David in the Bible who slew Goliath), who told him to slay his parents because they were out to get him. He tended to ramble on with incoherent statements from the Bible, and he also stated that cosmic rays were in control of people. At his arrest, he appeared to be expecting congratulations for what he had done rather than incarceration.

The court ordered a 90-day observation period in a maximum security hospital for the mentally ill to determine his sanity.

Neighbors and school officials could add little to explain his actions. He had dropped out of school at age 16. Neighbors felt that he was "weird" and had ordered their children not to associate with him. They reported that they sometimes saw him butchering birds. When they asked him why, he said he was being advised by Alfred Hitchcock (director of the film *The Birds*) to do this to prevent an attack.

Psychiatrists concluded that Dan was paranoid schizophrenic. It was felt his insanity was such that he would not be able to understand the nature of court proceedings connected with his offense. With this recommendation, the court committed him indefinitely to a maximum security psychiatric hospital.

"mental illnesses" in which personality changes result following brain deterioration from such causes as Alzheimer's disease, arteriosclerosis, chronic alcoholism, general paresis, AIDS, or serious brain damage caused by an accident. Common symptoms are loss of memory, listlessness, apathy, and deterioration of personal grooming habits. Szasz says these disorders can appropriately be considered "diseases," but they are diseases of the brain rather than diseases of the mind.

According to Szasz, the notion that people with emotional problems are mentally ill is as absurd as the belief that the emotionally disturbed are possessed by demons: "The belief in mental illness as something other than man's trouble in getting along with his fellow man is the proper heir to the belief in demonology and witchcraft. Mental illness exists or is real in exactly the same sense in which witches existed or were real."[8]

In actuality, there are three steps to becoming labeled mentally ill: (a) The person displays unwanted emotions (such as depression) or some strange, deviant behaviors; (b) the emotions or behaviors are not tolerated by family or local community, and as a result, the person is referred for an evaluation to a mental health professional; and (c) the mental health professional, usually a psychiatrist, happens to believe in the medical model and assigns a mental-illness label. Thomas Scheff and David Mechanic provide independent evidence that whether the family or community will tolerate the deviant behavior and whether the mental health professional believes in the medical model are more crucial in determining whether someone will be assigned a label of mentally ill than are the emotions or behaviors exhibited by the person.[9]

The point that Szasz and many other writers are striving to make is that people *do* have emotional problems, but they *do not* have a mystical mental illness. Terms that describe behavior are very useful—for example, depression, anxiety, obsession, compulsion, excessive fear, hallucinations, feelings of failure. Such terms describe personal problems that people have. But the medical terms are not useful because there is no distinguishing symptom that would indicate whether a person does or does not have the "illness." In addition, Caplan points out there is considerable variation among cultures regarding what is defined as a mental illness.[10] (Russia, for example, used to define protests against the government as a symptom of mental illness.) The usefulness of the medical model is also questioned because psychiatrists frequently disagree on the medical diagnosis to be assigned to those who are disturbed.[11]

In a dramatic study, psychologist David Rosenhan demonstrated that professional staff in mental hospitals could not distinguish "insane" patients from "sane" patients.[12] Rosenhan and seven "normal" associates went to 12 mental hospitals in five different states claiming they were hearing voices; all eight were admitted. After admission, these pseudopatients stated that the voices had stopped, and they behaved normally. The hospitals, unable to distinguish their "sane" status from the "insane" status of other patients, kept them hospitalized for an average of 19 days. All were then discharged with a diagnosis of "schizophrenia in remission."

The use of medical labels, it has been asserted, has several adverse effects.[13] People labeled mentally ill believe that they have a disease for which there may be no known "cure." The label gives people an excuse for not taking responsibility for their actions (for example, pleading innocent by reason of insanity). Because there is no known "cure," the disturbed frequently idle away their time waiting for someone to discover a cure rather than assuming responsibility for their behavior, examining the reasons for their problems, and making efforts to improve. Other undesirable consequences of being labeled mentally ill are that the individuals may lose some of their legal rights; may be stigmatized in social interactions as being dangerous, unpredictable, untrustworthy, or of "weak" character; and may find it difficult to secure employment or receive a promotion.[14]

The question of whether mental illness exists is indeed important. The assignment of mental-illness labels to disturbed people has substantial implications for how the disturbed will be treated, for how others will view them, and for how they will view themselves. Cooley's "looking-glass-self" approach crystalizes what is being said here.[15] The "looking glass" means we develop our self-concept in terms of how other people react to us. People are likely to respond to those labeled mentally ill as if they were mentally ill. As a result, those labeled mentally ill may well define themselves as being different or "crazy" and begin playing that role. Authorities who adhere to the interactional model raise a key question: "If we relate to people with emotional/behavioral problems as if they are mentally ill, how can we expect them to act in emotionally healthy and responsible ways?"

Compared to a physical illness, a diagnosis of a mental illness carries a greater stigma. In 1972 Senator Thomas Eagleton was forced to withdraw his candidacy for vice president on the Democratic ticket after it was revealed that he had received electroshock treatments for depression. The leaders of the Democratic party feared that the public would perceive someone who had once received psychiatric help as too "unstable" and "dangerous" to be in line for the presidency. On the other hand, Franklin Roosevelt had a physical disability resulting from polio, but he was elected president four times.

Szasz also argues that the mental-illness approach is used (perhaps unintentionally) as a means of control over people who do not conform to social expectations.[16] The former Soviet Union had a long history of labeling dissenters (including literary figures and intellectuals who would

Questioning the Usefulness of the Mental-Illness Concept

While working at a mental hospital, I was assigned the case of George, a 22-year-old male who had decapitated a 17-year-old female friend, Emily (not their real names). Two psychiatrists diagnosed him as schizophrenic, and a court found him "innocent by reason of insanity." He was then committed to a mental hospital.

Why did George do it? Labeling him as insane provides an explanation to the general public that he committed this tragic murder because he was "crazy." But does such a label explain why he killed Emily rather than killing someone else or committing some other bizarre act? Does the label explain what would have prevented him from committing this act? Does the label suggest the kind of treatment that will cure him? The answer to all these questions is, of course, no.

WHAT IS SCHIZOPHRENIA?

As noted earlier, schizophrenia is commonly defined as a psychotic condition characterized by disturbances of language and communication, thought, perception, affect, and behavior and lasting longer than 6 months. People who have Alzheimer's disease exhibit all these symptoms. Are they schizophrenic? No. What about the severely and profoundly mentally retarded who have a mental age of less than 2? They have these symptoms but are not considered schizophrenic. What about people who go into a coma following a serious accident? They also fit the definition but are not considered schizophrenic. The 22-year-old male who committed the bizarre homicide knew the act was wrong, was aware of what he was doing, was in contact with reality, and told me his reasons for doing what he did. Then why was *he* labeled schizophrenic?

Many authorities are now asserting that there is no definition of symptoms that separates people who have this "disease" from those who do not. I generally agree with Albert Ellis's assertion that the reasons for the occurrence of any deviant act can be determined by examining what the offender was thinking prior to and during the commission of the act.[a]

THE REASONS UNDERLYING THE SEXUAL ASSAULT AND MURDER

After George described what had happened, it was understandable (even though bizarre) why he had done what he did. His account also identified the specific problems he needed help with. He described himself as a very isolated person who, except for Emily, had no close relatives or friends. He came from a broken home and was raised by a series of relatives and in foster homes. Because of frequent moves, he attended a number of different schools and made no lasting friends. At age 20, George met Emily and dated her periodically for 2 years. She provided the only real meaning that he had in life. He held the traditional vision of marrying her and living happily ever after. However, a few months before the fatal day, he became very alarmed that he was going to "lose her." She encouraged him to date others, mentioned that she wanted to date others, and suggested that they no longer see as much of each other.

[a] Albert Ellis, *Reason and Emotion in Psychotherapy* (New York: Lyle Stuart, 1962).

George thought long and hard about how he could preserve the relationship. He also realized he had rather intense sexual tensions for which he had no outlet. Putting the two together, he naively concluded: "If I'm the first person to have sexual relations with her, she will forever feel tied to me." He therefore tried on several occasions to have intercourse, but she always managed to dissuade him. Finally, one afternoon during the summer, when he knew they would be alone together, he arrived at the following decision: "I *will* have sex with her this afternoon, even if I have to knock her unconscious." He stated that he knew such action was wrong but, "It was my last hope of saving our relationship. Without her, life would not be worth living."

He again tried to have sexual relations with Emily that afternoon, but she continued to discourage him. George then took a soda bottle and knocked her unconscious. He attempted to have coitus but was unsuccessful for reasons related to her physical structure. In an intense state of emotional and sexual excitement, he was unable to rationally consider the consequences of his actions. (All of us, at times, have done things while angry or in a state of intense emotional excitement that we would not have done in a calmer state.) At this point, he felt his whole world was caving in. When asked during an interview what he was thinking at this point, he stated, "I felt that if I couldn't have her, no one else would either." He sought and found a knife, became further carried away with emotions, and ended up slaying her. He knew it was wrong, and he was aware of what he was doing.

From talking with George (and identifying his thinking before and during this bizarre murder), I was able to pinpoint certain factors that led to the murder: his loneliness and isolation, his feeling that the romantic relationship was the only source of meaning in his life, his naive thinking that a forced sexual relationship would make Emily feel tied and attracted to him, his having no outlet for his sexual drives, and his jealous and possessive desires to go to extreme lengths to prevent her from developing a romantic relationship with another male. Such reasons help to explain why the bizarre behavior took place, whereas the label *schizophrenia* does not.

If the foregoing problems had been identified and treated prior to the murder, the slaying might have been prevented. What George needed was to find other sources of interest and other meaningful relationships in his life. Joining organizations in the community and developing hobbies may have helped. An appropriate sexual outlet probably would have also been helpful. Reducing the intensity of his jealous and possessive feelings, along with developing more mature attitudes toward romance and sexuality, might also have been preventative. These specific problems are the ones that will have to be addressed during his hospitalization. In no way do I feel that George should be excused for his actions, as implied by the term "innocent by reason of insanity." But he does need help for these problems. (In 10 or 12 years he will probably be released; if these problems are not rectified, he will be a danger to society upon his release.)

If you are wondering how anyone could reach a point at which he does something as bizarre as slaying someone he loves, remember that it is necessary to attempt to view the situation from the deviant person's perspective. You must try to consider all the circumstances, pressures, values, and belief systems of the deviant person.

(continued)

CASE
EXAMPLE 5.2   *(continued)*

Another example highlights the fact that practically anyone will do something bizarre when circumstances become desperate: Several years ago a passenger plane crashed in the Andes Mountains in the wintertime. A number of people were killed, but there were nearly 30 survivors. Rescue efforts initially failed to locate the survivors, who took shelter from the cold in the wreckage of the plane. The survivors were without food for over 40 days before they were finally rescued. During this time, they were faced with the choice of dying of starvation or cannibalizing those who had died. It was a desperate, difficult decision. (Psychologically, many people who commit a bizarre act feel they are facing a comparably desperate decision.) In this situation, all but one of the initial crash survivors chose cannibalism. The one who refused died of starvation.

Source: Adapted from an article written by Charles Zastrow, "When Labeled Mentally Ill," in *The Personal Problem Solver,* eds. Charles Zastrow and Dae H. Chang. © 1977. Used by permission of the publisher, Prentice-Hall/A division of Simon and Schuster, Englewood Cliffs, NJ.

be respected in this country) as mentally ill and then sending them to concentration camps or to insane asylums. In the past, psychiatrists in Russia often concluded that people who did not accept the Marxist–Leninist philosophy were psychologically impaired.

Are some psychiatrists using mental-illness labels to control the behavior of nonconformists in our country? Szasz asserts that they are and uses the example of homosexuality—listed as a mental disorder by the American Psychiatric Association until 1974. As another example, Szasz cites Dana L. Farnsworth, a Harvard psychiatrist and an authority on college psychiatric services:

> *Library vandalism, cheating and plagiarism, stealing in the college or community stores or in the dormitories, unacceptable or antisocial sexual practices (overt homosexuality, exhibitionism, promiscuity), and the unwise and unregulated use of harmful drugs are examples of behavior that suggest the presence of emotionally unstable persons. . . .*[17]

Mental-illness labels do have a "boundary" effect; they define what behaviors a society defines as "sick," with pressures then being put on citizens to avoid such behaviors. Szasz's point is that

a number of nonconformists are adversely affected by the use of the medical model to control their behavior.

Adherents to the interactional approach assert that mental illness is a myth. They maintain that people are labeled mentally ill for two main reasons: They may have an intense unwanted emotion, or they may be engaged in dysfunctional (or deviant) behavior. Assigning a mental-illness label to unwanted emotions or dysfunctional behaviors does not tell us how the emotions or behaviors originated, nor does it tell us how to treat such emotions and behaviors. The material presented later in this chapter on rational therapy does both: It gives us an approach for identifying the sources of unwanted emotions and dysfunctional behaviors and provides strategies for changing them.

LABELING AS THE CAUSE OF CHRONIC "MENTAL ILLNESS"

A question is frequently raised about Szasz's assertion that mental illness is a myth: "If you assert that mental illness doesn't exist, why do some people go through life as if they are mentally ill?" Thomas Scheff has developed a sociological theory that provides an answer.[18] Scheff's main hypothesis is that labeling is the most important determinant of people's displaying a chronic (long-term) mental illness.

Scheff begins by defining how he determines, for research purposes, who is mentally ill. Before giving his definition, he notes:

One source of immediate embarrassment to any social theory of "mental illness" is that the terms used in referring to these phenomena in our society prejudge the issue. The medical metaphor "mental illness" suggests a determinate process which occurs within the individual: the unfolding and development of disease. In order to avoid this assumption, we will utilize sociological, rather than medical, concepts to formulate the problem.[19]

He goes on to state that the symptoms of mental illness can be viewed as violations of social norms and that he uses the term *mental illness* only to refer to those assigned such a label by professionals (usually psychiatrists).

Scheff indicates that thousands of studies have been conducted that seek to identify the origins of long-term mental disorders. Practically all of this research has focused on internal causes (for example, metabolic disorders, unconscious conflicts, chemical imbalances, heredity factors). These research efforts have been based on medical and psychological models of human behavior. Yet, amazingly, in spite of this extensive investigation, the determinants of chronic mental disorders (for example, schizophrenia) are largely unknown.

Scheff suggests that researchers may be looking in the wrong direction. He asserts that the major determinants are not inside a person but in social processes—that is, in interactions with others. Here's a brief summary of his theory.

Everyone, at times, violates social norms and commits acts that could be labeled as symptoms of mental illness. For example, a person may occasionally get in fights with others, experience intense depression or grief, be highly anxious, use drugs or alcohol to excess, display a fetish, or commit a highly unusual or bizarre act.

Usually the person who has unwanted emotions or who commits deviant acts is not identified (labeled) as mentally ill. His or her emotions and actions are ignored, unrecognized, or rationalized in some other manner.

Occasionally, however, such norm violations are perceived by others as "abnormal." The offenders are then labeled mentally ill and consequently are related to as if they were mentally ill. Being highly suggestible to cues from others, they then begin to define and perceive themselves as mentally ill.

Traditional stereotypes define the mentally ill role, both for those who are labeled mentally ill and for the people they interact with. Those labeled mentally ill are often rewarded for enacting that social role. They are given sympathy and attention and are excused from holding a job, fulfilling other role requirements, and being held responsible for their wrongdoings.

In addition, those labeled mentally ill are punished for attempting to return to conventional roles. They are viewed with suspicion and implicitly considered to still be insane. They may have considerable difficulty obtaining employment or receiving a job promotion.

Such pressures and interactions with others gradually lead to changes in their self-concept; they begin to view themselves as different, as insane. Often a vicious circle is created. The more they enact the mentally ill role, the more they are defined and treated as mentally ill; the more explicitly they are defined as mentally ill, the more they are related to as if they are mentally ill, and so on. Unless this vicious circle is interrupted, it will lead to a career of long-term mental illness. Scheff's conclusion is that the labeling is the single most important determinant of chronic mental illness.

Accordingly, significant changes are needed in diagnostic and treatment practices. Mental health personnel are frequently faced with uncertainty in deciding whether a person has a mental disorder. An informal norm has been developed to handle this uncertainty: When in doubt, it is better to judge a well person ill than to judge an ill person well. This norm is based on two assumptions: (a) A diagnosis of illness results in only minimal damage to one's status and reputation. (b) Unless the illness is treated, it will become progressively worse. However, both these assumptions are questionable. Unlike medical treatment, psychiatric treatment can drastically change a person's status in the community; for example, it can remove rights that are difficult to regain. Furthermore, if Scheff is right about the adverse effects of mental-illness labeling, then the exact opposite norm should be established to handle uncertainty (when in doubt, do not label a person mentally ill). This would be in accord with the legal approach, "When in doubt, acquit" or "A person is innocent until proved guilty."

If labeling is indeed a major determinant of mental illness, then certain changes are called for in treating violators of social norms. One is to attempt to maintain and treat people with problems in their local community without labeling them mentally ill or sending them to a mental hospital where their playing the role of the mentally ill is likely to be reinforced. The field of mental health has, in the past several years, been moving in this direction. Another outgrowth of Scheff's theory would be increasing public education efforts to inform the general population of the nature of emotional/behavioral problems and the adverse effects that result from inappropriate labeling.

OTHER ISSUES

There are other issues at stake in the field of mental health. These include care for the homeless, the civil rights of those labeled mentally ill, the improper use of the insanity plea to excuse criminals from their actions, the use (or misuse) of drugs in "treating" supposedly mentally ill people, and the merits and shortcomings of managed mental health-care systems.

The Homeless

One of the population groups that has received considerable media attention is the homeless. Having hundreds of thousands of people homeless in the richest nation in the world is a national disgrace. The number of homeless Americans is large and growing larger. The exact number is unknown, but estimates range from 250,000 to over 3 million people.[20] Many of the homeless are living on the street, in parks, in subways, or in abandoned buildings. Food is often sought from garbage cans.

An estimated 25% to 50% of the homeless are thought to suffer from serious and chronic forms of mental illness.[21] Discharged from institutions without the support they need, tens of thousands of former patients live on the street in abominable conditions. Instead of providing support services for discharged patients, many states have a deinstitutionalization program of simply drugging people and dumping them into the street.

Such an approach is a far cry from what was envisioned 30 years ago when federal authorities embarked on an ambitious program to phase out large state hospitals and move the disturbed to more humane and convenient treatment in communities. This commendable goal has not been fulfilled. Federal, state, and local governments have failed to provide enough housing, transitional care, and job training to integrate patients into society. In many areas of the country, a revolving-door policy prevails: Patients are discharged from state hospitals, only to return to the hospitals again because of a lack of community support.

It is true that institutional care not only is expensive (over $50,000 per person per year[22]) but frequently also stifles the intellectual, social, and physical growth of patients. But tragically, the necessary supportive services have not been developed in most communities to serve discharged patients.

There are a variety of reasons for the large increase in the number of homeless. Deinstitutionalization of state mental hospitals is one cause. Cutbacks in social services by the federal government is another. Urban renewal projects have demolished low-cost housing in many areas. The shift from blue-collar jobs to service and high-tech jobs in our society has sharply reduced the demand for unskilled labor. Another factor has been a recent trend to ignore members of our

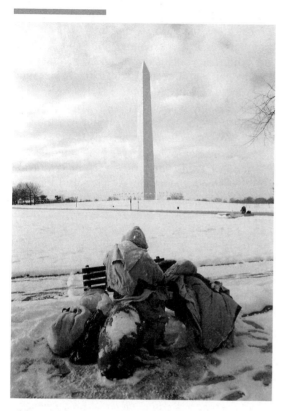

Although the number of homeless in America is unknown, estimates range from 250,000 to over 3 million people. Many sleep in streets, subways, parks, abandoned buildings, and cars. Our nation's capital is no exception.

society who are unable to fend for themselves. Most of the homeless are such because they cannot afford the housing that is available; our country does not have a commitment to a social policy of providing affordable housing to the poor. The majority of the homeless are not mentally ill, but simply too poor to afford available housing.

Solutions to the dismal conditions in which the homeless are living include low-cost housing, job training and placement programs, and community services for those with emotional problems. Is our society willing to provide the necessary resources to meet the needs of the homeless? Deplorably, the answer is, "No. Not at present."

Civil Rights

State laws have permitted the involuntary confinement of people in mental hospitals, which can be seen as an infringement of their civil right to liberty. Although state laws vary, in some jurisdictions, people can be hospitalized without their consent and without due process.[23] Often all that is required for confinement is the statement of a physician.[24]

When I worked at a hospital for the "criminally insane," there was a patient who was originally arrested on a disorderly conduct charge for urinating on a fire hydrant. Some neighbors thought he might be mentally ill, so the judge ordered that he be sent to a mental hospital for a 60-day observation period to determine his sanity. The hospital judged him "insane" and "incompetent to stand trial" on the charge. He was not considered a threat to himself or to others. But because of the hospital's finding, the judge confined him to a maximum security hospital for the criminally insane. When I met him there, he had already been hospitalized for 9 years—for committing an offense for which, if found guilty, he probably would only have been required to pay a small fine. Involuntary confinement has been a controversial practice for years.

Today, in most jurisdictions, persons cannot be involuntarily confined unless they commit illegal acts (such as aggravated assaults or suicide attempts) that demonstrate they are a threat either to themselves or to others. Such a policy provides some assurance that emotionally disturbed individuals' right to liberty will be safeguarded. But the policy also has been sharply criticized. Emotionally disturbed persons who provide warning signs of doing bodily harm to others cannot be involuntarily confined unless they actually commit an illegal act. As a result, the civil right of others to safety in our society is sometimes infringed upon.

Striking an acceptable balance between the disturbed person's right to liberty and society's right to safety and protection is complex. Throughout our nation's history, policies on this issue have swung back and forth on the continuum between these two sets of rights.

Another problem in some mental hospitals is that patients do not receive adequate treatment, even after several years of confinement. Lack of treatment became a civil rights violation when, in 1964, Congress established a statutory right to treatment in the Hospitalization of the Mentally Ill Act.[25]

Decisions about providing treatments such as electroconvulsive therapy (which has questionable value and may cause brain damage) also raise civil rights questions. The severely disturbed are often unable to make rational choices about their own welfare. Permission of relatives is sometimes obtained, but this still denies patients their fundamental rights.

These problems caused the President's Commission on Mental Health to recommend in 1978 that due process be followed in arriving at decisions involving enforced hospitalization and treatment.[26] Federal court decisions have also reflected these concerns; they have held that mental illness is not a sufficient basis for denying liberty and that hospitalized mental patients have a right to either adequate treatment or release.[27]

Plea of Innocent by Reason of Insanity

In 1979 a San Francisco jury found Dan White innocent by reason of insanity on charges of the premeditated murder of Mayor George Moscone and Supervisor Harvey Milk. This verdict was rendered even though testimony clearly showed that the murders had been carefully planned and carried out by White.[28] The general public was as shocked by the jury's decision as it had been by the crime. White was confined in a mental hospital for a few years and then released in 1984. (He subsequently committed suicide.)

In 1982 John Hinckley, Jr., was found innocent by reason of insanity for the attempted assassination of President Reagan a year earlier. Three other people were also injured by Hinckley in the assassination attempt. He is currently receiving treatment in a mental hospital.

In another case, Kenneth Bianchi (called the Hollywood "Hillside Strangler") was accused of murdering 13 women in the Los Angeles area and 2 more in Washington State in the 1970s. Six different psychiatrists examined him and came to three different conclusions about his mental state: Two judged him sane, two judged him insane, and two were undecided.[29]

Cases such as those of White, Hinckley, and Bianchi have forced the courts and psychiatrists to begin to examine more carefully the plea of innocent by reason of insanity. As indicated earlier, the terms *mental illness* and *mental health* are poorly defined. Mental illness (insanity) may not even exist. In a number of trials involving the insanity plea, it has become routine for the prosecuting attorney to use as witnesses those psychiatrists who are likely to judge the defendant "sane," whereas the defendant's attorney uses as witnesses those psychiatrists who are likely to arrive at an "insane" recommendation. An authority notes:

> *Among psychiatrists, there is nothing remotely approaching a consensus on what constitutes insanity. Moreover, psychiatrists themselves concede that they lack reliable means for determining whether a person was insane in any sense at the time of a crime. All too often, they must rely heavily on the accused's behavior and on what he tells them—two types of data that a shrewd defendant can carefully orchestrate.*[30]

Defendants are increasingly becoming aware that they can probably get a psychiatrist to label them insane by "acting crazy," such as by openly performing indecent acts or by claiming to hear voices.

The argument for eliminating the insanity plea is that people are literally using it to get away with murder and other serious felonies. Instead of forcing people to take responsibility for their felonies, the insanity plea excuses them for their crimes. The plea enables a clever defendant or attorney to seek refuge from criminal punishment.

When a person is acquitted by reason of insanity, she or he is generally sent to a mental institution. Under the law, a person is kept there until doctors determine he or she is no longer dangerous and a judge concurs. Sadly, the measures for determining "no longer dangerous" are as untrustworthy as those used to assign a mental-illness label.

For example, E. E. Kemper, III, spent 5 years in a hospital for the criminally insane after murdering his grandparents. Kemper convinced psychiatrists and the judge that he was cured by giving rational answers to a battery of psychological tests. (He had memorized the answers prior to the tests.) Three years after his release, he was again arrested for brutally killing eight women—including his mother.[31]

Psychiatrist Lee Coleman urges that the insanity defense be eliminated altogether to resolve this dilemma. Doing so would allow courts to deal with the guilt or innocence of an individual without interference from psychiatrists. Coleman states: "Victims are no less injured by one who is mentally sound and violent."[32] Coleman further urges that, if the convicted individual later wishes help for emotional or behavioral problems, he or she can then request it.

Because of the controversy over the insanity plea, a number of states have revised their laws surrounding it. One approach adopted by about 20 states is to have a two-step process in which the jury first determines whether the defendant is innocent or guilty. If the verdict is guilty, the jury then decides if that person is sane or insane. (If found insane, the defendant is usually sent to a maximum security mental hospital.) At least three states—Montana, Idaho, and Utah—have abolished the insanity defense entirely, but there's evidence that those who would have used the plea are now just found incompetent to stand trial and end up in the same hospitals.

Use of Psychotropic Drugs

Psychotropic drugs include tranquilizers, antipsychotic drugs (such as Thorazine), and antidepressants. Since their discovery in 1954, these drugs have been credited with markedly decreasing the number of patients in state and county hospitals from 550,000 in 1955 to about 100,000 at the present time.[33] Psychotropic drugs do not "cure" emotional problems but are useful in reducing high levels of anxiety, depression, and tension.

Americans make extensive use of psychotropic drugs, particularly tranquilizers, like Valium, Librium, and Miltown. Most general practitioners prescribe tranquilizers for the large number of patients who complain of tension and emotional upset. Lithium and Prozac have been found to be fairly effective in reducing depression in a number of clients and are now widely prescribed by physicians.

"Popping pills" (both legal and illegal) has become fashionable, but the dangers of excessive drug use include physical and psychological dependency and unwanted side effects. There is also the danger that, because drugs provide temporary symptom relief, users may avoid making the necessary changes in their lives to resolve the problems causing the anxiety, depression, or tension. Physicians face a dilemma in balancing the benefits of psychotropic drugs against the dangers of abuse, particularly when such drugs are sought by patients for extended periods of time. Because psychotropic drugs provide only temporary relief for a patient's *symptoms* (such as anxiety and depression), many authorities urge that patients also receive counseling or psychotherapy to help resolve the underlying emotional difficulties.

Managed Mental Health Care

Managed health care is a generic term used to describe a variety of methods of delivering and financing health-care services designed to contain the costs of service delivery while maintaining a defined level of quality of care. At its best, it is perceived as a system in which appropriate control, structure, and accountability enable the most efficient use of health resources to achieve maximal health outcome. (To date, there is a lack of agreement as to what is the "best" system.) At its worst, it is perceived as a system in which no real dollars are saved, and money is diverted to administrative operations and profits at the expense of needed patient services.

Health-care delivery is shifting from practice based on fee-for-service to managed care systems.

Many complex issues are raised as health-care delivery is shifting from practice based on fee-for-service to managed care systems.

An example of a managed care system is a health maintenance organization (HMO). Most U.S. corporations have now adopted a managed health benefit program in providing health insurance to their employees and family members.

Managed mental health care has become a component of managed health care, as the health insurance programs offered by employers to their employees and family members have provisions for the types of mental health services that are covered. There are a variety of ways to contain costs in managed health benefit programs for mental health services. Examples include:

■ Restrict the number of days covered for in-patient care.

■ Limit the number of visits for psychotherapy.

■ Limit the number of dollars per year for mental health care per person.

■ Limit the number of dollars per lifetime for mental health care per person.

■ Increase deductibles.

■ Increase copayments.

■ Require referral by a gatekeeper, such as the primary care physician.

■ Require approval on a case-by-case basis by a utilization review mechanism for the types and costs of services provided.

The introduction of managed mental health care has raised many complex issues, including:

■ To what degree does the design and implementation of a given delivery system work for or against the best interests of the client?

■ How is quality of care defined and who defines it?

■ What are the provisions for access to care for persons considered at high health risk? For example, there have been instances where a mental health provider has recommended in-patient care for a highly suicidal client, but the utilization review mechanism has denied reimbursement, with the client then subsequently taking his or her life![34]

■ Who has legitimate access to clients' mental health records? More review of care decisions and computerization means more sneaky eyes seeing personal mental health-care information. Complex issues surrounding confidentiality arise with managed care.

■ Do managed care efforts to streamline care and keep costs down lead to treating symptoms, not underlying causes? For example, prescribing drugs that provide symptom relief is cheaper than long-term psychotherapy.

■ Does managed care lead to a system in which those therapists who see more people in less time are rewarded, while those therapists who provide longer term care to fewer people are punished? "Yes!"

■ Since managed care systems have policies that limit expenses, coverage limits can be a heavy burden for people who need expensive medication permanently to treat such chronic mental disorders as bipolar disorder.

SOCIAL STRUCTURE AND MENTAL ILLNESS

Sociologists have conducted a number of studies on the relationships between social factors and the rate of mental illness. Questions they have tried to answer include: Is social-class status related to the rate of mental illness? Does illness occur more in urban areas, in suburbs, or in rural areas? Which age groups are more prone to be affected? Are men or women more likely to be affected? (As indicated earlier, there is a question as to whether mental illness exists. In this section, the term *mental illness* is used to refer to those labeled mentally ill.)

SOCIAL CLASS

A classic study was conducted in 1958 by A. B. Hollingshead and F. C. Redlich in New Haven, Connecticut.[35] The study examined the social-class status of patients who were treated for a mental illness in hospitals and in private and public agencies. The researchers used a socioeconomic scale ranging from Class I (highest) to Class V (lowest). The results showed that the rate of mental illness was significantly higher in the lower classes than in the upper classes. Class V had by far the highest rate, with schizophrenia 11 times more prevalent for Class V than for Class I if measured in terms of hospitalization rates. The study also found that the types of treatment and opportunities for rehabilitation for the lower classes were of poorer quality and less satisfactory than those for the upper classes.

A research project by William Rushing studied 4560 males admitted to mental hospitals in Washington, D.C.[36] As in the Hollingshead and Redlich study, hospitalization rates were found to vary inversely with class. Hospitalization rates were particularly high for the lowest class.

A third study was conducted in midtown Manhattan in the 1950s by Leo Srole and his associates.[37] The study involved conducting extensive interviews with 1660 randomly selected people to find out if they had ever experienced a nervous breakdown, sought psychotherapy, or shown neu-

rotic symptoms. The researchers gave the information to a team of psychiatrists, who rated each case on degree of psychiatric impairment. Almost 23% of the sample was considered "significantly" impaired in mental functioning, including many people not under treatment. In addition, psychological impairment was found to correlate closely with social class. Nearly one person in every two in the lowest class was considered psychologically impaired, whereas the rate fell to one in eight for the highest class.

These studies clearly suggest that the poor are more likely to be labeled mentally ill. A variety of explanations shed light on these results. Perhaps the poor are less likely to seek treatment when emotional problems first begin to develop; they therefore become mentally ill before receiving help. Perhaps they are under greater psychological stress. Perhaps their attitudes, values, educational histories, and living conditions make them more susceptible to becoming mentally ill. Perhaps mental illness leads to lower status.

Or there may be *no* actual difference in severity and rate of emotional problems among social classes. It is possible that psychiatrists are less likely to assign a mental-illness label to a person of higher status because of the stigma associated with the label. In addition, psychiatrists may have less understanding of the value systems of the poor and therefore be more likely to label behavior of lower-class patients as deviant or mentally ill.

A number of studies have also found social-class differences in quality of treatment of those labeled mentally ill.[38] Lower-class patients often receive lower-quality care (often just custodial care when hospitalized) and have lower rates of release when hospitalized in a mental institution.

URBANIZATION

There is some evidence that cities, particularly inner-city areas, have a higher rate of mental illness than rural areas.[39] This finding may be due to overcrowding and to the deteriorated quality of life—dirt, noise, crime, transportation problems, inadequate housing, unemployment, drugs—which create a higher level of emotional problems. Also, mental health facilities tend to be located in and around urban areas, which increases the probability that urban dwellers with emotional problems will be identified and treated.

AGE

The elderly are more likely than younger people to have emotional problems, particularly depression (which is partially due to the low status that the elderly have in our society; low status leads to a crushing sense of uselessness and isolation). Additionally, the elderly may experience disturbances associated with degeneration of brain cells from such causes as arteriosclerosis and chronic alcoholism.[40]

MARITAL STATUS

People who are single, divorced, or widowed have higher rates of mental disorder than married people. Unmarried men have somewhat higher rates than unmarried women.[41]

SEX

Men and women are equally likely to be treated, but the nature of the diagnosis varies. Women are more likely to be diagnosed as suffering from anxiety, depression, and phobias and to be hospitalized in a mental institution. Men are more likely to be diagnosed as having a personality disorder.[42]

The vast majority of psychiatrists are men, and there is evidence that psychiatrists are more apt to consider sexual promiscuity or aggressive behavior in women a mental disorder as compared to men.[43]

RACE

Compared with Whites, African Americans are more likely to be diagnosed as mentally ill, and their rate of hospitalization is substantially higher.[44] There are several sociological explanations for these trends. African Americans may be under greater psychological pressure due to discrimination. Or the higher rates may stem from their lower social status, as a greater proportion of people in the lower social classes are diagnosed mentally ill. Or because most psychiatrists are White, a lack of awareness of the lifestyles of African Americans may lead psychiatrists to more readily assign the label "mentally ill" to Blacks who may differ in class, status, cultural values, and cultural background.

TREATMENT

Brief History

Although the history of treatment for the emotionally disturbed is fascinating, it is also filled with injustices and tragedies. George Rosen explains that most societies have developed unique ways of viewing mental illness and treating those so labeled.[45] In some societies, deviants have been highly valued and even treated as prophets with supernatural powers. In others the emotionally disturbed have been viewed as evil and even feared as possessing demonic powers. In medieval times, for example, the emotionally disturbed were viewed as possessed by demons; they were "treated" by flogging, starving, and dunking in hot water to drive the devils out. During a brief period in our colonial history, certain disturbed individuals were viewed as "witches" and were burned at the stake. Prior to the 19th century, the severely disturbed in the United States were confined in "almshouses," received only harsh custodial care, and often were chained to the walls.[46]

In the 19th century, a few mental institutions in France, England, and the United States began to take a more humanitarian approach to treating the disturbed. Although the severely disturbed were still confined in institutions, they began to be viewed either as having an illness or as having an emotional problem. The physical surroundings were improved, and efforts were made to replace the harsh custodial treatment with a caring approach that recognized each resident as a person deserving respect and dignity. Unfortunately, these humanitarian efforts were not widely accepted, in part because they were considered too expensive. Most of the severely disturbed continued to be confined in overcrowded, unsanitary dwellings with inadequate care and diet.

In 1908 Clifford Beers's book *A Mind That Found Itself* was published.[47] Beers had been confined as a patient, and the book recounted the atrocities occurring in this "madhouse." The book reached a wide audience and sensitized the public to the emotional trauma experienced by those confined. Under Beers's leadership, mental health associations were formed that advocated the need for improved inpatient care and initiated the concept of outpatient treatment.

Between 1900 and 1920, Sigmund Freud developed his psychoanalytic theories about the causes and treatment of emotional problems. According to Freud, emotional problems were mental illnesses that resulted from early traumatic experiences, internal psychological conflicts, fixations at various stages of development, and unconscious psychological processes. Most members of the counseling professions (psychiatry, clinical psychology, social work) accepted, from the 1920s to the 1950s, Freud's and other psychoanalytic theorists' views with regard to diagnosing and treating the disturbed. Due to Freud's influence, the public adopted a more humanitarian approach to treating the disturbed.

However, in the 1950s, questions began to arise about the effectiveness of the psychoanalytic method. It was expensive and lengthy (an analysis took 4 or 5 years), and research studies began to show that the rate of improvement for those undergoing analysis was no higher than that for people receiving no treatment.[48] Since the 1950s, a variety of counseling approaches have been developed that reject most or all of the concepts underlying psychoanalysis; these newer approaches include behavior modification, rational therapy, reality therapy, transactional analysis, family therapy, feminist intervention, and client-centered therapy.[49]

Certain segments of the medical procession have continued to maintain, since the 19th century, that mental illness is akin to other physical illnesses. They assert that infectious diseases, genetic endowment, and metabolic imbalances are the causes of mental disorders.[50] However, only a few specific organic causes have been identified. General paresis, for instance, which is a progressive emotional disorder, has been linked to syphilis; pellagra, another disorder, has been found to result from a dietary deficiency.

EXHIBIT 5.3

Asylums and Total Institutions

In 1961 Erving Goffman wrote *Asylums,* which described life inside state mental hospitals. Goffman indicates that such mental hospitals are "total institutions." (Other total institutions are prisons, boot camps, monasteries, and convents.) In a total institution, a resident is cut off from society for appreciable periods of time and required to lead a regimented life. Inside an asylum, residents are stripped of their clothing and deprived of contact with the outside world. Total institutions seek to control residents fully and to resocialize and remake their lives. The fear of expulsion is often a major control mechanism. Long-term confinement in asylums usually causes people to lose their capacities to respond in an independent, rational fashion and undermines their ability to cope with the outside world.

Total institutions teach residents to accept the staff's view of right and wrong, eroding residents' capacities to think independently. Such actions as questioning the therapeutic value of treatment programs are taken not as signs of mental stability but as a symptom of sickness. The "good" patient, from the staff's point of view, is one who is undemanding, docile, and obedient. In general, mental hospitals downgrade patients' feelings of self-esteem and emphasize their failures and inadequacies. Uniform furniture and clothing, a regimented routine, and a custodial atmosphere encourage patients to be docile and unassertive. The use of the medical-model approach to emotional problems encourages patients to view themselves as sick and in need of help. Such "resocialization" actually hinders residents from making a successful return to society. There is a high probability that long-term hospitalization will do more harm than good. The film *One Flew over the Cuckoo's Nest* vividly illustrates the resocialization process described by Goffman.

Source: Erving Goffman, *Asylums: Essays on the Social Situation of Mental Patients and Other Inmates* (New York: Doubleday, 1961).

The notion that mental disorders are physiological led to certain medical treatments that now appear to be tragedies. In the 18th century, bloodletting was widely practiced. In the early 20th century, prefrontal lobotomies (surgical slashing of the frontal section of the brain) were performed to "remove" the mental illness. Lobotomies have little therapeutic value, cause lasting brain damage, and leave patients docile and retarded.

Current Trends

In the past 30 years, there have been two major developments in the treatment of the severely disturbed. The first was the discovery and use of psychoactive drugs, both tranquilizers and antidepressants. The initial hope was that such drugs would cure severe disturbances, but it was soon realized that they provide primarily symptom relief and thereby enable the disturbed person to be more accessible to other therapy programs and approaches.[51] The second development was deinstitutionalization. Mental health practitioners realized that mental hospitals, instead of "curing" the disturbed, were frequently perpetuating disturbed behavior via long-term hospitalization. That is, the disturbed were labeled mentally ill and came to define themselves as "different" and enact the insane role.[52] They also became adapted to the relaxed, safe life of a hospital; the longer they stayed, the more they perceived the outside world as threatening.

Mental health professionals now use hospitalization only for those whose emotional problems pose a serious threat to their own well-being or to that of others. Psychotherapy is the main treatment approach used in mental hospitals. In most cases now, hospitalization for an emotional problem is brief.

The concept of deinstitutionalization has brought about a significant expansion of services designed to meet the needs of the disturbed in their home community, including community-based mental health centers, halfway houses, rehabilitation workshops, social therapeutic clubs, and foster-care services for the disturbed.

A criticism of the deinstitutionalization approach has been that some communities have returned long-term hospitalized patients to society *without* developing adequate community-based support services. The result is that many of the patients who have been discharged are living with families, friends, or on the street and are receiving little or no counseling and/or medical services.

Recent investigations have revealed incidents of discharged mental patients living in squalor in unlicensed group homes and low-quality hotels.[53] Many are victims of crime, fire, and medical neglect. Some are fed rancid food and exposed to rats and cockroaches. Sometimes such former patients set fires and abuse others; a few commit homicide or suicide.

TREATMENT FACILITIES: COMMUNITY MENTAL HEALTH CENTERS

Treatment services for emotional/behavioral problems are provided by nearly every direct-service social welfare agency, including public welfare agencies, probation and parole agencies, penal institutions, school social services, family service agencies, adoption agencies, private psychotherapy clinics, sheltered workshops, social service units in hospitals, and nursing homes. However, in many communities, mental health centers are a primary resource for serving those with emotional problems.

Community mental health centers were given their impetus with the passage by the federal government of the Community Mental Health Centers Act of 1963. This act provided for transferring the care and treatment of the majority of "mentally ill" people from state hospitals to their home communities. The emphasis is on local care, with the provision of comprehensive services (particularly to underprivileged areas and people).

Other emphases are (a) early diagnosis, treatment, and return to the community; (b) location of centers "near and accessible to" the populations they serve; and (c) the provision of comprehensive care consisting of five basic components: inpatient care, outpatient care, partial hospitalization (that is, day, night, and weekend care), emer-

Many social agencies offer counseling and therapy to people with emotional problems. Art therapy is one activity these professionals use in working with children at a private medical center.

gency care, and consultation/education. Services provided are expected to relate to a wide range of problem areas and population groups, such as the disturbed, the elderly, minorities, and people with alcohol and other drug-related problems.[54]

Professionals in a community mental health center may include psychiatrists, social workers, psychologists, psychiatric nurses, specialized consultants, occupational and recreational therapists, paraprofessionals, and volunteers. Typical services include outpatient care, inpatient care, alcohol and chemical abuse treatment, work evaluation, occupational therapy, family and group therapy, transportation services, counseling of children and adults, crisis intervention (including 24-hour emergency care), community education, and field training of students in the helping professions.

Community mental health services have in recent years received increasing criticism. Studies have found that some community mental health services are ineffective and inadequate.[55] Patients still have high readmission rates and inadequate

levels of adjustment to the community.[56] Many centers have been ineffective in dealing with the personal and societal problems of large numbers of poor people, because many of these so-called comprehensive centers provide little more than traditional inpatient and outpatient care for middle-class patients.[57]

On the other hand, proponents of community mental health centers argue that the centers have shown impressive results. For example, their programs have reduced the number of people in state and county mental hospitals from 550,000 in 1955 to about 100,000 at the present time.[58]

SOCIAL WORK AND MENTAL HEALTH

Social workers were first employed in the mental health field in 1906 to take social histories of newly admitted patients to Manhattan State Hospital in New York City.[59] Since then they have been involved in providing a variety of preventative, diagnostic, and treatment services.

Over the years, there has been a shift in emphasis from treating the individual to treating the family. Social workers, psychologists, and psychiatrists now function interchangeably as individual, family, and group therapists. All three professional groups are also involved in designing and administering mental health programs. Other professionals involved in working as a team in mental health facilities include psychiatric nurses, occupational therapists, and recreational therapists.

The number of social workers providing mental health services in the United States is larger than the number of psychiatrists or clinical psychologists providing such services.[60] Many social agencies, in addition to community mental health centers, provide counseling and psychotherapy to people with emotional problems. Such agencies include schools, family counseling agencies, public welfare departments, hospitals, adoption agencies, and probation and parole departments. An increasing number of clinical social workers are opening private practices to provide individual, family, and group therapy for a variety of emotional problems. Increasingly, payments from public and private insurance programs reimburse social workers for providing therapy on a private basis.

The National Association of Social Workers (NASW) has been promoting state licensing (or registration) requirements to assure the public that social work practitioners, especially those in private practice, meet high standards of competency. All states have now enacted legislation to license social workers.

NASW has also established a national Registry of Clinical Social Workers. Requirements for membership are:

- A master's or doctoral degree in social work from a graduate school accredited by the Council on Social Work Education (CSWE).

- Two years or 3000 hours of postgraduate clinical social work experience, supervised by a clinical social worker with at least 2 years of experience.

- Active membership in the Academy of Certified Social Workers (ACSW) or a state license that requires an examination.[61]

At one time, the social work role in the mental health field was generally considered subordinate to psychiatry. But with a growing recognition that emotional problems are primarily problems in living rather than organic in nature, social workers are increasingly employed in agencies to provide counseling and psychotherapy without supervision by a psychiatrist.

The primary therapy approach used to treat people with emotional or behavioral problems is psychotherapy or counseling (I use these two terms interchangeably, as there do not appear to be clear-cut distinctions between the two). Counseling is a broad term covering individual, family, and group therapy. A skilled counselor has knowledge of (a) interviewing principles and (b) comprehensive and specific treatment approaches. The next section discusses these two areas and is designed to give you a "flavor" of what counseling is composed of. Additional theoretical material covering these two areas is presented in social work practice and field placement courses. Through role playing of contrived counseling situations and, later, through working with clients, social work students gain skill and confidence in putting this material into practice. Sharpening and further developing one's counseling skills do not end with acquiring a degree in a counseling field; they are ongoing, lifelong processes.

COUNSELING

Counseling services are provided by practically every direct-service social welfare agency. Some agencies, such as welfare departments and mental health centers, provide counseling services covering almost all emotional or interpersonal problems. Other more specialized agencies provide counseling designed for specific problems that require considerable background knowledge and training in using highly developed treatment techniques. (Such areas include drug abuse counseling, therapy for eating disorders, genetic counseling, and sex therapy.)

The capacity to counsel effectively is one of the key skills needed by social workers; in fact, it may be *the* most important skill. Acquiring in-depth skill at counseling in one area (for example, marriage or adoption counseling) prepares that person for counseling in other areas. Because this skill is transferable, undergraduate and graduate social work programs can take a generic (broad-based) approach to social work training. The emphasis is placed on in-depth training in counseling rather than on training in specialized counseling areas.

How to Counsel *

Counseling someone with personal problems is neither magical nor mystical. Although training and experience in counseling are beneficial, everyone has the potential of helping another by listening and talking through difficulties. Counseling with a successful outcome can be done by a friend, neighbor, relative, hairdresser, banker, or bartender, as well as by social workers, psychiatrists, psychologists, guidance counselors, and the clergy. This is not to say that everyone will be successful at counseling. Professional people, because of their training and experience, have a higher probability of being effective. But competence and empathy, rather than degrees or certificates, are the keys to desirable outcomes.

There are three phases to counseling: (1) building a relationship, (2) exploring problems in depth, and (3) exploring alternative solutions. Successful counseling gradually proceeds from one phase to the next, with some overlapping of the stages. For example, in many cases, while exploring problems, the relationship between the counselor and the counselee continues to de-

velop; while exploring alternative solutions, the problems are generally being examined in greater depth.

BUILDING A RELATIONSHIP
The following are guidelines for building a relationship with a client:

1. Seek to establish a nonthreatening atmosphere in which the counselee feels safe to communicate fully his or her troubles while feeling accepted as a person.

2. In initial contacts with the counselee, you need to "sell" yourself—not arrogantly, but as a knowledgeable, understanding person who may be able to help and who wants to try.

3. Be calm. Do not laugh or express shock when the counselee begins to open up about problems. Emotional outbursts, even if subtle, will lead the counselee to believe that you are not going to understand his or her difficulties, and she or he will usually stop discussing them.

4. Generally be nonjudgmental and non-moralistic. Show respect for the counselee's values, and do not try to sell your values. The values that work for you may not be best for someone else in a different situation. For example, if the counselee is premaritally pregnant, do not attempt to force your values toward adoption or abortion. Let the counselee decide on a course of action after a full examination of the problem and an exploration of the possible solutions.

5. View the counselee as an equal. Rookie counselors sometimes make the mistake of thinking that, because someone is sharing intimate secrets, the counselor must be very important; they then end up creating a superior/inferior relationship. If counselees feel that they are being treated as inferior, they will be less motivated to reveal and discuss personal difficulties.

6. Use "shared vocabulary." This does not mean using the same slang words or the same accent as the counselee. If the counselee sees your speech as artificial, it may seriously offend him or her. You should use words that the counselee understands and that are not offensive.

---

* This section on "How to Counsel" is reprinted from an article of the same title written by me in *The Personal Problem Solver*, Charles Zastrow and Dae Chang, eds. (Englewood Cliffs, NJ: Spectrum Books, 1977). Reprinted by permission of Prentice-Hall, Englewood Cliffs, NJ.

7. The tone of your voice should convey the message that you empathetically understand and care about the counselee's feelings.

8. Keep confidential what the counselee has said. All of us by nature have urges to share "juicy secrets" with someone else. But, if the counselee discovers that confidentiality has been violated, a working relationship may be quickly destroyed.

9. If you are counseling a relative or a friend, there is a danger that, because you are emotionally involved, you may get upset or into an argument with the other person. If that happens, it is almost always best to drop the subject immediately, as tactfully as possible. Perhaps, after tempers cool, the subject can be brought up again. Or it may be best to refer the counselee to someone else. Many professionals refuse to counsel friends or relatives because emotional involvement interferes with the calm, detached perspective that is needed to help clients explore problems and alternative solutions.

EXPLORING PROBLEMS IN DEPTH

Following are suggestions to guide counselors in helping clients explore problems in depth:

1. Many rookie counselors make the mistake of suggesting solutions as soon as a problem is identified, without exploring the problem in depth. For example, an advocate of abortions may advise this solution as soon as a single female reveals that she is pregnant. A counselor should take the time to discover whether this person is strongly opposed to abortions, really wants a baby, or intends to marry soon.

2. In exploring problems in depth, the counselor and counselee need to examine such areas as the extent of the problem, its duration, its causes, the counselee's feelings about the problem, and the physical and mental capacities and strengths the counselee has to cope with the problem, before exploring alternative solutions. For example, if a single female is pregnant, the counselor and counselee need to explore the following questions: How does the person feel about being pregnant? Has she seen a doctor? About how long has she been pregnant? Do her parents know? If so, what are

their feelings and concerns? Has the female informed her partner? What are his feelings and concerns? What does she feel is the most urgent situation to deal with first? Answers to such questions will determine the direction of counseling. The most pressing, immediate problem might to be to inform her parents, who may react critically, or it might be to secure medical services.

3. When a problem area is identified, a number of smaller problems may occur (for example, planning how to tell her partner, obtaining medical care, obtaining funds for medical expenses, deciding where to live, deciding whether to leave school or work during the pregnancy, deciding whether to keep the child, and making plans for what to do after the child is delivered or the pregnancy is terminated). Explore all these subproblems.

4. In a multiproblem situation, the best way to decide which problem to handle first is to ask the counselee which one she or he perceives as most pressing. If the problem can be solved, start with exploring that subproblem in depth and developing together a strategy for the solution. Success in solving a subproblem will increase the counselee's confidence in the counselor and thereby will further solidify the relationship.

5. Convey empathy, not sympathy. Empathy is the capacity to show that you are aware of and can to some extent feel what the counselee is feeling. Sympathy is also sharing of feelings, but it has the connotation of pity. The difference is subtle, but empathy is oriented toward problem solving, whereas sympathy usually prolongs problems. For example, if you give me sympathy when I'm depressed, I'll keep telling you my sad story over and over, each time having an emotional outpouring supported by your sympathy, without taking any action to improve the situation. This process only reopens old wounds and prolongs my depression.

6. "Trust your guts." The most important tool you have as a counselor is yourself (your feelings and perceptions). You should continually strive to place yourself in the client's situation (with the client's values and pressures). To use the earlier example, if the client is 17 years old, single, and

pregnant, and has parents who are very critical of the situation and want her to have an abortion, a competent counselor would continually strive to feel what she is feeling and to perceive the world from her perspective, with her goals, difficulties, pressures, and values. It probably never happens that a counselor is 100% accurate in placing himself or herself in the counselee's situation, but 70–80% is usually sufficient to gain an awareness of the counselee's pressures, problems, and perspectives. This information helps the counselor to determine what additional areas need to be explored, to decide what to say, and to figure out possible solutions. In other words, a counselor should ask "What is this person trying to tell me, and how can I make it clear that I understand not only intellectually but empathetically?"

7. When you believe that the client has touched on an important area of concern, you can encourage further communication by:

a. Nonverbally showing interest.
b. Pausing. Inexperienced counselors usually become anxious when there is a pause, and they hasten to say something—anything— to have conversation continue. This is usually a mistake, especially when it leads to a change in the topic. Pausing will also make the counselee anxious, give him or her time to think about the important area of concern, and then usually motivate him or her to continue conversation in that area.
c. Using neutral probes. Examples are: "Could you tell me more about it?" "Why do you feel that way?" "I'm not sure I understand what you have in mind."
d. Summarizing what the client is saying. You might offer: "During this past hour you made a number of critical comments about your spouse; it sounds like some things about your marriage are making you unhappy."
e. Reflecting feelings. Examples are: "You seem angry" or "You appear to be depressed about that."

8. Approach socially unacceptable issues tactfully. Tact is an essential quality of a competent counselor. Try not to ask a question in such a way that the answer will put the respondent in an embarrassing position. Suppose, for instance, you are counseling a male with poor personal hygiene who has been discharged from a variety of jobs and does not know why. The man explains that employers initially compliment him on his work productivity and then tend, a few weeks later, to discharge him without informing him why. After several possible explanations have been explored and eliminated, you as the counselor may tactfully say "I'm wondering if your personal appearance and hygiene may be a reason for the dismissals. I notice you haven't shaved for a few days, and I sense you may not have bathed for a few days either. Do you think this may be an explanation?" It's very important to confront clients with ineffective actions that are having substantial negative effects on their lives.

9. When pointing out a limitation that a counselee has, also mention and compliment him or her on any assets. Discussion of a limitation will literally make the counselee feel that something is being laid bare or taken away. Complimenting him or her in another area will give something back.

10. Watch for nonverbal cues. A competent counselor will generally use such cues to identify when a sensitive subject is being touched on, as the client will show anxiety by changing tone of voice, fidgeting, yawning, assuming a stiff posture, or appearing flushed.

11. Be honest. An untruth always runs the risk of being discovered. If that happens, the counselee's confidence in you will be seriously damaged and perhaps the relationship seriously jeopardized. But being honest goes beyond not telling lies. The counselor should always point out those shortcomings that are in the counselee's best interest to give attention to. For example, if someone is being fired from jobs because of poor grooming habits, this needs to be brought to his or her attention. Or, if a trainee's relationship skills and personality are not suited for the helping professions, that person needs to be "counseled out" in the interests of clients and in the trainee's own best interests.

12. Listen attentively to what the counselee is saying. Try to hear his or her words not from your perspective but from the counselee's. Unfortunately, some counselors are caught up in their own interests and concerns, and they do not "tune out" their own thoughts while the counselee is speaking. This guideline seems very simple, but it is indeed difficult for many to follow.

EXPLORING ALTERNATIVE SOLUTIONS

The following are guidelines for exploring alternative solutions with a client:

1. After (or sometimes while) a subproblem is explored in depth, the next step is for the counselor and the counselee to consider alternative solutions. In exploring alternative solutions, it is almost always best for the counselor to begin by asking something like "Have you thought about ways to resolve this?" The merits, shortcomings, and consequences of the alternatives thought of by the counselee should then be tactfully and thoroughly examined. If the counselee has not thought of certain viable alternatives, the counselor should mention these, and the merits and shortcomings of these alternatives should also be examined. For example, in the case of the unwed pregnant teenager, if she decides to continue the pregnancy to full term, possible alternatives for the subproblem of making plans for living arrangements include keeping the child, getting married, seeking public assistance, finding foster care after delivery, filing a paternity suit, placing the child for adoption, and obtaining the assistance of a close relative to help or care for the child.

2. The counselee usually has the right to self-determination—that is, to choose the course of action among possible alternatives. The counselor's role is to help the counselee clarify and understand the likely consequences of each available alternative but generally not to give advice or choose the alternative for the counselee. If the counselor were to select the alternative, there would be two possible outcomes: (1) The alternative may prove to be undesirable for the counselee, in which case the counselee will probably blame the counselor for the advice, and the future relationship will be seriously hampered. (2) The alternative may prove

to be desirable for the counselee. This immediate outcome is advantageous; but the danger is that the counselee will then become overly dependent on the counselor, seeking his or her advice for nearly every decision in the future and generally being reluctant to make decisions independently. In actual practice, most courses of action have desirable and undesirable consequences. For example, if the unmarried mother is advised to keep her child, she may receive considerable gratification from being with and raising the child, but at the same time she may blame the counselor for such possible negative consequences as long-term financial hardships and a restricted social life.

The guideline of not giving advice does *not* mean that a counselor should not suggest alternatives that the client has not considered. On the contrary, it is the counselor's responsibility to suggest and explore all viable alternatives with a client. A good rule to follow is that, when a counselor believes a client should take a certain course of action, this idea should be phrased as a suggestion ("Have you thought about . . . ?") rather than as advice ("I think you should . . . ").

3. Counseling is done *with* the counselee, not *to* or *for* the counselee. In general, the counselee should take responsibility for those tasks that she or he has the capacity to carry out, and the counselor should attempt to do only those that are beyond the capacities of the counselee. As with giving advice, doing things *for* counselees may create a dependency relationship. Furthermore, successful accomplishment of tasks by counselees leads to personal growth and better prepares them for taking on future responsibilities.

4. The counselee's right to self-determination should be taken away only if the selected course of action has a high probability of seriously hurting others or the counselee. For example, if it seems likely that a parent will continue to abuse a child or that a counselee will attempt to take his or her own life, intervention by the counselor is called for. For most situations, however, the counselee should have the right to select his or her alternative, even when the counselor believes that another alternative is a better course of action. Frequently, the counselee is in a better position to

know what is best for him or her; if the alternative is not the best, the counselee will probably learn from the mistake.

5. Attempt to form explicit, realistic "contracts" with counselees. When the counselee does select an alternative, he or she should clearly understand what the goals will be, what tasks need to be carried out, how to do the tasks, and who will carry out each of them. It is often desirable to build into the "contract" a time limit for the accomplishment of each task. For example, if the unmarried mother decides to keep her child and now needs to make long-range financial plans, this goal should be understood and specific courses of action decided on—seeking public assistance, seeking support from the alleged father, securing an apartment within her budget, and so on. Furthermore, who will do what task within a set time limit should be specified.

6. If the counselee fails to meet the terms of the "contract," do not punish, but do not accept excuses. Excuses let people off the hook; they provide temporary relief, but they eventually lead to more failure and to a failure identity. Simply ask "Do you still wish to try to fulfill your commitment?" If the counselee answers affirmatively, another deadline acceptable to the counselee should be set.

7. Perhaps the biggest single factor in determining whether the counselee's situation will improve is the motivation to carry out essential tasks. A counselor should seek to motivate apathetic counselees. One of the biggest reality shocks of inexperienced helping professionals is that many clients, even after making commitments to improve their situation, do not have the motivation to carry out the steps outlined.

8. One way to increase motivation is to clarify what will be gained by meeting the commitment. When counselees fulfill commitments, reward them verbally or in other ways. Avoid punishment if commitments are not met. Punishment usually increases hostility without positive lasting changes. It also serves as only a temporary means of obtaining different behavior; a person who is no longer under surveillance will usually return to the "deviant" behavior.

9. Sometimes the counselee lacks the confidence or experience to carry out certain tasks. In this case it is helpful to "role-play" the tasks. For example, if a pregnant unwed teenager wants help in deciding how to tell her partner about the pregnancy, role-playing the situation will assist her in selecting words and developing a strategy for informing him. The counselor can first play her role and model an approach, while she plays her partner's role. Then the roles should be reversed so that the teenager practices telling her partner.

Other helpful hints for counseling could be given here, but the basic format is to develop a relationship, explore problems in depth, and then explore alternative solutions. These guidelines are not to be followed dogmatically; they will probably work 70% to 80% of the time. Learn to trust your own feelings, perceptions, relationship capacities, and interviewing skills.

One final important guideline is that the counselor should refer the counselee to someone else, or at least seek a professional counselor to discuss the case with, for any of the following situations: if the counselor feels that she or he is unable to empathize with the counselee; if the counselor feels that the counselee is choosing alternatives (such as seeking an abortion) that conflict with the counselor's basic value system; if the counselor feels that the problem is of such a nature that she or he will not be able to help; and if a working relationship is not established. A competent counselor knows that she or he can work with and help some people but not all. If you encounter a client you feel you cannot help, it is in that person's best interests, as well as your own, to refer the client to someone else who can.

Comprehensive and Specialized Counseling Approaches

In addition to a good grasp of interviewing principles, an effective counselor needs a knowledge of comprehensive counseling theories and of specialized treatment techniques to diagnose precisely what problems exist and decide how to intervene effectively. There are a number of contemporary comprehensive counseling approaches: psychoanalysis, rational therapy, client-centered therapy, Adlerian psychotherapy, behavior modification, Gestalt therapy, reality therapy, transactional analysis, neurolinguistic programming, and encounter approaches.* These therapy approaches generally present theoretical material on (a) personality theory, or how normal psychosocial development occurs; (b) behavior pathology, or how emotional/behavioral problems arise; and (c) therapy, or how to change unwanted emotions and dysfunctional behaviors.

An effective counselor generally has a knowledge of several treatment approaches. Depending on the unique set of problems presented by the client, the counselor picks and chooses from his or her "bag of tricks" the intervention strategy that is likely to have the highest probability of success. In addition to comprehensive counseling approaches, there are a number of specialized treatment techniques for specific problems, such as assertiveness training for people who are shy or overly aggressive, relaxation techniques for people experiencing high levels of stress, specific sex therapy techniques for such difficulties as premature ejaculation or orgasmic dysfunction, and parent effectiveness training for parent–child relationship difficulties.† An effective counselor strives to gain a working knowledge of a wide variety of treatment techniques to increase the likelihood of being able to help clients.

For illustrative purposes, one comprehensive therapy approach, rational therapy, will be summarized.

RATIONAL THERAPY

The two main developers of rational therapy are Albert Ellis and Maxie Maultsby.[62] The approach potentially enables those who become skillful in

rationally analyzing their self-talk to control or get rid of any undesirable emotion or any dysfunctional behavior.

It is erroneously believed by most people that our emotions and our actions are determined primarily by our experiences (that is, by events that happen to us). On the contrary, rational therapy has demonstrated that the primary cause of all our emotions and actions is what we tell ourselves about what happens to us.

All feelings and actions occur according to the following format:

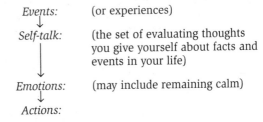

Events:	(or experiences)
↓	
Self-talk:	(the set of evaluating thoughts you give yourself about facts and events in your life)
↓	
Emotions:	(may include remaining calm)
↓	
Actions:	

An example will illustrate this process.

Event:	Cheryl, the 5-year-old daughter of Mr. and Mrs. Shaw, is playing with her brother and knocks over and breaks a lamp.
↓	
Mr. Shaw's self-talk:	"That lamp was our favorite. We bought it on our honeymoon— it's irreplaceable. This is awful."
	"Spare the rod and spoil the child. Some stiff discipline will make her shape up."
	"As head of this household, it's my duty to make her shape up. I'll teach her a lesson she'll never forget by giving her the spanking of her life."
	"She's always breaking things. I think this might have been intentional! I'll teach her to have respect for me and for our valuable items."
↓	
Emotions:	Anger, disappointment, frustration.
↓	
Actions:	Spanking and yelling at Cheryl, with the severity of the spanking bordering on abuse.

---

* A good summary of contemporary global counseling approaches is provided in Raymond Corsini and Danny Wedding (eds.), *Current Psychotherapies*, 5th ed. (Itasca, IL: F. E. Peacock, 1995) and Charles Zastrow, *The Practice of Social Work*, 6th ed. (Pacific Grove, CA: Brooks/Cole, 1999).

† A summary of specialized treatment techniques appears in Charles Zastrow, *The Practice of Social Work*, 6th ed. (Pacific Grove, CA: Brooks/Cole, 1999).

If, on the other hand, Mr. Shaw gives himself a different set of self-talk, his emotions and actions will be quite different:

Event:	Cheryl, the 5-year-old daughter of Mr. and Mrs. Shaw, is playing with her brother and knocks over and breaks a lamp.
Mr. Shaw's self-talk:	"This was a lamp we cherished, but I know she didn't break it intentionally. It was an accident. My getting angry at this point won't help."
	"I might have prevented this accident by informing Cheryl and our son that they can horse around indoors only in the rec room and in their bedrooms."
	"With young children, some accidents are bound to happen."
	"The most constructive thing I can do at this point is to say that I understand that it was an accident, that all of us are disappointed that the lamp broke, and that in the future their horsing around should be limited to the rec room and their bedrooms."
Emotions:	Some disappointment but generally remaining calm.
Actions:	Talking to the children in an understanding fashion and expressing his thoughts in line with his self-talk.

The most important point about the preceding processes is that our self-talk determines how we feel and act; by changing our self-talk, we can change how we feel and act. Generally we cannot control events that happen to us, but we have the power to think rationally and thereby change *all* of our unwanted emotions and ineffective actions.* This is the rehabilitative aspect of the conceptualization.[63]

The self-talk we give ourselves about specific events that happen to us is often based on a variety of factors, including our beliefs, attitudes, values, wants, motives, goals, and desires.[64] For example, the self-talk a married woman might give herself on being informed by her husband that he wants a divorce would be influenced by her desire (or lack of desire) to remain married, by her values and beliefs about being a divorcée, by her attitudes toward her husband, by her present goals (and whether getting a divorce would be consistent or inconsistent with them), and by her beliefs about the reasons her husband says he wants a divorce.

Another important point about self-talk is that, with repeated occurrences of an event, a person's emotional reaction becomes nearly automatic. That is, the person rapidly gives himself or herself a large set of self-talk gradually acquired through past experiences. For example, a few years ago, I counseled a woman who became intensely upset and depressed every time her husband came home intoxicated. In examining her emotional reactions, it became clear that, because of the repeated occurrences, she would rapidly tell herself the following on seeing him inebriated:

- "He's making a fool of himself and of me."

- "He's foolishly spending money we desperately need."

- "For the next few hours, I'm going to have to put up with his drunken talk and behavior. This is awful."

- "He loves drinking more than he loves me, because he knows I don't want him to get drunk."

- "Woe is me."

The use of rational therapy is demonstrated in Case Example 5.3.

---

* According to Maultsby, rational thinking and rational behavior (a) are consistent with the facts, (b) help you protect your life, (c) help you achieve your short- and long-term goals more quickly, (d) help you get out and stay out of significant trouble with other people, and (e) help you prevent significant unwanted emotions.

Using Rational Therapy: Coping with a Sexual Affair

A 21-year-old woman, Cindy, sought counseling after she was informed by her boyfriend, Jim, that a few months earlier he had become sexually involved with another woman, Linda. Jim and Cindy had dated fairly steadily for the past 2 years. Both were attending the same college. Prior to their summer break, they were having frequent arguments and decided not to see each during the summer. When they returned to college in the fall, they resumed their relationship. A few weeks later, Jim (after Cindy questioned him) informed her that he once had sex with Linda.

Cindy told the counselor that she wanted to better handle her unwanted emotions about this affair. After discussing her feelings in some depth, the counselor informed her that she could counter her undesirable emotions by doing a rational self-analysis (based on rational therapy). This involves writing down:

A. The facts and events that occurred.

B. The self-talk a person gives himself or herself.

C. The emotions a person experiences.

D. An examination of the statements in section A to determine whether they are factual or whether they belong in section B (a person's self-talk). This section is written *only* after sections A, B, and C are written.

E. Positive and rational self-talk challenges to the negative and irrational self-talk in section B (this segment is the main therapeutic part of the process).

F. The emotional and behavioral goals a person has.

For this process to be therapeutic, the person must practice replacing the irrational self-talk with rational self-talk. In writing a rational self-analysis (RSA), the person first writes in the left column the components A, B, and C; then he or she comes back to the beginning to write in the right column the components D, E, and F. The following RSA should be read with this A-B-C/D-E-F format in mind.

A	D
Facts and Events	*Factual Check of A*
My boyfriend, Jim, informed me that he had sexual relations with Linda, after a party at which they had both been drinking.	This is all factual. I know this because Jim told me himself. Jim and I are very close, and I know he would not lie to me.
B	**E**
My Self-Talk	*My Rational Debates of B*
B-1. It's not fair! How could Jim do such a thing to me?	E-1. Jim had sex with Linda. I'll just have to accept that. Because people are human and fallible,

it's a mistake to expect that I will always be treated with fairness by others. Besides, Jim and I had broken up, so I'm sure they didn't have me in mind when they did it. At the time they were sexually involved, neither Jim nor I had any commitment to each other. In truth, I also considered getting sexually involved this summer and perhaps would have if I had met the right guy.

B-2. That creep just had sex with Linda because he was horny.

E-2. Jim probably had sex with Linda for other reasons. I know he's not the type to "use" a woman merely for relief of his sexual tensions. It's also a mistake to label him a creep. No one is a creep. People are humans. If I mislabel him as a creep, it may lead me to view him in terms of an inaccurate label.

B-3. Jim and Linda had no good reasons for doing what they did. They only did it because they were both drunk. What a couple of jerks!

E-3. I do believe that alcohol had something to do with the fact that Jim and Linda had sex. I know for a fact that Jim becomes much less inhibited when he's had a few drinks. I don't know about Linda, though. The drinking can't be the only reason they had sex. Maybe they felt attracted to each other and wanted to have sex. I've got to remember that this summer Jim and I had no commitments to each other, and therefore I don't have the right to expect that he would be celibate to please me. Also, it's a mistake for me to refer to Jim or Linda as a "jerk." People are people.

(continued)

**CASE
EXAMPLE 5.3**   *(continued)*

B-4. Linda must be some kind of cheap tramp. Only a tramp would have sex with a guy she didn't love.

E-4. I don't even know Linda, so I shouldn't judge her like this. Furthermore, I have no way of knowing how Linda felt about Jim. Maybe she felt she loved him at the time. A woman isn't necessarily loose if she has sex with a guy.

B-5. Jim must think he's some kind of stud now.

E-5. Jim has told me that he has had sex with only two women. My idea of a "stud" is a guy who thinks he can have sex with any woman who comes along. I know Jim better than that. He doesn't think he could conquer any woman—nor would he try to.

B-6. Jim and I will never again be able to have a good sexual relationship of our own now that he has someone else to compare me to. I just know that he'll be thinking of Linda from now on.

E-6. Jim and I love each other. Jim told me that he does not love Linda. Just because Jim had sex with Linda does not mean our relationship will always be adversely affected. We can communicate easily during sex, and it has always been satisfying so far. It would be silly for Jim to compare our entire relationship to the one night he spent with Linda.

B-7. This is the worst thing that Jim could have done.

E-7. This is not the worst thing that Jim could have done. What he did was not a crime, like murder or rape, which would have been worse. The situation would be worse if Jim had slept with Linda while he was still seeing me. I'm glad to know that he would never do that.

B-8. Now that I know Jim had sex with Linda, our whole relationship will be ruined.

E-8. The fact that Jim had sex with Linda does not have to ruin our relationship. The event occurred in the past. It's over. Past sexual experiences should have no bearing on the future of our relationship. I want the relationship to continue, and I don't want to see it ruined.

B-9. I should never have broken up with Jim. Then he would never have slept with Linda. It's all my fault.

E-9. It's not my fault at all. I broke up with Jim because I felt it was the best thing to do at the time. I know Jim would not have been unfaithful to me had we still been dating, but we weren't dating at the time this happened. I had no way of knowing he would go to bed with Linda, and knowing would not have changed my decision to break up with him. It's not my fault because I wasn't even involved.

B-10. From now on, whenever I hear Linda's name mentioned, I'm going to have a fit! I won't be able to handle it!

E-10. When I hear Linda's name mentioned, I don't have to respond by having a fit. I can handle my feelings by being calm and not letting the mention of her name bother me.

C
My Emotions

I feel guilty, hurt, angry, upset, and jealous.

F
My Emotional and Behavioral Goals

I want to get over my unwanted emotions that I have had about this affair. I want to put this affair in our past. At the time it happened, Jim and I had no commitments to each other. What is important to Jim and me is our present and future relationship, not what happened one evening after Jim and I had broken up.

SUMMARY

Emotional and behavioral problems are two comprehensive labels covering an array of problems. All of us, at times, experience emotional and behavioral problems. Serious or severe emotional problems are sometimes labeled "mental illnesses."

The history of treatment for the emotionally disturbed is fascinating but also is filled with injustices and tragedies. In the past, the disturbed have been viewed in a variety of ways, ranging from prophets to evil people possessed by demonic powers. Recent major developments in treatment are the discovery and use of psychoactive drugs and the trend toward deinstitutionalization.

A major controversy is whether mental illness exists. Adherents of the medical approach believe that the disturbed person's mind is affected by some generally unknown internal condition. Critics of the medical model assert that disturbed people display a social deviation or have an emotional problem but do not have a disease of the mind. Further, the critics assert that mental-illness labels have no diagnostic or treatment value and frequently have an adverse effect.

The large number of homeless people in our nation is a national disgrace. Many of the homeless are thought to suffer from serious and chronic forms of mental illness. Discharged from mental institutions without the support they need, tens of thousands of former mental patients live on the street in abominable conditions.

Another major issue in the mental health field is civil rights concerns over involuntary confinement, inadequate treatment, and enforced use of treatments that have adverse side effects. Other issues include the usefulness of the innocent by reason of insanity plea, the extent to which psychotropic drugs should be used, and the adequacy of the services provided by local communities to emotionally disturbed individuals who are no longer (because of deinstitutionalization) being sent to state mental hospitals. The emergence of managed mental health-care systems raises a number of issues, including the extent to which such systems are restricting the provision of needed services to persons with emotional or behavioral difficulties.

Sociologists have found a number of associations between social factors and mental illness. Higher rates of diagnosed mental illness have been found in the lower socioeconomic classes, in inner cities as compared to rural areas, among the elderly, among unmarried people, and among African Americans as compared to Whites. Men and women are about equally likely to receive treatment; women are more likely to be diagnosed as suffering from anxiety, depression, and phobias and to be hospitalized. Men are more likely to be labeled as having a personality disorder. Lower-class patients often receive lower-quality care.

The main therapy approach used to treat people with emotional and behavioral problems is psychotherapy or counseling. Counseling services are provided by practically every direct-service social welfare agency. The ability to counsel others effectively is perhaps the most important skill needed by social workers. To be a competent counselor, it is essential to have a working knowledge of interviewing principles and of a wide range of treatment approaches. There are three distinct phases to counseling: building a relationship, exploring problems in depth, and exploring alternative solutions.

NOTES

1. Albert Ellis, *Reason and Emotion in Psychotherapy* (New York: Lyle Stuart, 1962).
2. William Kornblum and Joseph Julian, *Social Problems*, 8th ed. (Englewood Cliffs, NJ: Prentice Hall, 1995), p. 64.
3. Ibid., pp. 64–70.
4. D. L. Rosenhan and M. E. Seligman, *Abnormal Psychology*, 3rd ed. (New York: Norton, 1995), p. 54.
5. Ibid.
6. *DSM-IV* (*Diagnostic and Statistical Manual of Mental Disorders*), 4th ed. (Washington, DC: American Psychiatric Association, 1994).
7. Thomas S. Szasz, *The Myth of Mental Illness* (New York: Hoeber-Harper, 1961).
8. Thomas S. Szasz, "The Myth of Mental Illness," in *Clinical Psychology in Transition*, John R. Braun, comp. (Cleveland: Howard Allen, 1961), p. 27.

9. Thomas Scheff, *Being Mentally Ill* (Chicago: Aldine, 1966); David Mechanic, "Some Factors in Identifying and Defining Mental Illness," *Mental Hygiene,* 46 (Jan. 1962), pp. 66–74.

10. P. J. Caplan, *They Say You're Crazy* (Reading, MA: Addison-Wesley, 1995).

11. Ibid.

12. David L. Rosenhan, "On Being Sane in Insane Places," *Science,* 179 (Jan. 1973), pp. 250–257.

13. Rosenhan and Seligman, *Abnormal Psychology.*

14. Ibid.

15. Charles H. Cooley, *Human Nature and the Social Order* (New York: Scribner's, 1902).

16. Thomas S. Szasz, "The Psychiatrist as Double Agent," *Transaction,* 4 (Oct. 1967), p. 16.

17. Ibid., p. 17.

18. Scheff, *Being Mentally Ill.*

19. Ibid., p. 31.

20. Kornblum and Julian, *Social Problems,* pp. 84–87.

21. Ibid.

22. Ibid.

23. Rosenhan and Seligman, *Abnormal Psychology,* pp. 695–703.

24. Ibid., pp. 696–700.

25. The President's Commission on Mental Health, *Report to the President from The President's Commission on Mental Health,* vol. 1 (Washington, DC: U.S. Government Printing Office, 1978).

26. Ibid., pp. 69–72.

27. Rosenhan and Seligman, *Abnormal Psychology.*

28. "Psychiatric Testimony Clouds Justice in the Courtroom," *Freedom,* Feb. 1980, p. 1.

29. Ibid., p. 4.

30. "Behind Growing Outrage over Insanity Pleas," *U.S. News & World Report,* May 1979, p. 41.

31. Ibid., p. 42.

32. "Psychiatric Testimony Clouds Justice in the Courtroom," p. 4.

33. Kornblum and Julian, *Social Problems,* p. 85.

34. Rosenhan and Seligman, *Abnormal Psychology.*

35. August B. Hollingshead and Frederick C. Redlich, *Social Class and Mental Illness: A Community Study* (New York: Wiley, 1958).

36. William Rushing, "Two Patterns in the Relationship Between Social Class and Mental Hospitalization," *American Sociological Review,* 34 (Aug. 1969), pp. 533–541; Leo Srole, T. S. Langer, S. T. Michael, M. K. Opler, and T. A. L. Rennie, *Mental Health in the Metropolis: The Midtown Manhattan Study,* rev. ed. (New York: Harper & Row, 1975).

37. Srole et al., *Mental Health in the Metropolis.*

38. Kornblum and Julian, *Social Problems,* pp. 72–75.

39. Ibid., pp. 75–76.·

40. Rosenhan and Seligman, *Abnormal Psychology.*

41. Daniel J. Curran and Claire M. Renzetti, *Social Problems,* 3rd ed. (Boston: Allyn & Bacon, 1993), p. 484.

42. Kornblum and Julian, *Social Problems,* pp. 76–77.

43. Ibid., p. 77.

44. Ibid., p. 76.

45. George Rosen, *Madness in Society: Chapters in the Historical Sociology of Mental Illness* (New York: Harper & Row, 1969).

46. Ibid., pp. 172–195.

47. Clifford W. Beers, *A Mind That Found Itself* (New York: Longman, Green, 1908).

48. H. J. Eysenck, "The Effects of Psychotherapy: An Evaluation," *Journal of Consulting Psychology,* 11 (1955), pp. 319–324.

49. A good summary of these therapies is provided in Raymond Corsini and Danny Wedding, eds., *Current Psychotherapies,* 5th ed. (Itasca, IL: F. E. Peacock, 1995).

50. Miriam Siegler and Mumphrey Osmond, *Models of Madness, Models of Medicine* (New York: Harper & Row, 1974).

51. Joseph Mehr, *Human Services* (Boston: Allyn & Bacon, 1980), p. 88.

52. Erving Goffman, *Asylums: Essays on the Social Situation of Mental Patients and Other Inmates* (New York: Doubleday, 1961).

53. Rosenhan and Seligman, *Abnormal Psychology.*

54. Kornblum and Julian, *Social Problems,* pp. 82–83.

55. Rosenhan and Seligman, *Abnormal Psychology,* pp. 695–726.

56. Ibid.

57. Kornblum and Julian, *Social Problems,* pp. 82–86.

58. Ibid., p. 83.

59. Anthony J. Vattano, "Mental Health," in *Contemporary Social Work,* 2nd ed., Donald Brieland, Lela B. Costin, and Charles R. Atherton, eds. (New York: McGraw-Hill, 1980), p. 293.

60. Kornblum and Julian, *Social Problems,* p. 80.

61. National Association of Social Workers, *1993 Register of Clinical Social Workers,* 7th ed. (Washington, DC: NASW, 1993), pp. v–vi.

62. Ellis, *Reason and Emotion in Psychotherapy;* Maxie Maultsby, *Help Yourself to Happiness* (Boston: Marborough/Herman, 1975).

63. Maultsby, *Help Yourself to Happiness,* pp. 2–23.

64. Charles Zastrow, *You Are What You Think* (Chicago: Nelson-Hall, 1993).

FAMILY PROBLEMS
AND SERVICES
TO FAMILIES

Following a short introduction to various family forms throughout the world, this chapter will:

- Present a brief history of changes in the American family since colonial days.
- Describe current problem areas in the American family, including divorce, empty-shell marriages, family violence, and births outside of marriage.
- Describe current social services for family problems.
- Describe current issues involving family problems.

DIVERSE FAMILY FORMS

The family is a social institution that is found in every culture. A common definition of a family is "a group of people related by marriage, ancestry, or adoption who live together in a common household."[1] It should be noted that such a definition does not cover a number of living arrangements in which the members consider themselves to be a family, such as:

- A husband and wife raising two foster children who have been in the household for several years.
- Two lesbians in a loving relationship who are raising children born to one of the partners in a previous heterosexual marriage.
- A family unit in which one of the spouses is living away from home—perhaps because of military service or incarceration.
- A man and woman who have been living together for years in a loving relationship but have never legally married.

Clearly, a definition of the term *family* that encompasses all its diverse forms has not as yet been developed.

Families take a variety of forms in different cultures. In some societies, husband and wife live in separate buildings. In others, they are expected to live apart for several years after the birth of a child. In many societies, husbands are permitted to have more than one wife. In a few countries, wives are allowed to have more than one husband. Some cultures permit (and even encourage) premarital and extramarital intercourse.

Some societies have large communes where adults and children live together. There are also communes in which the children are raised separately from adults. In some cultures without communes, surrogate parents rather than the genetic parents raise the children. Some societies encourage certain types of homosexual relationships, and a few recognize homosexual as well as heterosexual marriages.

In many cultures, marriages are still arranged by the parents. Some societies do not recognize the existence of romantic love. Some cultures expect older men to marry young girls. Others expect older women to marry young boys. Some expect a man to marry his father's brother's daughter; others insist that he marry his mother's sister's daughter. Most societies prohibit the marriage of close relatives, yet a few subcultures encourage marriage between brothers and sisters or between first cousins. In a few societies, infants are married before they are born (if the baby is of the wrong sex, the marriage is dissolved). In some societies, a man, on marrying, makes a substantial gift to the bride's father; in others, the bride's father gives a substantial gift to the new husband.

People in each society generally feel strongly that their particular pattern is normal and proper; many feel the pattern is divinely ordained. Suggested changes in their particular form are usually viewed with suspicion and defensiveness; changes are often sharply criticized as being unnatural, immoral, and a threat to the survival of the family.

In spite of these variations, practically all family systems can be classified into two basic forms: the extended family and the nuclear family.

An *extended family* consists of a number of relatives living together, such as parents, children, grandparents, great-grandparents, aunts, uncles, in-laws, and cousins. The extended family is the predominant pattern in preindustrial societies.

Extended families, like this one in Bangladesh, are still the predominant pattern in many developing countries.

The members share various agricultural, domestic, and other duties.

A *nuclear family* consists of a married couple and their children living together. The nuclear family emerged from the extended family. Extended families tend to be more functional in agricultural societies in which many "hands" are needed. The nuclear family is more suited to the demands of complex industrialized societies because its smaller size and potential geographic mobility make it more adaptable to changing conditions—such as the need to relocate to obtain a better job.

In the United States and a number of other countries, a third family form is emerging: the single-parent family. Single-parent families are created in a variety of ways, such as by an unmarried person adopting a child, an unmarried woman giving birth to a child, and a married couple divorcing with one parent (usually the woman) as-

suming custody of the children. Single-parent families now constitute nearly 25% of all families in the United States.[2]

THE AMERICAN FAMILY: PAST AND PRESENT

The Family in Preindustrial Society

We often view the family as a stable institution in which few changes occur. Surprisingly, a number of changes have taken place since colonial and frontier days.

Prior to the 1800s, the economy in our country was predominantly agricultural. The majority of people lived on small farms in rural areas. In preindustrial society, transportation was arduous and travel was constricted. The family was nearly self-sufficient; most of what it consumed was produced on the farm. The house and the farm were the center of production. The most common family type was the extended family, with each member having specific roles and responsibilities. Because there were many tasks on small farms, the extended family was functional; it contained a number of family members to carry out those tasks.

Economic considerations influenced family patterns. Marriage was highly valued, as was having many children. A large family was needed to do all the tasks involved in planting and harvesting crops and in raising cattle and other animals. With more children, a married couple could cultivate more acreage and thereby become more profitable. Children were thus important economic assets. Parents wanted their sons to marry robust, industrious women who could substantially contribute to the work that needed to be done.[3]

John F. Cuber et al. have noted that preindustrial American society developed a *monolithic code* of cultural beliefs that was accepted by most people during this era.[4] A monolithic code permits only one acceptable pattern of behavior. Components of this code were:

1. Adults were expected to be married. Women were expected to marry in their teens or early twenties. Those who delayed marriage or did not ever marry were referred to as "old maids" and "spinsters."

2. Marriage was considered permanent—for life. Divorce was rare and highly disapproved of.

3. An individual was expected to place the welfare of the family unit ahead of his or her individual preferences. For example, an individual's choice about who she or he wanted to marry was considered less important than the parents' notions about what was best for the family as a unit.

4. Sexual relations were restricted to marriage. There was a double standard: Women who had premarital or extramarital affairs were more harshly criticized and stigmatized than men who did so.

5. Married couples were expected to have children. Children were not only considered an economic asset but were also viewed as a religious obligation, based on the biblical ethic of "be fruitful and multiply."

6. Parents were expected to take care of their children, whatever the cost. Children were expected to obey and honor their parents. When parents became partially disabled (for example, from old age), children were expected to care for them.

7. The father was the head of the family and made the important decisions. Women and children were expected to be subordinate to him. There were numerous advantages to being male. Women left their parents' home upon marriage and moved into the husband's home (usually near or in his parents' home). Male children were more highly valued than female children, partly because males would remain home after marrying. The woman's place was in the home, and she was expected to do the cooking, washing, cleaning, and a variety of other domestic tasks. Thus, American preindustrial society was clearly patriarchal.

These beliefs were so strongly held by most people that they were considered the morally decent way to live. To violate them was viewed as going against nature and against God's will. (As we'll see, remnants of this code still remain in American society.)

The Family in Industrial Society

The Industrial Revolution, which began roughly 200 years ago, greatly changed family life. Factories and large-scale business organizations replaced small family farms as centers of economic production. Urbanization accompanied industrialization, and most people now live in urban or semiurban areas. Products that were mass produced on assembly lines or produced using complex equipment and technology became much cheaper than those produced on small family farms or in small family shops.

As the family gradually began losing its economic-productive function, other changes followed. Fewer people were needed in families to fill essential economic roles. Smaller families became more functional for industrialized societies because they could more readily relocate to fill employment openings that arose.

Gradually there was a shift toward individualism. A key component of individualism is the belief that the desires of the individual should take precedence over those of the family. As a result, it became increasingly recognized that the choice of a mate should be based on personal preference, not family need.

In addition, with the loss of the economic-productive function, children became economic liabilities; that is, they did nothing to increase family income but still had to be clothed, fed, and sheltered. As a response, parents began having fewer children.

There have been numerous other changes. No longer is the wisdom of the elderly as highly valued, partly because children are now trained and educated in institutionalized settings. In a rapidly changing industrial society, the job skills of older workers often become obsolete. As a result, the elderly are less esteemed than they once were.

Gradually women won the right to vote, and in the past three decades, the feminist movement has been calling into question the "double standards" of sexual morality. Women are also seeking egalitarian relationships with men. An increasing number of women are entering the labor force and seeking employment in settings (such as police departments) that were once considered appropriate only for men. Sexuality is more openly discussed today, and there has been an increase in the rate of sexual relations outside of marriage.[5] However, recent concern about AIDS has led many adults to reduce their sexual contacts. (The chances of acquiring AIDS increase with the number of sexual partners one has.)

Still, remnants of the monolithic code remain. Some people continue to find it objectionable if a married couple divorce or choose not to have children, or if a single person becomes pregnant or decides never to marry.

In 1938 sociologist William Ogburn summarized changes in function the American family has undergone as a result of industrialization and technological advances:[6]

1. The economic-productive function has been lost. In most families, financial resources are now acquired outside the home.

2. The protective function has been lost. The protective function is now being met by such agencies as police departments, hospitals, insurance companies, and nursing homes.

3. The educational function has been sharply reduced. Schools, day-care centers, and Head Start programs have taken on much of this function.

4. The family is less likely to be the center for religious activity.

5. The recreational function has largely been reduced. Each family member is now more likely to join recreational groups outside the home.

6. The status recognition function has been sharply reduced. Individuals now receive recognition through their own achievements in organizations outside the family, such as at school, at work, and in social and religious groups.

7. The family has retained its affectional function. Members receive social and emotional gratification from the family and also have many of their companionship needs met by the family.

Most authorities agree with Ogburn's assessment that many of the functions of the American family have been lost or sharply reduced. It has been noted, however, that the modern family retains certain functions that Ogburn overlooked. Following are five essential functions that families perform to help maintain continuity and stability in modern industrial society.[7]

REPLACEMENT OF THE POPULATION

Every society must have some system for replacing its members. Because practically all societies consider the family as the unit in which children are produced, societies have defined the rights and responsibilities of the reproductive partners within the family unit. These rights and responsibilities help maintain the stability of society, although they are defined differently from one society to another.

CARE OF THE YOUNG

Children require care and protection until at least the age of puberty. The family is a primary institution for rearing children. Modern societies have generally developed supportive institutions to help in caring for the young—for example, medical services, day-care centers, parent training programs, and residential treatment centers.

SOCIALIZATION OF NEW MEMBERS

To become productive members of society, children must be socialized into the culture. Children are expected to acquire a language, to learn social values and mores, and to dress and behave within the norms of society. The family plays a major role in this socialization process. In modern societies, a number of other groups and resources are involved in this process. Schools, the mass media, peer groups, the police, movies, books, and other written materials are important influences in the socialization process. (Sometimes these different influences clash by advocating opposing values and attitudes.)

REGULATION OF SEXUAL BEHAVIOR

Failure to regulate sexual behavior would result in clashes between individuals due to jealousy and exploitation. Unregulated sexual behavior would probably also result in large numbers of births outside of marriage—children for whom no fathers could be held responsible. Every society has rules that regulate sexual behavior within family units. Most cultures, for example, have incest taboos, and most disapprove of extramarital sex.

SOURCE OF AFFECTION

Spitz has demonstrated that humans need affection, emotional support, and positive recognition from others (including approval, smiles, encouragement, and reinforcement for accom-

plishments).[8] Without such affection and recognition, a person's emotional, intellectual, physical, and social growth is stunted. The family is an important source for obtaining affection and recognition because members generally regard one another as among the most important people in their lives and gain emotional and social satisfaction from these relationships. (As noted earlier, Ogburn identified this function as the primary one remaining in modern families.)

This brief sketch of American family history shows that, although a number of changes have occurred, the family retains several important functions. We will now turn to an examination of problem areas for today's American family: divorce, empty-shell marriages, family violence, and births outside of marriage.

PROBLEMS IN THE FAMILY

Divorce

Our society places a higher value on romantic love than do most other societies. In cultures in which marriages are arranged by parents, love generally has no role in mate selection. In the United States, however, romantic love is a key factor in forming a marriage.

American children are socialized from an early age to believe in the glories of romantic love. "Love conquers all," it is asserted. Magazines, films, TV programs, and books continually portray "happy ending" romantic adventures. All of these breathtaking romantic stories suggest that every normal individual falls in love with that one special person, gets married, and lives happily ever after. This ideal rarely happens.

Nearly one of every two marriages ends in divorce.[9] This high rate has been gradually increasing; before World War I, divorce seldom occurred.

Divorce usually leads to a number of difficulties for those involved. First, those who are divorcing face many emotional concerns, such as a feeling that they have failed, doubt over whether

EXHIBIT 6.1

Romantic Love Versus Rational Love

Achieving a gratifying, long-lasting love relationship is one of our paramount goals. The experience of feeling "in love" is exciting, adds meaning to life, and gives us a good feeling about ourselves.

Unfortunately, few people are able to maintain a long-term love relationship. Most individuals encounter problems, like falling in love with someone who does not love them, falling out of love with someone after an initial stage of infatuation, being highly possessive of someone they love, or having substantial conflicts with the loved one because of differing sets of expectations about the relationship. Failures in love relationships are more often the rule than the exception.

The emotion of love is often viewed (erroneously) as a feeling over which we have no control. A number of common expressions (erroneously) connote or imply that love is a feeling beyond our control: "I *fell* in love." "It was love at first sight." "I just couldn't help it." "He swept me off my feet." It is more useful to think of the emotion of love as based primarily on our self-talk (that is, what we tell ourselves) about a person we meet. Romantic love can be diagramed as follows:

Event
Meeting or becoming acquainted with a person who has *some* of the overt characteristics you seek in a lover.

↓

Self-talk
"This person is attractive and personable and has *all* of the qualities I admire in a lover/mate."

↓

Emotion
Intense infatuation; a feeling of being romantically in love; a feeling of ecstasy.

Romantic love is often based on self-talk that stems from intense, unsatisfied desires and frustrations rather than on reason or rational thinking. Unsatisfied desires and frustrations include extreme sexual frustration, intense loneliness, parental and personal problems, and extensive desires for security and protection.

A primary characteristic of romantic love is to idealize the person with whom we are infatuated as "perfect"; that is, we notice that this person has some overt characteristics we desire in a lover and then conclude that this person has *all* the desired characteristics.

A second characteristic is that romantic love thrives on a certain amount of distance. The more forbidden the love, the stronger it becomes. The more social mores are threatened, the stronger the feeling. (For example, couples who live together and later marry often report that living together was more exciting and romantic.) The greater the effort required to be with each other (for example, traveling long distances), the more intense the romance. The greater the frustration (for example, loneliness or sexual needs), the greater the ecstasy.

The irony of romantic love is that, if an ongoing relationship is achieved, the romance usually withers. Through sustained contact, the person in love gradually comes to realize what the idealized loved one is really like—simply another human being with certain strengths and limitations. When this occurs, the romantic love relationship either turns into a rational love relationship or is found to have significant conflicts and dissatisfactions and then is terminated. For people with intense unmet needs, the latter occurs more frequently.

Romantic love thus tends to be temporary and based on make-believe. A person experiencing romantic love never loves the real person—only an idealized imaginary person.

(continued)

EXHIBIT 6.1   *(continued)*

Rational love, in contrast, can be diagrammed in the following way:

Event

While being aware of and comfortable with your own needs, goals, identity, and desires, you become well acquainted with someone who reflects, to a fair extent, the characteristics you desire in a lover or spouse.

↓

Self-talk

"This person has many of the qualities and attributes I seek in a lover or spouse. I admire this person's strengths, and I am aware and accepting of his (her) shortcomings."

↓

Emotion

Rational love.

The following are ingredients of a rational love relationship: (a) You are clear and comfortable about your desires, identity, and goals in life; (b) you know the other person well; (c) you have accurately and objectively assessed the loved one's strengths and shortcomings and are generally accepting of the shortcomings; (d) your self-talk about this person is consistent with your short- and long-term goals; (e) your self-talk is realistic and rational so that your feelings are not based on fantasy, excessive need, or pity; (f) you and this person are able to communicate openly and honestly so that problems can be dealt with when they arise and so that the relationship can continue to grow and develop; (g) you and the other are able to give and receive, show kindness and affection, and know and do what pleases the other person.

Because love is based on self-talk that causes feelings, it is we who create love. Theoretically, it is possible to love anyone by making changes in our self-talk. On the other hand, if we are in love with someone, we can gauge the quality of the relationship by analyzing our self-talk to determine the nature of our attraction and the extent to which our self-talk is rational and in our best interests.

---

they are able to give and receive love, a sense of loneliness, concern over the stigma attached to getting a divorce, worry about the reactions of friends and relatives, concern over whether they are doing the right thing by parting, and fear about whether they will be able to make it on their own. Many people who are considering separation feel trapped because they believe they can neither live with nor without their spouse. Dividing up the personal property is another matter that frequently leads to bitter differences of opinions. If there are children, there are concerns about how the divorce will affect them.

There are also other issues that need to be decided. Who will get custody of the children? (Joint custody is now an alternative; with joint custody, each parent has the children for part of the time.)

If one parent is awarded custody, controversies are likely to arise over visiting rights and child support payments. Each spouse often faces the difficulties of finding a new place to live, making new friends, doing things alone in a couple-oriented society, trying to make it on one's own financially, and thinking about the hassles connected with dating.

Going through a divorce is very difficult. People are less likely to perform their jobs well and are more likely to be fired during this time period.[10] Divorced people have a shorter life expectancy.[11] Suicide rates are higher for divorced men than for married men.[12]

Divorce per se is no longer automatically assumed to be a social problem, although some of its consequences still are. On the other hand, there is increasing recognition that in some marriages (in which there is considerable tension, bitterness, and dissatisfaction) divorce is sometimes a solution. It may be a concrete step that some people take to end the unhappiness and to begin a more productive and gratifying life. Further, there is increasing awareness that a divorce may be better for the children because they may no longer be subjected to the tension and unhappiness of a marriage that has gone sour.

The rising divorce rate does not necessarily mean that more marriages are failing. It may simply mean that more people in unhappy marriages are dissolving them rather than continuing to live unhappily.

REASONS FOR MARITAL HAPPINESS

There are many sources of marital breakdown: alcoholism, economic strife caused by unemployment or other financial problems, incompatibility of interests, infidelity, jealousy, verbal or physical abuse of spouse, and interference in the marriage by relatives and friends.

As noted earlier, many people marry because they believe they are romantically in love. If this romantic love does not grow into rational love, the marriage is likely to fail. Unfortunately, young people in our society are socialized to believe that marriage will bring them continual romance, resolve all their problems, and be sexually exciting, thrilling, and full of adventure. (Most young people need only look at their parents' marriage to realize such romantic ideals are seldom attained.) In actuality, living with someone in a marriage involves carrying out the garbage, washing dishes and clothes, being weary from work, putting up with one's partner's distasteful habits (for example, poor hygiene or belching), changing diapers, and dealing with conflicts over such things as finances and differences in sexual interests. *To make a marriage work, each spouse must put considerable effort into that relationship.*

Another factor that is contributing to an increasing divorce rate is the unwillingness of some men to accept the changing status of women. Many men still prefer a traditional marriage in which the husband is dominant and the wife plays a sup-

portive (subordinate) role as child-rearer, housekeeper, and the husband's and family's emotional support. Many women are no longer accepting such a status and are demanding egalitarian marriages in which making major decisions, doing the domestic tasks, raising the children, and bringing home paychecks are shared responsibilities.

Today about two-thirds of American women with children under 18 work outside the home.[13] These women are no longer as heavily reliant financially on their husbands. Women who are able to support themselves financially are more likely to seek a divorce if their marriages go sour.[14]

Another factor contributing to the increasing divorce rate is the growth of individualism. Individualism involves the belief that people should seek to actualize themselves, to be happy, to develop their interests and capacities to the fullest, and to fulfill their own needs and desires. The interests of the individual take precedence over those of the family. People in our society have increasingly come to accept individualism as a way to go through life. In contrast, people in more traditional societies and in extended families are socialized to put the interests of the group first, with their own individual interests viewed as less important. With America's growing belief in individualism, people who are unhappily married are much more likely to dissolve the marriage and seek a new life.

Yet another reason for the rise in the divorce rate is the growing acceptance of divorce in our society. With less stigma attached to divorce, more unhappily married people are now ending those marriages.

An additional factor in the increasing divorce rate is that modern families no longer have as many functions as did traditional families. Education, food production, entertainment, and other functions once centered in the family are now largely provided by outside agencies. Kenneth Keniston notes:

In earlier times, the collapse of a marriage was far more likely to deprive both spouses of a great deal more than the pleasure of each other's company. Since family members performed so many functions for one another, divorce in the past meant a farmer without a wife to churn the cream into butter or care for him when he was sick, and a mother without a husband to plow the fields and bring her the food to feed their children. Today, when emotional satisfaction is the bond that holds marriages together, the waning of love or the emergence of real incompatibilities and conflicts between husband and wife leave fewer reasons for a marriage to continue. Schools and doctors and counselors and social workers provide their supports whether the family is intact or not. One loses less by divorce today than in earlier times, because marriage provides fewer kinds of sustenance and satisfaction.[15]

Exhibit 6.2 identifies variables that predict whether a marriage will or will not last.

DIVORCE LAWS

In the past, society attempted to make the breakup of marriages almost impossible. One way it did this was through laws that made a divorce difficult to obtain. After one spouse petitioned the court for a divorce, there were long waiting periods before that divorce could be obtained. Divorce courts also followed the "adversary" judicial procedures in which the spouse seeking the divorce had to document that the other spouse was guilty of some offense, such as adultery, desertion, or cruel and inhuman treatment. In many cases, the actual reasons for the divorce (such as no longer finding the relationship satisfying) bore little relationship to the grounds on which the court allowed that divorce. Often the marital partners contrived a story that fit the legal requirements.

In most divorces, both partners contribute to the marital breakdown. Yet traditional divorce laws erroneously assumed that one partner was guilty and the other party innocent. Traditional divorce laws often intensified the trauma that both partners were undergoing and pitted the partners against each other. Moreover, the process was very expensive.

Because of these difficulties, most states have now passed "no fault" divorce laws, which allow the couple to obtain a divorce fairly rapidly by stating to the court that they both agree their marriage

EXHIBIT 6.2

Facts About Divorce

Age of spouses: Divorce is most likely to occur when the partners are in their twenties.

Length of engagement: Divorce rates are higher for those who had a brief engagement.

Age at marriage: People who marry at a very young age (particularly teenagers) are more likely to divorce.

Length of marriage: Most divorces occur within 2 years after marriage. There is also an increase in divorce shortly after the children are grown. This may occur partly because some couples wait until their children leave the nest before dissolving an unhappy marriage.

Social class: Divorce occurs more frequently at the lower socioeconomic levels.

Education: Divorce rates are higher for those with fewer years of schooling. Interestingly, divorce occurs more frequently when the wife's educational level is higher than the husband's.

Residence: Divorce rates are higher in urban areas than in rural areas.

Second marriages: The more often individuals marry, the more likely they are to get divorced again.

Religion: The more religious individuals are, the less likely they are to divorce. Divorce rates are higher for Protestants than for Catholics or Jews. Divorce rates are also higher for interfaith marriages than for intrafaith marriages.

Sources: William J. Goode, "Family Disorganization," in *Contemporary Social Problems*, 4th ed., Robert K. Merton and Robert Nisbet, eds. (New York: Harcourt Brace Jovanovich, 1976), pp. 511–556; Goode, *After Divorce* (New York: Free Press, 1956); Paul C. Glick, *American Families* (New York: Wiley, 1957); J. Richard Udrey, *The Social Context of Marriage*, 2nd ed. (Philadelphia: Lippincott, 1971); William Kornblum and Joseph Julian, *Social Problems*, 9th ed. (Upper Saddle River, NJ: Prentice Hall, 1998), pp. 359–361.

has irreparably broken down. (The adversary process is still available for any spouse who chooses to use it.)

Issues that are still often contested between the two partners in divorce proceedings involve the division of property, alimony or maintenance (a financial allowance paid to one spouse by the other for support after the divorce), child support payments, and custody of the children. In the past, courts invariably awarded the woman custody of the children, child support payments, and alimony (particularly if she was not employed). However, a large percentage of the men failed to make some, or all, of their child support and alimony payments, which left their former wives in dire financial straits.

Changes in sex roles and the increased employment of women have led to changes in divorce settlements. Most states have enacted legislation allowing courts to require that the woman make alimony payments to her former husband (although few courts have as yet issued such orders). Custody of the children is still generally given to the mother, although this assignment is no longer automatic. An increasing number of fathers are requesting custody of their children and are making it known that they resent the sexist bias of many courts, which assumes that a mother is better qualified to raise children.

A critical point about divorce is that, when it occurs, many of the costs are paid by society. In families of average income or less, the burden of divorce-related poverty falls on society as a whole. Examples of such costs include subsidized housing, public sector make-work jobs, and payments to lawyers who are involved in collecting support for women and children.

The recent willingness of courts to award custody to the father has a hidden cost to society. Fathers often threaten a protracted custody battle. As a result, mothers who want custody of their children without a fight are routinely forced to "barter" custody in exchange for reduced child support payments. Because such payments are so low, these women and their children then qualify for welfare. Richard Neely, a state supreme court justice, notes:

> Most of us begin with a political conviction that women ought to be equal to men economically, and then leap to a conclusion that they are. It then logically follows that women can support children as well as men and that whoever wants the children can pay for them.
>
> The fact is that women are much poorer than men, and this pattern appears highly resistant to change.[16]

Custody battles between fathers and mothers are becoming common in divorce cases. Typical custody battles may take as long as 2 years and cost thousands of dollars for attorneys, expert witnesses, and court costs. During this process, the parents are likely to use the children as "pawns" against each other. They bribe the children with large allowances, relax discipline, and indulge outrageous whims of their children. They may also try to turn their children against the other parent by "badmouthing" him or her. Custody battles are not only costly but also emotionally damaging to all family members.

In many states now, children over age 14 are allowed to select the parent with whom they wish to live if that parent is "fit." As a way of avoiding custody battles and the situation in which women barter reduced child support payments for custody, Richard Neely recommends that, for children under 14, custody be awarded to the primary caretaker parent, who is defined as:

> . . . the parent who: (1) prepares the food; (2) changes the diapers, dresses, and bathes the child; (3) takes the child to school, church, and other activities; (4) makes appointments with a doctor and generally watches over the child's health; and (5) interacts with the child's friends, the school authorities, and other adults engaged in activities that involve the child. It is not surprising that the "primary caretaker" is usually the mother, but that need not be the case.[17]

In 90% of divorce cases, the mothers are awarded custody of the children.[18] After the divorce, the mother's standard of living sharply declines, whereas the father's standard of living generally increases because he has fewer financial responsibilities.[19] Women are awarded alimony in only 15% of divorce cases.[20] When there are children, the fathers are usually required to pay child support, but the amounts awarded are generally insufficient to meet the financial needs of the children. In addition, many divorced fathers fail to pay the full amount of child support payments, and some do not make any court-ordered payments.[21] As a result, the income for the divorced mother and her children often plunges below the poverty level. In many case, taxpayers wind up supporting the mother and her children through the welfare system.[22]

In an effort to combat these problems, Congress mandated in the late 1980s that states enact legislation to withhold child support from the paychecks of all noncustodial parents (generally fathers). For example, Wisconsin passed legislation that the noncustodial parent pay a set percentage (based on the number of children) of his or her gross income for child support, which ranges from 17% for one child to 35% for five or more children. These child support payments are sent by the employer to the court that handled the divorce, and the court then sends a check to the custodial parent. Additional mechanisms that have been created to pressure the noncustodial parent to pay child support include: withholding the noncustodial parent's income tax refunds, reporting child support arrearages to consumer credit agencies, reporting the names of delinquent noncustodial parents in newspapers, and placing liens on delinquent noncustodial parents' property. Such mechanisms have reduced failure rates of the noncustodial parent to make child support payments, which increases the chances that the custodial parent (generally the mother) will have a steady income from child support.

Empty-Shell Marriages

In empty-shell marriages, the spouses feel no strong attachments to each other. Outside pressures keep the marriage together rather than feelings of warmth and attraction between the partners. Such outside pressures may include business reasons (for example, an elected official wanting to convey a stable family image), investment rea-

sons (for example, husband and wife may have a luxurious home and other property that they do not want to lose by parting), and outward appearances (for example, a couple living in a small community may remain together to avoid the reactions of relatives and friends to a divorce). In addition, a couple may believe that ending the marriage would harm the children or be morally wrong.

John F. Cuber and Peggy B. Harroff have identified three types of empty-shell marriages.[23] In a *devitalized relationship,* husband and wife lack excitement or any real interest in each other or their marriage. Boredom and apathy characterize this relationship. Serious arguments are rare.

In a *conflict habituated relationship,* husband and wife frequently quarrel in private, or they may also quarrel in public, or they may put up a façade of being compatible. The relationship is characterized by considerable conflict, tension, and bitterness.

In a *passive-congenial relationship,* both partners are not happy but are content with their lives and generally feel adequate. The partners may have some interests in common, but those interests are generally insignificant. The spouses contribute little to each other's real satisfactions. This type of relationship generally has little overt conflict.

The number of empty-shell marriages is unknown: It may be as high as (or even higher than) the number of happy marriages. The atmosphere in empty-shell marriages is usually joyless. Members do not share and discuss their problems or experiences with each other. Communication is kept to a minimum. There is seldom any spontaneous expression of affection. Children in such families are usually starved for love and reluctant to have friends over to visit because they are embarrassed about how their parents interact.

The couples in these marriages engage in few activities together and display no pleasure in each other's company. Sexual relations between the partners, as might be expected, are rare and generally unsatisfying. Outsiders may perceive that the partners (and often the children) appear insensitive, cold, and callous to each other. Yet closer observation will reveal that the spouses are highly aware of each other's weaknesses and sensitive areas, and they manage to mention them frequently to hurt each other.

William J. Goode compares empty-shell marriages to marriages that end in divorce:

> Most families that divorce pass through a state—sometimes after the divorce—in which husband and wife no longer feel bound to each other, cease to cooperate or share with each other, and look on one another as almost a stranger. The "empty shell" family is in such a state. Its members no longer feel any strong commitment to many of the mutual role obligations, but for various reasons the husband and wife do not separate or divorce.[24]

It is not known how many empty-shell marriages end in divorce. It is likely that a fair number eventually do. Both spouses must put considerable effort into making a marriage work to prevent an empty-shell marriage from gradually developing.

MARRIAGE COUNSELING

The primary social service for people who are considering a divorce or who have an empty-shell marriage is marriage counseling. (Those who do obtain a divorce may also need counseling to work out adjustment problems, such as adjusting to single life. Generally such counseling is one-on-one, but at times it may include the ex-spouse and the children, depending on the nature of the problem.)

Marriage counseling is provided by a variety of professionals, including social workers, psychologists, guidance counselors, psychiatrists, and members of the clergy. It is also provided (to a greater or lesser extent) by most direct social service agencies.

Marriage counselors generally use a problem-solving approach in which (a) problems are first identified, (b) alternative solutions are generated, (c) the merits and shortcomings of the alternatives are examined, (d) the clients select one or more alternatives to implement, and (e) the extent to which the problems are resolved by the alternatives is later assessed. Because the spouses "own" their problems, they are the primary problem solvers.

A wide range of problems may be encountered by married couples. For example, the couple may experience sexual problems, financial problems, communication problems, problems with relatives, conflicts of interest, infidelity, conflicts on how to discipline and raise children, or drug or alcohol problems. Marriage counselors attempt to have spouses precisely identify their problems and then use the problem-solving format to seek to resolve the issues. In some cases, couples may rationally decide that a divorce is in their best interest.

In marriage counseling, there is considerable effort by the counselor to see both spouses together during sessions. Practically all marital conflicts involve both partners and therefore are best resolved when both partners work together on resolving them. (If the spouses are seen separately, each spouse is likely to become suspicious of what the other is telling the counselor.) By seeing both together, the counselor can facilitate communication between the partners. (When spouses are seen individually, they are also more likely to exaggerate the extent to which their mate is contributing to the disharmony.) Joint sessions allow each partner the opportunity to refute what the other is saying. Only in rare cases is it desirable to hold an individual session with a spouse. For example, if one of the partners wants to work on unwanted emotions concerning a past incestuous relationship, it may be desirable to meet individually with that spouse. (When an individual session is held, the other spouse should be informed of why it is being held and what will be discussed.)

If some of the areas of conflict involve other family members (such as the children), it may be desirable to include these other members in some of the sessions. For example, if a father is irritated that his 14-year-old daughter is often disrespectful to him, the daughter may be invited to the next session to work on this subproblem.

ADDITIONAL MARRIAGE-RELATED SERVICES

Although marriage counseling and divorce counseling are the primary social services for resolving marital conflicts, other related services are available.

Premarital counseling services are designed for couples who are considering marriage. Such services help clients assess whether marriage is in their best interest and also help them to prepare for the realities of marriage. Conflicts that people are having while dating are also worked on, and other topics, such as birth control, are explored.

The self-help organization *Parents Without Partners* (PWP) serves divorced people, unwed mothers or fathers, and stepparents. It is partially a social group, but it is also an organization that helps members with the adjustment problems of raising a family alone.

A recent development in social services is *divorce mediation,* which helps divorcing spouses to resolve (as amicably as possible) such issues as dividing the personal property, deciding custody and child support issues, and working out possible alimony arrangements.

Some agencies are now offering *relationship workshops* and *encounter couple groups,* which are designed to help those who are dating or who are married to improve their relationships through sharing concerns and improving communication patterns.

Violence in Families

We tend to view the family as a social institution in which love and gentleness abound. Sadly, the opposite is often true, with violence pervasive in American families.

Beatings, stabbings, and assaults are common in many families. The extent of violence in families is largely unknown, as much of it is unreported. It is estimated that child abuse, spouse abuse, and other physical violence occur in more than half of all U.S. households.[25] An estimated 50 million people fall victim annually to physical harm at the hands of another family member.[26] Studies show that in 20% of child-abuse cases, a spouse is also abused.[27]

Violence in families is not limited to child abuse and spouse abuse. The number of children who assault their parents is greater than the number of children abused by their parents.[28] *Elder abuse* is increasingly receiving attention. This term refers to "the physical or psychological mistreatment of the elderly."[29] The perpetrator may be the son or daughter of the elderly victim, a caregiver, or some other person. Lewis and Joanne Koch provide one case example:

> *In Chicago, a 19-year-old woman confessed to torturing her 81-year-old father and chaining him to a toilet for seven days. She also hit him with a hammer when he was asleep: "I worked him over real good with it. Then after I made him weak enough, I chained his legs together. After that I left him and rested. I watched TV for a while."*[30]

The varied forms of mistreatment of the elderly are typically grouped into the following four categories:

■ *Physical abuse.* The infliction of physical pain or injury, including bruising, punching, restraining, or sexually molesting.

■ *Psychological abuse.* The infliction of mental anguish, such as intimidating, humiliating, and threatening harm.

■ *Financial abuse.* The illegal or improper exploitation of the victim's assets or property.

■ *Neglect.* The deliberate failure or refusal to fulfill a caregiving obligation, such as denial of food or health care or abandoning the victim.[31]

Violence between children is also common. Some children even use a weapon (such as a knife or a gun) when having conflicts with their siblings.

Patterns of family violence appear to be learned in families. Abused children (when they become adults and parents) are more likely to abuse their children. Also, adults abused as children by their parents who then become the primary caregivers for those parents are more likely to abuse their elderly parents.

The victims of family violence—battered children, battered parents, and battered wives—have common disadvantages. They are generally smaller in size, have less physical strength, and usually feel helpless in relation to the aggressors (primarily because they depend on their aggressors for physical, financial, and emotional support).

Before the 1960s, little attention was given to violence in families, partly because the family was viewed as a sacred institution and a private domain: What went on within families was viewed as a personal concern and the responsibility of family members alone—not outsiders. Over the past four decades, there has been an increasing awareness that violence in families is a major social problem.

Family fights constitute the largest single category of calls to police. The highest rate of police fatalities arises from responses to disturbance calls, and domestic violence cases make up a large proportion of such calls.[32] Suzanne Steinmetz and Murray Straus have noted: "It would be hard to find a group or an institution in American society in which violence is more of an everyday occurrence than it is within the family."[33] Violence not only causes physical harm in families; each incident also weakens the loyalty, affection, and trust among members that are basic to positive family functioning.

One explanation of why family violence occurs is based on the theory that frustration often provokes an aggressive response. A husband or wife who is frustrated at work may come home and take out that frustration on the spouse or the children. A young child frustrated by the action of a sibling may take a poke at him or her. Steinmetz and Straus observe: "In a society such as ours, in which aggression is defined as a normal response to frustration, we can expect that the more frustrating the familial and occupational roles, the greater the amount of violence."[34]

In another explanation, John O'Brien has noted that family members often use physical force to gain an advantage.[35] A parent spanks a child for disciplinary reasons. A sister may shove her brother out of the way in an attempt to obtain something they both want. O'Brien suggests that family members are likely to resort to physical force when other resources are nonexistent, diminished, or exhausted. Thus, an alcoholic husband who feels he has lost the respect of his family may resort to physical abuse as a last-ditch effort to assert his authority.

SPOUSE ABUSE

Spouse abuse, particularly wife beating, was unfortunately tolerated for many years but has now become an issue of national concern. The problem leaped into the spotlight in 1994 following the death of Nicole Brown Simpson, who was savagely stabbed to death, and her former husband (O. J. Simpson) was charged with the murder. At least eight times prior to her death, police had been called to the Simpson home after Nicole claimed she was battered by O. J.[36] (Two years later in a civil trial, O. J. was found guilty of murdering his wife and Ronald Goldman.)

It is not just wives who are abused. Husbands are slapped or shoved with about the same frequency as are wives.[37] The greatest physical damage, however, is usually suffered by women. Studies show that men cause more serious injuries largely because they are physically stronger.[38]

Over 10% of all murder victims are killed by spouses.[39] Women tend to endure cruelty and abuse much longer than men, at times because they feel trapped due to unemployment and financial insecurity. Spouse abuse is sometimes precipitated by the victim; that is, the recipient of the abuse may be the first to use verbal or physical violence in the incident.[40] However, the dominant theme in American spouse abuse is the systematic use of violence and the threat of violence by some men to "keep their wives in line." That is to say, there is a traditional belief held by some segments of our society that husbands have a right to control what their wives do and to force them to be submissive.

Domestic violence from husbands, male partners, or other family members happens so often that violence is the major cause of injury to women.[41] Injuries from woman battering are more common than those from rape, mugging, or even auto accidents.[42]

Incidents of physical abuse between spouses are not isolated, but tend to recur frequently in a marriage. Spouse abuse occurs as often among the well educated as among the less educated.[43]

Most wives who are severely beaten by their husbands do not seek to end the marriage. Wives are more likely to remain in the home if (a) the violence is infrequent, (b) they were abused by

Spouse abuse has become an issue of national concern and new services have been developed to treat domestic violence.

their parents when they were children, or (c) they believe they are financially dependent on their husbands.[44]

Many authorities believe spouse abuse is related to a norm of tolerating violence in American families. Straus notes:

> There seems to be an implicit, taken-for-granted cultural norm which makes it legitimate for family members to hit each other. In respect to husbands and wives, in effect, this means that the marriage license is also a hitting license.[45]

Several studies have found that a sizable number of both men and women believe it is appropriate for a husband to hit his wife "every now and then."[46]

Men batter women for a variety of reasons. Many men have a poor self-image; they are insecure about their worth as breadwinners, fathers, and sexual partners. They tend to have a stereotyped view of their wives as playing a submissive role and as needing to be controlled. Many men use alcohol and other drugs to excess and are much more likely to be violent when intoxicated or high.

In battered-spouse families, a cycle of violence tends to be continually repeated as follows: A battering incident occurs, and the wife sustains injuries. The husband feels remorse, but he also fears his wife may leave or may report the abuse to the police, so he tries to "honeymoon" her into thinking he is a good husband who won't abuse her again. (He may even send flowers, buy expensive gifts, or be overly attentive.) Gradually the "honeymoon" efforts on his part cease, and tensions about work or family matters again begin to build inside him. As the tension builds, a minor incident sets him off, often while he's intoxicated, and he again batters his wife. The battering/honeymoon/tension-building/battering cycle tends to be repeated again and again.

Abusive husbands often isolate their spouses and make them dependent. They try to make their wives sever ties with relatives and friends. They ridicule their wives' friends and relatives, and they usually create an embarrassing scene when the wife is with those friends or relatives. The wife then ends contact with friends and relatives to "keep peace." Abusive husbands make their wives dependent on them by continually ridiculing them, which lowers the women's self-esteem and leads them to play a submissive role. Husbands also create financial dependency, such as by creating barriers that prevent their wives from seeking high-paying employment.

A surprising number of battered women do not permanently leave their husbands for a variety of reasons. Many are socialized to play a subordinate role to their husbands, and the husbands use violence and psychological abuse to make them feel too inadequate to live on their own. Some women believe it is their moral duty to stick it out to the end—that marriage is forever, for better or for worse. Many hope (in spite of the continuing violence) that their husbands will change.

Some fear that, if they try to leave, their husbands will retaliate with even more severe beatings. A fair number do not view leaving as a viable alternative because they feel financially dependent. Many have young children and do not believe they have the resources to raise children on their own. Some believe the occasional beatings are better than the loneliness and insecurity connected with leaving. Some dread the stigma associated with separation or divorce. These women are captives in their own homes.

Fortunately, new services in recent years have been developed for battered women. Shelter homes for battered women and their children have been established in many communities. These shelters give abused women an opportunity to flee from their abusive situation. The women also generally receive counseling, assistance in finding a job, and legal help. Services to battered women now include "safety planning," which is an empowerment approach to help women develop a repertoire of resources to maintain their safety. In some areas, programs are also being established for the husbands. These programs include group therapy for batterers, anger management programs for batterers, marriage counseling for both spouses, and 24-hour hotlines that encourage potential spouse abusers to call when they are angry. (Unfortunately, many batterers refuse to participate in such programs.) Many communities also have public information programs (for example, short television announcements) to inform battered women that they have a legal right not to be abused and that there are resources to stop the abuse.

In an effort to treat domestic abuse as seriously as crimes between strangers, many states have enacted a domestic abuse law which requires police to make an arrest (of either spouse, but usually the husband) if physical abuse has occurred and injury or threat of further harm exists. Police face criminal or civil penalties under the law if they do not make a mandated arrest.[47]

As services for battered wives become more widely available, we may expect an increasing number of these women to flee from their homes and refuse to return until they have some guarantee of their safety.

CHILD ABUSE AND NEGLECT

Although definitions of child abuse and neglect vary somewhat from state to state, Alfred Kadushin and Judith Martin summarize these kinds of situations as including:

■ Physical abuse.

■ Malnourishment; poor clothing; lack of proper shelter, sleeping arrangements, attendance, or supervision. (Includes "failure to thrive" syndrome, which describes infants who fail to grow and develop at a normal rate.)

■ Denial of essential medical care.

■ Failure to attend school regularly.

■ Exploitation, overwork.

■ Exposure to unwholesome or demoralizing circumstances.

■ Sexual abuse.

■ Somewhat less frequently, the definitions include emotional abuse and neglect involving denial of the normal experiences that permit a child to feel loved, wanted, secure, and worthy.[48]

The consequences of child abuse and neglect can be devastating. Gelles notes:

Researchers and clinicians have documented physical, psychological, cognitive, and behavioral consequences of physical abuse, psychological abuse, sexual abuse, and neglect. Physical damage can range from death, brain damage, and permanent disabilities to minor bruises and scrapes. The psychological consequences can range from lowered sense of self-worth to severe psychiatric disorders, including dissociative states. Cognitive problems range from severe organic brain disorders to reduced attention and minor learning disorders. Maltreated children's behavioral problems can include severe violent and criminal behavior and suicide as well as inability to relate to peers.[49]

Physical Abuse. In the past 40 years, there has been considerable national concern about the "battered-child syndrome." The Children's Division of the American Humane Society conducted a nationwide survey of newspaper reports on child abuse and concluded:

The forms or types of abuse inflicted on these children are a negative testimony to the ingenuity and inventiveness of man. By far the greater number of injuries resulted from beatings with various kinds of implements and instruments. The hairbrush was a common implement used to beat children. However, the same purpose was accomplished with deadlier impact by the use of bare fists, straps, electric cords, TV aerials, ropes, rubber hoses, fan belts, sticks, wooden shoes, pool cues, bottles, broom handles, baseball bats, chair legs, and, in one case, a sculling oar. Less imaginative, but equally effective, was plain kicking with street shoes or with heavy work shoes.

Children had their extremities—hands, arms, and feet—burned in open flames as from gas burners or cigarette lighters. Others bore burn wounds inflicted on their bodies with lighted cigarettes, electric irons, or hot pokers. Still others are scalded by hot liquids thrown over them or from being dipped into containers of hot liquids.

Some children were strangled or suffocated by pillows held over their mouths or plastic bags thrown over their heads. A number were drowned in bathtubs, and one child was buried alive.

To complete the list—children were stabbed, bitten, shot, subjected to electric shock, were thrown violently to the floor or against a wall, were stamped on, and one child had pepper forced down his throat.[50]

The survey went on to report that these abused children incurred various kinds of injuries:

The majority had various shapes, sizes, and forms of bruises and contusions. There was a collection of welts, swollen limbs, split lips, black eyes, and lost teeth. One child lost an eye.

Broken bones were common. Some were simple fractures; others compound. There were many broken arms, broken legs, and fractured ribs. Many children had more than one fracture. One five-month-old child was found to have 30 broken bones in his little body.

The grimmest recital of all is the listing of internal injuries and of head injuries. The head injuries particularly were a sizable group. Both the internal injuries and the head injuries were responsible for a great many of the fatalities. In this group, we find damage to internal organs such as ruptured livers, ruptured spleens, and ruptured lungs. Injuries to the head were concussions or skull fractures, with brain hemorrhage and brain damage a frequent diagnosis.

This is indeed a grim, sad, sordid, and horror-filled recital of what happens to children in communities in almost every state of the Union.[51]

Physical abuse involves beating a child to the point at which some physical damage is done. The line between physical abuse and harsh parental discipline is difficult to define. Silver et al. note:

If a parent punishes a child with a belt, is it after the fourth slash with the belt that parental rights end and child abuse begins; is it after the belt raises a welt over two millimeters that it becomes abuse versus parental rights?[52]

Definitions of abuse vary. Some are narrow in scope, restricting abuse to actual serious injury sustained by the child; broader definitions include intent to harm the child and verbal abuse.

In the late 1960s, in response to a growing national concern about child abuse, all states adopted child-abuse and neglect-reporting laws. Such laws are essentially a case-finding device. They require professionals (such as physicians, social workers, counselors, hospital administrators, school administrators, nurses, and dentists) to report suspected cases of child abuse to certain specified agencies, such as the local police department and the county welfare department.

The true extent of child abuse is unknown. Accurate data are difficult to get for two reasons: the failure of citizens and professionals to report suspected cases and the reluctance of abused children to talk. Many battered children, believing their punishment is deserved, keep mute when interviewed by those who might help, and they develop negative self-images.

A significant result of child abuse is that violence breeds violence. George C. Curtis reports evidence showing that abused children may "become tomorrow's murderers and perpetrators of other crimes of violence."[53] When they become parents, there is also a high probability they will

CASE
EXAMPLE 6.1 **Physical Abuse and Murder**

Chicago—Jody Marie Olcott lived only 102 days. She died on November 16, 1994. The coroner's report showed that she had suffered more injuries than most people who live into late adulthood. Charged with second-degree murder in her death was her father, Malcom Olcott, age 34.

Jody Marie was born on August 5, 1994. Her unmarried parents lived together. Her mother, Judy Forbes, worked as a waitress. Her father was unemployed and felt considerable "pressure" over being unemployed and now having parental responsibilities.

Jody's first 2 months were quite normal. Her pediatrician saw her early in October and reported that she had gained nearly 2 pounds and appeared in good health. Shortly after that, Jody's nightmare began. The pathologist who examined Jody after her death noted that she suffered from at least five broken ribs caused about a month earlier by kicking or by punching with a fist.

The pathologist noted that about 10 days before her death she had received bruises to her head, chest, and left elbow. Also, at about the same time, she had received burn marks on her buttocks and her head. The district attorney acknowledged that Mr. Olcott had admitted (at the time of his arrest) to setting Jody on top of a space heater.

The pathologist's report also noted one of Jody's knees was broken, and the other was badly sprained, "possibly resulting from the child being picked up by her legs and then her legs being snapped." At the time of her death, Jody's weight had dropped to 6 pounds—1 pound less than when she was born.

The blow that caused Jody's death occurred during the night of November 15. Ms. Forbes was at her waitressing job at a fast-food restaurant. The district attorney stated that Mr. Olcott was feeling on edge with his financial and family responsibilities. He began drinking. Jody was crying, as she had done for the past several days (probably from the pain of all her injuries). Mr. Olcott stated he just couldn't take the incessant crying. He grabbed Jody and tossed her about 10 feet—hoping she'd land on the sofa. Jody missed the sofa and landed on her head on a hardwood floor. Mr. Olcott told the police that during the next few hours Jody stopped crying but appeared to have trouble breathing and sometimes vomited. When Ms. Forbes came home that evening, she found that Jody did not appear to be breathing. She called for an ambulance. Jody was pronounced dead on arrival, with the cause of death being a blood clot caused by a skull fracture. Ms. Forbes was asked by the police why she did not report the violence occurring to Jody over the past several weeks. Ms. Forbes stated, "Malcom told me if I went to the police, he would leave me and have nothing more to do with me."

become abusive parents.[54] Theoretically, abuse generates an unusually high degree of hostility, which, in future years, may be channeled into violence. A disproportionate number of rapists, murderers, robbers, and spouse abusers were child-abuse victims when they were younger. Abused children are high risks to become runaways, which exposes them to other kinds of victimization and sometimes results in their being involved in criminal activity, such as shoplifting, theft, or prostitution.

Although in rare cases abuse is nonrecurrent, generally it is repeated. Nonrecurrent abuse is usually difficult to document, as the abuser can contrive a plausible explanation for the one-time injuries received by the child.

Gelles reviewed studies on the characteristics of parents and caregivers who are most at risk of abusing their children and found:

■ Abuse was more likely to occur among parents with limited education and few employment skills, among non-White families, and among mother-headed, single-parent families.

■ In many of the families, there was evidence of "family discord" and stress due to limited financial resources. (It is possible that the higher incidence of abuse in the lower classes may partly result from the fact that middle- and upper-class parents are in a better position to conceal the abuse.)

■ Mothers are more likely to abuse their children than fathers. The reasons for this gender difference are probably related to the fact that mothers tend to spend more time with children, and mothers in our society are considered more responsible for the children's behavior than are fathers.

■ More than two-thirds of abused children are permitted to remain in their homes by protective services even after abuse is determined. (Protective services are described later in this chapter.)[55]

Physical Neglect. In contrast to child abuse, child neglect is more a problem of omission than of commission. Specific types of physical neglect include (a) child abandonment; (b) environmental neglect—letting a child live in filth, without proper clothing, unattended, unsupervised, or without proper nourishment; (c) educational neglect, in which a child is allowed to be excessively absent from school; and (d) medical neglect, in which no effort is made to secure needed medical care for the child. Although child neglect has received less national attention than child abuse, it is the most common situation in which protective services agencies must intervene.

In rare cases, such as child abandonment, the parent rejects the parental role. In most child-neglect cases, however, the parent inadequately performs the role. Kadushin and Martin define a typical neglectful mother as physically exhausted, mentally impoverished, emotionally deprived, and socially isolated.[56] Parental neglect is more likely to be found among those who are poverty stricken or who live on marginal incomes.

Vincent De Francis provides the following description of what a social worker encountered in investigating a neglect complaint:

> *What I saw as I entered the room was utter, stark disorganization. The room was a combined kitchen-dining room. At the other end of the room, two scrawny, owl-eyed, frightened children—a girl of about four and a boy of three—stared silently at me. Except for thin cotton undershirts, they were stark naked. They had sore crusts on their legs and arms. They were indescribably dirty, hair matted, body and hands stained and covered with spilled food particles. Sitting on a urine-soaked and soiled mattress in a baby carriage behind them was a younger child—a boy about two.*
>
> *The floor was ankle-deep in torn newspapers. There were feces in about a half-dozen spots on the floor, and the air was fetid and saturated with urine odor.*
>
> *There were flies everywhere. What seemed like giant roaches were crawling over the paper-strewn floor. The kitchen sink and gas stove were piled high with greasy and unwashed dishes, pots, and pans.*[57]

Emotional Neglect. Meeting a child's affectional needs is as important to normal growth and development as meeting his or her physical needs. Yet emotional neglect is difficult to define and document in the precise terms required by law.

The National Clearinghouse on Child Neglect and Abuse defines emotional neglect as:

> *. . . failure to provide the child the emotional nurturing or emotional support necessary for the development of a sound personality, as for example, subjecting the child to rejection or to a home climate charged with tension, hostility, and anxiety-producing occurrences which result in perceivable problems in children.*[58]

Interpreted broadly, the problem with this definition is that practically every parent at times is guilty of such neglect. Other definitions of emotional neglect encounter the same problem. Nevertheless, there is solid agreement that some

Is This Emotional Neglect?

The following case example raises a number of as-yet-unanswered questions surrounding emotional neglect.

Gary, age 9, was the only child of Mr. and Mrs. Jim N. The N. family lived in a suburb of a metropolitan area, and Gary's physical needs were adequately met. Yet Gary was not doing well in school. He repeated the first grade and now is repeating the third grade.

Gary was referred for psychological testing and was found to have a very low self-concept. His self-concept was so negative that he refused to study math for fear of failing and would not participate in any competitive games with peers. He instead preferred to play by himself, with toys appropriate to children of an age level of 5.

A home study found that Mr. N. was a stoic, unaffectional person who was seldom at home, as he spent long hours operating a service station he owned. Mrs. N. had such a distasteful personality and disposition that she was unable to hold a job and had no close friends. Below average in intellectual functioning, she completed only the ninth grade. In her interactions with Gary, she was observed to have a short tolerance level, to frequently berate and criticize him, and to call him "stupid" and "an idiot." Gary appeared somewhat fearful of her and tried to avoid interacting with her. Both parents refused to take parent effectiveness training or to receive counseling.

- Are Gary's personal problems (negative self-image) a result of interactions with his parents or of some other factors (for example, school environment, a past traumatic experience, or an inherited disposition)?

- Even if it is assumed that his problems are due to his parental interactions, how can this be proved in court?

- Would his personal problems be reduced or intensified if he were removed from his home and placed in foster care? For example, would moving him to a foster home lead him to feel rejected by his parents or to blame himself for the move because he erroneously assumed he was "bad"?

children do suffer from emotional neglect, even when they are adequately cared for physically.

Emotional neglect is very difficult to document in court. When emotional neglect is accompanied by physical neglect, protective services agencies make a case based on the physical neglect.

Sexual Abuse. Sexual abuse within families has in recent years become an issue of national concern. It is discussed at length in Chapter 7.

Unwholesome or Demoralizing Conditions. Children who are exposed to their parents' continued prostitution, criminal activity, drug addiction, and severe alcoholism are also considered in need of protective services. Such exposure is deemed injurious to the moral development of children.

Exploitation. This category involves forcing a child to work for unreasonably long hours or encouraging a child to beg, steal, or engage in prostitution.

Abusive and Neglectful Parents. No single cause can fully explain why parents abuse or neglect their children. Available research indicates that abusive and neglectful parents may have little in common. The following factors[59] have been found to be associated with parents who abuse their children:

- Some abusive parents were themselves abused as children. If not abused, they generally had a lack of stable love relationships in their childhood and an inadequate gratification of early emotional needs.

- Although abuse, like neglect, is more heavily concentrated among the lower classes, it is more randomly distributed through the population than is neglect.

- Frequently, one child in a family is singled out to be the target of the abuse. Many reasons appear to account for this. The child may be viewed as mentally slow or as a potential delinquent. Where there is marital conflict, one child may be chosen as the victim because of a resemblance to the disliked spouse. One child may cry more, be more hyperactive, or be more demanding of parental care. The child may be punished because he or she was conceived prior to marriage, is illegitimate, or is the result of an unwanted pregnancy.

- In some cases, the abused child contributes to the process by placing greater than normal burdens on parental patience by having severe temper tantrums; by having feeding, speech, or toilet-training problems; and/or by being restless, negative, unresponsive, listless, whiny, or fussy.

- The child who is the victim may, in disturbed families, be essential for the psychic stability of the family. It appears that some disturbed families need a "whipping boy" or "scapegoat" to maintain an equilibrium within the family. Sometimes when an abused child is removed, another is selected to be the victim and thereby fulfills the "stability" role.

- Abusive parents often show an absence of guilt, have a tendency toward social isolation, have a high level of overall aggressiveness, are prone to impulsivity, tend to have emotional problems, have feelings of inadequacy, and have a low tolerance of criticism.

- Environmental stress factors (for example, marital problems), economic pressures, and social isolation sometimes help trigger abuse.

- Abusive parents tend to believe in strict discipline and to view misbehavior by their children as willful, deliberate disobedience. Also characteristic is a high demand for the child to perform to gratify the parent.

- Alcohol/drug abuse plays an important contributing role in some cases.

The following factors[60] have been identified as associated with child neglect:

- The preponderance of families comes from the lower socioeconomic classes. Financial deprivation is a major contributing factor. Many also have inadequate housing.

- A high percentage (60% in some studies) are one-parent families, generally headed by a female.

- Neglectful parents frequently have an atypically large number of children.

- A fair number of neglectful mothers are below normal in intellectual capacity.

- Neglectful parents (particularly the mothers who have the most contact with children) are physically and emotionally exhausted, have health problems, are socially withdrawn or isolated, are frustrated, are apathetic, and lack hope. Such factors lead them to be "indifferent" toward their children.

- Neglectful parents tend to have been emotionally deprived during their early childhood years. Similar to abusive parents, they lacked stable affectional relationships when they were young. Such early childhood experiences appear to lead to later emotional inadequacies and then, when combined with severe financial and environmental stress, result in physical and emotional exhaustion.

- Neglectful parents are not without intrapsychic distress but are generally less emotionally disturbed than abusive parents. Similar to abusive parents, they tend to be socially isolated.

PROTECTIVE SERVICES

Under the concept of *parens patriae,* the state is ultimately a parent to all children. When the natural parents neglect, abuse, or exploit a child, the state has the legal right and responsibility to intervene. Protective services has been defined as "a specialized casework service to neglected, abused, exploited, or rejected children. The focus of the service is preventive and nonpunitive and is geared toward rehabilitation through identification and treatment of the motivating factors which underlie" the problem.[61]

Brief History. In colonial days, a child was regarded as chattel (an item of personal property). This gave parents the right to sell the child, exploit his or her labor, offer the child as a sacrifice, or even kill the child at birth. Although most communities regulated and restricted such behaviors, it was not until the era of industrialization that children were considered to have any rights. These rights have gradually been expanded. In the early 20th century, child labor laws were finally enacted, prohibiting parents from exploiting the labor of their children.

Agencies providing protective services in America trace their origin to the case of Mary Ellen in 1875.[62] Mary Ellen was severely beaten and neglected by the couple who had raised her since infancy. Concerned community citizens were unaware of any legal approach to protect her. In desperation, they appealed to the Society for the Prevention of Cruelty to Animals. (It's interesting to note that at this time organizations existed to protect animals, but not children.) Mary Ellen was brought to the court's attention by this society. She was given protection by the court and was placed with another family. The abusive couple were sentenced to prison. Following this dramatic case, the Society for the Prevention of Cruelty to Children was formed in New York. Gradually other such societies throughout the United States were formed, laws protecting children from abuse and neglect were enacted, and agencies providing protective services were established.

Almost from the start, protective services had two focuses: a law enforcement approach and a rehabilitative approach. The law enforcement focus emphasized punishment for the abusive or neglectful parents, whereas the rehabilitative approach emphasized the importance of helping the parents and keeping the family together rather than disrupting it. Throughout the 20th century, protective services have generally taken the rehabilitative approach.

Since the late 1960s, there has been a dramatic growth of interest in services to prevent and treat child abuse. With this interest came, in 1975, passage of Title XX to the Social Security Act, making protective services mandatory for each state and providing federal reimbursement for most costs. A federal Child Abuse Prevention and Treatment Act, passed in January 1974, provides direct assistance to states to help them develop child-abuse and child-neglect programs.

Processes in Protective Services. Extensive efforts have been made to encourage parents who have mistreated their children (or feel they may mistreat them) to request agency services voluntarily. Radio and TV announcements, along with posters, announce the availability of stress hotline services that parents may call in many communities.

Parents who mistreat their children, however, do not generally seek help. Currently, initiation of services most often results from the legal requirement of mandatory reporting by professionals of suspected abuse, physical neglect, sexual abuse, and emotional injury. The list of professionals required to report includes, among others, social workers, school personnel, doctors, day-care workers, counselors, legal personnel, nurses, and dentists. The agencies to which reports are made include the local police department, the county welfare department, and the county sheriff. The law grants civil and criminal immunity to the professionals required to make such reports and also specifies penalties for failure to report.

Each state has the legal right and responsibility to intervene when a child is abused, neglected, or exploited. This right and responsibility are delegated to protective services (in many states protective services is located within public welfare departments).

Case finding is almost always through a complaint referral. Complaints generally are filed by neighbors, relatives, or family friends—in addition to those professionals already mentioned who are required by law to report abuse. A complaint is a report of a possible neglect or abuse situation that needs exploration. The complainant may remain anonymous. Occasionally, unfounded complaints are made to harass a parent.

Some complainants feel guilty about making a report, and they are given reassurance that they are performing a very useful function that is necessary to protect and safeguard children. They are also informed that their identity (name) will not be revealed to the family against which the report has been made.

All complaints are then investigated by the protective services agency. Some agencies arrange for the initial visit by telephone. Others prefer an unannounced visit, which has the advantage of allowing the social worker to view the home environment in its day-to-day appearance. The initial approach is direct and frank. The social worker conveys that a concern about potential danger to a child has been expressed and needs to be explored; if a potential danger does exist, the worker's responsibility and interest are to be helpful to both the parents and their children.

The social worker attempts to obtain an objective and accurate description of the situation. Specific information relevant to the complaint is sought. For example, if the complaint is that a child appears malnourished and is frequently absent from school, specific questions are asked about the daily diet of the child, any illnesses he or she has had, and the specific dates and reasons why the child has been absent from school. Such details are necessary to determine whether the child is in fact in danger and what help (if any) is needed. The information is also essential as evidence if a petition is made to the court to remove the child from the home. Obtaining this information must be done tactfully because it is also important that the social worker try to develop a working relationship with the parents.

During this evaluation process, the social worker almost always attempts to see the child who allegedly has been endangered. If abuse or neglect exists, the objective is to convey to the parents that the focus of protective services is to prevent further neglect or abuse and to alleviate the factors that are now a danger to the child. Because many families charged with abuse or neglect have multiple problems, services may be far ranging (involving, for example, services related to health, education, finances, housing, counseling, employment, parent effectiveness training, day care, and so on).

When there is no evidence of neglect or abuse, the case may be closed after the initial interview. For families with serious problems, continued services may be provided for years.

If the child is clearly in danger (for example, is a victim of repeated severe abuse) or if the parents are unable or unwilling to make changes essential for the long-term well-being of the child, the youngster may have to be removed from the home. Protective services agencies view court action as "a means of protecting the child rather than prosecuting the parents."[63]

If the social worker decides it is necessary to remove the child from the home, the parents' voluntary consent is first sought. If it is not received, a petition is made to the court requesting that the child receive protection. (Court action is atypical in protective services; studies suggest that most cases are closed without it.)[64]

After a petition is filed, a preliminary hearing is held within a few weeks. Parents are permitted to be represented by an attorney, and the normal adversarial court procedures are followed. The social worker must support the petition with documented facts. The judge has the responsibility of protecting the rights not only of the child but also of the parents. At the preliminary hearing, the parents are asked if they will consent to or contest the petition. If they decide to contest and if evidence of abuse and neglect is substantiated, a trial is held.

In making a disposition, a number of avenues are open to the judge. She or he may decide that there is not sufficient evidence of neglect or abuse to warrant any action. Or the judge can place the child under supervision of the court while permitting him or her to remain at home. Such supervision puts pressure on the family to make needed changes, with the threat of the child being removed if the changes are not made. The judge also has the option of placing the child under protective legal custody. Under this arrangement, legal custody is assigned to a social agency, which then has the authority to remove the child if essential changes are not made. The judge can also terminate the parents' legal rights and place the child under guardianship of the agency. Under this disposition, the child is automatically removed from the home.

For children who are in imminent danger, many jurisdictions have provisions that allow either the protective services agency or the family court to remove the child immediately. Such children are then usually placed in a temporary foster home. When a child is removed for emergency reasons, a court hearing must be held within 24 hours to determine the appropriateness of the action. Unless the court is satisfied that protection of the child requires removal from the home, the child must be returned to his or her parents.

Involuntary Services. Protective services cannot withdraw from the situation if it finds that the parents are uncooperative or resistant. For most social services, clients are voluntary recipients. Protective services is one of the few services in which participation is involuntary (probation and parole are other examples).

Because protective services is involuntary, and because provision of services is based on an "outside" complaint, the recipients are likely to view the services as an invasion of privacy. The initial contact by the social worker may arouse hostility, be viewed as a threat to family autonomy, and perhaps raise some guilt about incidents in which the parents have mistreated their children in the past. Having one's functioning as a parent questioned and explored arouses substantial emotional feelings. Although the focus of protective services theoretically is rehabilitative and nonpunitive, protective services clients generally view the services as punitive and investigatory.

Some recipients of protective services remain hostile and resistant throughout the time services are provided. Others, in time, form a productive working relationship with the agency, in which case positive changes are much more likely to occur. A few individuals are cooperative from the beginning, perhaps because they recognize that their family needs help.

In working with parents who neglect or abuse their children, the social worker must show respect for the parents as people while in no way conveying acceptance of their mistreatment. The worker needs to convey empathy with their situation, be warm, and yet be firm about the need for positive changes. This approach is illustrated in the following interview:

> The C. family was referred to the child welfare agency by a hospital which treated the 6-year-old boy, Wade, for a broken arm suffered in a beating by his mother.
>
> Both parents said they whipped the children because they believed in firm discipline, and they challenged the worker's right to question this. Mr. C. again attempted to avoid the subject of Wade's beating by describing at length how strict his parents had been with him.
>
> Again the worker brought the conversation back to the C.'s own disciplinary practices by saying that children had to be dealt with firmly, but the injury of a child was a serious matter. He added, "I can understand that one may be so upset he has trouble controlling himself." Mrs. C. hesitatingly said, "I was so upset and too angry," and broke into tears. The worker replied that, if together they could try to understand why Mrs. C. gets so upset, perhaps the behavior would not continue. Mr. C., who had been silent for a while, said he realized it was serious and that he did not approve of Mrs. C. beating the children but did not know what to do. He had told her that this was bad for the youngsters, but she continued. Mrs. C. remarked that looking back on Wade's beating was a terrible experience. She did not realize she had injured him until his arm became swollen. She supposed it was her anger and her temper that did it. She would like to talk to someone and she does need help.[65]

The protective services worker must be ready to perform a variety of roles: teacher, enabler, adviser, coordinator of treatment, intervener, supporter, confidante, and expediter. The focus must be on constantly identifying concrete needs, selecting intervention approaches, and providing specific services. Workers must also be ready to collaborate with other professional groups: the doctors treating the child, schoolteachers, lawyers, and judges.

A wide variety of treatment resources are used in attempting to make the needed changes. Crisis nurseries, extended day-care centers, and emergency foster homes provide short-term shelter to relieve a potentially damaging crisis situation. Parent effectiveness training programs, group therapy, and family life education programs sometimes are useful in curbing the abuse or neglect. Homemakers relieve the frustrated, overburdened mother of some of the daily load of child care. Emergency relief funds are sometimes provided to meet immediate rent, heat, food, and electricity expenses. Behavior modification programs, such as modeling and role playing, have been used to change the behaviors of parents toward their children. "Emergency parents" have been used in some communities to go into a home and stay with a child who has been left unsupervised and unprotected. Psychotherapy and counseling have also been provided by protective services workers and other professionals. A self-help group, Parents Anonymous, is described in Exhibit 6.3. (Very few communities have the resources to provide all of these services. In many cities, the primary intervention resources available to protective services workers are their own counseling capacities and their ability to remove from the home children who are in danger.)

Kadushin and Martin have reviewed studies on the effectiveness of protective services and conclude:

> In summary, the evaluation studies suggest that the agencies have achieved some modest measure of success. The amount of change one might reasonably expect the agencies to effect must be assessed against the great social and personal deprivation characteristic of the client families. Even the modest success achieved may have been more than could have been expected initially.
>
> The resources available to treat these families are limited. The technology available to the worker in trying to effect change in such families is blunt and imprecise. . . .

> Scarce resources backed by a weak technology applied to a group of involuntary, disturbed clients resistive to change and living in seriously deprived circumstances would seem to guarantee the likelihood of limited success.[66]

Social workers have found protective services to be demanding. Burnout occurs at a higher rate among protective services workers than in many other social welfare areas.

Family Preservation Programs. With the implementation of mandatory child-abuse and child-neglect reporting in the 1960s, the number of reports of suspected abuse and neglect skyrocketed. In many cases where abuse or neglect was determined to be occurring, the maltreated children were placed in temporary placements—typically foster homes. By the end of the 1960s, there was increasing concern about the number of children in foster care and the cost. There was widespread questioning of both the need to remove so many children from their biological homes and the effectiveness of foster care as a means of dealing with abused or neglected children. As a result, intensive family preservation programs were developed as a mechanism for protecting children and preserving families.

Family preservation is a model of intervention developed specifically for work with families in which the placement of one or more of the children is imminent. Gelles describes family preservation services as follows:

> The essential feature is that family preservation services are intensive, short-term, crisis interventions. Services are provided in the client's home, although social workers do not actually move in. The length of home visit is variable—it is not confined to the "50-minute" clinical hour. Services are available 7 days a week, 24 hours a day, not just during business hours Monday through Friday. Caseloads are small—two or three families per worker. Soft services, such as therapy and education, and hard services, such as food stamps, housing, a homemaker, and supplemental Social Security, are available.[67]

Family preservation services are typically limited to 4 to 6 weeks.

EXHIBIT 6.3

Parents Anonymous (PA)

Self-help organizations (such as Alcoholics Anonymous, Parents and Friends of Lesbians and Gays, Overeaters Anonymous, and Weight Watchers) have had considerable rehabilitative success. One such group, Parents Anonymous (PA), has been particularly effective at helping individuals who have abused or neglected their children.

PA was established in 1970 in California by Jolly K., who was desperate to find help to meet her needs. For 4 years, she had struggled with an uncontrollable urge to punish her daughter severely. One afternoon she attempted to strangle the child. She sought help from the local child-guidance clinic and was placed in therapy. When asked by her therapist what she could do about this situation, she formed an idea: "If alcoholics can stop drinking by getting together, and gamblers can stop gambling, maybe the same principle would work for abusers, too."[a] With her therapist's encouragement, she formed Mothers Anonymous in 1970 and started a few local chapters in California. Now the organization has chapters in most areas of the United States and Canada, and the name has been changed to Parents Anonymous because fathers who abuse their children are also eligible to join.

PA uses some of the basic therapeutic concepts of Alcoholics Anonymous. It is a crisis intervention program that offers two main forms of help:

1. Regular group meetings in which members share experiences and feelings and learn to control their emotions better.

2. Personal and telephone contact among members during periods of crisis, particularly when a member feels a nearly uncontrollable desire to take his or her anger or frustration out on a child.

Parents may be referred to PA by a social agency (including protective services) or may be self-referrals who are aware they need help.

Cassie Starkweather and S. Michael Turner describe why some parents who abuse their children would rather participate in a self-help group than receive professional counseling:

It has been our experience that most [abusive] parents judge themselves more harshly than other more objective people tend to judge them. The fear of losing their children frequently diminishes with reassurance from other members that they are not the monsters they think they are.

Generally speaking, PA members are so afraid they are going to be judged by others as harshly as they judge themselves that they are afraid to go out [to] seek help. Frequently, our members express fears of dealing with a professional person, seeing differences in education, sex, or social status as basic differences that would prevent easy communication or mutual understanding.

Members express feelings of gratification at finding that other parents are "in the same boat." They contrast this with their feelings about professionals who, they often assume, have not taken out the time from their training and current job responsibilities to raise families of their own.[b]

PA emphasizes honesty and directness. In the outside world, parents who are prone to abuse their children learn to hide this problem because society finds it so detestable. In contrast, the goal in PA is to help parents admit and accept the fact that they are abusive. The term *abuse* is used liberally at meetings. PA has found that this insistence on frankness has a healthy effect. Parents are relieved because finally they have found a

(continued)

EXHIBIT 6.3   *(continued)*

group of people who are able to accept abusive parents for what they really are. Furthermore, it is only after they are able to admit they are abusive that they can begin to find ways to cope with this problem.

During PA meetings, parents are expected to say why they believe they are beating their child, and the members challenge one another to find ways to curb the abuse. Members also share constructive approaches that have been successful for them, and efforts are made to help one another develop specific plans for dealing with potentially abusive episodes. Members learn to recognize danger signs and then to take the necessary action to avoid committing abuse.

PA stresses protecting people's anonymity and confidentiality. This protection permits group members to discuss their experiences and asocial thoughts without risk of public disclosure. The fact that they are sharing their experiences with

other parents who have abused children assures their being able to "confess" without danger of humiliation, recrimination, or rejection.

Group members develop a sense of "oneness," and often the group becomes a surrogate family. Each member is given the phone numbers of all others in the group and is urged to reach for the phone instead of the child when feeling distressed. Members are gradually transformed into "lay professionals" who are able to help other abusers and who perceive themselves as skillful at this because they have, at one time, been child abusers.

The group leader or chapter chairperson is always a parent who at one time abused a child. Members can identify more readily with an abuser than they can with a professional therapist. Among the reasons PA is successful is that it diminishes the social isolation of abusive parents and provides them with social supports.

[a] Phyllis Zauner, "Mothers Anonymous: The Last Resort," in *The Battered Child*, Jerome E. Leavitt, ed. (Morristown, NJ: General Learning Press, 1974), p. 247.
[b] Cassie L. Starkweather and S. Michael Turner, "Parents Anonymous: Reflections on the Development of a Self-Help Group," in *Child Abuse: Intervention and Treatment*, Nancy C. Ebeling and Deborah A. Hill, eds. (Acton, MA: Publishing Sciences Group, 1975), p. 151.

Initial evaluations of intensive family preservation programs were uniformly enthusiastic. They were claimed to be successful in protecting the children involved and in saving costs by reducing placement of children outside the home. In recent years, however, there has been an increasing level of criticism of family preservation programs. Gelles concludes: "To date, no evaluation study that uses a randomly assigned control group has found that intensive family preservation programs reduce placement, costs or the risk of maltreatment."[68] There is a danger that failing to remove children who are being abused in a home actually places those children at risk of re-abuse or even fatal abuse.

Patrick Murphy describes one family preservation case that ended in tragedy:

In December 1991, the aunt of a 3-year-old girl told the family services department that her sister and her sister's lover had physically abused the child. State investigators confirmed the abuse: the child had bruises and rope burns on her body. Instead of bringing the case to court, the department provided a housekeeper and a social worker who between them went to the home a total of 37 times over the next 90 days. The housekeeper helped the mother clean up and make dinner. The social worker took her out for meals and shopping.

On March 7, 1992, the aunt telephoned the family services agency again, pleading that the child was still being abused. The agency ignored her. On March 17, the agency closed the case with a glowing report on how well the family was doing. Several hours later, the girl was dead. An autopsy revealed that boiling water had been poured on her genitals and that she had been struck on the head with a blunt instrument. Her body was covered with 43 scars, bruises and rope burns, most of which had been made in the previous few weeks. She weighed 17 pounds.[69]

Rights of Children versus Rights of Parents. Earlier in American history, the law guarded the rights of parents but gave little attention to the rights of children. In recent years, defining and protecting the rights of children have received national attention, as indicated by a variety of child advocacy efforts and the specification of various "bill of rights for children" proclamations. Protective services, particularly in contested court cases, encounters the problem of defining the respective rights of parents and children. The balance of rights between parents and children varies from community to community.[70]

Some of the situations in which this balance becomes an issue are the following. If parents, for religious reasons, are opposed to their child's receiving medication for a serious health problem, should the state intervene? Should the state intervene when an unmarried parent is sexually promiscuous yet is meeting his or her children's basic physical and emotional needs? Should the state intervene when a child is being raised in a homosexual environment or in a commune where lifestyles and mores are substantially different? Should the state intervene in families in which a child has serious emotional problems and the parents refuse to seek professional help? Should the state intervene in certain ethnic settings when educational needs are not being met? Should intervention occur when a father uses harsh discipline by whipping a child two or three times a week? Should the state intervene in families in which there is long-term alcoholism and serious marital discord? Should the state intervene when a child is living in filth, has ragged clothing, and seldom bathes, even though his or her emotional and social needs are being met?

Different workers, different judges, and different communities would probably disagree on what should be done. The reluctance to intervene may have tragic consequences, as indicated in the following case:

In 1953, a boy of 13 was referred to a children's court because of chronic truancy. A psychiatric examination established the fact that the boy was "drawn to violence" and represented "a serious danger to himself and to others." Psychiatric treatment was recommended by the psychiatrist and social workers concerned with the boy's situation. The mother refused to accept the recommendation and refused to bring the boy back for treatment. Should the mother have been forced to accept treatment for the boy? This is a question of limits of protection intervention. Nothing was done. Ten years later the boy, Lee Harvey Oswald, assassinated President Kennedy.[71]

Births Outside of Marriage

Women between the ages of 15 and 24 constitute about 40% of the total population of women of childbearing age—yet they account for roughly 70% of births outside of marriage.[72] More than a million teenage women become pregnant each year. Most of these pregnancies are unplanned and unwanted and result from misinformation or lack of access to birth control. Roughly 60% of these teenagers have babies, with the remainder ending the pregnancy through abortion or miscarriage.[73] Two of every five American women giving birth to their first child were not married when they became pregnant.[74] Four of five teenage marriages end in divorce; many of these marriages were preceded by a pregnancy.[75] For those who are unmarried when the child is born, over 90% decide to keep the baby rather than give it up for adoption.[76]

About 70% of African American babies are born to single women.[77] African American women have a substantially higher rate of birth outside of marriage than White women.[78] Coleman and Cressey give the following reasons for the high birthrate among single African American women:

> *Although the causes are not entirely clear, several factors stand out. First and foremost, blacks are much more likely to be poor than whites, and the illegitimacy rate is much higher among poor people from all ethnic groups. Second, the prejudice and discrimination that have been aimed at blacks for so many years have hit particularly hard at black males from poor homes. The extremely high rate of unemployment among this group makes it much harder to live up to the expectations of fatherhood, and fathers who feel inadequate to meet the needs of their families are far more likely to withdraw and leave their support to the welfare department. Third, the pattern of early pregnancy and single-parent homes has been passed down from one generation to the next in the black underclass.[79]*

The higher birthrates among single non-White women do not necessarily mean that unmarried non-Whites are more likely to be promiscuous. They may simply mean that non-Whites have less access to contraceptives, they may be less likely to seek an abortion, or they may be less likely to marry the father before the birth of the child.

Although teenage women represent roughly 25% of the population of childbearing age, they account for over 45% of all births outside of marriage.[80] These statistics emphasize that birth outside of marriage is a problem that is disproportionately faced by adolescents. Teenagers who marry when pregnant are nearly as likely to be single parents sometime in the future (due to divorce) as are those who are unmarried at the time of the child's birth.

Many adolescents are not adequately informed about the reproductive process and tend not to use contraceptives. Some teenage women think that, if they take a birth control pill once a week, they're okay; some believe it's safe to have sex standing up; some are afraid birth control will harm them or their future babies.[81]

Many unmarried mothers are simply not prepared—by education, work experience, or maturity—to undertake the dual responsibility of parenthood and economic support. As a result, society inevitably must contribute to the support of these children through public assistance payments and social welfare services.

Fifty years ago, both premarital intercourse and births outside of marriage were considered immoral in our society. (In fact, children born outside of marriage were labeled "illegitimate" and were usually stigmatized as much as the mother. The terms *illegitimate* and *illegitimacy* persist today, even though they stigmatize innocent people.) In the 1940s, Alfred Kinsey found, however, that high percentages of the population had experienced premarital intercourse.[82] Since the Kinsey studies, attitudes toward premarital intercourse have become more tolerant; today, few people are virgins when they marry.

Attitudes toward birth outside of marriage have also become somewhat more tolerant. Few parents now send their pregnant daughter off to a maternity home to avoid "disgracing" the family. However, we sometimes see the unusual situation in which parents tolerate premarital intercourse yet, if their daughter becomes pregnant, they strongly disapprove.

Why are births outside of marriage seen as a social problem by most Americans? There are many answers to this question. Some parents still feel "disgraced" if their daughter becomes pregnant. Some single pregnant women (and their parents) view it as a problem because difficult decisions need to be made about whether to end the pregnancy. If it is decided not to have an abortion, decisions need to be made about adoption, continued education or employment, a possible marriage, living arrangements, and perhaps welfare assistance. The father of the child must make decisions about his role and the extent to which he will seek to provide emotional and financial support.

Some people see birth outside of marriage as a social problem—a sign of a breakdown in the traditional family and a symptom of moral decay. Others assert that it is a problem mainly because the great majority of these children are born to women who are simply not yet prepared—by experience, education, or maturity—to be a parent or to provide for a family financially. Authorities who view birth outside of marriage as a problem for this reason are concerned about the effects on the child of being raised by a mother who is in many ways merely an older child herself. They are also concerned about the effects on the mother of trying to maintain a one-parent family with limited financial and personal resources. Finally, some authorities view birth outside of marriage as a problem because of the high cost to society of having to make welfare payments to large numbers of single-parent families (see Chapter 4).

Is the social stigma attached to birth outside of marriage functional? Certainly it is not to either the child or the mother. On the other hand, some authorities have argued that the stigma is functional to society because it discourages births outside of marriage and thereby helps perpetuate the nuclear family, which provides a structure for the financial support and socialization of children. In response to this view, it can be argued that this punitive approach may not be the optimal way to reduce the incidence of births outside of marriage. The Sex Information and Education Council of the United States (SIECUS) asserts that a more effective approach would involve quality educational programs about responsible sexuality. SIECUS asserts that the goals of sex education should be:

1. Information *To provide accurate information about human sexuality, including: growth and development, human reproduction, anatomy, physiology, masturbation, family life, pregnancy, childbirth, parenthood, sexual response, sexual orientation, contraception, abortion, sexual abuse, HIV/AIDS and other sexually transmitted diseases.*

2. Attitudes, values, and insights *To provide an opportunity for young people to question, explore, and assess their sexual attitudes in order to develop their own values, increase self-esteem, develop insights concerning relationships with members of both genders, and understand their obligations and responsibilities to others.*

3. Relationships and interpersonal skills *To help young people develop interpersonal skills, including communication, decision-making, assertiveness, and peer refusal skills, as well as the ability to create satisfying relationships. Sexuality education programs should prepare students to understand their sexuality effectively and creatively in adult roles. This would include helping young people develop the capacity for caring, supportive, non-coercive, and mutually pleasurable intimate and sexual relationships.*

4. Responsibility *To help young people exercise responsibility regarding sexual relationships, including addressing abstinence, how to resist pressures to become prematurely involved in sexual intercourse, and encouraging the use of contraception and other sexual health measures. Sexuality education should be a central component of programs designed to reduce the prevalence of sexually-related medical problems, including teenage pregnancies, sexually transmitted diseases including HIV infection, and sexual abuse.*[83]

Even with over 1 million teenagers becoming pregnant each year, the question of whether to provide sex education is still a controversial issue in many school systems. Apparently, many people believe sex education will lead to promiscuity and to teenage pregnancies. Advocates of sex education argue that such programs reduce the number of teenage pregnancies.

Health clinics located in or near high schools appear particularly effective in reducing the number of teenage pregnancies. Such clinics provide birth control information and also prescribe contraceptives for sexually active people.[84] Critics of this approach assert that making birth control information and contraceptives more readily available will simply increase sexual activity. The response of the health clinics to this criticism is that learning accurate information about human reproduction in an educational setting is more desirable than the alternative of receiving largely inaccurate information from peers on the street.

The peril of AIDS has given sex education in schools a major boost. The best way of stopping the transmission of AIDS is through quality sex

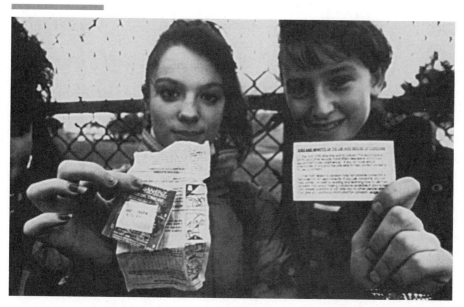

High schools in several U.S. cities are now freely distributing condoms to teenagers. This program has two objectives: to reduce teen pregnancy and to curb the spread of HIV.

education programs that provide accurate information on safe sex practices.[85]

One motivation for the passage of the 1996 welfare reform act was the desire to change policies that conservatives claim reward early childbearing by single mothers. The welform reform act denies public assistance payments to teenage mothers, except under the following conditions: States can provide payments to unmarried teenage parents only if a mother under 18 is living at home or in another adult-supervised setting and attends high school or an alternative educational or training program as soon as the child is 12 weeks old. The underlying reason behind denying welfare payments to most teenage mothers is to send a message to teenagers that having babies will not be financially rewarded; that is, conservatives hope this will discourage teenage women from becoming pregnant.[86] Most authorities who study this issue believe this reasoning is flawed; if the "welfare incentive" theory is accurate, then one would expect to find higher teenage birthrates in the states with the highest welfare payments, but this has never been true.[87]

SINGLE-PARENT SERVICES

Services to single women who become pregnant have become known as single-parent services. A high proportion of pregnant single women decide to carry the baby to full term and then keep the child. The scope of single-parent services extends from predelivery to postdelivery. Single-parent services are provided by certain public agencies (generally the public welfare department) and by private agencies (such as Catholic Social Services and Lutheran Social Services).

Typical single-parent services include:

■ *Alternatives counseling:* The pregnant single woman is helped to make decisions about carrying the baby to full term, having an abortion, keeping the child, terminating parental rights, deciding on foster placement, and undergoing adoption counseling. (Workers in single-parent services generally refrain from revealing their own values about abortion and the other alternatives to the clients because clients have the legal right to make their own decisions in these matters.)

■ *Physical and mental childbirth preparation:* Clients are informed about the effects of drug and alcohol abuse on the embryo. They are prepared for childbirth, given pre- and post-natal counseling, and provided with information on the effects of venereal diseases. Clients also receive mental and physical health counseling.

■ *Counseling on legal issues:* Areas covered include paternity action, procedures for termination of parental rights, legitimation and/or adoption procedures, rights to attend school, and procedures involved in receiving public assistance.

■ *Counseling on interpersonal relationships:* Such counseling focuses on the client's relationships with the alleged father, parents and other relatives, and significant others.

■ *Alternative living arrangements:* Alternatives include a maternity home, the home of parents or other relatives, and foster homes.

■ *Alleged-father counseling:* This involves informing him about his rights and responsibilities, counseling him on his concerns, and providing birth control counseling and perhaps premarital counseling.

■ *Family planning counseling:* Birth control information is provided for both parents, and perhaps referral to a family planning clinic is made.

■ *Educational and employment counseling:* Here, information is provided about remaining in educational programs (including home study programs) or about employment opportunities and work-training programs.

■ *Self-development counseling:* This may include a variety of areas such as identity formation, assertiveness training, sexual counseling, rape counseling, and so on.

■ *Financial and money management counseling:* This includes eligibility for public assistance, food stamps, and Medicare.

■ *Child care:* After a baby is born, single-parent services assists the mother in making child-care arrangements (such as day care) when needed. Such assistance may include financial assistance for child care.

■ *Child development counseling:* New parents receive counseling on caring for young children and meeting their physical, social, and emotional needs.

In providing social services to single parents, social workers seek first to establish a helping relationship (see Chapter 5). If the client is single and pregnant, the worker tries to convey that she (not her parents) has the right and responsibility to decide among the alternatives of carrying the child to delivery, having an abortion, keeping the baby after delivery, placing the baby in foster care, or putting the baby up for adoption. To help a client make such decisions, the worker uses a problem-solving approach. That is, he or she helps the client:

1. Define her problems.
2. Identify the alternatives.
3. Make a pro/con list for each alternative.
4. Evaluate the alternatives.
5. Select one or more alternatives.
6. Implement, and later evaluate, the alternatives that are chosen.

Most single parents decide to keep their baby, and the proportion making this decision has been increasing. The social stigma of single parenthood has weakened. In addition, unmarried single parents are not as conspicuous as they have been in the past because we now have single foster parents, single adoptive parents, and a large number of one-parent families following a divorce.*

---

*I do not want to take a position on whether, in general, unmarried mothers should keep their babies. Being a parent at a young age has some rewards. But it is certainly an immense responsibility. An unmarried mother often has little time to enjoy young adulthood. Dating, pursuing a career, and having the necessary funds to meet wants and desires are more or less restricted. Most workers in single-parent services feel that it is usually in the long-range best

Ursula Myers (a former supervisor of a single-parent unit at a social services agency) describes the small minority of single parents who decide to terminate parental rights:

> In our experience, the woman who terminates her parental rights is generally long-range goal, reality oriented. The stigma of single parenthood is for her perceptually more marked. She sees the coming child as an encumbrance or as totally out of place in her present and future world, her immediate culture, and her internal mental health system. She is usually aware that her pregnancy is untimely and that she cannot cope with the vital needs of an infant at this point in her life. The separation process can result in a broad spectrum of responses, all perfectly normal and human. Both or either parent may feel a sense of loss, grief, emptiness, and unreality. There may be a sense of relief and even pleasure at terminating for some, while others may become depressed and withdrawn. Some work through the grief process to a point of rational and emotional acceptance, while others may completely sever themselves from the pregnancy by "cutting out" that part of their lives and/or totally denying its reality.[88]

FOSTER CARE AND ADOPTION

If a single mother relinquishes her parental rights, the child is usually placed temporarily in foster care. Some single parents who are unsure about whether to give up parental rights may also place their child in foster care until they make a decision. (Foster care, as was discussed earlier, is also used for children who are removed from their parents for neglect or abuse.)

The goals of foster care are to protect the children, to rehabilitate the parents, and generally to return the children to their genetic parents as soon as it is feasible. Foster care is the temporary provision of substitute care for children whose parents are unable or unwilling to meet the child's needs in their own home. Except for emergency placement, legal custody of the child is usually transferred, by court action, from the child's parents to the agency responsible for foster placement. (Removal of a child from the parents' legal custody is carefully weighed by the court in an effort to protect the parents' rights while at the same time providing protection to the child.)

Foster parents face the difficult task of being expected to provide love and affection to foster children without becoming too emotionally attached. The placement is temporary, and separating is easier when strong emotional bonds have not been established between foster parents and foster children. One of the tragic aspects of some foster placements is that the genetic parents never attain the capacity to care for their children. If they do not relinquish parental rights, the children may end up being raised in a series of foster homes. When this happens, a serious question arises about whether a child's right to be raised in a stable, healthy environment is being preserved. Children who are shuffled among foster homes are likely to experience considerable emotional trauma over relating to and later separating from a variety of parental figures.

Agencies seek to attain quality care in foster placements by studying and selecting applicants for foster parenthood, licensing foster parents, and monitoring each home after a child is placed. While the children are in foster care, the genetic parents have visitation rights. In neglect and abuse cases, the hours of visitation are usually arranged through the court and supervised by the foster placement agency. Single parents who decide to relinquish their parental rights often choose not to visit the foster home because they are in the process of separating emotionally from their child.

If the genetic mother relinquishes her rights, the alleged father does not automatically receive custody of the child. He must first be adjudged the father of the child by a court of law. Then, to obtain custody, he must also convince the court of

interest of the child and the mother to consider placing the child for adoption. In working with unmarried mothers, however, workers in single-parent services seek to refrain from expressing their views. They instead seek to have the single mother carefully analyze the pros and cons of the available alternatives. Deciding whether to keep the baby is a very difficult, emotionally taxing responsibility.

his fitness and ability to care for the child. (If the mother decides to keep her child, she need not legally demonstrate her fitness.) For a child to be eligible for adoptive placement, both the genetic mother and the alleged father must relinquish their parental rights. In recent years, many more people have applied for adoptive parenthood than there are children available for adoption. In particular, there are many more applicants for White, healthy infants than there are available babies.

Adoptive placement agencies carefully study, select, and prepare for parenthood applicants who want a child. After a child is placed, the agency monitors the placement until it is finalized by court action. Courts generally wait several months after a child is placed before finalizing a placement. Only in very rare circumstances is a child removed from an adoptive home. The purpose of this waiting period is to ascertain, as thoroughly as possible, that the placement is working out well.

As fully as possible, the medical histories of both biological parents are compiled to provide physical health and genetic information to the adoptive parents. Efforts are also made by placement agencies to meet the wishes of the biological parents concerning the physical characteristics, religious affiliation, racial characteristics, and geographical location of the adoptive parents.

A recent trend in adoptions is "open adoption," whereby the genetic and adoptive parents become officially known to each other. (In the past, adoptive placement agencies usually did not tell the adoptive parents who the genetic parents were, nor did they tell the genetic parents who the adoptive parents were.) Some adoptive and genetic parents even maintain contact with each other. Another trend is for some adoptive children (when they become young adults) to seek out and make contact with their genetic parents.

Not all adoptions are arranged by state-licensed agencies. Although professionally frowned on, some attorneys (for a substantial fee) arrange adoptions for couples seeking a child. These attorneys sometimes pay a fee (which they charge to the adoptive couple) to the birth mother for carrying the pregnancy to term and then relinquishing parental rights.

SUMMARY

The family is a social institution that is found in every culture. Yet there are substantial variations in family patterns and forms. Most families throughout the world can be classified as either extended or nuclear. Our culture has moved from an extended family system (before the Industrial Revolution) to a nuclear family system. In a number of countries, a third family form, the single-parent family, is now emerging.

No society has ever existed without the institution of the family. Five essential functions performed by the modern family are replacing the population, caring for the young, socializing new members, regulating sexual behavior, and providing affection.

Four problems in the American family were examined: divorce, empty-shell marriages, family violence, and birth outside of marriage.

One of two marriages ends in divorce. Divorce per se is not a social problem, but the consequences sometimes are. Reasons for the high divorce rate in our society include the extensive emphasis on romantic love, the changing status of women (who are now increasingly more financially independent), the growth of individualism, the growing acceptance of divorce, and the loss of certain functions in the modern family.

In empty-shell marriages, the spouses feel no strong attachments to each other. Three types were described: devitalized relationships, conflict habituated relationships, and passive-congenial relationships. Some empty-shell marriages eventually end in divorce. Marriage counseling is the primary service available to spouses contemplating a divorce or to spouses with an empty-shell marriage.

Spouse abuse, child abuse, and elder abuse occur in more than half of all U.S. households. In the past four decades, family violence has become recognized as one of our major social problems.

With spouse abuse, the greatest physical damage is usually sustained by women. Although husbands are slapped or shoved with about the same frequency as wives, they are not controlled through violence to the extent that battered wives are. Spouse abuse appears to be related to a norm of tolerating violence in American families. A sizable number of men and women believe it is acceptable for a husband to occasionally hit his wife. Services (for example, shelter homes) are increasingly being developed in many communities for battered wives.

Large numbers of children are victims of child abuse or neglect. Physical abuse is dramatic and has received considerable national attention. Child neglect has received less national attention, even though it occurs more frequently than physical abuse. *Physical abuse, physical neglect,* and particularly *emotional neglect* are terms that are somewhat ambiguous and difficult to define precisely. The primary service designed to curb child abuse and neglect is protective services.

Premarital intercourse is fairly common and is now often tolerated in our society. If a single woman becomes pregnant, however, there may be considerable turmoil within families. Birth outside of marriage has become somewhat more accepted in our society, yet it is still viewed as a social problem. There is considerable variation in the reasons why it is viewed as a problem ranging from the assertion that it is a sign of the moral decay and collapse of the family to a concern about the difficulties that the single parent and her child will encounter. A disproportionately high number of births outside of marriage occur among teenagers, suggesting a need for quality educational programs about responsible sexuality. Single-parent services is the primary social service for women who are single and pregnant and for unmarried mothers and fathers.

NOTES

1. James W. Coleman and Donald R. Cressey, *Social Problems*, 6th ed. (New York: HarperCollins, 1996), p. 124.
2. Ibid., p. 126.
3. Philippe Aries, "From the Medieval to the Modern Family," in *Family in Transition*, Arlene S. Skolnick and Jerome H. Skolnick, eds. (Boston: Little, Brown, 1971), pp. 90–104.
4. John F. Cuber, Martha Tyler John, and Kenrick S. Thompson, "Should Traditional Sex Modes and Values Be Changed?" in *Controversial Issues in the Social Studies: A Contemporary Perspective,* Raymond H. Muessig, ed. (Washington, DC: National Council for the Social Studies, 1975), pp. 87–121.
5. Janet S. Hyde, *Understanding Human Sexuality,* 5th ed. (New York: McGraw-Hill, 1994).
6. William F. Ogburn, "The Changing Family," *The Family,* 19 (Jul. 1938), pp. 139–143.
7. George P. Murdock, *Social Structure* (New York: Free Press, 1949); Ogburn, "The Changing Family," pp. 139–143; William J. Goode, "The Sociology of the Family," in *Sociology Today,* Robert K. Merton, Leonard Broom, and Leonard J. Cottrell, eds. (New York: Basic Books, 1959); Talcott Parsons and Robert F. Bales, *Family, Socialization and Interaction Process* (Glencoe, IL: Free Press, 1995); Coleman and Cressey, *Social Problems,* pp. 124–128.
8. René Spitz, "Hospitalism: Genesis of Psychiatric Conditions in Early Childhood," *Psychoanalytic Study of the Child,* 1945, pp. 53–74.
9. Coleman and Cressey, *Social Problems,* p. 130.
10. Diane E. Papalia and Sally W. Olds, *Human Development,* 5th ed. (New York: McGraw-Hill, 1992), pp. 457–459.
11. Ibid.
12. Ibid., pp. 514–516.
13. William Kornblum and Joseph Julian, *Social Problems,* 9th ed. (Upper Saddle River, NJ: Prentice Hall, 1998), p. 359.
14. Ibid.
15. Kenneth Keniston, *All Our Children: The American Family under Pressure* (New York: Harcourt Brace Jovanovich, 1977), p. 21.
16. Richard Neely, "Barter in the Court," *The New Republic,* Feb. 10, 1986, p. 14.
17. Ibid., p. 17.
18. Coleman and Cressey, *Social Problems,* pp. 133–134.
19. Ibid.
20. Ibid.
21. Ibid.
22. Ibid.
23. John F. Cuber and Peggy B. Harroff, "Five Types of Marriage," in *Family in Transition,* Arlene S. Skolnick and Jerome H. Skolnick, eds. (Boston: Little, Brown, 1971), pp. 287–299.
24. William J. Goode, "Family Disorganization," in *Contemporary Social Problems,* 4th ed., Robert K. Merton and Robert Nisbet, eds. (New York: Harcourt Brace Jovanovich, 1976), p. 543.

25. Richard J. Gelles, *Intimate Violence in Families*, 3rd ed. (Thousand Oaks, CA: Sage Publications, 1997).
26. Ibid.
27. Ibid.
28. Ibid.
29. Coleman and Cressey, *Social Problems*, p. 564.
30. Lewis Koch and Joanne Koch, "Parent Abuse—A New Plague," *Parade*, Jan. 27, 1980, p. 14.
31. Gelles, *Intimate Violence in Families*, p. 116.
32. Coleman and Cressey, *Social Problems*, p. 136.
33. Suzanne K. Steinmetz and Murray A. Straus, *Violence in the Family* (New York: Dodd, Mead, 1974), p. 3.
34. Ibid., p. 9.
35. John O'Brien, "Violence in Divorce Prone Families," *Journal of Marriage and the Family*, 33 (Nov. 1971), pp. 692–698.
36. Steven V. Roberts, "Simpson and Sudden Death," *U.S. News & World Report*, Jun. 27, 1994, pp. 26–32.
37. Gelles, *Intimate Violence in Families*.
38. Ibid.
39. Ibid.
40. Ibid.
41. Ibid.
42. Ibid.
43. Ibid.
44. Murray A. Straus, Richard Gelles, and Suzanne Steinmetz, *Behind Closed Doors: A Survey of Family Violence in America* (Garden City, NY: Doubleday, 1979).
45. Ibid.
46. Gelles, *Intimate Violence in Families*.
47. Andrea Saltzman and Kathleen Proch, *Law in Social Work Practice* (Chicago: Nelson-Hall, 1990), pp. 296–307.
48. Alfred Kadushin and Judith A. Martin, *Child Welfare Services*, 4th ed. (New York: Macmillan, 1988), pp. 218–327.
49. Gelles, *Intimate Violence in Families*, p. 66.
50. Vincent De Francis, *Child Abuse—Preview of a Nation-wide Survey* (Denver: American Humane Association, Children's Division, 1963), pp. 5–6.
51. Ibid., p. 6.
52. Larry Silver et al., "Does Violence Breed Violence? Contribution from a Study of the Child-Abuse Syndrome," *American Journal of Psychiatry*, Sept. 1969, pp. 404–407.
53. George C. Curtis, "Violence Breeds Violence—Perhaps?" in *The Battered Child*, Jerome E. Leavitt, ed. (Morristown, NJ: General Learning Press, 1974), p. 3.
54. Gelles, *Intimate Violence in Families*.
55. Ibid.
56. Kadushin and Martin, *Child Welfare Services*, pp. 243–244.
57. Vincent De Francis, *Special Skills in Child Protective Services* (Denver: American Humane Association, 1958), p. 11.
58. American Humane Association, *National Analysis of Official Child Neglect and Abuse Reporting* (Denver: American Humane Association, 1978), p. 27.
59. C. Henry Kempe and Ray E. Helfer, *Helping the Battered Child and His Family* (Philadelphia: Lippincott, 1972); Kadushin and Martin, *Child Welfare Services;* Jerome E. Leavitt, *The Battered Child* (Morristown, NJ: General Learning Press, 1974); Gelles, *Intimate Violence in Families*.
60. Ibid.
61. Kadushin and Martin, *Child Welfare Services*, p. 218.
62. Sallie A. Watkins, "The Mary Ellen Myth: Correcting Child Welfare History," *Social Work*, 35, no. 6 (Nov. 1990), pp. 500–503.
63. Ellen Thomson, *Child Abuse—A Community Challenge* (Buffalo, NY: Henry Stewart, 1971), p. 44.
64. Gelles, *Intimate Violence in Families*.
65. Anna Mae Sandusky, "Services to Neglected Children," *Children*, Jan.–Feb. 1960, p. 24.
66. Kadushin and Martin, *Child Welfare Services*, p. 291.
67. Gelles, *Intimate Violence in Families*, p. 152.
68. Ibid., p. 153.
69. Patrick Murphy, "Family Preservation and Its Victims," *The New York Times*, Jun. 19, 1993, p. 21.
70. Gelles, *Intimate Violence in Families*.
71. Kadushin and Martin, *Child Welfare Services*, p. 315.
72. U.S. Bureau of the Census, *Statistical Abstract of the United States, 1997* (Washington, DC: U.S. Government Printing Office, 1997), pp. 73–76.
73. Ibid.
74. Ibid.
75. Ibid.
76. Ibid.
77. Ibid., p. 74.
78. Ibid.
79. James W. Coleman and Donald R. Cressey, *Social Problems*, 4th ed. (New York: Harper & Row, 1990), p. 136.
80. *Statistical Abstract of the United States, 1997*.
81. C. P. Green and K. Poteteiger, "Major Problems for Minors," *Society*, 1978, pp. 10–13.
82. Alfred C. Kinsey, W. B. Pomeroy, and C. E. Martin, *Sexual Behavior in the Human Male* (Philadelphia: Saunders, 1948); Alfred C. Kinsey, W. B. Pomeroy, C. E. Martin, and P. H. Gebhard, *Sexual Behavior in the Human Female* (Philadelphia: Saunders, 1953).

83. Sex Information and Education Council of the United States, *Guidelines for Comprehensive Sexuality Education* (New York: SIECUS, 1991).

84. Hyde, *Understanding Human Sexuality,* pp. 659–674.

85. Joseph P. Shapiro, "Teenage Sex: Just Say 'Wait,'" *U.S. News & World Report,* Jul. 26, 1993, pp. 56–59.

86. Kornblum and Julian, *Social Problems,* p. 369.

87. K. Luker, *Dubious Conceptions: The Politics of Teenage Pregnancy* (Cambridge, MA: Harvard University Press, 1996).

88. Ursula S. Myers, "Illegitimacy and Services to Single Parents," in *Introduction to Social Welfare Institutions,* 2nd ed., Charles Zastrow, ed. (Homewood, IL: Dorsey Press, 1982), p. 176.

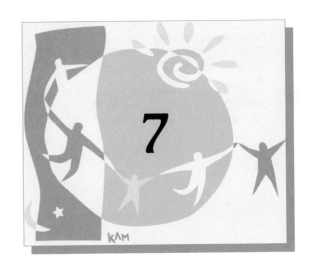

SEXUAL ORIENTATION, SEX VARIANCES, AND SEX COUNSELING

I regard sex as the central problem of life. . . . Sex lies at the root of life, and we can never learn to reverence life until we know how to understand sex.

—*Havelock Ellis*[1]

Amazingly, we were able to put a man in space before we learned to understand the physiology of sexual orgasms.[2] This chapter will:

- Present a brief look at sexual expression in history and in other cultures.
- Present a historical review of scientific studies of sexuality.
- Describe three types of sexual variances:
    1. Tolerated sex variances—behaviors such as premarital intercourse and masturbation, which are generally tolerated in our society.
    2. Structural sex variances—sexual actions such as homosexual behavior, which is disapproved of by some persons in our society yet has supportive social structures.
    3. Asocial sex variances—sexual behaviors such as incest and rape, which are highly disapproved of in our society and do not have supportive social structures.
- Discuss personal sexual concerns, including sexual difficulties such as premature ejaculation among males and painful intercourse among females.
- Briefly describe sex counseling and sex therapy.

SEX IN HISTORY AND IN OTHER CULTURES

Practically every conceivable sexual activity and conjugal arrangement, to some degree, has been socially acceptable to at least some people. Intercourse for procreation only, oral-genital relations, premarital sex, adultery, anal intercourse, monog-amy, polyandry (more than one husband), polyg-yny (more than one wife), homosexuality, lifelong celibacy—each has been a method of responding to sexual desire that has been socially approved by some human community. Not even incest, which is among the most widely prohibited of sexual relationships, has been universally tabooed.[3] Some ancient cultures encouraged incest in royal families as a way to maintain the wealth and power among a small number of people and as a way to ensure the purity of the royal line.

Male and female homosexuality in ancient Greece was not only acceptable but encouraged. There is a wide range of attitudes toward homosexuality in various cultures. At one extreme are societies that strongly disapprove of homosexual behavior for people of any age. In contrast, some societies tolerate homosexual behavior for children but disapprove of it in adults. Yet other societies actively force all their male members to engage in some homosexual behavior, usually in conjunction with puberty rites.[4] No matter how a particular society views homosexuality, the behavior always occurs in some individuals; thus, homosexuality is found in all societies.[5]

Societies differ considerably in their rules regarding premarital sex. Inhabitants of the Trobriand Islands encourage premarital sex because it is thought to be an important preparation for marriage. Some societies permit young boys and girls to play husband and wife even before puberty. In Asia the Lepcha society believes that girls need sexual intercourse to mature.[6] In contrast, in many Muslim and South American cultures, premarital chastity for women is highly revered: A female who has premarital sex is likely to be shamed and ostracized. However, in some other developing countries, some low-income parents sell their adolescent daughters as prostitutes, particularly to tourists.

There are some cultures in which rape is practically nonexistent, as among the Arapesh of New Guinea. In that society, males are socialized to be peaceful and nonaggressive. In contrast, in the Gussi tribe in Kenya, the rate of rape is several times higher than in the United States. In this tribe, both men and women are socialized to be

EXHIBIT 7.1

Sexuality in Mangaia

Mangaia is an island in the South Pacific. The Mangaians have elaborate rituals that use sex for pleasure and for procreation.

Mangaian boys around the age of 7 or 8 are instructed how to masturbate. At about age 13, they have a superincision ritual (in which a slit is made on the full length of the skin on the top part of the penis). This ritual initiates them into manhood. As part of this ritual, they are also given instruction in how to kiss, how to bring a female partner to orgasm several times before they have an orgasm themselves, and how to perform cunnilingus. Approximately 2 weeks later, each boy is introduced to sexual intercourse with an experienced woman. She demonstrates intercourse in various positions and further instructs him on how to delay ejaculation to have simultaneous orgasms with his partner.

Mangaian girls also receive sexual instruction from adult women. Thereafter, Mangaian boys and girls actively seek each other out, and many have coitus nearly every night. Teenage girls are raised to believe virility in a male is proof of his desire for her. In particular, a male is expected to be able to vigorously continue the in-and-out action of intercourse for 15 to 30 minutes or longer while the female moves her hips back and forth in a rhythmic motion. Any male who is unable to perform this act is looked down on.

By age 20, the average male is likely to have had ten or more female partners, and the average "nice" female will have had three or four successive male partners. Mangaian parents encourage such sexual experiences because they want their daughters and sons to find a marriage partner with whom they are sexually compatible. At around age 18, Mangaians typically have sex every night. Men are brought up to believe that bringing their partner to orgasm is one of the chief sources of sexual pleasures for a man.

Source: John C. Messinger, "The Luck of the Irish," and Donald S. Marshall, "Too Much in Mangaia," both in *Human Sexual Behavior*, D. S. Marshall and R. C. Suggs, eds. (New York: Basic Books, 1971).

aggressive and competitive—and women often resist sexual relations, even with their husbands.[7]

It has been fairly common throughout history for soldiers to rape the women of the societies they conquered. In the past, Eskimo husbands offered male guests the privilege of spending the night with their wives, and it was considered a serious insult for guests to refuse. White slave owners in U.S. history often prohibited their slaves from marrying, and some attempted to improve the characteristics of African American children by mating female slaves with an African American male who was considered to have desirable characteristics. Some persons with a cognitive disability in various societies have been sterilized in an effort to prevent them from having children. Hitler, in Nazi Germany in the 1930s and 1940s, mated women with certain soldiers in an effort to "breed" offspring with the characteristics he considered desirable.

Some parents in Europe believe that fathers should have intercourse with their daughters to teach them about sex, although this practice is most often viewed as an excuse for incest or sexual abuse. Although there is a myth in our society that the elderly do not and should not engage in sexual activity, many elderly people are sexually active and may have more than one partner. In many cultures, males greet each other with a kiss and a hug.

Sex-change operations have been occurring since the early 1930s. They became well publicized in 1952, when Christine Jorgensen announced to the world that she had undergone surgery to change her from being biologically male to biologically female. As is often the case with sexual matters that are little understood by the larger society, Jorgensen's surgery met with widespread disapproval. Nonetheless, several thousand people have since undergone such operations.[8]

Clearly, what is defined as acceptable and unacceptable sexual behavior varies from culture to culture and from one time period to another. Let's look briefly at the history of our changing sexual attitudes and mores.

Perhaps the major influence on the current attitudes toward sex in Western culture has been the Judeo-Christian tradition. The Old Testament approved of sexual intercourse only within marriage. The purpose of intercourse, it was asserted, should be only to conceive children. Judaism was somewhat more liberal, stating that heterosexual intercourse for pleasure within a marriage was not sinful. Masturbation, homosexuality, and all other sexual expressions outside of marriage were viewed as sinful.

Early Christianity endorsed the position that sex is evil and degrading and should be indulged in only by married couples and only for the purpose of procreation. This remains the official position of the Roman Catholic Church.

The Protestant Reformation, which began in the 16th century, advocated a strict and repressive sexual code. The Protestant ethic that emerged at the time emphasized the importance of hard work and asserted that it was morally wrong to engage in pleasurable activities of any kind. Denying sexual urges and refraining from sexual activities except to procreate were seen as virtues. A major immigrant group that began colonizing America in the 17th century, the Puritans, rigidly adhered to this ascetic (self-denial of pleasurable activities) life.

The views promulgated by the Protestant ethic became incorporated into what has become known as "Victorian morality." The name is derived from the reign of Queen Victoria of England.

EXHIBIT 7.2

Learning Sexual Behavior via Scripts

Sociologists have made a major contribution to our understanding of human sexuality by asserting that sexual behavior (as well as most other human behavior) is developed through learning "scripts." *Scripts* (as in a play) are plans that we learn and then carry around in our heads. These scripts enable us to conceptualize where we are in our activities and provide us with direction for completing those activities and accomplishing our goals. Scripts are also devices for helping us to remember what we have done in the past.

Sexual scripts result from elaborate prior learning in which we acquire an etiquette of sexual behavior. According to this script approach, little in sexual activity is spontaneous. Scripts tell us who appropriate sexual partners are, what sexual activity is expected, where and when the activity should occur, and what the sequence of the different sexual behaviors should be.

Scripts vary greatly from one culture to another. Hortense Powdermaker provides the following description of a script about female masturbation that is generally held by the Lesu of the South Pacific:

A woman will masturbate if she is sexually excited and there is no man to satisfy her. A couple may be having intercourse in the same house, or near enough for her to see them, and she may thus become aroused. She then sits down and bends her right leg so that her heel presses against her genitals. Even young girls of about six years may do this quite casually as they sit on the ground. The women and men talk about it freely, and there is no shame attached to it. It is a customary position for women to take, and they learn it in childhood. They never use their hands for manipulation.[a]

[a] Hortense Powdermaker, *Life in Lesu* (New York: Norton, 1933), pp. 276–277.

Victorian morality was prominent in the 19th and early 20th centuries. John Gagnon and Bruce Henderson note:

> The Puritan-dominated sex ethic became that of penny-pinching Adam Smith. . . . The moral values of the new middle classes, with their belief in hard work, delayed gratification, and avoidance of pleasure, including the sexual, were to triumph during the Victorian age, not only in England but in most of Western Europe.[9]

Victorian morality all but banished sexuality from discussion in respectable relationships. Modesty was stressed to the point of extreme prudishness. In polite conversations, simple anatomical terms such as *legs* or *breasts* were taboo; these body parts instead were referred to as limbs and bosoms. The limbs (legs) of tables were often covered by long tablecloths so that sexual feelings would not be aroused. Women did not get "pregnant"; they were "in a family way" and were expected to remain at home during their "condition." In Philadelphia men and women were not allowed to visit art galleries together for fear their modesty might be offended by the classical statues (on which fig leaves were added to the genital areas to minimize their offensiveness).[10]

Middle- and upper-class women, before marriage, were expected to be virgins. There were considered to be two types of females: The good women were virgins—undamaged property—who were fit to marry. The bad were "fallen women" who were sexually active premaritally. They were pitied but not consoled because their "fall" was attributed to their own weakness. They were no longer deemed fit to marry but were nevertheless considered available for nonmarital relations with men. A popular myth throughout this period held that men were inherently more sexual than women. This led to the development—still very prevalent today—of two standards of acceptable behavior (the so-called double standard). Although it was hoped that men would remain chaste, because of their "animal natures" they were seldom criticized for having premarital and extramarital relations. Prostitutes and lower-class women were proper outlets for men's excessive sexual urges, which were too beastly to impose on their wives. J. John Palen notes:

> From this division of women—good and bad, mothers and whores—came the double standard that implicitly allowed men to be sexually active but that forbade "nice girls" even to think about such things. Overt sexuality was condemned, while covert premarital or extramarital sex among men was tolerated as a necessary evil, given the male's more pressing sexual urges.[11]

Researchers have since found that the female sex drive is as strong as that of the male. Interestingly, even during the repressive years of the Puritan and Victorian eras, there were always certain segments advocating more liberal expressions of sexuality. For example, in the Victorian era, there was a profitable trade in erotic drawings and novels.

Since the early 1900s, there have been dramatic changes in sexual attitudes and behaviors. For example, recent surveys indicate most males and females in the United States have engaged in premarital intercourse by the age of 19, and most young women (ages 18 to 24) are not virgins at marriage.[12] One of the most striking features of the sexual revolution of the last few decades is the increased popularity of mouth-genital (oral-genital) sex.[13]

The 1970s in the United States were viewed as a time of sexual permissiveness and experimentation during which many people engaged in sexual behaviors that were previously uncommon. Since then there has been a partial reversal of this permissive trend, with a general movement toward fewer partners, more emphasis on long-term relationships, and a more gradual development of the sexual aspects of a relationship. This reversal has been attributed to a general dissatisfaction with sexual behavior divorced from intimacy, as well as to the very real threat of increased susceptibility to sexually transmitted diseases for persons who have sexual contact with multiple partners.[14] In the 1980s and 1990s, there was substantial publicity about seemingly new epidemics of sexually transmitted diseases, particularly genital herpes and AIDS. The AIDS epidemic has been likened to a modern-day plague. Cures have not yet been found for either genital herpes or AIDS. Publicity about AIDS and the realization that prevention cannot be guaranteed short of sexual abstinence or sexual monogamy with an uninfected partner have led millions of people to shift their patterns of sexual behavior by adding precautions (for example, using condoms). Several of the tenets of the sexual revolution, such as the belief that sexual intercourse between relative strangers could be enjoyed purely for recreational pleasure and without consequences, are being rejected in the face of new challenges.

At present, ambiguity and confusion abound over what ought to be the sexual code and behavior of Americans. On the conservative end of the spectrum are groups such as the Catholic Church and some fundamentalist religious organizations. They advocate that sex be for procreation only and restricted to heterosexual married people. Such groups express alarm that increased sexual permissiveness will destroy the moral fiber of the family and ultimately result in the destruction of our society.

At the liberal end of the spectrum are groups and individuals holding that sex can legitimately be enjoyed for recreation as well as for procreation. They assert that the ways in which sexuality is expressed should be of no concern except to those consenting adults who participate.

Repercussions of this liberal attitude are visible throughout society. Sexual topics are presented frankly and openly by the mass media, including television, magazines, and newspapers. Nudity is displayed in movies, in magazines, and on television. No longer are women who have premarital sex considered unfit for marriage. One factor that appears to have led to the increases in premarital and extramarital relations is the increased availability of birth control devices, particularly the pill.[15]

Because of the widely conflicting codes advocated by parents, peers, and other pressure groups in our society, many individuals go through considerable turmoil in arriving at a personal code of sexual behavior that they can be comfortable with and seek to live by.

FORMAL STUDY OF SEX

Prior to the 20th century, there were practically no scientific studies of sexuality. Since about 1900, the work of four social scientists has had profound effects on our understanding of human sexuality: Sigmund Freud, Alfred Kinsey, and the team of William Masters and Virginia Johnson.

Sigmund Freud

Sigmund Freud was a psychoanalyst who theorized in his writings (from 1895 to 1925) that the sex drive was a fundamental part of human life. Freud realized that many people had sexual conflicts. He made sexuality a central focus of his theories and defined most emotions and behaviors as being primarily sexual in nature. He interpreted "sexuality" broadly; he thought of it as including physical love, affectional impulses, self-love, love for parents and children, and friendship associations.

Freud advanced a number of controversial theories. He asserted that everyone, from birth on, has sexual interests. He stated that boys at an early age (around age 3) fall sexually in love with their mother and fear their father will discover this interest and then castrate them (a fear referred to as castration anxiety). Girls, on the other hand, at about the same age (age 3) fall sexually in love with their father. They discover that they do not have a penis, and their desire to have one leads to penis envy. Girls conclude that they lost their penis at an earlier age when their mother discovered their sexual interest in their father. That is, they believe their mother castrated them because of their love for their father. Girls also experience castration anxiety, but it stems from their belief that having been castrated makes them inferior to males.

Freud's notion that sexuality was a critical part of human development initially provoked shock and outrage. Before his time, it was thought that sexual interests played only a minor role in human development. Gradually his theories came to have a liberating effect, as sexuality slowly became recognized as playing a key role in personality development. Freud's theories also led to increased communication about sexuality and stimulated scientific investigations of this topic.

Perhaps Freud's greatest contribution was this change he effected on our attitudes toward sexuality. Unfortunately, he developed a number of hypotheses and advanced them as "truths" without scientifically testing their validity. Consequently, some of Freud's specific hypotheses about sexuality have been hotly disputed and widely challenged—for example, his hypotheses involving castration anxiety in boys and castration anxiety and penis envy in girls. In recent years, a storm of criticism of Freudian theory has arisen from feminists. Feminists are particularly offended by Freud's assumption that the female is biologically inferior to the male because she lacks a penis. They ask what is so intrinsically valuable about a penis that makes it better than a clitoris, a vagina, or a pair of ovaries? Feminists argue that psychoanalytic theory is essentially a male-centered theory that has adverse effects on women as it asserts females are biologically inferior to males.

Alfred Kinsey

In 1948 Alfred C. Kinsey, an American zoologist, published *Sexual Behavior in the Human Male,* which was based on interviews with 5300 White American men. This study investigated sexual practices and found that the actual sexual behavior of males differed substantially from the stated moral values of the time. One-third of the respondents had at least one homosexual experience since puberty; 83% had premarital relations; half of those who were married had extramarital affairs; and 92% had masturbated to orgasm.[16]

Five years later, in 1953, Kinsey published *Sexual Behavior in the Human Female,* which was based on interviews with 5940 White American women.[17] This study showed, to some extent, that the double standard was still operating. But it also found that women were not as asexual as was commonly thought. More than half of these respondents had premarital relations, and one-fourth of those who were married had extramari-

Pioneer sexologist Alfred Kinsey's studies revealed the discrepancy between Americans' sexual mores and their sexual practices.

tal relations. (It should be noted that Kinsey's studies lacked racial diversity in that he studied no people of color. Therefore, any conclusions he drew can be applied to White Americans only.)

Kinsey's findings were widely publicized by the mass media. For the first time, society was confronted with the wide gaps that existed between sexual mores and sexual practices. Kinsey's studies may have led people to become freer in their sexual behavior or at least to feel less guilt about sexual behavior that was inconsistent with traditional sexual mores. The studies certainly challenged the belief that women were basically uninterested in sex.

William Masters and Virginia Johnson

In 1957 William Masters and Virginia Johnson began their study of the physiology of human sexual response, which culminated in the publication of their classic text *Human Sexual Response*.[18] Their contribution to the scientific understanding of human sexual response has been enormous, and their findings have generally withstood the test of others' replications.

Masters and Johnson were the first to provide accurate information about the physiology of human sexual response based on laboratory observations of people's responses rather than their personal reports. Their findings destroyed a number of myths. Freud, for example, had asserted that vaginal orgasm in women was superior to clitoral orgasm. Masters and Johnson found that the clitoris was the organ having the most nerve endings (and therefore the area of greatest pleasure) in a female's genitals. The clitoris was essentially the main structure being stimulated in both clitoral orgasm and vaginal orgasm, and therefore there were no physiological differences between these orgasms. This finding enhanced the sex lives of many women who were fruitlessly searching for the vaginal orgasm—many of whom felt that they were inadequate or that they were missing out on something. Other important findings were that men and women are able to enjoy sexual activity into advanced age and that some women have numerous orgasms in succession.

On completion of this research, Masters and Johnson began to treat people with sexual dysfunctions, such as premature ejaculation in males and failure to achieve orgasm in females. They departed radically from the prevailing thinking of the day, which viewed sexual dysfunction as a byproduct of other individual or relationship problems. They identified the relationship of the two partners as the client, rather than one person or the other, and indeed required both partners to participate in the process of therapy. They did what many others had thought untenable—they dealt primarily with the sexual problem and treated people in short-term (2 weeks) therapy.

Extremely successful results were achieved, and their methods and outcomes were subsequently published in *Human Sexual Inadequacy*.[19] They also demonstrated there is no evidence that relief of a sexual problem led (as Freud asserted) to the formation of a replacement problem. Most contemporary forms of sex therapy are based on Masters and Johnson's original work.

VARIANCES RATHER THAN SEXUAL PROBLEMS

Human beings are capable of expressing their sexuality in an amazing variety of ways due to both biological determinants and learning. Everyone has some form of a sex drive, but how it is expressed is shaped by biological predispositions, rituals, acceptable role models, trial and error as to what is pleasurable and what is not, and the attitudes of others (parents, peers, teachers, and so forth). Gagnon and Henderson note that the learning of ways to express our sexuality is closely related to the process of forming our gender identity (our self-concept of maleness or femaleness):

> We assemble our sexuality beginning with gender identity, and we build upon that the activities we come to think of as fitting to ourselves. Our belief in what is correct and proper results more from our social class, religion, style of family life, and concepts of masculinity and femininity than from the specifically sexual things that we learn.[20]

One approach to studying the wide variety of sexual behaviors is the social problems approach. This approach seeks to classify as social problems any sexual behavior that differs from a norm to such a great extent that a significant number of people (or a number of significant people) feel that something should be done about it. This approach requires delineation of the code or norm of acceptability. However, there is no consensus about which sexual expressions are acceptable and which are not. In addition, as the Kinsey study showed, there is a vast difference between the purported sexual norms of society and people's actual sexual behavior.

Another shortcoming in using the social problems approach is that those acts that would be identified as social problems would then be stigmatized as "sick," "degenerate," or "perverted." During the Victorian era, our society suffered too much from the efforts of some to make value judgments about what is inappropriate sexual behavior. This text will not attempt to force any specific sexual code onto readers—too many other groups are still trying to do this. Instead of the term *social problems,* the term *sex variances* will be used to refer to sexual expressions that are of concern to certain segments of our society.

Definitions of acceptable and nonacceptable sexual behavior tend to change over time. Some behaviors that were once widely condemned are now generally accepted. Masturbation, for example, used to be viewed as sinful, immoral, and unhealthy but now is widely practiced and is recommended by sex therapists as a way to learn about one's sexuality. Not long ago, oral sex was considered immoral or wrong, but today many people engage in oral sex.[21]

It may be argued that laws in a society can be used to determine acceptable and unacceptable sexual expressions. Any sexual acts that are legally prohibited could therefore be identified as unacceptable. However, many of our present laws relating to sexual behaviors were enacted during the Victorian era and remain highly conservative. There is a considerable time lag between changes in laws relating to sexuality and changes in attitudes and norms about sexuality. Acts that are currently still illegal in at least some states include premarital sex, oral sex, masturbation, extramarital sex, cohabitation, and intercourse in any position other than the missionary position. Historically, severe penalties were imposed for those found guilty of "sex crimes." For example, the 17th-century Puritans made extramarital sex a crime punishable by death. Some states continue to have severe penalties for "sex crimes." For example, a Georgia statute specifies oral sex between consenting adults as a felony punishable by not less than 1 year or more than 20 years in jail.[22]

Laws, to some extent, are an indicator of how societies feel about certain sexual behaviors. For example, the stiff penalties for rape and child molestation suggest strong disapproval. Yet for the reasons just cited, laws cannot be used as the only measure of prevailing views about acceptable sexual behavior in a society.

TYPES OF SEXUAL VARIANCES

A useful classification of sexual variances is provided by William Kornblum and Joseph Julian, who identify three categories: tolerated sex variance, structural sex variance, and asocial sex variance.[23] Tolerated sex variances are sexual acts that are generally disapproved of but either serve a socially useful purpose and/or occur so often among a population with such low social visibility that few people are sanctioned for engaging in them. Structural sex variances are generally disapproved of by some people in our society, yet have supportive social structures. This category includes homosexuality, prostitution, and pornography. Asocial sex variances are behaviors that our society strongly disapproves of and that do not have supportive social structures. Behaviors in this category include incest and rape.

Tolerated Sex Variance

Behaviors such as masturbation, premarital intercourse, sex between consenting adults in a variety of positions, and heterosexual oral-genital contact may be considered tolerated sex variances. There are a few groups (such as certain fundamentalist religious groups) who assert that these acts are immoral and ought to be prohibited. Laws in some states prohibit such sexual behavior but are seldom enforced. Most segments of our society, however, tolerate these acts. Because these sexual behaviors tend to be tolerated, we will move on to examine structural sexual variances.

Structural Sex Variance: Homosexuality

Sexual behaviors in this category run counter to prevailing norms and legal statutes but have supportive social structures and are participated in by substantial numbers of people. Prostitution and pornography fit this description, but in this section, we will focus on homosexuality because in recent years it has generated the greatest interest among social workers.

Kornblum and Julian, who categorize homosexuality together with prostitution and pornography, emphatically state that they are not making a judgment about the desirability or undesirability of homosexuality.[24] Some segments of our society have viewed homosexual behavior as "deviant," "sick," or "unnatural." As we will see, research is increasingly confirming that sexual orientation is determined very early in life (before age 5) and may be biologically driven. Therefore, each person's response to sexual drives is highly individualized in what she or he experiences as "natural" behavior. Homosexuality thus represents a sexual variation, not a social problem.

There is a major difference between homosexuality and the other two structural sex variances (prostitution and pornography). Engaging in prostitution or using pornography appears to have primarily sociological and psychological determinants. In contrast, being gay or lesbian appears to have primarily biological determinants (as described later in this section). Similar to masturbation, homosexuality has been viewed negatively by some segments of our society, yet recent research indicates that both are natural expressions of sexual drives.[25]

HOMOSEXUALITY EXAMINED

A homosexual is a person whose sexual or erotic orientation is toward members of his or her same sex. We use this term to refer to an orientation rather than occasional sexual experimentation with someone of the same gender. Teenagers, in experimenting with sexuality, may, for example, have some homosexual experiences. People isolated from the other gender (in prisons, segregated schools, or the military) often have sexual experiences with members of their own sex. On the other hand, it is possible to be a homosexual without practicing homosexual behavior—by ignoring one's homosexuality, denying it, or simply pretending to be heterosexual.

Surveys have found that a majority of Americans regard homosexuality as "very obscene and vulgar" and as a "curable disease."[26] Homosexuals are also often viewed as harmful to American life. The negative view of homosexuality in this country is indicated by the array of derogatory slang terms for homosexuals. (Similar attitudes and different derogatory terms have been applied in the past to various ethnic minorities, including the Irish, Italians, African Americans, and Latinos.) Homosexuals have frequently been the victims of antigay hate crimes.[27] Many heterosexuals are *homophobic:* They have feelings of personal anxiety and disgust of homosexuals and seek to avoid contact with them.

Such negative attitudes can have considerable psychological impact on gay and lesbian people. It can be devastating to learn that a majority of Americans consider your natural interests and behaviors to be vulgar and obscene. Some homosexuals therefore seek to hide their sexual orientation, and they live in constant fear of being "outed." Some believe (often correctly) that discovery will result in being fired from their job or being ostracized by friends and relatives. Tragically, some gay and lesbian youths become so despondent that they commit suicide. The suicide rate of homosexual adolescents is significantly higher than that of heterosexual teenagers.[28] This is a sad and extreme example of the ultimate costs of bigotry.

There are several erroneous myths about homosexuality:

Myth 1: People are either homosexual or heterosexual.

Fact: Alfred Kinsey found that homosexuality and heterosexuality are not mutually exclusive categories. Most people have had sexual thoughts, feelings, and fantasies about members of the same sex as well as about members

EXHIBIT 7.3

The Continuum of Sexuality According to Kinsey

1	2	3	4	5	6	7
Exclusively heterosexual	Heterosexual with incidental homosexual experience	Heterosexual with substantial homosexual experience	Equal heterosexual and homosexual experience	Homosexual with substantial heterosexual experience	Homosexual with incidental heterosexual experience	Exclusively homosexual

Source: Adapted from Alfred C. Kinsey et al., *Sexual Behavior in the Human Male* (Philadelphia: Saunders, 1948), p. 638.

of the opposite sex. Kinsey proposed a seven-point rating scale to categorize sexuality, with exclusive heterosexuality at one end and exclusive homosexuality at the other (Exhibit 7.3). Kinsey noted:

> The world is not divided into sheep and goats. . . . Only the human mind invents categories and tries to force facts into pigeonholes. The living world is a continuum in each and every one of its aspects. The sooner we learn this concerning human sexual behavior, the sooner we will reach a sound understanding of the realities of sex.[29]

Myth 2: Homosexuality is universally disapproved of in all cultures.

Fact: Some cultures accept, and even encourage, homosexuality. A young male in ancient Greece was sometimes given a boy slave who served as a sexual partner until the boy was old enough to marry a woman. It was also common for older married men to form a homosexual relationship with a young boy. Today all males among the Siwans of North Africa are expected to engage in homosexual relationships throughout their lives.[30] Among the Aranda of central Australia, there are relationships between young boys and unmarried men, with these liaisons generally ending at marriage.[31]

Myth 3: Male homosexuals are generally "effeminate," and lesbians are generally "masculine." The stereotype is that male homosexuals are limp-wristed, talk with a lisp, and have a "swishy" walk; lesbians are believed to have short hair and to wear clothes that are normally worn by males.

Fact: Most homosexuals are indistinguishable in appearance and mannerisms from heterosexuals.[32] This myth probably comes from confusing homosexuality with transvestism—wearing the clothing of the opposite gender for sexual arousal. Transvestism and homosexuality are different: Most transvestites are heterosexual.[33] Interestingly, whereas our culture erroneously associates male homosexuality with effeminacy, the ancient Greeks and Romans associated homosexuality with aggressive masculinity (as among the Spartan warriors).

Hyde notes:

> The belief that gay men are feminine and that lesbians are masculine represents a confusion of two important concepts: gender identity *(sense of maleness or femaleness)* and sexual orientation *(heterosexual or homosexual)*. The gay person differs from the majority in who the erotic and emotional partner is, but the gay person does not typically differ from the majority in gender identity. That is the gay man chooses a partner of the same gender, but his identity is quite

definitely masculine. He thinks of himself as male and has no desire to be a female. The same holds true for the lesbian; although her erotic and emotional orientation is toward other women, she is quite definitely a woman and typically has no desire to be a man.[34]

Myth 4: Homosexuals are "sick" and different in personality characteristics from heterosexuals.

Fact: Clinical projective tests do not reliably distinguish between homosexuals and heterosexuals. Studies of homosexuals and heterosexuals have found no differences between the two groups in personality traits or in general adjustment.[35] The only difference is their sexual orientation.

Homosexuality was listed as a mental disorder by the American Psychiatric Association until 1973. For a number of years preceding 1973, homosexuals demonstrated at psychiatric conventions, demanding that homosexuality no longer be considered a mental disorder. In 1973, after several years of heated controversy, the board of trustees of the American Psychiatric Association voted to strike homosexuality from its official list of mental diseases. Thomas Szasz (a psychiatrist) asserted around this time that psychiatrists and others who labeled homosexuality an illness were merely taking the place of the church in identifying homosexuals and punishing them for their deviant sexual behavior.[36]

Myth 5: One partner in a homosexual liaison generally plays the "active" or masculine role in sexual activity and the other plays the "passive" or feminine role.

Fact: Most homosexuals play both roles and (similar to heterosexuals) experiment with a variety of arousal techniques. There is no single form of homosexual expression or identity. In reality there is as wide a divergence among homosexuals as among heterosexuals. Some married homosexuals enjoy intercourse with their spouses; a few are genuinely bisexual, enjoying the sex act with either male or female partners. Most married homosexuals are more comfortable in homosexual relationships but are married for the sake of domestic stability, companionship, and respectability. Some homosexuals candidly acknowledge their sexual orientation and live their homosexuality openly. Others are not willing to "come out" (publicly acknowledge their sexual orientation) as they fear they may then be discriminated against. Some homosexuals refuse to view themselves as homosexual primarily from abhorrence at being identified with a socially outcast minority.

The question is sometimes asked: "What do homosexuals do in bed?" Most of their activities are similar to those in which heterosexuals engage. Foreplay generally includes kissing, hugging, and petting. Male homosexuals may engage in mutual masturbation, oral-genital sex, interfemoral intercourse (in which one man's penis moves between the thighs of the other), and anal intercourse. Lesbians may engage in mutual masturbation, oral-genital sex, and more infrequently, tribadism (one partner lying on top of the other and making thrusting movements so that both receive genital stimulation); a rarer practice among lesbians is the use of a dildo by one female to stimulate the other.

Myth 6: Male homosexuals primarily seek out young boys.

Fact: Homosexuals are no more attracted to children than are heterosexuals, and homosexual child molesting is less common than its heterosexual counterpart. Most child molesting is done by heterosexual men and involves young girls.[37] Strangely, people who worry that homosexual male teachers will try to seduce young boys in a school do not seem to worry that heterosexual male teachers will try to seduce young girls—and the latter occurs much more frequently.

Myth 7: Gays and lesbians are to blame for AIDS, which is a punishment from God for their behavior.

Fact: Although gay males are a high-risk group for contracting the AIDS virus in our society, very few cases have been reported among lesbians.[38] (Gay men are at high risk for acquiring AIDS because of the transfer of body fluids that occurs during anal intercourse.) AIDS is a life-threatening disease not only for gay men. The growth in the spread of AIDS is currently fastest among heterosexuals.[39]

Homosexuals are not the cause of AIDS. Blaming this deadly disease on the group that, in the United States, has suffered and died most disproportionately from it is a classic and regrettable case of blaming the victims. Although it is true that the largest single risk group of people with AIDS is male homosexuals, it is ludicrous to assume they caused this health crisis. AIDS is caused by a virus. It is even more ludicrous to assert that male homosexuals would want to deliver the disease on the world after first spreading it among themselves. Quite to the contrary, the gay male community in the United States has been in the forefront of educating people about behavior that minimizes the transmission of the disease. Gay men have radically altered their sexual behavior patterns, as evidenced by a substantial drop in the rate of transmission of this disease among this group in the past few years. (Expanded material on AIDS is presented in Chapter 15.)

INCIDENCE OF HOMOSEXUALITY

Determining the extent of homosexuality is difficult. First, there are definitional problems because most people are not exclusively heterosexual or homosexual. Second, because of the stigma attached to homosexuality, some people are reluctant to acknowledge homosexual thoughts, feelings, or acts.

Kinsey found that 4% of White males and 2% of White females were exclusively homosexual—that is, never had sex with someone of the opposite sex. He further estimated that 37% of American males have had one or more homosexual experiences to orgasm and that 10% of American males have long periods of more or less exclusive homosexuality.[40] Other research has resulted in similar estimates.[41] After reviewing several studies, Janet Hyde concludes that the answer to the question "How many people are homosexual and how many are heterosexual?" is complex.

> Probably about 80 percent of men and 90 percent of women are exclusively heterosexual. About 2 percent of men and 1 percent of women are exclusively homosexual. And the remaining [men and women] have had varying amounts of both heterosexual and homosexual experience.[42]

The Ten Percent Society, a gay and lesbian organization, states that the incidence of homosexuality is 10%. Hyde notes:

> This statistic comes from no single study, but rather from an amalgamation of many. It represents those people whose orientation is predominantly homosexual, although they may have had some heterosexual experience. In view of the most recent surveys, the 10 percent figure may be a bit high, but it is probably not too far off.[43]

CAUSES OF HOMOSEXUALITY

People are often curious about the causes of homosexuality. Why are some people erotically attracted to members of the same gender and others to members of the other gender? Social, behavioral, and biological scientists have examined and argued this question for decades. Let's see what they have learned.

First, you cannot study the question of why one becomes homosexual without studying the larger question of what determines sexual object choice for anyone, heterosexual or homosexual. Why do we get aroused by a woman, or a woman with particular attributes, or a man of a certain body type? Is this something we've learned? Are we born with a "script" that determines our sexual object choice?

Many researchers and theoreticians have advanced hypotheses in an effort to explain this complex and important question. Some believe that the biology of an individual determines heterosexuality or homosexuality. Some studies have shown chemical differences between the two groups, but it is impossible to determine causation from the results of these studies. In other words, are the chemical differences between people responsible for this behavior, or does their behavior somehow alter their body chemistry?

Other theorists posit that childhood experiences determine heterosexuality or homosexuality. Here we have the causation question again. If we determined that a certain child had more sex play with a child of the same gender and grew to be a homosexual in adult life, can we say that this sex play led to homosexuality? Perhaps the increased sex play grew out of an inborn desire and erotic potential toward gratification from such play. That is, the behavior grew out of a predisposition toward homosexuality; the predisposition did not grow out of the behavior.

The most comprehensive study of this question to date was undertaken by researchers at the Alfred C. Kinsey Institute for Sex Research.[44] The researchers, Alan P. Bell, Martin S. Weinberg, and Sue Kiefer Hammersmith, studied 979 homosexual and 477 heterosexual men and women, gathering a large amount of information about their lives in an effort to determine critical and statistically significant differences between these two groups. They analyzed their data using a method called "path analysis," which enabled them to examine a large number of independent variables (such as parental traits, parent and sibling relationships, and gender conformity) to determine *causation* of sexual orientation and not merely association between variables. Their significant findings were as follows: (a) By the time boys and girls reach adolescence, their sexual orientation is likely to be determined, even though they may not yet have become sexually very active. (b) The homosexual men and women in the study were not particularly lacking in heterosexual experiences during their childhood and adolescent years. They were distinguished from their heterosexual counterparts, however, in finding such experiences ungratifying. (c) Among both the men and women in the study, there was a powerful link between gender nonconformity and the development of homosexuality. (Gender nonconformity refers to children who prefer engaging in activities generally associated in this culture with the other gender—for example, boys playing with dolls.)

What do these findings suggest? First, they show that sexual orientation is established early in life, perhaps long before adolescence. Although every person has the potential to behave sexually in the manner he or she chooses, one's true sexual orientation may be set before birth or at a very early age and then no longer be influenced by the environment. Many homosexually oriented people behave as if they are heterosexual in this society because there are so many sanctions against homosexuality. However, their preferred sexual partner, in the absence of these negative sanctions, would be someone of the same gender. Human beings certainly have the ability to respond sexually to people who are not their most preferred sexual partner, but to do so requires going against the current of their innermost inclinations. We can freely choose various behaviors; we cannot freely choose who or what "turns us on." The question of what causes a person's sexual orientation to be set (either as homosexual or heterosexual) before birth or at a very early age has not yet been answered. (Some people are naturally left-handed and others are naturally right-handed; it appears that some people are naturally heterosexual in orientation and others are naturally homosexual.)

The possibility that sexual orientation is more a matter of nature than of nurture got a boost in a 1991 study that reported differences in the brains of homosexual and heterosexual men. The research focused on the hypothalamus, the region of the brain thought to control sexual behavior. The results were striking. Certain groups of nerve cells in the hypothalamus were more than two times larger in heterosexual men than in homosexual men. The hypothalamus of a gay man appears to be closer in structure to that of a heterosexual woman than to that of a heterosexual man.[45]

Studies of separated twins were conducted in 1991 and 1993 at the Boston University School of Medicine. It was found that there was greater likelihood of both twins in a pair being homosexual if they were identical (shared the same genes) than if they were fraternal (did not share the same genes).[46] Another study in 1993 found additional evidence that homosexuality is genetically determined. Evidence of a "gay gene" was found when researchers studied the X chromosome in 40 pairs of homosexual brothers. In this group, 33 shared identical genetic markers in the tip of the X chromosome, suggesting with more than 99% certainty that the sexual orientation of the men was genetically influenced.[47]

LIFE AS A HOMOSEXUAL

Homosexual behavior between males is illegal in many states. Lesbianism (female homosexuality) is prohibited in fewer states than is male homosexuality. There appear to be several reasons for this: (a) Fewer females than males are homosexual. (b) Lesbians keep their sexual behavior more hidden and are not as likely to form obvious homosexual communities as are males. (c) Most legislators have been males and perhaps see male homosexuality as more of a threat to them than female homosexuality.

The Gay Liberation Movement has been seeking to change negative attitudes and end discriminatory acts toward homosexuals. Yet many people still view homosexuals as psychologically "sick"—as having a form of mental illness. (Until 1973 the American Psychiatric Association defined homosexuality as a mental illness.)

The Gay Liberation Movement is composed of groups such as the Gay Liberation Front, the National Gay Task Force, and the International Union of Gay Athletes. This social movement contends (along with many social scientists) that homosexuality is not a perversion or sickness but is simply a different lifestyle. Their arguments have met with mixed reactions. Some states have repealed antihomosexual legislation, and several cities have passed homosexual civil rights ordinances that prevent discrimination against police officers, teachers, and other city employees who have a homosexual orientation. Other cities and states have rejected bills that sought to ban discrimination against homosexuals.

When Bill Clinton was running for president in 1992, he promised to reverse the 50-year-old policy aimed at keeping homosexuals out of the military. After his election, he tried in 1993 to lift the ban by executive order but encountered strong resistance in the Pentagon and Congress. After

months of hearings and negotiations, Congress passed and Clinton signed a bill that has been referred to as "Don't ask, don't tell." New recruits to the military no longer can be asked by military personnel if they are homosexual; however, anyone who openly engages in homosexual conduct can be discharged. As part of the policy, the Pentagon promised to end purges of military personnel who keep their homosexuality private. (Some gay activists consider this policy as onerous as the original prohibition.) A legal battle is raging over the "Don't ask, don't tell" policy. Federal courts have split on the issue, and a Supreme Court test case seems inevitable.

In 1996 Congress passed, and President Clinton signed, the Defense of Marriage Act, which allows states to refuse to recognize gay marriages. (At the time of this writing, no state has passed legislation that legally recognizes same-sex marriages.) The Defense of Marriage Act prevents one partner in a homosexual relationship from claiming Social Security, veteran's, or other federal benefits in the event of the other's death or disability. It also bars gay and lesbian couples from filing joint income-tax returns, even if they live under the same roof and share everything else.

Courts are increasingly hearing cases involving gay rights issues. Some judges are supportive of gay rights issues, whereas others are not, as illustrated by the following two conflicting decisions (both of which were made in 1993). A federal judge in Virginia denied a lesbian mother custody of her son solely because of her sexuality; he awarded custody to the boy's grandmother. However, in Boston a state supreme court ruling made two lesbians the first gay couple to win approval to adopt a child in Massachusetts.[48]

Job discrimination against gays is legal in most states in the United States.[49] Such discrimination exists even though more than 80% of the public believe (in survey polls) gays should be protected from employment discrimination.[50]

Because of negative attitudes and discriminatory acts, some homosexuals go to extensive lengths to hide their sexual behavior. They fear discrimination and even loss of employment. They also fear the stigma and embarrassment that they and their families would receive if they "came out." Some homosexuals marry someone of the opposite sex and may even hide their homosexual encounters from their spouses. Leading a double life, with fear of criminal penalties if one's sexual orientation were discovered, is stress producing.

Many larger cities now have homosexual communities that provide an escape from the pressures of leading such a double life. These communities may offer recreational and leisure-time activities and may serve to socialize new entrants into the homosexual subculture. They are often located in a certain geographical area of a city and generally have shops, restaurants, and hotels that are owned and patronized primarily by homosexual customers. The "gay bars" are perhaps the most visible establishments in such communities. Gay bars provide opportunities for their clientele to drink, socialize, and find a sexual partner or a lover. Some gay bars look just like any other bar from the outside, while others have names (such as The Gay Closet) that indicate the clientele.

Unlike other minority-group members, homosexual girls and boys grew up as minorities even within their own families. People of color, for example, are socialized—trained—by their parents, older siblings, and relatives about functioning in a society that is likely to discriminate against them. Gay and lesbian youths have no such training ground, as most young homosexuals are raised in heterosexual families. This makes homosexually identified institutions (the most visible and approachable of which is the gay bar) very important in the life of the homosexual young adult. Most homosexuals patronize these gay bars for only a brief period (primarily while they are formulating their homosexual identity). After this phase, they generally prefer social contact with other homosexuals in environments where the focus is not on alcohol and superficial interactions.

There is a wide variation in homosexual lifestyles, as is true for heterosexuals. In addition, lesbians and male homosexuals differ somewhat in their sexual attitudes and practices. Lesbians are more likely to equate sex with love. They tend to engage in sex with fewer partners than do male homosexuals. Their relationships tend to last longer and to be based more on love and affection. Female homosexuals may be less likely to

Despite the negative and even hostile view many Americans still have of homosexuality, more gay men and women now openly acknowledge their sexual orientation.

acknowledge their sexual orientation publicly or to participate in a homosexual community.[51]

Lesbians are better able to conceal their sexual orientation because the public is less suspicious of two women living together or otherwise being close to each other. Most female homosexuals have had sexual relationships with men. Jack H. Hedblom notes: "The female homosexual does not prefer sex with a woman because she has had no experience with a man."[52]

A bisexual person's sexual orientation is toward both women and men (that is, toward members of the other and the same gender). The proponents of bisexuality argue that it has the advantage of allowing more variety in one's sexual and human relationships than either exclusive homosexuality or exclusive heterosexuality. On the other hand, some heterosexuals may devalue those who are known to be bisexual. In addition, persons who are bisexual may be viewed with suspicion or downright hostility by the gay community.[53] Some gays and lesbians view bisexuals as "fence-sitters" who betray the gay and lesbian movement as they can pretend to be "straight" when it is convenient and gay (or lesbian) when it is convenient.[54]

There is a diversity of bisexuals. Some bisexuals (referred to as 50:50 bisexuals) have equal preferences for men and for women. Some bisexuals have a preference for one gender but are accepting of sex with the other. Some are sequentially bisexual; they have only one lover at a time, sometimes a man and sometimes a woman. Some are simultaneously bisexual; they have both a male and a female lover at the same time. Some are transitory bisexuals who are passing through a bisexual phase on the way to becoming exclusively heterosexual or homosexual. Others are enduring bisexuals who maintain their bisexual preferences throughout their life span.

The specter of AIDS has had a tremendous impact on homosexual communities, particularly on gay men. Homosexual communities have been active in encouraging federal and state governments to (a) recognize the dangers of AIDS, (b) provide research funds to develop treatments for those who are infected with the AIDS virus, and (c) provide research funds to develop approaches to prevent the spread of AIDS.[55] Homosexual communities have also been advocates of safer sex practices, and many gay men have made responsible and dramatic changes in their sexual practices. Homosexual communities have also developed support systems for people with AIDS.

CURRENT ISSUES IN HOMOSEXUALITY

As mentioned earlier, a major issue is whether civil rights laws should be enacted to protect homosexuals from discrimination in housing, employment, military service, and other areas. Homosexuals argue that they are refused jobs in teaching, in the military, and in many private corporations. They also are commonly the targets of blackmailers who threaten to reveal their sexual orientation. They assert that legal protection for gay rights will not turn heterosexuals into homosexuals. Having long been the victims of abuse and exploitation, they now want the same protection that other minorities receive.[56]

Those who oppose civil rights laws for homosexuals assert that gays are not like other minority groups who are discriminated against based on physical characteristics (African Americans, women, persons with a disability). They believe that homosexuals choose their sexual orientation, which can be changed if they so desire. A number of other objections are also given by opponents: Legislation to protect gay rights would indicate approval of homosexual behavior, which in fact they consider unnatural. Permitting homosexuals to teach in school would unwisely expose children to homosexual attitudes and activities and would probably lead to increased homosexual experimentation. In addition, if sanctions were relaxed, homosexuality would flourish, the stability of the family would be threatened, birthrates would drop drastically, and society would be severely damaged. This is, of course, highly unlikely; with or without social sanctions, homosexuals constitute only a small minority of any society. And social support is unlikely to significantly increase behavior so basic to one's being as sexual orientation.

As can be seen, arguments on both sides of this issue are intense. And there are other concerns as well.

Some churches are now marrying homosexual couples who request this ceremony. These marriages are recognized by certain religious groups but not by state laws, which still prohibit homosexuals from marrying. Proponents of gay marriages assert that homosexuals ought to be permitted to receive the same personal gratifications and financial advantages through marriage that are available to heterosexuals. Opponents view these marriages as sacrilegious, as a violation of the purpose of marriage, and as a threat to the stability of the traditional family.

Related issues involve homosexuals' rights to adopt children and to retain custody of their own children after divorce. As we've seen, in some court cases, lesbian mothers have won custody of their children; in other cases, courts have decreed that lesbian behavior is sufficient evidence that a person is unfit to be a parent. At issue in homosexual adoptions and custody battles is whether homosexuals would pass on their sexual orientation to the child. Initial research findings suggest that this is unlikely.[57] We as a society continue to be confused about how sexual orientation might influence—if at all—other important aspects of life, such as child rearing or work performance.

In the past, psychotherapists who counseled homosexuals generally tried to switch their sexual orientation to homosexuality.[58] This goal was seldom achieved. Homosexuals often became more anxious and uncomfortable about their sexual orientation but continued to maintain homosexual behavior. The emphasis in counseling has shifted in recent years. Most therapists now help homosexuals to examine their concerns and arrive at a sexual identity they can be comfortable with. The majority of gays choose to continue their homosexual behavior, and counseling is then geared to helping them deal with discrimination and other concerns (such as whether to inform their relatives or employer and whether to "come out" in other ways).

Over time, our society has become more tolerant; years ago, efforts to suppress homosexuality were so strong that no newspaper even dared to print the word *homosexual.* Today this orientation is no longer an unmentionable deviancy. It is discussed on the airwaves, in newspapers and magazines, and in political debates. It is depicted in movies and on TV. Openly gay candidates for political office in the United States are increasingly being elected. Officially sanctioned support groups for gays are being established in high schools. Domestic partnerships between gay couples have been officially recognized in dozens of cities, and numerous corporations are granting partners of their homosexual employees the same benefits heterosexual spouses receive. Discrimination on the basis of sexual orientation is now illegal in several states and in nearly 100 cities and counties.

The two most prominent social work organizations in the United States (the Council on Social Work Education and the National Association of Social Workers) have identified gays and lesbians as populations at risk. These organizations also consider it the obligation of all social workers to work toward ending the discrimination and oppression experienced by gays and lesbians in our society.

Asocial Sex Variance

This category of sex variance refers to acts that elicit widespread, strong disapproval and do not have a social structure that supports them. Acts in this category include child molestation, incest, rape, voyeurism, and exhibitionism. People who engage in these behaviors usually act alone; that is, they do not have a social group that encourages and rewards their acts. All of these sex variances are prohibited by laws.

CHILD MOLESTATION

Child molestation is the sexual abuse of a child by an adult. Sexual abuse includes not only sexual intercourse (genital or anal) but also oral-genital contact, fondling, and behaviors such as exposing oneself to a child and photographing or viewing a child for the molester's erotic pleasure. Although legal definitions of various forms of sexual contact between older and younger people are clearly delineated in statute books, the central feature that makes the behavior abusive is that the sexual act is designed for the erotic gratification of the older, more powerful person. In child sexual abuse, the child is used as an object for the immediate gratification of another person, generally with no regard for the short- or long-term consequences for the child.

Child molestation is generally regarded as one of the most despicable sexual offenses in our society. The public fears—rightly—that this type of sexual abuse will destroy the innocence of the child and may lead to severe psychological trauma, interrupting the child's (and subsequent adult's) normal sexual development.

How extensive is child molestation? Many studies have been conducted to determine the incidence of child sexual abuse, and they indicate that approximately one in three girls and one in six boys have experienced sexual abuse.[59]

Over 90% of child molesters are males.[60] A number of factors partially explain this gender imbalance: (a) Men in our culture are socialized toward seeing sexuality as focused on sexual acts rather than as part of an emotional relationship. (b) Men are also socialized to be more aggressive and to believe that appropriate sexual partners are smaller and younger than themselves. In contrast, women are socialized to think that appropriate partners are larger and older than they are. (c) Finally, women in our culture are much more often caregivers of children and therefore are more attuned than men to children's emotional needs. A person who is closely involved since birth with taking care of a child is far less likely to view children in sexual ways than is someone who has had more incidental contact.

In the past few decades, there have been several well-publicized cases of child molestation. In 1979 John Wayne Gacy was arrested and convicted in Chicago for enticing 33 male adolescents into his home, sexually assaulting them, and then killing and burying them under his home. He was executed for these crimes in 1994. On March 11, 1977, Roman Polanski (a noted film director) was arrested in Los Angeles and charged with unlawful sexual intercourse, child molestation, supplying a minor with the drug Quaalude, oral copulation, sodomy, and rape via the use of drugs. A teenage girl was the alleged victim of these charges. After a plea bargain, he confessed to and was found guilty of only the first charge. While awaiting sentencing, he fled the United States and has never returned. In 1991 Jeffrey Dahmer in Milwaukee (who was on probation for molesting a 13-year-old boy in 1988) confessed to sexually assaulting, murdering, and dismembering 17 males, some of whom were teenagers. In 1993 Michael Jackson, the immensely popular singer, was accused of prolonged sexual contact with a 13-year-old boy; in 1994 the boy's parents withdrew a civil lawsuit for damages against Jackson after he paid them several million dollars.

Who are child molesters? The stereotype is that a molester is a stranger who lurks in the dark, waiting to pounce on a child who is walking or playing alone. The fact is that in most cases the offender is an acquaintance, friend, or relative.[61] (If the offender is a relative, the abuse is called incest.) Scores of parents, stepparents, scout leaders, child-care workers, and people from all walks of life have been found to be child molesters. Force is rarely used. The abuser generally gains sexual access to the child by manipulation and enticement rather than by use of a threat of force or harm. The nature of the abuse ranges on a continuum from inappropriate touching to actual intercourse.

In a small proportion of cases, the child may even initiate the contact. However, such initiation does not justify the adult's becoming an active participant and almost always indicates that the child has been sexually abused previously. (It is *always* the adult's responsibility for any abuse that occurs, and never the child's.)

A. Nicholas Groth has identified two categories of child molesters: fixated and regressed.[62] A *fixated* child molester's primary sexual object choice is children; he would always prefer a child as a sexual partner over an adult. These men are also known as pedophiles. Pedophilia is a sexual disorder characterized by recurrent sexual fantasies and urges or behaviors involving sexual activity with children.[63] A *regressed* child molester is a person whose usual sexual interest is in adult partners, but when faced with massive stress (marital difficulty, loss of job, a death in the family, and so on), he "regresses" emotionally (becomes a psychologically younger person) and acts out sexually toward children to meet his needs. Regressed child molesters generally seek female children as partners; fixated molesters are generally interested in male children. Most incest perpetrators are of the regressed type; they generally function well in society, are in a stable heterosexual relationship, but manage stress inappropriately by acting out sexually toward children. Some molesters have been found to engage in a variety of other inappropriate sexual behaviors, including voyeurism ("Peeping Toms"), exhibitionism, and even rape of adult women.[64] They apparently exercise little control over their sexual impulses; when a child becomes available, he or she becomes a victim.[65]

Even though the most attention in the media and among protective services workers is given to the sexual assault of girls in families (primarily incestuous relationships), recent research indicates that child molesters who abuse boys outside the home victimize children in far larger numbers. In an innovative study, Abel and his colleagues discovered that child molesters of boys reported an average (mean) of 150 victims, whereas child molesters of girls reported an average of 20 victims.[66] So why is less attention given to sexual abuse of boys as compared to abuse of girls? The most significant reason is that girls are far more likely to report sexual victimization, whereas boys often view being molested as reflecting an "unmasculine" weakness in themselves. It is thought by many authorities that child molestation of boys is the most underreported major crime in America.

How traumatic is molestation for the child? The factors that have the most emotional impact on child (and later adult) development seem to include (a) the relationship between the child and the adult (it is more damaging to the further development of trust to be abused by someone you are close to than by a stranger); (b) the frequency and duration of the abuse; (c) the actual sexual behaviors engaged in; (d) the number of perpetrators; (e) the reactions of other people if the abuse becomes revealed; (f) the child's general mental and emotional health and coping strategies; and (g) the availability and use of professional intervention by the victim, the abuser, and others (such as the parents). The most helpful interventions following child sexual abuse occur when all significant parties (professionals, parents, siblings, and so forth) believe the child's report, when the perpetrator takes full responsibility for his or her actions, and when the child has forums that promote understanding and healing at various stages in his or her later development.

INCEST

Incest is defined as sexual relations between blood relatives. Typically, the definition is extended to include sex between certain nonblood relatives, such as between a stepparent and a child. In the past, families generally attempted to hide this type of abuse, and it usually was not reported. Now, with an increased openness about human sexuality, there is a greater willingness for family members to seek professional help.

In the largest proportion of incest cases reported to the police, the sexual abuse is between father or stepfather and daughter.[67] However, most incest cases are never reported to the police. Brother/sister incest is actually the most common form.[68] This may or may not constitute sexual abuse. If the children are approximately the same age and the sexual activity is mutual and not coerced, this type of incest may be considered normal sexual experimentation. However, if the children are more than a few years apart in age, the potential exists for the younger child to be coerced into activity she or he is not comfortable with. At that point, consent no longer exists, and nonconsenting sex is sexual abuse.

Most often incest occurs in the child's home. The child is usually enticed or pressured, rather than physically forced, to participate. The age range of the abused child is from several months to adulthood, although most reports involve teenagers.[69] Children are unlikely to report the sexual abuse because they often have loyalties toward the abuser and realistically fear the consequences for themselves, for the abuser, and for the family.

Causes of Incest. Why does incest occur? Students of sexology have long known that people frequently use sexual behavior to achieve nonsexual rewards. For example, a teenage boy might wish to have intercourse with his girlfriend (sexual behavior) not primarily because he loves her or because he seeks sexual gratification but rather to enhance his status with his friends and therefore gratify his ego (nonsexual reward).

Adults who are threatened by and fearful of the rejection of other adults often turn for reassurance to children, who are nonthreatening and generally unconditionally loving. This need for acceptance can lead to the adult's initiating sexual behavior (especially if the adult had been sexually abused as a child, as is often the case) because many people view sexual behavior as the ultimate acceptance and ego validation. Most child molesters intend no harm to their victims; they are psychologically needy people who use children in their own battle for emotional survival.

Effects of Incest. Blair and Rita Justice have studied the consequences of incest at three different points in time: while the incest is going on, when the incest is discovered, and years after its occurrence.[70] It is important to bear in mind that incest is a symptom of a disturbed family system.

First we will look at the effects while the incest is occurring. A daughter who has sex with her father often gains special power over him; she controls a very important secret. The daughter can receive special privileges from the father, which makes the other siblings (and even the mother) jealous. Role confusion often occurs. The daughter is still a child, but at times she is a lover and an equal to her father. Victims are deprived of the opportunity to explore and discover their sexuality by themselves or with a peer partner of their choice. Instead, this normal sexual development is violated by an adult imposing his exploitative behavior. The daughter often does not know if her father is going to act as a parent or as a lover, so she is confused about whether she should respond to him as a child or as a sexual partner. The mother may become both a parent and a rival to her daughter. Siblings may also become confused about who is in charge and how to relate to their sister who is receiving special privileges. Fathers in an incestuous family may become jealous and overpossessive of their daughters.

As the daughter grows older, she wants to be more independent and to spend more time with other teenagers. Often she grows more resentful of her father's possessiveness. To make a break from the father, she may run away or tell someone about the incest. Or she may passively resist the father's rules, for example, by ignoring curfews.

In a small number of cases, the incest is discovered when the daughter becomes pregnant. (Genetically, incest may have adverse consequences as it leads to inbreeding. The offspring are more apt to have lower intelligence, physical performance difficulties, and genetic defects.[71]) At times the incest is discovered by the mother,

who then may try to stop it by reporting it to the police. (Sometimes the mother discovers the incest but remains quiet.)

If the incest is reported to the police and criminal charges are filed against the father, the entire family is usually caught up in a traumatic, time-consuming, confusing, and costly legal process. When there is legal involvement, the daughter is often subjected to embarrassing and humiliating interrogation. She may feel, at times, that her account of the incest is not believed. Or she may feel that blame is being placed on her rather than on her father. Once she is recognized as a victim of incest, she be approached sexually by other men who now view her as "fair game."[72] Often she is removed from the home to prevent further abuse. In addition, the mother and father suffer considerable embarrassment and humiliation. Their marriage may become so conflictful that it ends in divorce.

The long-term effects of incest vary from child to child. Younger children usually do not fully realize the significance of the sexual behavior and tend to suffer less guilt than adolescent victims. However, with young children there is always the danger that, as they grow older and learn about society's taboos against incest, they may start blaming themselves for having participated. Possible long-term effects on the daughter include low self-esteem, guilt, depression, and fear.[73]

The daughter may also become angry at both parents for not protecting her and at the father for exploiting her. Moreover, she may believe that she is somehow to blame for what happened; she may feel tainted by the experience and see herself as worthless or as "damaged goods." Because of her guilt and anger, she may in future years develop difficulties in expressing her sexuality and relating to men. She may feel unable to trust men because she was betrayed and severely hurt by her father, whom she deeply trusted. Some victims seek to blot out their pain and loneliness through self-destructive behavior such as prostitution, drug abuse, or suicide.

If the incest is ongoing and unreported and the victim is an older child, she may attempt to avoid the abuser by running away from home. If she flees, there is a strong possibility that she will become a prostitute to support herself, in part because she has been taught, dysfunctionally, that her sexuality is valued by men and is her most valuable asset. She is also likely to abuse drugs as a method of escaping the life situation she is trapped in.

Some victims during their childhood years seek to deny or suppress the traumas associated with incest. When they become adults, they may experience difficulties in developing relationships with others. Because relationships are founded on trust, and because the victims' fundamental trust in others (and therefore their ability to trust their own judgment of others) has been violated, they often fear making commitments to others in an attempt to protect themselves from further hurt. Many of these victims finally acknowledge as adults the traumas they experienced as children. Therapy is highly recommended for these adult victims to help them come to terms with the pain and suffering of having been violated by someone they trusted.

Treatment of Incest. Because incest is only one symptom of a disturbed family, treating these families is difficult and complex. In the past when incest was reported, the victim (usually a teenage girl) was generally placed in a foster home, further victimizing her. Such action was likely to reveal the sexual abuse to the local community. Often neighbors, relatives, and friends expressed shock and began shunning all members of the family. The disruption usually intensified the marital conflict between husband and wife and generally led to permanent dissolution of the family. In some instances, the husband was also prosecuted, which even further intensified the family conflicts.

In recent years, a number of social service agencies have been seeking to keep the family intact, particularly when all three of the members involved (husband, wife, and victim) express a desire to maintain the family. A typical intervention requires the father's removal from the home for a period of 6 months to 1 year, during which time all family members are involved in individual and group treatment. The incest perpetrator must acknowledge to his wife and daughter that he was entirely responsible for the sexual abuse, that he is sorry it happened, and that he will make the necessary lifestyle and value changes to ensure that the abuse will not recur. The nonabusing parent (typically the mother) is taught assertiveness. Intervention with the mother and daughter is geared toward improving their relationship, which is usually very damaged. The victim (typically the daughter) is helped to process her anger, guilt, and confusion. Eventually all family members are seen in therapy together to help them build, perhaps for the first time, a healthy, functional family system.

RAPE

Forced intercourse is a commonly committed violent crime in the United States. More than 90,000 cases are reported annually, and many more instances go unreported.[74] Victims of rape are hesitant to report the crime for a variety of reasons. They may feel that reporting the case will do them no good because they have already been victimized. They sometimes fear that they may be humiliated by the questions the police will ask. They are reluctant to press charges because they fear the reactions of the general public and of people close to them, including their boyfriends or husbands. Many fear that, if they report the offense, the rapist will try to attack them again. Some victims just want to try to forget about it. Others fail to report it because they do not want to testify in court. But perhaps the most common reason women fail to report sexual assault is that they feel—usually wrongly—that they somehow contributed to the rape's occurrence. This is especially true in the most frequent type of rape—that by an acquaintance.

In many states, rape is defined as a crime that only males can commit. Although the great majority of male rape victims are raped by men (frequently in prison settings), a few men are raped by women.[75] Research shows that men may respond with an erection in emotional states such as anger and terror.[76] Research indicates that men who have been raped by women experience a rape trauma syndrome that is very similar to the rape trauma syndrome (soon to be described) of female victims.

An unusual case of a woman raping a male occurred in Seattle. Mrs. Mary Kay Letourneau was a highly respected elementary school teacher. She was married, age 34, and the mother of four children. In 1997 she pleaded guilty to raping a 13-year-old boy who was a former student of hers. She acknowledged that she had a 6-month affair with this young teenager. She became pregnant by him and delivered a baby girl. In November 1997, a judge sentenced her to 6 months in jail and to 3-years participation in an outpatient sex offender treatment program for committing second-degree rape of a child. (A few months later, she violated the rules of probation by having contact with the teenager and was sentenced by a judge to prison for over 7 years.)

There is no profile that fits all rapists. They vary considerably in terms of motivation for committing the rape, prior criminal record, education, occupation, marital status, and so on. In a majority of cases, the rapist and his (or her) victim know each other on a first-name basis. A significant proportion of rapes are date rapes.

Rape is primarily an aggressive act and secondarily a sexual act. That is, it is a sexual expression of aggression, not an aggressive expression of sexuality. Many people wrongly believe that rape occurs because the rapist cannot control his sexual arousal or because he is "oversexed." Rape is, instead, the mismanagement of aggression; the rapist's gratification (if any) comes not from the sexual act but rather from the expression of anger or control through the extreme violation of another's body.

There are a number of typologies for classifying rapists, depending on numerous variables. One straightforward model was developed by A. Nicholas Groth,[77] who describes rapists as falling into one of three categories: the anger rapist, the power rapist, and the sadistic rapist.

The *anger rapist* performs his act to discharge feelings of pent-up anger and rage. He is brutal in the commission of his assault, using far more force than is necessary to gain sexual access to his vic-

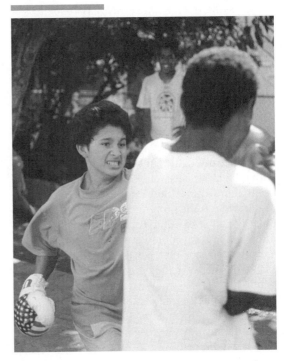

Our society socializes males to be aggressive and that aggression may then be used as proof of manhood.

tim. His aim is to hurt and debase his victim; forced sex is his ultimate weapon.

The *power rapist* is interested in possessing his victim sexually, not harming her. He acts out of underlying feelings of inadequacy and is interested in controlling his victim. He uses only the amount of force necessary to gain her compliance. Sometimes he will kidnap his victim and hold her under his control for a long period of time, perhaps engaging in sexual intercourse with her numerous times.

The *sadistic rapist* eroticizes aggression; that is, aggressive force creates sexual arousal in him. He is enormously gratified by his victim's torment, pain, and suffering. His offenses often are ritualistic and involve bondage and torture, particularly to the sexual organs.

We live in a society that promotes aggression and represses sexuality. In the United States, males are socialized to be aggressive, even in seeking sexual gratification. For example, men are often expected to play the "aggressive" role in sex. In our culture, sex and aggression are frequently confused and combined. In Swedish culture, where sexual information is readily available in the media but depictions of aggression are not, the incidence of rape is low. According to Janet Hyde, the confusion of sex and aggression in socialization practices may lead males to commit rape:

> It may be, then, that rape is a means of proving masculinity for the male who is insecure in his role. For this reason, the statistics on the youthfulness of rapists make sense; youthful rapists may simply be young men who are trying to adopt the adult male role, who feel insecure about doing this, and who commit a rape as proof of their manhood. Further, heterosexuality is an important part of manliness. Raping a woman is a flagrant way to prove that one is a heterosexual.[78]

(See Exhibit 7.4 for more about aggression and sexuality.)

Date Rape. In a study by Struckman-Johnson of female college students, 22% stated that they had been victimized by at least one incident of forced sexual intercourse on a date.[79] The study demonstrates that date rape is not a rare occurrence.

In some cases, date rape seems to result from the mistaken belief on the part of the man that, if he spends money on the woman, he is entitled to (or she is implicitly giving consent to) sexual rewards. The traditional view in dating relationships has been that, when the woman says "no," she really means "yes." Unfortunately, media depictions of this misinformation abound, from John Wayne movies to such classics as *Last Tango in Paris* and *Gone with the Wind*. For example, in the movie *The Quiet Man*, John Wayne plays a macho, quiet Irishman. He courts a feisty woman played by Maureen O'Hara, but to no avail. Only after beating up a mean rival, spanking the woman in front of the townspeople, and literally dragging her home does he win her compliance and cooperation. The underlying message seems to be that

EXHIBIT 7.4

Gang Rapes at Fraternities

Anthropologist Peggy Sanday analyzed a number of fraternity gang rapes that have been reported to the authorities. She concludes that such gang rapes have two consequences: (a) they promote strong bonds among the male offenders and (b) they debase the female victims and establish dominance over them. Usually the victim is drunk or is secretly drugged so that she is barely conscious. (When the gang rape occurs, many of the fraternity members are also intoxicated.) Sanday further concludes that fraternities in which gang rape occurs are essentially a subculture that socializes members to have sexist attitudes toward women and creates an environment in which gang rape is apt to occur. In such fraternities, the members are socialized to prize the loyalty to the group over their own values and mores. Sometimes, when cases of gang rape go to court, the male offenders state they had no idea that their activities were wrong or illegal.

In one fraternity investigated by Sanday, the intoxicated victims were raped successively by a series of members of the XYZ (name has been changed for confidentiality reasons) fraternity who stood in line to take their turn, much like cars in a train. The members called this practice the "XYZ express." Sanday concludes, "Social ideologies, not human nature, prepare men to abuse women" (p. 12).

Source: Peggy R. Sanday, *Fraternity Gang Rape* (New York: New York University Press, 1990).

"real men" obtain power, status, and sexual gratification by violating women sexually—a very dangerous message indeed!

Leon, a college student, described his thinking processes prior to a date rape:

> It's time for me to make my move. Tonight her every dream will come true when I show her

what it's like to be with a real man. It'll be the perfect ending to an evening she'll never forget. I knew that she was after more than dinner and dancing from the moment that I picked her up. I mean, check out that dress she's wearing, those fancy jewels, that sexy perfume, and those looks she has been giving me—they're unmistakable. Now that she has agreed to a nightcap at my place, we can end the evening in style. I'll just slide a little closer to her on the couch, slip my arm around her shoulder, and kiss her neck . . . Does she really think that moving away and saying "No!" will stop me? I guess all women play that game. I dropped a bundle on this date and now it's time for her to pay up. Boy, the guys will be impressed to know that I scored with such a classy number. Even if she wanted to, she couldn't stop someone as powerful as me. Besides, everyone knows that when a woman says "No!" she really means "Yes!"

The vast majority of date rapes go unreported. In fact, many of the female victims of sexual assault do not interpret the assault as such.[80] When the victims view themselves as being "in love" with the perpetrator, there is a tendency to see the rape as being within the realm of acceptable behavior.

Kanin studied 71 unmarried college men who were self-disclosed date rapists and compared them to a control group of unmarried college men.[81] The date rapists tended to be sexually predatory. When asked how frequently they attempt to seduce a new date, 62% of the date rapists said "most of the time," compared with 19% of the controls. The date rapists also were much more likely to report using a variety of manipulative techniques on their dates, including falsely professing love, getting the dates high on alcohol or other drugs, and falsely promising to go steady or get engaged.

Men need to learn that "no" means "no." Date-rape educational programs are needed in elementary, secondary, and college settings. Laws against date rape should be more vigorously enforced. And society (including the mass media) must stop glamorizing rape and instead report it as a serious crime that takes a devastating toll on its victims.

Effects on Victims. Ann Burgess and Lynda Holmstrom have found that rape generally constitutes a severe crisis for the victims and that aftereffects often persist for 6 months or longer.[82] They analyzed the reactions of 92 victims of forcible rape and labeled the series of emotional changes experienced by the victims the "rape trauma syndrome."[83]

This syndrome occurs in two phases: an acute phase and a long-term reorganization phase. The *acute phase* begins immediately after the rape (or attempted rape) and may last for several weeks. Victims have an expressive reaction in which they are likely to cry and have feelings of anger, fear, humiliation, tension, anxiety, and a desire for revenge. During this phase, victims also usually have periods of controlled reaction in which they mask or deny their feelings and appear calm, composed, or subdued. Victims undergo many physical reactions during this phase such as stomach pains, nausea, headaches, insomnia, and jumpiness. In addition, some women who had been forced to have oral sex reported irritation or damage to the throat. Some who had been forced to have anal intercourse reported rectal pain and bleeding. Two feelings were especially common: fear and self-blame. Many women feared future physical violence or continued to suffer from the fear of being murdered during the attack. The self-blame is related to the tendency on the part of the victim and others to "blame the victim." The women often spent hours agonizing over what they thought they had done to bring on the attack or over what they could have done to fight off the attacker. Common self-criticisms are, "If only I hadn't walked alone," "If only I had bolt-locked the door," "If only I hadn't worn that tight sweater," and "If only I hadn't been dumb enough to trust that guy."

The *long-term reorganization phase* follows the acute phase. At this point, victims may experience a variety of major disruptions. Some women who have been raped outdoors may develop a fear of going outdoors; others who have been raped indoors may develop a fear of being indoors. Some are unable to return to work, particularly if the rape occurred there. Some quit their job and remain unemployed for a long time. Many fear the

CHAPTER 7 ■ SEXUAL ORIENTATION, SEX VARIANCES, AND SEX COUNSELING **261**

rapist will find them and assault them again. To attempt to avoid this recurrence, they may move (sometimes several times), change their telephone number, or get an unlisted number. Some develop sexual phobias and have severe difficulties in returning to their regular sexual behaviors. In some cases, it takes several years before the victim returns to her previous lifestyle.

In addition, if the victim reports the rape, the police investigation and the trial (if it occurs) are further crises that are experienced. Police and the courts have a history of abusive and callous treatment of rape victims. The police have, at times, conveyed the idea that the victim was fabricating the assault or had willingly agreed to have sex but then changed her mind. The police often ask embarrassing questions about the details of the rape without showing much understanding or sympathy. In court it is common for the defense attorney to imply that the victim provoked the defendant. Victims are sometimes made to feel as if they are the ones who are on trial.

Of late, fortunately, many police departments have developed sensitive crime units with specially trained officers to intervene in cases of rape and child sexual assault. With such units, victims are less likely to be further victimized by authorities. Furthermore, a number of states have enacted "shield" evidence laws, which prohibit defense attorneys from asking questions about the victim's previous sexual experiences (except with the alleged rapist) during a rape trial. (In the past, defense attorneys sought to imply that the victim was promiscuous and therefore probably seduced the defendant.)

Because rape and its aftereffects are extremely traumatic, Burgess and Holmstrom urge counseling for victims to (a) provide support and allow the victims to vent their feelings, (b) lend support and guidance during the medical tests and police interrogation, (c) provide similar support during the trial, and (d) provide follow-up counseling for emotional reactions to the rape.[84]

Burgess and Holmstrom also note that, because a majority of rapes are not reported, many of the victims have a *silent rape reaction*.[85] Nonreporters not only fail to report the rape to the police, but many tell no one about it. They are likely to experience the same adjustment problems as victims who report the rape experience. However, the trauma for nonreporters is often intensified because they have no way of expressing or venting their feelings. Some nonreporters eventually seek professional counseling for other problems, such as depression, anxiety, or inability to have orgasms. Often such problems are then found to stem from the rape. Women who have had unreported rape experiences should be helped to talk about them so they can gradually learn to deal with the trauma. A number of communities now have rape crisis centers that provide counseling, medical services, and legal services to victims.

EXHIBITIONISM AND VOYEURISM

Exhibitionists and voyeurs are frequently referred to as "flashers" and "Peeping Toms," respectively. They are often considered nuisances rather than serious threats to society or to individuals. There is, of course, more alarm and disdain when exhibitionists disrobe in front of children. Having someone peek into our homes is also alarming. Of greater concern is the research finding that exhibitionists and voyeurs are also likely to engage in more assaultive sex offenses, such as sexual abuse of children and even rape.[86] This finding contradicts the traditional view that exhibitionists and voyeurs usually don't commit more harmful sexual acts.

To some extent, all of us have probably displayed our bodies to others, perhaps during nude swimming (skinny-dipping) or sunbathing. A number of years ago, streaking (running nude on college campuses and other places) was popular. "Mooning" (displaying one's buttocks in public) has been a common fad among high school and college students. However, the exhibitionist obtains a great deal of sexual arousal by exposing his genitals to unwilling strangers. The exhibitionist may be unable to become aroused by more normal expressions of sexuality and is often quite compulsive in his exposure behaviors. For him, exposure is not an occasional lark with the guys but a planned, frequently repeated activity.

Voyeurism is defined as watching people undress, viewing them in the nude, or observing

EXHIBIT 7.5

How to Attempt to Prevent Rape

There have been a number of suggestions to help women prevent rape and fight off an attacker. These suggestions include having and using secure locks on doors, not walking alone at night, and learning self-defense measures such as judo, aikido, tae kwon do (Korean karate), or jujitsu. Being assertive when saying "no" to unwanted sexual advances is particularly useful in preventing acquaintance rape.[a] Exercising regularly and keeping in shape are also recommended to give the potential victim the strength to fight back and the speed to run fast. Some experts recommend poking an attacker in the eyes or kneeing him in the groin. Other experts recommend that every woman have a psychological strategy to use if attacked, such as telling the rapist that she has cancer of the cervix or a sexually transmittable condition (such as being HIV-positive). If other preventative measures fail, some experts urge dissuading the attacker by regurgitating on him, which can be accomplished by sticking one's finger down one's throat. Another last-ditch strategy is to urinate on him.

It is important that each woman have a strategy, or set of defensive measures, she would seek to use if an attack occurred. No one type of advice can apply to all situations because the rapist may respond quite differently to the victim's fighting back, depending on whether he is primarily a power, anger, or sadistic rapist. Therefore, any woman who physically survives a rape should be viewed as having utilized a successful strategy.

On a broader sociological level, feminists urge a revision in our sex-role socialization practices. Margaret Mead has noted that rape does not occur in societies in which males are socialized to be nurturant rather than aggressive.[b] To reduce rape sharply, Janet S. Hyde recommends the following changes in socialization practices:

> *If little boys were not so pressed to be aggressive and tough, perhaps rapists would never develop. If adolescent boys did not have to demonstrate that they are hypersexual, perhaps there would be no rapists. . . .*
>
> *Changes would also need to be made in the way females are socialized, particularly if women are to become good at self-defense. Weakness is not considered a desirable human characteristic, and so it should not be considered a desirable feminine characteristic, especially because it makes women vulnerable to rape. . . . While some people think that it is silly for the federal government to rule that girls must have athletic teams equal to boys' teams, it seems quite possible that the absence of athletic training for girls has contributed to making them rape victims. . . .*
>
> *Finally, for both males and females, we need a radical restructuring of ideas about sexuality. As long as females are expected to pretend to be uninterested in sex and as long as males and females play games on dates, rape will persist.[c]*

---

[a] Janet S. Hyde, *Understanding Human Sexuality,* 5th ed. (New York: McGraw-Hill, 1994), p. 496.
[b] Margaret Mead, *Sex and Temperament in Three Primitive Societies* (New York: Morrow, 1935).
[c] Hyde, *Understanding Human Sexuality,* p. 498.

---

them performing sexual acts without their knowledge or consent. Everyone has probably found enjoyment at times in looking at pictures of people who are nude or seminude, going to nightclubs featuring nude dancers, going to X-rated movies, watching our sex partner undress, or observing the attractive physiques of others in public. Again, it should be noted that invasion-of-privacy voyeurism is demeaning and threatening to an unwilling victim.

Exhibitionism and voyeurism involve behaviors that differ in degree from the kinds of showing and looking that are considered normal in our society.

PERSONAL SEXUAL CONCERNS

At one time or another, everyone has sexual concerns. The kinds of sexual concerns are probably infinite, so only a few will be listed:

- A teenager may wonder whether to become sexually involved with someone he or she is dating.

- A male who had sex with a prostitute may be concerned he has contracted the AIDS virus.

- Adolescents may feel guilty about masturbating.

- A wife may feel guilty about having had an extramarital affair.

- Men may worry about premature ejaculation, failure to have an erection, or failure to become sexually aroused.

- Some women are concerned because they seldom have an orgasm.

- Persons married or dating over an extended period of time may become alarmed because their sex life appears to be becoming boring and routine.

- Some people may be unhappy with various sexual techniques and approaches used by their partners.

- Victims of rape or incest may still have unwanted emotions related to what happened to them.

- An admirer of someone of his or her own sex may wonder if this attraction has homosexual elements.

- Middle-aged people may fear losing their sexual capacities.

- Some may find intercourse painful.

- Some know their current sexual partner has had previous sexual experiences with others and feel angry or hurt.

SEX COUNSELING AND SEX THERAPY

Sex counseling and sex therapy are designed directly to resolve personal sexual concerns. *Sex counseling* is short-term, often crisis-oriented counseling directed toward the alleviation of some immediate sexual concern. *Sex therapy,* on the other hand, is somewhat longer term and tends to focus more on resolving specific sexual dysfunctions (such as premature ejaculation and erectile difficulties in men and failure to achieve orgasm and painful intercourse in women). Sex therapy involves several stages: problem identification, taking a sexual physical examination, information giving, history about the concern, assigning sexual exercises designed to resolve the dysfunction, and ongoing evaluation.[87] In actual counseling, the distinctions between sex counseling and sex therapy are not clear-cut. Sex counseling and sex therapy treatment programs are available in many communities. Social workers at most social service agencies occasionally counsel clients with sexual concerns. Private sex therapy centers, often based on the treatment programs pioneered by Masters and Johnson, provide services in many larger communities.

Jack Annon has developed an extremely useful conceptual scheme for treating personal sexual concerns.[88] Having found that very few persons with sexual concerns need intensive sex therapy, he advances a model with four levels of intervention:

1. Permission
2. Limited information
3. Specific suggestions
4. Intensive therapy

Most people can be treated at one of the first three levels of intervention.

CASE EXAMPLE 7.1   Sex Counseling for Seeking Meaning in Life Through Sex

Cassie, a 19-year-old fast-food restaurant employee, revealed to Maria Ricardo (social worker at a Planned Parenthood clinic) that she felt guilty and despondent upon "being used by men." She indicated that she had experienced a series of "one-night stands" and always felt guilty and depressed afterward. Ms. Ricardo probed into her feelings of guilt, and Cassie gradually revealed that her thoughts underlying her guilt feelings included: "I am promiscuous, which my religion says is immoral"; "I am letting men who don't love me use my body"; "I am giving myself to men whom I don't love, which is wrong"; and "I'm a bad person, a whore, for doing this."

Her feelings of being depressed after sex were also examined. Her thoughts underlying her depression were: "No one really cares about me as a person, only about my body"; "I am leading the kind of life I really don't want to lead"; "I am putting myself at risk for getting AIDS or some other STD [sexually transmitted disease]"; and "I give everything I have to these guys, and they don't even ask me out for a date afterward."

When asked by Ms. Ricardo to identify her thoughts prior to having sex that lead her to engage in intercourse, Cassie eventually stated: "At times I really like it, and enjoy and want sex" and "Sex is the one way I can get a guy interested in me." After reflecting on these reasons, Cassie concluded that she was using her sexuality as the primary way to attract men, which was leading to "one-night stands," putting her at risk for an STD, and resulting in her feeling guilty and depressed. Ms. Ricardo asked Cassie if her current way of seeking meaning in life was through dating and whether she was using sex to have dates. Cassie thought about this and gradually agreed. Ms. Ricardo then asked Cassie whether such a strategy was getting her what she wanted in life. Cassie indicated, "Definitely not. It is leading to one-night stands, which result in me feeling guilty and depressed."

The largest number of people can be treated at the first level simply by the helping professional giving accurate, well-placed "permission." *Permission* involves a kind of professional reassurance, letting clients know they are all right and normal, not sick or perverted. Many people at this level are not bothered by the sexual behavior they are engaging in but are more concerned about what other people think. These concerns may include masturbation, oral-genital sex, and sexual fantasies. It is important to note that permission involves helping clients first to understand it is to their benefit to engage in sexual activities they desire as long as they do not hurt themselves or infringe on the rights of others and then to assure them of their right *not* to engage in sexual behaviors that other people are urging. Lloyd Sinclair gives the following example of counseling at the permission level:

The client reports, "My wife and I hear a lot about oral sex. We just aren't interested in doing that. Do you think there's something wrong with us?" The counselor can give permission: "Sex is best when you're doing things you both want to do, not because of somebody else's expectations. I would encourage you to do what you both like, and if at some point you want to try oral sex, fine. But if you don't, that's fine too." [89]

Ms. Ricardo asked Cassie to do a homework assignment prior to their next meeting. It involved Cassie brainstorming and writing down a list of options (including some in which she may have little interest in pursuing) for how to feel better about herself and to identify other ways of finding meaning in life. Cassie came back the next week with the following list:

1. Wait until marriage to next have sex.
2. Wait to have sex until I meet someone I love—and who also loves me.
3. Take courses at the local community college in an effort to find, and prepare for, a career I'm interested in.
4. Volunteer at the nursing home that my grandmother is living in.

Ms. Ricardo explored these options with Cassie. She indicated that the option or options Cassie selects were up to her, as she is in the best position to know which would best suit her values, her current lifestyle, and her goals in life. For each option, Ms. Ricardo also discussed how Cassie is apt to feel about herself if she pursues that option. After considerable discussion, Cassie decided to pursue options 2 and 3. She seemed to feel good about her decisions.

Ms. Ricardo then asked Cassie if she would be interested in being tested for HIV. Cassie agreed to have the test, and the results came back negative 2 weeks later. Ms. Ricardo also discussed safer sex practices (such as using a condom) in the future when Cassie becomes romantically involved with someone. She also suggested that Cassie have another HIV test in about 6 months, just in case she was recently exposed to the AIDS virus. (For a person infected with HIV, it generally takes up to 6 months before enough antibodies are produced to be detected by an AIDS test. AIDS tests do not directly detect the virus, but only the antibodies a person's immune system develops to fight the virus.) Cassie agreed to take this additional AIDS test.

The second largest number of people need *limited information;* that is, specific factual information to alleviate their sexual concerns. Sinclair gives an example of providing limited information and its effects:

A sixty-eight-year-old client . . . had believed for as long as he could remember that human beings were capable of a certain number of orgasms in life, and no more. So he had rationed *them, always confining orgasm to a single intercourse experience each weekend. The therapist informed him that what he had believed was incorrect. In fact, he could enhance his ability to respond sexually by maintaining a frequency and regularity of response. Since this client re-*

ceived this information, he has been making up for a great deal of lost time.[90]

The third level of intervention is *specific suggestions.* A smaller number of clients benefit at this level than at each of the preceding levels. Prior to giving suggestions, the therapist takes a brief sexual history, including a description of the current concern, its onset and course, the client's views of the cause and maintenance of the concern, past treatment efforts and outcome, and current goals and expectations from treatment.[91] Such background information is very useful in determining which specific suggestions are apt to be the most useful in alleviating the sexual distress.

Specific suggestions are often given to treat performance difficulties. For example, a woman who finds intercourse painful due to lack of sexual arousal and lack of lubrication may benefit from suggestions encouraging the couple to spend more time on foreplay, helping her communicate to her partner those behaviors that are pleasurable to her, and advising her not to proceed to intercourse until she is lubricating.

For a male suffering from premature ejaculation, a specific suggestion is to briefly stop the stimulation to decrease the erection and thereby delay the orgasm. Another suggestion is for him or his partner to squeeze the penis in certain areas during an erection to decrease the erection and delay the orgasm. Yet another suggestion is to use touching experiences with one's partner without proceeding to intercourse, so that the male learns to enjoy such touching experiences and thereby delays orgasm.[92]

Annon's final level of intervention, *intensive therapy,* is needed by a very small number of persons with sexual concerns. At this level, the concerns are fairly complicated and involved. An example would be a married couple who no longer is having sexual intercourse, largely because the wife has never experienced orgasm and because the husband is now having difficulty maintaining an erection. Descriptions of intensive therapy[93] are beyond the scope of this text. It involves having clients receive physical examinations, taking an extensive sexual history of both partners, helping the partners communicate better with each other, conveying accurate information to the clients about the physiology of sex, assigning sexual exercises designed to resolve the concerns, and evaluating efforts made to resolve the concerns.

SUMMARY

Practically every conceivable sexual activity is socially acceptable to some groups of people. What is defined as acceptable and unacceptable sexual behavior varies from culture to culture and from one time period to another. Judeo-Christian values, the Puritan influence, and Victorian morality contributed in our history to repression of sexual expression. At present, ambiguity and confusion abound over what ought to be the sexual code and behavior of Americans. For the past several decades, our society has been undergoing a revolution in sexual values and mores. The work of four social scientists has had profound effects on our understanding of human sexuality: Sigmund Freud, Alfred Kinsey, and the team of William Masters and Virginia Johnson.

This text uses a social variance approach to examining sexual concerns rather than a social problems approach because there is as yet no general consensus about which sexual acts are acceptable and which are not. Three categories of sexual variances were discussed: tolerated sex variance, structural sex variance, and asocial sex variance. Tolerated sex variance includes masturbation, premarital intercourse, and heterosexual oral-genital contact between consenting adults.

Structural sex variance refers to acts that run counter to prevailing norms and legal statutes but at the same time have supportive social structures. Homosexuality, pornography, and prostitution are in this category. Homosexuality was discussed at some length.

Asocial sex variance includes acts that elicit strong disapproval and at the same time do not have a social structure that supports them. Acts in this category include incest, child molestation, rape, voyeurism, and exhibitionism.

Almost everyone experiences personal sexual concerns. For example, men may worry about premature ejaculation, and women may experience painful intercourse.

The social worker can be a helping agent to people suffering from sexual problems. The social worker is frequently called on to step out of her or his primary professional role to become a sex counselor. In this role, the worker performs short-term, often crisis-oriented counseling directed toward the alleviation of some immediate difficulty related to sex.

A useful model for counseling people with sexual concerns was developed by Jack Annon. This model has four levels of intervention: permission, limited information, specific suggestions, and intensive sex therapy.

In the past century, our country has made a number of changes in what are acceptable sexual attitudes and sexual behaviors.

NOTES

1. Havelock Ellis, *Sex and Marriage: Eros in Contemporary Life* (Westport, CT: Greenwood Press, 1977), p. 42.
2. David A. Schulz, *Human Sexuality* (Englewood Cliffs, NJ: Prentice Hall, 1979), p. 4.
3. Don Grubin, "Sexual Offending: A Cross Cultural Comparison," in *Annual Review of Sex Research*, vol. III, John Bancroft, Clive M. Davis, and Howard J. Ruppel, Jr., eds. (Lake Mills, IA: Society for the Scientific Study of Sex, 1993), pp. 201–217.
4. Janet S. Hyde, *Understanding Human Sexuality*, 5th ed. (New York: McGraw-Hill, 1994), p. 13.
5. Ibid.
6. John Gagnon and Bruce Henderson, *Human Sexuality: The Age of Ambiguity* (Boston: Little, Brown, 1975), p. 14.
7. Hyde, *Understanding Human Sexuality*, pp. 492–493.
8. Ibid., pp. 412–415.
9. Gagnon and Henderson, *Human Sexuality: The Age of Ambiguity*, p. 16.
10. J. John Palen, *Social Problems* (New York: McGraw-Hill, 1979), p. 544.
11. Ibid.
12. Hyde, *Understanding Human Sexuality*, pp. 322–324.
13. Ibid., p. 284.
14. Ibid.
15. Ibid., pp. 224–229.
16. Alfred C. Kinsey, W. B. Pomeroy, and C. E. Martin, *Sexual Behavior in the Human Male* (Philadelphia: Saunders, 1948).
17. Alfred C. Kinsey, W. B. Pomeroy, C. E. Martin, and P. H. Gebhard, *Sexual Behavior in the Human Female* (Philadelphia: Saunders, 1953).
18. William H. Masters and Virginia E. Johnson, *Human Sexual Response* (Boston: Little, Brown, 1966). For a layperson, an excellent summary is Ruth Brecher and Edward Brecher, *An Analysis of Human Sexual Response* (New York: Signet Books, 1966).
19. William H. Masters and Virginia E. Johnson, *Human Sexual Inadequacy* (Boston: Little, Brown, 1970). For a layperson, an excellent summary is Fred Belliveau and Lin Richter, *Understanding Human Sexual Inadequacy* (New York: Bantam Books, 1970).
20. Gagnon and Henderson, *Human Sexuality: The Age of Ambiguity*, p. 14.
21. Hyde, *Understanding Human Sexuality*, pp. 284–286.
22. Ibid., p. 636.
23. William Kornblum and Joseph Julian, *Social Problems*, 8th ed. (Englewood Cliffs, NJ: Prentice Hall, 1995), pp. 95–97.
24. Ibid., pp. 92–103.
25. Hyde, *Understanding Human Sexuality*.
26. Ibid., pp. 421–424.
27. Ibid., pp. 422–423.
28. Ibid., p. 439.
29. Kinsey et al., *Sexual Behavior in the Human Male*, p. 639.
30. Hyde, *Understanding Human Sexuality*, p. 13.
31. Thomas Sullivan, Kenrick Thompson, Richard Wright, George Gross, and Dale Spady, *Social Problems* (New York: Wiley, 1980), p. 537.
32. Hyde, *Understanding Human Sexuality*, p. 424.
33. Ibid.
34. Ibid.
35. Kornblum and Julian, *Social Problems*, p. 102.
36. Ibid., p. 100.
37. Hyde, *Understanding Human Sexuality*, p. 426.
38. Ibid.
39. Ibid.
40. Kinsey et al., *Sexual Behavior in the Human Male*; Kinsey et al., *Sexual Behavior in the Human Female*.
41. Hyde, *Understanding Human Sexuality*, pp. 436–438.
42. Ibid., pp. 437–438.
43. Ibid., p. 438.
44. Alan P. Bell, Martin S. Weinberg, and Sue Kiefer Hammersmith, *Sexual Preference* (Bloomington: Indiana University Press, 1981).
45. Charlene Crabb, "Are Some Men Born to Be Homosexual?" *U.S. News & World Report*, Sept. 9, 1991, p. 58.
46. William F Allman, "The Biology-Behavior Conundrum." *U.S. News & World Report*, Jul. 26, 1993, pp. 6–7.
47. Ibid., pp. 6–9.
48. Kim I. Mills, "Was 1993 'The Year of the Queer'?" *Wisconsin State Journal*, Jan. 1, 1994, p. 4A.
49. Hyde, *Understanding Human Sexuality*, pp. 636–638.
50. "Congress Defines Marriage: 1 Man, 1 Woman," *U.S. News & World Report*, Sept. 23, 1996, p. 19.
51. Karlein M. G. Schrewrs, "Sexuality in Lesbian Couples: The Importance of Gender," in *Annual Review of Sex Research*, vol. IV, John Bancroft, Clive M. Davis, and Howard Ruppel, Jr., eds. (Lake Mills, IA: Society for the Scientific Study of Sex, 1994), pp. 49–66.

52. Jack H. Hedblom, "The Female Homosexual: Social and Attitudinal Dimensions," in *Deviance: Studies in Definition, Management, and Treatment,* 2nd ed., Simon Dinitz, Russell R. Dynes, and Alfred C. Clarke, eds. (New York: Oxford University Press, 1975), p. 246.

53. Hyde, *Understanding Human Sexuality,* p. 453.

54. Ibid, p. 454.

55. Ibid.

56. Ibid., pp. 631–643.

57. Ibid., pp. 438–456.

58. Timothy F. Murphy, "Redirecting Sexual Orientation: Techniques and Justifications," *Journal of Sex Research,* 29 (1992), pp, 510–523.

59. Hyde, *Understanding Human Sexuality,* pp. 498–499.

60. Ibid., p. 490.

61. Ibid.

62. A. Nicholas Groth, "The Incest Offender," in *Intervention in Child Sexual Abuse,* Suzanne M. Sgroi, ed. (Lexington, MA: Lexington Books, 1982), pp. 215–239.

63. *Diagnostic and Statistical Manual of Mental Disorders, Fourth Edition (DSM-IV).* (Washington, DC: American Psychiatric Association, 1994), pp. 527–528.

64. G. G. Abel, J. V. Becker, J. Cunningham-Rathner, M. S. Mittelman, and J. L. Rouleau, "Multiple Paraphilic Diagnoses Among Sex Offenders," *Bulletin of the American Academy of Psychiatry and the Law,* 16, no. 2 (1988), pp. 153–168.

65. R. Karl Hanson, Rocco Gizzarelli, and Heather Scott, "The Attitudes of Incest Offenders," *Criminal Justice and Behavior,* 21, no. 2 (June 1994), pp. 187–202.

66. G. G. Abel, J. V. Becker, M. S. Mittelman, J. Cunningham-Rathner, J. L. Rouleau, and W. D. Murphy, "Self-Reported Sex Crimes of Nonincarcerated Parapheliacs," *Journal of Interpersonal Violence,* 2, no. 1 (1987), pp. 3–25.

67. Hyde, *Understanding Human Sexuality,* p. 500.

68. Ibid.

69. Ibid.

70. Blair Justice and Rita Justice. *The Broken Taboo: Sex in the Family* (New York: Human Sciences Press, 1979).

71. Hyde, *Understanding Human Sexuality,* p. 502.

72. Justice and Justice, *The Broken Taboo,* p. 177.

73. Judith Siegel, Jacqueline M. Golding, Judith A. Stein, M. Audrey Burnam, and Susan B. Sorenson, "Reactions to Sexual Assault," *Journal of Interpersonal Violence,* 5 (1990), pp. 229–246.

74. Thomas J. Sullivan, *Introduction to Social Problems,* 4th ed. (Boston: Allyn & Bacon, 1997), p. 329.

75. Hyde, *Understanding Human Sexuality,* p. 493.

76. Philip Sarrel and William Masters, "Sexual Molestation of Men by Women," *Archives of Sexual Behavior,* 11 (1982), pp. 117–132.

77. A. Nicholas Groth, *Men Who Rape* (New York: Plenum Press, 1979).

78. Hyde, *Understanding Human Sexuality,* p. 492.

79. Cindy Struckman-Johnson, "Forced Sex on Dates: It Happens to Men, Too," *Journal of Sex Research,* 24 (1988), pp. 234–241.

80. M. P, Koss et al., "Non-stranger Sexual Aggression: A Discriminant Analysis of the Psychological Characteristics of Undetected Offenders," *Sex Roles,* 12 (1985), pp. 981–992.

81. Eugene J. Kanin, "Date Rapists: Differential Sexual Socialization and Relative Deprivation," *Archives of Sexual Behavior,* 14 (1985), pp. 219–232.

82. Ann W. Burgess and Lynda Holmstrom, *Rape: Victims of Crisis* (Bowie, MD: Robert J. Brady, 1974).

83. Ann W. Burgess and Lynda Holmstrom, "Rape Trauma Syndrome," *American Journal of Psychiatry,* 131 (1974), pp. 981–986.

84. Ibid.

85. Ibid.

86. Abel et al., "Self-Reported Sex Crimes of Nonincarcerated Paraphiliacs," pp. 3–25.

87. For descriptions of sex therapy, see Fred Belliveau and Lin Richter, *Understanding Human Sexual Inadequacy,* and Lloyd G. Sinclair, "Sex Counseling and Therapy," in *The Practice of Social Work,* 6th ed., C. Zastrow, ed. (Pacific Grove, CA: Brooks/Cole 1999).

88. Jack S. Annon, *Behavioral Treatment of Sexual Problems* (Hagerstown, MD: Harper & Row, 1976).

89. Sinclair, "Sex Counseling and Therapy."

90. Lloyd G. Sinclair, "Sexual Counseling and Sex Therapy," in *Introduction to Social Welfare Institutions: Social Problems, Services, and Current Issues,* 3rd ed., C. Zastrow, ed. (Homewood, IL: Dorsey Press, 1986), p. 213.

91. Annon, *Behavioral Treatment of Sexual Problems,* p. 77.

92. For an extended discussion, see Richard L. Timmers, "For Men: Controlling Premature Ejaculation," in *The Personal Problem Solver,* C. Zastrow and D. H. Chang, eds. (Englewood Cliffs, NJ: Prentice Hall, 1977), pp. 97–105.

93. Annon, *Behavioral Treatment of Sexual Problems.*

DRUG ABUSE
AND DRUG
TREATMENT
PROGRAMS

Practically everyone has taken one or more drugs and, on a few occasions, used a drug to excess. A large proportion of our population, as we will see, currently abuses drugs. This chapter will:

- Define drugs and drug abuse.
- Provide a brief history of our drug-taking society.
- Present sociological theories of drug abuse.
- Describe drug subcultures.
- Summarize facts about and effects of commonly used drugs.
- Describe rehabilitation programs for drug abuse.
- Present suggestions for curbing drug abuse in the future.

DRUGS AND DRUG ABUSE

Pharmacologically, a drug is any substance that chemically alters the function or structure of a living organism.[1] This definition would include food, insecticides, air pollutants, water pollutants, acids, vitamins, toxic chemicals, soaps, and soft drinks. Obviously this interpretation is too broad to be useful. For our purposes, a definition based on context is more appropriate. In medicine, for example, a drug is any substance that is manufactured specifically to relieve pain or to treat or prevent diseases and other medical conditions.

In a social problems approach, a *drug* is any habit-forming substance that directly affects the brain and nervous system. It is a chemical that affects moods, perceptions, body functions, or consciousness and that has the potential for misuse because it may be harmful to the user.

Drug abuse is the regular or excessive use of a drug when, as defined by a group, the consequences endanger relationships with other people, are detrimental to the user's health, or jeopardize society itself. This definition identifies two key factors that determine what is considered drug abuse in a society: The first is the actual drug effects, and the second is a group's perception of the effects.

Society's perceptions of the ill effects of a drug are often inconsistent with the actual effects. In our society, moderate use of alcohol and tobacco is accepted by many Americans, even though moderate use of both can cause serious health problems. Excessive drinking of coffee (containing caffeine) is accepted in our society but can also lead to health problems. In the 1930s, our society was convinced that marijuana was a dangerous drug; it was said to cause insanity, crime, and a host of other ills. Now available evidence suggests that it may be no more dangerous than alcohol.[2] The occasional use of heroin has been thought for years to be highly dangerous, but evidence now indicates that occasional users suffer few health consequences and can lead productive lives.[3]

The dominant social reaction to a drug is influenced not only by the actual dangers of the drug but also by the social characteristics and motives of the groups that use it. Heroin is considered dangerous because its use has been popularly associated with inner-city residents and high crime rates. Society is generally accepting of the use of pills by middle-aged people to reduce stress and anxiety but less accepting of college students using the same pills "to feel good" and "to get high." Surprisingly, legal drugs (such as alcohol and tobacco) are more often abused and cause more harm in our society than illegal drugs.

One of the most widely used drugs today is aspirin. Millions of Americans use it to relieve pain and other discomforts. Taken in excessive amounts, however, aspirin can be harmful, causing gastrointestinal bleeding, ulcers, and other ailments.

Other over-the-counter drugs (those available without a physician's prescription) can be and are abused. Laxatives, for example, which are taken for constipation, can damage the digestive system. Large doses of vitamins A and D are toxic.

Prescription drugs are also frequently abused. Among the most abused prescription drugs are tranquilizers, painkillers, sedatives, and stimulants. Many Americans are obsessed with taking pills, and many prescription drugs have the potential to be psychologically and physiologically addicting. Drug companies spend millions in advertisements in an effort to convince consumers that there is something wrong with them—that they are too tense, that they are taking too long to fall asleep, that they should lose weight, that they are not "regular" enough—and that their medications will solve these problems. Unfortunately, many Americans accept this easy symptom-relief approach and end up depending on pills rather than making life changes to improve their health (such as learning stress reduction techniques, changing their diets, and deciding to exercise regularly).

Because a drug is legal and readily available does not mean it is harmless. Alcohol and tobacco are legal, but both may seriously damage our health. The rationale determining the acceptability of a drug is often illogical. Drugs favored by the dominant culture (such as alcohol in our society) are generally acceptable, whereas those favored by a small subculture are usually outlawed. It is interesting to note that in many parts of North Africa and the Middle East marijuana is a legal drug and alcohol is outlawed.[4] Our country imposes severe penalties on the use of cocaine, but in certain areas of the Andes Mountains that substance is legal and widely used.[5]

A characteristic of habit-forming drugs is that they lead to a *dependency,* with the user developing a recurring craving for them. This dependency may be physical, psychological, or both. When physical dependency occurs, the user will generally experience bodily withdrawal symptoms, which may take many forms and range in severity from slight tremblings to fatal convulsions. When psychological dependency occurs, the user feels psychological discomfort if use is terminated. Users also generally develop a *tolerance* for the drug, which means that they have to take increasing amounts over time to achieve a given effect. Some drugs (such as aspirin) do not create tolerance.

Drug addiction is somewhat difficult to define. In its broadest usage, the term refers to an intense craving for a particular substance. All of us have intense cravings—such as for ice cream, strawberry shortcake, potato chips, or chocolate. To distinguish drug addiction from other intense cravings, some authorities have erroneously defined drug addiction as the physiological dependency that a person develops after heavy use of a particular drug. Most addicts, however, experience

periods when they "kick" their physical dependency, yet their psychological craving continues undiminished; as a result, they soon return to using their drug of choice. It is therefore more useful to define drug addiction as the intense craving for a drug that develops after a period of physical dependency from heavy use.[6]

Why are Americans so involved in using and abusing drugs? There are numerous reasons: to feel good, to get high, to escape from reality, to obtain relief from pain or anxiety, and to relax or sleep. Drugs definitely meet a functional need (such as providing temporary relief from unwanted emotions) but can have serious side effects. On a broader level, many segments of our society encourage and romanticize the use of drugs. Senator Frank Moss, for example, comments on the role played by advertisements and commercials:

> It is advertising which mounts the message that pills turn rain to sunshine, gloom to joy, depression to euphoria, solve problems, and dispel doubt. Not just pills: cigarette and cigar ads; soft drinks, coffee, tea, and beer ads—all portray the key to happiness as things to swallow, inhale, chew, drink, and eat.[7]

A BRIEF HISTORY OF OUR DRUG-TAKING SOCIETY

When the Pilgrims set sail for America in 1620, they loaded on their ships 14 tons of water—plus 10,000 gallons of wine and 42 tons of beer.[8] Ever since, Americans have been widely using and abusing drugs.

During and after the Civil War, thousands of injured soldiers were treated with narcotics to relieve their pain; many became addicted. Narcotics addiction was a serious problem from the 1860s to the first decade of the 20th century. At the turn of the century, about 1% of the population was addicted to a narcotic drug—the highest rate in our history.[9] At that time, opiates (including heroin and morphine) were readily available for a variety of purposes. They were used to treat such minor ailments as stomach pains and to ease the discomfort of infants during teething. Pharmacies, grocery stores, and mail-order houses did a prosperous business in selling opiates. Such sales were legally stopped in 1914 by the Harrison Narcotics Act, which required that narcotic drugs be dispensed only through prescriptions by licensed physicians.

In colonial times, tobacco was a popular substance for chewing, and after 1870 its use for smoking increased greatly. For a brief time shortly after 1900, its sale was prohibited in 14 states because it was thought to be a "steppingstone" to alcohol use and to lead to sexual deviance, insanity, and impotence. The laws banning the sale proved ineffective and were repealed after World War I. Today tobacco is one of our most widely used—and abused—drugs, despite what we know about the health hazards of smoking.

Marijuana use has occurred throughout our history. In the mid-19th century, it was often smoked by writers and artists in the larger cities. Shortly after the beginning of the 20th century, Latinos and African Americans began smoking it. The drug was then thought to lead to "unruly" behavior, and the first laws prohibiting its use and distribution were passed in the South. The rest of the states soon enacted similar legislation. In 1937 the director of the Federal Bureau of Narcotics labeled marijuana the "assassin of youth." The mass media jumped on this campaign and began publishing stories stereotyping marijuana users as "crazed drug fiends." Later, to continue receiving funds for his bureau, the director asserted that marijuana was dangerous, as it was a "steppingstone" to narcotic drugs.[10] Marijuana, in the 1960s and 1970s, became increasingly popular among youths, college students, drug subcultures, and the general population. Its use and effects remain a controversial issue.

Alcohol use has continued unabated ever since the Pilgrims landed. The first governor of Massachusetts complained of excessive drunkenness in his colony, and since that time, there have always been some segments of American society that have viewed alcohol use as a social problem. The American Temperance Union was formed in the early 1800s. It was later followed by the Women's Christian Temperance Union, the Anti-Saloon League, and several other temperance organizations. Alcohol was viewed as responsible for many social ills: crime, the collapse of the family, and unemployment. Immigrants, the poor, and certain minority groups were the major consumers of alcohol at that time. Under pressure, several states passed legislation prohibiting the sale and distribution of alcoholic beverages in the latter half of the 19th century. By the start of World War I, nearly half the population resided in "dry" areas.

The 18th Amendment to the Constitution, which prohibited the sale of alcohol, was ratified in 1920. Prohibition had begun. But people continued to drink, and the law was virtually unenforceable. It gave impetus to organized crime. Moonshiners (people who distilled or sold liquor illegally) and speakeasies (places where illegal alcoholic beverages were sold) flourished. Prohibition became a political embarrassment, and the United States was a laughingstock around the world. In 1933 the 18th Amendment was repealed. Following Prohibition the use of alcohol became more widespread.[11] People in the middle and upper-middle classes also began drinking on a rather large scale. As a result, alcohol was no longer viewed as the scourge of society.

It is interesting to note that, whereas narcotics made a transition from respectability to disrepute in the past 100 years, alcohol made exactly the opposite transition.

SOCIOLOGICAL THEORIES OF DRUG ABUSE

A number of biological, psychological, and sociological theories have been advanced to explain drug abuse. Summarizing all of these theories is beyond the scope of this text, but three sociological theories will be presented for illustrative purposes: anomie theory, labeling theory, and differential association.

Anomie Theory

This theory stems largely from the work of Emile Durkheim[12] and Robert Merton.[13] Merton used anomie to explain deviant behavior. Anomie is a

In 1920 the 18th Amendment, which prohibited the sale of alcohol, was ratified and thus an era of speakeasies, bootleg liquor, and "bathtub" gin began. Here authorities display a confiscated still in 1925.

condition in which the acceptance of approved standards of conduct is weakened. Every society has both approved goals (such as making a lot of money) and approved means for attaining these goals (such as high-paying jobs). When certain members of society want these goals but have insufficient means for attaining them, a state of anomie results, and these individuals then seek to achieve the desired goals through deviant means. Applied to drug abuse, this theory asserts that, if people are prevented from achieving their goals, they may be "driven to drink" or to use other drugs. The drugs may be used as an escape—to avoid the suffering caused by failure to achieve goals—or they may be used as a substitute for the "highs" that users had originally hoped to experience from successfully accomplishing their goals.

Merton asserts that drug abuse can be reduced if society (a) sets realistic goals that people can attain and then (b) establishes legitimate means, available to everyone, for attaining these goals. However, anomie theory fails to explain drug abuse by people who appear to be achieving their goals.

Labeling Theory

This theory was developed by a number of researchers.[14] Labeling theorists view drug abuse as largely stemming from occasional users' being labeled "abusers." Initially, occasional users indulge in drug use that is disapproved of by others—such as getting drunk or smoking marijuana. These users do not at this point view themselves as abusers. However, if their use is discovered and made an issue by significant other people (such as parents, police, or teachers), and if they are then publicly labeled a "drunkard," "pothead," or "dope user," they are more closely watched. Under this closer surveillance, if they continue to occasionally be found using drugs, the label is gradually confirmed. Their significant others may begin to relate to them in terms of the label, causing these occasional users to view themselves as people who truly are whatever label is applied. When this happens, the occasional user is likely to embark on a "career" as a habitual drug abuser.

Labeling theory asserts that drug abuse can be reduced by avoiding labeling—that is, by refusing to treat occasional drug users as if they were "abusers." However, it fails to explain drug abuse among "closet alcoholics" and others who are already drug abusers before being labeled as such.

Differential Association

This theory, developed by Edwin Sutherland,[15] asserts that behavior is determined primarily by the values and actions that are considered important by the small, intimate groups one interacts with. Applied to drug abuse, differential association theory asserts that people will learn and take on the drug use norms of the small groups they associate with. These groups include family, neighborhood peer groups, and religious and social groups. Differential association has been used to explain differences in alcoholism rates among ethnic and religious groups.

There are, for example, marked differences in alcohol use patterns between the Irish, Italians, and Jews in the United States. The Italian subculture (both in Italy and in this country) widely accepts the moderate use of alcohol, particularly at mealtimes. Serving wine with meals is part of the dietary customs, which even the young participate in. Excessive drinking, however, is frowned on. As a result, although alcohol is widely used in the Italian community, drunkenness and alcoholism are relatively rare.[16]

Similarly, the Jewish community uses alcohol widely, including as a component in religious rituals. As with Italian families, the use of alcohol

in controlled social settings minimizes its potential negative effects. And because there are strong norms against drunkenness and abuse, alcoholism among American Jews is rare.[17]

In contrast, the Irish subculture tolerates periodic episodes of excessive drinking, particularly by single males. Such drinking is seen as a way to relieve tension and frustration. With such norms, there is a relatively high rate of alcoholism among Irish American males.[18]

It is, of course, possible for people to be resocialized into the drug use norms of another subculture. For example, a teenager raised in a family opposed to marijuana use may become attracted to a high school group that places a high value on smoking marijuana. This teenager may then, through the principles of differential association, become resocialized by this new group into using marijuana.

As noted, there are many other theories (including psychological and biological ones) concerning the causes of drug abuse.[19] No single theory is sufficient for identifying all causes, and each theory may or may not apply in any given case.

DRUG SUBCULTURES

A person's decision about whether to use a drug depends not only on his or her personality characteristics and family background but also on the attitudes of peers. These views determine which drugs are used, how often they are used, how much is used at any one time, and what other activities will be engaged in when drugs are used.

A group of peers who advocates the use of one or more drugs can be called a *drug subculture.* Most drug taking occurs in a social group that approves the use of the drug. In a classic study, "Becoming a Marijuana User," Howard Becker found that the peer group plays a crucial role in the individual's learning to smoke marijuana.[20] The group introduces the novice to smoking and teaches the new smoker to recognize the pleasant experiences associated with a "high." Membership in this drug subculture also encourages further drug use and instructs the newcomer to reject established norms and instead to accept the norms of this group.

Drug subcultures appear to function similarly in relation to different drugs. They are more likely to develop around the use of illegal rather than legal drugs. Use of alcohol (among teenagers), marijuana, heroin, LSD, PCP, and cocaine generally occurs in drug subcultures.

In many cities in the United States, a number of gangs (composed of juveniles and young adults) have formed and become involved in widespread use and distribution of illegal drugs. Frequently, gang members also engage in other crimes (such as thefts and burglaries) to financially support their drug habits.

Although drug subcultures are often dysfunctional for society, they do serve important functions for the user. They provide instruction on how to use the drug, including guidelines on the safety limits of dosages. They help handle adverse effects, assist in obtaining the drug, and provide protection from arrest when the drug is being used. They also provide a party-type atmosphere to enhance enjoyment of the effects of the drug.

FACTS ABOUT AND EFFECTS OF COMMONLY USED DRUGS

Depressants

In this section, we will examine the following drugs, which are classified as depressants: alcohol, barbiturates, tranquilizers, Quaalude, and PCP.

ALCOHOL

Alcohol is the most abused drug in American society. Still, its use is so accepted that few Americans view alcohol as a serious social problem. Social drinking is highly integrated into the customs of our society. In many areas of the country, the local pub is a center (particularly for men) for meeting and socializing with friends and neighbors. Going out and getting "high" or even "smashed" is a favorite pastime of college stu-

EXHIBIT 8.1

Jokes About Drunks

Jokes about drunks are common, which suggests that our society does not take alcohol abuse seriously. Here are two examples:

A man walked into a pub with a duck under his arm, and a drunk remarked, "What are you doing with that pig in here?" The man said, "That isn't a pig. It's a duck." The drunk said, "I was talking to the duck."

A drunk staggered out of a bar and started to get into her car. An officer stopped her and stated, "You don't really intend to drive that car home, do you?" The drunk replied, "Of course, officer; I'm in no condition to walk."

dents. Taverns and nightclubs are primary sites for meeting and entertaining dates. Businesses frequently use cocktail lounges to wine and dine customers. In some communities, it is the custom to have "a second church service" at a local wateringhole after the weekly church service is over. Because of the pervasiveness of alcohol in our society, this chapter will devote considerable attention to its use, abuse, and treatment.

Alcohol is a colorless liquid that is a component of beer, wine, brandy, whiskey, vodka, rum, and other intoxicating beverages. The average American over the age of 21 consumes an average of 33.2 gallons of beer, 2.7 gallons of wine, and 2.0 gallons of hard liquor a year.[21] The vast majority of American teenagers and adults drink alcohol.

Drinking has become so entrenched into our customs that, unfortunately, people who do not drink are sometimes viewed as "weird," "stuck up," or "killjoys" and are often assumed to have something wrong with them. The serving of alcoholic beverages is expected at many rituals and ceremonies for adults: weddings, birthday parties, Christmas parties, graduations, and the like. Some formal religious rites also include alcohol (for

TABLE 8.1

Drugs of Abuse: Facts and Effects

Drug	Dependency Potential		Tolerance	Duration of Effects (in hours)	Usual Methods of Administration
	Physical	Psychological			
Narcotics					
Opium	High	High	yes	3 to 6	Oral, smoked
Morphine	High	High	yes	3 to 6	Injected, smoked
Heroin	High	High	yes	3 to 6	Injected, sniffed
Depressants					
Alcohol	High	High	yes	1 to 12	Oral
Barbiturates	High	High	yes	1 to 16	Oral, injected
Tranquilizers	Moderate	Moderate	yes	4 to 8	Oral
Quaalude	High	High	yes	4 to 8	Oral
Stimulants					
Caffeine	High	High	yes	2 to 4	Oral
Cocaine	Possible	High	yes	2	Injected, sniffed
Crack	Possible	High	yes	2	Smoked
Amphetamines	Possible	High	yes	2 to 4	Oral, injected
Butyl nitrate	Possible	?	Probable	up to 5	Inhaled
Amyl nitrate	Possible	?	Probable	up to 5	Inhaled
Hallucinogens					
LSD	None	Degree unknown	yes	variable	Oral
Mescaline and peyote	None	Degree unknown	yes	variable	Oral, injected
Psilocybin-psilocyn	None	Degree unknown	yes	variable	Oral
PCP	None	Degree unknown	yes	variable	Oral, injected, smoked
Cannabis					
Marijuana	Degree unknown	Moderate	yes	2 to 4	Oral, smoked
Hashish	Degree unknown	Moderate	yes	2 to 4	Oral, smoked
Nicotine (tobacco)	High	High	yes	2 to 4	Smoked, chewed
Anabolic steroids	None	High	?	?	Oral

Possible Effects	Effects of Overdose	Withdrawal Symptoms
Euphoria, drowsiness, respiratory depression, constricted pupils, nausea	Slow and shallow breathing, clammy skin, convulsions, coma, possible death	Watery eyes, runny nose, yawning, loss of appetite, irritability, tremors, panic, chills and sweating, cramps, nausea
Slurred speech, disorientation, drunken behavior, loss of co-ordination, impaired reactions	Shallow respiration, cold and clammy skin, dilated pupils, weak and rapid pulse, coma, possible death	Anxiety, insomnia, tremors, delirium, convulsions, possible death
Increased alertness, excitation, euphoria, dilated pupils, increased pulse rate and blood pressure, insomnia, loss of appetite	Agitation, increase in pulse rate and blood pressure, loss of appetite, insomnia	Apathy, long periods of sleep, irritability, depression, disorientation
Increased alertness, excitation, euphoria, dilated pupils, increased pulse rate and blood pressure, insomnia, loss of appetite	Agitation, increase in body temperature, hallucinations, convulsions, tremors, possible death	Apathy, long periods of sleep, irritability, depression, disorientation
Excitement, euphoria, giddiness, loss of inhibitions, aggressiveness, delusions, depression, drowsiness, headache, nausea	Loss of memory, confusion, unsteady gait, erratic heartbeat and pulse, possible death	Insomnia, decreased appetite, depression, irritability, headache
Illusions and hallucinations, poor perception of time and distance	Longer, more intense "trip" episodes, psychosis, possible death	?
Euphoria, relaxed inhibitions, increased appetite, disoriented behavior, increased heart and pulse rate	Fatigue, paranoia, possible psychosis, time disorientation, slowed movements	Insomnia, hyperactivity and decreased appetite reported in a limited number of individuals
Increased alertness, excitation, euphoria, dilated pupils, increased pulse rate and blood pressure, insomnia, loss of appetite	Agitation, increase in pulse rate and blood pressure, loss of appetite, insomnia	Apathy, long periods of sleep, irritability, depression
Moodiness, depression, irritability	?	?

example, wine as the blood of Christ during Communion). Many popular songs highlight drinking. But it is not the use of alcohol at rituals and ceremonies that causes most problems. Because most American alcohol use is informal and relatively uncontrolled, it can easily become excessive without the safeguards that are built into the drinking patterns of many ethnic groups.

The type of alcohol found in beverages is ethyl alcohol. (It is also called grain alcohol because most of it is made from fermenting grain.) Many drinkers believe that alcohol is a stimulant because it relaxes tensions, lowers sexual and aggressive inhibitions, seems to facilitate interpersonal relationships, and usually leads those who have a few drinks to talk more. It is, however, very definitely a depressant to the central nervous system. Its chemical composition and effects are very similar to those of ether (an anesthetic used in medicine to induce unconsciousness).

Alcohol slows mental activity, reasoning ability, speech ability, and muscle reactions. It distorts perceptions, slurs speech, lessens coordination, and slows memory functioning and respiration. In increasing quantities, it leads to stupor, sleep, coma, and finally, death. A hangover (the aftereffects of too much alcohol) may cause headache, thirst, muscle aches, stomach discomfort, and nausea.

The effects of alcohol vary with the percentage of alcohol in the bloodstream as it passes through the brain. Generally, effects are observable when the concentration of alcohol in the blood reaches one-tenth of 1%. Five drinks (each containing 1 ounce of 86-proof alcohol, 12 ounces of beer, or 3 ounces of wine) in 2 hours will result in a blood alcohol concentration of one-tenth of 1% for a 120-pound person. (The heavier the person, the more drinks it takes to increase the level of alcohol in the blood.) Table 8.2 shows the effects of increasing percentages of alcohol in the blood.

In 1990 scientists discovered that women's stomachs are less effective than men's at breaking down alcohol; as a result, women generally become intoxicated more quickly. Men have in their stomachs substantially more dehydrogenase (an enzyme) than do women. This enzyme breaks down much of the alcohol in the stomach before

TABLE 8.2

Percentages of Alcohol in the Blood and Its Effects

Alcohol	Effects
.05%	Lowered alertness and a "high" feeling
.10	Decreased reactions; reduced coordination (legally drunk in most states)
.20	Massive interference with senses and motor skills
.30	Perceptions nearly gone; understanding nearly gone
.40	Unconsciousness
.50	Potential death

Sources: Adapted from Oakley S. Ray, *Drugs, Society, and Human Behavior* (St. Louis: Mosby, 1972), p. 86; Erich Goode, *Drugs in American Society* (New York: Knopf, 1972), pp. 142–143.

it reaches the bloodstream. This finding may also help explain why medical complications, including cirrhosis of the liver, anemia, and gastrointestinal bleeding, develop more rapidly in alcoholic women than in alcoholic men.[22]

Who Drinks? The primary factors related to whether an individual will drink and how much alcohol a drinker will use include socioeconomic factors, gender, age, religion, urban–rural residence, and geographic region.[23]

▪ *Socioeconomic factors:* College-educated people are more likely to drink than are those with only a high school education. Young men at the highest socioeconomic level are more likely to drink than young men at lower socioeconomic levels. However, drinkers at the lower socioeconomic levels are more likely to drink excessively than those at higher socioeconomic levels.

▪ *Gender:* Men are more likely to use and abuse alcohol than are women. Still, recent decades have seen a dramatic increase in alcoholism among adult women. Why? One explanation is that cultural taboos against heavy drinking among women have weakened. Another explanation is that increased drinking is related to the changing roles of women in our society.

■ *Age:* Older people are less likely to drink than younger people, even if they were drinkers in their youth. Heavy drinking is most common at ages 21 to 30 for men and ages 31 to 50 for women.

■ *Religion:* Nonchurchgoers drink more than regular churchgoers. Heavy drinking is more common among Episcopalians and Catholics, whereas conservative and fundamentalist Protestants are more often nondrinkers or light drinkers.

■ *Urban–rural residence:* Urban residents are more likely to drink than rural residents.

■ *Geographic region:* People who live in the Northeast and along the West Coast are more apt to drink than people who live in the South and Midwest.

In the last two decades, there has been a decline in drinking, especially of hard liquor, in many segments of the American public.[24] For example, some business executives have switched from having martini luncheons to jogging and working out. In recent years, the federal government has put considerable financial pressure on states to raise the legal drinking age to 21 or else have federal highway funds withheld. Practically all states have now raised the drinking age to 21. Secondary schools, colleges, and universities have initiated alcohol awareness programs. Many businesses and employers offer Employee Assistance Programs, which are designed to provide treatment services to alcoholics and problem drinkers. Drunk-driving laws have become stricter, and police departments and the courts are more vigorously enforcing these laws. Organizations such as Mothers Against Drunk Driving (MADD) and Students Against Drunk Driving (SADD) have been fairly successful in creating greater public awareness of the hazards of drinking and driving. A cultural norm seems to be emerging that it is no longer stylish to have too much to drink. Despite these promising trends, however, rates of alcohol use and abuse in the United States remain extremely high.

Reasons for Drinking. As discussed earlier, social patterns influence people to drink in a wide variety of situations, such as at happy hours, before and after dinner, and at parties.

There are also individual reasons for drinking. Some people drink because alcohol acts as a "social lubricant," relaxing them so that they feel more at ease interacting with others. Some drink simply to relax. Others use alcohol as a kind of anesthetic, to dull the pain of living and to take their minds off their problems. Some excessive drinkers seek a continual "buzz" to avoid facing life. Others drink occasionally to get "high." Some insomniacs drink so that they will sleep (often they pass out). Drinking before a flight is common for persons with a fear of flying because alcohol has a tranquilizing effect. Also, people often drink to temporarily get rid of unwanted emotions such as loneliness, anxiety, depression, feelings of inadequacy, insecurity, guilt, and resentment.

Alcoholism is a rather imprecise term because there is no clear-cut distinction between a problem drinker and an alcoholic. Nevertheless, a useful definition of alcoholism is *the repeated and excessive use of alcohol to the extent that it is harmful to interpersonal relations, to job performance, or to the drinker's health.*

Whether a person will be labeled an alcoholic depends to a large extent on the reactions of his or her employers, family, friends, associates, and community. For example, the "drier" the community in which one lives, the less alcohol and the fewer the problem incidents involving alcohol it takes for someone to be defined as an alcoholic.

People's reactions to drinking vary considerably. Some individuals can drink large amounts quite regularly while appearing sober—although their driving is affected, and they may have a high likelihood of becoming alcoholic in the future. Some people drink heavily without experiencing hangovers, although hangovers are functional because they let people know they have ingested too much alcohol and discourage further binges. Generally, as we've seen, the greater the weight of the drinker, the more she or he can consume before becoming intoxicated.

Many alcoholics who stop drinking must abstain *totally;* if they start again, they will have a

CASE EXAMPLE 8.1   Courts Have Gotten Tougher on Drunk Drivers

Prior to the 1980s, courts tended to be very lenient with drunk drivers involved in serious traffic accidents. Societal values then held that being intoxicated was a condition that to a considerable extent excused drunk drivers from being held responsible for the damage they caused. There has been a major change in the 1980s and 1990s on this issue.

Larry Mahoney was a 34-year-old father who was described by a friend as "somebody who wouldn't hurt anybody for the world." On Sunday evening, May 14, 1988, while drunk, Larry climbed into his pickup truck and drove the wrong way down a Kentucky interstate. He had 0.24% alcohol in his blood—more than twice Kentucky's statutory level. He slammed head-on into an old school bus carrying 67 passengers, mainly teenagers, on a church outing from Radcliff, Kentucky. Twenty-four teenagers and three adults were killed in this crash, the worst alcohol-related traffic accident in U.S. history. Larry Mahoney was charged with "capital murder," which carries the death penalty.

In December 1989, Mahoney was found guilty of 27 counts of second-degree manslaughter, 27 counts of first-degree wanton endangerment, 12 counts of first-degree assault, 14 counts of second-degree wanton endangerment, and 1 count of drunken driving. He was sentenced to 16 years in prison. This lengthy sentence is one more indication that the court system is taking a tougher stand on drunk driving.

Many states have enacted legislation to immediately suspend the driver's license of offenders and have mandated jail terms for repeat offenders. Also, many states now mandate instant suspension of the driver's license for individuals failing, or refusing to take, a breath test.

Sources: "Kentucky's Textbook Case in Drunk Driving," *U.S. News & World Report,* May 30, 1988, pp. 7–8; "Man Sentenced in Fatal Church Bus Accident," *Wisconsin State Journal,* Feb. 24, 1990, p. 3A.

compulsive, uncontrollable urge to go on a series of binges. Because of this, Alcoholics Anonymous asserts that "Once an alcoholic, always an alcoholic." There is some evidence (highly controversial) that certain alcoholics can, after treatment, return to social drinking.[25] However, this finding has been highly criticized by a number of treatment organizations because it has led some alcoholics who had quit drinking to try to drink lightly, with the result that they immediately returned to excessive drinking.

There are over 15 million alcoholics in the United States, and each one affects at least four other people close to him or her—including spouse, family, or employer. Approximately two of three alcoholics are male, but the proportion of female alcoholics has risen in the past 20 years.[26] Contrary to popular stereotypes, only an estimated 5% are "skid-row bums."[27] Most are ordinary people.

Some people become alcoholic quite soon after they start drinking. Others may drink for 10, 20, or 30 years before becoming addicted. An alcoholic may be only psychologically dependent on alcohol, but most are also physically dependent.

Health Problems Caused by Alcohol. The life expectancy of alcoholics is 10 to 12 years lower than that of nonalcoholics.[28] There are several reasons for this. Alcohol, over an extended period of time, gradually destroys liver cells, leaving scar tissue in their place. When the scar tissue is extensive, a medical condition called cirrhosis of the liver occurs. This condition is the eighth most frequent cause of death in the United States (about 25,000 deaths per year).[29]

Alcohol has no healthy food value, although it contains a high number of calories. Heavy drinkers, as a result, have a reduced appetite for nutritious food, frequently suffer from vitamin deficiencies, and are highly susceptible to infectious diseases.

Heavy drinking also causes kidney problems, contributes to a variety of heart ailments, is a factor that leads to diabetes, and also appears to contribute to cancer. It is a contributing cause of ulcers and impotency in males. In addition, heavy drinking is associated with over 10,000 suicides annually.[30] Death can occur from drinking an excessive amount of alcohol—for example, from depression of the respiratory system or from the drinker choking on vomit while unconscious.

Interestingly, for some as-yet-unknown reason, the life expectancy for light to moderate drinkers exceeds that for nondrinkers.[31] Perhaps an occasional drink helps people relax and thereby reduces the likelihood of life-threatening stress-related illnesses.

Combining alcohol with other drugs can have disastrous and sometimes fatal effects. Sometimes two drugs taken together have a *synergistic* interaction, meaning that they create an effect much greater than either would produce alone. For example, sedatives like barbiturates (often found in sleeping pills) or Quaaludes, when taken with alcohol, can so depress the central nervous system that a coma or even death may result.

Other drugs tend to have an *antagonistic* response to alcohol, meaning that one drug negates the effects of the other. Many doctors now caution patients not to drink while taking certain prescribed drugs because the alcohol will reduce, or even totally negate, the beneficial effects of these drugs.

Whether drugs will interact synergistically or antagonistically depends on a wide range of factors: the properties of the drugs, the amounts

EXHIBIT 8.2

Polydrug Abuse Is a Serious Problem

Notables such as Elvis Presley, John Belushi, River Phoenix, and former First Lady Betty Ford were dependent on two or more drugs. Polydrug abuse contributed to the early deaths of Presley, Belushi, and Phoenix. Betty Ford publicly acknowledged that she was dependent on Valium, alcohol, and the medication she was taking for arthritis. She received treatment at the Naval Hospital in Long Beach, California. Later she was instrumental in founding the Betty Ford Clinic for treatment of substance abuse problems. A number of celebrities have voluntarily acknowledged receiving treatment at the Betty Ford Clinic.

taken, the user's tolerance to them, the amount of sleep the user has had, the kind and amount of food that has been eaten, and the user's overall health. The interactive effects may be minimal one day and extensive the next.

Withdrawal from alcohol once the body is physically addicted may lead to delirium tremens (DTs) and other unpleasant reactions. The DTs are characterized by rapid heartbeat, uncontrollable trembling, severe nausea, and profuse sweating.

Drinking and Driving. Alcohol is a significant contributing factor in approximately half of all automobile fatalities and in many serious automobile injuries.[32] Each year over a million people in the United States are arrested for driving under the influence of alcohol.[33] One of the most noted persons to die in an alcohol-related accident was Princess Diana of Britain, age 36, who died in August 1997. The driver of the car, Henri Paul, was legally drunk when the crash occurred in a tunnel in Paris, France. Mothers Against Drunk Driving, an organization that was formed several years ago, is having considerable success in getting states to enact and enforce stricter drunk-driving laws. In addition, the news media (particularly television and radio) have been airing public service programs and announcements to educate the public about the consequences of drunk driving.

Alcohol and Crime. About one-eighth of all arrests for minor crimes are alcohol related: public drunkenness, violations of liquor laws, disorderly conduct, and vagrancy.[34]

Alcohol is also a contributing factor in many major crimes. In a majority of homicides, aggravated assaults, sexual crimes against children, and sexually aggressive acts against women, the offender had been drinking.[35] This is not to say that alcohol is the main cause of these crimes. However, it appears to be a contributing factor that increases the likelihood of such crimes.

Effects of Alcohol Abuse on the Family. In the past, if there was a problem drinker in the family, it was almost always the husband. Now the likelihood is increasing that it could be the wife or one (or more) of the teenagers.

Heavy drinking is a contributing factor to many family problems: child abuse, child neglect, spouse abuse, parent abuse, financial problems, unemployment of wage earners, violent arguments, and unhappy marriages. Marriage to an alcoholic often ends in divorce, separation, or desertion. Children of an alcoholic parent have higher rates of severe emotional and physical illnesses.[36]

Sharon Wegscheider indicates that members of alcoholic families tend to assume roles that both protect the chemically dependent person from taking responsibility for his or her behavior and actually serve to maintain the drinking problems. She identifies several roles that are typically played by family members in addition to the chemically dependent person: the chief enabler, the family hero, the scapegoat, the lost child, and the mascot.[37]

The chief enabler's main purpose is to assume the primary responsibility for the family functioning. The abuser typically continues to lose control and relinquishes responsibility. The chief enabler, on the other hand, takes on more and more responsibility and begins making more and more family decisions. A chief enabler is often the parent or spouse of the chemically dependent person.

Conditions in families of chemically dependent people often continue to deteriorate as the dependent person loses control. A positive influence is needed to offset the negative. The family hero fulfills this role. The family hero often is the "perfect" person who does well at everything he or she tries. The hero works very hard at making the family appear to be functioning better than it is. In this way, the family hero provides the family with self-worth.

Another typical role played by someone in the chemically dependent family is the scapegoat. Although the alcohol abuse is the real problem, a family rule may mandate that this fact be denied and the blame be placed elsewhere. Frequently, another family member is targeted with the blame. The scapegoat often behaves in negative ways (for example, gets caught for stealing, runs away, becomes extremely withdrawn), which draws the spotlight to him or her. The scapegoat's role is to distract attention away from the dependent person and onto something else. This role helps the family avoid addressing the problem of chemical dependency.

Often there is also a lost child in the family. This is the person who seems rather uninvolved with the rest of the members yet never causes any trouble. The lost child's purpose is to provide relief to the family from some of the pain it is suffering. At least there is someone in the home who neither requires much attention nor causes any stress. The lost child is simply there.

Finally, chemically dependent families often have someone playing the role of mascot. The mascot is the person who probably has a good sense of humor and appears not to take anything seriously. Despite how much the mascot might be suffering inside, he or she provides a little fun for the family.

In summary, alcoholism is a problem affecting the entire family. Each member is suffering over the dependency, yet each assumes a role in order to maintain the family's status quo and to help the family survive. Family members are driven to maintain these roles, no matter what.

EXHIBIT 8.3

Fetal Alcohol Syndrome

Prior to the 1940s, it was thought that the uterus was a glass bubble that totally separated the fetus from the outside world and fully protected the fetus from whatever drugs the mother happened to be using. Since then, medical science has learned that chemical substances are readily transferred from the mother's uterine arteries, across the placental membrane, into the baby's umbilical vein, and then to the baby's entire body.

When a pregnant woman drinks any alcoholic beverage (including beer and wine), the alcohol easily crosses the placenta, and the fetus attains blood alcohol levels that are similar to those in the mother. Heavy alcohol consumption by pregnant mothers can cause a variety of conditions in the new baby that, taken together, have been labeled fetal alcohol syndrome. These conditions include mental retardation and developmental delays, overall growth retardation before and after birth, and various congenital malformations of the face, head, skeleton, and heart. These babies are more likely to be born prematurely, to have a low birth weight, to be hyperirritable, and to have neurological defects and poor muscle tone. They also have a higher infant mortality rate. The chances of microcephaly (a condition in which the baby has a small brain and skull and is mentally retarded) are increased.

The more alcohol a pregnant woman ingests, the greater the probability that her baby will have fetal alcohol syndrome. Studies suggest that, if a pregnant woman has five or more drinks at any one time, her baby will have a 10% chance of developing fetal alcohol syndrome. If she drinks lightly over a prolonged period, the syndrome may also occur. An average of 1 ounce per day results in a 10% risk; an average of 2 ounces per day results in a 20% risk.

The U.S. Public Health Service recommends that pregnant women not drink alcohol. Just as a mother would not give a glass of wine to her newborn, she should not give it to her unborn baby. It is not just alcohol, but other drugs (such as tobacco, marijuana, cocaine, and heroin) during pregnancy also endanger the unborn child.

Sources: Mike Samuels and Mary Samuels, "Pregnancy: How Smoking and Drugs Endanger Baby," *Wisconsin State Journal,* Jul. 2, 1986, sec. 2, p. 1; Diane E. Papalia and Sally W. Olds, *Human Development,* 6th ed. (New York: McGraw-Hill, 1995), p. 76.

Alcohol and Industry. Alcoholism costs business and industry billions of dollars annually. This figure reflects losses in terms of sick leave, absenteeism, missed or late work assignments, and on-the-job accidents.

Alcoholism Gene Theory. Alcoholism has long been assumed to be caused by *both* environmental and genetic factors. There has been considerable controversy in recent years, however, concerning the alcoholism gene theory.

Alcoholism has been found to run in families. In addition, children of alcoholic (biological) parents who are adopted at an early age have a significantly higher chance of becoming alcoholic than do children in the general population.[38]

Researchers in 1990 reported pinpointing a gene in people prone to alcoholism—a finding that adds weight to the argument that alcoholism is a disease and not a moral weakness or willful misconduct.[39] The researchers, Ernest Noble and Kenneth Blum, stated that a particular gene on a chromosome previously linked with alcoholism was far more common in alcoholics than in nonalcoholics. Researchers previously had implicated three chromosomes as possibly having a role in alcoholism, but no one had identified any single gene on these chromosomes as the culprit. (Chromosomes are threadlike structures of thousands of individual genes, the "fingerprints" of DNA that carry each cell's hereditary blueprint. A person's traits are determined by the nearly 100,000 genes in each cell.)

The gene pinpointed by Noble and Blum has two alternative forms called "A-1 allele" and "A-2 allele." The researchers looked at both alternative forms of the gene in brain matter from the cadavers of 70 subjects, 35 alcoholics and 35 nonalcoholics. The A-1 allele was found to have a high association with alcoholism, and the A-2 allele was found to be associated with nonalcoholism. The A-1 allele was present in 69% of the alcoholics but in only 20% of the nonalcoholics. (The study suggests, but does not conclusively prove, the existence of an alcoholism gene. Because there is not a 100% association between the A-1 allele and alcoholism, other factors—including the environment—could play a role in causing the problem.) The researchers conclude that the rare form of the gene (that is, the A-1 allele) may make those possessing it more prone to alcoholism, but they remain cautious about the implications of these findings.

Previous studies suggesting an association between genes and such diseases as bipolar disorder and schizophrenia have not held up to further scrutiny. If the A-1 allele does turn out to be linked to alcoholism, a test for this allele could identify individuals at high risk before they become addicted to alcohol. The disease may be brought on by a number of genes. Having identified one of the genes would allow scientists to map the chemical pathways to alcoholism and to devise drugs to alter them. Such drugs, for example, could reduce the craving for liquor, giving alcoholics a means of recovery.

Several months after the release of the Noble and Blum study, an investigation by David Goldman cast doubt on the earlier finding linking a particular gene with alcoholism.[40] The Goldman team studied genes from the white blood cells of living people—40 alcoholics compared with a control group of 127 nonalcoholics chosen in a random manner. The A-1 allele was present in 38% of alcoholics and in 30% of the random group—a statistically insignificant difference.

These conflicting results lead to the conclusion that the extent to which genetics contributes to alcoholism is unclear.

Avoiding Treatment for Alcoholism.   Many alcoholics (perhaps the majority) do not seek help because they *deny* they have a drinking problem. In an attempt to prove they can drink like any other person, they wind up sneaking drinks, excusing their drinking behavior, or blaming others ("If you had a job like mine, you'd drink too!"). There are many reasons why alcoholics refuse to admit the severity of their condition. Alcoholism is highly stigmatized. It is viewed as a disease, and alcoholics may not want to perceive themselves as "sick." Some see alcohol as essential to their lives. They socialize through drinking and are able to relax, fall asleep, or escape from their problems. Thus, they may choose to keep drinking even though they know it is ruining their health, destroying their reputation in the community, getting them fired at a variety of jobs, and breaking up their family. In many ways, alcohol becomes their "best friend," which they refuse to abandon—even if it kills them.

If an alcoholic is to be helped, this denial of their problem must be confronted. (We will discuss denial further in the section on rehabilitation programs.)

BARBITURATES

Barbiturates, which are derived from barbituric acid, depress the central nervous system. Barbiturates were first synthesized in the early 1900s, and there are now over 2500 different varieties. They are commonly used to relieve insomnia and anxiety, to treat epilepsy and high blood pressure, and to relax patients before or after surgery. Barbiturates are illegal unless obtained by a physician's prescription.

Taken in sufficient doses, barbiturates have effects similar to strong alcohol. Users experience relief from inhibitions, have a feeling of euphoria, feel "high" or in good humor, and are passively content. However, these moods can change rapidly to gloom, agitation, and aggressiveness. Physiological effects include slurred speech, disorientation, staggering, confusion, drowsiness, and impaired coordination.

Prolonged heavy use of barbiturates can cause physical dependency, with withdrawal symptoms similar to those of heroin addiction. Withdrawal is accompanied by body tremors, cramps, anxiety, fever, nausea, profuse sweating, and hallucinations. Many authorities believe barbiturate addiction is more dangerous than heroin addiction, and it is considered more resistant to treatment than heroin addiction. Abrupt withdrawal can cause fatal convulsions. One forensic pathologist noted: "Show me someone who goes cold turkey (the sudden and complete halting of drug use) on a bad barbiturate habit, and I'll show you a corpse."[41]

Barbiturate overdose can cause convulsions, coma, poisoning, and sometimes death. Barbiturates are particularly dangerous when taken with alcohol because the alcohol acts synergistically to magnify the potency of the barbiturates. Accidental deaths due to excessive doses are frequent. Often the user becomes groggy, forgets how much has been taken, and continues to take more until an overdose level has been reached. Barbiturates are also the most popular suicide drug. A number of famous people (for example, Marilyn Monroe) have fatally overdosed on barbiturates.

Generally, barbiturates are taken orally, although some users inject them intravenously. Use of barbiturates, like alcohol, may lead to traffic fatalities.

TRANQUILIZERS

Other depressants are the drugs classified as tranquilizers. Common brand names are Librium, Miltown, Serax, Tranxene, and Valium. They reduce anxiety, relax muscles, and act as sedatives. Users have a moderate potential of becoming physically and psychologically dependent. Tranquilizers are usually taken orally, and the effects last 4 to 8 hours. Side effects include slurred speech, disorientation, and behavior resembling intoxication. Overdoses are possible and result in cold and clammy skin, shallow respiration, dilated pupils, weak and rapid pulse, coma, and possibly death. Withdrawal symptoms are similar to those from alcohol and barbiturates: anxiety, tremors, convulsions, delirium, and sometimes death.

QUAALUDE AND PCP

Both Quaalude and PCP are depressants. (PCP also produces effects similar to those of hallucinogens.)

Methaqualone (better known by its patent name, Quaalude) resembles barbiturates and alcohol in its effects, although it is chemically different. It has the reputation of being a "love drug" because users believe it makes them more eager for sex and enhances sexual pleasure. These effects probably stem from the fact that it lowers inhibitions (similar to alcohol and barbiturates). Quaaludes also reduce anxiety and give a feeling of euphoria. Users can become both physically and psychologically dependent. Overdose can result in convulsions, coma, delirium, and even death. Most deaths occur when the drug is taken together with alcohol, which vastly magnifies its effects. Withdrawal symptoms are severe and unpleasant. Abuse of the drug may also cause hangovers, fatigue, liver damage, and temporary paralysis of the limbs.

The technical name for PCP is phencyclidine, and its street name is "angel dust." PCP was developed in the 1950s as an anesthetic, but this medical use soon ended because patients displayed symptoms of severe emotional disturbance after receiving it. PCP is legal today only for tranquilizing elephants and monkeys, which apparently do not experience the adverse side effects.

PCP is used primarily by young people who are unaware of its hazards. It is usually smoked, often after being sprinkled on a marijuana "joint." It may also be sniffed, swallowed, or injected. PCP is a very dangerous drug. It distorts the senses, disrupts balance, and leads to an inability to think clearly. Larger amounts of PCP can cause a person to become paranoid, can lead to aggressive behavior (even violent murder), and can create temporary symptoms of a severe emotional disturbance. Continued use can lead to the development of a prolonged emotional disturbance. Overdose may result in coma or even death.

EXHIBIT 8.4

Date-Rape Drugs

In the mid-1990s, Rohypnol became known as the date-rape drug. A number of women in the mid-1990s were sexually assaulted after the drug was slipped into one of their drinks (both alcoholic and nonalcoholic). Rohypnol often causes blackouts, with complete loss of memory. Female victims of being slipped the drug and then raped often cannot remember any details of the crimes.

Rohypnol is a sedative, related to Valium, but ten times stronger. It is legally available in more than 60 countries for severe insomnia but is illegal in the United States (many drugs—such as cocaine and heroin—are, too, but are widely used and abused). Much of the illegal Rohypnol in the United States is smuggled in from Mexico and Colombia.

Rohypnol is also popular with teens and young adults (both males and females) who like to combine it with alcohol for a quick punch-drunk hit. Another reason for its popularity is that it's relatively inexpensive, often being purchased on the street for $1 to $5 per pill. In some jurisdictions, drivers are now tested for Rohypnol when they

appear drunk but register a low alcohol level. (Rohypnol is also addictive, and there is a potential for lethal overdosing.)

Because of the ease through which Rohypnol can be slipped into a drink, rape crisis centers are urging women *never* to take their eyes off their drinks. In 1997 the marketer of Rohypnol, Hoffmann-LaRoche, announced it intended only to sell a new version that would cause any liquid that it is slipped into to have a blue color. Even with this change, people (particularly women) need to beware. Other sedatives have similar effects!

Gamma hydroxy butyrate (GHB) is another drug that is increasingly being used as a date-rape drug. GHB is a central nervous system depressant that is approved as an anesthetic in some countries. It can be readily made at home from a mixture of chemicals purchased in stores normally used in cleaning, such as lye. Just 1 gram of this liquid home brew provides an intoxicating experience equivalent to 26 ounces of whiskey. Similar to Rohypnol, GHB is slipped into a drink of intended victims.

Research has not as yet concluded whether PCP induces physical or psychological dependency. The drug has a potential to be used (and abused) extensively because it is relatively easy to prepare in a home laboratory and because the ingredients and recipes are widely available. An additional danger of PCP is that even one-time users sometimes have flashbacks in which hallucinations are reexperienced, even long after use has ceased. It may be that many accidents and unexplained disasters are caused by someone's previous use of PCP or some other undetectable hallucinogenic substance.

Stimulants

In this section, we will examine the following drugs classified as stimulants: caffeine, amphetamines, cocaine and crack, amyl nitrate and butyl nitrate.

CAFFEINE

Caffeine is a stimulant to the central nervous system. It is present in coffee, tea, cocoa, Coca-Cola, and many other soft drinks. It is also available in tablet form (for example, No-Doz).

Practically all Americans use caffeine on a daily basis. It reduces hunger, fatigue, and boredom and improves alertness and motor activity. The drug appears to be addictive because many users develop a tolerance for it. A further sign that it is addictive is that heavy users (for example, habitual coffee drinkers) will experience withdrawal symptoms of mild irritability and depression. Excessive amounts of caffeine cause insomnia, restlessness, and gastrointestinal irritation and can even, surprisingly, cause death.

Because caffeine has the status of a "nondrug" in our society, users are not labeled criminals, there is no black market for it, and no subculture is formed to give support in obtaining and using the drug. Because caffeine is legal, its price is low compared to that of other drugs. Users are not tempted to resort to crime to support their habit. Some authorities assert that our approach to caffeine should serve as a model for the way we react to other illegal drugs (such as marijuana) that, they feel, are no more harmful than caffeine.[42]

AMPHETAMINES

Amphetamines are called "uppers" because of their stimulating effects. When prescribed by a physician, they are legal. Some truck drivers have obtained prescriptions to stay awake and alert during a long haul, with a few becoming addicted. Dieters have received prescriptions to help them lose weight and have also found that the pills tend to give them more self-confidence and buoyance. College students have used them to stay awake and alert while studying. Others who have used amphetamines to increase alertness and performance for relatively short periods of time include athletes, astronauts, and executives. Additional nicknames for these drugs are *speed, ups, pep pills, black beauties,* and *bennies.*

Amphetamines are synthetic drugs. They are similar to adrenalin, a hormone from the adrenal gland that stimulates the central nervous system. The better known amphetamines include Dexedrine, Benzedrine, and Methedrine. Physical reactions to amphetamines are extensive: Consumption of fat stored in body tissues is accelerated, heartbeat is increased, respiratory processes are stimulated, appetite is reduced, and insomnia is

common. Users feel euphoric and stronger and have an increased capacity to concentrate and to express themselves verbally. Prolonged use can lead to irritability, deep anxiety, and an irrational persecution complex that can provoke sudden acts of violence.

Amphetamines are usually taken orally in tablet, powder, or capsule form. They also can be sniffed or injected. "Speeding" (injecting the drug into a vein) produces the most powerful effects but also the greatest harm. An overdose can cause a coma, with possible brain damage, and in rare cases death may occur. Speeders may develop hepatitis, abscesses, convulsions, hallucinations, delusions, and severe emotional disturbances. Another danger is that, when sold on the street, the substance may contain impurities that are additional health hazards.

An amphetamine high is often followed by mental depression and fatigue. Continued amphetamine use leads to psychological dependency. It is unclear whether amphetamines are physically addicting because the withdrawal symptoms are uncharacteristic of withdrawal from other drugs. Amphetamine withdrawal symptoms include sleep disturbances, apathy, decreased activity, disorientation, irritability, exhaustion, and depression. Some authorities see these withdrawal symptoms as indicative of physical addiction.[43]

One of the legal uses of certain amphetamines is in the treatment of hyperactivity in children. Hyperactivity (also called hyperkinesis) is characterized by a short attention span, excessive motor activity, restlessness, and shifts in moods. Little is known about the causes of this condition. As children become older, the symptoms tend to disappear, even without treatment. Interestingly, some amphetamines (Ritalin is a popular one) have a calming and soothing effect on children; the exact opposite effect occurs when Ritalin is taken by adults. It should be noted that treatment of "uncontrollable" children with amphetamines has frequently been abused. Some of the children for whom Ritalin is prescribed are not really hyperactive. They are normal children who simply refuse to submit to what their teachers and parents

CASE EXAMPLE 8.2 Tragic Cocaine Overdoses

On June 17, 1986, Len Bias, an All-American forward from the University of Maryland, was the Boston Celtics' first pick in the National Basketball Association draft. He was the second player chosen overall. The Celtics was his favorite team, and he looked forward to signing a contract for around $1 million per year. Two days later, he was partying and died of heart failure induced by cocaine intoxication.

Eight days after the death of Len Bias, Don Rogers was celebrating at his bachelor party. He was to be married the next day. Rogers was a professional football player for the Cleveland Browns. He had played at UCLA and was the Browns' number-one pick in the 1984 college draft. That year he was selected as the Defensive Rookie of the Year in the American Football Conference. Rogers died at his bachelor party of heart failure induced by cocaine intoxication.

---

consider appropriate childhood behavior. As a result, these children are labeled "problem children" and are introduced into the world of taking a mood-altering drug on a daily basis.

An amphetamine that has had increasing illegal use in recent years is methamphetamine hydrochloride, known on the street as "meth" or "ice." In liquid form, it is often referred to as "speed." Under experimental conditions, cocaine users often have difficulty distinguishing cocaine from methamphetamine hydrochloride. There is a danger this drug may be increasingly abused, as its "high" lasts longer than that from cocaine and the drug can be synthesized relatively easily in laboratories from products that are sold legally in the United States. Methamphetamine hydrochloride (Desoxyn) is legally used to treat obesity as one component of a "last-resort" weight-reduction regimen. There is, however, a serious side effect of this drug when used for weight reduction: The user's appetite returns with greater intensity after the drug is discontinued.

COCAINE AND CRACK

Cocaine is obtained from the leaves of the South American coca plant. It has a chic status in this country and is rapidly replacing other illegal drugs in popularity. Although legally classified as a narcotic, it is in fact not related to the opiates from which narcotic drugs are derived. It is a powerful stimulant and antifatigue agent.

In the United States, cocaine is generally taken by sniffing and absorbed through the nasal membranes. The most common method is sniffing through a straw or a rolled-up bank note; this is known as "snorting." It may also be injected intravenously, and in South America the natives chew the coca leaf. It may be added in small quantities to a cigarette and smoked. Cocaine has been used medically in the past as a local anesthetic, but other drugs have now largely replaced it for this purpose.

Cocaine constricts the blood vessels and thereby leads to increased strength and endurance. It also is thought by users to increase creative and intellectual powers. Other effects include a feeling of euphoria, excitement, restlessness, and a lessened sense of fatigue. Some users of cocaine claim that it heightens or restores their virility and enables them to prolong intercourse for long periods.[44]

Larger doses or extended use may result in hallucinations and delusions. A peculiar effect of cocaine abuse is *formication*—the illusion that ants, snakes, or bugs are crawling on or into the skin. Some abusers have such intense illusions that they literally scratch, slap, and wound themselves trying to kill these imaginary creatures.

Physical effects of cocaine include increased blood pressure and pulse rate, insomnia, and loss of appetite. Frequent users may experience weight loss or malnutrition due to appetite suppression. Physical dependency on cocaine is considered a low to medium risk. However, the drug appears to be psychologically habituating; withdrawal usually results in intense depression and despair, which drive the person back to taking the drug.[45] Additional effects of withdrawal include apathy, long periods of sleep, extreme fatigue, irritability, and disorientation. Serious tissue damage to the nose can occur when large quantities of cocaine are "sniffed" over a prolonged time period. Regular use may result in habitual sniffling and sometimes leads to an anorexic condition. High doses can cause agitation, increased body temperature, and convulsions. A few people who overdose may die if their breathing and heart functions become too depressed.

Crack (also called "rock") is obtained from cocaine. The inert ingredients are separated from the cocaine by mixing it with water and ammonium hydroxide. The water is then removed from the cocaine base by means of a fast-drying solvent, usually ether. The resultant mixture resembles large sugar crystals, similar to rock sugar. Crack is highly addictive. Some authorities claim that one use is enough to lead to addiction. Users generally claim that, after they have finished one dose, they immediately crave another.

Crack is usually smoked, either in a specially made glass pipe or mixed with tobacco or marijuana in a cigarette. The effects are similar to those of cocaine, but the "rush" is more immediate, and the drug gives an intensified high and has an even greater orgasmic effect.

An overdose is more common when crack is injected than when it is smoked. Withdrawal effects include an irresistible compulsion to have the drug, as well as apathy, long periods of sleep, irritability, extreme fatigue, depression, and disorientation.

Communal use of needles spreads AIDS. Cocaine and crack can have serious effects on the heart, straining it with high blood pressure, with interrupted heart rhythm, and with raised pulse rates. Cocaine and crack may also damage the liver. Severe convulsions can cause brain damage, emotional problems, and sometimes death. Smoking crack may also damage the lungs.

AMYL NITRATE AND BUTYL NITRATE

Amyl nitrate ("poppers") is prescribed for patients who risk certain forms of heart failure. It is a volatile liquid that is sold in small bottles. When the container is opened, the chemical begins to evaporate (similar to gasoline). If the vapor is sniffed, the user's blood vessels are immediately dilated, and there is an increase in heart rate. These physical changes create feelings of mental excitation ("head rush") and physical excitation ("body rush"). The drug is legal only by prescription, but (as with many other drugs) illicit dealers readily obtain and distribute it.

Butyl nitrate is legally available in some states without a prescription and has an effect similar to that of amyl nitrate. Trade names under which it is sold are Rush and Locker Room. Similar to amyl nitrate, the vapor is sniffed. It is available at some sexual aid and novelty stores.

Both these drugs have been used as aphrodisiacs and as stimulants while dancing. The drugs have some short-term, unpleasant side effects that may include fainting, headaches, and dizziness. A few deaths have been reported due to overdoses. Both these drugs are classified as stimulants.

Narcotics

The most commonly used narcotic drugs in the United States are the opiates (such as opium, heroin, and morphine). The term *narcotic* means "sleep inducing." In actuality, drugs classified as narcotics are more accurately called analgesics, or painkillers. The principal effect produced by narcotic drugs is a feeling of euphoria.

The opiates are all derived from the opium poppy, which grows in many countries. Turkey, Southeast Asia, and Colombia have in our recent past been major sources of the opiates. The drug opium is the dried form of a milky substance that oozes from the seed pods after the petals fall from

EXHIBIT 8.5

Crack Babies

In recent years, crack cocaine use by pregnant women has sharply increased. As a result, hundreds of thousands of babies have been born who have been adversely affected by their mother's crack use.

Cocaine causes the blood vessels in a pregnant woman to constrict, thus reducing the vital flow of oxygen and other nutrients to the fetus. Because fetal cells multiply swiftly in the first months, an embryo deprived of a proper blood supply by a mother's early and continuous use of cocaine is likely to suffer an adverse cognitive impact. At birth such babies may look quite normal, but they are likely to be undersized, and the circumference of their heads tends to be unusually small—a trait associated with lower IQ scores. Only the most intensive care after birth will give these babies a fighting chance to have a "normal" life.

In rare cases during the latter months of pregnancy, heavy crack use can lead to an embolism (a clot) that lodges in a fetal vessel and completely disrupts the blood supply to an organ or a limb. The result will be a deformed arm or leg, a missing section of an intestine or kidney, or various other deformities.

Cocaine exposure affects brain chemistry as well. The drug alters the actions of neurotransmitters, the messengers that travel between nerve cells and help control a person's mood and responsiveness. Such changes may explain the behavioral problems, including impulsiveness and moodiness, seen in cocaine-exposed children as they mature.

Some pregnant women repeatedly use crack cocaine in combination with other drugs. This increases the chances that the fetus will be affected because the other drugs can also damage the baby.

The children born to pregnant mothers who used crack cocaine have become known as "crack babies" and "crack kids." A few such children have

A nurse cares for an infant abandoned by a crack-addicted mother.

severe physical deformities from which they will never recover. In others the damage can be more subtle, showing up as behavioral problems that may sabotage the children's schooling and social development. Many of these youngsters look and act like other children, but their early exposure to cocaine makes them less able to overcome negative influences, such as a disruptive home life.

Crack children often require exhaustive and expensive medical treatment. Some grow up in dysfunctional families and increasingly display behavioral and emotional disorders as they grow older. The injury during gestation is often com-

(continued)

EXHIBIT 8.5   *(continued)*

pounded after birth by an environment of ne-glect, poverty, and violence. Many crack-addicted mothers continue using the drug, even after giving birth to drug-impaired children.

How can crack babies be helped? What seems to work is a combination of the social services carrot and the legal stick. That is, the best way to rescue a crack child is to rescue the mother as well. Successful programs for the addicted mothers offer a variety of assistance, beginning with detoxification, then extending to pediatric services for the child, psychological and job counseling for the mother, and extensive parenting classes. Crack

children often need extensive medical services, social services, and specialized educational services. All of these services need to be backed up with the threat of legal intervention, including the threat of removal of the child to foster care through the protective services system.

Some studies have shown that cocaine-exposed infants can catch up in weight, length, and head circumference by 1 year of age.[a] They may also be able to catch up in other ways. So it is important for people who care for such children and for policymakers not to give up on them. They can be helped after birth.

---

[a] Diane E. Papalia and Sally W. Olds, *Human Development,* 6th ed. (New York: McGraw-Hill, 1995), pp. 77–78.

the purple or white flower. Opium has been used for centuries.

Morphine is the main active ingredient of opium. It was first identified in the early 1800s and has been used extensively as a painkiller. Heroin was first synthesized from morphine in 1874. It was once thought to be a cure for morphine addiction but later was also found to be addicting. Heroin is a more potent drug than morphine.

Opium is usually smoked, although it can be taken orally. Morphine and heroin are either sniffed (snorted) or injected into a muscle or a vein (called "mainlining"), which maximizes the drugs' effects.

Opiates affect the central nervous system and produce feelings of tranquility, drowsiness, or euphoria. They also generate a sense of well-being, which makes pain, anxiety, or depression seem unimportant. Tony Blaze-Gosden notes:

It has been described as giving an orgasmlike rush or flash that lasts briefly but memorably. At the peak of the euphoria, the user has a feeling of exaggerated physical and mental comfort and wellbeing; a heightened feeling of buoyancy

and bodily health, and a heightened feeling of being competent, in control, capable of any achievement, and being able to cope.[46]

Overdoses can cause convulsions, coma, and in rare cases, death by respiratory failure. All opiates are now recognized as highly addictive.

Heroin is the most widely abused opiate. In addition to the aforementioned effects, heroin slows the functioning parts of the brain. The user's appetite and sex drive tend to be dulled. After an initial feeling of euphoria, the user generally becomes lethargic and stuporous. Contrary to popular belief, most heroin users take the drug infrequently and do not as a rule become addicted.[47]

Opiate addiction occurs when the user takes the drug regularly for a period of time. Whether addiction will occur depends on the opiate taken, the strength of the dosages, the regularity of use, the characteristics of the user, and the length of time taken. Addiction can occur within a few weeks. Users rapidly develop a tolerance and may eventually need a dose that is up to 100 times stronger than a dose that would have been fatal during the initiation to the drug.[48]

The withdrawal process is very unpleasant. Symptoms include chills, cramps, sweating, nervousness, anxiety, runny eyes and nose, dilated pupils, muscle aches, increased blood pressure, severe cramps, nausea, and fever. Most addicts are obsessed with securing a fix to avoid these severe withdrawal symptoms.

Addiction to opiates is extremely difficult to break, partly because intense craving for the drug may recur periodically for several months afterward.

Most opiate addicts are under age 30, of low socioeconomic status, and poorly educated. A disproportionate number are African Americans. Distribution and addiction to narcotic drugs occur primarily in large urban centers.

When heroin was first discovered in the late 1800s, it was initially used as a painkiller, as a substitute for people addicted to morphine, and as a drug taken by many to experience euphoria. A fair number of people became addicted, and in the early 1900s, laws were passed to prohibit its sale, possession, and distribution.

Heroin abuse continues to be regarded by some Americans as our most serious drug problem. This stereotype does not appear warranted because only a tiny fraction of the U.S. population has ever tried heroin. The number of people addicted to heroin is minuscule compared to the number addicted to alcohol or tobacco. In addition, drugs such as alcohol and barbiturates contribute to many more deaths.

One reason why heroin retains its reputation is that users are thought to be "dope fiends" who commit violent crimes and reject the values of contemporary society. Addicts, however, are unlikely to commit such violent crimes as rape or aggravated assault. They are more likely to commit crimes against property (shoplifting, burglary, pickpocketing, larceny, and robbery) to support their habit.[49] Prostitution for female addicts is also common. Because the severe withdrawal symptoms begin about 18 hours after the last fix, addicts who have experienced these symptoms will do almost anything to avoid them.

Unsanitary injections of heroin may cause hepatitis and other infections. Communal use of needles can spread AIDS. Also, the high cost of maintaining a heroin habit—often over $100 daily—may create huge financial problems for the user.

Because the price of illicit narcotic drugs is so high, organized crime has made huge profits in the smuggling and distribution of these drugs. Often narcotics are diluted with dangerous impurities, which pose serious health hazards for the users.

Hallucinogens

Hallucinogens were popular as psychedelic drugs in the late 1960s. These drugs distort the user's perceptions, creating hallucinatory impressions of "sights and sounds" that do not exist. The four hallucinogens most commonly used in this country are mescaline (peyote), psilocybin, psilocin, and LSD. All are taken orally—swallowed in capsule form, eaten on a sugar cube, or licked from the back of a stamp.

Peyote is derived from a cactus plant. Mescaline is the synthetic form of peyote. Psilocybin and psilocin are found in approximately 90 different species of mushrooms (called "magic mushrooms"). Both peyote and psilocybin have had a long history of use among certain Native American tribes. Members of the Native American Church, a religious organization, have won the legal right to use peyote on ceremonial occasions.[50]

The most popular hallucinogen is LSD (lysergic acid diethylamide). LSD is a synthetic material derived from a fungus (ergot) that grows on rye and other plants. It is one of the most potent drugs known; a single ounce will make up to 300,000 doses.

The effects of LSD vary greatly depending on the expectations and psychological state of the user and on the context in which it is taken. The same person may experience differing reactions on different occasions. Users report "seeing" sounds and "hearing" colors. Colors may seem unusually bright and shift kaleidoscopically, and objects may appear to expand and contract. LSD users become highly suggestible and easily manipulated, including sexually.

Bizarre hallucinations are also common. The experience may be peaceful or may result in panic. Some users have developed severe emotional disturbances that resulted in long-term hospitalization. Usually a "trip" will last 8 to 16 hours. Physical reactions include increased heartbeat, goose bumps, dilated pupils, hyperactivity, tremors, and sweating. Aftereffects include acute anxiety or depression. Flashbacks sometimes occur after the actual drug experience. They may happen at any time and place, with no advance warning. If the user is driving a car when a flashback occurs, the condition could be life threatening for everyone in the vicinity. Users develop tolerance to the drug very rapidly, with larger doses being needed in the future to achieve the desired effects. Cessation of use, even for a few days, will restore sensitivity to the drug, enabling the user to again take smaller quantities to experience the effects.

The effects and dangers of mescaline, psilocybin, and psilocin are similar to those of LSD. LSD is, however, the most potent of the hallucinogens.

Tobacco

The use of tobacco has now become recognized as one of the most damaging drug habits in the United States. Smoking can cause emphysema, cancer of the mouth, ulcers, and lung cancer. Users have a reduced life expectancy. Smoking significantly increases the risk of strokes and heart disease, particularly in women who use birth control pills.[51] Smoking by a pregnant woman sometimes leads to miscarriages, premature births, and underweight infants. Yet in spite of these widely publicized hazards, about 25% of Americans continue to smoke.[52]

Tobacco is the number-one killer drug, contributing to far more deaths than all other drugs combined.[53] It is estimated to lead to 40,000 deaths per year in the United States.[54] This is more than double the number of deaths caused by alcohol abuse and hundreds of times the number of deaths caused by cocaine.[55] Most of these deaths result from heart disease and lung cancer due to cigarette smoking. However, over 2000 deaths per

year result from fires caused by smoking.[56] There is also substantial evidence that "passive smoking" (breathing the smoke from others' cigarettes, cigars, or pipes) is hazardous to health. One source of such evidence is the finding that young children whose parents smoke have a higher incidence of pneumonia and other respiratory disorders than young children whose parents do not smoke.[57]

The attitudes of Americans toward tobacco use are gradually becoming more negative. Increasingly, we are viewing tobacco as a dangerous drug, and nonsmokers are perceiving smokers as pariahs. Some authorities are now predicting that cigarettes will eventually be outlawed in many countries.

In 1988 the Surgeon General of the United States, C. Everett Koop, declared that tobacco is as addictive as heroin or cocaine.[58] Koop defined people who are addicted to tobacco as drug addicts.

Tobacco is highly habit forming. Nicotine, the primary drug in tobacco, has remarkable capacities; it can act as a depressant, a stimulant, or a tranquilizer. Smokers quickly develop a tolerance for nicotine and gradually increase consumption to one or two packs or more a day.

There are special clinics and a variety of other educational and therapeutic programs to help people quit smoking. Tobacco is a very habit-forming drug. Withdrawal from use leads people to become restless, irritable, and depressed and to have an intense craving to smoke. Studies show that only a minority of smokers who make determined efforts to quit actually succeed.[59]

In the biggest civil settlement in U.S. history, tobacco companies agreed in 1998 to pay over $240 billion to the 50 states to settle claims against the industry for health-care costs blamed on tobacco-related illnesses. The payments to the states are distributed over 25 years (payments begin in 2000). Some of the funds will go to a foundation to study how to reduce teen smoking. A major objective of the deal is to discourage children from smoking by restricting advertising and by imposing sharp limits on the ways that cigarettes are marketed.

Marijuana

Marijuana ("grass" or "pot") comes from the hemp plant *Cannabis sativa*. This plant grows throughout the world, and its fibers are legally used to produce rope, twine, paper, and clothing.

The main use of the plant now, however, centers on its dried leaves and flowers—marijuana—and on its dried resin—hashish. Both marijuana and hashish may be taken orally but are usually smoked. Hashish is several times more potent than marijuana.

The effects of marijuana (and hashish) vary, as with any other drug, according to the mood and personality of the user, the circumstances, and the quality of the drug. Marijuana has sedative properties and creates in the user a sense of relaxed well-being and freedom from inhibition. There may also be mild hallucinations that create a dreamy state in which the user experiences fantasies. Smokers become highly suggestible and may engage in actions (such as sexual activities) they might otherwise avoid. The drug may induce feelings of joyousness, hilarity, and sociability. It may lead to talkativeness, disconnected ideas, a feeling of floating, and laughter. Sometimes marijuana intensifies sensory stimulation, creates feelings of enhanced awareness and creativity, and increases self-confidence.

The threat of physical dependency is rated low; the threat of psychological dependency is rated moderate. Withdrawal, however, may be very unpleasant, with the user suffering from insomnia, hyperactivity, and loss of appetite.

The short-term physical effects of marijuana are minor: a reddening of the eyes, dryness of the throat and mouth, and a slight increase in heart rate. There is some evidence that continued use by young teenagers will result in their becoming apathetic, noncompetitive, and uninterested in school and other activities.

Frequent users may have impairments of short-term memory, concentration, judgment, and coordination. They may find it difficult to read, to understand what they read, or to follow moving objects with their eyes. Users may feel confident that their coordination, reactions, and perceptions are quite normal while they are still experiencing the effects of the drug; under these conditions, such activities as driving a vehicle may have tragic consequences to them and to others. Marijuana use by pregnant women may also contribute to malformations in fetuses, much like the effects of alcohol use.

An overdose of the active ingredients of cannabis can lead to panic, fear, confusion, suspiciousness, fatigue, and sometimes, aggressive acts. One of the most frequently voiced concerns about marijuana is that it will be a "steppingstone" to other drugs. About 60% of marijuana users "progress" to other drugs.[60] However, other factors, such as peer pressure, are probably more crucial determinants of which mind-altering drugs people will " advance" to using.

The attempt to restrict marijuana use through legislation has been described as a "second prohibition,"[61] with similar results: A large number of people are using the drug in disregard of the law. The unfortunate effect of laws that attempt to regulate acts (crimes, as defined by law) without victims is that they criminalize the private acts of many people who are otherwise law abiding. They also foster the development of organized crime and the illicit drug market.

For years heated debates have raged about the hazards of long-term marijuana use. Some studies claim that it causes brain damage, chromosome damage, irritation of the bronchial tract and lungs, and a reduction in male hormone levels. These findings have not been confirmed by other studies, and the controversy rages on.[62]

In 1982 the National Academy of Science completed an extensive 15-month study on marijuana. The investigation found no evidence that marijuana causes permanent changes in the nervous system and concluded that the drug probably does not break down human chromosomes. It also found that marijuana may be useful in treating glaucoma, asthma, certain seizure disorders, and spastic conditions and in controlling severe nausea caused by cancer chemotherapy.

The study warned, however, that the drug presents a variety of short-term health risks and justifies "serious national concern." One of the reversible short-term health effects is impairment of motor coordination, which adversely affects driving or machine-operating skills. The drug also impairs short-term memory, slows learning abilities, and may cause periods of confusion and anxiety. There was evidence that smoking marijuana may affect the lungs and respiratory system in much the same way that tobacco smoke does and may be a factor in causing bronchitis and precancerous changes.

Thus, the study found some evidence that marijuana may lead to certain adverse long-term health problems. The major recommendation was that "there be a greatly intensified and more comprehensive program of research into the effects of marijuana on the health of the American people." [63]

In 1996 voters in California and Arizona approved the medical use of marijuana (for example, for treating symptoms of AIDS, cancer, and other diseases). However, the Clinton administration threatened sanctions against doctors who prescribed it. In 1997 a panel of experts convened at the National Institutes of Health stated that marijuana shows promise in treating painful symptoms of some diseases and urged its medical use to be studied further. [64] The controversy continues.

Anabolic Steroids

Anabolic steroids are synthetic derivatives of the male hormone testosterone. Although steroids have been banned for use by athletes in sporting competition, they are still used by some athletes, bodybuilders, and teenagers who want to look more muscular and brawny. From early childhood, many boys have been socialized to believe that the ideal man looks something like Mr. Universe. Such well-known athletes as Olympic sprinter Ben Johnson and Seattle Seahawks linebacker Brian Bosworth are known to have taken the steroid shortcut to muscularity and increased running speed. [65]

Some young male bodybuilders use steroids to promote tissue growth and to endure arduous workouts, routinely flooding their bodies with 100 times the testosterone they produce naturally. [66] Most steroid users are middle class and White.

Steroid-enhanced physiques are a hazardous prize. Steroids can cause temporary acne and bald-

ing, upset hormonal production, and can damage the heart and kidneys. Doctors suspect that they may also contribute to liver cancer and atherosclerosis. [67] For teens the drugs can stunt growth by accelerating bone maturation. Male steroid users have also experienced shrinking of the testicles, impotency, yellowing of the skin and eyes, and development of female-type breasts. In young boys, steroids can have the effect of painfully enlarging the sex organs. In female users, the voice deepens permanently, breasts shrink, periods become irregular, the clitoris swells in size, and hair is lost from the head but grows on the face and body.

Steroid drug users are prone to moodiness, depression, and irritability and are likely to experience difficulty in tolerating stress. Some formerly easygoing males display raging hostility after prolonged use, ranging from being obnoxious to continually provoking physical fights. Some users become so depressed that they commit suicide.

Steroid users generally experience considerable difficulty in terminating use of the drugs. One reason is that bulging biceps and ham-hock thighs soon fade when steroid use is discontinued. Concurrent with the decline in muscle mass is the psychological feeling of being less powerful and less "manly." Most users who try to quit wind up back on the drugs. A self-image that relies on a steroid-enhanced physique is difficult to change.

REHABILITATION PROGRAMS

Rehabilitation programs for alcohol abuse are very similar to those for most other drugs. We'll begin by looking closely at the treatment of alcoholism.

Alcohol Treatment Programs

As mentioned earlier, before an alcoholic can be helped, his or her denial of the problem must be confronted. If the alcoholic cannot or does not do so, the confrontation can be arranged by family members, friends, employers, or alcohol counselors—or by all of these together. Tim Bliss briefly describes guidelines for this confrontation:

> In confronting the alcoholic, documentation of incidents that occurred while drinking becomes extremely important. This is particularly important because the alcoholic may have blackouts. These are periods of amnesia as opposed to passing out or unconsciousness. Both are due to excessive drinking. Many times during confrontation it is important that the entire family be present to reinforce the incident. In documenting the incident, one should be instructed to write down the date and time, and to be as specific as possible in describing the situation. The counselor can be present during this confrontation to act as a facilitator; however, the primary responsibility in breaking through denial is with the spouse, family, or employer.
>
> Many times the practicing alcoholic has been threatened with divorce, job discipline, and so on. It is important not to continue these threats; action must occur if the alcoholic continues to drink after confrontation.[68]

If the alcoholic continues to deny that a problem exists, there are some guidelines for what family members should and should not do. "Nagging" the alcoholic will only increase family arguments and may provoke the alcoholic into verbally or physically abusing someone, particularly when he or she is inebriated. Family members often make the mistake of assuming they are responsible for getting the alcoholic to stop drinking, and they feel guilty or frustrated if the person continues to drink. They, however, do not *own* the drinking problem; the alcoholic is the one responsible for the drinking and is the one who determines whether he or she will stop drinking. When a person is drunk, yelling and screaming at him or her will accomplish nothing (except perhaps to make other family members more upset). What is more productive for the other family members is to isolate themselves from the alcoholic when she or he is drunk—perhaps by going shopping, taking a walk, or if need be, locking themselves in a room.

There are three self-help groups that family members can attend. Al-Anon is for spouses and other family members of alcoholics. The program reaches out to people affected by another person's drinking regardless of whether the alcoholic recognizes his or her problem. It helps members learn the facts about alcoholism and ways to cope with an alcoholic. Alateen is for teenage children of alcoholics and helps adolescents to understand alcoholism and to learn effective ways to cope with problems. Adult Children of Alcoholics helps adults cope with issues they are still struggling with that largely stem from being raised in an alcoholic family.

If the alcoholic does acknowledge a drinking problem, many treatment programs are available. The best-known and most successful program is Alcoholics Anonymous, which is further described in Exhibit 8.6.

There appear to be several reasons why such self-help groups are successful. The members have an intrinsic understanding of the problem that helps them to help others. Having experienced the misery and consequences of the problem, they are highly motivated and dedicated to find ways to help themselves and others who are fellow sufferers. The participants also benefit from the "helper therapy principle"; that is, the helper gains psychological rewards by helping others.[69] Helping others leads the helper to feel "good" and worthwhile and also enables the helper to put his or her own problems into perspective by seeing that others have problems that are as serious, or even more serious. From the viewpoint of the new member who is still drinking, having people around who have successfully stopped provides role models of abstinence and gives them reason to believe that they too can break the grip of alcohol abuse.

At one time, intoxicated people were just thrown into jail to sober up. (Unfortunately, this is still happening in some places.) Many communities, however, have now switched to a treatment approach.

Most alcohol treatment facilities offer both inpatient and outpatient programs. Outpatient treatment usually serves clients who have the potential to stop using alcohol while living at home. If the client is unable to live at home or is still drinking excessively, inpatient treatment will usually be

EXHIBIT 8.6

Alcoholics Anonymous

In 1929 Bill Wilson was a stock analyst. When the stock market crashed that year, he lost most of his money and turned to alcohol. A few years later, his doctor warned him that his continued drinking was jeopardizing his health and his life. Bill W. underwent what he perceived as a spiritual experience, and he made a commitment to stop drinking. He also discovered that, through discussing his drinking problem with other alcoholics, he was helped to remain sober. One of the people he talked with was Robert Smith, an Ohio doctor and also an alcoholic. Together they formed Alcoholics Anonymous (AA), a self-help group composed of recovering alcoholics.

AA stresses the following precepts: (a) confessing to the group that one has a drinking problem, (b) recounting to the group past experiences with the drinking problem and plans for handling the problem in the future, and (c) phoning another member of the group whenever one feels an intense urge to drink. The person called will do whatever can be done to keep the caller "dry," including coming over to stay with the person until the urge subsides.

Today AA has chapters in over 100 countries. Local chapters (around 25 people per chapter) meet once or twice a week for discussions. These sessions resemble traditional group therapy but without the presence of a trained professional leader.

Bill W. and Dr. Bob, as they were known within AA, remained anonymous until their deaths. Local chapters still follow procedures similar to the original ones—the sharing of similar experiences in order to abstain from taking the first drink (which is "one too many") and the thousandth (which is "not enough").

AA is widely recognized as the treatment approach that has the best chance of helping an alcoholic. Testimony to its value is that hundreds of other self-help groups with treatment principles based on the AA model have now been formed to deal with other personal problems—for example, Overeaters Anonymous, Narcotics Anonymous, Prison Families Anonymous, Debtors Anonymous, Gamblers Anonymous, Emotions Anonymous, Emphysema Anonymous, Adult Children of Alcoholics, and many more.

---

recommended. Those who go through an inpatient program receive subsequent follow-up treatment on an outpatient basis. Inpatient treatment can last anywhere from a few days to 3 months, depending on the patient's problems and the treatment program. Inpatient treatment is usually intense, including one-on-one therapy, group therapy, an orientation to Alcoholics Anonymous, and occupational and recreational therapy. Outpatient treatment is not as intense, usually lasts from 3 to 6 months, and offers the same forms of treatment.

Outpatient and inpatient services are provided in some medical hospitals, in drug rehabilitation centers, and in community mental health centers.

Many communities also have halfway houses that serve the alcoholic who is unable to live with family members but is not yet ready to live alone.

Most larger companies now sponsor alcohol treatment programs (as a component of Employee Assistance Programs, described in Chapter 11) for their employees. These programs seek to identify problem drinkers in their early stages and then intervene before severe problems arise. The problem drinkers are referred to appropriate community resources. If the employee uses such help, there are no adverse work consequences. Considerable pressure may be placed on the employee to participate, with the threat of eventual discharge

Therapy with a Heroin Addict

Tim Bliss, a drug counselor, describes the following efforts to treat an addict:

Many times the drug counselor feels he or she isn't making any progress in the recovery process of the heroin addict. Counseling the heroin addict takes a special type of counselor—one who can walk the walk and talk the talk so to speak. To counsel, first off, it takes an extreme amount of dedication, concentration, and effort.

The client I worked with was a 30-year-old black, married male with three children. The history was as follows. The client will be referred to as Bob. Bob was raised in an urban area; he was the middle child and seemingly led a normal childhood. As he reached his early teens, he got more and more involved with drinking and drugs. He graduated from high school and went into the army soon after graduation. This is where many problems arose. Bob had several bouts with the army ranging from insubordination to disorderly conduct. He started chipping [occasionally using] heroin and became quite involved in the drug culture overseas in Germany. He then married a white German woman and brought her back to the United States, where they have lived for the past 10 years. Bob then became involved in an armed robbery and claimed he was innocent; yet he spent three years in prison. After his prison time ended, Bob secured a job at a local factory; this lasted approximately one and one-half years at which time he was fired for excessive absenteeism. The excessive absenteeism was a result of episodic drinking and drug abuse.

Prior to Bob's going to prison, he was involved in the Black Panthers [a militant black separatist organization]. What was interesting was that he was married to a white, which had to be a conflict with Bob.

In general Bob seemingly had quite a conflict being black. He wanted at times to be white, and yet at other times wanted to be married to a black instead of a white.

Bob became increasingly involved with drugs, and in time developed a habit with heroin. This led to his involvement in both the criminal justice system and treatment.

Fortunately, there was a federal grant at this time that could divert criminal justice clients to alcohol or drug treatment centers. Bob became involved in a local alcohol treatment center while on probation. However, due to the fact that he was a heroin addict, treatment was ineffective. Within a very short period of time after discharge, Bob was back to "junk." He was then involved in another armed robbery and this time was facing 7 to 10 years for several counts of armed robbery and burglary. At this point I became involved with the client. Bob was out on bond and was awaiting his court date. Throughout this time period Bob was seen on an outpatient treatment basis. Urine drug screens were taken, and all turned up negative for opiates for about four weeks. Then Bob started chipping . . . heroin [again]. A therapeutic community which treated heroin addicts had been contacted to arrange an intake interview with Bob. The therapeutic community was a six- to nine-month intensive inpatient treatment program. Their philosophy was that the drug of choice was only a symptom and what needed to be changed was the lifestyle.

The court date was finally reached, and it was time for Bob to "face the music." The therapeutic community had interviewed Bob, and he was accepted into their program. I had arranged for a psychologist to run a series of tests on Bob to determine statistically his chances for succeeding in treatment. The results of this testing were that Bob would have one-third of a chance of succeeding in treatment, one-third not succeeding, and one-third of no change at all. Obviously statistics were against Bob, but in outpatient treatment he had demonstrated that he was sincere and did want to change. So with that, this counselor and Bob's probation officer felt treatment was the best alternative rather than incarceration. The presiding judge was approached with this alternative, and he accepted it. However, Bob was found guilty, so the judge imposed a stayed sentence of seven years to be served if Bob did not successfully complete treatment.

The following week Bob was transferred to the therapeutic community. He stayed there approximately six months, at which time the community voted that he be terminated, unsuccessfully completing treatment. Bob was voted out for a number of reasons: (1) he wasn't following instructions when reprimanded by staff, (2) overall he was an extremely bad influence on the rest of the community as he was always gaming people, not being able to be honest with himself or others, (3) he was breaking cardinal rules, which meant that when he would get angry other members of the community were actually afraid to be around him as they were afraid he might get physically violent. The incident that resulted in Bob's termination was that he was reprimanded for an incident that involved a female client. Supposedly Bob had intercourse with the female, and the female admitted this to staff in one of the community's "cop to" groups. (A "cop to" simply means people in the community who have done something wrong, or are feeling guilty, talk about it in one of these groups.)

The staff told Bob he was on a communication ban (no talking) the following day; they also requested he wear a five-foot sign with some writing on it. This kind of reprimand might seem ineffective or silly to some of us; however, it is quite effective in an atmosphere like a therapeutic community, especially on a long-term basis. Bob didn't follow through the next day, and a vote was taken; he was transferred to the county jail where he would await a decision by the probation officer, the judge, and the original referring agent.

We had decided Bob was still amenable to treatment. However, this would entail a more highly structured treatment environment, a facility that dealt more with the hard-core heroin addict.

Meanwhile Bob was becoming increasingly bitter sitting in jail thinking about what had occurred, and also becoming anxious due to the fact he was facing seven years in prison.

The probation officer and original treatment staff involved with Bob found a treatment facility that would be most favorable to any kind of successful treatment for Bob. The judge also went along with this.

Bob, after about two weeks of sitting in jail, was transferred on a Friday afternoon to this treatment facility. Friday evening he called his wife and absconded from treatment. He has not been heard of since, and consequently his probation has been revoked. When caught, he will be sent to prison.

I have heard unofficial reports that he is still around, back to heroin in his old way of life.

(continued)

CASE
EXAMPLE 8.3   *(continued)*

This is not a success story, obviously, but all too often that's all we ever hear. The field is challenging; however, this case history is also a real part of treatment, that oftentimes a therapist has to realize his or her own limitations and accept reality as it is. Not everyone is a success, and no matter what you do, you can't change that. All we can do is seek as much knowledge about the field as possible and utilize every tool available to motivate clients in changing their behavior. Only after this can we say "I gave it my best shot, and that's all there is."

Source: From "Drugs—Use, Abuse, and Treatment," by Tim Bliss in *Introduction to Social Welfare Institutions,* by Charles Zastrow, pp. 315–316. Copyright © 1978 by The Dorsey Press. Reprinted by permission of Brooks/Cole Publishing Company, a division of Thomson Publishing, Pacific Grove, CA 93950.

if she or he refuses help and continues to display lowered work productivity due to drinking.

Most therapists now believe that alcohol is used to meet some need—the need for socialization, relaxation, escape, and so on. If treatment is to be successful, it must provide alternatives for satisfying these needs: by helping the alcoholic to find a new circle of friends, to learn other ways to relax, to learn to handle life's problems better—whatever may be the unique needs of the drinker. This theory of *functional need equivalents* has been applied to addictions in addition to alcohol abuse.

Other Drug Treatment Programs

There is a stereotype that "once an addict, always an addict." This attitude has hampered efforts to rehabilitate those who are chemically dependent. Statistical evidence in the past tended to confirm this myth. More recent evidence, however, suggests that drug addicts *can* successfully kick their habits. Martin Kasindorf found, for example, that American soldiers addicted to heroin in Vietnam could successfully terminate use on returning home.[70]

Physical dependency on practically any drug can be ended with a detoxification program. Generally, the user will undergo some intense and highly painful withdrawal symptoms for the first few days or even for a few weeks. Psychological dependency is more difficult to end. Because drugs meet psychological needs, they are functional. Users receive certain psychic rewards (feelings of relaxation, euphoria, more alertness, less pain, escape from reality and problems). The psychological needs met by taking a drug are often unique to each user. To end the dependency, it is necessary for treatment programs to discover what psychological needs are being met for each user and then teach the user new (drug-free) ways to meet those needs.

INPATIENT PROGRAMS

Community mental health centers, specialized chemical abuse rehabilitation centers, and some medical hospitals provide inpatient treatment programs. Detoxification lasts from 24 hours to 3 weeks, depending on the severity of withdrawal. Additional inpatient care lasts 2 to 3 more weeks in a chemically free environment. Inpatient care is designed for those chemically dependent individuals who are unable to end the dependency while remaining in the community. Inpatient treatment is highly expensive; it may cost $10,000 or more for a 30-day stay.

OUTPATIENT PROGRAMS

Outpatient care, which is usually less intense than inpatient care, generally lasts 3 to 6 months. It is designed for people who no longer need inpatient care, as well as for those who have a good chance of terminating their habit without having to be hospitalized. Outpatient care consists of counseling, medical services, and vocational services. Such services are provided by community mental health centers, specialized rehabilitation centers for treating chemical abuse, medical hospitals, and outpatient clinics for chemical abuse.

SELF-HELP PROGRAMS

Modeled after Alcoholics Anonymous, there are many self-help programs for abusers. They include Narcotics Anonymous, Synanon, Potsmokers Anonymous, Pills Anonymous, Delancey Street Foundation, and Renaissance Project.[71]

THERAPEUTIC COMMUNITIES

These are long-term residential treatment programs, with patients usually staying from 12 to 18 months. Therapeutic communities emphasize making lifestyle changes so that the person will learn to find rewards for staying drug free and to function more appropriately in society. Tim Bliss further describes the focus:

> The environment is one of constant confrontation that aims at breaking down walls that cover up the real person. An individual might, for example, come on as a "tough guy" as a result of leading the street life. Actually, this image needs to be broken down. Feelings that are painful (for example, loneliness, fear, depression) are allowed to be expressed, eventually allowing the individual to be honest with himself or herself, and thus not needing to wear a mask.

> Many graduates of therapeutic communities remain in close contact for support purposes. It is difficult to measure the success of these programs because there is a high rate of dropouts. However, for those that graduate there is evidence they are successful in obtaining employment and remaining chemically free.[72]

HALFWAY HOUSES

Halfway houses assist those who have been hospitalized (and detoxified) to reenter the community at their own pace. They also serve those who are psychologically dependent and want to kick a habit but do not need to be hospitalized. Halfway houses provide counseling services (both one-to-one and group) to help residents remain drug free and work on resolving other personal problems they face. Residents also receive vocational training, assistance in finding a job, and room and board. Many halfway houses employ staff who were former addicts. Recovered drug abusers are often more effective than professional staff in relating to the residents and in breaking down the barriers of denial, anger, isolation, and hostility that addicts feel. Former addicts also provide a model, since they are evidence that addiction is a curable disease. Halfway houses emphasize the importance of residents' assuming responsibility for their actions and behaviors.

TREATMENT USING DRUGS

Analogous to the use of Antabuse with alcoholics (see Exhibit 8.7), some chemicals are used in therapeutic programs to treat certain drug addictions.

Methadone, which has received considerable publicity, is used to treat heroin addiction. Methadone is a synthetic narcotic and is sufficiently similar to heroin to satisfy the addict's physical craving. It prevents the anguish of heroin withdrawal symptoms but does not induce a high. Methadone thus allows a heroin addict to function fairly normally in a community. (It is usually not effective for heroin users who are unwilling to give up their "high.")

Methadone itself is addictive. Moreover, it does not cure addicts of their addiction to heroin. It simply *maintains* addicts in their communities without their having to use heroin. Methadone is controversial, and many authorities object to treating heroin addicts by making them dependent on another drug.

Methadone is available (legally) only through approved programs. In the first few weeks of treatment, addicts are usually required to report daily to the treatment center to receive their dose. As with any other drug that is in demand, an illicit market has developed in methadone. Some heroin addicts use methadone to tide them over when they cannot obtain heroin; others sometimes seek to treat themselves by taking methadone instead of heroin. As with heroin, an overdose of methadone can result in death.

EXHIBIT 8.7

Antabuse Treatment

Antabuse, developed in Copenhagen in 1947, is a drug that is useful for helping an alcoholic stay sober. When taken, it makes a patient's system react adversely to even small quantities of alcohol. Shortly after a person drinks an alcoholic beverage, Antabuse causes intense flushing, increased pulse rate, and nausea, often to the point of vomiting.

Before beginning treatment, the patient is detoxified. Then the drug is administered for several consecutive days, along with small doses of alcohol. The small amounts of alcohol are used to help the patient recognize the strong and uncomfortable effects that will occur while drinking.

Antabuse is not a cure-all for drinking because the reasons for drinking still remain. An alcoholic, if she or he chooses, can simply stop taking the drug and resume drinking. However, Antabuse is useful as part of a comprehensive treatment program involving counseling, vocational and social rehabilitation, and AA. By taking Antabuse, a person is forced to remain sober and is thereby more likely to respond to other therapies.

Scientists have also developed narcotic antagonists that prevent opiate (morphine and heroin) users from experiencing euphoria. Two of the best-known opiate antagonists are Naloxone and Cyclazocine. These drugs prevent addicts from feeling the euphoria they crave and thereby help motivated addicts to kick the habit.

Understanding and Treating Codependency

Codependent people are so trapped by a loved one's addiction that they lose their own identity in the process of obsessively managing the day-to-day trauma created by the addict. Codependency is unhealthy behavior learned amid chaos. Some codependents are as dysfunctional as the addict, if not more so. Living with addiction triggers excessive caregiving, suppression of one's own needs, feelings of low self-worth, and strained relationships.

Many codependents grow up in a dysfunctional family. (Some are adult children of alcoholics.) They marry or become romantically involved with someone who abuses alcohol or some other drug. To some extent, the addict fills the need of the codependent—to be a caregiver, to feel inferior, and so on. Codependency can thus be viewed as a normal reaction to abnormal stress.

The addict may terminate the use of his or her drug of choice, but the codependent's dysfunctional behaviors generally continue, unless he or she receives treatment. There are a variety of treatment approaches for codependents: individual psychotherapy, group therapy, and self-help groups (such as Al-Anon, Adult Children of Alcoholics, and Codependents Anonymous). For many codependents, treatment involves recognition that they have a life and an identity separate from the addict, that the addict alone is responsible for his or her substance abuse, and that their life and the addict's will improve by terminating their caregiving and enabling behaviors. Through treatment, many codependents regain (or gain for the first time) their own identity and banish the self-destructive habits that sabotage their happiness.

SUGGESTIONS FOR CURBING DRUG ABUSE IN THE FUTURE

It is, of course, important to treat current drug abusers. But perhaps it is even more important to prevent nonabusers from becoming abusers. This section discusses six preventative approaches: educational programs, prevention of illegal drug trafficking across borders, employee drug-testing programs, stricter laws and enforcement, decriminalization of drug use, and the British approach.

Teens address an anti-drug rally. D.A.R.E. is a police-sponsored program designed to educate elementary school children about drug abuse prevention.

Educational Programs

More programs are appearing that give students as well as the general public a realistic understanding of drug use and abuse. Quality programs teach (a) what effects commonly used drugs produce, (b) how to recognize signs of abuse, (c) how to responsibly decide when and when not to use drugs, (d) how to help someone who overdoses, (e) how to help friends and relatives who are abusing drugs, (f) what treatment resources and programs are available in the community, (g) what to do if you think you may have a drug problem, (h) what to do if a relative or friend refuses to acknowledge his or her drug problem, and (i) how to help abusers learn drug-free ways of meeting their psychological needs.

Educational programs in the past often used scare tactics such as showing pictures of fatal automobile crashes after drug use, suggesting that drug users end up on "skid row," and indicating that experimenting with small quantities of drugs would forever ruin the users' lives. Such tactics

are now viewed as ineffective. The young see their parents, other adults, and peers using drugs (particularly alcohol) without dire consequences (generally). These alarmist approaches wound up destroying the credibility of the educators.

Fortunately, books, curriculum guides for teachers, and audiovisual materials now available paint a more realistic picture of drug use and abuse.

In the past two decades, the mass media and the schools have launched major campaigns to prevent drunk driving, alcohol abuse, smoking, and illegal drug use. Extensive drug abuse prevention programs are now underway in elementary schools, middle schools, high schools, and colleges. These programs, which are tailored to the age level of the students at which they are targeted, include McGruff, the Crime Dog, at the kindergarten level; D.A.R.E. (Drug Abuse Resistance Education), a police-sponsored program, at the elementary school level; and various clubs, retreats, and lock-ins at middle and high school levels. They use a variety of approaches, including pointing out the risks of drug use, providing accurate information on drugs and their effects, offering instructions on how to assertively say "no" to peer pressure to use drugs, providing enjoyable drug-free activities, and enhancing students' self-esteem.

With drug and alcohol abuse increasingly portrayed in the media and in the schools as risky and dangerous rather than glamorous and fashionable, overall drug and alcohol use appears to be declining for adults.[73] It is highly unlikely that the United States will ever become drug-free. Certain drugs do have valid medical use. But the abuse of drugs can and should be curbed.

One reason why the United States has one of the highest rates of drug abuse in the world is the erroneous view that "there's a pill for everything." Americans tend to believe that medical technology can solve every ill the body encounters, and we use this belief to absolve ourselves of the responsibility of maintaining a healthy lifestyle. At the same time, the tendency to self-medicate is a common response when we feel worthless, "stressed out," or mistreated by society. In a culture where medication is so much the norm (a view that is boosted by advertising from the massive alcohol, pharmaceutical, and tobacco industries), it is easy to turn to drugs, alcohol, or tobacco as a way of relieving stress or forgetting about one's all-too-real problems. Public education is definitely needed to convey that drug use does not *solve* life's problems—it *intensifies* them.

Prevention of Illegal Drug Trafficking Across Borders

Small-time drug dealers often make enormous profits, middle-level dealers frequently become millionaires, and the top drug barons are billionaires. Clearly, illegal drug trade across borders of countries is a big, highly profitable endeavor. One way of combating the illegal drug trade is to take the kind of action that will put drug barons out of business.

The United States and other countries have spent millions of dollars trying to prevent illegal drugs from being smuggled across borders. A few

drug shipments are confiscated, and a few transporters of drugs are arrested. But drug barons are generally successful in finding increasingly creative ways to smuggle drugs across borders. If drug trafficking across borders is to be stopped, more effective steps need to be taken.

One way to combat drug trafficking across borders would be for all the countries of the world to agree among themselves to treat this activity as an international crime, indictable by international law.

An international court to administer this law could be established as a division of the United Nations. This court could have an investigative force with the authority to enter drug-producing countries to gather evidence against the drug barons who are masterminding the production, manufacture, and distribution of illegal drugs across borders. Countries would be expected to arrest and extradite for trial to this international court any individuals indicted for masterminding drug trafficking across borders. Those found guilty could be penalized with a life sentence, with no chance of parole. The United Nations could be empowered to impose trade sanctions against any country that refused to arrest and extradite indicted drug barons. (No country can survive today without international trade and finance.) In addition, armed forces of the United Nations could be made available to those governments that are too weak to combat the private armies employed by some of the notorious drug barons.

The U.S. government appears to be stepping up efforts to put drug barons in foreign countries out of business. The U.S. government has given financial and other assistance to other governments (such as in Mexico and in Colombia) to help in arresting and extraditing drug barons to this country to face drug trafficking charges.

Employee Drug-Testing Programs

In 1986 the President's Commission on Organized Crime recommended that both government and private industry launch drug-testing programs for employees. The commission asserted that such examinations would help curb a drug abuse epidemic that drains billions of dollars annually from American society and erodes the nation's quality of life.[74]

A number of major U.S. companies require applicants or employees to provide urine for an analysis that can detect the use of such drugs as cocaine, marijuana, heroin, and morphine. The tests are also given in the military, in a few sensitive federal agencies, and in many drug-treatment facilities. Local governments in many communities are now requiring random drug testing of employees in certain job categories, such as bus drivers.

Professional baseball, basketball, and football organizations also have drug-testing programs. For example, the National Football League requires all players to take a mandatory urine test prior to the start of the regular season and two unscheduled tests during the regular season. If a player tests positive, he is first required to receive treatment. If he relapses twice (as identified by three positive tests over a period of time), he is permanently banned from the league. The National Basketball Association and the National Football League have already banned several players for repeated drug violations.

Drug-testing programs are recommended in the interest of safety, health, and increased productivity. The programs are a clear signal that companies are serious about addressing the hazards caused by drugs. Employees who test positive are generally given an opportunity to enter treatment programs. If further drug tests reveal continued use of illegal drugs, the employee is usually discharged.

Opponents of drug testing assert that such programs violate civil liberties, including the Constitution's ban on unreasonable searches.[75]

Stricter Laws and Enforcement

It is clear from public opinion polls that the most popular approach to curbing drug abuse is enactment of stricter laws and more rigid enforcement of laws involving drug abuse. In the past two decades, a variety of such laws have been passed.

In 1984 federal legislation was enacted that placed considerable pressure on states to raise the minimum drinking age to 21 years; states that do not comply risk losing federal matching funds for highways. Most states have reduced the legal alcohol levels required for conviction of drunken driving and toughened penalties for driving while intoxicated. With regard to tobacco, most states have passed "clean indoor air" laws, requiring nonsmoking areas in restaurants and, in many cases, banning smoking entirely in public places. To combat illegal drugs, various state and local governments established a policy of confiscating property (such as cars or boats) used to carry or store drugs, even small amounts of marijuana for personal use. As we've seen, drug testing in the workplace is becoming more widespread.

Have these efforts worked? Drug, alcohol, and tobacco use appears to be declining in our society. But it's hard to tell how much of the current decline is due to stricter laws and enforcement and how much is due to increased awareness of the risks of drug and alcohol abuse and smoking.

Decriminalization of Drug Use

Over the past century, a number of laws have prohibited the use of a variety of drugs. Penalties for violators have become harsher. Yet the proportion of the population using drugs remains high, and jails and prisons are filled with people who have been arrested for drug law violations. Drug legislation makes possession of illegal drugs a crime with penalties in some cases equivalent to or in excess of those for such criminal acts as grand larceny and second-degree murder. In the past, states have sentenced people for up to 25 years—and even life—for selling or giving small quantities of marijuana to another person. Such harshness discredits the criminal justice system and contributes to disrespect for the law.

Until recently, drug legislation in this country has been designed to punish users rather than to treat abusers or to prevent use of drugs. Does it really do any good to arrest and jail (sometimes weekly) habitual drunks?

The public's general lack of accurate information about drugs has led to irrational fears about drug use and abuse. For example, there is the fear that use of marijuana will always be a stepping-stone to use of narcotic drugs. There are unwarranted fears about the negative effects of such drugs as heroin and opium. These irrational fears have led citizens to demand that harsh legislation be enacted to attempt to curb the use of drugs.

However, it is increasingly recognized that punitive legislation often does not work. Prohibition demonstrated that outlawing alcohol would not end its use. In an analogous vein, laws prohibiting the use of other drugs have been largely responsible for the enormous growth of organized crime and the illicit drug trade. Prison wardens cannot even keep drugs out of their own prisons.

A number of authorities are now urging that drug laws be revised to emphasize treatment rather than punishment of addicts and to make penalties for the possession of drugs more consistent with the actual dangers. It seems irrational to send to prison (at a huge expense to taxpayers) a person who possesses one joint of marijuana (a drug that may be less dangerous than alcohol).

Changes in certain drug laws in the past two decades are emphasizing rehabilitation and reducing harsh penalties for the sale and possession of certain drugs. Many of these revisions have centered on marijuana.

In 1972 the National Commission on Marijuana and Drug Abuse recommended changes in state and federal laws regarding marijuana. The commission urged that the private possession of marijuana for personal use and the distribution of small amounts without profit to the distributor no longer be considered offenses.[76] Since this 1972 report, a number of states have passed laws decriminalizing the use of marijuana.[77]

Laws have also been passed mandating that those arrested for public drunkenness receive treatment rather than simply being thrown into jail. In some areas of the country, individuals who acknowledge that they are addicted to a hard drug (such as heroin) are now given treatment without risking arrest or incarceration. Such programs are experimental and often controversial.

The Netherlands decriminalized drugs in 1976. Drug users and small-time dealers are not prosecuted, whereas large drug dealers and those who sell to minors are. Since 1976 the consumption rate of marijuana and hashish has declined, and the use of other drugs has not increased.[78] The Netherlands has fewer hard drug addicts than other Western European countries.[79] It has far less of a drug problem and a lower death rate due to drug overdose than the United States.[80] The Netherlands also has a very low incidence of AIDS among intravenous drug users.[81] It treats drug addiction as a health problem instead of a crime. This approach creates an atmosphere in which addicts can openly acknowledge their drug abuse and seek treatment for their addiction and associated health problems.

Whether the approach used in the Netherlands would work in this country is questionable. A value system has developed in the Netherlands that tolerates the moderate use of drugs and encourages those with a serious drug problem to seek treatment. There is a danger that decriminalizing illegal drugs in this country would lead to increased experimentation with hard-core drugs. If a value system that encourages drug abusers to seek treatment does not develop (as it has in the Netherlands), then there is an imminent danger that the use and abuse of drugs currently categorized as illegal will sharply increase.

The British Approach

As noted, the United States in the 20th century has primarily used a punitive approach with anyone found guilty of possessing or using prohibited drugs. In contrast, the British for many years have avoided labeling drug users as criminals and have viewed drug use as a disease that should be treated. Because of this rehabilitative emphasis, the British have formulated a very different set of laws and government policies to curb drug abuse. The British regard narcotic addicts as "sick" instead of "criminal." Rather than sending narcotic addicts to prison, they allow them to buy drugs at a low cost. If the addict cannot pay, she or he is given the drug free of charge. The system does not allow the addict to have an unlimited supply of narcotics. Extensive precautions are taken to carefully regulate the distribution of narcotic drugs.

The British program applies to heroin, morphine, and cocaine. (It does not involve marijuana, barbiturates, amphetamines, or hallucinogens.) To qualify, the narcotics user must demonstrate to a physician certified by the government that she or he is an addict. The person is then officially registered as an addict and receives a steady supply of the drug. The dosage is not enough to produce a "high" but is sufficient to prevent withdrawal symptoms. There is a central registry, so it is difficult for addicts to register with more than one clinic to obtain duplicate supplies. If a registered addict is discovered to be receiving a narcotic drug from more than one source, she or he is prosecuted. Anyone found possessing a narcotic who is not a registered addict is also prosecuted. Efforts are made to rehabilitate the addicts. For example, with heroin addicts the amount of heroin that is given is gradually decreased or the addicts are switched to methadone.

The British approach appears to be working well. The rate of addiction is far lower than in the United States, and the illicit market is far smaller and less profitable. British addicts don't require vast amounts of money to support their habits, and as a result they commit fewer property crimes. Organized crime has little profit incentive to smuggle narcotics into the country, so there are few narcotics available for nonaddicts to experiment with. Because the prescription drug is of uniform strength and is distributed in small dosages, narcotics overdosing is rare. The prescription drug does not contain impurities, thereby minimizing drug fatalities and other health hazards. In addition, a higher percentage of British addicts (compared to American addicts) are able to keep their jobs and be productive.[82]

Whether the British system would work in this country is questionable. The idea of giving heroin and other drugs to addicts runs counter to American values that people should not be drug dependent, that users should be punished to deter others, and that the government should not be involved in distributing potentially harmful drugs.

With organized crime's strong position in this country, there is also the danger that it could gain access to the government's supply of drugs and sell them to nonaddicts at inflated prices. However, because the British system is so successful, it certainly warrants careful consideration for adaptation here.

SUMMARY

A drug is any habit-forming substance that directly affects the central nervous system; it affects moods, perceptions, bodily functions, or consciousness. Drug abuse is the regular or excessive use of a drug when, as defined by a group, the consequences endanger relationships with others, are detrimental to a person's health, or jeopardize society itself. The dominant social reaction to a drug is influenced not only by the actual dangers of the drug but also by the social characteristics and motives of the groups that use it. Legal drugs are abused more often and cause more harm in our society than illegal drugs. Many drugs produce psychological or physical dependency (addiction) or both. Often users develop a tolerance for a drug, which means that they need steadily increasing dosages. Drug addiction is the intense craving for a drug that develops after a period of physical dependency from heavy use.

Social costs of drugs include property crime (generally committed to support a habit), automobile accidents, economic losses, health problems, disrespect for the law, family disruption, spouse and child abuse, financial crises for users, and adverse psychological effects on individuals.

Our society romanticizes and encourages the use of several drugs through commercials, films, books, and TV programs. Widely advertised drugs include alcohol, tobacco, caffeine, and over-the-counter drugs.

The most commonly used drugs include depressants (alcohol, barbiturates, tranquilizers, Quaalude, PCP), stimulants (caffeine, amphetamines, cocaine, crack, amyl nitrate, butyl nitrate), narcotics (opium, heroin, morphine), hallucinogens (peyote, psilocybin, psilocin, LSD), tobacco, marijuana, and anabolic steroids. Alcohol is by far the most widely abused drug in our society.

Treatment programs for drug abuse include inpatient and outpatient services provided by community mental health centers, some medical hospitals, and specialized chemical abuse rehabilitation centers. Additional programs include self-help groups, halfway houses, and therapeutic communities.

Drug abuse will probably never cease in this country, but the extent of the abuse can certainly be reduced. Punitive laws, as Prohibition demonstrated, do not deter drug use for many people and often encourage the development of organized crime and an illicit drug market. Suggestions for curbing abuse include expanding quality educational programs that give accurate information about drugs, indicting drug barons who mastermind the production and distribution of illegal drugs, using employee drug-testing programs, enacting stricter laws and increasing enforcement activity against violations involving drug abuse, and decriminalizing drug use to encourage a treatment approach rather than a punitive approach.

NOTES

1. *Webster's New Collegiate Dictionary* (Springfield, MA: Merriam-Webster, 1990).
2. William Kornblum and Joseph Julian, *Social Problems*, 8th ed. (Englewood Cliffs, NJ: Prentice Hall, 1995), p. 142.
3. Howard Abadinsky, *Drug Abuse: An Introduction* (Chicago: Nelson-Hall, 1989), pp. 90–97.
4. Ibid., pp. 54–58.
5. Ibid.
6. James W. Coleman and Donald R. Cressey, *Social Problems*, 5th ed. (New York: HarperCollins, 1993), p. 304.
7. Quoted in Earle F. Barcus and Susan M. Jankowski, "Drugs and the Mass Media," *The Annals of the American Academy of Political and Social Science*, 417 (1975), p. 89.
8. Ian Robertson, *Social Problems*, 2nd ed. (New York: Random House, 1980), p. 438.
9. Leon G. Hunt and Carl D. Chambers, *The Heroin Epidemics* (New York: Spectrum Books, 1976).
10. Alfred R. Lindesmith, *The Addict and the Law* (Bloomington: Indiana University Press, 1965), p. 228.
11. Joseph Gusfield, *Symbolic Crusade: Status Politics and the American Temperance Movement* (Urbana: University of Illinois Press, 1963).
12. Emile Durkheim, *Suicide: A Study in Sociology*, trans. John Spaulding and George Simpson (New York: Free Press, 1951).
13. Robert Merton, *Social Theory and Social Structure*, 2nd ed. (New York: Free Press, 1968).
14. See Charles H. Cooley, *Human Nature and the Social Order* (New York: Scribner's, 1902); Howard S. Becker, *Outsiders: Studies in the Sociology of Deviance* (New York: Free Press, 1963).
15. Edwin H. Sutherland and Donald R. Cressey, *Principles of Criminology*, 7th ed. (Philadelphia: Lippincott, 1966).
16. Kornblum and Julian, *Social Problems*, pp. 134–135.
17. Ibid.
18. Ibid.
19. For a review of these theories, see Abadinsky, *Drug Abuse: An Introduction*, pp. 111–136.
20. Howard S. Becker, "Becoming a Marijuana User," *American Journal of Sociology*, 59 (Nov. 1953), pp. 235–242.
21. Kornblum and Julian, *Social Problems*, p. 132.
22. "Why Liquor Is Quicker for Women," *U.S. News & World Report*, Jan. 22, 1990, p. 13.
23. The material in this section is summarized from studies that were reviewed in Kornblum and Julian, *Social Problems*, pp. 134–136.
24. Ibid., p. 135.
25. See David J. Armor, J. Michael Polich, and Harriet G. Stambul, *Alcoholism and Treatment* (New York: Wiley Interscience, 1978).
26. Kornblum and Julian, *Social Problems*, pp. 132–133.
27. Ibid., pp. 133–134.
28. Ibid., p. 136.
29. Ibid., p. 137.
30. Ibid.
31. John E. Farley, *American Social Problems*, 2nd ed. (Englewood Cliffs, NJ: Prentice Hall, 1992), p. 237.
32. Kornblum and Julian, *Social Problems*, p. 137.
33. Ibid.
34. Ibid.
35. Ibid., pp. 137–138.
36. Ibid., p. 138.
37. Sharon Wegscheider, *Another Chance: Hope and Health for the Alcoholic Family* (Palo Alto, CA: Science & Behavior Books, 1981).
38. Brenda C. Coleman, "Study Adds to Alcoholism Gene Theory," *Wisconsin State Journal*, Apr. 18, 1990, p. 1A.
39. Ibid.

40. Brenda C. Coleman, "Alcoholism Gene May Not Be Key," *Wisconsin State Journal,* Dec. 26, 1990, p. 3A.

41. Wayne W. Dunning and Dae H. Chang, "Drug Facts and Effects," in *The Personal Problem Solver,* Charles Zastrow and Dae H. Chang, eds. (Englewood Cliffs, NJ: Spectrum Books, 1977), p. 177.

42. John Timson, "Is Coffee Safe to Drink?" *Human Nature,* Dec. 1978, pp. 57–59.

43. Abadinsky, *Drug Abuse: An Introduction.*

44. Tony Blaze-Gosden, *Drug Abuse* (Birmingham, Great Britain: David & Charles Publishers, 1987), p. 99.

45. Abadinsky, *Drug Abuse: An Introduction.*

46. Blaze-Gosden, *Drug Abuse,* p. 95.

47. Abadinsky, *Drug Abuse: An Introduction,* pp. 90–97.

48. Ibid.

49. Ibid., pp. 14–22.

50. Robertson, *Social Problems,* p. 450.

51. Abadinsky, *Drug Abuse: An Introduction.*

52. Timothy Noah, "A Hit or a Miss for Mr. Butts?" *U.S. News & World Report,* Jun. 30, 1997, pp. 22–24.

53. Ibid., p. 22.

54. Ibid.

55. Ibid.

56. Ibid.

57. Ibid.

58. Lynn Rosellini, "Rebel with a Cause: Koop," *U.S. News & World Report,* May 30, 1988, pp. 55–63.

59. Noah, "A Hit or a Miss for Mr. Butts?"

60. "About Marijuana," *Hope Health Letter,* 14, no. 4 (Apr. 1991), p. 7.

61. John Kaplan, *Marijuana: A New Prohibition* (New York: World, 1970).

62. National Academy of Sciences, *Marijuana and Health* (Washington, DC: U.S. Government Printing Office, 1982).

63. Ibid.

64. Warren E. Leary, "Panel Recommends Marijuana Studies," *Wisconsin State Journal,* Feb. 21, 1997, p. 2A.

65. A. Toufexis, "Shortcut to the Rambo Look," *Time,* Jan. 30, 1989, p. 78.

66. Ibid.

67. Ibid.

68. Tim Bliss, "Drugs—Use, Abuse, and Treatment," in *Introduction to Social Welfare Institutions,* Charles Zastrow, ed. (Homewood, IL: Dorsey Press, 1978), p. 301.

69. Frank Riessman, "The 'Helper Therapy' Principle," *Journal of Social Work,* Apr. 1965, pp. 27–34.

70. Martin Kasindorf, "By the Time It Gets to Phoenix," *New York Times Magazine,* Oct. 26, 1975, p. 30.

71. For descriptions of these self-help groups, see Thomas J. Powell, *Self-Help Organizations and Professional Practice* (Silver Spring, MD: NASW, 1987).

72. Bliss, "Drugs—Use, Abuse, and Treatment," p. 314.

73. Kornblum and Julian, *Social Problems,* pp. 135–136.

74. "A Test-Tube War on Drugs?" *U.S. News & World Report,* Mar. 17, 1986, p. 8.

75. Alvin P. Sanoff, "Baseball's Drug Menace," *U.S. News & World Report,* Mar. 17, 1986, p. 57.

76. National Commission on Marijuana and Drug Abuse, *Drug Use in America: Problem in Perspective,* Second Report (Washington, DC: U.S. Government Printing Office, Mar. 1973).

77. Kornblum and Julian, *Social Problems,* pp. 152–154.

78. Thomas J. Sullivan, *Introduction to Social Problems,* 4th ed. (Needham Heights, MA: Allyn & Bacon, 1997), p. 386.

79. Ibid.

80. Ibid.

81. Ibid.

82. Ibid., p. 387.

CRIME, JUVENILE DELINQUENCY, AND CORRECTIONAL SERVICES

Being victimized by crime is the social problem that many Americans are most concerned about. Types of crimes include murder, battery, aggravated assault, burglary, theft, arson, forcible rape, drug trafficking, and white-collar crime. What can be done to prevent these and other offenses? This chapter will:

- Discuss the nature and extent of crime.
- Present crime causation theories.
- Describe types of crime.
- Describe the criminal justice system (the police, the courts, and the correctional system).
- Suggest ways to reduce crime and delinquency.
- Discuss the role of social work in providing correctional services.

NATURE AND EXTENT OF CRIME

What Is Crime?

A *crime* is simply an act committed or omitted in violation of a law. A *law* is a formal social rule that is enforced by a political authority. Usually the state (or the power elite that controls the state) specifies as crimes those acts that violate certain strongly held values and norms. Not all behaviors that violate norms are prohibited by law; in some cases, informal processes such as social disapproval regulate norm violations. For example, a swimmer's failure to aid a drowning person is not a criminal act, although it is usually considered morally wrong.

Norms and values change over time, and therefore so do laws. When norms change, there is often a time lag before laws based on the outdated norms are changed. Some areas still have obsolete laws that prohibit card playing on Sundays and sexual intercourse (even between married couples) in any position other than the missionary position. Certain norms and values differ among cultures and societies; therefore, so do laws. In many Arab countries, the use of alcohol is illegal but the use of marijuana is acceptable; in the United States the reverse is generally the law.

Everyone, at one time or another, has violated some law. Whether a violator becomes a convicted offender depends on a number of factors, including whether he or she is arrested, how forcefully the prosecuting attorney wants to present the case, how effective the defense attorney is, whether there are witnesses, and how the offender presents himself or herself in court.[1]

With thousands of laws on the books, police, prosecuting attorneys, and judges have considerable discretion over which laws to ignore, which to enforce, and how strongly to enforce them. This discretionary power offers many opportunities for criminal justice officials to choose whom to arrest and whom to release. The act of applying the law often involves issues of political power and favorable treatment for certain groups and classes. Because this power usually resides with the White middle and upper classes, the poor and minority groups are often (intentionally or unintentionally) treated more harshly. For example, authorities are substantially less vigorous in enforcing white-collar crime than they are in enforcing vagrancy laws in middle- and upper-class neighborhoods. (The middle- and upper-power structure generally seeks to enforce vagrancy laws "to keep bums and other undesirables off the streets, or at least out of respectable neighborhoods."[2])

How Extensive Is Crime?

Crime is one of the most serious problems facing our nation. Former President Richard Nixon on several occasions called crime our "number-one enemy" and remarked that "we must declare war against it." (Ironically, Nixon and many of his top administrative officials later faced criminal charges—with some imprisoned—in connection with the Watergate affair.*)

---

*The Watergate affair involved a break-in in the early 1970s at the Democratic National Committee headquarters (housed in the Watergate building in Washington, D.C.) by persons who were clandestinely employed to help reelect Nixon. Nixon and some of his top aides then committed a

TABLE 9.1

Number of Reported Serious Crimes, 1996

Crime	Number
Arson	(Statistics unavailable)
Murder	19,650
Forcible rape	95,770
Robbery	537,050
Aggravated assault	1,029,810
Burglary	2,501,500
Larceny-theft	7,894,600
Motor vehicle theft	1,395,200
Total	13,473,580

Source: Crime in the United States, 1996: Uniform Crime Reports (Washington, DC: U.S. Government Printing Office, 1997), p. 61.

EXHIBIT 9.1

Crime Clock: Frequency of Reported Crimes in the United States

Murder—one every 27 minutes
Forcible rape—one every 6 minutes
Robbery—one every 59 seconds
Aggravated assault—one every 31 seconds
Violent crime—one every 19 seconds
Motor vehicle theft—one every 23 seconds
Burglary—one every 13 seconds
Larceny-theft—one every 4 seconds
Property crime—one every 3 seconds

Source: Crime in the United States, 1996: Uniform Crime Reports (Washington, DC: U.S. Government Printing Office, 1997), p. 4.

The most comprehensive statistical summary of crime in the United States is the annual publication of the *Uniform Crime Reports* (UCR) by the FBI. This report lists the crimes and arrests in this country as reported by law enforcement agencies.

One part of this report is the Serious Crime Index, which is constructed to show the amount of, and trends in, serious crime. The Serious Crime Index is composed of four types of property crimes (burglary, larceny-theft, motor vehicle theft, and arson) and four types of crimes against people (willful homicide, forcible rape, aggravated assault, and robbery). Over 13 million Serious Crime Index offenses are reported to law enforcement agencies in the United States.[3] These offenses for 1996 are listed in Table 9.1.

It is generally agreed that serious violent crime has reached alarming proportions in the United States. Many Americans feel unsafe in their own neighborhood at night, and a high proportion own guns, largely for self-protection.[4] Exhibit 9.1 demonstrates graphically why people are so fearful today.

How does the crime rate in the United States compare to the rates in other countries? This question is difficult to answer for a couple of reasons. Different countries define their crimes in somewhat different ways—for example, prostitution is a crime in some countries but not in others. In addition, many other countries do not collect accurate statistics on the extent of crime in their homeland. There is, however, one crime that every country defines in the same way and for which they collect accurate data. That crime is murder.

The United States has by far the highest rate of murder of any industrialized nation. The murder rate in the United States is five times higher than in Canada and seven and one-half times higher than in Europe.[5] Coleman and Cressey give the following explanation for the high level of violence in the United States:

> *The high level of violence in America is often seen as a holdover from the rowdy days of frontier expansion. According to this view, violence became a way of life as an unending stream*

---

variety of offenses in an effort to cover up this break-in. Nixon was eventually forced to resign from the presidency after the coverup was revealed.

of settlers fought among themselves and with native peoples for land and profit. . . . Furthermore, America is an extremely wealthy nation, but, compared with other Western countries, it has a bigger gap between the rich and the poor and inferior welfare and social programs. Thus, those at the bottom of the social hierarchy tend to be more frustrated and desperate, and more resentful of those who possess the wealth they are denied.[6]

Who Is Arrested?

Those who are arrested for crimes are disproportionately likely to be males, young, members of a racial minority, and city residents.

Males are arrested about four times as often as females.[7] (Only in juvenile runaway and prostitution cases are females arrested more often.) There are two major reasons why males are more often arrested. One is sex-role socialization, which encourages males to be more aggressive and daring, whereas females are encouraged to be more passive and conforming to rules and norms. The second reason is the tendency of police officers and the courts to deal more leniently with female offenders.[8] However, in the past two decades, crime among females has been increasing faster than that among males,[9] which may be a negative side effect of women's challenging their traditional sex roles.

Young people appear to commit far more than their share of crime, including the crimes that are classified by the FBI as most serious—rape, murder, robbery, arson, burglary, aggravated assaults, auto theft, and larceny. In 1996, of all arrests 32% were under age 21 and 45% were under age 25.[10] A partial explanation of the high arrest rate among juveniles and young adults is that they may be less skillful than older adults in avoiding arrest. In addition, they tend to commit crimes (such as auto theft) that are highly visible to the police. Even when all these factors are taken into account, it is still the case that the young commit more crimes than the old.

There are differences in arrest rates among various racial and ethnic groups. Chinese Americans and Japanese Americans have the lowest ar-

rest rates in the country.[11] The arrest rate for African Americans is three times higher than for Whites.[12] One reason for this higher rate is that a higher proportion of the African American population is poor or unemployed, and there are high correlations between poverty (and unemployment) and the types of crime classified by the FBI as most serious. An additional reason for the higher arrest rate among certain minority groups may be racial prejudice. A number of studies have shown that the probability of arrest, prosecution, conviction, and incarceration for an offense decreases as the social status of the offender increases. In one study, judges were given fact sheets on a hypothetical case and asked to recommend an appropriate sentence. The fact sheets contained the following information:

> *"Joe Cut," 27, pleaded guilty to battery. He slashed his common-law wife on the arms with a switchblade. His record showed convictions for disturbing the peace, drunkenness, and hit-run driving. He told a probation officer that he acted in self-defense after his wife attacked him with a broom handle. The prosecutor recommended not more than five days in jail or a $100 fine.*[13]

Half the fact sheets identified "Joe Cut" as White, and the other half identified him as African American. The judges who thought he was White recommended a sentence of 3 to 10 days, whereas those who thought he was African American recommended a sentence of 5 to 30 days.

Kornblum and Julian describe another factor that contributes to higher arrest rates among African Americans:

> *Still another factor that is thought to contribute to high rates of crime among blacks is family disorganization, especially the rapid increase in the number of female-headed families. Such families lack male role models with legitimate jobs, leaving open the possibility that children will be influenced by others in the community, including individuals who engage in criminal activities.*[14]

A majority of reported crimes and reported arrests are in large cities, as compared to suburbs and rural areas.[15] Within large cities, crime tends to occur in sections that are changing rapidly and that have a high concentration of low-income and transient inhabitants. Arrest rates are substantially lower in more stable, higher-income, residential areas. Crime is lower in the suburbs than in the cities and lower still in the rural areas.[16]

How Accurate Are Official Crime Statistics?

As described earlier, the Federal Bureau of Investigation annually compiles the *Uniform Crime Report* (UCR), based on data from law enforcement agencies throughout the country on crimes committed and arrests made. The Serious Crime Index is a part of the UCR.

There are a number of problems connected with this index. Actual crime rates are substantially higher than the official rates. Kornblum and Julian estimate that crimes reported to the police account for about 33% of actual offenses and about 50% of violent crimes.[17] Victims often do not report crimes to the police because (among other reasons) they feel that nothing can be done.[18] As indicated in Exhibit 9.2, most crimes go unsolved.

The Serious Crime Index focuses on crimes that are more likely to be committed by people of lower social and economic status. It does not reflect the types of crimes typically committed by higher-income groups: fraud, false advertising, corporate price fixing, bribery, embezzlement, industrial pollution, tax evasion, and so on. If white-collar crimes were included in the Serious Crime Index, and if law enforcement authorities were more vigorous in enforcing such laws, the profile of a typical criminal would very likely be older, wealthier, whiter, and more suburban than suggested by the Serious Crime Index.

Self-report studies, in which respondents are asked anonymously the details of any crimes they may have committed, reveal that "close to 100 percent of all persons have committed some kind of offense, although few have been arrested."[19] In what way, then, do those who are arrested differ from those who are not? For one thing, those who are not caught tend to commit a crime only rarely,

EXHIBIT 9.2

Does Crime Pay? Quite Often!

Violent crimes include murder, rape, robbery, and aggravated assault. There are over 4 million violent crimes committed each year in the United States, but only a tiny fraction of criminals are put behind bars.

For every 100 violent crimes:

Only 42 are reported to police

Only 17 people are arrested

Only 5 people are convicted

Only 4 people are sent to prison/jail

Source: Ted Gest, "The Real Problems in American Justice," *U.S. News & World Report,* Oct. 9, 1995, pp. 54–55.

whereas those who are arrested tend to break the law more frequently. Perhaps a better explanation, however, lies in the types of crimes committed. Those arrested may be committing the kinds of crimes that are more strictly enforced by law enforcement agencies. The poor, for example, may be more likely to commit high-risk, low-yield crimes such as larceny, burglary, or robbery. In contrast, the wealthier are more likely to commit low-risk, high-yield crimes such as income tax evasion and false advertising.

In the past 20 years, there have been dramatic increases in the number of crimes committed as cited in the Serious Crime Index. Yet it is uncertain what this rate increase actually represents. Perhaps crime victims are reporting more offenses. Or perhaps the increase is due to improvements in police-reporting practices; police departments are increasingly using computers, clerical personnel, and statisticians to improve the accuracy of their reports.

Strictly speaking, the Serious Crime Index is not fully comparable among jurisdictions. At times it is even inconsistent from one year to the next within the same reporting unit. A major reason for this difficulty is that each of the 50 states has its own unique criminal code. For example, an offense that is classified as burglary in one state may be classified as larceny or robbery in another; what is classified as sexual assault in one state may be considered a less serious offense in another. Because states occasionally make changes in their criminal codes, inconsistencies may arise from one year to the next within the same reporting unit because of changes in definitions of offenses. Furthermore, individual officers interpret the law differently as they carry out their duties.

Finally, crime statistics are at times manipulated by the police and public officials. Data may be skewed to show higher rates of crime, perhaps to help document the need for a federal or state grant or to politick for a budget increase in personnel or facilities. More often than not, however, police and public officials are under considerable pressure to keep the crime rate low. By manipulating statistics, they can reclassify certain serious crimes into different, less serious categories.

In summary, the Serious Crime Index of the FBI provides an indication of the rates and trends of certain crimes in the United States. Yet these statistics overlook white-collar crime, are affected by police-reporting practices, and must be viewed against the fact that many crimes are unreported. It further appears that the poor, the undereducated, and minorities have been the victims not only of selective law enforcement but also of misleading statistics on crime. Some sociologists have contended that, because higher-income classes are far more involved in white-collar crime (which is often ignored by law enforcement agencies), they may actually have a higher rate of crime than the lower classes.[20]

CRIME CAUSATION THEORIES

A variety of theories about the causes of crime have been advanced by several disciplines. Space limitations permit only a summary of the more promi-

EXHIBIT 9.3

Prominent Theories of Crime

Theory	Approximate Date of Origin
Early theories	
Demonology	Nonliterate societies
Classical/Neoclassical	1775
Marxist–Leninist	1850
Physical and mental trait theories	
Phrenology	1825
Lombrosian	1900
Mental deficiency	1900
Morphological	1920
Psychological theories	
Psychoanalytic	1900
Psychodynamic problem solving	1920
Frustration-aggression	1950
Self-talk	1975
Sociological theories	
Labeling	1900
Differential association	1939
Societal control	1950
Deviant subcultures	1955
Anomie	1957
Critical	1995

nent theories. Exhibit 9.3 identifies these prominent theories along with their approximate dates of origin. As you read about each of these theories, ask yourself the following questions: Is this theory helpful in explaining why a person committed a rape (or burglary, murder, drug-trafficking offense, aggravated assault, kidnapping, embezzlement, and so on)? Is the theory useful in suggesting a correctional plan to prevent a recurrence of the offense?

Early Theories

Three of the earliest theories on the causes of crime were *demonology,* the *classical/neoclassical theory,* and the *Marxist–Leninist theory.*

DEMONOLOGY

For centuries many nonliterate societies conceived of crime as caused by evil spirits. This belief is commonly referred to as *demonology.* It was thought that those who engaged in deviant behavior were possessed by the devil. The only way to cure the criminal act was to remove the evil spirit through prayer, through a ritual, or by torture (sometimes to the point of death). This theory is no longer prominent, partly because scientific study has found no evidence that lawbreakers are possessed by evil spirits. Remnants of the theory remain, however, as seen in satanic cults, rock lyrics with satanic themes, and movies (such as *Friday the 13th* and *The Exorcist*) depicting people possessed by demons.

CLASSICAL AND NEOCLASSICAL THEORY

The classical and neoclassical schools were based on hedonistic psychology. Classical theory asserted that a person makes a decision about whether to engage in criminal activity based on the anticipated balance of pleasure and pain. Each individual was assumed to have a free will and to act solely on the basis of the anticipated hedonistic calculations. Advocates of this school considered this to be a full and exhaustive explanation of causality. Applied to corrections, this approach urged that clear-cut punishments be assigned to each offense so the prospective offender could calculate anticipated pleasures and pains. The penalties assigned were to be slightly more severe than anticipated pleasures to discourage criminal activity. The neoclassical school accepted the basic notion of hedonistic calculations but urged that children and "lunatics" be exempt from punishment because of their inability to calculate pleasures and pain responsibly. Judicial discre-

tion was also urged for certain mitigating circumstances (for example, an offense now referred to as involuntary manslaughter).

Although correctional systems in the 19th century were based primarily on the neoclassical approach, classical/neoclassical theory has waned in popularity. Some elements of it can still be found in our legal/judicial system—particularly the emphasis on using punishment to deter crime. The theory has been severely criticized because it does not allow for other causes of crime and because the punitive approach it advocates has not been very successful in curbing further criminal activity. In addition, hedonistic psychology ignores the fact that much human behavior is determined by values and morals rather than by the pleasure-versus-pain calculation.

MARXIST–LENINIST THEORY

Marxist–Leninist theory assumes that all crime results from the exploitation of workers and from intense competition among people. Crime disappears, according to neo-Marxists, when society achieves a "classless" status. The basic tenet of communism is, "From each according to his ability, to each according to his need." Socialist countries (such as Cuba and North Korea) have in the past sought to formulate their societies on the principles advocated by Karl Marx. Class differentials are much less prominent in socialist countries as compared to capitalist nations.

Although Marx asserted that crime would be sharply reduced in socialist countries because there would be less class conflict, substantial criminal activity does occur in these countries. (The extensiveness of criminal activity is difficult to determine because these countries publish almost no crime-rate reports.) The continued existence of crime in socialist countries is not taken by socialists as evidence that the theory is defective; rather, it is explained as being the result of old capitalistic traditions and ideologies and the imperfect application of Marxist theory. (Many socialist countries in recent years have been discarding Marxist principles and are moving toward incorporating capitalistic incentives into their economies.)

Physical and Mental Trait Theories

You may have noticed in Exhibit 9.3 that the first "physical and mental trait theory," *phrenology*, actually originated before Marxist–Leninist theory. Although it falls chronologically into the category of "early theories," it is more closely related to "trait theories" and will be discussed in this section along with three other trait theories: the *Lombrosian*, the *mental deficiency*, and the *morphological* theories.

PHRENOLOGY

Phrenology was popular until the turn of the 20th century. Phrenologists maintained that criminal behavior was related to the size and shape of the human skull. They closely scrutinized the grooves, ridges, and number of bumps on a skull. The shape of the brain, which was influenced by the shape of the skull, was thought to be sufficient to predict criminal activity. Although there were isolated incidents in which offenders with "criminal prone" skulls were treated more harshly than other offenders, this approach was not widely incorporated into correctional systems. Scientific studies have found no evidence of correlations between criminal behavior and the shape of the skull.

LOMBROSIAN THEORY

Around the beginning of the 20th century, biological/constitutional theories were popular. The prototype of such theories was Cesare Lombroso's theory of the "born criminal." This school maintained that a criminal inherits certain physical abnormalities or stigmata, such as a scanty beard, low sensitivity to pain, distorted nose, large lips, or long arms. The more such stigmata a person had, the more he or she was thought to be predisposed to a criminal career. People with several stigmata were thought to be unable to refrain from criminal activity unless their social environment was unusually favorable. The theory that criminals have distinct physical characteristics was refuted by Charles Goring, who found no significant physical differences in a study comparing several thousand criminals with several thousand noncriminals.[21]

MENTAL DEFICIENCY THEORY

The mental deficiency theory replaced the Lombrosian school when the latter fell into disrepute. Mental deficiency theory asserted that criminal behavior resulted from "feeblemindedness," which was alleged to impair the capacity to acquire morality and self-control or to appreciate the meaning of laws. As mental tests became standardized and widely used, it was discovered that many criminals achieved average or above-average intelligence scores. The theory waned in popularity in the 1930s. Neither the Lombrosian nor the mental deficiency approach had a lasting, significant effect on corrections.

MORPHOLOGICAL THEORY

Closely related to the mental deficiency and Lombrosian theories is morphological theory, which asserted that there is a fundamental relationship between psychological makeup and physical structure. The most popular variant of this theory was William Sheldon's, developed in the 1940s. Sheldon described three body categories: endomorph (obese), mesomorph (muscular), and ectomorph (lean). To the mesomorph he ascribed an unusual propensity to criminal activity. Sheldon did not assert that mesomorphs were inherently criminally prone. Rather, he asserted that this physique was associated with a distinctive type of temperament, characterized by such traits as love of physical adventure, abundance of restless energy, and enjoyment of exercise. Mesomorphy thus produced energetic, aggressive, and daring types of individuals, such as generals, athletes, and politicians, as well as criminals. Morphological approaches like Sheldon's are still popular in southern European and South American countries. Scientific studies, however, have found little evidence that muscular people are more likely to commit crimes than people who are lean or overweight.

Psychological Theories

Psychological theories about crime attribute its causes to the criminal's thought processes, which are seen as relatively unrelated to overall societal conditions. These theories include the *psychoanalytic, psychodynamic problem-solving, frustration-aggression,* and *self-talk* approaches to understanding criminal behavior.

PSYCHOANALYTIC THEORY

Psychoanalytic theory is not a single coherent theory but a variety of hypotheses developed by psychoanalysts since the turn of the 20th century from the pioneering work of Sigmund Freud. Generally, these theories postulated that delinquent behavior results when the restraining forces in the superego (one's conscience and self-ideal) and the ego (mediator among the superego, the id, and reality) are too weak to curb the instinctual, antisocial pressures from the id (source of psychic energy). Human nature was seen as largely determined by id instincts, which were basically antisocial and immoral in character. This theory postulated that current behavior was largely controlled by early childhood experiences. Deviant behavior was viewed as stemming from unconscious conflicts, fixations, and repressed traumatic experiences.

The psychiatric school, of which psychoanalysis is a large component, has had a significant influence on corrections because it asserts that some offenders commit illegal acts because they are insane. Criminal justice systems frequently call on psychiatrists to determine the "sanity" of accused offenders. If someone is judged by the court to be "innocent by reason of insanity," he or she is sent to a mental hospital, instead of to a jail, to recuperate.

Psychiatry has also classified individuals into numerous categories in terms of their "mental" functioning. One category, *sociopath,* has had considerable relevancy for corrections. A sociopath is a person who is thought to have no moral constraints against engaging in criminal activity, doing so whenever it is personally advantageous, even though others may be hurt.

Since 1950, Thomas Szasz and others have seriously questioned the medical-model approach to emotional problems and have asserted that mental illness is a myth.[22] Szasz believes that people have emotional problems, but not a "disease of the mind," as implied by the medical model (see Chapter 5). Courts, however, continue to use the mental-illness model.

Psychoanalytic theory is increasingly falling into disfavor. One reason is the finding that people with emotional problems who undergo psychoanalysis are no more likely to improve than a comparable group who receives no therapy.[23]

PSYCHODYNAMIC PROBLEM-SOLVING THEORY

Psychodynamic problem-solving theory views deviant behavior as contrived by the personality as a way of dealing with some adjustment problem. The problem is generally perceived as a conflict among various ingredients of the personality: wishes, drives, fears, strivings, loyalties, codes of ethics, and so on. Situational factors are generally deemphasized.

A serious shortcoming of the theory is that it is often extremely difficult (if not impossible) to determine precisely which wishes, drives, fears, or ethics motivated someone to commit a crime. For example, the following internal desires have all been advanced as motivations for committing rape: unfulfilled sexual desires, a desire for violence, and feelings of inferiority. All are theorized to be temporarily alleviated during rape as the offender feels a sense of power and superiority. When a sexual assault occurs, it is nearly impossible to determine the extent to which each of these internal desires contributed to the assault. Frequently, when using this theory, only speculations can be made about why a crime occurred, as few "tools" exist to check the accuracy of the speculations.

FRUSTRATION-AGGRESSION THEORY

Frustration-aggression theory asserts that frustration often provokes an aggressive response. Thus, violence is seen as a way to release the tension produced by a frustrating situation. An unemployed husband, unable to pay the bills or find a job, for example, may beat his wife. Some authorities viewed the burning and rioting in our inner cities in the 1960s as a reaction by African Americans to the frustration of living in a society that promises equality but does not provide it.

| CASE EXAMPLE 9.1 | Self-Talk Theory: A Presidential Assassination Attempt |

On March 30, 1981, President Ronald Reagan was shot in Washington, D.C., by a .22-caliber bullet, which pierced the left side of his chest and collapsed his left lung. Also injured was a secret service agent, a Washington policeman, and White House press secretary James Brady. Fortunately, all four men survived. Arrested for this assassination attempt was John W. Hinckley, Jr., 25, the son of a multimillionaire Colorado oil executive.

Born into wealth, John Hinckley has been described as a loner and a drifter, a misfit who craved fame. In high school, Hinckley was an average student but had few friends. He went to college for 7 years off and on but never graduated. His father was a self-made millionaire, and his brother was vice president of his father's firm. His family members were known as strong Reagan supporters.

John Hinckley became infatuated with actress Jodie Foster, although they had never met. In the film *Taxi Driver*, Jodie Foster played a teenage prostitute. The film was about a disturbed loser (played by Robert DeNiro) who stalks a political figure. This film appears to have influenced Hinckley's assassination attempt, as he wrote in an unmailed letter to Ms. Foster:

> I would abandon this idea of getting Reagan in a second if I could only win your heart and live out the rest of my life with you, whether it be in total obscurity or whatever. I will admit to you that the reason I'm going ahead with this attempt now is because I just cannot wait any longer to impress you. . . .
>
> Jodie, I'm asking you to please look into your heart and at least give me the chance with this historical deed to gain your respect and love.[a]

Apparently, John Hinckley shot the president because he believed that such an action would impress Jodie Foster and lead to a relationship with her.

When attorneys, judges, police officers, and other criminal justice officials search for the motive for an offender committing a crime, they are really searching to identify the cognitions (that is, the self-talk) that led the offender to commit a crime.

[a]John S. Lang, "John Hinckley—A Misfit Who Craved Fame," *U.S. News & World Report*, Apr. 13, 1981, p. 26.

Frustration-aggression theory provides an explanation for only violent crimes. It does not attempt to explain other kinds of criminal behavior, such as prostitution, fraud, and forgery.

SELF-TALK THEORY

Self-talk theory is a psychological approach for identifying the underlying motives for committing a crime.[24] According to this theory, the reasons for any criminal act can be determined by examining what the offender was thinking prior to and dur-

ing the time the crime was committed (see Case Example 9.1). A shortcoming of the theory is that, when offenders discuss what they were thinking during a crime, they often seek to slant what they reveal in a socially acceptable way.

Sociological Theories

Sociological theories focus on societal factors that influence people to commit crimes. For ease in understanding these theories, we will examine them out of chronological order (see Exhibit 9.3) as follows: *differential association theory, anomie theory, deviant subcultures theory, societal control theory, labeling theory,* and *critical theory.*

DIFFERENTIAL ASSOCIATION THEORY

Edwin Sutherland, perhaps the best-known criminologist in contemporary sociology, advanced his famous theory of differential association in 1939. The theory asserts that criminal behavior is the result of a learning process that primarily occurs in small, intimate groups—family, neighborhood peer groups, friends, and so on. In essence, "A person becomes delinquent because of the excess of definitions favorable to violation of law over definitions unfavorable to violation of law."[25] Whether a person decides to commit a crime is based on the nature of present and past associations with significant others. People internalize the values of the surrounding culture. When the environment includes frequent contact with criminal elements and infrequent contact with noncriminal elements, a person is likely to engage in delinquent or criminal activity.

Past and present learning experiences in intimate personal groups thus define whether a person should violate laws; for those deciding to commit crimes, the learning experiences also include the choice of which crimes to commit, the techniques of committing these crimes, and the attitudes and rationalizations for committing these crimes. Thus, a youth whose most admired person is a member of a gang involved in burglaries or drug trafficking will seek to emulate this model, will receive instruction in committing these crimes from the gang members, and will also receive approval from the gang for successfully committing these crimes.

The theory does little to explain such crimes as arson and embezzlement, in which the offender often has no exposure to others who have committed such crimes.

ANOMIE THEORY

Robert Merton applied anomie theory to crime.[26] This approach views criminal behavior as resulting when an individual is prevented from achieving high-status goals in a society. Merton begins by noting that every society has both approved goals (for example, wealth and material possessions) and approved means for attaining these goals. When certain members of society share these goals but have insufficient access to approved means for attaining them, a state of anomie results. (Anomie is a condition in which acceptance of the approved standards of conduct is weakened.) Unable to achieve the goals through society's legitimately defined channels, they then seek to achieve them through illegal means.

Merton asserts that higher crime rates are likely to occur among groups that are discriminated against (that is, groups that face additional barriers to achieving the high-status goals). These groups include the poor and racial minorities. Societies with high crime rates (such as the United States) differ from those with low crime rates because, according to Merton, they tell all their citizens they can achieve, but in fact they block achievement for some people.

Anomie theory has difficulty explaining why white-collar crime (which is committed primarily by individuals who are seldom discriminated against) is perhaps the most common type of crime committed in this country.[27]

DEVIANT SUBCULTURES THEORY

Deviant subcultures theory is another explanation for crime. This theory asserts that some groups develop their own attitudes, values, and perspectives, which support criminal activity. Walter Miller, for example, argues that American lower-class culture is more conducive to crime than middle-class culture.[28] He asserts that lower-class culture is organized around six values—trouble, toughness, excitement, fate, smartness (ability to con others), and autonomy—and allegiance to these values produces delinquency. Miller concludes the entire lower-class subculture is deviant in the sense that any male growing up in it will accept these values and almost certainly violate the law.

Albert Cohen advanced another subculture theory.[29] He contended that gangs develop a delinquent subculture that offers solutions to the problems of young male gang members. A gang gives them the chance to belong, to amount to something, to develop their masculinity, and to fight

A new member of a female street gang in East Los Angeles undergoes a violent initiation into the group. According to one theory, gangs develop delinquent subcultures that solve the status problems of working-class adolescents, especially those rejected by middle-class society.

middle-class society. In particular, the delinquent subculture, according to Cohen, can effectively solve the status problems of working-class boys, especially those who are rejected by middle-class society. Cohen contends that the main problems of working-class boys revolve around status.

As with the previous theories, deviant subculture theories are unable to explain white-collar crime and other crimes committed by the middle and upper classes.

SOCIETAL CONTROL THEORY

Control theories ask the question, "Why do people *not* commit crimes?" Theories in this category assume that all of us would "naturally" commit crimes and therefore must be constrained and

controlled by society from breaking the law. Control theorists have identified three factors for preventing crime. One is the internal controls that build up through the process of socialization; a strong conscience and a sense of personal morality prevent most people from breaking the law. A second factor is a strong attachment to small social groups (for example, the family), which is thought to prevent individuals from breaking the law because they fear rejection and disapproval from the people who are important to them. A third factor (taken from the classical school) is that people do not break the law because they fear arrest and incarceration.

Control theories assume that basic human nature is asocial or evil. Such an assumption has

CASE EXAMPLE 9.2   The Saints and the Roughnecks: A Study Showing the Effects of Labeling and of Expectations of Significant Others

William Chambliss, in a dramatic study, examined factors affecting delinquency within two groups of adolescents at the same high school. One group was composed of middle- and upper-class boys (the Saints), and the other was composed of lower-class boys (the Roughnecks). The Saints were often truant from school, harassed citizens and the police, openly cheated on exams, vandalized homes, drank excessively, and drove recklessly. Teachers, school officials, and the police largely ignored their acts because they were viewed as basically good boys. They were almost never arrested by the police, and hardly anything negative appeared in their school records. These youths were regarded as harmless pranksters, were allowed to "sow their wild oats," and were expected to succeed in life. Interestingly, the success expectations appeared to be a major factor in determining their futures; practically all of the Saints went on to college and white-collar careers.

On the other hand, the Roughnecks, who committed fewer, although similar, offenses, were labeled "deviants." Because they didn't have cars as the Saints did, the Roughnecks were confined to an area where they were more easily recognized and substantially more often arrested. The police and school officials expected that they would fail—and they did. These "delinquents" did poorly in school and went on to low-status jobs or criminal careers.

One additional factor that led to fewer arrests for the Saints was their apologetic nature whenever they were stopped by a police officer. They were polite and penitent and pled for mercy when stopped. In contrast, there was a high level of dislike and distrust between the police and the Roughnecks. When stopped by police, they came across as "tough" kids who displayed disdain and hostility—and as a consequence were more frequently arrested.

This study of the Saints and Roughnecks demonstrates that both labeling and the expectations of significant others can have a substantial effect on behavior.

Source: William Chambliss, "The Saints and the Roughnecks," *Society,* 2, no. 11 (Nov.–Dec. 1973), pp. 24–31.

---

never been proved. Theories that perceive humans as having an evil nature are unable to explain altruistic and other "good" deeds performed by people.

LABELING THEORY

Labeling theorists, similar to differential association theorists, assert that criminals *learn* to break the law. Labeling theory focuses on the process of branding people as criminals and on the effects of such labeling. Contrary to control theory, this theory holds that labeling a person as a delinquent or a criminal encourages rather than discourages criminal behavior.

Charles Cooley developed a labeling theory with his "looking glass self-concept."[30] This theory argues that people develop their self-concept (sense of who and what they are) in terms of how others relate to them, as if others were a looking glass or mirror. For example, if a neighborhood identifies a young boy as a "troublemaker" or "delinquent," neighbors are likely to relate to the youth as if he were not to be trusted. They may accuse him of delinquent acts, and they will label his semidelinquent and aggressive behavior "delinquent." This labeling process also results in a type of prestige and status for the boy, at least from his peers. In the absence of objective ways to gauge whether he is, in fact, a "delinquent," the youth will rely on the subjective evaluations of others. Thus, gradually, as he is related to as a "delinquent," he begins to perceive himself in that way and enacts the delinquent role.

Labeling theory is unable to explain why some offenders stop committing crimes after being arrested and convicted.

CRITICAL THEORY

This theory argues that the capitalist economic system is the root cause of our crime problem. Supporters of this theory assert that capitalism fosters crime by encouraging, and even requiring, the exploitation of one group by another and by promoting the selfish quest for personal gain as if it were the inevitable goal of all human behavior.[31] (Readers will note the similarities of this theory to Marxist–Leninist theory, which was described earlier.) Critical theory fails to explain why crime occurs in communist societies, which do not have a capitalist economic system.

Usefulness of Theories

These theories identify some of the reasons why crime occurs, especially why crime rates are higher within some groups than within others. One of the most important questions in criminology is, "Do these theories identify the reasons why an offender committed a specific crime (for example, an aggravated rape)?" The answer, unfortunately, is that most theories are not very useful in identifying the causes for specific crimes. Also, they are not very useful in explaining why one individual commits forgery, another commits rape, and yet another burglarizes someone. Without knowing why a crime occurs, it is extremely difficult to develop an effective rehabilitation approach to curb repeat offenders.

Theories that attempt to explain all types of crime have a built-in limitation. Crime is a comprehensive label covering a wide range of offenses, including purse snatching, auto theft, rape, check forgery, prostitution, drunkenness, possession of narcotics, and sexual exhibition. Obviously, because the natures of these crimes vary widely, the motives or causes underlying each must vary widely. Therefore, it is unlikely that any theory can adequately explain the causes of all crimes. It may be more productive to focus on developing more limited theories that attempt to identify the causes of specific offenses (for example, drunkenness, incest, auto theft, rape, or fraud) rather than to develop additional comprehensive theories.

Now let's take a detailed look at specific types of criminal offenses.

TYPES OF CRIME

We tend to think that crime is a well-defined phenomenon and to have stereotyped views about who criminals are. Actually, criminal offenses and the characteristics of lawbreakers are almost as varied as noncriminal offenses and law abiders. Many diverse forms of behaviors are classified as crimes, with the only major common thread being a violation of a criminal statute. Because it is impossible to look at all crimes, we will examine the more important ones. Keep in mind that the following categories are not mutually exclusive.

Organized Crime

Organized crime is a large-scale operation. Illegal activities are carried out as part of a well-designed plan developed by a large organization seeking to maximize its overall profit. Activities that lend themselves to organized crime include illegal gambling, drug dealing, fencing (receiving and selling stolen goods), prostitution, bootlegging, and extortion (in the form of selling protection). Large-scale operations are more cost efficient than small-scale operations in certain illegal activities. For example, in drug trafficking, drugs are smuggled into a country and distributed on a large scale, with corrupt officials paid off to reduce the risks of arrest and prosecution.

It appears the most organized crime efforts start on a small scale, generally with one small organization that carries on a particular crime, such as extortion or gambling. The group then expands to control this activity within a given neighborhood or city by absorbing or destroying the competition. Eventually the organization expands its activities into other crimes and begins to operate in larger regions or even nationwide.

A major characteristic of organized crime is that many of its activities are not predatory (such as robbery, which takes from its victims). Instead, organized crime generally seeks to provide to the public desired goods and services that cannot be obtained legally (drugs, gambling, prostitution, loan money). For its success, organized crime relies on public demand for illegal services.

Because of the obvious emphasis on secrecy in organized crime, only limited information is available about the extent of offenses, the leaders and members of organized crime, or the nature of the internal organization.

Organized crime in the United States is thought to revolve primarily around the Mafia (also called the Cosa Nostra). Its leadership is Italian American, with the lower ranks drawn from a variety of other ethnic groups. The Mafia developed largely during the 1920s and 1930s, when criminal groups organized to supply illegal alcohol during Prohibition. It has grown into a loose network of American regional syndicates or groups. These syndicates coordinate their efforts through a "commission" composed of the heads of the most powerful "families."[32] At the head of each family is a "don," who has absolute authority over the family unless overruled by the commission. Each don is assisted by an underboss and a counselor. Next in the hierarchy are "lieutenants," each of whom supervises a group of "soldiers" who are involved in illegal enterprises. Contrary to public opinion, the Mafia is not an international syndicate of Sicilian lawbreakers; rather, it is a network of syndicates that were developed and organized in this country. The *Godfather* books and films paint a fairly realistic picture of the structure and operations of organized crime.

The costs to society and to our economy from organized crime are enormous. Through gambling and drug traffic, the lives of many individuals and their families are traumatized. Labor racketeering and infiltration of legitimate businesses lead to higher prices for goods, lower-quality products, the forced closing of some businesses, the establishment of monopolies, the unemployment of workers, misuse of pension and welfare benefits, and higher taxes. Through corruption of public officials (a necessary component of many illegal ventures), organized crime leads to public cynicism about the honesty of politicians and the democratic process. It also leads to higher taxes and mismanagement of public funds.

In the 1980s and 1990s, the FBI made immense progress in its battle against organized crime. The heads of many of the nation's Mafia families were indicted, convicted, and incarcerated. In addition, thousands of organized crime members were arrested and convicted of a variety of offenses. Experts credit this breakthrough to a number of factors. The FBI now devotes a significant proportion of its workforce to combating organized crime[33] and has been making increased use of electronic eavesdropping. The FBI also is working more closely with state law enforcement authorities and with Italy to curb organized crime. Recently law enforcement agencies have been successful in getting large numbers of gang members to violate the traditional code of *omertà*—conspiracy of silence. Fearing lengthy stays in prison, where they could be vulnerable to mob-ordered murders, many underworld figures are joining a witness-protection effort that provides informants with new identities (including fake biographies) and homes in a different area of the country.

Despite these efforts, no one sees an end to the mob's influence anytime soon. Many of the old leaders are being replaced by a "new breed" of leadership, who have a greater familiarity with the world of high finance and legitimate business. Organized crime is developing new marketplace scams, including counterfeiting consumer credit cards and airline tickets, bootlegging gasoline (thereby avoiding payment of federal and state gasoline taxes), and selling fraudulent tax shelters.[34] In addition, new organizations unassociated with the Mafia are emerging to import and distribute illegal drugs.[35]

Let's examine the major crime efforts: gambling, drug trafficking, loan sharking, infiltrating legitimate businesses, labor racketeering, and prostitution.

GAMBLING

Illegal gambling takes place on a wide scale and generates enormous profits. Illegal operations include lotteries, off-track betting, illegal casinos, "numbers," and dice games. Such operations can be located practically anywhere—in a restaurant, garage, tavern, apartment complex, or even on business premises.

DRUG TRAFFICKING

Drug trafficking is an industry that makes billions of dollars annually in the United States. With such profits, it is little wonder that organized crime is involved in the importation and distribution of drugs such as cocaine, heroin, marijuana, crack, amphetamines, and hallucinogens. A recent trend in the illicit drug trade in the United States is the growth of new organizations unassociated with older crime "families." Some of these new organizations have ethnic group identities, such as Colombian, Chinese, Vietnamese, Puerto Rican, African American, or Russian.[36]

LOAN SHARKING

This crime involves lending money at interest rates above the legal limit. Interest rates have been reported to go as high as 150% a week.[37] Syndicated crime can ensure repayment by the threat of violence. Major borrowers from loan sharks include gamblers who need to cover losses, drug users, and small-business owners who are unable to obtain credit from legitimate sources.

INFILTRATING LEGITIMATE BUSINESSES

The huge profits from illegal activities provide organized crime with the capital to enter into legitimate operations, including the entertainment industry, banking, insurance, restaurants, advertising firms, bars, the automotive industry, and real estate agencies—to name but a few.

Infiltrating legitimate business provides organized crime with tax covers for its members, gives them a certain respectable status in the community, and offers additional profit-making opportunities. With its cash reserves, a syndicate can temporarily lower prices and bankrupt competitors. It can also use strong-arm tactics to force customers to buy its goods and services.

LABOR RACKETEERING

This activity involves the systematic extortion of money from labor unions and businesses. Racketeers can extort money from union members by forcing them to pay high union dues and fees in order to obtain and secure employment. Racketeers can shortchange employees by paying less than union wages and by misusing the union's pension and welfare funds. Finally, racketeers can extort money from employers by forcing them to make payoffs for union cooperation (for example, to avoid a strike).

PROSTITUTION

Because prostitutes offer a service for which some people are willing to pay high prices, prostitution can be a highly profitable endeavor, which makes it appealing to organized crime. Mobsters serve as brokers for prostitutes and customers and also protect them from arrest and prosecution by bribing law enforcement officials. Organized crime has also gotten involved in other sex-related forms of crime, such as the illegal distribution of pornographic films and magazines.

White-Collar Crime

John Johnson and Jack Douglas have noted that the most costly—and perhaps the most frequent—crimes are committed by "respectable" middle-class and upper-class citizens.[38] White-collar crimes are work-related offenses committed by people of high status.[39]

Offenses against customers include false advertising, stock manipulation, violations of food and drug laws, release of industrial waste products into public waterways, illegal emissions from industrial smokestacks, and price-fixing agreements. In the 1980s and early 1990s, there was

Kepone—A Case Example of Industrial Pollution

In the late 1970s, Life Science Products Company and Allied Chemical Corporation were found guilty of safety violations in producing Kepone and of contaminating the James River in Virginia with Kepone through dumping. Kepone is a chemical pesticide and a hydrocarbon similar to DDT. (DDT has been banned from use because of the adverse side effects it produces in humans and wildlife.)

Life Science was producing Kepone in Hopewell, Virginia, in the mid-1970s, under contract for Allied Chemical. Hopewell is a small town located on the James River. On July 23, 1975, a Virginia health official, Dr. Robert Jackson, inspected the facilities of Life Science. He was appalled at what he found. The "plant" consisted of a metal building and an abandoned service station. Safety precautions were virtually non-existent. Kepone dust was everywhere in the town—in the air and on the soil. Traffic on streets was slowed by Kepone dust when the wind blew.

Examinations of employees revealed a number of medical problems and the danger that other disorders such as cancer might develop in the future from exposure to the chemical. The most common symptom was called "Kepone shakes," in which the entire body shook. Other symptoms included difficulty in breathing, tension, skin rash, and psychological disorientation. The plant was immediately closed. Yet further examination revealed additional alarming disclosures. Kepone was found to cause cancer in rodents, to cause reproductive problems and infertility in birds, and to have the potential to kill both rodents and birds—and perhaps also humans. It was also discovered that 100,000 pounds of waste products containing Kepone had been dumped into the James River. The James empties into Chesapeake Bay, which has since been found to be contaminated with Kepone.

The governor of Virginia closed the lower James River to fishing in 1975 after the contamination was revealed. Unfortunately, Kepone accumulates in fish. If the fish are eaten by humans, the chemical can cause cancer, liver problems, and reproductive problems. The Virginia fishing industry lost at least $10 million in 1976 alone. Many businesses associated with the fishing industry have since been forced to close.

A particular difficulty with Kepone is that it is bioaccumulative, which means the body retains all that it consumes rather than passing it off in wastes. Therefore, the greater the exposure, the greater the accumulation in the body and the greater the probability of future disorders, such as cancer. The long-term effects of Kepone contamination are as yet unknown.

A number of criminal and civil suits were filed against Life Science, the city of Hopewell, and Allied. The city of Hopewell was fined $10,000. Life Science was fined $3.8 billion and went bankrupt. Allied Chemical was fined $13.4 million. (Allied's fine was reduced to $5 million, with Allied pledging another $8 million for cleanup efforts.) As is often the case with white-collar crime, no one served a prison sentence.

extensive fraud in the savings and loan industry that led to the industry's collapse. The federal government had to cover many of the losses. It cost taxpayers an estimated $500 billion, with large amounts of unprotected savings also lost by individual investors.[40] This savings and loan scandal helps to illustrate that white-collar crimes cost more money than all other types of crimes put together.[41]

The case of stock speculator Ivan Boesky provides a classic example of white-collar crime. Boesky personally made over $100 million on illegal insider trading (acting on information not available to the public). Brokers who possess inside information (such as knowledge of an impending corporate merger or a change in the financial condition of a company that will affect the price of its stock) are prohibited from profiting from that information themselves or from selling it to others who may be able to profit from it. In 1986 Boesky admitted his illegal activities, paid the Securities and Exchange Commission $100 million in fines and illicit profits, and was later convicted of conspiracy to file false documents with the federal government. Boesky's crimes precipitated a wave of additional allegations of insider trading, which have rocked the financial community in recent years. For these multimillion-dollar offenses, Boesky was imprisoned only 2 years.

Embezzlement is an offense in which an employee fraudulently converts some of the employer's funds for personal use through altering company records. Embezzlers who take large sums of money are usually thought to be respectable citizens and trusted employees. They are often motivated by financial problems that their regular income cannot handle, such as gambling debts, financial demands of a lover or spouse, and extensive medical bills for a relative.[42] Sullivan et al. note: "Embezzlers rationalize their theft by convincing themselves that they are merely 'borrowing' the money, that their employers are really crooks who deserve to lose the money, or that the employers will not miss the funds."[43]

Embezzlement occurs at all levels of business, from a clerk stealing from petty cash to the presi-

White-collar crimes are more costly than all other types of crimes. At $3.4 billion, Charles Keating's Lincoln Savings and Loan was the most costly savings and loan failure in U.S. history. Keating was convicted of fraudulently marketing junk bonds to tens of thousands of Lincoln customers and arranging sham real estate transactions to inflate Lincoln's profits. He served 5 years of a 12½ year sentence, only to have his convictions tossed out on legal technicalities.

dent of a company stealing large investment sums. Many cases go undetected or unprosecuted. Often an informal arrangement is worked out whereby the embezzler agrees to pay back the amount stolen and seeks employment elsewhere—a solution that is often more effective than prosecution for recovering the stolen funds. Because a scandal involving employee dishonesty threatens the employer's public image and hurts future business, companies often prefer to handle the offense informally and privately.

Other examples of white-collar crime include income tax evasion, expense-account fraud, misuse of government funds by business organizations, corporate bribes, and computer-related crime. The latter involves illegal use of computer technology. People who have access to a personal computer, a modem, and the correct password can transfer millions of dollars anywhere in the world.

American society, unfortunately, is generally tolerant of white-collar crime. A pickpocket who repeatedly steals small sums of money will likely go to prison, whereas someone who repeatedly fails to report large earnings on income tax returns is unlikely to face prosecution. This acceptance of white-collar crime appears to be due largely to the attitude that the victim is a large, impersonal organization (for example, the government or a large corporation) that will be unaffected. People who would never think of taking an item from a private home might feel no qualms about stealing "souvenirs" (towels, sheets, ashtrays) from hotels.

White-collar crime raises serious questions about our conceptions of crime and criminals. It suggests that crime is not necessarily concentrated among the young, the poor, and racial minorities and in our inner cities. Why, in our society, are burglars and pickpockets severely punished and stigmatized, whereas white-collar criminals who commit far more costly offenses are seldom prosecuted or viewed as criminals? Could it be due to the power structure of our society, in which the middle and upper classes define their own offenses as "excusable," but those committed by powerless groups as "intolerable"?

Victimless Crimes

With most crimes, there is an identifiable victim, as with embezzlement or robbery. However, there are several crimes in which no one suffers, except perhaps the person who willfully decides to engage in the illegal activity. Victimless crimes include prostitution, vagrancy, pornography, gambling, drunkenness, curfew violations, loitering, drug abuse, fornication, and homosexuality between consenting adults. (Some of these actions are illegal in certain jurisdictions and legal in others.) Laws that make such behaviors criminal are designed to regulate people's private lives rather than to protect some citizens from others. The laws exist because powerful groups within society regard these acts as "undesirable."

The United States invests enormous resources in controlling victimless crime, as evidenced by arrest statistics. Nearly one-fourth of all arrests annually involve victimless crimes.[44] Organized crime makes much of its money from victimless crimes by providing illegal goods and services for which customers willingly pay. Prohibition is the classic example; organized crime supplied illegal alcoholic beverages at wildly inflated prices.

Because victimless crimes are considered less serious (by at least some segments of the population) and because these crimes consume excessive money and time that police and the courts could devote to reducing more serious crime, there have been efforts to decriminalize or repeal some of these laws. Alexander Smith and Harriet Pollack state:

> For every murderer arrested and prosecuted, literally dozens of gamblers, prostitutes, . . . and derelicts crowd our courts' dockets. If we took the numbers runners, the kids smoking pot, and winos out of the criminal justice system, we would substantially reduce the burden on the courts and the police. . . . Moral laws that do not reflect contemporary mores or that cannot be enforced should be removed from the penal code through legislative action because, at best, they undermine respect for the law.[45]

Criminal penalties for such crimes may also do more harm than good. For example, treating someone arrested for homosexual activity as a hardened criminal may well damage the person's self-concept and status in the community. Criminal penalties may also force the offenders to form a subculture to continue their illegal activity with greater safety. Such subcultures (for instance, of homosexuals and drug users) serve to separate them even further from the rest of society.

Sex Offenses

Sex offenses include forcible rape, prostitution, soliciting, statutory rape, fornication, sodomy, homosexuality, adultery, and incest.

In most states, only males are legally liable for rape by force. Forcible rape is a highly underreported crime, with less than one-quarter of the victims reporting the assault to the police.[46] Why? In about half of the cases, the attacker is a friend or acquaintance of the victim; therefore, some victims think police action will only create more interpersonal problems. Many victims are reluctant to report the offense because they believe (perhaps realistically) they have nothing to gain and more to lose by making a report, including social embarrassment, interrogation by sometimes unsympathetic law enforcement officials, and humiliating public testimony in court about the offense. A danger to society of underreporting rape is that the rapist is less likely to fear apprehension and thus more likely to seek out other victims.

Statutory rape involves sexual contact between a male who is of a legally responsible age (usually 18) and a female who is a willing participant but is below the legal age of consent (16 in some states and 18 in others). In most states, females are not defined as being liable for committing statutory rape. In some states, a charge of statutory rape can be made on the basis of sexual contact other than sexual intercourse (such as oral-genital contact).

There is considerable variation in homosexuality laws among states. Most states still define male homosexual acts between consenting adults as illegal, although some states have legalized such relations. Some states that prohibit male homosexuality between consenting adults do not prohibit such acts between adult females. (Homosexuality is further discussed in Chapter 7.)

Increased attention is now being given to sexual abuse of children. Such abuse includes sexual intercourse (genital or anal), masturbation, oralgenital contact, fondling, and exposure. There is no unambiguous definition of sexual abuse. Sexual intercourse with children is definitely abuse, but other forms of contact are more difficult to judge as abusive. At some point, hugging, kissing, and fondling become inappropriate. Abus-ers may be parents, older siblings, extended relatives, friends, acquaintances, or strangers. (Sexual abuse is discussed in greater length in Chapter 7.)

Certain sex offenses (such as incest, rape, and homosexual contact with a minor) incite considerable repugnance among the general public, which results in harsh punishments for offenders. Unfortunately, less attention is given to helping the victims cope with their exploitation or to rehabilitating the offenders.

Homicide and Assault

Criminal homicide involves the unlawful killing of one person by another. Criminal assault is the unlawful application of physical force on another person. Most homicides are unintended outcomes of physical assaults. People get into physical fights because one (or both) is incensed about the other's actions and decides to retaliate. Provoking actions may include ridicule, flirting with the other's spouse or lover, and failure to repay a debt. Fighting is often an attempt by one or both to save face when challenged or degraded. Homicides frequently are "crimes of passion," occurring during a violent argument or other highly charged emotional situation.

Yet some homicides are carefully planned and premeditated, including most gangland killings, killings to obtain an inheritance, and mercy killings. Homicides are also associated with robberies, during which the victim, the robber, or a law enforcement official may be shot.

Contrary to public stereotypes, the majority of murders occur between relatives, friends, and acquaintances.[47] Because of the overt physical damage from assault and homicide, these crimes generate the most fear. The police have a higher arrest rate (around 70%) in homicide cases than with any other crime—partly because they devote extensive attention to murders and partly because the questioning of the victim's friends, neighbors, and relatives usually identifies the killer.[48] Alcohol is frequently an important contributing factor in murders and assaults, as slightly over half of all those in prison for violent crimes report they were under the influence of alcohol or other drugs at the time of their offense.[49]

Murder and the Fall of an American Hero

Orenthal James (O. J.) Simpson was born and raised on Connecticut Street in Potrero Hill, a poor neighborhood in San Francisco, which O. J. once described as "your average Black ghetto." His father, Jimmy, a custodian and cook, left home when O. J. was 5. Jimmy was a homosexual who died of AIDS in 1985. O. J.'s mother, Eunice, worked long hours as a hospital orderly to support her four children.

As a youth, O. J. joined gangs, picked fights, stole hubcaps, shot craps, and played hookey from school. After a gang fight at age 15 landed him briefly in jail, Lefty Gordon, the supervisor of the local recreational center, arranged for baseball great Willie Mays to meet with O. J. The meeting left a lasting impression on O. J., who stated, "He made me realize that we all have it in ourselves to be heroes."

O. J. Simpson

O. J. applied himself to football. He didn't have the grades for a 4-year school, so he attended City College of San Francisco, where he set records as a running back. In his junior year, he transferred to the University of Southern California. O. J. led USC to two Rose Bowls, and in his senior year, he won the Heisman Trophy, given annually to the best player in college football.

After his triumphs at USC, O. J. was drafted by the National Football League. In 1973, while playing halfback for the Buffalo Bills, he broke the single-season rushing record held by Jim Brown.

Theft

This category of crime refers to illegally taking someone's property without the person's consent. Offenses range from pickpocketing and burglary to sophisticated multimillion-dollar swindles. Thieves range from grocery store clerks who take small amounts of food to people who concoct highly professional confidence schemes to swindle others out of thousands of dollars.

The most successful thieves (labeled professional thieves by the noted criminologist Edwin H. Sutherland[50]) engage in confidence games, forg-

ery, expert safecracking, counterfeiting, extortion (for example, blackmailing others who are involved in illegal acts), and organized shoplifting. Most such crimes require that professional thieves appear personable and trustworthy and that they be good actors to convince others that they are somebody who they are not. Professional thieves use sophisticated, nonviolent techniques. Their crimes are carefully planned, and they tend to steal as a regular business. They define themselves as thieves, have a value system supportive of their career, and often are respected by their colleagues and by law enforcement officials. Because of their

The world of advertising in the 1970s was searching for a "breakthrough Black man" who had the right look, the right smile, and the right nickname. O. J. was it. His magnetic image won him several lucrative advertising contracts.

Even before his retirement from pro football after 11 seasons, he started acting in movies and on TV. He became a sports broadcaster for NBC and ABC. He was also inducted in the football Hall of Fame.

But apparently there was another side to O. J. Simpson. A married man with two children, he met Nicole Brown, a very attractive teenager. Shortly after she turned 19, they began living together. Eventually they married, had two children of their own, and lived a glamorous life in their West Los Angeles mansion. However, on at least eight occasions, police were called to their home to settle domestic fights. In 1989, after one particularly brutal fight, witnesses said O. J. had repeatedly screamed "I'll kill you!" The Los Angeles city attorney filed charges against Simpson for wife beating, and he pleaded no contest.

In 1992 Nicole and O. J. finally divorced. Afterward they continued to see each other, and O. J. hoped for a reconciliation. But in the spring of 1994, friends say Nicole shattered O. J.'s dreams by telling him she had decided not to reconcile.

During the evening of June 12, 1994, Nicole Simpson was brutally stabbed to death outside her condominium. Also brutally stabbed to death was Ronald Goldman, a friend of hers who reportedly was returning a pair of sunglasses she had left earlier in the evening at the restaurant in which he worked.

A few days later, O. J. was arrested and charged with these murders. In 1995 a jury in a criminal trial proceeding found O. J. innocent of these two murders. In 1996 a jury in a civil court proceeding found O. J. responsible for the wrongful deaths of Nicole Brown and Ronald Goldman, and he was ordered to pay over $30 million in damages to the families of these two victims.

---

cunning and skill, they seldom are arrested. They often justify their activities by claiming that they are simply capitalizing on the fact that all people are dishonest and would probably also be full-time thieves if they had sufficient skills.

Semiprofessional thieves engage in armed robberies, burglaries, holdups, and larcenies that do not involve much detailed planning. Some semiprofessional thieves work alone, holding up service stations, convenience stores, liquor stores, and the like. Semiprofessionals often wind up spending substantial portions of their lives in prison because they commit the types of crimes that are harshly punished by courts. They also tend to be repeat offenders for similar crimes. Often they define themselves as products and victims of a corrupt and unjust system, having started their careers in low-income and ghetto neighborhoods. They adjust fairly well in prison because other inmates often have similar backgrounds, lifestyles, and views on life. However, as a group they are poor parole risks.[51]

Amateur thieves are individuals who steal infrequently. In contrast to professional and semiprofessional thieves, these individuals generally define themselves as respectable law-abiding citizens. Their criminal acts tend to be crude, unsophisticated, and unplanned, with some offenders being juveniles. Examples of offenses by this group include stealing from employers, shoplifting, stealing an unguarded bicycle, taking an auto for a joyride, taking soda from a truck, and breaking into a home to take CDs or beer. Businesses and industries suffer substantial losses from amateur thieves who are either employees or customers.

Juvenile Delinquency

CRIME AMONG YOUTHS

According to official crime statistics, 19% of all people arrested are under age 18.[52] A fair number of these arrests are for crimes that have already been discussed—thefts, robberies, assaults, and rapes. Yet one reason why juveniles have such a high arrest rate is that a majority of the arrests are for status offenses—that is, acts that are defined as illegal if committed by juveniles but not if committed by adults. Status offenses include being truant, having sexual relations, running away from home, being ungovernable, violating curfew, and being beyond the control of parents.

Police arrests of lower-class juveniles are far higher than for middle- and upper-class juveniles.[53] This is partly due to the fact that police are more inclined to arrest lower-class juveniles than middle- and upper-class juveniles.[54] After reviewing a number of studies on the relationships between delinquency and poverty, Kornblum and Julian conclude that these two variables are interrelated in a complex manner. Middle- and upper-class juveniles tend to commit nuisance crimes at about the same rates as lower-class youths, but lower-class youths commit higher rates of serious crimes, such as homicide.[55]

GANGS

Juvenile gangs have existed for many decades in the United States and in other countries. In recent years in the United States, there have been increases in the number of gangs, the number of youths belonging to gangs, gang youth drug involvement, and gang violence. Violent, delinquent urban gang activity has become a major social problem in the United States. The scientific knowledge base about delinquent gangs is very limited. Longres notes:

No consensus exists for a definition of a youth gang. In addition, no agreed upon recording system exists, and no data on gang offenses are collected in systematic ways by disinterested agencies. Furthermore, attempts to eradicate gangs through social service and criminal justice programs have met with little success.[56]

The inadequacy of the knowledge base about delinquent gangs is a major obstacle to developing effective intervention strategies with this population. There have been numerous definitions of gangs, but no consensus exists on their distinguishing characteristics.[57] The lack of consensus is indicated by the numerous and diverse categories that have been used by different investigators to classify gangs: corner group, social club, conflict group, pathological group, athletic club, industrial association, predatory organization, drug addict group, racket organization, fighting-focused group, defensive group, unconventional group, criminal organization, turf group, heavy metal group, punk rock group, satanic organization, skinhead, ethnic or racial group, motorcycle club, and scavenger group.[58]

An illustration of a categorization is provided by Morales, who classified youth gangs into four types: criminal, conflict, retreatist, and cult/occult.[59]

Criminal gangs have as a primary goal material gain through criminal activities, including theft of property from people or premises, extortion, fencing, and drug trafficking (especially of rock cocaine).

Conflict gangs are turf oriented. They engage in violent conflict with individuals of rival groups that invade their neighborhood or commit acts that they consider degrading or insulting. Respect is highly valued and defended. Latino gangs often fall into this category. Sweeney notes that the Code of the Barrio mandates that gang members watch out for their neighborhood and be willing to die for it.[60]

Retreatist gangs focus on getting "high" or "loaded" on alcohol, cocaine, marijuana, heroin, or other drugs. Individuals tend to join this type of gang to secure continued access to drugs. In contrast to criminal gangs that become involved with drugs for financial profit, retreatist gangs become involved with drugs for consumption.

Cult/occult gangs engage in devil or evil worship. *Cult* refers to systematic worshiping of evil or the devil; *occult* implies keeping something secret or hidden or a belief in supernatural or mysterious powers. Some occult groups place extensive emphasis on sexuality and violence, believing that, by sexually violating an innocent child or virgin, they have defiled Christianity. Not all cult/occult gangs are involved in criminal activity. Unlike the other three gang types, which are composed primarily of juveniles, the majority of occult groups are composed of adults.

Contradictions abound in conceptualizing delinquent gangs. Gangs are believed to be composed largely of ethnically homogeneous adolescents (African American, Latino, and Asian youths); yet some gangs composed of White youths exist. Most gang members are believed to be between ages 12 and 18, yet recent evidence indicates some gangs include and may be controlled by adults.[61] Gangs are believed to be composed of males; yet some gangs have female members, and a few gangs consist exclusively of females.[62] Gangs are believed to be primarily involved in drug trafficking; yet some delinquent gangs have other illegal foci, such as burglary, robbery, larceny, or illegal drug consumption. Gang activity is thought to be primarily located in large inner-city areas; yet gang activity is flourishing in many smaller cities and in some suburbs.[63]

At the present time, there are inadequate statistical data on the number of gangs, the number and characteristics of members, and their criminal activities. Longres notes:

> Statistics on gangs and their criminal behavior are not obtained easily. Many cities have gang control units that collect data but do not report them in any systematic way. Even when such data are obtained, they are difficult to interpret because no uniform definition of gang offenses exists, no recording system has been in place long enough to discern trends, and arrest data from police departments may reflect bias. Additionally, no uniform definition of a gang-related offense exists across police jurisdictions even within the same state, city, or county.[64]

Spergel presents documentation that gangs primarily develop in those local communities that are often socially disorganized and/or impoverished.[65] Gang members typically come from families where the parents lack effective parenting skills, where the school systems give little attention to students who are falling behind in their studies, where youths are exposed to adult crime groups, and where youths feel there is practically no opportunity to succeed through the legitimate avenues of education and a good paying job. Spergel asserts that youths join gangs for many reasons—security, power, money, status, excitement, and new experiences—particularly under conditions of social deprivation or community instability. In essence, he presents a community disorganization approach to understanding the attraction of joining a gang.

In a very real sense, a delinquent gang is created because the needs of youths are not being met by the family, neighborhood, or traditional community institutions (such as the schools, police, and recreational and religious institutions). Some useful changes suggested by Spergel are reduced access to handguns; improved educational resources; access to recreation, job training, jobs, family counseling, drug rehabilitation, and mobilization of community groups and organizations to restrain gang violence (such as neighborhood watch groups). Social policy changes are also needed at state and national levels to funnel more resources to urban centers. Funds are needed to improve the quality of life for city residents, including youths, so that the needs of youths are met in ways other than through gang involvement.[66]

THE CRIMINAL JUSTICE SYSTEM

The criminal justice system consists of the police, the courts, and the correctional system. It is perceived by many Americans as cumbersome, ineffective, irrational, and unjust, fostering a perception that "crime does pay." Some segments of the population are suspicious of the police and believe that they abuse their powers. Other segments, particularly the middle and upper classes, see the police as unduly hampered in their work by cumbersome arrest and interrogation procedures designed to protect the civil rights of suspected offenders.

Courts are sharply criticized for their long delays in bringing cases to conclusion and for their sentencing procedures. Many Americans believe that courts are not harsh enough on offenders. Courts are also criticized for (a) varying widely in the harshness of sentences meted out for apparently similar offenses and (b) giving harsh sentences to "ordinary offenders" but light fines to white-collar offenders.

Prisons, too, have been sharply criticized, as they are viewed as failing to rehabilitate their populations. The rate of recidivism (that is, return to crime) is alarmingly high. Over half of those released from prison later return after being convicted of another crime.[67] Indeed, far from rehabilitating inmates, prisons are accused of being schools for crime.

In all societies, criminal justice systems face a conflict between two goals: crime control and due process. The crime-control goal involves the need to curb crime and protect society from lawbreakers. It emphasizes speedy arrest and punishment for those who commit crimes. The due-process goal involves the need to protect and preserve the rights and liberties of individuals. Some societies are police states that use strong-arm tactics to control their citizens, displaying little concern for individual rights. At the other extreme are societies in which individuals flagrantly break the law, with the government having neither the power nor the respect of its citizens to uphold the law. American society seeks to strike a balance between the conflicting goals of crime control and due process, but the struggle is constant. At times the same individual may seek to have one goal emphasized in one situation but the conflicting goal emphasized in a different setting. For example, a homeowner may want speedy justice when her house is burglarized but may seek to use all the due-process protections when accused of income tax evasion.

We will now take a closer look at each of these three components of the criminal justice system.

The Police

Police officers are the gatekeepers for the criminal justice system. Whom they arrest determines whom the courts and corrections will have to deal with. As we have seen, nearly everyone commits an occasional crime. Police cannot arrest everyone, or the jails, courts, and prisons would be overloaded and our society would collapse. Therefore, police exercise considerable discretion in which laws they vigorously enforce and which types of offenders they arrest. For example, police are more likely to arrest lower-income than middle-income youths.

Only a small part of a police department's effort is directly focused on making arrests. Police officers classify as "criminal" only about 10% to 20% of the calls and incidents they handle on a given day.[68]

David Peterson has noted that the role of a police officer is usually best conceptualized as that of a "peace officer" or even "social worker" rather than as a "law enforcement officer":

> A prominent theme in the literature dealing with the work behavior of the police stresses that the role of the uniformed patrol officer is not a strict legalistic one. The patrol officer is routinely involved in tasks that have little relation to police work in terms of controlling crime. His activities on the beat are often centered as much on assisting citizens as upon offenses; he is frequently called upon to perform a "supportive" function as well as an enforcement function. Existing research on the uniformed police officer in field situations indicates that more than half his time is spent as an amateur social worker assisting people in various ways. Moreover, several officers have suggested that the role of the uniformed patrol officer is not sharply defined and that the mixture of enforcement and service functions creates conflict and uncertainties for individual officers.[69]

Service functions of police may include giving first aid to injured people, rescuing trapped animals, and directing traffic. When police do perform law enforcement functions, they squarely face trying to achieve the proper balance between the crime-control model and the due-process model. There is considerable pressure to swiftly apprehend certain lawbreakers—murderers, rapists, and arsonists. Yet they are expected to perform according to the due-process model so that the legal rights of those arrested are not violated. James Coleman and Donald Cressey note: "Police officers operate more like diplomats than like soldiers engaged in a war on crime."[70]

In many areas of the nation, police do not have sufficient resources to do their job effectively. Often there is also considerable hostility toward police officers. Part of this hostility may result from the fact that everyone commits an occasional crime; people may be suspicious of police officers because they fear possible apprehension. In addition, some people (particularly the poor and minority group members) have been harassed by being picked up for crimes they clearly did not commit and by being subjected to long "third-degree" interrogations. Also, some hostility toward the police stems from well-publicized incidents of police corruption (for example, taking bribes), particularly in larger cities.

The Courts

HOW THE COURTS WORK

Criminal justice in the United States is an adversary system. That is, a prosecuting attorney first presents the state's evidence against a defendant, and that defendant, presumed innocent until proved guilty, then has an opportunity to refute the charges with the assistance of a defense attorney.

Contrary to public opinion, over 90% of convictions in the United States are obtained not in court but through plea bargaining between the prosecuting attorney and the defendant, who is often represented by a defense attorney in the plea-bargaining process.[71] For a plea of guilty, a suspect may receive a more lenient sentence, have certain charges dropped, or have the charge reduced to a less serious offense. Plea bargaining is

not legally binding in court, but the judge usually goes along with the arrangement. Plea bargaining is highly controversial. It does save taxpayers considerable expense because court trials are costly. But it may in some cases circumvent due-process protections if an innocent person charged with some serious offense is pressured into pleading guilty to a reduced charge.

There are four key positions in a court: the prosecuting attorney, the defense attorney, the judge, and the jury.

Prosecuting attorneys have considerable discretionary authority in choosing whether to seek a conviction for those arrested and how vigorously to prosecute a defendant. Prosecuting attorneys are either elected or appointed to office and are therefore political figures who must periodically seek reelection or reappointment. Therefore, they seek to prosecute most vigorously the cases they perceive the community is most concerned about. Prosecuting attorneys usually focus police departments' attention on which violations will be further processed by the criminal justice system.

Defense attorneys are supposed to represent their clients' interest before the criminal justice system. Impoverished individuals are provided, at the state's expense, a court-appointed attorney. The skills and competency of the defense attorney are major factors in determining whether a defendant will be found innocent or guilty if there is a trial. The wealthy not only can retain the best attorneys but also can afford additional resources (such as private investigators) to help prepare a better defense.

Sometimes the poor are shortchanged by court-appointed defense attorneys, who tend to be young, inexperienced practitioners, or less competent older lawyers, who resort to this type of practice in order to survive professionally. Because these defense attorneys depend on the good opinion of their legal colleagues (including judges and prosecuting attorneys) to stay in practice, the client's best interest sometimes receives secondary priority.[72]

If a defendant is prosecuted for a minor offense, the case is generally presented before a lower-court judge without a jury. For a serious offense, the defendant first receives a preliminary hearing, which is solely for the benefit of the suspect. At the hearing, the prosecutor presents evidence against the suspect, and the judge decides whether that evidence is sufficient to warrant further legal proceedings. If the evidence is insufficient, the suspect is discharged. If the evidence is sufficient, the accused is held over to await a court trial. (Often the held-over cases are then decided by plea bargaining before they go to trial.)

A jury is supposed to be a cross section of the community. However, there is a tendency for retired persons, housewives with grown children, and the unemployed—those who are not inconvenienced by the duty—to be overrepresented on juries. Juries use the standard of reasonable doubt to decide if the prosecution has provided enough evidence for conviction. To obtain the conviction of a defendant charged with a crime, all 12 members of the jury must vote "guilty." A hung jury occurs when a jury is unable to reach a decision. Because of group pressure, only rarely does a lone juror produce a hung jury.

Under the bail system, accused people are allowed to deposit money or credit with the court to obtain a release from jail while awaiting trial. Bail is designed to ensure that the suspect will appear for trial. The amount of bail is set by the court and varies according to the offense and the judge's attitudes toward the suspect. The bail system severely discriminates against the poor. Anyone unable to raise enough money must stay in jail while awaiting trial, which may take several months. Those who cannot post bail have less opportunity to prepare a good defense because they are locked up. Also, their case is further prejudiced when they do appear in court because they are brought into the courtroom in handcuffs and often without proper grooming. Being locked up before trial is a form of punishment that runs counter to the notion that the suspect is innocent (and should be treated as such) until proved guilty. In some cases, a suspect spends more time in jail awaiting trial than she or he spends in jail if found guilty.

After defendants have been found guilty or have pleaded guilty, they return to the courtroom for sentencing. Judges usually have fairly wide discretion in assigning sentences; for example, they can place one murderer on probation, commit another to prison, and in those states where capital punishment is legal, order the execution of a third. Judges base their sentences on such factors as the seriousness of the crime, the motives for the crime, the background of the offender, and their attitudes toward the offender.

Judges vary greatly in the extent to which they send convicted offenders to prison, use probation, or assign fines. Concern about disparities in sentences has grown in recent years. Coleman and Cressey note:

> Judges and other sentencing authorities are on the spot. They are supposed to give equal punishments, no matter what the social status of the defendants involved. Yet they are supposed to give individual punishments because the circumstances of each crime and the motivations of each criminal are always different and a just punishment for one burglar or car thief may be completely inappropriate for another. . . . As judges try to satisfy these conflicting demands, they are bound to be denounced as unfair. The judge's task, like the police officer's task, is to walk a thin line between the crime control model and the due process model, balancing demands for repressing crime against demands for human rights and freedom.[73]

JUVENILE COURTS

The first juvenile court was established in Cook County, Illinois, in 1899. The philosophy of the juvenile court is that it should act in the best interests of the child, as parents should act. In essence, juvenile courts have a treatment orientation. Adult criminal proceedings focus on charging the defendant with a specific crime, on holding a public trial to determine whether the defendant is guilty as charged, and on sentencing the defendant if he or she is found guilty. In contrast, the focus in juvenile courts is on the current psychological, physical, emotional, and educational needs of children, as opposed to punishment for misdeeds. Reform or treatment of the child is the goal, even though the child or his or her family may not necessarily agree that the court's decision is in the child's best interests.

Of course, not all juvenile court judges live up to these principles. In practice, some juvenile judges focus more on punishing than on treating juvenile offenders. There is also a danger that court appearances by children can have adverse labeling effects. A Supreme Court decision in the famous Gault case of May 15, 1967, restored to juveniles procedural safeguards that had been ignored—including notification of charges, protection against self-incrimination, confrontation, and cross-examination.[74] There is currently considerable effort to have juvenile probation officers provide informal supervision for youths who commit "minor" violations. With informal supervision, youthful offenders receive counseling and guidance and do not appear in court.

Correctional Systems

Current correctional systems in the United States and throughout the world contain conflicting objectives. Some components are punishment oriented, whereas others are treatment oriented. A manifestation of this confusion is the existence, side by side, of correctional programs intended primarily for deterrence and retribution and other programs designed to reform offenders. Only rarely do punitive and treatment components complement each other. Generally, the two components, when combined, result in a system that is ineffective and inefficient in curbing criminal activity. In the past two decades, correctional systems have moved toward a more punitive approach.

THE PUNITIVE APPROACH

Throughout history various approaches have been used to punish offenders. These methods include physical torture, social humiliation, financial penalties, exile, the death penalty, and imprisonment.

Physical Torture. Most societies have at one time or another used this method. Specific examples of corporal (bodily) punishment have included stocks, whipping, flogging, branding, hard labor, confinement in irons and cages, arm twisting, and mutilation of body parts. Corporal punishment was particularly popular during the medieval period. Virtually no types of corporal punishment are assigned today by European or U.S. courts.

Social Humiliation. Reducing the social status of an offender is another method of punishment. This approach flourished in the 16th and 17th centuries, and remnants exist today. Specific techniques included some that also had corporal-punishment facets: the stocks, the pillory, the ducking stool, branding, and the brank. (The brank was a small cage that was placed over the offender's head. It had a bar that was inserted into the mouth of the offender to prevent him or her from talking; occasionally this bar had spikes in it.) Some of these punishments were temporary—for example, the stocks—whereas others had a permanent effect on the offender—for example, branding. One of the objectives of the permanent method was to deter future crime by publicly humiliating offenders. However, the techniques frequently had the opposite effect, as they overtly labeled the offender, thereby making it difficult for him or her to secure employment and earn a living in a law-abiding manner.

Deprivation of civil rights is another approach that has been used for centuries to humiliate the convicted offender socially. The principal rights that are taken away from convicted felons by most states in this country are (a) the right to vote while in prison or while on probation or parole; (b) the right to hold public office; (c) the right to practice certain professions, such as the law; and (d) the right to own or possess firearms.[75]

Financial Penalties. The use of fines in criminal law became widespread in this country about a century ago and is now by far the most frequent court approach to punishing offenders. More than 75% of all penalties imposed at present are fines.[76] The advantages of a fine are: (a) it provides revenue to the state; (b) it costs the state almost nothing to administer, especially in comparison to the cost of imprisonment; (c) the amount of the fine can easily be adjusted to the enormity of the offense, the reaction of the public, and the wealth and character of the offender; (d) it inflicts a material type of suffering; and (e) it can easily be paid back if the alleged offender is later found innocent. A serious disadvantage is that it is highly discriminatory toward the poor, who have less ability to pay. Sweden has found a way to curb this discrimination by the creation of day fines, in which the offender pays the equivalent of the amount earned in a specified number of days of work rather than a flat amount as a fine.

Courts are also increasingly requiring, in their sentencing decisions, that the offender make restitution payments to the victim that are in line with the amount of injury. This kind of reaction to crime is more treatment oriented, as it attempts to give the offender an opportunity to "make good." Restitution is, of course, also advantageous to the victim. Restitution and reparation are used most frequently for minor offenses. Generally, the offender is placed on probation, with restitution being a condition of probation. Some of the work of probation departments now involves acting as a collection agency to obtain restitution payments from probationers.

Exile. Almost all societies have exiled certain offenders, particularly political criminals. Deportation on a large scale, however, has been used only since about the 16th century. The United States has been deporting alien criminals for decades. In addition, many counties and municipalities in the United States give people accused or convicted of a crime a set number of hours to "get out and stay out" of their jurisdiction.

Death Penalty. The extent to which the death penalty has been used and the methods for executing offenders have varied considerably in different societies. Criminals have been hanged, electrocuted, shot, burned, gassed, drowned, boiled in oil, broken at the wheel, guillotined, stoned, put in an iron coffin, pierced with a sharp stake, stabbed with a sword, and poisoned. In essence, almost every lethal method has at one time or another been used by some society.

The death penalty has been used in the United States throughout most of our history. In colonial America, "witches" in some communities were burned at the stake. While the West was being developed, individuals who stole a horse or committed certain other crimes were sometimes shot or hanged (sometimes by a lynch mob or a "kangaroo court"). From the time of the Civil War until the recent past, African Americans in the South who were thought to have committed a serious crime against Whites (for example, rape) were sometimes lynched. Gas chambers, firing squads, lethal injections, hangings, and electric chairs are the current methods of execution used in the United States.

From 1967 to 1977, the death penalty was not used in this country, partly due to U.S. Supreme Court decisions that ruled the penalty unconstitutional. In October 1976, the Supreme Court changed its position on this issue and ruled that states may execute murderers under certain guidelines. On January 17, 1977, Gary Gilmore was the first person in a decade to be executed, and the sensational case attracted national attention. Gilmore was convicted of ruthlessly killing several people. Since 1977 the number of offenders executed annually in the United States has gradually been increasing. The continued use of the death penalty remains a controversial national issue.

The primary argument for using the death penalty for certain crimes is that it is assumed to have a deterrent effect. This assumption is questionable, as statistics generally do *not* show a corresponding decrease in serious crime rates when a country adopts the death penalty.[77] Also, there is no clear-cut evidence that, when a country discontinues use of the death penalty, there will be an increase in serious crimes.[78] Additional arguments for use of the death penalty are that (a) some crimes (such as brutal, premeditated murder) are so abominable that the offender deserves the ultimate punishment and (b) it is less expensive to society to put hardened criminals to death than to incarcerate them for life. (In reality, executing someone has been more expensive than lifetime incarceration as huge amounts of legal expenses have been incurred on the appeals that precede an execution.)

Arguments against use of the death penalty are as follows: (a) it constitutes cruel and unusual punishment, being the ultimate punishment; (b) if the convicted person is later found innocent, the penalty is irreparable; (c) the "eye for an eye" approach is inconsistent with civilized, humanitarian ideals; (d) the "right to life" is a basic right that should not be infringed on; and (e) the death penalty appears to be assigned in a discriminatory manner (African Americans and Latinos are proportionately much more likely than Whites to be sentenced to death).

Imprisonment. The penal system currently plays an enormous role in our society. Thousands of people are incarcerated each year. As noted, the recidivism rate (return to prison after release) is estimated to be over 50%, which raises questions about the effectiveness of prisons in curbing future criminal activity.[79] Since 1970 several large-scale prison revolts (for example, Attica Prison, in New York, in 1971 and New Mexico State Penitentiary in 1980) have raised the concern of the general public.

Conditions within prisons prior to the 20th century were deplorable. Frequently the young were placed with hardened criminals, and women were not separated from men. Only custodial care was provided, often with "hard-labor" work projects. There were a number of prison reform studies from 1700 to 1850 that criticized within prisons the use of intoxicating liquors, sexual orgies, gambling, and the personal lewdness of security officers. Some prisons kept inmates in solitary confinement for months at a time, and corporal punishment was frequently used.

Since 1800 prisons have become more specialized. Jails are used for shorter sentences and for those awaiting trial. Separate institutions have been built for the young, for women, and for those labeled as criminally insane. Prisons also have various degrees of security: maximum, moderate, and minimum. Special programs have been developed to meet individual needs of inmates (for example, alcohol and drug abuse programs, educational and vocational training, medical and dental programs, and recreational programs).

Prisons are still distasteful and sometimes physically dangerous institutions. There is now the danger of AIDS being transmitted by sexual assaults in prison. However, in the past 100 years, the horrors of prison life have been somewhat reduced. In addition to rehabilitative programs, strides have been made in safeguarding civil rights of inmates, abandoning long-term solitary confinement, improving methods of discipline, promoting contact between inmates and the outside world, providing libraries, reducing the monotony of prison life, and improving diet, ventilation, and cleanliness within the facilities. Gone are such humiliating approaches as shaving the head, chaining inmates, issuing striped clothing, and using the ball and chain. Also, corporal-punishment methods, such as whipping, are no longer officially approved. The most severe punishment that remains for many prisoners is their constant fear of being victimized by their fellow inmates.

Since 1975 there has been a dramatic increase in the number of people sentenced to prison by the courts.[80] Part of this increase is due to the mushrooming of drug-related convictions, including drug trafficking convictions. Another reason is that our society has become more conservative and therefore is demanding a more punitive approach (imprisonment) to handling convicted offenders. As a result of the increased use of imprisonment, many prisons are currently overcrowded. An alternative to imprisonment that is used for less serious criminal offenders is home confinement with the use of electronic surveillance monitors to ensure that the convicted offenders remain at home.

The first American institution built specifically to house juvenile offenders was opened in New York City in 1825. There are now over 300 state and local training schools for juveniles. It has always been contended that such institutions are not prisons, but schools to educate and reform the young. However, until the recent past, most were best described as prisons in terms of functions, methods of discipline, and daily routine. Even today a few are still prison oriented. One of the most significant developments in juvenile institutions was cottage-type architecture, which provides a more homelike setting. The first such juvenile homes were established in Massachusetts and Ohio in 1858. These settings facilitate, but do not necessarily ensure, a treatment orientation.

Objectives of Incarceration. The conflict between the punitive approach and the treatment approach to corrections is strikingly clear in our penal system. Until a few centuries ago, the purpose of incarceration was strictly to punish an offender. From 1900 to 1970, there was an increased emphasis on treatment and a shift away from punishment. There were several reasons for this shift. Practically all prisoners return to society, and it was concluded that punitive approaches alone do not produce the desired reformation. Locking a person in an artificial environment, without providing rehabilitative programs, does not sufficiently prepare that person to be a productive citizen on his or her return. Moreover, in this era of accountability, the 50% recidivism rate is unacceptable, especially because the annual cost of incarceration per inmate is more than $30,000.[81]

In the 1980s and 1990s, however, the pendulum has swung back to using a more punitive approach in our prison system. Increased concerns about community protection and the effects of crime on victims and a greater emphasis on wanting criminals to pay for their crimes have been factors that have led to a shift away from the treatment approach.

The specific objectives for imprisonment are: (a) to reform offenders so they will no longer commit crimes; (b) to incapacitate criminals so they cannot commit crimes for a period of time, thereby protecting society; (c) to achieve retribution for the victim and, to some extent, for the state; and (d) to serve as a warning to the general public, thereby having a deterrent effect. A major problem with these objectives is that some components conflict with others. The infliction of pain and suffering is aimed at meeting the retribution and deterrence objectives, but most punitive approaches are counterproductive in terms of having reformative value.

There are also some dangers with using imprisonment. Association with other offenders may result in inmates learning additional lawbreaking techniques. Moreover, incarceration may label the offender as a "lawbreaker." According to labeling theory, if convicted offenders are related to as "dangerous, second-class citizens who are law vi-

olators," they may begin to perceive themselves as being "law violating."[82] Once they perceive themselves as law violators, labeling theory asserts they will then play that role upon their release.

In addition, as Sutherland and Cressey note, "Hatred of the criminal by society results in hatred of society by the criminal."[83] Relating to criminals as being dangerous, segregating them, and making them keep their distance (both while they are incarcerated and following their release) may force them into a career of criminal activity.

A third danger of long-term imprisonment is "institutionalization." Some prisoners, especially those who have had problems in adjusting to outside society, may eventually prefer prison life to outside society. After several years, they may actually feel more comfortable being confined (with their basic needs met) than having to return to the world outside, which will have undergone substantial change since their entry into prison. They will also have established a circle of friends within the prison from whom they receive respect. If they encounter problems on their return to society (for example, being unemployed and broke), they may yearn at some level to return to prison.

THE TREATMENT APPROACH

There are literally hundreds of treatment programs in the corrections system. Space limitations prevent an exhaustive discussion of these programs, but a brief summary of major approaches will be covered in this section. It is necessary, however, to remember that the punitive approach has the continuous effect of decreasing the efficiency and effectiveness of treatment programs.

Individualized treatment for offenders has been increasingly popular since the 19th century. It developed as a reaction to the classical school, which advocated uniform penalties for criminals. Throughout history, however, there has been a dual standard of justice, with the rich and politically influential being (a) much less likely to be charged with a crime; (b) much less likely to be found guilty when accused because of their "character," position in society, and better legal representation; and (c) much less likely to receive a severe sentence if found guilty.

Counseling. Both one-to-one counseling and group counseling are used in prisons and by probation and parole officers. The aim is to identify the specific problems of each offender (including the reasons that motivated him or her to become involved in criminal activity) and then to develop programs for solving these problems. The inmate's needs may be extensive and numerous, including medical, psychological, and financial issues; drug use and abuse patterns; family and peer relationships; housing; education; vocational training; and employment. Attention is also given to the criminal's attitudes, motives, group and peer relationships, and rationalizations regarding criminality.

The effectiveness of counselors (social workers, probation and parole officers, psychologists, vocational rehabilitation counselors) is somewhat mitigated by their "dual" role perception by offenders. Some inmates view them as true helpers, whereas others view them as authority figures in control of rewards and punishments. Offenders with the second perception are reluctant to discuss socially unacceptable needs and motives or to establish a close relationship for fear that information divulged will be used against them.

Prison Education. Education in prison has two objectives: (a) to give inmates formal academic training comparable to schools and (b) to resocialize inmates' attitudes and behaviors. To accomplish these objectives, prisons use TV programs, movies, libraries, lectures, classroom instruction in academic subjects (covering elementary, secondary, and sometimes even college material), religious programs, group discussions, and recreational programs. However, the bitter attitude that most inmates have toward prison and the prison administration often interferes with their accomplishing educational objectives.

Vocational Training. The objective of these programs is to give inmates a job skill suitable to their capacities that will prepare them for employment on release. The quality of such programs in institutions throughout the country varies greatly. In many prisons, vocational training is defined as the maintenance work of the institution: laundry, cooking, custodial work, minor repairs, dishwashing. For a period of time, vocational training was considered the main component of rehabilitation, but now rehabilitation is seen as covering many other areas.

Prison Labor. The idea that prisoners should perform work has always existed. Originally, labor in prisons was seen as a method of punishment. England, for example, for a long time had inmates carry a cannonball on treadmills that had a meter measuring the number of units of work produced. For each meal, inmates had to produce a certain number of units. Additional units were assigned for misconduct.

Currently there are two conflicting conceptions of work: (a) it should be productive and train inmates for employment upon their release and (b) it should be hard, unpleasant, or monotonous for retributive purposes. The second view is still rationalized by some authorities as also having a reformative function; it is thought to teach discipline, obedience, and conformity and to develop an appreciation for avoiding criminal activity.

Convict labor has been used for building roads, running agricultural farms, fighting fires, conducting insect control programs, doing lumber-camp work, doing laundry, making state license plates, and performing a wide variety of other tasks. Work and educational release programs in jails and in some prisons allow release of inmates during the day so they may work or attend school while being locked up in the evening.

Good Time. Good-time legislation permits a prison review board to release a prisoner early if she or he has maintained good conduct. Most good-time laws specify that, for every month of acceptable behavior, a certain number of days will be deducted from the sentence. Good-time laws are designed to make inmates responsible for their conduct, to provide an incentive for good conduct and rehabilitation efforts, and to reduce discipline problems within prisons.

Indeterminate sentences, which were first established in the 1800s, have similar objectives. Many sentences are indeterminate, with a minimum and a maximum limit on the amount of time an inmate can be incarcerated. In recent years, however, a movement to return to determinate sentencing has gained considerable support.

Parole and Probation. Parole is the conditional release of a prisoner serving an indeterminate or unexpired sentence. It is granted by an administrative board (parole board) or by an executive. Parolees are considered "in custody" and are required to maintain acceptable conduct and avoid criminal activity. Parole is designed both to punish (certain behavior is restricted, and there is a threat of return to prison) and to treat the offender (a parole officer generally counsels and helps the parolee meet his or her needs).

Probation is granted by the courts. It involves suspending the sentence of a convicted offender and giving him or her freedom during good behavior under the supervision of a probation officer. Probationers are viewed as undergoing treatment. There is, however, the threat of punishment; if the conditions of probation are violated, the offender will be sent to prison. Similar to parole, probation contains reformation and retribution components.

Probation and parole officers have a dual role responsibility: a police role and a rehabilitative role. The probation and parole officer functions in the "police" or authority role by closely monitoring the activities of probationers and parolees to observe whether they are violating laws or violating the conditions of their parole/probation. Those being supervised are continually aware that the probation/parole officer has the authority to initiate procedures to revoke the probation/parole, which will send them to prison. Many probationers and parolees are distrustful of the criminal justice system and are therefore wary of anyone (including probation and parole officers) associated with this system.

This police role conflicts at times with the second primary function of probation and parole officers: the rehabilitative role. For rehabilitation to be most effective, the counselee must trust the counselor, must feel free to reveal socially unacceptable attitudes and activities to the counselor, and must form a close working relationship with the counselor. Obviously, those probationers and parolees who view their supervising officer primarily in the police role are likely to avoid forming a counseling relationship with that person.

HOW TO REDUCE CRIME AND DELINQUENCY

The heading of this section may be inappropriate. Societies have been trying for centuries to reduce crime through a number of different approaches, yet the rate of crime seems to fluctuate independently of direct crime-suppression efforts. About 30 years ago, former President Nixon declared war on crime, and the federal government has since spent billions trying to curb crime. Yet the rate continues to increase. The prospects for reducing crime in the future remain uncertain because we do not as yet know enough about how to prevent people from committing crimes or how to reform them after they do. Nevertheless, this section will summarize major approaches that have been advanced to improve the situation. (You will note that some of the proposals are contradictory.) We will consider three general areas:

1. Increasing or decreasing sentences.
2. Reforming the correctional system.
3. Preventing crime in the first place.

Increasing or Decreasing Sentences

There are conflicting opinions concerning the appropriateness of various sentences as related to the crime committed. Suggestions to improve the effects of various sentences include shortening the times between arrest, conviction, and punishment; imposing harsher sentences; permanently imprisoning repeat offenders; increasing prosecution of white-collar criminals; creating uniform sentences; decriminalizing victimless offenses; and imposing stricter gun control.

INSTITUTING SWIFT AND CERTAIN PUNISHMENT

It is generally agreed that the deterrent value of punishment decreases as the time lag between the crime and the eventual punishment increases. Only a fraction of those who commit crimes are arrested, and only a fraction of those arrested are ever found guilty. All too often, crime does pay—particularly white-collar crime and organized crime. Criminal court proceedings commonly drag on for months and even years. During this time, offenders use due-process maneuvers in the hope that public anger over their crimes will dissipate and they will either be found innocent or have the charges reduced. Swifter action in catching, convicting, and punishing a greater percentage of lawbreakers will, it is argued, lead to greater respect for the law and curb crime. The argument against swifter action is that it would conflict with due-process protections and might result in a higher number of innocent people being arrested, convicted, and incarcerated.

IMPOSING HARSHER SENTENCES

This approach is also based on the assumption that punishment has a deterrent effect. Advocates demand longer prison sentences and increased use of capital punishment. The reasoning is that lengthier sentences will reduce crime because criminals obviously cannot victimize citizens when they are locked up.

Opponents of this approach claim that longer sentences may increase crime rates rather than reduce them. Because practically all people sent to prison return to society, lengthier sentences may simply increase the bitterness of those serving time, reduce their respect for our laws and criminal justice system, and give them extended training in breaking the law through association with other hardened criminals. Opponents also note that imprisonment is expensive for society; it costs more per year to send someone to prison than to college.

SEPARATING REPEAT OFFENDERS FROM SOCIETY

Crimes of violence (arson, rape, armed robbery, murder) are of particular concern to society, as are certain other offenses, such as repeated hard-drug trafficking. According to some authorities, repeated arrests and convictions for these offenses demonstrate that the offenders are so dangerous that protection of society must become the primary concern. It is further asserted that, because past efforts at reformation have not been effective, future efforts are not likely to be either. For repeat offenders of serious crimes, we should just "throw away the key." Our courts are in fact heading in this direction by locking up "repeaters" for longer periods of time.

A particular problem with this proposal is that serious crimes of violence are often committed by juveniles. As we've seen, juvenile courts use a "child-saving" approach: Their main focus is not on the nature of the crime but on treatment or rehabilitation. A number of states now allow juveniles arrested for homicide and other violent crimes to be charged and tried as adults. In adult court, convicted juveniles can then be given sentences commensurate with the seriousness of their offenses.

Advocating that repeat lawbreakers who commit serious crimes be locked up for long periods is an admission of rehabilitation failure. On the other hand, it is a proclamation that potential victims have rights too and that their rights take priority over the rights of repeaters.

GETTING TOUGHER ON WHITE-COLLAR CRIME

In the early 1970s, many high-ranking officials in the Nixon administration (which was pledged to "law and order") were accused of committing such offenses as illegal wiretapping, tax fraud, destruction of evidence, misappropriation of campaign funds, extortion, bribery, conspiracy to pervert the course of justice, and conspiracy to violate civil rights. Many of these officials were convicted but received very light sentences (often in special federal prisons referred to as "resorts") in comparison to the harsher sentences given to ordinary burglars and thieves. Former President Nixon was pardoned by President Gerald Ford prior to facing criminal charges. The Watergate scandal aroused a major discussion about the mild way in which white-collar crime is handled in our society. Yet today, white-collar crime is still largely ignored or glossed over by the police, the courts, and the correctional system. (It should be noted that organized crime is also increasingly involved in white-collar type offenses.)

It has been argued that more vigorous arrests, prosecution, and sentencing of white-collar crime and organized crime would lead to increased respect for the law by all citizens and would reduce crime. But that would require the White power structure in our society to encourage the police and the courts to arrest and prosecute its own members. In actuality, that power structure is more interested in prosecuting the crimes that are committed by members of the powerless groups in our society.

CREATING UNIFORM SENTENCES

As noted earlier, there are wide variations in sentences imposed on different convicted offenders for the same crime. If justice is to be equal for all, then variables such as the economic status, race, and gender of the offender should not influence his or her sentence. Sentencing one murderer to death while putting another on probation undermines respect for the law and the criminal justice system. One way to reduce the disparity in sentences is to make them subject to appeal; currently the harshness of a sentence cannot be appealed. A second way is to take legislative action to reduce the latitude that is given to judges in imposing sentences for each type of conviction.

The move toward greater uniformity in sentencing in recent years does address somewhat the need for equality of treatment, but it also reduces the opportunity for individualized justice, which is a hallmark of our system. In addition, more uniform sentences (especially the imposition of mandatory minimums) has increased the average length of stay in prisons and contributed to prison overcrowding.

DECRIMINALIZING VICTIMLESS OFFENSES

Prohibition is the classic example of creating problems by outlawing a victimless activity. Prohibition made it a crime to manufacture, distribute, or drink alcohol. Police spent substantial time and resources trying to enforce this law but were largely unsuccessful. Instead, Prohibition led to bootlegging and fostered the rise of organized crime.

Today, victimless crimes are still with us—gambling, marijuana use, fornication, and prostitution, to name just a few. If such actions were decriminalized, immense resources in money and time could be diverted to confronting the crimes that do have victims. There is some movement to decriminalize certain offenses; for example, Nevada now allows prostitution in a few counties. In the past decade, police departments have been less vigorous in making arrests for smoking marijuana, and there are efforts to decriminalize this activity in several states. Gambling laws are beginning to undergo change, as some states have now set up legal gambling activities, such as lotteries, casinos, and parimutuel betting on horse races and dog races.

IMPOSING STRICTER GUN CONTROL

In the past 40 years, John F. Kennedy, Robert Kennedy, Martin Luther King, Jr., Anwar Sadat, and John Lennon were killed by shootings. In 1981 there were assassination attempts on President Reagan and on the pope. Over 19,000 homicides and over 500,000 robberies are committed annually in the United States.[84] Many homicides and armed robberies involve the use of a handgun.

There are an estimated 60 million handguns in the United States—one handgun for every two homes and one for every four citizens.[85] The number of Americans killed by handguns exceeds the number of Americans killed in wars declared by the United States in the 20th century.[86] States that have a higher proportion of guns have higher rates of homicides, suicides, and deaths during domestic disputes.[87] A number of special-interest groups have advocated an end to the sale of handguns except for approved and limited purposes.

It appears that Congress and the federal government are moving in the direction of imposing stricter gun controls. In 1993 the Brady Bill was enacted, which requires that gun buyers wait 5 business days and undergo a background check by police. (The Brady Bill was named in honor of James Brady, former presidential press secretary who was shot and severely wounded in the 1981 assassination attempt on President Reagan.) Supporters and opponents of the Brady Bill agree that the enactment of this bill will not stop the majority of criminals from obtaining firearms. In 1994 Congress passed, and President Clinton signed, a crime bill banning 19 types of assault-style firearms, which are used primarily to rapidly kill a number of people.

The major opposition to passing stricter gun control laws comes from the gun lobby (a coalition of several powerful organizations including the National Rifle Association) that is funded by sports enthusiasts and firearms manufacturers.

Reforming the Correctional System

Perhaps the first step in improving the correctional system is to clarify its presently conflicting objectives, some of which are punitive in nature and others of which are treatment oriented. When the general public and public officials are confused about what the primary objective for incarceration should be, prison administrators and inmates will also be confused, making rehabilitation difficult.

If our society decides that retribution, deterrence, and vengeance should be the primary goals, then we can expect a continued high rate of recidivism and continued high crime rates because those being punished will become increasingly bitter and hostile toward society. However, from a social benefits viewpoint, the primary objective of a correctional system should be to curb future criminal activity of incarcerated offenders in the least expensive way. The current prison system is not only ineffectual in preventing recidivism, but it is also expensive. The national average per capita cost for institutionalization of adult felons is many times greater than the cost of probation services to adults.

If the correctional system had rehabilitation as its primary objective, a number of changes would occur. For example, sentencing of wrongdoers is now based primarily on the nature of their past deeds. If a convicted person has previously committed serious felonies, a long incarceration is likely. A reformative approach would, instead, focus on identifying ways to curb the supervisee's (or offender's) tendency to break the law. Involved in this identification process would be an assessment of the reasons why the person is committing crimes and a determination of how the offender can legally obtain what he or she wants. Needed services would then be specified, and the responsibilities of the supervisee would be identified—such as maintaining or securing employment, enrolling in an educational or vocational program, receiving counseling or family therapy, undergoing medical or drug treatment, paying debts, and/or making restitution. Removal from society would generally be used only after the supervisee failed to meet the requirements of the supervision plan (for example, restitution) or when the supervisee was a definite threat to society.

Let's consider two examples that illustrate this approach.

1. A 17-year-old female runs away from home, has very limited employment and educational skills, and therefore turns to prostitution for financial reasons. Instead of assigning fines after each arrest, would it not make more sense to identify her needs (such as financial needs, educational needs, need for legal employment that pays her more than prostitution, and need to resolve the conflicts with her parents) and then provide her with services to meet these needs?

2. A 32-year-old male is arrested for burglarizing 43 homes in wealthy neighborhoods over a span of 4 months. The man is unemployed, and he states that he committed the burglaries to support his cocaine habit. Instead of sending him directly to prison at taxpayers' expense, authorities could identify his needs (such as job training, employment, and drug treatment) and then provide

him with services to meet those needs. As part of such a rehabilitative approach, he would be required (over a realistic period of time) to make restitution to the victims. He would be informed that additional convictions or any other failure on his part to fulfill the terms of the rehabilitative plan would result in a lengthy prison sentence.

With this approach, supervisees would become acutely aware that they have the choice and the responsibility to decide which of two avenues to pursue: continuation of criminal activity (resulting in a lengthy prison sentence) or a more law-abiding, productive, and respectable future. If they choose the latter, they would be given access to services (for example, counseling and vocational training) available to assist them, but they would also be made aware of the responsibility and effort required on their part.

With more than 1 million people behind bars, the United States imprisons a higher proportion of its population than any other nation.[88] Marc Mauer notes:

> *The same policies that have helped make us a world leader in incarceration have clearly failed to make us a safer nation. We need a fundamental change of direction, towards proven programs and policies that work to reduce both imprisonment and crime. We've got to stop jailing and start rehabilitating.*[89]

DIVERSION PROGRAMS

Labeling theory suggests that the criminal justice system perpetuates crime by branding offenders and interacting with them as if they were delinquents and criminals. Diversion programs have therefore been developed in a number of communities to divert first-time or minor offenders from entering the criminal justice system; as an alternative, they receive services from community agencies.

One such program is "deferred prosecution," which some communities now provide. Adults who are arrested for the first time for a minor offense (such as shoplifting) are referred by either a judge or a prosecuting attorney to deferred prosecution prior to standing trial. Deferred prosecu-

tion programs provide, over a period of several weeks, small-group sessions that are geared to helping the members refrain from committing additional crimes. The case is dismissed if the defendant (a) pays for any damages, (b) is not re-arrested while participating in the program, and (c) attends all the group meetings.

Many diversion programs focus on keeping juveniles out of juvenile courts and criminal courts by instead referring them to treatment programs handled by community agencies. Juveniles, for example, may be referred for counseling (from social workers, probation officers, or psychologists); they may receive help for emotional or family problems; or they may receive help with schoolwork.

Many communities have Scared Straight programs, which were initially developed at a prison in Rahway, New Jersey. Juveniles who have committed offenses are taken to visit a prison, where inmates harshly describe prison life. Prison conditions are also observed firsthand. The objective is to expose juveniles to the realities of life in prison so that the threat of imprisonment will motivate them to stop breaking the law. It is not yet certain, however, that this exposure has a deterrent effect on juveniles.

TRANSITIONAL PROGRAMS

A variety of transitional programs are now offered to offenders. While in jail or prison, a person may be allowed to work in the community during the daytime. School-release programs allow inmates to attend college or a technical school during the day. Halfway houses have been used as an alternative to sending a person to prison; they allow residents to work or go to school in their home community. Halfway houses have also been used to help inmates just released from prison to readjust to society. If offenders misbehave while in halfway houses, there is the threat of being sent back to jail or prison.

A goal of transitional programs is for inmates to maintain and develop strong ties to the non-criminal elements in their home community. The programs seek to reduce or alleviate the negative effects of incarceration and provide opportunities and resources for rehabilitation.

Preventing Crime

Theoretically, there are four ways to prevent crime:

1. Make the punishment for violating a law so severe that lawbreakers will be deterred from committing crimes. Studies on the use of capital punishment, however, suggest that even this severest penalty does not deter crime.

2. Keep the convicted lawbreakers in prison. Such an approach would be very expensive—especially since practically everyone occasionally commits a crime.

3. Change the economic, social, and political conditions that breed crime. Among the numerous proposals that have been advanced are: improve family life; improve the educational system to make education an exciting, growth-producing experience for students; end racial discrimination; provide equal opportunities for achieving success for all citizens, including the poor and minority groups; provide full employment and a decent living wage for all able-bodied people; improve housing conditions and living conditions in our inner cities; and curb alcohol and drug abuse.

4. Educate the general public on how to avoid becoming a victim of crime. This fourth approach will be discussed in some detail and involves reducing opportunities for crime to occur. This approach is highlighted because it is one everyone should be aware of and participate in.

Dae Chang describes this approach, which developed from victimology, an area of study in criminology:

> Research shows that much crime—and by far the greatest portion of street crime and burglary—is the result of opportunity and luck rather than of careful and professional planning.
>
> Someone sees an "opportunity"—in an open window, an empty house, a person alone in a dark alley—and acts on it. Muggers look for likely victims, not specific individuals, burglars, for a house they can enter, not a particular address. Preselected targets frequently are chosen precisely because they are seen as "easy marks."
>
> Who is the victim of a crime? What causes crime? Who causes crime? There are some startling answers to these questions. In the majority of cases, the victim contributes, and in some cases is a major cause of a criminal act. All of us are potential victims. We frequently present the criminal or an individual with an invitation to commit a crime. We entice him, advertise to him, coax him, give him the opportunity, and even implant the idea into his head. Through our carelessness, open disregard for our personal possessions, forgetfulness, attitudes, vanity, etc., we frequently invite someone to commit a criminal act either directly at ourselves or to our possessions. We also invite bodily harm upon ourselves by our actions in public and private. Our habits, attitudes, dress, etc. all are signals to the people who would be enticed into crime.[90]

In effect, one must ask oneself, "Is what I'm currently doing, or failing to do, making me vulnerable to becoming a victim of a crime?" Exhibit 9.4 presents a number of specific precautions to prevent becoming a crime victim.

SOCIAL WORK AND THE CRIMINAL JUSTICE SYSTEM

Role of Social Work

The primary focus of social work in the criminal justice system has been on the correctional component. Social workers have frequently been employed as probation and parole officers, as social workers in a prison, and as social workers at a correctional halfway house. There are only a few police departments that employ social workers to provide social services to individuals and families with whom police come in contact.

To a lesser extent, social workers have been employed in programs that are primarily preventative (as composed to correctional) in nature. For example, in the juvenile gang arena, a wide variety of programs have attempted to reduce delinquent gang activities. These have included detached worker programs, in which workers join gangs and seek to transform antisocial into prosocial

EXHIBIT 9.4

Precautions to Prevent Becoming a Crime Victim

AT HOME

- Bolt doors and windows, and use exterior lighting to frustrate burglary techniques.

- Engrave identification numbers on possessions to curb fencing of stolen property.

- If you leave home for part of the evening, make it look as though someone is home. Leave some lights and music on. Or leave the television on, keeping it low so that it sounds as if people are inside talking or the family is home watching TV.

- Double-secure sliding-glass doors by placing lengths of metal rod or wooden dowels in the lower tracks to prevent the doors from being opened.

- Put in exterior lighting over front and back doors. Also, cut back shrubbery that might be used to hide intruders.

- If you hear someone breaking in at night, let the intruder know you have heard the noise, but avoid a confrontation. Chances are the person will leave as fast as possible. If you confront the intruder unexpectedly, you could get hurt. Instead, yell, "Get the shotgun!"—even if you are alone. Or yell to the neighbors or call the police.

- One of the best places to have a strong dead-bolt lock is on the inside of your bedroom door.

- A dog that barks a lot may deter an intruder. The yapping of the dog will make the intruder wary that someone else will hear the barking, so the intruder will probably exit in a hurry.

- Do not leave the key to your home under the doormat, in the mailbox, or on top of the door ledge.

- Be cautious about inviting door-to-door salespeople into your home. Many communities now require salespeople to carry an identification card.

- Do not leave possessions on lawns or in your driveway at night. If left, bicycles, barbecue grills, power tools, and lawn mowers are easily removed.

- Do not leave important papers, expensive jewelry, or large sums of money at home. Rent a bank security deposit box, which protects valuables not only from burglars but also from fires and natural disasters.

- When going on an extended vacation, arrange for a friend to check your home every few days. Do not let newspapers or mail pile up. The post office will hold your mail at no cost while you are away. Inexpensive timers can be purchased to activate lights, radios, or TVs to give the impression you are home.

- When you expect a visitor and are unable to be home, do not leave a telltale note outside: "Welcome—will be back at 8 P.M. Walk in and make yourself at home. Door is unlocked." Burglars readily accept such invitations.

- Women are advised to list only their last name and initials on mailboxes and in phone directories.

IN AN AUTOMOBILE

- Flashy equipment on autos will invite theft or break-ins. If you have mag wheels, a stereo tape deck, CB radio, fancy wheel covers, and other expensive gadgets, your car will draw attention. The place you park your car can be an invitation for it to be stolen or broken into. Always lock your car, put valuables in the trunk, and never leave the key in the ignition.

- If you leave your car someplace for a few days (for example, at an airport), it will be nearly

(continued)

EXHIBIT 9.4   *(continued)*

theft-proof if you pull the center wire out of the distributor in addition to locking the car and taking the keys. (Before pulling the wire, make sure you know how to put it back!)

■ Remove identification from key chains so that, if your keys are lost or stolen, no one knows what the keys will open.

■ Do not hitchhike or pick up hitchhikers. Hitchhiking has led to a significant number of robberies and assaults. If you cannot avoid hitchhiking, be very selective as to whom you ride with.

IN PUBLIC

■ Avoid carrying large sums of money. If forced to do so, take along a second wallet containing three or four bills and some expired credit cards, which you can give a thief if confronted.

■ When in a crowd, place your wallet in a safe place (for example, front pocket, a waist pocket, or a buttoned back pocket) to frustrate pickpocketing efforts.

■ Never leave a purse unattended.

■ Avoid going into a dark parking lot. It may be cheaper to call a taxi than risk being mugged.

■ There are a variety of approaches to avoid becoming a victim of rape, including physical techniques of self-defense (for example, the martial arts) and distasteful approaches (for example, vomiting or urinating on the rapist, informing the potential rapist you have tested positive for HIV, sharply squeezing the genitals of the rapist, and poking your fingers into the rapist's eyes). Women should become familiar with these approaches and select a few that they would be comfortable with and prepared to use should an attack occur.

---

attitudes and behaviors; drug treatment programs for gang members who have a chemical addiction; programs to support and strengthen families, particularly single-parent families in urban areas; programs to prevent dropping out of school and to provide academic support (such as mentoring programs); and family preservation programs (see Chapter 6 for a description).

Many probation and parole officers are trained in social work. One of the important responsibilities of a probation and parole officer is to prepare a presentence report. This is a social history of the offender that is prepared to help guide the judge in sentencing. A sample presentence report appears in Case Example 9.5.

In the field of corrections, there are two important factors influencing treatment: custody-treatment conflict and offenders' "con games." Social workers need to understand how these factors operate.

Factors Influencing Treatment

CUSTODY-TREATMENT CONFLICT

In prison settings, administrators emphasize custody. Over 90% of the money spent in such institutions goes for custody.[91] When custody policies clash with treatment programs, treatment almost always comes in second. Prison administrators are primarily concerned with preventing escapes, curbing riots, and calming internal disruptions. New social workers in prison settings soon realize rehabilitation is not the primary focus.

Social workers in prisons, and those who work as probation and parole officers, are often viewed by offenders as part of the larger authoritarian bureaucracy that caught and convicted them. Many offenders are distrustful of social workers because they feel the social workers are "monitoring" or "policing" them.

CASE EXAMPLE 9.5   Presentence Report

Walworth County Court
June 23, 1998

Name: James LaMartina

Address: 408 Walnut St.
Delavan, WI 54987

Legal Residence: Same

Age: 34

Date of Birth: 5-8-64

Sex: Male

Race: Caucasian

Citizenship: U.S.A.

Education: 11th grade

Marital Status: Married

Dependents: Two (wife and
a 4-year-old son)

Soc. Sec. No.: 393-42-9067

FBI No.: 287 1237

Detainers or Charges Pending:
None

Offense: Second-degree sexual assault

Penalty: Imprisoned not more than 10 years
and/or fined not more than $10,000

Plea: Guilty on 6-10-94

Verdict:

Custody: Posted bail of $5000

Prosecuting Attorney: Richard Jorgenson,
Assistant District Attorney

Defense Counsel: Donald Hauser

OFFENSE: OFFICIAL VERSION

Officers Karen Davenport and David Erdmier stated they arrested Mr. LaMartina in
Lakeland County Park at 12:30 A.M. on June 5, 1998, for having sexual intercourse
with a 17-year-old minor. Mr. LaMartina and the minor were in the back seat of the
offender's car and were reported to be unclothed.

Mr. LaMartina stated he had met the woman in Don's Hillside Tavern earlier in the
day. He stated that this was the first time he had met her and did not know her age—
he assumed she was an adult. A check with Donald Leesburg, owner of the tavern,
indicated that Mr. LaMartina was a frequent patron of the tavern but that the woman
was not a regular patron. The owner further stated that the night of June 5, 1998, was
busy. He noted that Mr. LaMartina was there earlier that evening, but the owner was
unaware whether Mr. LaMartina had met this woman at the tavern.

The minor appeared intoxicated at the time of the arrest. Her driver's license the
night of the arrest revealed her age to be 17 years and 2 months. She was returned
home by the police to her parents, who were very angry; Officers Davenport and Erdmier had to restrain the father from physically hitting her.

DEFENDANT'S VERSION OF OFFENSE

Mr. LaMartina stated that he frequently stopped at Don's Hillside Tavern after work with fellow workers from the construction company he has worked with for the past 6 years. Mr. LaMartina stated that this evening was the first time he had met this woman. He mentioned he began buying drinks for her and for the two other women friends she was with. He stated that she had drunk considerably more than he had. He emphasized that he assumed she was at least 21 years of age (the legal drinking age in this state).

Around midnight he asked her if she wanted a ride home, which she accepted. He drove instead to Lakeland County Park, where he emphasized she willingly agreed to go to the back seat with him and willingly became sexually involved. When asked whether he had become sexually involved with other women, Mr. LaMartina became defensive and refused to answer.

PRIOR RECORD

Date	Offense	Disposition
9-7-90	Disorderly conduct	$80 fine
10-11-94	Driving motor vehicle while under the influence	$310 fine and group dynamics course

PERSONAL HISTORY

The defendant was born in Fort Atkinson, Wisconsin, on May 8, 1964, the older of two children. His parents were dairy farmers. He attended public schools and completed the 11th grade. He received mainly Cs and Ds in school and left school to help on the farm. He had a number of friends in school and was active in several sports, including the high school varsity basketball and baseball teams.

The defendant's father, Leonard, died following a stroke when the defendant was 22 years of age. His mother, Loretta, is still living on the family farm in rural Jefferson County. The defendant ran the farm for 6 years after his father's death and then sold the cattle in order to work for Johnstone's Road Construction Company. The farm appeared to be only marginally successful when the defendant had dairy cattle. The defendant still plants and harvests crops on the farm.

The defendant's sister, Janine, is 28 years of age and has been married for the past 6 years to Dennis Richter, a dairy farmer in Dane County.

Mr. LaMartina has been married for the past 8 years to Sue Heinz (maiden name). Sue is 32 years of age and graduated from Milton College 10 years ago. She taught elementary school for the first 4 years of their marriage but has not taught school for the past 4 years—since their son, Tim, was born. She and James LaMartina have lived in the LaMartinas' farmhouse since their marriage.

Sue LaMartina separated from her husband shortly after she heard he was arrested. She and her son are now staying with her parents. She has ambivalent feelings about

(continued)

CASE EXAMPLE 9.5 *(continued)*

her husband. She stated that he can be a good father and husband, but she is intensely irritated about his drinking and about his staying out late at night with his "cronies." She stated that she suspected he may occasionally have been having affairs with other women, but this incident is "the last straw." She stated that she is seeing a counselor at the mental health center, has contacted an attorney, and is contemplating a divorce.

Mr. LaMartina stated that he does not want a divorce and appears sincerely remorseful about the family problems he has created. He stated that if he and his wife can reconcile, he will change his ways. He will not stay out late or become involved with other women. Mr. LaMartina has asked his wife to attend marriage counseling with him, but she indicated she is still too emotionally hurt and embarrassed to be able to discuss the incident.

There is some evidence that Mr. LaMartina has been drinking to excess for several years. Mr. LaMartina denies this, but his frequent stops after work at a tavern and his past arrest record suggest otherwise. The future of his marriage, however, appears to be a more immediate problem needing attention.

EVALUATIVE SUMMARY

The defendant is a 34-year-old male who entered a plea of guilty to second-degree sexual assault. The defendant was arrested for having sexual intercourse with a 17-year-old woman he met, apparently for the first time, earlier that evening at a tavern. The defendant apparently did not know the woman was a minor. The defendant's wife has separated from him following this arrest and is contemplating a divorce. The defendant expressed considerable remorse about the embarrassment and domestic strife he has caused.

Mr. LaMartina has a 4-year-old son and has no prior felony arrest record. He may at times drink to excess. He completed 11 years of schooling and has run a dairy farm. For the past 6 years, he has been a road construction worker. His employer reports that he is dependable and has been a good worker.

RECOMMENDATION

It is recommended that the defendant be fined and placed on probation. If placed on probation, the defendant expresses willingness to seek counseling for his domestic problems. This counseling should also at some future time explore whether he has a drinking problem. The future of his marriage, however, needs first attention.

Respectfully submitted,

Ralph Franzene
Probation and Parole Officer
State of Wisconsin

OFFENDERS' "CON GAMES"

Since the 1930s, the criminal justice system has promoted both individual and group therapy. Prison administrators and directors of probation and parole programs have required offenders to participate in treatment programs. Obviously, compelling clients to submit to treatment interventions can inhibit establishment of rapport with offenders. Yet enforced treatment is commonplace in corrections.

Offenders are highly skilled at "conning" professional staff through persuasion, deceit, and manipulation. Most convicted offenders disdain correctional staff. This disdain is strengthened when they see therapy forced on them. Inmates realize that they must participate in such activities as individual and group counseling in order to have a good record. If imprisoned on an indeterminate sentence (as is common in most states), a good record will get them released on parole sooner. If they are on probation or parole, offenders may see their participation in "treatment" programs as a way to get the probation/parole officer to do things for them or to overlook minor violations of the rules for probation and parole.

The social worker should be aware that many offenders who request professional assistance have no genuine interest in self-improvement but are seeking to manipulate the worker.

SUMMARY

Crime is one of the most serious problems facing our nation. Serious, violent crime has reached alarming proportions. In addition, the criminal justice system (the police, the courts, and prisons) is perceived as relatively ineffective in curbing crime.

Everyone, at one time or another, has violated some laws. Those arrested for crimes are disproportionately likely to be male, young, a member of a racial minority, and a city resident. If white-collar crime and organized crime were more vigorously prosecuted, the "typical" criminal would more likely be older, White, and a suburban resident.

Official crime statistics are inaccurate for a variety of reasons. Many crimes go unreported. Police and courts vigorously enforce only certain crimes. Police-reporting practices are affected at times by political considerations, such as reclassifying serious offenses as less serious to attempt to make police departments appear more effective in curbing serious crimes. In terms of number of people victimized and financial costs to society, it appears that white-collar crime is our most serious type. Yet it is less vigorously enforced by the police and the courts.

A variety of theories about the causes of crime have been advanced. These theories identify some of the reasons crime occurs. But we do not have a complete understanding of all the reasons for crime. With the crime rate continuing to increase, it is also clear that we do not as yet know how to reduce crime effectively.

Current correctional systems throughout the world reflect conflicting objectives; some components are punishment oriented, whereas others are treatment oriented. Generally, the two components, when combined, result in a system that is confusing and ineffective in curbing criminal activity. There is a danger that prisons may serve as schools for crime and may have a labeling effect that leads to future criminal activity.

A number of proposals have been advanced for reducing crime, including administering swift and certain punishment, imposing harsher sentences, separating repeat offenders from society, getting tougher on white-collar crime, creating uniform sentencing, decriminalizing victimless offenses, imposing stricter gun control, reforming the correctional system to emphasize the treatment approach, increasing use of diversion and transitional programs, and educating citizens on how to avoid becoming crime victims. Some of these proposals contradict others. Although each proposal has some research support, no proposal has conclusively been proved valid in reducing crime.

The ways in which societies have punished convicted offenders are as atrocious as the atrocities offenders have inflicted on victims. The "eye for an eye" retributive approach generally is ineffective in curbing future crime.

NOTES

1. Vincent N. Parrillo, John Stimson, and Ardyth Stimson, *Contemporary Social Problems*, 2nd ed. (New York: Macmillan, 1989), pp. 127–158.
2. William Kornblum and Joseph Julian, *Social Problems*, 9th ed. (Upper Saddle River, NJ: Prentice Hall, 1998), pp. 156–181.
3. *Crime in the United States, 1996: Uniform Crime Reports* (Washington, DC: U.S. Government Printing Office, 1957), p. 5.
4. Donald Baer, "Guns," *U.S. News & World Report*, May 8, 1989, pp. 20–25.
5. James W. Coleman and Donald R. Cressey, *Social Problems*, 6th ed. (New York: HarperCollins, 1996), p. 400.
6. Ibid.
7. Kornblum and Julian, *Social Problems*, p. 174.
8. Ibid., p. 175.
9. Ibid.
10. *Crime in the United States, 1996*, pp. 224–225.
11. Kornblum and Julian, *Social Problems*, p. 178.
12. Ibid.
13. Donald Jackson, "Justice for None," *New Times*, Jan. 11, 1974, p. 51.
14. William Kornblum and Joseph Julian, *Social Problems*, 6th ed. (Englewood Cliffs, NJ: Prentice Hall, 1989), p. 175.
15. *Crime in the United States, 1996*.
16. Coleman and Cressey, *Social Problems*, p. 397.
17. Kornblum and Julian, *Social Problems*, 9th ed., pp. 164–166.
18. Ibid.
19. Coleman and Cressey, *Social Problems*, p. 397.
20. H. E. Pepinsky and R. Quinney, *Criminology as Peacemaking* (Bloomington: Indiana University Press, 1991).
21. Charles Goring, *The English Convict* (London: His Majesty's Stationery Office, 1913).
22. Thomas Szasz, *The Myth of Mental Illness* (New York: Hoeber-Harper, 1961).
23. H. J. Eysenck, "The Effects of Psychotherapy," *International Journal of Psychiatry*, 1 (1965), pp. 97–144.
24. Charles Zastrow and Ralph Navarre, "Self-Talk: A New Criminological Theory," *International Journal of Comparative and Applied Criminal Justice*, Fall 1979, pp. 167–176.
25. Edwin H. Sutherland and Donald R. Cressey, *Criminology*, 8th ed. (Philadelphia: Lippincott, 1970), p. 10.
26. Robert K. Merton, *Social Theory and Social Structure* (New York: Free Press, 1968), p. 232.
27. John M. Johnson and Jack Douglas, eds., *Crime at the Top: Deviance in Business and the Professions* (Philadelphia: Lippincott, 1978).
28. Walter B. Miller, "Lower Class Culture as a Generating Milieu of Gang Delinquency," *Journal of Social Issues*, 14 (1958), pp. 5–19.
29. Albert Cohen, *Delinquent Boys: The Culture of the Gang* (New York: Free Press, 1955).
30. Charles Cooley, *Human Nature and the Social Order* (New York: Scribner's, 1902).
31. Gary Cavendar, "Alternative Approaches: Labeling and Critical Perspectives," in *Criminology: A Contemporary Handbook*, Joseph F. Sheley, ed. (Belmont, CA: Wadsworth, 1995), pp. 186–199.
32. Stewart Powell, Steven Emerson, and Orr Kelly, "Busting the Mob," *U.S. News & World Report*, Feb. 3, 1986, pp. 24–31.
33. Kornblum and Julian, *Social Problems*, 9th ed., pp. 170–171.
34. Powell, Emerson, and Kelly, "Busting the Mob," pp. 24–31.
35. Ibid.
36. Coleman and Cressey, *Social Problems*, pp. 390–391.
37. Kornblum and Julian, *Social Problems*, 9th ed., pp. 170–171.
38. Johnson and Douglas, *Crime at the Top*.
39. Edwin H. Sutherland, *White Collar Crime* (New York: Dryden Press, 1949), p. 9.
40. Kornblum and Julian, *Social Problems*, 9th ed., p. 168.
41. Coleman and Cressey, *Social Problems*, p. 392.
42. Kornblum and Julian, *Social Problems*, 9th ed., p. 168.
43. Thomas Sullivan, Kenrick Thompson, Richard Wright, George Gross, and Dale Spady, *Social Problems* (New York: Wiley, 1980), p. 586.
44. *Crime in the United States, 1996*.
45. Alexander B. Smith and Harriet Pollack, "Crimes Without Victims," *Saturday Review*, Dec. 4, 1971, pp. 27–29.
46. Janet S. Hyde, *Understanding Human Sexuality*, 5th ed. (New York: McGraw-Hill, 1994), p. 483.
47. Kornblum and Julian, *Social Problems*, 9th ed., p. 166.
48. Coleman and Cressey, *Social Problems*, p. 386.

49. Ibid., p. 387.

50. Edwin H. Sutherland, *The Professional Thief* (Chicago: University of Chicago Press, 1937).

51. Charles H. McCaghy and Stephen A. Cernkovich, *Crime in American Society,* 2nd ed. (New York: Macmillan, 1987), pp. 245–247.

52. *Crime in the United States, 1996,* p. 224.

53. Kornblum and Julian, *Social Problems,* 9th ed., p. 394.

54. Ibid.

55. Ibid.

56. J. F. Longres, "Youth Gangs," in *Encyclopedia of Social Work: 1990 Supplement* (Silver Spring, MD: NASW, 1990), p. 320.

57. A. P. Goldstein, *Delinquent Gangs: A Psychological Perspective* (Champaign, IL: Research Press, 1991).

58. Ibid.

59. Armando Morales, "Urban Gang Violence," in *Social Work: A Profession of Many Faces,* 5th ed., Armando Morales and Bradford W. Sheafor, eds. (Boston: Allyn & Bacon, 1989), pp. 419–421.

60. T. A. Sweeney, *Streets of Anger: Streets of Hope* (Glendale, CA: Great Western, 1980), p. 86.

61. C. R. Huff, "Gangs in the United States," in *The Gang Intervention Handbook,* A. P. Goldstein and C. R. Huff, eds. (Champaign, IL: Research Press, 1993).

62. Longres, "Youth Gangs," p. 323.

63. Goldstein, *Delinquent Gangs.*

64. Longres, "Youth Gangs," p. 325.

65. I. A. Spergel, *The Youth Gang Problem: A Community Approach* (New York: Oxford University Press, 1995).

66. Ibid.

67. Coleman and Cressey, *Social Problems,* p. 408.

68. Ibid., p. 406.

69. David M. Peterson, "The Police Officer's Conception of Proper Police Work," *The Police Journal,* 47 (1974), pp. 102–108.

70. Coleman and Cressey, *Social Problems,* p. 406.

71. Ibid., pp. 406–407.

72. Don C. Gibbons, *Society: Crime and Criminal Behavior,* 5th ed. (Englewood Cliffs, NJ: Prentice Hall, 1987), p. 439.

73. Coleman and Cressey, *Social Problems,* p. 407.

74. Alan Neigher, "The Gault Decision: Due Process and the Juvenile Court," *Federal Probation,* 31, no. 4 (Dec. 1967), pp. 8–18.

75. George F. Cole, *The American System of Criminal Justice,* 6th ed. (Pacific Grove, CA: Brooks/Cole, 1992), pp. 506–513.

76. Ibid., pp. 532–537.

77. Kornblum and Julian, *Social Problems,* 9th ed., pp. 183–184.

78. Ibid.

79. Coleman and Cressey, *Social Problems,* p. 408.

80. Ibid., p. 409.

81. Kornblum and Julian, *Social Problems,* 9th ed., p. 187.

82. Cooley, *Human Nature and the Social Order.*

83. Sutherland and Cressey, *Criminology,* p. 354.

84. *Crime in the United States, 1996.*

85. Coleman and Cressey, *Social Problems,* p. 412.

86. "Guns, Guns, Guns," *NBC News Summer Showcase,* Jul. 5, 1988.

87. Ibid.

88. Coleman and Cressey, *Social Problems,* p. 409.

89. Marc Mauer, quoted in "Prison Ratio Highest in U.S.," *Wisconsin State Journal,* Jan. 5, 1991, p. 3A.

90. Dae H. Chang, "How to Avoid Becoming a Victim of Crime," in *The Personal Problem Solver,* Charles Zastrow and Dae H. Chang, eds. (Englewood Cliffs, NJ: Prentice Hall, 1977), pp. 348–349.

91. Kornblum and Julian, *Social Problems,* 9th ed., pp. 187–193.

10

PROBLEMS IN EDUCATION AND SCHOOL SOCIAL WORK

In 1957 the United States and the Soviet Union were involved in an unofficial race to be first to place a satellite in orbit. The race became a symbol of international honor and prestige. The Soviets won when they successfully launched *Sputnik I* into orbit. Why did the United States lose? There were numerous reasons. However, the general public blamed the American educational system for neglecting subjects that were vital to national survival. For example, one outspoken critic, Max Rafferty, stated, "Instead of offering a four-year program of studies in mathematics, history, foreign languages, and other disciplines [high schools] encourage students to divert themselves with ceramics, stagecraft, table decorating, upholstering, and second-year golf." [1] Following these events, the American educational system was called on to emphasize mathematics, natural science, and other courses that would enable our country to successfully compete with the Soviets.

This chapter will:

- Summarize problems that school systems currently face.

- Present proposals for improving education.

- Discuss ideas for improving educational opportunities for children of low-income and minority families.

- Summarize the functions of school social workers and describe several role models for school social work practice.

PROBLEMATIC AREAS IN EDUCATION

The educational system has frequently been asked to resolve and alleviate social problems. For example, it is currently being called on to help reduce racism and sexism by developing new curricula designed to change the attitudes of school-age children. (The school setting is one of the few places where real integration of the races is likely to occur.) The educational system is expected to provide students of low-income families with the education and job-training skills that will enable them to escape from a life of poverty. It must identify and refer for treatment those children who have emotional or learning problems and those who abuse alcohol and other drugs. The school system is a mechanism for conveying antidelinquent values. In addition, it is required to refer to protective services any children who are suspected of being physically abused, neglected, or sexually abused.

Sometimes the educational system is perceived as a social problem itself because it is not meeting the expectations of society. Education is in a crisis of controversy and indecision. The self-confidence, morale, and motivation of teachers are often low. Some schools have been accused of perpetuating, rather than alleviating, social inequality for the poor and for minorities. Although recent improvements have occurred, student scores on achievement tests are substantially lower than they were 35 years ago. [2] Some inner-city schools are so victimized by vandalism and violence that students and teachers are as concerned with survival as with education.

The educational system in our country faces a number of crises. This section will examine the following problems: the question of the quality of education, the issue of equal access to a quality education, confusion about the goals of education, and intolerable working conditions in some school settings.

The Question of Quality

A number of indicators raise questions about the quality of education in the United States. Mean SAT (Scholastic Aptitude Test) scores of high school students on the verbal-reasoning section and on the mathematics-reasoning section have declined almost steadily over the last three decades. The SAT is taken annually by about 1 million high school students. From the mid-1950s to the mid-1960s, the scores were fairly constant, ranging from 472 to 478 on the verbal-reasoning section and from 495 to 502 on the mathematics-reasoning section. In the second half of the 1960s, both scores began to decline and continued to do so until around 1980, when the mean verbal score was 424 and the mean mathematics score was 466. Since 1980 there has been a slight increase, although scores are still significantly below what they were 35 years ago.[3]

In 1996 the U.S. Department of Education released the results of the Third International Mathematics and Science Study.[4] This study compared 41 industrialized nations according to math and science tests taken by eighth-graders. American eighth-graders ranked 28th in math tests and 17th in science tests. (The top three in math were Singapore, Korea, and Japan; the top three in science were Singapore, Czech Republic, and Japan.)

It is estimated that at least 3 million adult Americans cannot read or write at all.[5] Furthermore, more than ten times that number are "functionally illiterate"; that is, they cannot perform many of the reading, writing, and math tasks necessary to satisfactorily function in an industrial society.[6] The growing need for an educated workforce in our increasingly complex technological society has accentuated the problem of illiteracy.

In tests of geographic knowledge, students in the United States rank dead last among students tested who live in industrialized nations.[7] In a recent study, young people (age 18 to 24) from Canada, France, Germany, Japan, Mexico, and Sweden knew more about the U.S. population than young Americans did.[8]

In 1993 the U.S. Department of Education released the results of a survey showing that nearly half of all adult Americans read and write so poorly that they have trouble holding decent jobs.[9] The survey found that nearly half of all Americans over age 15 cannot write a short letter explaining a billing error or use a calculator to figure out the difference between a sale price and a regular price.

The National Commission on Excellence in Education summarized the educational problem in the United States as follows: "The educational foundations of our society are presently being eroded by a rising tide of mediocrity that threatens our very future as a nation and a people."[10]

Two explanations have been offered for the decline in student achievement in the United States, neither of which has been proven. One holds the school systems responsible, whereas the other places the cause in societal changes.

The first explanation asserts that school systems responded to the protests of the 1960s by changing their curricula. At that time, there were nationwide protests against racial inequality, the Vietnam War, and the role of traditional institutions (such as education) in our society. In response, many school systems reduced the number of required courses and gave students greater choice in course selections. As a result, for many students there was a decline in the amount of time spent in courses designed to teach basic skills. Such softening of the school curriculum, it has been asserted, led to the decline in achievement scores.

The second explanation focuses on societal changes since the mid-1960s. Students now spend much more time watching television—more time, in fact, than at any other activity except sleeping. Because children watch television more, they spend less time reading books and therefore do not read or write as well. Furthermore, with the advent of the computer age, youngsters are spending much of their time playing computer games and thereby devoting *even less* time to reading and writing. There have also been changes in the family. The proportion of single-parent families has risen dramatically. Also, in two-parent families, *both* parents are now more likely to be employed outside the home. Thus, parents may be less involved with the school system and may not monitor their children's homework assignments as closely. A similar assertion (not yet proven) is that there has been an increase in the proportion of dysfunctional families. Being raised in a dysfunctional family not only adversely impacts academic performance but also generates personal problems that sometimes lead to anger, violence, or substance abuse.

Whatever the reason or reasons, there is considerable pressure on school systems to make changes so that students will improve their basic skills of reading, writing, and arithmetic.

Equal Access to Quality Education

An egalitarian society has a responsibility to provide equal opportunity for a high-quality education to all its citizens. Our society has generally failed to meet this responsibility, especially with respect to minority groups and the poor.

A number of studies have found social class to be the single most effective predictor of achievement in school.[11] Students from the middle and upper classes tend to achieve higher grades, stay in school longer, and get higher scores on standardized achievement tests. There are two primary explanations for this relationship; one focuses on family background and the other on school systems.

The family background explanation ascribes the inequality to the fact that lower-class children live in a very different environment from middle- and upper-class children. The theory asserts that lower-income homes tend to have fewer magazines, newspapers, and books. Parents usually have less education and are less likely to act as role models to encourage reading in their children. Because lower-class families tend to be larger and to be headed by a single parent, it is said, their children receive less guidance and educational encouragement. Because of such factors, poor children may be less likely to view education as a means of achieving in society and less likely to develop educational goals. Further, poor children are more likely to be hungry and undernourished, which also inhibits their motivation to learn. In contrast, middle- and upper-class families tend to place a higher value on education and therefore put more time and effort into helping their children do homework in order to do well in school.

School systems are primarily geared for educating middle- and upper-class students. Youngsters who live in wealthy tax districts benefit from having more money spent on their schools than students who live in poorer districts. Nearly 50% of the funds for public schools in this country come from local school district taxes.[12] Because most of this money is derived from property

taxes, school districts with numerous expensive homes have much more revenue for their schools. (Roughly 40% of public school revenues comes from state taxes, and 10% comes from federal taxes.)[13]

In Illinois, for example, the richest districts spend about six times as much per student as the poorest districts.[14] In New York State, the richest districts spend nearly eight times as much as the poorest.[15]

Ironically, those who live in poorer school districts generally pay a higher percentage of the assessed value of their property in taxes than people who live in wealthier districts. One study on education concluded:

> It is unconscionable that a poor man in a poor district must often pay local taxes at higher rates for the inferior education of his child than the man of means in a rich district pays for the superior education of his child. Yet, incredibly, that is the situation today in most of the 50 states.[16]

Most teachers have middle-class backgrounds, which may mean they are better able to establish relationships with middle- and upper-income children, with whom they have more in common. There is also evidence that teachers expect less of poor children academically and behaviorally than they expect of middle- and upper-class children. In turn, low-income students tend to respond to such expectations by underachieving and misbehaving.[17] Thus, the expectation becomes a self-fulfilling prophecy.

Many school systems place students in one of several different tracks or ability groups. In high school, the so-called most promising are placed in college preparatory courses, whereas others go into "basic" or vocational classes. Lower-class and minority students are much more likely to be placed in the basic or vocational track[18] and are not exposed to college-oriented math, science, and literature.

In addition, because such students have little contact with college-bound students, they are less likely to aspire to a college education. Without a

The Pygmalion Effect

According to Greek mythology, Pygmalion was a king of Cyprus who made a female figure of ivory. Aphrodite, the Greek goddess of love and beauty, brought the statue to life for him. Robert Rosenthal and Lenore Jacobson performed an intriguing experiment to demonstrate that teachers' expectations of students can increase students' IQ scores. They called this self-fulfilling prophecy the Pygmalion Effect.

These experimenters began by giving a standard IQ test to students in 18 classrooms of an elementary school. (The teachers were told that the test was the Harvard Test of Inflected Acquisition—no such test exists.) The researchers then randomly selected 20% of the students and informed their teachers that the test results predicted remarkable progress for these students in the coming school year. When the students were retested 8 months later, those who had been expected to be remarkable achievers showed a significantly greater increase in IQ scores than the others. The researchers concluded that this increase was due to the higher expectations of the teachers, who then worked more intensively with these students. If the expectations of teachers do indeed affect student achievement and IQ test scores, lower-class and minority students may be at a disadvantage; most teachers are White, middle-class, and have a tendency to expect less from lower-class and minority students.

Source: Robert Rosenthal and Lenore Jacobson, *Pygmalion in the Classroom* (New York: Harper & Row, 1969).

college education, they have very limited opportunities to obtain high-paying jobs.

The small proportion of low-income and minority students who do pursue a college education generally do not have the financial resources to attend prestigious colleges and universities. Also, they have more difficulty competing academically with wealthier students, partly because they have to work (at least part time) to offset some of their expenses.

Minority students are particularly likely to have inferior educational opportunities. Until 1954 Blacks attended segregated schools in the South that were markedly inferior to those attended by Whites. In 1954 the U.S. Supreme Court, in *Brown v. Board of Education*, ruled that racial segregation in public schools was unconstitutional. Although *de jure* (legal) segregation ended, *de facto*

(actual) segregation remained in many communities with significant proportions of non-Whites.

Schools in such communities tend to remain segregated because housing is segregated. To deal with this problem, the Supreme Court ruled that school districts must seek racial balance in schools. In many districts, school busing is used to attain a racial balance. Studies indicate that segregation has been reduced *within* school districts but has increased *between* districts.[19] This increase is largely due to "White flight"—that is, Whites leaving the inner cities and moving to suburbs. In some communities, courts have ordered busing between school districts, and some Whites have responded by sending their children to private schools. Chicago's public schools are a classic example of de facto segregation. Some authorities have called this the worst school district in

Three decades of school busing have failed to deliver the benefits promised. In 1974, police had to escort buses in Boston on the third day of court-ordered busing to counter the intense opposition.

the country. The city's public school system is about 90% non-White, whereas the private school system is primarily White.[20]

Ironically, today there is less racial segregation of schools in the South than in other parts of the United States, and the North has become the most heavily segregated region in the country.[21] Much of northern school segregation is due to housing segregation.

Surveys have found that most Americans now favor school integration, but most African Americans and Whites are opposed to busing programs to achieve integration.[22] In many large cities (such as Baltimore, Chicago, Cleveland, and Detroit), public schools are approaching 90% minority enrollment.[23]

Three decades of school busing have failed to deliver all the benefits its boosters hoped for and its critics demanded. Scores of studies generally agree that White students do not suffer academically from school integration via busing.[24] Integration via busing appears to improve the academic performance of African American students, but mainly in the primary grades, not in junior high or high school.[25]

There have been other benefits of integration via busing. African Americans who attended elementary and high schools with Whites are substantially more likely to attend White-majority colleges, get jobs in desegregated workplaces offering higher pay, and have White friends as adults.[26] Also, African American students who go to integrated suburban schools rather than segregated city schools are less likely to drop out of high school, get in trouble with the police, drop out of college, or bear a child before age 18, and they are more likely to have White friends and live in integrated neighborhoods.[27] Whites also benefit from attending school with African American students because they learn more about diversity and tend to more thoroughly confront their racial stereotypes.[28]

Are the benefits of school busing worth the costs? This is a very complex issue, and as yet there is no definitive answer. The financial costs of busing children from one school district to another are high. Many authorities in both White and non-White neighborhoods are now increasingly arguing that it would be better to use the money currently spent on busing to improve school facilities. Critics also note that busing is inconsistent with the concept of neighborhood schools (in which the schools in the neighborhood become centers for educational, social, and recreational interaction for residents in a community). Critics also assert that busing for integration purposes almost always becomes a major obstacle for parental involvement in the school system due to the long distances between schools and residences. (Extensive parental involvement is associated with higher quality educational achievement of students; parental involvement leads to teachers, parents, and school administrators working together to improve school facilities and to develop innovative programs to instruct students.[29]) As noted in Chapter 12, African American leaders, recent U.S. presidents, and prominent educational authorities are moving away from advocating busing to achieve integration.

Have desegregation programs decreased racial prejudice? Research shows mixed results. Some studies show a decrease in prejudice, whereas others show that prejudice remains the same or even intensifies.[30] In communities in which desegregation takes place in an atmosphere of cooperation and goodwill, prejudice tends to be reduced. However, desegregation programs that are court ordered in an atmosphere of antagonism and misunderstanding are unlikely to reduce prejudice. In recent years, the Supreme Court appears to be less aggressive in mandating that busing be used to achieve desegregation. For instance, the Court has stated that there must be proof that schools are intentionally discriminating against minority students before busing is ordered.

In 1991 the Supreme Court declared that busing to achieve integration, when ordered, need not continue indefinitely, although the Court did not say precisely how long is enough. The ruling allows communities to end court-ordered busing if they can convince a judge they have done everything "practicable" to eliminate "vestiges of past discrimination" against minorities. In many inner cities, minority students continue to be segregated in dangerous, crowded, and inferior schools.

Urban Latinos and African Americans are not the only ones who have inferior educational opportunities: Native Americans, Alaskan Eskimo, and migrant workers also lack access to high-quality schools. Many Native Americans attend reservation schools, which are inferior in quality.

For Latinos, bilingual/bicultural education is an issue of intense debate. (There is also controversy about whether Black English should be taught in inner-city schools that have high proportions of African American students.) With bilingual/bicultural education, students are taught wholly or partly in their native language until they can speak English fairly fluently, and in some cases longer. One side argues that preserving the culture and language of minorities is a worthwhile (or essential) goal of public education. The opposing side believes that minority students will be best prepared to compete effectively in American society if they are "immersed" in English-language instruction; moreover, bilingual (using Black English or Spanish) education is expensive and reinforces separateness because it is a factor in keeping people of color living in ethnic communities.

Given all these factors, it is not surprising that there are significant differences in educational achievement between Whites and African Americans and between Whites and Latinos. Latinos and African American students are substantially more likely to drop out of high school as compared to Whites.[31] Latinos and African Americans (as compared to Whites) have substantially higher rates of functional illiteracy—that is, unable to read or write a simple sentence in any language.[32] (There are very few jobs in our society for the functionally illiterate.)

Confusion About the Goals of Education

There is agreement that school systems should teach the basic skills of reading, writing, and arithmetic. However, considerable controversy exists over what other values, knowledge, and skills schools should teach.

■ Feminists criticize school systems for teaching and perpetuating sexism—for example, by discouraging females from pursuing careers in science and math (technologically oriented college majors often receive the highest paying jobs in our society).

■ There is controversy over the extent to which school systems should offer educational programs to prevent sexual assaults and date rapes.

■ Controversy exists over what roles the schools should play in educating students about sexual harassment and intervening to prevent harassment.

- Schools have been criticized for helping to perpetuate the class system.

- There is considerable disagreement about the extent to which sex education should be taught in the school system.

- There is disagreement on whether prayers should be allowed in public schools, even though the Supreme Court has ruled that prayers in public schools violate the principle of separation of Church and State.

- There is disagreement about the emphasis that should be placed on teaching such subjects as music, sports, and home economics.

- There is disagreement on the extent to which school systems should be used to combat racism, stop drug abuse, prevent unwed pregnancies, help people with a disability, and reduce delinquency.

- There is controversy over whether schools should focus more on developing the creative thinking capacities of students or on teaching academic content.

- Now that the threat of AIDS has arisen, there is controversy over whether school systems should offer information on contraceptive methods that help to prevent AIDS.

- There is controversy regarding what school systems should teach about homosexuality.

In recent years, there has been a conservative trend in our society that has been expressed as a "back-to-basics" movement in school systems. Educational conservatives are opposed to schools being experimental, custodial (for the emotionally disturbed), or recreational facilities and to their offering "frill" and elective courses or "social services" such as sex education. This movement is calling for the establishment of clear standards of achievement for students, "criteria mastery" as the basis for grade promotion, participation by students in varsity sports only when certain grade levels are achieved, increased attention to academic subjects and to the teaching of "core values," more testing and homework, longer school

hours, and sterner discipline. The movement also urges that teachers receive salary increases based on merit rather than seniority (the underlying assumption is that such a system would motivate teachers to do a better job in the classroom).

There are controversies, however, within the back-to-basics movement. Are goals such as "learning to get along with others" and "communicating effectively" components of a "basic" education? Are "the basics" the same for all students?

A variety of other questions have been raised about education. Should private schooling be financially supported by refunding to those families who send their children to private schools the amounts they spend on public education through taxes? Should public colleges and universities collect more of their funds through higher student tuitions (which makes it more difficult for students of low-income families to attend)? What changes in school curricula need to be made to train students for the high-technology jobs that are opening up in our society? Clearly there is a need for increased consensus on the priorities and goals in education.

Intolerable Working Conditions for Some Teachers

In surveys, half of all teachers say that, if they had the opportunity to choose careers again, they would not select teaching.[33] Many factors contribute to disenchantment with teaching: low pay, low prestige, inadequate preparation, increased alternative job opportunities for women, and intolerable working conditions. College graduates can earn substantially more money in many other areas: accounting, engineering, computer science, or sales, for example.

Intolerable working conditions in school systems include some teachers in secondary schools being threatened by students and even being physically attacked. In some schools, teachers spend as much time trying to keep peace and order (baby-sitting) as they do teaching. There are high

Low pay, low prestige, inadequate preparation, and poor working conditions are just a few of the reasons many teachers feel disenchanted with their profession.

rates of drug and alcohol abuse among students, and teachers are forced to confront this issue, often without much preparation. Many school districts have insufficient instructional supplies. High student-to-teacher ratios are another concern—the more students, the more difficult it is for teachers to give individualized instruction.

A 1998 study of violence in schools found that 20% of American middle schools and high schools reported at least one serious crime (such as rape or robbery) in 1997. Public schools nationwide experienced (in 1997) more than 11,000 fights in which weapons were used, 4,000 rapes and other sexual assaults, and 7,000 robberies.[34]

Many teachers do not feel adequately prepared to teach protective behavior (such as how to protect oneself against sexual assaults), alcohol and drug abuse education, and similar topics.

An amazing statistic is that fewer than one in five new teachers is still in the profession after 10 years[34]; many leave because of the distressing

working conditions. The United States ranks last of all the major industrialized nations in how generously it compensates its teachers.[35]

STRATEGIES TO IMPROVE EDUCATION

Michael Rutter and his associates evaluated a number of high schools and concluded what most parents already know: "Schools do indeed have important impact on children's development, and it does matter what school a child attends."[36] Rutter found that the best schools required more homework, maintained high academic standards, had well-understood and well-enforced discipline standards, and yet created a comfortable and supportive atmosphere for students.[37] This section will examine four proposals for improving the school system: increased incentives for teachers, improvement of the curriculum, parental choice of schools, and extension of the school year.

Increase Incentives for Teachers

Perhaps the only way to encourage more high-quality college students to enter the teaching profession, and to raise the morale of existing teachers, is to increase incentives for teaching. Incentives might include increased pay, expanded in-service training, provision of sufficient school supplies, increased availability for classroom use of high-tech equipment (computers, film and videotape equipment), and improved working conditions.

A controversial recommendation is the creation of a "master teacher" rank that would recognize and reward ability and dedication to teaching. There is growing evidence that superior teaching can have immense positive effects on students. Pedersen and Faucher found a high correlation between outstanding first-grade teaching and later adult success of students, all of whom came from an inner-city neighborhood.[38] Master teachers would be paid substantially more and have added responsibilities, such as curriculum design and supervision of new teachers. Teachers' unions have generally opposed the concept, fearing that criteria other than ability and dedication (such as favoritism) will be used in making such selections. Unions also tend to be opposed to higher pay and promotion based on merit because the merit concept conflicts with the preferred union concept of basing pay on seniority.

Improve the Curriculum

If few new resources are required, practically everyone is in favor of this proposal. However, a major question is: In what directions should the curriculum be improved? As noted earlier, considerable confusion exists as to the goals of a quality education. In the 1960s and early 1970s, there was criticism of the rigidity and authoritarianism in schools, which led to increases in the number of electives in high schools and colleges and a reduction in the number of basic "academic" classes. Alternative schools were created for students who found traditional schools to be "stifling." History and social studies classes were revised to include content on significant contributions made by Native Americans, African Americans, Latinos, and other minority groups. New courses were developed that attempted to make schoolwork more relevant to the lives of minority students.

In the 1980s and 1990s, concern has shifted. There is a focus on the decline in academic achievement, and school systems are returning to stiffer academic programs. In fact, many of the requirements for basic academic courses that were dropped in the 1960s and early 1970s have been reinstated. In the 1980s and 1990s, there has been a move toward teaching basic skills (reading, writing, and arithmetic) and away from teaching electives (sociology, psychology, or specialized areas of literature and history). As part of this movement, children are also taught to respect authority, be patriotic, and lead moral lives. Some schools have reestablished strict dress codes and sought to curb unconventional behavior.

At the same time, a critical-thinking movement is taking place, which focuses on developing the thinking capacities of students. This approach encourages students to make observations and to critically analyze issues. It stresses class discussions and downplays lectures, emphasizes critical analysis over rote learning, and advocates assessing student understanding through use of essay tests rather than objective tests. In some ways, the critical-thinking movement conflicts with the back-to-basics movement. The latter places greater emphasis on learning and remembering facts; the former asserts that memorizing is much less important than developing thinking capacities.

In 1994 the Goals 2000 Educate America Act was passed by Congress and signed by President Clinton. The law was a sweeping reform program that established the first-ever national goals in the United States for education. The act was intended to make American students more competitive in the world economy and to give parents a way to

EXHIBIT 10.1

Schools Without Failure

In 1969 William Glasser wrote *Schools Without Failure* (New York: Harper & Row), which has had considerable impact on improving teaching. Glasser's concepts are as relevant today as they were three decades ago. The major concepts of Glasser's approach are summarized as follows.

Glasser believes that a major problem of school systems is that they are organized in such a way that most students experience failure. He is critical of schools for a variety of reasons. Getting an A is considered the paramount goal in schools; because only a few students get a majority of A's, most do not feel successful. Memorizing is more highly valued than developing thinking capacities. (He believes education is the process of developing thinking capacities.) Glasser asserts that thinking (including creative, artistic, and fun uses of students' brains) is drastically downgraded in schools. Also, schools do not deal with real-life problems faced by children. Relevancy is frequently absent from the curriculum; as a result, children do not transfer classroom learning to problem solving outside of school and thus do not gain the motivation to learn.

Glasser notes:

Unless we can provide schools where children, through a reasonable use of their capacities, can succeed, we will do little to solve the major problems of our country. We will have more social disturbances, more people who need to be kept in jails, prisons, and mental hospitals, more people who need social workers to take care of their lives because they feel they cannot succeed in this society and are no longer willing to try. (p. 6)

For a child to succeed in this world, she or he has to develop a positive identity (sense of self). Children who develop a failure identity are unlikely to succeed. Instead, they are likely to become angry, depressed, alienated, lonely, or hostile and may express their failure identity through delinquency, withdrawal, or development of emotional disturbances.

Glasser theorizes that there are two needs that must be met for establishment of a positive or success identity: love and self-worth. If these two needs are unmet, then the child will develop a failure identity. If these two needs are met, the child will develop a success identity and will pay off society many times over by being a responsible, contributing citizen.

Because home conditions in many families are less than desirable, many children do not receive the love or the sense of self-worth that they need. When they cannot fulfill their needs at home, Glasser asserts, they must have the opportunity to do so at school, or they will develop a failure identity. Because every child attends school, schools are in a unique position to identify children who are starting to develop a failure identity.

Teachers need to be better trained in identifying children with failure identities. Colleges of education should provide more content on identifying these children and also should put greater emphasis on developing the relationship capacities of education majors.

Glasser asserts that perhaps the greatest strength of a quality teacher is the ability to form positive relationships with students. Teachers need to convey that each student has a sense of self-worth. Teachers must also convey that they sincerely care about the well-being of each student. Those students identified as beginning to develop a failure identity need to be referred to Pupil Services for help, or the teacher needs to find a way to make the classroom a success experience for these (and all other) students.

Glasser recommends that more emphasis be placed on the teaching of personal development:

(continued)

EXHIBIT 10.1   *(continued)*

being assertive, learning to solve life's problems, improving relationships, handling unwanted emotions, learning to express one's sexuality responsibly, learning to handle stress, and so on.

Group problem-solving meetings should be held daily in classes. Such meetings would focus on identifying alternatives for solving the problems that students are encountering at school and in their lives. The topics to be discussed would often be brought up by the students themselves (for example, relationship difficulties they are having with someone). Such discussions should take place in a supportive, positive atmosphere. Blaming and fault finding should be minimized or eliminated entirely. The atmosphere needs to be one in which everyone's opinion is equally valued.

According to Glasser, students should not be separated into tracks because those placed in lower-level tracks are likely to view themselves as failures. He also recommends abolishing the current grading system of A-B-C-D-F and replacing it with a system of competency criteria for each course. For example, in a mathematics course, a student would have to perform a predetermined level of mathematical computations to pass the course. Students who achieve these standards would receive a P (for pass) on their report card. Students who do superior work and who help other students may be awarded an S (for superior work). Students who do not achieve the standards would not receive any grade, and no records would be kept of classes that students do not pass. For basic academic courses, students would be required to repeat the classes until they successfully achieve the established competency levels.

---

define educational excellence and measure their local school systems by it. Participation by states was voluntary, but the act provided powerful incentives, in the form of educational grants, for school systems to seek to upgrade their classrooms. The eight national goals to be met by the year 2000 are as follows:

1. *All children in America will start school ready to learn.*

2. *The high school graduation rate will increase to at least 90%.*

3. *American students will leave grades 4, 8, and 12 having demonstrated competency in English, math, science, history, and geography. Every school in America will ensure that all students learn to use their minds well so they will be prepared for responsible citizenship, further learning, and productive employment.*

4. *American students will be first in the world in science and math.*

5. *Every adult will be literate.*

6. *Every school in America will be free of drugs and violence and will offer a disciplined environment.*

7. *Schools will encourage parental involvement in education.*

8. *Schools will promote professional training for teachers.*[39]

Very little progress (if any) has been made in implementing these goals. Conservatives attacked the goals as a "federal power grab" and "an attempt to have government determine official knowledge."[40] Local school boards (who have considerable control over what is taught in their school systems) have a tradition of wanting to set their own policies of what is taught. For all practical purposes, there are now few initiatives to achieve the Goals 2000. Americans agree that our educational system needs to be improved, but there is vast disagreement on what the curriculum goals should be.

Allow Parental Choice of Schools

Under a parental choice system, not only are parents entitled to enroll their children in public schools outside their geographic district, but state tax dollars go to the school that wins the enrollment. By creating market incentives, the thinking goes, academically superior schools should thrive, while inferior schools would either have to improve their performance or face bankruptcy. A voucher system is usually used for implementing a parental choice system; the voucher system is a program in which the government gives vouchers to students that may be used to pay for education at any school that they or their parents choose.

Parental choice of schools is currently being tried in a number of states, including Minnesota, Iowa, Nebraska, and Arkansas. Initial findings indicate that the reasons parents and students opt out of one school and for another are often unrelated to academics.[41] In some cases, the parents select schools with lower educational standards to increase the chances that their son or daughter will graduate—or will graduate with higher grades. Other parents pick schools near their work for convenience reasons. Some parents select schools that will increase the chances of their son or daughter playing on a varsity sports team. In many cases, transportation problems force parents to select the school closest to their home.

A major problem with parental choice of schools is that it has the potential to undermine the neighborhood school concept. This concept holds that the neighborhood school should be a center of community living, with its facilities used by both youngsters and adults for a variety of purposes: education, recreation, leisure activities, social gatherings, sporting events, and community meetings. If parents in a neighborhood send their children to different schools, the neighborhood school will not become a center of community life.

Another drawback of parental choice is that many children are not in a position to travel to faraway schools. These children (some of whom are already educationally disadvantaged) may then be "left behind" in the worst districts, which become further impoverished as money follows students to better-financed schools.

Extend the School Year

Elementary and secondary schools in the United States are in session an average of 180 days a year. In contrast, Japan's schools are in session an average of 240 days a year. As a result, Japanese students attending 12 years of school receive the equivalent of about 16 years of schooling in the United States.[42] Comparisons with other advanced nations show a similar disparity.[43]

In 1994 the National Education Commission on Time and Learning (NECTL) found that high schools in the United States require students to spend barely 41% of classroom time on academic subjects.[44] As Little notes, "The typical high school student's schedule—1st period: Driver's ed.; 2nd period: AIDS awareness; 3rd period: Counseling—is looking less and less like a classical education."[45] The NECTL found that high school students in the United States spend only 3 hours a day on English, science, math, civics, languages, or history—half of what is spent on academic courses in Germany, France, and Japan.[46] In 1994 this commission recommended boosting class time spent on these basic academic subjects to an average of 5½ hours per day; it also strongly recommended extending the nation's school year.[47]

A strong case can be made for extending the school year. In a review of 100 research projects, Toch found that in nine of ten instances student achievement rises with the amount of time in class.[48] Toch notes:

A study of students taking an international math test found that Japanese students had studied 98 percent of the precalculus and calculus topics on the test, while their U.S. counterparts had been taught only 50 percent. Half of the Japanese performed as well as the top 5 percent of Americans.[49]

Research also reveals that students lose a lot of ground educationally by letting their minds lie fallow during the summer. Teachers spend on average the whole first month of the fall semester

EXHIBIT 10.2

Academic Time Requirements

Over 4 years, the average hours required for academic subjects[a] in high school classrooms are listed below.

Country	Average Hours
Germany	3528
France	3280
Japan	3170
United States	1460

[a] The academic subjects were defined to be English, science, mathematics, civics, languages, and history.

Source: Rod Little, "The Endangered Summer Vacation," *U.S. News & World Report,* May 16, 1994, p. 12.

reteaching material forgotten over the summer.[50] The problem is particularly acute for students from impoverished families, who often have fewer opportunities to learn during the summer. One study found that affluent students gain an average of 1 month of knowledge during the summer, whereas disadvantaged students lose 3 to 4 months.[51] Extending the school year into the traditional summer break would also assist working parents who have to deal with child-care arrangements during the daytime.

TOWARD EQUAL EDUCATIONAL OPPORTUNITY

As we've seen, educational opportunities are often lacking for minorities and the poor in this country. Nearly everyone agrees that there should be equal educational opportunity for all. But there is considerable disagreement on how this can be achieved. Three proposals for progressing toward equal educational opportunity are:

1. Reforming school financing so that an equal amount of money is spent on each student's education

2. Establishing special compensatory educational programs for disadvantaged students

3. Integrating students from different ethnic backgrounds into the same school

Reform of School Financing

Schools in wealthy districts tend to receive considerably more money per student than schools in poor districts. At the present time, a majority of the revenue for school districts in practically all states comes from local property taxes. Decaying inner cities are especially hard-pressed to finance school systems, and many schools in these areas are inferior.

There is growing opposition in the United States to using property tax dollars as the primary source of revenue for funding school systems. Taxpayers on fixed incomes (such as the retired elderly) are increasingly unable to pay large annual increases in their property tax bills. In 1993 taxpayers in Michigan voted to abolish using property tax revenues to fund the public school system in that state. In 1994 voters in Michigan approved a constitutional amendment to raise the state sales tax and cigarette tax as the primary sources of supporting the state's schools. One result of this action in Michigan is movement toward equalizing among school districts the amount of money spent on each student's education.[52] Will other states follow this approach?

Another suggestion for equalizing the amount of money spent on each student's education is for the federal government to pay for all primary and secondary education, giving the same amount of money per student to each school. Critics of this approach assert that schools in this country have excelled because of local control and involvement. If the funding shifted to the federal government, critics say, the result would be greater federal control and increased red tape, meaning that a huge federal bureaucracy would undoubtedly evolve.

Compensatory Education

Many authorities believe that special programs and extra assistance would improve achievement levels of the poor and minorities. A variety of programs already exist.

Project Head Start gives preschool instruction to disadvantaged children. Evaluations of the results of Head Start indicate that students who attend are better prepared for starting first grade than disadvantaged students who do not attend Head Start.[53] Unfortunately, the benefits of the program tend to diminish after the students no longer receive services. Coleman and Cressey indicate that disadvantaged students keep benefiting when they continue to receive extra help from programs such as Title I of the Elementary and Secondary Education Act.[54] They conclude:

> Don't stop the programs after only a few years. Disadvantaged students should continue to receive help as long as they need it, which in many cases would probably be until their final years of high school. . . . It would certainly take a lot more money to provide help for all the students in all grades who need it, but such an investment would pay enormous dividends in terms of a healthier, more competitive economy, lower rates of crime and welfare dependency, and, most important, a more just society.[55]

Most school districts have Pupil Services departments that seek to assess the academic, social, and emotional needs of children who are not progressing well in school. Once an assessment of a child is completed, programs are developed to meet the unique learning needs of the child. A wide variety of services may be provided depending on the identified needs. There are special classes for the emotionally disturbed and for those with learning disabilities. Counseling is sometimes provided. Some students are referred for drug abuse, and some are referred for visual or hearing difficulties. Pupil Services departments are staffed by a variety of professionals—school psychologists, social workers, and guidance counselors. In 1975 Congress passed the Education for All Handicapped Children Act, now known as PL 94-142. This law addresses the numerous physical, developmental, learning, and social-emotional problems that hamper the education of children. In sweeping legislation, the law mandated that all school districts identify students with these problems and then develop specialized programs to meet their needs. Unfortunately, many low-income school districts, because of financial constraints, have not been able to meet the objectives of this bill.

In many states, programs are being developed to prevent children from dropping out of school. Some school districts have dropout rates approaching 50%, and the national average is over 10%.[56] Dropping out represents an enormous loss to those individuals and to society because of lost potential productivity. The estimated lifetime earnings of high school graduates are over $200,000 higher than those of dropouts.[57] Programs for "at-risk" students are a response to the need to help high school students stay in school and learn practical job skills.

Some elementary and secondary school systems now have reading, writing, and arithmetic programs during the summer for students who need assistance in these areas. A variety of compensatory educational programs have been established at the college level as well. These include noncredit courses in English and mathematics, tutoring, and various testing programs. Many colleges have special provisions for the admission of minority students who do not meet standard admission requirements, and these students are encouraged to utilize the educational opportunity programs that are available. (Students who attended inferior elementary and secondary school systems in inner cities are often two to four grade levels behind in reading, writing, and arithmetic and therefore need educational opportunity programs to have a chance to succeed in college.)

Educational opportunity programs have become an accepted part of most colleges and universities. A stickier question involves special admissions of minority students to graduate and professional schools. Supporters believe that these affirmative action admissions are attempts to compensate for the inferior school systems and other discriminations that minorities have been subjected to in the past. On the other hand, because

A music classroom in New York City reflects current efforts to achieve equal educational opportunity. Children with disabilities in a Brooklyn school have the opportunity to participate in such classes in part because of recent legislation mandating that school districts develop specialized programs to meet their needs.

competition is intense for the limited admissions into these schools, White students complain that they are the victims of reverse discrimination—that they are being rejected even though their entrance exam scores are higher than those of some minority students who are accepted. The legal status of this affirmative action policy has not as yet been fully resolved.

Effective Integration

As discussed earlier, school busing has been used to attempt to integrate students within school districts. Many Whites in large cities have responded by moving to suburbs or sending their children to private schools. Some big cities, through court orders, are experimenting with merging suburban school districts with inner-city school districts and then busing children within each district. The extent to which such merging will occur is questionable. There is a major problem with distance, as some suburban communities are so far from

inner cities that students would have to spend a large part of their day on a bus. Most White parents in suburbs would not raise serious objections to a small number of inner-city children being bused to their schools in the suburbs. However, most suburbanites (fearing potential violence and a lower-quality education) would object to their children being bused to inferior school systems in inner cities. Many White parents, if faced with such a court order, would probably respond by placing their children in private schools.

The ideal way to integrate neighborhood schools is through integration of residential areas, so that neighborhood schools are then automatically integrated. Such integration would provide ongoing opportunities for interracial cooperation and friendships for children and for adults. The chances of this proposal working, however, are minute. People of different ethnic and racial groups generally are reluctant to live together in the same neighborhood. In addition, many members of minority groups cannot afford to live in affluent neighborhoods, and White residents of such neighborhoods object to having low-cost housing built in their communities.

Another possible avenue toward integration is through the use of "magnet" schools in cities. Magnet schools are ones that offer special courses, programs, or equipment. Examples would be a fine arts middle school or high school and a school emphasizing curriculum in the area of computer science. Proponents of magnet schools hope that placing such schools in inner-city areas would draw students from suburbs because of the excellent educational opportunities they could offer.

The prospects of significant federal help for inner-city schools in the near future are not bright. In this era of trying to reduce the federal deficit through budget cutbacks, the chances of the enactment of a bold new federal program to channel resources to financially distressed school districts are remote.

John E. Farley summarizes the significance to all Americans of providing equal educational opportunities for minorities and the poor:

> If the overall effectiveness of the educational system is poor, American productivity will suffer, and our standard of living will likely fall in our increasingly competitive world. Likewise, if we fail the large and growing proportion of our young people who are African American, Hispanic, or from low-income homes of any race, the result will be the same. Failing to educate those who account for such a large and growing share of the future labor force will have a similar destructive impact on America's productivity and its standard of living.[58]

SCHOOL SOCIAL WORKERS: A RESPONSE TO CRISIS *

Given the problems within the educational system and the societal difficulties that schools have been asked to erase, it is not surprising that spe-

---

*This section was written especially for this text by Don Nolan, MSSW, school social worker.

cialists, such as school social workers, have become part of the school system. School social work is a relatively new role. Before 1960 there were few school social workers, and they were employed primarily by large urban school systems (for example, New York City and Chicago). In fact, one of the earliest books on school social workers was first published in 1955.[59] School social work, then, must be discussed within the context of its evolving role.

Before doing this, however, it is necessary to have a method of analyzing behavior so that we have an initial base for understanding the nature of children's problems in schools. It is a practical necessity for any school social worker to understand the dynamics of behavior because social workers have been and will continue to be closely involved with problematic behavior in children. In 1975 Congress enacted PL 94-142 (the Education for All Handicapped Children Act). This statute mandates that each local school district must provide full and appropriate educational opportunities to all children with a disability. Much of the definition of social work services offered in PL 94-142 specifies (a) defining the nature of social or behavioral problems, (b) using individual or family counseling skills, and (c) using other resources to make an impact on behavioral, emotional, and social problems.

In the summer of 1997, Congress reauthorized PL 94-142. This act continues to mandate a system of identifying and developing programs for children with special educational needs.

The Nature of Behavior

We will begin with the premise that behavior is purposeful—that we do things for a reason. We may not always know exactly why we are doing something because we don't analyze each of our behaviors. But we always respond to a given situation with a set of beliefs, with a history of past attempts to solve a problem, and within the context of our present environment.[60]

In using his rational-emotive behavior therapy, Albert Ellis looks at behavior within the context of what he calls its ABCs. In essence, he says that B—a belief system composed of attitudes, interpretations, and emotions—is always juxtaposed between an activating situation, A, and a consequence, C.[61] This belief system is based, no matter what our age, on opinions we have about ourselves and others in relation to our perceptions about our place in the larger world. The person, then, can decide on a course of action given certain circumstances. Children, like adults, do not act in a random fashion. They act in relation to a decision they have made about the consistency and stability of their relationships with adults and other children. There are antecedents of behavior that often depend on *decisions* they have made about their abilities, not on their *actual* abilities. Thus, although it may seem that a girl is misbehaving when she approaches new situations, in reality she may have decided from past experience that she will have little success in the task and is thus acting up because she does not want to face the fear of another failure. The child has made a decision, although it may be based on what can be termed a *mistaken belief system*.[62] She wrongly assumes that failure means she is worthless and that trying is not important. To understand how to alter that self-perception, one must look more closely at some primary goals of behavior.

Rudolf Dreikurs postulated that the force behind every human action is a goal. We all know some of what we want, although often we do not consciously act on those goals but rather on unanalyzed means of achieving them. It is possible to understand the psychological motivation of the child if one develops diagnostic skills to analyze four goals of misbehavior: attention getting, power seeking, revenge seeking, and assuming a disability.[63] Some children try to get attention, to always be the focal point for others, because they believe that otherwise they are worthless. Other children attempt to prove their power in the belief that only if they can do what they want and defy adult pressure can they be important. Still others may seek revenge: The only means by which they feel significant is to hurt others, just as they feel hurt by them. Others may display actual or imaginary disabilities in order to be left alone so that nothing is demanded of them. The crucial point is that,

whatever deviant behaviors children display, there are always reasons for them.

Anyone who has worked extensively with children, in any situation, can readily remember youngsters who were acting out these goals. For example, Ted, who is constantly in front of the teacher interrupting and is always calling attention to himself by "forcing" the teacher to repeatedly reprimand him, is clearly seeking attention. Juan, who is usually confrontational, who is noncompliant to reasonable requests from the teacher, and who rejects praise and social reinforcers from the teacher, is in a power struggle. Noriko, who physically injures others and who usually puts others and herself down, is probably seeking revenge for some perceived wrong. Odell, who is withdrawn, who sinks down in his desk, who is shy with classmates, and who fears new situations, is probably displaying a disability.

We must, of course, be careful not to overgeneralize or analyze too quickly, and we must remember that the child could be displaying these behaviors because of dysfunctional family patterns or because of medical or psychiatric problems. Behavior is complicated and can be deceptive at times. However, if we use the goals-of-behavior construct, with its philosophy of purposeful behavior and actions, we have a starting point for responding to these behaviors. Thus, given a general philosophy of behavior as it applies to the educational system, we can talk about specific ways of intervening to solve problems.

Traditional School Social Work Roles

Because many school systems have never had social workers on their staff, the responsibility for elucidating the many roles of social work and the potential value of these functions often remains with the new school social worker. This will be a long and at times frustrating process, for any fundamental change in basic system services will affect the balance and direction of all services. Consequently, the social worker must be in a position to prove that the change she or he brings will ultimately benefit the system and thus be worth the uneasiness that the other staff will feel in adjusting to a new person in a different and challenging role. Persistence and what Albert Ellis terms self-awareness (being perceptive and accepting of one's strengths and limitations) will be needed initially.[64]

Let's look at some traditional roles for school social work practice: caseworker, group worker, truant officer, counselor, and parent liaison.

CASEWORKER

Intervention has always been the essence of social work. Social workers have responded with a variety of methods to the problems caused by the complexities of modern society. Casework, traditionally, has been one of the first methods used in any given area; it encompasses the more clinical and best-known aspects of social work. Basically, social workers have had to prove their worth; that is, they have had to prove that they do something different from what was already being done. Because social workers have substantial training in family dynamics, they can analyze and diagnose common problems in the dysfunctional family. This is a skill that others in the typical school system do not have, and thus it is viewed as an area of particular expertise for the school social worker.

Consider the case of Mike, age 10, who had a number of problems. He was physically aggressive toward other children and was prone to act with outbursts of emotion and anger when put in new or different situations. He had virtually no coping skills and came to school after weekends or vacations in an angry, violent mood. The family consisted of five children and his mother. His father was no longer living at home but visited on occasion. Mike's emotional problems, and particularly his violent attitudes, were accentuated after these visits. In addition, Mike wore dirty, unkempt clothing, which always seemed either too small or much too big. Mike's behavior in class was, of course, a problem. His goals of misbehavior were a combination of attention seeking and power seeking. In an attempt to change this behavior pattern, the social workers, using a casework strategy, (a) made a referral to the county department of social services to make sure that the family was getting all services that were available—for example, homemaking, medical services, and counseling; (b) modified Mike's behavior at school by devising a system of reinforcers that were important to him; (c) made sure that Mike had an opportunity for success in academic areas in school by helping the teacher to individualize for Mike's needs; (d) tried to help the mother understand that Mike should not be put in situations in which he had to adopt a negative attitude toward adults; and (e) contacted the father about his relationship to his son. All of this takes considerable time and energy. In casework a consistent, organized, step-by-step approach is used. Casework thus becomes a one-to-one involvement with a family in an attempt to solve a problem.

Now let's look at Phyllis, age 6, who had a hearing disability. She was in a special education program 4 days a week. There were a number of problems: noncompliant behaviors when Phyllis knew what was wanted of her, a difficulty in communicating in any way, and a number of medical problems. The caseworker decided that a home intervention program was necessary. Consistency was needed in the sign language program between home and school. Behavior management was lacking in the home, for Phyllis was not expected to do anything there; the only demands were bathroom skills. The parents needed help in developing reasonable goals and expectations for Phyllis and then following through on a program. Medically, Phyllis needed extensive diagnostic work at a nearby hospital. The caseworker made contact with the hospital, arranged for a meeting, and then made sure that follow-up came from the hospital. Again, the social worker set specific goals and followed them in an attempt to solve a multitude of problems. Much of the emphasis in the caseworker model is on doing things that teachers are not prepared for and do not have the time to do. The goals are not strictly educational but have the purpose of enabling children to achieve in school.

GROUP WORKER

As casework came to be considered outmoded in some areas of social work practice,[65] school social workers found another method of intervening in school problems: group work. Essentially, the rationale was that the social worker could influence the lives and educational success of too few people when using the casework approach. A group approach also assumes that, by sharing experiences, students can put their own problems in perspective and can learn new strategies for resolving school-related and personal problems. A few examples of a group approach follow.

Ms. Tanner's fifth-grade class was a problem for her. Specifically, four boys regularly would not listen, clowned around, and did little work in class. In fact, they were doing less well academically than in the past year and were starting to go around as a group, often getting into trouble on the playground. An intervention strategy was designed: the creation of groups as a means of solving these problems. Two groups of five boys were created, with two of the "problem" boys in each group. The groups worked in specific high-interest areas; for example, one group worked on a science project that involved creating a metric unit for the third grade, while the other studied the principles of flight and aerodynamics, making kites, paper airplanes, and wooden models. There were a number of planned goals for each group. First, the social worker wanted to create new friendships and show the disruptive children models of more appropriate behavior that could be as rewarding as attention-getting behavior. Second, cooperation was fostered in conjunction with the principles of peer pressure. All children worked toward step-by-step, cooperative goals; unless all helped, none could reach their goal. Finally, the social worker wanted everyone—the target boys, their peers in the class, and their teacher—to realize that the boys could be productive and successful so that both the teacher's and students' perceptions would be altered. The social worker also discussed with Ms. Tanner how individual programming could be used to provide additional successful educational experiences for these four boys.

In another case, group experience involved high school freshmen who were failing in their initial coursework. Study habits, poor motivation, and a negative attitude toward school success were the main concerns. In this case, the social worker organized a group of students who took a special course focused on ways of studying. The course was named "Ten Ways to Beat the System" and was structured in a way that allowed the student to learn enjoyable ways to become successful in school. At the same time, a number of older students were organized to meet informally with the freshmen to discuss some positive aspects of high school that the younger students could look forward to. In addition, these upperclassmen offered guidance about which teachers to avoid and which teachers they could expect a fair deal from.

Many school districts are now offering a variety of groups that are often led by social workers. Examples include *assertiveness training* for students who are shy or nonassertive, *anger control* for students who frequently lose their temper or are aggressive, *relationship building* for students who have love relationship problems, *coping with loss* for students whose parents divorce or who have experienced the death of a loved one, *student assistance programs* for students who are using or abusing alcohol or other drugs, and *school-age mothers* for students who are pregnant or are raising a child.

TRUANT OFFICER

Social workers in the school have performed a number of other roles, including that of truant officer. Often the truant officer functions as an advocate for the child. There are times when acting as an agent of social control (the law, the system) need not be looked at negatively. A case in point is a multiproblem family with three boys in high school. Although none of the boys had reached the legal age after which school was no longer compulsory, the parents decided to keep the boys at home so they could help the father in his job as a farmhand. The boys had mentioned to different teachers that they feared this was about to happen, but they were afraid to tell their father that they wanted to stay in school. The social worker was able to intervene in this case by using the truancy laws to inform the parents that they had no choice but to send their sons to school. In this case, the undesirable role of truant officer was transformed into one that was advantageous for the children involved. It was also a means of helping to promote the concept of equal access. Given the high truancy and dropout rates in larger cities, the approach of combining the services of truant officers with creative or alternative approaches to education can benefit children.

COUNSELOR AND PARENT LIAISON

The social worker as a counselor and/or parent liaison or parent trainer is also a fairly common role in school social work. Often teachers will expect the school social worker to be the liaison between themselves and parents. And it is frequently assumed that the social worker will defend and justify the actions or educational planning of the teacher. This can cause somewhat strained relations between the social worker and the rest of the teaching staff, especially when a worker agrees with a parent that the school system ought to make changes in its educational programs to better serve the children. This role requires a lot of tact and prior planning, as well as a relatively assertive view toward expanding social work services.

In the role of counselor, the social worker brings a number of skills to the situation. As school social work services have developed, there has been a trend toward perceiving the social worker as a therapist rather than as an academic counselor. This distinction has been more than semantic because advanced professional (master's degree) training has greatly increased the diagnostic and psychological skills of school social workers relative to other school professionals (such as guidance counselors). Thus, a school social worker can be seen as both a specialist in the diagnosis of emotional difficulties in children and as the support staff person with the most extensive psychiatric and medically based training.

Newer Social Work Roles

In essence, role development and expansion are of critical concern to school social workers. When they join a school system, a number of expectations and specific job-related demands will be placed on them. There are bound to be conflicts because the older roles encompassing casework, group work, counselor, or parent liaison may not provide enough flexibility to meet the demands of the change effort. As a result, school social workers have adapted by developing newer approaches to their role. We'll now look at seven of these newer approaches: advocate, behavioral specialist, mental health consultant, alcohol and other drug abuse specialist, multidisciplinary team member, violence prevention specialist, and systems change specialist.

ADVOCATE

Recently one of the most provocative roles for the social worker has become that of advocate.[66] In the school setting, an advocate is someone who understands and is not intimidated by large complicated systems and can help a family or child in facing the educational bureaucracy of dealing with other social systems.

This can be a particularly useful role when working with families who are not well acquainted with the educational system. For instance, in an early education program that is geared to helping prekindergarten children who show evidence of developmental delay, the social worker can use the advocate role to help the parents understand their rights under the law, including their rights to appeal program decisions if they feel the programs do not fit the needs of their child. The social worker can explain who is teaching what materials and why this should help the child progress. She or he can be the person who follows the child in the program so that the parents can have contact with someone they have rapport with and with whom they feel comfortable asking questions. The social worker can also be the person who makes them aware of applicable medical or social service agencies that are available to give them a better knowledge of their child or offer supportive services when these are needed. The social worker can be a person to talk to about the complexities, difficulties, fears, or guilt associated with raising a child who in some way is different from other children.

Another more general function is to advocate for parents as a group in meetings with teachers, administrators, or school boards. An example might be in the area of homework. Academic expectations have dramatically increased in the past decade, such that much of what was high school algebra and biology are now commonly taught in seventh and eighth grades. Teaching staffs need to understand that there are many parents who cannot tutor their children in their homework once the children are beyond sixth or seventh grade. Instead of complaining about lack of parental help, teachers and administrators need assistance in developing more creative ways of helping students, such as peer helpers, study skill groups, and/or extra time for students to meet with the teacher before or after class. Thus, a combination of all of these functions expands the role of home liaison and enables the advocate to meet needs that have not previously been met in the school context.

BEHAVIORAL SPECIALIST

There has been a trend at some major universities toward training school social workers in one discrete, highly recognizable skill. Within this context, emphasis is often put on the social worker's becoming a behavioral specialist, a person who understands and can systematically apply behavior modification. Within the schools, a knowledge of how to alter behavior has immediate and long-term applicability. Using behavioral skills, the social worker can provide guidance in general learning principles as applied to overall teaching and can develop specific programs for children who are having difficulty adjusting to the normal classroom routine. The following is a case example.

Phillip, age 9, was having difficulty paying attention and was usually noncompliant to directions. His teacher was having trouble understanding his behavior and motivating him to be involved in usual classroom activities—for example, doing independent work in math and reading, participating in small-group activities, and cooperating in play arrangements. A social worker with behavioral training was asked to intervene. After observing the antecedents of the noncompliant behavior and recording baseline data of on-task or attending behaviors in nonacademic situations,[67] the social worker was able to put together a program. The program included (a) the planned use of social reinforcers (praise from the teacher); (b) a reward system built around interest in science (other work had to be done before the work

in science could begin); and (c) a system that involved ignoring Phillip's verbal noncompliance while reinforcing compliance with praise and tangible rewards, such as permitting him to help with a special project. In this way, Phillip's behaviors were changed in a relatively short time.

MENTAL HEALTH CONSULTANT

A school social worker can also function as a mental health consultant to the other staff. Curriculum today is no longer as simple as reading, writing, and arithmetic (if this ever was the case). Although there is currently substantial concern about teaching the "basics" in education, teachers must still seek to improve old curriculum and develop new materials and new teaching styles. Because social workers have training in the social psychology of individual behavior, they can serve as consultants to the mental health and human relations aspects of curriculum and to teaching style. With this focus, the social worker plays a preventative role, seeking to help teachers motivate students via stimulating materials. She or he can help create a teaching approach that is not threatening but intriguing, questioning, and supportive of the process of learning. Naturally, the social worker would also be involved in helping teachers to individualize education—to devise materials and teaching styles that meet the needs of all children, no matter what their current academic level.

The social worker can help create a systematized approach to monitoring progress and then create new techniques to facilitate remediation when necessary. To accomplish these goals, it may be necessary to organize brainstorming sessions with all the teachers or to begin an investigation of the materials available on a number of topics.

In this way, social workers can help provide guidance in curriculum development, with an overall emphasis on human relations. The inclusion of specific human relations goals in teaching has often been overlooked, even though many problems in the schools (such as trouble on the playground and problems with special and regular education classes) can be seen as directly attributable to a lack of human relations materials. Children need to learn that "different is okay," that cultural or racial differences can be enjoyed rather than feared, that all people deserve respect as human beings, and that values are learned concepts that can be changed.[68] School social workers, because of their training and unique place in the school, can provide the perspective needed to devise such a curriculum and help create systems for implementation.

Another more complex role in this area, and one which requires advanced training, is to help evaluate whether children might have significant emotional or psychiatric difficulties. There has been a significant increase in the number of children who have been diagnosed by the medical and/or child psychological disciplines as having attention deficit hyperactivity disorder (ADHD) or other emotional/behavioral disorders (such as a major depression or bipolar disorder). Because of the unique skills and roles of the school social worker, he or she can be a liaison to the mental health and/or medical community by making appropriate referrals and by assisting in follow-up care. Often parents will be confused about their child's behavioral or emotional development. Parents will then need assistance in understanding what may be "naughty behavior" or "going through a stage" as opposed to behaviors that indicate the possibility of a more serious problem. It is imperative in these latter situations that the child and the parents be referred to qualified specialists or clinics and that communication then take place between mental health providers and schools. It is equally important that teachers receive assistance in understanding the nature of child psychiatric problems and how to help affected children.

ALCOHOL AND OTHER DRUG ABUSE SPECIALIST

Drug use and abuse continue to be a major problem in our society. From the days of Prohibition, various segments of society have addressed the "evils" of alcohol and other drug use. Today, with the tragic loss of lives associated with drunk driving and with the much-publicized drug-overdose deaths of sports and entertainment figures, there is a growing realization of the need for drug prevention programs. Programs having a punitive interventive focus have not been successful. Thus,

there has been a recent emphasis on prevention, and schools have become the mechanism for drug prevention programs.

Because schools generally do not have trained specialists in this area, many school districts have hired school social workers to consult with parents and to refer students who are abusing drugs to appropriate inpatient or outpatient treatment centers. Social workers, because of their knowledge of chemical dependency, their training in interviewing, their skills in interacting with parents, and their knowledge of community resources, have become the logical choice to spearhead the development of prevention programs. They have also been asked to become curriculum specialists in this area. Thus, as part of their overall responsibilities, many school social workers help develop teaching curriculum on drug use and abuse for elementary, middle, and high schools. In this respect, social workers are responding to changes in society and in the family, as education seeks to accomplish more and more societal goals.

Many school districts have developed intervention programs for students who either have become chemically dependent or are concerned about the possibility of this occurring. Student Assistance Programs (SAPs), often led by school social workers, offer a group approach in this area. Groups for students who have returned from alcohol or other drug treatment centers, groups for students who want to know more about the mood-altering effects of alcohol and other drugs, and groups for students who are concerned about others' use of chemicals have become commonplace in many schools. There may also be groups for students affected by others' (such as parents') use of alcohol or other drugs.

MULTIDISCIPLINARY TEAM MEMBER

Another role of the social worker that is gaining increasing popularity involves using his or her skills in conjunction with other members on a team. The school social worker may join with other professionals (psychologist, speech therapist, special education teacher, physical therapist, and regular education teacher) to determine the special educational needs and particular programming appropriate for certain children. This is an area of implementation of PL 94-142, with the group of professionals commonly called an M-team (multidisciplinary team). In this case, the social worker might be involved (a) with an initial assessment of the child and the family, with special emphasis on family functioning and the child's social and adaptive skills; (b) with the parents clinically, either through family counseling and role analysis or through training in special techniques, such as behavior modification or crisis intervention; or (c) in teacher observation, training, and support.

The point here is that the social worker acts as part of a team—as a member with certain discrete skills and knowledge—and in conjunction with the team seeks to alleviate problems. Although this may appear to be a somewhat constricting role, in that other methods may seem to offer more independence, it can be a useful way to find gaps in services and to decrease overlap among individual skills. It has its advantages, especially if one is responsible for a school (or a school system) with a large population. One particular advantage is the learning that takes place for the social worker as she or he interacts with other professionals on the team.

A somewhat different type of multidisciplinary team is "team consultation" provided by a pupil service team. Similar to the multidisciplinary team, this team has members from many disciplines—in fact, often the same members as the previously described M-team. However, this team consultation approach differs in that it is a consultation/prevention resource to teachers. Instead of a child being formally referred as a client with a potential emotional/behavioral disability, the pupil service team seeks to find ways to help the child, the teacher, or the parents immediately. An illustration of a prevention effort by this type of multidisciplinary team is the team consulting with teachers on how to work more effectively with children who have been diagnosed as having attention deficit hyperactivity disorder.

VIOLENCE PREVENTION SPECIALIST

Schools are often said to be a microcosm of the larger society. In many of our cities, violence toward others has become a major problem, and it

is not limited to adults. Offenses committed by juveniles have become more serious in nature. In many inner cities, gangs have become such a destructive force that some school districts now have instituted dress codes in an attempt to counter the influence of gang symbols (the wearing of certain apparel or colors is thought to be a factor in developing and maintaining a "gang identity"). Student violence against teachers has also increased, creating a climate in some schools of fear and intimidation. Police liaison officers are now common in many schools.

Violence prevention is yet another area where schools have traditionally not employed specialists. Some 30 to 40 years ago, in a slower-paced and more stable society, the school principal would usually enforce whatever discipline was necessary. (The principal often solicited parent cooperation in administering strict, often punitive, consequences to students who violated school rules.) Today gangs have become the "family" of far too many teens. The use of such drugs as crack and cocaine has caused an increase in addictive behaviors and aggression toward others. The methods of maintaining behavioral control in schools have changed, and school social workers are in a unique position to again demonstrate leadership and knowledge of human behavior.

Teachers need to develop more effective ways of working with students who are prone to become violent or aggressive. School social workers can help train teaching staff to become effective in nonviolent intervention techniques. For example, teachers can be instructed in helping students to learn anger-control techniques. Students can be taught how to reframe their angry thought processes so that they express their anger in assertive and nonviolent ways rather than in aggressive ways. They can also be instructed in how to walk away from a potential fight, and they can learn indirect ways of expressing their anger (such as by hitting a punching bag or by jogging). Teachers who have learned to guide students in anger-control techniques also regain a sense of "being in charge."

Another example of an effective technique for reducing student violence is peer mediation, whereby students mediate their interpersonal conflicts. School social workers develop a training plan to teach a core group of students the skills of active listening, compromising, and problem solving. Through training and supervision, this core group can then mediate conflicts that occur in the school, potentially preventing smaller disagreements from becoming violent conflicts. The influence of the social worker is then greatly enhanced, as many more students are ultimately "seen" through the core group of trained students.

Another approach to minimize school violence is the formation of violence-prevention teams formed from the police department, schools, and youth-serving agencies. Too often, agencies and schools are involved only in intervention efforts. Because of their unique position and skills and because of the system coordination expectations in their job, school social workers can take a leadership role in developing a team effort for the prevention of violence that uses the resources and energies of professionals from many systems.

SYSTEMS CHANGE SPECIALIST

Allen Pincus and Anne Minahan postulate that the focus of social work practice should be the interaction between people and systems in the social environment.[69] If we look at schools as a natural access point for families (most families must deal with schools at some point in their existence), social workers should be able to perform a unique role in the schools. Given the complex nature of society today, most people need to enhance their problem-solving abilities. Social workers can help in this regard by linking people to systems and improving existing service and delivery mechanisms. This role model can involve situations of equal access or integration, the development of programs to deal with changing family patterns, or issues relating to the quality of education. Schools are a critical link in the total societal resource system. Indeed, the neighborhood school is often the system with which the average citizen feels most comfortable. Thus, we must examine our schools and look for the inadequacies in their educational structure. The questions we need to answer are: What do we really need to determine success for the student? How can we use the materials and personnel in the most efficient way? Through a system of assessing present data, determining goals, and forming active systems for the purpose of exercising influence, one can answer these questions and ultimately build a better, more accessible, more demand-based school program.

The social worker has a large role to play in this process, for he or she can become an organizer, a leader, a catalyst toward change, a liaison for the needs and wishes of the families, and a specialist in devising systems to meet change-oriented goals. Typical focuses are on discovering (a) the particular deficiencies in the school and the community, (b) the under- or unserved population, and (c) the programs that are needed to get children back in school and to curb juvenile delinquency. Another focus might be to analyze the interaction among the components in the systems in schools, or between the schools and the county departments of social services, to see, for example, whether these components are really working together or if they have underlying assumptions that work at cross-purposes.

As a systems change specialist, a social worker is an institutional change agent, a person analyzing ongoing programs and proposed new programs. The systems change approach seeks to change the goals of the traditional school social worker. The traditional goals were to help the child adapt to the school, to use the learning opportunities available, and to modify student behavior or parent–child relationships to alleviate problems in the school. With the systems approach, the goals are to analyze which parts of the system are activating stress in a given situation and then to alter that system so that equilibrium is again maintained. One must find and prioritize targets for change, acknowledging that different approaches must be used to solve different problems.

This approach should become clearer if we analyze a typical problem (see Case Example 10.2) that might be referred to a school social worker. By reevaluating and refocusing the problem, the systems change specialist makes the goals clearer and more meaningful.

Another example of the systems change role relates to the previously discussed issues of alcohol use and abuse by students. Using a systems

CASE
EXAMPLE 10.2   An Example of the Systems Change Role

John is a 10-year-old boy in a special education class. He is in that class because he is considerably behind the rest of his age group in reading and math. He also demonstrates some behavioral problems, particularly in stressful situations. He has not yet been termed EMR (educable mentally retarded), but as he gets older and does less well academically, he may ultimately be tested and found to have an IQ in the educable range. He is involved in a specialized program called mainstreaming, whereby he is placed in a regular class for physical education, music, art, and social studies. In the beginning of the year, there was hope for further mainstreaming into remedial reading and math, but behavioral problems have interfered. A referral has been sent to the school social worker asking that a behavioral program be started and that mainstreaming be stopped until further reassessment can be done. If the goal is only to put a "Band-aid" on the problem, it would be relatively easy to start a behavioral program and withdraw the child from the situation. Seemingly, everyone could accept this "solution," but what would it do for John's learning?

Another way of approaching the problem, using a systems change role, is to form a group composed of the teacher, the support personnel, and the principal to discuss mainstreaming as a general educational goal and to form flexible school policies regarding it. Forming a better mainstreaming program in which John can be successful becomes the main goal, as the assumption is that other students are encountering similar difficulties and will also benefit from any change. At the same time, the social worker must provide a support system for the regular education teacher involved with John. This could include (a) giving the teacher some general suggestions regarding behavioral management that are applicable to many children, (b) helping to find curriculum materials that are interesting to John and applicable to the rest of the group, (c) forming a group of students around John who would display good modeling behaviors, (d) writing a contract with John in which he could agree to certain limited goals for himself within the classroom, and (e) making sure through classroom discussion in human relations that John has the potential for friendships in the regular education class. The social worker could also support the special education teacher and continue to give reinforcement for mainstreaming students. Finally, he or she could make John's parents aware of the benefits of mainstreaming so that they could talk about it at home and generally tell John how desirable they thought it was. John's parents could then be more actively involved in his education, which would help to increase John's motivation to learn. Another goal would be to use this (or some other successful) mainstreaming effort to encourage more mainstreaming of additional students with other teachers.

Using this model, the social worker is designing a planned change approach and recognizing motivations for change and problems resulting from change. John is the focus for a much larger problem and is not *the* problem. He is the *access point* for the interconnection among a number of systems: regular education teachers, special education teachers, children with behavioral problems, and children with learning disabilities. As far as the school social worker is concerned, John is a catalyst for the creation of a system that will better serve many children.

modality, a school social worker might focus on seeking to change a community's acceptance of teen use of alcohol. A change effort could involve the social worker forming a group of concerned community leaders, such as representatives from the clergy, the police, business, social services, service clubs such as the Rotary, parents, teens, and others to develop a plan to increase community knowledge of the dangers of alcohol use. The ultimate goal is to decrease teen use of alcohol by strategies such as: improved parental supervision of teens, increased police enforcement of current laws, parent networks to decrease home parties, and community development of alternative activities to teen drinking. An advantage of this approach is that substantially more teens and their families will potentially benefit than if the school social worker meets on a one-to-one basis with teens who are using or abusing alcohol.

SUMMARY

Education, which in the past has been called on to resolve a variety of social problems, is now recognized as a social problem itself. Education is currently facing a variety of crises and problems.

There are a number of indicators that raise questions about the quality of education in this country. For example, scores on the Scholastic Aptitude Test, which is taken annually by high school seniors, are significantly lower than they were 35 years ago.

A second problematic area is that school systems are providing inferior educational opportunities for the poor and for members of minority groups. Less money is spent per student on education in low-income school districts and in school districts in which high proportions of minority students live. In our society, academic achievement is highly correlated with socioeconomic status.

A third problematic area is that there is considerable confusion about the desirable goals of education. There is agreement that schools should teach the basic skills of reading, writing, and arithmetic. However, there is controversy among different interest groups concerning the other learning goals that education should strive to attain.

A fourth problematic area is intolerable working conditions for teachers in some school settings. Intolerable conditions include low pay and low prestige, drug and alcohol abuse among students, physical threats and assaults from some students, insufficient instructional supplies, and high student-to-teacher ratios.

Four proposals for improving education in this country are to increase incentives for teachers, to improve the curricula, to allow parents to choose the school to which they will send their children, and to extend the school year. One of the controversial proposed incentives for teaching is the creation of master-teacher positions that would reward excellence in teaching. A major problem with seeking to improve the curriculum is a lack of agreement about what the curriculum should teach students. Under the parental choice of schools approach, it is theorized that market incentives would be created whereby academically superior schools would thrive and inferior schools would have to improve or face bankruptcy.

Three proposals were presented for seeking to work toward equal education opportunities for low-income and minority students: (a) reform school financing to spend an equal amount of money on each student's education, (b) establish special compensatory educational programs for disadvantaged students, and (c) integrate students from different ethnic and racial backgrounds into the same schools.

There are several role models for school social work practice. Traditional roles include those of caseworker, group worker, truant officer, counselor, and parent liaison. Newer roles include advocate, behavioral specialist, mental health consultant, alcohol and other drug abuse specialist, multidisciplinary team member, violence prevention specialist, and systems change specialist.

School social workers cannot solve all of the problems in education. Difficulties with integration, differences over goals, problems with the quality of the teaching staff, and changing roles and expectations in the family are all very complex and demanding problems. However, new ideas and creative approaches can be developed within the role of a systems change specialist, who can help the educational system address the problems of education and ultimately seek solutions.

NOTES

1. Quoted in William Kornblum and Joseph Julian, *Social Problems,* 6th ed. (Englewood Cliffs, NJ: Prentice Hall, 1988), p. 394.
2. James W. Coleman and Donald R. Cressey, *Social Problems,* 6th ed. (New York: HarperCollins, 1996), pp. 103–104.
3. Ibid.
4. "The Learning Lag: You Can't Blame TV," *U.S. News & World Report,* Dec. 2, 1996, p. 16.
5. Coleman and Cressey, *Social Problems,* p. 103.
6. Ibid.
7. Ibid., p. 105.
8. Ibid.
9. "If U Cn Reed Thiz Storie . . . ," *U.S. News & World Report,* Sept. 20, 1993, p. 10.
10. Quoted in Coleman and Cressey, *Social Problems,* p. 105.
11. Coleman and Cressey, *Social Problems,* p. 95.
12. "Michigan's Model," *U.S. News & World Report,* Mar. 28, 1994, p. 16.
13. Ibid.
14. Coleman and Cressey, *Social Problems,* p. 96.
15. Ibid.
16. Manley Fleischman et al., *The Fleischman Report on the Quality, Cost, and Financing of Elementary and Secondary Education in New York State* (New York: Viking Press, 1974), p. 57.
17. John E. Farley, *American Social Problems,* 2nd ed. (Englewood Cliffs, NJ: Prentice Hall, 1992), pp. 448–455.
18. Ibid., pp. 448–464.
19. Coleman and Cressey, *Social Problems,* pp. 98–100.
20. Jerelyn Eddings, "Second Thoughts About Integration," *U.S. News & World Report,* Jul. 28, 1997, p. 32.
21. Ibid.
22. Ibid.
23. Ibid.
24. Ibid.
25. Ibid.
26. L. Tye, "Study: U.S. Retreats on Integration," *Wisconsin State Journal,* Jan. 12, 1992, p. 9A.
27. Ibid.
28. Ibid.
29. Coleman and Cressey, *Social Problems,* pp. 98–101.
30. L. Tye, "Study: U.S. Retreats on Integration," p. 9A.
31. Coleman and Cressey, *Social Problems,* p. 100.
32. Ibid.
33. Ibid., p. 114.
34. Robert Burns, "20% of Middle Schools, High Schools Had at Least One Serious Crime in '97," *Wisconsin State Journal,* Mar. 20, 1998, p. 2A.
35. Coleman and Cressey, *Social Problems,* pp. 114–115.
36. Michael Rutter and associates, quoted in W. William Salgank, "British Study Finds Sharp Differences in Schools," *Los Angeles Times,* Nov. 22, 1979, part VIII, pp. 1–2.
37. Michael Rutter, *15,000 Hours: Secondary Schools and Their Effects on Children* (Cambridge, MA: Harvard University Press, 1979).
38. Eigil Pederson and Therese Annette Faucher, with William W. Eaton, "A New Perspective on the Effects of First-Grade Teachers on Children's Subsequent Adult Status," *Harvard Educational Review,* 48 (1978), pp. 1–31.
39. "Education Reform Signed," *Wisconsin State Journal,* Apr. 1, 1994, p. 2A.
40. Thomas Toch, "The Case for Tough Standards," *U.S. News & World Report,* Apr. 1, 1996, pp. 52–56.
41. "The Uncertain Benefits of School Choice," *U.S. News & World Report,* Nov. 6, 1989, pp. 79–81.
42. Rod Little, "The Endangered Summer Vacation," *U.S. News & World Report,* May 16, 1994, p. 12.
43. Ibid.
44. Ibid.
45. Ibid.
46. Ibid.
47. Ibid.
48. Thomas Toch, "The Perfect School," *U.S. News & World Report,* Jan. 11, 1993, pp. 60–61.
49. Ibid.
50. Ibid.
51. Ibid.
52. "Michigan's Model," *U.S. News & World Report,* p. 16.
53. Coleman and Cressey, *Social Problems,* p. 109.
54. Ibid., pp. 108–109.
55. Ibid., p. 109.
56. Ibid., p. 100.
57. William Kornblum and Joseph Julian, *Social Problems,* 8th ed. (Englewood Cliffs, NJ: Prentice Hall, 1995), p. 380.
58. Farley, *American Social Problems,* p. 480.
59. See Mildred Sikkema, "The School Social Worker Serves as a Consultant," *Casework Papers* (New York: Family Service Association of America, 1955), pp. 75–82.
60. Alan Guskin and Samuel Guslan, *A Social Psychology of Education* (Reading, MA: Addison-Wesley, 1970), pp. 1–3.

61. Albert Ellis, *Humanistic Psychotherapy* (New York: McGraw-Hill, 1973), pp. 55–69.

62. Edward Jones and Harold Gerard, *Foundations of Social Psychology* (New York: Wiley, 1967), pp. 83–92.

63. Rudolf Dreikurs, Bernice Grunwald, and Floy Pepper, *Maintaining Sanity in the Classroom* (New York: Harper & Row, 1971), pp. 17–21.

64. Ellis, *Humanistic Psychotherapy*, pp. 129–133.

65. Joel Fisher, "Is Casework Effective?" *Social Work*, 18 (Jan. 1973), pp. 5–21.

66. See Mary J. McCormick, "Social Advocacy: A New Dimension in Social Work," *Social Casework*, 51 (Jan. 1970), pp. 3–11.

67. For a more detailed discussion of behavior modification, see Beth Sulzer and G. Roy Mayer, *Behavior Modification Procedures for School Personnel* (New York: Holt, Rinehart & Winston, 1972).

68. Sidney Simon, *Values Clarification* (New York: Hart, 1972), pp. 20–21.

69. Allen Pincus and Anne Minahan, *Social Work Practice: Model and Method* (Itasca, IL: F. E. Peacock, 1973), pp. 3–9.

WORK-RELATED PROBLEMS AND SOCIAL WORK IN THE WORKPLACE

A question that is commonly asked when two strangers meet is, "What do you do for a living?" Work is a central focus in our lives. Work not only enables us to earn money to pay bills, but it can also provide a sense of self-respect, a circle of colleagues and friends, and a source of self-fulfillment. A challenging job can help us to grow intellectually, psychologically, and socially. Work also largely determines our place in the social structure. We are, to a great extent, defined by our work.

In our society, we value the "work ethic"; that is, we consider work to be honorable, productive, and useful. Unemployed, able-bodied people are often looked down on. This chapter will:

- Present a brief history of work.

- Describe three major problems involving work: alienation, unemployment, and occupational health hazards.

- Summarize current efforts and proposed new approaches to combat these problems.

- Describe social work in the workplace, which is an emerging field of social work practice.

A BRIEF HISTORY OF WORK

Work has not always been so esteemed. The ancient Greeks, for example, viewed work as a curse imposed on humanity by the gods. Work was thought to be an unpleasant and burdensome activity that was incompatible with being a citizen and developing one's mind. The Greeks therefore used slaves and justified slavery on the grounds that it freed citizens to spend their time in philosophic contemplation and cultural enrichment. Aristotle remarked: "No man can practice virtue who is living the life of a mechanic or laborer."[1]

Although the Romans viewed commercial banking as acceptable employment, practically all other occupations were considered vulgar and demeaning.

The ancient Hebrews viewed work ambivalently. On the one hand, they regarded it as a drudgery or a grim necessity. On the other hand, they saw it as an expression of love for God.

The early Christians also were ambivalent toward work. They viewed working as doing penance for Original Sin. (The Christian interpretation of the Bible asserts that Original Sin began with Adam and Eve disobeying God in the Garden of Eden.) But they also believed that people needed to work to make their own living and to help those in need.

The Protestant Reformation, which began in the 17th century, brought about profound changes in social values concerning work. Work became highly valued for the first time. One of the Protestant reformers, Martin Luther, asserted that labor was a service to God. Since that time, work has continued to be viewed as honorable and as having religious significance.

Another Protestant reformer, John Calvin, had an even more dramatic effect on changing social views toward work. Calvin preached that work is the will of God. Hard work, good deeds, and success at one's vocation were taken to be signs that one was destined for salvation. God's will was that people should live frugally (that is, spend very little money) and should use profits from work to invest in new ventures, which in turn would bring in more profits for additional investments, and so on. Idleness or laziness came to be viewed as sinful. One religious group that was heavily influenced by Calvin's teachings was the Puritans. The Puritans also developed a strong ascetic lifestyle—that is, the practice of denying worldly pleasures as a demonstration of religious discipline. Calvin's teachings were widely accepted and formed a new cultural value system that became known as the Protestant ethic. This ethic has three core values: hard work, frugality, and asceticism.

The values advanced by the Protestant ethic have continued throughout our history. For example, Benjamin Franklin cleverly praised these values in several axioms:

A penny saved is a penny earned.

Time is money.

After industry and frugality, nothing contributes more to the raising of a young man than punctuality.

EXHIBIT 11.1

Max Weber and the Protestant Ethic

In 1904 the German sociologist Max Weber published what has become one of the most provocative theories in sociology. In *The Protestant Ethic and the Spirit of Capitalism,* Weber asserted that the Protestant ethic encouraged and made possible the emergence of capitalism. Weber theorized that the ideas of puritanism (advocated by Martin Luther and John Calvin) provided the value system that led to the transformation from traditional society to the Industrial Revolution.

Weber noted that puritan Protestantism embraced the doctrine that people were divinely selected for either salvation or damnation. There was nothing people could do to alter their fate. No one knew for sure whether she or he was destined for eternal salvation or eternal damnation. However, people looked for signs from God to suggest their fate. Because they also believed that work was a form of service to God, they concluded that success at work (making profits) was a sign of God's favor. They therefore worked very hard to accumulate as much wealth as possible.

Because the Protestant ethic viewed luxury and self-gratification as sinful, the profits acquired were not spent on luxuries. Instead, profits were reinvested into new ventures to increase incomes.

Such new ventures included building factories and developing new machines. Thus, according to Weber, the Industrial Revolution began, and capitalism was born.

Source: Max Weber, *The Protestant Ethic and the Spirit of Capitalism,* rereleased (New York: Scribner's, 1958).

He who sits idle . . . throws away money.

Waste neither time nor money; an hour lost is money lost.[2]

Former President Nixon, in a speech on welfare reform, declared that labor had intrinsic value, that it had a strong American tradition, and that it was consistent with religious teachings. Nixon added: "Scrubbing floors and emptying bedpans have just as much dignity as there is in any work done in this country—including my own. . . . Most of us consider it immoral to be lazy or slothful."[3]

Although we no longer value the frugal, ascetic lifestyle of puritanism, we still believe strongly in the ethic of hard work. An able-bodied person, to gain approval from others, is expected to be employed (or at least to be receiving job training). People on welfare are often looked down on. There remains a strong link between amount of income and sense of personal worth. The more people are paid, the more highly they are regarded by others and the more highly they regard themselves.

People in low-status jobs are generally unable to form a satisfying identity from their jobs. Having an assembly-line job, for example, often leads workers to view themselves as personally insignificant. They routinely perform the same task day in and day out—such as attaching nuts to bolts. Many such workers feel embarrassed about not having a better job.[4]

Because our work has immense effects on our self-concept, having a degrading, boring, and dehumanizing job can damage our psychological well-being. We judge ourselves not only by how much we earn but also by whether our job is challenging and satisfying and helps us to grow and develop.

TRENDS IN THE AMERICAN WORKFORCE

Since the turn of the 20th century, unions have generally been growing in power in this country, which has led to significant pay increases and fringe benefits for employees. Since 1980, however, the power balance between unions and management has shifted more toward management. In a number of businesses, management has been asking that employees take zero wage increases (or even pay cuts), with the threat of moving the business elsewhere or closing the doors permanently. Employees have generally chosen, with considerable reluctance, to accept management's offers rather than to strike and risk losing their jobs.

In the 20th century, the nature of work and the composition of the workforce have changed radically in our society. Eight changes seem especially prominent: the increase in white-collar workers, the emergence of an employee society, specialization, changes in the sex and age composition of the workforce, the emphasis on intrinsic rewards, the emphasis on high technology, the growth of low-paying jobs, and outsourcing in a global factory.

Increase in White-Collar Workers

In colonial times, most people made a living working on small farms, either their own or someone else's. We have since moved from an agricultural economy to a modern industrial economy.

In 1990, 27% of the labor force were farm workers, and 18% were white-collar workers. In 1995 only 2% were farm workers, and 58% were white-collar workers.[5] The immense productivity of our industrial system has made it possible for 2% of the workforce to feed all of us! Farm workers (farmers, farmhands, and farm managers), once the largest occupational group, are now one of the smallest.

White-collar workers (professionals, clerical personnel, sales personnel, managers), once the smallest occupational group, are now the largest. This group surpassed blue-collar workers in terms of numbers in 1956.[6]

Work in industrial societies can be grouped into three categories: primary, secondary, and tertiary.

Primary industry is the gathering or extracting of undeveloped natural resources, such as farm-ing, mining, or fishing. In the early stages of industrialization, most workers are employed in this category.

Secondary industry involves turning raw materials into manufactured goods, such as processed food, steel, and automobiles. In the middle stages of industrialization, most workers are employed in this category. Most of these workers are blue-collar workers.

Tertiary industry involves service activities of one kind or another, such as dental care, medical services, automobile maintenance, sales, and pest control. In advanced societies such as ours, most workers are employed in service activities, primarily in white-collar jobs. Now, over 60% of our workforce is employed in tertiary industry.[7] Work in this category is generally cleaner and more pleasant than work in primary and secondary industries.

Emergence of an Employee Society

No longer are Americans likely to be self-employed, as they generally were in colonial times. Less than 10% of the workforce now classify themselves as self-employed.[8] A few small-business owners, small family-owned farms, independent shopkeepers, and independent carpenters and artists still remain. But small owner-operated businesses increasingly are finding it difficult to compete against well-organized corporations and businesses. The vast majority of workers are employed by someone else: large corporations, the government, and so forth. Even physicians, who once were largely self-employed as general practitioners, now generally work for a medical clinic or some other organization.

Specialization

The 1850 census listed a total of only 323 distinct job titles in the United States.[9] There are now over 35,000 job titles—more than 100 times as many different occupations.[10] Some of the unusual jobs one can choose for a career are clock winder, tea taster, and water smeller. With this extensive

Workers assemble a B-1 bomber. Today the vast majority of workers are employed by large corporations, government, or some other organization.

specialization, production of goods is now fragmented into repetitive and monotonous tasks, with each worker contributing only a small portion of the final product. A worker on an assembly line commented:

> The assembly line is no place to work, I can tell you. There is nothing more discouraging than having a barrel beside you with 10,000 bolts in it and using them all up. Then you get a barrel with another 10,000 bolts, and you know every one of those 10,000 bolts has to be picked up and put in exactly the same place as the last 10,000 bolts.[11]

Specialization has contributed substantially to the development and provision of highly sophisticated products and services. But it has also created problems. Workers find it difficult to take pride in

their work when they realize they are merely a replaceable adjunct to a machine or a process and when they contribute only a small part to the final product. Such specialization often results in job dissatisfaction. Those who are trained for a single narrowly defined job that later becomes obsolete are often without marketable skills for other openings. Specialization has also created problems of worker cooperation and coordination for managers of organizations. Our society has become highly interdependent because of specialization. With interdependency, disruption in one work area may gravely affect the whole economy. In 1997, for example, employees of United Parcel Service (UPS) went on strike for about a week, seriously disrupting the U.S. economy, which is heavily dependent on products being transported by mail.

Changes in the Sex and Age of the Labor Force

The labor force consists of people 16 years of age and over who are employed or who are actively seeking work (the unemployed). There have been some significant trends in the composition of the labor force.

Older men are becoming less likely to be in the labor force. In 1954, 40% of males over age 65 were in the labor force, but by 1995 only 16% in this category were in the labor force.[12] Employers are reluctant to hire older workers when younger workers with more recent training are available at lower salaries. Job obsolescence and myths about the unproductivity of older workers also make it difficult for unemployed older workers to be hired.

Women are increasingly entering the labor force. In 1900 only 20% of all adult women were in paid employment, compared to over 55% at present.[13] Women, however, still tend to be employed in the less prestigious, lower-paying positions (as will be discussed further in Chapter 13).

Two groups that have historically had high rates of unemployment or received low pay if employed have been minority group workers and teenage workers. Unemployment rates are particularly high for non-White teenagers; in some cities, more than 50% of people in this category are unemployed.[14] Women who work full time are paid, on the average, only about two-thirds of what men who work full time are paid.[15] Non-White women, subjected to double discrimination, earn even less.

Emphasis on Intrinsic Rewards

Intrinsic rewards come from the nature of the work itself. Work that offers intrinsic rewards is fulfilling and challenging, helps one grow socially and emotionally, contributes to physical fitness, promotes a sense of accomplishment through the use of one's talents, generates a feeling of self-respect, provides interest and enjoyment, offers an opportunity to meet new friends, and so on. In the past, people took a job primarily for its extrinsic rewards—a paycheck that would enable them to pay their bills. In the last 30 years, workers have become increasingly concerned about the intrinsic rewards prospective jobs will provide.[16]

Emphasis on High Technology

Our society's economy is becoming increasingly based on high technology, such as computers and advanced communication systems. Automation and robots are now doing more of the work that was previously done by blue-collar workers.

Technology is a double-edged sword. Every major technological innovation has both freed humans from previous hardships and created new, unanticipated problems. For example, the development of nuclear power is an important source of energy, but a nuclear mishap has the potential to kill thousands (and even millions) of people. Technology can be defined as the totality of means used to provide objects necessary for human comfort and sustenance. Daniel Bell defines technological change as "the combination of all methods (apparatus, skills, organization) for increasing the productivity of labor and capital."[17]

Technological innovations are causing major changes in the type of work available to Americans. Blue-collar and agricultural jobs are declining, and jobs in high-technology fields (such as computers and communications) are increasing. People who are laid off or discharged in industries (such as the steel industry) in which jobs are declining face immense obstacles in obtaining employment that pays comparable wages. On the other hand, people who are trained for high-tech positions have excellent career opportunities. In the employment market, technological advances are a boon for some and a disaster for others. Automobile executives welcome the coming of robots to the assembly line because robots are cutting production costs. Unemployed assembly-line workers with home mortgages are cursing the use of robots.

There is a growing concern among many educational, political, and civil rights leaders that, as we come to depend increasingly on computers and other technological innovations, only a select portion of the population will have the skills needed to function well in our society. Those who lack

Multinational companies can take advantage of cheap labor by having products made and assembled in developing countries and then sold in the United States and elsewhere.

such skills may find themselves trapped in lower-class positions.

The Growth of Low-Paying Jobs

Despite the increase in the total number of jobs in the American economy in the 1980s and 1990s, average wage and salary income (adjusted for inflation) declined in most industries.[18] A major reason for this trend has been the extensive growth in low-wage jobs. For example, there has been extensive expansion of minimum wage jobs in the fast-food industry. There has also been significant expansion of part-time employment (that is, jobs offering fewer than 35 hours of work per week). More part-time jobs are now created each month than full-time jobs.[19] Employers are also more likely now, as compared to two decades ago, to hire temporary employees (for example, limited term positions).[20] By hiring part-time and temporary employees, employers avoid paying many

fringe benefits (such as health-care insurance and retirement plans). Another reason for the growth in low-paying jobs is a continued shift of the labor force out of manufacturing and into service jobs. As plants have closed and manufacturing jobs have been exported to less developed countries, displaced workers have been forced to accept jobs in services and trade, which have twice the proportion of low-wage jobs as the manufacturing sector.[21] Many manufacturing corporations in the 1990s emphasized *downsizing* their number of full-time employees.

Outsourcing in a Global Factory

Multinational corporations (corporations headquartered in one country that pursue business activities in one or more foreign countries) are transforming the world's economy with "global factories." Such corporations are no longer confined to producing their products in just one

CASE
EXAMPLE 11.1   Job Dissatisfaction

Mary and Robert Buyze met in college and were married shortly after Mary graduated in 1991. Bob had graduated a year earlier. Bob majored in history and Mary in psychology. Both shared the American dream of having a home in the suburbs, a motorboat, and two cars. Because both had graduated from college, they were optimistic that they were well on their way. They fantasized about taking a yearly trip to such places as Acapulco, Europe, Jamaica, and Hawaii.

It is now 6 years later. Bob is 29 and Mary is 28. They have yet to take a trip and now have two young children. They are deeply in debt, having tried to buy much of their dream with credit. They purchased a run-down "starter" home with two bedrooms that was advertised as a "fixer's delight." Unexpected repairs to the furnace, the roof, and the plumbing have plunged them even deeper into debt, as have medical expenses, food, and clothing for the family.

What is even sadder is that they both have jobs they dislike. Bob has been a life insurance salesman for a small company for the past three and a half years. Bob states:

> I took the job because I couldn't find anything else. There were no job openings for historians when I graduated, so I took a variety of odd jobs, none of which I enjoyed. I was a truck driver, manager of a pizza place, taxicab driver, car salesman—and much of the time I was unemployed.
>
> I hoped when I took this job that I would finally be able to make good money. It just hasn't worked out. I hate selling insurance. Most of the time, I randomly call people from the telephone directory and urge them to buy a policy. It's like begging for money for a charity. I absolutely despise having to put myself in a position of peddling policies—and being nice and charming to people who at times end up slamming the phone down and hurting my eardrum. But I have no choice. I've got so many bills to pay that I can't afford not to work. I also hate to see Mary having

country. High-speed transportation enables these corporations to get raw materials and finished products from one location to another anywhere in the world. Such transportation systems enable multinational companies to take advantage of the supply of cheap labor in developing countries. For example, U.S. baseball manufacturers send the materials for their product—yarn, leather covers, cement, and thread—to Haiti, where baseballs are assembled for wages far below those paid for similar work anywhere in the United States.

Outsourcing is the practice of locating plants that produce products for American markets in Third World nations where the corporation can take advantage of lower wage rates. Outsourcing in effect "exports" manufacturing jobs from the

United States to the Third World. (Some authorities have referred to this phenomenon as deindustrialization in the United States.)

PROBLEMS IN THE WORK SETTING

Alienation

Alienation has a specific sociological meaning: *the sense of meaninglessness and powerlessness that people experience when interacting with social institutions they consider oppressive and be-*

to work with the kids so young. But again, we have no choice. What really hurts is that both of us are slaving away at jobs we don't like. Yet, with all the bills we have to pay, we hardly are able to buy Christmas presents.

Mary is a clothing store clerk. She also was unable to get a job in her field (psychology). After graduating, she worked for 2 years as a typist, which paid about the same as her present job—slightly above the minimum wage. She quit being a typist shortly before their first child (Rob) was born; she disliked secretarial work even more than her present job. A few months after Rob's birth, she began working part time in the job she now holds full time. Mary states:

> *When I was in college, I guess I was too idealistic. I expected to get a challenging job that would help me grow as a person and also pay well. That just hasn't happened. What I earn now is very little, especially after having to pay the baby-sitter. This job at times is boring, especially during the months when business is slow. November and December are just the opposite—we're running all the time, and I'm exhausted by the end of the day. It's feast or famine. But my day doesn't end when I leave the store. I've got cooking, washing, and cleaning to do—plus trying to find time to spend with the children. The last 4 years since the kids were born have been a nightmare—changing diapers, getting up in the middle of the night, taking care of sick kids. Don't get me wrong—I wouldn't trade them in, but some days I really wonder where I went wrong. What really hurts is that we have almost nothing to show for our efforts.*
>
> *I tell you, some mornings I'm so worn out when I get up and so unhappy with work that tears roll out of my eyes when I drive to work. What's just as bad is that I know that Bob hates his job as much as I do. Increasingly, when he has a bad day, he drinks too much—and that is worrying me more and more. I'm in a dead-end job with no chance for advancement, and I can't afford to give it up. Is this all there is to life?*

yond their control. The term *worker alienation* was originally used by Karl Marx. (Perhaps because Marx has been associated with communism, the subject of worker alienation has tended to be neglected in our country.) Marx suggested that worker alienation occurs largely because workers are separated from ownership of the means of production and from any control over the final product of their labor. They thus feel powerless and view their work as meaningless. Marx described alienation as follows:

> *In what does this alienation consist? First, that work is external to the worker, that it is not part of his nature, that consequently he does not fulfill himself in his work but denies himself, has*

> *a feeling of misery, not well-being, does not develop freely a physical and mental energy, but is physically exhausted and mentally debased. . . . His work is not voluntary but imposed, forced labor. . . . Finally, the alienated character of work for the worker appears in the fact that it is not his work but work for someone else, that in work he does not belong to himself but to another person.*[22]

According to Marx, specialization is a major cause of alienation. With specialization workers are forced to perform an unfulfilling task repeatedly. Because people use only a fraction of their talents, work becomes an enforced, impersonalized activity rather than a creative venture.

Marx believed that worker alienation would eventually lead to such discontent that the workers would band together and revolt against owners. Another reason workers would revolt is that they would realize they were exploited by the dominant class, who prosper from their toil.

Marx's prediction of a class revolution has not come true in the United States. Marx did not foresee the effectiveness of collective bargaining and new technology in improving the conditions of workers during the 20th century. Interestingly, even workers in socialist countries such as China and Cuba experience considerable alienation. (Marx had predicted that there would be less alienation in socialist countries.)

It may be that much of the alienation that Marx attributed to capitalistic societies was really caused by industrialism. Workers in this country, contrary to what Marx predicted, continue to have basic trust and faith in the American capitalistic system. Many workers have made financial investments in stocks, bonds, real estate, savings, and so forth. To a significant extent, they are also part of the dominant class. Marx saw only a struggle between two classes—owners and workers. He did not foresee considerable overlap between these classes, nor did he foresee the development of a large middle class that tends to include both investors and workers. Because of Americans' faith in our system and their disdain of communism, it is highly unlikely that there will be a class revolution in our country in the foreseeable future.

In fact, the working class has not successfully staged a socialist revolution in any industrialized country. The socialist revolutions that have occurred—in the former Soviet Union, China, Cuba, and so forth—have all taken place in developing or preindustrial countries. It is important to note that even China and, especially, Russia are increasingly using the profit motive (a key component of capitalism) as an incentive to work and as a method to stimulate their economies.

In addition, it appears that Marx's theories about the evils of a capitalistic economy are being rejected by many of the societies (such as the former Soviet Union and Poland) that tried to establish economic systems based on Marxist principles. These countries have concluded that, unless they use capitalistic incentives, they cannot motivate their citizens to produce at desired rates. Some authorities are now asserting that Marx's theories about economic production have been tried and tested and have been found to have failed miserably. In terms of productivity, the economies of Eastern Europe that have been based on Marx's theories have fallen far behind those of Western Europe (which have been using capitalistic incentives). In 1990 posters of Karl Marx bearing the caption, "Workers of the World! Forgive me" were selling widely in eastern Germany.[23] (Marx had coined the slogan, "Workers of the World! Unite.")

PRESENT SOURCES OF ALIENATION

Alienation has many sources. Specialization has led workers to feel that they have meaningless jobs and are contributing insignificantly to the business. It is difficult, for example, for assembly-line workers to take pride in producing an automobile when they only attach an ignition wire.

Working for a large business or corporation and knowing that you can readily be replaced leads to feelings of powerlessness and lowered self-esteem. Not being involved in the decision-making process and being aware that supervisors do not want workers to "make waves" also lead to feelings of powerlessness and meaninglessness.

In some businesses, machines have been developed to do most of the work. This automation (for example, assembly lines in the auto industry) has led workers to feel they are insignificant cogs in the production process. Even the pace at which they work is controlled by the assembly-line machinery. Jobs that offer little opportunity to be creative also contribute to alienation. Such jobs include typist, receptionist, janitor, garbage collector, assembly-line worker, or telephone operator. Most American workers do not hold jobs they had planned for; they are doing what they do for such reasons as "simple chance" or "lack of choice." As a result, many people feel trapped in their jobs.[24]

Alienation also derives from jobs that do not provide opportunities to learn, a sense of accomplishment, or the chance to work with compatible people. Many authorities believe that alien-

CASE EXAMPLE 11.2 The Hawthorne Effect

In 1927 in Chicago, the Hawthorne Works of the Western Electric Company began a series of experiments designed to discover ways to increase worker satisfaction and productivity. Hawthorne Works primarily manufactured telephones, with the plant operating on an assembly-line basis. Workers needed no special skills in this production process and performed simple repetitive tasks. The employees were not unionized. Management speculated that, if they found ways to increase job satisfaction, the employees would work more efficiently and productivity would increase.

The company tested a number of factors potentially related to productivity. These factors included rest breaks, better lighting, changes in the number of work hours during the day, changes in the wages paid, improved food facilities, and so on.

The results were surprising. Productivity increased, as expected, with improved working conditions. But it also increased when working conditions worsened. (One way that working conditions were worsened was by substantially dimming the lighting.) The finding that productivity increased when working conditions worsened was unexpected and led to additional study to find an explanation.

The investigators discovered that participation in the experiments was extremely attractive to the workers. They felt they had been selected by management for their individual abilities, and so they worked harder, even when working conditions became less favorable. There were additional explanations. The workers' morale and general attitude toward work improved, as they felt they were receiving special attention from management. By participating in this study, they were able to work in smaller groups, and they also became involved in making decisions. Working in smaller groups allowed them to develop a stronger sense of solidarity with their fellow workers. Being involved in decision making decreased feelings of meaninglessness and powerlessness about their work.

The results of this study have become known as the "Hawthorne effect" in sociological and psychological research. The Hawthorne effect holds that, when subjects know they are participants in a study, this awareness may lead them to behave differently and thereby substantially influence the results of the study.

Source: Fritz J. Roethlisberger and William J. Dickson, *Management and the Worker* (Cambridge, MA: Harvard University Press, 1939).

---

ation leads to acts of disruption in the production process—work of poor quality, high rates of absenteeism, and vandalism or theft of company property.

Dissatisfaction with one's job is a useful indicator of alienation at work. Studies on job satisfaction show wide differences, according to vocation, in worker satisfaction with their jobs. Many jobs are simply dull. For workers who already earn enough to live adequately, additional income cannot always offset the meaninglessness of such jobs.

CONFRONTING ALIENATION AND JOB DISSATISFACTION

One of the best-known efforts to increase worker satisfaction and productivity was that of Hawthorne Works, a division of Western Electric Company in Chicago. The results were surprising, as described in Case Example 11.2.

Many employers have become aware that job dissatisfaction reduces efficiency and productivity. There are a number of ways to increase job satisfaction. The first step is to find out precisely what the workers are dissatisfied about. Then changes can be made. In one job setting, workers may be most concerned about safety conditions (as in coal mining); in another they may be most concerned about boring, repetitive work (as on an assembly line); in another it may be wages (as for jobs that pay only the minimum wage); in yet another it may be lack of recognition (as for clerical workers who make their supervisors look good).

A wide variety of changes can be made to improve job satisfaction. The following list is far from exhaustive:

- Find ways to make the work challenging and interesting.

- Provide opportunities for career advancement.

- Provide in-service training on relevant aspects of the work—for example, stress management programs for stressful jobs.

- Increase wages, salaries, and fringe benefits.

- Involve workers in the decision-making process.

- Have social get-togethers to help improve group morale.

- Give workers more of the profits through a profit-sharing program.

- Have a reward system to recognize significant contributions made by workers.

- Institute employee policies that generate a sense of job security.

- Allow workers some control over their schedules—for example, through flexitime. Workers are more satisfied in jobs in which they feel they have some decision-making responsibilities and some control over their work schedules. They don't like punching a time clock, whereas flexitime is appealing. The idea behind flexitime is to have most workers present during the busiest time of the day but to leave the remaining hours up to the discretion of the workers. Those who want to start earlier, so they can leave earlier, can do so. Those who

want to come in later and stay later also have this option. In some places, it is possible with flexitime to work 4 days a week (10 hours per day) and thereby have an extra day off.

Many government agencies and private companies are now on flexitime. Although supervisors have found it is more difficult to coordinate work schedules when using flexitime, absenteeism declines and productivity increases under such a program.

- Make the work setting as free of hazards as possible.

- Have promotion-from-within policies, training programs, personnel policies that ensure equal opportunity for advancement and education, and good physical facilities and conveniences (lounges, cafeterias, gyms, and the like).

A variety of programs involve employees in *participative management.* For example, in *consultive management,* managers consult with their employees (either individually or in small groups) and encourage them to think about job-related issues and contribute their own ideas before decisions are made. *Democratic management* goes even further; it systematically allows employee groups to make a number of major decisions. An example of democratic management is the practice of allowing work teams to hire, orient, and train new employees. *Self-managing teams* are a subcategory of democratic management; they are autonomous work groups that are given a high degree of decision-making authority and are expected to control their own behavior and work schedules, with compensation usually based on the team's overall productivity.

Quality circles are work-improvement task forces in which managers and employees meet regularly to allow employees to air grievances (which in itself has a ventilating effect in reducing job dissatisfaction), to identify problems that hinder productivity, and to offer suggestions for alleviating these concerns. *Suggestion programs* are formal procedures to encourage employees to recommend work improvements, often in writing; in many companies, employees whose suggestions result in cost savings receive monetary awards. *Stock trusts* allow employees to buy or receive

EXHIBIT 11.2

Theory Y: Improving Productivity and Job Satisfaction

Douglas McGregor categorized management thinking and behavior into two types—Theory X and Theory Y.

Theory X managers view employees as incapable of much growth. Employees are perceived as having an inherent dislike for work, and it is presumed that they will attempt to evade work whenever possible. Therefore, X-type managers believe they must control, direct, force, or threaten employees to make them work. Employees are also viewed as having relatively little ambition. Theory X managers believe employees seek to avoid taking on new responsibilities and prefer to be directed. X-type managers therefore spell out job responsibilities carefully, set work goals without employee input, use external rewards (such as money) to force employees to work, and punish employees who deviate from established rules. Because Theory X managers reduce responsibilities to a level at which few mistakes can be made, work usually becomes so structured that it is monotonous and distasteful. The assumptions of Theory X are, of course, inconsistent with what behavioral scientists assert are effective principles for directing, influencing, and motivating people.

In contrast, *Theory Y managers* view employees as wanting to grow and develop by exerting physical and mental effort to accomplish work objectives to which they are committed. Y-type managers believe that internal rewards, such as self-respect and personal improvement, are stronger motivations than external rewards (money) and punishment. A Y-type manager also believes that, under proper conditions, employees will not only accept responsibility but seek it. Most employees are assumed to have considerable ingenuity, creativity, and imagination for solving the organization's problems. Therefore, employees are given considerable responsibility in order to test the limits of their capabilities. Mistakes and errors are viewed as necessary phases of the learning process, and work is structured so that employees can have a sense of accomplishment and growth.

Employees who work for Y-type managers are generally more creative and productive, experience greater work satisfaction, and are more highly motivated than employees who work for X-type managers. Under both management styles, expectations often become self-fulfilling prophecies.

Source: Douglas McGregor, *The Human Side of Enterprise* (New York: McGraw-Hill, 1960).

---

stock in the company, thereby becoming partial owners; a benefit of stock trusts is that they act as an incentive for higher productivity among employees. *Employee ownership* occurs when employees provide the capital to purchase control of an existing company; employee ownership generally increases employee interest in the company's financial success and acts as an incentive for workers to remain with the company.[25]

A number of American companies have increased productivity by conducting "climate surveys," in which workers are asked to vent their concerns and to criticize their jobs. Sometimes such surveys identify problematic situations that can be improved through relatively minor changes. Even when the problems cannot be resolved, work tensions are often temporarily reduced just by allowing workers to let off steam.

Theory Y managers have been found to substantially improve productivity and job satisfaction, as compared to Theory X managers (see Exhibit 11.2).

CASE EXAMPLE 11.3

American Dream Becomes Economic Nightmare Through Unemployment

Lorraine and Jim Dedrick thought they had it made. They had a five-bedroom, stone-foundation home on a lake, a landscaped yard, two well-behaved children, a car, a van, a motorboat, and a sailboat. The home, the vehicles, and the boats were bought on time payments. Because both were working, they were confident that they could easily make the monthly payments. Mrs. Dedrick describes what happened.

My husband worked at Dana Corporation (a car- and truck-axle manufacturing plant). He was a crew supervisor and was making over $37,000 a year. I was, and still am, a legal secretary.

When the layoffs started in spring 1993, we didn't think it would touch Jim. He had 6 years of seniority. But by March of 1994, we knew a layoff was inevitable. Dana Corporation was not doing well financially. When the layoff came in June of 1994, we weren't surprised.

At first we weren't worried. Jim thought it would be nice to have a summer off and looked forward to doing some fishing and some fixing up around the house. Because he was 39 years old and had worked steadily since he was 18, I also thought a few months' break would do him good. He was of course able to draw unemployment benefits, and with my salary I was certain we could get by. Surely Dana Corporation would recover, and he would be called back in the fall.

In late summer, however, a rumor started and quickly spread throughout the plant that Dana was going to close its plant. In September they announced the plant was going to close.

Both of us immediately became alarmed. Jim started looking for other work in earnest. Unfortunately, there were no comparable jobs in the area.

Jim applied at many different jobs but had no luck. I know of nothing worse than to see a once-proud, secure person come home each evening with the look on his face that he has once again been rejected. Jim began developing stomach problems from the rejections, and I started having, and still have, tension headaches. We used to go out a lot, laugh, and have a good time. Now we not only cannot afford it, but we no longer have an interest.

Jim grabbed at every straw. He even went to apply for jobs in Milwaukee and Chicago. In the last year, he appears to have aged 10 years.

Unemployment

THE COSTS OF UNEMPLOYMENT

As illustrated in Case Example 11.3, unemployment can have devastating effects. Most obviously, it reduces (sometimes to below poverty levels) the amount of income that a family or single person receives. Short-term unemployment, especially when one receives unemployment compensation (described in Chapter 4), may have only minor consequences. But long-term unemployment inflicts numerous problems.

Harold Wilensky found that long-term unemployment often leads to extreme personal isolation. Work is a central part of many people's lives. When unemployment occurs, work ties are sev-

In February of 1995, his unemployment benefits ended. Bill collectors began hounding us. We soon depleted all our savings. We got so many calls from bill collectors that we took out an unlisted telephone number. Never before were we unable to pay our bills.

The months since February have been hell. Increasingly we have gotten into arguments. Whenever I bring my check home, Jim has a pained look on his face, as he feels he's not doing his share. I try to tell him that it's not his fault, but whenever we talk about it, he appears hurt and becomes angry.

At the end of February, he began to advertise by word of mouth that he was an independent carpenter. He's good with his hands. Unfortunately, the few jobs he got have as yet not even paid for the extra tools he's had to buy. It has only gotten us deeper into debt.

When I drive to work, the tears often fall. It's my only time alone. Driving home I often cry as I think about our situation and know I'll have to face Jim's sad look.

We don't associate much with friends now. They either pity us or have that arrogant "I told you so" look in response to our optimism when Jim was first laid off.

It just doesn't look like Jim is going to be able to get a job in this area. Next week he's going to Atlanta—we've heard there are a lot of job openings there.

Dennis, our 12-year-old son, is alternately sad and angry about the possibility of leaving this area. He's got a lot of friends and loves to go boating, fishing, and sailing. Having to take your son away from something he really loves is one of the most difficult things I'll probably ever have to do.

Karen, our daughter who's 15, really had a bad year at school. Her grades fell, and when we asked her why, she said, "What's the use in studying—won't help in getting a job." That remark hurt deeply, probably because it may have a ring of truth in it.

It looks like we're going to have to give up our dream house on this lake. (Tears came to Mrs. Dedrick as she spoke.) We've lived here for the past 5 years and really loved it. This is our first real home. We've added on a patio, a bedroom, and enlarged the living room. We also spend a lot of time in painting and fixing it up. It's really become a part of us. If Jim gets a job in Atlanta, we'll be forced to sell. We checked what market prices are, and there's no way we're going to get what we put into this house.

A few years ago, we thought we were starting to live the American dream. This past year and a half has been hell. Here we are broke, unhappy, and about to lose our home. At our age, starting life over is almost more than we can take.

ered. As a result, many of the unemployed see friends less, cease participating in community life, and become increasingly isolated.[26]

D. D. Braginsky and B. M. Braginsky found that long-term unemployment causes attitude changes that persist even after reemployment.[27] Being laid off (or fired) is often interpreted by the unemployed as a sign of being incompetent and worthless. Self-esteem is lowered, they are likely to experience depression, and they feel alienated from society. Many suffer deep shame and avoid their friends. They feel dehumanized and insignificant and see themselves as an easily replaced statistic. They also tend to lose faith in our political and economic system, with some blaming the political system for their problems. Even when they find new jobs, they do not fully recover their self-esteem.

Harvey Brenner found a strong association between unemployment and emotional problems. During an economic recession, mental hospital admissions increase. The suicide rate increases, indicating an increase in depression. Also higher during times of high unemployment are the divorce rate, the incidence of child abuse, and the number of peptic ulcers (a stress-related disease).[28] Just the threat of unemployment can lead to emotional problems.

In many cases, the long-term unemployed are forced to exhaust their savings, sell their homes, and become public assistance recipients. A few turn to crime, particularly the young. The unemployed no longer enjoy the companionship of their fellow workers. They often experience feelings of embarrassment, anger, despair, depression, anxiety, boredom, hopelessness, and apathy. These feelings may lead to alcoholism, drug abuse, insomnia, stress-related illnesses, marital unhappiness, and even violence within the family. The work ethic is still prominent in our society: When people lose their jobs, they devalue themselves and also miss the sense of self-worth that comes from doing a job well.

As more and more women have entered the labor force, the consequences of unemployment for single women with children have assumed ever-greater importance. Newman found that middle-class women who experience divorce "typically have to make do with 29 to 39 percent of the family income they had before divorce."[29] When these women are in the labor force and experience unemployment, it is often difficult for them to support their families while looking for new jobs. Typically they had interrupted their careers for marriage and child rearing, and they now find themselves less competitive in the labor market than men who have been working more or less continuously.

Widespread unemployment also sharply cuts government tax revenues. When tax revenues are reduced, federal departments are forced to cut services at a time when the services are most needed. Such cuts further add to alienation and despair.

High unemployment also leads to high rates of underemployment. Underemployment occurs when people are working at jobs below their level of skill. College graduates, for example, may be forced to take unskilled road construction work or become clerical workers.

WHO ARE THE UNEMPLOYED?

In the past two decades, the national unemployment rate has ranged from 4% to 11%. Official statistics are compiled by the Bureau of Labor Statistics. The bureau, usually monthly, makes a survey of households randomly selected from the total population.

Virtually all of us will be unemployed at some point during our working years. There is some variation from time to time in the groups that are most vulnerable to unemployment. In the late 1970s and early 1980s, unemployment was particularly high among steel workers and automobile workers. In the mid-1970s, PhDs in the liberal arts and social sciences had high unemployment rates. In the early 1980s, the housing industry was in a slump, and there were high unemployment rates among carpenters and construction workers. In the middle and late 1980s, there were high rates of unemployment among workers in the petroleum production industry. In the 1990s, businesses and corporations were downsizing their workforces, including administrative positions; as a result, there were high unemployment rates among middle-level managers.

Some groups have chronically high unemployment rates. These groups include African Americans and Latinos, teenagers, women, older workers, the unskilled, the semiskilled, and persons with a disability.

High unemployment among African Americans and Latinos is partly due to racial discrimination. Unfortunately, there is truth in the cliché that minorities are "last to be hired, first to be fired." Another reason for high unemployment is due to their lower average level of educational achievement, which leaves them unqualified for many of the available jobs. (Lower educational levels and lack of marketable job skills are largely due to *past* discrimination.)

High unemployment among women also stems partly from discrimination. Many employers (most of them men) are still inclined to hire a man before a woman, and many jobs are still erroneously thought to be "a man's job." Women have also been socialized to seek lower-paying jobs, to not be competitive with men, and to believe their place is in the home and not in the workforce (see Chapter 13 for a fuller discussion).

Myths about older workers—age 40 and over—make it more difficult for them to obtain a new job if they become unemployed. They are *erroneously* thought to be less productive, more difficult to get along with, more difficult to train, clumsier, more accident prone, less healthy, and more prone to absenteeism than younger workers (see Chapter 14 for a further discussion of these myths, along with a review of research studies that refute these stereotypes). An additional problem for unemployed older workers is that younger people are often available at salaries far below what the older applicants were paid at their last job.

Unemployment is high for teenagers and young people. This is partly because many of them have not received the training that would provide them with marketable skills.

Employers are willing to hire unskilled workers when they have simple repetitive tasks to be performed. But unskilled workers are the first to be laid off when there is a business slump. These workers can readily be replaced if business picks up. Highly skilled workers are more difficult to replace. Also, employers have much more invested in skilled workers, as they have spent more time in training them.

Blue-collar workers are more affected by economic slumps than white-collar workers. Industries that employ large numbers of blue-collar workers—housing, road construction, manufacturers of heavy equipment such as tractors, the auto industry—are quickly and deeply hit by recessions and often forced to lay off workers. As noted earlier, the number of blue-collar jobs is decreasing, whereas white-collar jobs are increasing. A major reason for this decline is *automation*, whereby the system of production is increasingly controlled by means of self-operating machinery. Examples of automation include the automobile assembly line and direct-dial telephone (which displaced thousands of telephone operators). Robots are now replacing workers in a number of industries, particularly for doing simple repetitive tasks.

Persons with a disability have very high unemployment rates. There are many stereotypes that contribute to these high rates, as described at some length in Chapter 16. There is a tendency in our society to conclude that because a person has a disability in one area he or she also has other disabilities. For example, those with a physical disability are sometimes thought to be less intelligent and less effective in social interactions. Numerous studies have found that when people with a disability are hired, they usually dispel all of the negative myths that surround them.[30] Kornblum and Julian conclude:

> An overwhelming majority prove to be dedicated, capable workers; they have only a slightly higher than average absentee rate, and their turnover rate is well below average. They are neither slower nor less productive than other workers and have excellent safety records.[31]

REASONS FOR THE HIGH UNEMPLOYMENT RATE

The reasons for the high unemployment rate in this country are numerous and complex. First, it should be noted that, even when a society has "full employment," there will always be some people capable of working who are temporarily unemployed. Some people will be changing jobs. Some recent graduates or dropouts have not as yet found a job. Some people who have had prolonged illness could be starting to look for a job. For these reasons, most countries generally consider full employment to exist when the unemployment rate does not exceed 2% to 3% of the workforce. Unfortunately, the unemployment rate in the United States in recent years has been considerably higher than this figure.

In many areas of the country, there are more people in the workforce than there are available jobs. Automation in many industries has reduced the number of workers needed and made certain job skills (such as blacksmithing) obsolete. Planting and harvesting machines in agriculture, for example, have drastically reduced the number of people needed in producing food. Picking beans, digging potatoes, and picking cotton and corn once required large numbers of workers, but such work is now done by machines.

From the end of World War II until around 1965, there was a "baby boom," when large numbers of children were born. For the past 35 years, these baby-boom children have been growing up and entering the labor force in large numbers. The last few decades have also seen women being liberated from the cultural expectation that they should remain at home. Millions of females are now employed or seeking full- or part-time work. This increase in the number of workers seeking employment has added to the unemployment rate.

As discussed earlier, outsourcing in a global factory is exporting manufacturing jobs from the United States to the Third World. For example, global sportswear companies headquartered in the United States are paying young girls and women in Indonesia less than $2 *per day* to assemble shoes that will be exported and sold in the United States.[32]

Another factor involves foreign trade. A decrease in orders of American products for foreign customers forces U.S. companies to cut back their production and, often, to lay off workers.

Excessively dry summers in our country sharply reduce the amount of food produced. The law of supply and demand therefore drives up the price of available food. Consumers are less able to buy other products, and companies are then forced to cut back production and lay off workers.

High interest rates make it too costly for consumers to buy homes, automobiles, and other expensive items that are normally purchased with a loan. The demand for such items goes down, and again businesses have to cut back production and lay off workers.

Still another major reason for the high unemployment rate in this country is that we have a structural unemployment problem; that is, large numbers of unemployed people are not trained for the positions that are open. In recent years, many blue-collar jobs have disappeared (as in the steel industry), while high-skill jobs have opened in other areas (such as in the high-tech field of computers). As people become trained for current positions, the employment needs of our economy will again shift; thus, there will continue to be disharmony between skills needed for vacant positions and skills held by unemployed people.

FACTORS THAT REDUCE UNEMPLOYMENT

Many factors increase the number of jobs and thereby reduce the unemployment rate. Lower interest rates encourage consumers to purchase more items through loans and with credit. Consumers buy more, stimulating companies to produce more to meet the demand and thus to hire more people. Lower interest rates have a direct effect on businesses. Companies often borrow money to purchase capital items (for example, additional machinery to produce their goods or buildings to expand the business) to increase production. When interest rates are lower, businesses borrow more money to increase production, which usually creates additional jobs.

Wars almost always reduce the unemployment rate. Some workers are drafted, and their former jobs become available for people who are unemployed. Furthermore, it takes many additional jobs to provide the military with the products needed to fight a war—bullets, bombs, tanks, fighter planes, food, medicine, and so on.

Businesses and governments in many other countries take a much more paternalistic approach to employees and to ensuring that there will be jobs for those who are unemployed. In the United States, when an economic slump occurs, businesses usually lay off workers. By contrast, in Japan businesses are much less likely to lay off workers; indeed, they seek to have their employees spend their entire working lives with the same company. Governments in many other countries attempt, when there is an economic slump, to create jobs for those who are unemployed. Germany, for example, pays the unemployed to receive work training.

The development of new products opens up many new jobs. The invention of the automobile, airplane, television, computer, hair dryer, and refrigerator created jobs not only for factory workers but also for managers, repair personnel, sales personnel, insurance personnel, and so on.

CONFRONTING UNEMPLOYMENT

Economists agree that the ideal way to overcome unemployment is through increased economic growth. They disagree, however, about the causes of a sluggish economy and about the best way to stimulate an economy.

Rapid economic growth, however, is a mixed blessing. It historically has had adverse effects on the natural environment because it leads to more rapid consumption of scarce resources (see Chapter 17). Once again we see that a solution to one problem often creates or aggravates another problem; in sociological terms, the solution has both functional and dysfunctional aspects.

In the early 1980s, the economy was in a slump, with high unemployment and high inflation rates. President Reagan stimulated the economy through a tax cut to individuals and to businesses. The tax cut gave individuals more buying power and businesses additional money to reinvest to increase production. Reagan's plan worked: The economy was stimulated, production increased, more jobs were created, and the unemployment rate went down. Reagan's plan also included immense cuts in federal spending for social welfare programs and for educational programs. The cuts were designed to reduce the inflation rate. (Big spending by the federal government has often been blamed as a major contributor to inflation.) For the most part, Reagan's plan worked. The economy was again stimulated, and the rates of unemployment and inflation were cut nearly in half. Unfortunately, massive tax cuts (along with sharp increases in military spending) led to other problems: a huge federal deficit that threatens to increase the inflation rate in the future and cuts in social programs that have increased the rates of poverty, homelessness, hunger, and a variety of other social problems.

Economics is a complicated and complex area. Certainly it is a mistake to assume that tax cuts will always stimulate the economy and lead to reductions in unemployment and inflation. For example, a case can be made that high rates of inflation and unemployment in the 1970s were due to rising oil prices, and drops in these rates in the 1980s were due not to tax cuts but to declining oil prices. Petroleum is the major source of energy in producing practically all goods. When the price of petroleum goes up, the cost of production increases, which raises the price of all commodities and results in inflation. With inflation, the public cannot buy as much, which results in an oversupply of goods. Industries then lay off workers, which increases the unemployment rate. When the price of petroleum goes down, the cost of producing goods goes down, which reduces prices and thereby reduces the rate of inflation. Also, the public can purchase more goods at lower prices, which reduces the supply of available goods. Industries are then stimulated to produce more goods, which they do by hiring more employees—thus reducing the unemployment rate.

Another proposal to reduce unemployment is for the government to be a "last resort" employer. Those who are unemployed and unable to find jobs in the private sector would be hired by the government. The work to be performed would ideally be useful to society—for example, building and repairing highways, planting trees, and providing services in agencies (such as recreational services to youths in high-delinquency areas). Working for the government in such capacities could also provide workers with job skills that would increase their opportunities in the private sector.

Another proposal is for the government to subsidize private companies to maintain their payrolls (instead of laying people off) during economic recessions. A number of foreign governments do this.

Geographically, there have always been areas of high unemployment, and areas that are booming and needing more workers. It has been suggested that the government could take a more active role in identifying geographic areas where employers are seeking employees, publicizing what jobs are available in these regions, and providing assistance in paying relocation expenses for unemployed workers who are willing to move from areas of high unemployment.

Another proposal is for the government to expand its role in providing job training to the unskilled and semiskilled and to those workers whose skills have become obsolete. Germany, as an example, not only provides such work training but also usually pays workers during the weeks or months they are learning new job skills.

Critics of the last four proposals argue that extensive government efforts in any of these areas would sharply increase government spending and thereby increase the rate of inflation. They also maintain that government-supplied jobs would merely be a stopgap measure that would not solve the overall problem of joblessness. According to these critics, government should not be in the business of creating "make-work" jobs.

Occupational Health Hazards

A number of occupational health hazards affect workers. These include on-the-job accidents, work-related illnesses, and job stress.

ON-THE-JOB AND WORK-RELATED HEALTH HAZARDS

Every year in the United States, about 10,000 workers are killed on the job, and nearly 2 million suffer disabling injuries from work accidents.[33] Proponents of occupational health have widened their focus to include illnesses as well as accidents, and they have also concentrated on preventing work-related diseases rather than merely treating or compensating workers for them. Over 100,000 Americans die of job-related diseases each year.[34]

Occupations that have high rates of injuries from accidents (some of which are fatal) are shipbuilding and repairing, meat packing, mobile-home construction, timber cutting and logging, aviation, asbestos insulation, structural metal work, electric power line and cable installation and repair, mining, fire fighting, roofing, farming, and law enforcement.

An example of a hazardous work site is the farm. Farmers, their families, and the workers they employ operate a wide range of heavy equipment. Often they are not carefully trained in the safe operation of that equipment. As a result, we hear frequent reports of people who are fatally injured when a tractor overturns. On-the-job accidents are common on farms. An even graver danger for farmworkers comes from pesticides and herbicides that are misused or overused. More farmworkers are poisoned by chemicals than are injured in farm accidents.[35]

Other industries have serious health hazards. Cotton dust levels are a threat in the textile and cottonseed-oil industries. Continued inhalation of cotton dust in the mill air causes brown-lung disease or byssinosis, which is irreversible and fatal. Although brown-lung disease was recognized in the 18th century, it was not until 1968 that it was officially classified as an occupational illness. (Company owners did not want official recognition of the disease because they did not want to pay compensation for those workers who became ill.) Even after official recognition, it took another 8 years of pressure from labor groups (such as the Amalgamated Clothing and Textile Workers Union) to force the government to set standards for allowable levels of cotton dust. Company owners were reluctant to have standards set because of the cost of remodeling buildings and purchasing the necessary equipment to meet these standards. They also argued that it might be more profitable to close the plants and relocate in foreign countries where governments are less safety conscious and they could hire workers at much lower wages.

Currently, one of the most controversial occupational hazards is the use of nuclear power for energy purposes. A number of nuclear power plants have already been built. In 1979 an accident at the nuclear plant at Three Mile Island in Pennsylvania released small amounts of radioactive particles into the air. Although thousands of people in the surrounding area were evacuated, authorities feared a serious threat from the released radioactivity. In 1986 an accident at the nuclear power plant in Chernobyl, Russia, released massive amounts of radioactivity into the atmosphere. More than 20 people died within a few days, and thousands now face the possibility of an early death due to radiation exposure. These accidents have raised a worldwide concern about the dangers of using nuclear energy to produce electricity.

A serious problem involving occupational hazards is that some substances take years before their deadly effects appear. Asbestos is a prime example. Asbestos is a mineral that has multiple uses, from construction to beer brewing. It has been handled by workers in a wide range of industries. Two decades ago, it was discovered that employees who had worked extensively with asbestos later became high risks to develop cancer. It was not only the workers who were in danger, but also their spouses and children who were exposed to clinging asbestos particles on the workers' clothes. The government is now advising persons who have been exposed to asbestos to undergo periodic medical examinations for early detection and treatment of cancer.

Asbestos workers die from lung cancer at a rate more than seven times that of the general public.[36] Mesothelioma was once a rare form of cancer; it attacks the abdominal organs and the lining of the lungs and is usually fatal. This type of cancer has now become relatively common among asbestos workers. Manufacturers and insurers had known for half a century that asbestos workers were dying prematurely from mesothelioma, but it was not until the mid-1970s that this became public knowledge.

Asbestos may be only the tip of the iceberg. There are over 2400 suspected carcinogens (cancer-causing substances). Only a few of them have been so designated and regulated by the government.[37]

Rubber workers are exposed to a variety of carcinogens and are dying of cancer of the prostate, cancer of the stomach, leukemia, and other cancers of the blood and the lymph-forming tissues.[38]

Steelworkers, especially those handling coal, are becoming victims of lung cancer at excessive rates. Workers exposed to benzidine and other aromatic amines (often used in producing dyestuffs) have excessively high rates of bladder cancer. Dry cleaners, painters, printers, and petroleum workers are exposed to benzene, which is a known leukemia-producing agent. Miners of iron ore, uranium, chromium, nickel, and other industrial metals fall victim to a variety of occupationally related cancers. Insecticide workers, farmworkers, and copper and lead smelter workers are exposed to inorganic arsenic, a carcinogen that results in high rates of lymphatic cancer and lung cancer.

One of the gravest health dangers involves the chemical industry. This industry was born amid the technological innovations of World War II and has been rapidly growing ever since. Chemicals are now involved in the manufacture of practically every product we use—our clothing, the processed food we eat, the soaps we wash with, our televisions, and our automobiles. A number of these chemicals have been found to cause certain diseases, such as cancer, birth defects, heart problems, nervous disorders, weight loss, and sterility. (DDT will be described in Chapter 17; it is a chemical that has been found to be a carcinogen.) There is some evidence that saccharin (used in the past in diet soft drinks) may be a carcinogen. Because new chemicals are being introduced at the rate of one every 20 minutes,[39] it is extremely difficult to determine the hazards of all the chemicals currently in use, not to mention those that will be discovered and used in the future.

It is extremely difficult to prove that a substance causes cancer. Scientists disagree about how much evidence is needed to document a causal relationship. In addition, cancer and certain other diseases (such as respiratory disorders) can take several years to appear after exposure. When a segment of the population has a high incidence of cancer, it is often difficult to identify the cancer-causing substances they were exposed to years earlier.

Simply documenting that certain chemicals are hazardous does not automatically mean they will be taken off the market. For example, there is solid evidence that tobacco is a health hazard, yet many Americans continue to smoke.

When given the choice of being unemployed or working in an industry that is a recognized health hazard (such as coal mining or the textile industry), people often elect to work. Because of the high cost of meeting safety standards, businesses commonly drag their feet in complying with government regulations and sometimes threaten to relocate to other countries when the government pressures them. In many occupational areas, such as textile mills, there is considerable controversy regarding what should be considered "safe" levels of exposure to substances.

In the past three decades, the federal government has become increasingly involved in seeking to reduce occupational illnesses. In 1970 it passed the Occupational Safety and Health Act, which established two new organizations to combat occupational hazards. The Occupational Safety and Health Administration (OSHA) was created in the Department of Labor to establish health standards for industry. The National Institute for Occupational Safety and Health (NIOSH) was created in the Department of Health and Human Services to research occupational hazards.

In 1976 the federal government enacted the Toxic Substances Control Act, which established systems and guidelines for screening and controlling dangerous substances. With the rapid development of chemicals and other substances, OSHA and NIOSH face formidable tasks in testing the effects of all of these substances and in setting and enforcing safety limits for substances found to be health hazards.

JOB STRESS

Most standard textbooks in medicine attribute anywhere from 50% to 80% of all diseases to stress-related or psychosomatic origins.[40] One of the main sources of stress is job pressures. Practically any job has stresses. Some of the more stressful jobs are inner-city schoolteacher, police officer, air traffic controller, medical intern, and fire fighter (see Exhibit 11.3). (Stress is further described in Chapter 15.) The list of stress-related illnesses includes bronchial asthma, peptic ulcer, ulcerative colitis, mucous colitis, hay fever, arthritis, hyperthyroidism, enuresis, hypertension, alcoholism, insomnia, cancer, migraine headache, impotency, atopic dermatitis, amenorrhea, and chronic constipation. Stress is also one of the causes of emotional disorders.

Employers are becoming increasingly aware of the cost of stress to employees and to their businesses: absenteeism, low productivity, short- and long-term stress-related illnesses, job alienation and job dissatisfaction, marital difficulties, and emotional disorders. Therefore, many com-

EXHIBIT 11.3

The 20 Most Stressful Jobs

1. Inner-city schoolteacher
2. Police officer
3. Air traffic controller
4. Medical intern
5. Firefighter
6. Waiter/waitress
7. Assembly-line worker
8. Customer service representative
9. Securities trader
10. Newspaper editor
11. Advertising executive
12. Public relations specialist
13. Middle-level manager
14. Salesperson
15. Attorney
16. Urban bus driver
17. Roofer
18. Real estate agent
19. Politician
20. Banker

Source: "Stressed Out?" *Wisconsin State Journal*, Sept. 3, 1996, p. 2C.

panies are sponsoring stress management programs to help their employees learn to reduce stress through techniques such as meditation, relaxation, hypnosis, exercise programs (such as jogging), time management, biofeedback, and hobbies.[41]

SOCIAL WORK IN THE WORKPLACE

Social work in the workplace has had a variety of other titles in recent years, including industrial social work, occupational social work, and employee assistance. No term has yet emerged as "preferred." In this section, we will primarily use the terms *social work in the workplace* and *occupational social work*.

Occupational social work is generally viewed as a new and emerging specialization. Social workers in the past decade have been employed in industry in increasing numbers and in a variety of settings and roles. However, the roots of occupational social work go back in time much farther than most people realize.

A Brief History

In the late 1800s, there was a welfare movement in American business. Programs and services were developed to help employees in work-related areas as well as with personal or domestic problems (such as marital conflicts). This movement grew steadily into the 1920s. By 1926, 80% of the 1500 largest companies in the United States had at least one type of welfare program for employees.[42]

The welfare movement emerged at this time for several reasons. Businesses were growing so large that personal contact between personnel and labor was practically nonexistent. In addition, an increasing percentage of the labor force was made up of women and non-English-speaking immigrants whom management did not understand. Employee turnover, employee sabotage, and the development of labor organizations also stimulated management's interest in the welfare movement. The threat of government regulation in the area of employee welfare also influenced businesses to take action.

The programs that were developed during this welfare movement required staff to provide the services. The positions that emerged became known as social secretaries, welfare secretaries, or social welfare secretaries. With little previous knowledge on which to draw, these secretaries developed methods and techniques through experimentation. One popular approach was that of group work. It was soon discovered that the formation of groups benefited employees in both work- and nonwork-related areas. For example, groups that formed for socialization or recreation fostered employee morale, which was reflected in work production and attitude. In addition to working directly with the employees, these secretaries performed many administrative duties such as handling pension and insurance programs.

The number of positions of welfare secretaries declined sharply in the 1930s for several reasons.[43] Labor leaders tended to oppose such positions because they felt the secretaries were antiunion. (All too often, management urged welfare secretaries to mold employees into loyal workers and to fight unionization.) Laborers came to react negatively to the paternalistic character of the position. With the Great Depression in the 1930s, many businesses were forced to cut back on welfare programs.

Aspects of the welfare secretary's role still exist. Many of these functions are now included in what is called personnel or human relations services, such as handling grievances, linking employees who need help with available resources, and processing health insurance and pensions.

In the 1960s and early 1970s, large corporations developed training programs for inexperienced, long-term unemployed people, including members of minority groups. Directors of these training programs learned that many of the trainees needed help in a variety of areas, such as child care, interpersonal skills, family problems, personal problems, and adequate housing and transportation. In the past three decades, industries have increasingly been employing social workers to provide services in these areas.

The development of employee assistance programs (EAPs) has also been a major factor in the emergence of occupational social work. The EAP movement had its roots in the development of alcoholism programs in the 1930s and 1940s. Originally these programs were operated by industrial physicians or were informal programs staffed by recovering alcoholics. Employee assistance programs now focus primarily on the restoration of employees' job performance when alcohol or other drug abuse, emotional or personal problems, or changes in the nature of a job have interfered. Occupational social work is now sometimes erroneously considered synonymous with EAP. However, EAP is essentially a specific performance-focused program, whereas (as we will see) occupational social work is much broader in scope.

There are now thousands of EAPs across the United States. They are staffed by people with a variety of backgrounds: social work, psychology, counseling, medicine, nursing, alcohol and drug abuse counseling, business administration, economics, and management.[44] The professional staff members of EAPs have generally completed some specialized training in alcohol and drug abuse counseling, mental health, and/or employee assistance programming.

The Present Status of Social Work in the Workplace

Businesses and industries perceive occupational social work as an emerging area for social work practice. Many social work programs have added content on occupational social work in their curricula for social work students who want a career in industry. Occupational social work has the potential to become one of the higher-paying areas for social work practice because most businesses and industries have considerable financial resources.

Common job titles used to describe the functional positions of occupational social workers in business and industrial settings are employee assistance program coordinator, employee counselor, substance abuse service coordinator, affirmative action officer, employee resources manager, occupational safety and health officer, community relations consultant, corporate relocation officer, training consultant, charitable allocations analyst, human resources policy adviser, career planning and development counselor, urban affairs adviser, outplacement specialist, and coordinator of corporate health and wellness programs. In a newly emerging field, there is always considerable confusion over what the specific tasks and functions of the professionals should be. This is particularly true in occupational social work.

Social workers might help employees deal with problems in the following areas: child care, financial problems, family problems, retirement planning, affirmative action, alienation, legal problems, health problems, mental health problems, alcohol and substance abuse, and recreation problems. Social workers might become involved in providing training and staff development programs. They might serve as advocates in developing programs to combat hazardous working conditions. They might design and implement stress management programs. They might provide consultation regarding the physical or social environment within the company. They might help strikers meet basic needs. They might become involved in community relations—for example, acting as a representative of the business in fund-raising and/or planning for community services. They might propose new job designs to replace boring, tedious, assembly-line work. Thus, occupational social workers have many more functions than simply being involved in operating direct-service programs. Paul Kurzman and Sheila Akabas note:

> Social workers may . . . be called on to consult with management on its human resource policy, donations to tax-exempt activities, collective bargaining demands, or other dimensions of emerging corporate efforts at social responsibility. Professionals may be expected to analyze legislation, administer health and welfare benefit systems, or assist in developing programs designed to attract unorganized workers to trade union membership.[45]

Leo Perlis, longtime community relations director of the American Federation of Labor–Congress of Industrial Organizations, cautions that an occupational social worker needs knowledge of labor–management relations to avoid direct involvement in the adversarial relationship between labor and management.[46] (Occupational social workers should not make the mistake of many welfare secretaries who became identified with the side of management.)

A number of other professionals in industry are already providing services similar to those of occupational social work, so questions of turf are arising. Such other professionals include psychiatrists, psychologists, drug and alcohol counselors, nurses, and experts in personnel management. It would seem that the profession of social work needs to develop models of occupational social work that will clarify to management, labor, and other helping professionals what it can realistically provide.

Businesses and industries do not provide social services for humanitarian reasons. Social workers in the workplace are expected to be accountable by demonstrating that their services promote improved productivity and reduce tardiness and absenteeism and make it easier to retain members of the company's workforce, many of whom have received expensive training.

There are at least five ways in which social services may be sponsored in business and industry:

1. Sponsorship by management in companies with or without a union.

2. Sponsorship by the union.

3. Sponsorship by both management and labor, with social workers employed by management and dually monitored by both management and labor.

4. Private consultantships by social workers under contract to union or management to provide services to workers and/or the organization.

5. Sponsorship by a community mental health center or family service agency that has a specific contractual arrangement with the company.[47]

Research is needed to identify the merits and shortcomings of each of these approaches to sponsorship.

Employee Assistance Programs

Most social services in the workplace are currently provided by EAPs. Social work practitioners are the primary professional group that provides staff for EAPs.[48] As noted earlier, other professionals (such as psychologists and guidance counselors) may also be employed by EAPs. In addition to being located in businesses and industries, EAPs are mandated in federal government agencies and many city and county governments, as well as in the military.

It is essential that EAPs operate outside the disciplinary system of an organization. Donald Brieland, Lela Costin, and Charles Atherton describe the importance of employees' feeling free to use EAP services without adverse reactions from management:

Employees ideally should come for help in the early stages of difficulties but are understandably reluctant to share information that management could use against them. Therefore, we have seen that employees tend to conceal problems from both management and fellow workers. After they are referred by management or by a supervisor or union steward for help, the employee may feel labeled as a problem. If they are confronted by management, they fear loss of their job or discrimination in promotion. Managers have similar fears about revealing their own personal problems. Sometimes getting help is specified as a condition for retaining a job. Workers have to be convinced of the ultimate value of getting help.[49]

It is also essential for employees to be aware that what they say to EAP staff will remain confidential; otherwise they will be reluctant to discuss their personal concerns and circumstances openly. Sometimes management finds confidentiality a difficult concession to make because it is paying the bill, but there is no other way to establish trust with employees. Brieland, Costin, and Atherton note:

Social workers in industry need a written agreement to guarantee that the services they provide will be confidential and also to spell out the guidelines for referral to other community resources. . . .

Management or supervisors who refer the employee should be concerned with job performance but not with diagnosis. If they detect problems they expect some response. One way to handle the issue is to submit a statement indicating that the employee was in contact with the EAP and to provide a brief statement of general progress later.[50]

The primary services provided by EAPs are alcohol and drug abuse counseling, counseling for emotional difficulties, family counseling, career counseling and education, credit counseling, and retirement planning. Each of these areas will be briefly described.

ALCOHOL AND DRUG ABUSE COUNSELING

The major focus of EAPs has been on alcohol and drug abuse. It is well recognized that alcohol and drug abuse costs businesses and industries millions of dollars in productivity each year through lower-quality work, absenteeism, tardiness, and deterioration of well-trained employees. EAPs tend to view alcoholism and other drug use as a disease and to emphasize total sobriety or total abstinence rather than a reduction in use. Alcoholics Anonymous and Narcotics Anonymous are also promoted in the treatment process. Inpatient hospital treatment is sometimes used, but outpatient efforts are preferred because they cost less and because they do not involve loss of work time. Some EAPs provide treatment to those who are chemically dependent, whereas other EAPs serve as brokers by arranging for treatment with other resources.

Students seeking a career in social work in the workplace are advised to become knowledgeable about drug and alcohol abuse through coursework and probably a field internship in the treatment of chemical dependency. Employees who have a chemical dependency that is affecting their work are generally offered treatment by EAP staff; such treatment is paid for by the employer (generally through health insurance programs). Employees who refuse treatment encounter the risk of being fired.

COUNSELING FOR EMOTIONAL DIFFICULTIES

EAPs also provide services to employees who have emotional problems, such as depression. As with alcohol and drug abuse treatment, EAP staff either provide treatment services for emotional difficulties or serve as brokers by arranging for treatment with other resources.

FAMILY COUNSELING

Brieland, Costin, and Atherton summarize the primary family problems that EAPs become involved in:

Stresses involving the spouse and other family members are an important concern. Not only does the employee take family problems to the workplace but he or she brings workplace problems home and displaces them on family members. Marriage counseling and child care are the most common needs. Separation and divorce take their toll in stress on the job. Child abuse and family violence increasingly come to the attention of the assistance program. These behaviors may lead to criminal prosecution. If publicity results, assault may lead to rejection in the workplace, even though no sentence results.[51]

EAPs either provide counseling in these areas or refer employees and their families to other therapists. If the family dispute involves court action, as in the case of spouse abuse, the court may ask the employer to provide an evaluation, which is then often conducted by staff of the EAP.

Financial problems for families are usually created when employees are laid off. EAP staff may help employees to obtain unemployment benefits. Because layoffs may contribute to increased drinking and to child and spouse abuse, EAPs can provide counseling and referral services for such difficulties during layoffs. For employees who need child care, EAPs may play a broker role in helping to link them with child-care services.

CAREER COUNSELING AND EDUCATION

EAPs have become involved in two areas of career counseling: helping employees to set and achieve specific career goals and helping them to learn and use stress management techniques. In the first area, EAPs may administer, or arrange for, aptitude tests. They may also help employees to understand the promotion and advancement opportunities within the company. EAPs help employees to enroll in educational programs that enhance their physical and mental health and increase their skills on the job. Many companies provide or pay for training that will facilitate promotion. Some companies will also pay for courses that increase employees' assertiveness, personal adjustment, self-understanding, and problem-solving capacities. (Many EAPs are reluctant to provide assistance to employees who are seeking a job outside the company.)

EAPs also provide, or arrange for, workshops and seminars on stress management techniques. Such techniques include: using relaxation exercises, hypnosis, time management, or positive thinking; developing hobbies and exercise programs; improving interpersonal relationships; learning to solve problems; and establishing a positive sense of self. Employees who are experiencing burnout or severe job stress may receive counseling by EAP staff or be referred elsewhere for therapy.

CREDIT COUNSELING

Many EAPs have become involved in providing assistance to employees who are having financial difficulties and need credit counseling. One aspect of this involves debt counseling, in which the workers receive assistance in renegotiating their payments to creditors over a longer period of time. They are also encouraged to make a commitment to defer further credit purchases until the financial burden is reduced. Often they also receive financial counseling on developing a budget to meet their financial needs.

In some states, creditors can claim part of the debtor's wages through legal garnishment. In such cases, the employer must deduct a portion of the employee's wages, which is then paid to the creditor to pay off the debt. This process reveals the credit problems to the employer. (Some employers may view a worker with bad credit as a problematic employee and may then discharge her or him.) EAP staff members may get involved in cases of legal garnishment to help employees straighten out their financial circumstances.

Some EAPs also provide financial planning assistance to employees who are burdened with alimony and child support payments.

RETIREMENT PLANNING

In recent years, employees have shown increased interest in retirement planning. EAPs can arrange retirement-planning workshops and seminars for employees. A wide variety of programs can be explained, including Social Security benefits, IRA plans, pension plans, profit-sharing plans, stock option plans, and tax-sheltered annuity plans.

EAP staff should be knowledgeable about the retirement plans available from the firm in order to help individuals make intelligent decisions. EAP staff may also provide assistance to employees nearing retirement. Such employees need to plan not only for their financial needs but also for what they will do to maintain a high level of positive mental and physical activity.

Occupational social work appears to be a challenging new growth area for social work. But careful planning is needed to avoid the mistakes that led to the demise of welfare secretaries. Because there are over 100 million workers in the United States, employees and their families constitute a massive target population. Business and industry could hire every graduating social worker and hardly dent their payrolls.[52]

SUMMARY

The major social problems involving work are alienation, unemployment, and occupational health hazards. Alienation is the sense of meaninglessness and powerlessness that many people feel about their jobs.

Work is highly esteemed in our society. Under the influence of the Protestant ethic, work has become a moral obligation. It is also a source of self-respect and an opportunity to form friendships, and it may be a source of self-fulfillment and an opportunity to use one's talents. To a large extent, our work determines our social status and defines who we are. Before the Protestant Reformation, work was denigrated and even considered a curse by some societies.

There have been significant changes or trends in the nature of work and the composition of the workforce in the past few decades. The number of white-collar workers has increased, and the number of farmers and blue-collar workers has decreased. Most workers are now employees rather than self-employed. Work is increasingly becoming specialized, and considerable automation is occurring. More women are entering the labor force, and older male workers are increasingly becoming unemployed. Workers are now seeking intrinsic rewards (rewards that come from the nature of the work itself). Our economy emphasizes high technology. Those who are well educated in high-tech areas have a promising future, whereas the unskilled face increased prospects of being trapped in the lower socioeconomic class. In the past two decades, there has been extensive growth in low-paying jobs. There has also been a trend to outsource manufacturing jobs to Third World countries. (Some authorities have referred to this phenomenon as deindustrialization in the United States.)

Alienation appears to be a serious problem for many workers. Sources of alienation include specialization, automation, lack of involvement in the decision-making process, performance of routine and repetitive tasks, and lack of opportunity to be creative or to use one's talents fully. Alienation may lead to poor-quality work, absenteeism, job turnover, and low productivity. Job dissatisfaction is one measure of alienation. Available studies indicate conflicting results about how satisfied American workers are with their jobs. A number of techniques have been proposed for reducing worker alienation and job dissatisfaction.

In the past two decades, the unemployment rate has ranged between 4% and 11%, which is considered high. Long-term unemployment has serious adverse effects: depletion of savings, loss of self-respect, loss of friends, isolation, and feelings of embarrassment, anger, despair, depression, anxiety, boredom, hopelessness, and apathy. It may be a factor leading to emotional problems, suicide, alcoholism, and stress-related illnesses.

Groups that have chronically high rates of unemployment are African Americans and Latinos, teenagers, women, older workers, the unskilled, the semiskilled, and persons with a disability. The reasons for high unemployment among these groups, as well as among the total workforce, are numerous and complex.

Economists agree that the ideal way to cure unemployment is through rapid economic growth.

They disagree, however, about the causes of a sluggish economy and about the best ways to stimulate it.

There are three main occupational health hazards: on-the-job accidents, conditions that lead to work-related physical diseases (for example, breathing cotton dust in the textile industry leads to brown-lung disease), and job stress. The large number of untested chemicals that are increasingly being used may pose the greatest health danger in the future. Many chemical substances have a delayed reaction in which an illness (such as cancer) appears several years after exposure.

Social work in the workplace is an emerging field for social work practice. Most social services in the workplace are currently provided by employee assistance programs (EAPs). EAP services include alcohol and drug abuse counseling, counseling for emotional difficulties, family counseling, career counseling and education, credit counseling, and retirement planning.

NOTES

1. Aristotle, *Politics*, Book 3, sec. V, Benjamin Jowett, trans. (Oxford: Clarendon Press, 1945).
2. Quoted in Thomas Sullivan, Kenrick Thompson, Richard Wright, George Gross, and Dale Spady, *Social Problems* (New York: Wiley, 1980), p. 300.
3. Quoted in Ian Robertson, *Social Problems*, 2nd ed. (New York: Random House, 1980), p. 87.
4. James W. Coleman and Donald R. Cressey, *Social Problems*, 6th ed. (New York: HarperCollins, 1996), pp. 37–41.
5. William Kornblum and Joseph Julian, *Social Problems*, 8th ed. (Englewood Cliffs, NJ: Prentice Hall, 1995), p. 420.
6. Ibid.
7. Ibid.
8. Coleman and Cressey, *Social Problems*, p. 36.
9. Seymour Wolfbein, *Work in American Society* (Glenview, IL: Scott, Foresman, 1971), p. 45.
10. Coleman and Cressey, *Social Problems*, p. 420.
11. Charles R. Walker and Robert Guest, *Man on the Assembly Line* (Cambridge, MA: Harvard University Press, 1952), pp. 54–55.
12. American Association of Retired Persons, *A Profile of Older Americans, 1996* (Washington, DC: AARP, 1996), p. 12.

13. U.S. Bureau of the Census, *Statistical Abstract of the United States, 1997* (Washington, DC: U.S. Government Printing Office, 1997), p. 398.

14. Coleman and Cressey, *Social Problems*, pp. 38–39.

15. Ibid., pp. 302–304.

16. Kornblum and Julian, *Social Problems*, pp. 416–427.

17. Daniel Bell, *The Coming of Post-Industrial Society: A Venture in Social Forecasting* (New York: Basic Books, 1973), pp. 188–195.

18. Coleman and Cressey, *Social Problems*, p. 420.

19. Ibid., pp. 420–421.

20. Ibid.

21. Ibid., p. 421.

22. Karl Marx, *Selected Writings in Sociology and Social Philosophy*, T. B. Bottomore, trans. (New York: McGraw-Hill, 1964), p. 47.

23. Charles Fenyvesi, "Trade Marx," *U.S. News & World Report*, Mar. 12, 1990, p. 23.

24. Karen Ball, "Most Jobs Aren't What We Planned," *Wisconsin State Journal*, Jan. 12, 1990, p. 1A.

25. Keith Davis and John W. Newstrom, *Human Behavior at Work*, 8th ed. (New York: McGraw-Hill, 1989), pp. 232–249.

26. Harold L. Wilensky, "Work as a Social Problem," in *Social Problems*, Howard Becker, ed. (New York: Wiley, 1966), p. 129.

27. D. D. Braginsky and B. M. Braginsky, "Surplus People: Their Lost Faith in Self and System," *Psychology Today*, Aug. 1975, p. 70.

28. Harvey Brenner, *Mental Illness and the Economy* (Cambridge, MA: Harvard University Press, 1973).

29. K. Newman, *Falling from Grace* (New York: Free Press, 1988), p. 202.

30. Kornblum and Julian, *Social Problems*, pp. 42–43.

31. Ibid., p. 43.

32. Thomas J. Sullivan, *Social Problems*, 4th ed. (Needham Heights, MA: Allyn & Bacon, 1997), p. 61.

33. Kornblum and Julian, *Social Problems*, p. 429.

34. Coleman and Cressey, *Social Problems*, p. 41.

35. Ibid.

36. Ibid.

37. Kornblum and Julian, *Social Problems*, pp. 429–430.

38. Ibid.

39. Ibid.

40. Brian L. Seaward, *Managing Stress*, 5th ed. (Boston: Jones & Bartlett, 1994).

41. Ibid.

42. Philip R. Popple, "Social Work Practice in Business and Industry, 1875–1930," *Social Service Review*, 55 (Jun. 1981), pp. 257–269.

43. Normal L. Wyers and Malina Kaulukukui, "Social Services in the Workplace: Rhetoric vs. Reality," *Social Work*, 29 (Mar.–Apr. 1984), pp. 167–172.

44. Nan Van Den Bergh, "Employee Assistance Programs," *Encyclopedia of Social Work*, 19th ed. (Washington, DC: NASW, 1995), pp. 842–849.

45. Paul A. Kurzman and Sheila H. Akabas, "Industrial Social Work as an Arena for Practice," *Social Work*, 26 (Jan. 1981), p. 53.

46. Leo Perlis, "The Human Contract in the Organized Workplace," *Social Thought*, 3 (Winter 1977), p. 49.

47. "Industrial Social Work Movement Expanding," *NASW News*, 23 (Feb. 1978), p. 7.

48. Van Den Bergh, "Employee Assistance Programs," p. 842.

49. Donald Brieland, Lela B. Costin, and Charles R. Atherton, *Contemporary Social Work*, 3rd ed. (New York: McGraw-Hill, 1985), p. 334.

50. Ibid., pp. 342–343.

51. Ibid., p. 343.

52. Van Den Bergh, "Employee Assistance Programs."

RACISM, ETHNOCENTRISM, AND STRATEGIES FOR ADVANCING SOCIAL AND ECONOMIC JUSTICE

W e see ethnic and racial conflict—riots, beatings, murders, and civil wars—nearly every time we turn on the evening news. In recent years, there have been clashes resulting in bloodshed from Northern Ireland to Bosnia, from Iraq to Israel, and from the United States to South America. Practically every nation with more than one ethnic group has had to deal with ethnic conflict. The oppression and exploitation of one group by another are particularly ironic in democratic nations because these societies claim to cherish freedom, equality, and justice. In reality, in all societies, the dominant group that controls the political and economic institutions rarely agrees to share (equally) its power and wealth with other groups. This chapter will:

- Define and describe ethnic groups, ethnocentrism, racial groups, racism, prejudice, discrimination, oppression, and institutional discrimination.

- Outline the sources of prejudice and discrimination.

- Summarize the effects and costs of discrimination and oppression.

- Present background material on racial groups: African Americans, Latinos, Native Americans, and Asian Americans.

- Outline strategies for advancing social and economic justice.

- Describe social work's commitment to ending racial discrimination and oppression.

- Forecast the pattern of race and ethnic relations in the United States in the future.

ETHNIC GROUPS AND ETHNOCENTRISM

An ethnic group has a sense of togetherness, a conviction that its members form a special group, and a sense of common identity or "peoplehood." Barker defines an *ethnic group* as:

A distinct group of people who share a common language, set of customs, history, culture, race, religion, or origin.[1]

Practically every ethnic group has a strong feeling of *ethnocentrism*, which is "an orientation or set of beliefs that holds one's own culture, ethnic or racial group, or nation is superior to others."[2] Ethnocentrism leads members of ethnic groups to view their culture as the best, as superior, as the one that other cultures should adopt. Ethnocentrism also leads to prejudice against foreigners, who may be viewed as barbarians, uncultured people, or savages.

Feelings of ethnic superiority within a nation are usually accompanied by the belief that political and economic domination by one's own group is natural, morally right, in the best interest of the nation, and perhaps also God's will. Ethnocentrism has been a factor in leading to some of the worst atrocities in history, such as the American colonists' nearly successful attempt to exterminate Native Americans and Adolf Hitler's mass executions of over 6 million European Jews, and millions more gypsies, people with disabilities, and other minority group members.

In interactions between nations, ethnocentric beliefs sometimes lead to wars and serve as justifications for foreign conquests. At practically any point in the last several centuries, at least a few wars have occurred between nations in which one society has been seeking to force its culture on another or to eradicate another culture. For example, Israel has been involved in bitter struggles with Arab countries in the Middle East for more than four decades over territory ownership. Bosnians, Serbs, Croats, and others are fighting for domination in what was once Yugoslavia.

RACE AND RACISM

Although a racial group is often also an ethnic group, the two groups are not necessarily the same. A *race* is believed to have a common set of physical characteristics. But the members of a racial group may or may not share the sense of togetherness or identity that holds an ethnic group together. A group that is both a racial group and an ethnic group is Japanese Americans; they are thought to have some common physical characteristics and also have a sense of "peoplehood." On the other hand, White Americans and White Russians are of the same race, but they hardly have a sense of togetherness. In addition, there are ethnic groups that are composed of a variety of races. For example, a religious group (such as Roman Catholics) is sometimes considered an ethnic group and is composed of members from diverse racial groups.

In contrast to ethnocentrism, racism is more likely to be based on physical differences than on cultural differences. *Racism* is "stereotyping and generalizing about people, usually negatively, because of their race; commonly a basis of discrimination against members of racial minority groups."[3] However, similar to ethnocentric ideologies, most racist ideologists assert that members of other racial groups are inferior. Some White Americans in this country have gone to extreme and morally reprehensible limits to seek to attain greater control and power over other racial groups.

PREJUDICE, DISCRIMINATION, AND OPPRESSION

Barker defines *prejudice* as:

> *An opinion about an individual, group, or phenomenon that is developed without proof or systematic evidence. This prejudgment may be favorable but is more often unfavorable and may become institutionalized in the form of a society's laws or customs.*[4]

Prejudice, in regard to race and ethnic relations, is making negative prejudgments. Prejudiced people apply racial stereotypes to all or nearly all members of a group according to preconceived notions of what they believe the group to be like and how they think the group will behave. Racial prejudice results from the belief that people who have different skin color and other physical characteristics also have innate differences in behaviors, values, intellectual functioning, and attitudes.

The word *discrimination* has two very different meanings. It may have the positive meaning of "the process of distinguishing between two objects, ideas, situations or stimuli."[5] However, in minority group relations, it is "the prejudgment and negative treatment of people based on identifiable characteristics such as race, gender, religion, or ethnicity."[6] Racial or ethnic discrimination involves denying to members of minority groups equal access to opportunities, residential housing areas, membership in religious and social organizations, involvement in political activities, access to community services, and so on.

Prejudice is a combination of stereotyped beliefs and negative attitudes, so that prejudiced individuals think about people in a predetermined, usually negative, categorical way. Discrimination involves physical actions—unequal treatment of people because they belong to a category. Discriminatory behavior often derives from prejudiced attitudes. Robert Merton, however, notes that prejudice and discrimination can occur independently. He describes four different "types" of people:

1. *The unprejudiced nondiscriminator,* in both belief and practice, upholds American ideals of freedom and equality. This person is not prejudiced against other groups and, on principle, will not discriminate against them.

2. *The unprejudiced discriminator* is not personally prejudiced but may sometimes, reluctantly, discriminate against other groups because it seems socially or financially convenient to do so.

3. *The prejudiced nondiscriminator* feels hostile to other groups but recognizes that law and social pressures are opposed to overt discrimination. Reluctantly, this person does not translate prejudice into action.

4. *The prejudiced discriminator* does not believe in the values of freedom and equality and consistently discriminates against other groups in both word and deed.[7]

An example of an unprejudiced discriminator is the owner of a condominium complex in an all-White middle-class suburb who refuses to sell a condominium to an African American family because of fear (founded or unfounded) that the sale would reduce the value of the remaining units. An example of a prejudiced nondiscriminator is a personnel director of a fire department who believes Latinos are unreliable and poor firefighters but complies with affirmative action efforts to hire and train Latinos.

It is very difficult to keep personal prejudices from eventually leading to some form of discrimination. Strong laws and firm informal social norms are necessary to break the causal relationship between prejudice and discrimination.

Discrimination is of two types: de jure and de facto. *De jure* discrimination is legal discrimination. The so-called Jim Crow laws in the South gave force of law to many discriminatory practices against African Americans, including denial of the right to trial, prohibition against voting, and prohibition against interracial marriage. Today, in the United States, there is practically no de jure discrimination because such laws have been declared unconstitutional.

De facto discrimination refers to discrimination that actually exists, whether legal or not. Acts of de facto discrimination often result from powerful informal norms that are discriminatory. Marlene Cummings gives an example of this type of discrimination and urges victims to confront it assertively:

> Scene: department store. Incident: Several people are waiting their turn at a counter. The person next to be served is a black woman; however, the clerk waits on several white customers who arrived later. The black woman finally demands service, after several polite gestures to call the clerk's attention to her. The clerk proceeds to wait on her after stating, "I did not see you."

> The clerk is very discourteous to the black customer; and the lack of courtesy is apparent, because the black customer had the opportunity to observe treatment of the other customers. De facto discrimination is most frustrating . . . ; the customer was served. Most people would rather just forget the whole incident, but it is important to challenge the practice even though it will possibly put you through more agony. One of the best ways to deal with this type of discrimination is to report it to the manager of the business. If it is at all possible, it is important to involve the clerk in the discussion.[8]

Barker defines *oppression* as:

> The social act of placing severe restrictions on a group or institution. Typically, a government or political organization that is in power places these restrictions formally or covertly on oppressed groups so that they may be exploited and less able to compete with other social groups.[9]

Oppression is the unjust or cruel exercise of authority or power. Members of minority groups in our society are frequently victimized by oppression from segments of the White power structure. Oppression and discrimination are closely related, as all acts of oppression are also acts of discrimination.

Racial and Ethnic Stereotypes

Barker defines *stereotypes* as:

> Preconceived and relatively fixed ideas about an individual, group, or social status. These ideas are usually based on superficial characteristics or overgeneralizations of traits observed in some members of the group.[10]

Racial and ethnic stereotypes involve attributing a fixed and usually inaccurate or unfavorable conception to a racial or ethnic group. Stereotypes are closely related to the way we think, as we seek to perceive and understand things in categories. We need categories to group things that are similar in order to study them and to communicate about them. We have stereotypes about many categories, including mothers, fathers, teenagers, communists, Republicans, schoolteachers, farmers, construction workers, miners, politicians, Mormons, and Italians. These stereotypes may contain some useful and accurate information about a member in any category. Yet each member of any category will have many characteristics that are not suggested by the stereotypes and is apt to have some characteristics that run counter to some of the stereotypes.

Racial stereotypes involve differentiating people in terms of color or other physical characteristics. For example, historically there was the erroneous stereotype that Native Americans become easily intoxicated and irrational when using alcohol. This belief was then translated into laws that prohibited Native Americans from buying and consuming alcohol. A more recent stereotype is that African Americans have a natural ability to play basketball and certain other sports. While at first glance, such a stereotype appears complimentary to African Americans, it has broader, negative implications. The danger is that, if people believe the stereotype, they may also feel that other abilities and capacities (such as intelligence, morals, and work productivity) are also determined by race. In other words, believing this positive stereotype increases the probability that people will also believe negative stereotypes.

Racial and Ethnic Discrimination

Gunnar Myrdal pointed out that minority problems are actually majority problems.[11] The White majority determines the place of non-Whites and other ethnic groups in our society. The status of different minority groups varies in our society because Whites apply different stereotypes to various groups; for example, African Americans are viewed and treated differently from Japanese. Elmer Johnson notes, "Minority relationships become recognized by the majority as a social problem when the members of the majority disagree

as to whether the subjugation of the minority is socially desirable or in the ultimate interest of the majority."[12] Concern about discrimination and segregation has also received increasing national attention because of a rising level of aspiration among minority groups who demand (sometimes militantly) equal opportunities and equal rights.

Our country was supposedly founded on the principle of human equality. The Declaration of Independence and the Constitution assert equality, justice, and liberty for all. Yet in practice, our society has always discriminated against minorities.

From its earliest days, our society has singled out certain minorities to treat unequally. Barker defines a *minority* as:

> A group, or a member of a group, of people of a distinct racial, religious, ethnic, or political identity that is smaller or less powerful than the community's controlling group.[13]

The categories of people who have been singled out for unequal treatment in our society have changed somewhat over the years. In the late 1800s and early 1900s, people of Irish, Italian, and Polish descent were discriminated against, but that discrimination has been substantially reduced. In the 19th century, Americans of Chinese descent were severely discriminated against. However, this also has been declining for many decades.

As time passes, new minorities are recognized as the victims of discrimination. For example, women, persons with a disability, and homosexuals have always been discriminated against, but only in the past 35 years has there been extensive national recognition of this discrimination.

Race as a Social Concept

Ashley Montague considers "race" to be one of the most dangerous and tragic myths in our society.[14] Race is erroneously believed by many to be a biological classification of people. Yet there are no clearly delineating characteristics of any "race," and no "racial" group has unique or distinctive genes. Throughout history the genes of different societies and racial groups have been intermingled. In addition, biological differentiations of racial groups have gradually been diluted through such sociocultural factors as changes in preferences of desirable characteristics in mates, effects of different diets on those who reproduce, and such variables as wars and diseases in selecting those who will live and reproduce.[15]

In spite of definitional problems, it is necessary to use racial categories in the social sciences because race has important (though not necessarily consistent) social meanings for people. To have a basis for racial classifications, a number of social scientists have used a social, rather than a biological, definition. A social definition is based on the way members of a society classify one another by physical characteristics. For example, a frequently used social definition of an African American is anyone who either displays overt Black physical characteristics or is known to have a Black ancestor.[16] The sociological classification of races is indicated by different definitions of a race among various societies. In the United States, anyone who is not "pure White" and is known to have a Black ancestor is considered to be Black, whereas in Brazil, anyone who is not "pure Black" is classified as White.[17]

Race, according to Ashley Montague, becomes a dangerous myth when it is assumed that physical traits are linked with mental traits and cultural achievements.[18] Every few years, it seems, some noted scientist stirs the country by making this erroneous assumption. For example, Herrnstein and Murray asserted that Whites, on the average, are more intelligent, as IQ tests show that Whites average scores of 10 to 15 points higher than African Americans.[19] Herrnstein and Murray's findings have been sharply criticized by other authorities as falsely assuming that IQ is largely genetically determined.[20] These authorities contend that IQ is substantially influenced by environmental factors, and it is likely that the average achievement of African Americans, if given similar opportunities to realize their potentialities, would be the same as Whites. Also, it has been charged that IQ tests are racially slanted. The tests ask the kinds of questions that Whites are more familiar with and thereby more apt to answer correctly.

Elmer Johnson summarizes the need for an impartial, objective view of the capacity of different racial groups to achieve:

> Race bigots contend that, the cultural achievements of different races being so obviously unlike, it follows that their genetic capacities for achievement must be just as different. Nobody can discover the cultural capacities of any population or race . . . until there is equality of opportunities to demonstrate the capacities.[21]

Most scientists, both physical and social, now believe that, in biological inheritance, all races are alike in every significant way. With the exception of several very small, inbred, isolated nonliterate tribes, all racial groups appear to show a wide distribution of every kind of ability. All important race differences that have been noted in personality, behavior, and achievement appear to be due to environmental factors.

Many Americans classify themselves as "mixed-race" or "multiracial," as they have parents of different races. Tiger Woods (a noted golfer), for example, has a multiracial background, with a Caucasian, African American, Native American, and Asian heritage.

Institutional Racism and Institutional Discrimination

In the last three decades, institutional racism has become recognized as a major problem. Institutional racism refers to discriminatory acts and policies against a racial group that pervade the major macrosystems of society, including the legal, political, economic, and educational systems. Some of these discriminatory acts and policies are illegal, while other are not. Barker defines *institutional racism* as:

> Those policies, practices or procedures embedded in bureaucratic structures that systematically lead to unequal outcomes for people of color.[22]

In contrast to institutional racism is the term *individual racism*, which Barker defines as:

The negative attitudes one person has about all members of a racial or ethnic group, often resulting in overt acts such as name-calling, social exclusion, or violence.[23]

Carmichael and Hamilton make the following distinction between individual racism and institutional racism:

When white terrorists bomb a black church and kill five black children, that is an act of individual racism, widely deplored by most segments of society. But when in the same city . . . five hundred black babies die each year because of the lack of proper food, shelter, and medical facilities, and thousands more are destroyed and maimed physically, emotionally, and intellectually because of conditions of poverty and discrimination in the black community, that is a function of institutional racism.[24]

Institutional discrimination is "prejudicial treatment in organizations based on official policies, overt behaviors, or behaviors that may be covert but approved by those in power."[25]

Discrimination is built, often unwittingly, into the structure and form of our society. The following examples reflect institutional racism:

- A family counseling agency with branch offices assigns its less skilled counselors and thereby provides lower-quality services to an office located in a minority neighborhood.

- A public welfare department encourages White applicants to request funds for special needs (for example, clothing) or to use certain services (for example, day care and homemaker services), whereas non-White clients are not informed (or are less enthusiastically informed) of such services.

- A public welfare department takes longer to process the requests of non-Whites for funds and services.

- A police department discriminates against non-White staff in terms of work assignments, hiring practices, promotion practices, and pay increases.

- A real estate agency has a pattern of showing White homebuyers houses in White neighborhoods and African American homebuyers houses in mixed or predominantly African American areas.

- A bank and an insurance company engage in redlining, which involves refusing to make loans or issue insurance in areas with large minority populations.

- A probation and parole agency tends to ignore minor rule violations by White clients but seeks to return non-White parolees to prison for similar infractions.

- A mental health agency tends to label non-White clients "psychotic" while ascribing a less serious disorder to White clients.

- White staff at a family counseling center are encouraged by the executive board to provide intensive services to clients with whom they have a good relationship (often White clients) and are told to give less attention to clients "they aren't hitting it off well with" who may be disproportionately non-White.

And what are the results of institutionalized racism? The unemployment rate for non-Whites has consistently been over twice that for Whites. The infant mortality rate for non-Whites is nearly twice as high as for Whites. The life expectancy for non-Whites is several years less than for Whites. The average number of years of educational achievement for non-Whites is considerably less than for Whites.[26]

There are many examples of institutional racism in school systems. Schools in White suburbs generally have better facilities and more highly trained teachers than schools in minority neighborhoods. Minority families are, on the average, less able to provide the hidden costs of "free" education (higher property taxes in the neighborhoods where the best schools are located, transportation, class trips, clothing, and supplies), and therefore, their children become less involved in the educational process. Textbooks generally glorify the White race and give scant attention to minorities. Jeannette Henry writes about the effects of history textbooks on Native American children:

> What is the effect upon the student, when he learns from his textbooks that one race, and one alone, is the most, the best, the greatest; when he learns that Indians* were mere parts of the landscape and wilderness which had to be cleared out, to make way for the great "movement" of white population across the land; and when he learns that Indians were killed and forcibly removed from their ancient homelands to make way for adventurers (usually called "pioneering goldminers"), for land grabbers (usually called "settlers"), and for illegal squatters on Indian-owned land (usually called "frontiersmen")? What is the effect upon the young Indian child himself, who is also a student in the school system, when he is told that Columbus discovered America, that Coronado "brought civilization" to the Indian people, and that the Spanish missionaries provided havens of refuge for the Indians? Is it reasonable to assume that the student, of whatever race, will not discover at some time in his life that Indians discovered America thousands of years before Columbus set out upon his voyage; that Coronado brought death and destruction to the native peoples; and that the Spanish missionaries, in all too many cases, forcibly dragged Indians to the missions?[27]

Even in school districts that use busing to attempt to achieve integration, institutional discrimination may occur. One method of discriminating is to use a track system. Most White children are placed in an "advanced" track, receiving increased educational attention from teachers, while most non-White children are placed in a "slower learner" track, receiving less educational attention.

Our criminal justice system also has elements of institutional racism. The justice system is supposed to be fair and nondiscriminatory. The very name of the system, *justice*, implies fairness and equality. Yet in practice, there is evidence of racism. Although African Americans constitute only about 12% of the population, they make up nearly 50% of the prison population. (There is considerable debate about the extent to which this is due to racism as opposed to differential crime rates by race.) The average prison sentence for murder and kidnapping is longer for African Americans than for Whites. Nearly half of those sentenced to death are African Americans.[28] Police departments and district attorneys' offices are more likely to vigorously enforce the kinds of crimes committed by lower-income groups and minority groups than those by middle- and upper-class White groups. Poor people (a disproportionate number of non-Whites are poor) are substantially less likely to be able to post bail. As a result, they are forced to remain in jail until their trial, which may take months or sometimes more than a year to come up. Unable to afford the expenses of a well-financed defense (including the prices charged by the most successful criminal defense teams), they are more likely to be found guilty.

Causes of Racial Discrimination and Oppression

No single theory provides a complete picture of why racial discrimination and oppression occur. The sources of discrimination are both internal and external to those who are prejudiced. We'll now look at several explanations for this behavior.

PROJECTION
Projection is a psychological defense mechanism by which we attribute to others characteristics that we are unwilling to recognize in ourselves. Many people have personal traits they dislike. They have an understandable desire to get rid of such traits, but this is not always possible. These people may then "project" some of these traits onto others (often to some other group in society), thus displacing the negative feelings they would otherwise

---

*The term *Indian* was originally used by early European settlers to describe the native populations of North America. Because of its nonnative derivation and the context of cultural domination surrounding its use, many people, particularly Native Americans, object to the use of the word. The term *Native American* is now generally preferred.

direct at themselves. In the process, they reject and condemn those onto whom they have projected the traits.

For example, a minority group may serve as a projection of a prejudiced person's fears and lusts. People who view African Americans as lazy and preoccupied with sex may be projecting their own internal concerns about their industriousness and their sexual fantasies onto another group. It is interesting to note that, although some Whites view Blacks as promiscuous, sexually indiscreet, and immoral, historically it has generally been White men who pressured Black women (particularly slaves) into sexual encounters. Perhaps these White males felt guilty about their sexual desires and adventures and dealt with their guilt by projecting their own lusts and sexual conduct onto African American males.

FRUSTRATION-AGGRESSION

Another psychic need satisfied by discrimination is the release of tension and frustration. All of us at times become frustrated when we are unable to achieve or obtain something we desire. Sometimes we strike back at the source of our frustration, but many times direct retaliation is not possible. For example, we may be reluctant to tell our employers what we think of them when we feel we are being treated unfairly because we fear repercussions.

Some frustrated people displace their anger and aggression onto a scapegoat. The scapegoat may not be limited to a particular person but may include a group of people, such as a minority group. Like people who take out their job frustrations on their spouses or family pets, some prejudiced people vent their frustrations on minority groups. (The term *scapegoat* derives from an ancient Hebrew ritual in which a goat was symbolically laden with the sins of the entire community and then chased into the wilderness. It "escaped"—hence the term *scapegoat*. The definition was gradually broadened to apply to anyone who bears the blame for others.)

INSECURITY AND INFERIORITY

Still another psychic need that may be satisfied by discrimination is the desire to counter feelings of insecurity or inferiority. Some insecure people feel better about themselves by putting down another group; they then can tell themselves that they are "better than" those people.

AUTHORITARIANISM

One of the classic works on the causes of prejudice is *The Authoritarian Personality,* by T. W. Adorno et al.[29] Shortly after World War II, these researchers studied the psychological causes of the development of European fascism and concluded that there was a distinct type of personality associated with prejudice and intolerance. The *authoritarian personality* is inflexible and rigid and has a low tolerance for uncertainty, has a great respect for authority figures and quickly submits to their will, and highly values conventional behavior while feeling threatened by unconventional behavior in others. To reduce this threat, this personality type labels unconventional people as "immature," "inferior," or "degenerate" and thereby avoids any need to question his or her own beliefs and values. The authoritarian personality views members of minority groups as unconventional, degrades them, and expresses authoritarianism through prejudice and discrimination.

HISTORY

There are also historical explanations for prejudice. Charles F. Marden and Gladys Meyer note that the racial groups now viewed by prejudiced White people as being second class are ones that have been conquered, enslaved, or admitted into our society on a subordinate basis.[30] For example, Africans were imported as slaves during our colonial period and stripped of human dignity. Native Americans were conquered, and their culture was viewed as inferior. Mexicans have been allowed to enter this country primarily to do seasonal low-paying farmwork.

COMPETITION AND EXPLOITATION

Our society is highly competitive and materialistic. Individuals and groups compete daily to acquire more of the available goods. These attempts to secure economic goods usually result in a struggle for power. In our society, Whites have historically sought to exploit non-Whites. As just mentioned, they have conquered, enslaved, or admitted non-

Whites into our society on a subordinate basis. They then use their powers to exploit non-Whites through cheap labor—for example, as sweatshop factory laborers, migrant farmhands, maids, janitors, and bellhops.

Members of the dominant group know they are treating the subordinate group as inferior and unequal. To justify such discrimination, they develop an ideology (set of beliefs) that their group is superior and that it is right and proper for them to have more rights, goods, and so on. Often they assert that God divinely selected their group to be dominant. Furthermore, they assign inferior traits (lazy, immoral, dirty, stupid) to the subordinate group and conclude that the minority need and deserve less because they are biologically inferior.

SOCIALIZATION PATTERNS

Prejudice is also a learned phenomenon, transmitted from generation to generation through socialization processes. Our culture has stereotypes of what different racial group members "ought to be" and how they "ought to behave" in relationships with members of certain outgroups. These stereotypes provide norms against which a child learns to judge people, things, and ideas. Prejudice, to some extent, is developed through the same processes by which we learn to be religious and patriotic, to appreciate and enjoy art, or to develop our value system. Racial prejudice, at least in certain segments in our society, is thus a facet of the normative system of our culture.

BELIEF IN THE ONE TRUE RELIGION

Some people are raised to believe that their religion is the one true religion and that they will go to heaven, whereas everyone who believes in a different religion is a heathen who will go to eternal damnation. A person with such a belief system comes to the conclusion that he or she is one of "God's chosen few," which leads that person to value himself or herself over "heathens." Feeling superior to others often leads such a person to devalue "heathens" and then treat them in an inferior way. The influence of the "one true religion" has led to an extensive number of wars between societies that each thought its religion was superior. These societies thought they were justified in

spreading their chosen religion through any possible means, including physical force, which has resulted in wars.

An excellent question to ponder is, "If a social worker believes his or her religion is the one true religion, can that social worker fully accept clients who are members of some other religious faith?" The belief in the one true religion may be one of the most crucial determinants in developing an attitudinal system of racial prejudice.

THE EYE OF THE BEHOLDER

No one of these theories explains all the causes of prejudice, which has many origins. Taken together, however, they identify a number of causative factors. All these theories assert that the causative factors of prejudice are in the personality and experiences of the person holding the prejudice, not in the character of the group against whom the prejudice is directed.

A novel experiment documenting that prejudice does not stem from contact with the people toward whom it is directed was conducted by Eugene Hartley. He gave his participants a list of prejudiced responses to Jews and African Americans and to three groups that did not even exist: Wallonians, Pireneans, and Danireans. Prejudiced responses included statements such as, "All Wallonians living here should be expelled." The respondents were asked to state their agreement or disagreement with these prejudiced assertions. The experiment showed that most of those who were prejudiced against Jews and African Americans were also prejudiced against people whom they had never met or heard anything about.[31]

THE EFFECTS AND COSTS OF DISCRIMINATION AND OPPRESSION

Racial discrimination is a barrier in our competitive society to obtaining the necessary resources to lead a contented and comfortable life. Being a victim of discrimination is another obstacle which has to be overcome. Being discriminated against due to race makes it more difficult to obtain adequate housing, financial resources, a quality education, employment, adequate health care and other services, equal justice in civil and criminal cases, and so on.

Discrimination also has heavy psychological costs. All of us have to develop a sense of identity about who we are and how we fit into a complex, swiftly changing world. Ideally, it is important that we form a positive self-concept and strive to obtain worthy goals. Yet as we have noted before, according to Cooley's "looking glass self," our idea of who we are and what we are is largely determined by the way others relate to us.[32] When members of a minority group are treated by the majority group as if they are inferior, second-class citizens, it is substantially more difficult for them to develop a positive identity. Thus, people who are the objects of discrimination encounter barriers to developing their full potential as human beings.

Young children of groups who are the victims of discrimination are likely to develop low self-esteem at an early age. African American children who have been subjected to discrimination prefer White dolls and White playmates over Black.[33]

Pinderhughes has noted that the history of slavery and oppression of African Americans, combined with racism and exclusion, has produced a "victim system":

A victim system is a circular feedback process that exhibits properties such as stability, predictability, and identity that are common to all systems. This particular system threatens self-esteem and reinforces problematic responses in communities, families and individuals. The feedback works as follows: Barriers to opportunity and education limit the chance for achievement, employment, and attainment of skills. This limitation can, in turn, lead to poverty or stress in relationships, which interferes with adequate performance of family roles. Strains in family roles cause problems in individual growth and development and limit the opportunities of families to meet their own needs or to organize to improve their communities. Communities limited in resources (jobs, education, housing, etc.) are unable to support families properly and the community all too often be-

comes an active disorganizing influence, a breeder of crime and other pathology, and a cause of even more powerlessness.[34]

Discrimination also has high costs for the majority group. It impairs intergroup cooperation and communication. Discrimination also is a factor in contributing to social problems among minorities (for example, high crime rates, emotional problems, alcoholism, and drug abuse), all of which have cost billions of dollars in social programs. Albert Szymanski argues that discrimination is a barrier to collective action (such as unionization) among Whites and non-Whites (particularly people in the lower income classes) and therefore is a factor in perpetuating low-paying jobs and poverty.[35] Less affluent Whites who could benefit from collective action are hurt.

The effects of discrimination are even reflected in life expectancy. The life expectancy of non-Whites is 6 years less than that of Whites in the United States.[36] The fact is that non-Whites tend to die earlier than Whites because they receive inferior health care, food, and shelter.

Finally, discrimination in the United States undermines some of our nation's political goals. Many other nations view us as hypocritical when we advocate human rights and equality. To make an effective argument for human rights on a worldwide scale, we must first put our own house in order by eliminating racial and ethnic discrimination. Few Americans realize the extent to which racial discrimination damages our international reputation. Non-White foreign diplomats to America often complain about being victims of discrimination, as they are mistaken for being members of American minority groups. With most of the nations of the world non-White, our racist practices severely damage our influence and prestige.

BACKGROUND OF RACIAL GROUPS

The largest racial group in the United States is the White race, which is the majority group, both in numbers (about 76% of the population[37]) and in power. African Americans compose about 12%

of the population,[38] and Latinos compose about 9%.[39] The other non-White groups constitute about 3% of our population and primarily include Native Americans and people of Japanese, Chinese, and Filipino descent. There are also small numbers of the following non-White groups: Aleuts, Asian Indians, Eskimo, Hawaiians, Indonesians, Koreans, and Polynesians. In educational attainment, occupational status, and average income, most of these non-White groups are clearly at a disadvantage as compared with the White groups. (The two major non-White groups that now approach Whites in socioeconomic status are Japanese Americans and Chinese Americans.)

African Americans

The United States has always been a racist nation. Although our country's founders talked about freedom, dignity, equality, and human rights, the economy of the United States prior to the Civil War depended heavily on slavery.

Many slaves came from cultures that had well-developed art forms, political systems, family patterns, religious beliefs, and economic systems. However, because their culture was not European, slave owners viewed it as being of "no consequence" and prohibited slaves from practicing and developing their art, language, religion, and family life. For want of practice, their former culture soon died in the United States.

The life of a slave was harsh. Slaves were viewed not as human beings but as chattel to be bought and sold. Long, hard days were spent working in the field, with the profits of their labor going to their White owners. Whippings, mutilations, and hangings were commonly accepted White control practices. The impetus to enslave Blacks was not simply racism; many Whites believed that it was to their economic advantage to have a cheap supply of labor. Cotton growing, in particular, was thought to require a large labor force that was cheap and docile. Marriages between slaves were not recognized by the law, and slaves were often sold with little regard to marital and family ties. Throughout the slavery period and even afterward, African Americans were discouraged from demonstrating intelligence, initiative,

or ambition. For a period of time, it was even illegal to teach them to read and write.

Some authorities have noted that the opposition to the spread of slavery preceding the Civil War was due less to moral concern for human rights and equality than to the North's fears of competition from slave labor and the rapidly increasing migration of free Blacks to the North and West.[40] Few Whites at that time understood or believed in the principle of racial equality—not even Abraham Lincoln, who thought Blacks were inferior to Whites. In 1858 in a speech in Charleston, Illinois, Lincoln asserted:

> I will say, then, that I am not, nor ever have been in favor of bringing about in any way the social and political equality of the white and black races; that I am not, nor ever have been, in favor of making voters or jurors of Negroes, nor of qualifying them to hold office, nor to inter-marry with White people . . . and inasmuch as they cannot so live, while they do remain together there must be the position of superior and inferior, and I as much as any other man am in favor of having the superior position assigned to the White race.[41]

Following the Civil War, the federal government failed to develop a comprehensive program of economic and educational aid to African Americans. As a result, most of them returned to economic dependency on the same planters in the South who had held them in bondage. Within a few years, laws were passed in the southern states prohibiting interracial marriages and requiring racial segregation in schools and public places.

A rigid caste system in the South hardened into a system of oppression known as "Jim Crow." The system prescribed how African Americans were supposed to act in the presence of Whites, asserted White supremacy, embraced racial segregation, and denied political and legal rights to African Americans. Those who opposed Jim Crow were subjected to burnings, beatings, and lynchings. Jim Crow was used to "teach" African Americans to view themselves as inferior and to be servile and passive in interactions with Whites.

World War II opened up new employment opportunities for African Americans, who migrated

EXHIBIT 12.1

The Africentric Perspective and Worldview

African American culture has numerous components. It has elements from traditional African culture; elements from slavery, reconstruction, and subsequent exposure to racism and discrimination; and elements from "mainstream" White culture. An emerging perspective is the *Africentric perspective,*[a] which acknowledges African culture and expressions of African beliefs, values, institutions, and behaviors. It recognizes that African Americans have retained, to some degree, a number of elements of African life and values.

The Africentric perspective holds that the application of Eurocentric theories to explain the behavior and ethos of African Americans is often inappropriate. Eurocentric theories of human behavior reflect concepts that were developed in European and Anglo-American cultures. Eurocentric theorists have historically vilified people of African descent and other people of color. Such theorists have explicitly or implicitly claimed that people of African descent were pathological or inferior in their social, personality, or moral development.[b] The origins of this denigration can be found in the slave trade, as slave traders and owners were pressed to justify the enslavement of Africans. The

fallout of Eurocentric theories is the portrayal of the culture of people of African descent as "uncivilized" and as having contributed practically nothing of value to world development and human history.

The Africentric perspective seeks to dispel the negative distortions about people of African ancestry by legitimizing and disseminating a *worldview* that goes back thousands of years and that exists in the hearts and minds of many people of African descent today. The concept of worldview involves one's perceptions of oneself in relation to other people, objects, institutions, and nature. It focuses on one's view of the world and one's role and place in it. The worldviews of African Americans are shaped by unique and important experiences, such as racism and discrimination, an African heritage, traditional attributes of the African American family and community life, and a strong religious orientation.

The Africentric perspective also seeks to promote a worldview that will facilitate human and societal transformation toward moral, spiritual, and humanistic ends and that seeks to persuade people of different cultural and ethnic groups that

(continued)

to the North in large numbers. Greater mobility afforded by wartime conditions led to upheavals in the traditional caste system. Awareness of disparity between the ideal and the real led many people to try to improve race relations, not only for domestic peace and justice but also to answer criticism from abroad. With each gain in race relations, more African Americans were encouraged to press for their rights.

A major turning point in civil rights history was the 1954 U.S. Supreme Court decision in *Brown* v. *Board of Education,* which ruled that racial segregation in public schools was unconstitutional.

Since then there have been a number of organized efforts by both African Americans and certain segments of the White population to secure equal rights and opportunities for minorities. Attempts to change deeply entrenched racist attitudes and practices have produced much turmoil: the burning of our inner cities in the late 1960s,* the assas-

---

*On April 4, 1968, Martin Luther King, Jr., was killed by a White assassin's bullet. His death helped trigger extensive rioting in 40 cities; in many places, whole blocks were burned down.

EXHIBIT 3.7 *(continued)*

they share a mutual interest in this regard. The Africentric perspective rejects the idea that the individual can be understood apart from others in his or her social group. It emphasizes a collective identity that encourages sharing, cooperation, and social responsibility.

The Africentric perspective also emphasizes the importance of spirituality, which includes one's moral development and attaining meaning and identity in life. The Africentric perspective views oppression and alienation as the major sources of human problems in the United States. Oppression and alienation are not only generated by prejudice and discrimination, but also by the European worldview that teaches people to see themselves primarily as material, physical beings seeking immediate pleasure for their physical, material, or sexual desires. It is further asserted that this European worldview discourages spiritual and moral development.

The Africentric perspective has been used to provide explanations of the origins of specific social problems. For example, violent crimes by youths are thought to be a result of the limited options and choices they have to advance themselves economically. Youths seek a life of street crime as a logical means to cope with, and protect against, a society that practices pervasive employment discrimination (associated with minimum wages, layoffs, lack of opportunities for education or training, and a wide gap between the rich and the poor). These youths calculate mentally that they can make more money from a life of street crime than from attending college or starting a legitimate business with little start-up capital. Turning to a life of crime is also thought more likely to occur in a society that uses the European worldview, which deemphasizes spiritual and moral development, as individuals then have little or no awareness of collective and social responsibility.

The Africentric perspective values a more holistic, spiritual, and optimistic view of human beings. It supports the "strengths perspective" and "empowerment" concepts of social work practice, which are described later in this chapter.

[a] W. Devore and E. G. Schlesinger, *Ethnic-Sensitive Social Work Practice*, 4th ed. (Needham Heights, MA: Allyn & Bacon, 1996).

[b] J. H. Schiele, "Afrocentricity: An Emerging Paradigm in Social Work Practice," *Social Work*, 41 (May 1966), pp. 284–294.

sination of Martin Luther King, Jr., and clashes between militant Black groups and the police. There have also been significant advances. Wide-ranging legislation has been passed, protecting civil rights in areas such as housing, voting, employment, and the use of public transportation and facilities. During the riots in 1968, the National Advisory Commission on Civil Disorders warned that our society was careening "toward two societies, one Black, one White—separate and unequal." [42]

America today is not the bitterly segregated society that the riot commission envisioned. African Americans and Whites now more often work together and lunch together—yet few really count each other as friends.

Four of five African Americans now live in metropolitan areas, over half of them in our central cities. [43] American cities are still largely segregated, with African Americans primarily living in African American neighborhoods. In recent years, the main thrust of the civil rights movement among African Americans has been economic equality. The economic gap between African Americans and Whites continues to be immense. African American families are three times as likely as White families to fall below the poverty line. [44]

Since the early 1950s, the African American unemployment rate has been approximately twice that of Whites. Unemployment is an especially severe problem for African American teenagers, whose rate of unemployment is substantially higher than for White youths and has run as high as 50%.[45]

We, as a nation, have come a long way since the U.S. Supreme Court's decision in 1954. But we still have a long way to go before we eliminate African American poverty and the oppression they are subjected to. Living conditions in African American inner cities remain as bleak as they were when our inner cities erupted in the late 1960s. Dissatisfaction with living conditions in the 1960s led African Americans in many inner-city areas to torch and burn down numerous buildings—these buildings were largely owned by White absentee landlords.

Two developments have characterized the socioeconomic circumstances of African Americans in the past 30 years. A middle class has emerged that is better educated, better paid, and better housed than any group of African Americans that has gone before it. However, as this group moves to better neighborhoods, they leave behind those who are living in poverty. The group that has been left behind generates a disproportionate share of the social pathology that is associated with the inner city, including high rates of crime, unemployment, drug abuse, school dropouts, births outside of marriage, and families receiving public assistance.

Over half of all African American children are raised in single-parent families.[46] However, many African American children in single-parent families are living in family structures composed of some variation of the extended family. Many single-parent families move in with relatives during adversity, including economic adversity. In addition, African American families of all levels rely on relatives for their children while they work.

While it is a reality that many African American families are headed by single mothers, it would be a serious error to view such family structures as inherently pathological. A single parent with good parenting skills, along with a supportive extended family, can lead to healthy family functions.

Schaefer summarizes five strengths identified by the National Urban League that allow African American families to function effectively in a racist society:

1. Strong kinship bonds. *Blacks are more likely than Whites to care for children and the elderly in an extended family network.*

2. A strong work orientation. *Poor Blacks are more likely to be working, and poor Black families often include more than one wage earner.*

3. Adaptability of family roles. *In two-parent families, the egalitarian pattern of decision making is the most common. The self-reliance of Black women who are the primary wage earners best illustrates this adaptability.*

4. A high achievement orientation. *Working-class Blacks indicate a greater desire for their children to attend college than working-class Whites. Even a majority of low-income African Americans desire to attend college.*

5. A strong religious orientation. *Black churches since the time of slavery have been the source of many significant grassroots organizations.*[47]

Solomon noted that "black culture contains elements of 'mainstream' white culture, elements from traditional African culture, and elements from slavery, reconstruction and subsequent exposure to racism and discrimination."[48]

Subcultures of African Americans have vocabularies and communication styles that differ from those of dominant White culture. Young children raised in these subcultures often have difficulty understanding the English spoken in schools. African American dialects appear to be the result of a creolized form of English that was at one time spoken on southern plantations by slaves.[49] (A *creolized* language is a speaker's native language that is based on two or more other languages.)

Present-day African American English is a combination of the linguistic remnants of its southern plantation past and a reflection of the current African American sociocultural situation. As such, it is important to recognize it as a dialect in its own right, not as just a distortion of standard English. Most adult African Americans are bilingual, being fluent in an African American dialect and in standard English.

Religious organizations that are predominantly African American have tended to focus not only on spirituality but also on social action efforts to combat racial discrimination. Many prominent African American leaders, such as Martin Luther King, Jr., and Jesse Jackson, have been members of the clergy. African American churches have served to develop leadership skills. They have also functioned as social welfare organizations to meet basic needs, such as clothing, food, and shelter. These churches have been natural support systems for troubled Black individuals and families.

Many African Americans have had the experience of being negatively evaluated by school systems, social welfare agencies, health-care institutions, and the justice system. Because of their past experiences, African Americans are likely to view such institutions with apprehension. Schools, for example, have erroneously perceived African Americans as less capable of developing cognitive skills. These perceptions often become a self-fulfilling prophecy. If African American children are expected to fail in school, teachers may put forth less effort in challenging them to learn. The children may then also put forth less effort to learn, resulting in a lower level of achievement.

Latinos

Latinos are Americans of Spanish origin. They constitute diverse groups bound somewhat together by their language, culture, and ties to Roman Catholicism. This broad categorization includes Mexican Americans (Chicanos), Puerto Ricans, Cubans, people from Central and South America and the West Indies, and others of Spanish origin (Figure 12.1). The Latino population is growing at five times the rate of the rest of the population.[50] There are three main reasons for this rapid growth: a tendency to have large families, a

FIGURE 12.1

Percentage Distribution of Latinos in the United States by Land of Origin

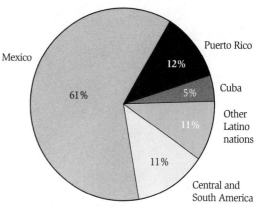

Source: Richard T. Schaefer, *Racial and Ethnic Groups,* 6th ed. (Boston: Little, Brown, 1996), p. 253.

continual inflow of immigrants (particularly from Mexico), and the high proportion of Latinos in this country who are of child-bearing age.

MEXICAN AMERICANS

The largest Latino group in the United States is Mexican Americans. Although many Americans are unaware of the fact, Mexican Americans have had a long history of settlement and land ownership in what is now the United States. In the 1700s and 1800s, there were a number of small Latino communities in what later became the American Southwest—in areas that have since gained statehood (including Texas, Arizona, New Mexico, and California). These early Latinos were generally small landholders. In the 1800s, Whites moved into these regions, and competition for good land became fierce. Many Mexican Americans had their land taken away by large White-owned cattle and agricultural interests. Texas was once part of Mexico. In 1836 the settlers (including many of Spanish descent) staged a successful insurrection against the Mexican government and formed an independent republic. In 1845 Texas

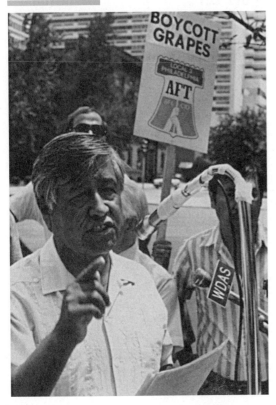

César Chávez formed the first successful labor union to represent migrant workers nearly 30 years ago. His nationwide boycotts of table grapes picked by underpaid workers and contaminated with pesticides have inspired other collective action by Chicanos.

was annexed to the United States. As a consequence, many of the Mexican settlers became U.S. citizens.

Since the 1850s, there has been a steady migration of Mexicans to the United States, with a number of immigrants entering this country illegally. The average income in Mexico is much lower than in the United States, so the quest for higher wages and a better life has lured many Mexicans to this country.

Relations between Whites and Mexican Americans have on occasion become vicious and ugly. Similar to Black-White confrontations, there have been many riots between Whites and Mexican Americans.

Many Mexican Americans live in barrios (Spanish-speaking sections of U.S. cities that have become ghettos) in cities such as Los Angeles, Denver, and Chicago. Although some are moving up in socioeconomic status, most have low-paying jobs.

A smaller number of Mexican Americans are employed in temporary seasonal work, largely on farms. Some migrate north in the summer to be farm laborers and return to the Southwest in the fall. In terms of acculturation and assimilation, these migrant workers are among the least "Americanized" of all ethnic groups.[51] They are reluctant to seek help from social agencies, partly because of their pride and partly because of language and cultural barriers.

An increasingly large segment of this ethnic group is becoming involved in the "Chicano" movement. Chicanos are Americans of Mexican origin who resent the stereotypes that demean Mexican Americans—particularly the image of laziness, because many are performing some of the hardest physical labor in our society. The origin of the word *Chicano* is not clear, but until the last generation it was a derogatory term Whites used for Mexican Americans. Now the word and the people have come full circle, and *Chicano* has taken on a new, positive meaning. The Chicano movement asserts that social institutions must become more responsive to the needs of Chicanos. Chicano-studies programs have been developed at a number of universities.

The civil rights activities of African Americans have provided encouragement for the Chicanos' militant stance. In addition, second- and third-generation Mexican Americans have fewer ties to Mexico than did their elders, and they are oriented more toward the majority American culture in terms of aspirations and goals. Yet similar to African Americans, Mexican Americans generally have low-paying jobs, high rates of unemployment, and high levels of poverty. They also have high rates of infant mortality, low levels of educational attainment, and high levels of substandard housing. Their standard of living is no better than that of African Americans.

Chicano men, as contrasted to Anglo men, have been described as exhibiting greater pride in their maleness.[52] *Machismo*—a strong sense of masculine pride—is highly valued among Chicano men and is displayed by males to express dominance and superiority. Machismo is demonstrated differently by different people. Some may seek to be irresistible to women and to have a number of sexual partners. Some resort to weapons or fighting. Some interpret machismo to mean pride in one's manhood, honor, and ability to provide for one's family. Others boast of their achievements, even those that never occurred. Recent writers have noted that the feminist movement, urbanization, upward mobility, and acculturation are contributing to the decline of machismo.[53] Chicanos also tend to be more "familistic" than Anglos. Familism is the belief that the family takes precedence over the individual. Schaefer notes:

> *Familism is generally regarded as good . . . as an extended family provides greater emotional strength at times of family crisis. The many significant aspects of familism include: (1) the importance of the* compadrazo *(godparent-godchild relationship); (2) the benefits of financial dependency on kin; (3) the availability of relatives as a source of advice; and (4) active involvement of the elderly within the family.*[54]

In the 1970s and 1980s, César Chávez unionized migrant workers in California, organized several strikes, and led successful nationwide boycotts of fruit and vegetables picked by underpaid workers. Powerful White economic interests made several violent attempts to break these strikes. Chávez's campaigns provided an example and incentive for other collective action by Chicanos. The future is likely to see Chicanos becoming an increasingly powerful political force with which to be reckoned.

PUERTO RICANS

After World War II, many Puerto Ricans migrated to the mainland United States, largely because of population pressure and insufficient job opportunities on the island. Although they are found in all the states, they have settled mainly in New York City, New Jersey, Illinois, Florida, California, Penn-sylvania, and Connecticut. Those migrating from Puerto Rico were from the higher socioeconomic classes in their home society. Although their earnings on the mainland are higher than in Puerto Rico, they have experienced lower job status than Anglos and many live in substandard housing.

For Puerto Ricans, the Spanish culture has been dominant, but they have also been influenced by the Taino, American, African, and European cultures. In Puerto Rico, status is based on culture or class, not skin color, and interracial marriages are common. On entering the mainland United States, many Puerto Ricans understandably become puzzled by the greater emphasis given to skin color here.

The island of Puerto Rico is in a commonwealth arrangement with the United States, and citizenship was extended to Puerto Ricans living on the island by the Jones Act of 1917.[55] As a commonwealth, its people have privileges and rights different from those on the mainland. They are subject to military service, selective service registration, and all federal laws. Yet they cannot vote in presidential elections and have no voting representation in Congress. Puerto Ricans pay a local income tax but no federal income tax. There is currently considerable controversy in Puerto Rico as to whether the island should seek independence from the United States, seek statehood, or remain a commonwealth.

Richard Schaefer summarizes the current status of Puerto Ricans:

> *The Puerto Rican people share many problems with other subordinate groups: poor housing, inadequate health care, weak political representation, and low incomes. Like Chicanos, they have a language and cultural tradition at variance with that of Anglo society. The dominant society has removed some barriers to achievement by Spanish-speaking people in the United States but public concerns grow about bilingual and bicultural programs. Chicanos and Puerto Ricans are poorly represented among key decision makers in both corporate offices and governmental agencies. Both Chicanos and Puerto Ricans, however, are close to or are actually in their home country, a situation that facilitates maintaining a rich cultural tradition. Hispanics'*

ability to maintain their original identity and solidarity means they have not been as compelled as European immigrants to assimilate White American customs and values.

The situation of Puerto Ricans is unique. Those on the island must resolve the issues of its political relationship to the mainland and the proper pace and emphasis of economic development. Those migrating to the mainland must adapt to a social definition of race different from that on the island and adjust to a system that leaves some Puerto Ricans in an ambiguous social position.[56]

CUBANS

Most Cuban Americans are recent migrants to the United States. Many are political refugees, having fled Cuba following the takeover of the government by Fidel Castro in 1959. Many of these Cuban Americans are well educated and have managerial or professional backgrounds. Large numbers have settled in southern Florida, particularly in the Miami area.

In 1980 Castro opened the doors of his socialist island, and over 100,000 more Cubans fled to this country. Many of these latest arrivals were from the lower class, some of whom had been imprisoned in Cuba for a variety of crimes. (Castro apparently sent them to the United States to reduce the costs of the correctional system in Cuba.) Many of these most recent arrivals have also settled in southern Florida, where they have experienced confrontations with Euro-Americans, a high rate of crime, and other adjustment problems.

Native Americans

When Columbus first came to America in 1492, there were about 1 million Native Americans grouped into more than 600 distinct societies.[57] Tribal wars between groups were common, and there were wide variations among tribes in customs, culture, lifestyle, languages, and religious ceremonies. The Whites gradually expanded their settlement, moving westward and slowly usurping native land. Colonists and pioneers adopted a policy that amounted to deliberate extermination of Native Americans. The saying "The only

good Indian is a dead Indian" became popular. Whites took their lands away, depleted the buffalo herds on which many tribes depended for survival, slaughtered tribes, and indirectly killed many others by leading forced marches in freezing weather and bringing diseases and famine.[58] Unable to mobilize a common defense, all native tribes were defeated by 1892.

In 1887 Congress passed the General Allotment Act, which empowered Congress unilaterally to revise treaties made with Native Americans. This action opened the way for land-hungry Whites to take productive native land. From 1887 to 1928, the land held by Native Americans decreased from 137 million acres to 50 million acres, with most of the remaining property being some of the least productive real estate in the country.[59]

Contact with the White culture has undermined Native Americans' traditional living patterns. It has been said that "the buffalo are gone"— meaning that Native Americans can no longer sustain themselves through hunting and fishing. Segregation to reservations has further damaged their pride and sense of self-worth. Government programs now attempt to meet subsistence needs, but they also serve to pauperize Native Americans. Native Americans on reservations have high rates of suicide, alcoholism, illiteracy, poverty, homicide, child neglect, and infant mortality.

Earlier in the 20th century, the plight of Native Americans was largely ignored because of their isolation on remote reservations. Through the Bureau of Indian Affairs (BIA), they received the most paternalistic treatment by the government of all minorities. For many years, the BIA had programs designed to destroy Native American culture, religion, and language. Today the bureau has become a symbol of frustration and despair.[60]

In the 1960s and 1970s, the plight of the Native Americans received national attention, and many Whites became actively involved in their problems. In the past, films depicted the "glorious" victories of the Whites over "savages." Now we know that early White settlers exploited the Native Americans by taking away their land and destroying their way of life.

During most of the 20th century, Native Americans have not been very active in civil rights

In the 1970s, the militant American Indian Movement demanded that government pay attention to their grievances. Some 20 years later, AIM's national director Clyde Bellecourt discussed plans to protest Native American mascots and racism in sports at the 1992 Super Bowl.

activities. However, in the 1960s and 1970s, there were some organized efforts to make changes. Like African Americans and Chicanos, Native Americans staged some widely publicized demonstrations, such as one at Wounded Knee, South Dakota, in the 1970s.

In 1978 the U.S. Congress enacted the Indian Child Welfare Act (PL 95-608), which seeks to protect Native American families and tribes. Recognizing that Native American children are the most important resource of the tribes, the act establishes federal standards for involuntary removal of Native American children from their families and provides a legal mechanism for tribes to assume jurisdiction over Native American children who have been involuntarily removed by state and local authorities. The act is therefore designed to promote the security and stability of Native American families and tribes. When a child is removed from a Native American family, the tribe must be notified, and preference must be given to placing the child with relatives, tribal members, or other Native American families. Despite this critical piece of federal legislation, many Native American children continue to be placed in foster care or for adoption with non-Native American families.[61] A significant hindrance to the implementation of PL 95-608 is the lack of awareness of social workers concerning the act's mandates.

High rates of poverty and other social problems continue among Native Americans. Schaefer notes:

> *Another enemy of the Native American people is their disunity: full-bloods are pitted against mixed-bloods, reservation residents against city dwellers, tribe against tribe, conservative against militant. This disunity reflects the diversity of cultural backgrounds and historical experiences represented by the people collectively referred to as Native Americans. This disunity is also counterproductive when it comes to confronting a central government.[62]*

Some tribes are taking legal action to recover land that was illegally usurped from them. The Nonintercourse Act of 1870 stated that any land transaction between Indians and others not approved by Congress is null and void. Many such transactions were not ratified by Congress. Some tribes have brought legal claims for land and for rights to minerals and rivers, and some of these claims have already been upheld. Two tribes in Maine have won their claim to half the land in the state. In Alaska, Native Americans have been awarded $1 billion and 40 million acres of land in compensation for illegal seizures of their territory in the past.[63]

In recent years, Native American tribes have opened gambling casinos in many states. These casinos have become very popular and highly profitable. (Recent court decisions about federal treaties with Native Americans permit substantial tax breaks on these profits.) Many Native

American tribes who are operating casinos are using some of the profits to fund social and educational programs for their tribal members.

Asian Americans

Asian Americans in the United States include the Japanese, Chinese, Filipinos, Koreans, Burmese, Hmongs, Indonesians, Guamanians, Samoans, South Vietnamese, and Thais. A large number of South Vietnamese immigrated to this country in the mid-1970s following the Vietnam War. Contrary to a popular stereotype, Asians are not homogeneous. Each ethnic group has its own history, religion, language, and culture. These Asian American groups also differ in terms of group cohesion, levels of education, and socioeconomic status. Just as it is wrong to view all Europeans as the same, it is an error to view all Asians as a single entity.

Like other disenfranchised groups, Asian Americans are victimized by discrimination. Immediate problems include housing, education, income maintenance, unemployment and underemployment, health care, and vocational training and retraining. Because of language and cultural barriers, many needy Asians (particularly new immigrants and the elderly) do not seek services to which they are entitled. The two most prominent Asian groups in this country are Japanese Americans and Chinese Americans.

JAPANESE AMERICANS

Until 1900 few Japanese migrants came to the United States, partly because of legal restrictions against their migration and partly because of the unfriendly reception they received in this country.

After the turn of the century, Japanese migration increased. Immigrants settled primarily on the West Coast. By 1941 (when Pearl Harbor was attacked), there were few distinctive Japanese American settlements outside the West Coast other than in New York City and Chicago. During World War II, Japanese Americans' loyalty was viewed with intense suspicion, and they severely felt the impact of prejudice, war hysteria, and the denial of certain civil rights. On March 2, 1942, the commander of the Western Theater of Operations established "relocation centers" (concentration camps) to which Japanese Americans living on the West Coast were sent. The confused policies of our nation during this war are indicated by the fact that 33,000 Japanese Americans served in the armed forces for the United States, while 110,000 Japanese Americans were confined in concentration camps.[64] Not only were their civil rights violated, but they also were forced to sell their property. (In comparison, Americans of German or Italian descent were not similarly persecuted, even though the war was fought against Germany and Italy as well as Japan.) Following the war, the return of Japanese Americans to the West Coast met with some initial opposition, but among Whites a counterreaction soon developed that emphasized fair play and acceptance.

Since 1946 Japanese Americans have settled in other parts of the country, and their socioeconomic status is now approaching that of Whites. Japanese Americans now have a higher level of educational achievement than White Americans.[65]

An act of Congress in 1988 granted $20,000 to each of the Japanese Americans who were interned during World War II. This act is a hopeful signal of greater intergroup cooperation in the future.

CHINESE AMERICANS

In the 1800s, the Chinese were encouraged to immigrate to the United States to do mining, railroad construction, and farm work. These immigrants soon encountered hostility from some Whites, particularly in western states, because of their willingness to work for low wages. Their racial and cultural distinctiveness also made them targets for scapegoating, especially during periods of high unemployment. Charles Henderson et al. describe the extent to which Chinese Americans were subjected to racism during this time period:

> *Racism against Asians is shown in the 1854 decision of the California Supreme Court in* The People *vs.* Hall. *The appellant, a white Anglo-American, had been convicted of murder upon the testimony of Chinese witnesses. Was such evidence admissible? The judge ruled that Asians should be ineligible to testify for or against a white man. This ruling opened the*

floodgate for anti-Chinese abuse, violence, and exploitation. Group murders, lynchings, property damage, and robbery of the Chinese were reported up and down the West Coast. Because of the harsh treatment of the Chinese, any luckless person was described as not having a "Chinaman's chance." [66]

In the early 1900s, Chinese Americans were concentrated largely on the West Coast, but since the 1920s, they have tended to disperse throughout the nation. They have settled in large cities, and many live in Chinatowns in cities such as Los Angeles, San Francisco, New York, Boston, and Chicago.

The struggles of China against Japan before and during World War II brought about a more favorable image of Chinese Americans. Nevertheless, some discrimination continues. They have been subjected to less discrimination in Hawaii than on the mainland, as Hawaii is much closer to being a pluralist society than the rest of the country. Chinese Americans now have a higher level of educational achievement than White Americans.[67] Although Chinese Americans still tend to intramarry, they are now more likely to marry a member of another racial group than was true in the past. An increasing number are also moving out of Chinatowns to live in suburbs and in other areas.

STRATEGIES FOR ADVANCING SOCIAL AND ECONOMIC JUSTICE

Social justice is an ideal condition in which all members of a society have the same basic rights, protection, opportunities, obligations, and social benefits.[68] Economic justice is also an ideal condition in which all members of a society have the same opportunities for attaining material goods, income, and wealth. A wide range of strategies have been developed to reduce racial and ethnic discrimination and oppression, thereby advancing social and economic justice. These strategies include the following: mass media appeals, strategies to increase interaction among the races, civil

rights laws, activism, school busing, affirmative action programs, confrontation of racist remarks and actions, confrontation of the problems in inner cities, minority-owned businesses, and grassroots organizations.

Mass Media Appeals

Newspapers, magazines, radio, and television at times present information designed to explain the nature and harmful effects of prejudice and to promote harmony among humanity. The mass media are able to reach large numbers of people simultaneously. By expanding public awareness of discrimination and its consequences, the media can counteract the influence of racial extremists. But the mass media have limitations in changing prejudiced attitudes and behaviors; they are primarily providers of information and seldom have a lasting effect in changing deep-seated prejudices through propaganda. Broadcasting such platitudes as "all people are brothers and sisters" and "prejudice is un-American" is not very effective. Highly bigoted people are often unaware of their own prejudices. Even if they are aware of them, they generally dismiss mass media appeals as irrelevant or as propaganda. However, the mass media probably have had a significant impact in reducing discrimination by showing non-Whites and Whites harmoniously interacting in commercials, on news teams, and on other TV fare.

Greater Interaction Among the Races

Increased contact among races is not in itself sufficient to alleviate racial prejudice. In fact, increased contact may, in some instances, highlight intergroup differences and increase suspicions and fear. George Simpson and J. Milton Yinger reviewed a number of studies and concluded that prejudice is likely to be increased when contacts are tension-laden or involuntary.[69] Prejudice is likely to subside when individuals are placed in situations in which they share characteristics in nonracial matters (for example, as coworkers, fellow soldiers, or classmates). Equal-status contacts, rather than inferior–superior contacts, also reduce prejudices.[70]

Civil Rights Laws

In the past 30 years, equal rights have been legislated in employment, voting, housing, public accommodation, and education. A key question is, "How effective are laws in curbing racial discrimination and reducing racial prejudice?"

Proponents of civil rights legislation make certain assumptions. The first is that new laws will reduce discriminatory behavioral patterns. The laws define what was once "normal" behavior (discrimination) as now being "deviant" behavior. With time, attitudes are expected to change and become more consistent with the forced nondiscriminatory behavior patterns.

A second assumption is that the laws will be enforced. Civil rights laws enacted after the Civil War were seldom enforced and gradually eroded. It is also unfortunately true that some officials will find ways of evading the intent of the law by eliminating only the extreme, overt symbols of discrimination without changing other practices. Thus, the enactment of a law is only the first step in the process of changing prejudiced attitudes and practices. However, as Martin Luther King, Jr., noted, "The law may not make a man love me, but it can restrain him from lynching me, and I think that's pretty important."

Activism

The strategy of activism attempts to change the structure of race relations through direct confrontation of discrimination and segregation policies. Activism employs three types of politics: the politics of creative disorder, the politics of disorder, and the politics of escape.[71]

Politics of creative disorder operate on the edge of the dominant social system and include school boycotts, rent strikes, job blockades, sit-ins (for example, at businesses that are alleged to discriminate), public marches, and product boycotts. This type of activism is based on the concept of nonviolent resistance. A dramatic illustration of nonviolent resistance involved Rosa Parks (see Case Example 12.1). The famous Montgomery bus boycott that her behavior provoked had an even more important psychological impact: It suggested that people of color had rights equal to those of Whites and that united nonviolent resistance could overturn discriminatory laws.[72]

Politics of disorder reflect alienation from the dominant culture and disillusionment with the political system. Those discriminated against resort to mob uprising, riots, and other forms of violence.

In 1969 the National Commission on Causes and Prevention of Violence reported that 200 riots had occurred in our inner cities in the previous 5 years.[73] In the early 1980s, there were riots in Miami and in some other inner cities. In 1992 there were devastating riots in Los Angeles following the acquittal of four White police officers who had been charged with using excessive force in arresting Rodney King, an African American; the brutal arrest had been videotaped. Most of these riots have involved minority group aggression against White-owned property.

Politics of escape are characterized by passionate rhetoric about how minorities are being victimized. But because the focus is not on arriving at solutions, the rhetoric is not productive, except perhaps for providing an emotional release.

The principal value of activism or social protest seems to be the stimulation of public awareness of certain problems. The civil rights protests in the 1960s made practically all Americans aware of the discrimination to which non-White groups were being subjected. As a result, at least some of the discrimination has ceased, and race relations have improved. Continued protest beyond a certain (admittedly indeterminate) point, however, appears to have little additional value.[74]

School Busing

Housing patterns in many large metropolitan centers have led to de facto segregation; that is, African Americans and certain other racial minorities live in one area, and Whites live in another. This segregation has affected educational opportunities for racial minorities. Non-White areas have fewer financial resources; as a result, educational

| CASE | Rosa Parks's Act of Courage As a Spark |
| EXAMPLE 12.1 | for the Civil Rights Movement |

On December 1, 1955, Rosa Parks was waiting for a bus in Montgomery, Alabama. She was in a hurry because she had a lot of things to do. When the bus arrived, she got on without paying attention to the driver. She rode the bus often and was aware of Montgomery's segregated seating law that required African Americans to sit at the back of the bus.

Rosa Parks

In those days in the South, Black people were expected to board the front of the bus, pay their fare, and then get off and walk outside the bus to reboard at the side door near the back. But she noted that the rear was already crowded, with standing room only. Black passengers were even huddled on the back steps of the bus. It was apparent to Rosa that it would be all but impossible to reboard at the back. Besides, bus drivers sometimes drove off and left Black passengers behind, even after accepting their fares. Rosa Parks spontaneously decided to take her chances. She paid her fare in the front of the bus, walked down the aisle, and took a seat in the area reserved for Whites. At the second stop, a White man got on and had to stand.

The bus driver saw the White man standing and ordered Rosa Parks to move to the back. She refused, thinking, "I want to be treated like a human being." Two police officers were called, and they arrested her. She was taken to city hall, booked, fingerprinted, jailed and fined. Her arrest—and subsequent appeal all the way to the U.S. Supreme Court—served as a catalyst for a year-long boycott of the city's buses by Blacks, who composed 70% of all bus riders. The boycott inspired Martin Luther King, Jr., to become involved. It ended when the Supreme Court declared Montgomery's segregated seating laws unconstitutional. Rosa Parks's unplanned defiance of that law sparked the civil rights movement. This movement not only promoted social and economic justice for African Americans but also inspired other groups to organize to advocate for their civil rights. These groups include other racial and ethnic groups, women, the elderly, persons with a disability, and gays and lesbians.

Source: Marie Ragghianti, "I Wanted to Be Treated Like a Human Being," *Parade,* Jan. 19, 1992, pp. 8–9.

quality is often substantially lower than in White areas. In the past three decades, courts in a number of metropolitan areas have ordered that a certain proportion of non-Whites be bused to schools in White areas and that a certain proportion of Whites be bused to schools in non-White areas.

The objectives are twofold: to provide equal educational opportunities and to reduce racial prejudice through interaction. In some areas, school busing has become accepted and appears to be meeting the stated objectives. In other areas, however, the approach is highly controversial and has exacerbated racial tensions. Busing in these areas is claimed to (a) be very expensive; (b) destroy the concept of the "neighborhood school," whereby the facility serves as a recreational, social, and educational center of the community; and (c) result in lower-quality education. A number of parents in these areas feel so strongly about busing that they are sending their children to private schools. In addition, some have argued that busing increases "White flight" from neighborhoods where busing has been ordered. As a result, in some communities, busing programs that once carried Black students to White schools now simply move them from one Black neighborhood to a school system that predominately has Black students.[75]

Busing children a long distance is very costly and uses funds that could otherwise be spent to improve the quality of education. Busing reduces local control and interest in schools, and it makes it less practical for parents to become involved in school affairs because the school is less accessible.

Surveys indicate a majority of Americans (including a large number of African Americans) oppose busing for integration purposes.[76] The main reason for the growing opposition toward busing is that it often has not raised the educational achievements of students of color.[77] As a result, it is unlikely there will be a resurgence of political support for expanding efforts to promote busing for integration purposes.

School busing to achieve integration was vigorously pursued by the court system and the Justice Department in the 1970s. In 1981 the Reagan administration stated that it would be much less active in advocating busing as a vehicle to achieve integration. The Bush and Clinton administrations have also been fairly inactive in promoting school busing. In the past decade, there has been less emphasis in many communities on using busing to achieve integration. In 1991 the U.S. Supreme Court ruled that busing to achieve integration, when ordered, need not be continued indefinitely. The ruling allows communities to end court-ordered busing by convincing a judge they have done everything reasonable to eliminate discrimination against African Americans. School busing for integration purposes is discussed further in Chapter 10.

Affirmative Action Programs

Affirmative action programs provide preferential hiring and admission requirements (for example, admission to medical schools) for minority applicants. The programs apply to all minority groups, including women. They require employers to (a) make active efforts to locate and recruit qualified minority applicants and (b) in certain circumstances, have hard quotas under which specific numbers of minority members must be accepted to fill vacant positions (for example, a university with a high proportion of White male faculty members may be required to fill half of its faculty vacancies with women and members of other minority groups). Affirmative action programs require that employers demonstrate, according to a checklist of positive measures, that they are not guilty of discrimination.

A major dilemma with affirmative action programs is that preferential hiring and quota programs create reverse discrimination, in which qualified majority group members are sometimes arbitrarily excluded. There have been several successful lawsuits involving reverse discrimination. The best-known case to date has been that of Alan Bakke, who was initially denied admission to the medical school at the University of California, Davis, in 1973. He alleged reverse discrimination because he had higher grades and higher scores on the Medical College Admissions Test than several minority applicants who were admitted under the university's minorities quota policy. In 1978 his claim was upheld by the U.S. Supreme Court in a precedent-setting decision.[78] The Court ruled that strict racial quotas are unconstitutional, but it did not rule against the use of race as one among many criteria in making admissions decisions.

Charles Henderson et al. summarize some of the views of Whites and minority groups about affirmative action:

> The minority worker in white agencies often asks himself: "Why have I been hired?" . . . The worker may meet resistance from white colleagues if he or she is a product of "affirmative action," seen by some white people as simply "reverse discrimination." Whites may be quick to say that competence is what

counts. Blacks perceive this as saying that they are not competent. Considering the many ways in which whites have acquired jobs, blacks wonder why competence is now suggested as the only criterion for employment. For every white professional who may dislike affirmative action to compensate for past exclusions and injustices, there is a black professional who feels that it is tragic that organizations have had to be forced to hire minorities.[79]

Supporters of affirmative action programs note that the White majority expressed little concern about discrimination when its members were the beneficiaries instead of the victims. They also assert that there is no other way to make up rapidly for past discrimination against minorities, many of whom may presently score slightly lower on qualification tests simply because they did not have the opportunities and the quality of training that the majority group members have had.

Affirmative action programs raise delicate and complex questions about achieving equality through preferential hiring and admissions policies for minorities. Yet no other means has been found to end obvious discrimination in hiring and admissions.

Gaining admission to educational programs and securing well-paying jobs are crucial elements in the quest for integration. The history of immigrant groups that have "made it" (such as the Irish, the Japanese, and the Italians) suggests that equality will be achieved only when minority group members gain middle- and upper-class status and thus become an economic and political force to be reckoned with. The dominant groups then become pressured into modifying their norms, values, and stereotypes. For this reason, a number of authorities have noted that the elimination of economic discrimination is a prerequisite for achieving equality and harmonious race relations.[80] Achieving educational equality among races is also crucial because lower educational attainments lead to less prestigious jobs, lower incomes, lower living standards, and the perpetuation of racial inequalities from one generation to the next.

In the mid-1990s, the future of affirmative action became a hotly debated national issue. In the 1996 presidential campaign, several Republican presidential hopefuls urged that affirmative action programs be ended. A *Wall Street Journal/ NBC News* survey found that two of three Americans were opposed to affirmative action.[81]

The assault on affirmative action gathered strength from a slow-growth economy, stagnant middle-class incomes, and corporate downsizing, all of which make the question of who gets hired —or fired—more volatile. Minority candidates who receive positions that are perceived by other workers as the result of affirmative action are often viewed by the other workers with suspicion, which sometimes results in toxic tension in the workplace. Critics note that such tension has not brought us a color-blind society (which was the hope), but instead has brought us an extremely color-conscious society. As a result, critics assert that affirmative action is now a highly politicized and painful remedy that has stigmatized many of those it was meant to help. Affirmative action is now perceived by many in our society as a system of preferences for the unqualified. Critics further assert that affirmative action may have been necessary 30 years ago to ensure that minority candidates received fair treatment to counter the social barriers to hiring and admission that stemmed from centuries of unequal treatment. But today such programs are no longer needed. They maintain it is wrong to discriminate against White males for the sole reason of making up for the injustices that somebody's great-grandfather may have done to somebody else's great-grandfather. They believe it is wrong for the daughter of a wealthy African American couple to be given preference in employment over the son of a homeless alcoholic who happens to be White.

Supporters of affirmative action assert, "If we abandon affirmative action, we return to the old-boys' network." They believe affirmative action has helped a number of women and people of color to attain a good education and higher-paying positions, and thereby to remove themselves from the ranks of the poor. They maintain that, in a society where racist and sexist attitudes remain, it is necessary to have affirmative action to give women and people of color a fair opportunity at attaining a quality education and well-paying jobs.

In 1996 voters in the state of California passed Proposition 209, which explicitly rejects the idea that women and other minority group members receive special consideration when applying for jobs, government contracts, or university admission. This affirmative action ban became law in California in August 1997. In addition, a number of lawsuits have been filed objecting to reverse discrimination. If the courts rule in favor of those filing the lawsuits, the power of affirmative action programs will be sharply reduced. In November 1997, the U.S. Supreme Court rejected a challenge to the California law that ended racial and gender preferences in that state. This Supreme Court action clears the way for other states and cities to ban affirmative action.

Is there a middle ground for the future of affirmative action? Zuckerman recommends:

The vast majority of Americans would probably accept a return to the original notion of affirmative action—an aggressive outreach to minorities to make sure they have a fair shot. They would probably see a social benefit in accepting that racial justice might be relevant in a tie-breaker case, or might even confer a slight advantage. The goal must be a return to policies based on evenhandedness for individuals rather than for groups. Then employers can concentrate on whether a minority applicant is the right person for the job rather than being moved by whether the applicant looks litigious. All employees could take it for granted that they had a fair shot.[82]

Confrontation of Racist and Ethnic Remarks and Actions

Jokes and sarcastic remarks related to race help shape and perpetuate racist stereotypes and prejudices. It is important that both Whites and non-Whites tactfully but assertively indicate that they do not view such remarks as humorous or appropriate. It is also important that people tactfully and assertively point out the inappropriateness of racist actions by others. Such confrontations have a consciousness-raising effect, making explicit the belief that subtle racist remarks and ac-

tions are discriminatory and harmful. Gradually these confrontations will reduce racial prejudices and actions.

Noted author, lecturer, and abolitionist Frederick Douglass stated:

Power concedes nothing without a demand—it never did, and it never will. Find out just what people will submit to, and you've found out the exact amount of injustice and wrong which will be imposed upon them. This will continue until they resist, either with words, blows, or both. The limits of tyrants are prescribed by the endurance of those whom they oppress.[83]

Minority-Owned Businesses

Many people aspire to run their own business. Running one's own business is particularly attractive to many members of minority groups. It means an opportunity to increase one's income and wealth. It is also a way to avoid some of the racial and ethnic discrimination that occurs in the work world, such as the "glass ceiling" that blocks the promotion of qualified minority workers.

Since the 1970s, federal, state, and local governments have attempted to assist minority-owned businesses in a variety of ways. Programs have provided low-interest loans to minority-owned businesses. Set-aside programs stipulate that government contracts must be awarded to a minimum proportion, usually 10% to 30%, of minority-owned businesses. Some large urban areas have created enterprise zones that encourage employment and investment in blighted neighborhoods through the use of tax breaks. The number of minority-owned businesses has slowly been increasing; yet only a small fraction of the total number of people classified as a member of a minority group has benefited from government support of minority-owned businesses.[84]

Confrontation of the Problems in Inner Cities

It is difficult to find the right adjectives to describe the dismal living conditions in inner cities. The following apply: decaying, inhuman, dreadful, distasteful, shocking, and degrading. Inner cities are primarily inhabited by the poor, the elderly, and members of minority groups, particularly African Americans and Hispanics. Many inner cities have an ethnic concentration, such as African American, Mexican American, Cuban, or Puerto Rican.

Inner cities have high rates of crime, illiteracy, births out of marriage, single-parent households, mental illness, suicide, drug and alcohol abuse, unemployment, infant mortality, rape, aggravated assault, and delinquency. High proportions of the residents are on welfare. Many services are inferior in inner cities. Schools are inferior, streets are narrow and often filled with potholes. Police and fire protection services are inadequate to meet the needs of the neighborhoods.

The housing is crowded, decaying, and much of it is substandard. Heat in winter is often inadequate. Many units lack adequate plumbing. Broken windows, peeling paint, and doors hanging off their hinges are common sights. Minority group members inhabit much of this substandard housing because most cannot afford an alternative and because discrimination makes it difficult to relocate, even for those whose incomes would enable them to move.

One of the factors that is leading to the decline of inner cities is the sharp decline of blue-collar jobs in our society. Many blue-collar jobs are unskilled or semiskilled jobs that require less training and education than white-collar and service jobs. The employable in inner cities have in the past largely held blue-collar jobs. For a neighborhood to resist deterioration, a minimal economic base must be maintained. As blue-collar jobs decline and the quality of municipal services (such as transportation and public schools) deteriorates, faith in community restoration and revitalization fades.

Inner cities are a national disgrace. Our country is the richest and most powerful in the world, yet we have been unable to improve living conditions in our inner cities.

Our country has tried a variety of approaches to improve inner-city living conditions. Programs and services include work training, job placement, financial assistance through public welfare, low-interest mortgages to start businesses, Headstart,

drug and alcohol treatment, crime prevention, housing, rehabilitation, day-care services, health-care services, and public health services.

One of the most comprehensive undertakings to assist inner cities was the Model Cities Program, which was part of the War on Poverty in the 1960s. Several inner cities were targeted for this massive intervention. The program involved tearing down dilapidated housing and constructing comfortable living quarters. Salvagable buildings were renovated. In addition, these Model City projects had a variety of programs that provided job training and placement, health-care services, social services, and educational opportunities. The results were more than depressing. The communities have again become slums. Living conditions are as bleak, or bleaker, than at the start of the Model City interventions.[85]

To date, all programs that have been tried have had, at best, only short-term success. No other conclusion can be made. Inner cities continue to have abysmal living conditions. In the 1980s and 1990s, the federal government, at least for the time being, appears to have given up trying to improve living conditions, as federal programs for inner cities have either been eliminated or sharply cut back. Poverty and dependency on welfare are becoming a lifestyle in inner cities and are being passed from one generation to another.

In 1996 federal legislation was enacted that is dismantling the AFDC program. This legislation, known as the Personal Responsibility and Work Opportunity Reconciliation Act, will have a major impact (probably adverse) in inner cities. The entire concept of poor families being entitled to basic human and health services as a basic right is shifting back to the assumption that charity and a paid job can respond more cheaply to local social problems than public services can. The new legislation calls for the following: (a) Each state sets its own rules and amounts for financial assistance. The federal government will provide block grants to states to assist in financing the programs that are developed. (b) Recipients of financial benefits will receive no more than 2 years of assistance without working, and there will be a 5-year lifetime limit on benefits for adults. What will happen to poor parents who are unable to support their children after the time limit on financial benefits ends? Will these families become homeless, turn to crime, or have their children removed from the home by the state?

Our society, for better or worse, is a materialistic one. The two main legitimate ways to acquire material goods are through a good education and a high-paying job. But it appears to many inner-city residents that prospects are bleak for getting a good education (when only inferior schools exist in their areas) or a high-paying job (when they have few marketable job skills). As a result, many turn to illegitimate ways to get material goods (shoplifting, drug trafficking, robbery, and con games). Many have also turned to immediate gratifications (including sex and drug highs). Their value system includes being dependent on the government through welfare for a substandard lifestyle.

One approach that has been suggested to combat these problems is to use birth control technology to stabilize (and perhaps even slightly reduce) the population size of inner cities. Residents of large cities could be encouraged to have only one child. Sex education programs in schools could be expanded to teach responsible sexual behavior. Birth control information and services could be provided by the government at no cost to recipients. Increased taxes might be levied on those who had more than one or two children. Health clinics (which provide free birth control information and services) could be located in every inner-city high school. Mothers and their teenage daughters who are receiving welfare benefits might be given higher monthly grants for voluntarily using effective birth control methods. If effective contraceptives are developed for males, teenage male children who are receiving welfare benefits could also be given higher monthly grants for using effective contraceptives.

Such a proposal is designed to gradually reduce the number of children on welfare, to reduce the poverty that is passed from one generation to another, and to seek to strengthen inner-city families. With smaller families on welfare, the parents should be better able to provide higher quality care to the children they presently have.

There are a number of criticisms of this proposal. There is a strong value in our country that holds that every person has a right to be a natural parent to as many children as he or she desires. Some religions, such as the Roman Catholic Church, strongly object to birth control. Encouraging welfare recipients to use birth control is viewed by many as "non-White genocide" (a higher percentage of non-Whites receive welfare assistance, and a policy of encouraging welfare recipients to practice birth control would thereby have the greatest impact on the birthrates of non-Whites).

Our society has tried a variety of programs in the past to combat the problems faced by inner-city residents. All past programs have largely failed to improve our inner cities. At the present time, our federal government has a laissez-faire approach, and conditions are deteriorating in many of our inner cities. Will our country try an unpopular program such as using birth control technology to stabilize population size in inner cities? Or are there other workable alternatives? One alternative is the development and support of grassroots organizations.

Grass Roots Organizations

A promising alternative solution to inner-city problems is grassroots organizations, which can effect positive, long-lasting changes in a variety of settings, including inner cities. Grassroots organizations are community groups composed of residents who work together to improve their surroundings. (It may be that lasting changes can be made only in neighborhoods whose residents are inspired to improve their community.) Case Example 12.2 is a description of a successful grassroots effort.

ETHNIC-SENSITIVE SOCIAL WORK PRACTICE

Traditionally, professional social work practice has used the medical model for the delivery of services. This is a deficit model that focuses on identifying problems within a person. The medical model largely ignores environmental factors that

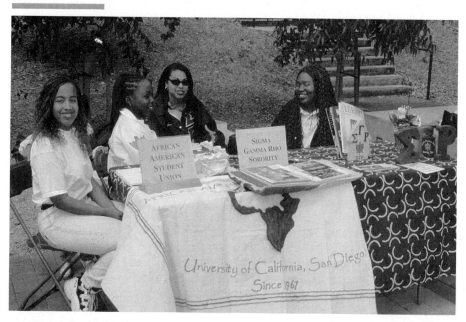

Ethnic-sensitive practice includes the concept of empowerment and the strengths perspective, which focus on the positive resources and abilities of individuals and groups. For example, organized efforts, such as student unions, fraternities, and sororities, can help consolidate a group's focus on academic success and achievement.

impact the person-in-situation. A major shortcoming of a deficit model is that it ignores strengths and resources. (When one emphasizes only the shortcomings of a person, that person's self-esteem is apt to be severely affected negatively, as that person is likely to define him- or herself in terms of the shortcomings and, in the process, overlook strengths and resources.)

Ethnic-sensitive practice seeks to incorporate understanding of diverse ethnic, cultural, and minority groups into the theories and principles that guide social work practice.[86] It is based on the view that practice must be attuned to the values and dispositions related to clients' ethnic group membership and social class position. Ethnic-sensitive practice requires that social workers have an in-depth understanding of the effects of oppression on racial and ethnic groups.

Another important conceptual framework is the "dual perspective."[87] This concept is derived from the view that all people are a part of two sys-

tems: (a) the dominant system (the society that one lives in), which is the source of power and economic resources, and (b) the nurturing system, composed of the physical and social environment of family and community. The dual perspective concept asserts that the adverse consequences of an oppressive society on the self-concept of a person of color can be partially offset by the nurturing system.

Ethnic-sensitive practice believes that social workers have a special obligation to be aware of and seek to redress the oppression experienced by ethnic groups. It assumes that each ethnic group and its members have a history with roots in the past that have a bearing on the members' perceptions of current problems. For example, the individual and collective history of many African Americans leads to the expectation that family resources will be available in times of trouble.[88]

Ethnic-sensitive practice, however, assumes the present is most important. For example, many

CASE EXAMPLE 12.2   Cochran Gardens: A Successful Grassroots Organization

Cochran Gardens was once a low-income housing project typical of many deteriorating housing projects in large urban areas. It was filled with rubbish, graffiti, and broken windows, and its residents were plagued by frequent shootings, crime, and drug trafficking.

Bertha Gilkey grew up in this housing project. Had it not been for her, this neighborhood might have continued to deteriorate. As a youngster, Gilkey believed the neighborhood could improve if residents worked together. As a teenager, she attended tenant meetings in a neighborhood church. When she was 20 years old, she was elected to chair this tenants' association. The neighborhood has since undergone gradual, yet dramatically positive, changes.

Gilkey and her group started with small projects. They asked tenants what realistically achievable things they really wanted. There was a consensus that the housing project needed a usable laundry room. The project's previous laundry rooms had all been vandalized, and the only working laundry room in the project had no locks. In fact, the entry door had been stolen. Bertha and her group requested and received a door from the city housing authority. The organization then held a successful fundraiser for a lock. Next the group held a fund-raiser for paint, and that too was a success. The organization then painted the laundry room. The residents were pleased to have an attractive, working facility, and its presence increased their interest in joining and supporting the tenants' association. The group then organized to paint the hallways, floor by floor, of the housing project. Everyone who lived on a floor was responsible for being involved in painting their hallway. Gilkey states:

Kids who lived on the floor that hadn't been painted would come and look at the painted hallways and then go back and hassle their parents. The elderly who couldn't paint prepared lunch, so they could feel like they were a part of it too.[a]

The organization continued to initiate and successfully complete new projects to spruce up the neighborhood. Each success inspired more and more residents to take pride in their neighborhood and to work toward making improvements. In the process, Gilkey and the tenants' organization also reintroduced a conduct code for the

[a] Quoted in Harry C. Boyte, "People Power Transforms a St. Louis Housing Project," *Occasional Papers* (Chicago: Community Renewable Society, Jan. 1989), p. 5.

Mexican American and Puerto Rican women currently feel tension as they attempt to move beyond traditionally defined gender roles into the mainstream as students and paid employees.[89]

Ethnic-sensitive practice introduces no new practice principles or approaches. Instead, it urges the adaptation of prevailing therapies, social work principles, and skills to take account of ethnic reality. Regardless of which practice approach is used, two concepts and perspectives that are emphasized are empowerment and the strengths perspective.

Empowerment

This concept has been defined as "the process of helping individuals, families, groups, and communities increase their personal, interpersonal, socioeconomic, and political strength and influence toward improving their circumstances."[90] In work-project. A committee formulated rules of behavior and elected monitors on each floor. The rules specified no loud disruptions, no throwing garbage out of the windows, and no fights. Slowly, residents got the message, and living conditions improved, one small step at a time.

The building was renamed Dr. Martin Luther King, Jr., Building. (Symbols are important in community development efforts.) The organization also held a party and a celebration for each successfully completed project.

Another focus of Gilkey's efforts was to reach out to children and adolescents. Positive behaviors were highlighted. The young people wrote papers in school on "what I like about living here." In art class, they built a cardboard model of the housing project that included the buildings, streets, and playground. These efforts were designed to build the self-esteem of the young people and to instill a sense of pride in their community.

Today Cochran Gardens is a public housing project with flower-lined paths, trees, and grass—a beautiful and clean neighborhood filled with trusting people who have a sense of pride in their community. The high-rise buildings have been completely renovated. There is a community center, and there are tennis courts, playgrounds, and townhouse apartments to reduce density in the complex. Cochran Gardens is managed by the tenants. The association (now named Tenant Management Council) has ventured into owning and operating certain businesses: a catering service, day-care centers, health clinics, and a vocational training program.

The Cochran Gardens success story has been based on the principles of self-help, empowerment, responsibility, and dignity. Gilkey states:

> *This goes against the grain, doesn't it? Poor people are to be managed. What we've done is cut through all the bullshit and said it doesn't take all that. People with degrees and credentials got us in this mess. All it takes is some basic skills. . . . If we can do it in public housing, it can happen anywhere.*[b]

Clearly, it makes sense for our federal, state, and city governments to seek to improve inner-city conditions by encouraging and supporting (including financially) grass-roots efforts.

[b] Ibid.

Source: Harry C. Boyte, "People Power Transforms a St. Louis Housing Project," *Occasional Papers* (Chicago: Community Renewable Society, Jan. 1989), pp. 1–5.

---

ing with an ethnic or racial group, empowerment counters the negative image or stereotypes of a group, which have been rendered through a long history of discrimination, with a positive value or image and an emphasis on the ability of each ethnic group member to influence the conditions of his or her life. Empowerment counters hopelessness and powerlessness with an emphasis on the ability of each person to address problems competently, beginning with a positive view of one-

self. Empowerment counters oppression and poverty by helping ethnic groups and their members to increase their ability to make and implement basic life decisions.

Strengths Perspective

The strengths perspective is closely related to empowerment. The strengths perspective seeks to identify, use, build, and reinforce the abilities and strengths that people have in contrast to the pathological perspective, which focuses on their deficiencies. It emphasizes people's abilities, interests, aspirations, resources, beliefs, and accomplishments.

For example, some strengths of African Americans in the United States include the more than 100 predominantly African American colleges and universities; fraternal and women's organizations; and social, political, and professional organizations. Many of the schools, businesses, churches, and organizations that are predominantly African American have developed social service programs such as family support services, mentoring programs, food and shelter services, transportation services, and educational and scholarship programs. Through individual and organized efforts, self-help approaches and mutual aid traditions continue among African Americans. African Americans tend to have strong ties to immediate extended family. They tend to have a strong religious orientation, a strong work and achievement orientation, and egalitarian role sharing.[91]

Social workers have an obligation to work vigorously toward ending racial and ethnic discrimination and advancing social justice. The social work professional needs to recognize the reality of practice in a culturally diverse environment. Social workers do have many of the prejudices and misperceptions of the general society, and the tendency to use one's own prejudices and stereotypes poses dangers for the well-meaning practitioner. For example, a social worker assigned to a Native American client might perceive the client's quietness as a sign that the client is being uncooperative or that the client is fully agreeing with the worker. It is possible that neither assumption is accurate. As a general rule, a Native American will not challenge or correct a worker who is off track because to do so would violate "noninterference." Noninterference is a basic value of Native American culture; it asserts that one should handle unwanted attempts at intervention with withdrawal—emotional, physical, or both.[92]

Another response pattern of White social workers that is counterproductive with Native Americans is the attempt to maintain direct eye contact.

Such face-to-face eye contact is considered rude and intimidating by many Native Americans.[93]

A bilingual practitioner working in a Chicano community may not understand all aspects of the language. For example, the special language of the barrio often contains words with a variety of connotations that differ from formal Spanish.[94] As a consequence, the worker who does speak Spanish must be acutely alert to the possibility that words may have very different meanings for clients living in a barrio.

In summary, a worker dealing with diverse cultural groups must (a) acquire a knowledge of self, including one's stereotypes, values, feelings, attitudes, and beliefs; (b) acquire a knowledge of the culture and the characteristics of the people with whom one is working; (c) acquire an understanding of the unique effects that standard counseling and intervention approaches will have on the client group; and (d) learn to challenge and change the stereotypic perceptions that one has of the client group.

It is a mistake for a social worker to conclude that working effectively with a different cultural group presents insurmountable barriers and obstacles. In actuality, the similarities between worker and clients almost always outweigh the dissimilarities.

The major professional social work organizations have in the past few decades taken strong positions to work toward ending racial discrimination and oppression. The National Association of Social Workers, for example, has lobbied for the passage of civil rights legislation. The NASW Code of Ethics (see the appendix) has an explicit statement that:

> Social workers should act to prevent and eliminate domination, exploitation, and discrimination against any person, group or class on the basis of race, ethnicity, national origin, color, age, religion, sex, sexual orientation, marital status, political belief, mental or physical disability, or any other preference, personal characteristic, or status.

The Council on Social Work Education (CSWE) requires in its accreditation standards for baccalaureate and master's programs that content on racism be included throughout the social work curriculum. Professional social work education is committed to preparing social work students to understand and appreciate cultural and social diversity. Students are taught to understand the dynamics and consequences of oppression, and they learn to use intervention strategies to combat social injustice, oppression, and their effects. CSWE also has an accreditation standard that prohibits racial discrimination and mandates affirmative action programs in social work educational programs. There is an Association of Black Social Workers, which has been very active in combating racial prejudice and discrimination.

THE FUTURE OF AMERICAN RACE AND ETHNIC RELATIONS

The 1980s and 1990s were a struggle for minorities as they tried to hold onto past gains in the face of reactions against minority rights. Vowing to take "big government" off the back of the American people and to strengthen the economy by giving businesses the incentive to grow and produce, the Reagan administration (1980–1988) largely removed the federal government from its traditional role as initiator and enforcer of programs to guarantee minority rights. The Bush administration (1988–1992) continued to follow a similar strategy. The federal government under the Reagan and Bush administrations asserted that private businesses were in the best position to correct the problems of poverty and discrimination. (Because businesses generally profit from paying low wages, most companies in the 1980s and early 1990s did not aggressively seek to improve the financial circumstances and living conditions of minorities.) Perhaps because of the federal government's shift in policies, minorities were less active in the 1980s and 1990s (as compared to the 1960s and 1970s) in using the strategy of activism. In the 1980s and 1990s, minority groups were expe-

riencing difficulties in maintaining the gains they had achieved two decades earlier in the job market through affirmative action and Equal Employment Opportunity programs. Bill Clinton, elected president in 1992, ran on a platform that promised a more active role by the federal government in promoting social and economic justice for all racial and ethnic groups in this country.

Bill Clinton's views on resolving social problems are consistent with a moderate (middle-of-the-road) to liberal orientation. His liberal proposals that would have benefited populations-at-risk included a health insurance program for all Americans and significantly expanded educational and training programs for individuals on welfare to help them become self-supporting.

The move toward liberalism in the early 1990s may, however, have been short-lived. In the congressional elections of 1994, the Republicans won majority control of both the Senate and the House of Representatives. (This was the first time in 40 years that Republicans held a majority in the House.) Most of these Republicans have a conservative political agenda that includes components such as shifting spending from crime prevention to prison construction, eliminating affirmative action programs, reducing spending for many social welfare programs, and reducing the amount of taxes paid by high-income individuals. Such proposals (if enacted into law) will probably widen the income gap between the rich and the poor and result in a severe reduction of services to populations-at-risk.

It is clear that minorities will assertively, and sometimes aggressively, pursue a variety of strategies to change racist attitudes and actions. Counteractions by certain segments of the White dominant society are also likely to occur. (Even in the social sciences, every action elicits a reaction.) For example, in recent years, there has been increased membership in organizations that advocate White supremacy (such as the Ku Klux Klan).

Minorities have been given the hope of achieving equal opportunity and justice, and it is clear that they will no longer submit to a subordinate status. Obviously we will see continued struggles to achieve racial equality.

What will be the pattern of race relations in the future? Milton Gordon has outlined three possible patterns of intergroup relations: Anglo-conformity, the melting pot, and cultural pluralism:

Anglo-conformity *assumes the desirability of maintaining modified English institutions, language, and culture as the dominant standard in American life. In practice, "assimilation" in America has always meant Anglo-conformity, and the groups that have been most readily assimilated have been those that are ethnically and culturally most similar to the Anglo-Saxon group.*

The melting pot *is, strictly speaking, a rather different concept, which views the future American society not as a modified England but rather as a totally new blend, both culturally and biologically, of all the various groups that inhabit the United States. In practice, the melting pot has been of only limited significance in the American experience.*

Cultural pluralism *implies a series of coexisting groups, each preserving its own tradition and culture, but each loyal to an overarching American nation. Although the cultural enclaves of some immigrant groups, such as the Germans, have declined in importance in the past, many other groups, such as the Italians, have retained a strong sense of ethnic identity and have resisted both Anglo-conformity and inclusion in the melting pot.*[95]

Members of some European ethnic groups (such as the British, French, and Germans) have assimilated the dominant culture of the United States and are now integrated. Other European ethnic groups (such as the Irish, Italians, Polish, and Hungarians) are now nearly fully assimilated and integrated.

Cultural pluralism appears to be the form that race and ethnic relations are presently taking. There has been a renewed interest on the part of a number of ethnic European Americans in expressing their pride in their own customs, religions, and linguistic and cultural traditions. We see slogans like, "Kiss Me. I'm Italian," "Irish Power," and "Polish and Proud." African Americans, Native Americans, Latinos, and Asian Americans are demanding entry into mainstream America—but

not assimilation. They want to coexist in a plural society while preserving their own traditions and cultures. This pride is indicated by slogans such as "Black Is Beautiful" and "Red Power." These groups are finding a source of identity and pride in their own cultural backgrounds and histories.

Some progress has been made toward ending discrimination since the *Brown* v. *Board of Education* Supreme Court decision in 1954. Yet equal opportunity for all people in the United States is still only a dream, as Martin Luther King, Jr., noted in his famous speech in 1963:

I say to you today, my friends, though, even though we face the difficulties of today and tomorrow, I still have a dream. It is a dream deeply rooted in the American dream. I have a dream that one day this nation will rise up, live out the true meaning of its creed: "We hold these truths to be self-evident, that all men are created equal."

I have a dream that one day on the red hills of Georgia sons of former slaves and the sons of former slave-owners will be able to sit down together at the table of brotherhood. I have a dream that one day even the state of Mississippi, a state sweltering with the heat of injustice, sweltering with the heat of oppression, will be transformed into an oasis of freedom and justice.

I have a dream that my four little children will one day live in a nation where they will not be judged by the color of their skin, but by the content of their character.

When we allow freedom to ring—when we let it ring from every city and every hamlet, from every state and every city, we will be able to speed up that day when all of God's children, black men and white men, Jews and Gentiles, Protestants and Catholics, will be able to join hands and sing in the words of the old Negro spiritual, "Free at last, Free at last, Great God Almighty, We are free at last."[96]

SUMMARY

Our country has always been racist and ethnocentric, but there has been progress in the past four decades in alleviating prejudice and discrimination. Yet we cannot relax. Discrimination continues to have tragic consequences for those who are its victims. Individuals who are targets of discrimination are excluded from certain types of employment, educational and recreational opportunities, certain residential housing areas, membership in certain religious and social organizations, certain political activities, access to some community services, and so on. Discrimination is also a serious obstacle to developing a positive self-concept and has heavy psychological and financial costs. Internationally, racism and ethnocentrism severely damage our credibility in promoting human rights.

Race is primarily a social concept rather than a biological concept. No "racial" group has any unique or distinctive genes. A social definition is based on the way in which members of a society classify one another by physical characteristics.

Prejudice is an attitude, whereas discrimination involves actions. Discrimination is often based on prejudice, although either may occur independently of the other. Oppression is the unjust or cruel exercise of authority or power.

Racial and ethnic discrimination is largely a social problem of Whites who tend to be the primary discriminators in power. (This does not mean, however, that only Whites must work to end discrimination; the effort must be an interracial one.)

Theories about the sources of discrimination and oppression involve projection, frustration-aggression, insecurity and inferiority, authoritarianism, historical explanations, competition and exploitation, socialization processes, and the belief that there is only one true religion. Institutionalized racism is pervasive in our society and involves discrimination that is built into our social institutions, such as the legal system, politics, employment practices, health care, and education.

There are numerous White and non-White groups in our nation, each with a unique culture, language, and history and with special needs. This uniqueness needs to be understood and appreciated if we are to progress toward racial and ethnic equality.

Strategies for advancing social and economic justice include mass media appeals, increased interaction among races, civil rights legislation, pro-

tests and activism, school busing, affirmative action programs, minority-owned businesses, confrontation of racist and ethnic remarks and actions, confrontation of the problems in inner cities, and grassroots organizations.

Three possible patterns of intergroup race and ethnic relations in the future are Anglo-conformity, the melting pot, and cultural pluralism. Cultural pluralism is the form that race and ethnic relations are presently taking and may well take in the future.

As a profession, social work has an obligation to work vigorously toward ending racial and ethnic discrimination and oppression and thereby advancing social and economic justice. Social workers have an obligation to implement the principles of ethnic-sensitive practice.

NOTES

1. Robert Barker, ed., *The Social Work Dictionary*, 3rd ed. (Washington, DC: NASW, 1995), p. 124.
2. Ibid., p. 125.
3. Ibid., p. 313.
4. Ibid., p. 291.
5. Ibid., p. 103.
6. Ibid.
7. Robert Merton, "Discrimination and the American Creed," in *Discrimination and National Welfare*, Robert M. MacIver, ed. (New York: Harper, 1949).
8. Marlene Cummings, "How to Handle Incidents of Racial Discrimination," in *The Personal Problem Solver*, Charles Zastrow and Dae H. Chang, eds. (Englewood Cliffs, NJ: Prentice Hall, 1977), p. 200.
9. Barker, *The Social Work Dictionary*, p. 265.
10. Ibid., p. 366.
11. Gunnar Myrdal, *An American Dilemma* (New York: Harper, 1962), p. 144.
12. Elmer H. Johnson, *Social Problems of Urban Man* (Homewood, IL: Dorsey Press, 1973), p. 344.
13. Barker, *The Social Work Dictionary*, p. 236.
14. Ashley Montague, *Man's Most Dangerous Myth: The Fallacy of Race*, 4th ed. (Cleveland: World, 1964).
15. Johnson, *Social Problems of Urban Man*, p. 350.
16. Richard T. Schaefer, *Racial and Ethnic Groups*, 5th ed. (New York: HarperCollins, 1993).
17. Paul Ehrlich and Richard Holm, "A Biological View of Race," in *The Concept of Race*, Ashley Montague, ed. (New York: Free Press, 1964), p. 82.
18. Montague, *Man's Most Dangerous Myth*.

19. R. J. Herrnstein and C. Murray, *The Bell Curve: The Reshaping of American Life by Differences in Intelligence* (New York: Free Press, 1994).

20. G. R. LeFrancois, *The Lifespan*, 5th ed. (Belmont, CA: Wadsworth, 1996).

21. Johnson, *Social Problems of Urban Man*, p. 50.

22. Barker, *The Social Work Dictionary*, p. 189.

23. Ibid., p. 185.

24. S. Carmichael and C. V. Hamilton, *Black Power: The Politics of Liberation in America* (New York: Vintage Books, 1967).

25. Barker, *The Social Work Dictionary*, p. 189.

26. William Kornblum and Joseph Julian, *Social Problems*, 8th ed. (Englewood Cliffs, NJ: Prentice Hall, 1995).

27. Jeanette Henry, *The Indian Historian*, 1 (Dec. 1967), p. 22.

28. Kornblum and Julian, *Social Problems*.

29. T. W. Adorno, E. Frenkel-Brunswik, D. J. Devinson, and R. N. Sanford, *The Authoritarian Personality* (New York: Harper & Row, 1950).

30. Charles F. Marden and Gladys Meyer, *Minorities in American Society* (New York: American Book, 1962).

31. Eugene Hartley, *Problems in Prejudice* (New York: King's Crown Press, 1946).

32. C. H. Cooley, *Human Nature and the Social Order* (New York: Scribner's, 1902).

33. J. W. Coleman and D. R. Cressey, *Social Problems*, 5th ed. (New York: HarperCollins, 1993).

34. E. Pinderhughes, "Afro-American Families and the Victim System," in *Ethnicity and Family Therapy*, M. McGoldrick, J. K. Pearce, and J. Giordana, eds. (New York: Guilford Press, 1982).

35. Albert Szymanski, "Racial Discrimination and White Gain," *American Sociological Review*, 41 (Jun. 1976), pp. 403–414.

36. Kornblum and Julian, *Social Problems*.

37. Richard T. Schaefer, *Racial and Ethnic Groups*, 6th ed. (New York: HarperCollins, 1996), p. 7.

38. Ibid.

39. Ibid.

40. Charles H. Henderson and Bok-Lim Kim, "Racism," in *Contemporary Social Work*, Donald Brieland, Lela Costin, and Charles Atherton, eds. (New York: McGraw-Hill, 1975), p. 180.

41. Excerpted from a speech by Abraham Lincoln in Charleston, IL, in 1858, as reported in Richard Hofstader, *The American Political Tradition* (New York: Knopf, 1948), p. 116.

42. Quoted in David Gelman, "Black and White in America," *Newsweek*, Mar. 7, 1988, p. 19.

43. Schaefer, *Racial and Ethnic Groups*, pp. 238–240.

44. Ibid., pp. 226–228.

45. Ibid.

46. Ibid., p. 235.

47. Ibid., pp. 235–236.

48. B. B. Solomon, "Social Work with Afro-Americans," in *Social Work: A Profession of Many Faces*, 3rd ed., A. Morales and B. W. Sheafor, eds. (Boston: Allyn & Bacon, 1983), p. 420.

49. J. L. Dillard, *Black English: Its History and Usage in the United States* (New York: Random House, 1972).

50. Schaefer, *Racial and Ethnic Groups*, pp. 252–254.

51. Ibid., pp. 278–298.

52. Ibid., p. 294.

53. Ibid.

54. Ibid., pp. 294–295.

55. Ibid., p. 304.

56. Ibid., p. 320.

57. Johnson, *Social Problems of Urban Man*, p. 349.

58. Dee Brown, *Bury My Heart at Wounded Knee* (New York: Holt, Rinehart & Winston, 1971).

59. Helen M. Crampton and Kenneth K. Keiser, *Social Welfare: Institution and Process* (New York: Random House, 1970), p. 104.

60. Schaefer, *Racial and Ethnic Groups*, pp. 161–162.

61. Communication with Mace J. Delosme, Arcata, CA.

62. Schaefer, *Racial and Ethnic Groups*, p. 185.

63. Ian Robertson, *Social Problems*, 2nd ed. (New York: Random House, 1980), p. 218.

64. Johnson, *Social Problems of Urban Man*, p. 349.

65. Schaefer, *Racial and Ethnic Groups*, pp. 385–391.

66. Charles Henderson, Bok-Lim Kim, and Ione D. Vargus, "Racism," in *Contemporary Social Work*, 2nd ed., Donald Brieland, Lela Costin, and Charles Atherton, eds. (New York: McGraw-Hill, 1980), p. 403.

67. Schaefer, *Racial and Ethnic Groups*, pp. 362–370.

68. Robert L. Barker, *The Social Work Dictionary*, 3rd ed. (Silver Spring, MD: NASW, 1995), p. 354.

69. George E. Simpson and J. Milton Yinger, *Racial and Cultural Minorities*, 3rd ed. (New York: Harper & Row, 1965), p. 510.

70. Thomas Sullivan, Kenrick Thompson, Richard Wright, George Gross, and Dale Spady, *Social Problems* (New York: Wiley, 1980), p. 437.

71. Johnson, *Social Problems of Urban Man*, pp. 374–379.

72. Cummings, "How to Handle Incidents," p. 197.

73. Sullivan et al., *Social Problems*, p. 438.

74. Ibid., p. 439.

75. Jerelyn Eddings, "Second Thoughts About Integration," *U.S. News & World Report*, Jul. 28, 1997, p. 32.

76. Ibid.

77. Ibid.

78. Allan P. Sindler, *Bakke, DeFunis and Minority Admissions: The Quest for Equal Opportunity* (New York: Longman, Green, 1978).

79. Henderson et al., "Racism," p. 403.

80. Kornblum and Julian, *Social Problems.*

81. S. V. Roberts, "Affirmative Action on the Edge," *U.S. News & World Report,* Feb. 13, 1995, pp. 32–39.

82. M. B. Zuckerman, "Fixing Affirmative Action," *U.S. News & World Report,* Mar. 20, 1995, p. 112.

83. Quoted in Cummings, "How to Handle Incidents," p. 201.

84. Schaefer, *Racial and Ethnic Groups.*

85. Ibid.

86. W. Devore and E. G. Schlesinger, *Ethnic-Sensitive Social Work Practice,* 4th ed. (Needham Heights, MA: Allyn & Bacon, 1996).

87. D. G. Norton, "Diversity, Early Socialization, and Temporal Development: The Dual Perspective Revisited," *Social Work,* 38, no. 1 (1993), pp. 82–90.

88. Devore and Schlesinger, *Ethnic-Sensitive Social Work Practice.*

89. Ibid.

90. Barker, *The Social Work Dictionary,* p. 120.

91. A. Billingsley, *Climbing Jacob's Ladder: The Enduring Legacy of African-American Families* (New York: Simon & Schuster, 1993).

92. Jimm G. Good Tracks, "Native American Noninterference," *Social Work,* 18 (Nov. 1973), pp. 30–34.

93. Ronald G. Lewis and Man Keung Ho, "Social Work with Native Americans," *Social Work,* 20 (Sept. 1975), pp. 378–382.

94. Dolores G. Norton, "Incorporating Content on Minority Groups into Social Work Practice Courses," in *The Dual Perspective* (New York: Council on Social Work Education, 1978).

95. Milton Gordon, "Assimilation in America: Theory and Reality," *Daedalus,* 90 (Spring 1961), pp. 363–365.

96. Jim Bishop, *The Days of Martin Luther King, Jr.* (New York: Putnam, 1971), pp. 327–328.

13

SEXISM
AND EFFORTS
FOR ACHIEVING
EQUALITY

Women who work full time are paid only about three-fourths as much as men who work full time.[1] Jobs held mainly by women (such as nurse or elementary school teacher) are paid at rates that average 20% less than those for equivalent jobs held mainly by men.[2] The average female college graduate is paid about the same as the average male high school graduate.[3] The average working White woman is paid less than the average working African American man, and the average working African American woman (subjected to double discrimination) earns least of all.[4] In families with a female householder and no spouse present, 37% live below the poverty line, compared to 12% of all families.[5] This chapter will:

- Present a history of sex roles, sexism, and sexual harassment.
- Describe traditional sex-role expectations.
- Examine whether there is a biological basis for sexism.
- Describe traditional sex-role socialization practices.
- Examine the consequences of sexism on males and females.
- Describe the sex-role revolution in our society.
- Present strategies for achieving sexual equality.
- Summarize social work's commitment to combating sexism.

HISTORY OF SEX ROLES AND SEXISM

In almost every known society, women have had lower status than men.[6] Women have been bound by more social restrictions and have consistently received less recognition for their work than have men. Women have been regarded differently than men, not only biologically but also emotionally, intellectually, and psychologically. Double standards have often existed for dating, for marriage, and for social and sexual conduct.

Most religions (including Judaism, Christianity, Hinduism, and Islam) in their traditional doctrines ascribe inferior status to women. This tradition continues in most countries, even though women attend religious services more often, hold firmer religious beliefs, pray more often, and are more active in church programs.[7] Many societies have concluded that it is divinely ordained that women should play a secondary and supportive role to men. In many Christian religions, women cannot become ministers or priests. Some orthodox Jewish men offer a daily prayer of thanks to God for not having made them a woman. In almost all houses of worship, God is referred to as "He."

Hunting and gathering societies provide insight into the processes that have resulted in women's lower status. Such societies usually lived in small bands consisting of several mating couples and their dependents. Men generally were the hunters, and women were the gatherers of nuts, plants, and other foods. There are several explanations for this role differentiation. Males were supposedly better suited to hunting because they were physically stronger and could run faster. The infant mortality rate was very high in these bands, so it was necessary for the women to be pregnant or nursing throughout most of their child-bearing years to maintain the size of the band. The need to tend to children largely prevented women from leaving the camp for days at a time to hunt large game. Even though women often gathered more food than men obtained through hunting, the male's hunting activities were viewed as more prestigious.

Women spent much of their adult lives pregnant, nursing infants, and raising children. Because they were forced to remain around the home, they were also assigned the "domestic tasks" of cooking, serving, and washing. Once these sex roles became part of tradition, the distinctions were perceived not only as practical but also as "natural."

Gradually more behavior patterns were added to these sex-role distinctions. Because men were trained at hunting, these skills led them to be recognized as the defenders of their band in case of attack from other groups. Child-rearing patterns

EXHIBIT 13.1

The Ideal Wife, According to Buddhism

Most traditional religions hold that women should have a submissive and supportive role to men. For example, Buddhism asserts that the ideal wife should be:

> . . . like a maid-servant. She serves her husband well and with fidelity. She respects him, obeys his commands, has no wishes of her own, no ill-feeling, no resentment, and always tries to make him happy.[a]

---

[a] *The Teaching of Buddha* (Tokyo: Kosaido, 1966), p. 448.

---

were developed to teach boys to value aggression and to be leaders. Girls, on the other hand, were taught to be passive and dependent and to provide emotional support to the males.

Before the Industrial Revolution, practically all societies had come to assign distinct roles to men and women. Females generally performed domestic and child-rearing activities, whereas males were involved in what were then considered the productive* (such as hunting and economic support) and protective functions for the family. Women in preindustrial societies also engaged in food production and economic support, such as making clothes, growing and harvesting garden crops, and helping on the farm. But their specific responsibilities were often viewed as inferior and requiring fewer skills.

The 19th-century Industrial Revolution brought about dramatic changes in sex roles. Men, instead of working on a small farm, left the home

to work in a factory or other setting to provide economic support. The economic role of women declined because they were no longer performing economically productive tasks. Women's roles became increasingly defined as child rearing and housework. But the amount of time required to perform these functions declined for several reasons. Families had fewer children. With compulsory education, older children went to school. Gradually, labor-saving devices reduced the need for women to perform time-consuming domestic tasks (baking bread, canning vegetables, and washing). As the traditional roles of women began to change, some females started to pursue activities (for example, outside employment) that had traditionally been reserved for men. With these changes, sex roles began to blur.

The struggle for women's rights in the United States has been going on for nearly two centuries. In the early 19th century, women who were working for the abolition of slavery complained that they, too, were denied such rights as voting. (An 1840 antislavery conference even refused to seat women, as the male delegates gave impassioned speeches about the moral imperative to end slavery.)

In 1848 two feminists, Susan B. Anthony and Elizabeth Stanton, organized the first women's rights caucus, which was held in the state of New York.[8] These early leaders demanded suffrage (the vote for women) and the reform of many laws that were openly discriminatory toward women. It took over 70 years, until 1920, to pass the 19th Amendment to the Constitution, which gave the vote to women. The suffrage movement was marked by jailings of feminist militants and fierce controversy. Many feminists equated winning the right to vote with achieving sexual equality. As a result, after 1920 the "women's movement" was nearly dormant for the next 40 years.

In the early 1900s, some modern birth control techniques became available. This advance gave women greater freedom from the traditional roles of child rearing and housework.

During World War II, large numbers of women were employed outside the home for the first time, to fill the jobs of men who had been drafted into

---

*The use of the term *productive* indicates the higher status that was assigned to the role of men. In actuality, the roles of women were as, or even more, "productive" in completing essential tasks.

EXHIBIT 13.2

Female Genital Mutilation: An Extreme Example of Sexism

Female circumcision, or more accurately, female genital mutilation (FGM), is commonplace in more than half of the African countries and in parts of the Middle East. The details of FGM vary somewhat from culture to culture and from region to region, but the basics are the same.

Shannon Brownlee and Jennifer Seter describe FGM as follows:

Sometime between infancy and adulthood, all or part of a girl's external genitalia is cut away with a knife or razor blade, usually with no anesthetic. In most cases, the clitoris and the labia minora are removed. In the most extreme form, known as infibulation, the external labia are also scraped and stitched together with thread or long thorns, leaving only a tiny opening for urine and menstrual blood. The opening must be widened on the woman's wedding night.

The pain lasts far longer than the operation. Many of the 85 million to 110 million women who have endured FGM suffer ill effects ranging from reduced or lost sexual sensation to infections, persistent pain, painful intercourse, infertility, and dangerous childbirth. The purpose is to diminish sexual appetite, in order to maintain a girl's virginity—and thus her marriageability.[a]

Anthropologists believe that the first clitoridectomies, like chastity belts, were a means for husbands to ensure that their children were truly their own; FGM reduces a woman's interest in sex and thus in extramarital affairs. Today young women in many African countries who have not undergone the procedure are shunned as oversexed, unmarriageable, and unclean. Currently FGMs are usually performed by select older women, who are held in high esteem in their societies.

Feminist organizations in the United States tend to view FGM as the gender oppression to end all oppressions. Yet most international human rights organizations have been slow to condemn the practice, arguing that it is inappropriate to interfere with other people's cultural practices.

[a] Shannon Brownlee and Jennifer Seter, "In the Name of Ritual," *U.S. News & World Report,* Feb. 7, 1994, pp. 56–58.

the military. At that time, over 38% of all women 16 years of age and over were employed outside the home, causing a further blurring of traditional sex roles.[9]

The 1960s saw a resurgence of interest in sex-role inequality for a variety of reasons. The civil rights movement had a consciousness-raising effect that made people more aware of and concerned about inequalities. This movement to curb racial discrimination through social action also served as a model, suggesting to a number of concerned women that sexual discrimination also could be alleviated through social action. More women attended college and thereby became more informed about inequalities. As females moved into new occupational positions, they became increasingly aware of discriminatory practices. Moreover, there was an explosion of research suggesting that sex-role differences were not innately determined but were in fact the result of socialization patterns that were discriminatory toward women.

One such study was conducted in 1955 by John Money, J. G. Hampson, and J. L. Hampson on hermaphrodites.[10] A hermaphrodite is a person who is born with both male and female sexual characteristics but is labeled either a male or a female at birth and then related to according to the gender on the birth certificate. These researchers did *not* find a significant correlation between physical characteristics and the hermaphrodites' own feelings about their sexual identities. These people were fulfilling the sex-role expectations of their labeled gender, although their observable anatomical characteristics often tended to place them in the other category. This research raised questions about the biological determination of sex roles.

Other studies have found dramatic differences in socialization patterns between males and females. Boys are given more sports equipment and task-oriented toys (like construction sets) to play with, whereas girls are given dolls and toys relating to marriage and parenthood.[11] During the first few months of life, girls receive more distal stimulation (like looking and talking) from their parents, whereas boys receive more proximal stimulation (like rocking and handling).[12] Fathers tend to play more aggressively with sons than with daughters.[13] But American sex-role socialization practices are not universal. In some Middle Eastern societies, males are reared to be more emotional and sensitive than females; females tend to be more impassive and practical.[14] In Sweden most heavy-machine operators are women.[15] In Russia most physicians are women.[16]

Betty Friedan, in her 1963 book *The Feminine Mystique*, provided the ideological base for the resurgence of the women's movement.[17] The term *feminine mystique* referred to the negative self-concept, lack of direction, and low sense of self-worth among women. The book served as a rallying point for women and led Friedan and others to form the National Organization for Women (NOW) in 1966. Today NOW is the largest women's rights group in the country and an influential political force. NOW and other women's groups have been working to end sexual discrimination, to achieve sexual equality, to end sexual double standards, and to improve the self-identity of women.

The Civil Rights Act of 1964, intended primarily to end racial discrimination, also prohibited discrimination on the basis of gender. However, a number of states have laws that discriminate against women and reinforce prejudices against them. For example, some states still have statutes that assign longer sentences to women than men for the same crimes on the assumption that female offenders require more rehabilitation.[18] (Conversely, many states treat women offenders more leniently than men on the assumption that women require the state's protection. For example, in many states, women must volunteer for jury duty or they will not be called.[19] Such laws and practices are forms of reverse discrimination.)

In 1972 the Equal Rights Amendment (ERA) received congressional approval but required ratification by three-fourths (38) of the states to become the 27th Amendment to the Constitution. The ERA stated: "Equality of rights under the law shall not be denied or abridged by the United States or any state on account of sex." Time ran out on the ERA in 1982 when, after 10 years of extensive political action, it narrowly failed to gain the support of enough states to be ratified.

Emotions ran high on both sides of the question of ERA ratification. Proponents asserted that it would be an important legal step toward true gender equality for women.[20] Opponents argued that passage of the ERA would mean that women could be drafted into the armed forces, would lose preferential treatment in divorce actions, and would become equally liable for alimony, child support, and spouse support. They asserted that labor laws giving preferential treatment to women would need to be revised, such as limits on the amount of weight women may lift on the job. Opponents also argued that "maternity leaves" would have to be made available to husbands who want to stay home with a newborn child.[21] A number of women concluded that the ERA would be more detrimental than beneficial to females, and they actively opposed its passage.

A variety of statutes have been passed to prevent sex discrimination. The federal Equal Pay Act of 1963 and a number of similar state laws require equal pay for equal work. As mentioned earlier, the Civil Rights Act of 1964 outlaws discrimination on the basis of race, color, sex, or religion. Executive Order 11246, as amended by Executive

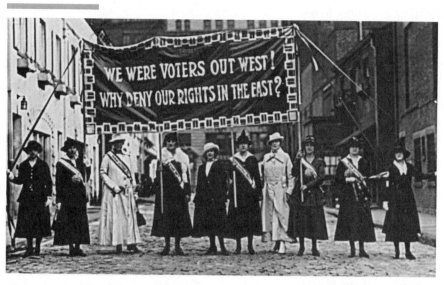

The primary goal of these suffragettes—equal voting rights in national and state elections—has been a reality for over 70 years. But in spite of affirmative action programs and other important gains of the 1970s and 1980s, full political and economic parity between men and women is yet to come.

Order 11375 on October 13, 1967, forbids sex discrimination by federal suppliers and contractors and provides procedures for enforcement. In addition, numerous court decisions have set precedents establishing the illegality of sex discrimination in hiring, promotions, and rates of pay.[22] Several landmark decisions have required employers to pay female employees millions of dollars in compensation for past wage discriminations.[23] In 1988, for example, the State Farm Insurance Company in California agreed (in a multimillion-dollar settlement) to pay damages and back wages to thousands of women who had been refused jobs as insurance agents over a 13-year period. The women had been told that a college degree was required for agents, even though men were hired without degrees.[24]

The Equal Credit Act of 1974 bars discrimination on the basis of marital status or gender in credit transactions. A number of states have passed laws prohibiting discrimination against pregnant women in hiring, training, and promo-

tion.[25] Despite these laws, acts, and precedents, however, substantial illegal sex discrimination still occurs, which women often have to fight on a case-by-case basis. For example, some high schools prohibit pregnant or married girls from attending classes, although unmarried fathers and married boys are allowed to attend.

Affirmative action programs apply to women as well as to certain racial minorities. Women are considered a minority group because for generations they have been subjected to discrimination and have been denied equal opportunities.

The following employers are required to have affirmative action programs: government contractors and suppliers, recipients of government funds, and businesses engaged in interstate commerce. Affirmative action applies primarily to job vacancies. Employers must demonstrate active efforts to locate and recruit minority applicants (defined to include women), must demonstrate positive efforts to increase the pool of qualified applicants (for example, special training programs for minorities), must give hiring preference to minority applicants, and in some cases must set hard quotas that specify numbers of minority members that must be accepted to fill vacant positions. The clout of affirmative action programs is in the threat of loss of government funds if employers do not have such programs effectively in place. (As noted in Chapter 12, the recent active backlash against affirmative action programs could curtail their effectiveness.)

SEXUAL HARASSMENT

Sexual harassment entails repeated and unwanted sexual advances. It has recently become recognized as a form of sex discrimination. Most of the victims are women; men rarely are the objects of unwanted sexual advances.

Paul Horton et al. identify some of the victims of sexual harassment:

> *Sexual harassment is an ancient practice. Attractive female slaves were routinely bought as sex playthings, and domestic servants were often exploited. If the Victorian housemaid denied her bed to a lecherous master, he dismissed her; if she admitted him, she soon became pregnant and disgraced, and his wife dismissed her. Either way, she lost!*
>
> *Sexual harassment can be found anywhere, but is likely to be a problem only where men have supervisory or gatekeeper power over women. The "casting couch" is a well-known feature of show business, and women in many occupations can escape unwelcome attentions only by quitting their jobs, often at a sacrifice. Sexual harassment on the campus has also surfaced, with many female graduate students claiming that senior professors claimed sexual privileges as the price for grades, degrees, and recommendations.*[26]

The definition of what is and what is not sexual harassment is somewhat vague. Repeated, unwanted touching is certainly harassment. A 1986 U.S. Supreme Court decision broadened the definition. Today a hostile work environment in which a woman feels hassled or degraded because of constant unwelcome flirtation, lewd comments, or obscene joking *may* be sufficient grounds for a lawsuit.[27] A number of colleges and universities in recent years have defined sexual harassment to include consenting sexual relationships between faculty and adult students. The rationale is that students are in a lower power position and may suffer adverse consequences if they refuse.

Sexual harassment (see Exhibit 13.3) is distinct from flirtation, flattery, a request for a date, and other acceptable behavior occurring in the workplace or the classroom. It is also distinct from other forms of harassment that do not involve conduct of a sexual nature. Sexual harassment is a type of sexual coercion that relies on the power of the perpetrator to affect the victim's economic or academic status and does not necessarily involve physical force. According to U.S. law, sexual harassment is a form of sexual discrimination in employment and education that is prohibited by Title VII of the Civil Rights Act of 1964. Sexual harassment is defined as:

> *Unwelcome sexual advances, requests for sexual favors, and other verbal or physical conduct of a sexual nature constitute sexual harassment when 1.) submission to such conduct is made either explicitly or implicitly a term or condition of an individual's employment; 2.) submission to or rejection of such conduct by an individual is used as a basis for employment decisions affecting such an individual; or 3.) such conduct has the purpose or effect of unreasonably interfering with an individual's work performance or creating an intimidating, hostile, or offensive working environment.*[28]

Sexual harassment almost always involves elements of unequal power and coercion. Although most victims are women, sexual harassment can be directed at either males or females. Repeated incidents of sexual harassment generally result in a hostile, intimidating, or anxiety-producing work or educational environment.

Those found guilty of sexual harassment are subject to reprimand, dismissal, demotion, and other consequences at their place of employment.

EXHIBIT 13.3

Types of Sexual Harassment

Sexual harassment falls into three categories: verbal, nonverbal, and physical. The following examples may represent sexual harassment if the behavior is clearly unwelcomed and not reciprocated.

VERBAL

- Sexual innuendo ("So you're majoring in packaging? I love your packaging.")
- Suggestive comments ("Those jeans really fit you well.")
- Sexual remarks about a person's clothing, body, or sexual activities ("I noticed you lost weight. I'm glad you didn't lose your gorgeous chest, too.")
- Sexist insults or jokes or remarks that are stereotypical or derogatory to members of the opposite sex ("Women should be kept barefoot, pregnant, and at the edge of town.")
- Implied or verbal threats concerning one's grades or job ("It's simple. If you want to pass this course, you have to be nice to me, and sex is the nicest thing I can think of.")
- Sexual propositions, invitations, or other pressures for sex ("My office hours are too limited. Why don't you drop by my house tonight? We'll have more privacy and time to get to know each other.")
- Use of employment position to request dates or sexual favors.

NONVERBAL

- Visual sexual displays; unwanted display of pornographic pictures, posters, cartoons, or other materials
- Body language (such as leering at one's body or standing too close)
- Whistling suggestively
- Mooning or flashing
- Obscene gestures
- Actions that involve gender-directed favoritism or disparate treatment

PHYSICAL

- Patting, pinching, and any other inappropriate touching or feeling
- Bra-snapping
- Brushing against the body
- Grabbing or groping
- Attempted or actual kissing or fondling
- Coerced sexual intercourse
- Attempted or actual sexual assault

Unfortunately, even a successful protest sometimes further victimizes the victim. She must endure the unpleasantness of pursuing the complaint, and she may be viewed by some as having invited the advances. Some women who protest eventually are forced to seek a new job because of the discomfort they feel in the old workplace.

In recent years, corporate America has received several wake-up calls on sexual harassment. For example, in 1994 a San Francisco jury awarded a legal secretary $7.1 million in punitive damages after finding that her former employer failed to stop an attorney in the firm from harassing her.

In 1998 Astra AB in Boston agreed to pay nearly $10 million to over 70 women to settle claims that its president and other executives replaced older female employees with beautiful, young single women who were then pressured into having sex. Also in 1998 Mitsubishi Motors agreed to pay a record $34 million to 350 women to settle allegations that women on the assembly line at its Illinois factory were groped and insulted and that managers did nothing to stop it.

In June 1998, the U.S. Supreme Court ruled than an employer could be held liable when a supervisor sexually harasses a worker, even if the employee's job is not harmed. (However, if a company has a strong program in place to prevent and discipline harassment, that company has, according to the Supreme Court, some measure of protection from sexual harassment lawsuits.)

TRADITIONAL SEX-ROLE EXPECTATIONS

Sex roles are learned patterns of behavior that are expected of the sexes in a given society. Sex-role expectations, which define how men and women are to behave and how they are to be treated by others, are based largely on stereotypes. *Stereotyping* involves attributing of fixed and usually inaccurate and unfavorable qualities to a category of people. Stereotyping makes it easier for discrimination (unequal treatment) to occur.

American women traditionally are expected to be affectionate, passive, conforming, sensitive, intuitive, and dependent—"sugar and spice and everything nice." They are supposed to be concerned primarily with domestic life, to be nurturing, to love to care for babies and young children, to fuss over their personal appearance, and to be self-sacrificing for their family. They should not appear ambitious, aggressive, competitive, or more intelligent than men. They should be ignorant about and uninterested in sports, economics, and politics. Also, they are not supposed to initiate relationships with men but are expected to

EXHIBIT 13.4

Traditional Stereotypes of a Businessman and a Businesswoman

- He's aggressive; she's pushy.
- He's good at details; she's picky.
- He loses his temper because he's so involved in his job; she's bitchy.
- When he's depressed (or hung over), everyone tiptoes past his office; she's moody so it must be her "time of the month."
- He follows through; she doesn't know when to quit.
- He's confident; she's conceited.
- He stands firm; she's hard.
- He has judgments; she's prejudiced.
- He's a man of the world; she's "been around."
- He drinks because of excessive job pressure; she's a lush.
- He isn't afraid to say what he thinks; she's mouthy.
- He exercises authority diligently; she's power mad.
- He's close-mouthed; she's secretive.
- He's a stern taskmaster; she's hard to work for.
- He climbed the ladder to success; she slept her way to the top.

Source: Author unknown.

be tender, feminine, emotional, and appreciative when in these relationships.

There are also a number of traditional sex-role expectations for males in our society: A male is expected to be tough, fearless, logical, self-reliant, independent, and aggressive. He should have definite opinions on the major issues of the day and make authoritative decisions at work and at home. He is expected to be strong—a sturdy oak—and never to be depressed, vulnerable, or anxious. He is not supposed to be a "sissy"—to cry or openly display emotions that suggest vulnerability. He is expected to be the provider, the breadwinner. He should be competent in all situations, physically strong, athletic, confident, daring, brave, and forceful. He should be in a position to dominate any situation—to be a "Rambo" or a "Clint Eastwood."[29] He is supposed to initiate relationships with women and be dominant in these relationships. Men who are supported by their wives, or who earn less than their wives, are likely to experience feelings of shame and inadequacy.

Even very young boys are expected to be masculine. Parents and relatives are far more concerned when a boy is a "sissy" than when a girl is a "tomboy." A tomboy is expected to outgrow her "masculine" tendencies, but it is feared that a sissy will never fare well in our competitive society and may even become homosexual. (The right of a boy to wear his hair long had to be won in many court battles in this country, whereas hardly anyone is concerned when a girl wears her hair short.)

IS THERE A BIOLOGICAL BASIS FOR SEXISM?

Let's examine the sexist ideology that assumes the differences between men and women are the result of biology—that anatomy equips men to play an active and dominant role in the world and women to play a passive and secondary role.

There are certain biological differences between men and women. Of course, there are the obvious anatomical, sexual, and reproductive differences. There are also hormonal differences. Each sex has both male and female hormones, but women have higher levels of female hormones and males have higher levels of male hormones. Research on some animal species (which may or may not be applicable to humans) has shown

that, if male hormones are injected into females, the females have a heightened sex drive and become more aggressive.[30] Scientists, however, see this hormonal difference as playing only a minor role in humans. This is because human behavior patterns are almost entirely learned, whereas behavior patterns in lower animals are more influenced by hormonal factors.[31]

Men, on the average, are taller and heavier than women and have greater physical strength. Women can tolerate pain better and have greater physical endurance (except in short-term feats of strength).[32] In most respects, women are physically healthier.[33] Females are less susceptible to most diseases and on the average live longer. Males have higher rates of fetal and infant mortality. Male fetuses can inherit a greater number of sex-linked weaknesses: Over 30 disorders have been found exclusively among males, including hemophilia, certain types of color blindness, and webbing of the toes.

Soon after birth, female babies tend be more content and less physically active.[34] As children develop, other differences appear, but it has not yet been determined whether the identified differences are due to inherited or learned factors. Girls learn to talk and read at an earlier age; they also become more docile and dependent and seem more intellectually mature (most remedial education classes have a large majority of boys). Boys are superior in elementary school on tasks requiring spatial, mechanical, and analytic ability, whereas girls are superior at tasks involving verbal capacities and numerical computation.[35] The basis for these differences is uncertain. Girls, for example, may be better at reading and language because they are encouraged to spend more time with adults and to read rather than to engage in competitive sports or similar activities.

There is considerable research supporting the position that sex-role differences are due primarily to socialization patterns. John Money and his associates examined cases in which parents wanted a girl so badly that they raised a male to be a girl, or vice versa.[36] The study found that children will play the role that they are socialized to learn

Are sex roles determined by biology? Or are human behavior patterns almost entirely learned and therefore flexible?

rather than the gender role outlined by traditional sex-role expectations. Money concluded that children are "psychosexually neuter at birth" and that sex role is independent of physiological sex.

The fact that there are wide variations in sex-role expectations among cultures also suggests that sex roles are learned rather than biologically determined. (If all cultures defined sex-role expectations similarly, this would suggest a biological basis for sex-role distinctions.) Let's consider a few examples. Most cultures expect women to do most of the carrying of heavy objects, whereas in this country and in most European countries men are expected to do most of the lifting and carrying of heavy objects. In some societies, unlike ours, the men do most of the cooking. Not so long ago in Europe, it was the males who wore stockings, perfume, and silks. Men in Scotland still wear kilts (skirts). Among the Maoris and the Trobrianders, it is the women who are expected to take the initiative in sexual activity.[37]

Margaret Mead, in a classic study, examined sex-role expectations in three tribes in New Guinea. She found that one tribe required both males and females to behave in a way we would define as "masculine"; a second required both to behave in a "feminine" fashion; and the third had the females act "masculine" and the males act "feminine." Mead concluded that sex-role expectations are determined primarily by cultural learning experiences (see Exhibit 13.5).

SEX-ROLE SOCIALIZATION

In the United States, sex-role socialization starts shortly after birth. Baby girls are dressed in pink, and baby boys are dressed in blue. Babies are given sex-related toys. Boys are bounced on the knee and handled roughly, whereas girls are cooed over. A child becomes aware that he is a "boy" or

EXHIBIT 13.5

Sex-Role Expectations Are Culturally Determined

In her classic study *Sex and Temperament in Three Primitive Societies,* Margaret Mead refuted the notion that sex-role expectations are biologically determined. The study was conducted among three tribes in New Guinea in the early 1930s. Mead demonstrated that many characteristics Americans classify as typically female or male are defined differently in these tribes.

Both sexes among the Arapesh would seem feminine to us. Both men and women are gentle, nurturant, and compliant. The personalities of males and females in this society are not sharply differentiated. Both girls and boys learn to be unaggressive, cooperative, and responsive to the needs and wants of others. Relations between husband and wife parallel the traditional mother–child relations in our society, with the Arapesh husband often seeing his role as providing training to his much younger wife.

In contrast, among the Mundugamor, both sexes would seem masculine to us. Both are headhunters and cannibals, are nonnurturant and aggressive, and actively initiate sexual involvement.

The most interesting society studied was the Tchambuli, which virtually reverses our traditional sex-role expectations and stereotypes. The men spend much more time than the women in grooming and decorating themselves and in painting, carving, and practicing dance steps. In contrast, the women are efficient, impersonal, unadorned, managerial, and brisk. They are the traders and have most of the economic power.

Mead concludes:

We no longer have any basis for regarding such aspects of behavior as sex linked. . . . Standardized personality differences between the sexes are . . . cultural creations to which each generation, male or female, is trained to conform.

Source: Margaret Mead, *Sex and Temperament in Three Primitive Societies* (New York: Morrow, 1935).

she is a "girl" long before noticing anatomical differences between the sexes.[38] Lawrence Kohlberg notes that children make basic decisions (based on what others tell them) that they are boys or girls and then select those activities that significant others (people that they view as important to them) define as conforming to this self-concept.[39]

Many parents go to great lengths to socialize their young children according to sex-role expectations. Little boys are given toy trucks to play with, and girls are given dolls. Boys are encouraged to play ball; girls are urged to play house. Ruth Hartley notes:

Girls gain approval . . . by doing the rather undemanding things that are expected of them. . . . A girl need not be bright as long as she is docile

and attractive. . . . This kind of treatment is likely to produce rather timid, unventuresome, unoriginal, conformist types.[40]

Young girls in many families are still raised by their parents to be mothers and homemakers and/or are encouraged to seek low-status, low-paid employment. The early socialization of boys, according to Hartley, is quite different:

Almost from birth the boy has more problems to solve autonomously. In addition, he is required to limit his interest at a very early age to sex-appropriate objects and activities, while girls are permitted to amble their way to a similar status at a more gradual and natural pace. . . . He is challenged to discover what he should do by being told what he should not do, as in the most frequently employed negative sanction, "Don't be a sissy!" . . . Interest in girlish things is generally forbidden and anxiety-provoking in American boyhood. . . . The boy is constantly open to a challenge to prove his masculinity. He must perform, adequately and publicly, a variety of physical feats that will have very little utility in most cases in adulthood. He is constantly under pressure to demonstrate mastery over the environment, and, concomitantly, to suppress expression of emotion.[41]

Boys are encouraged to play more competitive games than girls and to be outgoing and aggressive, whereas young girls are encouraged to be passive and reserved.[42] Young children are impressionable. Such sex-role stereotyping often becomes a self-fulfilling prophecy. According to Charles Cooley's "looking glass self-concept," people will come to view themselves as others relate to them.[43]

Research shows that some females are actually taught to fear success and achievement and to "play dumb" in order to "boost the male ego."[44] To be feminine, girls must display softness, helplessness, tenderness, understanding, and be generally nonassertive. Thus, adolescent and adult females are put in a double bind due to *femininity/ achievement incompatibility*.[45] There is a traditional view in our society that a woman cannot be both feminine and achievement oriented. (Of course, this traditional view is an arbitrary one that has been a factor in leading women to play a submissive role; there is nothing intrinsically incompatible about femininity and achievement.)

A significant part of the socialization process occurs in school. Girls are often channeled into sewing, typing, and cooking classes, whereas boys are channeled into such classes as woodworking, printing, and mechanics. Although 83% of grade-school teachers are female, close to 90% of the principals are male.[46] Thus, children see men in superior decision-making positions and women in subordinate positions.

A review of over 100 studies by the American Association of University Women found that:

■ Although girls and boys start school with similar levels of skill and confidence, by the end of high school girls trail boys in science and math test scores.

■ Teachers pay less attention to girls than to boys.

■ Reports of sexual harassment of girls are increasing.

■ Textbooks still ignore or stereotype women and girls and omit discussions of pressing problems such as sexual abuse.

■ Some tests are biased against females and thereby limit their chances of obtaining scholarships.

■ African American girls are particularly likely to be ignored or rebuffed in schools.[47]

Since boys are given more encouragement to be independent and assertive, they are more likely to act up and get into trouble.[48] Perhaps for this reason, studies of teacher–student interaction have found that boys get more attention from teachers than do girls.[49] Myra Sadker and associates put it this way, "Boys are the central figures . . . and girls are relegated to second-class participation."[50] Partly because of such socialization practices in school systems, males are much more apt when they enter college to major in fields such as science, mathematics, and engineering, which are most likely to lead directly to high-paying careers.

Textbooks in preschool, elementary, junior high, and high school portray female characters as more passive and dependent and less creative than males.[51]

Guidance counselors generally advise students to pursue careers not just on the basis of their abilities, but also on the basis of traditional sex-role expectations. For example, a young girl who excels at math may be encouraged to be a teacher, whereas a young boy with equal skills may be urged to consider engineering. Janet Chafetz comments on such counseling practices:

Counselors defend such practices on the basis of what youngsters may "realistically" expect to face in the future: marriage, child care, and a lack of opportunity in a number of career fields for females, and the need to support a family at the highest income and status levels possible for males. "Realism," however, has always been an excuse for maintaining the status quo, and it is no different in the case of sex role stereotypes. If, for instance, females do not prepare to enter previously masculine fields, such fields will remain male-dominated, allowing another generation of counselors to assure girls that females can't work in them. In addition, it is questionable whether counselors' notions of "reality" in fact keep pace with reality. There is undoubtedly a lag between expanding opportunities and changing sex role definitions on the one hand, and counselors' awareness of these phenomena on the other.[52]

Even contemporary theories in psychology describe women as more passive and emotional, lacking in abstract interests, and as having an instinctive tenderness for babies.[53] Although masculinity and femininity are largely learned roles, contemporary psychological theories subtly imply (erroneously) that sex-role differences are genetically determined. Sigmund Freud's theory of the development of the female personality is probably the most sexist and outrageous. According to Freud, young girls discover that their genitals differ from boys', which leads them to have "penis envy." Because of this difference, girls conclude that they are biologically inferior to males and then develop a passive, submissive personality as a way to adjust to interactions with males, whom they view as superior.[54]

There are many sexist implications built into the English language. The words we select greatly influence our interpretation of reality. The use of sexist language has been a significant factor in defining and maintaining the position of males as dominant in our society, with females assigned a supportive or submissive role. The following words and phrases portray males as dominant: *mankind, manned, manpower, chairman, congressman, businessman, mailman, salesman, foreman, policeman, the best man for the job,* and *man*

and wife. There are other examples of how sexism has infiltrated the English language. Books in the past tended (there has been considerable improvement in recent years) to use the pronoun "he" to refer in a generic sense to a person when the gender is unspecified. On reaching adulthood, a man becomes "Mr." for the remainder of his life; this is a polite term that makes no reference to the status of a man's personal life. On the other hand, a woman starts as a "Miss" and then becomes a "Mrs." upon marriage, which clearly identifies her marital status. (The modern-day use of "Ms." is a desired nonsexist alternative term.) In addition, traditional customs assume a woman will, upon her marriage, use her husband's last name (instead of her maiden name).

The mass media, particularly in advertising, also play an important role in sex-role socialization. Women are frequently portrayed in commercials as being wives, mothers, or sex objects or as obsessed with getting a date. They used to be portrayed as invariably less intelligent and more dependent than men and were hardly ever shown in executive positions. Some TV ads still depict women in traditional sex-role stereotypes such as delighting in waxing their floors or in discovering a new detergent to get their families' white clothes whiter. Fortunately, changes are occurring in the mass media's portrayal of women, reflecting changes in our society. Many commercials are now even reversing traditional roles. Because the mass media are important socialization vehicles, they can assist in changing attitudes about "proper" sex roles in the future.

CONSEQUENCES OF SEXISM

Sexism is prejudice or discrimination against women. Although females represent a numerical majority in our society, they are considered a minority group because they are victims of discrimination on many fronts and have unequal access to valued resources.

EXHIBIT 13.6

Consequences of Sexist Traditions: Rape and Murder of Wives in India

Fifteen-year-old Baskar was married in July 1997 to a stranger selected by her conservative Muslim family. As is traditional in India, Baskar's family sent a dowry (consisting of a refrigerator, furniture, and other household goods) to the family of the groom. However, the family could not afford one item that the groom had demanded—a motorcycle. On her wedding night, her drunken husband and three of his male friends took turns beating her and raping her, forcing her to crouch on all fours (simulating a motorcycle) as they victimized her.

A few years earlier, a young bride was burned to death because her in-laws were unhappy over her dowry. More than 5000 women are killed every year in India because their in-laws consider the dowries they receive inadequate. Only a small percentage of the rapists and killers over dowry disputes are ever punished, due to tradition. Reena Bannerjee, a women's rights activist who works with dowry disputes and rape victims, commented, "The position of women is so low that men consider them lower than the shoes they wear."

Source: Hema Shukla, "Women Seek Justice in a Land Where Their Voices Are Stifled," *Wisconsin State Journal,* Aug. 2, 1997, p. 10A.

Effects on Occupation and Income

Women tend to be concentrated in the lower-paying, lower-status positions: secretaries, child-care workers, receptionists, typists, nurses, hairdressers, bank tellers, cashiers, and file clerks. Men tend to be concentrated in higher-paying positions: lawyers, judges, engineers, college teachers, physicians, and dentists (see Table 13.1).

As noted earlier, full-time working women are paid about three-fourths of what full-time working men are paid.[55] Even though sex discrimination laws have been passed, job discrimination continues to be found in a number of studies.[56]

Women hold fewer than 10% of the nation's elective offices.[57] There has never been a woman president or vice president in the United States. The vast majority of senators and representatives in Congress are men. It is a rarity when a woman is elected governor in a state. Men still control the political processes to nominate candidates and to campaign for their election. The potential political clout of women, however, is immense because they constitute a majority of the nation's voters.[58]

Women hold only 2% of the top management positions in American corporations and just 6% of the seats on corporate boards of directors.[59] Even successful female executives often complain about an invisible "glass ceiling" that seems to lock them out of the key positions of power. One study, based on interviews with 100 male and female executives from three major U.S. corporations, concluded that there was a clear double standard in promotions and that women had to perform significantly better than their male counterparts to get ahead.[60]

About two-thirds of the women who work outside the home in the United States are employed in the "women's ghetto" positions of housekeepers, secretaries, receptionists, telephone operators, clerks, and so on.[61] And overall, women earn less income than men in practically every job category.[62] Even in the armed forces, where pay levels are standardized, it is less likely that women will receive additional flight pay, combat pay, or hazardous duty pay.[63] It is true that differences in income between men and women by job category are due partly to seniority (men earn more because they've held their jobs longer), but studies taking seniority into account have found that women tend to receive less pay for doing the same job.[64]

There are probably many reasons for these occupational and income differences between men and women. Female children are socialized to seek lower-paying occupations and careers. For example, boys are encouraged to be lawyers and

TABLE 13.1

Employment Positions Held by Women

Position	Percentage Held by Women
Dental assistants	99.1
Secretaries	98.6
Child-care workers	97.1
Receptionists	96.9
Typists	94.8
Cleaners, servants	93.6
Registered nurses	93.3
Teachers' aides	92.1
Hairdressers, cosmetologists	91.1
Bookkeepers	91.1
Telephone operators	90.5
Bank tellers	90.1
Elementary school teachers	83.3
Librarians	82.7
Maids, housemen	81.8
General office clerks	80.8
Cashiers	78.1
Waiters, waitresses	77.9
File clerks	77.6
Social workers	68.5
Psychologists	61.4
Food service workers	56.6
Authors	54.1
Financial managers	54.0
College teachers	43.5
Natural scientists	29.3
Lawyers, judges	29.0
Physicians	26.4
Architects	16.7
Police officers	15.8
Dentists	13.7
Engineers	8.5
Firefighters	2.1

Source: U.S. Bureau of the Census, *Statistical Abstract of the United States, 1997* (Washington, DC: U.S. Government Printing Office, 1997), pp. 410–412.

doctors, whereas girls are encouraged to be teachers and secretaries. Men and women are also "sex typed" for various jobs: Males seeking employment are encouraged by prospective employers to apply for higher-status positions, whereas women are encouraged to apply for lower-level positions.[65] Then there is the tendency for our society

to assign lower pay to job categories in which women are concentrated: receptionists, secretaries, and typists. Nonetheless, lower pay for women holding the same jobs as men indicates that there are discriminatory practices occurring even after women are hired.

Paul Horton and Gerald Leslie provide additional reasons, stemming from sex-role socialization, for the job and income disparity between men and women:

> *Motivation for career advancement is difficult to measure, and rash generalization is dangerous. Yet there are good reasons to suspect that intense career ambitions have been less common among women than among men. Beginning in early socialization, most girls are trained to please and charm others; most boys are trained to impress and outdistance others. Boys are trained to dominate and lead; girls, to submit and follow. Boys are taught to make demands upon others; girls learn to serve others' needs. Boys are praised for their strength; girls, for their prettiness and graciousness. As adults, men in our society are evaluated primarily according to their career success ("Meet my son, the doctor"), while women have been evaluated primarily according to their skill in human relationships ("She has a handsome husband and three darling children"). Husbands who knowingly neglected their families to pursue career advancement (moonlighting, night school, weekends working at the office) were praised for their ambition, while wives who allowed their careers to interfere with family life were scolded and scorned. A woman's spectacular success might alienate men, and much has been written about the avoidance-of-success syndrome in women. . . . This all has contributed to a lower level of career expectation among women than among men.*[66]

Effects on Human Interactions

The effects of sexism on human interactions are immense. Let's look at some examples.

Parents place more social restrictions on teenage daughters than on teenage sons. Daughters cannot stay out as late, their friends are more closely monitored, they are less likely to be given the family car for going out, and they are discouraged from participating in athletics.

Women are pressured to have the "Miss America" look—well-developed busts, shapely figures, and attractive features. Women who are judged less attractive, according to current American stereotypes, receive less attention from males, find it more difficult to get dates, and may even have less success at obtaining higher-status employment. The psychological costs are particularly severe when a woman reaches middle age. Socialized into believing her main function is child rearing and her main asset is her physical attractiveness, she often watches with despair as both her children and her youth leave her.

There are many double standards for male and female social interactions. If teenage boys are sexually active, they are viewed as "studs," whereas sexually active teenage girls may be called derogatory names. To a greater extent, males are allowed to be aggressive and to use vulgar language. There are social restrictions that discourage women from entering certain nightclubs and other places of entertainment. Married women who have an affair are usually subjected to more disapproval than are married men who do.

In male–female interactions, there is a tendency for the male to seek to be dominant and for the female either to seek an egalitarian relationship or to be manipulated into being submissive. For example, in dating, the male usually is expected to ask the female for a date and to choose what they will do on the date. Also, males often try to be "macho"; some females find that, to receive positive reinforcement and social acceptability, they must play along by being submissive, passive, or "feminine." When both husband and wife are working, the wife usually leaves her job and follows her husband to a new geographic area when he gets a job transfer.[67]

Often there are power struggles between males and females related to sex-role expectations. Marriage counselors are now seeing many couples in which the husband wants his wife to play a traditional role: stay at home, raise the children, and do the housework. If a wife does work, the husband often demands that the job not interfere with her doing the domestic tasks. He also perceives her job as a "second income" in contrast to a "career." Wives who want egalitarian relationships and who are becoming increasingly aware of the negative effects of sex-role stereotyping are likely to experience conflict with husbands who want them to fulfill the traditional wife role.

Women experience more depression and greater dissatisfaction in marriage than men.[68] Women are expected to make most of the adjustments necessary to keep the marriage intact. Middle-aged women frequently suffer severe depression when many of their tasks as mothers and homemakers are phased out—especially if they do not have outside jobs.[69] Research demonstrates that employed wives are happier than full-time homemakers.[70] Women who are extensively battered by their husbands, yet continue to live in these circumstances for years, sadly document the extent to which some women feel trapped by social arrangements that perpetuate their dependency and submission.

Matina Horner found that many women are motivated to avoid success because they fear that, the more ambitious and successful they are, the less feminine they will appear in their interactions with men.[71]

Sex-role stereotypes also contribute to women being treated as sex objects by some men and to women being sexually harassed at work, at school, and in other settings.

Of course, it is not just female stereotypes that cause difficulties in human interaction. Males also experience problems in living up to the "Clint Eastwood" image (described earlier). It is almost impossible for any male to meet such expectations. Yet there are considerable pressures on males to try—or suffer the consequences. Take the example of Senator Edmund Muskie in the Democratic presidential primary campaign in 1968. Senator Muskie was the leading candidate for the nomination. Then a newspaper in New England made some derogatory accusations about his wife and Muskie reacted by breaking down and crying in public. Very quickly the American public concluded that Muskie did not have the emotional stability to be president, and his popularity plummeted in the polls. Deborah David and Robert Brannon describe another example:

> A friend explained to me that he broke down and cried in front of a colleague at the office after some personal tragedies and office frustrations. He explained, "The news of my crying was all over the office in an hour. At first, no one said anything. They just sort of looked. They couldn't handle the situation by talking about it. Before this, only girls had cried. One of the guys did joke, 'Hear you and Sally been crying lately, eh?' I guess that was a jibe at my masculinity, but the 'knowing silence' of the others indicated the same doubts. What really hurt was that two years later, when I was doing very well and being considered for a promotion, it was brought up again. My manager was looking over my evaluations, read a paragraph to himself, and said, 'What do you think about that crying incident?' You can bet that was the last time I let myself cry."[72]

Ruth Hartley notes that sex-role socialization of boys inevitably leads to personal conflicts in later years:

> The boy is not adequately socialized for adulthood. . . . The boy is conditioned to live in an all-masculine society, defining his own self-image by rejecting whatever smacks of femininity. In adulthood, he will have to adjust to a heterosexual work world, perhaps even take orders from a female, a species he has been taught to despise as inferior. Finally, the emphasis on repression of the emotions, the high value of stoicism, leaves the boy wholly unprepared for the emotional closeness and intimate personal interaction now more and more expected of a lover and a spouse.[73]

Men frequently feel they must put their careers first and thereby sharply limit the interactions and satisfactions received in being husbands and fathers. In contrast, women are traditionally expected to put their roles as wives and mothers first and thereby limit their growth, capacities, and satisfactions in other areas.

Men in this country are disadvantaged before the law in several areas. In some jurisdictions, husbands are legally required to provide financial support for their families, and failure to do so is grounds for divorce by the wife. If a marriage breaks up, most courts grant custody of the children to the wife. In child custody battles, the father bears a heavier burden of proof that he is a fit parent than does the mother, and only in cases in which the mother is demonstrably negligent is the father's claim seriously considered. Alimony is much more frequently awarded to wives, even when both spouses can support themselves. Several men's groups have now formed in various regions of the country to advocate for equal treatment of men in these legal areas.

Sex-role stereotyping probably also plays a key role in the following statistics.[74] Men are four times more likely than women to commit suicide, are substantially more likely to be involved in violence, and commit far more crimes. Alcoholics and drug addicts are primarily men. Males also have higher rates of stress-related illnesses, such as heart disease, ulcers, and hypertension. The life expectancy for men in our society is several years less than for women. This shorter life expectancy stems partly from the pressures they face to succeed financially and from the fact that they are socialized not to vent their emotions. As a result, they experience more psychological stress, which leads to higher rates of stress-related illnesses and thus a shorter life span.

Because of male stereotypes, many men view themselves as failures when they cannot meet the financial needs of their families. Some men are badly beaten in fights because they felt they could not walk away and still be "real men." Many women find it frustrating to interact with men who are unable to be honest and open about their feelings. Not being able to live up to the "model man" image makes many men unhappy, depressed, and unfulfilled. Clearly, sex-role stereotyping has huge costs (financial, social, and personal) not only for women but also for men.

RECENT DEVELOPMENTS AND A LOOK TO THE FUTURE

There is currently a sex-role revolution occurring in our society. Men as well as women are becoming aware of the negative effects of sex-role distinctions. Increasingly we see courses on this topic in high schools, vocational schools, and colleges. More and more women are entering the labor force. The proportion of employed females to employed males is about 45 to 55.[75]

Women are becoming more involved in athletics than they were in the past, and they are entering certain types of competition previously confined to males. Women are now playing basketball, football, baseball, and volleyball. There are increasing numbers of women in track and field events, swimming, boxing, wrestling, weightlifting, golf, tennis, and stock-car racing.

In 1983 Sandra Day O'Connor became the first woman justice on the U.S. Supreme Court. In 1984 Geraldine Ferraro was the first woman selected to be a vice presidential candidate for a major political party.

Women are also pursuing a number of professions and careers that previously were nearly all male: military officers, engineers, lawyers, judges, firefighters, physicians, dentists, accountants, administrators, police officers, managers. Entering these new professions often has presented obstacles. Carl Glassman, for example, reports that women police officers receive stares from other citizens and are often viewed with suspicion by male partners.[76] (Male police partners fear that women may break under pressure, may not be able to subdue and handcuff a resisting offender, and may not be able to control disorderly males and several other types of violent situations. Male officers tend to feel both hostile and protective toward female officers, and one

Women are advancing in areas in which their presence was all but unthinkable just a few years ago. Barbara Harris blesses her congregation after being ordained as the first female bishop in the history of the Episcopal Church.

woman's failing is often held up as an indictment against all the rest.)

Human interactions are also changing, with more women being assertive and seeking out egalitarian relationships with males. To some extent, men are also (more slowly) beginning to realize that sex-role stereotypes limit the opportunities open to them in terms of emotional expression, interpersonal relationships, occupations, and domestic activities. Coleman and Cressey note:

Advocates of the men's movement argue that current gender roles are just as harmful to men as they are to women, but in different ways. They particularly object to the ideal of masculinity that holds that "real" men must always be strong, self-controlled, and successful. The effort to live up to this impossible ideal (or at least to appear to live up to it) leaves many men feeling anxiety-ridden and isolated.[77]

A men's movement is slowly becoming more prominent in our society. Some men are concerned that women tend to see them as "success objects," as women are substantially more apt than men to believe that a well-paying job is an essential requirement for selecting a spouse.[78] Men are also concerned that when a divorce occurs, many courts routinely assume that the mother will make the better parent. As a result, the mother is usually given custody of the children, with the father having to pay to support them and often given only limited visitation rights in return. The men's movement also asserts that some feminists have a tendency toward "male bashing"; they claim such feminists perpetuate negative stereotypes of men and blame men for problems that are actually created by historical forces beyond the control of any person or group.

Sex-role stereotypes have been costly to society. They have prevented a number of people from assuming more productive roles and have resulted in the expenditure of substantial resources on emotional and physical problems generated by these stereotypes.

Men also are taking on new roles and entering new careers. It is becoming increasingly common for men to accept equal responsibility for domestic tasks and for child rearing. In addition, we are now seeing more male nurses, secretaries, childcare workers, nursery school teachers, and flight attendants.[79]

In the past three decades, millions of Americans have begun to change their ideas about the "naturalness" of sex roles. Traditional discriminations are coming to be perceived as an irrational system that threatens women with lifelong inferiority and wasted potential and restricts men to the role of always being competitive, aggressive, and emotionally insensitive.

Our society is slowly moving toward gender equality, but as we have seen earlier in this chapter, substantial gender inequality continues to exist. If men and women achieve sexual equality in our society, what will be the effects? Kornblum and Julian speculate:

One obvious answer is that society's supply of talent in every segment of the work force would increase. More men would participate in traditionally female fields. . . . Breaking down the occupational barriers that separate women and men would also help them relate to each other as equals. Also, because fewer men would be the sole support for their families, there would be more flexibility in working life: Men and women would be freer to leave their jobs if they were unhappy with them, and in general there would be greater sharing of economic and homemaking responsibilities. This would reduce the pressures that exist for men to "succeed" and for women to remain dependent. The most important result of true sexual equality, then, may be simply that people would be free to be themselves.[80]

Some feminists and social scientists have urged that men and women be socialized to be flexible in their role playing and to express themselves as human beings rather than in traditional feminine or masculine ways.[81] This idea is called "androgyny," from *andro* (male) and *gyne* (female). The notion is to have people explore a broad range of role-playing possibilities and express emotions and behaviors without regard to sex-role stereotypes. People thus are encouraged to pursue tasks and careers at which they are most competent and with which they are most comfortable and to express the attitudes and emotions they really feel. If a male wants to be a cook or an elementary school teacher and a female wants to be a soldier or an athlete—and they're good at it—then it is functional for society if both develop their talents and are allowed to achieve everything they're capable of.

EXHIBIT 13.7

Strategies for Achieving Sexual Equality

Sexual equality does not imply a "unisex" world. Advocates of sexual equality are not urging that men and women use the same public bathroom facilities, dress the same, or play professional football and hockey together. What they *are* advocating is the equal treatment of the sexes (for example, in employment) and the elimination of traditional sex-role stereotyping. No role, behavior, aptitude, or attitude should be limited to one sex alone. True sexual equality simply means that people would be free to be themselves.

To achieve sexual equality, we must take action in many areas, some of which are summarized as follows:

■ We must put an end to the motherhood myth, which holds that women are most fulfilled as mothers.

■ Fathers must share equally in child rearing and in domestic tasks. This does not mean that men should do exactly half of each domestic task; rather, husband and wife should communicate with each other about how best to allocate family responsibilities. Women cannot compete equally with men in the work world if they also are required to assume all of the traditional child-rearing and homemaker responsibilities.

■ Additional day-care provisions are needed for working mothers and fathers, particularly for one-parent families. Without quality day-care arrangements, many mothers who want to work are prevented from doing so.

■ Laws preventing sex discrimination need to be enforced, and laws in matters in which legal discrimination still exists need to be enacted. (For example, women still sometimes have a more difficult time obtaining a bank loan.) Sex discrimination laws are also needed to protect men in certain matters (such as in alimony and child custody).

■ Dysfunctional sex-role socialization practices should be ended. Children should be reared to

(continued)

SEXISM AND SOCIAL WORK

Females have held, and currently do hold, a number of leadership positions in social work, serving as deans of graduate schools, chairs of undergraduate social work programs, directors of agencies, and presidents of national, state, and local social work organizations. There have also been a vast number of female authors of social work texts and professional journal articles. However, overall, males predominate in leadership positions in social work.

Because 69% of social workers are female, there is the notion that social work is a female-dominated profession.[82] Some different statistics suggest otherwise. Gibelman and Schervish analyzed the demographics of NASW's membership and found that "male social workers disproportionately hold managerial positions, assume such positions earlier in their careers, and earn more money in these positions than do their female counterparts."[83] Female social workers earn about 80 cents for every dollar earned by male social workers.[84] Huber and Orlando surveyed social workers holding master's degrees and found:

Male social workers who responded to a survey reported receiving about $8,000 more annually than female social workers. Differences persisted

EXHIBIT 13.7   *(continued)*

take on the roles, attitudes, and behaviors they desire and for which they have aptitudes and interests, rather than having boys raised to be "masculine" and girls to be "feminine." Parents and teachers should learn to relate to each child as an *individual,* not as a *male* or a *female.*

■ Assertiveness training programs should be used more extensively to help both men and women effectively express themselves and gain skills in countering sex-role stereotypes.

■ Advertisers who still portray women only as homemakers or as sex objects should start to portray the sexes more equally.

■ Consciousness-raising groups need to be expanded to reach more men and women. Such groups are now being held largely with women to help them become more aware of sex-role stereotypes, to help them establish a better self-concept, and to foster contact with others who are working to end sexism.

■ Continued development of such services as shelters for battered women, rape crisis cen-

ters, abortion counseling, family planning services, and marriage and sexual counseling is needed if people are to develop their capacities fully.

■ School counselors and teachers should help students to make career decisions based on their abilities, not on their gender.

■ Girls and boys should be encouraged to take vocational courses they desire (cooking, shop, typing, printing) without regard to gender.

■ Publishers should put an end to sex-role stereotyping and portray females and males in a variety of roles—such as males performing domestic tasks and women being pilots and physicians.

■ Laws should be enacted demanding that both government and private business organizations abide by the principles of comparable worth. Women have the right to receive equal pay or have pay equity for doing work comparable to that which men traditionally do. (This concept is described more fully at the end of this chapter.)

---

when other factors were controlled: age, years of experience, number of hours worked per week, method of practice (administrative versus direct practice), and field of practice (for example, children and families versus mental health).[85]

Social Work's Response to Women's Issues

There is evidence that the profession is responding to women's issues. In 1973 the Delegate Assembly of NASW added sexism to poverty and racism as basic concerns and priorities for the

profession. The Council on Social Work Education (CSWE) has required in accreditation standards for baccalaureate and master's programs that content on women's issues be included throughout the curriculum. CSWE also has an accreditation standard that prohibits gender discrimination in social work educational programs and mandates affirmative action programs for women administrators, faculty, students, and staff in social work educational programs.

The NASW Legal Defense Fund has provided financial support in sex discrimination cases. In addition, NASW supported the Equal Rights Amendment and is working on other issues related to sexism.

In practice there is some truth that social work has an emphasis on serving women because a majority of social work clients are women. About three-fourths of all people receiving public assistance and welfare payments are females.[86] Because women still primarily care for children, they are the main users of child welfare services. They are more likely to seek and receive counseling, and they are the major consumers of services for the aged. In addition, females are the primary consumers of family planning, pregnancy counseling, abortion services, rape crisis services, services from shelters for battered wives, and displaced homemaker services.

There are a number of reasons why more women than men are social work clients. For one thing, women outnumber men in the United States. Julia B. Rauch identifies another reason: "Most women in this country are socialized to accept weakness and dependence with more ease than men. The role of client is compatible with behaviors expected of women but is not congruent with men's expectations of themselves."[87] Women tend to need more services because poverty is a problem that disproportionately affects them; women who work full time are paid substantially less than men who work full time. Women also have higher rates of unemployment and are much more likely to be single heads of households.

Rauch summarizes a number of additional reasons why women are more likely to be social work clients:

> . . . teenage and unwanted pregnancies, post-partum depression, and sexual dysfunction; the need, resulting from the concentration of parenting functions in women's hands, for services for mothers who abuse or neglect their children and for the mothers of emotionally disturbed, learning disabled, mentally retarded, blind, or otherwise handicapped children; women's vulnerability to wife abuse and rape; the limitations of the wife-mother role and the "empty nest" syndrome; the practical and emotional stresses for women of separation or divorce and the difficulties of raising children alone; and the norm that

> women marry older men, which, in combination with women's longer life expectancy leads to widowhood and the stresses of bereavement, loss of the role of wife, and loneliness.[88]

It is important for social workers to understand that the traditional socialization process and the sex-role stereotypes in our society account for many of the problems that confront female, as well as male, clients. Workers should be skilled in helping clients to actualize themselves and to overcome rigid sex-role stereotypes. As noted earlier, many interaction problems between males and females in our society are consequences of sex-role stereotyping. One therapy approach that is widely used to help both men and women express themselves more effectively and gain skills in countering sex-role stereotypes is assertiveness training (described later in this chapter). Consciousness-raising groups, largely with women, are helping clients to become more aware of sex-role stereotypes, to establish a better self-concept, and to foster contact with others who are also working to end sexism.

The growing awareness of sexism and women's issues has led to the provision of improved services to groups that had been largely ignored: victims of rape, battered wives, women seeking abortions, husbands and wives with marital concerns, people with sexual dysfunctions, single-parent households headed by women, and displaced homemakers.[89]

The Feminist Perspective on Therapy

Female social work authors have made substantial contributions to developing the feminist perspective on therapy. This perspective has been explored by a number of writers, including Nan Van Den Bergh and L. Cooper.[90]

Feminism is a multifaceted concept that is difficult to accurately define. Barker has defined it as "the social movement and doctrine advocating legal and socioeconomic equality for women."[91] Barker further defines "feminist social work" as "the integration of the *values*, skills, and knowledge of social work with a feminist orientation to help individuals and society overcome the emotional and social problems that result from *sex discrimination*."[92] Barker has also defined "feminist therapy":

> *A psychosocial treatment orientation in which the professional (usually a woman) helps the client (usually a woman) in individual or group settings to overcome the psychological and social problems largely encountered as a result of* sex discrimination *and sex role stereotyping. Feminist therapists help clients maximize potential, especially through* consciousness-raising, *eliminating sex stereotyping, and helping them become aware of the commonalities shared by all women.*[93]

The following nine principles of feminist intervention have been identified.[94]

1. A client's problems should be viewed within a sociopolitical framework. Feminist intervention is concerned with the inequitable power relationships between women and men and is opposed to all "power-over" relationships, regardless of gender, race, class, age, and so on. Such relationships lead to oppression and domination. Feminism seeks to change all social, economic, and political structures based on relationships between "haves" and "have-nots." Another way of stating this principle is that "personal is political." Van Den Bergh comments:

> *This principle maintains that what a woman experiences in her personal life is directly related to societal dynamics that affect other women. In other words, an individual woman's experiences of pejorative comments based on sex and of blocked opportunities are directly related to societal sexism. For ethnic minority women, racism and classism also are factors that affect well being.*[95]

A primary distinguishing characteristic of feminist treatment is helping the client to analyze how her problems are related to systematic difficulties experienced by women in a sexist, classist, and racist society.

2. Traditional sex roles are pathological, and clients need encouragement to free themselves from traditional gender-role bonds. Traditionally, women have been socialized to fill a "learned helplessness" role. Van Den Bergh describes the effects of such sex-role stereotyping:

> *Sex-role stereotypes suggest that women should be submissive, docile, receptive, and dependent. The message is one of helplessness; that women cannot take care of themselves and are dependent upon others for their well being. This sets up a dynamic in which a woman's locus of control is external to her self, preventing her from believing that she can acquire what she needs on her own in order to develop and self-actualize. In other words, oversubscription to sex-role stereotypes engenders a state of powerlessness in which a woman is likely to become involved in situations where she becomes victimized. . . . For example, because young girls are socialized to be helpless, when they become women they tend to have a limited repertoire of responses when under stress; e.g., they respond passively.*[96]

In feminist treatment, clients are helped to see that, by internalizing traditional sex roles, they have set themselves up to play passive, submissive roles and to experience low self-esteem and self-hatred. The feminist approach encourages clients to make their own choices and to pursue the tasks and goals they desire rather than being constrained by traditional sex roles.

3. Intervention should focus on client empowerment. Van Den Bergh describes the empowerment process:

> *Helping women to acquire a sense of power, or the ability to affect outcomes in their lives, is a crucial component of feminist practice. Empowerment means acquiring knowledge, skills, and resources that enhance an individual's ability to control her own life and to influence others. Traditionally women have used indirect, covert techniques to get what they want, such*

as helplessness, dependency, coyness, and demureness.[97]

Empowerment can be fostered in a variety of ways: (a) by helping the client to define her own needs and clarify her personal goals so that she can then derive a sense of purposefulness; (b) by providing the client with education and access to resources; (c) by helping the client to believe that the ability to change lies within herself—that alterations in her life will result only from her own undertakings; and (d) by focusing on the identification and enhancement of the client's strengths rather than pathologies. Empowered women are ones who have learned to control their environments in order to get what they need.

4. The self-esteem of clients should be enhanced. Self-esteem and self-confidence are essential for empowerment. The worker should seek to be an encouraging person (as described in Chapter 4), helping clients to identify and recognize their unique qualities and strengths. Many clients with low self-esteem tend to blame themselves for everything that is wrong. For example, a battered woman typically blames herself for being battered. Such clients need to look more realistically at those areas for which they are blaming themselves and feeling guilt so they can distinguish where their responsibility for dysfunctional interactions ends and other individuals' begins.

5. Clients should be encouraged to develop their identity (sense of self) based on their own strengths, attributes, interests, and achievements. It is a serious mistake for women to define themselves in terms of their husbands or boyfriends, their children, their friends, or their relatives. Women need an independent identity that is not based on their relationships with others.

6. Clients need to value other women and to develop social support systems with them. In a society that devalues women, it is all too easy for some females to view other females as insignificant. With social support systems, women can vent their concerns and share their experiences and the solutions they've found to similar problems. They can serve as brokers in identifying resources, and they can provide emotional support and nurturance to one another.

7. Clients need to find an effective balance between work and personal relationships. Feminist intervention encourages both women and men to share in the nurturant aspects of their lives and in providing economic resources.

8. The nature of the relationship between practitioner and client should approach equality as much as possible. Feminist practitioners view themselves not as experts in resolving clients' problems but as catalysts in helping clients empower themselves. Feminist practitioners seek to eliminate dominant–submissive relationships. On this topic, Van Den Bergh notes:

> *Obviously, there is an innate power differential between practitioner and client because the former has expertise and training as an "authority." However, the feminist admonition is to avoid abusing that status; "abuse" in this sense might be, for example, taking all credit for client change, or using terminology and nomenclature that are difficult for the client to understand.*[98]

9. Clients should be helped to express themselves assertively. (The steps in assertiveness training are described in Exhibit 13.8.) As indicated earlier, many women are socialized to be passive and nonassertive. Through individual and group counseling, clients can become more assertive, which will increase their self-confidence and self-esteem. They will be better able to communicate their thoughts, feelings, and opinions. Also, learning to express oneself is an important component in empowerment.

Many women feel anger over being victimized by sex discrimination and gender stereotyping. Some of these women turn their angry feelings inward, which often results in depression. Assertiveness training can help such women recognize that they have a right to be angry; it can also help them identify and practice constructive ways of expressing their anger (that is, assertively rather than aggressively).

EXHIBIT 13.8

Assertiveness Training

Do you handle put-downs well? Are you reluctant to express your feelings and opinions openly and honestly in a group? Are you frequently timid when interacting with people in positions of authority? Do you react constructively to criticism? Do you sometimes explode in anger when things go wrong, or are you able to remain calm? Do you find it difficult to maintain eye contact when talking? If you are uncomfortable with someone smoking near you, do you express your feelings? Are you timid in arranging a date or social event? For anyone who has trouble in any of these situations, there is, fortunately, a useful technique—assertiveness training—that enables people to become more effective in interpersonal interactions.

Assertiveness problems range from extreme shyness, introversion, and withdrawal to inappropriate rage that results in alienating others. A nonassertive person is often acquiescent, fearful, and afraid of expressing his or her real, spontaneous feelings in a variety of situations. Frequently, resentment and anxiety build up, resulting in general discomfort, feelings of low self-esteem, tension headaches, fatigue, and perhaps a destructive explosion of temper, anger, and aggression. Some people are overly shy and timid in nearly all interactions. Most of us, however, encounter occasional problems in isolated matters in which it would be to our benefit to be more assertive. For example, a bachelor may be quite effective and assertive in his job as a store manager but still be awkward and timid while attempting to arrange a date.

There are three basic styles of interacting with others: nonassertive, aggressive, and assertive. Characteristics of these styles have been summarized by Robert Alberti and Michael Emmons:

In the non-assertive style, *you are likely to hesitate, speak softly, look away, avoid the issue,*
agree regardless of your own feelings, not express opinions, value yourself "below" others, and hurt yourself to avoid any chance of hurting others.

In the aggressive style, *you typically answer before the other person is through talking, speak loudly and abusively, glare at the other person, speak "past" the issue (accusing, blaming, demeaning), vehemently expound your feelings and opinions, value yourself "above" others, and hurt others to avoid hurting yourself.*

In the assertive style, *you will answer spontaneously, speak with a conversational tone and volume, look at the other person, speak to the issue, openly express your personal feelings and opinions (anger, love, disagreement, sorrow), value yourself equal to others, and hurt neither yourself nor others.*[a]

EXAMPLES OF BEHAVIOR

You are driving with an acquaintance to another city to attend a conference. The acquaintance lights up a pipe, and you soon find the smoke irritating and the odor somewhat stifling. What are your choices?

1. Nonassertive response: You attempt to carry on a "cheery" conversation for the 3-hour trip without commenting about the smoke.

2. Aggressive response: You become increasingly irritated, finally exploding, "Either you put out that pipe, or I'll put it out for you—the odor is sickening."

3. Assertive response: You look directly at the acquaintance and in a firm, conversational tone state, "The smoke from your pipe is irritating me. I'd appreciate it if you put it away."

---

[a] Robert E. Alberti and Michael L. Emmons, *Stand Up, Speak Out, Talk Back!* (New York: Pocket Books, 1975), p. 24.

(continued)

EXHIBIT 13.8 *(continued)*

At a party with friends, during small-talk conversation, your husband gives you a subtle put-down by stating, "Wives always talk too much." What do you do?

1. Nonassertive response: You don't say anything but feel hurt and become quiet.

2. Aggressive response: You glare at him and angrily ask, "John, why are you always criticizing me?"

3. Assertive response: You carry on as usual, wait until the drive home, and then calmly look at him and say, "When we were at the party tonight, you said that wives always talk too much. I felt you were putting me down when you said that. What did you mean by that comment?"

BEING ASSERTIVE

Simply stated, assertive behavior is expressing yourself without hurting or stepping on others. Assertiveness training is designed to help us realize, feel, and act on the assumption that we have the right to be ourselves and to express our feelings freely. Assertive responses generally are not aggressive responses. The distinction between these two types of interactions is important. If, for example, a wife has an overly critical mother-in-law, aggressive responses by the wife would include ridiculing the mother-in-law, intentionally doing things that she knows will upset the mother-in-law (not visiting, serving the type of food the mother-in-law dislikes, not cleaning the house), urging the husband to tell his mother to "shut up," and getting into loud verbal arguments with the mother-in-law. On the other hand, an effective assertive response would be to counter criticism by saying: "Jane, your criticism of me deeply hurts me. I know you're trying to help me when you give advice, but I feel when you do that you're criticizing me. I know you don't want me to make

mistakes. But to grow, I need to make my own errors and learn from them. If you want to help me the most, let me do it myself and be responsible for the consequences. The type of relationship that I'd like to have with you is a close, adult relationship and not a mother–child relationship."

The steps for learning to become more assertive are as follows:[b]

1. Examine your interactions. Are there situations that you need to handle more assertively? Do you at times hold opinions and feelings within yourself for fear of what would happen if you expressed them? Do you occasionally lash out angrily at others? Studying your interactions is facilitated by keeping a diary for a week or longer. Record the situations in which you acted timidly, those in which you were aggressive, and those that you handled assertively.

2. Select those interactions in which it would be to your benefit to be more assertive. They may include situations in which you were overpolite or overly apologetic. Or perhaps you were timid and allowed others to take advantage of you, at the same time harboring feelings of resentment, anger, embarrassment, fear of others, or self-criticism for not having the courage to express yourself. Overly aggressive interactions in which you exploded in anger or walked over others also need to be dealt with. For *each* set of nonassertive or aggressive interactions, you can become more assertive, as shown in the next steps.

3. Concentrate on a specific incident in the past in which you were either nonassertive or ag-

---

[b] These self-training steps are a modification of assertiveness training programs developed by Robert E. Alberti and Michael L. Emmons, *Your Perfect Right,* 7th ed. (San Luis Obispo, CA: Impact, 1995), and by Herbert Fensterheim and Jean Baer, *Don't Say Yes When You Want to Say No* (New York: Dell, 1975).

(continued)

EXHIBIT 13.8   *(continued)*

gressive. Close your eyes for a few minutes and vividly imagine the details, including what you and the other person said and how you felt at the time and afterward.

4. Write down and review your responses. Ask yourself the following questions to determine how you presented yourself:

   a. Eye contact: Did you look directly at the other person with a relaxed, steady gaze? Looking down or away suggests a lack of self-confidence. Glaring is an aggressive response.

   b. Gestures: Were your gestures appropriate, free-flowing, and relaxed? Did they emphasize your messages effectively? Awkward stiffness suggests nervousness; other gestures (such as an angry fist) signal an aggressive reaction.

   c. Body posture: Did you show the importance of your message by directly facing the other person, by leaning toward that person, by holding your head erect, and by sitting or standing appropriately close?

   d. Facial expressions: Did your facial expressions show a stern, firm pose consistent with an assertive response?

   e. Voice tone and volume: Was your response stated in a firm, conversational tone? Shouting may suggest anger. Speaking softly suggests shyness, and a cracking voice suggests nervousness. By tape recording and listening to your voice, you can practice increasing or decreasing the volume.

   f. Speech fluency: Did your speech flow smoothly, clearly, and slowly? Rapid speech or hesitation in speaking suggests nervousness. Tape recording assertive responses that you want to try out for problem situations is a way to improve fluency.

   g. Timing: Were your verbal reactions to a problem situation stated at the most ap-

propriate time for you and the other person to review the incident? Generally, spontaneous expressions are best, but certain situations should be handled at a later time (for example, challenging some of your boss's erroneous statements in private rather than in front of a group she or he is making a presentation to).

   h. Message content: For a problem situation, which of your responses were nonassertive or aggressive, and which were assertive? Study the content and consider why you responded in a nonassertive or aggressive style.

5. Observe one or more effective models. Watch the verbal and nonverbal approaches that are assertively used to handle the type of interactions with which you are having problems. Compare the consequences of their approach and yours. If possible, discuss their approach and their feelings about using it.

6. Make a list of various alternative approaches for being more assertive.

7. Close your eyes and visualize yourself using each of these alternative approaches. For each approach, think through what the full set of interactions would be, along with the consequences. Select an approach, or combination of approaches, that you believe will be most effective for you to use. Through imagery, practice this approach until you feel comfortable that it will work for you.

8. Role-play the approach with someone else, perhaps a friend or counselor. If certain segments of your approach appear clumsy, awkward, timid, or aggressive, practice modifications until you become comfortable with the approach. Obtain feedback from the other person about the strengths and shortcomings of your approach. Compare your interactions to the verbal/nonverbal guidelines for assertive

(continued)

EXHIBIT 13.8 *(continued)*

behavior in Step 4. It may be useful for the other person to model through role playing one or more assertive strategies, which you would then, by reversing roles, practice using.

9. Repeat Steps 7 and 8 until you develop an assertive approach that you believe will work best for you and that you are comfortable with.

10. Use your approach in a real-life situation. The previous steps are designed to prepare you for the real event. Expect to be somewhat anxious when first trying to be assertive. If you are still too fearful of attempting to be assertive, repeat Steps 5 through 8. For those few individuals who fail to develop the needed confidence to try out being assertive, professional counseling is advised because expressing yourself effectively in interactions with others is essential for personal happiness.

11. Reflect on the effectiveness of your effort. Did you remain calm? Getting angry at times is a normal human emotion, and it needs to be expressed. However, the anger should be expressed in a constructive, assertive fashion. When expressed in a destructive, lashing-out fashion, it violates the rights of others. Considering the nonverbal/verbal guidelines for assertive behavior discussed in Step 4, what components of your responses were assertive, aggressive, and nonassertive? What were the consequences of your effort? How did you feel after trying out this new set of interactions? If possible, discuss how you did in regard to these questions with a friend who may have observed the interactions.

12. Expect some success but not complete personal satisfaction with your initial efforts. Experiencing personal growth and interacting more effectively with others will be a continual learning process. Quite appropriately, "pat yourself on the back" for the strengths of your approach—you earned it. But also note the areas in which you need to improve, and use the foregoing steps for improving your assertiveness efforts.

These steps systematically make sense but are not to be followed rigidly. Each person has to develop a process that works best for himself or herself.

The structure of this technique is relatively simple to understand. Considerable skill (common sense and ingenuity), however, is needed to determine what will be an effective assertive strategy when a real-life situation arises. The joy and pride derived from being able to express oneself assertively are truly life enriching.

Source: From "How to Become More Assertive," by Charles Zastrow, pp. 236–240, in Charles Zastrow and Dae H. Chang (eds.), *The Personal Problem Solver.* Copyright © 1977 by Prentice Hall, Englewood Cliffs, New Jersey.

FUTURE DIRECTIONS OF THE WOMEN'S MOVEMENT

Within the women's movement, there is currently much debate over policy directions. Coleman and Cressey note:

As in other social movements, all feminists do not agree on the best ways to win their objec-tives. The liberal feminists are the largest group in the movement, and their approach is the predominant one in the National Organization for Women (NOW). Drawing on the values of freedom and individual liberty that are central to the liberal tradition, these feminists call for a vigorous government attack on all forms of prejudice and discrimination. The liberal feminists nonetheless have their critics both inside and outside the movement. To the left are the social-

ist feminists, *who argue that the exploitation of women arises from the capitalist system and that only fundamental changes in our economic institutions can liberate women.* Radical feminists *focus more on the social arena, calling for a "women-centered" culture to replace the current pattern of patriarchal (male-dominated) society. At the same time, all feminists are criticized by those who feel that they are undermining the family and traditional social values.*[99]

The conservative trend of the 1980s and early 1990s jeopardized some of the progress that feminists made during the 1960s and 1970s. Both President Reagan and Nancy Reagan, as well as most members of the Reagan cabinet, opposed the Equal Rights Amendment, and it eventually failed to be ratified. The conservative movement and the Reagan and Bush administrations put less emphasis on enforcing affirmative action programs and actively opposed the concept of setting quotas for the percentage of minorities that must be hired by employers. There also were cuts in a number of social programs that the women's movement vigorously supported, such as funding for public day care, sex education, and contraception.

Bill Clinton, who was elected president in 1992 and reelected in 1996, has a more liberal orientation than Reagan and Bush. His wife, Hillary, has been very active in policymaking decisions and is viewed by many as a role model for contemporary women. President Clinton has appointed a number of feminists to high-level government positions and has supported the feminist position on several social issues, such as the abortion debate and universal health insurance coverage.

The National Organization for Women (NOW) has been united in its determination to fight efforts to prohibit abortions. The women's movement views access to abortions as a basic right of women to decide what happens to their bodies and to their lives.

Women burdened by unwanted children often become dependent on their partners or on public assistance and find it very difficult to compete with men in the job market. In a key 1989 abortion decision, *Webster* v. *Reproductive Health Services*, the U.S. Supreme Court gave indications that it may be backing away from its previous position, passed down in *Roe v. Wade* in 1972, which held that women had a right to obtain an abortion in the first trimester of their pregnancy.[100] This 1989 decision gave states the right to pass certain laws regulating abortions. The broader effect of the Court's decision is to throw this hot political issue back to state legislatures. Feminists are hopeful that Clinton will have the opportunity to appoint justices with pro-choice views to the Supreme Court, thereby preserving the basic provisions of *Roe v. Wade.*

There is a debate in the women's movement about whether traditional roles held by women should be devalued. Advocates for modern roles emphasize equality and careers, yet some leaders of NOW assert that the role of homemaker should be given equal respect.

One of the directions that the women's movement is taking is to seek help for single-parent families, particularly low-income, female-headed families. There has been a feminization of poverty in this country, and an increasing proportion of poor people are women. It is almost impossible for single mothers to be "financially equal" to males in the job market when day care is highly expensive and when women who work full time are paid considerably less than men who work full time. The women's movement is certain to continue to advocate for increased financial support by the federal government for child care.

The women's movement has also been advocating for "comparable worth." Comparable worth involves the concept of "equal pay for comparable work" rather than "equal pay for equal work." Comparable worth asserts that the intrinsic value of different jobs, such as that of a secretary or plumber, can be measured. Those jobs that are evaluated to be of comparable value should receive comparable pay. If implemented, it is believed that the concept will reduce the disparities in pay between women and men who work full time. Jobs held mainly by women pay an average of 20% below equivalent jobs held mainly by men.[101] Some states (such as Wisconsin and Washington) have initiated efforts to develop comparable worth programs for state employees.

Another direction that the women's movement is taking is to encourage and support female candidates for public offices at federal, state, and local levels. The women's movement recognizes that achieving social equality depends partly on moving toward political equality.

The women's movement has made important gains in improving the status of women in our society in the past three decades. It is clear that its general thrust toward equality will continue.

SUMMARY

In almost every known society, women have had lower status than men. Women have traditionally been assigned housework and child-rearing responsibilities and have been socialized to be passive, submissive, and feminine. The socialization process and sex-role stereotyping have led to a number of problems. There is sex discrimination in employment, with men who work full time being paid substantially more than women who work full time. There are double standards of conduct for males and females. There are power struggles between males and females because men are socialized to be dominant in interactions with women, whereas women often seek egalitarian relationships. Sex-role stereotyping and the traditional female role have led women to be unhappier in marriages and to be more depressed than men.

Sex-role stereotyping is pervasive in our society, with aspects being found in child-rearing practices, the educational system, religion, contemporary psychological theories, our language, the mass media, the business world, marriage and family patterns, and our political system.

The women's movement, which had a resurgence in the 1960s, is working to eliminate sex-role stereotypes and is revolutionizing the socialization process. A number of laws forbidding sex discrimination have been enacted. Women as well as men are now pursuing new careers and are taking on roles and tasks that run counter to traditional sex stereotypes. The androgyny notion is gaining strength. Androgynous people explore a broad range of role-playing possibilities and express emotions and behaviors without regard to sex-role stereotypes.

Interestingly, the women's movement also has had many payoffs for males. Men experience extreme difficulties and encounter many problems in trying to fulfill the stereotypes of the model-man role—to always be dominant and strong, to never be depressed or anxious, to hide emotions, to be the provider, to be self-reliant and aggressive, and to never cry. Men are gradually realizing that this stereotypical role limits their opportunities in terms of interpersonal relationships, occupations, emotional expression, and domestic activities. Sex-role stereotyping has huge costs for women, for men, and for society. True sexual equality simply means that people would be free to be themselves.

The social work profession has made commitments to eliminate sexism, both within its own ranks and in the broader society. Although 69% of practicing social workers are female, more males are concentrated in administrative and other leadership positions in social work. Most social work clients are women. Social workers need to become skilled in helping clients to actualize themselves and to stop being negatively influenced by sex-role stereotypes.

NOTES

1. William Kornblum and Joseph Julian, *Social Problems*, 8th ed. (Englewood Cliffs, NJ: Prentice Hall, 1995), p. 294.
2. Ibid.
3. U.S. Bureau of the Census, *Statistical Abstract of the United States, 1997* (Washington, DC: U.S. Government Printing Office, 1997).
4. Ibid.
5. Ibid., p. 478.
6. Jean Stockard and Miriam M. Johnson, *Sex Roles* (Englewood Cliffs, NJ: Prentice Hall, 1980), pp. 19–42.
7. Kornblum and Julian, *Social Problems*, p. 310.
8. Thomas Sullivan, Kenrick Thompson, Richard Wright, George Gross, and Dale Spady, *Social Problems* (New York: Wiley, 1980), p. 452.
9. Francine D. Blair, "Women in the Labor Force: An Overview," in *Women: A Feminist Perspective,*

Jo Freeman, ed. (Palo Alto, CA: Mayfield, 1979), p. 272.

10. John Money, J. G. Hampson, and J. L. Hampson, "An Examination of Some Basic Sexual Concepts: The Evidence of Human Hermaphroditism," *Bulletin of the Johns Hopkins Hospital*, 1955, pp. 301–309.

11. H. L. Rheingold and K. V. Cook, "The Contents of Boys' and Girls' Rooms As an Index of Parents' Behavior," *Child Development*, 46 (June 1975), p. 461.

12. Eleanor Maccoby and Carol Jacklin, *The Psychology of Sex Differences* (Stanford, CA: Stanford University Press, 1974).

13. Ibid.

14. Clarice Stasz Stoll, ed., *Sexism: Scientific Debates* (Reading, MA: Addison-Wesley, 1973).

15. Warren Farrell, *The Liberated Man* (New York: Random House, 1975).

16. Kornblum and Julian, *Social Problems,* p. 297.

17. Betty Friedan, *The Feminine Mystique* (New York: Dell, 1963).

18. Kornblum and Julian, *Social Problems,* p. 314.

19. Ibid.

20. Paul R. Horton, Gerald R. Leslie, and Richard F. Larson, *The Sociology of Social Problems,* 9th ed. (Englewood Cliffs, NJ: Prentice Hall, 1988), p. 252.

21. Sullivan et al., *Social Problems,* pp. 475–476.

22. Kornblum and Julian, *Social Problems,* pp. 311–312.

23. Ibid., pp. 300–310.

24. Ibid., pp. 300–308.

25. "ERA Stalled, but Women Make Piecemeal Gains," *U.S. News & World Report,* Aug. 20, 1979, p. 56.

26. Horton et al., *The Sociology of Social Problems,* p. 261.

27. Amy Saltzman, "Hands Off at the Office," *U.S. News & World Report,* Aug. 1, 1988, pp. 56–58.

28. D. A. Charney and R. C. Russell, "An Overview of Sexual Harassment," *American Journal of Psychiatry,* 151, no. 1 (Jan. 1994), p. 11.

29. Deborah S. David and Robert Brannon, eds., *The Forty-Nine Percent Majority: The Male Sex Role* (Reading, MA: Addison-Wesley, 1976).

30. Stockard and Johnson, *Sex Roles,* pp. 133–147.

31. Richard C. Friedman, Ralph M. Richart, and Raymond L. Vande Wiehe, eds., *Sex Differences in Behavior* (New York: Wiley, 1974).

32. See Shirly Weitz, *Sex Roles: Biological, Psychological, and Social Foundations* (New York: Oxford University Press, 1977); Betty Yorburg, *Sexual Identity: Sex Roles and Social Change* (New York: Wiley, 1974); Michael Teitelbaum, ed., *Sex Roles: Social and Biological Perspectives* (New York: Doubleday/Anchor, 1976).

33. Ibid.

34. Maccoby and Jacklin, *The Psychology of Sex Differences.*

35. Ibid.

36. John Money, Joan Hampson, and John Hampson, "Imprinting and the Establishment of Gender Role," *Archives of Neurology and Psychiatry,* 77 (Mar. 1967), pp. 333–336; see also John Money and Anke A. Ehrhardt, *Man and Woman, Boy and Girl* (New York: New American Library, 1974); Richard Green, *Sexual Identity Conflict in Children and Adults* (Baltimore: Penguin, 1975).

37. Clellan S. Ford and Frank Beach, *Patterns of Sexual Behavior* (New York: Harper & Row, 1951).

38. Allan Katcher, "The Discrimination of Sex Differences by Young Children," *Journal of Genetic Psychology,* 87 (Sept. 1955), pp. 131–143.

39. Lawrence Kohlberg, "A Cognitive-Developmental Analysis of Children's Sex-Role Concepts and Attitudes," in *The Psychology of Sex Differences,* Maccoby and Jacklin, eds., pp. 82–173.

40. Ruth E. Hartley, "American Core Culture: Changes and Continuities," in *Sex Roles in Changing Society,* Georgene H. Seward and Robert C. Williamson, eds. (New York: Random House, 1970), pp. 140–141.

41. Ibid., p. 141.

42. Sullivan et al., *Social Problems,* pp. 460–465.

43. Charles H. Cooley, *Social Organization* (New York: Scribner's, 1909).

44. Matina Horner, "Fail: Bright Women," *Psychology Today,* Nov. 1969, pp. 36–38; Vivian Gornick, "Why Women Fear Success," *Ms.,* Spring 1972, pp. 50–53.

45. Janet S. Hyde, *Understanding Human Sexuality,* 5th ed. (New York: McGraw-Hill, 1994), pp. 385–394.

46. *Statistical Abstract of the United States, 1997,* p. 41.

47. American Association of University Women, *How Schools Shortchange Women: The A.A.U.W. Report* (Washington, DC: A.A.U.W. Educational Foundation, 1992).

48. James W. Coleman and Donald R. Cressey, *Social Problems,* 6th ed. (New York: HarperCollins, 1996), p. 300.

49. Ibid.

50. Myra Sadker, David Sadker, and Susan S. Klein, "Abolishing Misconceptions About Sex Equity in Education," *Theory into Practice* 25 (Autumn 1986), p. 220.

51. Coleman and Cressey, *Social Problems,* p. 302.

52. Janet S. Chafetz, *Masculine, Feminine or Human? An Overview of the Sociology of Sex Roles* (Itasca, IL: F. E. Peacock, 1974).

53. Kornblum and Julian, *Social Problems,* p. 309.

54. Sigmund Freud, *A General Introduction to Psychoanalysis* (New York: Boni & Liveright, 1924).

55. Kornblum and Julian, *Social Problems,* p. 294.

56. Ibid., pp. 300–301.
57. Coleman and Cressey, *Social Problems,* p. 305.
58. Ibid.
59. Ibid., pp. 304–305.
60. Ann M. Morrison, "Up Against a Glass Ceiling," *Los Angeles Times,* Aug. 23, 1987, sec. 1, p. 3.
61. Kornblum and Julian, *Social Problems,* pp. 300–303.
62. Coleman and Cressey, *Social Problems,* pp. 302–303.
63. Hyde, *Understanding Human Sexuality.*
64. Coleman and Cressey, *Social Problems,* p. 303.
65. Hyde, *Understanding Human Sexuality.*
66. Horton et al., *The Sociology of Social Problems,* p. 258.
67. Ibid.
68. Kornblum and Julian, *Social Problems,* p. 304.
69. Hyde, *Understanding Human Sexuality.*
70. Ibid.
71. Matina S. Horner, "Femininity and Successful Achievement: A Basic Inconsistency," in *Feminine Personality and Conflict,* Judith M. Bardwich, ed. (Pacific Grove, CA: Brooks/Cole, 1970).
72. David and Brannon, *The Forty-Nine Percent Majority,* pp. 53–54.
73. Hartley, "American Core Culture," p. 142.
74. U.S. Bureau of the Census, *Statistical Abstract of the United States, 1997.*
75. Ibid.
76. Carl Glassman, "How Lady Cops Are Doing," *Parade,* Jul. 27, 1980, pp. 4–5.
77. Coleman and Cressey, *Social Problems,* p. 313.
78. Ibid., p. 309.
79. *Statistical Abstract of the United States, 1997,* pp. 410–413.
80. Kornblum and Julian, *Social Problems,* p. 313.
81. Hyde, *Understanding Human Sexuality.*
82. *Statistical Abstract of the United States, 1997,* p. 410.
83. M. Gibelman and P. H. Schervish, "The Glass Ceiling in Social Work: Is It Shatterproof?" *AFFILIA,* 8, no. 4 (1993), p. 443.

84. B. Lott, *Women's Lives: Themes and Variations in Gender Learning,* 2nd ed. (Pacific Grove, CA: Brooks/Cole, 1994).
85. Ruth Huber and Betty P. Orlando, "Persisting Gender Differences in Social Workers' Incomes: Does the Profession Really Care?" *Social Work,* 40, no. 5 (Sept. 1995), p. 585.
86. Julia B. Rauch, "Gender As a Factor in Practice," in *Social Work: A Profession of Many Faces,* Armando Morales and Bradford W. Sheafor, eds. (Boston: Allyn & Bacon, 1989), 340–342.
87. Ibid., p. 342.
88. Ibid., pp. 343–344.
89. Ketayun H. Gould, "Sexism," in *Contemporary Social Work,* 2nd ed., Donald Brieland, Lela Costin, and Charles Atherton, eds. (New York: McGraw-Hill, 1980), pp. 427–428.
90. Nan Van Den Bergh and L. B. Cooper, "Feminist Social Work," in *The Encyclopedia of Social Work* (Washington, DC: NASW, 1987), pp. 610–618.
91. R. L. Barker, *The Social Work Dictionary,* 3rd ed. (Washington, DC: NASW, 1995), p. 135.
92. Ibid.
93. Ibid.
94. Van Den Bergh and Cooper, "Feminist Social Work," pp. 610–618; Nan Van Den Bergh, "Feminist Treatment for People with Depression," in *Structuring Change,* K. Corcoran, ed. (Chicago: Lyceum, 1992), pp. 95–110; K. K. Kirst Ashman and G. H. Hull, Jr., *Understanding Generalist Practice* (Chicago: Nelson-Hall, 1993), pp. 422–463.
95. Van Den Bergh, "Feminist Treatment for People with Depression," p. 103.
96. Ibid., p. 101.
97. Ibid., p. 104.
98. Ibid.
99. Coleman and Cressey, *Social Problems,* pp. 313–314.
100. Hyde, *Understanding Human Sexuality.*
101. Kornblum and Julian, *Social Problems,* p. 294.

14

AGING
AND
GERONTOLOGICAL
SERVICES

The plight of the elderly, so long overlooked, has now become recognized as a major social problem in the United States. The elderly face a number of social and personal problems: high rates of physical illness and emotional difficulties, poverty, malnutrition, lack of access to transportation, low status, lack of a meaningful role in our society, and inadequate housing. To a large extent, the elderly are a "recently discovered" minority group. Like other minority groups, they are victims of job discrimination, are excluded from the mainstream of American life on the basis of supposed group characteristics, and are subjected to prejudice that is based on erroneous stereotypes. This chapter will:

- Describe the specific problems faced by the elderly.
- Explore the causes of these problems.
- Discuss current services to meet these problems.
- Note gaps in current services.
- Describe the role of social work in providing services to the elderly.
- Discuss social and political changes needed to improve the status of the elderly.

AN OVERVIEW

Throughout time some tribal societies have abandoned their enfeebled old. The Crow, Creek, and Hopi Indians, for example, built special huts away from the tribe where the old were left to die. The Eskimo left their incapacitated elderly in snowbanks or forced them to paddle away in a kayak. The Siriono of the Bolivian forest simply left them behind when they moved on in search of food.[1] Even today the Ik of Uganda leave the elderly and disabled to starve to death.[2] (Generally, the primary reason tribal societies have been forced to abandon the elderly is scarce resources.)

Although we might consider these customs shocking and barbaric, have we not also abandoned the elderly? We encourage them to retire when many are still productive. All too often, when a person retires, his or her status, power, and self-esteem are lost. Also, in a physical sense, we seldom have a place for large numbers of older people. Community facilities—parks, subways, libraries—are oriented to serving children and young people. Most housing is designed and priced for the young couple with one or two children and an annual income in excess of $30,000. If the elderly are not able to care for themselves (and if their families are unable to care for them), we "store" them away from society in nursing homes. Moreover, we do little to relieve the financial problems of the elderly; one-fifth of them have incomes close to or below the poverty line.[3] (In a sense, our abandonment of the elderly is more unethical than that of tribal societies who are motivated by survival pressures; we don't have such serious survival problems.)

A "RECENTLY DISCOVERED" MINORITY GROUP

Our society's treatment of the elderly has only recently come to be viewed as a major social problem. In effect, the elderly are a recently discovered minority group. Like other minority groups, they are subjected to job discrimination. The most striking example of age discrimination has been the practice of mandatory retirement, whereby people are forced to leave their jobs once they reach a certain age.

The legal retirement age used to be 65. In 1978 Congress enacted legislation that raised the age to 70 for most jobs. Then, in 1986, Congress (recognizing that mandatory retirement was overtly discriminatory against the elderly) outlawed most mandatory retirement policies.

The elderly are discriminated against in many ways. Older workers are erroneously believed to be less productive. Unemployed workers in their fifties and sixties have greater difficulty finding new jobs and remain unemployed much longer than younger unemployed workers. The elderly are given no meaningful role in our society.

**CASE
EXAMPLE 14.1** **The Best Years of Your Life—Retirement**

Tom Townsend had been with the ironworks plant for 42 years. Being promoted to supervisor 16 years ago had fulfilled his dreams, and there was nothing he wanted more than to be on the job and managing his crew. He has been married to Laura for the past 37 years. At first their marriage had some rough moments, but Laura and Tom grew accustomed to and comfortable with each other over the years. They have a traditional view of the role of women in society. Her main job has always been to maintain the home. They have two grown children who have moved away and now have homes of their own.

Life was at the factory for Tom. He didn't have time to develop other hobbies and interests, nor was he interested in picnics or socials. When he had time off from work, he used it to repair things around the house and to "tool up" for getting back to work. Television replaced talk in his home, and Tom usually spent weekends watching a variety of sports programs.

On May 18, Tom turned 70. The company marked the occasion with a retirement dinner that was well attended. Tom and Laura were there, along with their children and families, the members of Tom's crew and their wives, and the company managers and their wives. At first everyone was a little anxious because these people did not often get together with one another socially. The dinner, however, went fairly well. Tom was congratulated by everyone, received a gold watch, and made appropriate remarks about his years with the company. After a few more cocktails, everyone went home. Tom was feeling sentimental, but also quite good about himself because everyone was acknowledging his contributions.

Tom awoke at 7 o'clock the next morning—the usual time for him to get ready for work. Then it hit him. He was retired, with nowhere to go and no reason to get up. His life at the plant was over. What should he do now? He didn't know.

He spent the next week following Laura around the house, getting on her nerves. At times he complained about feeling useless. Twice he commented that he wished he were dead. He went back to the plant to see his men, but they were too busy to talk. Besides, Bill, who had been promoted to supervisor, delighted in showing Tom how the department's productivity had increased and bored Tom with his plans for making changes to increase production further.

Long walks didn't help much, either. As he walked, he thought about his plight and became more depressed. What was he going to do? What could he find to occupy his time meaningfully? He looked into a mirror and saw his receding hairline and numerous wrinkles. More and more, he started to feel a variety of aches and pains. He thought to himself, "I guess I'm just a useless old man." He wondered what the future would hold. Would his company pension keep pace with increasing bills? Would he eventually be placed in a nursing home? What was he going to do with the remainder of his life? He just didn't know.

Ours is a youth-oriented society that devalues old people. We glorify the body beautiful and physical attractiveness and thereby shortchange the elderly. Older persons are viewed as "out of touch with what's happening," and therefore, their knowledge is seldom valued or sought. It is also erroneously believed that intellectual ability declines with age. Research shows, however, that intellectual capacity, barring organic problems, remains essentially unchanged until very late in life.[4]

The elderly are misperceived as senile, conservative, resistant to change, inflexible, incompetent, and burdensome to the young. Given opportunities, elderly individuals usually prove such prejudicial concepts wrong.

The elderly generally react to prejudice against them in the same way that racial and ethnic minorities react—by displaying self-hatred and by being self-conscious, sensitive, and defensive about their social and cultural status.[5] (Cooley's looking glass self-concept suggests that, if individuals frequently receive negative responses from others, they will eventually come to view themselves negatively.)

DEFINITIONS OF LATER ADULTHOOD

Kornblum and Julian describe some of our myths and stereotypes about the elderly:

> Popular culture characterizes old people as senile, lacking in individuality, tranquil, unproductive, conservative, and resistant to change. These beliefs persist despite abundant evidence to the contrary.[6]

On the other hand, the mass media portray some retired people as always traveling and playing golf, sunning themselves in warm climates in the winter, and being in good health and free of money worries. For the "young aging," particularly those in upper-income groups, there is some validity to this stereotype. But it is not the experience of most of the elderly in our society.

EXHIBIT 14.1

Age Need Not Be a Barrier to Making Major Contributions

- At 77 Ronald Reagan was president of the United States.
- At 80 George Burns received his first Academy Award for his role in *The Sunshine Boys*.
- At 81 Benjamin Franklin mediated the compromise that led to the adoption of the U.S. Constitution.
- At 82 Winston Churchill finished his four-volume text *A History of the English-Speaking Peoples*.
- At 88 Konrad Adenauer was chancellor of Germany.
- At 88 Michelangelo designed the Church of Santa Maria degli Angeli.
- At 89 Arthur Rubinstein gave a critically acclaimed recital at Carnegie Hall in New York City.
- At 89 Albert Schweitzer was directing a hospital in Africa.
- At 90 Pablo Picasso was producing engravings and drawings.
- At 91 Eamon de Valera was president of Ireland.
- At 93 George Bernard Shaw wrote a play entitled *Farfetched Fables*.
- At 100 Grandma Moses was still painting.

Source: U.S. News & World Report, Sept. 1, 1980, pp. 52–53.

The social and physical needs of the elderly have only recently been recognized. In earlier societies, few people survived to advanced ages. Life expectancy has increased dramatically in the United States since the turn of the 20th century—up from 49 years in 1900 to 76 years at present.[7]

Also, in most other societies, in contrast to ours, the elderly had some meaningful role to perform—as arbitrators and advisers, as landowners and leaders, as repositories of the wisdom of the tribe, as performers of tasks within their capabilities.

Chronological age is very important to us. Our passage through life is partially governed by our age. Chronological age dictates when we are deemed old enough to go to school, drive a car, marry, or vote. Our society has also generally selected 65 as the beginning of old age.

Members of nonliterate tribes often do not know how old they are. Old age is determined by physical and mental conditions, not by chronological age. And their definitions of old age are more accurate than ours. Everyone is not in the same mental and physical condition at age 65. Aging is an individual process that occurs at different rates in different people, and social-psychological factors may retard or accelerate the physiological changes.

The process of aging is called *senescence*. Senescence affects different people at different rates. In addition, the rates of change in various body processes affected by aging vary among people. Visible signs of aging include the appearance of wrinkled skin, graying and thinning of hair, and stooped or shortened posture from compressed spinal disks.

As a person ages, blood vessels, tendons, the skin, and connective tissue lose their elasticity. Hardening of blood vessels and stiffening of joints occur. Bones become brittle and thin; hormonal activity and reflexes slow down. Many of the health problems faced by the elderly result from a general decline of the circulatory system. Reduced blood supply impairs mental sharpness, interferes with balance, and reduces the effectiveness of the muscles and body organs. The probability of strokes and heart attacks also increases.

As a person ages, the muscles lose some of their strength, and coordination and endurance become more difficult. There is also a decline in the functioning of organs such as the lungs, the kidneys, and to a lesser extent, the brain. As senescence proceeds, hearing and vision capacities decline, food may not taste the same, the sense of touch may become less acute, and there may be a loss of memory of recent and past events. Fortunately, the degree to which one's body loses its vitality can be influenced by one's lifestyle. People who are mentally and physically active throughout their younger years remain more alert and vigorous in their later years.

A key fact to remember about senescence is that no dramatic decline need take place at one's 65th birthday—or at any other age. We are all slowly aging throughout our lives. The rate at which we age depends on many factors. Most elderly people are physically active and mentally alert. Unfortunately, in reading about the process of aging, you may get the impression that both the physical functioning and the mental functioning of the elderly person are reduced to a minimal level. This is seldom the case. Although functioning may slow somewhat, it remains at a high enough level to enable most elderly persons to be physically active and mentally alert.

There is growing evidence that many of the effects of aging are neither irreversible nor inevitable. Rather, several of the supposed effects of aging are due largely to the inactivity that is often associated with aging. Learning to reduce stress, along with exercising and maintaining a healthful diet, can reverse, or at least hold in abeyance, many of the effects thought to be caused by aging. In one study, a group of 70-year-old inactive men participated in a daily exercise program, and at the end of a year, they had regained the physical fitness levels of 40-year-olds.[8]

In defining "old age," the federal government generally uses a chronological cutoff point—age 65—to separate elderly adults from others. There is nothing magical or particularly scientific about 65. In 1883 the Germans set age 65 as the criterion of aging for the world's first modern social security system for the elderly.[9] When the Social Security Act was passed in 1935, the United States also selected 65 as the eligibility age for retirement benefits based on the German model.

The elderly are an extremely diverse group, spanning a 30- to 35-year age range. This large range, by itself, leads to considerable diversity. Just as there are substantial differences between

TABLE 14.1

Number and Percentage of U.S. Population Age 65 and Older

	Year					
	1900	1950	1970	1980	1990	2000ᵃ
Number of older people (in millions)	3	12	20	25	31	35
Percentage of total population	4	8	9.5	11	12	13

ᵃ Percentages for 2000 are projected.
Source: United States Bureau of the Census, *Statistical Abstract of the United States, 1997* (Washington, DC: U.S. Government Printing Office, 1997).

20-year-olds and 50-year-olds, there are generally vast differences between those age 65 and those age 95.

An Increasing Elderly Population

There are now over ten times as many people age 65 and older as there were at the turn of the 20th century (see Table 14.1). There are several reasons for the phenomenal growth of the older population. The improved care of expectant mothers and newborn infants has reduced the infant mortality rate, and vaccinations have prevented many life-threatening childhood illnesses, allowing an increased proportion of those born to live to adulthood. New drugs, better sanitation, and other medical advances have increased the life expectancy of Americans.

Another reason for the increasing proportion of the elderly is that the birthrate is declining—fewer babies are being born, while more adults are reaching later adulthood. After World War II, a baby boom lasted from 1947 to 1960. Children born during these years flooded schools in the 1950s and 1960s. Then they moved into the labor market. After 1960, there was a baby bust, a sharp decline in birthrates. The average number of children per woman went down from a high of 3.8 in 1957 to the current rate of about 2.0.[10]

The increased life expectancy along with the baby boom followed by the baby bust will significantly increase the median age of Americans in future years. The median age is increasing dramatically. The long-term implications are that the United States will undergo a number of cultural, social, and economic changes.

The "Old Old"—The Fastest-Growing Age Group

As medical science makes strides in treating and preventing heart disease, cancer, strokes, and other killers, an increasing percentage of the elderly are living into their eighties, nineties, and beyond. People age 85 and over constitute, proportionately, the fastest-growing age group in the United States.

The older population is getting older. In 1995 the 65–74 age group (18.8 million) was 8 times larger than in 1990, but the 75–84 age group (11.1 million) was 14 times larger and the 85+ age group (3.6 million) was 29 times larger.[11]

We are witnessing "the graying of America," also called "the aging of the aged." This population revolution is occurring rather quietly in our society.

Those who are age 85 and over will present a number of problems and difficult decisions for our society. Alan Otten notes:

It is these "oldest old"—often mentally or physically impaired, alone, depressed—who pose the major problems for the coming decades. It is they who will strain their families with demands for personal care and financial support. It is they who will need more of such community help as Meals on Wheels, homemaker services, special housing. It is they who will require the extra hospital and nursing-home beds that will further burden federal and state budgets.

And it is they whose mounting needs and numbers already spark talk of some sort of rationing of health care. "Can we afford the very old?" is becoming a favorite conference topic for doctors, bioethicists and other specialists.[12]

Many of the old old suffer from a multiplicity of chronic illnesses. Common medical problems include arthritis, heart conditions, hypertension, osteoporosis (brittle bones), Alzheimer's disease, incontinence, hearing and vision problems, and depression.

The older an elderly person becomes, the higher the probability that she or he will become a resident of a nursing home. Although only about 5% of the elderly are currently in a nursing home, nearly one of four of those age 85 and over is living in a nursing home.[13] The cost to society for this care is high—over $30,000 a year per person.[14]

Despite the widespread image of families dumping aged parents into nursing homes, most frail elderly still live outside institutional walls with a spouse, a child, or a relative as the chief caregiver. Some middle-aged people are now encountering simultaneous demands to put children through college and to support an aging parent in a nursing home. (The term *sandwich generation* has recently been coined to refer to middle-aged parents who are caught in the middle of trying to meet the needs of both their aging parents and their children.)

With people retiring at age 65 or 70 and then living to age 85 or 90, the number of years spent in retirement can be considerable. To maintain the same standard of living after retiring will require immense assets.

Rising health-care costs and superlongevity have ignited controversy over whether to ration health care to the very old. For example, should people over age 75 be prohibited from receiving liver transplants or kidney dialysis? Discussion of euthanasia (the practice of killing individuals who are hopelessly sick or injured) has also been stirring increased debate. In 1984 Governor Richard Lamm of Colorado made the controversial statement that the terminally ill have a duty to die. Dr. Eisdor Fer stated:

The problem is age-old and across cultures. Whenever society has had marginal economic resources, the oldest went first, and the old people bought that approach. The old Eskimo wasn't put on the ice floe; he just left of his own accord and never came back.[15]

PROBLEMS FACED BY THE ELDERLY

We have a personal stake in improving the status and life circumstances of the elderly. They are what we are becoming. If we do not face and solve the problems of the elderly *now,* we will be in dire straits in the future. Let's examine some of these problems.

Low Status

We have generally been unsuccessful in finding anything important or satisfying for the elderly to do. In most nonliterate societies, the elderly were respected and viewed as useful to their people to a much greater degree than is the case in our society. Industrialization and the growth of modern society have robbed the elderly of high status. Prior to industrialization, older people were the primary owners of property. Land was the most important source of power; therefore, the elderly controlled much of the economic and political power. Now people earn their living primarily in the job market. The vast majority of the elderly own little land and are viewed as providing no salable labor.

Later Adulthood Is the Age of Recompense

The following case example illustrates that how we live in our younger years largely determines how we will live in our later years.

LeRoy was a muscular, outgoing teenager. He was physically bigger than most of his classmates and starred in basketball, baseball, and football in high school. In football he was chosen all-state linebacker in his senior year. At age 16 he began drinking at least a six-pack of beer each day, and at 17 he began smoking. Because he was an athlete, he had to smoke and drink on the sly. But LeRoy was good at conning others, and he found it fairly easy to smoke, drink, party, and still play sports. That left little time for studying, but LeRoy was not interested in that anyway. He had other priorities. He received a football scholarship and went on to college. He did well in football and majored in partying. His grades suffered, and, when his college eligibility for football was used up, he dropped out. Shortly thereafter he married Rachel Rudow, a college sophomore. She soon became pregnant and dropped out of college.

LeRoy was devastated after leaving college. He had been a jock for ten years, the envy of his classmates. Now he couldn't find a job with status. After a variety of odd jobs, he signed on as a road construction worker. He liked working outdoors and also liked the macho-type guys he worked, smoked, drank, and partied with.

He had three children with Rachel, but he was not a good husband. He was seldom home, and, when he was, he was often drunk. After a stormy seven years of marriage (including numerous incidents of physical and verbal abuse), Rachel moved out and got a divorce. She and the children moved to Florida with her parents so that LeRoy could not continue to harass her and the children. LeRoy's drinking and smoking increased. He was smoking over two packs a day, and he sometimes drank a quart of whiskey also.

A few years later he fathered an out-of-wedlock child for whom he was required to pay child support. At age 39 he married Jane, who was only 20. They had two children together and stayed married for six years. Jane eventually left him, because she became fed up with being belted around when LeRoy was drunk. LeRoy now had a total of six children to help support, and he seldom saw any of them. He continued to drink and also ate to excess. His weight went up to 285 pounds, and by age 48 he was no longer able to keep up with the other road construction workers. He was discharged by the company.

The next several years saw LeRoy taking odd jobs as a carpenter. He didn't earn much, and he spent most of what he earned on alcohol. He was periodically embarrassed by being hauled into court for failure to pay child support. He also was dismayed because he no longer had friends who wanted to get drunk with him. When he was 61, the doctor discovered that he had cirrhosis of the liver and informed LeRoy that he wouldn't live much longer if he continued to drink. Since LeRoy's whole life centered around drinking, he chose to continue. LeRoy also noticed that he had less energy and frequently had trouble breathing. The doctor indicated that he probably had damaged his lungs by smoking and now had a form of emphysema. The doctor lectured LeRoy on the need to stop smoking, but LeRoy didn't heed that advice either. His health continued to deteriorate, and he lost 57 pounds. At age 64, while drunk, he fell over backward and fractured his skull. He was hospitalized for three and a half months. The injury permanently damaged his ability to walk and talk. He now is confined to a low-quality nursing home. He is no longer allowed to smoke or drink. He is frequently angry, impatient, and frustrated. He has no friends. The staff detests working with him; his grooming habits are atrocious, and he frequently yells obscenities. LeRoy frequently expresses a wish to die to escape his misery.

ElRoy, LeRoy's brother, has lived a vastly different life. ElRoy had a lean, almost puny muscular structure and did not excel at sports. LeRoy was his parents' favorite and had dazzled the young females in school and in the neighborhood. ElRoy had practically no dates in high school and was viewed as a prude. He did well in math and in the natural sciences. He spent much of his time studying and reading. He also liked taking radios and electrical appliances apart. At first he got into trouble because he was not skilled enough to put them back together. However, he soon became known in the neighborhood as someone who could fix radios and electrical appliances.

ElRoy went on to college and studied electrical engineering. He had no social life but graduated with good grades in his major. He went to graduate school and earned a master's degree in electrical engineering. On graduation, he was hired as an engineer by Motorola in Chicago. He did well there and in four years was named manager of a unit. Three years later he was lured to RCA with an attractive salary offer. The group of engineers he worked with at RCA made some significant advances in television technology.

At RCA ElRoy began dating a secretary, Elvira McCann, and they were married when he was 36. Life became much smoother for ElRoy after that. He was paid well and enjoyed annual vacations with Elvira to such places as Hawaii, Paris, and the Bahamas. ElRoy and Elvira wanted to have children but could not. In ElRoy's early forties they adopted two children, both from Korea. They bought a house in the suburbs and also a sailboat. ElRoy and Elvira occasionally had some marital disagreements, but generally they got along well. In their middle adult years, one of their adopted sons, Kim, was tragically killed by a drunk driver. That death was a shock and very difficult for the whole family to come to terms with. But the intense grieving gradually lessened, and after a few years ElRoy and Elvira put their lives back together.

Now, at age 67, ElRoy is still working for RCA and loving it. In a few years he plans to retire and move to the Hawaiian island of Maui. ElRoy and Elvira have already purchased a condominium there. Their surviving son, Dae, has graduated from college and is working for a life insurance company. ElRoy is looking forward to retiring so he can move to Maui and get more involved in his hobbies of photography and model railroads. His health is good, and he has a positive outlook on life. He occasionally thinks about his brother and sends him a card at Christmas and on his birthday. But, since ElRoy never had much in common with LeRoy, he seldom visits him.

Source: From *Understanding Human Behavior and the Social Environment,* 2nd edition, pp. 441–442, by Charles Zastrow and Karen Kirst-Ashman. Copyright © 1990 Nelson-Hall Publishers, Chicago. Reprinted by permission.

EXHIBIT 14.2

High Status for the Elderly in China, Japan, and Other Countries

For many generations, the elderly in Japan and China have experienced higher status than the elderly in the United States. In both countries, the elderly are integrated into their families much more than in this country. In Japan more than 75% of the elderly live with their children, while in the United States most of the elderly live separately from their children.[a]

The elderly in Japan are accorded respect in a variety of ways. For example, the best seats in a home are apt to be reserved for the elderly, cooking tends to cater to the tastes of the elderly, and individuals bow to the elderly.

However, Americans' images of the elderly in Japan and China are somewhat idealized. The elderly, although more revered than in the United States, are not as revered and idealized as American stereotypes. Japan is now becoming more urbanized and Westernized. As a consequence, the proportion of the elderly living with their children is decreasing, and the elderly there are now often employed in lower-status jobs.[b]

What factors are associated with whether the elderly are accorded a position of high status in a culture? Five factors have been identified:

1. Older persons are recognized as having valuable knowledge.

2. Older persons control key family and community resources.

3. The culture is more collectivistic than individualistic.

4. The extended family is a common family arrangement in the culture, and older persons are integrated into the extended family.

An elderly Japanese American man celebrates his 102nd birthday with members of the Japanese American community. Traditionally, the elderly in Japan are accorded great respect and status.

5. Older persons are permitted and encouraged to engage in useful and valued functions as long as possible.[c]

---

[a] John W. Santrock, *Life-Span Development*, 5th ed. (Madison, WI: Brown & Benchmark, 1995).
[b] Ibid., p. 562.
[c] Ibid.

In earlier societies, the elderly were also valued because of the knowledge they possessed. Their experiences enabled them to supervise planting and harvesting and to pass on knowledge about hunting, housing, and craft making. They also played key roles in preserving and transmitting the culture. But the rapid advances of science and technology have tended to limit the value of the elderly's knowledge; books and other "memory-storing" devices have rendered the elderly less valuable as storehouses of culture and records.

There are other reasons why the status of the elderly has declined over time. Children no longer learn their future profession or trade from their parents; instead, these skills are acquired through institutions, such as the school system. In addition, the children of the elderly are no longer dependent on their parents for their livelihood; they make their living through a trade or profession that is independent of their parents. Finally, the elderly no longer perform tasks that are viewed as essential by society: Often the older workers' skills are viewed as outmoded even before these individuals retire.

The low status of the elderly is closely associated with *ageism,* which refers to discrimination and prejudice against people simply because they are old. Today many people react negatively to the elderly. Ageism is like sexism or racism because it involves intolerance and unfair treatment of all members of a particular social category.

Ageism is evident in our everyday language, by the use of terms that no racial or ethnic group would ever accept: "old buzzard," "old biddy," "old fogey." From a rational view, ageism makes no sense; those who delight in discriminating against the elderly will one day be old themselves. If you believe that "old age is ugly," you probably are guilty of ageism.

Early Retirement

Maintaining a high rate of employment is a major goal in our society. In many occupations, the supply of labor exceeds the demand. An often-used remedy for the oversupply of available employees is the encouragement of earlier retirement. Forced retirements often create financial and psychological burdens that retirees usually face without much assistance or preparation.

Our massive Social Security program supports early retirement, which can come as early as age 62. Pension plans of some companies and unions make it financially attractive to retire as early as age 55. Perhaps the extreme case is the armed forces, which permit retirement on full benefits after 20 years' service as early as age 38.

Many workers who retire early supplement their pension by taking another job, usually of lower status. Nearly 90% of Americans 65 years of age and older are retired, even though many are intellectually and physically capable of working.[16]

Early retirement has some advantages to society, such as reducing the labor supply and allowing younger employees to advance faster. But there are also some serious disadvantages. For society the total bill for retirement pensions is already huge and still growing. For the retiree, it means facing a new life and status without much preparation or assistance. Although our society has developed formal institutions to prepare the young for the work world, it has not developed comparable avenues for preparing the elderly for retirement. Being without a job in our work-oriented society is often a reality shock for older people.

In our society, we still view a person's worth partly by his or her work. People often develop their self-image (their sense of who they are) in terms of their occupation—"I am a teacher," "I am a barber," "I am a doctor." Because the later years generally provide no exciting new roles to replace the occupational roles lost on retirement, a retiree cannot proudly say, "I am a . . ." Instead, she or he must say, "I *was* a good . . ." The more a person's life revolves around work, the more difficult retirement is likely to be.

Retirement often removes people from the mainstream of life. It diminishes their social contacts and their status and places them in a *roleless role.* Individuals who were once valued as salespeople, plumbers, accountants, or secretaries are

EXHIBIT 14.3

Disengagement Theory: Response of Individuals and Society to Aging

In 1961 Elaine Cumming and William E. Henry coined the term *disengagement* to refer to a process whereby people respond to aging by gradually withdrawing from the various roles and social relationships they occupied in middle age.[a] Such disengagement is claimed to be functional for the individual because he or she is thought to gradually lose the energy and vitality to sustain all the roles and social relationships held in younger years.

The term *societal disengagement* has been coined to refer to the process whereby society withdraws from the aging person.[b] It is allegedly functional for our society—which values efficiency, competition, and individual achievement—to disengage from the elderly, who have the least physical stamina and the highest death rate. Societal disengagement occurs in a variety of ways: Older people may not be sought out for leadership positions in organizations, their employers may try to force them to retire, their children may no longer want them involved in making family decisions, and the government may be more responsive to meeting the needs of people who are younger. (Actually, societal disengagement is often unintended and unrecognized by society.) Many elderly persons do not handle forced role losses well. Some even try to escape with alcohol, drugs, or suicide.

With reference to the two terms just explained, *disengagement theory* hypothesizes a mutual disengagement or withdrawal between the individual and society. Disengagement theory has stimulated considerable interest and research. There is a good deal of controversy over whether disengagement is functional for the elderly and for our society. Research has found that some people undeniably do voluntarily disengage as they grow older. Yet disengagement is neither a universal nor an inevitable response to aging. Contrary to disengagement theory, most older people maintain extensive associations with friends. Most also maintain active involvements in organizations (such as church groups, fraternal organizations, and unions). Some elderly persons, after retiring, develop new interests, expand their circle of friends, do volunteer work, and join clubs. Others *rebel* against society's stereotypes and refuse to be treated as if they had little to offer society. Many of these people are marshaling political resources to force society to adapt to their needs and skills.

A severe criticism of societal disengagement theory is that it can be used to justify both ageism and society's failure to help the elderly maintain meaningful roles. Disengagement theory may, at best, be merely a description of the problems we must confront as we try to combat ageism.

In contrast to the disengagement theory of aging is the activity theory. It asserts that, the more physically and mentally active the elderly are, the more successfully they will age. There is considerable evidence that being physically and mentally active will help to maintain the physiological and psychological functions of the elderly. Whereas disengagement theory expects the elderly to slow down, activity theory urges them to remain physically and mentally active.

[a] Elaine Cumming and W. E. Henry, *Growing Old: The Process of Disengagement* (New York: Basic Books, 1961), p. 6.
[b] Robert C. Atchley, *Aging: Continuity and Change* (Belmont, CA: Wadsworth, 1983), p. 97.

now considered noncontributors in a roleless role on the fringe of society.

Several myths about the older worker have been widely accepted by both employers and the general public. Older workers are thought to be less healthy, clumsier, more prone to absenteeism, more accident prone, more forgetful, and slower in task performance.[17] Research has shown that these myths are erroneous. Older workers have lower turnover rates, produce at a steadier rate, make fewer mistakes, have lower absenteeism rates, have a more positive attitude toward their work, and have fewer on-the-job injuries than younger employees.[18] However, if the older worker does become ill, she or he usually takes somewhat longer to recover.[19]

Even though employers can no longer force a worker to retire, many exert subtle pressures on their older employees. Adjustment to retirement varies for different people. Retirees who are not worried about money and who are healthy are happier in retirement than those who miss their income and do not feel well enough to enjoy their leisure time. Many recent retirees relish the first long stretches of leisure time they have had since childhood. After a while, however, they may begin to feel restless, bored, and useless. Schick found that the most satisfied retirees tend to be physically fit people who are using their skills in part-time volunteer or paid work.[20]

Retirement appears to have little effect on physical health, but it sometimes affects mental health. Bossé, Aldwin, Levenson, and Ekerdt found that retirees are more likely than workers to report depression, obsessive-compulsive behavior, and physical symptoms that had no organic cause.[21] Workers who are pressured to retire before they want may feel anger and resentment, and may feel out of step with younger workers. Also, workers who defer retirement for as long as possible because they enjoy their work may feel that no longer working is an immense loss after they have been pressured to retire.

On the other hand, some people's morale and life satisfaction remain stable through both working and retirement years. The effect of retirement on the lives of people has positive consequences for some and negative consequences for others.

The two most common problems associated with retirement are adjusting to a reduced income and missing one's former job. Those who have the most difficulty in adjusting tend to be rigid or overly identify with their work by viewing their job as their primary source of satisfaction and self-image. Those who are happiest are able to replace job prestige and financial status with values stressing self-development, personal relationships, and leisure activities.

The "golden age" of leisure following retirement appears to be largely a myth. Lawton found that life in retirement is likely to be sedentary, with TV viewing and sleep outranking such traditional leisure-time activities as gardening, sports, clubs, and other pastimes.[22] Many of the elderly are poorly educated, which makes them less likely to enjoy reading or activities that focus on learning or self-improvement. A sharp reduction in income, fear of crime, lack of transportation, and reduced mobility also contribute to the sedentary lifestyle of the elderly.

It would seem far better if workers who are still productive could stay on the job longer on a part- or full-time basis rather than pensioned off or forced to take another job of lower status. (This perspective will be expanded on later in this chapter.)

Societal Emphasis on Youth

Our society fears aging and old age more than most other societies do. Our emphasis on youth is indicated both by our dread of getting gray hair and wrinkles or becoming bald and by the pleasure we experience when someone guesses our age to be younger than it actually is. We place a high value on change and newness. European societies, on the other hand, place a higher value on preserving traditional customs and lifestyles. Our society also emphasizes mobility, action, and energy. We like to think we are doers.

But why this emphasis on youth in our society? The reasons are not fully clear. There appear to be several factors. Industrialization has resulted in a demand for laborers who are energetic and agile and have considerable strength. Rapid advances in technology and science have made past knowledge and certain specialized work skills (for example, that of a blacksmith) obsolete. Competition has always been a cornerstone of our society, reinforced by Darwin's notions on evolution and the survival of the fittest. The mass media portray youthfulness and a beautiful physique as highly valued in our society, and the advertising industry seeks to sell a variety of diet programs and products, numerous cosmetics, and a variety of exercise equipment and programs that claim to give the consumer a more youthful image.

Health Problems and Costs of Health Care

Old age is a social problem partly because of the high costs of health care. Most of the elderly have at least one chronic condition, and many have multiple conditions. The most frequent health problems are arthritis, hypertension, hearing and visual impairments, heart disease, orthopedic impairments, sinusitis, cataracts, diabetes, and tinnitus (a sensation of hearing ringing or other noises).[23] Older persons visit their doctors more frequently, spend a higher proportion of their income on prescribed drugs, and are hospitalized for longer periods than younger people. As might be expected, the health status of the old old (85 and over) is worse than that of the young old.

The medical expenses of an elderly person average more than four times those of a young adult.[24] This is partly because the elderly suffer much more from long-term illnesses, such as cancer, heart problems, diabetes, and glaucoma.[25]

Of course, the physical process of aging (senescence) contributes to health problems. However, research in recent years has demonstrated that social and personal stresses also play a major role in causing diseases. The elderly face a wide range of stressful situations: loneliness, death of friends and family members, retirement, changes in living arrangements, loss of social status, reduced income, and a decline in physical energy and physical capacities. Medical conditions may also result from substandard diets, inadequate exercise, cigarette smoking, and excessive alcohol intake. Flynn notes:

> Studies of long-living peoples of the world show that neither heredity nor low prevalence of disease is a significant determinant of longevity. Four other factors are much more likely to predict long-term survival: (1) a clearly defined and valued role in society; (2) a positive self-perception; (3) sustained, moderate physical activity; and (4) abstinence from cigarette smoking. Studies in this country indicate that secure financial status, social relationships, and high education are also important.[26]

(Health care for the elderly is discussed further in Chapter 15.)

Financial Problems

Many elderly persons live in poverty. A fair number lack adequate food, essential clothes and medicines, and perhaps even a telephone. One-fifth of the elderly have incomes close to or below the poverty line.[27] Only a small minority have substantial savings or investments.

The importance of financial security for the elderly is emphasized by Sullivan et al. as follows:

> Financial security affects one's entire lifestyle. It determines one's diet, ability to seek good health care, to visit relatives and friends, to maintain a suitable wardrobe, and to find or maintain adequate housing. One's financial resources, or lack of them, play a great part in finding recreation (going to movies, plays, playing bridge or bingo, etc.) and maintaining morale, feelings of independence, and a sense of self-esteem. In other words, if an older person has the financial resources to remain socially independent (having her own household and access to transportation and medical services), to continue contact with friends and relatives, and to maintain her preferred forms of recreation, she is going to feel a great deal better about herself and others than if she is deprived of her former style of life.[28]

Financial problems among the elderly are compounded by the high cost of health care, as previously discussed. Another factor is inflation, which is especially devastating to those on fixed incomes. Most private pension benefits do not increase after a worker retires. For example, if annual living costs rise at the rate of 7%, a person on a fixed pension would in 20 years be able to buy only one-fourth as many goods and services as she or he could at retirement.[29] Fortunately, in 1974 Congress enacted an "automatic escalator" clause in Social Security benefits, providing a 3% increase in payments when the Consumer Price Index (CPI) increases a like amount.

Subgroups of the elderly population with high proportions of members living in poverty include African Americans, Latinos, women, and persons living alone or with nonrelatives (as compared to those living with family).[30]

The Social Security system was never designed to be the main source of income for the elderly. It was originally intended as a form of insurance that would *partially supplement* other assets when retirement, disability, or death of a wage-earning spouse occurred. Yet many elderly do not have investments, pensions, or savings to support them in retirement, and therefore, Social Security has become their major or sole source of income.

The U.S. Social Security system was developed in 1935. The system was fairly solvent until recently. During its first few decades, more money was paid into the system from Social Security taxes imposed on employers and employees than was paid out. This was due largely to the fact that life expectancy was only about 60 years of age. The life expectancy rate, however, has gradually increased to 76.[31] There is now a danger that the Social Security system will soon be paying out more than it takes in. Social Security taxes have increased sharply in recent years, but with the old old being the fastest-growing age group and with the proportion of the elderly increasing in our society, the system may go bankrupt. Some projections have the fund being depleted around 2020.

The *dependency ratio* is the ratio between the number of working people and the number of nonworking people in the population. With the elderly proportion of the population increasing, nonworkers will represent a ballooning burden on workers. Authorities predict that by the year 2020 the dependency ratio will decline from the current level of about 3 workers for every nonworking person to a ratio of about 2 to 1.[32]

Clearly, serious problems exist with the system. First, as already noted, the benefits are too small to meet the financial needs of the elderly. With payments from Social Security, an estimated 80% of retirees now live on less than half of their preretirement annual incomes. The monthly payments from Social Security are generally below the poverty line.[33] Second, it is unlikely that the monthly benefits will be raised much because the amount of Social Security taxes paid by employees is already quite high.

The nation faces some hard choices about how to keep the system solvent in future years. Benefits might be lowered, but this would even further impoverish recipients. Social Security taxes might be raised, but there is little public support for this, as the maximum tax rate has already increased more than tenfold since 1970 (about $400 in 1970 to about $5000 at the present time per employee).[34]

Loss of Family and Friends

Elderly persons who are single are generally less well off than those who are married. The longer life span of women has left nearly 60% of women over age 65 without a spouse.[35] Gordon Moss and Walter Moss comment about the value of marriage for older persons:

> They now have much more time for and are more dependent upon each other. Some marriages cannot handle this increased togetherness, but those that can become the major source of contentment to both partners. . . . A good marriage, or a remarriage, provides the elderly person with companionship and emotional support, sex, the promise of care if he is sick, a focus for daily activities, and frequently greater financial independence. Sex roles often blur, and the husband actively helps in household chores.[36]

EXHIBIT 14.4

Alzheimer's Disease

Tony Wilkins is 68 years old. Two years ago, his memory began to falter. As the months went by, he even forgot what his wedding day to Rose had been like. His grandchildren's visits slipped from his memory in 2 or 3 days.

The most familiar surroundings have become strange to him. Even his friends' homes seem like places he has never been before. When he walks down the streets in his neighborhood, he frequently becomes lost.

Tony is now quite confused. He has difficulty speaking and can no longer perform such elementary tasks as balancing his checkbook. At times Rose, who is taking care of him, is uncertain whether he knows who she is. All of this is very baffling for Tony. Until he retired 3 years ago, he had been an accountant and had excelled at remembering facts and details.

Tony has Alzheimer's disease. Although the disease sometimes strikes in middle age, most sufferers are over 65. Estimates of its prevalence ranges from 2% to 10% of all people over 65 and from about 13% to 50% of people 85 and over.[a] The statistics indicate the disease affects the old old to a greater extent than the younger old.

Alzheimer's disease is a degenerative brain disorder that causes gradual deterioration in intelligence, memory, awareness, and ability to control bodily functions. In its final stages, Alzheimer's leads to progressive paralysis and breathing difficulties. The breathing problems often result in pneumonia, the most frequent cause of death for Alzheimer's victims. Other symptoms include irritability, restlessness, agitation, and impairments of judgment.

Over a period lasting from as few as 5 years to as many as 20, the disease destroys brain cells. The changes in behavior displayed by those afflicted show some variation. Brownlee notes:

One sufferer refuses to bathe or change clothes, another eats fried eggs without utensils, a third walks naked down the street, a fourth has the family's beloved cats put to sleep, while yet another mistakes paint for juice and drinks it. The outlandish acts committed by Alzheimer's patients take as many forms as there are people who suffer the disease. Yet, in every case, the bizarre behavior serves as a sign that the sufferer is regressing towards unawareness, a second childishness.[b]

The most prominent early symptom of Alzheimer's is memory loss, particularly for recent events. Other early symptoms (which are often overlooked) are a reduced ability to play a game of cards, reduced performance at sports, and sudden outbreaks of extravagance. More symptoms then develop—irritability, agitation, confusion, restlessness, and impairments of concentration, speech, and orientation. As the disease progresses, the symptoms become more disabling. Caregivers eventually have to provide 24-hour supervision, which is a tremendous burden. As the disease progresses in its final stages, nursing home placement is often necessary. Near the end, the patient usually cannot recognize family members, cannot understand or use language, and cannot eat without help.

Brownlee describes the mental and physical trauma that caregivers and family members of those afflicted experience:

They live in a private hell, one that cannot be discussed with neighbors and friends in too much detail because the details are so devastating. They grieve even as their loved ones plunge them into a maelstrom of unreality, where mothers streak through the living room wearing nothing but a shower cap and garter belt

(continued)

EXHIBIT 14.4 *(continued)*

and grandfathers try to punch their baby granddaughters.[c]

In addition, the patient's inability to reciprocate expressions of caring and affection robs relationships of intimacy.

Diagnosing the disease is difficult because the disorder has symptoms that are nearly identical to other forms of dementia. The only sure diagnosis at the present time is observation of tissue deep within the brain, which can be done only by autopsy after death. Doctors usually diagnose the disease in a living person by ruling out other conditions that could account for the symptoms.[d]

Researchers in recent years have made tremendous strides in identifying the causes of Alzheimer's disease. As of 1997, three different genes have been linked to causing the disease, and there may be additional genes associated with it. Yet having one or more of these genes does not always result in the development of this disorder. Therefore, researchers believe there must be some as yet unidentified "triggers" such as viral infections, biochemical deficiencies, high levels of stress, toxic poisons, exposure to radiation, and nutritional deficiencies. Scientists are now aware that genetic tendencies are a contributing factor because relatives of Alzheimer's patients have an increased risk of having the disease in the future.[e]

Scientists are also investigating other hypotheses as to what triggers Alzheimer's. One intriguing clue comes from the finding that victims of Down syndrome (a severe form of mental retardation due to a chromosome defect) who survive into their thirties frequently develop symptoms indistinguishable from those of Alzheimer's. Another recent clue is the discovery of fragments of amyloid in brains of persons who died from the disorder. Amyloid is a very tough protein that in normal amounts is necessary for cell growth throughout the body. Some researchers hypothesize that abnormal patches of this protein in the brain set up a chain reaction that progressively destroys brain cells. This amyloid protein is an abnormal product formed from a larger compound called amyloid precursor protein, or APP.

Researchers are now seeking to develop a test to detect Alzheimer's disease in its early stages. If they are successful, people will be better able to plan for their future care and make arrangements for their families while they still retain control of their mental faculties. Furthermore, if in fact Alzheimer's disease results from an accumulation of the amyloid protein and if the early accumulation of this protein can be detected, then it is likely that drugs can be developed to treat the disorder by blocking the formation of amyloid in the brain.[f]

At the present time, there is no cure for the disease. Patients with Alzheimer's receive some relief from drugs that reduce depression and agitation and help them sleep. Both vitamin E and selegiline (a drug used to treat Parkinson's disease) seem to slow the progress of Alzheimer's disease. Exercise, physical therapy, proper nourishment, and proper fluid intake are also beneficial. Memory aids assist somewhat in everyday functioning. Especially helpful to patients and their families are emotional and social support provided by groups and professional counseling.

[a] Diane Papalia and Sally W. Olds, *Human Development*, 6th ed. (New York: McGraw-Hill, 1995), p. 541.

[b] S. Brownlee, "Alzheimer's: Is There Hope?" *U.S. News & World Report*, Aug. 12, 1991, pp. 40–49.

[c] Brownlee, "Alzheimer's: Is There Hope?" p. 48.

[d] L. L. Heston and J. A. White, *Dementia* (New York: W. H. Freeman, 1983).

[e] Papalia and Olds, *Human Development*, pp. 539–542.

[f] S. S. Sisodia, E. H. Koo, K. Beyreuthe, A. Unterbeck, and D. L. Price, "Evidence That B-Amyloid Protein in Alzheimer's Disease Is Not Derived by Normal Processing," *Science*, 248 (Apr. 27, 1990), pp. 492–495.

EXHIBIT 14.5

Triple Jeopardy: Being Female, African American, and Old

The poverty rate for elderly females is almost double that of elderly males.[a] Many immigrant ethnic groups in our society traditionally have relegated the woman's role to family maintenance when younger African American females have been victimized by both sexism and racism. Despite their positive status in the African American family and the African American culture, African American women over the age of 70 are the poorest population group in the United States.[b] Three of five elderly African American women live alone, and most of them are widowed.[c] The poverty rate of this age group is related to ageism, sexism, and racism. In the past, these women tended to hold very low-paying jobs, some of which were not even covered by Social Security or, in the case of domestic service, were not apt to be reported by the employer even though the reporting is legally required.

Although many of these women are struggling (financially, socially, and physically), Edmonds notes they have shown remarkable adaptiveness, resilience, coping skills, and responsibility.[d] Extension of family networks helps them cope with the bare essentials of living and gives them a sense of being loved. African American churches have provided avenues for meaningful social participation, social welfare services, feelings of power, and a sense of internal satisfaction. These women have also tended to live together in ethnic minority communities, giving them a sense of belonging. They have also tended to adhere to the American work ethic and have viewed their religion as a source of strength and support. Nonetheless, the income and health of older African American women (as well as that of other ethnic minority individuals) are important concerns in our aging society.

[a] John W. Santrock, *Life-Span Development*, 5th ed. (Madison, WI: Brown & Benchmark, 1995), p. 560.

[b] Ibid.

[c] Ibid.

[d] M. Edmonds, "The Health of the Black Aged Female," in *Black Age*, Z. Harel, E. A. McKinney, and M. Williams, eds. (Newbury Park, CA: Sage Publications, 1990).

The elderly person's life becomes more isolated and lonely when close friends and relatives move away or die. Of course, later adulthood is a time when close friends are most likely to die.

The needs of aging parents can present some painful dilemmas for their children, especially if the parents are poor or in ill health. The children may have families of their own, with heavy demands on their time and finances. For people on tight budgets, deciding how to divide their resources among their parents, their own children, and themselves can be agonizing. Some face the difficult question of whether to maintain a parent within their home, to leave the parent living alone, to place the parent in a nursing home, or to place the parent in some other type of housing for the elderly (such as a group home).

Substandard Housing

We hear so much about nursing homes that few people realize 95% of the elderly do not live in nursing homes or in any other kind of institution.[37] About 77% of all elderly males are married and live with their wives.[38] Because females tend to outlive their spouses, about 40% of women over age 65 live alone.[39] Nearly 80% of older married couples maintain their own households—in apartments, mobile homes, condominiums, or their own houses.[40] When the elderly do not maintain their own households, they most often live in the homes of relatives, primarily one of their children.

The elderly who live in rural areas generally have higher status than those in urban areas. People living on farms can retire gradually. Also, people whose income is in land, rather than in a job, can retain importance and esteem to an advanced age.

However, about three-quarters of our population reside in urban areas, where the elderly often live in poor-quality housing.[41] At least 30% of the elderly live in substandard, deteriorating, or dilapidated housing.[42] Often the urban elderly live in inner-city hotels or apartments with inadequate living conditions. Their neighborhoods may be decaying and crime-ridden, which makes them easy prey for thieves and muggers.

Fortunately, many mobile-home parks, retirement villages, assisted living residences, and apartment complexes geared to the needs of the elderly have been built throughout the country. Such housing communities provide a social center, security/protection, sometimes a daily hot meal, and perhaps a little help with maintenance.

Transportation

Only the more affluent and physically vigorous elderly can afford the luxury of owning and driving a car. The lack of convenient, inexpensive transportation is a problem faced by most older citizens.

Crime Victimization

Because of their reduced energy, strength, and agility, the elderly are vulnerable to being victimized by crime, particularly robbery, aggravated assault, burglary, larceny, vandalism, and fraud. Many older persons live in constant fear of being victimized, although reported victimization rates for the elderly are actually lower than those for younger people. The true victimization rates for the elderly may be considerably higher than official crime statistics indicate because many older

individuals feel uneasy about becoming involved with the legal and criminal justice systems. Therefore, they may fail to report some of these crimes. Also, some elderly people are afraid of retaliation from the offenders if they report the crimes.

Sadly, some of the elderly are hesitant to leave their homes for fear that they will be mugged or that their homes will be burglarized while they are away.

Sexuality in Later Adulthood

There is a common misconception that older people lose their sexual drive. An older male who displays sexual interest is labeled a "dirty old man." When two older people exhibit normal heterosexual behavior, someone may comment, "Aren't they cute?" Yet many older people have a strong sexual interest and a satisfying sex life.[43] Sexual capacities, particularly in women, show little evidence of declining with age, and a large percentage of both elderly men and elderly women are capable of sexual relations.[44]

Noted sex researchers William Masters and Virginia Johnson see no reason why sexual activity cannot be enjoyed by the elderly.[45] If sexual behavior does decline, it probably is due more to social reasons than to physical reasons. According to Masters and Johnson, the major deterrents to sexual activity when one is older are the lack of a partner, overindulgence in drinking or eating, boredom with one's partner, attitudes toward sex (such as the erroneous belief that sex is inappropriate for the elderly), poor physical or mental health, attitudes toward menopause, and fear of poor performance.[46]

The attitudes of the younger generations frequently create problems for the elderly. A widow or widower may face strong opposition to remarrying from other family members. Negative attitudes are often strongest when an elderly person becomes interested in someone younger who will become an heir if the older person dies. The elderly are sometimes informed that they should not be interested in members of the opposite sex and that they should not establish new sexual relationships when they have lost a mate.

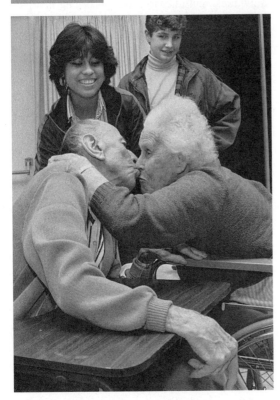

Residents of a private care facility share a kiss. Sexual capacities show little evidence of declining with age.

Fortunately, attitudes toward sexuality in later adulthood are changing. Merlin Taber notes:

With the changing attitudes of younger people to alternatives to the traditional family, some older people are finding informal arrangements for living together attractive. The couple who do not have a marriage ceremony can share all the companionship and sexual satisfactions without upsetting inheritance rights and retirement benefits. When they become aware of it, their children may accept such a pattern because they find it preferable to remarriage. We have no idea of the numbers that are involved, but the old as well as the young have new options as societal norms change. The popularity of living together without marriage will probably increase.[47]

Malnutrition

The elderly are the most uniformly undernourished segment of our population.[48] There are a number of reasons for chronic malnutrition among the elderly: transportation difficulties in getting to grocery stores; lack of knowledge about proper nutrition; lack of money to purchase a well-balanced diet; poor teeth or lack of dentures, which can greatly limit one's diet; lack of incentive to prepare an appetizing meal when one is living alone; and inadequate cooking and storage facilities.

Depression and Other Emotional Problems

The older person is often a lonely person. Most people 70 years of age or older are widowed, divorced, or single. When someone has been married for many years and his or her spouse dies, a deep sense of loneliness usually occurs that seems unbearable. The years ahead often seem full of emptiness. It is not surprising, then, that depression is the most common emotional problem of the elderly. Symptoms of depression include feelings of uselessness, of being a burden, of being unneeded, of loneliness, and of hopelessness. Somatic symptoms of depression include loss of weight and appetite, fatigue, insomnia, and constipation. It is often difficult to determine whether such somatic symptoms are due to depression or to an organic disorder.

Depression can alter the personality of an elderly person. Depressed people may become apathetic, withdrawn, and show a slowdown in behavioral actions. An elderly person's reluctance to respond to questions is apt to be due to depression rather than to the contrariness of old age.[49]

Those who have unresolved emotional problems in earlier life will generally continue to have them when older. Often these problems will be intensified by the added stresses of aging.

Two major barriers to good mental health in the later years are failure to bounce back from psychosocial losses (such as the death of a loved one) and failure to have meaningful life goals.

Later adulthood is a time when there are drastic changes thrust on the elderly that may create emotional problems: loss of a spouse, loss of friends and relatives through death or moving, poorer health, loss of accustomed income, and changing relationships with children and grandchildren.

Unfortunately, there is an erroneous assumption that *senility* and *mental illness* are inevitable and untreatable. On the contrary, the elderly respond well to both individual and group counseling.[50] In addition, even many 90-year-olds show no sign of senility. Senility is by no means an inevitable part of growing old.

Elderly males have the highest suicide rate of any age group in the United States.[51] Although the elderly make up about 13% of the population, about 25% of reported suicides occur in this age group.[52] The suicide rate of White men in their eighties is three times that of men in general.[53] There are a variety of reasons why the elderly have a high rate of suicide, including declining health, loss of status, reduced income, and lack of relationships with families and friends. The higher suicide rate for elderly males is thought to be due to the fact that males are more apt than females in our society to make work the central focus of their lives; once they retire, many no longer see a reason for living.

Death

Preoccupation with death—and particularly with the circumstances surrounding it—is an ongoing concern of the elderly. They see their friends and relatives dying, and they dread the disability, pain, and long periods of suffering that may precede death. They generally hope for a death with dignity; in their own homes, with little suffering, with mental faculties intact, and with families and friends nearby. The elderly also worry about the costs of their final illness, the difficulties they may cause others by the manner of their death, and the financial resources to permit a dignified funeral.

In our society, we tend to wall off the dying with silence. (Perhaps we do so to avoid having to confront our own mortality.) In hospitals great efforts are made to separate the dying from the living. Often the medical staff attempts to shield the dying person from awareness of his or her impending death. Families, too, begin to treat the patient differently when they know the end is near. (This different treatment often subtly informs the dying that death is imminent.)

A number of authorities have urged our society to treat death more openly.[54] Such openness would enable dying persons to prepare for death better, perhaps by having additional time to reassess their lives. It would also give the dying person more time to become accepting of death and to make financial arrangements, such as drawing up a will. It would give family members time to make necessary arrangements (including financial), as well as time to redress old wrongs and heal misunderstandings. We all need to face, and to come to terms with, our own eventual death. The popularity of courses in death and dying on college campuses shows that people feel a need to become more psychologically comfortable with facing death.

People in nonliterate societies were generally better prepared for death than we are. Margaret Mead notes:

> In peasant communities where things didn't change and where people died in the beds they were born in, grandparents taught the young what the end of life was going to be. So you looked at your mother, if you were a girl, and you learned what it was like to be a bride, a young mother. Then you looked at your grandmother and knew what it was like to be old. Children learned what it was to age and die while they were very small. They were prepared for the end of life at the beginning.[55]

(Unfortunately, in our society, many of us seek to deny our own deaths, even though we are all "terminal" from birth.)

In the modern United States, most people die in nursing homes or hospitals, surrounded by medical staff.[56] Such deaths often occur without dignity.

Fortunately, the hospice movement allows the terminally ill to die with dignity—to live their final weeks in the way they want. Hospices originated in the Middle Ages among European religious groups who welcomed sick, tired, or hungry

EXHIBIT 14.6

Ethical Issue: Should Assisted Suicide Be Legalized?

The technology of life-support equipment can keep people alive almost indefinitely. Respirators, artificial nutrition, intravenous hydration, and so-called miracle drugs not only sustain life but also trap many of the terminally ill in a degrading mental and physical condition. Such technology has raised a variety of ethical questions. Do people who are terminally ill and in severe pain have a right to die by refusing treatment? Increasingly, through "living wills," patients are able to express their wishes and refuse treatment. However, does someone in a long-term coma who has not signed a living will have a right to die? How should our society decide when to continue and when to stop life-support efforts? Courts and state legislatures are presently working through the legal complexities governing death and euthanasia.

Should assisted death, or assisted suicide, be legalized? As of 1998, only the Netherlands permitted physicians to give qualifying terminally ill patients a lethal dose of drugs. There is considerable controversy about assisted suicide in the United States. Hemlock Society founder Derek Humphry has written a do-it-yourself suicide manual that has become a best-seller. (The Hemlock Society promotes active voluntary euthanasia.) Michigan doctor Jack Kevorkian has made national news by building a machine to help terminally ill people end their lives and by assisting a large number of them to do so.

In the Netherlands, an informal, de facto arrangement made with prosecutors over 25 years ago allows physicians there to help patients die, as long as certain safeguards are followed. The patient, for example, has to be terminally ill, in considerable pain, and mentally competent; she or he must also repeatedly express a wish to die.

Oregon's Death with Dignity Act was passed by voters in 1994. It allows doctors to prescribe lethal drugs at the request of terminally ill patients who have less than 6 months to live. Doctors may only prescribe a lethal dose, not administer it.

People in favor of assisted suicide argue that unnecessary long-term suffering is without merit and should not have to be endured. They argue that people have a right to a death with dignity, which means a death without excessive emotional and physical pain and without excessive mental, physical, and spiritual degradation. They see assisted suicide as affirming the principle of autonomy—upholding the individual's right to make decisions about his or her dying process. Allowing the option of suicide for the terminally ill is perceived as the ultimate right of self-determination.

Opponents assert that suicide is unethical and is a mortal sin for which the deceased cannot receive forgiveness. They view assisted suicide as assisted murder. They maintain that modern health care can provide almost everyone a peaceful, pain-free, comfortable, and dignified end to life. Opponents believe that most terminally ill persons consider suicide not because they fear death but because they fear dying—pain, abandonment, and loss of control—all of which the hospice is designed to alleviate. Horror stories of intense suffering are most often the tragic results of medical mismanagement, they feel. Moreover, assisted-suicide legislation could easily result in the philosophy that the terminally ill have a *duty* to avoid being a financial and emotional burden to their families and to society. A health-care system intent on cutting costs could give subtle, even unintended, encouragement to a patient to die. Relatives of a terminally ill person receiving expensive

(continued)

EXHIBIT 14.6 *(continued)*

medical care may put pressure on the person to choose physician-assisted suicide to avoid eroding the family's finances. There is concern that, if competent people are allowed to seek death, then pressure will grow to use the treatment-by-death option with adults in comas or with others who are mentally incompetent (such as the mentally ill and those who have a severe cognitive disability). Finally, many people worry that, if the "right to die" becomes recognized as a basic right in our society, then it can easily become a "duty to die" for the elderly, the sick, the poor, and others devalued by society.

Some authorities have sought to make a distinction between active euthanasia (assisting in suicide) and passive euthanasia (withholding or withdrawing treatment). In many states, it is legal for physicians and courts to honor a patient's wishes not to receive life-sustaining treatment.

A case of passive euthanasia involved Nancy Cruzan. On January 11, 1983, when this Missouri woman was 25, her car overturned. Her brain lost oxygen for 14 minutes following the accident, and for the next several years she was in a "persistent vegetative state," with no hope of recovery. A month after the accident, her parents, Joyce and Joe Cruzan, gave permission for a feeding tube to be inserted. In the months that followed, however, the parents gradually became convinced there was no point in keeping Nancy alive indefinitely in such a hopeless condition.

In 1986 they were shocked when a Missouri state judge informed them that they could be charged with murder for removing the feeding tube. The Cruzans appealed the decision all the way to the U.S. Supreme Court, requesting the Court to overturn a Missouri law that specifically prohibits withdrawal of food and water from hope-

lessly ill patients. In July 1990, the Supreme Court refused the Cruzans' request that their daughter's tube be removed but ruled that states could sanction the removal if there is "clear and convincing evidence" that the patient would have wished it. Cruzan's family subsequently found other witnesses to testify that Nancy would not have wanted to be kept alive in such a condition.

A Missouri judge decided that the testimony met the Supreme Court's test. The tube was disconnected in December 1990, and Nancy Cruzan died several days later, on December 26.

At the present time, 10,000 Americans are in similar vegetative conditions, unable to communicate. Many of these individuals have virtually no chance to recover. Right-to-die questions will undoubtedly continue to be raised in many of these cases.

In June 1997, the U.S. Supreme Court ruled that terminally ill people do not have a constitutional right to doctor-assisted suicide. The Court upheld laws in New York and Washington State that make it a crime for doctors to give life-ending drugs to mentally competent but terminally ill patients who no longer want to live. The judges in their ruling made it clear their decision does not permanently attempt to resolve the assisted-suicide issue, and they in fact urged debate on this issue to continue.

Do you believe that the terminally ill have a right to die by refusing treatment? Do you believe that assisted suicide should be legalized? If you had a terminally ill close relative who was in intense pain and asked you to assist her or him in acquiring a lethal dose of drugs, how would you respond? Would you be willing to help? Or would you refuse?

EXHIBIT 14.7

Some Programs for the Elderly

- *Medicare:* Helps pay the medical and hospital expenses of the elderly (described in Chapter 15).

- *Old Age, Survivors, Disability, and Health Insurance:* Provides monthly payments to eligible retired workers (described in Chapter 4).

- *Supplemental Security Income:* Provides a minimum income for the indigent elderly (described in Chapter 4).

- *Medicaid:* Pays most medical expenses for low-income people (described in Chapter 15).

- *Food stamps:* Offset some of the food expenses for low-income people who qualify (described in Chapter 4).

- *Nursing Home Ombudsman Program:* Investigates and acts on concerns expressed by residents in nursing homes.

- *Meals on Wheels:* Provides hot and cold meals to housebound recipients who are incapable of obtaining or preparing their own meals but who can feed themselves.

- *Retired Senior Volunteer Program (RSVP):* Seeks to match work and service opportunities with the elderly volunteers seeking them.

- *Foster Grandparent Program:* Pays the elderly for part-time work in which they provide individual care and attention to ill and needy children and youths.

- *Service Corps of Retired Executives (SCORE):* Provides consulting services to small businesses. This program enables retired executives to retain meaningful functions in our society.

- *Senior citizens' centers, golden-age clubs, and similar groups:* Provide leisure-time and recreational activities for the elderly.

- *Special bus rates:* Reduce bus transportation costs for the elderly.

(continued)

---

travelers.[57] Hospices today are located in a variety of setting—in a separate unit of a hospital, in a building independent of a hospital, or in the dying person's home. Medical services and social services are provided, and extensive efforts are made to allow the terminally ill to spend their remaining days as they choose. Hospices sometimes have educational and entertainment programs, and visitors are common. Pain relievers are used extensively so that patients can live out their final days in relative comfort.

Hospices view the disease, not the patient, as terminal. The emphasis is on helping patients to use the time that is left rather than on trying to keep people alive as long as possible. Many hospice programs are set up to assist patients to live their remaining days in the home of their family. In addition to medical and visiting-nurse services, hospices have volunteers who help the patient and family members with services such as counseling, transportation, insurance forms and other paperwork, and respite care for family members. After patients die, many hospices offer bereavement services for the survivors.

Parent Abuse

Parent abuse refers to abuse of elderly parents by their children. It occurs most often when the parents live with the children or are dependent on

EXHIBIT 14.7 *(continued)*

- *Property tax relief:* Available to the elderly in many states.

- *Special federal income-tax deduction:* For people over 65.

- *Housing projects for the elderly:* Built by local sponsors with financial assistance provided by the Department of Housing and Urban Development.

- *Reduced rates at movie theaters and other places of entertainment:* Often offered voluntarily by individual owners.

- *Home health services:* Provide visiting-nurse services, physical therapy, drugs, laboratory services, and sickroom equipment.

- *Nutrition programs:* Provide meals for the elderly at group "eating sites." (These meals are generally provided four or five times a week and usually are lunchtime meals. These programs improve the nutrition of the elderly and offer opportunities for socialization.)

- *Homemaker services:* Provided in some communities to take care of household tasks that the elderly are no longer able to do for themselves.

- *Day-care centers for the elderly:* Provide activities that are determined by the needs of the group. (This service gives the family some relief from 24-hour care. Programs such as home health services, homemaker services, and day-care centers prevent or postpone institutionalization.)

- *Telephone reassurance:* Provided by volunteers, often older people, who telephone elderly people who live alone. (Such calls are a meaningful form of social contact for both parties and also ascertain whether any accidents or other serious problems have arisen that require emergency attention.)

- *Nursing homes:* Provide residential care and skilled nursing care for the elderly who cannot take care of themselves or whose families can no longer take care of them.

them. This problem is described in more depth in Chapter 6.

CURRENT SERVICES

The problems of the elderly are coming into the public spotlight. Many state governments now have an office on aging, and some municipalities and counties have established community councils on aging. A number of universities have established centers for the study of gerontology, and nursing, medicine, sociology, social work, architecture, and other disciplines and professions have established fields of study on gerontology. (*Ger-*

ontology is the scientific study of aging and the problems of the elderly.) Government research grants encourage gerontological study by academicians. Publishers are now producing books and pamphlets to educate the public about the elderly, and a few high schools are offering courses to help teenagers understand the elderly and their circumstances.

Present services and programs for the elderly are principally "maintenance" in nature; that is, they are primarily designed to meet basic physical needs. Nonetheless, there are a number of programs, often federally funded, that provide needed services to the elderly. A few of these are briefly described in Exhibit 14.7.

Older Americans Act of 1965

The Older Americans Act of 1965 created an operating agency (Administration on Aging) within the Department of Health, Education and Welfare.* This law and its amendments are the bases for financial aid by the federal government to assist states and local communities in meeting the needs of the elderly. The act was designed to secure the following for the elderly:

1. An adequate income.
2. Best possible physical and mental health.
3. Suitable housing.
4. Restorative services for those who require institutional care.
5. Opportunity for employment.
6. Retirement in health, honor, dignity.
7. Pursuit of meaningful activity.
8. Efficient community services.
9. Immediate benefit from research knowledge to sustain and improve health and happiness.
10. Freedom, independence, and the free exercise of individual initiative in planning and managing their own lives.[58]

Although these objectives are commendable, the reality is that the goals have not been realized for many of our elderly.

Nursing Homes

Nursing homes were created as an alternative to expensive hospital care and are substantially supported by the federal government through Medicaid and Medicare. Over 1.6 million older people now live in extended-care facilities, making nursing homes a billion-dollar industry.[59] There are more patient beds in nursing homes than in hospitals.[60]

_____
*This department was renamed the Department of Health and Human Services in 1980.

Nursing homes are classified according to the kind of care they provide. At one end of the scale are residential homes that offer primarily room and board, with some nonmedical care (such as help in dressing). At the other end of the scale are nursing-care centers that provide skilled nursing and medical attention 24 hours a day. The more skilled and extensive the medical care given, the more expensive the home. The costs per resident average more than $3000 per month.[61] Although only a small percentage of the elderly live permanently in nursing homes (about 5%), many more spend some time convalescing in them.

One scandal after another characterizes care in some nursing homes. Patients have been found lying in their own feces or urine. In some nursing homes, the food is so unappetizing that some residents refuse to eat it. Some homes have serious safety hazards. In some homes, boredom and apathy are common among staff as well as residents. A number of nursing homes fail to meet food sanitation standards and have problems administering drugs and providing personal hygiene for residents.[62]

Donald Robinson conducted a nationwide investigation of nursing homes and concluded: "I learned that the majority of nursing homes are safe, well-run institutions that take good care of the sick people entrusted to them. Some are superb."[63] Robinson also noted a number of horrors and abuses in some of the homes. The abuses included giving new and unapproved drugs to patients without their consent, giving patients heavy doses of tranquilizers to keep them docile, stealing funds from patients, submitting phony cost reports to Medicare, and charging patients thousands of dollars to gain admission to a home. There were also instances of sexual abuse of patients by staff members.[64]

At present, people of all ages tend to be prejudiced against nursing homes, even those that are well run. Frank Moss describes the elderly person's view of nursing homes: "The average senior citizen looks at a nursing home as a human junkyard, as a prison—a kind of purgatory, halfway between society and the cemetery—or as the first step of an inevitable slide into oblivion."[65] To some degree there is reality to the notion that nursing homes are places where the elderly wait to die.

The cost of care for impoverished nursing home residents is largely paid by the Medicaid program (described in Chapter 15). Since the federal government has set limits on what will be reimbursed under Medicaid, other problems may arise. There may be an effort to keep salary and wage levels as low as possible and the number of staff to a minimum. A nursing home may postpone repairs and improvements. Food is apt to be inexpensive such as macaroni and cheese, which is high in fats and carbohydrates. Congress has mandated that every nursing home patient on Medicaid is entitled to a monthly personal spending allowance. The homes have control over these funds, and some homes keep this money.

A danger of nursing home care is the potential abuse of the residents by staff members. In a telephone survey of 577 nurses and nurses' aides, Pillemer and Moore heard many instances of abuse by staff.[66] Over one-third of the respondents stated they had seen other staff members physically abusing patients—pushing, shoving, pinching, hitting, or kicking them; throwing things at them; or restraining them more than necessary. Ten percent acknowledged committing one or more of these acts themselves. Psychological abuse was even more common, with 81% of the respondents indicating they had seen other staff members yelling at patients, insulting them, swearing at them, isolating them unnecessarily, threatening them, or refusing to give them food. Forty percent of the respondents acknowledged committing such abuse themselves!

Complaints about the physical facilities of nursing homes include not enough floor space or too many people in a room. The call light by the bed may be difficult to reach, or the toilets and showers may not be conveniently located. And the building may be in a state of decay.

While the quality of nursing home care ranges from excellent to awful, nursing homes are needed, particularly for those requiring round-the-clock

EXHIBIT 14.8

Community Options Program: Providing Alternatives to Nursing Home Placement

Community Options Programs (COP) is an innovative program in Wisconsin to provide alternatives to nursing home placement. COP is funded by the state and federal governments and is administered by county social services departments.

To qualify for the program, a person must have a long-term or irreversible illness or disability and be a potential or current resident of a nursing home or of a facility for persons with a developmental disability. The person must also have income and assets that are below the poverty line. If these eligibility guidelines are met, a social worker and a nurse assess applicants for their social and physical abilities and disabilities to determine the types of services needed.

If an alternative to nursing home placement is available, financially feasible, and—most important—preferred by an applicant, a plan for services is drawn up and a start date for in-home or in-community services is determined.

A wide variety of services may be provided as alternatives to placement in nursing homes. Typical services include homemaker services, visiting-nurse services, home-delivered meals, adult foster care, group home care, assisted living care, and case management. COP is a coordinated program that makes use of a number of resources from a variety of agencies. Wisconsin has found that the program is not only cost effective in comparison to the high cost of nursing home care but is also preferred over nursing home care by service recipients. (A number of other states are now offering COP or similar programs.)

health care for an extended time. If nursing homes were abolished, other institutions such as hospitals would have to serve the elderly. Life in nursing homes need not be bad. Where homes are properly administered, residents can expand their life experiences.

The ideal nursing home should be lively (with recreational, social, and educational programming), safe, hygienic, and attractive. It should offer stimulating activities and opportunities to socialize with people of both sexes and all ages. It should offer privacy so that (among other reasons) residents can be sexually active. It should offer a wide range of therapeutic, social, recreational, and rehabilitative services. The best-quality care tends to be provided by larger nonprofit facilities that have a high ratio of nurses to nurses' aides.[67]

At present only 5% of the elderly population reside in nursing homes. However, it is estimated that one of every five of us who live beyond age 65 will spend part of our life in a nursing home.[68]

SOCIAL WORK AND THE ELDERLY

Social work education is taking a leading role in identifying the problems of the elderly and is developing gerontological specializations within the curricula. Social workers are a significant part of the staff of most agencies serving the elderly. Some states, for example, are now requiring that each nursing home employ a social worker.

Some of the services in which social workers have expertise in providing to the elderly are the following:

■ *Brokering services.* In any community, there are a wide range of services available, but few people are knowledgeable about the array of services or the eligibility requirements. The elderly are in special need of this "broker" service because some have difficulty with transportation and communication and others may be reluctant to request needed assistance to which they are entitled.

■ *Case management or care management services.* Social workers are trained to assess the social service needs of a client and the client's family. When appropriate, the social worker case manages by arranging, coordinating, monitoring, evaluating, and advocating for a package of multiple services to meet the often complex needs of an elderly client. Common functions of most case management programs for the elderly include: case finding, prescreening, intake, assessment, goal setting, care planning, capacity building, care plan implementation, reassessment, and termination.

■ *Advocacy.* Because of shortcomings in services to the elderly in our society, social workers need at times to advocate for needed services for the elderly.

■ *Individual and family counseling.* Counseling interventions focus on examination of the elderly client's needs and strengths, the family's needs and strengths, and the resources available to meet the identified needs.

■ *Grief counseling.* The elderly are apt to need counseling for role loss (such as retirement or loss of self-sufficiency), loss of a significant other (such as a spouse, a child, or an adult sibling), and loss due to chronic health or mental health conditions.

■ *Adult day-care services.* Social workers provide individual and family counseling, outreach and broker services, supportive services, group work services, and care planning services for the elderly being served by adult day-care services.

■ *Crisis intervention services.* Social workers providing crisis intervention seek to stabilize the crisis situation and connect the elderly person and the family to needed supportive services.

■ *Adult foster care services.* Foster care and group homes are designed to help the older person remain in the community. Social workers providing foster care match foster families with an older person and monitor the quality of life for those living in foster care settings.

■ *Adult protective services.* Social workers in adult protective services assess if adults are at risk for personal harm or injury owing to the actions (or inactions) of others. At-risk circumstances include physical abuse, material (financial) abuse, psychological abuse, and neglect (in which caregivers withhold medications or nourishment or fail to provide basic care). If abuse or neglect is determined, then adult protective services workers develop, implement, and monitor a plan to stop the maltreatment.

■ *Support and therapeutic groups.* In some settings, social workers facilitate the formation of support groups and therapeutic groups for the elderly or for family members (some of whom may be caregivers). Support and therapeutic groups are useful for such issues as adjusting to retirement, coping with illnesses such as Alzheimer's disease, dealing with alcohol or other drug abuse, coping with a terminal illness, and coping with depression and other emotional difficulties.

■ *Respite care.* Social workers are involved with the recruitment and training of respite care workers as well as identifying families in need of these services. When an older person requires 24-hour at-home care, respite services allow caregivers (such as the spouse or other family members) time away from caregiving responsibilities, which alleviates some of the stress involved in providing care around the clock.

■ *Transportation and housing assistance.* Social workers operate as brokers for finding appropriate housing in the community and for arranging safe transportation services.

■ *Social services in hospitals and nursing homes.* Social workers in these settings provide: assessment of social needs; health education for the older person and the family; direct services (such as counseling) to the elderly person, the family, and significant others; advocacy; discharge planning; community liaison; participation in program planning; consultation on developing a therapeutic environment in the facility; and participation in developing care plans that maximize the older person's potential for independence.

The reader will note that there is some overlap in these descriptions of services provided by social workers to the elderly. Because the elderly population is the most rapidly growing age group in our society, it is anticipated that services to the elderly will significantly expand in the next few decades. This expansion will generate a number of new employment opportunities for social workers.

THE EMERGENCE OF THE ELDERLY AS A POWERFUL POLITICAL FORCE

In spite of all the maintenance programs that are now available, the key problems of the elderly remain to be solved. A high proportion of older people do not have meaningful lives, respected status, adequate income, transportation, good living arrangements, a healthy diet, or adequate health care.

Our society has made gains in combating many kinds of prejudice, but ageism is still prevalent. Gordon and Walter Moss comment: "Just as we are learning that black can be beautiful, so we must learn that gray can be beautiful, too. In so learning, we may brighten the prospects of our own age."[69]

In the past, prejudice has been most effectively countered when those discriminated against joined together for political action. It therefore seems apparent that, if major changes in the elderly's role in our society are to take place, similar action will be needed.

Older people are, in fact, becoming increasingly involved in political activism—and in some cases, even radical militancy. Two prominent organizations are the American Association of Retired Persons and its affiliated group, the National Retired Teachers Association. These groups, among others, are lobbying for the interests of the elderly at local, state, and federal levels of government.

An action-oriented group that has caught the public's attention is the Gray Panthers. This organization argues that a fundamental flaw in our society is the emphasis on materialism and the consumption of goods and services rather than on improving the quality of life for all citizens (including the elderly). The Gray Panthers are seeking to end ageism and to advance the goals of human freedom, human dignity, and self-development. This organization advocates social action techniques, including getting the elderly to vote as a bloc for their concerns. The founder of the group, Maggie Kuhn, stated, "We are not mellow, sweet old people. We have got to effect change, and we have nothing to lose."[70]

There are clear indications that the politics of age have arrived. The elderly are one of the most politically organized and influential groups in the United States. The past 35 years have seen some significant steps toward securing a better life for the elderly: increased Social Security payments, enactment of Medicare and Medicaid programs, the emergence of hospices, and the expansion of a variety of other programs. With the clout of this powerful political bloc, additional changes to improve the status of the elderly in our society can be expected.

DEVELOPMENT OF SOCIAL ROLES FOR THE ELDERLY

It is essential for our society to find a meaningful, productive role for the elderly. At present, many companies' early retirement programs and society's stereotypic expectations of the elderly often result in older citizens' being unproductive, inactive, dependent, and unfulfilled. There are several steps that can be taken to provide productive roles for older people.

The elderly who want to work and are still performing well should be encouraged to continue working well past age 65 or 70, even if only half time or part time. Two elderly people working half time could be allowed to fill a full-time position. New roles might also be created for the elderly as consultants after they retire in the areas in which they possess special knowledge and expertise. For those who do retire, there should be

educational and training programs to help them develop their interests and hobbies (such as photography) into new sources of income.

Working longer would have a number of payoffs for the elderly and for society. Older people would continue to be productive, contributing citizens; they would have a meaningful role; they would continue to be physically and mentally active; they would have higher self-esteem; and they could break down the stereotypes of the elderly being unproductive and a financial burden on society. And importantly, they would be paying into the Social Security system rather than drawing from it.

Objections to such a system may be raised by those who maintain that some of the elderly are no longer productive. This may be true, but some younger people are also unproductive. What is needed to make the proposed system work is realistic, objective, and behaviorally measurable levels of performance. Individuals at any age who do not meet those standards would be informed about the deficiencies and given training to improve. If the performance levels still were not met, discharge would be used as a last resort. (For example, if a tenured faculty member's performance is inadequate—as measured by students' course evaluations, peer faculty evaluations of teaching, record of public service, record of service to the department and to the campus, and record of publications—she or he would be informed of the deficiencies. Training and other resources to meet standards should be offered. If the performance then does not improve to acceptable levels, dismissal proceedings would be initiated. Some colleges and universities are now moving in this direction.)

Another objection that has been voiced about this new system is that the elderly have worked most of their lives and therefore deserve to retire and live in leisure with a high standard of living. It would be nice if the elderly really had this option. However, that is not realistic. Most older citizens do not have the financial resources after retiring to maintain a high standard of living. The only real options in our society are to work and thereby maintain a higher standard of living or to retire and have a lower standard of living.

Some progress is being made in keeping the elderly in productive roles. Most members of the U.S. Supreme Court and many members of Congress are over age 70. In addition, a number of organizations have been formed to promote the productivity of the elderly. Three examples are the Retired Senior Volunteer Program, the Service Corps of Retired Executives, and the Foster Grandparent Program.

The *Retired Senior Volunteer Program (RSVP)* offers people over age 60 the opportunity of doing volunteer service to meet community needs. RSVP agencies place volunteers in hospitals, schools, libraries, day-care centers, courts, nursing homes, and a variety of other organizations.

The *Service Corps of Retired Executives (SCORE)* offers retired businesspeople an opportunity to help owners of small businesses and managers of community organizations who are having management problems. Volunteers receive no pay but are reimbursed for out-of-pocket expenses.

The *Foster Grandparent Program* employs low-income older people to help provide personal, individual care to children who live in institutions. (Such children include those who have a severe cognitive disability, those who are emotionally disturbed, and those who have a developmental disability.) Foster grandparents are given special assignments in child care, speech therapy, physical therapy, or as teacher's aides. This program has been shown to be of considerable benefit to both the children and the foster grandparents.[71] The children served become more outgoing and enjoy improved relationships with peers and staff. They have increased self-confidence, improved language skills, and decreased fear and insecurity. The foster grandparents have an additional (although small) source of income, increased feelings of vigor and youthfulness, an increased sense of personal worth, a feeling of being productive, and a renewed sense of personal growth and development. For society, foster grandparents provide a vast pool of relatively inexpensive labor that can be used to do needed work in the community.

The success of these programs illustrates that the elderly can be productive in both paid and volunteer positions. In regard to using elderly volunteers in agencies, Robert Atchley makes the following recommendations to increase the opportunities for successful outcomes:

> *First, agencies must be flexible in matching the volunteer's background to assigned tasks. If the agency takes a broad perspective, useful work can be found for almost anyone. Second, volunteers must be trained. All too often agency personnel place unprepared volunteers in an unfamiliar setting. Then the volunteer's difficulty confirms the myth that you cannot expect good work from volunteers. Third, a variety of placement options should be offered to the volunteers. Some volunteers prefer to do familiar things; others want to do anything but familiar things. Fourth, training of volunteers should not make them feel that they are being tested. This point is particularly sensitive among working-class volunteers. Fifth, volunteers should get personal attention from the placement agency. There should be people (perhaps volunteers) who follow up on absences and who are willing to listen to the compliments, complaints, or experiences of the volunteers. Public recognition from the community is an important reward for voluntary service. Finally, transportation to and from the placement should be provided.*[72]

In a 1990 study, a surprisingly large number of recent retirees said they would like to be back at work.[73] Of recent retirees, half are satisfied, a quarter are unable to work because of their health or family situations, and a quarter (about 2 million people) say they would prefer working again over retirement.

PREPARATION FOR LATER ADULTHOOD

Growing old is a lifelong process. Turning 65 does not interrupt the continuities in what a person has been, presently is, and will be. Recognition of this fact should reduce the fear of growing old. For people of modest means who have prepared thoughtfully, later adulthood can be a period, if not of luxury, then at least of reasonable comfort and pleasure.

Our lives depend largely on our goals and our motivations to achieve those goals. How we live prior to retiring will determine whether later adulthood will be a nightmare or a dream. There are a number of areas we should attend to in our younger years:

■ *Health:* A sound exercise plan and periodic health examinations are crucial to the prevention of chronic health problems. Also critically important in maintaining health is learning and using techniques to reduce psychological stress (see Chapter 15).

■ *Finances:* Saving money for later years is important, as is learning to manage or budget money wisely.

■ *Interests and hobbies:* Psychologically, people who are traumatized most by retirement are those whose self-image and life interests center around their work. Individuals who have meaningful hobbies and interests look forward to retirement so they can devote more of their time to these enjoyable activities.

■ *Self-identity:* People who are comfortable and realistic about who they are and what they want out of life are better prepared, including in later years, to deal with stresses and crises that arise.

■ *A view toward the future:* A person who dwells on the past or rests on past laurels is likely to find the later years depressing. On the other hand, a person who looks to the future is able to find new challenges and new satisfactions in later years. Looking toward the future involves planning for retirement, including deciding where you want to live and what you want to do with your free time.

■ *Effective problem solving:* If a person learns to cope effectively with crises in younger years, these coping skills will remain when the person is older. Effective coping involves learning to approach problems realistically and constructively.

SUMMARY

Aging is an individual process that occurs at different rates in different people. Chronological age is not an accurate measure of how physically fit or mentally alert an elderly person is.

People 65 and older now compose over one-tenth of our population. The old old are the fastest-growing age group in our society. The elderly encounter a number of problems in our society: low status, lack of a meaningful role, the social emphasis on youth, health problems, financial problems, loss of family and friends, inadequate housing, transportation problems, restrictive attitudes about expressing their sexuality, malnutrition, crime victimization, and emotional problems such as depression and concern with circumstances surrounding dying. A majority of the elderly depend on Social Security as their major source of income. Yet monthly payments are inadequate, and the system is no longer financially sound.

A wide array of services are available to older people, but these are primarily geared to maintaining the elderly, often at or only slightly above a subsistence level of existence. Services provided in many of our nursing homes are inadequate, and the level of care in some of these homes has been sharply criticized. Nursing homes have also been criticized as being "storage centers" for the elderly so that members of our society can avoid coming face to face with their own mortality.

Although the level of care needs to be substantially improved, nursing homes are needed for the elderly who cannot take care of themselves and/or for those whose families can no longer provide care. Most older persons, however, do not need nursing homes for permanent care or shelter. (It is not generally known that 95% of the elderly live independently or with relatives, not in nursing homes.)

To provide the elderly with a productive, meaningful role in our society, it is suggested that they be encouraged to work (either in paid jobs or as volunteers) as long as they are productive and have an interest in working to maintain their standard of living. Empowering the elderly to be productive in their lives would have a number of personal payoffs for them and would also be highly beneficial to society.

In many ways, the elderly are victims of ageism. Social workers play numerous roles in serving the elderly, including that of an advocate to secure system changes that will better serve the elderly. Increasingly, the elderly are becoming politically active and are organizing to improve their status. In the future, there are likely to be a number of social, economic, and political changes that will improve the status of the elderly.

NOTES

1. Gordon Moss and Walter Moss, *Growing Old* (New York: Pocket Books, 1975), p. 18.
2. Colin M. Turnbull, *The Mountain People* (New York: Simon & Schuster, 1972).
3. American Association of Retired Persons, *A Profile of Older Americans: 1996* (Washington, DC: AARP, 1996).
4. Diane E. Papalia and Sally W. Olds, *Human Development*, 6th ed. (New York: McGraw-Hill, 1995), pp. 543–550.
5. Milton L. Barron, "The Aged as a Quasi-Minority Group," in *The Other Minorities*, Edward Sagarin, ed. (Lexington, MA: Ginn, 1971), p. 149.
6. William Kornblum and Joseph Julian, *Social Problems*, 8th ed. (Englewood Cliffs, NJ: Prentice Hall, 1995), p. 334.
7. American Association of Retired Persons, *A Profile of Older Americans: 1996*, p. 1.
8. Joan Arehart-Triechel, "It's Never Too Late to Start Living Longer," *New York*, Apr. 11, 1977, p. 38.
9. Thomas Sullivan, Kenrick Thompson, Richard Wright, George Gross, and Dale Spady, *Social Problems* (New York: Wiley, 1980), pp. 335–370.
10. U.S. Bureau of the Census, *Statistical Abstract of the United States, 1997* (Washington, DC: U.S. Government Printing Office, 1997).
11. American Association of Retired Persons, *A Profile of Older Americans: 1996*, p. 1.
12. Alan S. Otten, "Ever More Americans Live into 80s and 90s, Causing Big Problems," *The Wall Street Journal*, Jul. 30, 1984, p. 1.
13. Papalia and Olds, *Human Development*, p. 569.
14. Ibid., pp. 569–570.
15. Eisdor Fer, quoted in Otten, "Ever More Americans Live into 80s and 90s, Causing Big Problems," p. 10.
16. American Association of Retired Persons, *A Profile of Older Americans: 1996*, p. 11.
17. Kornblum and Julian, *Social Problems*, p. 336.
18. Ibid.
19. Ibid.
20. F. L. Schick, ed., *Statistical Handbook on Aging Americans* (Phoenix, AZ: Oryz, 1986).
21. R. Bossé, C. M. Aldwin, M. R. Levenson, and D. J. Ekerdt, "Mental Health Differences Among Retirees and Workers: Findings from the Normative Aging Study," *Psychology and Aging 2* (1987), pp. 383–389.
22. M. P. Lawton, "Leisure Activities for the Aged," *Annals of the American Academy of Political and Social Science*, 438 (1978), pp. 71–79.
23. American Association of Retired Persons, *A Profile of Older Americans: 1996*, p. 13.
24. Ibid., p. 14.
25. Ibid.
26. Marilyn L. Flynn, "Aging," in *Contemporary Social Work*, 2nd ed., Donald Brieland, Lela Costin, and Charles Atherton, eds. (New York: McGraw-Hill, 1980), p. 353.
27. American Association of Retired Persons, *A Profile of Older Americans: 1996*, p. 10.
28. Sullivan et al., *Social Problems*, pp. 357–358.
29. Kornblum and Julian, *Social Problems*, pp. 343–346.
30. American Association of Retired Persons, *A Profile of Older Americans: 1996*, pp. 10–11.
31. *Statistical Abstract of the United States, 1997*.
32. Kornblum and Julian, *Social Problems*, pp. 343–345.
33. Ibid.
34. Ibid., pp. 343–344.
35. American Association of Retired Persons, *A Profile of Older Americans: 1996*, p. 3.
36. Moss and Moss, *Growing Old*, p. 47.
37. American Association of Retired Persons, *A Profile of Older Americans: 1996*, pp. 3–4.
38. Ibid., p. 3.
39. Ibid.
40. Ibid., pp. 3–4.
41. Ibid., p. 5.
42. Ibid., pp. 3–5.
43. Janet S. Hyde, *Understanding Human Sexuality*, 5th ed. (New York: McGraw-Hill, 1994).
44. Ibid.
45. William H. Masters and Virginia E. Johnson. "The Human Sexual Response: The Aging Female and the Aging Male," in *Middle Age and Aging*, L. Neugarten, ed. (Chicago: University of Chicago Press, 1968).
46. Ibid., p. 269.

47. Merlin Taber, "The Aged," in *Contemporary Social Work*, Donald Brieland, Lela Costin, and Charles Atherton, eds. (New York: McGraw-Hill, 1975), p. 359.

48. Papalia and Olds, *Human Development.*

49. B. M. Newman and P. R. Newman, *Development Through Life: A Psychosocial Approach* (Pacific Grove, CA: Brooks/Cole, 1995).

50. R. C. Atchley, *Social Forces and Aging*, 5th ed. (Belmont, CA: Wadsworth, 1988), pp. 8–10.

51. *Statistical Abstract of the United States, 1997.*

52. Ibid.

53. Ibid.

54. See, for example, Elisabeth Kübler-Ross, *On Death and Dying* (New York: Macmillan, 1969); R. E. Kavanaugh, *Facing Death* (Los Angeles: Nash, 1972).

55. Margaret Mead, "Dealing with the Aged: A New Style of Aging," *Current*, no. 136 (Jan. 1972), p. 44.

56. Carol Staudacher, *Beyond Grief* (Oakland, CA: New Harbinger, 1987).

57. Sullivan et al., *Social Problems*, p. 363.

58. *Older Americans Act of 1965, As Amended, Text and History* (Washington, DC: U.S. Department of Health, Education and Welfare, November 1970).

59. American Association of Retired Persons, *A Profile of Older Americans: 1996*, p. 4.

60. *Statistical Abstract of the United States, 1997.*

61. Ibid.

62. Kornblum and Julian, *Social Problems.*

63. Donald Robinson, "The Crisis in Our Nursing Homes," *Parade*, Aug. 16, 1987, p. 13.

64. Ibid.

65. Frank Moss, "It's Hell to Be Old In the U.S.A.," *Parade*, Jul. 17, 1977, p. 9.

66. K. Pillemer and D. W. Moore, "Abuse of Patients in Nursing Homes: Findings from a Survey of Staff," *Gerontologist*, 29 (1989), pp. 314–320.

67. Ibid.

68. Papalia and Olds, *Human Development.*

69. Moss and Moss, *Growing Old*, p. 79.

70. Quoted in Robert N. Butler, *Why Survive? Being Old in America* (New York: Harper & Row, 1975), p. 341.

71. Robert C. Atchley, *The Social Forces in Later Life: An Introduction to Social Gerontology*, 2nd ed. (Belmont, CA: Wadsworth, 1977), p. 267.

72. Ibid., p. 81.

73. Tamar Lewin, "Many Retirees Tire of Leisurely Lives, Seek New Jobs," *Wisconsin State Journal*, Apr. 22, 1990, p. 1A.

HEALTH
PROBLEMS
AND MEDICAL
SOCIAL
SERVICES

Health and happiness are what we want most in life. Wealthy people who develop a chronic illness often say they would, if given a choice, relinquish their riches for a return to health. Most Americans now consider proper medical care a basic human right for which society should pay if an individual cannot. The view that health care is a basic right rather than a privilege is of relatively recent origin. For example, in 1967 the president of the American Medical Association still asserted that health care should be available only to those who could afford it.[1] The view of health care as a right was expressed by former President Richard Nixon in his "Health Message of 1971":

Just as our National Government has moved to provide equal opportunity in areas such as education, employment, and voting, so we must now work to expand the opportunity for all citizens to obtain a decent standard of medical care. We must do all we can to remove any racial, economic, social, or geographic barriers that now prevent any of our citizens from obtaining adequate health protection. For without good health, no man can fully utilize his other opportunities.[2]

This chapter will:

- Briefly describe the health-care system in the United States.
- Summarize problems in health care: profit orientation, limited attention to preventative medicine, unequal access to health services, health care for the elderly, AIDS, unnecessary and harmful medical services, use of life-sustaining equipment, and the high cost of medical care.
- Discuss efforts to resolve these problems.
- Outline a number of proposed policies and programs to combat these problems.
- Describe medical social work.

PHYSICAL ILLNESSES AND THE HEALTH-CARE SYSTEM

There are hundreds of thousands of different medical conditions ranging in severity from a minor scratch to a terminal illness. The causes are also nearly infinite: accidents, infections, birth defects, viruses, bacteria, the aging process, stress, poor nutrition, and so on.

Medical services in this country are organized into four basic components: physicians in private practice, group outpatient settings, hospital settings, and public health services.[3]

Physicians in individual or solo practice are, proportionately, more often found in rural than in urban areas. Such a physician is usually a general practitioner who is trained to provide treatment for the more common medical ailments. Supervision of general practitioners is minimal or nil; they are primarily accountable only to patients. Except through referrals for consultation and occasional use of laboratories and hospitals, a physician in private practice works in relative isolation from colleagues.

Group outpatient settings can be organized in several ways. A group of general practitioners may share facilities, such as a waiting room, examining rooms, and a laboratory. Or each physician within a group may have a different specialty and complement the skills of the others. Because medical knowledge and treatment techniques have become so vast and diverse, it is now impossible for a physician to have in-depth knowledge of all areas. Another type of outpatient setting is one in which a third party (a university, union, business, or factory) employs a group of physicians to provide medical care for its constituency. In still another type, a group of doctors with the same specialty (for example, neurological surgery) provide services in the same facility.

A third subsystem of health care is the hospital setting, which has a wide range of laboratory facilities, specialized treatment equipment, inpatient care facilities, and highly skilled technicians. Hospitals employ diverse and numerous medical personnel. A hospital is generally the center of the medical-care system in communities. Because of the spiraling costs of hospital care and the lack of sufficient beds, many communities are now building nursing homes and convalescent homes for people who require fairly extensive medical care but not inpatient hospital attention.

Public health services are organized on five levels: local (city or county), regional, state, national, and international. The majority of public health services to a community are provided through local health programs. The priorities in public health keep changing; as success is achieved in dealing with one problem, other problems emerge that demand attention. Public health services have virtually eliminated a number of communicable diseases in this country, such as tuberculosis, polio, and smallpox.

The focus of public health services is primarily preventative in nature. Services provided through local health departments include: (a) health counseling to families regarding family planning, prenatal and postpartum care, growth and development, nutrition, and medical care; (b) skilled nursing care and treatment to the acute and chronically ill; (c) physical rehabilitation to patients with strokes, arthritis, and similar medical conditions; (d) school health services to public and parochial institutions and liaison services among home, school, and community; (e) disease prevention and control; (f) immunization services; (g) referral of families and individuals to make maximum use of available community resources; (h) environmental sanitation, which involves developing and enforcing codes, rules, and regulations designed to maintain and/or improve conditions in the environment that affect health (this activity covers a broad area, including air and water pollution, food protection, waste material disposal, and sanitation of recreation facilities); (i) maintenance of an index of all area births, deaths, marriages, and current communicable diseases; and (j) health education and information services to stimulate the public to recognize existing health problems. In the United States, the vast majority of health-care services are private

rather than public (that is, administered by the government).

PROBLEMS IN HEALTH CARE

The health-care system in the United States faces a number of problems. These include a service orientation versus profit orientation, limited attention to preventative medicine, unequal access to health services, low-quality health care for the elderly, AIDS, unnecessary or harmful care, use of life-sustaining equipment, and the high cost of medical care.

Service Orientation versus Profit Orientation

Most Americans believe that the only focus of health care is to keep people healthy by preventing diseases, illnesses, and impairments from occurring and by restoring to health as rapidly as possible those who do become ill. If this were the only objective, the health-care system would not receive very high grades. There are a number of countries that have a higher life expectancy than the United States, including Australia, Austria, Belgium, Canada, France, Italy, Japan, the Netherlands, Spain, Sweden, Switzerland, and the United Kingdom.[4] Life expectancy is highly correlated with the quality of health care in a society. As a population's health improves because of better medical care and improved living conditions, the average age to which its members live rises. (On the other hand, the life expectancy in the United States is more than double that of some developing countries. For example, it is 76 in the United States, but only 34 in Uganda.[5])

Another indicator of the quality of health care is the infant mortality rate. Again, many other countries have a lower infant mortality rate than the United States, including Australia, Austria, Belgium, Canada, Denmark, France, Germany, Japan, the Netherlands, Spain, Sweden, Switzerland, and the United Kingdom.[6] The higher the rate at which newborns live in a country is directly correlated with the quality of health care provided to newborns and their mothers. (The infant mortality rate in the United States is, however, much lower than in developing countries; in the United States, the infant mortality rate is about 8 per 1000 live births, while in Afghanistan it is about 150 per 1000 live births.[7]) The infant mortality rate is determined by the number of deaths of children under 1 year of age per 1000 live births in a calendar year.

The objectives of health-care providers in the United States are not only to restore and maintain health but also to make a profit. There are numerous statistics documenting that the system is prospering. Many of our more than 7000 hospitals are among the most modern in the world. Physicians have the highest median income of any occupational group. They earn several times more than the average wage earner. The mean income of physicians is about $200,000 per year.[8] The average daily cost for a hospital bed has gone from $74 in 1970 to over $900 in 1997.[9] One of the most profitable small businesses in this country is the private medical practice. Among the most profitable intermediate-sized businesses are nursing homes. The pharmaceuticals industry, involving the manufacture and sale of drugs, has been one of the most profitable large industries in the country.

The United States spends more money on health care (in both absolute and proportionate terms) than any other country. Medical costs constitute 15% of our total production of goods and services.[10]

Consumers seeking immediate and inexpensive health care in our country are often frustrated and angered over high costs and delays. Access is particularly difficult in low-income neighborhoods in cities and smaller rural communities because health-care facilities tend to be located in affluent urban and suburban neighborhoods. The late Robert F. Kennedy described the health-care system in the United States as "a national failure" that is "providing poor quality care at high costs."[11]

Other industrialized nations regard medical care as a social service. This philosophy is based

TABLE 15.1

Ten Leading Causes of Death in the United States

Rank	Percentage of Total Deaths
1. Heart disease	32.0
2. Cancer	23.3
3. Stroke	6.8
4. Chronic obstructing pulmonary disease	4.5
5. All accidents	3.9
6. Pneumonia and influenza	3.6
7. Diabetes	2.6
8. Suicide	1.3
9. Chronic liver disease and cirrhosis	1.1
10. Kidney diseases	1.0

Source: U.S. Bureau of the Census, Statistical Abstract of the United States, 1997 (Washington, DC: U.S. Government Printing Office, 1997), p. 94.

on the premise that the kind of care you receive depends on the kind of illness you have. In contrast, in the United States, the kind of medical care you receive depends not only on your illness but also on how much money you are able and willing to spend.

Emphasis on Treatment Rather Than on Prevention

Most of the major causes of death today in the United States are chronic diseases: heart disease, cancer, cerebrovascular disease (such as strokes), obstructive pulmonary disease, and the like (Table 15.1). Chronic diseases progress and persist over a long period of time. They may exist long before we are aware of them because often there are no symptoms in the early stages and because we tend to ignore early symptoms. Social, psychological, and environmental factors are important influences in the progression of these diseases. Heart disease, for example, is known to be associated with a diet high in saturated animal fats (beef, butter, and cheese), lack of consistent and vigorous exercise, heavy smoking, and stress.

A major problem is that modern medicine is oriented toward crisis medicine, which is geared to treating people *after they become ill.* The crisis approach is effective in coping with some types of medical conditions, such as acute problems (for example, injuries, influenza, or pneumonia). Unfortunately, with chronic diseases, once the symptoms manifest themselves, much of the damage has already been done, and it is often too late to effect a complete recovery. To curb the incapacitating effects of chronic diseases, the health-care delivery system needs to emphasize the prevention of illness before extensive damage occurs. To date, preventative medicine has had a lower priority than crisis-oriented medicine in terms of research funding, the allocation of health-care personnel, and the construction of medical facilities. (There is more profit in treatment programs than in prevention programs.) This emphasis on treatment violates the common-sense notion that "an ounce of prevention is worth a pound of cure."

The kinds of health problems that we have in this country stem largely from our lifestyles. Millions of Americans smoke, drink, or eat to excess. Smoking is a serious health hazard. It has been linked to a long list of diseases, including heart disorders, ulcers, lung cancer, and emphysema. The death rate for heavy smokers (two or more packs a day) is double that for nonsmokers.[12] Some authorities now believe that nicotine is more addictive than heroin or cocaine.[13] Secondhand smoke (breathing in the smoke from someone else who is smoking) is now recognized as a dangerous carcinogen.[14]

The health hazards of alcohol abuse are described at length in Chapter 8. The life expectancy of alcoholics is 10 to 12 years lower than that of nonalcoholics.[15]

Our diet is another aspect of lifestyle that has a profound impact on health and life expectancy. We eat too many fatty foods (such as red meat) and not enough fruits, vegetables, and whole-grain products. Our sugar consumption should be reduced and the fiber in our diet increased.[16] In

EXHIBIT 15.1

Health Practices and Longevity

The following ten health practices have been found to be positively related to good health and longevity:

1. Eating breakfast
2. Eating regular meals and not snacking
3. Eating moderately to maintain normal weight
4. Exercising moderately
5. Not smoking
6. Drinking alcohol moderately or not at all
7. Sleeping regularly 7 to 8 hours a night
8. Avoiding the use of illegal drugs
9. Learning to cope with stress
10. Leading a healthy sexual life

Source: Diane E. Papalia and Sally W. Olds, *Human Development,* 5th ed. (New York: McGraw-Hill, 1992), pp. 372–373.

addition, we love high-calorie food and have a major tendency to overeat, both of which cause the serious problem of obesity. Research has found that obesity is associated with a variety of health problems, including high blood pressure, high cholesterol levels, heart disease, and diabetes.[17] One-third of all Americans are now estimated to be overweight.[18]

Medical research shows that regular exercise is essential to good health. Exercise reduces significantly the risk of heart disease, which is the leading cause of death in the United States.[19] Regular exercise is one of the best predictors of overall longevity; yet the majority of Americans do not exercise regularly.[20] An often quoted minimum guideline for exercise is 30 minutes a day at least three or four times per week.

Environmental factors also pose health risks. Our air and water are filled with thousands of toxic chemicals (caused by emissions from autos and

EXHIBIT 15.2

Understanding and Reducing Stress

Miller and Smith document that rational and positive thinking has a major impact in promoting healing and maintaining health and that irrational and negative thinking is a major determinant of stress-related illnesses. (Thinking is irrational if it does one or more of the following: is inconsistent with objective reality, hampers you in protecting your life, hampers you in achieving short- and long-term goals, causes significant trouble with other people, and leads you to feel unwanted emotions.) Stress-related physiological and psychological disorders have now become our number one health problem.[a]

A simplified description of the effect of our thinking processes in creating stress-related illnesses is outlined as follows:

Stressor {
Events or experiences
↓
Certain kinds of *self-talk*
(For example, "This is a very dangerous situation.")
}

↓

Stress {
Emotions
(Such as tenseness, anxiety, worry, alarm)

↓

Physiological reactions
The alarm stage of the general stress reaction will occur. The physiological changes of this alarm stage include an accelerated heart and pulse rate, shallow respiration, perspiring hands, tenseness of the neck and upper back, a rise in red blood count for fighting infection, increased metabolism, and secretion of pro-inflammatory hormones.[b] The physiological reactions that most students experience prior to giving a speech before a group illustrate the components of this alarm stage.
}

↓

Stress-related disorders
(If the emotional and physiological reactions are intensive and long term, a stress-related disease is apt to develop—such as an ulcer, migraine headache, diarrhea, heart problems, digestive problems, cancer, hypertension, branchial asthma, hay fever, arthritis, enuresis, certain skin problems, constipation.) According to the above formula, there are two components of a "stressor": (a) the event and (b) the self-talk that we give ourselves about that event. *Stress* is the emotional and physiological reaction to a *stressor*. Self-talk plays a key role in producing stress. The self-talk approach enables us to understand how positive (as well as negative events) can lead to a stress reaction. For example:

Positive event
Receiving a promotion

↓

Self-talk
"I now will have additional responsibilities that I may or may not be able to handle."
"If I fail at these new responsibilities, I will be fired and will be a failure. My career plans will never be realized."
"This promotion will make others in the office jealous."
"I'm in big trouble."

↓

Emotion
Worry, tension, anxiety

↓

Physiological reaction
Alarm stage of the general stress reaction

↓

Stress-related disorder
After a prolonged period of self-talk worries, a stress-related illness—such as ulcers or high blood pressure—develops.

Stress can be reduced in three primary ways. One way is to identify irrational and negative self-

(continued)

EXHIBIT 15.2   *(continued)*

talk and then give yourself rational self-challenges (see Chapter 5 for examples of this approach). A second way is to become involved in activities that you enjoy, which will lead you to stop your irrational thinking and instead focus on events you view more positively. For example, if you enjoy golf, playing golf will lead you to stop thinking about your day-to-day problems and instead lead you to think about the enjoyable experiences as-

sociated with golfing. Activities that are likely to stop your irrational thinking include hobbies, entertainment events, jogging and other exercise programs, biofeedback programs, muscle relaxation exercises, and meditation.[c] A third way to reduce stress is to change the event that is producing it (for example, taking a job that you view as having less pressure).

[a] Lyle H. Miller and Alma D. Smith, *The Stress Solution* (New York: Pocket Books, 1993).
[b] Hans Selye, *The Stress of Life* (New York: McGraw-Hill, 1965).
[c] These stress-reducing techniques are described in Charles Zastrow, *The Practice of Social Work,* 6th ed. (Pacific Grove, CA: Brooks/Cole, 1999).

factories) that create health hazards, such as cancer and emphysema. The fatality rate from automobile crashes is staggeringly high. Many such accidents are caused by driving while intoxicated.

Physicians often treat the symptoms of chronic illnesses rather than the underlying causes. Patients who are tense or anxious are prescribed tranquilizers rather than receiving therapy to reduce the psychological stress that is causing the tension. Patients who are depressed are prescribed antidepressant medication rather than being counseled to determine the underlying reasons for the depression. Patients with stress-related disorders (for example, ulcers, migraine headaches, insomnia, diarrhea, digestive problems, hypertension) are often prescribed medication rather than receiving therapy to change certain aspects of their lifestyles that would reduce the underlying psychological stress, which is a major factor in producing such problems.

In recent years, holistic programs, which are preventative in nature, have been established in industry, in hospitals, in school settings, in medical clinics, and elsewhere. Holistic medicine recognizes that our thinking processes function together with our body as an integrated unit, and it focuses on both our physical and psychological functions. The major determinants of most illnesses are our

lifestyles (including exercise patterns, diet, sleep, and particularly, stress reaction patterns) . Holistic medicine instructs people in proper exercises, proper diet, and techniques to reduce psychological stress in order to maintain health and curb the development of chronic disorders.

Thomas McKeown emphasized the responsibility that each person has (although it is often not recognized) in maintaining good health:

> The role of individual medical care in preventing sickness and premature death is secondary to that of other influences, yet society's investment in health care is based on the premise that it is the major determinant. It is assumed that we are ill and are made well, but it is nearer the truth to say that we are well and are made ill. Few people think of themselves as having the major responsibility for their own health. . . .
>
> The public believes that health depends primarily on intervention by the doctor and that the essential requirement for health is the early discovery of disease. This concept should be replaced by recognition that disease often cannot be treated effectively, and that health is determined predominately by the way of life individuals choose to follow. Among the important influences on health are the use of tobacco, the misuse of alcohol and drugs, excessive or

unbalanced diets, and lack of exercise. With research, the list of significant behavioral influences will undoubtedly increase.[21]

Unequal Access to Health Services

The use and availability of medical care are directly related to socioeconomic class and race. For example, the average life expectancy of white males is about 8 years longer than that for African American males, and the average life expectancy for white females is about 7 years longer than for African American females.[22] In addition, the infant mortality rate for African Americans is more than twice that for whites.[23] Nonwhites have higher rates of practically every illness than whites[24]; a number of factors help explain this difference, as nonwhites have less access to health care, are exposed to discrimination in a variety of ways, and are apt to receive a lower quality of health care from the health-care delivery system.

Membership in a lower social class is also correlated with higher rates of illnesses. The poor are seriously ill more frequently and for longer periods of time. They have higher rates of untreated illnesses and higher mortality rates for almost all illnesses. Contrary to popular belief, the highest rates of heart disease occur among the lowest salaried, not among top-level executives and managers.[25] (Stress levels may in fact be higher among the poor, who continually face psychological stress from financial crises. Differences in diet, exercise, and lifestyle patterns may also be factors.)

Of course, these higher rates of illness among the poor are largely attributable to their inability to afford private, high-quality medical care. Because of the profit motive, health-care services are located primarily in affluent urban areas and in suburbs. The poor who live in small rural areas or in urban, low-income regions therefore have much more difficulty in gaining access to medical care, especially if they have transportation barriers. In the United States, health-care services are provided on a *fee-for-service* basis. As a result, a two-tier system now exists; the upper tier serves the wealthy with high-quality care, and the lower tier serves the poor with inferior care.

When poor people do decide to seek treatment (often they wait until they are seriously ill), they tend to visit a clinic rather than a private or family physician. At the clinic, they may feel self-conscious about their appearance. Frequently they must wait for hours in crowded waiting rooms and generally receive impersonal care. A trusting relationship with a physician seldom develops. Doctors generally come from the middle and upper classes and therefore may face barriers in establishing rapport with low-income and nonwhite patients. Seham notes:

> In general, health professionals have little—if any—understanding of the lifestyle of the poor. For a doctor to advise a patient who is living in poverty to increase his intake of protein, without helping him to work out how to do it, is useless. Similarly, to suggest to a working mother that she come to the clinic for weekly treatments, when the clinic hours coincide with her working hours, is tantamount to not providing treatment at all.[26]

Being poor promotes poor health. The poor cannot afford to eat properly, so inadequate diet makes them more susceptible to illnesses. They are more likely to live in the most polluted areas, so they are more susceptible to cancer, emphysema, and other respiratory diseases. They cannot afford proper housing, have less heat in the wintertime, and are more exposed to disease-carrying rodents and garbage. Their lives are more stress filled, particularly with respect to financial concerns. They are less likely to know about and use preventative health approaches. They are less likely to seek early treatment that would prevent a serious disorder from developing. Because they are sometimes treated with hostility and contempt by physicians and other medical personnel, they are likely to avoid seeking medical help.

Low-Quality Health Care for the Elderly

As noted in Chapter 14, the proportion of the elderly in our society is increasing dramatically, and the old old (age 85 and over) are our fastest-

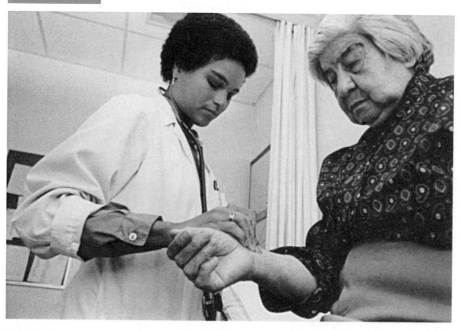

Most physicians today specialize in treating the young. The scarcity of doctors trained in geriatrics has compounded the crisis in health care for the elderly.

growing age group. Today there is a crisis in health care for the elderly for a variety of reasons.

The elderly are much more likely to have long-term illnesses. In the 1960s, the Medicare and Medicaid programs were created to pay for much of their medical expense. However, in the 1980s, the Reagan and Bush administrations decided that the government could no longer pay the full costs of that care. As a result, cuts were made in eligibility for payments and limits were set for what the government will pay for a variety of medical procedures.[27]

Physicians are trained primarily in treating the young and are often less interested in serving the elderly. Accordingly, when the elderly become ill, they may not receive quality medical care. For example, Hugh Downs, in an ABC news report, described the case of an 82-year-old woman who was shuffled from one hospital to another over a 3-month period and finally dumped in a county hospital, where she eventually died of a single grossly neglected bedsore. Downs notes:

The revolution of longer life has produced a new complex of critical medical needs, needs this nation does not yet seem prepared to meet. For example, there seems little prospect that there will be anything like the numbers of geriatricians needed to care for the elderly. It's a field still avoided by young doctors. Because of the complicated problems of the aging, there is a need for more health evaluation services and more psychiatric and rehabilitation assistance. Even for the limited efforts we now make, funding has always been meager.

The new era of the longevity revolution is already bringing with it multiplying health problems to which our society remains largely blind . . . and within this nation's vast medical complex, many old who could be helped are left adrift, trapped, their needs unrecognized.[28]

Medical conditions of the elderly are often misdiagnosed because doctors lack the specialized training to recognize the unique medical conditions of old people. Many of the elderly who are seriously ill do not get medical attention. One of the reasons physicians are less interested in treating the elderly is that the Medicare program sets reimbursement limits on a variety of procedures. With younger patients, the fee-for-service system is much more profitable.

There also are restrictions on hospital payments under Medicare. In the past, the payment system covered the full cost of the patient's expenses. However, to curtail rampant costs, the federal government in the 1980s set flat payments for each category of illness. These categories are called "diagnostic related groups" (DRGs). With this system, instead of reimbursing hospitals for the actual cost of treating Medicare patients, the government now pays a set fee for each medical condition. If a hospital spends less on a patient than the fixed amount, it makes money; if it spends more, it must absorb the loss. A perverse, unintended consequence of DRGs is that many seriously ill elderly patients are discharged prematurely.[29] Hospitals that have a social conscience and continue to treat the elderly beyond the length of time allowed by the DRG regulations must cover the expenses themselves and thereby risk bankruptcy.

The elderly who live in the community often have transportation difficulties in getting medical care. Those living in nursing homes sometimes receive inadequate care because health professionals are not interested in providing high-quality medical care for patients who no longer have much time to live. Medical care for our elderly is becoming a national embarrassment.

AIDS

Acquired immune deficiency syndrome (AIDS) is a contagious, presently incurable disease that destroys the body's immune system. AIDS is caused by the human immunodeficiency virus (HIV), which is transmitted from one person to another primarily during sexual contact or through the sharing of intravenous drug needles and syringes.

AIDS made national headlines in 1985 when it was revealed that actor Rock Hudson had contracted the disease. (Hudson died a few months after public release of the story.) National concerns about this disease were spurred again in 1991, when Magic Johnson (a prominent basketball player) announced that he had tested HIV positive (see Exhibit 15.3).

A virus is a protein-coated package of genes that invades a healthy body cell and alters the normal genetic apparatus of the cell, causing it to reproduce the virus. In the process, the invaded cell is often killed. The HIV virus falls within a special category of viruses called *retroviruses,* so named because they reverse the usual order of reproduction within the cells they infect. HIV invades cells involved in the body's normal process of protecting itself from disease, and it causes these cells to produce more of the virus. Apparently HIV destroys normal white blood cells, which are supposed to fight off diseases invading the body. As a result, the body is left defenseless and can fall prey to other infections. The virus devastates the body's immune or defense system so that other diseases occur and eventually cause death. Without a functioning immune system to combat germs, the affected person becomes vulnerable to bacteria, fungi, malignancies, and other viruses that may cause life-threatening illnesses, such as cancer, pneumonia, and meningitis.

In recent years, it has become clear that more than one virus is linked with the development of AIDS. The first virus to be identified, and the one that causes the largest number of AIDS cases, has been designated as human immunodeficiency virus type 1 (HIV-1). This virus appears to be the most virulent member of the growing family of AIDS and AIDS-related viruses. HIV is a formidable enemy in that it is constantly changing, or mutating, and is present in multiple strains. To simplify our discussion of AIDS in the following pages, we will refer to the infectious agent simply as HIV.

HIV is a tiny delicate shred of genetic material. As far as scientists know, it can live only in a very limited environment. It prefers one type of cell—the T-helper cell in human blood. Outside of blood and other bodily fluids, the virus apparently dies.

Documented ways in which the AIDS virus can be transmitted are by having sexual intercourse

EXHIBIT 15.3

Magic Johnson, an American Hero, Joins the Battle Against the AIDS Virus

On November 18, 1991, millions of people throughout the world were stunned when Earvin "Magic" Johnson announced at a news conference that he had contracted the AIDS virus. He also announced his retirement from the Los Angeles Lakers and the National Basketball Association after 12 superb seasons. He added, "I will now become a spokesman for the HIV virus."

Thirteen years earlier, Magic Johnson made his first appearance in the public eye by leading Michigan State University, as a sophomore, to the NCAA (National Collegiate Athletic Association) championship. At 6 feet 9 inches, he could play every position, including center.

In his 12 years with the Los Angeles Lakers, he led the Lakers to five world championships and, in the process, acquired three Most Valuable Player awards. Magic Johnson is not only one of the most talented individuals ever to play basketball, he is also charismatic and has an appealing smile. A few days after the news conference, Johnson indicated he believes he became infected with the virus from sexual intercourse with a female. He further acknowledged that over the years he has had a large number of female partners.

A few days after Johnson's news conference, he appeared on the *Arsenio Hall Show* and stated, "You don't have to feel sorry for me because if I die tomorrow, I've had the greatest life." His main message to Hall's audience and to the general public was: "Practice safe sex, start using condoms and be aware. . . . Please put your thinking caps on and put your caps on down there" (gesturing below his belt).

In 1991 fears about the disease ran rampant. Johnson triggered a storm of criticism when he tried to stage a professional basketball comeback in 1992 for possibly endangering the health of his teammates and other players. In February 1996, Johnson ended his retirement and returned to play for the Los Angeles Lakers. His comeback unleashed bear-hugs from his teammates and an avalanche of support from across the country. The change in public opinion about his comeback in 1996 versus 1992 is a remarkable sign of growing compassion and understanding by the public of persons infected by HIV. (Johnson retired at the end of the 1996 season "on his own terms.")

with someone who has HIV, by using hypodermic needles that were also used by someone who has the virus, and by receiving contaminated blood transfusions or other products derived from contaminated blood. Babies can contract the AIDS virus before or at birth from their infected mothers and through breast milk.

HIV has been isolated in semen, blood, vaginal secretions, saliva, tears, breast milk, and urine. Only blood, semen, vaginal secretions, and to a much lesser extent, breast milk have been iden-

tified as capable of transmitting the AIDS virus. Many experts doubt whether there is enough of the virus present in tears and saliva for it to be transmitted in these fluids. Experts rule out casual kissing or swimming in pools as a means of contracting AIDS. Sneezing, coughing, crying, and shaking hands also have not proven to be dangerous. Only the exchange of body fluids (for example, through anal, oral, or genital intercourse) permits infection. The virus is very fragile and cannot survive long without a suitable environment,

AIDS has generated a host of highly controversial issues. Some people view Jon Parker (above) as a hero; Parker has given over 50,000 clean hypodermic needles to drug addicts to help combat the spread of AIDS. Other people feel that the distribution of needles to addicts condones and promotes intravenous drug abuse.

and it is not able to penetrate the skin. In sum, evidence has not shown that AIDS can be spread through any type of casual contact. You cannot get AIDS from doorknobs, toilets, or telephones. Also, it does not appear that HIV can be transmitted by blood-sucking insects such as mosquitos or ticks.

Few lesbians have contracted AIDs. Lesbians are at low risk unless they use intravenous drugs or have unsafe sexual contact with people in high-risk groups. Female-to-female transmission is possible, however, through vaginal secretions or blood.

Women who use sperm from an infected donor for artificial insemination are also at risk of infection. Donors should be screened by licensed sperm banks as a preventative measure.

After an individual is exposed to the virus, it usually becomes inactive. Once it is in the body,

it apparently needs help to stay active. Such help might include the person's history of infections with certain other viruses, generally poor health, the abuse of certain recreational drugs (such as butyl nitrite), malnutrition, and genetic predisposition. For those who do develop AIDS, the mortality rate is very high.

In the early 1980s, the AIDS virus was transmitted in some cases through blood transfusions. Today the blood used in transfusions is tested for the presence of antibodies to the AIDS virus, making transmission in this way unlikely. Because antibodies do not form immediately after exposure to the virus, a newly infected person may unknowingly donate blood after becoming infected but before his or her antibody test becomes positive.

Most people infected by HIV will eventually develop AIDS. The length of time between initial infection of HIV and the appearance of AIDS symptoms is called the incubation period for the virus. The average incubation period (prior to the development of recent drugs) was estimated to be 7 to 11 years.[30] There is considerable variation, however, ranging from a few months (particularly for babies who are HIV positive) to 20 years or more.

The drug AZT (azidothymidine) has been found to delay the progress of the disease in some people. First synthesized in 1964 and initially developed as a cancer drug, AZT helps to extend life and provide hope. It does not cure AIDS, and there are some serious difficulties with the drug. AZT or Retrovir (its brand name) must be taken every 4 hours both night and day. People often experience very uncomfortable side effects. These include nausea, headaches, anemia, lowered white blood cell counts, liver function changes, kidney effects, and bone marrow damage. The longer the drug is taken, the more likely the person is to experience side effects with increasing severity. Additionally, the drug is very difficult to manufacture, involving 17 chemical steps plus 6 more steps to make it marketable. The result is scarcity and high costs. Nonetheless, the existence of a drug which at least can delay the effects of such a devastating disease has provided hope and has fought the black curtain of pessimism that has shrouded AIDS.

Other drugs to combat the AIDS virus are being developed. In 1991 the Food and Drug Administration approved DDI (didanosine) for treatment of adults and children with advanced AIDS who cannot tolerate or are not helped by AZT.[31] In 1995 and 1996, the Food and Drug Administration approved several drugs called protease inhibitors, which fight HIV by snipping an enzyme the virus needs before it can infect human blood cells. Researchers see signs that combining AZT with some of these protease inhibitors is delaying substantially the progression of AIDS in people who are HIV infected.[32]

A major health problem involves people who are HIV positive but have no symptoms of AIDS. Most of these individuals have not been tested for the AIDS virus and therefore are unaware they have it. They may then infect others, although they experience no life-threatening symptoms themselves. The following is a summary of high-risk factors in contracting AIDS:

■ Having multiple sex partners without using safe sex practices (such as using condoms). The risk of infection increases according to the number of sexual partners, male or female. In considering the risks of acquiring AIDS, a person should heed the warning, "When you have sex with a new partner, you are going to bed not only with this person but also with all this person's previous sexual partners."

■ Sharing intravenous needles. HIV may be transmitted by reusing contaminated needles and syringes.

■ Having anal intercourse with an infected person.

■ Having sex with prostitutes. Prostitutes are at high risk because they have multiple sex partners and often are intravenous drug users.

Sexually active heterosexual adolescents and young adults are increasingly becoming a high-risk group for contracting HIV. Persons in this age group tend to be sexually active with multiple sex partners. The risk of male-to-female transmission through sexual intercourse is higher than that of female-to-male. As noted, the risk of woman-to-woman transmission through sexual contact appears low. Although multiple exposures to HIV infection through sexual intercourse are not necessary for transmission, multiple sexual partners increase the likelihood that transmission will occur.

Lloyd describes the ways in which sexual transmission of HIV can be prevented or reduced:

Only two methods of completely preventing sexual transmission have been identified: (1) abstaining from sex or (2) having sexual relations only with a faithful and uninfected partner. The risk of infection through sexual intercourse can be reduced by practicing what has been called "safe sex," which is using a condom for all sexual penetration (vaginal, oral, and anal) whenever there is any doubt about a sexual partner's HIV status; engaging in nonpenetrative sexual activity; limiting the number of sexual partners;

and avoiding sexual contact with people such as prostitutes who have had many partners.[33]

Many people believe that any contact with someone who is HIV positive will guarantee illness and death. Such fears are not justified. Body fluids (such as fresh blood, semen, urine, and vaginal secretions) infected with the virus must enter the bloodstream for the virus to be transmitted from one person to another. Male homosexuals account for so many AIDS cases because they are likely to engage in anal intercourse. Anal intercourse often results in a tearing of the lining of the rectum, which allows infected semen to get into the bloodstream. Sharing a needle during mainlining a drug with someone who is carrying the virus is also dangerous because it involves transmission of blood. A small amount of the previous user's blood is often drawn into the needle and then injected directly into the bloodstream of the next user.

At the present time, there is no evidence that the virus can be spread by "dry" mouth-to-mouth kissing. There is a theoretical risk of transmitting HIV through vigorous "wet" or deep tongue kissing, as infected blood may be transmitted from one person to the other.

Several tests have been developed to determine if a person has been exposed to the virus. These tests do not directly detect the virus—only the antibodies a person's immune system develops to fight the virus. Two of the most widely used tests are called the ELISA and the Western blot, ELISA stands for Enzyme-Linked Immunosorbent Assay. ELISA can be used in two important ways. First, it can screen donated blood to prevent the AIDS virus from being transmitted by blood transfusions. Second, individuals who fear they may be carriers of the virus can be tested. For a person who has been infected with HIV, it generally takes 2 to 3 months before enough antibodies are produced to be detectable by the test.

ELISA is an extremely sensitive test and is therefore highly accurate in detecting the presence of antibodies. It rarely gives a negative result when antibodies are present. However, it has a much higher rate of false positive. That is, it may indicate that antibodies are present when in reality they are not. Therefore, it is recommended that positive results on the ELISA be confirmed by another test called the Western blot or immunoblot. This latter test is much more specific and less likely to give a false positive. Since the Western blot is expensive and difficult to administer, it can't be used for mass blood screening, as can the ELISA.

It must be emphasized that neither test can determine if a person already has AIDS or will actually develop it. The tests establish only the presence of antibodies that indicate exposure to the virus.

The origin of AIDS is unknown, although there have been a variety of speculations. (We probably never will be able to identify the origin, particularly now that AIDS has spread throughout the world.)

Persons with the AIDS virus are now classified as being either HIV asymptomatic (without symptoms of AIDS) or HIV symptomatic (with symptoms). HIV particularly invades a group of white blood cells (lymphocytes) called T-helper cells or T-4 cells. These cells in turn produce other cells, which are critical to the body's immune response in fighting off infections. When HIV attacks T-4 helper cells, it stops them from producing immune cells that fight off disease. Instead, HIV converts T-4 cells so that they begin producing HIV. Eventually the infected person's number of healthy T-4 cells is so reduced that infections cannot be fought off.

Once a person is infected with HIV, several years usually go by before symptoms of AIDS appear. Initial symptoms include dry cough, abdominal discomfort, headaches, oral thrush, loss of appetite, fever, night sweats, weight loss, diarrhea, skin rashes, tiredness, swollen lymph nodes, and lack of resistance to infection. (Many other illnesses have similar symptoms, so it is irrational for persons to conclude they are developing AIDS if they have some of these symptoms.) As AIDS progresses, the immune system is less and less capable of fighting off "opportunist" diseases, making the infected person vulnerable to a variety of cancers, nervous system degeneration, and infections caused by other viruses, bacteria, parasites, and fungi. Ordinarily, opportunistic infections are not life threatening to people with healthy immune systems, but they can be fatal to people with AIDS, whose immunological functioning has been severely compromised.

The serious diseases that afflict persons with AIDS include Kaposi's sarcoma (an otherwise rare form of cancer that accounts for many AIDS deaths), pneumocystic carinii pneumonia (a lung disease that is also a major cause of AIDS deaths), and a variety of other generalized opportunistic infections, such as shingles (herpes zoster), encephalitis, severe fungal infections that cause a type of meningitis, yeast infections of the throat and esophagus, and infections of the lungs, intestines, and central nervous system. The incidence of tuberculosis, a disease once nearly eradicated in the United States, has escalated in recent years due largely to the epidemic of HIV infection and AIDS.

Initially, HIV infection was diagnosed as AIDS only when the immune system became so seriously impaired that the infected individual developed one or more severe, debilitating diseases, such as Kaposi's sarcoma or pneumocystic carinii pneumonia. However, on April 1, 1992, the Centers for Disease Control broadened its definition of AIDS; now anyone who is infected with HIV and has a helper T-cell count of 200 cells per cubic millimeter of blood or less is said to have AIDS, regardless of other symptoms that person may or may not have. (Normal helper T-cell counts in healthy people not infected with HIV range from 800 to 900 per cubic millimeter of blood.)

AIDS as a syndrome is not any one specific disease. It simply makes those infected by the virus increasingly more vulnerable to any disease that might come along. The process of AIDS involves a continuum whereby those affected become more and more vulnerable to devastating diseases.

In some patients, AIDS may attack the nervous system and cause damage to the brain. This deterioration, called AIDS-dementia complex, occurs gradually over a period of time (sometimes a few years). Several specific intellectual impairments may result from AIDS. These include in-

ability to concentrate, forgetfulness, inability to think quickly and efficiently, visuospatial problems that make it difficult to get from place to place or to perform complex and simultaneous tasks, and slowed motor ability. It is interesting that language capacity and the ability to learn, difficulties that characterize people with Alzheimer's disease, do not seem to be affected.

Contrary to popular belief, people who are HIV positive can live for an indeterminately long time. Gavzer summarizes the characteristics that long-term AIDS survivors tend to have:

- *They are realistic and accept the AIDS diagnosis but do not take it as a death sentence.*

- *They have a fighting spirit and refuse to be "helpless-hopeless."*

- *They are assertive and have the ability to get out of stressful and unproductive situations.*

- *They are tuned in to their own psychological and physical needs, and they take care of them.*

- *They are able to talk openly about their illness.*

- *They have a sense of personal responsibility for their health, and they look at the treating physician as a collaborator.*

- *They are altruistically involved with other persons with AIDS.*[34]

There are a fortunate group of HIV infected persons—some scientists call them long-term nonprogressors—who show no measurable signs of AIDS for 10 or more years and who have a stable, near normal count of T-cells. Only about 5% of HIV-infected people fit this description.[35] Do their immune systems have a way of combating HIV? If a combative agent is identified, might it be replicated and then given as a treatment to others who are HIV infected? Scientists are now investigating these important questions.

As noted, at this time there is no cure for AIDS, and there are a multitude of hurdles to overcome in combating the disease. AIDS is caused by a form of virus. Even with modern technology, we don't know how to cure a virus. The common cold is also caused by a virus; although pharmaceutical companies have spent millions of dollars on research in the hopes of finding an effective treatment for colds, none has yet been found. Currently, extensive research is being undertaken to better understand, prevent, and fight AIDS.

Prevention can be pursued in two major ways. First, people can abstain from activities and behaviors that put them at risk for contracting the disease. Second, scientists can work on developing a vaccine to prevent the disease, just as there are vaccines that prevent polio and measles. A vaccine might either block the virus from attacking a person's immune system or bolster the immune systems so that HIV is unable to invade it.

Former Surgeon General C. Everett Koop makes the following recommendations to avoid getting the AIDS virus.

The most certain way to avoid getting the AIDS virus and to control the AIDS epidemic in the United States is for individuals to avoid promiscuous sexual practices, to maintain mutually faithful monogamous sexual relationships and to avoid injecting illicit drugs.[36]

It is advisable to use a condom when having sexual intercourse with a new partner until you are certain the person is not HIV positive. You cannot acquire AIDS from someone who is not infected by HIV.

In June 1998, the U.S. Supreme Court ruled that people infected by HIV (including those having AIDS) are covered by the 1990 Americans with Disabilities Act, which protects those with a disability against discrimination in jobs, housing, and public accommodations.

Unnecessary or Harmful Care

As indicated earlier, one of the objectives of the health-care system is to make a profit. All too often, this happens by using unnecessary diagnostic and treatment approaches—ordering diagnostic tests that are unnecessary, prescribing drugs and other medications that are unnecessary, and performing unneeded operations.

The poor and nonwhites, as noted earlier, are more likely to be victimized by inferior care, as are women. The health-care industry is male dominated, with men holding most of the prestigious, high-paying, and powerful positions. Men account for 78% of today's physicians, whereas 94% of the registered nurses are women.[37] Almost all dentists are men, whereas practically all dental hygienists and dental assistants are women.[38] The health-care system in the United States is clearly dominated by men in authority positions who tell women supportive staff what to do.

In recent years, the number of cesarean births has grown from 5% to 25% of all births, giving the United States the highest rate of such births.[39] Sullivan notes:

Some cesareans, of course, are medically justified, but there is much suspicion that some are performed for the convenience of medical personnel, to protect against malpractice suits, or because doctors and hospitals are reimbursed more for surgical births. In any event, the mother loses control of the birth process when it becomes overly medicalized. Over the years, then, male dominance in medicine has meant that men have been the "authorities" telling women about their own bodies, and what the men told the women sometimes did more to bolster inaccurate stereotypes or line the pockets of physicians than to benefit the health of women.[40]

The medical procedure that is among those most likely to be performed unnecessarily is a hysterectomy, which is the surgical removal of all or part of the uterus. It is estimated that one-third of all hysterectomies over the years were medically unnecessary.[41]

With regard to unnecessary, and even harmful, care, Susan Dentzer notes:

Experts estimate that up to one third of all medical services performed in the U.S. are of questionable value and may even be harmful. In effect, as much as $200 billion spent on health last year could have been poured down a rat hole, and 50,000 Americans may have died from procedures they didn't need.[42]

Thousands of deaths and hundreds of thousands of hospitalizations occur annually from reactions to antibiotics and other prescribed drugs. A large number of people each year become addicted to tranquilizers and to pain-killing drugs prescribed by physicians. Thousands of people die each year from complications after undergoing unnecessary surgery. No surgery is without its risks. Even with such a simple operation as a tonsillectomy, 2 of every 1000 patients die.[43]

Why does harmful treatment occur? One reason is that physicians make a profit from prescribing unnecessary treatment—and such treatment sometimes leads to complications. Another reason is that it is conservatively estimated that about 10% of the nation's physicians are incompetent and should have their licenses revoked.[44] Unfortunately, most patients are unable to judge the professional competency of their doctors.

Suing has become a national pastime, particularly malpractice suits in the medical field. The large number of successful suits documents the common existence of harmful treatment. At the same time, the possibility of a malpractice suit arising from failure to make a correct diagnosis because an unlikely procedure was *not* used leads many physicians to routinely order more costly diagnostic tests than are likely to be needed.

Controversy over the Use of Life-Sustaining Equipment

Medical technology has made dramatic advances in this century. Today we can keep alive for months, and in many cases years, people who in the past would have died.

Even after a person's brain has stopped functioning, technology can keep the respiratory processes, the heart, the liver, and other vital organs functioning for months. The lives of those who are terminally ill can be prolonged for substantial periods of time, but they may experience considerable pain and will be in a deteriorated condition. Many controversial issues have arisen about the use of life-sustaining technology. How should death now be defined, since vital functions can be

kept going even when the brain is dead? Some lawsuits have already been filed in organ donor cases in which organs allegedly were removed before the donor was deceased. Should the lives of the terminally ill be prolonged when there is practically no hope for recovery and the patients are in severe pain? Should society seek to keep alive people who are so severely and profoundly retarded that they cannot (and will never be able to) walk or sit up? Should abortion be mandatory if major genetic defects are detected in the fetus? When should life-prolonging efforts be used, and when should the patient be allowed to die? If terminally ill persons who are in severe pain want to end their life by suicide, should they be legally allowed to—and should others (such as physicians and close relatives) be legally allowed to assist in such suicides?

Because of the adverse consequences of being kept alive indefinitely when there is no hope of recovery, an increasing number of people are signing "living wills." In a living will, a person stipulates in writing that, if he or she becomes physically or mentally disabled from a life-threatening illness in which there is no reasonable expectation of recovery, she or he wants to be allowed to die and not be kept alive by artificial means. A living will is not binding, but it conveys a patient's wishes to those (such as relatives and attending physicians) who must make a decision about whether to use life-sustaining equipment. To complement living wills, a number of states have enacted legislation enabling adults to authorize (by filling out a Power of Attorney for Health Care form) other individuals (called health-care agents) to make health-care decisions on their behalf should they become incapacitated.

The President's Commission for the Study of Ethical Problems in Medicine and Biomedical and Behavioral Research recommended in 1981 that all states define death as occurring when either of the following is judged to have taken place: (a) the reversible cessation of circulatory and respiratory functions (this is essentially the definition used in the past) or (b) irreversible cessation of all functions of the entire brain, including the brain stem (this is a new definition). In adopting the "whole brain concept," the commission rejected a more controversial argument that death should be deemed to occur when "higher-brain functions" (those controlling consciousness, thought, and emotions) are lost. Patients who have lost higher-brain functions but retain the brain-stem functions can persist for years in a chronic vegetative state. Many states have now incorporated this definition of death into their statutes.

The High Cost of Medical Care

Health-care costs have risen dramatically in the past 35 years. Expenditures on health care as a percentage of this country's total production of goods and services increased from 5.6% in 1960 to 14.6% in 1996.[45] These high costs are now recognized as a matter of national concern. There are many reasons why health expenses are so high and continue to increase more rapidly than the rate of inflation.

First, as we've seen, one of the objectives of the health-care system is to make a profit. There are few controls designed to keep fees and prices down. Although the United States uses a marketplace approach to health care, ill consumers are not in a position to shop around for medical treatment. If they are suffering, their priority is to feel better, so they are willing to pay whatever a doctor chooses to charge. Most patients are not even informed before receiving treatment what the physician will charge. Fees for doctors' services are not advertised and therefore are not subjected to the competition that exists elsewhere in marketplace systems. Physicians have successfully established a public image in which they are so revered that most patients will sit for an hour in a waiting room without complaining and will be reluctant to ask questions about charges before receiving treatment. (The same individuals don't hesitate to voice their frustrations about having to stand in line for 5 minutes at a checkout counter in a store.)

Another factor in the high cost of health care is dramatic technological advances in life-saving treatment interventions. New equipment, along with the cost of highly skilled personnel to operate it, is expensive. Thirty-five years ago, we did not have cobalt machines, heart pacemakers, artificial heart valves, and microsurgical instruments that enable doctors to perform surgery under a microscope. Coleman and Cressey note that there are huge profits in developing new medical procedures and new drugs, and as a result, attention has been diverted away from less expensive (and often more effective) techniques of preventative medicine.[46] Klein and Castleman assert, "The processes that drive medical research toward expensive treatments also turn it away from preventive measures that do not hold the promise of corporate profit."[47]

Yet another reason is the increased life span of Americans. Now a larger proportion of our population is old, and the elderly require more health care than younger people. Many technically and professionally trained groups (such as nurses and physical therapists) are demanding salaries consistent with their training and responsibilities. These higher salaries are reflected, of course, in the overall costs of medical treatment.

Another contributor is the fact that third-party financing is increasingly paying medical bills. Historically, medical bills were primarily charged to and paid by consumers. Now most bills are charged to and paid by third parties, including private insurance companies and the public Medicare and Medicaid programs. Physicians are more likely to recommend expensive diagnostic and treatment procedures if they feel such procedures will not be a financial burden to the patient. Third-party payments also tempt some physicians to perform surgeries that may be unnecessary.

The increase in malpractice suits is also a contributing factor. Juries in many cases have awarded large settlements when malpractice is judged to have occurred. Physicians are required by law to carry malpractice insurance, with annual premiums ranging from $5000 to over $90,000, depending on a variety of factors—including geographic area and field of practice.[48] (Neurosurgeons and anesthesiologists are often charged the highest rates because their fields are considered "high risk.") These premium costs are, of course, passed on to consumers.

The tendency toward increased specialization by doctors is another factor. At present, about 90% of physicians have a specialty.[49] The growth of medical knowledge has encouraged specialization; it is impossible today for a physician to be an expert in all medical areas. However, specialists charge more than general practitioners to receive compensation for their additional training and expertise. Specialization also raises costs because patients often are required to consult with (and pay) two or more physicians for each illness that they have. (A serious additional problem caused by specialization is that medical care becomes impersonal, dehumanized, and fragmented because patients now rarely establish a trusting, long-term relationship with one physician.)

Hospital care is extremely expensive. Hospitals compete with one another to offer the most prestigious and expensive equipment, which often leads to a duplication of expensive and seldom-used technology. And hospitals, similar to physicians, are not subjected to fees set by consumers on a supply-and-demand basis. Patients generally are not able to shop around for the hospital they want to go to.

Hospitals, physicians, nursing home operators, and drug companies are politically powerful. Health-care providers are represented by such influential organizations as the American Medical Association, the Pharmaceutical Manufacturers Association, the American Hospital Association, and the American Association of Medical Schools. Health-care providers appear, at least at present, to have clout to prevent changes in health care that would sharply restrict their profits.

FINANCING MEDICAL CARE

Medical expenses are paid for by private insurance, through governmental programs, and by direct payments from the individual to the health-care provider. In 1996 private insurance paid 34% of the total costs for health care, the consumer paid 22%, and the government paid 44%.[50] Most of the 44% of the federal government's health-care bill is paid through Medicaid and Medicare. (The

EXHIBIT 15.4

How Should Financial Resources Be Allocated?

Fiscal conservatives argue that our society cannot afford widespread use of medical technology to prolong the lives of people who will not be productive in the future. They point to cases such as that of Geri D., which they say is proof that too much money is already being spent in some health-care situations.

At 5 months of age, Geri D. is in a residential facility for persons with a severe developmental disability. The annual cost there is over $100,000. Geri was born prematurely with multiple medical problems, including cardiovascular dysfunctions. Lifesaving technology kept her alive. She has a profound cognitive disability—she will never be able to sit up, a developmental milestone that children of average intelligence achieve at 6 months of age. Already, over $250,000 has been spent on this child. By the time she becomes a young adult, more than $2 million will have been spent on keeping her alive.

With medical advances, our society will face increasingly difficult issues regarding where financial resources should be used.

government also participates in the health insurance of federal employees, provides medical programs for families of members of the armed forces, and supports Veterans Administration hospitals.)

Medicaid

This program was established in 1965 by an amendment (Title XIX) to the Social Security Act. Medicaid provides medical care primarily for recipients of public assistance. It enables states to make direct payments to hospitals, doctors, medical societies, and insurance agencies for services provided to those on public assistance. The federal government shares the expense with states on a

55% to 45% basis. Medical expenses that are covered include diagnosis and therapy performed by a surgeon, physician, and dentist; nursing services in the home or elsewhere; and medical supplies, drugs, and laboratory fees.

Under the Medicaid program, benefits vary from state to state. The original legislation encouraged states to include coverage of all self-supporting people whose marginal incomes made them unable to pay for medical care. However, this inclusion was not mandatory, and "medical indigence" has generally been defined by states to provide Medicaid coverage primarily to recipients of public assistance.

Although the stated purpose of Medicaid was to assure adequate health care to the nation's poor and near poor, the program actually covers fewer than half of all poor families.[51] This is because the federal government has restricted eligibility in order to cut costs. In the past, hospitals supported the uninsured by charging paying patients more. But after years of soaring costs, government and private insurers have rebelled against "costshifting" by setting limits on what they will pay for services provided in hospitals. Many hospitals, unable to support the cost of indigent care, are turning these patients away. *A two-tiered system of health care is emerging in this country based on the ability to pay.*[52]

Medicare

The elderly are most afflicted with illnesses yet least able to pay for medical care. People over age 65 now make up 13% of the population, and the percentage is increasing each year. Over four times as many dollars are spent per capita on health care for the elderly as for hospital or nursing care.[53] Therefore, in 1965 Congress enacted Medicare (Title XVIII of the Social Security Act). Medicare helps the elderly pay the high cost of health care. It has two parts: hospital insurance (Part A) and medical insurance (Part B). Everyone age 65 or older who is entitled to monthly benefits under the Old Age, Survivors, Disability, and Health Insurance program gets Part A automatically, without paying a monthly premium. Practically everyone in the United States age 65 or older is eligible for Part B. Part B is voluntary, and beneficiaries are charged a monthly premium. Disabled people under age 65 who have been getting Social Security benefits for 24 consecutive months or more are also eligible for both Part A and Part B, effective with the 25th month of disability.

Part A—hospital insurance—helps pay for time-limited care in a hospital, in a skilled nursing facility (home), and for home health visits (such as visiting nurses). Coverage is limited to 150 days in a hospital and to 100 days in a skilled nursing facility. If patients are able to be out of a hospital or nursing facility for 60 consecutive days following confinement, they are again eligible for coverage. Covered services in a hospital or skilled nursing facility include the cost of meals and a semiprivate room, regular nursing services, drugs, supplies, and appliances. Part A also covers home health care on a part-time or intermittent basis if beneficiaries meet the following conditions: They are homebound, in need of skilled nursing care or physical or speech therapy, and services are ordered and regularly reviewed by a physician. Finally, Part A covers up to 210 days of hospice care for a terminally ill Medicare beneficiary.

Part B—supplementary medical services—helps pay for physicians' services, outpatient hospital services in an emergency room, outpatient physical and speech therapy, and a number of other medical and health services prescribed by a doctor, such as diagnostic services, X-ray or other radiation treatments, and some ambulance services.

Each Medicare beneficiary can choose coverage from an "alphabet soup" of health plans. This variety includes preferred provider organizations, provider service organizations, point of service plans, private fee-for-service plans, and medical savings accounts. (It is beyond the scope of this text to give detailed descriptions of these plans.)

Private Insurance

All health-care costs are rapidly rising, including the costs of health insurance. People who are not covered through group plans at their place of employment are increasingly finding it difficult to purchase private health insurance. An estimated 40 million Americans do not have health insurance.[54] Kornblum and Julian note:

> Contrary to what many people in the United States believe, the majority of the uninsured are full-time and part-time workers and their children. The very poor who are out of the labor force qualify for Medicaid, and the elderly are eligible for Medicare. Young people who are subject to frequent periods of unemployment, and minority workers who are employed at jobs with no health benefits, are especially likely to be uninsured.[55]

IMPROVING THE CURRENT SYSTEM

Practically everyone agrees that the rising costs of medical care are a threat to any family's financial security and, on a broader scale, to the economic stability of our society. Yet there is no consensus on specific measures that should be taken to hold down costs and to resolve the other problems that have been identified in this chapter. Some of the specific suggestions advocated by authorities in the field will be briefly summarized.

Holding Down Costs

A number of proposals to hold down health-care costs have been suggested. They include the following:

■ Increase the number of admissions to medical schools in order to train more doctors. Larger numbers of doctors could reduce difficulties in gaining access to health care and encourage competition among physicians in attracting patients, which could lead to reductions in fees.

■ Expand outpatient facilities (such as emergency care facilities that are open not only during the day but also during evening hours and on weekends) so that illnesses can be detected and

treated early, thereby preventing the development of more serious and costly medical conditions.

■ Permit doctors to advertise their services and fees. Other professionals, such as attorneys and dentists, are increasingly doing this. Such competition may result in fee reductions.

■ Encourage (through fellowships and scholarships) medical students to become general practitioners rather than specialists.

■ Expand outpatient treatment facilities so that more illnesses can be treated without hospitalization.

■ Train more physician assistants and paramedics to treat routine illnesses (for example, flu and colds), to provide preventative services, and to provide treatment in geographical areas without physicians.

■ Encourage patients to seek a second opinion before consenting to an operation to reduce unnecessary surgeries. Many insurance programs are now paying the fees for a second opinion.

■ Expand and encourage the use of generic drugs. Generic drugs are nonpatent drugs that have the same chemical composition as patent drugs. The main differences between generic and patent drugs are that the latter carry a trade name and cost considerably more.

Preventative Medicine and Managed Care

Prevention programs usually are cost saving in the long run. Several specific suggestions have been made for expanding the scope of preventative medicine.

Educational programs should be expanded in schools and among the general public to inform people how much our lifestyles (diet, handling of stress, exercise patterns, amount of sleep, hygiene habits) determine when we will become ill and what illnesses we will develop. Educational programs are also needed to help people recognize that, when they become ill, they are important participants in the treatment process; their attitudes, emotions, diet, and hygiene patterns will greatly influence their recoveries. Most Americans, unfortunately, believe that physicians have nearly magical powers, and they rely exclusively on doctors to cure them.

The federal government is encouraging the use of Health Maintenance Organizations (HMOs) as an alternative to other private insurance plans. The present health-care system is primarily curative in focus; it concentrates on illness and injury rather than on prevention. At the present time, most private health insurance policies do not cover periodic screening examinations but only provide coverage when a person is actually sick or injured. Such a model rewards providers of health services for treating illnesses but not for preventing them.

HMOs, in contrast, are prepaid health-care insurance plans that emphasize prevention. Subscribers pay a fixed annual sum, usually in installments, and in return receive comprehensive care. HMOs vary in size and structure but generally include physicians (both general practitioners and specialists) who provide a wide range of services—diagnostic, treatment, and hospital and home care. An HMO program operates similarly to an insurance program. Subscribers pay a fee (often the fee is paid by the subscriber's employer), and the HMO pays for all medical expenses that arise. Because HMO revenues are fixed, their incentives are to keep patients well because they benefit from patient wellness, not sickness. Their entire cost structure is geared to preventing illness and, failing that, to promoting rapid recovery through the least costly services consistent with maintaining quality. In contract to pay-for-service insurance plans, the HMO's financial incentives tend to encourage the least utilization of high-cost forms of care and also tend to limit unnecessary procedures.

In comparison to fee-for-service health insurance plans, HMO plans have been found to: (a) reduce the use of inpatient hospital care from 15% to 40%, (b) lower overall health-care costs by 15% to 20%, and (c) provide quality of care that is better or at least equal.[56]

It is crucial that incentives be found throughout the health-care system to focus on prevention and cost reduction, as HMOs do. Numerous public and private employers have chosen to provide HMO programs for their employees. HMOs have been successful in reducing overall health-care costs per patient, partly because they emphasize prevention.

HMOs, Medicare, and Medicaid compose the system of managed care in the United States. The growth in managed care programs has been phenomenal; in 1970 there were about 30 different plans, and there are now over 1500.[57] The majority of Americans with health insurance are now covered by a managed care program.[58] Managed care, in one sense, has turned the system upside down, from one in which payments tempted doctors to do too much to a system in which payments tempt them to do too little. Under the old system, patients did their doctor a favor by being sick, as the doctor was paid for providing treatment. In the new economics of managed care and HMOs, the relationship has been reversed, as most plans pay physicians a fixed fee per registered member regardless of how much treatment each patient needs. As a result, a chronically sick person is a liability for the HMO and the physician.[59]

HMOs have recently been criticized for the following practices and procedures:

■ Their 24-hour limits on hospital maternity stays.

■ The "gag clauses" prohibiting doctors from speaking freely about the range of treatments available to their patients.

■ The huge corporate bonuses paid to HMO executives.

■ Sensational cases of patients being denied care. (For example, a young mother in California died because her HMO did not approve a referral to a specialist.)

■ Patients having to jump through bureaucratic hoops to receive authorized care. (For example, an elderly man in Florida was presented with a $30,000 bill by his HMO because he failed to get emergency room authorization for care for his wife who suffered a cerebral hemorrhage. She later died from the hemorrhage.)

■ Patients having fewer choices among doctors and hospitals.

- Doctors being required to prescribe medicines from lists of cheaper drugs.

- Patients having to battle the HMO bureaucracy to get the treatment they feel they need, as HMOs have utilization review panels that review patients' records and decide which treatments the health plan will cover.

- Doctors becoming frustrated because the utilization review panels occasionally mandate a different treatment program for some patients than what the attending physician believes is optimal.[60]

As managed care expands in the United States, the merits and shortcomings of this system will increasingly be debated.

Additional Health-Care Proposals

Several other suggestions for resolving current health-care problems have been made. They include the following:

- Incentives need to be developed to encourage physicians to practice in rural areas and in low-income urban areas. One approach is to give stipends that would help pay the expenses of medical students in exchange for a requirement that recipients practice for a few years in areas currently underserved by physicians.

- More nonwhite students should be admitted to medical schools. These students after graduation tend to serve nonwhite communities.

- More female students need to be admitted to medical and dentistry schools to counter our health-care system's male domination.

- Further guidelines need to be established regarding when heroic life-sustaining measures should be used and when "the plug should be pulled." The high cost of keeping alive people who will never again be productive is raising some national concerns about euthanasia—so-called "mercy killing." The issues surrounding assisted suicide also need to be resolved.

- Colleges and universities need to expand existing programs and develop new programs to meet the emerging health-care needs of the elderly. Physicians and other health-care professionals (nurses, social workers, physical therapists, and so on) should receive training in diagnosing and treating the medical conditions of older citizens. Incentives need to be developed to encourage health-care professionals to work with the elderly.

- Sex education and AIDS education must start at the lowest grade possible as part of any health and hygiene program. People need to be informed of the importance of safer sex (such as using condoms).

- Offices, factories, and other work sites should develop a plan for educating the workforce and accommodating people with AIDS. Employees who are HIV positive and those who have AIDS should not be discriminated against but should be dealt with as are any other workers with a chronic illness.

Establishing a National Health Insurance Program in the United States

This country does not as yet have a national health insurance program. Great Britain, Canada, and many other countries do have a plan (Exhibit 15.5) in which public tax dollars are used to pay for medical care for all citizens. In the past three decades, some members of Congress and organizations have pressed for a public health insurance program. Many people subscribe to private insurance plans, which are available primarily to employed persons and their families. Those who are either marginally employed or unemployed are generally not covered by health insurance.

Hospitals cannot survive without assured income for services provided. Physicians, as well, need to be paid for their services. Alarmingly, 40 million Americans are without private or government-sponsored health insurance.[61]

There are several reasons why a national health insurance plan is needed. The rapid rise in health and insurance costs makes it impossible for the poor, for those of marginal income, and even for middle-class families to pay for insurance or extensive medical bills. The poor who are not

EXHIBIT 15.5

The British System: A Comparison

About five decades ago, Great Britain created a health-care system that has been described as "social medicine." The program illustrates that there are ways of providing health care other than our marketplace, for-profit system.

In the British system, medical care is provided as a public service, similar to the way in which elementary and secondary education is provided here. Most physicians are employed by the British government, which owns and operates the clinics, hospitals, and other facilities.

Every individual selects and registers with a physician. Most doctors are general practitioners who see patients at their office and, when needed, make house calls. Each physician receives a basic salary paid by the government and an additional small annual fee based on the number of patients on his or her register. (This fee is the same whether a person sees the physician 50 times a year or not at all.) Doctors' incomes, then, depend on the number of people who register with them, not on the amount or kind of treatment they provide. There are some specialists in Great Britain to whom general practitioners may refer cases for consultation and treatment. General practitioners earn, on the average, less than half of what American doctors earn.

Physicians are allowed to take private, fee-paying patients if they desire. (A few doctors serve only private patients.) In addition, some individuals (generally the wealthy) choose to receive private physician and hospital care, which, of course, they pay for. The quality of public care is generally about the same as that of private care, although private patients generally get faster appointments for nonemergency medical care, and private hospital rooms are generally more spacious and pleasant in appearance.

The British system provides free medical care to any person in the country—including visitors

(continued)

covered by Medicaid cannot pay for even moderate medical expenses; as a result, they often forgo early treatment and develop more serious medical conditions. Medicare covers short-term hospitalization expenses for the elderly but not long-term expenses. Extensive medical treatment can wipe out substantial savings and force a family deeply into debt, thereby dramatically changing its standard of living and lifestyle.

Starting with Franklin Roosevelt, every president except Ronald Reagan and George Bush has proposed a national health insurance program—without any being passed. The result is that the United States is the only industrialized nation lacking a comprehensive national medical insurance system.[62] A variety of national programs have in the past been advanced by Democratic and Republican legislators, administration officials, organized labor, representatives of private insurance companies, and the American Medical Association. In January 1991, the National Association of Social Workers proposed a national health-care plan that is similar in many respects to the British health-care system.[63]

President Clinton in 1993 proposed a national health insurance program that would have provided universal coverage for all Americans; he assigned this program the highest priority of his administration. Clinton's proposal was hotly debated by Congress in 1994, and several other alternative plans were proposed in Congress and also intensely debated. However, no proposal received

EXHIBIT 15.5 *(continued)*

who have a medical emergency. Practically all costs (for doctor visits, surgery, hospital rooms and meals, ambulance services, diagnostic tests, and essential medical supplies such as eyeglasses and wheelchairs) are paid by the government. There is a small charge for any prescription drug, even though the actual cost may be many times higher. There also is a small charge for each dental visit. (Persons over age 65 and under age 16 are excused from these fees.) Individuals do have to pay for purely cosmetic services such as face-lifts or gold fillings.

This health-care system is financed through taxes. British opinion polls show that around 80% of the public approve of the National Health Service. Health care in Great Britain is the most highly rated government service. The system is also supported by the medical profession and by both political parties. In terms of costs, the system appears more efficient than ours. The per-person cost of health care in Great Britain is less than half of that in the United States. Britons also appear to be healthier than Americans on a number of indicators: They live longer, have a lower infant mortality rate, and spend less time in hospitals.

The main complaint that Britons have about this public health-care system is that there are long waiting lists for treatment of nonemergency medical problems, such as minor illnesses. Patients sometimes must wait days, and in some cases even months, for treatment. Emergency problems such as heart attacks or broken arms receive immediate attention.

Great Britain's historical tradition in health care is different from ours. The primary focus of their system is service, whereas ours has both a service and a profit orientation. It is uncertain whether the British system would work in our country. Our medical profession, which has considerable vested interest in maintaining its high profits, would probably be successful in sabotaging efforts to establish a similar system in this country.

Sources: Judith Randa, "Health Service Is 30 and British Still Love It," New York *Daily News,* July 5, 1978, p, 36; James W. Coleman and Donald R. Cressey, *Social Problems,* 6th ed. (New York: HarperCollins, 1996), p. 251.

sufficient support to attain congressional passage. The main concern was the high cost of a national health insurance program.

Proposals for national health insurance have been of three major types. In the public approach, government agencies would collect funds (for example, from employers and employees) and pay the claims. In the mixed public–private approach, health insurance funds would be collected by the federal government and disbursed by private insurance companies. In the private approach, tax credits would be given to individuals for the purchase of private health insurance.

The main objection to national health insurance revolves around the cost to taxpayers and the effect such an expensive new program would have on the economy. There is concern that such a program would escalate the costs of health care in a manner similar to what has happened with Medicare and Medicaid.

MEDICAL SOCIAL WORK

Many public and private social welfare agencies (such as public welfare departments, adoption agencies, family service agencies, neighborhood centers, and probation and parole departments) are perceived as primary settings for social workers. They are *primary* because they are often managed by social workers and because social

Medical social workers provide direct casework with patients and their families as well as group work, consultation, and training of other professionals.

work is their primary service. Hospitals, medical clinics, and schools are, on the other hand, *secondary* settings because their primary service is not social work. But this secondary focus does not reduce their importance for social work because health care and education serve a vital function and expend a substantial proportion of our national resources. Because social workers are not administratively in charge of secondary settings, problems related to status and influence sometimes arise. In such settings, it is important for social workers to learn to work with those in control. American doctors are the highest-paid professional group in our society, and they tend to expect a status consistent with their salary. Some allied health professionals who work with physicians state that many doctors expect "Godlike" respect.

The main setting for medical social work is the hospital. Dr. Richard C. Cabot first introduced social services into the Massachusetts General Hos-

pital in Boston in 1905. Now almost every hospital has a social services department. In fact, a social services department is required by the American Hospital Association as a condition for accreditation.[64] Social workers provide not only direct casework with patients and their families but also group work with certain patients, consultation, and training of other professionals. They also are involved in planning and policy development within the hospital and with various health agencies. At times medical social workers teach medical school courses in which they convey their professional knowledge of the sociopsychological components of illnesses and of the treatment process.

It is becoming increasingly recognized that psychological processes are causative factors in nearly every illness—in stress-related illnesses, alcoholism, depression, drug addiction, heart conditions, hypertension, and susceptibility to viruses, bacteria, and other infections. The patient's emotions and motivation for recovery also substantially affect the treatment process. Sexually transmitted diseases (including AIDS) and cirrhosis of the liver, for instance, may evoke feelings of shame and guilt because of the stigma attached to these illnesses. People with heart conditions need to learn how to relax, avoid continued stressful conditions, and follow a prescribed diet. A miscarriage may result in a wide variety of emotional reactions that need to be dealt with. Adjusting to a chronic or permanent disability also evokes a variety of negative psychological reactions. Medical treatment teams depend on social workers to attend to social and psychological factors that are either contributing causes of medical ailments or side effects of a medical condition.

Physicians consider social work an allied medical discipline. Along with doctors, nurses, and other therapists, social workers take part in the study, diagnosis, and treatment-planning processes for patients. A medical social worker frequently obtains important information on the living conditions, environment, habits, personality, and income of patients. Because physicians are no longer as well acquainted with patients, such information is often vital in arriving at a diagnosis and a treatment plan. Through interviews with the patient and members of his or her family the worker gains a perspective on the social and emotional components of the illness and how these components may affect treatment.

In medical social work (now often referred to as social work in the health field), a wide variety of problems and situations are encountered. Social workers engage in the following activities:

- Helping terminally ill patients and their families cope.

- Counseling women who have had a mastectomy.

- Helping a low-income wife from a distant area find lodging in the community while her husband undergoes heart surgery.

- Counseling people who are so depressed they are contemplating suicide.

- Helping a single woman who has just become a mother to plan for the future.

- Providing genetic counseling for a young couple who gave birth to a child with a cognitive disability.

- Helping an executive of a large company make plans for the future following a severe heart attack.

- Counseling a woman about her emotional reactions following a miscarriage or a stillbirth.

- Being a support person to a hospitalized person with AIDS and to his or her friends and relatives.

- Finding living arrangements that will provide some medical attention for people who no longer need to be hospitalized.

- Counseling alcoholics and drug addicts or making appropriate referrals to other agencies.

- Counseling patients who are apprehensive about undergoing surgery.

- Helping someone suddenly struck with a permanent disability to adjust and make plans for the future.

- Meeting with relatives and friends of patients to help interpret the nature of the medical condition and perhaps to solicit their help in formulating a treatment plan to facilitate recovery.

- Counseling someone with emphysema on how to stop smoking.

- Counseling a rape victim concerning her psychological reactions.

- Informing relatives about the medical condition of someone who has just had a severe automobile accident.

While dealing with such problems and situations, the social worker is almost always a member of a medical team headed by a physician.

The job of a social worker in the health field is a dynamic one that requires continued study. With the dramatic expansion of new therapy approaches for medical conditions (for example, organ transplants, new prescription drugs, extensive new surgery techniques), it is essential that medical social workers keep informed about new technological approaches.

CASE EXAMPLE 15.1   An Illustration of Medical Social Work

Janet Ely was hospitalized to have a hysterectomy because she had a tumor in her uterus. She is an attractive, single, 22-year-old woman.

Before the surgery, the nursing staff noted that she was apprehensive, depressed, and anxious. Following the operation, Ms. Ely became even more agitated and withdrawn. Her physician, again, fully answered her questions related to her hysterectomy. However, Ms. Ely appeared very concerned and confused about her future, making statements such as, "No one will ever marry me now," "Life isn't worth living," "My family doesn't care about me—no one does," and "Oh, well, I'm going to die soon anyway." At this point, her doctor asked Ms. Ely if she would be willing to discuss her concerns with the social worker at the hospital, Vicki Vogel, and she indicated she would.

Ms. Vogel met with Ms. Ely on 5 of the remaining 7 days of her hospitalization. Ms. Ely had a number of problems, primarily involving plans for her future. She had alienated nearly all her relatives when, at age 17, she quit school in her senior year and began living with her 20-year-old boyfriend. A year and a half later, her boyfriend discovered that she was having an affair with another man and demanded that she leave. She went to live with the other man and became rather heavily involved in drinking and experimenting with drugs. A year ago, Ms. Ely left this man and moved to this area. She is now living with a divorced man.

Ms. Ely continued to have a number of questions related to her hysterectomy: Would her sex life be changed? Might the cancer recur? Would the hysterectomy affect her future as a woman? Can a person be orgasmic following a hysterectomy? Ms. Vogel attempted to provide some answers and also arranged for Debra Nass (a 32-year-old woman who had a hysterectomy three and a half years ago) to talk with Ms. Ely. Although some uncertainty remained (for example, the possible recurrence of a malignancy), Ms. Ely became more comfortable about having undergone the hysterectomy after talking to Ms. Nass.

However, Ms. Ely had a number of questions that she felt she needed to look at. She wondered why, when people were nice to her, she sometimes was "rotten" to them. For instance, she had lived with two different men, and each time she continued to have sexual relationships with other men. She also wondered what the future held for her. She was not skilled at a trade or a profession and did not know what kind of a career, if any, she desired. She was very confused about what she wanted out of life and also admitted that she had occasional blackouts from heavy drinking.

These problems were briefly discussed with Ms. Vogel. The focus of social services at this hospital, however, was limited to short-term crisis counseling. Because these complicated problems indicated that longer-term counseling was needed, Ms. Vogel suggested, and Ms. Ely agreed to, a referral to the mental health center in the area.

Several months later, Ms. Vogel heard from a friend of hers that Ms. Ely had gotten engaged but "on the spur of the moment" moved with another man to live on the West Coast.

Thus, the immediate psychological crisis situation surrounding the hysterectomy appears to have been resolved. However, problems remain in Ms. Ely's relationships with others.

Social work in hospitals tends to be short term and crisis oriented because there is generally a fairly rapid turnover of patients. Social workers are often involved in discharge planning (for example, making arrangements for patients to return to their families or to a convalescent home). In recent years, there has been a trend throughout the country to reduce the length of hospital stays to cut the costs of hospitalization. This trend has increased the importance of discharge planning (and thus of the services of social workers) in hospitals.

At times hospital social workers must act as advocates to ensure that the rights of patients are secured and that their needs are best served. Although social workers in medical settings are involved primarily in direct services to patients and their families, there are occasions when they engage in activity planning, administration of programs (for example, directing a hospice program so that terminal patients can live their final months in dignity), research, and education of other professionals.

The development of specialized clinics and programs—for providing genetics counseling; abortion services; family planning; services to people with AIDS or to people who are HIV positive; services to rape victims; services to the terminally ill; and treatment for alcoholics, drug abusers, and people with eating disorders—has created new opportunities for social workers in the health field. Sometimes these programs are located in offices away from hospitals. Nursing homes also are increasingly employing social workers.

One of the emerging fields of practice for social workers is combating AIDS. Social workers are getting involved in advocating for programs that will assist in reducing discrimination against those who are HIV positive or who have AIDS. They are also involved in counseling those who test HIV positive and in providing services in hospitals, nursing homes, and hospices to those who have AIDS. Social workers have become case managers for many people with AIDS. The case manager works with the AIDS patient, her or his loved ones, providers of care, and payers of health-care expenses to make certain that pressing medical, financial, social, and other needs are met and to ensure that the most cost-effective care possible is provided. In serving people with AIDS, the trend is to have more and more of the medical care delivered outside the hospital or nursing home, often at home or in an outpatient clinic.

There is also a trend for group medical clinics, individual practitioners, family practice clinics, and prepaid health clinics to employ social workers as part of a team in diagnosing and treating patients. Increasingly, social workers in such settings are working with high-risk groups, playing a preventative as well as a therapeutic role. High-risk groups include teenage mothers, women requesting abortions, drug and alcohol abusers, people undergoing organ transplants, severely depressed or highly anxious people, people under stress, people attempting suicide, amputees, and individuals with an eating disorder.

COUNSELING THE TERMINALLY ILL

One of the most difficult tasks of doctors, nurses, social workers, and other allied professionals in the health field is to help a terminally ill patient deal with dying. Death is a frightening event, and the fear of death is felt universally in all cultures.

Most people in our society die in a hospital. This setting, in itself, is one of the primary reasons why dying is so hard. Health professionals are committed to recovery—to healing. When someone is found to have a terminal illness, medical personnel experience a sense of failure. In some cases, health professionals may feel guilty that they cannot do more or that they might have made a mistake that contributed to the terminal illness. Many health professionals are not comfortable in counseling the terminally ill. They feel insecure and do not know what to say or do. Often they have not come to terms with their own mortality; that is, they have not come to see death as an integral part of their lives. If a professional person views death as a frightening, horrible, taboo topic, she or he will never be able to face it calmly and helpfully with a patient.

EXHIBIT 15.6

Five Stages of Dying in the Terminally Ill

The following stages identified by Dr. Elisabeth Kübler-Ross have been found to be a valuable paradigm in understanding a terminally ill person's behavior:

Stage 1: Denial. "It can't be." "No, not me." "There must be a mistake." This is generally the first reaction when a person learns she or he has a terminal illness. Dr. Kübler-Ross believes such a reaction is functional because it helps cushion the impact that death will soon be inevitable.

Stage 2: Rage and anger. "Why me!" "Look at the good things I've done and still need to do for the members of my family." "This just isn't fair!" Patients resent the fact that they will soon die while others remain healthy and alive. God is frequently a special target of the anger during this stage, as God is viewed as unfairly imposing a death sentence. Dr. Kübler-Ross believes that such anger is permissible and inevitable. And she adds, "God can take it."

During this stage, family and hospital staff frequently experience difficulty in coping with the anger, which is displaced in many directions. The patient may charge that the doctor is incompetent,

that the hospital surroundings are inhumane, that the nurses are unconcerned about people, that there is too much noise, and so on. The underlying reasons generating the patient's anger need to be remembered during this stage. Reacting personally or angrily to the patient's anger will only feed into that hostile behavior. During this stage, conveying to the patient that she or he is an important person who is worthy of respect, time, and understanding will usually lead to a reduction of angry demands.

Stage 3: Bargaining. "I realize my death is inevitable, but if I could just live 6 months more I could. . . ." During this stage, patients come to accept their terminal illness but try to strike bargains (frequently with God) for more time. They promise to do something worthwhile or to be good in exchange for another month or year of life. Dr. Kübler-Ross indicates that even agnostics and atheists sometimes attempt to bargain with God during this stage.

Stage 4. Depression. "Yes, it will soon be over." "It's really sad, but true." The first phase of this stage is when the patient mourns things not done,

(continued)

Dr. Elisabeth Kübler-Ross (perhaps the foremost authority on death and dying in our era) has identified five stages that terminally ill patients may go through[65] (see Exhibit 15.6). These stages are not absolute; not everyone goes through every stage according to the sequence described. (Some patients never advance beyond the first or second stage, and some patients vacillate from stage to stage.)

The one thing that usually persists through all five stages is hope—hope for a "miracle" cure. All terminally ill patients seem to have a little bit of

hope and are supported and nourished by it, especially during their most difficult times. With respect to hope, the desired direction in counseling is to be honest with the patient about the probable outcome while allowing the person to hope for the million-to-one chance of recovery.

To work with the terminally ill requires maturity, which comes only from experience. The most important communication is the "door-opening interview," in which the counselor conveys verbally and nonverbally to the dying patient that she or he is ready and willing to share the dying person's

EXHIBIT 15.6 *(continued)*

past losses, and wrongs committed. This type of depression is frequently exacerbated by guilt or shame about acts of omission or commission. Counseling during this phase generally focuses on helping the patient to resolve feelings of guilt and shame. In some cases, this may involve helping family members to make realistic plans for their future and to reassure the patient that vital unfinished situations are being taken care of.

The second phase of this stage is when the patient enters a state of "preparatory grief," in which she or he is getting ready for the inevitable by taking into account impending losses. During this stage, the patient should not be encouraged to be cheerful; this would interfere with the necessity for the patient to contemplate his or her impending death. During this phase, the patient generally becomes quiet and does not want to see visitors. The patient is in the process of losing everything and everybody she or he loves. If the patient is allowed to express this sorrow, final acceptance of death will be much easier. In addition, the patient will be grateful to those who are able to sit quietly nearby, without telling him or her not to be sad. According to Dr. Kübler-Ross, when a dying patient no longer continues to request to see some-

one to discuss his or her situation, it is a sign that unfinished business is completed and the patient has reached the final stage.

Stage 5: Acceptance. "I will soon pass on, and it's all right." Dr. Kübler-Ross describes this final stage as "not a happy stage, but neither is it unhappy. It's devoid of feelings but it's not resignation; it's really a victory." During this stage, visitors often are not desired because the patient no longer is in a talkative mood. Communications with a counselor may become more nonverbal than verbal. Patients may just want to hold the counselor's hand—to sit together in silence with someone who is comfortable in the presence of a dying person.

Dr. Kübler-Ross notes that some patients continue grieving about their terminal illness without ever reaching the final stage of acceptance. She also notes that not everyone will progress through these stages as presented here. There is often considerable movement back and forth among stages. For example, a patient may go from denial to depression, to rage and anger, back to denial, then to bargaining, then to depression, and so on.

Sources: Elisabeth Kübler-Ross, *On Death and Dying* (New York Macmillan, 1969); Elisabeth Kübler-Ross, ed., *Death: The Final Stage of Growth* (Englewood Cliffs, NJ: Prentice Hall, 1975).

concerns without fear and anxiety. A prerequisite is that the counselors have an attitude toward their own death with which they are comfortable.

Mwalimu Imara views dying as potentially the final stage of growth and gives a number of suggestions on how to come to terms with one's own dying.[66] Having a well-developed sense of identity (that is, a sense of who you are) is an important step. (Chapter 2 in this text discusses ways to develop a positive identity.) This requires arriving at realistic life goals that you will have pride in achieving. Without a blueprint of what will give

meaning and direction to our lives, we will experience our lives as fragmented and aimless.

Imara indicates that a dying patient at the stage of acceptance corresponds to a person with a healthy identity. An individual who comes to accept a terminal illness has also arrived at a fairly well-thought-out sense of himself or herself. Death is the final stage of growth in that the patient finally develops a unified sense of self and accepts imminent death. (Ideally, people will develop a healthy identity long before the final crisis and thus be fairly prepared before that crisis arises.)

According to Imara, all of us experience separations and pains throughout life that lead to personal growth—for example, leaving family to attend kindergarten, leaving high school to seek work or attend college, leaving work and friends to seek a better position in a different geographical area, and experiencing romantic and perhaps marital separations. Imara indicates that "abandoning old ways and breaking old patterns is like dying, at least dying to old ways of life for an unknown new life of meaning and relationships. But living without change is not living at all, not growing at all."[67] Making changes in our lives also creates fears and anxieties in us. But if such changes lead to personal growth, we will be better prepared to face new challenges and new changes. Through a willingness to risk the unknown, we undertake the search for ourselves. Overcoming fears and anxieties that arise from current challenges (and learning more about ourselves through these experiences) helps prepare us for the fears and anxieties that will arise when we learn that our death is near.

SUMMARY

There are a number of problems with our health-care system. In contrast to other industrialized countries in which health care is viewed as having a service orientation, the health-care system in the United States has the dual (and sometimes conflicting) objectives of providing service and making a profit. The system is indeed prospering. The United States is now spending substantially more per capita on health care than are other industrialized nations. Yet a number of other countries have lower infant mortality rates and longer life expectancies than ours. Such statistics suggest that other countries are providing health care that is as good as (or better than) ours at a lower cost.

Our health-care system is focused on treating people *after* they become ill; little attention is given to preventing illnesses. It is increasingly being recognized that our lifestyles (including exercise, diet, sleep patterns, and stress reaction patterns) largely determine whether illness will occur

and also influence the recovery process when an illness does occur. People need to realize that they, and not their physicians, have the major responsibility for their own health.

The poor and racial minorities have higher rates of illnesses and shorter life expectancies for a variety of reasons. Largely because of the profit motive, low-income areas in cities and rural areas are generally underserved by health-care services.

The profit motive has also led to the use of unnecessary treatment approaches, including diagnostic tests, medication and drugs, and surgeries. A more devastating problem is receiving harmful care. It is estimated that 10% of practicing physicians are incompetent.

Health care for the elderly is becoming a national disgrace. Many older citizens lack access to quality care. Medical conditions of the elderly are often misdiagnosed, and treatment is often inadequate.

AIDS has emerged as a major health problem. The two primary ways in which it is transmitted from one person to another are through sexual contact and through sharing of intravenous needles. There are many misconceptions about AIDS that have led those who are HIV positive and those who have AIDS to be shunned and discriminated against.

The use of life-sustaining technology has raised a number of questions. Should such equipment be used to prolong the life of someone who is terminally ill and in considerable pain? How should death be defined? Should society seek to keep alive people who have such a profound cognitive disability that they will never be able to walk or even sit? Can society afford to continue to expand the use of such costly life-sustaining equipment? Should physician-assisted suicide for the terminally ill who want to die be legalized?

The high costs of medical care have become an issue of national concern. Illnesses now can threaten a family's financial stability. The high costs are also a threat to the economic stability of our country. There are a variety of reasons why medical expenses are so high, including the profit-making focus, high costs of technological advances, increased life expectancies of people, third-party financing, inadequate health-care planning, proliferation of malpractice suits, and increased specialization by doctors.

A number of possibilities are available to resolve each of these problems. Some suggestions include increasing admissions to medical schools to train more doctors, permitting doctors to advertise their services and fees, training more physician assistants and paramedics, expanding use of generic drugs, encouraging patients to seek a second opinion before consenting to an operation, developing more preventative medical programs, expanding the use of health maintenance organizations, and developing a national health insurance program.

Health care is a secondary setting for social work. In such a setting, social workers generally function as members of a team, and they need to learn to work with those in charge. Medical treatment teams are increasingly dependent on social workers to attend to sociopsychological factors that are either contributing causes of illnesses or side effects of a medical condition that must be dealt with to facilitate recovery. As a member of a medical team, social workers have an important role in diagnosing and treating medical conditions.

A social worker in the health field needs skills and knowledge about how to counsel people with a wide variety of medical conditions. Counseling the terminally ill requires a high level of emotional maturity, a well-thought-out identity, and a high level of competency in counseling.

NOTES

1. Joseph Julian, *Social Problems,* 3rd ed. (Englewood Cliffs, NJ: Prentice Hall, 1980), p. 25.
2. Richard Nixon, "Health Message of 1971," Feb. 18, 1971, White House.
3. William Kornblum and Joseph Julian, *Social Problems,* 8th ed. (Englewood Cliffs, NJ: Prentice Hall, 1995), pp. 28–61.
4. Ibid., p. 29.
5. Ibid.
6. Ibid.
7. Ibid.
8. U.S. Bureau of the Census, *Statistical Abstract of the United States, 1997* (Washington, DC: U.S. Government Printing Office, 1997).
9. Ibid.
10. James W. Coleman and Donald R. Cressey, *Social Problems,* 6th ed. (New York: HarperCollins, 1996), p. 248.
11. Quoted in John A. Denton, *Medical Sociology* (Boston: Houghton Mifflin, 1978), p. 65.
12. Coleman and Cressey, *Social Problems,* p. 224.
13. Ibid.
14. Ibid.
15. Kornblum and Julian, *Social Problems,* p. 136.
16. Coleman and Cressey, *Social Problems,* p. 223.
17. Ibid.
18. Ibid., p. 224.
19. Ibid., p. 223.
20. Ibid.
21. Thomas McKeown, "Determinants of Health," *Human Nature,* 1 (Apr. 1978), p. 66.
22. Kornblum and Julian, *Social Problems,* p. 32.
23. Ibid.
24. Ibid.
25. Ibid., p. 33.
26. Max Seham, *Blacks and American Medical Care* (Minneapolis: University of Minnesota Press, 1973), pp. 22–23.
27. "Growing Old in America," ABC News Program Transcript (New York: Journal Graphics, Dec. 28, 1985).
28. Ibid., p. 11.
29. Ibid.
30. G. A. Lloyd, "HIV/AIDS Overview," in *Encyclopedia of Social Work,* 19th ed. (Washington, DC: NASW, 1995).
31. C. Scanlan, "New AIDS Drug Wins OK by FDA," *Wisconsin State Journal,* Oct. 10, 1991, p. 3A.
32. S. Brink, "Beating the Odds," *U.S. News & World Report,* Feb. 12, 1996, pp. 60–68.
33. G. A. Lloyd, "AIDS and HIV: The Syndrome and the Virus," *Encyclopedia of Social Work: 1990 Supplement* (Silver Spring, MD: NASW, 1990), p. 25.
34. B. Gavzer, "Why Do Some People Survive AIDS?" *Parade,* Sept. 18, 1988, p. 5.
35. Brink, "Beating the Odds," pp. 60–68.
36. C. Everett Koop, *Surgeon General's Report on Acquired Immune Deficiency Syndrome* (Washington, DC: U.S. Department of Health and Human Services, 1987), p. 27.
37. Thomas J. Sullivan, *Social Problems,* 4th ed. (Needham Heights, MA: Allyn & Bacon, 1997), p. 146.
38. Ibid.
39. Ibid., p. 147.
40. Ibid., pp. 147–148.
41. Ibid., p. 148.
42. Susan Dentzer, "America's Scandalous Health Care," *U.S. News & World Report,* Mar. 12, 1990, p. 25.
43. Ibid.

44. Paul B. Horton, Gerald R. Leslie, and Richard F. Larson, *The Sociology of Social Problems,* 10th ed. (Englewood Cliffs, NJ: Prentice Hall, 1991), p. 232.

45. *Statistical Abstract of the United States, 1997.*

46. Coleman and Cressey, *Social Problems,* pp. 249–250.

47. Jeffrey Klein and Michael Castleman, "The Profit Motive in Breast Cancer," *Los Angeles Times,* Apr. 4, 1994, p. B7.

48. Coleman and Cressey, *Social Problems,* p. 250.

49. Kornblum and Julian, *Social Problems,* p. 36.

50. *Statistical Abstract of the United States, 1997.*

51. Kornblum and Julian, *Social Problems,* p. 37.

52. Ibid., pp. 32–33.

53. American Association of Retired Persons, *A Profile of Older Americans: 1996* (Washington, DC: AARP, 1996).

54. Kornblum and Julian, *Social Problems,* p. 37.

55. Ibid.

56. Dorothy P. Rice, "Health Care: Financing," in *Encyclopedia of Social Work,* 19th ed. (Washington, DC: NASW, 1995), p. 1171.

57. Susan Brink and Nancy Shute, "Are HMOs the Right Prescription?" *U.S. News & World Report,* Oct. 13, 1997, pp. 60–64.

58. Ibid.

59. Ibid.

60. Ibid.

61. Kornblum and Julian, *Social Problems,* p. 37.

62. Coleman and Cressey, *Social Problems,* p. 251.

63. "National Health Care and NASW Plan," *The Wisconsin Social Worker,* 17, no. 2 (Mar.–Apr. 1991), p. 1.

64. Donald Brieland, Lela B. Costin, and Charles R. Atherton, *Contemporary Social Work* (New York: McGraw-Hill, 1975), p. 123.

65. Elisabeth Kübler-Ross, *On Death and Dying* (New York: Macmillan, 1969).

66. Mwalimu Imara, "Dying As the Last Stage of Growth," in *Death: The Final Stage of Growth,* Elisabeth Kübler-Ross, ed. (Englewood Cliffs, NJ: Prentice Hall, 1975), pp. 147–163.

67. Ibid., p. 148.

PHYSICAL
AND MENTAL
DISABILITIES
AND
REHABILITATION

There are an estimated 50 million people with a disability in the United States—nearly one of five people.[1] Persons with a disability include those who:

Are temporarily injured (from severe burns, injuries to the back or spine, broken limbs).

Have a chronic physical disability (including people who use canes, crutches, walkers, braces, or wheelchairs; the mobility-impaired elderly; and people with illnesses such as severe cardiovascular disorder, cerebral palsy, chronic arthritis, and AIDS).

Have a hearing disability.

Have a visual disability.

Have a mental disability (including an emotional disorder, a cognitive disability,* or a severe learning disability).[2]

This chapter will:

- Provide a brief history of rehabilitation practices and of the ways different cultures have treated persons with a disability.

- Define and describe developmental disabilities.

- Describe different levels of cognitive disability and summarize the causes.

- Discuss our society's reactions to disabilities.

- Identify current services for persons with a disability.

- Summarize the roles of social workers in working with clients who have a disability and their families.

HISTORY OF REHABILITATION PRACTICES

Society's willingness to help persons with a disability has been determined largely by the per-

---

* Because the term *mental retardation* has negative connotations, the term *cognitive disability* will instead be used in this text.

ceived causes of the disability, existing medical knowledge, and general economic conditions. Ancient and modern religious faiths (including Christianity) have at times been an aid and at other times a detriment to viewing those with a disability as "people." Attitudes have ranged from perceiving persons with a disability as possessed by demons to viewing them as saintlike, with the community having a responsibility to care for them.

The early Greeks promoted the philosophy of the unity of body and soul, with a blemish on one signifying a blemish on the other.[3] This philosophy led to a negative attitude toward those with a disability. The extreme implication of this doctrine was found in Sparta, where "the immature, the weak, and the damaged were eliminated purposefully."[4] Centuries later the Romans also put to death some people with a disability who were considered "unproductive."[5] In ancient history, there were almost no organized efforts to meet the needs of persons with a cognitive disability. In early Greece and in the Roman Empire, mental illness was seen as stemming from demons entering the body, with exorcism being the primary treatment.[6]

During the Middle Ages, disabilities were seen either as the result of demonic possession or as God's punishment.[7] Modern Judeo-Christian values of charity and humanitarian treatment were generally absent during this period, partly as a result of poor economic conditions. About the only employment provided by feudal lords for persons with a disability was that of court jester, a position considered suitable for those with a cognitive or physical disability.[8] The mentally ill continued to be viewed as possessed by demons, and cruelty was advocated and used to punish and drive out the demons.

The Elizabethan English Poor Laws of 1601 provided financial support for the involuntarily unemployed (including persons with a disability). These Poor Laws were the first major secular-based relief effort for the poor and persons with a disability.[9]

In early colonial America, conditions were not yet suitable for the development of rehabilitation programs. The colonists were barely able to earn a living from the soil; also, disability was viewed as the result of God's punishment.[10]

In the 19th century, gradual recognition was given to the needs of persons with a disability in the United States. The first programs to help these people were developed around that time.

Thomas Gallaudet opened the first school for educating the deaf in this country in 1817 in Hartford, Connecticut.[11] Gallaudet demonstrated that the deaf could be taught to read and speak, which led to the opening of other schools for the deaf. The first school for the blind was opened in 1832 in Massachusetts.[12] The first sheltered-type work situation for the employment of the blind was established in 1850 in Massachusetts.[13]

Cognitive disability, before and during the early part of the 19th century, was thought to be inherited and therefore incurable.[14] In the first half of the 1800s, most persons with a cognitive disability "were relegated to lunatic asylums, poorhouses, almshouses, or local jails."[15] Interest in providing services to persons with a cognitive disability began in France, especially after the physician Jean Itard made considerable progress over a 5-year period in the early 1800s in educating a 12-year-old "wolf child" found in a forest. The boy was diagnosed as having a severe level of cognitive disability. When found, he was unsocialized and walked on all fours.[16] The philosophy of providing services to persons with a cognitive disability gradually spread to this country. In 1848 the first residential school for persons with a cognitive disability was established in Barge, Massachusetts.[17]

Unfortunately, the orientation toward persons with a cognitive disability in the latter half of the 19th century switched from one of education and training to one of custodial care. A major reason for this change was the popularity of Social Darwinism, which asserted that it was far better for society to allow the poor and the weak to perish than to sustain their existence and encourage their proliferation through government-supported programs.[18] Persons with a cognitive disability were viewed as having defective genetic strains; as a result, sterilization was used extensively at the end of the 19th century.[19]

The first hospitals for the mentally ill were built in this country in the 1850s and 1860s.[20] Before this time, as Dorothea Dix had documented, the mentally ill were either kept "out of sight" in the homes of their families or confined in almshouses and local jails.[21] The living conditions of almshouses and mental hospitals were deplorable.

Until the latter half of the 19th century, persons with a physical disability were either taken care of by their family or placed in almshouses. Toward the end of the 19th century, these persons began to benefit from medical advances: antiseptic surgery, orthopedic surgery, heat and water therapy, braces, and exercise programs.[22] Around that same time, public funds began to be used for the education and training of children with a disability.[23]

The charity organization movement during the latter part of the 19th century created a structure not only for future social work practices but also for vocational rehabilitation casework.[24] These early organizations had a rehabilitation rather than a maintenance focus. The movement also advocated extensive investigation of each case and the use of individualized treatment determined by the needs of each client. Unfortunately, the volunteers who provided the services for charity organizations operated from the premise that the causes of poverty and of disabilities had moral roots; thus, the primary way to help was to urge those with a disability to become active members in a church (with the church then providing some social services).[25]

During the late 19th and early 20th centuries, few precautions were taken by industries to improve worker safety. As a result, a large number of people developed disabilities from poor working conditions and industrial accidents. To meet the tolls being taken by the Industrial Revolution, the first workers' compensation law was passed in 1910 in New York.[26]

In the early 20th century, large numbers of unskilled rural youths began flocking to cities seeking employment. There were also increasing numbers of dislocated industrial workers who needed retraining. Therefore, the federal government passed the Smith-Hughes Act in 1917, which made federal monies available for vocational education programs and created the Federal Board of Vocational Education.[27] In 1918 the Soldier's

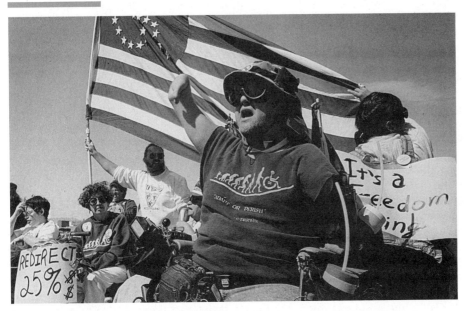

Members of Americans Disabled for Attendant Care Today (ADAPT) campaign for a change in funding practices. They believe public money should be transferred from payments for institutional care, particularly nursing home care, to community or home-based care.

Rehabilitation Act was passed, which was a program designed to rehabilitate veterans who had a disability.[28]

The federal Social Security Act of 1935 established the permanency of rehabilitation programs and instituted public assistance programs for the blind and for the disabled. The Barden-LaFollette Act of 1943 extended rehabilitation services to the mentally ill and to persons with cognitive disabilities.[29]

During World War II, there was a severe labor shortage, which provided work opportunities to people with a disability. These persons were able to demonstrate to thousands of employers that, if placed in an appropriate job, they could perform well. This growing realization led in 1945 to the establishment of the President's Committee on Employment of the Handicapped.[30] After World War II, a number of other federal programs underscored society's growing belief that those with a disability could be productive workers and should

be given the opportunities and training to demonstrate their work capacities.[31]

Spurred by the civil rights movement of the 1950s and 1960s, a new minority group began to be heard in the late 1960s and 1970s. Persons with a physical disability began speaking out, marching forth, and demanding equal rights. They have been seeking (including through legislation and lawsuits) an end to job discrimination, limited educational opportunities, architectural barriers, and societal discrimination. In 1973 Congress passed the Vocational Rehabilitation Act, one section of which prohibits discrimination against persons with a disability by any program or organization receiving federal funds. Included in this legislation is an affirmative action policy (described in Chapter 12) in which employers who receive federal funds must demonstrate extensive efforts to hire those with a disability.

In 1990 Congress passed, and President Bush signed into law, the Americans with Disabilities

Act. This act prohibits discrimination against persons with a disability either in hiring or by limiting access to public accommodations (such as restaurants, stores, museums, and theaters). The law requires that new public buildings be accessible by persons with a disability and that barriers in existing public buildings be removed if the changes can be accomplished without much difficulty or expense. Advocates of the law call it the most significant civil rights legislation since the 1964 act prohibiting discrimination based on race.[32]

The 20th century has seen the development of numerous programs and technological advances to help persons with a disability. Yet, as will be discussed, much remains to be done in changing society's attitudes toward persons with a disability and in helping them to live satisfying and productive lives. Increasingly, people with a disability are receiving improved services that facilitate the development of their capacities.

DEVELOPMENTAL DISABILITIES

Developmental disability is a relatively recent term, and many people erroneously believe it to be synonymous with cognitive disability. However, it is a broader term that includes not only cognitive disabilities, but also a variety of other conditions that occur before age 22 and hinder development. These conditions include epilepsy, infantile autism, cerebral palsy, and some cases of dyslexia (a learning disability).

The Rehabilitation, Comprehensive Services, and Developmental Disabilities Act (PL 95-602) of 1978 defines developmental disability as follows:

> *Developmental disability means a severe, chronic disability of a person which is attributable to a mental or physical impairment or combination of mental and physical impairment and*
>
> ■ *is manifest before twenty-two years of age*
> ■ *is likely to continue indefinitely*

> ■ *results in substantial functional limitations in three or more of the following areas of major life activity:*
>
> *self-care*
> *receptive and expressive language*
> *learning*
> *mobility*
> *self-direction*
> *capacity for independent living*
> *economic self-sufficiency*
>
> ■ *and reflects the person's need for a combination and sequence of special, interdisciplinary, or generic care, treatment or other services which are of lifelong or extended duration and individually planned and coordinated.*[33]

Autism

Perhaps the most puzzling developmental disability is infantile autism. As yet the causes of this disorder are unknown. David Rosenhan and Martin Seligman offer the following description:

> *The essential feature of **autism** is that the child's ability to respond to others does not develop within the first thirty months of life. Even at that early age, gross impairment of communicative skills is already quite noticeable, as are the bizarre responses these children make to their environment. They lack interest in and responsiveness to people, and they fail to develop normal attachments. In infancy, these characteristics are manifested by their failure to cuddle, by lack of eye contact, or downright aversion to physical contact and affection. These children may fail entirely to develop language, and if language is acquired, often it will be characterized by **echolalia**—the tendency to repeat or echo immediately or after a brief period precisely what one has just heard—or **pronominal reversals**—the tendency to use "I" where "you" is meant, and vice-versa. Such children also react very poorly to change, either in their routines or in their environments.*[34]

Autism occurs in about 4 children per 10,000, about the same frequency as deafness and twice that of blindness.[35] With regard to gender differences, boys outnumber girls by about three to one.[36] The disorder does not appear related to race or socioeconomic class.[37] One promising method of treating the disorder is a *direct structured educational approach,* which focuses on improving the specific cognitive, motor, and perceptual disabilities of these children. Long-term follow-up studies of autistic children indicate that the prognosis for them is questionable. Close to 60% are unable to lead an independent life as adults.[38] Only one in six will improve sufficiently to hold a job.[39] A majority of autistic adolescents and young adults are placed in residential facilities.

Cognitive Disability

The largest subcategory of developmental disabilities is cognitive disability. It is a disorder that afflicts 3 of 100 children, two-thirds of whom are boys.[40] The disorder is somewhat difficult to define precisely or diagnose accurately. The difficulty occurs because defining the concept of intelligence (which is at the core of cognitive disability) is problematic. The American Association on Mental Deficiency provides this definition:

> *It is characterized by significantly subaverage intellectual functioning, existing concurrently with related limitations in two or more of the following applicable adaptive skill areas: communication, self-care, home living, social skills, community use, self-direction, health and safety, functional academics, leisure, and work. Mental retardation manifests before age eighteen.*[41]

LEVELS OF COGNITIVE DISABILITY

The various levels of cognitive disability, and the percentages of people affected at these levels, are shown in Table 16.1. The IQ scores for this table are based on the Wechsler Intelligence Test. We'll now look at the functioning of people at these various levels.

Mild Cognitive Disability. Persons at this level develop communication and social skills similar to other people's. Their cognitive disability is often not recognized until they are in the third or fourth

TABLE 16.1

Levels of Cognitive Disability

Level	Percentage of People with This Level of Cognitive Disability	Wechsler IQ Score
Mild	85	50–70
Moderate	10	35–49
Severe	4	20–34
Profound	1	Below 20

Source: David L. Rosenhan and Martin E. P. Seligman, *Abnormal Psychology,* 3rd ed. (New York: Norton, 1995), p. 626.

grade, when they begin to have serious academic difficulties. With help they can acquire academic skills beyond the sixth-grade level. Other than intellectual functioning, their needs and abilities are indistinguishable from those of others. Special education programs in school often enable these children to acquire the vocational skills needed for performing unskilled and semiskilled jobs. As adults, many are employed and live somewhat independently.

Moderate Cognitive Disability. Children at this level learn to talk and communicate during the preschool years. Unlike other children, however, they have difficulties in learning social customs. They are unlikely to ever perform beyond second-grade level in academic subjects. Some have poor motor coordination. As adults they can learn to contribute to their own support by working at semiskilled or unskilled tasks in protected settings; many live in group homes.

Severe Cognitive Disability. People at this level have major difficulties in communicative speech, and before the age of 5 they display considerable evidence of motor coordination problems. At special schools, they may learn to talk, and they can be trained in elementary hygiene. As adults they may be able to perform simple and unskilled job tasks under supervision in a protected setting.

Most reside in group homes or in residential institutions.

Profound Cognitive Disability. People at this level display severe disabilities in adaptive behavior. During the preschool years, they are able to master only the simplest motor tasks. Later some development of motor skills may occur, and they may learn some elementary self-care skills. This level of cognitive disability is often associated with severe physical deformities and central nervous system difficulties. Health and resistance to diseases are often poor. Life expectancy is substantially shortened. Children and adults at this level usually need custodial care.

CAUSES OF COGNITIVE DISABILITY

Hundreds of causes of cognitive disability have been identified, and we'll summarize some of the major ones. It should be noted that not everyone who is exposed to some of these factors will automatically experience a cognitive disability. For example, a majority of children whose mothers drank heavily during gestation do not have a cognitive disability.

Cultural/Familial Cognitive Disability. Accounting for about two-thirds of all cognitive disabilities,[42] this category stems from genetic and environmental influences. The vast majority of people in this category have a mild or moderate level of cognitive disability. Many of them have parents and siblings who also have a cognitive disability, suggesting that at least part of the disability is passed on through the genes.

The second major contributor to this type of cognitive disability is the restricted environment in which the individuals in this category live and develop. People who are raised in poverty have a much higher probability of experiencing this type of cognitive disability. Rosenhan and Seligman note:

Lower-class mothers are more likely to give birth to premature infants with low birth weights, and low birth weight is a risk factor for retardation. Children from impoverished backgrounds also face a number of postnatal environmental challenges to intellectual growth. Some of these children ingest toxic levels of lead by eating fragments of lead-based paint that peel off the walls of the old buildings in which they live. In turn, exposure to lead is associated with retarded intellectual growth. In addition, children from lower-class families are more likely than upper-class children to be malnourished, to receive poor health care, and to suffer from a variety of illnesses across childhood. Such an environment inhibits the full development of the intellectual abilities a child does have.[43]

Environmental influences include poor prenatal care, frequent accidents, infections, poor health habits, malnutrition, and lack of stimulation. With cultural/familial cognitive disability, it is nearly impossible to determine for each affected person how much of the cognitive disability is due to genetic variables and how much is due to environmental variables.

Gestational Disorders. Infants born prematurely (before 37 weeks of gestation) are at increased risk of having a cognitive disability. Many metropolitan centers have specialized clinics for pregnant women who are known to be at high risk of premature delivery, and most hospitals have neonatal intensive care units for infants who are born prematurely. These facilities reduce the risk of neurological damage as a result of gestational problems.

Toxemia. Toxic (poisonous) substances in the blood during the gestation period pose a risk for both the pregnant woman and the fetus. Such substances include prescription drugs, cocaine and other illegal drugs, nicotine (from smoking), and alcohol.

A toxic disorder that has received considerable publicity is fetal alcohol syndrome (FAS). It is associated with heavy drinking (generally considered to be five or six drinks on occasion) during the gestation period. Pregnant women who occasionally have one or two drinks also place their fetus at some risk for FAS, which is characterized by facial and cranial abnormalities, possible heart defects, delayed physical and intellectual development, joint and limb anomalies, decreased weight of the fetus, and increased risk of stillbirth.[44]

The risk of toxemia can be substantially reduced if pregnant women receive early, regular, and specialized care during pregnancy. Pregnant women should follow their physician's advice about which medications to take, and which to avoid, during pregnancy.

Infections During Gestation. Certain infections that pregnant women contract may place the fetus at risk for having a cognitive disability. One of these infections, rubella (also called German measles), can result from the mother's exposure to the virus during the first trimester of pregnancy. The affected fetus is also at higher risk of being born with other congenital abnormalities, such as deafness, blindness, heart anomalies, and microcephalus. Mass immunization programs now provide child-bearing women protection against rubella. Blood tests are also available to determine the level of protection a woman has against the virus; those who are unprotected can then become immunized before pregnancy.

Another infection of pregnant women that can prove devastating for the fetus is syphilis. Syphilis infection, like rubella, is passed on to the fetus through the placenta. The affected fetus is likely to be born with many physical anomalies in addition to a cognitive disability.

A virus that is affecting an increasing number of babies is the AIDS virus. Infants can be infected during gestation, at birth, or after birth from milk from an HIV-positive mother. AIDS infants tend to have a life expectancy of only a few years.

Postnatal Cerebral Infection. A variety of viral and bacterial diseases, such as encephalitis and meningitis, can cause severe and irreversible brain damage, particularly if not treated in the early stages of infection. The AIDS virus may also lead to brain deterioration in older children and adults.

Chromosome Abnormalities. The best-known and most common disorder in this category is Down syndrome. This condition arises because there are 47 chromosomes, rather than the usual 46, in the cells of those affected. The disorder does not appear to be inherited, although the reason for this chromosome abnormality is not presently known.

The disorder occurs in children born to mothers of all ages but with higher frequency in children born to mothers over age 35. The risk of the disorder is about 1 in 1500 for children born to mothers in their twenties; it increases to 1 in 40 when the mother is over 40 when the child is born.[45]

Down syndrome children and adults generally experience a moderate to severe level of cognitive disability. Their eyes are almond shaped and slanted, and they tend to have a round face. Many of those affected also have physical anomalies, which may include heart lesions and gastrointestinal difficulties.

There are a variety of other chromosomal abnormalities that may occur. In 1991 scientists discovered the gene that causes fragile X syndrome.[46] This gene was located on the X chromosome. Fragile X syndrome is the most common inherited form of cognitive disability. (Down syndrome is more common but does not run in families.) Symptoms of fragile X syndrome can range from mild learning disability to a severe level of cognitive disability, with serious behavioral problems. Some carriers are completely normal but can pass the gene that produces the syndrome to later generations. Fragile X syndrome is incurable. It occurs in 1 in 1000 males and 1 in 600 females.[47]

Through a test called amniocentesis, prenatal detection of Down syndrome, other chromosome defects, and some metabolic disorders is possible. Although some small risk of miscarriage is involved, amniocentesis is a fairly simple procedure. A needle is inserted through the abdomen and into the uterus, and amniotic fluid is extracted for chromosome or chemical studies. The procedure should be performed in the first trimester of pregnancy if the mother is known to be at risk for having a child with a specific chromosome or metabolic condition. The test is recommended if the pregnant woman has a complicated medical or gestational history.

Another test, called chorionic villi sampling (CVS), has recently been developed to help identify certain fetal abnormalities. The test can be performed in a physician's office as early as the fifth week of gestation (which is several weeks earlier than amniocentesis can first be used). CVS is relatively simple to perform and under some conditions is a viable alternative to amniocentesis.

Metabolic Disorders. Phenylketonuria (PKU) is perhaps the best-known metabolic disease. The affected infant cannot metabolize phenylalanine, an essential building block of protein in food. As a result, phenylalanine and its derivative, phenyl pyruvic acid, build up in the body and rapidly poison the central nervous system, causing irreversible brain damage. About a third of such children cannot walk, about two-thirds never learn to talk, and more than half have a profound level of cognitive disability.[48] PKU results from the action of a recessive gene that is inherited from each parent. At present no test exists to identify the recessive gene in the parents. However, affected babies can be identified by a simple test of the urine about 3 weeks after birth. Once identified, the infants can be placed on a diet that controls the level of phenylalanine in their system until age 6, at which time the brain is nearly fully developed and their chances of surviving with normal intelligence and health are good.

Lipid storage disorders include Tay-Sachs disease, Hunter's syndrome, and Hurler's syndrome. These disorders involve a progressive degenerative process due to the accumulation of fatty substances in the cells that eventually leads to the death of the affected individuals. These conditions are inherited, and as yet effective treatment has not been developed. The incidence, however, has been greatly reduced through genetic counseling programs and prenatal diagnosis.

Disorders of Unknown Prenatal Influence. Of the numerous disorders in this category, two of the better known are hydrocephalus and microcephalus. Hydrocephalus involves a condition in which there is an increased amount of cerebrospinal fluid within the skull that will, unless treated, cause an enlargement of the skull. Neurosurgical techniques are now available that prevent brain damage by decreasing the pressure that causes it.

Microcephalus is a condition in which there is a reduced circumference of the head. In some cases, it may result from an inherited disorder; in other cases, it may result from fetal or neonatal brain damage.

Trauma to the Brain. Injury to the brain can occur at any time during prenatal, perinatal, or postnatal development. During the prenatal period, one source of injury is X rays that the pregnant woman may have during gestation. If the fetus's brain is exposed to the X rays, a severe level of cognitive disability may occur.

During the prenatal and perinatal periods, brain injury can result from deprivation of oxygen (anoxia) or from insufficient oxygen (hypoxia) to maintain functioning of the brain tissue. Such conditions destroy brain cells and may result in a cognitive disability. Shortage of oxygen may occur for a variety of reasons, including a knotted umbilical cord, premature separation of the placenta, or difficult birth as a result of a breech position.

Postnatal damage can result from an almost infinite number of causes. Brain injury can occur from a blow to the head while boxing or fighting, bicycle and automobile accidents, near drowning, football injuries, falls from a horse, battering by a parent, or any other damage to the head.

These diverse causes of cognitive disability illustrate how fragile human life is. We are all one accident or one infection away from experiencing a severe cognitive disability. In reviewing the multitude of sources, Maureen Foster addresses the concerns of prospective parents:

> *The temptation is to think that with all the possibilities of having a retarded child, it is impossible to believe that one could have a baby who is normal and healthy and stays that way through the entire developmental period. The risk of having a retarded child is low, and every prospective parent should approach parenthood with optimism. . . . Although precautions can be taken to decrease the chances of retardation, it can and does occur every day in families in which early and excellent prenatal care was sought, in which the mother stayed away from all agents known or suspected to be toxic, in which no illness occurred during the gestational period, and in which the birth was uncomplicated.*[49]

SOCIETY'S REACTIONS TO DISABILITIES

Our culture places a high value on having a beautiful body. We work out at health clubs, and we spend large proportions of our incomes on clothes, cosmetics, hair stylists, and special diets to look more attractive. Beauty is erroneously identified with goodness and ugliness with evil. Movies, television, and books portray heroes and heroines as physically attractive and villains as ugly. Snow White, for example, was lovely, whereas the evil witch was horrible looking. Children are erroneously taught that being physically attractive will lead to the good life, whereas having unattractive features is a sign of being inferior. Richardson found that young children rated people with a disability as "less desirable" than people without a disability.[50]

Unfortunately, this emphasis on the body beautiful has caused persons with a disability to be the objects of cruel jokes and has occasionally led them to be either shunned or treated as inferior. According to C. H. Cooley, if persons with a disability are related to as if they are inferior, second-class citizens, they are likely to come to view themselves as inferior and to have a negative self-concept.[51] Our society needs to reassess its values about the perfect physique. It would seem that other traits ought to be more important: honesty, integrity, a pleasant personality, responsibleness, kindness, and helpfulness.

Wright has noted that the emphasis on beautiful bodies has also led society to believe that persons with a disability "ought" to feel inferior.[52] She has coined the term *the requirement of mourning* for this expectation of society. A person who spends a great deal of time, money, and effort to be physically attractive psychologically wants a person with a disability to mourn the disability because the "body beautiful" person needs feedback that it is worthwhile and important to strive to have an attractive physique.

Another consequence of this misplaced emphasis is that persons with a disability are sometimes pitied as being less fortunate and given sympathy. Many persons with a disability decry receiving pity and being patronized. They seek to be treated as equals.

Asch and Mudrick have noted that persons with a disability are stigmatized and often treated as "not quite human" or "not normal."[53] The fear and aversion to disability that most people have often lead them to fear and reject people with a disability.[54] (Social workers have to recognize their own apprehensions of impairment to become effective change agents in combating prejudices against those with a disability.)

There is also a tendency in our society to conclude that a person with one kind of disability will have other kinds of disabilities. Nancy Weinberg has noted that people talk louder in the presence of someone who is blind, erroneously assuming that people who cannot see also have hearing problems.[55] Individuals with a physical disability are also erroneously assumed at times to have a cognitive disability. A 22-year-old college student in a wheelchair describes one example of this tendency:

> I'm in church with my father and my father is standing beside me and I'm in a wheelchair. I'm relatively intelligent, but I'm disabled. I'm sitting there like anyone else. And somebody comes up to my father and they're about as far away from me as from him and they say to my father, "How's he doing?" "Well he's looking pretty good." And I just want to kick him in the stomach.[56]

Receiving such responses from others may lead those with a physical disability to believe they are less intelligent and less effective in social interactions.

Studies have found that many people cut short their interactions with persons who have a disability.[57] They are uncomfortable when a person with a disability is near because they are uncertain about what is appropriate and inappropriate to say and they fear offending the person. Usually they do not want to make any direct remarks about the disability. People show their discomfort in a variety of ways—through abrupt and superficial conversations, fixed stares away from the person with a disability, compulsive talking, or an artificial seriousness. Individuals with a disability are sensitive to such insincere interactions. Fred David describes a few encounters that produce interactional strains:

> I get suspicious when somebody says, "Let's go for a uh, ah [imitates confused and halting speech] push with me down the hall," or something like that. This to me is suspicious because it means that they're aware, really aware, that there's a wheelchair here, and that this is probably uppermost with them. . . . A lot of people in trying to show you that they don't care that you're in a chair will do crazy things. Oh, there's one person I know who constantly kicks my chair, as if to say "I don't care that you're in a wheelchair. I don't even know that it's there." But that is just an indication that he really knows it's there.[58]

Persons with a disability detest being treated as socially different simply because of their disability. It is important that all of us respect persons who have a disability for a variety of reasons, one of which is that all of us have a vested interest in creating a society that respects persons who have a disability. As we grow older, we almost certainly will eventually develop one or more disabilities, perhaps in hearing, in vision, in mobility, or in having a chronic illness. Right now, we are just an accident away from one.

CURRENT SERVICES

A number of programs provide funds and services to persons with a disability. Some of these are federally funded and administered at state or local levels.

Rehabilitation Centers

Rehabilitation centers serving those with a mental or physical disability provide a variety of services, generally including vocational evaluation, sheltered employment, work adjustment training, counseling services, and placement services. (This type of rehabilitation center used to be called a sheltered workshop.)

VOCATIONAL EVALUATION
Clients are assessed on the basis of work behavior, physical capacities, social interaction, psychological functioning, and vocational goals and interests. Emphasis is on identifying the client's vocational assets and limitations. (In recent years, some rehabilitation centers have made a policy change. They now consider their "clients" to be "workers" or "employees." This shift has created a more efficient, work-oriented environment and helped the "employees" maximize their capacities for productive work.)

SHELTERED EMPLOYMENT
These programs provide a work environment for individuals who are unable to secure or maintain jobs in the community. Clients are paid (often below the minimum-wage level) for work produced. Work tasks derive from various subcontract jobs from other industries in the community and allow for long-term vocational development and possible placement into competitive employment. There is periodic evaluation of clients' progress in meeting rehabilitation objectives to ensure maximum vocational and personal development.

WORK ADJUSTMENT TRAINING
Vocational training experiences are provided to clients who are not yet ready for competitive employment following their initial vocational evaluation. The program is conducted in a work setting, using various types of subcontract jobs secured from industries in the community. The employment is designed to train individuals in developing good work skills and appropriate behavior on the job. Counselors are available to discuss problems, to assist learning new tasks, and to teach better work habits.

COUNSELING SERVICES
Counseling services include individual, group, parent, and vocational guidance. Individual counseling stresses work and intervention goals applied to mutually determined problem areas. Group counseling focuses on peer interaction and development of social skills. Parent counseling acquaints parents with rehabilitation objectives, thus providing support in the home for the total

Special Olympic events foster pride and self-worth for children and adults with developmental disabilities.

rehabilitation program. Exposure to the work world, development of job-seeking skills, and identification of realistic goals are the major emphases of vocational counseling.

PLACEMENT SERVICES

These programs assist clients in securing competitive employment. First, clients' work habits and skills are assessed. Then they receive training in searching for a job, applying for a job, and holding a job. Counselors then seek, together with clients, to place the clients with local employers.

After placement, contact is maintained for a period of time to deal with any adjustment problems that may arise. At many work sites in the community, counselors serve as job coaches (often for a few weeks) to assist the clients in learning and performing the tasks of the positions for which they have been hired.

Educational Programs

Historically, many public schools either refused to serve children with a severe disability or segregated them in special programs. In 1975 Congress enacted the Education for All Handicapped Children Act. This statute mandates that all local school districts provide full and appropriate educational opportunities to all children, including those with a disability. An individualized educational program designed to meet the unique needs of each child must be developed to provide instruction in the least restrictive environment that is feasible. The intent is to "mainstream" children with a disability so that they can participate as much as possible in regular educational programs. Most school districts now have "special educational programs" designed to meet the educational needs of children with a cognitive disability, emotionally disturbed children, children with learning disabilities, and children with a physical disability. Many states have schools for children with a hearing disability and for those with a visual disability. Often these specialized schools also provide statewide consultation for young children.

Residential Programs

GROUP HOMES, HALFWAY HOUSES, AND NURSING HOMES

A number of these facilities provide living arrangements for children and adults with a disability who, for a variety of reasons, are unable to live with their families.

RESIDENTIAL TREATMENT CENTERS

Centers that provide residential care and treatment include mental hospitals, residential treatment centers for the emotionally disturbed, and centers for those with a developmental disability.

The average length of stay varies among facilities and may range from several days to permanent care. Some of these residential facilities also serve clients on an outpatient basis, providing diagnostic, evaluative, and planning services.

DAY-CARE CENTERS

These centers provide day-care services to children with a cognitive disability, to the emotionally disturbed, and to children with a physical disability. The centers not only give the parents some relief time but also provide training in self-help, socialization, homemaking, communication, and leisure-time activities.

HOSPITAL SERVICES

Hospitals provide a variety of rehabilitation services for those with a disability, such as medical services, physical therapy, and speech therapy. For individuals who are severely injured or have a serious chronic illness, hospitals are often the entry point into the rehabilitation system.

Home Services

MEALS ON WHEELS

This program provides hot and cold meals to housebound recipients who are incapable of obtaining or preparing their own meals but who can feed themselves.

HOME HEALTH SERVICES

These programs provide visiting nurse services, drugs, physical therapy, laboratory services, and sickroom equipment.

HOMEMAKER SERVICES

In some communities, homemakers are available to do household tasks that persons with a disability are unable to do for themselves.

Federal and State Assistance Programs

VOCATIONAL REHABILITATION FUNDING

Federal funding programs for rehabilitation have developed gradually in this country. Two of the key statutes were the Vocational Rehabilitation Act Amendments of 1954 and the Rehabilitation Act of 1975.[59] At present there are federal matching funds available to states for basic rehabilitation programs at the matching rate of 80% federal and 20% state. Individuals are eligible for vocational rehabilitation services if they have a mental or physical disability that substantially interferes with their capacity to obtain employment and if there is a reasonable expectation that services will enable them to obtain employment. Potential clients receive medical testing free of charge to assess the extent of their disability and to check their overall health. Rehabilitation counselors employed by the state review these results. Applicants found eligible may then receive, at state and federal expense, a variety of services:

- Special equipment, such as hearing aids, guide dogs, wheelchairs, canes, or prosthetics.
- Special training in such areas as sign language, vocational training, reading, or social adjustment. This training may take place at a rehabilitation center, at a vocational school, at a public or private college, or on the job.
- Money for transportation and living expenses during the training period.
- Medical, surgical, and other services that will reduce the extent of the client's impairment.
- Individual counseling and guidance.
- Assistance in finding a suitable job and essential equipment, licenses, tools, or stock for a small business.
- Follow-up to smooth the client's entrance into employment.

Under this program, states are able to set priorities for categories of eligible clients who will be served when financial resources are limited. For example, states may assign a higher priority to clients who need medical restoration than to those who need psychological counseling. Each state also has the option of deciding whether an economic means test should be used to determine whether the applicant is entitled to certain services.

The amendments in 1992 to the Rehabilitation Act require that the services financed be aimed at individuals with the most severe disabilities. In addition to providing funds for the traditional rehabilitation areas of job counseling, retraining, and prosthetic and other assistive devices, the amendments authorize funding for "supported employment"—a service model in which a person with a severe disability works in a private-sector job with a "job coach" who eases the transition to independent employment.

MEDICAID

This program (described in Chapter 15) covers medical expenses for low-income people.

OLD AGE, SURVIVORS, DISABILITY, AND HEALTH INSURANCE

This is a social insurance program (described in Chapter 4) for those who are no longer able to work following several years of covered employment.

SUPPLEMENTAL SECURITY INCOME

This is a public assistance program (described in Chapter 4) for low-income persons with a physical or mental disability.

FOOD STAMPS

This program (described in Chapter 4) offsets some of the food expenses for low-income people who qualify.

WORKERS' COMPENSATION PROGRAM

Workers injured or disabled on the job, and surviving dependents of workers who die as a result of such injury, are provided financial assistance to compensate for lost wages and to pay the cost of any required medical or rehabilitative care.

People with permanent disabilities arising from work injuries may receive a lump sum or a monthly payment in perpetuity from workers' compensation. Workers' compensation is not a federal program; laws in every state require employers to purchase workers' compensation insurance to cover the claims made by injured workers.

ROLES OF SOCIAL WORKERS

Social workers come in contact with persons with a disability in two general ways.

First, they encounter persons with a disability in settings in which the primary service focus is something other than rehabilitation. For example, workers at family counseling agencies usually see families with marital and interpersonal problems. One or more of these family members may have a disability. The disability may be unrelated to the family problems, or it may be an important contributing factor. In the latter case, the social worker's role is to help the family assess and understand the nature and impact of the disability and then develop effective strategies for handling the difficulties associated with the disability.

Second, social workers may be employed in settings that primarily serve persons with a disability, such as rehabilitation centers, nursing homes, general hospitals, day-care centers for persons with a disability, rehabilitation hospitals, and specialized schools (such as schools for persons with a visual disability).

Rehabilitation for persons with a physical or mental disability can be defined as restoration to the fullest physical, mental, social, vocational, and economic usefulness of which they are capable.[60] Programs focus on vocational training, vocational counseling, psychological adjustment, medical and physical restoration, and job placement. Clients, of course, differ in which of these services are needed. Some clients require help in all of these areas.

A wide range of professionals provide rehabilitation services: physicians, nurses, clinical psychologists, physical therapists, psychiatrists, occupational therapists, recreational therapists, vocational counselors, speech therapists, hearing therapists, industrial arts teachers, social workers, special education teachers, and prosthetists. Most of these therapists focus on the physical functioning of the clients, whereas social workers focus primarily on their social functioning. In most rehabilitation settings, a team approach is used.

The major functions of social workers in rehabilitation settings are discussed in the following sections.

Counseling Clients

Counseling in this context involves helping clients adjust to their disability and to the rehabilitation programs at the agency. A wide range of problems may be covered: personal, interpersonal, family, financial, vocational adjustment, and educational adjustment.

Counseling Families

In some rehabilitation settings, the social worker is involved primarily in working with the family and not with the client, especially if the client is a young child. Counseling with the family involves helping them to understand the nature of the disability and the prognosis, to make the essential adjustments to help the client, and to deal with personal and interpersonal concerns associated with the disability. In such a role, a worker provides information, comfort, understanding, counseling on specific concerns, and sometimes referral services.

Taking Social Histories

A social history contains information about the client's family background and present status. It includes information about what the client's family life was like before contact with the agency, what it is like now, and what it will probably be like in the future. A social history contains a history of the disability, positive and negative reactions of family members to the disability, significant family relationships, summary of strengths and weaknesses within the family for handling the disability, information on social skills of the client, a history of the client's functioning at school and at work, a history of services provided in the past, and a summary of the problems associated with the disability and concerns of family members (see Case Example 16.1). Information for the so-

cial history is gathered from the client, from family members, and from case records of other social and medical agencies that the client has had contact with.

Serving as Case Manager

As a case manager, a social worker coordinates needed services provided by a number of agencies, organizations, or facilities to clients. A person with a disability may require extensive services and resources, including those provided by systems of health care, mental health, rehabilitation, education, housing, employment, and other related systems. Because of the pervasive needs of clients with a disability, it is vital that one of the service providers, typically a social worker, be designated as case manager. Such an arrangement assigns responsibility for planning and orchestrating the delivery of services in a systematic and timely manner. As a case manager, the worker may provide services to a client in a variety of roles, including broker, advocate, counselor, teacher, community organizer, coordinator, and planner. Case managers assess the comprehensive needs of clients, connect them to appropriate services, and ensure that those services are provided effectively.

Serving as Liaison Between the Family and the Agency

Keeping the lines of communication open is essential in any human service setting. In a rehabilitation setting, social workers generally have the responsibility to serve as liaison between the agency staff and the family. At times a worker arranges meetings between the staff and the family to discuss the client's disability, factors affecting rehabilitation, and future plans and services. In a hospital setting, it is the physician's responsibility to explain the particular medical condition to the client, but a social worker often discusses the implications of the medical condition with the client and the family. Implications covered include the likely effect the disability will have in the future

<table>
<tr><td>

**CASE
EXAMPLE 16.1**

</td><td>

Social History of a Client at a Vocational Testing Division of a Rehabilitation Center

</td></tr>
</table>

Hillside Vocational Training Center
Columbus, Ohio

Name: Jim Frey

Date of Birth: 6-30-79

Address: 550 S. Adams, Columbus

Telephone: 478-2346

Religion: Lutheran

Occupation: Unemployed

Race: Black

Marital Status: Single

Height: 5'10"

Weight: 180

Reason for Testing. On April 30, 1996, Jim Frey was involved in an automobile accident with his older brother, Bob. Bob was killed in the accident, and Jim's spine was severed. Jim was hospitalized for 3 months, spent 5 more months convalescing in a nursing home, and since that time has been living with his parents. Jim is paralyzed from the waist down. Following the accident he was also severely depressed. He was referred to this agency by Lakeland Counseling Center, an agency that Jim and his parents have been receiving counseling from. Jim's depression has gradually decreased, and he is now seeking testing and vocational counseling to explore career opportunities.

Family Background and Early History. Jim's father, Donald Frey, has been an insurance salesman for the past 27 years. His mother, Joan Frey, has been a real estate broker for the past 14 years. Both Mr. and Mrs. Frey appear very concerned about their son's future, and both stated they are willing to do whatever they can to help. The Freys live in a middle-class neighborhood and have a home that is clean and well kept. The Freys appeared to have considerable respect for each other and a good relationship.

The only children that the Freys had were Jim and Bob, with Bob being 2 years older. The Freys reported that both their children did well academically in school, and each had a number of friends. The boys were both active in intramural sports, with Bob being a second-string player on the basketball team in his junior and senior years. The most serious trouble that either of the boys had gotten into prior to the accident was Bob being arrested for setting off firecrackers around the 4th of July 5 years ago.

The automobile accident occurred late one evening after Jim and Bob had left a party in which alcoholic beverages were served. Their car hit a bridge abutment. Bob was killed instantly. The parents reported they were extremely distraught following this accident and felt their whole world had been shattered. They indicated they had few friends they socialized with, as they spent most of their time prior to the accident with their work and their children. They received counseling for grief and depression for 18 months from Lakeland Counseling Center. They indicated they discontinued counseling when the person they were seeing made a job transfer to the West Coast.

For nearly the past 2 years, Mr. and Mrs. Frey have been caring for Jim at home. Mrs. Frey indicated she has taken a leave of absence from her real estate position in order to care for her son. They acknowledged that caring for Jim has been "taxing," as he has been quite depressed and has required considerable physical attention. Only recently has he been able to get into and out of a wheelchair without assistance. The parents still mourn the loss of Bob but are increasingly becoming optimistic with the progress that Jim has been making, including a decrease in his depression, increased physical agility, and now a motivation to receive training for a career.

School Performance. Jim attended Franklin Elementary School, Stevens Junior High, and Randal High School. At the time of his accident, Jim was a senior. He was near graduation but as yet has not completed the coursework. School records show that Jim generally received *A*s and *B*s, with a few *C*s. Jim had an intelligence test in his sophomore year in which he achieved a score of 122. Before the accident, Jim was planning to attend college. He reportedly had a number of friends, and most continued to visit him for the first several months following the accident. But as time passed and as Jim's depression continued, his friends gradually stopped coming by to see him. At present he has no close friends.

General Health. Until the accident, his health was generally good. He had a hernia operation at age 10 and a broken collarbone at age 12. During the accident, Jim suffered a severed spine and is now partially paralyzed. He also had a variety of cuts from glass that required over 80 stitches. Since the accident, he at times has experienced considerable pain connected with his injury and has been prone to catch flus and colds. Medical reports indicate Jim received intensive physical therapy while at the hospital and while convalescing in the nursing home. On returning to his home, Jim's parents were instructed on giving him a variety of exercises.

Dating History. Jim indicated he dated a number of young women before the accident. At the time of the accident, he was dating someone steadily (during his senior year). At first this person showed considerable interest in Jim and his circumstances. However, Jim stated that after a few months she started dating others, and her interest in continuing their relationship rapidly declined.

Employment History. Jim was a paperboy for a few years. Before the accident, he worked part-time as a busboy at a restaurant. He has not worked since the accident.

Prior Contact with Social Agencies. Jim was hospitalized in 1996 for 3 months at St. Mary's Hospital. Records show he received extensive physical therapy and counseling for depression from the social work staff. Following this hospitalization, he was transferred to Countryside Nursing Home, where he continued to receive physical therapy and counseling. Jim had fallen asleep on the fateful night when his brother

(continued)

CASE EXAMPLE 16.1 *(continued)*

was killed. For months after that, he was depressed and continued to feel guilty because he felt that, if he had stayed awake, he might have kept his brother awake. (The police concluded that the accident occurred after Bob had fallen asleep.) Jim also has been depressed over the breakup with his girlfriend, over the loss of other friends, and particularly over the shattered hopes and expectations for his future. After Jim returned home, his parents made arrangements with the referring agency (Lakeland Counseling Center) for Jim to receive counseling associated with his depression and also focused on his future. Reports received from Lakeland Counseling Center also indicated that his parents have expressed concerns in the past year that Jim may be drinking beer and other alcoholic beverages to excess.

General Impressions. Jim has made gradual progress in putting his life back together since his auto accident some 3 years ago. At times he is still somewhat depressed, but he now is making efforts to stop brooding about his past and is motivated to improve his situation. He is looking forward to the test results at the center, since he wants to receive training for a career. At the present time, he is uncertain which career he desires to pursue and is uncertain which vocations or professions he is qualified to pursue. He is articulate and personable and appears to possess a high intellect. He has expressed a strong interest in graduating from high school and wonders whether he might have the capacities and financial resources to attend college. His parents appear supportive of his desires to seek a higher education and stated they would be willing and able to provide some financial support.

Jim stated he is also interested in learning to drive and hopes to be able to secure a driver's license and an auto with assistive devices that would enable him to drive.

Jim's drinking was discussed with him. He stated that he may at times drink to excess, but he said this only happens when he is bored or depressed or has nothing to do. It would seem that Jim's drinking is a potential difficulty that should be monitored.

Jim has the support and encouragement of his parents. Jim's present optimism about his future is indeed a positive sign. However, it is important for him to realize that testing is only the first step. Jim hopes to acquire the necessary training, employment, and financial resources to live independently of his parents. Although his parents are supportive, there are occasional conflicts between Jim and his parents, such as over his drinking. Jim may occasionally get discouraged when he encounters obstacles to arriving at the goals that he has set. It is at these times that he may need continued counseling to prevent the return of a long-term depression.

Respectfully submitted,

Frank Lia
Social Worker

on the capacity of the affected person to function at work, at school, in social situations, and within the family. To be an effective liaison, a social worker in a rehabilitative setting needs a basic knowledge of a variety of medical conditions and of medical terminology as well as an awareness of the implications of these medical conditions for emotional, physical, and social functioning.

Being a Broker

Often a social worker functions to link families with other community resources. To be an effective broker, a worker needs a knowledge of other community services, including the programs provided, eligibility requirements, and admission procedures. Clients may need a variety of services from other community agencies, such as financial assistance, wheelchairs, prosthetic services, day-care services, special job training, visiting nurse services, and transportation.

Doing Discharge Planning

In some rehabilitation settings, such as hospitals, social workers have major responsibility for discharge planning. If a client is unable to return home, arrangements must be made for placement in some other setting, such as a nursing home or a group home. Social workers often help clients and their families prepare for returning to the home or to some other facility. In this capacity, the social worker may arrange for financial aid and for such specialized care as home health care, day care, physical therapy, and job training.

REACTIONS TO HAVING A DISABILITY

To work effectively with persons with a disability and their families, the social worker must understand and deal with the emotional reactions to the disability. Clients and their families experience a variety of reactions on being informed that a disability exists.

The reactions that a person has on becoming aware that she or he (or a member of the family) has a disability are centered around the realization that a loss has occurred. For example, when parents become aware their young daughter has a cognitive disability, they are likely to mourn the loss of having a "normal" child. When a loss occurs, people go through a grieving process.

Nearly all of us are currently grieving about some loss that we have had. It might be the end of a romantic relationship, a move away from friends and parents, the death of a pet, failure to get a grade we wanted, or the death of someone close. The reactions that a person has when a disability occurs are analogous to these feelings of loss. Examples of disability-related losses include the following: a couple is informed that their 1-year-old daughter has a cognitive disability; a 20-year-old male learns that he will be paralyzed for the rest of his life as the result of an auto accident; a couple is told that their 6-month-old son has cerebral palsy; a 33-year-old business executive has a massive heart attack and is informed that he will have to make major changes in his lifestyle; a husband learns that his wife will have a severe visual disability following an accident at work; a 26-year-old woman is told that she has multiple sclerosis; a 28-year-old farmer is informed that his leg must be amputated following a tractor accident; a couple discovers that their 2-year-old son has a severe hearing disability; a 17-year-old high school student learns that she has rheumatoid arthritis; a 27-year-old actor hears that he has tested HIV positive. This list could go on and on.

The Grieving Process

It is a mistake to believe that grieving over a loss should end in a set amount of time, such as 6 months, 1 year, or 3 years. The "normal" grieving process is often the life span of the griever. When we first become aware of a loss of very high value, we are likely to grieve intensively—to cry, be depressed, be in a state of shock, and so on. Gradually we will have hours, then days, then weeks, then months when we will not dwell on the loss and will not grieve. However, there will always be something that reminds us of the loss (such as anniversaries of when it occurred), and we will grieve again. The intense grieving periods will, however, gradually become shorter in duration, occur less frequently, and decrease in intensity.

Two important models of the grieving process have been advanced: the Kübler-Ross model and the Westberg model. Some people who are grieving believe the Kübler-Ross model better describes the process, whereas others assert that the Westberg model more accurately describes their feelings. These models help us to understand the grief we feel from *any* loss we experience.

In both of these models, Kübler-Ross and Westberg note the following: (a) Some people continue to grieve and never reach the final stage (acceptance in the Kübler-Ross model and affirming reality in the Westberg model) and (b) one should not rigidly believe that everyone will progress through these stages as diagramed. There is often considerable movement back and forth in these stages. For example, in the Kübler-Ross model, a person may go from denial to depression, to anger and rage, back to denial, then to bargaining, then to depression, back to anger and rage, and so on.

Acceptance is the final phase in Elisabeth Kübler-Ross's model of the grieving process.

KÜBLER-ROSS MODEL

In *On Death and Dying*, Kübler-Ross describes five stages of dying that terminally ill people typically proceed through.[61] These five stages (summarized in Chapter 15) include denial, rage and anger, bargaining, depression, and acceptance. In my experience, *all* clients typically display these five stages when confronted with evidence that they have a personal problem—including a disability.

Stage 1: Denial ("No, not me."). During this stage, clients tell themselves, "No, this can't be," "There must be a mistake," "This just isn't happening." It is difficult for clients (or the families of clients) to admit they have a disability, and they may often (erroneously) perceive themselves as sinful, weak, or irresponsible. In our society, which glorifies "the body beautiful," acknowledging that a disability exists is often erroneously interpreted by clients as indicating that they are less important or worthy. In addition, recognizing that a disability exists means acknowledging that

one's life will have to change. When such change becomes inevitable, clients often mourn the loss of what used to be. For example, a young, successful businesswoman may need to change her whole life following a heart attack, including pursuing some other career with fewer pressures. Denial is often important and necessary because it helps cushion the impact of the client's awareness that change is inevitable.

Stage 2: Rage and Anger ("Why me?"). Clients (or their families) resent the fact that others remain the same while they are afflicted with a disability. They feel it is "unfair." Also, they may resent the fact that relatives, old friends, and others are doing the things that they can no longer do. Anyone may be the target of clients' anger, including the social worker who confronts them with the reality of their disability.

Stage 3: Bargaining ("Yes, me, but . . ."). During this stage, clients begin to accept the existence of

FIGURE 16.1

Westberg Model of the Grieving Process

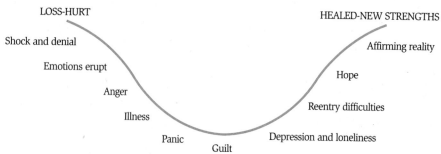

Source: Granger Westberg, *Good Grief* (Philadelphia: Fortress Press, 1962).

the disability but will bargain for a wide variety of things: getting a second opinion, substituting cigar smoking for cigarette smoking for someone who has emphysema, working 2 more weeks to organize things at the office before taking an extended period of relaxed recovery for someone who has had a heart attack, and so on. Clients promise to be good or to do something in exchange for another week or month before they accept the alternatives presented to them for change. Or they hope that there will be scientific breakthroughs that will fully cure their disability.

During the bargaining stage, clients will usually try to change a few circumstances in their lives, hoping that these changes will miraculously eliminate the disability. Parents of a child with a severe cognitive disability may hope, for example, that increased training and education will enable their child, in several years' time, to be of "normal" intelligence.

Stage 4: Depression ("Yes, me."). Clients (and their families) at this stage have stopped denying the existence of their disability. Their anger has subsided, and they no longer try to bargain. They understand the nature of their disability and realize they will need to make changes in their lives. However, they as yet are not ready to put forth the efforts to improve their circumstances. They tend to brood about having a disability and convey an attitude of "Woe is me," "How awful this is," and

"Poor me." Often they blame themselves for having the disability. They mourn about how it will affect their future, and they mourn the loss of what they will have to change in their lives.

Stage 5: Acceptance ("I have a problem, but it's all right; I can."). Clients now, for the first time, make a concerted effort to minimize the effects of the disability and to put their lives back together. They have the attitude of "I can do it." There is hope. Fear and apprehension are still present but very much reduced. Only when clients reach this stage are they ready to work on a rehabilitation program.

WESTBERG MODEL

The Westberg model[62] of the grieving process is diagrammed in Figure 16.1.

Shock and Denial. Many people, when informed about a tragic loss, are so numb and in such a state of shock that they are practically devoid of feeling. It could be that, when emotional pain is unusually intense, the system temporarily "blows out." As a result, the person hardly feels anything and thus acts as if nothing has happened. Denial is a way of avoiding the impact of a tragic loss.

Emotions Erupt. As the realization of the loss becomes evident, the person expresses pain through sobs or screams or through gentle tears or deep sighs.

EXHIBIT 16.1

How to Cope with Grief

If you are grieving, try whichever of the following suggestions you believe will be most useful.

- Crying is an acceptable and valuable expression of grief. Cry as you feel the need. Crying releases the tension that is part of grieving.

- Talking about your loss and your plans for the present and the future is very constructive. Sharing your grief with friends, family, the clergy, or a professional counselor is advisable. You may want to become involved with a group of people who are having similar experiences. Talking about your grief eases loneliness, allows you to vent your feelings, and helps you to accept your loss and make constructive plans for the present and the future. Talking with close friends gives you a sense of security and brings you closer to others you love. Talking with others who have similar losses helps put your problems into perspective; you will see that you are not the only one with problems, and you will feel good about yourself when you assist others in handling their losses.

- Disabilities often cause us to examine and question our faith or philosophy of life. Do not become concerned if you begin questioning your beliefs. Talk about them. For many people, a religious faith provides help in accepting the loss.

- Writing out a rational self-analysis of your grief will help you to identify irrational thinking that is contributing to the grief. (Chapter 5 explains how to write a rational self-analysis.) Once your irrational thinking is identified, you can relieve much of your grief through rational challenges to your irrational thinking.

- Try not to dwell on how unhappy you feel. Become involved and active in life around you. Do not waste your time and energy on self-pity.

- If there are certain days of the year when you tend to grieve deeply (such as an anniversary of a disabling automobile accident), spend these days with family and friends who will give you support.

- You may feel that you have nothing to live for and may even think about suicide. Understand that many people who encounter severe losses feel this way. Seek to find assurance in the fact that a sense of purpose and meaning will return.

- Intense grief is very stressful, and stress can lead to a variety of illnesses, such as headaches, colitis, ulcers, colds, and flus. If you become ill, seek a physician's help and tell the doctor that your illness may be related to grief you are experiencing.

- Intense grief may also lead to sleeplessness, sexual difficulties, loss of appetite, or overeating. You may find you have little energy and cannot concentrate. All of these reactions are normal. Seek to focus on the fact that eventually a sense of purpose and meaning will return to your life. Such a return happens for practically everyone who suffers a serious loss.

- Seek during your grief to eat a balanced diet, to get ample rest, and to exercise moderately. Every person's grief is unique. If you are experiencing unusual physical reactions (such as nightmares), try not to become overly alarmed.

- Medication should be taken sparingly and only under the supervision of a physician. Avoid trying to relieve your grief with alcohol or other drugs. Many drugs are addictive and may stop or delay the necessary grieving process.

- Recognize that guilt, real or imagined, is a normal part of grief. Parents who have a child

(continued)

EXHIBIT 16.1 *(continued)*

with a disability often feel guilty about things they have done or about things they think they should have done. If you are experiencing intense guilt, share it with friends or with a professional counselor. It might also be helpful to write a rational self-analysis on the guilt (see Chapter 5). Learn to forgive yourself. If you didn't make mistakes, you wouldn't be human.

■ You may find that friends and relatives appear to be shunning you. If this is happening, they are probably uncomfortable around you because they do not know what to say or do. Take the initiative and talk with them about your loss. Tell them about ways in which you would like them to be supportive to you.

■ If possible, put off making major decisions (changing jobs, moving away, and so on) until you become more emotionally relaxed. When you're highly emotional, you're likely to make unwise decisions.

Anger. At some point, the person usually experiences anger. It may be directed at God for causing the loss. The anger may stem partly from the unfairness of the loss. If a child is born with a disability or later develops a disability, it is not uncommon for the parents at times to become angry at the child for having the disability and for complicating their lives.

Illness. Because grief is stress producing, stress-related illnesses are likely to develop, such as colds, flus, ulcers, tension headaches, diarrhea, rashes, insomnia, and so on.

Panic. Realizing that she or he does not feel like the "old self," the grieving person may panic and even worry about going insane. Nightmares, unwanted emotions that appear uncontrollable, and physical illnesses contribute to the panic. A variety of fears may develop. The person with a disability may fear the reactions of others. Parents may fear that their siblings will suffer from having a brother or sister with a disability, that they will be unable to deal with the burdens of caring for a child with a disability, or that both they and their child will be the target of ridicule.

Guilt. The grieving person may blame himself or herself for having done something that contributed to the loss or disability or may feel guilty for not having done something that might have prevented it. If a child is born with a disability, the mother may wonder, "Could this have been caused by my smoking or drinking during pregnancy?" This tendency to blame oneself is reinforced by the questions asked by professionals. For example, the mother may be asked, "Did you smoke during the pregnancy? Did you have a serious fall or illness? Did you drink? What pills did you take?" (Although these questions need to be asked, professionals should be careful about how they are phrased because they can have devastating effects.)

Depression and Loneliness. At times the grieving person will feel very sad about the disability or loss and have feelings of isolation and loneliness. She or he may withdraw from others who don't seem supportive or understanding.

Reentry Difficulties. At this point, the grieving person makes efforts to put his or her life back together. Reentry problems are likely to arise. The person may resist letting go of attachments to the past, and loyalties to memories may hamper reentry.

Hope. Gradually hope of putting one's life back together returns and begins to grow.

Affirming Reality. The old feeling of having control of one's life returns. The reconstructed life is not the same as the old, and memories of the loss remain. But the reconstructed life is viewed as "okay."

Facilitating the Grieving Process

The Kübler-Ross and Westberg paradigms can help social workers better understand why clients are reacting in various ways to their disabilities. It is important that workers help clients identify those emotions that are interfering with a habilitative or rehabilitative program. Strategies can then be developed to counter those emotions that are interfering with progress. For example, a mother of a child born with Down syndrome may feel guilty because she thinks she caused the problem by lifting too much during her pregnancy. The social worker can arrange for a physician or a genetics counselor to explain the etiology of the disorder and to assure her that her concerns over lifting heavy objects had nothing to do with causing the Down syndrome.

Kübler-Ross's and Westberg's paradigms may not always apply to young children. Children born with a disability generally are not initially aware of their condition. Awareness gradually develops through interacting with others over a lengthy period of time. Children with a disability come to learn that they are different and that others often place negative values on their disability. In the following excerpt from an autobiography, Christy Brown, born with cerebral palsy, describes some of his feelings. Christy Brown used to ride in a wagon that was pulled by his brothers and sisters, but when it broke, he was unable to get around.

Christy Brown's dawning awareness of his disability at the age of ten made him realize he was different and he began to consider himself through the eyes of a "cripple."

I was now just ten, a boy who couldn't walk, speak, feed, or dress himself. I was helpless, but only now did I begin to realize how helpless I really was. I still didn't know anything about myself: I knew nothing beyond the fact that I was different from others. I didn't understand what made me different or why it should be I. . . .

I couldn't reason this out. I couldn't even think clearly about it. I could only feel it, feel it deep down in the very core of me, like a thin sharp needle. . . .

Up to then I had never thought about myself. True, there had come sometimes a vague feeling that I wasn't like the others, an uneasy sort of stirring in my mind that came and went. But it was just one dark spot in the brightness of things; and I used to soon forget it. . . .

Now it was different. Now I saw everything, not through the eyes of a little boy eager for fun and brimming with curiosity, but through those of a cripple, a cripple who had only just discovered his own affliction.

I looked at Peter's hands. They were brown, steady hands with strong, square fingers, hands that could clasp a hurley firmly or swing a chestnut high into the air. Then I looked down

at my own. They were queer, twisted hands,
with bent, crooked fingers, hands that were
never still, but twitched and shook continually
so that they looked more like two wriggling
snakes than a pair of human hands.

I began to hate the sight of those hands, the
sight of my wobbly head and lopsided mouth.[63]

Christy's awareness of his disability involved
four steps: (a) an avoidance of thinking about himself and his disability, (b) a vague sense that he
was different from others, (c) a critical incident—
not being able to go out—that forced him to acknowledge that he had a disability, and (d) self-
deprecation because of his disability.

There is a tendency for parents to overindulge
and overprotect a child with a disability. They give
the child less responsibility, place fewer limits on
unwanted behaviors, indulge personal whims of
the child, and are reluctant to punish the child,
partly because of their sympathy for the suffering
the child is undergoing. Children become aware
of this special status and sometimes use this sympathy to manipulate those around them. Louise
Baker describes how she manipulated others at
age 8, shortly after a leg was amputated following
an automobile accident:

Even before I left the hospital my sudden power
over people was showing itself. First of all, with
completely unconscious brilliance, I chose rather
inspired subjects to discuss during my five days
of postoperative delirium. I rambled on fever-
ishly but with moving feeling about a doll with
real golden hair and blue eyes that opened and
closed. I even conveniently mentioned the awe-
some price and just where such a doll might be
purchased, and I sighed over my father's attested
poverty which prevented him from buying this
coveted treasure. . . . The news spread: "The
poor little crippled child in the hospital . . .
wants a doll. . . ." When I left the hospital it
took two cars to transport my loot.

Very soon after I came home from the hos-
pital I realized that all I had to do was mumble
the magic words. . . "I'll never be able to run
again, will I?" This sad little speech—then
the moment was ripe to make almost any
demand. . . .

Three months before, I was a reasonably
well-mannered child . . . now I was a precocious
gold-digger, and anyone was fair game.[64]

When clients or members of their family are
reacting (emotionally or behaviorally) in ways that
substantially interfere with the rehabilitation process, social workers have a responsibility to confront them about this tactfully. Sometimes a considerable amount of evidence will have to be
presented, perhaps over a period of time, before
clients and family members will acknowledge that
certain reactions are intensifying the negative effects of the disability. Once the acknowledgment
occurs, strategies for changing the reaction patterns can be discussed, and one or more approaches may be selected and implemented to
eliminate the destructive patterns.

SUMMARY

Persons with a disability include those who are
temporarily injured, those with a chronic physical
disability, those with a hearing or visual disability,
those who have an emotional disorder, those with
a cognitive disability, those with a learning disability, and those with degenerative illnesses and
chronic health disorders.

Developmental disabilities include cognitive
disability, infantile autism, epilepsy, cerebral palsy,
and a variety of other conditions that occur before
age 22 and that hinder development. There are
hundreds of illnesses and medical conditions that
have been identified as contributing causes of cognitive disability.

Throughout history the willingness of societies
to care for the needs of those with a disability has
always been largely determined by the perceived
causes of the disability, the existing medical
knowledge, and the general economic conditions.
In the past, disability was often viewed as a result
of demonic possession or of God's punishment.

In the 20th century, our society has made
progress in better understanding the needs of persons with a disability and in designing services to
meet these needs. Yet there is still a general lack

of acceptance of persons with a disability; it is often related to our emphasis on the "body beautiful" in our society. Persons with a disability are still frequently pitied, shunned, or made the brunt of jokes. Our society has yet to learn that persons with a disability are people who want to be treated as peers. (All of us are only an accident away from having a disability.) Until persons with a disability are given an opportunity, not only legally but also socially, to be treated as peers, social services will be only partially effective. Ideally, persons with a disability should be limited only by the physical or mental restrictions of their disability. Sadly, the psychological and social obstacles faced by these persons are often greater than their actual physical or mental limitations. Our society has yet to learn that a person with a disability is a person—a person who happens to have a disability.

Social workers are only one of numerous groups of professionals who provide services to persons with a disability. The roles of social workers in providing rehabilitative services include counseling persons with a disability, counseling family members, gathering information through social histories, serving as case managers, serving as liaisons between the family and the agency, being brokers, and doing discharge planning.

Another role of the social worker is to help persons with a disability and their family members to change emotional and behavioral reactions that are interfering with the rehabilitative process. Two useful paradigms summarize emotional, behavioral, and physiological reactions to having a disability: the Kübler-Ross model and the Westberg model. Both models conceptualize the reactions in terms of the disability being perceived as a loss by the affected person.

NOTES

1. U.S. Bureau of the Census, *Statistical Abstract of the United States, 1997* (Washington, DC: U.S. Government Printing Office, 1997).
2. Ibid.
3. G. L. Dickinson, *Greek View of Life* (New York: Collier Books, 1961), p. 95.
4. S. Nichtern, *Helping the Retarded Child* (New York: Grosset & Dunlap, 1974), p. 14.
5. J. F. Garrett, "Historical Background," in *Vocational Rehabilitation of the Disabled*, D. Malikin and H. Rusalem, eds. (New York: New York University Press, 1969), pp. 29–38.
6. J. C. Coleman, *Abnormal Psychology and Modern Life*, 3rd ed. (Glenview, IL: Scott, Foresman, 1964).
7. C. E. Obermann, *A History of Vocational Rehabilitation in America* (Minneapolis: Dennison, 1964).
8. L. Kanner, *A History of the Care and Study of the Mentally Retarded* (Springfield, IL: Charles C. Thomas, 1964), p. 6.
9. M. Judge, "A Brief History of Social Services, Part I," *Social and Rehabilitation Record*, 3, no. 5 (Sept. 1976), pp. 2–8.
10. Stanford Rubin and Richard Roessler, *Foundations of the Vocational Rehabilitation Process* (Baltimore: University Park Press, 1978), p. 4.
11. A. F. Tyler, *Freedom's Ferment* (New York: Harper & Row, 1962), pp. 294–296.
12. J. Lenihan, "Disabled Americans: A History," *Performance*, 27 (1977), Bicentennial issue (Washington, DC: The President's Committee on Employment of the Handicapped).
13. Obermann, *A History of Vocational Rehabilitation in America*, p. 333.
14. L. M. Dunn, "A Historical Review of the Retarded," in *Mental Retardation*, J. Rothstein, ed. (New York: Holt, Rinehart & Winston, 1961), pp. 13–17.
15. Obermann, *A History of Vocational Rehabilitation in America*, p. 80.
16. Kanner, *A History of the Care and Study of the Mentally Retarded*, pp. 36–38.
17. Ibid., p. 39.
18. Rubin and Roessler, *Foundations of the Vocational Rehabilitation Process*, pp. 12–13.
19. Ibid., pp. 13–14.
20. Lenihan, "Disabled Americans: A History," pp. 28–37.
21. Tyler, *Freedom's Ferment*, p. 306.
22. Rubin and Roessler, *Foundations of the Vocational Rehabilitation Process*, pp. 8–9.
23. Ibid., pp. 10–11.
24. R. Lubove, *The Professional Altruist* (Cambridge, MA: Harvard University Press, 1965).
25. Ibid.
26. Obermann, *A History of Vocational Rehabilitation in America*, p. 121.
27. Rubin and Roessler, *Foundations of the Vocational Rehabilitation Process*, pp. 22–23.
28. Obermann, *A History of Vocational Rehabilitation in America*, pp. 155–157.
29. R. Thomas, "The Expanding Scope of Service," *Journal of Rehabilitation*, 36, no. 5 (1978), pp. 37–40.

30. Rubin and Roessler, *Foundations of the Vocational Rehabilitation Process,* pp. 30–32.

31. Ibid., pp.32–45.

32. Gregory Spears, "Bush Inks Disabled Rights Bill," *Wisconsin State Journal,* July 27, 1990, p. 5A.

33. William E. Kiernan and Jack A. Stark, eds. *Pathways to Employment for Adults with Developmental Disabilities* (Baltimore: Brooks, 1986), pp. 12–15.

34. David L. Rosenhan and Martin E. P. Seligman, *Abnormal Psychology,* 3rd ed. (New York: Norton, 1995), p. 633.

35. Ibid., p. 638.

36. Ibid.

37. Ibid.

38. Ibid., pp. 640–641.

39. Ibid., p. 640.

40. Ibid., p. 624.

41. Ibid.

42. Ibid., p. 630.

43. Ibid., pp. 630–631.

44. Diane E. Papalia and Sally W. Olds, *Human Development,* 6th ed. (New York: McGraw-Hill, 1995), pp. 74–76.

45. Rosenhan and Seligman, *Abnormal Psychology,* p. 628.

46. Daniel Q. Haney, "Retardation Gene Discovered," *Wisconsin State Journal,* May 30, 1991, p. 1A.

47. Ibid.

48. Rosenhan and Seligman, *Abnormal Psychology,* p. 629.

49. Maureen O'Gorman Foster, quoted in *Introduction to Social Welfare,* 4th ed., Charles Zastrow, ed. (Belmont, CA: Wadsworth, 1992), p. 515.

50. S. Richardson et al., "Cultural Uniformity in Reaction to Physical Disabilities," *American Sociological Review,* 26 (April 1961), pp. 241–247.

51. C. H. Cooley, *Human Nature and the Social Order* (New York: Scribner's, 1902).

52. Beatrice A. Wright, *Physical Disability: A Psychological Approach* (New York: Harper & Row, 1960), p. 259.

53. Adrienne Asch and Nancy R. Mudrick, "Disability," in *Encyclopedia of Social Work,* 19th ed. (Washington, DC: NASW, 1995), p. 753.

54. Ibid.

55. Nancy Weinberg, "Rehabilitation," in *Contemporary Social Work,* 2nd ed., Donald Brieland, Lela Costin, and Charles Atherton, eds. (New York: McGraw-Hill, 1980) p. 310.

56. Ibid.

57. R. Kleck, H. Ono, and A. H. Hastorf, "The Effects of Physical Deviance upon Face-to-Face Interaction," *Human Relations,* 19 (1966), pp. 425–436.

58. Fred David, "Deviance Disavowal: The Management of Strained Interaction by the Visibly Handicapped," in *The Other Side: Perspectives on Deviance,* Howard S. Becker, ed. (New York: Free Press, 1964), p. 123.

59. Rubin and Roessler, *Foundations of the Vocational Rehabilitation Process,* pp. 32–44.

60. Ibid.

61. Elisabeth Kübler-Ross, *On Death and Dying* (New York: Macmillan, 1969).

62. Granger Westberg, *Good Grief* (Philadelphia: Fortress Press, 1962).

63. Christy Brown, *The Story of Christy Brown* (New York: Pocket Books, 1971), p. 72.

64. Louise Baker, *Out on a Limb* (New York: Whittlesly House, 1946), pp. 4–5.

OVERPOPULATION, MISUSE OF THE ENVIRONMENT, AND FAMILY PLANNING

roblems associated with overpopulation and despoiling of the environment threaten to reduce the quality of human life throughout the world. The seriousness of these problems is illustrated by the fact that some nations are contemplating the enactment of compulsory sterilization laws. This chapter will:

- Describe the problems associated with rapid population growth throughout the world.
- Discuss pollution and misuse of the environment.
- Summarize current efforts to curtail the growth of the world's population and to preserve the environment.
- Outline proposals that have been advanced for population control and for environmental protection in the future.
- Provide suggestions for what each of us can do to save the earth.
- Describe the role of social work in family planning.

THE POPULATION CRISIS

There are now about 6 billion people living on earth.[1] In 1930 there were 2 billion. The world's population is increasing at the rate of 185 people a minute, 11,100 an hour, 266,400 a day, and 97.2 million a year[2] (see Table 17.1). The dangers of runaway population growth can be viewed in historical perspective by looking at the world's population in units of 1 billion people. It took all of human history until 1850 for the world's population to reach 1 billion, but the next unit of 1 billion was added in only 80 years (1850–1930). The unit after that was in 30 years (1930–1960), and the next occurred in only 15 years (1960–1975). Since 1975, 2 billion people have been added.[3]

Assuming a continued doubling rate of 40 years, by 2040 there will be 12 billion people. If this growth continued for 900 years, there would be 60 *million billion* people! This means that there would be about 100 people for each square yard of the earth's surface, including both land and water.[4]

TABLE 17.1

Doubling Times of the World's Population

Date	Estimated World Population	Time Required for Population to Double (in years)
8000 B.C.	5 million	
1650 A.D.	500 million	1500
1850	1 billion	200
1930	2 billion	80
1975	4 billion	45
2015	8 billion	40

Sources: Paul R. Ehrlich, *The Population Bomb* (New York: Ballantine, 1971); Werner Fornos, *Gaining People, Losing Ground* (Washington, DC: Population Institute, 1987).

Doubling Time and Population Growth

The rate at which the population doubles in a country, and in the world, has immense consequences. Doubling time is based on the extent to which the birthrate exceeds the death rate. Doubling times have a compound effect. Just as interest dollars earn interest, people added to the population produce more people. Table 17.2 shows the relationship between the annual population growth rate and the doubling time of the population. Thus, what seems a small population growth rate of 1.9% per year (the current rate in the world) leads to a dramatic doubling time of 40 years. With an annual growth rate of 1.9%, over 95 million people are added to the world's population annually.[5]

Doubling Time and Developing Countries

The countries experiencing the most severe doubling-time problems are the "developing countries" (also called Third-World nations), which are

TABLE 17.2

Rate of Population Growth and Doubling Time

Annual Percentage Increase	Doubling Time (in years)
1.0	70
2.0	35
3.0	24
4.0	17

Source: Paul Ehrlich, *The Population Bomb* (New York: Ballantine, 1971), p. 10.

just beginning to industrialize. Sadly, population growth is greatest in the countries that can least afford increases—that is, the countries that need to spend their resources on improving their economic conditions. Developing countries have over two-thirds of the world's population and doubling times of about 20 to 35 years.[6] They tend to have primitive and inefficient agriculture, small gross national products, and high illiteracy rates. Their populations spend most of their time trying to meet basic subsistence needs, and many people are starving in these countries.

Developing countries are characterized by high birthrates and declining death rates. The trend in the past has been that, when a country begins to industrialize, the death rate drops (people live longer) while the birthrate remains high for a substantial period of time. The result is rapid population growth. Unfortunately, developing countries, where people's living conditions most need improvement, are precisely the nations whose populations are increasing so rapidly that most people are scarcely better off than they were a generation ago. Nine of every ten people added to the world's population are born in the poorer, developing countries.[7] Third-World countries are much more likely than industrial countries to have a population explosion.

The population crisis in the world today is not due to families having more children than they did in the past; family size has not increased. However, more people are living to the age of fertility and beyond. In effect, more babies are growing to maturity to produce babies themselves. This change is due to several factors: advances in medicine, sanitation, and public health and the increased capacity to reduce the effects of famines, floods, droughts, and other natural disasters.

Lee Rainwater has noted that "the poor get children."[8] There is a vicious circle involving rapid population growth and poverty. Rapid population growth places an increasing strain on a nation's ability to feed and clothe its growing masses, which leads to poverty. Poverty, in turn, leads to a high birthrate, which leads to further population growth. Former World Bank President Robert S. McNamara warned: "Short of thermonuclear war itself, rampant population growth is the gravest issue the world faces over the decades ahead."[9]

Developed or industrialized countries have doubling times in the 50- to 200-year range.[10] In the United States in recent years, the birthrate has steadily decreased and is nearing a zero-population-growth rate (an average of two children per family). The basic reason for the longer doubling time in developed countries is that people decide to have fewer children (for financial and other reasons). The average cost of raising a child from birth to age 18 in the United States is estimated to be $161,000 in low-income families, $225,000 in middle-income families, and $315,000 in upper-income families.[11] Developed nations are characterized by both low birthrates and low death rates.

The slower doubling times in industrialized countries in no way indicate that these nations are not part of the problem. If one looks at consumption rates of raw materials, they are the major culprit. The United States, for example, uses about one-third of all the raw materials consumed each year but has less than one-fifteenth of the world's population.[12] Americans are therefore using five times their "fair share" of raw materials. People in the United States also consume, on the average, four times as much food per person as inhabitants of developing countries.[13]

Werner Fornos noted in 1987 that most of the population growth in the future will occur in the

FIGURE 17.1

Age/Sex Population Pyramids:
Industrialized and Developing Country Models

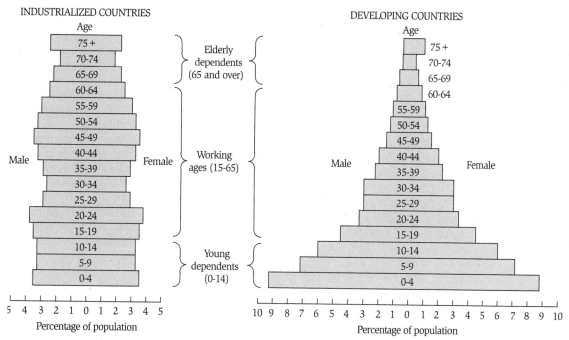

Industrialized countries have three or four adults of economically productive ages for each dependent child. When an industrialized country's children grow up and reproduce, the population structure will change only a little.

Developing countries have one (or fewer) adult of economically productive age for each dependent child. When the developing country's children grow up and reproduce, a population explosion will occur.

urban centers of the developing (Third-World) countries:

> The population of the Third World as a whole is increasing by a significant 2.1 percent each year, but the population of the Third World's cities is growing by a swift 3.5 percent annually—fully three times as fast as the industrialized world's urban centers. Africa's cities are growing fastest, at a runaway 5 percent each year. The slum squatter settlements associated with these centers are growing at twice the rate of the cities themselves.[14]

In many developing countries, families average seven or eight children.[15] As a result, these coun-

tries are increasingly populated by the young. Figure 17.1 indicates that one result of this younger population is that developing countries are much more likely than industrialized countries to have a population explosion.

An Optimal Population Size

A common question is, "What is the capacity of the world to support people?" To say that the population is too large or too small implies there is an optimal size, but no exact figure could accurately be considered the ideal population for the world.

EXHIBIT 17.1

Compulsory Sterilization Laws

Overpopulation is now recognized as one of the severest problems affecting the preservation of the quality of human life. Some countries are now seriously considering enacting compulsory sterilization laws to control rapid population growth. One such country is India. In 1976 Maharashtra (a state in India) passed a compulsory sterilization law to limit family size. The law required all males under age 55 and all females under age 45 to be sterilized within 180 days of the birth of their third living child. Prison terms of up to 2 years could be assigned to those who failed to comply, although offenders were generally sterilized and then paroled. From April 1976 through December 1976, more than 7 million sterilizations reportedly were performed. This law was rescinded with the fall of Prime Minister Indira Gandhi's government in 1976. Nevertheless, it illustrates the desperation some countries feel to alleviate the pressures of unwanted population growth.

Source: "Maharashtra Passes Family Size Limitation Measure," *Intercom*, 9 (Sept. 1976), p. 5; Lynn C. Landman, "Birth Control in India: The Carrot and the Rod?" *Family Planning Perspectives*, 9 (May–Jun. 1977), p. 102.

Many variables and values would enter into specifying an optimal world population size, including preservation of a certain standard or quality of life, rate of consumption of nonrenewable raw materials, future technological breakthroughs in finding new energy and food sources, maintenance of "safe" levels of clean air and water, and public acceptance of the government's role (perhaps compulsory) in population control. The industrialized nations, with their high-consumption and high-waste economies, are using up more of the earth's raw materials and generating more pollution than are developing countries. Because

of consumption rates, adding 1 million people to industrialized countries is comparable to adding 30 million people to developing countries.[16]

With regard to the question of whether the earth is already overpopulated, Paul Ehrlich and Anne Ehrlich note:

> *The key to understanding overpopulation is not population density but the numbers of people in an area relative to its resources and the capacity of the environment to sustain human activities; that is, to the area's* carrying capacity. *When is an area overpopulated? When its population can't be maintained without rapidly depleting nonrenewable resources (or converting renewable resources into nonrenewable ones) and without degrading the capacity of the environment to support the population. In short, if the long-term carrying capacity of an area is clearly being degraded by its current human occupants, that area is overpopulated.*
>
> *By this standard, the entire planet and virtually every nation is already vastly overpopulated.*[17]

Problems of Overpopulation

A wide range of problems are associated with overpopulation. These include too little food, too little water, economic problems, international terrorism, crowding, immigration issues, too little energy, and shortages of other nonrenewable resources.

TOO LITTLE FOOD

An estimated half-billion people today are undernourished—that is, slowly starving—and another billion are malnourished.[18] Malnourishment during childhood years can have devastating effects. It delays physical maturity, impairs brain development, reduces intelligence, and may produce dwarfism. An undernourished adult is listless, apathetic, and unable to work as vigorously as a well-fed adult. A number of diseases are caused directly by dietary deficiency, including beriberi, rickets, and marasmus. Malnutrition also lowers resistance to disease, so the malnourished are likely to have a number of other health problems.

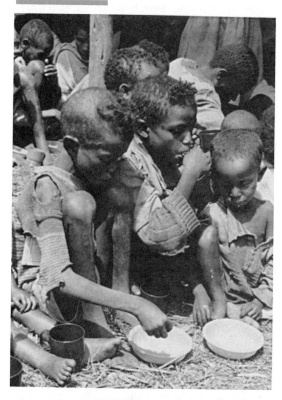

Ethiopian children are fed at a relief camp. Up to 20 million people, mostly children in developing countries, die of starvation each year.

The danger of epidemics is always high in overpopulated areas where people are malnourished. In addition, the damage of malnutrition is passed from one generation to the next, as babies born to malnourished mothers are weaker and in poorer health than the babies of well-fed mothers.[19]

Even in the United States, many people are undernourished, with some dying of starvation.[20] In approximately the time it takes to read this sentence, four people will die (three of them children) from malnutrition.[21] The brain of an infant grows to 80% of its adult size within the first 3 years of life. If supplies of protein are inadequate during this period, the brain stops growing, and the damage is irreversible; such children suffer permanent cognitive disabilities.[22]

More than 200 years ago (in 1798), Thomas Malthus asserted that population growth, if left unchecked, would outstrip the food supply.[23] Malthus theorized that uncontrolled population growth increases in powers of 2: 1, 2, 4, 8, 16, 32, 64—that is, in a geometric ratio. In contrast, the food supply cannot possibly increase that fast. At best, the food supply increases in a steady additive fashion: 1, 2, 3, 4, 5, 6, 7—that is, in an arithmetic ratio. Inevitably, according to Malthus, population growth overtakes the growth in food supplies. Therefore, either population has to be controlled by society, or starvation, hunger, and poverty will be the unavoidable fate of most of the world's people. The fact that widespread starvation and poverty are indeed common in many countries today provides some evidence of the validity of Malthusian theory.

There has been an ongoing, heated controversy among scientists over whether technology will be able to substantially increase the world's food supply. Some scientists claim that we have already reached the limit, and technology is no longer able to increase the food supply to meet the needs of even a slowly growing world population. Others are predicting that future technology will provide food for a population ten times as large as our current one.[24]

Which side is right? The verdict is not yet in. A few decades ago, a technological breakthrough led to a dramatic improvement in much more food produced per acre by new strains of wheat and rice. This "green revolution," however, requires increased use of fertilizers and water. Fertilizers are becoming scarce and more expensive, and many developing countries cannot afford costly irrigation systems.

Research on increasing the food supply is also taking other approaches. One effort is to investigate the feasibility of cultivating the tropical rain forests of Africa, South America, and Indonesia. These areas have large amounts of sunshine and water but poor soil (requiring large quantities of fertilizer) and severe insect infestations. Another effort is geared to finding new ways to harvest fish and plant life from the sea. The sea contains huge quantities of food, much of which is currently distasteful. Not only does more food need to be produced, but food distribution systems must be improved. In the United States, it is more than ironic that farmers are producing more food than Americans can consume, yet an estimated 30 million people in the country do not have enough to eat.[25]

TOO LITTLE WATER

Somewhat surprisingly, fresh water is also in short supply in the world. Of the world's water, 97% is salt water; only 3% is fresh water.[26]

Developed nations use substantially more water per person than developing nations. It has been estimated that an African uses 0.8 gallon of water a day, compared to 270 gallons for a New Yorker.[27]

ECONOMIC PROBLEMS

In industrialized countries, rapid population growth reduces the standard of living and the quality of life by reducing the average per capita income.[28] Because birthrates are consistently higher among the lower-income groups, there are additional social and economic strains. Some authorities openly express alarm that high birthrates among poorer classes may lead to a reduction in average educational achievement and provide a threat to the values espoused by the middle and upper classes. Rapid population growth also leads to other problems: massive unemployment, air and water pollution, traffic jams, inadequate and insufficient housing, and so on.

Economic problems are even more serious in developing nations. Economic progress tends to be canceled out by the increased population. For poor countries to industrialize requires that the inhabitants invest (through either public or private funds) in capital items such as factories, tractors, and industrial equipment. Many developing nations do not even have the funds to provide adequate food for their people. Inability to invest in capital items practically guarantees that they will be unable to improve their people's standard of living.

Lack of funds also creates educational and political problems. Developing countries have a high proportion of school-age children but do not have the resources to provide enough schools. For example, Dr. Benson Morah describes the situation in Nigeria: "You have schools with 70 children in the classrooms, there are children sitting in the windows, children carrying their chairs to school."[29] As a result, in many countries a majority of children do not attend school. Illiteracy and lack of training further lock the inhabitants into poverty.

In addition, people who are poorly housed, hungry, and miserably clothed are likely to view the government as the protector of the rich and the oppressor of the poor. Such conditions often lead to political unrest, revolutions, and civil wars—as have been common in Africa, Asia, and South America.

The gap in living standards between industrialized and developing countries is wide and growing wider. In 1997, for example, the average per capita gross income was about $20,000 in the United States; in some developing nations, it was less than $500.[30]

INTERNATIONAL TERRORISM

Rapid population growth is a factor that contributes to civil unrest, violence, and international strife. Overpopulation leads to higher unemployment, rapid urbanization, declining public health, environmental degradation, economic stagnation, and a large youthful population. Young people in Third-World countries are in destitute poverty and have little hope for a better future; yet at the same time, they have a gnawing awareness that people in industrialized nations are much more affluent. Such conditions create an "Aspiration Bomb." Many young people see violence and terrorism as their only avenue for achieving a better life.

In a report on population, the U.S. National Security Control noted:

> Recent experience, in Iran and other countries, shows that this younger age group, frequently unemployed and crowded into urban slums, is particularly susceptible to extremism, terrorism, and violence as outlets for frustration. On balance, these factors add up to a growing potential for social unrest, political instability, mass migrations, and possible conflicts over control of land and resources.[31]

Werner Fornos makes the following comments about the perils of the "Aspiration Bomb":

Fully 60 percent of the Third World is under 20 years of age; half are 15 years or less. These population pressures create a volatile mixture of youthful aspirations that when coupled with economic and political frustrations help form a large pool of potential terrorists.

The "Aspiration Bomb" may well present a greater threat to U.S. security than the atomic bomb. This is because while there is always the hope that mutual deterrence or common sense will preclude the use of nuclear weapons, there is no such countervailing influence against the violence and frustration embodied in the Aspiration Bomb.[32]

CROWDING

Crowding has been described as a person's subjective judgment that he or she has insufficient space. A number of studies have investigated the effects of crowding on animals. John Calhoun placed rats in laboratory pens and allowed them to breed until their number rose far beyond that found in their natural environment. Several behavioral changes took place. Many females became infertile, others began to abort, and some that bore offspring did not adequately care for their young.[33]

In other studies, overcrowding among animals has led them to become irritable, overly aggressive, nervous, inattentive to grooming, and messy, with some even resorting to cannibalism. In many cases, such negative behaviors continued when the animals were returned to a normal environment.[34]

Although animal research is suggestive, it is not necessarily applicable to humans. The effects of crowding on people have not been sufficiently researched. Some authorities believe it is a factor that leads to crime, emotional problems, incest, child abuse, suicide, violence, dirty streets, and polluted air. Other authorities assert that increases in these behaviors are due not to overcrowding but to poverty and to the breakdown in traditional values. Nonetheless, we should remember that *a delicate balance often exists between a population and an environment, and this balance can be drastically changed by a slight increase in population.* For example, adding one or two fish to a fully populated aquarium may result in a shortage of oxygen that kills most of the fish.[35]

IMMIGRATION ISSUES

Overpopulation also intensifies issues related to immigration. *Immigrate* means to enter a country of which one is not a native for permanent residence. Throughout the world, people living in poor nations dream of moving to the richer countries. Immigration to the United States has reached levels unmatched since early in the century. Other affluent countries have also experienced an influx of people from poorer nations.

It is often said that the United States is a nation of immigrants. Since the earliest days of European settlement, North America has attracted people from all over the world. Some, like the black slaves from Africa, were brought here against their will. Most other groups came in search of freedom from oppression and economic opportunities. In the past two centuries, millions of immigrants of different religions, races, cultures, and political views have come to the United States. This diversity is one of the attributes and strengths of American culture. The immense variety of dress, diet, and music in our society can be traced to the contributions of immigrants from many different cultures and nations.

Immigration has also contributed to some of the social problems that plague American society. Immigration has resulted in ethnic and racial conflict, exploitation of illegal aliens, competition among different ethnic groups for a "piece of the pie," and the stresses and costs associated with educating and caring for new arrivals.

The presence of illegal aliens (also called undocumented immigrants) is one of the most complex social issues in our country. The number of undocumented immigrants currently in the United States is unknown, as is the number of new arrivals each year. By far the largest percentage of undocumented immigrants are Mexicans and Central Americans.

The effects of illegal residents on the economy of the United States has been a topic of heated debate for decades. Some authorities argue they take jobs away from native-born residents. Other authorities believe they are a boon to our economy as they perform distasteful work that U.S. citizens are reluctant to do—such as harvesting garden crops on their knees. They also maintain some industries by accepting lower wages and inferior working conditions. The survival of such industries stimulates growth in associated services, thereby creating more jobs. During economic recessions, undocumented immigrants are generally laid off or discharged more readily than citizens; they thereby help cushion the native-born population from economic uncertainty.

A highly controversial issue related to immigration is whether people who test positive for the HIV virus should be allowed into the United States. As of this writing, individuals who are HIV positive are allowed to enter. (For most of the 1980s and part of the 1990s, they were prohibited from entering.)

Undocumented immigrants are easily exploited by ruthless individuals who know that the immigrants cannot complain to authorities when they have been victimized. (If they went to the authorities, their illegal status might be discovered, which would subject them to deportation.) Although many undocumented immigrants are working in the United States, their employment is now illegal. In 1986 Congress passed the Immigration Reform and Control Act, under which employers are subject to civil penalties ranging from $250 to $10,000 for each illegal alien they hire.

The vast majority of the immigrants who arrive in the United States settle in only a few cities and regions, such as the metropolitan areas of New York City, Los Angeles, Miami, and Chicago. The phenomenon of *chain migration* is the primary cause of this urban concentration. The term refers to the tendency of immigrants to migrate to areas where relatives and others from their home communities are already living. These relatives and acquaintances share the immigrants' culture and language (or dialect) and are available to help the immigrants adjust to the new surroundings. The clusters of immigrants in large cities greatly add to the costs of services in these areas, such as education, health care, job training, public housing, and adult English-language classes.

Now, as in the past, much of the opposition to immigration is based on racial and ethnic prejudice because most of the immigrants to the United States in recent decades have been people of color and non-Europeans. But there is a legitimate question as to whether immigrants raise the unemployment rate by adding to the competition for a limited number of jobs.

Sudden surges of political refugees or illegal immigrants may create special problems. For example, in 1980 Fidel Castro released a number of prisoners and residents of mental hospitals in Cuba; many of these individuals fled to southern Florida, particularly Miami. The influx taxed governmental services in southern Florida and also spurred several serious outbreaks of racial violence in the area during the 1980s.

In 1997 the respected National Academy of Sciences/National Research Council released a landmark report entitled *The New Americans: Economic, Demographic, and Fiscal Effects of Immigration.* The report concluded immigration has a very small impact on the U.S. economy: "The costs to native-born workers are small, and so are the benefits."[36] The report found that immigrants have no negative effects on the wages of most Americans. There is one exception: the very low skilled. Workers with less than a high school degree (who represent about 15% of the workforce) earn wages that are somewhat lower (about 5%) than they would without competition from low-skilled immigrants. The study found that the other losers are taxpayers in California, Florida, Texas, and a few other states where most immigrants live. Taxpayers in these states end up paying more in taxes for the government services (primarily health care and public schools) used by the newcomers. The study also found that immigrants generate a growing share of taxes the longer they are here; the study concluded each additional immigrant and his or her descendants provide $80,000 in extra tax revenues over their lifetimes[37] (see Table 17.3).

TOO LITTLE ENERGY

The world's consumption of energy has doubled every 12 years in our recent history.[38] Over nine-tenths of all energy is provided by fossil fuel sources: oil, coal, and natural gas. Natural gas sources are rapidly being depleted. The domestic supply of oil in the United States is incapable of meeting our needs, and therefore, this country is heavily dependent on foreign sources.

The United States, with less than 5% of the world's people, uses a quarter of all the energy consumed each year; all the industrialized nations combined hold only 25% of the world's people but use an estimated 85–90% of the energy consumed each year.[39]

It has been estimated that the world's petroleum and natural gas reserves will be substantially depleted within a century.[40] New sources of energy that work as well as fossil fuel sources will have to be found.

SHORTAGES OF OTHER NONRENEWABLE RESOURCES

The world's mineral resources also contain elements that are essential for industrial production. These essential elements include copper, lead, zinc, tin, nickel, tungsten, mercury, chromium, manganese, cobalt, molybdenum, aluminum, platinum, iron, and helium. Consumption of these minerals is occurring so rapidly that reserve sources will eventually be depleted, expensive mining of low-quality ores will have to be undertaken, and substitutes will have to be found. As the developing countries continue to industrialize, the demand for these nonrenewable minerals will far exceed the supply.

The Theory of Demographic Transition

As noted, rate of population growth is highest in developing countries. Researchers have observed that growth rates tend to decrease and then stabilize after a fairly high level of industrialization has been achieved. This observation is assumed to be true about population growth in general, and the assumption is called the *theory of demographic transition*. This transition is thought to take place in three stages:

1. *Preindustrial agricultural societies.* In this stage, there is a fairly stable population size.

TABLE 17.3

The Bottom Line on Immigration

Impact on State and Local Treasuries	Impact on Federal Treasury	Total Impact
−$25,000	+$105,000	+$80,000

These figures are arrived at by adding the taxes that an immigrant and his or her descendants are likely to pay over their lifetimes, while subtracting the costs of the government services they are likely to use. The result is that each immigrant produces a net revenue gain to government, with the federal government getting most of the benefit and state and local treasuries losing. In addition, immigrants with higher educations are a greater benefit to government treasuries as indicated below:

Less Than High School	High School Graduate	More Than High School	Overall
−$13,000	+$51,000	+$198,000	+$80,000

Source: National Academy of Sciences, *The New Americans: Economic, Demographic, and Fiscal Effects of Immigration* (Washington, DC: National Research Council, 1997).

The societies have both high birthrates and high death rates.

2. *Developing societies that are beginning to industrialize.* In such societies, the birthrates remain high, but the death rates drop, leading to a rapid increase in the population. The death rates drop because these societies develop the medical capacities to keep people alive and increase the average life span.

3. *Developed industrial societies.* Such societies have both low birthrates and low death rates, resulting in a stable population once again. The low birthrates are thought to be due to people voluntarily limiting the number of children they have. Parents decide to have fewer children to maintain a higher standard of living for themselves and their children.

The theory of demographic transition gives hope that, as developing countries continue to industrialize, their high population growth rates will eventually decrease and then stabilize. However, the concept of demographic transition is merely a theoretical model. It is a summary statement of what happened in the United States and in many other industrialized nations. Because some past societies have had this demographic history does not necessarily mean that current developing nations will repeat the same patterns.

A variety of factors, including religious and cultural values, can affect the rate of population growth. In Japan, for example, certain values rapidly accelerated passage through the second stage in the demographic transition. At the end of World War II, Japan was a developing nation with a high birthrate. Two variables thrust Japan into the third stage of demographic transition. First, there was a general consensus that population control was needed. Second, abortion was not considered immoral (as it was in Western societies). As a result, from 1947 to 1957, the birthrate in Japan dropped from 34 children per 1000 to 14 per 1000, one of the sharpest declines on record. During this decade, half of all conceptions were terminated by abortion.[41] It is doubtful that such a rapid transition could be achieved in countries with cultural traditions that encourage large families.

With regard to stabilizing population growth, Ian Robertson notes:

> The question is not whether population will stabilize—it will. If the global population exceeds the carrying capacity of the earth, death rates will rise and halt population growth. The issues are whether stability will result from a decrease in birth rates or an increase in death rates, how long it will take before stability occurs, and how many people will be here when this finally happens. The prospect of a demographic transition offers the hope that if certain preconditions are met, population growth rates in the developing world will be reduced by a decline in birth rates rather than the grim alternative.[42]

At present, tragically, most developing countries have become lodged in a "holding pattern" in the middle stage of demographic transition, with high birthrates and lowered death rates.[43] The longer these countries remain in this stage, the more the size of their populations will swell and the more difficult it will become for them to industrialize and complete the "demographic transition."

Problem Attitudes and Values

The Roman Catholic Church still objects to using any birth control approach except the rhythm method. In many countries, widely accepted values encourage parents to have large families. Abortions are still a controversial issue in our society. And many Americans believe that population growth is *not* a major issue requiring immediate attention.[44] With such attitudes and values, it is clear that overpopulation is not recognized as one of our most serious problems.

With regard to attitudes toward the use of birth control, Ehrlich and Ehrlich note:

> We shouldn't delude ourselves: the population explosion will come to an end before very long. The only remaining question is whether it will be halted through the humane method of birth control, or by nature wiping out the surplus. We realize that religious and cultural opposition to birth control exists throughout the world; but we believe that people simply don't understand the choice that such opposition implies. Today, anyone opposing birth control is unknowingly voting to have the human population size controlled by a massive increase in early deaths.[45]

Two Countries with Severe Population Problems

India and China are two countries with immense overpopulation problems. If the population growth rate in the world is not curbed, most countries will face similar conditions in the future.

INDIA

With an area about one-third the size of the United States, India has a population over three times the size of ours; it is approaching 1 billion people.[46] About 25 million babies are estimated to be born in India each year.[47]

India is also one of the world's poorest nations, with a per capita income of $250 per year.[48] Many of its citizens are malnourished and starving. The average Indian has a daily food intake of about 2000 calories. (The minimum requirement for staying healthy is about 2300 to 2500 calories.) In some states in India, more than 100 of every 1000 babies die due to inadequate antenatal care and delivery services, low levels of immunization among children, and a substantial proportion of high-risk births.[49]

In 1952 India became the first country in the world to adopt a public family planning program to reduce the birthrate. At first the program was poorly funded. In 1956, for example, total expenditures amounted to 1¢ per year for every 20 people. The principal contraceptive method that was promoted was the rhythm method, which is one of the least effective approaches. In the 1960s, vasectomies and the intrauterine device (IUD) were added to the techniques used. At the end of the 1960s, oral contraceptives were also added, although vasectomies and IUDs remain the preferred methods.

Although the birthrate has declined somewhat in India, birth control devices have not reduced the rate to the zero-growth level. A major reason is that most people using birth control techniques decide to do so only after they already have a large family.[50]

In 1976 the Indian government under Indira Gandhi decided to promote a more aggressive population control strategy. Public educational programs were developed to try to persuade Indians that their main problem was not too little food but too many people. The federal government threatened to dismiss civil service employees who had more than three children. Individual states were asked to pass bills requiring compulsory sterilization of parents after the birth of their third child. As we saw in Exhibit 17.1, one state, Maharashtra, passed such a law and began compulsory sterilization.

In 1977, however, Mrs. Gandhi received a crushing electoral defeat, partly because of her government's record on civil liberties and partly because of the unpopularity of the population control programs. Following her defeat, the compulsory sterilization law in Maharashtra was rescinded.

At India's current growth rate of 1.7% annually, India's population will soon exceed 1 billion.[51] India is projected to surpass China in population size by the year 2050, as India's growth rate is substantially higher than China's.[52]

More than 80% of all Indians are Hindus. Hindu husbands frequently will not permit their wives to use contraceptives until they have produced at least two sons.[53] An additional 11% of the population are Muslims. Some Muslim religious leaders denounce birth control of any kind, but especially sterilization, because cutting the body is a violation of religious law.[54] The obsession for sons is so strong in India that, in order to prevent abortions of unwanted female fetuses, national law prohibits physicians from telling a pregnant woman the sex of the unborn child.[55]

Will India continue to race toward starvation and famine, or will it find politically acceptable approaches to controlling its population growth and begin to raise the standard of living for its citizens? Answers to such questions are of vital significance to all developing countries (and will also have substantial consequences for the rest of the world).

CHINA

In terms of sheer size, China's population surpasses that of India. China already has over 1 billion people—nearly one-fifth the world's entire population.[56]

China's attitude about population growth has varied with time. For many years, the government considered its huge population an important military resource in any conflict with the former Soviet Union or the United States. Furthermore, it urged other developing nations to take the same view. As is common with many developing nations, China's standard of living is low, and much of the farming and factory work is done by hand.

Poor harvests and resulting food shortages (along with changes in the top leadership and a closer relationship with the United States) have convinced the Chinese government that population control is essential. The leaders are now promoting the view that limiting family size will

Afternoon traffic jams the streets in Calcutta. At its current annual growth rate of about 2%, India will have a population of over 1 billion by the end of the 20th century.

improve the health and living conditions of all its citizens and will also liberate women from traditional restrictions. Propaganda posters advertise that an education and a good career are more easily attained with a small family.

Prior to the present policies on family size, Chinese women averaged three children each.[57] In 1980 China's government established a one-child-per-family policy. It raised the minimum legal age of marriage by 2 years, to 22 for men and 20 for women. In some higher-density areas, this minimum age is even older; in Beijing it is 28 for men and 25 for women.[58] (A higher minimum age for marriage is correlated with a smaller average family size.[59]) To have a large family is now regarded as disrespectful to the Communist party and to the country.

Women who become pregnant after the birth of their first child are sometimes pressured to have an abortion. China has also established a number of economic and social incentives for couples to have no more than one child, including income bonuses, priority consideration in urban housing assignments, subsidies in health care, promises of higher pensions, and private vegetable gardens for city residents. For couples who have more than two children, there are also disincentives, such as possible wage deduction to fund welfare programs.

China has greatly slowed its growth rate with these policies. China's current growth rate is down to about 1.1%—an extremely low rate for what is still a poor agricultural nation.[60] It is clear that China is now committed to an all-out effort to stabilize the size of its population, which is good news for the future of China (and for the rest of the world).

Yet new problems have emerged. Some fears have surfaced about the possibility of an emerging generation of spoiled and self-centered only children. Also, if the one-child policy were fully

achieved, China would become a society without brothers, sisters, uncles, or aunts.[61] Chinese peasants have traditionally placed a high value on having sons, who live with the extended family throughout their lives. Daughters, on the other hand, are expected to move in with their husband's family and are therefore considered more of a burden than an asset. Having a son is also viewed as vitally important in continuing the family's name and heritage. As a result, the one-child policy has caused a startling increase in female infanticide because couples then are able, without government opposition, to attempt another pregnancy in the hope of having a male child. The pace of childbearing in China has decelerated faster than in any other large developing country.[62]

Another problem related to female infanticide in China is that today there are nearly three men for every two women.[63] This statistic poses some obvious problems for unmarried Chinese men.

In recent years, China has opened its doors to the West, inviting tourists and Western technology and investments. Undoubtedly there will be rapid technological, social, cultural, and lifestyle changes. History suggests that such changes will be accompanied by political turmoil. (For example, in the 1970s, the Shah of Iran established governmental policies and programs to facilitate industrialization, using funds from the sale of its crude oil to foreign countries. These rapid changes led to political unrest, civil war, and the eventual ouster of the shah.) The future changes in China will have immense implications for the rest of the world.

Will coercive population control policies such as those in India and China eventually be needed in the United States? Ehrlich and Ehrlich note:

> We must hope that our government doesn't wait until it too decides that only coercive measures can solve America's population problem. One must always keep in mind that the price of personal freedom in making childbearing decisions may be the destruction of the world in which your children or grandchildren live. How many children a person has now has serious social consequences in all nations, and therefore is a legitimate concern of society as a whole.[64]

ENVIRONMENTAL PROBLEMS

Higher concentrations of people in an area usually intensify environmental problems. In this section, we will examine the following issues: despoilment of the land, waste disposal (including radioactive and solid waste), air pollution, radioactive leaks from nuclear power plants, nuclear war, water pollution, acid rain, and general pollutants.

Despoilment of the Land

The scenic beauty of our land—as well as its long-term economic value—is being spoiled by a variety of short-term human efforts: strip mining of coal, oil drilling, clearing trees and forests, building highways, constructing oil pipelines, overgrazing by cattle and sheep, dumping garbage, littering, and erecting highway billboards. In nature there is often a delicate balance among the elements: Some fertile land needs trees and grass to retain moisture and fertility; grass-eating animals need grass to survive; carnivorous animals need the grass-eating animals; some birds need seed and insects; other birds feed on small animals or larger animals that have died; all are in need of water. Upsetting this balance often leads to destruction. Dinosaurs once ruled the earth, but all died from some as-yet-unknown environmental change. The Sahara Desert, fewer than 20,000 years ago, was a luxuriant forest. Overgrazing by domesticated sheep and goats and clearing of the forests were major factors in destroying the area.[65]

Deforestation is caused almost entirely by humans who log trees to get lumber and fuel and intentionally destroy the forests to make room for the farms and cities demanded by a growing population. Every year the world loses an area of tropical forest land that is comparable to the size of Wisconsin.[66] At this rate, virtually no tropical forests will be left in 30 or 40 years.[67] If the rain forests are destroyed, over a million unique species of animals and plants will die with them.[68]

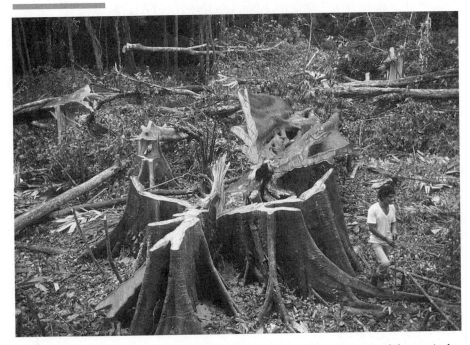

Deforestation causes a huge upset to the delicate balance of the elements. If the tropical rain forests are destroyed, over a million unique species of animals and plants may become extinct.

Paul and Anne Ehrlich describe what happens when forests are cleared:

Numerous animals that depend on the trees for food and shelter disappear. Many of the smaller forest plants depend on the trees for shade; they and the animals they support also disappear. With the removal of trees and plants, the soil is directly exposed to the elements, and it tends to erode faster. Loss of topsoil reduces the water-retaining capacity of an area, diminishes the supply of fresh water, causes silting of dams, and . . . flooding. . . . Deforestation . . . reduces the amount of water transferred from ground to air by the trees in the process known as "transpiration." This modifies the weather downwind of the area, usually making it more arid and subject to greater extremes of temperature.[69]

Some areas of the world are losing several inches of topsoil each year because of poor management that exposes the land to water and wind erosion. This is particularly alarming in light of the fact that it takes 300 to 1000 years to produce 1 inch of topsoil under favorable conditions.[70] Each year 25 billion tons of topsoil are lost, primarily by erosion and by being washed into the sea.[71]

Forests, water, and soil are renewable resource systems that have "carrying capacities"—that is, levels at which they can provide maximum yields without injuring their capacity to repeat those yields. We can chop down only a certain number of trees in a forest each year without destroying the forest's capacity to replace those trees. Human populations in many parts of the world have grown so large that they are beginning to exceed the "carrying capacities" of their environments.[72]

Sometimes the environment is despoiled by human accidents. The worst and most expensive oil spill in the United States occurred in March 1989 in Prince William Sound in Alaska. The petroleum tanker Exxon *Valdez* struck rocks, puncturing a huge hole in the vessel. Nearly 11 million gallons of crude oil spilled into the water. Exxon spent $2 billion trying to clean up the crude oil but recovered only 5–9% of the oil spilled. Millions of birds, animals, fish, and plants were killed. Local fishing industries, along with many other industries that depended on marine commerce in this area, were ruined.[73]

Sometimes the environment is intentionally despoiled by humans. Prior to being forced out of Kuwait in 1991 during the Gulf War, President Saddam Hussein of Iraq ordered his military forces to set 600 oil wells in Kuwait on fire. Billions of dollars of oil reserves were destroyed, skies were blackened for months, and the persistent smoke and fires had severe adverse effects on the quality of life for humans and animals in the region.

Waste Disposal

As yet our country does not have a safe way of disposing of radioactive waste material. Solid waste disposal also poses major problems.

RADIOACTIVE WASTES

The United States now has over 100 nuclear power plants and plans to build more in the future.[74] A danger is that nuclear power plants generate radioactive nuclear wastes, and disposing of radioactive wastes is a complex problem. In large doses, radiation from these wastes can cause death; small doses may lead to cancer or birth deformities. These wastes are particularly hazardous because they remain radioactive for as long as 300,000 years. The Nuclear Regulatory Commission has considered various proposals for disposing of these wastes: firing them into space by rockets, burying them at sea, burying them in solid rock formations, and burying them in the deepest abandoned mines that can be found. An ultimate solution has not as yet been found. Such wastes are now generally put in concrete tanks and buried. A serious danger is that these tanks are built to last only for a couple of hundred years, not for the needed thousands.

Radioactive wastes remain boiling hot for years. Leakage from some of these waste tanks has already occurred. In 1974 one leaked for 51 days

and raised the radiation count substantially above the minimum acceptable levels.[75] A crucial question is, with our current ways of disposing of nuclear wastes, "Are we creating a lethal problem for the future?"

SOLID WASTE DISPOSAL

So much public concern is focused on radioactive waste disposal that we sometimes overlook another serious disposal problem: good old-fashioned trash. Each year Americans junk billions of tons of wastes: food, glass, paper, plastics, cans, paints, dead animals, abandoned cars, old machinery, and a host of other things. We are often referred to as a "consumer society." More accurately, we are a throwaway society.

Solid wastes are ugly, unpleasant, and odorous. They pollute water that circulates through them and provide breeding grounds for rats and other noxious pests.

The two principal methods of solid waste disposal are landfills (that is, burying in the ground) and incineration. Many garbage-dumping areas, particularly in small towns, do not meet the sanitary standards set by the federal government.[76] In addition, improperly designed municipal incinerators are major contributors to urban air pollution.

TOXIC WASTES

Toxic wastes, or residues, are a major problem. Toxic wastes result from the production of pesticides, plastics, paints, and other products. These wastes have typically been buried in pits or ditches. The famous case of Love Canal, near Niagara Falls (see Exhibit 17.2), arose when toxic residues that had been dumped into the unfinished canal seeped into the surrounding area and contaminated both the soil and the water.

Air Pollution

Air pollution is most severe in large, densely populated industrial centers. Some cities (such as Los Angeles) occasionally have such dense smog that, even on clear days, there is a haze over the city. Moreover, not only is city air polluted; the entire atmosphere of the earth is affected to some degree.

EXHIBIT 17.2

Tragedy at Love Canal

Love Canal was once a pleasant neighborhood of tree-lined streets in the city of Niagara Falls, New York. Up until the late 1970s, hardly anyone was concerned that the area had once been a chemical dumping ground. Over a 25-year period ending in 1953, Hooker Chemicals and Plastic Corporation had buried 20,000 tons of toxic substances in leaky drums. Among the chemicals dumped was highly lethal dioxin. In the late 1970s, it was noted that the residents of Love Canal had substantially higher rates of birth defects, cancer, miscarriages, chromosome damage, kidney failure, and death.

The neighborhood—homes, schools, and parks—had been built above the dump site. Families noted that bluish-black substances sometimes oozed through the ground. The substances were discovered to be toxic. Dumped pesticides and other poisons had polluted the groundwater, seeping up through the earth and into basements, creating hazardous vapors. Tests in certain basements found 80 different toxic chemicals to be present. It was also thought that contamination was occurring from eating home-grown garden vegetables.

In 1980 the Environmental Protection Agency conducted tests in the area and found it to have dangerously high levels of toxic substances. The residents of Love Canal were eventually evacuated. In 1991, after extensive cleanup, some houses in the Love Canal area were declared habitable again.

Environmental experts acknowledge that the Love Canal disaster is not an isolated problem. Of the nearly 50,000 toxic-chemical dumps in the United States, more than 1000 are considered potential health hazards.

Sources: "Living with Uncertainty: Saga of Love Canal Families," *U.S. News & World Report*, Jun. 2, 1980, p. 32; William Kornblum and Joseph Julian, *Social Problems*, 8th ed., Englewood Cliffs, NJ: Prentice Hall, 1995, p. 517.

HEALTH EFFECTS AND EXTENT OF AIR POLLUTION

Not only does air pollution rot windshield wiper blades and nylon stockings, blacken skies and clothes, damage crops, and corrode paint and steel, it also kills people. Death rates are higher whenever and wherever smog occurs, especially for the very old, the very young, and those with respiratory ailments. Pollution contributes to a higher incidence of pneumonia, emphysema, lung cancer, and bronchitis. A 1952 London smog disaster was directly linked to some 4000 deaths. And such disasters are of substantially less significance than the far-reaching effects of day-to-day living in seriously polluted cities. Every day, New York City residents inhale enough cancer-producing substances to equal two packs of cigarettes.[77] Also, poor visibility caused by smog is recognized as a major factor in both airplane and automobile accidents.

Each year in the United States, we release into the air tons of pollutants, including carbon monoxide, hydrocarbons, oxides of nitrogen, oxides of sulfur, soot, and ashes. Cars emit many of these pollutants, industrial centers (particularly pulp and paper mills, petroleum refineries, chemical plants, and iron and steel mills) add a large share, and so do trash incineration and the burning of fuel for heating homes and offices.[78]

Air pollution is believed to contribute to the deaths of at least 50,000 Americans every year.[79] Valleys and closed air basins are more likely to have air pollution than plains and mountains. In the former areas, the air can become especially bad when a layer of warmer air moves over a layer of cooler air and seals in pollutants that would ordinarily rise into the upper atmosphere; this condition is known as *temperature inversion*.

AIR POLLUTION AND ENVIRONMENTAL CHANGES

Air pollution may also be breaking down the earth's protective ozone layer. This layer surrounds the earth from an altitude of 8 to 30 miles above sea level and screens out many of the harmful rays from the sun. Some studies suggest that fluorocarbon gases (commonly used in refrigerating systems and aerosol spray cans) may be destroying the ozone layer.[80] If it is breaking down, there reportedly will be sharp increases in skin cancer and crop failure as well as changes in the world's climate. When these studies became public knowledge, the use of fluorocarbon spray cans by American consumers dropped sharply (demonstrating that individuals acting in concert can and do make a difference). Manufacturers responded to this drop in sales by developing spray cans without fluorocarbons. However, fluorocarbons are still used in coolants in refrigerators and air conditioners, for making plastic foams, and as cleaning solvents for microelectronic circuitry. Under certain conditions, these compounds escape into the atmosphere, rise high into the stratosphere, and set off chemical reactions that rapidly destroy ozone.

Air pollutants have the potential to alter the earth's atmosphere and climate in other ways as well. For example, some scientists are concerned that a buildup of carbon dioxide in the atmosphere could produce a "greenhouse" effect; that is, the carbon dioxide could trap heat near the earth's surface, raising the average temperature. Such overheating, even by just a few degrees, could melt polar icecaps and lead to incredible flooding of coastal areas around the world. Other scientists predict that the opposite may occur; that is, air pollutants could reflect sun rays away from the earth. The earth would then become cooler and perhaps enter into a new Ice Age.[81] The greenhouse effect is largely due to the burning of fossil fuels (such as coal and petroleum), which emit carbon dioxide into the atmosphere. Some evidence that came to light in the 1980s suggests that the world's climate is getting warmer—a finding about which some scientists have expressed grave concerns.[82] Changing temperatures could also change rainfall patterns, which could turn the American Midwest and other major agricultural areas into dust bowls.

Radioactive Leaks from Nuclear Power Plants

We've already discussed one of the problems associated with nuclear energy: radioactive wastes. Another nuclear energy problem is the potential for radioactive leaks into the atmosphere. In the United States, there have been numerous malfunctions at nuclear power plants that have resulted in the release of minor amounts of radioactivity into the air.[83] In 1979 over 200,000 residents had to be evacuated from the area surrounding the power plant at Three Mile Island, Pennsylvania. Radioactive leakage from a damaged reactor caused fear that an explosion might occur. In 1986 an explosion did occur at a nuclear power plant in Chernobyl, Ukraine (see Exhibit 17.3).

Nuclear War

On the morning of August 6, 1945, adults in Hiroshima, Japan, were preparing to go to work. An American bomber was spotted overhead. Seconds later it dropped an atomic bomb, which exploded 2000 feet above the center of the city. The destruction was devastating. The heat and force of the blast killed tens of thousands of people almost instantly. It also released radiation, which eventually killed over 100,000 more people.[84] Numerous bombs have since been built that are 1600 times more powerful than the one that destroyed Hiroshima.[85]

One of the greatest dangers to the survival of civilization is nuclear war. A nuclear war would have devastating effects on the environment and, according to many authorities, could end human civilization. Russia and the United States have the nuclear capacity to destroy each other several times over. Many other nations also possess nuclear bombs or are seeking to develop nuclear warheads or purchase them from other countries.[86]

If a nuclear war occurred, life forms located nearby would be killed instantly. Anyone or anything that initially survived would face death from a variety of sources. (Exposure to radiation may cause cancer and a variety of other fatal medical conditions.) Some scientists predict that survivors would face a "nuclear winter," in which a cloud of soot would block the sun over much of the earth, pushing temperatures far below freezing and preventing the growth of most foods. Another worry is that the ozone layer would break down. Clearing of the cloud of soot would cause intense sun rays to penetrate humans and animals, resulting

EXHIBIT 17.3

Nuclear Power Plant Explosion in Chernobyl, Ukraine

In spring 1986, there was an explosion and fire at a nuclear power plant in Chernobyl, Ukraine. The explosion blew the top off the reactor and sent a radioactive plume across large parts of the former Soviet Union and much of Eastern and Western Europe. The 4000°F fire burned in the reactor's graphite core for over a week before it was extinguished. Within a few weeks after the disaster, over 20 people had died from massive doses of radiation. It is feared that exposure to smaller amounts of radiation will result in early deaths for tens of thousands of other people from cancers of the bone marrow, breast, and thyroid.

The disaster occurred at a highly vulnerable place. Eighty miles from the site is the city of Kiev, which has a population of over 2 million. Chernobyl is also near the breadbasket area of Russia; nearly half of that country's winter wheat is grown there. Much of the grass and animal feed in the area was contaminated with radioactive particles. Such accidents have alerted the public to the dangers of nuclear power plants and have slowed the growth of nuclear energy use. Whether to expand or curtail the development of nuclear plants is an international issue. It is an issue that illustrates the complexity of trying to choose between energy needs and physical safety, especially when experts are in sharp disagreement about the technological risks. Those exposed to radioactivity in Chernobyl would, if given a choice, undoubtedly opt for less energy over the current reality that they are now more likely to bear children with birth defects and more likely to die early from cancer.

in skin cancer and other disorders. Another danger is that crops would be affected by radioactivity and would be potentially dangerous as food sources. Quite possibly, the initial survivors would face a slow, painful death. Their quality of life could slip to depths at which they would grub out a brute-like, barely human existence. The social infrastructure would unravel; that is, the industrial, educational, agricultural, transportation, health-care, political, and communication systems would cease to function. Those who did survive would also face intense psychological stress from grief, despair, disorientation, hopelessness, and anger.[87]

How can a nuclear war be averted? This is perhaps one of the most important questions facing civilization. Fortunately, the chances of an all-out nuclear war appear to have lessened in recent years, primarily because of the improvement in relationships between the former Soviet Union and the United States. Prior to the 1990s, these two superpowers were unable to agree on a nuclear disarmament plan. As a result, both countries built and stockpiled nuclear weapons that had the capacity to destroy each other several times over.

Only after Russia rejected communism and started to move toward a democratic form of government around 1990 were the two superpowers willing to trust each other sufficiently to make progress in reducing nuclear warheads. In 1993 Russia and the United States signed the START (Strategic Arms Reduction Treaty) agreement, which substantially reduced U.S. and Russian stockpiles of long-range nuclear missiles.[88] A major reason for this more cooperative relationship was the easing of mutually hostile ideologies. Once Russia moved toward democracy and away from a state-controlled economy, it became less ideologically opposed to the United States. At the same time, Russia's move toward democracy led the United States to give up its perception of Russia as "the evil empire." (This term was used by President Reagan in 1984 in referring to the former Soviet Union.)

Even though the threat of a nuclear holocaust resulting from the Cold War between the United States and the Soviet Union has greatly diminished, the possibility exists that nuclear bombs will be obtained (and perhaps used) by nations in unstable areas of the world, such as in the Middle East and by North Korea. There is also the danger that radioactive materials will be stolen (or bought) by terrorist groups and converted into low-grade nuclear bombs. In 1994 German police arrested a Russian smuggler with over 300 grams of plutonium in his baggage; it turned out to be a sample from 4 kilograms of plutonium that were being offered for sale for $250 million.[89] Such concerns suggest it is premature to celebrate the end of the threat of a nuclear holocaust.

Water Pollution

Over two-thirds of the earth's surface is covered by water. Water is continually cleansing itself by evaporating, forming clouds, and raining back to the earth. Unfortunately, people are contaminating the water supply faster than it can cleanse itself. As the population grows in a particular area, so does industry, which pours into the water a vast array of contaminants: detergents, sulfuric acid, lead, hydrofluoric acid, ammonia, and so on. Increased agricultural production also pollutes water with insecticides, herbicides, and nitrates (from fertilizers). The result is the spread of pollution in creeks, streams, and lakes; along coastlines; and—most seriously—in ground water, where purification is almost impossible. Water pollution poses the threat of disease epidemics such as hepatitis and dysentery as well as poisoning by exotic chemicals. Some rivers and lakes are now so polluted that they cannot support fish and other organisms that require relatively clean, oxygen-rich water. These lakes and rivers are accurately described as "dead."

The United States has the dubious distinction of being the only country in the world with a river that has been called a fire hazard. So many industrial chemicals, oils, and other combustible pollutants have been dumped into the Cuyahoga River in Ohio that it has twice caught on fire.[90]

Human waste is also a major contributor to water pollution. The sewage from New York City alone produces 5 million cubic yards of sludge a year, which is dumped into the ocean and now covers over 15 square miles of ocean bottom.[91] An even bigger source of pollution is waste from oil refining, food processing, animal feedlots, textile and paper manufacturing, and other industries. Of the world's rural populations, 86% (more than 2 billion people) lack adequate clean water.[92]

A study by the Natural Resources Defense Council concluded that 20% of the drinking water in the United States is not adequately treated for bacteria, toxic chemicals, parasites, and other pollutants. The study also found that 14% of the U.S. population drinks water from companies that have been caught violating federal water standards within the previous 3 years.[93]

Acid Rain

There is a growing concern over acid rain. Formed from emissions from automobiles and industrial plants, acid rain has become a serious problem in eastern Canada, in the northeastern United States, and in many other countries.[94] It is created when sulfur and nitrogen oxides in emissions combine with moisture in the air to form sulfuric and nitric acids. Acid rain is killing fish in lakes and streams and is reducing the number of plant nutrients in the ground, thereby making soil less fertile. It has also damaged timber and may eventually start affecting synthetic structures, including classic architecture and sculptures. Scientists estimate that 50,000 lakes in the United States and Canada are now so polluted by acid rain that fish populations have been either destroyed or severely damaged.[95]

General Pollutants

Some substances—such as chlorinated hydrocarbons, lead, mercury, and fluorides—reach us in so many ways that they are considered *general pollutants*. Of the chlorinated hydrocarbons, DDT was used the longest but is now banned. DDT is a synthetic insecticide; chemically it breaks down slowly, and it will last for decades in soil. Unhappily, the way DDT circulates in ecosystems leads to a concentration in carnivores (including humans); that is, it becomes increasingly concentrated as it is passed along a food chain. Following World War II, DDT was widely used as an insecticide until research with laboratory animals showed that it affects fertility, causes changes in brain functioning, and increases the incidence of cancer.[96]

The long-term effects of DDT (and of many other general pollutants) are still unknown. The substance is poisonous and may (or may not) lead to subtle physiological changes. An important question is: Among the thousands of chemicals currently being used, which ones will have unknown toxic side effects?

Radioactive wastes and certain poisons such as DDT also pose serious problems because of biological magnification. With this process (mentioned previously), the concentration of the substance increases as it ascends in the food chain. For example, Richard Curtis and Elizabeth Hogan found in a study of the Columbia River in the western United States that, although the radioactivity of the water was at such low levels that it was nonhazardous, the radioactivity of river-related biological life forms was much higher and potentially hazardous:

> . . . the radioactivity of the river plankton was 2,000 times greater; the radioactivity of the fish and ducks feeding on the plankton was 15,000 and 40,000 times greater, respectively; the radioactivity of young swallows fed on insects caught by their parents in the river was 500,000 times greater; the radioactivity of the egg yolks of water birds was more than a million times greater.[97]

The radioactivity was thought to be due to isotopes released into the river from the nuclear power plant at Hanford, Washington.

DDT, many other pesticides, and radioactive material are cumulative poisons; that is, they are retained in the tissues of the organisms that consume them rather than excreted back into the environment. Thus, one never loses the poison of previous exposure, and future exposures compound the potential danger to the individual. In 1984 the National Academy of Sciences released a report stating that little or nothing is known about the effects on humans of 80% of the 48,500 different chemicals in use because very little research has been conducted in this area.[98]

The use of pesticides by American farmers also has a number of adverse consequences. An article in *Newsweek* noted:

> It's a bit of the devil's bargain. In exchange for using $3 billion worth of pesticides yearly,

> American farmers reap $12 billion worth of crops that might otherwise be lost to weeds and insects. Without the chemicals, millions of people might face food shortages. On the other hand, less than 1 percent of the poisons reach their target pests; the rest wind up as contaminants in water, residues on produce and poisonous fallout on farm workers. Worldwide, the compounds fatally poison an estimated 10,000 people a year and injure 400,000 more. Uncounted millions more may be at increased risk for cancer, reproductive problems and birth defects due to low-level, chronic exposure. We can't seem to do without pesticides; but can we live with their consequences?[99]

Chronic lead poisoning is also serious; it leads to loss of appetite, weakness, and apathy. It also causes lesions of the neuromuscular system, the circulatory system, the gastrointestinal tract, and the brain. Exposure to lead comes from a variety of sources: pesticides, lead pipes, and lead-contaminated food and water. Perhaps the most hazardous instance is when children eat paint containing lead. Most household paints today do not contain lead, but the danger still exists with older buildings and furniture that were painted with lead-based paint. Even when these buildings are painted over with lead-free paint, peeling may expose the original lead-based ones.

Exposure to high concentrations of mercury can cause blindness, deafness, loss of coordination, severe mental disorders, or even death. Mercury is added to the environment in many ways: It may leak into the water from industrial processes that produce chlorine; it is emitted by the pulp and paper industry; it is a primary ingredient of agricultural fungicides. Also, small amounts are released when fossil fuels are burned.

WHAT NEEDS TO BE DONE

Up to now, we've merely been describing several national and international problems: overpopulation, food and water shortages, economic problems, international terrorism, crowding, energy shortages, shortages of nonrenewable resources, despoilment of the land, radioactive and solid waste disposal, toxic wastes, air pollution, radioactive leaks from nuclear power plants, nuclear war, water pollution, acid rain, and general pollutants. Now we'll look at a number of recommendations for confronting overpopulation and environmental problems.

Confronting Overpopulation

Limiting population growth will have a major positive effect on all of the problems discussed in this chapter. If the world's population growth is reversed to approach a zero-growth rate—or even a negative rate—it may give us the necessary time to find solutions to other problems. Limiting population growth is a key factor in maintaining our current quality of life. Ehrlich and Ehrlich noted in 1990:

> *Earth cannot long sustain even 5.3 billion people with foreseeable technologies and patterns of human behavior. If civilization is to survive, population* shrinkage *below today's size eventually will be necessary.*[100]

How can the size of the population be limited? Dr. Paul Ehrlich suggests that, as the most affluent and influential superpower, the United States should become a model for population control by (a) setting a goal of a stable optimum population size for our country and displaying our determination to achieve this goal rapidly and (b) reversing our government's current "reward" system for having children. Specific measures include:

- No longer allowing income-tax deductions for children.
- Placing a luxury tax on layettes, diapers, cribs, expensive toys, and diaper services.
- Rewarding small families by such measures as giving "responsibility prizes" to each man who has a vasectomy after having two children.
- Subsidizing adoptions and simplifying adoption procedures.
- Guaranteeing the right of any woman to have an abortion.

- Enacting a federal law to require sex education in schools, including material on the need for regulating the birthrate and on techniques of birth control.
- Developing new contraceptives that are reliable and easy to use and do not have harmful side effects.[101]

Bernard Berelson compiled a list of other proposals to control population:

- Adding temporary sterilants to water or food supplies, with doses of an antidote carefully rationed by the government to produce the desired population size (such sterilants are not yet in existence).
- Making sterilization of men with three or more living children compulsory.
- Raising the minimum age for marriage.
- Providing benefits (money, goods, or services) to couples who do not bear children for extended time periods.
- Requiring that foreign countries establish effective population control programs before *any* foreign aid will be provided.[102]

Some of these proposals appear too radical for most Americans to accept, and they conflict with the moral and ethical values of many citizens. But will we reach such an overpopulation crisis that they may be necessary in the future? Many developing nations are now instituting sex education and family planning programs, which (at least temporarily) are showing evidence of lowering birthrates. Ideally, the population control measures recommended by Berelson can be avoided.

A developing country that has had success in reducing the rate of population growth is Indonesia. It launched its national family planning program in the 1960s. Initially, Indonesia focused its efforts on informing its people (including the country's conservative religious leaders) of the problems associated with overpopulation and the advantages of a smaller family. The government's next effort shifted to making contraceptives available to everyone who wanted them. This effort was careful to respect the conservative sexual attitudes of most Indonesians. (For example, there was very little effort to promote the use of condoms because most Indonesians associate them with prostitution.) The government now offers incentives for the long-term use of contraceptives, including subsidies for government employees, valuable agricultural products, and even complimentary trips to Mecca (the holiest site of the Islamic religion). As a result of these efforts, Indonesia's birthrate has declined by about 45% in the last two decades.[103] Its current annual growth rate is about 1.6%, which is significantly lower than most other developing countries.[104]

Ehrlich, Ehrlich, and Holdren provide an elegant summary of the need to establish a worldwide vision of the future of the human race:

> Perhaps the major necessary ingredient that has been missing from a solution to the problems of both the United States and the rest of the world is a goal, a vision of the kind of Spaceship Earth that ought to be and the kind of crew that should man her. Society has always had its visionaries who talked of love, beauty, peace, and plenty. But sometimes the "practical" men have always been there to praise smog as a sign of progress, to preach "just" wars, and to restrict love while giving hate free rein. It must be one of the greatest ironies of the history of the human species that the only salvation for the practical men now lies in what they think of as the dreams of idealists. The question now is: can the self-proclaimed "realists" be persuaded to face reality in time?[105]

The Abortion Controversy

If the world's population continues to grow at or near its present rate, the current debate over voluntary abortions may pale compared to controversies that will be generated if compulsory population control measures are needed.

The abortion controversy has been going on for three decades, but it was heightened in January 1973, when the U.S. Supreme Court, in a 7-2 decision, overruled state laws that prohibited or restricted a woman's right to obtain an abortion during the first 3 months of pregnancy. Suing under the assumed name of Jane Roe, a Texas resident argued that her state's law against abortion denied her a constitutional right. The Court agreed that the right of personal privacy includes the right to decide whether to have an abortion. However, the Court held that such a right is not absolute and that states have the authority to impose restrictions after the third month. This decision, known as *Roe* v. *Wade,* also allowed states to prohibit abortions in the last 10 weeks of pregnancy (a time when there is a good chance that the fetus will live), except when the life or health of the mother is endangered.

In 1977 Congress passed, and President Carter signed into law, the so-called Hyde Amendment (named for its original sponsor, Representative Henry Hyde from Illinois). This amendment prohibits Medicaid spending for abortions except when a woman's life would be endangered by childbirth or in cases of promptly reported rape or incest. In June 1980, this amendment was upheld as constitutional in a 5-4 vote by the U.S. Supreme Court. The ruling means that the federal government and individual states do not have to pay for most abortions for women on welfare.

The Hyde Amendment is significant because more than one-third of the legal abortions performed in the United States between 1973 and 1977 were for women on welfare.[106] The passage of the amendment illustrates the strength of the anti-abortion forces in this country. Is it fair for middle- and upper-class women to have more access to abortions than lower-income women?

With the election of President Reagan in 1980, there was a move toward conservatism in our society. Certain groups, such as the Catholic Church and right-to-life groups, have been strongly urging that a constitutional amendment be passed to prohibit abortions, except in cases where the woman's life is endangered.

During the Reagan and Bush administrations from 1980 to 1992, some liberal Supreme Court judges retired and were replaced by more conservative judges. As a result, the Supreme Court gradually assumed a more conservative (pro-life) position on the abortion issue. The waning of the Supreme Court majority recognizing a woman's right to an abortion became clear in a 1989 decision, *Webster* v. *Reproductive Health Services.* The

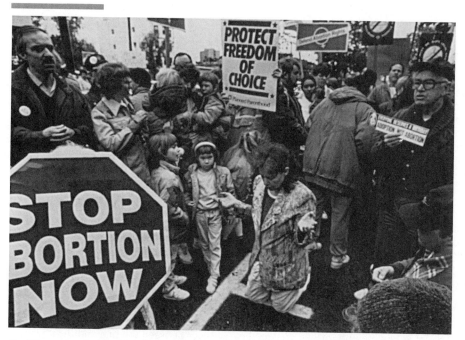

Pro-life or pro-choice? Abortion is probably the single most divisive public issue today.

Supreme Court upheld a restrictive Missouri law that (a) prohibited state employees from assisting in abortions and prohibited abortions from being performed in state-owned hospitals and (b) banned abortions of *viable* fetuses. (The Missouri law viewed fetuses as viable if the woman was believed to be 20 or more weeks pregnant and a viability test showed the fetus could live.) The broader effect of the Court's decision was to throw the hot-potato issue of abortion back to state legislatures, many of which debated a variety of abortion bills.

In 1992 Bill Clinton was elected president. He had adhered to a pro-choice position on the abortion issue. President Clinton has had the opportunity to appoint a few liberal judges to the Supreme Court. As of the late 1990s, it appears that the Court is likely to continue to uphold the basic provisions of *Roe* v. *Wade*.

Waldman, Ackerman, and Rubin summarize significant information on abortions in the United States. Roughly 1.4 million women have abortions each year. About 80% are unmarried or separated,

and over 40% have had at least one previous abortion. Catholic women have them at a higher rate than do Protestant women. It is estimated that 43% of the women in the United States will have an abortion in their lifetime.[107]

The major objection to permitting abortions is based on perceptions of moral principles. The Catholic Church views abortion as one of the most important current moral issues. This church and various right-to-life groups condemn abortions as being synonymous with murder. They assert that life begins at conception—that there is no phase during pregnancy in which there is a distinct, qualitative difference in the development of the fetus. The Catholic Church views abortion as acceptable only when it is done to save the physical life of the mother. This type of abortion is justified on the principle of "double effect," which holds that a morally evil action (performing an abortion) is allowable when it is the side effect of a morally good action (saving the life of the mother). (Exhibit 17.4 summarizes the arguments both for and against legal abortion.)

EXHIBIT 17.4

Legal Abortion: Arguments Pro and Con

Against Legal Abortion	In Favor of Legal Abortion
Human life begins at conception: therefore, abortion is murder. Even scientists have not reached a consensus on any other point in fetal development that can be considered the moment the fetus becomes a person. Life is a matter of fact, not religion or values.	The belief in personhood at conception is a religious belief held by the Roman Catholic Church. Most Protestant and Jewish denominations regard the fetus as a potential human being, not a full-fledged person, and have made position statements in support of legal abortion. When the unborn becomes a person is a matter of religion and values, not absolute fact.
We must pass a constitutional amendment to protect unborn babies from abortion. To say that the law will not be followed and therefore should not be made is like saying laws against murder should be repealed because people still get murdered.	No law has ever stopped abortion, and no law ever will. The issue is not whether abortions will be done, but whether they will be done safely, by doctors, or dangerously, by back-alley butchers or by the women themselves. History has shown that anti-abortion laws are uniquely unenforceable and do not prevent abortions.
Medicaid should not pay for abortion. It is wrong to try to eliminate poverty by killing the unborn children of the poor. Tax money should not be used for the controversial practice of aborting unwanted children. The decision not to have children should be made before one gets pregnant.	The original intent of Medicaid was to equalize medical services between the rich and the poor and to help the poor become independent and self-sufficient. To make them ineligible for abortion defies justice, common sense, and rational policy. Women burdened by unwanted children cannot get job training or go to work and are trapped in the poverty/welfare cycle. Neither abortion nor childbirth should be forced on poor women.
If you believe abortion is morally wrong, you are obligated to work for the passage of a "human life" amendment to the Constitution.	Many people who are personally opposed to abortion, including most Roman Catholics, believe it is wrong to impose their religious or moral beliefs on others.
The right of the unborn to live supersedes any right of a woman to "control her own body."	For women to have equality with men, they must be autonomous and free to make an abortion decision. If women lose the right to have an abortion, their lives and lifestyles would substantially be determined by men and impregnation.
The "abortion mentality" leads to infanticide, euthanasia, and the killing of disabled and elderly people.	In countries where abortion has been legal for years, there is no evidence that respect for life has diminished or that legal abortion leads to the killing of any people. Infanticide, however, is prevalent in countries where the overburdened poor cannot control their childbearing and was also prevalent in Japan before abortion was legalized.
Abortion causes psychological damage to women.	The Institute of Medicine of the National Academy of Sciences has concluded that abortion is not associated with a detectable increase in the incidence of

(continued)

EXHIBIT 17.4 *(continued)*

Against Legal Abortion	In Favor of Legal Abortion
	mental illness. The depression and guilt feelings reported by some women are usually mild, temporary, and outweighed by feelings of relief. Such negative feelings would be substantially lessened if anti-abortion advocates were less vehement in expressing their beliefs. Women choosing abortion should be informed of the risks and benefits to the procedure and should decide for themselves what to do.
Women have abortions for their own convenience or on "whim."	Right-to-life advocates dismiss unwanted pregnancy as a mere annoyance. The urgency of women's need to end unwanted pregnancy is measured by their willingness to risk death and mutilation, to spend huge sums of money, and to endure the indignities of illegal abortion. Women have abortions only when the alternative is unendurable. Women take both abortion and motherhood very seriously.
In a society in which contraceptives are so readily available, there should be no unwanted pregnancies and therefore no need for abortion.	No birth control method is perfectly reliable, and for medical reasons many women cannot, or will not, use the most effective methods. Contraceptive information and services are not available to all women, particularly to teenagers, the poor, and rural women.
Abortion is not the safe and simple procedure we're told it is.	Before the 1973 Supreme Court rulings, illegal abortion was the leading cause of maternal death and mutilation. Having a legal abortion is medically less dangerous than giving birth.
Doctors make large profits from legal abortions.	Legal abortion is less costly and less profitable than illegal abortion was. Many legal abortions are done in nonprofit facilities. If it's not improper to "make money" on childbirth, it is not wrong to earn money by performing legal abortions.
Parents have the right and responsibility to guide their children to important decisions. A law requiring parental notification of a daughter's abortion would strengthen the family unit. (Many states have now passed parental consent laws that are consistent with this argument.)	Many teenagers voluntarily consult their parents, but some simply will not. Forcing the involvement of unsympathetic, authoritarian, or very moralistic parents in a teen's pregnancy (and sexuality) can damage the family unit beyond repair. Some family units are already under so much stress that knowledge of an unwed pregnancy could be disastrous.
Pro-abortionists are antifamily. Abortion destroys the American family.	The unwanted child of a teenage mother has little chance to grow up in a normal, happy American home. Instead, a new family is created: a child and her child, both destined for a life of poverty and hopelessness. Legal abortion helps women limit their families to the number of children they want and can afford, both emotionally and financially, and reduces the number of children born unwanted. Pro-choice is definitely profamily.

If abortions were prohibited again, women would seek illegal abortions as they did in the past. Performed in a medical clinic or hospital, an abortion is a relatively safe operation, but performed under unsanitary conditions, perhaps by an inexperienced or unskilled abortionist, the operation is extremely dangerous and may even imperil the life of the woman. When abortions are illegal, some women attempt to self-abort. Self-induced abortions can be extremely dangerous. Women have tried such techniques as severe exercise, hot baths, and pelvic and intestinal irritants and have even attempted to lacerate the uterus with such sharp objects as hatpins, nail files, and knives.

Opponents of abortion argue that the "right to life" is basic and should in no way be infringed on. Proponents of abortion counter this view by arguing that there may be a more basic right than the right to life: the preservation of the quality of life. Given the overpopulation problem and the fact that abortion is an effective population control technique (in some countries, the number of abortions is approaching the number of live births), some authorities argue that abortion is a necessary measure (although less desirable than contraception) to preserve the quality of life. Unless life has quality, the right to life is meaningless.

Providing Family Planning Services

Family planning services are obviously essential programs for preventing unwanted pregnancies. Such services include birth control information and contraceptives, pregnancy testing, HIV testing and counseling, testing and counseling about other sexually transmitted diseases, sex education, abortion counseling and abortions, counseling on child spacing, sterilization information and operations, infertility counseling, and preparation for parenthood.

GOVERNMENTAL PROGRAMS

National family planning programs involve governmental efforts to lower birthrates by funding programs that provide birth control information and services. With family planning programs,

families voluntarily decide whether to limit the number of children they have. Most countries, including both developing and developed nations, now have official family planning programs. This is a remarkable achievement, because 45 years ago no developing country had such a program. (In fact, 45 years ago, several countries had programs with the opposite objective—to increase the birthrate and the rate of immigration.) Concern about world population growth clearly is a recent phenomenon.

Despite these advances, only a few countries have established population control policies. (Population control is the deliberate regulation of the size of the population by society. Family planning, in contrast, is the regulation of births by individual families.) As we noted, India's population control program included a sterilization policy that was soon retracted after the ruling party failed to be reelected. Whether India will attempt to enact another population control policy is unclear; future population growth may be a decisive factor in determining whether such action is necessary.

Until President Lyndon Johnson's 1965 State of the Union Address, family planning was not considered a proper concern for our government. In that address, President Johnson stated that $5 spent on family planning was worth $100 invested in some other area of world economic development. In 1966 the federal government developed regulations that, for the first time, allowed federal funds to provide family planning services to welfare clients on a voluntary basis. The avowed purpose of this policy (which was widely criticized) was not phrased in terms of family planning goals. Rather, the stated objectives were to reduce the welfare burden by lowering the illegitimacy rate and to break the poverty cycle by decreasing the transmission of poverty from one generation to another.

The National Center for Family Planning Services was established by the passage of the Family Planning Services and Population Research Act of 1970. This act recognized that family planning was part of the delivery of comprehensive health services for all. In 1972 Congress mandated that family planning services be provided to all welfare recipients who desired them. At that time, contraceptive policy changes were also made, lifting restrictions on marital status and age for receiving birth control information and devices.

PRIVATE AGENCIES

In the United States, most family planning services in the past were provided by private agencies and organizations. The largest and best-known organization is Planned Parenthood. Founded by Margaret Sanger in 1916 with the opening of the first birth control clinic in Brooklyn, the organization now has clinics throughout the nation. Planned Parenthood offers the following: (a) medical services—physical examinations, Pap tests, urine and blood tests, screening for sexually transmitted diseases, all medically approved methods of contraception, and pregnancy testing; (b) counseling services—infertility, premarital, contraceptive, pregnancy, and sterilization for males and for females; and (c) educational services—sex education, contraceptive information (including effectiveness and side effects of the varied approaches), and breast self-examinations. (Table 17.4 shows a ranking of the effectiveness of various contraceptives in preventing pregnancies.)

Family planning services are now available in practically all areas in the United States from a variety of public and private organizations, including health departments, hospitals, physicians in private practice, Planned Parenthood affiliates, and other agencies such as community action groups and free clinics.

THE FUTURE

Violence against abortion clinics and family planning clinics has escalated in recent years. Antiabortion groups have picketed clinics, with the objective being to stop patients from using clinic services. Clinic physicians and other staff often receive threatening phone calls and have their own homes picketed. Abortion clinics, staff, and patients have been subjected to a number of incidents of violence involving bombings, arsons, vandalisms, burglaries, assaults, death threats, kidnappings, and stalkings. Violent tactics by anti

TABLE 17.4

Ranking of Effectiveness of Birth Control Methods in Preventing Pregnancies

Method	Number of Pregnancies per 100 Women During 1 Year of Use
1. Abstinence	0
2. Norplant implant	0.09
3. Depo-Provera	0.3
4. Sterilization	0.4
5. IUD	0.8
6. Condom	12
7. Diaphragm	18
8. Cervical cap	18
9. Withdrawal	19
10. Natural family planning (rhythm)	20
11. Contraceptive foam and suppositories	21
12. Vaginal pouch (female condom)	21

Note: After the first five listed methods, the risk of pregnancy for sexually active users sharply increases. (Sterilization for women, tubal ligation, is nearly 100% effective, although in very rare cases, the tubes may rejoin.)

Source: Facts About Birth Control (New York: Planned Parenthood Federation of America, 1997).

abortion supporters have even included incidents of shooting and killing staff at abortion clinics. It is ironic that some fringe elements of the right-to-life movement have resorted to murder to seek to force their views on others. Will such violence continue to escalate in the United States in the future?

The United States needs to resolve a number of family planning issues before it can have an effective national policy on family planning. Currently there is considerable controversy about a number of issues associated with family planning: sex education in schools, provision of birth control information and devices for teenagers, approaches

EXHIBIT 17.5

RU-486: An Abortion Pill

RU-486, a pill that induces abortion early in pregnancy, was developed and introduced in France. This pill is now widely used in France, Great Britain, Sweden, and China to induce abortions. RU-486 acts by impeding a hormone (progesterone) that is necessary for a fetus to stay implanted in the uterus. The pill, which works only until 7 weeks after conception, is effective about 85% of the time. For its effectiveness to reach 96%, it must be followed by a dose of prostaglandin, a substance that induces uterine contractions. Proponents envision a day when a woman who wants to end a suspected pregnancy can merely take a pill in the privacy of her own home, thereby avoiding demonstrators outside abortion clinics.

A small percentage of users experience some adverse side effects of RU-486, including heavy bleeding and nausea. (Surgical abortions also pose some risks—from anesthesia, infections, and damage to the cervix and uterus.)

RU-486 is also a highly effective morning-after pill that appears to prevent implantation of the fertilized egg in the wall of the uterus. RU-486 may also be effective in treating breast and ovarian cancer (two of the biggest killers of women). It has also been used to treat endometriosis, a leading cause of female infertility.

The right-to-life movement was successful in the late 1980s and early 1990s in keeping RU-486 from being legally distributed in the United States. The Food and Drug Administration banned the pill in 1989 after being pressured by anti-abortion groups. The pro-life movement has said it will call for boycotts against any company that seeks to market RU-486 in the United States.

In 1994 the U.S. government announced that an agreement had been reached with France's Roussel Uclaf, the company that originally patented the drug, permitting testing of the pill on 2000 American women. Will RU-486 be licensed for use in the United States?

Source: Lauran Neergaard, "Agreement Clears Way for Abortion Drug in U.S.," *Wisconsin State Journal*, May 17, 1994, p. 1A.

---

to prevent HIV and other sexually transmitted diseases, and abortions (including the issue of whether the federal government should pay for abortions for those who cannot afford them).

If problems associated with overpopulation continue to intensify, a national policy of population control may need to be developed. Several authorities are predicting dire consequences for the future of the world unless population control measures are implemented immediately. Other authorities discount overpopulation concerns and predict that technological advance will prevent cataclysmic effects from rapid population growth. If the latter authorities are mistaken, we may be forced in a few years to apply population

control measures that now seem unethical and "inhumane."

Werner Fornos strongly urges the United States to fund international programs designed to slow population growth in developing countries:

If Americans now feel anguish over witnessing the recent human suffering and needless deaths in Ethiopia, just imagine a world in which virtually the entire Third World will be wracked by vast poverty and human misery. . . .

And if Americans are now troubled by the specter of instability, revolution, and authoritarianism in the Third World, they have only to imagine the consequences of inaction, because the fragile seed of democracy cannot survive long in societies with escalating misery, crippled economies, and dying environments.

In shaping the federal budget, the U.S. Congress must ask not only how much it will cost to fund population programs, but also what will be the cost of not funding them.[108]

Confronting Environmental Problems

Although environmental problems are very serious, it would be a mistake to assume that the environment is heading for catastrophe. In the late 1960s, the public began to wake up to the environmental problems we face. Dozens of organizations have since been formed (many of them with international memberships) that are working on everything from saving wild animals to recycling aluminum cans to developing new sources of energy.

Since the 1960s, there has been progress in a number of areas. Air quality has improved. Less sewage is being dumped into water. Most automobiles have emission control devices. Life expectancy in the United States has been rising, which is an indirect measure that environmental living conditions may be improving. Relationships between the United States and Russia have improved, which reduces the chances for a nuclear war. Obviously, however, much more needs to be done.

Energy development, preservation of the environment, and economic growth are interdependent problems. Programs that advance one of these causes often aggravate the others. For example, the development of nuclear power plants led to the explosion in Chernobyl that may shorten the lives of tens of thousands of people who were exposed. Devices that clean exhaust from automobiles reduce air pollution but also decrease fuel economy and thereby more rapidly deplete oil reserves. Strip mining of coal increases available energy supplies but despoils the scenery. Effective environmental programs in the future will need to strike a balance among our competing objectives.

Environmentalists have been waging a political and educational campaign that has not only increased public awareness of environmental concerns but also prompted passage of significant legislation to protect the nation's air, land, and water. For example, the Clean Air Act of 1970 established the Environmental Protection Agency (EPA) and empowered it to set and enforce standards of environmental quality. However, since the 1980s, political opposition to environmental concerns intensified. For example, some of the largest corporations in the world have sought to drill oil wells and dig mines in fragile wilderness areas or have sought to "get the government off their back" when they spewed pollutants into the air and water.[109] These businesses have spent millions of dollars to persuade the government to let them pursue such activities. Since the 1980s, environmentalists have struggled to preserve the gains made in the 1970s. Environmentalists, however, do not have the financial resources that large corporations do. Therefore, it is crucial for those concerned about preserving our environment to be aware of political issues in this area and to express their views to government leaders.

It is clear that in the future our environmental problems are not going to disappear on their own. In fact, left alone, existing problems are likely to increase, and new ones will arise. What can be done? Actions needed include changing values from consumption to conservation and developing new sources of energy.

CHANGING VALUES

We must realize that bigger is not necessarily better. We need to focus on preserving and conserving our resources rather than consuming them. George Ritzer notes:

We need a reorientation of American culture, a reorientation that may already be underway. Basically, we need to move away from a system that values things growing constantly bigger and better. We are no longer able to master and subdue all that surrounds us. Rather, we must learn to live more harmoniously with our environment. We need to learn to value and protect our environment rather than seeing it as something to be exploited, raped and despoiled. Most importantly, we need to accept the idea that we are approaching the limits of what the environment can yield to us. At best, we can expect a steady state, at worst a marked decline in our style of life. . . . We need, in other words, to focus on, and invest in, resources that we can renew rather than the current propensity to exploit such nonrenewable resources as coal and oil.[110]

The move toward conserving resources can be put into action in a variety of ways. Garbage can be used as fuel for running mills to make recycled paper. Water in communities can be purified again and again, so that it can continually be reused without being discharged into a river, lake, or ocean. Homes can be better insulated to conserve heat. Smaller cars can be driven at more energy-efficient speeds. People can ride trains and buses instead of cars. Newspapers, aluminum (especially cans), tin, cardboard, magazines, plastic, paper, and glass can be recycled to reduce the amount of solid-waste materials. Recycling a 4-foot stack of newspapers saves a 40-foot pine tree.[111] Aluminum recycling saves 95% of the energy needed to make new cans from raw materials.[112] Using recycled glass to make new glass reduces the amount of air and water pollution by 50% to 60% compared to producing glass from silica.[113] Our society needs to use the conservation measures that are already available. Each of us can make a difference in combating the environmental problems on this planet! (See Exhibit 17.6.)

People in this country appear to be increasingly aware that all of us have a responsibility to preserve the environment. There is a growing interest in Earth Day, which was founded on April 22, 1970, and is recognized annually.[114] The pesticide DDT has been banned.[115] The United States has cut sulfur dioxide emissions (from 1970 to 1994) by 28%.[116] Auto emissions have been cleaned up dramatically: Catalytic converters cut hydrocarbons by as much as 87%, carbon monoxide by an average of 85%, and nitrogen oxides by 62%.[117] Lead has been removed from gasoline. Emissions of lead into the air dropped by 96% between 1970 and 1994, and overall lead levels

in the average American's blood dropped by one-third since 1976.[118]

Since the late 1980s, economic and political values have changed significantly in Eastern European countries. These changes have largely been based on former Soviet President Mikhail Gorbachev's concepts of *glasnost* and *perestroika.* Glasnost refers to greater openness and increased freedoms for people in the Eastern Bloc countries. Perestroika involves economic, social, and political reforms in these countries. Based on these principles, a number of these nations have rejected communism and are moving toward establishing democracies. There is optimism that such restructuring will lead to improved relationships between Western and Eastern nations. If this happens, less money would need to be allocated for defense. Will the savings lead to more available funds to combat environmental destruction and overpopulation? Will Western and Eastern nations now work cooperatively to overcome the problems that severely impact all inhabitants of this planet? Slow but gradual progress is occurring in these areas.

FINDING NEW SOURCES OF ENERGY

Reduction of pollution, population, and energy consumption will not alter the fact that much of our current energy comes from nonrenewable fuel sources. Sooner or later, we will have to find new sources of energy. In the meantime, it is crucial that all countries set a priority on conserving the earth's nonrenewable fuel sources. Ehrlich and Ehrlich summarize an approach for conserving fuel in the United States:

The United States could start by gradually imposing a higher gasoline tax—hiking it by one or two cents per month until gasoline costs $2.50 to $3.00 per gallon, comparable to prices in Europe and Japan. The higher fuel price would create a powerful incentive for people to buy and drive smaller, more fuel-efficient cars and use energy-efficient alternative forms of transportation. It would make driving safer once the majority of automobiles were smaller, help preserve crumbling highways and bridges, reduce air pol-

lution and acid precipitation, and slow global warming—among other benefits.[119]

Possible new sources of energy are nuclear energy, synthetic fuel, and solar energy.

Nuclear Energy. Nuclear energy is a potential solution to the energy shortage, but concerns over the safety of nuclear power plants have slowed construction of them. In March 1979, a near-disaster at the nuclear plant at Three Mile Island in Pennsylvania increased these concerns. Radioactive steam escaped, and there was a danger of a meltdown that probably would have killed many people in the area from lethal overdoses of radiation. The April 1986 explosion in Chernobyl was a much more serious accident; tens of thousands of inhabitants were exposed to radioactivity and face the threat of a shortened life span.

Such accidents emphasize that safety in any nuclear power plant cannot be taken for granted. Nuclear energy out of control has the potential for large-scale disaster. A major question is whether future development of nuclear energy is worth the risks.

Synthetic Fuel. In 1980 the federal government passed legislation to create and finance a synthetic-fuel industry. The raw materials for synthetic fuel are in oil shale formations, coal deposits, and gooey-tar sands. The term *synthetic fuel* is actually a misnomer because its components have the same carbon base as crude oil. Coal, for example, will become gas if it is pulverized and then mixed with oxygen and steam under extreme heat. Shale is a dark-brown, fine-grained rock that contains carbon. Production problems are considerable; it is estimated that it takes 1.7 tons of shale to produce a barrel of oil and that it takes a ton of coal to produce two barrels of oil.[120] Whether synthetic fuel can be cost effective remains a major question. A few years after the initiation of the synthetic-fuel program, a temporary glut of crude oil occurred worldwide. Partly as a result of this glut, synthetic-fuel efforts have been postponed or discontinued. When another shortage of crude oil occurs, programs to develop synthetic fuel may again be initiated.

On a positive note, it is estimated that the United States has a 600-year supply of the raw materials for synthetic fuel.[121]

Solar Energy. Solar energy is another potential solution to the world's energy crisis. Thousands of U.S. homes and offices are getting all or part of their heating and cooling from the sun.[122] Even the White House has a solar water-heating system on its roof. Another potential use of sunlight is direct conversion to electricity with photovoltaic cells, but at present this process is too expensive to be used widely. Solar energy is really an imitation of nature because all energy ultimately comes from the sun.

SOCIAL WORK AND FAMILY PLANNING

Social workers are concerned about overpopulation—about the problems it is creating now and the even greater problems it may create in the future. In almost every social service agency, social workers come in contact with clients who want and need family planning information. Social workers also must respond to controversial issues: providing abortion information and making referrals, responding to those who advocate involuntary sterilization of people who have a severe inherited disability, and setting up family planning clinics in high schools so that contraceptive information and devices are more readily accessible to teenagers.

Social workers are increasingly employed in settings in which the primary service is family planning. Many roles in family planning are well suited for social workers: premarital counseling; pregnancy counseling; provision of contraceptive information including effectiveness and side effects of the varied approaches; sex education services; counseling about sexually transmitted diseases; AIDS education and counseling; abortion counseling; infertility counseling; and community planning efforts to develop family planning services and create a community atmosphere that

EXHIBIT 17.6

What *You* Can Do to Help Save Planet Earth

You can make a difference! If everyone takes small steps, major improvements will occur. The following are simple things that you and your family members can do to help the earth:

- Use mugs instead of paper cups, washable cotton towels instead of paper towels, and cloth napkins rather than paper napkins.

- Use both sides of sheets of paper.

- To minimize solid waste, buy products in bulk or products that have the least amount of packaging. Packaging accounts for an amazing 50% of our trash (U.S. output of garbage equals 400,000 tons every day).

- At the market, use paper bags (which you can recycle) instead of plastic bags. Plastics tend to be nonbiodegradable; they do not break down into innocuous materials.

- Buy products that are recyclable, reliable, repairable, refillable, and/or reusable. Avoid disposables. The new buzzword in waste management is "source reduction," which means buying wisely to minimize the consequences of consumption.

- Grow some of your own food, organically when possible. Plant deciduous shade trees (trees whose leaves fall off) that protect south- and west-facing windows from sun in summer but allow it in during winter. Plant and maintain trees, bushes, or shrubbery. Trees and shrubbery consume carbon dioxide and thereby reduce air pollution.

- Avoid use of styrofoam cups, which tend to be nonbiodegradable.

- To save water, install sink faucet aerators and water-efficient showerheads. Such adjustments cut water use up to 80% without a noticeable decrease in performance. Repair leaky faucets.

- Take showers of fewer than 5 minutes instead of baths.

- Do not run water continuously when brushing your teeth or shaving.

- Consider ultra-low flush toilets, which use 60–90% less water than conventional models. Conserve water by placing a brick or a jug of water in the toilet's water tank.

- Where possible, use fluorescent bulbs rather than incandescent bulbs. Fluorescent bulbs use considerably less energy.

- Use cloth diapers for babies. Disposable diapers annually account for 18 billion tons of trash that, because of plastic content, will take 500 years to decompose. In addition, disposable diapers in landfills frequently contain fecal matter, which can harbor viruses (such as hepatitis) that may trickle into water supplies.

- Turn down the thermostat at night and when the house is empty. Close off and do not heat or cool unused rooms. Wear a sweater instead of turning up the heat. Keep windows (especially near thermostats) tightly shut.

- Turn the thermostat on the water heater down to 120°.

- When possible, use a clothesline instead of a dryer.

- Reduce the use of hazardous chemicals in your home. For example, instead of using ammonia-based cleaners, use a mixture of distilled vinegar, salt, and water for surface cleaning, and use baking soda and water for the bathroom.

- Don't buy motorized or electric tools or appliances when hand-powered ones are available. This includes lawn mowers. (Mowing a lawn with an old-fashioned mower is also good exercise.)

(continued)

EXHIBIT 17.6 *(continued)*

■ To conserve energy, wash clothes and other materials in warm water and rinse in cold water.

■ Open blinds during the day for heat from the sun during cold weather, and close them at night to conserve heat. Close blinds during the day in hot weather to reduce air-conditioning costs.

■ Bike, walk, carpool, or use public transit. If at all possible, try to live close to your work and shop close to home.

■ Get a low-cost home energy audit from your utility company for suggestions for conserving energy.

■ Check caulking around windows and doors, and add it where needed.

■ Use latex paints (which are considerably less toxic to the environment) rather than oil-based paints.

■ Buy and use cars that are fuel efficient. Keep your car well tuned so that it is fuel efficient. (Burning 1 gallon of gasoline produces nearly 20 pounds of carbon dioxide, which is a major source of the greenhouse effect that contributes to global warming.)

■ Avoid use of aerosols and other products containing chlorofluorocarbons (CFCs). CFCs are depleting the protective ozone layer in the atmosphere. Such depletion has already led to sharp increases in rates of skin cancer caused by the sun's rays.

■ Reduce food wastes, which are major contributors to garbage. Whenever possible, compost food wastes.

■ Stop the delivery of junk mail. Your local post office will give you the address and instructions for writing to Direct Mail Marketing Association in New York City to request an end to junk mail delivery.

■ Buy products that are made out of recycled paper. Buying recycled paper helps create a market for it.

■ Do not litter.

■ Cut the grass tall on your lawn. Short grass requires more water. Water lawns at night or early in the morning rather than during direct sunlight. (Watering in direct sunlight is wasteful because much of the water evaporates.)

■ Recycle motor oil. Used oil is highly destructive to the environment when dumped and also is likely to contaminate nearby water supplies.

■ Use soap detergents that are low in phosphates. Phosphates are toxic.

■ Use dry cleaning sparingly because it is done with toxic chlorinated solvents.

■ Be cautious in using chipboard, plywood, insulation, carpeting, and upholstery; they contain or can create toxic formaldehyde gas.

■ Avoid purchasing products made from endangered species—for example, ivory, tortoise shells, and reptile skin.

■ Buy eggs in paperboard cartons instead of plastic foam cartons (which tend to be nonbiodegradable).

■ Purchase meat, poultry, and other products that are wrapped in paper rather than plastic.

■ Buy beverages in aluminum cans or glass bottles, and buy food in glass containers with metal lids instead of plastic. Return the bottles, cans, and glass for recycling.

■ Do not put toxic waste products into garbage containers. If deposited into landfills, such products can trickle into nearby water reserves.

■ Keep fireplace dampers closed (to reduce heat loss) unless there's a fire.

Sources: "A User's Guide to Saving the Planet," CBS television show, broadcast nationally on April 19, 1990; "What You Can Do to Help Earth," *Wisconsin State Journal,* Apr. 22, 1990, p. 1H.

is accepting of family planning as a legitimate service.

There are several reasons for anticipating that family planning services will be expanded in future years, thereby creating new career opportunities for social workers. The general public is becoming increasingly aware of the dangers of overpopulation. There has been a growing acceptance in our society of contraceptives. The specter of AIDS has led to greater awareness that AIDS education and sex education are widely needed.

Social workers are being hired in specialized agencies that deal with family planning. These include Planned Parenthood, maternal and child health clinics, and agencies providing abortions and abortion counseling.

School social workers have become increasingly involved in family planning activities in connection with sex education for sexually active teenagers. Social workers in single-parent units of social services departments (also called public welfare or human services departments) also provide family planning services. Other settings in which social workers counsel on family planning include pediatrics and gynecology departments in hospitals and clinics, child welfare agencies, and residential treatment facilities for teenagers.

Unfortunately, very few undergraduate and graduate social work programs have family planning courses. A number of programs do provide some family planning instructional units in other courses.

YOUR FUTURE IN COMBATING HUMAN PROBLEMS

This text has described social work and social welfare. A major thrust has been to illustrate the social problems and the diverse fields of practice in which social workers and other human service professionals seek to combat human problems. Through case examples, I've tried to show some of the frustrations and gratifications encountered in social work practice. All of this information is designed to help you make a career decision about

whether social work is a profession you want to pursue.

Test your interest by answering these questions:

1. Do you enjoy working closely and intensely with people?

2. Do you think you could cope with failure?

3. Do you think you would be willing to acquire the knowledge, skills, and values necessary to make life more meaningful to individuals, groups, families, organizations, and communities?

4. Do you think you would like a profession dedicated to social change and to combating social injustice?

If you honestly can answer "yes" to each of these questions, you may well have the potential to become an effective social worker.

Whether or not you decide to pursue a career in social work, the material in this text on social problems and social services will give you a framework for making responsible citizenship decisions. As a voter, you help decide which political officials will be elected to work for the expansion or the curtailment of social welfare services. You have the opportunity to be a volunteer for a human service agency, to serve on boards and committees of agencies, to participate in fund-raisers for human service programs, to become involved in legislative processes that address human issues, and to influence others in daily interactions about controversial social welfare issues. Changes in the structure and functioning of the social welfare system are inevitable. You can work for the improvement of human living conditions. As John F. Kennedy, in his 1961 Presidential Inaugural Address, so eloquently stated, "Ask not what your country can do for you. Ask what you can do for your country."[123]

SUMMARY

Problems associated with overpopulation and misuse of the environment are very serious and may have an adverse, dramatic effect on the quality of life in the future. The world's population has tripled in size since 1930. At current growth rates, the population will again double in the next 40 years. Already we are experiencing resource crises. Some of the problems associated with over-population and misuse of the environment are:

- Too little food. At present a large proportion of the people in the world are undernourished, and many are starving.

- Too little water. Fresh water is in short supply.

- Economic problems. Overpopulation lowers the average per capita income, reduces the standard of living, and often leads to political turmoil.

- International terrorism. Rapid population growth is a factor that contributes to civil unrest, violence, and international strife.

- Crowding. There is some evidence that the subjective feeling of insufficient space may be a factor in such problems as crime, emotional disturbances, suicide, violence, incest, and child abuse.

- Immigration issues. Immigration has resulted in ethnic and racial conflict, economic competition among different nationality groups, exploitation of undocumented immigrants, and the stresses and costs associated with education and caring for new arrivals.

- Too little energy. We currently have an energy crisis. Fossil fuel resources (oil, coal, and natural gas), which provide over nine-tenths of the world's energy consumption, are rapidly being depleted.

- Depleted mineral resources. Essential elements such as copper, zinc, iron, and manganese are increasingly becoming short in supply.

- Despoiling of the land. Coal strip mining, oil drilling, deforestation, and overgrazing by cattle and sheep not only are unsightly but also cause devastating environmental damage when the delicate balance among nature's elements is interrupted.

- Radioactive wastes. As yet we have not found a safe way to dispose of nuclear wastes, which may create lethal problems in the future.

- Garbage. Increased consumption increases throwaways, the disposal of which often leads to air pollution, water pollution, and other undesirable environmental effects.

- Air pollution. In large industrial centers, air pollution is a health hazard. There are also growing concerns about the gradual depletion of the ozone layer, about the greenhouse effect, and global warming.

- Water pollution. Water pollution is also a serious health hazard; some rivers and lakes are now so polluted that they cannot support fish and other organisms.

- Acid rain. Acid rain has damaged timber and is killing fish in lakes and streams.

- Radioactive leaks from nuclear power plants. Leaks and accidents at nuclear power plants in the Ukraine and in the United States raise the question of whether nuclear energy is worth the risks.

- Nuclear war. The number of countries that have nuclear warheads is increasing, which makes nuclear war an ever-greater threat to civilization.

- General pollutants. Increasingly, we are becoming aware of the harmful effects of such pollutants as lead, mercury, DDT, and other chlorinated hydrocarbons.

Unless the size of the world's population is brought under control, these problems will intensify. A number of proposals have been advanced to curtail the growth of the world's population, some of which, if implemented, would radically change current lifestyles. Proposals include subsidizing adoptions, expanding sex education in schools, developing safer contraceptives, enforcing compulsory sterilization of adults who have two or more children, raising the minimum age of marriage, no longer allowing tax deductions for children, making birth control information and devices more available, and making abortions more accessible. If nations are not successful in controlling the birthrate through voluntary family planning, pressure will mount for countries to adopt population control programs.

It is essential that we confront our environmental problems. Two primary actions that are needed are changing values toward conserving resources and developing new sources of energy, such as solar energy.

Family planning services are crucial to population control. Social workers are increasingly being employed in settings that offer family planning services. Family planning appears to be an emerging career field for social work, as many roles are well suited for social workers: premarital counseling, pregnancy counseling, provision of contraceptive information, sex education services, abortion counseling, counseling on sexually transmitted diseases, and community planning efforts to further develop family planning services.

All of us can take steps to help save our earth. Whatever happens to the earth will surely affect everyone. This chapter (and this text) ends with challenging you to work for the improvement of human living conditions.

NOTES

1. Thomas J. Sullivan, *Social Problems*, 4th ed. (Needham Heights, MA: Allyn & Bacon, 1997), pp. 434–435.
2. Ibid.
3. James W. Coleman and Donald R. Cressey, *Social Problems*, 6th ed. (New York: HarperCollins, 1996), p. 479.
4. Paul R. Ehrlich, *The Population Bomb* (New York: Ballantine, 1971), p. 4.
5. Sullivan, *Social Problems*, pp. 434–436.
6. Werner Fornos, *Gaining People, Losing Ground* (Washington, DC: Population Institute, 1987), p. 57.
7. William Kornblum and Joseph Julian, *Social Problems*, 8th ed. (Englewood Cliffs, NJ: Prentice Hall, 1995), pp. 472–479.
8. Lee Rainwater, *And the Poor Get Children* (Chicago: Quadrangle Books, 1960).
9. Quoted in Donald C. Bacon, "Poor vs. Rich: A Global Struggle," *U.S. News & World Report*, Jul. 31, 1978, p. 57.
10. Fornos, *Gaining People, Losing Ground*, pp. 38–61.
11. R. V. Kail and J. C. Cavanaugh, *Human Development* (Pacific Grove, Ca: Brooks/Cole, 1996), p. 363.
12. Kornblum and Julian, *Social Problems*, pp. 472–479.
13. Paul Ehrlich and Anne Ehrlich, *The Population Explosion* (New York: Simon & Schuster, 1990), pp. 34–36.
14. Fornos, *Gaining People, Losing Ground*, p. 7.
15. Ibid.
16. Ehrlich and Ehrlich, *The Population Explosion*.
17. Ibid., pp. 38–39.
18. Coleman and Cressey, *Social Problems*, p. 485.
19. Ibid.
20. Ibid., pp. 485–487.
21. Ehrlich and Ehrlich, *The Population Explosion*.
22. Ian Robertson, *Social Problems*, 2nd ed. (New York: Random House, 1980), p. 41.
23. Thomas R. Malthus, *On Population*, Gertrude Himmelfarb, ed. (New York: Modern Library, 1960), pp. 13–14. (Original edition published 1798)
24. Coleman and Cressey, *Social Problems*, pp. 485–487.
25. Ibid.
26. Paul R. Ehrlich and Anne H. Ehrlich, *Population, Resources, Environment* (San Francisco: W. H. Freeman, 1970), p. 65.
27. "Warning: Water Shortages Ahead," *Time*, Apr. 4, 1977, p. 48.
28. Fornos, *Gaining People, Losing Ground*, pp. 7–23.
29. Quoted in Fornos, *Gaining People, Losing Ground*, p. 10.
30. U.S. Bureau of the Census, *Statistical Abstract of the United States, 1997* (Washington, DC: U.S. Government Printing Office, 1997).
31. Quoted in Fornos, *Gaining People, Losing Ground*, pp. 20–21.
32. Fornos, *Gaining People, Losing Ground*, p. 21.
33. John B. Calhoun, "Population Density and Social Pathology," *Scientific American*, 206 (Feb. 1962), pp. 139–148.
34. Joseph Julian, *Social Problems*, 3rd ed. (Englewood Cliffs, NJ: Prentice Hall, 1980), p. 502.
35. Ibid.
36. Paul Glastris, "The Alien Payoff," *U.S. News & World Report*, May 26, 1997, p. 20.
37. Ibid., p. 21.
38. Coleman and Cressey, *Social Problems*, p. 518.
39. Ibid.
40. Ibid., pp. 518–519.
41. Irene B. Taeuber, "Japan's Demographic Transition Reexamined," *Population Studies*, 14 (Jul. 1960), p. 39.
42. Robertson, *Social Problems*, p. 43.
43. Fornos, *Gaining People, Losing Ground*, p. 5.
44. Ibid.
45. Ehrlich and Ehrlich, *The Population Explosion*, p. 17.
46. "25 Million Births in India Each Year," *Popline*, Jul.–Aug. 1997, p. 3.
47. Ibid.

48. Ibid.
49. Ibid.
50. Ibid.
51. Ibid.
52. Ibid.
53. "India's Program Stresses Role of Women," *Popline,* 12 (Mar.–Apr. 1990), p. 3.
54. Ibid.
55. Ibid.
56. Coleman and Cressey, *Social Problems,* pp. 495–497.
57. Ibid.
58. Ibid.
59. Ibid.
60. Ibid.
61. Fornos, *Gaining People, Losing Ground,* p. 42.
62. Ehrlich and Ehrlich, *The Population Explosion,* pp. 205–209.
63. Coleman and Cressey, *Social Problems,* p. 495.
64. Ehrlich and Ehrlich, *The Population Explosion,* p. 207.
65. Ibid.
66. Coleman and Cressey, *Social Problems,* p. 511.
67. Ibid.
68. Ibid.
69. Ehrlich and Ehrlich, *The Population Explosion,* pp. 205–209.
70. Fornos, *Gaining People, Losing Ground,* pp. 45–46.
71. Ibid.
72. Ibid., p. 13.
73. David Foster, "Hidden Oil Soils Alaska's Coast," *Wisconsin State Journal,* Mar. 22, 1990, p. 2A.
74. Coleman and Cressey, *Social Problems,* p. 514.
75. Robertson, *Social Problems,* p. 71.
76. Kornblum and Julian, *Social Problems,* pp. 516–517.
77. Julian, *Social Problems,* p. 528.
78. Coleman and Cressey, *Social Problems,* pp. 507–509.
79. Ibid., p. 508.
80. Ibid.
81. Ibid., pp. 508–509.
82. Ibid., p. 509.
83. Ibid.
84. Kornblum and Julian, *Social Problems,* pp. 533–535.
85. Ibid., p. 534.
86. Ibid., pp. 533–535.
87. Orr Kelly, "Nuclear War's Horrors: Reality vs. Fiction," *U.S. News & World Report,* Nov. 28, 1983, pp. 85–86.
88. Barry Schwied, "U.S., Russia Seal Missile Deal," *Wisconsin State Journal,* Jan. 4, 1993, p. 1A.
89. Coleman and Cressey, *Social Problems,* p. 515.
90. Kornblum and Julian, *Social Problems,* pp. 515–516.
91. Coleman and Cressey, *Social Problems,* p. 510.
92. Vincent Parrilo, John Stimson, and Ardyth Stimson, *Contemporary Social Problems,* 2nd ed. (New York: Macmillan, 1989), p. 501.
93. Coleman and Cressey, *Social Problems,* p. 511.
94. Ehrlich and Ehrlich, *The Population Explosion,* pp. 123–124.
95. Ibid.
96. Ehrlich, *The Population Bomb,* pp. 31–35.
97. Richard Curtis and Elizabeth Hogan, *Perils of the Peaceful Atom* (New York: Ballantine, 1969), p. 194.
98. "Chemical Dangers May Be Unknown," *Wisconsin State Journal,* Mar. 3, 1984, p. 1.
99. "Silent Spring Revisited," *Newsweek,* Jul. 14, 1986, p. 72.
100. Ehrlich and Ehrlich, *The Population Explosion,* p. 238.
101. Ehrlich, *The Population Bomb,* pp. 127–145.
102. Bernard Berelson, "The Present State of Family Planning Programs," *Studies in Family Planning,* 57 (Sept. 1970), p. 2.
103. Coleman and Cressey, *Social Problems,* p. 497.
104. Ibid.
105. Paul R. Ehrlich, Anne H. Ehrlich, and John P. Holdren, *Human Ecology: Problems and Solutions* (San Francisco: W. H. Freeman, 1973), p. 279.
106. "Abortion Foes Gain Victory," *Wisconsin State Journal,* Jul. 1, 1980, sec. 1, p. 1.
107. Steven Waldman, Elise Ackerman, and Rita Rubin, "Abortions in America," *U.S. News & World Report,* Jan. 19, 1998, pp. 20–25.
108. Fornos, *Gaining People, Losing Ground,* pp. 106–107.
109. Kornblum and Julian, *Social Problems,* pp. 521–526.
110. George Ritzer, *Social Problems,* 2nd ed. (New York: Random House, 1986), p. 556.
111. "Don't Throw a Good Thing Away," *Policyholder News,* 23, no. 1 (Spring 1990), p. 3.
112. Ibid.
113. Ibid.
114. Steven Thomma, "Some Problems Solved Since Earth Day in '70, But Now We Face New Troubles," *Wisconsin State Journal,* Apr. 22, 1994, p. 1D.
115. Ibid.
116. Ibid.
117. Ibid.
118. Ibid.
119. Ehrlich and Ehrlich, *The Population Explosion,* pp. 219–220.
120. "Fuels for America's Future," *U.S. News & World Report,* Aug. 13, 1979, p. 33.
121. Ibid.
122. Ibid.
123. Quoted in James A. Henretta, W. Elliot Brownlee, David Brody, and Susan Ware, *America's History* (Chicago: Dorsey Press, 1987), p. 875.

APPENDIX

CODE OF ETHICS OF THE NATIONAL ASSOCIATION OF SOCIAL WORKERS *

OVERVIEW

The National Association of Social Workers Code of Ethics is intended to serve as a guide to the everyday professional conduct of social workers. This code includes four sections. Section one, Preamble, summarizes the social work profession's mission and core values. Section two, Purpose of the Code of Ethics, provides an overview of the code's main functions and a brief guide for dealing with ethical issues or dilemmas in social work practice. Section three, Ethical Principles, presents broad ethical principles, based on social work's core values, that inform social work practice. The final section, Ethical Standards, includes specific ethical standards to guide social workers' conduct and to provide a basis for adjudication.

PREAMBLE

The primary mission of the social work profession is to enhance human well-being and help meet basic human needs of all people, with particular attention to the needs and empowerment of people who are vulnerable, oppressed, and living in poverty. An historic and defining feature of social work is the profession's focus on individual well-being in a social context and the well-being of society. Fundamental to social work is attention to the environmental forces that create, contribute to, and address problems in living.

Social workers promote social justice and social change with and on behalf of clients. 'Clients' is used inclusively to refer to individuals, families, groups, organizations, and communities. Social workers are sensitive to cultural and ethnic diversity and strive to end discrimination, oppression, poverty, and other forms of social injustice. These activities may be in the form of direct practice, community organizing, supervision, consultation, administration, advocacy, social and political action, policy development and implementation, education, and research and evaluation. Social workers seek to enhance the capacity of people to address their own needs. Social workers also seek to promote the responsiveness of organizations, communities, and other social institutions to individuals' needs and social problems.

The mission of the social work profession is rooted in a set of care values. These care values, embraced by social workers throughout the profession's history, are the foundation of social work's unique purpose and perspective:

- Service
- Social justice
- Dignity and worth of the person
- Importance of human relationships
- Integrity
- Competence

The constellation of these core values reflects what is unique to the social work profession. Core values, and the principles which flow from them, must be balanced within the context and complexity of the human experience.

PURPOSE OF THE CODE OF ETHICS

Professional ethics are at the core of social work. The profession has an obligation to articulate its basic values, ethical principles, and ethical standards. The NASW Code of Ethics sets forth these values, principles, and standards to guide social workers' conduct. The code of ethics is relevant to all social workers and social work students, regardless of their professional functions, the settings in which they work, or the populations they serve.

This NASW Code of Ethics serves six purposes:

- The code identifies core values on which social work's mission is based.
- The code summarizes broad ethical principles that reflect the profession's core values and establishes a set of specific ethical standards that should be used to guide social work practice.
- The code of ethics is designed to help social workers identify relevant considerations when professional obligations conflict or ethical uncertainties arise.
- The code provides ethical standards to which the general public can hold the social work profession accountable.
- The code socializes practitioners new to the field to social work's mission, values, ethical principles, and ethical standards.
- The code articulates standards that the social work profession itself can use to assess whether social workers have engaged in unethical conduct. NASW has formal procedures to adjudicate ethics complaints filed against its members.* In subscribing to this code social workers are required to cooperate in its implementation, participate in NASW adjudication proceedings, and abide by any NASW disciplinary rulings or sanctions based on it.

This code offers a set of values, principles, and standards to guide decision making and conduct when ethical issues arise. It does not provide a set of rules that prescribe how social workers should act in all situations. Specific applications of the code must take into account the context in which it is being considered and the possibility of conflicts among the code's values, principles, and standards. Ethical responsibilities flow from all human relationships, from the personal and familial to the social and professional.

Further, the code of ethics does not specify which values, principles, and standards are most important and ought to outweigh others in instances when they conflict. Reasonable differences of opinion can and do exist among social workers with respect to the ways in which values, ethical principles, and ethical standards should be rank-ordered when they conflict. Ethical decision making in a given situation must apply the informed judgment of the individual social worker and should also consider how the issues would be judged in a peer review process where the ethical standards of the profession would be applied.

---

*For information on NASW adjudication procedures, see *NASW Procedures for the Adjudication of Grievances.*

Ethical decision making is a process. There are many instances in social work where simple answers are not available to resolve complex ethical issues. Social workers should take into consideration all the values, principles, and standards in this code that are relevant to any situation in which ethical judgment is warranted. Social workers' decisions and actions should be consistent with the spirit as well as the letter of this code.

In addition to this code, there are many other sources of information about ethical thinking that may be useful. Social workers should consider ethical theory and principles generally, social work theory and research, laws, regulations, agency policies, and other relevant codes of ethics, recognizing that among codes of ethics social workers should consider the NASW Code of Ethics as their primary source. Social workers also should be aware of the impact on ethical decision making of their clients' and their own personal values, cultural and religious beliefs, and practices. They should be aware of any conflicts between personal and professional values and deal with them responsibly. For additional guidance social workers should consult relevant literature on professional ethics and ethical decision making, and seek appropriate consultation when faced with ethical dilemmas. This may involve consultation with an agency-based or social work organization's ethics committee, regulatory body, knowledgeable colleagues, supervisors, or legal counsel.

Instances may arise where social workers' ethical obligations conflict with agency policies, relevant laws, or regulations. When such conflicts occur, social workers must make a responsible effort to resolve the conflict in a manner that is consistent with the values, principles, and standards expressed in this code. If a reasonable resolution of the conflict does not appear possible, social workers should seek proper consultation before making a decision.

This code of ethics is to be used by NASW and by other individuals, agencies, organizations, and bodies (such as licensing and regulatory boards, professional liability insurance providers, courts of law, agency boards of directors, government agencies, and other professional groups) that choose to adopt it or use it as a frame of reference. Violation of standards in this code does not automatically imply legal liability or violation of the law. Such determination can only be made in the context of legal and judicial proceedings. Alleged violations of the code would be subject to a peer review process. Such processes are generally separate from legal or administrative procedures and insulated from legal review or proceedings in order to allow the profession to counsel and/or discipline its own members.

A code of ethics cannot guarantee ethical behavior. Moreover, a code of ethics cannot resolve all ethical issues or disputes, or capture the richness and complexity involved in striving to make responsible choices within a moral community. Rather a code of ethics sets forth values, ethical principles, and ethical standards to which professionals aspire and by which their actions can be judged. Social workers' ethical behavior should result from their personal commitment to engage in ethical practice. This code reflects the commitment of all social workers to uphold the profession's values and to act ethically. Principles and standards must be applied by individuals of good character who discern moral questions and, in good faith, seek to make reliable ethical judgments.

ETHICAL PRINCIPLES

The following broad ethical principles are based on social work's core values of: service, social justice, dignity and worth of the person, importance of human relationships, integrity, and competence. These principles set forth ideals to which all social workers should aspire.

VALUE: *Service*

Ethical Principle: *Social workers' primary goal is to help people in need and to address social problems.*

Social workers elevate service to others above self-interest. Social workers draw on their knowledge, values, and skills to help people in need and to address social problems. Social workers are encouraged to volunteer some portion of their professional skills with no expectation of significant financial return (pro bono service).

VALUE: *Social Justice*

Ethical Principle: *Social workers challenge social injustice.*

Social workers pursue social change, particularly with and on behalf of vulnerable and oppressed individuals and groups of people. Social workers' social change efforts are focused primarily on issues of poverty, unemployment, discrimination, and other forms of social injustice. These activities seek to promote sensitivity to and knowledge about oppression, and cultural and ethnic diversity. Social workers strive to ensure equality of opportunity, access to needed information, services, resources, and meaningful participation in decision making for all people.

VALUE: *Dignity and Worth of the Person*

Ethical Principle: *Social workers respect the inherent dignity and worth of the person.*

Social workers treat each person in a caring and respectful fashion, mindful of individual differences and cultural and ethnic diversity. Social workers promote clients' socially responsible self-determination. Social workers seek to enhance clients' capacity and opportunity to change and to address their own needs. Social workers are cognizant of their dual responsibility to clients and to the broader society. They seek to resolve conflicts between clients' and the broader society's interests in a socially responsible manner consistent with the values, ethical principles, and ethical standards of the profession.

VALUE: *Importance of Human Relationships*

Ethical Principle: *Social workers recognize the central importance of human relationships.*

Social workers understand that relationships between and among people are an important vehicle for change. Social workers engage people as partners in the helping process. Social workers seek to strengthen relationships among people in a purposeful effort to promote, restore, maintain, and enhance the well-being of individuals, families, social groups, organizations, and communities.

VALUE: *Integrity*

Ethical Principle: *Social workers behave in a trustworthy manner.*

Social workers are continually aware of the profession's mission, values, ethical principles, and ethical standards, and practice in a manner consistent with them. Social workers act honestly and responsibly and promote ethical practices on the part of the organizations with which they are affiliated.

VALUE: *Competence*

Ethical Principle: *Social workers practice within their areas of competence and develop and enhance their professional expertise.*

Social workers continually strive to increase their professional knowledge and skills and to apply them in practice. Social workers should aspire to contribute to the knowledge base of the profession.

ETHICAL STANDARDS

The following ethical standards are relevant to the professional activities of all social workers. These standards concern: (1) social workers' ethical responsibilities to clients, (2) social workers' ethical responsibilities to colleagues, (3) social workers' ethical responsibilities in practice settings, (4) social workers' ethical responsibilities as professionals, (5) social workers' ethical responsibilities to the profession, and (6) social workers' ethical responsibilities to the broader society.

Some of the standards that follow are enforceable guidelines for professional conduct and some are more aspirational in nature. The extent to which each Standard is enforceable is a matter of professional judgment to be exercised by those responsible for reviewing alleged violations of ethical standards.

1. Social Workers' Ethical Responsibilities to Clients

1.01 COMMITMENT TO CLIENTS

Social workers' primary responsibility is to promote the well-being of clients. In general, clients' interests are primary. However, social workers' responsibility to the larger society or specific legal obligations may on limited occasions supersede the loyalty owed clients and clients should be so advised. (Examples include when a social worker is required by law to report that a client has abused a child or has threatened to harm self or others.)

1.02 SELF-DETERMINATION

Social workers respect and promote the right of clients to self-determination and assist clients in their efforts to identify and clarify their goals. Social workers may limit clients' right to self-determination when, in their professional judgment, clients' actions or potential actions pose a serious, foreseeable, and imminent risk to themselves or others.

1.03 INFORMED CONSENT

(a) Social workers should provide services to clients only in the context of a professional relationship based, when appropriate, on valid informed consent. Social workers should use clear and understandable language to inform clients of the purpose of the service, risks related to the service, limits to service because of the requirements of a third-party payor, relevant costs, reasonable alternatives, clients' right to refuse or withdraw consent, and the time frame covered by the consent. Social workers should provide clients with an opportunity to ask questions.

(b) In instances where clients are not literate or have difficulty understanding the primary language used in the practice setting, social workers should take steps to ensure clients' comprehension. This may include providing clients with a detailed verbal explanation or arranging for a qualified interpreter and/or translator whenever possible.

(c) In instances where clients lack the capacity to provide informed consent, social workers should protect clients' interests by seeking permission from an appropriate third party, informing clients consistent with their level of understanding. In such instances social workers should seek to ensure that the third party acts in a manner consistent with clients' wishes and interests. Social workers should take reasonable steps to enhance such clients' ability to give informed consent.

(d) In instances where clients are receiving services involuntarily, social workers should provide information about the nature and extent of services, and of the extent of clients' right to refuse service.

(e) Social workers who provide services via electronic mediums (such as computers, telephone, radio, and television) should inform recipients of the limitations and risks associated with such services.

(f) Social workers should obtain clients' informed consent before audiotaping or videotaping clients, or permitting third party observation of clients who are receiving services.

1.04 COMPETENCE

(a) Social workers should provide services and represent themselves as competent only within the boundaries of their education, training, license, certification, consultation received, supervised experience, or other relevant professional experience.

(b) Social workers should provide services in substantive areas or use intervention techniques or approaches that are new to them only after engaging in appropriate study, training, consultation, and/or supervision from persons who are competent in those interventions or techniques.

(c) When generally recognized standards do not exist with respect to an emerging area of practice, social workers should exercise careful judgment and take responsible steps—including appropriate education, research, training, consultation, and supervision—to ensure the competence of their work and to protect clients from harm.

1.05 CULTURAL COMPETENCE AND SOCIAL DIVERSITY

(a) Social workers should understand culture and its function in human behavior and society, recognizing the strengths that exist in all cultures.

(b) Social workers should have a knowledge base of their clients' cultures and be able to demonstrate competence in the provision of services that are sensitive to clients' culture and to differences among people and cultural groups.

(c) Social workers should obtain education about and seek to understand the nature of social diversity and oppression with respect to race, ethnicity, national origin, color, sex, sexual orientation, age, marital status, political belief, religion, and mental or physical disability.

1.06 CONFLICTS OF INTEREST

(a) Social workers should be alert to and avoid conflicts of interest that interfere with the exercise of professional discretion and impartial judgment. Social workers should inform clients when a real or potential conflict of interest arises and take reasonable steps to resolve the issue in a manner that makes the clients' interests primary and protects clients' interests to the greatest extent possible. In some cases, protecting clients' interests may require termination of the professional relationship with proper referral of the client.

(b) Social workers should not take unfair advantage of any professional relationship or exploit others to further their personal, religious, political, or business interests.

(c) Social workers should not engage in dual or multiple relationships with clients or former clients in which there is a risk of exploitation or potential harm to the client. In instances when dual or multiple relationships are unavoidable, social workers should take steps to protect clients and are responsible for setting clear, appropriate, and culturally sensitive boundaries. (Dual or multiple relationships occur when social workers relate to clients in more than one relationship, whether professional, social, or business. Dual or multiple relationships can occur simultaneously or consecutively.)

(d) When social workers provide services to two or more persons who have a relationship with each other (for example, couples, family members), social workers should clarify with all parties which individuals will be considered clients and the nature of social workers' professional obligations to the various individuals who are receiving services. Social workers who anticipate a conflict of interest among the individuals receiving services, or who anticipate having to perform in potentially conflicting roles (for example, when a social worker is asked to testify in a child custody dispute or divorce proceedings involving clients), should clarify their role with the parties involved and take appropriate action to minimize any conflict of interest.

1.07 PRIVACY AND CONFIDENTIALITY

(a) Social workers should respect clients' right to privacy. Social workers should not solicit private information from clients unless it is essential to providing service or conducting social work evaluation or research. Once private information is shared, standards of confidentiality apply.

(b) Social workers may disclose confidential information when appropriate with a valid consent from a client, or a person legally authorized to consent on behalf of a client.

(c) Social workers should protect the confidentiality of all information obtained in the course of professional service, except for compelling professional reasons. The general expectation that social workers will keep information confidential does not apply when disclosure is necessary to prevent serious, foreseeable, and imminent harm to a client or other identifiable person or when laws or regulations require disclosure without a client's consent. In all instances, social workers should disclose the least amount of confidential information necessary to achieve the desired purpose; only information that is directly relevant to the purpose for which the disclosure is made should be revealed.

(d) Social workers should inform clients, to the extent possible, about the disclosure of confidential information and the potential consequences and, when feasible, before the disclosure is made. This applies whether social workers disclose confidential information as a result of a legal requirement or based on client consent.

(e) Social workers should discuss with clients and other interested parties the nature of confidentiality and limitations of clients' right to confidentiality. Social workers should review with clients circumstances where confidential information may be requested and where disclosure of confidential information may be legally required. This discussion should occur as soon as possible in the social worker–client relationship and as needed throughout the course of the relationship.

(f) When social workers provide counseling services to families, couples, or groups, social workers should seek agreement among the parties involved concerning each individual's right to confidentiality and obligation to preserve the confidentiality of information shared by others. Social workers should inform participants in family, couples, or group counseling that social workers cannot guarantee that all participants will honor such agreements.

(g) Social workers should inform clients involved in family, couples, marital, or group counseling of the social worker's, employer's, and/or agency's policy concerning the social worker's disclosure of confidential information among the parties involved in the counseling.

(h) Social workers should not disclose confidential information to third party payors, unless clients have authorized such disclosure.

(i) Social workers should not discuss confidential information in any setting unless privacy can be assured. Social workers should not discuss confidential information in public or semipublic areas (such as hallways, waiting rooms, elevators, and restaurants).

(j) Social workers should protect the confidentiality of clients during legal proceedings to the extent permitted by law. When a court of law or other legally authorized body orders social workers to disclose confidential or privileged information without a client's consent and such disclosure could cause harm to the client, social workers should request that the court withdraw or limit the order as narrowly as possible and/or maintain the records under seal, unavailable for public inspection.

(k) Social workers should protect the confidentiality of clients when responding to requests from members of the media.

(l) Social workers should protect the confidentiality of clients' written and electronic records and other sensitive information. Social workers should take reasonable steps to ensure that clients' records are stored in a secure location and that clients' records are not available to others who are not authorized to have access.

(m) Social workers should take precautions to ensure and maintain the confidentiality of information transmitted to other parties through the use of computers, electronic mail, facsimile machines, telephones and telephone answering machines, and other electronic or computer technology. Disclosure of identifying information should be avoided whenever possible.

(n) Social workers should transfer or dispose of clients' records in a manner that protects clients' confidentiality and is consistent with state statutes governing records and social work licensure.

(o) Social workers should take reasonable precautions to protect client confidentiality in the event of the social worker's termination of practice, incapacitation, or death.

(p) Social workers should not disclose identifying information when discussing clients for teaching or training purposes, unless the client

has consented to disclosure of confidential information.

(q) Social workers should not disclose identifying information when discussing clients with consultants, unless the client has consented to disclosure of confidential information or there is a compelling need for such disclosure.

(r) Social workers should protect the confidentiality of deceased clients consistent with the preceding standards.

1.08 ACCESS TO RECORDS

(a) Social workers should provide clients with reasonable access to records concerning them. Social workers who are concerned that clients' access to their records could cause serious misunderstanding or harm to the client should provide assistance in interpreting the records and consultation with the client regarding the records. Social workers should limit client access to social work records, or portions of clients' records, only in exceptional circumstances when there is compelling evidence that such access would cause serious harm to the client. Both the client's request and the rationale for withholding some or all of the record should be documented in the client's file.

(b) When providing clients with access to their records, social workers should take steps to protect the confidentiality of other individuals identified or discussed in such records.

1.09 SEXUAL RELATIONSHIPS

(a) Social workers should under no circumstances engage in sexual activities or sexual contact with current clients, whether such contact is consensual or forced.

(b) Social workers should not engage in sexual activities or sexual contact with clients' relatives or other individuals with whom clients maintain a close, personal relationship where there is a risk of exploitation or potential harm to the client. Sexual activity or sexual contact with clients' relatives or other individuals with whom clients maintain a personal relationship

has the potential to be harmful to the client and may make it difficult for the social worker and client to maintain appropriate professional boundaries. Social workers—not their clients, their clients' relatives, or other individuals with whom the client maintains a personal relationship—assume the full burden for setting clear, appropriate, and culturally sensitive boundaries.

(c) Social workers should not engage in sexual activities or sexual contact with former clients because of the potential for harm to the client. If social workers engage in conduct contrary to this prohibition or claim that an exception to this prohibition is warranted due to extraordinary circumstances, it is social workers—not their clients—who assume the full burden of demonstrating that the former client has not been exploited, coerced, or manipulated, intentionally or unintentionally.

(d) Social workers should not provide clinical services to individuals with whom they have had a prior sexual relationship. Providing clinical services to a former sexual partner has the potential to be harmful to the individual and is likely to make it difficult for the social worker and individual to maintain appropriate professional boundaries.

1.10. PHYSICAL CONTACT

Social workers should not engage in physical contact with clients where there is a possibility of psychological harm to the client as a result of the contact (such as cradling or caressing clients). Social workers who engage in appropriate physical contact with clients are responsible for setting clear, appropriate, and culturally sensitive boundaries that govern such physical contact.

1.11 SEXUAL HARASSMENT

Social workers should not sexually harass clients. Sexual harassment includes sexual advances, sexual solicitation, requests for sexual favors, and other verbal or physical conduct of a sexual nature.

1.12 DEROGATORY LANGUAGE

Social workers should not use derogatory language in their written or verbal communications to or about clients. Social workers should use accurate and respectful language in all communications to and about clients.

1.13 PAYMENT FOR SERVICES

(a) When setting fees, social workers should ensure that the fees are fair, reasonable, and commensurate with the service performed. Consideration should be given to the client's ability to pay.

(b) Social workers should avoid accepting goods or services from clients as payment for professional services. Bartering arrangements, particularly involving services, create the potential for conflicts of interest, exploitation, and inappropriate boundaries in social workers' relationships with clients. Social workers should explore and may participate in bartering only in very limited circumstances where it can be demonstrated that such arrangements are an accepted practice among professionals in the local community, considered to be essential for the provision of service, negotiated without coercion, and entered into at the client's initiative and with the client's informed consent. Social workers who accept goods or services from clients as payment for professional services assume the full burden of demonstrating that this arrangement will not be detrimental to the client or the professional relationship.

(c) Social workers should not solicit a private fee or other remuneration for providing services to clients who are entitled to such available services through the social workers' employer or agency.

1.14 CLIENTS WHO LACK DECISION-MAKING CAPACITY

When social workers act on behalf of clients who lack the capacity to make informed decisions, social workers should take reasonable steps to safeguard the interests and rights of those clients.

1.15 INTERRUPTION OF SERVICES

Social workers should make reasonable efforts to ensure continuity of services in the event that they are interrupted by factors such as unavailability, relocation, illness, disability, or death.

1.16 TERMINATION OF SERVICES

(a) Social workers should terminate services to clients, and professional relationships with them, when such services and relationships are no longer required or no longer serve the clients' needs or interests.

(b) Social workers should take reasonable steps to avoid abandoning clients who are still in need of services. Social workers should withdraw services precipitously only under unusual circumstances, giving careful consideration to all factors in the situation and taking care to minimize possible adverse effects. Social workers should assist in making appropriate arrangements for continuation of services when necessary.

(c) Social workers in fee-for-service settings may terminate services to clients who are not paying an overdue balance if the financial contractual arrangements have been made clear to the client, if the client does not pose an imminent danger to self or others, and if the clinical and other consequences of the current non-payment have been addressed and discussed with the client.

(d) Social workers should not terminate services to pursue a social, financial, or sexual relationship with a client.

(e) Social workers who anticipate the termination or interruption of services to clients should notify clients promptly and seek the transfer, referral, or continuation of services in relation to the clients' needs and preferences.

(f) Social workers who are leaving an employment setting should inform clients of appropriate options for the continuation of service and their benefits and risks.

2. Social Workers' Ethical Responsibilities to Colleagues

2.01 RESPECT

(a) Social workers should treat colleagues with respect, and represent accurately and fairly the qualifications, views, and obligations of colleagues.

(b) Social workers should avoid unwarranted negative criticism of colleagues with clients or with other professionals. Unwarranted negative criticism may include demeaning comments that refer to colleagues' level of competence or to individuals' attributes such as race, ethnicity, national origin, color, age, religion, sex, sexual orientation, marital status, political belief, mental or physical disability, or any other preference, personal characteristic, or status.

(c) Social workers should cooperate with social work colleagues and with colleagues of other professions when it serves the well-being of clients.

2.02 CONFIDENTIALITY WITH COLLEAGUES

Social workers should respect confidential information shared by colleagues in the course of their professional relationships and transactions. Social workers should ensure that such colleagues understand social workers' obligation to respect confidentiality and any exceptions related to it.

2.03 INTERDISCIPLINARY COLLABORATION

(a) Social workers who are members of an interdisciplinary team should participate in and contribute to decisions that affect the well-being of clients by drawing on the perspectives, values, and experiences of the social work profession. Professional and ethical obligations of the interdisciplinary team as a whole and of its individual members should be clearly established.

(b) Social workers for whom a team decision raises ethical concerns should attempt to resolve the disagreement through appropriate channels. If the disagreement cannot be resolved, social workers should pursue other avenues to address their concerns, consistent with client well-being.

2.04 DISPUTES INVOLVING COLLEAGUES

(a) Social workers should not take advantage of a dispute between a colleague and employer to obtain a position or otherwise advance the social worker's own interests.

(b) Social workers should not exploit clients in a dispute with a colleague or engage clients in any inappropriate discussion of a social worker's conflict with a colleague.

2.05 CONSULTATION

(a) Social workers should seek advice and counsel of colleagues whenever such consultation is in the best interests of clients.

(b) Social workers should keep informed of colleagues' areas of expertise and competencies. Social workers should seek consultation only from colleagues who have demonstrated knowledge, expertise, and competence related to the subject of the consultation.

(c) When consulting with colleagues about clients, social workers should disclose the least amount of information necessary to achieve the purposes of the consultation.

2.06 REFERRAL FOR SERVICES

(a) Social workers should refer clients to other professionals when other professionals' specialized knowledge or expertise is needed to serve clients fully, or when social workers believe they are not being effective or making reasonable progress with clients and additional service is required.

(b) Social workers who refer clients to other professionals should take appropriate steps to facilitate an orderly transfer of responsibility. Social workers who refer clients to other professionals should disclose, with clients' consent, all pertinent information to the new service providers.

(c) Social workers are prohibited from giving or receiving payment for a referral when no professional service is provided by the referring social worker.

2.07 SEXUAL RELATIONSHIPS

(a) Social workers who function as supervisors or educators should not engage in sexual activities or contact with supervisees, students, trainees, or other colleagues over whom they exercise professional authority.

(b) Social workers should avoid engaging in sexual relationships with colleagues where there is potential for a conflict of interest. Social workers who become involved in, or anticipate becoming involved in, a sexual relationship with a colleague have a duty to transfer professional responsibilities, when necessary, in order to avoid a conflict of interest.

2.08 SEXUAL HARASSMENT

Social workers should not engage in any sexual harassment of supervisees, students, trainees, or colleagues. Sexual harassment includes sexual advances, sexual solicitation, requests for sexual favors, and other verbal or physical conduct of a sexual nature.

2.09 IMPAIRMENT OF COLLEAGUES

(a) Social workers who have direct knowledge of a social work colleague's impairment which is due to personal problems, psychosocial distress, substance abuse, or mental health difficulties, and which interferes with practice effectiveness, should consult with that colleague when feasible and assist the colleague in taking remedial action.

(b) Social workers who believe that a social work colleague's impairment interferes with practice effectiveness and that the colleague has not taken adequate steps to address the impairment should take action through appropriate channels established by employers, agencies, NASW, licensing and regulatory bodies, and other professional organizations.

2.10 INCOMPETENCE OF COLLEAGUES

(a) Social workers who have direct knowledge of a social work colleague's incompetence should consult with that colleague when feasible and assist the colleague in taking remedial action.

(b) Social workers who believe that a social work colleague is incompetent and has not taken adequate steps to address the incompetence should take action through appropriate channels established by employers, agencies, NASW, licensing and regulatory bodies, and other professional organizations.

2.11 UNETHICAL CONDUCT OF COLLEAGUES

(a) Social workers should take adequate measures to discourage, prevent, expose, and correct the unethical conduct of colleagues.

(b) Social workers should be knowledgeable about established policies and procedures for handling concerns about colleagues' unethical behavior. Social workers should be familiar with national, state, and local procedures for handling ethics complaints. These include policies and procedures created by NASW, licensing and regulatory bodies, employers, agencies, and other professional organizations.

(c) Social workers who believe that a colleague has acted unethically should seek resolution by discussing their concerns with the colleague when feasible and when such discussion is likely to be productive.

(d) When necessary, social workers who believe that a colleague has acted unethically should take action through appropriate formal channels (such as contacting a state licensing board or regulatory body, NASW committee on inquiry, or other professional ethics committees).

(e) Social workers should defend and assist colleagues who are unjustly charged with unethical conduct.

3. Social Workers' Ethical Responsibilities in Practice Settings

3.01 SUPERVISION AND CONSULTATION

(a) Social workers who provide supervision or consultation should have the necessary knowledge and skill to supervise or consult appropriately and should do so only within their areas of knowledge and competence.

(b) Social workers who provide supervision or consultation are responsible for setting clear, appropriate, and culturally sensitive boundaries.

(c) Social workers should not engage in any dual or multiple relationships with supervisees in which there is a risk of exploitation of or potential harm to the supervisee.

(d) Social workers who provide supervision should evaluate supervisees' performance in a manner that is fair and respectful.

3.02 EDUCATION AND TRAINING

(a) Social workers who function as educators, field instructors for students, or trainers should provide instruction only within their areas of knowledge and competence, and should provide instruction based on the most current information and knowledge available in the profession.

(b) Social workers who function as educators or field instructors for students should evaluate students' performance in a manner that is fair and respectful.

(c) Social workers who function as educators or field instructors for students should take reasonable steps to ensure that clients are routinely informed when services are being provided by students.

(d) Social workers who function as educators or field instructors for students should not engage in any dual or multiple relationships with students in which there is a risk of exploitation or potential harm to the student. So-

cial work educators and field instructors are responsible for setting clear, appropriate, and culturally sensitive boundaries.

3.03 PERFORMANCE EVALUATION

Social workers who have the responsibility for evaluating the performance of others should fulfil such responsibility in a fair and considerate manner, and on the basis of clearly stated criteria.

3.04 CLIENT RECORDS

(a) Social workers should take reasonable steps to ensure that documentation in records is accurate and reflective of the services provided.

(b) Social workers should include sufficient and timely documentation in records to facilitate the delivery of services and to ensure continuity of services provided to clients in the future.

(c) Social workers' documentation should protect clients' privacy to the extent that is possible and appropriate, and should include only that information that is directly relevant to the delivery of services.

(d) Social workers should store records following the termination of service to ensure reasonable future access. Records should be maintained for the number of years required by state statutes or relevant contracts.

3.05 BILLING

Social workers should establish and maintain billing practices that accurately reflect the nature and extent of services provided, and by whom the service was provided in the practice setting.

3.06 CLIENT TRANSFER

(a) When an individual who is receiving services from another agency or colleague contacts a social worker for services, the social worker should carefully consider the client's needs before agreeing to provide services. In order to minimize possible confusion and conflict, social workers should discuss with potential clients the nature of their current relationship with other service providers and the implications, including possible benefits or risks, of entering into a relationship with a new service provider.

(b) If a new client has been served by another agency or colleague, social workers should discuss with the client whether consultation with the previous service provider is in the client's best interest.

3.07 ADMINISTRATION

(a) Social work administrators should advocate within and outside of their agencies for adequate resources to meet clients' needs.

(b) Social workers should advocate for resource allocation procedures that are open and fair. When not all clients' needs can be met, an allocation procedure should be developed that is non-discriminatory and based on appropriate and consistently applied principles.

(c) Social workers who are administrators should take reasonable steps to ensure that adequate agency or organizational resources are available to provide appropriate staff supervision.

(d) Social work administrators should take reasonable steps to ensure that the working environment for which they are responsible is consistent with and encourages compliance with the NASW Code of Ethics. Social work administrators should take reasonable steps to eliminate any conditions in their organizations that violate, interfere with, or discourage compliance with the Code of Ethics.

3.08 CONTINUING EDUCATION AND STAFF DEVELOPMENT

Social work administrators and supervisors should take reasonable steps to provide or arrange for continuing education and staff development for all staff for whom they are responsible. Continuing education and staff development should address current knowledge and emerging developments related to social work practice and ethics.

3.09 COMMITMENTS TO EMPLOYERS

(a) Social workers generally should adhere to commitments made to employers and employing organizations.

(b) Social workers should work to improve employing agencies' policies and procedures, and the efficiency and effectiveness of their services.

(c) Social workers should take reasonable steps to ensure that employers are aware of social workers' ethical obligations as set forth in the NASW Code of Ethics and their implications for social work practice.

(d) Social workers should not allow an employing organization's policies, procedures, regulations, or administrative orders to interfere with their ethical practice of social work. Social workers should take reasonable steps to ensure that their employing organizations' practices are consistent with the NASW Code of Ethics.

(e) Social workers should act to prevent and eliminate discrimination in the employing organization's work assignments and in its employment policies and practices.

(f) Social workers should accept employment or arrange student field placements only in organizations where fair personnel practices are exercised.

(g) Social workers should be diligent stewards of the resources of their employing organizations, wisely conserving funds where appropriate, and never misappropriating funds or using them for unintended purposes.

3.10 LABOR–MANAGEMENT DISPUTES

(a) Social workers may engage in organized action, including the formation of and participation in labor unions, to improve services to clients and working conditions.

(b) The actions of social workers who are involved in labor–management disputes, job actions, or labor strikes should be guided by the profession's values, ethical principles, and ethical standards. Reasonable differences of opinion exist among social workers concerning their primary obligation as professionals during an actual or threatened labor strike or job action. Social workers should carefully examine relevant issues and their possible impact on clients before deciding on a course of action.

4. Social Workers' Ethical Responsibilities As Professionals

4.01 COMPETENCE

(a) Social workers should accept responsibility or employment only on the basis of existing competence or the intention to acquire the necessary competence.

(b) Social workers should strive to become and remain proficient in professional practice and the performance of professional functions. Social workers should critically examine, and keep current with, emerging knowledge relevant to social work. Social workers should routinely review professional literature and participate in continuing education relevant to social work practice and social work ethics.

(c) Social workers should base practice on recognized knowledge, including empirically-based knowledge, relevant to social work and social work ethics.

4.02 DISCRIMINATION

Social workers should not practice, condone, facilitate, or collaborate with any form of discrimination on the basis of race, ethnicity, national origin, color, age, religion, sex, sexual orientation, marital status, political belief, or mental or physical disability.

4.03 PRIVATE CONDUCT

Social workers' should not permit their private conduct to interfere with their ability to fulfill their professional responsibilities.

4.04 DISHONESTY, FRAUD, AND DECEPTION

Social workers should not participate in, condone, or be associated with dishonesty, fraud, or deception.

4.05 IMPAIRMENT

(a) Social workers should not allow their own personal problems, psychosocial distress, legal problems, substance abuse, or mental health difficulties to interfere with their professional judgment and performance or jeopardize the best interests of those for whom they have a professional responsibility.

(b) Social workers whose personal problems, psychosocial distress, legal problems, substance abuse, or mental health difficulties interfere with their professional judgment and performance should immediately seek consultation and take appropriate remedial action by seeking professional help, making adjustments in workload, terminating practice, or taking any other steps necessary to protect clients and others.

4.06 MISREPRESENTATION

(a) Social workers should make clear distinctions between statements made and actions engaged in as a private individual and as a representative of the social work profession, a professional social work organization, or of the social worker's employing agency.

(b) Social workers who speak on behalf of professional social work organizations should accurately represent the official and authorized positions of the organizations.

(c) Social workers should ensure that their representations to clients, agencies, and the public of professional qualifications, credentials, education, competence, affiliations, services provided, or results to be achieved are accurate. Social workers should claim only those relevant professional credentials they actually possess and take steps to correct any inaccuracies or misrepresentations of their credentials by others.

4.07 SOLICITATIONS

(a) Social workers should not engage in uninvited solicitation of potential clients who, because of their circumstances, are vulnerable to undue influence, manipulation, or coercion.

(b) Social workers should not engage in solicitation of testimonial endorsements (including solicitation of consent to use a client's prior statement as a testimonial endorsement) from current clients or from other persons who, because of their particular circumstances, are vulnerable to undue influence.

4.08 ACKNOWLEDGING CREDIT

(a) Social workers should take responsibility and credit, including authorship credit, only for work they have actually performed and to which they have contributed.

(b) Social workers should honestly acknowledge the work of and the contributions made by others.

5. Social Workers' Ethical Responsibilities to the Social Work Profession

5.01 INTEGRITY OF THE PROFESSION

(a) Social workers should work toward the maintenance and promotion of high standards of practice.

(b) Social workers should uphold and advance the values, ethics, knowledge, and mission of the profession. Social workers should protect, enhance, and improve the integrity of the profession through appropriate study and research, active discussion, and responsible criticism of the profession.

(c) Social workers should contribute time and professional expertise to activities that promote respect for the value, integrity, and competence of the social work profession. These activities may include teaching, research, consultation, service, legislative testimony, presentations in the community, and participation in their professional organizations.

(d) Social workers should contribute to the knowledge base of social work and share with colleagues their knowledge related to practice, research, and ethics. Social workers should seek to contribute to the profession's literature and to share their knowledge at professional meetings and conferences.

(e) Social workers should act to prevent the unauthorized and unqualified practice of social work.

5.02 EVALUATION AND RESEARCH

(a) Social workers should monitor and evaluate policies, the implementation of programs, and practice interventions.

(b) Social workers should promote and facilitate evaluation and research in order to contribute to the development of knowledge.

(c) Social workers should critically examine and keep current with emerging knowledge relevant to social work and fully utilize evaluation and research evidence in their professional practice.

(d) Social workers engaged in evaluation or research should consider carefully possible consequences and should follow guidelines developed for the protection of evaluation and research participants. Appropriate institutional review boards should be consulted.

(e) Social workers engaged in evaluation or research should obtain voluntary and written informed consent from participants, when appropriate, without any implied or actual deprivation or penalty for refusal to participate, without undue inducement to participate, and with due regard for participants' well-being, privacy, and dignity. Informed consent should include information about the nature, extent, and duration of the participation requested and disclosure of the risks and benefits of participation in the research.

(f) When evaluation or research participants are incapable of giving informed consent, social workers should provide an appropriate explanation to them, obtain the participant's assent, and obtain consent from an appropriate proxy.

(g) Social workers should never design or conduct evaluation or research that does not use consent procedures, such as certain forms of naturalistic observation and/or archival research, unless rigorous and responsible review of the research has found it to be justified because of its prospective scientific yield, educational, or applied value and unless equally effective alternative procedures that do not involve waiver of consent are not feasible.

(h) Social workers should inform participants of their rights to withdraw from evaluation and research at any time without penalty.

(i) Social workers should take appropriate steps to ensure that participants in evaluation and research have access to appropriate supportive services.

(j) Social workers engaged in evaluation or research should protect participants from unwarranted physical or mental distress, harm, danger, or deprivation.

(k) Social workers engaged in the evaluation of services should discuss collected information only for professional purposes and only with persons professionally concerned with this information.

(l) Social workers engaged in evaluation or research should ensure the anonymity or confidentiality of participants and the data obtained from them. Social workers should inform participants of any limits of confidentiality, the measures that will be taken to ensure confidentiality, and when any records containing research data will be destroyed.

(m) Social workers who report evaluation and research results should protect participants' confidentiality by omitting identifying information unless proper consent has been obtained authorizing disclosures.

(n) Social workers should report evaluation and research findings accurately. They should not fabricate or falsify results and should take steps

to correct any errors later found in published data using standard publication methods.

(o) Social workers engaged in evaluation or research should be alert to and avoid conflicts of interest and dual relationships with participants, should inform participants when a real or potential conflict of interest arises, and should take steps to resolve the issue in a manner that makes participants' interests primary.

(p) Social workers should educate themselves, their students, and colleagues about responsible research practices.

6. Social Workers' Ethical Responsibilities to the Broader Society

6.01 SOCIAL WELFARE
Social workers should promote the general welfare of society, from local to global levels, and the development of people, their communities, and their environment. Social workers should advocate for living conditions conducive to the fulfillment of basic human needs and promote social, economic, political, and cultural values and institutions that are compatible with the realization of social justice.

6.02 PUBLIC PARTICIPATION
Social workers should facilitate informed participation by the public in shaping social policies and institutions.

6.03 PUBLIC EMERGENCIES
Social workers should provide appropriate professional services in public emergencies, to the greatest extent possible.

6.04 SOCIAL AND POLITICAL ACTION
(a) Social workers should engage in social and political action that seeks to ensure that all persons have equal access to the resources, employment, services, and opportunities that they require in order to meet their basic human needs and to develop fully. Social workers

should be aware of the impact of the political arena on practice, and should advocate for changes in policy and legislation to improve social conditions in order to meet basic human needs and promote social justice.

(b) Social workers should act to expand choice and opportunity for all persons, with special regard for vulnerable, disadvantaged, oppressed, and exploited persons and groups.

(c) Social workers should promote conditions that encourage respect for the diversity of cultures and social diversity within the United States and globally. Social workers should promote policies and practices that demonstrate respect for difference, support the expansion of cultural knowledge and resources, advocate for programs and institutions that demonstrate cultural competence, and promote policies that safeguard the rights of and confirm equity and social justice for all people.

(d) Social workers should act to prevent and eliminate domination, exploitation, and discrimination against any person, group, or class on the basis of race, ethnicity, national origin, color, age, religion, sex, sexual orientation, marital status, political belief, mental or physical disability, or any other preference, personal characteristic, or status.

PHOTO CREDITS

INDEX

AA. *See* Alcoholics Anonymous
Abel, G. G., 255
Abortion, 26, 34, 229, 481, 602–606, 608
Absolute approach to poverty, 134–135
Academy of Certified Social Workers (ACSW), 184
Acceptance stage of grieving, 549, 573
Accountability, 112
Acid rain, 599
Ackerman, Elise, 603
ACSW. *See* Academy of Certified Social Workers
Activism. *See also* Justice, strategies for advancing; Social
    action role
    civil rights movement, 436, 437
    elderly people, 513–514
    people with disabilities, 556
    as social work role, 75
Acute phase of rape trauma syndrome, 260
Addams, Jane, 46, 47
Administration, 54–55
Adoption, 231–232
    and abortion, 26
    homosexual parents, 37, 252–253
    Native American children, 433
    transracial, 37
Adorno, T. W., 422
Adult Children of Alcoholics, 296
Adult day care, 512
Advocate role, 58, 59, 75, 376–377, 512
AFDC. *See* Aid to Families with Dependent Children
Affirmative action programs, 370–371, 438–440,
    457–458, 481
African Americans, 424–429
    and crime, 313, 318, 421
    and death penalty, 339
    drug use, 292
    and education, 360–362
    elderly people, 502
    and emotional/behavioral problems, 180
    and Great Society, 21
    health, 526
    and intelligence, 419
    poverty, 137, 427
    self-esteem, 424
    single parenthood, 226–227, 428
    stereotypes, 418, 422
    and stigmatization of welfare, 21, 147
    strengths perspective, 428, 446
    transracial adoption, 37
    unemployment, 400, 428
Africentric perspective, 426–427
Age. *See also* Ageism; Elderly people
    and alcohol use, 279
    and crime, 313
    of parents, 34–35
    and unemployment, 401
    and work, 390
Ageism, 401, 486, 488, 495

TO THE OWNER OF THIS BOOK:

We hope that you have found *Introduction to Social Work and Social Welfare*, seventh edition, useful. So that this book can be improved in a future edition, would you take the time to complete this sheet and return it? Thank you.

School and address: _____

Department: _____

Instructor's name: _____

1. What I like most about this book is: _____

_____

_____

2. What I like least about this book is: _____

_____

_____

3. My general reaction to this book is: _____

_____

4. The name of the course in which I used this book is: _____

_____

5. Were all of the chapters of the book assigned for you to read? _____

    If not, which ones weren't? _____

6. In the space below, or on a separate sheet of paper, please write specific suggestions for improving this book and anything else you'd care to share about your experience in using the book.

_____

_____

_____

_____

Optional:

Your name: _____ Date: _____

May Brooks/Cole • Wadsworth quote you, either in promotion for *Introduction to Social Work and Social Welfare,* seventh edition, or in future publishing ventures?

Yes: _____ No: _____

Sincerely,

Charles Zastrow

IN-BOOK SURVEY

At Brooks/Cole • Wadsworth, we are excited about creating new types of learning materials that are interactive, three-dimensional, and fun to use. To guide us in our publishing/development process, we hope that you'll take just a few moments to fill out the survey below. Your answers can help us make decisions that will allow us to produce a wide variety of videos, CD-ROMs, and Internet-based learning systems to complement standard textbooks. If you're interested in working with us as a student Beta-tester, be sure to fill in your name, telephone number, and address. We look forward to hearing from you!

In addition to books, which of the following learning tools do you currently use in your counseling/human services/social work courses?

_____ **Video** _____ in class _____ school library _____ own VCR

_____ **CD-ROM** _____ in class _____ in lab _____ own computer

_____ **Macintosh® disks** _____ in class _____ in lab _____ own computer

_____ **Windows® disks** _____ in class _____ in lab _____ own computer

_____ **Internet** _____ in class _____ in lab _____ own computer

How often do you access the Internet? _____

My own home computer is:

_____ Macintosh _____ DOS _____ Windows _____ Windows 95

The computer I use in class for counseling/human services/social work courses is:

_____ Macintosh _____ DOS _____ Windows _____ Windows 95

If you are NOT currently using multimedia materials in your counseling/human services/social work courses, but can see ways that video, CD-ROM, Internet, or other technologies could enhance your learning, please comment below:

_____

_____

_____

Other comments (optional): _____

_____

Name _____ Telephone _____

Address _____

School _____

Professor/Course _____

You can fax this form to us at (800) 522-4923; e-mail to: info@wadsworth.com; or detach, fold, secure, and mail.

FOLD HERE

BUSINESS REPLY MAIL

FIRST CLASS   PERMIT NO. 34   BELMONT, CA

POSTAGE WILL BE PAID BY ADDRESSEE

SOCIAL WORK MARKETING ASSISTANT
WADSWORTH PUBLISHING COMPANY
10 DAVIS DRIVE
BELMONT, CALIFORNIA 94002

FOLD HERE